Child Development and Education

Fourth Edition

Teresa M. McDevitt
University of Northern Colorado

Jeanne Ellis Ormrod
University of Northern Colorado (Emerita)
University of New Hampshire

Merrill
Upper Saddle River, New Jersey
Columbus, Ohio

Library of Congress Cataloging-in-Publication Data

McDevitt, Teresa M.

   Child development and education / Teresa M. McDevitt, Jeanne Ellis Ormrod. — 4th ed.
     p. cm.
   Includes bibliographical references and index.
   ISBN 978-0-13-713383-3
  1. Child development. 2. Adolescent psychology. 3. Educational psychology. I. Ormrod,
Jeanne Ellis. II. Title.

   LB1115.M263 2010
   305.231—dc22   2008039375

Vice President and Editor in Chief: Jeffery W. Johnston
Publisher: Kevin M. Davis
Development Editor: Christina Robb
Permissions Coordinator: Rebecca Savage
Editorial Assistant: Lauren Carlson
Senior Managing Editor: Pamela D. Bennett
Senior Project Manager: Mary Harlan
Project Coordination: Mary Tindle, S4Carlisle Publishing Services
Senior Art Director: Diane Lorenzo
Cover Image: SuperStock
Cover Design: Candace Rowley
Photo Coordinator: Lori Whitley
Media Producer: Autumn Benson
Media Project Manager: Rebecca Norsic
Senior Operations Supervisor: Matthew Ottenweller
Operations Specialist: Laura Messerly
Vice President, Director of Sales & Marketing: Quinn Perkson
Marketing Manager: Jared Bruckner
Marketing Coordinator: Brian Mounts

This book was set in Garamond by S4Carlisle Publishing Services. It was printed and bound
by Courier Kendallville, Inc. The cover was printed by Phoenix Color Corp.

Photo credits appear on page P-1, following the Subject Index.

Pearson® is a registered trademark of Pearson plc
Merrill® is a registered trademark of Pearson Education, Inc.

Pearson Education Ltd., London
Pearson Education Singapore, Pte. Ltd.
Pearson Education Canada, Inc.
Pearson Education–Japan
Pearson Education Australia PTY, Limited

Pearson Education North Asia, Ltd., Hong Kong
Pearson Educación de Mexico, S.A. de C.V.
Pearson Education Malaysia Pte. Ltd.
Pearson Upper Saddle River, New Jersey

Merrill
is an imprint of

www.pearsonhighered.com

10 9 8 7 6 5 4 3
ISBN-13: 978-0-13-713383-3
ISBN-10:   0-13-713383-9

Dedication

To our parents,
Rita and John McDevitt and Nancy and James Ellis,
who inspired our interest in education

Teresa M. McDevitt (left) is a psychologist with specializations in child development and educational psychology. She received a Ph.D. and M.A. in child development from Stanford University's Psychological Studies in Education program, an Ed.S. in educational evaluation from Stanford University, and a B.A. in psychology from the University of California, Santa Cruz. Since 1985 she has served the University of Northern Colorado in a variety of capacities—in teaching courses in child and adolescent psychology, human development, educational psychology, program evaluation, and research methods; in advisement of graduate students; in administration and university governance; and in research and grant writing. Her research focuses on child development, families, and teacher education. She has published articles in such journals as *Child Development, Learning and Individual Differences, Child Study Journal, Merrill-Palmer Quarterly, Youth and Society,* and *Science Education,* among others. She has gained extensive practical experiences with children, including raising two children with her husband and working in several positions with children—as an early childhood teacher of toddlers and preschool children, an early childhood special education teacher, and a volunteer in school and community settings. Teresa enjoys spending time with her children and husband and, when she has the chance, traveling internationally with her family.

Jeanne Ellis Ormrod (right) is an educational psychologist with specializations in learning, cognition, and child development. She received a Ph.D. and M.S. in educational psychology at The Pennsylvania State University and an A.B. in psychology from Brown University; she also earned licensure in school psychology through postdoctoral work at Temple University and the University of Colorado, Boulder. She was Professor of Educational Psychology at the University of Northern Colorado from 1976 until 1998, when she moved east to return to her native New England. She is now affiliated with the University of New Hampshire, where she occasionally teaches courses in educational psychology and research methods. She is the author or coauthor of several other Merrill/Pearson Education books, including *Educational Psychology: Developing Learners; Essentials of Educational Psychology; Human Learning; Case Studies: Applying Educational Psychology;* and *Practical Research.* She has worked as a middle school geography teacher and school psychologist and has conducted research in cognitive development, memory, problem solving, spelling, and giftedness. When Jeanne is not teaching, writing, reading professional books and journals, or spending time with her three grown children, she enjoys racquetball, boating, and travel with her husband to diverse cultural settings.

Preface

As psychologists and teacher educators, we have been teaching child and adolescent development for many years. A primary goal in our classes has been to help students translate developmental theories into practical implications for teaching and caring for youngsters with diverse backgrounds, characteristics, and needs. In past years, the child development textbooks available to our students were typically quite thorough in their descriptions of theory and research, but they generally offered few concrete suggestions for working with infants, children, and adolescents.

With this book, now in its fourth edition, we bridge the gap between theory and practice. We draw from innumerable theoretical concepts, research studies conducted around the world, and our own experiences as parents, teachers, psychologists, and researchers to identify strategies for promoting young people's physical, cognitive, and social-emotional growth. Like the third edition, this book focuses on childhood and the adolescent years and draws implications that are primarily educational in focus. As we wrote the fourth edition, we took to heart requests from readers that we offer succinct descriptions of concepts that are truly central to understanding how children and adolescents develop. Users of previous editions will note, for example, that our introductory overviews have been made more concise and transitions between sections have been shortened. We also responded to suggestions that we create a layout that would help readers proceed smoothly through the various sections. The result of our efforts, we hope, is a cleaner, less cluttered layout that keeps readers moving steadily through core concepts. In addition, we placed artifacts, tables, photographs, and references to videos and exercises strategically to enrich readers' understanding of essential ideas, and we gathered several exercises at the end of each chapter to deepen readers' insights into the developmentally appropriate education and care of children and adolescents.

We addressed other suggestions as well. We had received feedback that readers needed to learn more about research foundations in the field of child development, to which we responded by identifying representative research articles for analysis in MyEducationLab, a new and comprehensive online resource that also contains *Building Teaching Skills and Dispositions* exercises, practice quizzes, *Activities and Applications*, videos for analysis, and supplementary readings. We also reorganized the order of chapters slightly to clarify that family, culture, and community are important foundations for children, and we increased our attention to social-emotional development by adding a chapter on the development of morality and interpersonal behaviors. Finally, we addressed readers' increasing interest in children's growth in diverse settings by systematically expanding coverage of children's distinct experiences in different cultures, ethnicities, and economic backgrounds. We hope that the outcome of our efforts is a valuable resource for prospective teachers and other educational professionals.

Several features of the book make it different from other comprehensive textbooks about child and adolescent development. In particular, the book

- Continually relates abstract theories to educational practices in schools
- Not only describes but also *demonstrates* developmental phenomena
- Guides observations of children and adolescents
- Facilitates analysis of what children and adolescents say, do, and create
- Offers concrete strategies for effective teaching of, and working with, children and adolescents

In the next few pages, we provide examples of how the book accomplishes these goals.

The Only Comprehensive Development Text Written Specifically for Educators

This book focuses on the concepts and principles that are important to both developmental theorists and educational practitioners. More so than any other text, *Child Development and Education* spells out the practical implications of developmental theory and research and provides concrete applications for those who teach and work with children and adolescents. The result is a text that is uniquely useful to those who are interested in the practical applications of developmental scholarship.

Development and Practice

Accommodating Children from Culturally and Linguistically Diverse Backgrounds

- **Think about how cultural beliefs and practices serve adaptive functions for children.**
  A third-grade teacher notices that few of the children are willing to answer her questions about common pets, even though it is clear from her individual conversations with them that they have pets and know the answers. She discovers that bringing attention to oneself is not appropriate in the children's culture and so modifies her style to allow for group responses.
- **Build on children's background experiences.**
  A teacher asks her class of inner-city African American children to translate a poem written in a local dialect by an African American scholar. She puts words to the poem on an overhead transparency and asks children to translate each line into Standard English. In doing so, she cultivates a sense of pride about knowing two language systems (Ladson-Billings, 1994).

forms small groups that will work on different aspects of the project, such as collecting data about public opinions, identifying relevant community agencies, and contacting local officials who might be willing to speak to the class. The teacher is careful to form groups that are each comprised of children from various neighborhoods and ethnic groups.
- **Expose youngsters to successful models from various ethnic backgrounds.**
  A high school teacher invites several successful professionals from minority groups to speak with her class about their careers. When some youngsters seem interested in particular career paths, she arranges for them to spend time with these professionals in their workplaces.
- **Be neutral, inclusive, and respectful regarding children's religious practices.**

Development and Practice

In addition to discussing applications throughout the text itself, we provide *Development and Practice* features that offer concrete strategies for facilitating children's development. To help readers move from research to practice, each strategy is followed by an example of a professional using that strategy in a classroom or other setting. You will find examples of the *Development and Practice* feature on pages 96, 208, and 222 of this text.

Observation Guidelines

To work productively with children and adolescents, one must first be able to draw appropriate inferences from their behavior. Knowledge of developmental concepts and principles provides an essential lens through which professionals must look if they are to understand children. One of the foundational goals of this text is to help educators observe developmental nuances in the infants, children, and adolescents with whom they work. To this end, throughout the book we include *Observation Guidelines* tables. As you can see on pages 84–85, 98, 200, and 209, these tables offer specific characteristics to look for, present illustrative examples, and provide specific recommendations for practitioners.

Observation Guidelines

Assessing Cognitive Advancements in Infants and Toddlers

Characteristic	Look For	Example	Implication
Repetition of Gratifying Actions	· Repetition of actions involving the child's own body · Repetition of actions on other objects · Evidence that the child repeats an action because he or she notices and enjoys it	Myra waves her arms, stops, and waves her arms again. She makes a sound and repeats it, as if she enjoys listening to her own voice.	Provide a variety of visual, auditory, and tactile stimuli; for instance, play "This little piggy" with an infant's toes, hang a mobile safely over the crib, and provide age-appropriate objects (e.g., rattles, plastic cups). Be patient and responsive when infants repeat seemingly "pointless" actions (e.g., dropping favorite objects).
Exploration of Objects	· Apparent curiosity about the effects that different behaviors have on objects · Use of multiple behaviors (feeling, poking, dropping, shaking, etc.) to explore an object's properties · Use of several sensory modalities (e.g., seeing, listening, feeling, tasting)	Paco reaches for his caregiver's large, shiny earring. The caregiver quickly removes the earring from her ear and holds its sharp end between her fingers while Paco manipulates the silver loop and multicolored glass beads that hang from it.	Provide objects that infants can explore using multiple senses, making sure the objects are free of dirt and toxic substances and are large enough to prevent swallowing.

Applying Concepts in Child Development

The exercises in this section will help you consider the implications of children's experiences with families, cultures, and communities for your work.

Case Study

Four-Year-Old Sons

Read the case and then answer the questions that follow it.

A common behavior displayed by preschoolers is asking a lot of *why* questions. Consider how two mothers of 4-year-old boys interpret their sons' incessant questioning. Elizabeth describes her son Charles as

. . . mouthing off; just always mouthing off. Whenever I say anything to him, he asks me "Why?" Like I say we're going to the store and he says "Why?" Or I tell him "Don't touch the bug 'cuz it's dead" and he says "Why?" Like he's just trying to get me mad by never listening to me. He never accepts what I say. He mouths off all the time instead of believing me. It's like he just wants to tease me. You know, he tests me. (Belenky, Bond, & Weinstock, 1997, pp. 129–130)

In contrast, Joyce describes her son Peter this way:

Well, you know, he's got such an active mind, always going; like he's never satisfied with just appearances—he's always trying to figure out how things tick, why they do. So if I ask him to do something or tell him to do something, he's always asking why. He really wants to understand what's

the goal—what's the purpose—how come? He's really trying to piece the world all together . . . and understand it all. It's wonderful. Or if I say, "We're going to the store," he wants to know why. He's real interested in figuring out how one thing leads to another. It's great, because sometimes he helps me realize that I haven't really thought through why I'm saying what I am. And so we do think it through. (Belenky et al., 1997, p. 130)

- How do the two mothers interpret their sons' questions differently? How might their interpretations help us to predict their disciplinary styles?
- How might Elizabeth and Joyce have developed their particular parenting styles?
- What kinds of educational opportunities might these mothers create at home for their children? What might teachers do to encourage each mother's involvement at school?

Once you have answered these questions, compare your responses with those presented in Appendix A.

Applying Concepts in Child Development

New to this edition is a chapter-ending section called *Applying Concepts in Child Development* (see, for example, pages 105–107 and 228–231). Included in this section are concluding case studies that provide readers with an opportunity to apply chapter content, Interpreting Children's Artifacts and Reflections features that give readers practice in evaluating and interpreting children's work and statements, and Developmental Trends Exercises that provide scenarios connected to developmental concepts and allow readers to practice applying their knowledge of development.

The Difference Between Reading About Development and Seeing It in Diverse Contexts

Another central focus of this text is the frequent illustration of developmental concepts and principles using the experiences of children and adolescents from diverse family, cultural, and socioeconomic backgrounds. Authentic case studies begin and end each chapter, and there are often separate, shorter vignettes within the chapter body. In addition to these types of illustrations, the text, much more than any similar text, makes frequent use of real artifacts from children's journals, sketchbooks, and schoolwork. The actual work of children and adolescents makes developmental concepts and principles meaningful to educators and other practitioners. More than any other text, *Child Development and Education* brings these concepts and principles to life.

Case Study: Cedric and Barbara Jennings

"I got a B in physics! I can't believe it."

He begins ranting about the cheating in his class, about how he thinks a lot of other kids cheated. . . . Barbara remembers that he mentioned something about this a week ago—but she dismissed the whole matter.

Squeezed into a school desk next to him, she wants to tell Cedric that it doesn't matter. None of it. Some small hubbub about cheating and grades is meaningless now that he's been admitted to Brown, the top college acceptance of any Ballou student in years.

But, of course, he knows all that, too. And the more dismissive her look, the more rabid he becomes. Then she gets it: it's about her watching over him, defending him, always being there. ". . . I mean, what are *we* going to do?!" he shouts at the end of his furious soliloquy about what's right and fair and just.

She's up. "Well, Lavar [she usually calls him by his middle name], we'll just have to go have a word with that teacher." A second later, they're stomping together through the halls, headed for the physics classroom of an unsuspecting Mr. Momen. They find that he is alone. He turns and offers greetings as they enter, but Cedric launches right in—the whole diatribe, offered with added verve from his rehearsal with his mom. . . .

Case Studies

Each chapter begins with a case study and related questions that illustrate and frame chapter content. A chapter-ending case provides readers with an additional opportunity to apply chapter content. The questions that accompany each of these end-of-chapter cases help the reader in this application process; examples of answers to these questions appear in Appendix A. The ending case study analyses may be especially useful in helping future teachers prepare for the *Praxis™ Principles of Learning and Teaching* tests and other licensure exams. You will find examples of the case studies on pages 105 and 228–229.

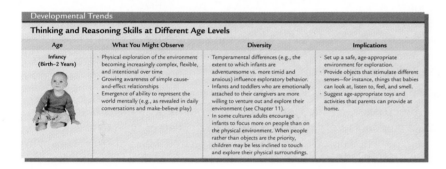

Developmental Trends			
Thinking and Reasoning Skills at Different Age Levels			
Age	What You Might Observe	Diversity	Implications
Infancy (Birth–2 Years)	· Physical exploration of the environment becoming increasingly complex, flexible, and intentional over time · Growing awareness of simple cause-and-effect relationships · Emergence of ability to represent the world mentally (e.g., as revealed in daily conversations and make-believe play)	· Temperamental differences (e.g., the extent to which infants are adventuresome vs. more timid and anxious) influence exploratory behavior. · Infants and toddlers who are emotionally attached to their caregivers are more willing to venture out and explore their environment (see Chapter 11). · In some cultures adults encourage infants to focus more on people than on the physical environment. When people rather than objects are the priority, children may be less inclined to touch and explore their physical surroundings.	· Set up a safe, age-appropriate environment for exploration. · Provide objects that stimulate different senses—for instance, things that babies can look at, listen to, feel, and smell. · Suggest age-appropriate toys and activities that parents can provide at home.

Developmental Trends Tables

Six-year-olds often think and act differently than 11-year-olds do, and 11-year-olds can, in turn, be quite different from 16-year-olds. Most chapters have one or more *Developmental Trends* tables that highlight the developmental differences that readers are apt to observe in infancy (birth–2 years), early childhood (2–6 years), middle childhood (6–10 years), early adolescence (10–14 years), and late adolescence (14–18 years). The diversity of potential observations is highlighted, and implications for practice are offered. See pages 87–88 and 225 for examples.

Interpreting Children's Artifacts and Reflections

Interpreting Children's Artifacts and Reflections features give readers practice in evaluating and interpreting children's work and statements. You will find examples of this feature in the chapter-ending section called Applying Concepts in Child Development, as well as within chapters (see pages 105–106, 230, and 267). Not only does this feature provide readers with additional authentic illustrations of chapter content, but it also offers readers an opportunity to apply their knowledge of child development in an authentic context. And since interpreting real children's work is a core assessment task of those who educate children and adolescents, this feature gives readers direct, concrete practice in assessment.

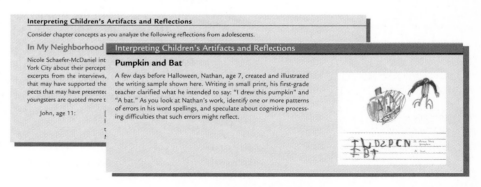

Interpreting Children's Artifacts and Reflections

Consider chapter concepts as you analyze the following reflections from adolescents.

In My Neighborhood

Nicole Schaefer-McDaniel int[...] York City about their percept[...] excerpts from the interviews, that may have supported the[...] pects that may have presented youngsters are quoted more t[...]

John, age 11:

Interpreting Children's Artifacts and Reflections

Pumpkin and Bat

A few days before Halloween, Nathan, age 7, created and illustrated the writing sample shown here. Writing in small print, his first-grade teacher clarified what he intended to say: "I drew this pumpkin" and "A bat." As you look at Nathan's work, identify one or more patterns of errors in his word spellings, and speculate about cognitive processing difficulties that such errors might reflect.

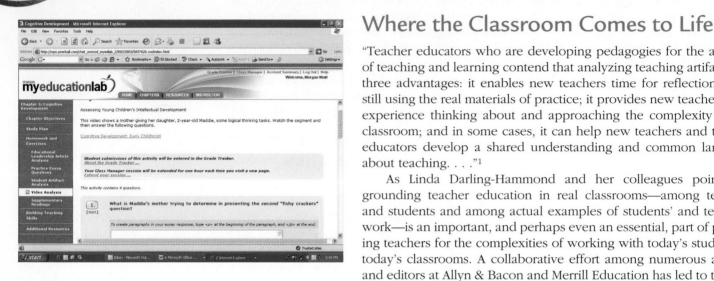

Where the Classroom Comes to Life

"Teacher educators who are developing pedagogies for the analysis of teaching and learning contend that analyzing teaching artifacts has three advantages: it enables new teachers time for reflection while still using the real materials of practice; it provides new teachers with experience thinking about and approaching the complexity of the classroom; and in some cases, it can help new teachers and teacher educators develop a shared understanding and common language about teaching. . . ."[1]

As Linda Darling-Hammond and her colleagues point out, grounding teacher education in real classrooms—among teachers and students and among actual examples of students' and teachers' work—is an important, and perhaps even an essential, part of preparing teachers for the complexities of working with today's students in today's classrooms. A collaborative effort among numerous authors and editors at Allyn & Bacon and Merrill Education has led to the creation of a Web site that provides instructors and students with the context of real classrooms and artifacts that research on teacher education tells us is so important. Through authentic in-class video footage, interactive activities, examples of authentic teacher and student work, and more, **MyEducationLab** offers instructors and students a uniquely valuable teacher education tool.

MyEducationLab is easy to use! Wherever the MyEducationLab logo appears in the margins or elsewhere in the text, readers can follow the simple link instructions to access the MyEducationLab resource that corresponds with the chapter content. For each textbook chapter you will find most or all of the following resources:

MyEducationLab

Observe how 10-year-old Kent easily conserves number but has difficulty with abstract proverbs in the "Cognitive Development: Middle Childhood" video.

- **Study Plan**
  - **Chapter Objectives:** Give students targets to shoot for as they read and study.
  - **Quiz:** Allows students to test their mastery of each chapter objective. Not only does the quiz provide subtest scores for each objective, but it also explains why responses to particular items are correct or incorrect.
  - **Review, Practice, and Enrichment:** Deepen students' understanding of particular concepts and principles of the chapter by providing interactive exercises or text excerpts. Detailed feedback is available to students for the exercises, allowing them to see why answers are correct or incorrect.

- **Activities and Applications**. Feedback for these exercises is available *only to instructors*.
  - **Interpreting Children's Artifacts and Reflections:** Give students additional experience interpreting artifacts.
  - **Developmental Trends Exercises:** Give students a chance to apply chapter concepts to fill in the blanks in the chapter-ending Developmental Trends table.
  - **Application Exercises:** Provide students with the opportunity to apply the concepts and principles of child development in a variety of short scenarios.
  - **Practice Essay Questions:** Give students practice answering essay questions similar to those they might find on a quiz or a test.
  - **Artifact Analyses:** Ask students to apply chapter concepts in analyzing written work or oral responses to interview questions.

[1]From *Preparing Teachers for a Changing World*, by L. Darling-Hammond and J. Bransford (Eds.), 2005, p. 427. San Francisco: John Wiley & Sons.

- **Video Analyses:** Present video clips of children and teachers in action, and ask students to apply chapter concepts in drawing conclusions.
- **Supplementary Readings:** Provide new information that extends understanding of chapter concepts.
- **Supplementary Readings Exercises:** Give students an opportunity to build on chapter concepts with activities related to advanced readings.
- **Understanding Research Exercises:** Increase students' understanding of how recent and classic investigations in child development contribute to knowledge about chapter topics, and deepen their understanding of developmental research methods.

- **Video Examples:** Allow students to explore topics—such as memory, friendship, and families—from the perspective of children from various age groups. The opportunity to see children and adolescents at different levels of development perform the same task or talk about a topic (e.g., what it means to be a friend) is unique and extremely powerful in demonstrating developmental differences. The video clips, formerly available on the CD set accompanying the third edition, are available here and have been supplemented with many other clips.

- **Building Teaching Skills and Dispositions exercises:** Provide scaffolded practice in a particular aspect of teaching, perhaps in observation, assessment, or sensitivity to diverse cultures. A final quiz tests mastery of the application. Feedback for the final quiz is available *only to instructors.*

MyEducationLab is easy to use, which is essential to providing the greatest benefit to students. Visit www.myeducationlab.com for a demonstration of this exciting new online teaching resource.

Increased Attention to the Diversity of Children's Experiences

Greater concern for the diversity of children's experiences is evident in new material on the cultural experiences of children (e.g., experiences of children from immigrant families in Chapter 3, cultural diversity in pregnancy and birth experiences in Chapter 4, cultural diversity in Chapter 7, English language learners in Chapter 9, cultural contexts of attachments and emotions in Chapter 11, ethnic identity in Chapter 12, and a substantial increase in the number of artifacts, figures, and cases from children from diverse backgrounds throughout the book).

Thoroughly Updated Research on Children's Development

This edition has been extensively revised with hundreds of new citations. Every chapter has important updates; examples include additions or substantive revisions with regard to developmental theories in Chapter 1, qualitative research methods in Chapter 2, parenting styles in Chapter 3, genetics in Chapter 4, brain development and obesity in Chapter 5, neo-Piagetian and Vygotskian approaches in Chapter 6, basic cognitive processes in Chapter 7, the Cattell-Horn-Carroll theory of intelligence in Chapter 8, development of a second language in Chapter 9, visual-spatial thinking in Chapter 10, attachments in older children and in school settings in Chapter 11, identity in children from diverse backgrounds in Chapter 12, achievement goals and attribution retraining in Chapter 13, contemporary perspectives on Kohlberg's theory and school violence and safety in Chapter 14, and cyberbullying and homeless youth in Chapter 15.

Additional Chapter on Social-Emotional Development

In the preceding edition we included a discussion of moral development in our chapter on motivation and self-regulation. In the current edition we give moral development its own chapter (Chapter 14), where we can better relate this aspect of development to trends in prosocial behavior and aggression. Adding this chapter has enabled us to include a new section, "Creating a Safe School Environment," in which we present strategies for minimizing and addressing violence on school grounds.

The following online supplements to the textbook are available for downloading at www.pearsonhighered.com. Simply click on "Educators," enter the author, title, or ISBN, and select this textbook. Click on the "Resources" tab to view and download the available supplements.

Online Instructor's Manual

This manual (ISBN: 0-13-713384-7) contains an outline of the primary chapter headings and sections, with a corresponding list of instructional materials to be used in each section; and suggestions and resources for learning activities, supplemental lectures, group activities, and handouts. Each element has been carefully crafted to provide opportunities to support, enrich, and expand on what students read in the text.

Online Test Bank and TestGen

The Online Test Bank (ISBN: 0-13-713385-5) contains an average of 60 items per chapter. These test items are categorized and marked as either lower-level items that ask students to identify or explain concepts they have learned or higher-level items that require students to apply their knowledge of developmental concepts and research to specific classroom situations. The online computerized test bank software (TestGen) (ISBN: 0-13-713390-1) allows instructors to create and customize exams. TestGen is available in both Macintosh and PC/Windows versions.

Online PowerPoint® Slides

The Online PowerPoint slides (ISBN: 0-13-713386-3) include key concept summaries, outlines, and other graphic aids to enhance learning. They are designed to help students understand, organize, and remember concepts and developmental theories.

Online Blackboard® and WebCT Course Cartridges

Available for both Blackboard (ISBN: 0-13-713388-X) and WebCT (ISBN: 0-13-713392-8), the online course cartridges contain the content of the Test Bank available for use on either online learning application.

MyEducationLab

A new online learning tool, MyEducationLab, available at www.myeducationlab.com, offers quizzes to test mastery of chapter objectives; Review, Practice, and Enrichment exercises to deepen understanding; Activities and Applications to foster usage of chapter concepts; Video Examples of children in action; and Building Teaching Skills and Dispositions exercises to provide interactive practice applying the core principles and concepts of child development.

The Videotape Package

Double-Column Addition: A Teacher Uses Piaget's Theory   (ISBN: 0-13-751413-1) Second graders construct creative strategies for adding and subtracting two-digit numbers and reveal a true understanding of place value.

A Private Universe   (ISBN: 0-13-859646-8) This video illustrates the pervasiveness of misconceptions in high school students and in graduates and faculty at Harvard University about the seasons of the year and the phases of the moon. One student's explanations are portrayed both before and after instruction. Questions probing her reasoning after instruction reveal she still holds some of her prior misconceptions.

Acknowledgments

Although we are listed as the sole authors of this textbook, in fact many individuals have contributed in significant ways to its content and form. Our editor, Kevin Davis, recognized the need for an applied child development book and nudged us to write one. Kevin has been the captain of our ship throughout all four editions of the book, charting our journey and alerting us when we drifted off course. We thank Kevin for his continuing encouragement, support, insights, task focus, and high standards.

We have been equally fortunate to work with Julie Peters (development editor for the first and second editions), Autumn Benson (development editor for the third edition), and Christie Robb (development editor for the fourth edition). Julie, Autumn, and Christie have seen us through the day-to-day challenges of writing the book—for instance, offering creative ideas for improving the manuscript, locating artifacts to illustrate key concepts, pushing us to condense when we were unnecessarily wordy, insisting that certain concepts be clarified and illustrated, overseeing the content and quality of the book's increasingly sophisticated online Web site, being a willing ear whenever we needed to vent our frustrations, and, in general, coordinating our writing efforts until books went into production. We thank Julie, Autumn, and Christie for their advice, support, and good humor, and also for their willingness to drop whatever else they were doing to come to our assistance at critical times.

Others at both Merrill Education and S4Carlisle Publishing Services have also been key players in bringing the book to fruition. Lorretta Palagi worked diligently to keep the manuscript focused, concise, and clear. Mary Tindle and Mary Harlan guided the manuscript through the production process; without a complaint, they let us continue to tweak the book in innumerable small ways even as production deadlines loomed dangerously close. Becky Savage secured permissions for the excerpts and figures we borrowed from other sources and was flexible and dependable when we added to our list at the eleventh hour. Lori Whitley sifted through many piles of photos to identify those that could best capture key developmental principles in a visual form. Marketing whizzes Brian Mounts, Quinn Perkson, and Jared Bruckner helped us get out the word about the book. Pearson Education sales representatives across the country offered us encouragement and relayed invaluable recommendations they had heard from instructors using the book.

We are also deeply indebted to the creators of videos available on MyEducationLab. Jayne Downey, who coordinated production of many of the videos, shared our desire to represent children and adolescents in a natural and positive light so that adults could understand them more deeply and sympathetically; among the many tasks she undertook were to recruit children and families, secure the services of interviewers, draft questions and set up tasks for children, film children in their homes, edit video clips, and interpret children's thoughts and actions. Stuart Garry brought his technological know-how, in-depth knowledge of developmental theory, artistic talents, and keen attention to producing Jayne's videos. Others were vital contributors as well. Jason Cole expertly programmed the software package. We extend our appreciation to Greg Pierson, Director of University Schools, and to Keli Cotner, Director of the Campus Child Care Center at the University of Northern Colorado, for granting permission and assistance to Jayne Downey in filming classrooms and facilities. Dana Snyder and Kelle Nolke, teachers at University Schools, kindly assisted with videotaping in their classroom; Dana Snyder also permitted her own lessons to be taped. We also acknowledge the excellent job done by interviewers Stacey Blank, Tara Kaysen, Addie Lopez, Laura Sether, and Lisa Blank. The children and families were especially generous in allowing Jayne and the interviewers to come into their homes and film the children. We are grateful that numerous other individuals affiliated with Pearson Education permitted us to use their footage of children in our exercises.

Finally, we are indebted to two individuals for their exemplary work in the development and design of MyEducationLab. Autumn Benson helped us locate videos and other materials for this fabulous new online resource for the book. Gail Gottfried drew on her wealth of knowledge about both child development and pedagogy as she wrote instructional objectives, practice quiz items, Understanding Research exercises, and other activities and exercises for each chapter of the book. Gail also developed new items for the test bank for this edition.

Children, Adolescents, Teachers, and Other Professionals Equally important contributors to the book were the many young people and practitioners who provided the work samples, written reflections, other artifacts, and verbal responses that appear throughout the 15 chapters and in MyEducationLab. The work of the following young people contributed immeasurably to the depth and richness of our discussions:

Davis Alcorn	Rachel Foster	Marianne Kies	Amber Rossetti
Jacob Alcorn	Tina Ormrod Fox	Sarah Luffel	Bianca Sanchez
Curtis Alexander	Eddie Garcia	Jessica Lumbrano	Daniela Sanchez
Kyle Alexander	Palet Garcia	Krista Marrufo	Corwin Sether
David Alkire	Veronica Garcia	Steven Merrick	Alex Sheehan
Geoff Alkire	James Garrett III	Margaret Mohr	Connor Sheehan
Brenda Bagazuma	Amaryth Gass	Tchuen-Yi Murry	Aftyn Siemer
Andrew Belcher	Andrew Gass	Mike Newcomb	Karma Marie Smith
Katie Belcher	Tony Gass	Malanie Nunez	Alex Snow
Kayla Blank	Dana Gogolin	Dustin O'Mara	Sam Snow
Madison Blank	Ivy Gogolin	Alex Ormrod	Connor Stephens
Brent Bonner	Kenton Groissaint	Jeff Ormrod	Megan Lee Stephens
Diamond Bonner	Acadia Gurney	Shir-Lisa Owens	Joe Sweeney
Ricco Branch	Amanda Hackett	Isiah Payan	Emma Thompson
Marsalis Bush	Jared Hale	Isabelle Peters	Grace Tober
Eric Campos	Cody Havens	Michelle Pollman	Sarah Toon
Leif Carlson	Tyler Hensley	Laura Prieto-Velasco	David Torres
Zoe Clifton	Elisabet Deyanira	Cooper Remignanti	Joseph Torres
Wendy Cochran	Hernandez	Ian Rhoades	Samuel Torres
Jenna Dargy	Lauryn Hickman	Talia Rockland	Madison Tupper
Noah Davis	Sam Hickman	Oscar Rodriguez	Danielle Welch
Shea Davis	William Hill	Elizabeth Romero	Brady Williamson
Mayra de la Garza	Brandon Jackson	Corey Ross	Joey Wolf
Brandon Doherty	Rachel Johnson	Katie Ross	Lindsey Woollard
Daniel Erdman	Jordan Kemme	Trisha Ross	Anna Young

We also thank the children in the first- and second-grade classroom of Dana Snyder and Kelle Nolke at the Laboratory School, Greeley, Colorado (now University Schools).

To ensure that we included children's work from a wide variety of geographic locations and backgrounds, we contacted organizations north and south, east and west to obtain work samples that would reflect ethnic, cultural, and economic diversity. We want to thank these individuals for their assistance and coordination efforts: Don Burger at Pacific Resources for Education and Learning (PREL), Michelle Gabor of the Salesian Boys' and Girls' Club, Rita Hocog Inos of the Commonwealth of the Northern Mariana Islands Public School System, Bettie Lake of the Phoenix Elementary School District, Heidi Schork and members of the Boston Youth Clean-Up Corps (BYCC), and Ann Shump of the Oyster River School District. Furthermore we thank the many teachers, counselors, principals, and other professionals—a child welfare case worker, a neurologist, a public health educator—who were so helpful in our efforts to identify artifacts, anecdotes, dialogues, and professional strategies to illustrate developmental concepts; key among them were Janet Alcorn, Rosenna Bakari, Trish Belcher, Paula Case, Michael Gee, Jennifer Glynn, Evie Greene, Diana Haddad, Betsy Higginbotham, Betsy Hopkins, Dinah Jackson, Jesse Jensen, Mike McDevitt, Erin Miguel, Michele Minichiello, Andrew Moore, Dan Moulis, Tina Ormrod Fox, Annemarie Palincsar, Kellee Patterson, Elizabeth Peña, Jrene Rahm, Nancy Rapport, Gwen Ross, Karen Scates, Cindy Schutter, Karen Setterlin, Jean Slater, Julie Spencer, Nan Stein, Sally Tossey, Pat Vreeland, and Cathy Zocchi.

Colleagues and Reviewers In addition, we received considerable encouragement, assistance, and support from our professional colleagues. Developmentalists and educational psychologists at numerous institutions around the country have offered their careful and insightful reviews of one or more chapters. We are especially indebted to the following reviewers of this edition:

Patricia Ashton, University of Florida
Irene Bersola-Nguyen, California State University–Sacramento
Teresa K. DeBacker, University of Oklahoma
Kathleen Fite, Texas State University
William Gray, University of Toledo

Kathy Nakagawa, Arizona State University
Terry Nourie, Illinois State University
Rob Weisskirch, California State University–Monterey Bay
Andrew R. Whitehead, East Stroudsburg University of Pennsylvania

We continue to appreciate the guidance of reviewers for earlier editions of the book. These individuals helped guide our early efforts:

Karen Abrams, Keene State College
Jan Allen, University of Tennessee
Lynley Anderman, University of Kentucky
David E. Balk, Kansas State University
Thomas M. Batsis, Loyola Marymount University
Doris Bergen, Miami University
Donna M. Burns, The College of St. Rose
Heather Davis, University of Florida
Teresa K. DeBacker, University of Oklahoma
Deborah K. Deemer, University of Northern Iowa
Karen Drill, University of Illinois at Chicago
Eric Durbrow, The Pennsylvania State University
William Fabricius, Arizona State University
Daniel Fasko, Morehead State University
Sherryl Browne Graves, Hunter College
Michael Green, University of North Carolina–Charlotte
Glenda Griffin, Texas A&M University
Deborah Grubb, Morehead State University
Linda L. Haynes, University of South Alabama
Melissa Heston, University of Northern Iowa
James E. Johnson, The Pennsylvania State University
Joyce Juntune, Texas A&M University
Michael Keefer, University of Missouri–St. Louis
Judith Kieff, University of New Orleans

Nancy Knapp, University of Georgia
Carol A. Marchel, Winthrop University
Mary McLellan, Northern Arizona University
Sharon McNeely, Northeastern Illinois University
Kenneth Merrell, University of Iowa
Marilyn K. Moore, Illinois State University
Tamera Murdock, University of Missouri–Kansas City
Bridget Murray, Indiana State University
Kathy Nakagawa, Arizona State University
Virginia Navarro, University of Missouri–St. Louis
Larry Nucci, University of Illinois–Chicago
Jennifer Parkhurst, Duke University
Sherrill Richarz, Washington State University
Kent Rittschof, Georgia Southern University
Linda Rogers, Kent State University
Richard Ryan, University of Rochester
Sue Spitzer, California State University, San Bernardino
Benjamin Stephens, Clemson University
Bruce Tuckman, The Ohio State University
Kathryn Wentzel, University of Maryland–College Park
Andrew R. Whitehead, East Stroudsburg University of Pennsylvania
Allan Wigfield, University of Maryland–College Park
Thomas D. Yawkey, The Pennsylvania State University.

Increasingly, we have heard from colleagues at other institutions who have taken the time to let us know what they think about the book and how it might be improved. We are grateful for such very helpful feedback. In addition, faculty and administrators at the University of Northern Colorado—especially Marlene Strathe, Steven Pulos, Randy Lennon, Kathy Cochran, Allen Huang, Mark Alcorn, Eugene Sheehan, and Kay Norton—unselfishly provided information, advice, resources, and time.

Our Families   Finally, our families have been supportive and patient over the extended period we have been preoccupied with reading, researching, writing, and editing. Our children gave of themselves in anecdotes, artwork, and diversions from our work. Our husbands picked up the slack around the house and gave us frequent emotional boosts and comic relief. Much love and many thanks to Eugene, Connor, and Alex (from Teresa) and to Richard, Tina, Alex, and Jeff (from Jeanne).

T.M.M.
J.E.O.

Brief Contents

part 1
Foundations in Child Development

chapter 1
Making a Difference in the Lives of Children
and Adolescents   2

chapter 2
Using Research to Understand Children and
Adolescents   32

chapter 3
Family, Culture, and Community   62

part 2
Biological Development

chapter 4
Biological Beginnings   108

chapter 5
Physical Development   144

part 3
Cognitive Development

chapter 6
Cognitive Development:
Piaget and Vygotsky   192

chapter 7
Cognitive Development:
Cognitive Processes   232

chapter 8
Intelligence   272

chapter 9
Language Development   312

chapter 10
Development in the Academic Domains   354

part 4
Social and Emotional Development

chapter 11
Emotional Development   402

chapter 12
Development of Self and Social
Understandings   442

chapter 13
Development of Motivation
and Self-Regulation   480

chapter 14
Development of Morality and
Interpersonal Behaviors   516

chapter 15
Peers, Schools, and Society   552

appendix A
Analyses of the Ending Case
Studies   A-1

appendix B
Analyses of Ending Artifacts   B-1

Glossary   G-1

References   R-1

Name Index   N-1

Subject Index   S-1

Photo Credits   P-1

Contents

part 1
Foundations in Child Development

chapter 1

Making a Difference in the Lives of Children and Adolescents   2

Case Study: Tonya   3
The Field of Child Development   4
   Three Developmental Domains   5
   Effects of Context on Development   5
Basic Issues in Development   5
   Nature and Nurture   5
   Universality and Diversity   8
   Qualitative and Quantitative Change   9
   Applying Basic Lessons from Child Development   10
Theories of Child Development   11
   Biological Theories   11
   Behaviorism and Social Learning Theories   12
   Psychodynamic Theories   13
   Cognitive-Developmental Theories   13
   Cognitive Process Theories   14
   Sociocultural Theories   15
   Developmental Systems Theories   15
   Taking an Eclectic Approach   16
Developmental Periods   17
   Infancy (Birth–2 Years)   19
   Early Childhood (2–6 Years)   20
   Middle Childhood (6–10 Years)   21
   Early Adolescence (10–14 Years)   22
   Late Adolescence (14–18 Years)   22
From Theory to Practice   23
   Applying Knowledge of Child Development in the Classroom and Community   27
   Strengthening the Commitment   28
Summary   28
Applying Concepts in Child Development   29
Case Study: Latisha   29

chapter 2

Using Research to Understand Children and Adolescents   32

Case Study: Jack's Research   33
Principles of Research   34
   Ethical Protection of Children   34
   The Scientific Method   34
   Research Participants   35

Analyzing Developmental Research   36
   Data Collection Techniques   36
   Research Designs   42
   Becoming a Thoughtful Consumer of Research   45
Gathering Data as an Educator   49
   Increasing the Accuracy of Conclusions About Children   50
   Observing Children   50
   Listening to Children   54
   Interpreting Assessments and Artifacts   55
   Conducting Action Research   56
   Ethical Guidelines for Teacher-Researchers   58
Summary   59
Applying Concepts in Child Development   59
Case Study: The Study Skills Class   59

chapter 3

Family, Culture, and Community   62

Case Study: Cedric and Barbara Jennings   63
Cradles of Child Development   64
   Family   64
   Culture   65
   Community   65
   Considering Children's Origins in the Classroom   66
Family Structures   68
   Mothers and Fathers   69
   Divorcing Parents   70
   Single Parents   71
   Parents and Stepparents   71
   Extended Family   72
   Adoptive Parents   73
   Foster Care   73
   Other Heads of Family   74
   Accommodating Diverse Family Structures   75
Family Processes   76
   Families' Influences on Children   76
   Children's Influences on Families   80
   Risk Factors in Families   83
   Forming Partnerships with Families   84
Children in a Diverse Society   92
   Children's Experiences in Diverse Groups   92
   Community Resources   100
   Working with Children from Low-Income Families   102
Summary   104
Applying Concepts in Child Development   105
Case Study: Four-Year-Old Sons   105

part 2
Biological Development

chapter 4

Biological Beginnings   108
Case Study: Birthing the Baby   109
Genetic Foundations of Child Development   110
  Structure of Genes   110
  Operation of Genes   111
  Formation of Reproductive Cells   112
  Genetic Basis of Individual Traits   114
  The Awakening of Genes   118
  The Blending of Heredity and Environment   119
  Acknowledging Nature and Nurture in Children's
    Lives   120
Prenatal Development   121
  Phases of Prenatal Growth   121
  Medical Care   125
  Supporting Parents, Protecting Babies   130
Birth of the Baby   133
  Preparation for Birth   133
  The Birth Process   134
  Medical Interventions   135
  Enhancing Parents' Sensitivity to Newborn
    Infants   138
Summary   141
Applying Concepts in Child Development   141
Case Study: Understanding Adam   141

chapter 5

Physical Development   144
Case Study: The Softball League   145
Principles of Physical Development   146
The Brain and Its Development   149
  Structures and Functions   150
  Developmental Changes in the Brain   152
  Applications of Research on Brain
    Development   155
Physical Development During Childhood   159
  Infancy (Birth–Age 2)   159
  Early Childhood (Ages 2–6)   159
  Middle Childhood (Ages 6–10)   161
  Early Adolescence (Ages 10–14)   162
  Late Adolescence (Ages 14–18)   165
Physical Well-Being   165
  Eating Habits   166
  Physical Activity   171
  Rest and Sleep   174
  Health-Compromising Behaviors   176
Special Physical Needs   182
  Chronic Illness   182
  Serious Injuries and Health Hazards   184
  Physical Disabilities   185
  Promoting Physical Well-Being in All
    Children   185

Summary   187
Applying Concepts in Child Development   187
Case Study: Lucy   187

part 3
Cognitive Development

chapter 6

Cognitive Development:
Piaget and Vygotsky   192
Case Study: Museum Visit   193
Piaget's Theory of Cognitive Development   194
  Key Ideas in Piaget's Theory   195
  Piaget's Stages of Cognitive Development   197
  Current Perspectives Related to Piaget's
    Theory   203
  Key Ideas in Neo-Piagetian Theories   205
  Applying the Ideas of Piaget and His
    Followers   207
Vygotsky's Theory of Cognitive Development   210
  Key Ideas in Vygotsky's Theory   211
  Current Perspectives Related to Vygotsky's
    Theory   215
  Applying the Ideas of Vygotsky and His
    Followers   219
Comparing Piagetian and Vygotskian
  Perspectives   224
  Common Themes   224
  Theoretical Differences   226
Summary   228
Applying Concepts in Child Development   228
Case Study: Adolescent Scientists   228

chapter 7

Cognitive Development:
Cognitive Processes   232
Case Study: How the United States Became a
  Country   233
Basic Cognitive Processes   234
  Key Ideas in Information Processing Theory   234
  Sensation and Perception   236
  Attention   238
  Working Memory and the Central Executive   239
  Long-Term Memory   240
  Thinking and Reasoning   242
  Facilitating Basic Cognitive Processes   243
Metacognition and Cognitive Strategies   245
  Learning Strategies   247
  Problem-Solving Strategies   248
  Metacognitive Awareness   249
  Self-Regulated Learning   251
  Epistemological Beliefs   252
  Cultural Diversity in Metacognition   253

Promoting Metacognitive and Strategic Development 254
Adding a Sociocultural Element to Information Processing Theory 258
  Intersubjectivity 258
  Social Construction of Memory 259
  Collaborative Use of Cognitive Strategies 259
  Enhancing Information Processing Through Social Interaction 260
Children's Construction of Theories 260
  Children's Theories of the Physical World 261
  Facilitating Children's Theory Construction 263
Comparing and Critiquing Contemporary Approaches to Cognitive Development 263
Exceptionalities in Information Processing 266
  Learning Disabilities 266
  Attention-Deficit Hyperactivity Disorder 266
  Working with Children Who Have Information Processing Difficulties 267
Summary 268
Applying Concepts in Child Development 269
Case Study: The Library Project 269

chapter 8

Intelligence 272
  Case Study: Gina 273
  Defining Intelligence 273
  Theoretical Perspectives of Intelligence 274
    Spearman's g 274
    Cattell-Horn-Carroll Theory of Cognitive Abilities 275
    Gardner's Multiple Intelligences 277
    Sternberg's Triarchic Theory 278
    Distributed Intelligence 279
  Measuring Intelligence 280
    Tests of General Intelligence 280
    Specific Ability Tests 285
    Dynamic Assessment 286
    Assessing the Abilities of Infants and Young Children 286
  Effects of Heredity and Environment on Intelligence 288
    Evidence for Hereditary Influences 288
    Evidence for Environmental Influences 290
    How Nature and Nurture Interact in Their Influence on Intelligence 292
  Developmental Trends in IQ Scores 293
  Group Differences in Intelligence 295
    Gender Differences 295
    Socioeconomic Differences 296
    Ethnic and Racial Differences 297
  Critique of Current Perspectives on Intelligence 298
  Implications of Theories and Research on Intelligence 300
  Exceptionalities in Intelligence 303
    Children Who Are Gifted 303
    Children with Intellectual Disabilities 305

Summary 308
Applying Concepts in Child Development 309
Case Study: Fresh Vegetables 309

chapter 9

Language Development 312
  Case Study: Mario 313
  Theoretical Perspectives of Language Development 314
    Early Theories: Modeling and Reinforcement 314
    Nativism 315
    Information Processing Theory 316
    Sociocultural Theory 317
    Functionalism 317
    Critiquing Theories of Language Development 318
  Trends in Language Development 320
    Semantic Development 321
    Syntactic Development 324
    Development of Listening Skills 328
    Development of Speaking Skills 331
    Development of Pragmatics 336
    Development of Metalinguistic Awareness 339
  Development of a Second Language 342
    The Timing of Second-Language Learning 342
    Bilingualism 343
    Teaching a Second Language 344
  Diversity in Language Development 346
    Gender Differences 346
    Socioeconomic Differences 346
    Ethnic Differences 346
  Exceptionalities in Language Development 347
    Specific Language Impairments 347
    Sensory Impairments and Language Development 349
  Summary 350
  Applying Concepts in Child Development 351
  Case Study: Boarding School 351

chapter 10

Development in the Academic Domains 354
  Case Study: Phyllis and Benjamin Jones 355
  Reading Development 356
    Emergent Literacy 356
    Letter Recognition and Phonological Awareness 357
    Word Recognition 358
    Reading Comprehension 359
    Metacognition in Reading 360
    Diversity in Reading Development 361
    Promoting Reading Development 364
  Writing Development 367
    Handwriting 368
    Spelling 368
    Syntax and Grammar 369
    Composition Skills 369
    Metacognition in Writing 370

Diversity in Writing Development 370
Promoting Writing Development 372
Mathematics Development 373
Number Sense and Counting 373
Mathematical Concepts and Principles 374
Basic Arithmetic Operations 374
More Advanced Problem-Solving Procedures 378
Metacognition in Mathematics 378
Diversity in Mathematics Development 379
Promoting Development in Mathematics 382
Science Development 383
Children's Theories About the Biological and Physical Worlds 383
Scientific Reasoning Skills 384
Metacognition in Science 385
Diversity in Science Development 385
Promoting Development in Science 387
Development in Other Academic Domains 389
History 389
Geography 390
Art 391
Music 393
Using Content Area Standards to Guide Instruction 394
Summary 398
Applying Concepts in Child Development 399
Case Study: Beating the Odds 399

part 4
Social and Emotional Development

chapter 11
Emotional Development 402

Case Study: Merv 403
Erikson's Theory of Psychosocial Development 404
Lessons Learned from Life's Challenges 404
Contemporary Perspectives on Erikson's Theory 406
Attachment 407
Developmental Course of Children's Attachments 408
Individual Differences in Children's Attachments 410
Origins of Attachment Security 411
Multiple Attachments 414
Attachment Security and Later Development 415
Implications of Attachment Research 416
Emotion 419
Developmental Changes in Emotions 419
Group Differences in Emotions 423
Promoting Children's Emotional Development 425
Temperament and Personality 428
Elements of Temperament and Personality 428
Helping Children Be Themselves 431

Supporting Children and Adolescents with Emotional and Behavioral Problems 435
Common Emotional and Behavioral Disorders 435
Supporting Youngsters with Emotional and Behavioral Problems 437
Summary 438
Applying Concepts in Child Development 439
Case Study: The Girly Shirt 439

chapter 12
Development of Self and Social Understandings 442

Case Study: Felita 443
Sense of Self 444
Effects of Children's Sense of Self 445
Factors Influencing Sense of Self 446
General Trends in Children's Sense of Self 447
Changes in the Self over Childhood and Adolescence 449
Diversity in Sense of Self 454
Enhancing Children's Sense of Self 462
Social Cognition 466
Understanding What Others Think 466
Factors Promoting Social Understandings 469
Diversity in Social Cognition 472
Fostering the Development of Social Cognition 474
Summary 475
Applying Concepts in Child Development 476
Case Study: Joachín's Dilemma 476

chapter 13
Development of Motivation and Self-Regulation 480

Case Study: Making Kites 481
Extrinsic and Intrinsic Motivation 482
Factors Affecting Extrinsic Motivation 482
Factors Affecting Intrinsic Motivation 483
Development of Goals 487
Achievement Goals 488
Social Goals 489
Future Aspirations 490
Coordinating Multiple Goals 490
Development of Attributions 491
Origins of Attributions 493
Diversity in Motivation 495
Gender Differences 495
Cultural and Ethnic Differences 496
Motivating Children and Adolescents 498
Self-Regulation 503
Developmental Trends in Self-Regulation 504
Conditions That Foster Self-Regulation 506
Diversity in Self-Regulation 507
Promoting Self-Regulation 508
Summary 512
Applying Concepts in Child Development 513
Case Study: Derrika 513

chapter 14

Development of Morality and Interpersonal Behaviors   516

Case Study: Changing the World, One City at a Time   517

Moral Reasoning and Behavior   518

Kohlberg's Theory of Moral Development   518

Developmental Trends in Morality   521

Factors Affecting Moral Development   524

Diversity in Moral Development   525

Promoting Moral Development   528

Interpersonal Behaviors   530

Interpersonal Behaviors at Different Ages   530

Development of Prosocial Behavior and Aggression   534

Diversity in Interpersonal Behaviors   539

Creating a Safe School Environment   545

Summary   548

Applying Concepts in Child Development   548

Case Study: Gang Mediation   548

chapter 15

Peers, Schools, and Society   552

Case Study: Sharing at the Zoo   553

Peers   554

Functions of Peer Relationships   554

Peer Acceptance   555

Friendships   556

Social Groups   561

Romance and Sexuality   564

Schools   571

The School as a Community   571

Socialization in Schools   573

Transitions to New Schools   575

Society   577

Services for Children and Adolescents   578

Television and the Interactive Technologies   581

Summary   586

Applying Concepts in Child Development   586

Case Study: Aaron and Cole   586

appendix A

Analyses of the Ending Case Studies   A-1

appendix B

Analyses of Ending Artifacts   B-1

Glossary   G-1

References   R-1

Name Index   N-1

Subject Index   S-1

Photo Credits   P-1

Special Features

The Only Comprehensive Development Text Written Specifically for Educators

Development and Practice

Engaging in Developmentally Appropriate Practice with Infants, Children, and Adolescents   26
Getting a Flavor for Conducting Research as a Teacher   57
Making Schools Family Friendly   91
Accommodating Children from Culturally and Linguistically Diverse Backgrounds   96
Showing Sensitivity to the Needs of Newborn Infants   138
Accommodating the Physical Needs of Infants and Children   163
Accommodating the Physical Needs of Adolescents   165
Facilitating Discovery Learning   208
Scaffolding Children's Efforts at Challenging Tasks   222
Providing Appropriate Stimulation for Infants   244
Getting and Keeping Children's Attention   245
Addressing the Unique Needs of Gifted Children and Adolescents   306
Maximizing the Development of Children and Adolescents with Intellectual Disabilities   307
Promoting Listening Skills in Young Children   331
Working with English Language Learners   345
Working with Children Who Have Specific Language Impairments   348
Working with Children Who Have Hearing Impairments   350
Promoting Phonological Awareness and Letter Recognition in Young Children   359
Promoting Effective Reading Comprehension Strategies   361
Offering Warm and Sensitive Care to Infants and Toddlers   417
Encouraging Social Perspective Taking   474
Helping Children Meet Their Social Goals   501
Encouraging and Supporting Students at Risk   504
Teaching Self-Regulation Skills   512
Teaching Social Skills   544
Easing School Transitions   577
Enhancing Students' Before- and After-School Experiences   581

Observation Guidelines

Learning from Children and Adolescents   51
Identifying Family Conditions   84–85
Identifying Cultural Practices and Beliefs   98
Indicators of Health in Newborn Infants   140
Assessing Physical Development in Infancy   160
Assessing Health Behaviors of Children and Adolescents   181
Assessing Cognitive Advancements in Infants and Toddlers   200
Assessing Piagetian Reasoning Processes in Children and Adolescents   209
Observing the Cognitive Aspects of Young Children's Play   223
Assessing Cognitive Processing and Metacognition   265
Seeing Intelligence in Children's Daily Behavior   302
Identifying Cultural Differences in Sociolinguistic Conventions   337
Assessing Emergent Literacy in Young Children   358
Assessing Young Children's Attachment Security   412
Assessing the Emotions of Children and Adolescents   420–421
Noticing Temperament in Infants and Toddlers   429–430
Observing Indicators of Children's Self-Perceptions   460–461
Recognizing Intrinsic Motivation in Children's Behaviors   488
Observing the Social Aspects of Young Children's Play   531
Assessing Children's Prosocial Development   537
Noticing Children's Level of Peer Acceptance   557

The Difference Between Reading About Development and Seeing It In Diverse Contexts

Case Studies

Tonya   3–4
Latisha   29
Jack's Research   33
The Study Skills Class   59
Cedric and Barbara Jennings   63–64
Four-Year-Old Sons   105
Birthing the Baby   109–110
Understanding Adam   141–142
The Softball League   145
Lucy   187–188
Museum Visit   193
Adolescent Scientists   228–229
How the United States Became a Country   233
The Library Project   269
Gina   273
Fresh Vegetables   309
Mario   313
Boarding School   351

Phyllis and Benjamin Jones   355
Beating the Odds   399
Merv   403–404
The Girly Shirt   439
Felita   443–444
Joachin's Dilemma   476
Making Kites   481
Derrika   513
Changing the World, One City at a Time   517–518
Gang Mediation   548–549
Sharing at the Zoo   553–554
Aaron and Cole   586–587

Developmental Trends

Accomplishments and Diversity at Different Age Levels   24–25
The Family's Concerns for Children of Different Ages   87–88
Prenatal Development   132
Physical Development at Different Age Levels   167–168
Chronic Health Conditions in Children and Adolescents   183–184
Thinking and Reasoning Skills at Different Age Levels   225
Basic Information Processing Characteristics at Different Age Levels   246
Cognitive Strategies and Metacognitive Understandings at Different Age Levels   255–256
Intelligence at Different Age Levels   294
Language Skills at Different Age Levels   340–341
Reading at Different Age Levels   362–363
Writing at Different Age Levels   371
Mathematics at Different Age Levels   379–380
Science at Different Age Levels   386
Emotional and Personal Development at Different Age Levels   433
Sense of Self at Different Age Levels   463
Social Cognition at Different Age Levels   470
Motivation at Different Age Levels   498
Moral Reasoning and Behavior at Different Age Levels   523
Interpersonal Skills at Different Age Levels   542–543
Peer Relationships at Different Age Levels   570–571

Interpreting Children's Artifacts and Reflections

James's Changes, Big and Small   30
I Went to Davis's House   60
In My Neighborhood   105–106
My Baby is Real!   129
Horses by Nadia   142
I Can See Clearly Now, My Brain is Connected   154
How Many Can I Do Today?   173
MyPyramid Worksheet by Alex   188
Fish in a Boat   230
Pumpkin and Bat   267
Interview with Aletha   270
Sunflower   301
Solar System   303–304

Jermaine's Life   309–310
Figure of Speech   351
Pseudowriting Samples   368
Arithmetic Errors   375
The Pet Who Came to Dinner   400
I Love Mommy   409
Paint Me Like I Am   439–440
Comparing Self-Descriptions   448
Hermit Crab   453
Two Histories   477
Tears of Pearls   513–514
Remembering 9/11 549
This Is Who I Am   567
Teachers at Work   587–588

Basic Developmental Issues

Illustrations in the Three Domains   11
Considering Family, Culture, and Community   67
Biological Beginnings   125
Physical Development   176
Contrasting Piaget and Vygotsky   227
Contrasting Contemporary Theories of Cognitive Development   264
Contrasting Theories of Intelligence   281
Contrasting Contemporary Theories of Language Development   319
Developmental Progressions in the Academic Domains   395–396
Attachment and Emotional Development   427
Comparing Sense of Self and Social Cognition   471
Contrasting Extrinsic and Intrinsic Motivation   494
Comparing Prosocial Behavior and Aggression   540
Social Contexts of Child Development   585

New Innovative Learning Technology

Activities and Applications exercises referenced on pages 16, 30, 56, 60, 97, 106, 136, 142, 143, 169, 188, 205, 230, 252, 270, 300, 310, 345, 351, 352, 389, 400, 415, 440, 457, 477, 492, 514, 536, 549, 550, 576, 587, and 588.
Building Teaching Skills and Dispositions exercises referenced on pages 26, 56, 69, 120, 171, 217, 249, 250, 301, 344, 364, 423, 474, 497, 511, 546, and 561.
Video Examples referenced on pages 20, 21, 22, 23, 36, 37, 38, 39, 42, 65, 66, 112, 115, 118, 135, 136, 139, 146, 148, 154, 155, 159, 161, 169, 172, 174, 182, 195, 196, 198, 201, 202, 203, 204, 207, 208, 214, 217, 223, 228, 236, 238, 243, 248, 256, 257, 258, 285, 287, 304, 320, 321, 330, 332, 333, 334, 336, 338, 344, 345, 350, 357, 361, 365, 366, 367, 372, 378, 385, 409, 410, 414, 423, 445, 448, 454, 468, 484, 485, 490, 505, 519, 521, 531, 532, 538, 539, 572, 579, and 583.

Child Development and Education

Making a Difference in the Lives of Children and Adolescents

When Mary Renck Jalongo thinks back to her years as a novice teacher, one student often comes to mind:

Not only was she big for her age, she was older than anyone else in my first-grade class because she had been retained in kindergarten. Her name was Tonya and she put my patience, my professionalism, and my decision making on trial throughout my second year of teaching. Tonya would boss and bully the other children, pilfer items from their desks, or talk them into uneven "trades."

Matters worsened when I received a . . . note from a parent. It read, "This is the fourth time that Tommy's snack cake has been taken from his lunch. What are you going to do about it?"

What I did was to launch an investigation. First, I asked if anyone else was missing items from lunchboxes and discovered that many other children had been affected. Next, I tried to get someone to confess—not in the way that *my* teachers had done it, by sitting in the room until the guilty party or an informant cracked, but simply by asking the perpetrator to leave a note in my classroom mailbox. My classroom was antiquated, but it included an enclosed hallway, now equipped with coat racks and shelves that led to a restroom. Apparently, while I was preoccupied teaching my lessons, a child was stealing food. Three days later, several other children reported that they had seen Tonya "messing around people's lunchboxes." I asked her, but she denied it. At recess, I looked in her desk and found it littered with empty food wrappers. Then Tonya and I discussed it again in private and examined the evidence.

I consulted my principal about what to do. He suggested that I punish her severely; a month without recess seemed warranted, he said. I thought it might be better to call her mother, but they had no telephone and the principal assured me that, based on her failure to attend previous school functions, Tonya's mother would not come to school. Then I said I would write a note and set up a home visit. He strongly advised against that, telling me that Tonya's mother had a disease, that the house was a mess, and that she had a live-in boyfriend.

All these things were true, but I understand them differently now. Tonya's mother had lupus and was at a debilitating stage of the disease that prevented her from working, much less maintaining a spotless home. Tonya's family now consisted of mother, unofficial stepfather (also permanently disabled), and a three-year-old brother. They lived on a fixed income, and Tonya qualified for free lunches.

As a first-year teacher [at this school], I was reluctant to go against the principal's wishes, but I did draw the line at harsh punishment. When I asked Tonya *why* she took things from the other children's lunches, she simply said, "'Cause I was hungry." I asked her if she ate breakfast in the morning, and she said, "No. I have to take care of my little brother before I go to school." I asked her if having breakfast might solve the problem and she said, "Yes. My aunt would help." And so, my first big teaching problem was solved by an eight-year-old when instead of foraging for food each morning, Tonya and her brother walked down the block to her unmarried aunt's house before school and ate breakfast.

There was still the matter of repairing Tonya's damaged reputation with the other children, who had accumulated a variety of negative experiences with her and had labeled her as a thief. I stood with my arms around Tonya's shoulder in front of the class and announced that Tonya had agreed not to take things anymore, that she could be trusted, and that all was well.

Two weeks later, a child's candy bar was reported missing, and the class was quick to accuse Tonya. I took her aside and inquired about the missing candy bar. "No," she said firmly, "I didn't eat it." As I defended Tonya's innocence to her peers, I noticed how Tonya, the child who had learned to slouch to conceal her size, sat up tall and proud in her seat.

I must confess that I was wondering if Tonya might be lying when Kendra, the child who reported the stolen candy bar, said she was ill and wanted to go home. Then, with a candor only possible in a young child, Kendra said, "I have a stomachache, and you want

Case Study:
Tonya

Outline:

Case Study: Tonya

The Field of Child Development

Basic Issues in Development

Theories of Child Development

Developmental Periods

From Theory to Practice

Summary

Applying Concepts in Child Development

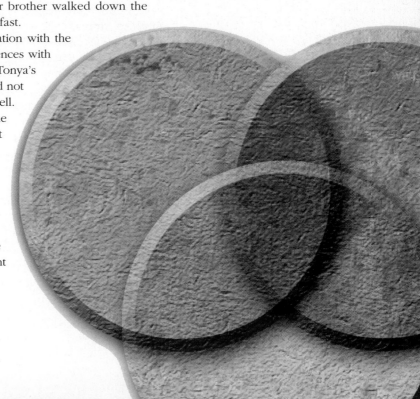

to know why? Because I just remembered that *I* ate my candy bar on the bus this morning." (Jalongo, Isenberg, & Gerbracht, 1995, pp. 114–116)[a]

- What kind of impact did Mary Jalongo have on Tonya's life?

- How did Mary draw on her understanding of child development as she worked with Tonya?

[a]From *Teachers' Stories: From Personal Narrative to Professional Insight* (pp. 114–116), by M. R. Jalongo, J. P. Isenberg, & G. Gerbracht, 1995, San Francisco: Jossey-Bass. Copyright © 1995 by Jossey-Bass, Inc. Reprinted with permission of John Wiley & Sons, Inc.

Mary Jalongo made a difference in Tonya's life. By drawing on her knowledge of child development, Mary was able to understand that Tonya could grow and change if given sensitive, loving care and age-appropriate instruction. By encouraging Tonya and her brother to eat breakfast with their aunt, Mary helped meet Tonya's physical needs and paved the way for closer ties to extended family. By repairing Tonya's damaged reputation with the other children, Mary helped Tonya earn their acceptance. Feeling comfortable physically and secure emotionally, Tonya was better prepared to tackle academic challenges and develop a healthy sense of who she was and how she fit into the world around her. Thanks, in part, to Mary Jalongo's thoughtful intercession, Tonya would ultimately thrive.[1]

The Field of Child Development

The study of human development helps us understand how human beings change from the time of conception, through maturation into adulthood, and on into old age and death. This book covers the early part of the human journey—beginning at conception and including prenatal growth, birth, infancy, childhood, and adolescence. The field of **child development** seeks to identify and explain persistent, cumulative, and progressive changes in the physical, cognitive, and social-emotional development of children and adolescents.

As you will learn throughout this book, a child's developmental journey is guided by three factors:

- *Nature*—the genetic inheritance affecting the child's growth
- *Nurture*—the influence of the environment in which the child lives
- *The child's own activity*—the child's choices, mental processes, emotional responses, and behaviors

As you will also discover in your reading, development includes changes that are common to most children and adolescents as well as those that are specific to particular individuals. At times, we will talk about changes that nearly everyone undergoes, such as acquiring complex language skills and developing consideration for other people's feelings. At other times, we will discuss changes that differ considerably among youngsters. For example, over time, some children spontaneously develop effective study skills, but others do not unless they have explicit instruction in such strategies.

To describe the many factors that contribute to children's growth, scholars of child development draw from many academic disciplines. In this book, our descriptions of children's development draw on research primarily in psychology but also in biology, sociology, anthropology, and the applied fields of early intervention, education, child and family studies, juvenile justice, counseling, social work, and medicine. We emphasize research that is relevant to children's education and experiences in schools.

Our primary goal in this book is to help you support healthy, optimal development in children and adolescents. We pursue this goal by focusing on two specific objectives. First, we want you to learn how children and adolescents think, feel, and act at various ages. This information can help you understand the individual children and adolescents with whom you work. Second, we want you to be able to apply what you learn in your classroom, school, and community. You can use practical ideas from the field of child development in your instruction, classroom routines, and ongoing relationships with children and adolescents.

child development
Study of the persistent, cumulative, and progressive changes in the physical, cognitive, and social-emotional development of children and adolescents.

[1]Tonya blossomed into a healthy, well-adjusted young woman, developing a talent in music, joining a choir, graduating from high school, and raising a loving family of her own (M. R. Jalongo, personal communication, June 12, 2007).

Three Developmental Domains

The study of child development is organized into three domains, or broad areas of study: physical development, cognitive development, and social-emotional development. **Physical development** is concerned with the biological changes of the body and the brain. It includes genetics, a fetus's growth in the mother's womb, the birth process, brain development, and the acquisition of such motor skills as throwing a ball and using scissors. It also encompasses behaviors that promote and impede health and environmental factors that influence physical growth. **Cognitive development** refers to the changes that occur in children's reasoning, concepts, memory, and language—changes that are cultivated by children's experiences in families, schools, and communities. **Social-emotional development** includes changes in emotions, self-concept, motivation, social relationships, and moral reasoning and behavior—advancements that depend in large part on children's interactions with other people.

Although the three domains may appear to be independent areas, they are in fact closely interrelated. For example, an increase in the ability to look at situations from multiple perspectives (a cognitive ability) enhances social skills. Thus, in their everyday work with children, educators often address more than one domain at a time. For instance, an elementary teacher might follow a period of quiet reading with a physically active social studies lesson, and a high school chemistry teacher could raise questions about both scientific matters and moral issues when discussing an industry's release of toxins into the community's groundwater.

Effects of Context on Development

All areas of development depend on the **context** of children's lives—children's experiences in families, schools, neighborhoods, community organizations, cultural and ethnic groups, and society at large. Child development research has shown, for example, that some sort of "family" or other cluster of close, caring relationships is a critical condition for optimal development. Schools, too, play a significant role in development, not only by fostering cognitive skills but also by communicating messages about children's abilities and worth and by providing an arena in which children can practice social skills.

In preparing to teach or in some other way care for children, you are about to become a vital part of the developmental context of young people. Your role in that context will be strengthened by a thorough foundation in child development. As you can see in Figure 1-1, this book provides such a foundation in its coverage of the three areas of development (physical, cognitive, and social-emotional domains), the contexts in which children and adolescents grow, and the research methods that reveal youngsters' developmental journeys.

Basic Issues in Development

In their attempts to explain the changes that take place during childhood, child development theorists have grappled with, but not yet resolved, three key issues. First, they wonder how strongly heredity and environment influence development. Second, they speculate about the developmental paths that are true for everyone or, conversely, unique to individuals. Third, they debate about the developmental changes that can be characterized as major transformations or, alternatively, as a series of gradual trends. Let's now look more closely at these three issues, which are referred to as questions of (a) nature and nurture, (b) universality and diversity, and (c) qualitative and quantitative change.

Nature and Nurture

In the study of development, **nature** refers to the inherited (genetic) characteristics and tendencies that influence development. **Nurture** consists of the environmental conditions that influence development. Nature and nurture are necessary partners in a child's development.

Nature creates both common human traits and individual differences among children. Some inherited characteristics appear in virtually everyone. For instance, almost all children have the capacity to learn to walk, understand language, imitate others, use simple tools, and draw inferences about how other people view the world. Other inherited characteristics vary

physical development
Systematic changes of the body and brain and age-related changes in motor skills and health behaviors.

cognitive development
Systematic changes in reasoning, concepts, memory, and language.

social-emotional development
Systematic changes in emotions, self-concept, motivation, social relationships, and moral reasoning and behavior.

context
The broad social environments, including family, schools, neighborhoods, community organizations, culture, ethnicity, and society at large, that influence children's development.

nature
Inherited characteristics and tendencies that affect development.

nurture
Environmental conditions that affect development.

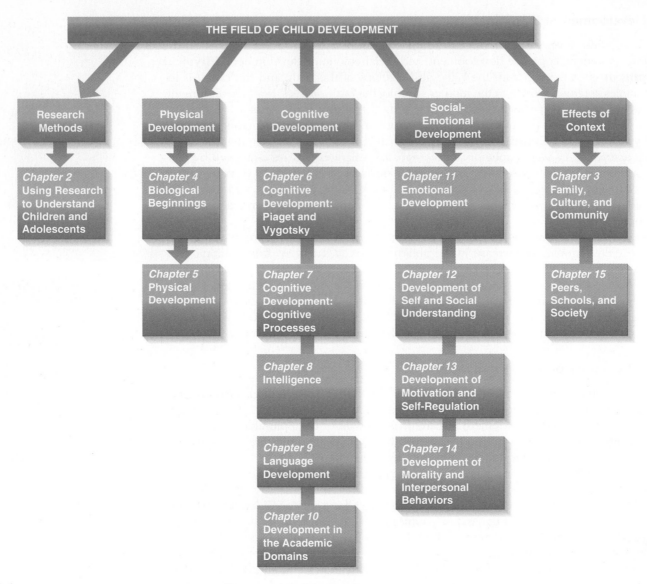

Figure 1-1

Overview of the book.

among people. Children's stature, eye color, and facial appearance are largely determined by heredity. Children's **temperaments**—their characteristic ways of responding to emotional events, novel stimuli, and their own impulses—seems to be affected by their individual genetic makeup (Rothbart & Bates, 2006). Similarly, being slow or quick to learn from instruction and everyday experiences has some genetic basis (Petrill et al., 2004).

Heredity is powerful, but it has limits. The effects of heredity depend very much on the child's developmental level, health, activity, and exposure to environmental substances. Whereas some hereditary instructions, such as the chromosomes that determine sex, exert an influence from the beginning, other instructions emerge only gradually through the process of **maturation,** the genetically guided changes that occur over the course of development. For example, genetic instructions for new motor abilities come into play only after the child gains experience and acquires an increasingly complex brain.

Children's experiences in the environment affect all aspects of their being, from the health of their bodies to the curiosity of their minds. *Nurture* affects children's development through multiple channels: physically through nutrition, activities, and stress; intellectually through informal experiences and formal instruction; and socially through adult role models and peer relationships. With good environmental support, children thrive. However, nurture faces limits, too. Even the best environments cannot overpower every possible defective gene. And, unfor-

temperament
A child's characteristic ways of responding to emotional events, novel stimuli, and personal impulses.

maturation
Genetically guided changes that occur over the course of development.

tunately, the conditions of nurture are *not* always *nurturing*. For example, children who grow up in an abusive family must rely on people outside the family for stable, affectionate care.

Historically, many theorists saw nature and nurture as separate and rival factors. Some theorists believed that biological factors are ultimately responsible for growth. Other theorists assumed that children become whatever the environment shapes them to be. In recent decades, developmental theorists have come to realize that nature and nurture are both important and that they intermesh dynamically in the lives of children. Consider the following principles of how nature and nurture exert separate and combined effects:

Expert coaching (nurture) can enhance children's inherited abilities (nature).

- ***The relative effects of heredity and environment vary for different areas of development.*** Some abilities are strongly influenced by genetically controlled systems in the brain. For example, the abilities to distinguish among various speech sounds and grammatical structures develop without formal training under a wide range of environmental conditions (Gallistel, Brown, Carey, Gelman, & Keil, 1991; R. A. Hayes & Slater, in press; Marean, Werner, & Kuhl, 1992; Soderstrom, Kemler Nelson, & Jusczyk, 2005). In contrast, abilities in traditional school subject areas (e.g., reading, geography) and advanced artistic and physical skills (e.g., playing the piano, playing competitive soccer) rely heavily on instruction and practice (Bruer, 1999; Ericsson, 2003; Schraw, 2006).

- ***Inherited tendencies make individual children more or less responsive to particular environmental influences.*** Because of their genetic makeup, some children are easily affected by certain conditions in the environment, whereas others are less affected (Rutter, 1997). For example, children who are, by nature, inhibited may be quite shy around other people if they have few social contacts. However, if their parents and teachers encourage them to make friends, expect them to act in age-appropriate ways, or enroll them in child care where they are exposed to unfamiliar peers, otherwise shy children may become more socially outgoing (Arcus, 1991; Kagan & Fox, 2006). In contrast, children who have more extroverted temperaments may be sociable regardless of the environment in which they grow up: They will persistently seek out peers with whom they can talk, laugh, and play.

- ***The environmental context may play a greater role in development when conditions are extreme rather than moderate.*** When youngsters have experiences typical for their culture and age-group, heredity often plays a strong role in their individual characteristics. Thus, when children grow up with adequate nutrition, a warm and stable home environment, and appropriate educational experiences, heredity affects how quickly and thoroughly they acquire new skills. But when they have experiences that are quite unusual—for instance, when they experience extreme deprivation—the influence of environment outweighs that of heredity (D. C. Rowe, Almeida, & Jacobson, 1999). For example, when children grow up deprived of adequate nutrition and stimulation, they may fail to develop advanced intellectual skills, even though they had the potential for such development when they were born (Plomin & Petrill, 1997; D. C. Rowe, Jacobson, & Van den Oord, 1999).

- ***Timing of environmental exposure matters.*** When children are changing rapidly in any area, they are especially prone to influence by the environment. For example, early in a mother's pregnancy, her use of certain drugs may damage her future offspring's quickly growing organs and limbs. Just prior to birth, exposure to the same drugs may adversely affect the baby's brain, which at that point is forming neurological connections that will permit survival and the ability to learn in the outside world.

In a few cases environmental stimulation *must* occur during a particular period for an emerging ability to become functional (Blakemore, 1976; Hubel & Wiesel, 1965). In such cases there is a *critical period* for stimulation. For example, at birth, certain areas of the brain are tentatively reserved for processing visual patterns—lines, shapes, contours, depth, and so forth. In virtually all cases, infants do encounter adequate stimulation to preserve these brain circuits. However, when cataracts are present at birth and not removed for a few years, a child's vision is obstructed, and areas of the brain that otherwise would be devoted to vision lose some of this capacity (Bruer, 1999).

In many and probably most other developmental areas, however, children may be most receptive to a certain type of stimulation at one point in their lives but be able to benefit from it to some degree later as well. Many theorists use the term **sensitive period** when referring

sensitive period
A period in development when certain environmental experiences have a more pronounced influence than is true at other times.

to such a long time frame of heightened sensitivity to particular environmental experiences. During early childhood, children are naturally predisposed to tune in to the sounds, structure, and meaning of language, suggesting a sensitive period for learning language. Sensitive periods appear to be more common than critical periods, reflecting nature's fortunate practice of giving children many extended chances to learn important skills. Educators frequently work with children who are delayed in literacy and other academic competencies, and in such situations educators can realistically expect to make meaningful progress if they address missing experiences, monitor children's progress, and communicate their expectations for children's success.

• *Children's natural tendencies affect their environment.* In addition to being affected by nature and nurture, children's growth is influenced by their own behaviors. Youngsters make many choices, seek out information and, over time, refine their knowledge and beliefs (Flavell, 1994; Piaget, 1985). For example, children often request information ("What *cooperate* mean, Mommy?") and experiences ("Uncle Kevin, can I play on your computer?"). Children even help create environments that intensify their genetic tendencies. For example, children with irritable dispositions might pick fights, creating a more aggressive climate in which to grow.

As children get older, they become increasingly able to seek stimulation that suits their tendencies. For example, imagine that Marissa has an inherited talent for verbal skills, such as acquiring new vocabulary words and comprehending stories. As a young child, Marissa depends on her parents to read to her. As she grows older, Marissa chooses her own books and begins to read to herself. Marissa's experience would suggest that genetic tendencies become more powerful as children grow older—an expectation that is in fact consistent with genetic research (Plomin & Spinath, 2004; Scarr & McCartney, 1983).

Universality and Diversity

Developmental changes that occur in just about everyone are said to reflect a certain degree of **universality.** For instance, unless physical disabilities are present, all young children learn to sit, walk, and run, almost invariably in that order. Other developmental changes are highly individual, reflecting **diversity.** As an illustration, the first words of some children are social gestures such as "bye-bye," and only later do these children add words for objects and actions. Other children initially learn words for objects and physical properties and later add social expressions.

Theorists differ in their beliefs regarding the extent to which developmental accomplishments are universal among all human beings or unique to particular individuals. Some propose that maturation and shared genes create universality in development (e.g., Gesell, 1928). They point out that despite widely varying environments, virtually all human beings acquire fundamental motor skills, proficiency in language, the ability to inhibit immediate impulses, and so on. Certain consistencies in children's environments provide an additional route to universality. In all corners of the world, children observe that objects always fall down rather than up and that people often get angry when someone intentionally hurts them.

Yet other theorists have been impressed by diversity in child development. Many of these theorists view the environment (nurture) as weighing heavily in how we develop. They propose that factors as global as the historical period of one's upbringing and as personal as one's family relationships help to shape development (Baltes, Lindenberger, & Staudinger, 2006). Some of these theorists also see *culture* as a significant source of diversity: Children differ in the competencies they acquire based on the particular tools, communication systems, and values that they regularly encounter (Rogoff, 2003; Wertsch & Tulviste, 1994).

Earlier we mentioned that the relative influences of nature and nurture vary from one area of development to another. The same is true for universality and diversity. For instance, development tends to be more universal in some aspects of physical development, such as the sequences in which puberty unfolds. In other areas, such as in many aspects of cognitive and social-emotional development, diversity tends to be more prevalent. Yet there is always *some* diversity, even in physical development. Obviously, children vary in height, weight, and skin color, and some are born with physical disabilities or become injured.

Although some developmental states are universal, others (e.g., tastes in clothing and music) reflect diversity in children's talents, temperaments, and experiences. Art by Ricco, age 13.

universality
In a particular aspect of human development, the commonalities seen in the way virtually all individuals progress.

diversity
In a particular aspect of human development, the varied ways in which individuals progress.

Throughout the book you will find instances of developmental universality, but just as often, you will see divergence among developmental pathways.

Qualitative and Quantitative Change

Sometimes development reflects dramatic changes in the essence or under- lying structure of a characteristic. Such major reorganizations are called **qualitative changes.** For instance, when children learn to run, they pro- pel their bodies forward in a way that is distinctly different from walking— they are not simply moving faster. When they begin to talk in two-word sentences rather than with single words, they are, for the first time, using rudimentary forms of grammar. But not all development involves dramatic change. In fact, development frequently occurs as a gradual progression, or *trend,* with many small additions and modifications to behaviors and thought processes. These progressions are called **quantitative changes.** For ex- ample, children grow taller gradually over time, and with both age and ex- perience they slowly learn about such diverse realms as the animal kingdom and society's rules for showing courtesy.

Teachers need to keep in mind not only typical age trends but also diversity in children's abilities and developmental progress.

Stage theories.   Theorists who emphasize qualitative changes often use the term **stage** to refer to a period of development characterized by a particular way of behaving or thinking. According to a **stage theory** of development, individuals progress through a series of stages that are qualitatively different from one another.[2]

Most stage theories are *hierarchical.* In other words, each stage is seen as providing the essential foundation for stages that follow. For example, after observing children in a wide variety of logical tasks and thought-provoking situations, psychologist Jean Piaget proposed a stage theory to describe the development of logical thinking and reasoning. His observa- tions led him to conclude that as infants, children interact with the world primarily through trial-and-error behavior. As children mature, they begin to represent, symbolically "manipu- late," and make mental predictions about objects and actions in the world around them. They know, for example, that a rubber ball will bounce when they drop it on a wooden floor. Later they begin to derive logical deductions about concrete, real-world objects and situations. And once they reach adolescence, they become capable of thinking systematically about abstract ideas—for instance, by thinking about the unseen physical factors (e.g., *momentum, gravity*) influencing a ball's bounce.

Another eminent stage theorist, Erik Erikson, focused on a set of primary developmen- tal tasks that individuals face at different points in their lives. During their infancy and early childhood years, youngsters learn first to trust others and then to act self-sufficiently. In their adolescent and adult years, people form *identities* that define who they are and later form intimate relationships with others. In Erikson's theory, stages are "soft": People do not fully replace earlier developments with new modes of thinking (Kohlberg, Levine, & Hewer, 1983). Instead, earlier struggles persist—and sometimes intrude—into new challenges. For exam- ple, a young adult who has failed to develop a clear identity may enter romantic relation- ships with considerable confusion (J. Kroger, 2003).

Many stage theories assume *universal* progressions: All children are thought to go through the same sequence of changes, although the ages at which individual children pass through each stage vary according to the environment. Piaget was a strong believer in uni- versal progressions in children's thinking. In contrast, Erikson believed that people deal with and resolve the social-emotional dilemmas in their lives in distinctly individual ways.

Over the years, developmental psychologists have offered a variety of stage theories to ex- plain children's development. However, research does not entirely support the idea that young people proceed through one stage at a time or that they always move in the same direction

qualitative change
Relatively dramatic developmental change that reflects considerable reorganization or modification of functioning.

quantitative change
Developmental change that involves a series of minor, trendlike modifications.

stage
A period of development characterized by a qualitatively distinct way of behaving or thinking.

stage theory
Theory that describes development as involving a series of qualitatively distinct changes.

[2]Note that developmentalists use the term *stage* in a somewhat narrower way than other people use it in everyday speech. Parents and caregivers often make comments like "He's at the terrible twos stage." Such comments reflect the idea that children are behaving typically for their age-group. When developmental scholars say a child is in a certain stage, they generally are assuming that the child is undergoing a series of age-related qualitative transformations.

(e.g., Ceci & Roazzi, 1994; K. W. Fischer & Bidell, 2006; Kurtines & Gewirtz, 1991; Metz, 1995). For example, a 9-year-old girl may show an advanced ability to plan ahead while playing chess (her hobby), but may have difficulty planning ahead while writing a complex essay (an unfamiliar activity). Nor do stage progressions always appear to be universal across cultures and educational contexts (e.g., Glick, 1975; S.-C. Li, 2007; J. G. Miller, 2007). For example, youngsters raised in vastly different cultures often learn to think in significantly different ways (Rogoff, 2003). Given these and other research findings, few contemporary developmental theorists support strict versions of stage theories (Parke, Ornstein, Rieser, & Zahn-Waxler, 1994).

Many theorists now believe that qualitative changes do exist—not as inevitable, universal, and hierarchical patterns, but rather as dynamic states of thinking and acting that evolve as children mature and try new things. It is obvious, for example, that the actions of adolescents differ from those of 2-year-old children. Fifteen-year-olds are not simply taller and more knowledgeable about the world; they go about their day-to-day living in qualitatively different ways. Maturation-based developments, such as the brain's increases in memory capacity, plus ever-expanding knowledge and experience, permit both gradual and occasionally dramatic changes in thinking and behaving (Case & Okamoto, 1996; Flavell, 1994).

Applying Basic Lessons from Child Development

As you read this book, you will find that the three basic developmental issues of nature and nurture, universality and diversity, and qualitative and quantitative change surface periodically within individual chapters. They are also presented in Basic Developmental Issues tables in each chapter. The first of these tables, "Illustrations in the Three Domains," provides examples of how the basic developmental issues are reflected in the domains of physical, cognitive, and social-emotional development.

Much of developmental research deals with these three basic issues. Keeping them in mind as you learn about how children and adolescents progress in specific domains will help you understand development more fully. But these big ideas also have several general implications for your work with children:

● *To best help children, keep in mind the influences of both nature and nurture on growth and development.* A child's fate is never sealed—it always depends on care from adults and the child's own efforts. Again and again, nurture matters. But so does nature. How children respond to instruction and guidance depends, in part, on their genetic inheritance. So when children show unusual talents, you can foster these talents. And when children's natural inclinations become stumbling blocks to positive growth, you can provide extra support.

● *To better understand children's capabilities and needs, become familiar with general developmental trends and common variations.* General trends at a particular age level affect the daily work of educators. For example, an elementary teacher familiar with Piaget's theory knows that young children have difficulty with abstract ideas and so arranges many concrete, hands-on experiences when teaching academic concepts. At the same time, many variations in developmental pathways—the timing, appearance, and nature of changes—are normal and to be expected. By growing familiar with the developmental diversity among children, you can learn to give individual youngsters the specific support they need.

● *When assessing children's development, look for both quantitative and qualitative changes.* As you teach children academic concepts, the benefits of physical activity, ways to get along with peers, and so on, you might find that children often learn information in a quantitative fashion. That is, they soak up facts and skills rapidly and incrementally. You can support such learning by exposing children to rich and varied resources. On other occasions children might need to revamp their basic ways of thinking before they can progress. Some of the momentum for qualitative change comes from the child, but teachers and other professionals can support new ways of thinking by exposing children to increasingly sophisticated reasoning. For example, a class discussion about school rules can prompt children to realize that breaking rules not only leads to punishment (an understanding that typically comes early in life) but also upsets other people (a later acquisition). With this new insight, many children become more considerate of others.

As you work with children, you will most certainly marvel at the complex ways these three basic developmental issues manifest themselves. Such issues have also intrigued the

Basic Developmental Issues

Illustrations in the Three Domains

Issue	Physical Development	Cognitive Development	Social-Emotional Development
Nature and Nurture	Nature guides the order and timing in which specific parts of the brain are formed. Genetic factors also determine certain individual dispositions, such as a tendency toward thinness or a susceptibility to diabetes. All growth depends on nurture. The effects of nutrition on health and the impact of training on athletic performance show that nurture can actively direct the course of development (Chapters 4 and 5).	Some aspects of intelligence, learning, and language seem to be genetically based. However, many contemporary theorists emphasize the significance of environmental influences (nurture), such as informal learning experiences, adult modeling and mentoring, family relationships, and formal schooling (Chapters 3, 5, 6, 7, 8, 9, and 10).	Individual differences in temperament appear to be partly controlled by heredity (nature). Environmental influences (nurture) are evident in the development of self-esteem and motivation. Becoming aggressive, on the one hand, or helpful and empathic on the other, occurs due to the combined influences of nature and nurture (Chapters 11, 12, 13, and 14).
Universality and Diversity	The emergence of key physical features (e.g., gender-specific characteristics appearing during puberty) is universal. Diversity is evident in the ages at which children and adolescents undergo key physical developments, as well as in their general state of physical health (Chapter 5).	The basic components of human language (e.g., an ability to combine words using grammatical rules) and learning (e.g., the mechanisms that allow new information to be compared to previous experiences) are universal. Diversity is evident in the fact that some children have more effective ways of learning and remembering academic information than do others (Chapters 6, 7, 8, and 9).	The need for peer affiliation represents a universal aspect of development in children and adolescents. However, there are considerable individual differences in the kinds of social groups that young people join (Chapter 15).
Qualitative and Quantitative Change	Some aspects of physical development (e.g., transformations during prenatal development and at puberty) reflect dramatic qualitative change. Most of the time, however, physical development occurs gradually as a result of many small changes (e.g., young children slowly grow taller) (Chapters 4 and 5).	Children's logical reasoning skills show some qualitative change; for instance, children acquire new, more sophisticated ways of solving problems. Quantitative change occurs as children gradually gain knowledge in various academic disciplines (Chapters 6, 7, and 10).	Some evidence suggests that with appropriate social experience, children's understanding of morality undergoes qualitative change, often in conjunction with changes in logical reasoning ability. In a more quantitative manner, children gradually come to understand how other people's minds work and discover that others' knowledge, beliefs, and desires may be different from their own (Chapters 12 and 14).

scholars who have proposed theoretical models of children's development. We turn now to a number of especially influential theories.

Theories of Child Development

To guide their hypotheses and questions, research methods, and interpretations of data, developmental scholars construct **theories,** organized systems of principles and explanations regarding particular phenomena. Seven theoretical approaches have dominated academic discussions of child development since the field emerged. We examine them here, one by one, and then refer to them selectively in later chapters as they become relevant to particular topics.

Biological Theories

The adaptive ability of children's bodies to support their survival, growth, and learning is the focus of **biological theories.** When heredity increases children's chances for survival, genes

theory
Organized system of principles and explanations regarding a particular phenomenon.

biological theory
Theoretical perspective that focuses on inherited physiological structures of the body and brain that support survival, growth, and learning.

for particular tendencies are passed on to the next generation. For example, our ancestors' children had to be prepared to form bonds with protective caregivers; without such bonds, they did not survive their early years, mature into adulthood, and go on to pass on their own genes to offspring. Thus children are now biologically predisposed to form attachments with primary caregivers.

Historically, biological theories emphasized the *maturation* of children's bodies and motor abilities (e.g., Gesell, 1928). Early theorists compiled detailed charts of the typical times that children learned to sit, crawl, reach for objects, and so forth. According to this view, children walk when they are physiologically ready, and puberty begins when a biological clock triggers the appropriate hormones. In some instances maturation establishes sensitive periods for learning in particular domains. For instance, Italian physician and educator Maria Montessori (1870–1952) noticed that infants are perceptive of order and details in the physical world and that young children eagerly soak up details about language (Montessori, 1936, 1949). In the many Montessori schools now in existence in North America and Western Europe, teachers are urged to become careful observers of children's natural tendencies and to provide stimulating materials that entice children to engage in educational activities specifically suited to their current developmental needs.

A limitation of many early biological perspectives was that they largely overlooked the effects of children's experiences on development. In contrast, contemporary biological theorists emphasize that genes are flexible instructions that blend with environmental experiences to affect the child. Thus biological perspectives are now more balanced in their regard for nature, nurture, and children's activity (Bjorklund, 2003; Gottlieb, Wahlsten, & Lickliter, 2006).

Two key principles that a practitioner can take away from biological theories are that (a) children's maturational levels impose limits on their abilities and interests and (b) children's physical abilities serve valuable functions for them, such as permitting their growth and age-appropriate exploration. Understanding youngster's natural inclinations can help teachers and other practitioners provide appropriate activities, structure, and guidance. For example, if you accept the idea that preschool children are predisposed to be physically active, you will understand that they need regularly scheduled time outdoors in safely equipped playgrounds.

Behaviorism and Social Learning Theories

Whereas biological theorists see heredity (nature) as the principal driving force behind development, advocates of behaviorism and social learning theories propose that developmental change is largely due to environmental influences (nurture). Conducting research with humans and other species (e.g., dogs, rats, pigeons), these theorists have shown that many behaviors can be modified through environmental stimuli. As a proponent of a perspective known as **behaviorism**, American psychologist B. F. Skinner (1904–1990) suggested that children actively "work" for rewards, such as food, praise, or physical contact, and tend to avoid behaviors that lead to punishment (Skinner, 1953, 1957). Other behavioral theorists have revealed how children learn emotional responses to certain stimuli (e.g., fear of dogs) based on their unique experiences with those stimuli (e.g., receiving a painful dog bite).

A serious limitation of behaviorism is that it focuses exclusively on children's visible, external behaviors, with little consideration for how internal thought processes might influence those behaviors. In contrast, contemporary **social learning theories** portray children's beliefs and goals as having crucial influences on children's actions. Researchers and theorists in the social learning tradition have shown that behavior is not just a response to a reward or punishment in the immediate environment. Children can anticipate the consequences of their actions and choose their behaviors accordingly, whether or not they have ever been rewarded or punished for particular actions. Moreover, children (and adults as well) learn a great deal by observing what other people do and what consequences (e.g., rewards and punishments) follow those behaviors.[3]

Numerous practical applications have been derived from behaviorism and social learning theory, and you will encounter many of them as you read this book. For now, let's look at two

behaviorism
Theoretical perspective in which children's behavioral and emotional responses change as a direct result of particular environmental stimuli.

social learning theory
Theoretical perspective that focuses on how children's beliefs and goals influence their actions and how they often learn by observing others.

---

[3]In recent years social learning theory has increasingly incorporated thought processes into its explanations of learning; accordingly, it is sometimes called *social cognitive theory*.

overarching principles. First, environmental stimuli, such as rewards and punishments, clearly do influence children's actions and feelings. Mary Jalongo, in the opening case study, realized that punishing Tonya harshly for stealing would do Tonya more harm than good. Second, children's actions are affected by what they see others doing. For example, children often imitate others' behaviors, whether those behaviors are desirable (e.g., the hoop shots of a famous basketball player) or undesirable (e.g., a teacher's condescending actions toward the school custodian).

Psychodynamic Theories

Psychodynamic theories focus on the interaction between certain internal conflicts and the environment. These theories assert that early experiences play a critical role in later characteristics and behavior. They typically focus on social and personality development and, often, on abnormal development.

The earliest psychodynamic theorist, Sigmund Freud (1856–1939), was an Austrian physician who argued that young children continually find themselves torn by sexual and aggressive impulses, on the one hand, and desires to gain approval from parents and society, on the other (Freud, 1905, 1910, 1923). Freud proposed that as an outgrowth of their personal motives and social experiences in families, children progress through a series of qualitatively distinct stages, ideally learning to channel their impulses in socially appropriate ways. Another psychodynamic theorist, Erik Erikson (1902–1994), who was born in Germany and eventually moved to the United States, suggested that people grow as a result of resolving their own internal struggles. Compared to Freud, Erikson focused less on sexual and aggressive impulses and more on other parts of the developing personality, such as desires to feel competent and sure of one's own identity (Erikson, 1963).

Psychodynamic perspectives have made a lasting contribution by highlighting the significance of children's social-emotional needs. Several psychodynamic ideas remain influential today: Early social experiences can direct later development; forceful and repeated efforts may be needed to dislodge children from an unhealthy path; and children wrestle with particular issues during certain phases of life.

A significant weakness of psychodynamic theories has been the difficulty of supporting claims with research data. For one thing, it is difficult to verify what internal conflicts a particular person might have, in part because many of an individual's conflicts are presumed by psychodynamic theorists to be subconscious. If we ourselves are not consciously aware of a conflict, we are unlikely to talk about that conflict with another person. In addition, generalizations cannot necessarily be made from the studies that the theorists themselves conducted. For example, Freud developed his ideas from in-depth interviews with troubled adults—individuals whose childhoods did not necessarily reflect typical developmental pathways. Critics point out that desires to restrain sexual urges (Freud's theory) and define one's personal identity (Erikson's theory) may be principal motives for some people but not others. Finally, research has refuted several ideas central to psychoanalytical perspectives. For example, Freud recommended that children perform mildly aggressive acts as a way to release inborn aggressive tendencies, yet research indicates that encouraging such acts can actually *increase* aggressive behavior (A. P. Goldstein, 1999; Mallick & McCandless, 1966).

Despite these serious problems, psychodynamic theories do remind educators that children often have mixed and confusing emotions. Adults can help children by teaching them to express their feelings in ways that both honestly reflect their experiences and are acceptable to other people.

Cognitive-Developmental Theories

Cognitive-developmental theories emphasize thinking processes and how they change, qualitatively, over time. According to these views, children play an active role in their own development: They seek out new and interesting experiences, try to understand what they see and hear, and work actively to reconcile any discrepancies between new information and what they previously believed to be true. Through these reflections, children's thinking becomes increasingly logical and abstract with age.

The earliest and best-known cognitive-developmental theorist was Swiss scientist Jean Piaget (1896–1980). With a career that spanned decades and spawned thousands of research

Children develop, in part, by actively seeking out new and interesting experiences. Art by Margot, age 6.

psychodynamic theory
Theoretical perspective that focuses on how early experiences and internal conflicts affect social and personality development.

cognitive-developmental theory
Theoretical perspective that focuses on major transformations to the underlying structures of thinking over the course of development.

studies around the world, Piaget focused primarily on children's cognitive development (Piaget, 1928, 1929, 1952a, 1952b). Using detailed observations, in-depth interviews, and ingenious experimental tasks, Piaget investigated the nature of children's logical thinking about such topics as numbers, physical causality, and psychological processes. Another prominent cognitive-developmental theorist, American psychologist Lawrence Kohlberg (1927–1987), is known for his extensive research on moral reasoning (Kohlberg, 1963, 1984).

Piaget, Kohlberg, and their colleagues have suggested that taking a developmental perspective means looking sympathetically at children and understanding the logic of their current level of thinking. Although adult-like reasoning may be the eventual, desired outcome for young people, cognitive developmentalists believe that it is a mistake to hurry children beyond their current capacities—that one cannot simply make a child think in ways beyond his or her current cognitive stage. They also believe that adults who try to push children beyond their current stage create unnecessary stress and fail to take advantage of the reasoning skills of which children *are* capable.

Many cognitive-developmental ideas are well regarded by the current generation of developmental scholars. For example, contemporary child development experts recognize that children's thinking often reflects a reasonable attempt to make sense of novel and puzzling information. However, cognitive-developmental theories have also undergone vigorous critiques. A central criticism is that researchers rarely find that children's development reflects clear-cut stage progressions. Instead, children often move back and forth between more and less sophisticated ways of thinking. Critics point out, for example, that simply because children do not think abstractly about a particular topic does not mean that they are *incapable* of abstract reasoning, especially with the support of an adult. As we mentioned in our earlier discussion of stage theories, children are sometimes able to reason at a very high level in certain areas, while simultaneously being incapable of advanced reasoning in other areas.

Perhaps the most important principle for education that emerges from cognitive-developmental theories is that teachers need to understand children *as children*. To facilitate children's learning, educators must listen closely to children's conversations, permit children to actively explore their environment, observe their actions, and gently probe them about their ideas. Only when adults understand children's thinking can they hope to enhance it.

Cognitive Process Theories

Cognitive process theories focus on basic thinking processes. For instance, cognitive process theorists examine how people interpret and remember what they see and hear and how these processes change during childhood and adolescence.

Cognitive process researchers conduct detailed analyses of what children think and do. For instance, they have studied the eye movements of children scanning pictures, the length of time children take to read various kinds of text, and children's strategies for completing puzzles. Such analyses are guided by clear models of how children attend to information, find it meaningful, and use it later. Cognitive process theories now dominate much of the research in cognitive development.

Recent research by American psychologist Robert Siegler illustrates the cognitive process approach. Siegler has found that children often spontaneously use a variety of different strategies when first learning to complete tasks in arithmetic. For instance, in solving the problem "2 + 4 = ?" children may count on their fingers, starting with the first number and then counting from there ("two . . . then three, four, five, six—six altogether"), or simply recall the number fact "2 + 4 = 6" from memory. The same versatility is present as children begin to tackle such other tasks as telling time, spelling, and reading. Children's general tactic of trying out a range of solutions and repeating procedures that seem effective is often quite adaptive for them (Siegler, 2006; Siegler & Alibali, 2005).

A key contribution of cognitive process theories has been to describe children's thinking with painstaking detail, but critics suggest that there is a price to pay for taking such a focused view of specific processes. Cognitive process researchers can easily overlook the larger issue of *why* children think as they do. For instance, cognitive process approaches often neglect the social-emotional factors and contexts of children's lives, factors that many other modern developmental theorists consider significant.

cognitive process theory
Theoretical perspective that focuses on the precise nature of human mental operations.

Another contribution of cognitive process theories has been the wealth of concrete, research-tested instructional strategies they have provided. Many teachers have found these strategies and applications to be quite helpful. For example, as we will discover in Chapter 7, cognitive process theories offer techniques for keeping children's attention, making the most of children's limited memory capabilities, and challenging children's misconceptions on particular topics.

Sociocultural Theories

Cognitive developmentalists and cognitive process theorists have focused squarely on how intellectual skills develop within an individual. By and large, both have paid little attention to the roles played by the broader social and cultural context within which individuals live. **Sociocultural theories,** on the other hand, try to explain the impact of social and cultural systems on development. These theories see development as the process of children becoming full adult participants in the society into which they are born.

Russian psychologist and educator Lev Vygotsky (1896–1934) is the pioneering figure credited with advancing our knowledge of how children's minds are shaped by everyday experiences in social settings. Having studied the learning and tool use of both children and adults, Vygotsky concluded that people learn by taking part in everyday cultural activities and gradually assuming higher levels of responsibility (Vygotsky, 1962, 1978). For example, when children learn to use an alphabet and number system, their minds are transformed, and they come to think about words, language, and numerical patterns in entirely new ways. Because different cultures impart different ways of thinking about and performing daily tasks, they teach different writing systems, scientific concepts, religious beliefs, and so on; thus children's thoughts and behaviors develop in culturally specific ways.

The last two decades have seen a virtual explosion of research conducted within sociocultural perspectives (Markus & Hamedani, 2007). This recent research is often well received by teachers because it focuses on real children in real settings and gives teachers a sense of the tangible steps they can take to support children's learning. Another strength of sociocultural theories is that they show concretely how specific cultural groups encourage children to use distinctly different modes of thinking.

As with any theoretical approach, however, sociocultural theories have limitations. Sociocultural theorists have described children's thinking with less precision than have theorists working within cognitive process perspectives. In some cases theorists have taken for granted that children learn important skills simply by taking part in an activity; in reality, however, some children merely go through the motions and take little responsibility for completing a task.

Sociocultural theories offer important applications for educators and other adults. A key principle is that children learn by being engaged in authentic adult tasks (Gauvain, 2001). For example, students in classrooms learn to read, write, perform basic mathematical operations, analyze a body of data, and think critically about social and economic problems. With the assistance of teachers and classmates, children begin to tackle real-world tasks that were previously beyond their capabilities.

Sociocultural perspectives also offer implications as to how children's cultural practices at home influence their learning and behavior at school. Almost every classroom includes children from diverse cultural backgrounds, making it vitally important to communicate rules for classroom behavior clearly and explicitly. Teachers can find ways to reach out to the range of cultures they serve, such as by inviting children's families to share some aspects of their family traditions and history with the classroom.

From the perspective of sociocultural theories, children and adolescents learn a lot from participating in routine, purposeful activities with adults.

sociocultural theory
Theoretical perspective that focuses on children's learning of tools, thinking processes, and communication systems through practice in meaningful tasks with other people.

developmental systems theory
Theoretical perspective that focuses on the multiple factors, including systems inside and outside children, that combine to influence children's development.

Developmental Systems Theories

Developmental systems theories help clarify how multiple factors combine to promote child development. A child's body is an active, living *system,* an organized assembly of parts that work together to keep the child alive and growing. The child is also part of a physical environment and a member of multiple, interconnected social systems (Baltes et al., 2006; K. W. Fischer & Bidell, 2006; Lerner, 2002; Thelen & Smith, 2006). The child's own activity contributes to changes in and among these various systems.

Urie Bronfenbrenner (1917–2005), a native of Russia and immigrant to the United States at age 6, is undoubtedly the most widely known developmental systems theorist. In his *bioecological model* of human development, Bronfenbrenner described the interacting effects of children's environments, which include their immediate and extended families, neighborhoods, schools, parents' workplaces, the mass media, community services, and political systems and policies (Bronfenbrenner, 1979, 2005; Bronfenbrenner & Morris, 2006). In the bioecological model, children partly determine their own environment by demonstrating their natural and acquired skills and temperaments (e.g., the child who is quiet and reflective triggers a different style of instruction from the teacher than does the child who is disruptive and inattentive). Thus a reciprocal relationship exists between the child and his or her environment. In fact, there is a dynamic relationship among all systems in which a child develops. For example, if parents and teachers develop mutually respectful relationships, they may exchange information and together magnify their support for a child. If parent-teacher relationships are poor, adults may blame one another for a struggling child's limitations, with the result that no one teaches the child needed skills. Because the child, parent, teachers, and other people in the environment are themselves maturing and responding to ongoing events, relationships affecting the child also undergo change with time.

Bronfenbrenner believed that the child's relationships with parents and other close family members are of utmost importance (Bronfenbrenner & Morris, 2006). Yet children clearly have influential relationships with people outside the family. In our introductory case Mary Jalongo played an important role in Tonya's life because she expressed her faith in Tonya and took a few practical steps. Teachers, peers, and neighbors regularly endorse the strong values children have learned at home and in other cases compensate for inadequate affection or troubled family relationships (Criss, Pettit, Bates, Dodge, & Lapp, 1992; Crosnoe & Elder, 2004). Contemporary developmental systems theorists suggest that educators can exert the greatest beneficial effect on children by considering the full range of strengths and risks children experience in their family relationships, ethnic affiliations, cultural beliefs and practices, peer contacts, and neighborhood resources (Spencer, 2006; see Figure 1-2).

The power of developmental systems theories is that they capture it all—nature, nurture, and the child's own activity. Ironically, the integrative character of these theories also creates their weaknesses. It is difficult to make predictions about any single factor in development because the effects of each factor are so intertwined with other elements of the developmental context.

Like other theoretical perspectives, developmental systems theories offer valuable ideas that can guide teachers in their interactions with children. Children's experiences are constantly changing in families, schools, and peer groups, and educators must adjust their services to the complex circumstances affecting children's adjustment. For example, youngsters can change dramatically after a major transition (e.g., moving to a new school, encountering a bully in the school yard), requiring educators to keep tabs on youngsters' evolving perceptions and feelings. Educators can also form close relationships with children, supplementing support that may or may not be offered at home.

Taking an Eclectic Approach

Table 1-1 summarizes the seven theoretical perspectives. With so many theories, it is tempting to ask, Which one is right? The answer is that, to some extent, they all are. Each perspective provides unique insights that no other approach can offer. At the same time, no single theory can adequately explain all aspects of child development, and increasingly, theorists themselves find they must draw from more than one camp to do justice to all we know about child development. In a sense, any theory is like a lens that brings certain phenomena into sharp focus but leaves other phenomena blurry or out of the picture. We urge you to take an eclectic attitude as you read about the variety of theoretical explanations you find in this book, looking for the most useful ideas each theory has to offer.

MyEducationLab

Gain practice in analyzing how family, friends, and teachers can play important complementary roles for children by completing an Understanding Research exercise in Chapter 1's Activities and Applications section in MyEducationLab at www.myeducationlab.com.

Figure 1-2

A child develops in a complex environment. Access to multiple interacting environmental systems provides opportunities for growth. The family is crucially important, ideally loving the child and offering daily informal lessons on becoming a productive member of society. Others interacting with the child regularly, including teachers, peers, and neighbors, also play foundational roles in the child's life. Some social settings and individuals, such as employers and family friends, typically give the parents needed financial and emotional support and thus indirectly help the child. The child is also affected by the prevailing customs and practices of society. The child, in turn, actively influences family members and other people based on his or her physical appearance, developmental abilities, temperament, intellectual skills, and behavior. The child, the environment, and the interactions among these various systems exhibit constant change and adaptation.
Based on Bronfenbrenner, 2005; Bronfenbrenner & Morris, 2006.

Developmental Periods

We can make our task of exploring child development more manageable by dividing the developmental journey into specific time periods. Age cutoffs are somewhat arbitrary, yet we know that children act in very different ways at specific age levels. In our discussions of various domains, we usually consider five periods: infancy (birth–2 years), early childhood (2–6 years), middle childhood (6–10 years), early adolescence (10–14 years), and late adolescence (14–18 years). Here we summarize each period, identifying the typical needs and accomplishments of youngsters and their implications for teachers and other practitioners. As we do, we refer you to some of the video clips in MyEducationLab.

MyEducationLab

Many videos in the Video Examples section of each chapter in MyEducationLab (www.myeducationlab.com) can help you see connections between concepts in child development and the experiences of real children and adolescents.

Table 1-1   Theories of Child Development

Theoretical Perspectives	Positions	Basic Developmental Issues	Representative Theorists[a]
Biological Theories	Investigators focus on genetic factors, physiological structures and functions of the body, and inborn psychological processes that help the child adapt and survive in the environment. As an illustration, preschool children in one investigation were more attentive to stories after outdoor recess breaks than before these breaks, possibly because sustained outdoor play rejuvenates children both physically and intellectually (Holmes, Pellegrini, & Schmidt, 2006).	*Nature and Nurture*: Characteristics and behaviors that enhance an individual's chances for survival and reproduction are supported by genetic instructions. Adequate nutrients, supportive social relationships, and exploration in the physical environment are essential to normal growth. *Universality and Diversity*: Universally, children form bonds with caregivers, express themselves with language, infer other people's intentions and feelings, and use tools. Diversity in physical characteristics and ability occurs through variations in genes and experience. *Qualitative and Quantitative Change*: Qualitative changes are seen in the emergence of sexual characteristics at puberty and with sensitive periods of development. In other respects the child grows gradually, reflecting many quantitative transformations.	Charles Darwin Arnold Gesell Maria Montessori Konrad Lorenz John Bowlby Mary Ainsworth Sandra Scarr Robert Plomin David Bjorklund Susan Gelman Henry Wellman
Behaviorism and Social Learning Theories	Investigators focus on environmental stimuli and learning processes that lead to behavioral change. For example, after an adult asked children with poor eating habits to set goals related to healthful eating habits, the children consumed more vegetables and fruit juice (the request and goals were the stimuli, the increase in consumption of vegetables and juice was the behavioral change) (Cullen et al., 2004).	*Nature and Nurture*: Emphasis is on nurture. When children act, the environment may respond with rewards or punishments. Children modify their actions based on their experiences, goals, and beliefs about whether an action will lead to desirable or undesirable consequences. *Universality and Diversity*: Children typically work for some common rewards (e.g., food, praise, physical contact). Because environments vary in how they respond to children's actions, diversity in behavior is expected. *Qualitative and Quantitative Change*: Development is quantitative: Children undergo countless incremental changes in behaviors.	B. F. Skinner John B. Watson Ivan Pavlov Sidney Bijou Donald Baer Albert Bandura
Psychodynamic Theories	Investigators focus on how early experiences and internal conflicts affect social and personality development. For example, in an investigation in which divorced parents and their children were studied over a 10-year period, researchers detected the emergence of factions and sibling rivalries that were based, in part, on unconsciously held allegiances to different parents (Wallerstein & Lewis, 2007).	*Nature and Nurture*: Sexual and aggressive urges are inborn. Family and society affect how children control and express instinctual urges; social relationships also affect children's basic trust in others and perceptions of themselves as individuals. *Universality and Diversity*: Universally, children struggle with strong feelings (e.g., aggression and sexuality, according to S. Freud) and personal challenges (e.g., the belief that they can or cannot make things happen, according to Erikson). Relationships with other people are highly varied and result in diversity in resolutions to life's challenges. *Qualitative and Quantitative Change*: Through a series of qualitatively distinct stages, children learn to resolve mixed feelings.	Sigmund Freud Anna Freud Erik Erikson
Cognitive-Developmental Theories	Investigators focus on major transformations in the cognitive structures that underlie thinking. For instance, in considering children's social perspective taking, one researcher found that young children focused on their own concrete views of an event, whereas older children and adolescents were able to consider how several individuals could see a single event from several valid points of view (Selman, 1980).	*Nature and Nurture*: Children are biological organisms strongly motivated to make sense of their personal worlds (nature). Access to a reasonably complex physical and social environment is vital to development (nurture). Young people actively contribute to their own intellectual development. *Universality and Diversity*: Universality is emphasized. Variations among youngsters are most common at the highest stages of development, which may depend on particular kinds of experiences (e.g., exposure to a puzzling phenomenon or moral dilemma, particular kinds of instruction). *Qualitative and Quantitative Change*: Children's thinking undergoes defined transformations in the very essence of reasoning; new ways of thinking build on previous structures but are increasingly abstract and systematic. Quantitative additions to the knowledge base occur within stages.	Jean Piaget Bärbel Inhelder Lawrence Kohlberg David Elkind Robbie Case John Flavell

Table 1-1   Theories of Child Development (continued)

Theoretical Perspectives	Positions	Basic Developmental Issues	Representative Theorists[a]
Cognitive Process Theories	Investigators focus on the precise nature of human cognitive operations. For example, in one study adolescents who participated in debates with their peers and received instruction in how to make counterarguments acquired more sophisticated reasoning and argumentation skills (Kuhn & Udell, 2003).	*Nature and Nurture*: Both nature and nurture are important. Children are born with basic capacities to perceive, interpret, and remember information; these capacities change with brain maturation, experience, and reflection. *Universality and Diversity*: The desire to make sense of the world is universal. Diversity is present in the kinds of educational experiences children have and, to some degree, in their natural intellectual talents. *Qualitative and Quantitative Change*: The methods by which children perceive, interpret, and remember information gradually change in both qualitative and quantitative ways.	David Klahr Deanna Kuhn Robert Siegler Ann L. Brown Henry Wellman Susan Gelman John Flavell Robbie Case
Sociocultural Theories	Investigators focus on acquisition of tools, communication systems, intellectual abilities, and social-emotional skills through practice in meaningful tasks with other people. For example, in one study children's ability to plan their informal activities (such as deciding what to do after school, what to eat for breakfast, and what to watch on television) improved over the elementary years and depended somewhat on their cultural background (Gauvain & Perez, 2005).	*Nature and Nurture*: Emphasis is on nurture. Children learn to use tools favored by their families and communities as they take part in meaningful tasks with others (nurture). However, being a social and cultural being is part of children's genetic inheritance (nature). *Universality and Diversity*: All children learn language, beliefs espoused in their communities, practical life skills, and so on. However, variation is present in the particular tools that various cultures and societies use. *Qualitative and Quantitative Change*: Children gradually take on responsibility in social groups. As children become increasingly able to regulate their own thinking, they shift qualitatively in how they carry out tasks. For example, having been taught basic mathematical systems and rules of writing, young people can eventually use these tools independently and appropriately during academic lessons.	Lev Vygotsky A. R. Luria James Wertsch Barbara Rogoff Patricia Greenfield Mary Gauvain Jerome Bruner Michael Cole
Developmental Systems Theories	Investigators focus on the multiple factors and systems that interact in children's development. For example, in one study, a wide range of factors were associated with hours children slept at night, including children's own activities (e.g., excessive television viewing was associated with relatively little sleep), family functioning (e.g., eating family meals together on weekdays was associated with relatively long sleep), and demographic factors (e.g., older African American children slept fewer hours than did children from other groups) (Adam, Snell, & Pendry, 2007).	*Nature and Nurture*: Multiple factors inside the child (nature) and outside the child (nurture) combine to influence developmental patterns. The child's own activity is also an essential factor in development. *Universality and Diversity*: Developmental changes occur in all individuals from conception to death. Some changes are common at particular ages, yet individual children may face slightly different obstacles when acquiring new abilities. The particular challenges children encounter depend heavily on historical events and life circumstances. *Qualitative and Quantitative Change*: Most change is quantitative, but shifts in action occur that result in entirely new ways of behaving. For example, a baby may use her arm to swat awkwardly at a toy and later learn to pick it up with a precise, effective finger grip.	Urie Bronfenbrenner Arnold Sameroff Richard Lerner Kurt Fischer Esther Thelen Gilbert Gottlieb Paul Baltes

[a]Several theorists have contributed to two or more theoretical perspectives. For example, John Flavell and Robbie Case have made important contributions to both cognitive-developmental and cognitive process theories, Albert Bandura has made contributions to social learning and cognitive process perspectives, and Henry Wellman and Susan Gelman have conducted research referring to biological functions and cognitive processes.

Infancy (Birth–2 Years)

Infancy is a truly remarkable period. It is a time when basic human traits, such as emotional bonds with other people, nonverbal communication, language expression, and motor exploration of the physical environment, burst onto the scene.

A newborn baby is completely dependent on others. But a baby is equipped with an arsenal of skills—including a distinctive cry, physical reflexes, an interest in human faces, and a brain alert to novelty and sameness—that elicit comfort and stimulation from caregivers. In a matter of weeks, the baby smiles broadly during good-humored exchanges with a caregiver. As the caregiver responds warmly and consistently, attachment grows.

During the first 2 years, many dramatic developmental changes occur.

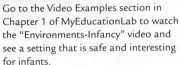

MyEducationLab

Go to the Video Examples section in Chapter 1 of MyEducationLab to watch the "Environments-Infancy" video and see a setting that is safe and interesting for infants.

A sense of security nourishes infants' desire to learn. Babies want to know everything: what car keys taste like, what older family members do in the kitchen, and what happens when they drop a bowl of peas. Infants' growing facility with language builds on interests in concrete experiences, such as a parent's laughter and the sensation of warm water in the bathtub.

Intellectual curiosity fuels babies' drive to use physical skills. Babies reach, crawl, and climb to get objects they desire. The urge to explore coincides with a budding sense of mastery ("I *can* do it!") and independence ("*I* can do it!"). Emotional reactions, such as a legitimate fear of heights and uneasiness in the presence of strangers, constrain physical exploration and occasionally prompt withdrawal.

Professional viewpoints. Caregivers who work effectively with infants realize that each baby is unique, develops at his or her own rate, and is hungry for loving interaction. Such caregivers emphasize *quality* of care, giving individualized, responsive, and affectionate attention to growing babies and their families (Chazan-Cohen, Jerald, & Stark, 2001).

In addition, knowledgeable infant caregivers design the physical environment so that infants can explore objects and their surroundings freely. The "Environments: Infancy" video in MyEducationLab shows one setting where crawling infants can speed up and down cushioned ramps, and walking infants (*toddlers*) can swagger around open spaces.[4] When infants stumble, furniture poses little threat because it has been crafted with soft, rounded edges. Caregivers also design environments to foster infants' cognitive and social abilities. In the video, notice a mirror that attracts attention; colorful toys with complex textures that beg to be touched; mobiles over cribs that encourage inspection; a tunnel that invites entering, exiting, and playing peekaboo games; and simple books to be examined while cuddling with a caregiver in a rocking chair.

High-quality early care prepares an infant for the expanded learning opportunities of early childhood. The infant is ready to venture from the caregiver's lap.

Early Childhood (2–6 Years)

Early childhood is a period of incredible creativity, fantasy, and play. Preschool-aged children see life as a forum for imagination and drama: They reinvent the world, try on new roles, and work hard to play their parts in harmony with one another.

Language and communication skills develop rapidly during early childhood. New vocabulary, sensitivity to communication rules, and facility with syntax (grammar) are noticeable advancements. Language builds on daily increases in knowledge about the world and, especially, the habits and patterns of daily life.

Physical changes are apparent as well. High levels of energy radiate from preschool-aged children's activities. The cautious movements of infancy give way to fluid rolling, tumbling, running, and skipping.

Socially and emotionally, preschoolers are often endearing, trusting, and affectionate. They become progressively more interested in others, eagerly spend time with playmates, infuse fantasy into play, and contend with aggressive and self-centered impulses.

Professional viewpoints. Effective teachers of young children inspire and channel children's natural energy. They are respectful of young children's curiosity, spontaneity, and desire to try on new roles.

Environments for young children can be designed to encourage the active and purposeful learning that is advocated by the National Association for the Education of Young Children (NAEYC) (1997). For example, in the "Environments: Early Childhood" video in MyEducationLab, you can see a classroom where children draw and paint creatively. Play structures encourage children to climb, hide, and see one another. Tables and chairs make it possible for children to sit and talk together during mealtimes and

Preschool children learn a lot from handling concrete objects, using their imaginations, and talking with others.

[4]Appreciation is extended to Greg Pierson, University Schools, and Keli Cotner, Campus Child Care Center, both of Greeley, Colorado, for granting permission to film their facilities.

group activities. A dramatic play area, furnished with kitchen appliances and dress-up clothes, encourages imagination. Elsewhere in the room children can sit and look at books and take turns on a computer. Mats let children recharge their batteries with rest; a separate bathroom area is available for toilet needs and hand washing. Outdoors, children can scoot on vehicles, ride bicycles, and play in the sand.

Given ample chances to explore the environment and converse with others, young children gain valuable knowledge about themselves and their world. They become ready to complete the realistic tasks of middle childhood.

Middle Childhood (6–10 Years)

Middle childhood is a time of sustained attention to real-world activities. Although pretending is not abandoned, it plays less of a role than it did earlier.[5] Instead, children invest effort in mastering the customs, tools, and accumulated knowledge of their community and culture. For example, in Western cultures children of this age often learn to read and write, apply rules in games and sports, care for younger brothers and sisters, and use computer technology.

Serious commitments to peers, especially to playmates of the same age and gender, also emerge during middle childhood. Friendships are important, and children learn much from spending time together and from getting into—and out of—scuffles. Children also begin to compare their performance to that of others: Why do I have fewer friends than Maria does? Am I good enough to be picked for the baseball team? When they routinely end up on the losing side in such comparisons, children are more hesitant to try new challenges.

In the elementary school years, children internalize many admonishments they've heard repeatedly ("Don't play near the river," "Keep an eye on your little brother"). They gain a sense of what is expected of them, and most are inclined to live up to these expectations. Rules of games and classroom conduct become important. Basic motor skills are stable during middle childhood, and many children gain proficiency in athletic skills.

Middle childhood is a time of sustained attention to realistic tasks.

Professional viewpoints.   In middle childhood, children do their best thinking when they are familiar with a topic and can rely on concrete objects to bolster their reasoning. Teachers can nurture children's skills by encouraging children to sort and analyze objects and events; gain proficiency in basic elements of reading, writing, mathematics, science, and other subjects; and focus on the connections between the academic concepts they are learning and the things they already know (National Council for Accreditation of Teacher Education, 2000).

You can see a classroom that provides tangible support for children's academic learning in the "Environments: Middle Childhood" video in MyEducationLab. For example, maps are visible in several places, suggesting the importance of the world's geography. Frequently used words are posted on cabinets for children to refer to while writing. Small objects can be manipulated, counted, and classified according to shape and other properties. Books, a computer, chalkboards, and other resources are available to extend children's learning. Tables and chairs permit group work, and sofas encourage relaxation while reading.

Having learned to think systematically, children are ready for some particularly challenging tasks: growing an adult body and speculating on what it means to hold a job, date, become intimate, and raise a family. This transition between childhood and adulthood takes time and effort, and there are growing pains along the way.

[5]Many children retain qualities typical of early childhood, such as an interest in pretend play, until age 8 or older, which has led the NAEYC to classify children from birth until age 8 as "young children" (NAEYC, 1997). In this book we have used age 6 as the cutoff between early and middle childhood. Although age 6 is somewhat arbitrary, it marks the typical age for first grade, during which time schools introduce an academic curriculum. We also wanted to distinguish the middle childhood period from the early adolescent period, since some youngsters (girls in particular) begin the first phases of puberty as early as age 8 or 9.

MyEducationLab

Go to the Video Examples section in Chapter 1 to watch the "Environments-Early Childhood" video and observe a setting that encourages creative movement, pretend play, and hands-on learning in young children

MyEducationLab

Go to the Video Examples section in Chapter 1 of MyEducationLab to watch the "Environments-Middle Childhood" video and view a setting that supports children's academic learning with concrete objects, displays of language rules, tables and chairs for group work, couches for relaxed reading, and other resources.

Early and late adolescence bring many physical, cognitive, and social-emotional changes.

Early Adolescence (10–14 Years)

In early adolescence, youngsters slowly lose their childlike bodies and make strides toward reproductive maturation. Physical changes are accompanied by equally dramatic reorganizations in learning processes and relationships with parents and peers.

The physical changes of puberty are orderly and predictable, but boys and girls alike often experience them personally as puzzling, disconcerting events. Young adolescents sometimes look and feel awkward, and hormonal changes, coupled with accelerating expectations from adults, can lead to mood swings. In addition, adolescents reflect on their changing selves and worry about how their peers perceive them. They wonder: What are they thinking of me? Am I one of the "cool" kids? Peers become a sounding board through which adolescents seek assurance that their appearance and behaviors are acceptable.

Adolescents begin to think in a far-reaching, logical, and abstract manner. The interests of young adolescents broaden well beyond family and peer group. Feeling powerful and idealistic, adolescents challenge the existing order, wondering why schools, governments, and the earth's ecosystem cannot be improved overnight.

Diversity is present in every developmental phase, but individual differences are especially pronounced in early adolescence. Although the physical changes of puberty occur in a fairly predictable manner, the ages at which they emerge can vary considerably from one individual to the next. Thus not all young adolescents begin puberty during the 10- to 14-year age range. Some, girls especially, may begin puberty before 10. Others, boys in particular, may not begin puberty until the end of this age span.

Professional viewpoints. The National Middle School Association (NMSA) offers guidelines for meeting the developmental needs of young adolescents at school (NMSA, 2003). First, every student should be supported by one adult (an *adviser*) who keeps an eye on the student's academic and personal development, perhaps within the context of a "home base" period or other group meeting time. The adviser-student relationship, when stable and positive, can help young adolescents weather the rapid developmental changes they are likely to experience. In addition, NMSA suggests that large middle schools be subdivided into smaller units (e.g., "houses") in which students share several classes and get to know the group's classmates and teachers. NMSA also advocates teaching techniques that are varied, engaging, and responsive to students' cultural backgrounds, prior knowledge, and individual talents.

Several environments designed to meet the developmental needs of young adolescents are shown in the "Environments: Early Adolescence" video in MyEducationLab. Classrooms are equipped with a rich array of instructional resources, including clocks, an easel, chalkboards, maps, binders, and a computer. Adolescents' artwork, papers, and a diorama are displayed for all to admire. A code of conduct reminds adolescents to treat themselves, others, and the environment with kindness and respect. A small room with two desks is set aside for private conversations with familiar adults. Hallways are clean and uncluttered, school colors are prominent, and rows of lockers give adolescents places to store personal supplies and congregate between classes.

First steps toward maturity are often hesitant ones. With affection from parents and teachers, young adolescents gradually gain confidence that the adult world is within reach.

Late Adolescence (14–18 Years)

As teenagers continue to mature, they lose some of the gawky, uneven features of early adolescence and blossom into attractive young adults. And resembling young adults, older adolescents often feel entitled to make decisions. Common refrains often include the word *my*: "It's *my* hair, *my* body, *my* clothes, *my* room, *my* education, *my life!*"

Late adolescence can be a confusing time to make decisions due to the abundance of mixed messages that society communicates. For instance, teenagers may be encouraged to ab-

MyEducationLab

Go to the Video Examples section in Chapter 1 of MyEducationLab to watch the "Environments-Early Adolescence" video and see a setting that encourages young adolescents to focus on academic learning, work together in groups, talk privately with advisors, and follow a code of conduct emphasizing kindness and respect.

stain from sexual activity, yet they continually encounter provocative sexual images in the media. Similarly, parents and teachers urge healthy eating habits, yet junk food is everywhere—in vending machines at school, at the refreshment stand at the movie theater, and often in kitchen cabinets at home.

Fortunately, many high school students make wise decisions. They try hard in school, gain work experience, and refrain from seriously risky behaviors. Others, however, are less judicious in their choices: They experiment with alcohol, drugs, sex, and violence and in general think more about here-and-now pleasures than long-term consequences.

Peer relationships remain a high priority in late adolescence. Affiliations with age-mates can have either a good or bad influence, depending on typical pastimes of the group. At the same time, most adolescents continue to savor their ties with trusted adults and preserve fundamental values championed by parents and teachers, such as the importance of a good education and the need to be honest and fair.

Individual differences in academic achievement are substantial during the high school years. Indeed, wide variations in students' abilities are among the biggest challenges faced by high schools today. Some low-achieving students drop out of high school altogether, perhaps to shield themselves from the stigma of academic failure. Many of the low achievers who stay in school hang out with students who share their own pessimistic views of education.

Professional viewpoints.   Older adolescents, who are beginning to take on grown-up responsibilities, need intelligent, behind-the-scenes support from adults. The National Association of Secondary School Principals (2004) urges schools to become student-centered and personalized in their services.

School environments can help meet adolescents' needs for personalized attention by doing several things. As you can see in the "Environments: Late Adolescence" video in MyEducationLab, classrooms can sometimes be arranged so students face one another, making it hard for anyone to remain anonymous. Of course, physical arrangements must be adapted to instructional formats, and what matters more than layout is that teachers communicate affection, respect, and high expectations to *all* adolescents. In the science classrooms in this clip, numerous types of equipment, resources, and materials are present; these can be used flexibly to meet individual learning needs. Statements of responsibility and citizenship are posted on a wall. A mural contains images appealing to a range of interests, including music, drama, and athletics. The message seems to be that *everyone* belongs here.

The five periods of development just identified appear in Developmental Trends tables throughout the book. These tables summarize key developmental tasks, achievements, and variations at different age levels. In addition, they suggest implications for teachers and other practitioners who work with young people in each developmental period. The first of these tables, "Accomplishments and Diversity at Different Age Levels" on the next two pages, gives an overview of the domains of physical, cognitive, and social-emotional development.

From Theory to Practice

The practical applications in this book build on a single basic principle: Children are nurtured most effectively when adults understand how children *generally* progress but also show sensitivity to children's *individual* needs. In other words, teachers engage in **developmentally appropriate practice,** instruction and caregiving adapted to the age, characteristics, and developmental progress of individual youngsters.

Developmentally appropriate practice enables growing children to be active learners, recognizes that adult-level functioning is not always either realistic or valuable for children to imitate, and encourages children to work together in an ethical and democratic fashion (Kohlberg & Mayer, 1972). Developmentally appropriate practice also represents an optimistic expectation that children *can* grow in positive directions.

By knowing the characteristics and thinking abilities of children at a particular age, adults can offer generally effective instruction and services. By further considering the individuality of children and the cultural differences that inevitably affect children's perceptions, values, beliefs, priorities, and traditions, educators can meet the needs of individual children (Mena & Eyer, 2007). Development and Practice features, which appear throughout the book, provide

MyEducationLab

Go to the Video Examples section in Chapter 1 of MyEducationLab to watch the "Environments-Late Adolescence" video and see a setting that encourages adolescents to become proficient in primary subjects, achieve deeper understandings in areas of personal interest, and follow a code of conduct emphasizing responsibility and citizenship.

developmentally appropriate practice
Instruction and other services adapted to the age, characteristics, and developmental progress of individual children.

Developmental Trends

Accomplishments and Diversity at Different Age Levels

Age	What You Might Observe	Diversity	Implications
Infancy (Birth–2 Years) 	**Physical Development** · Motor skills that include rolling over, sitting, crawling, standing, walking · Growing ability to reach, grab, manipulate, and release objects · Rudimentary self-feeding by the end of infancy **Cognitive Development** · Ability to distinguish among different faces (beginning in the first month) · Rapid growth in communication, including crying, using gestures and facial expressions, synchronizing attention with caregivers, babbling, forming one-word sentences, constructing multiple-word sentences · Ability to imitate simple gestures with a model present, moving to complex imitation of actions and patterns from memory · Increasing ability to remember people and things out of sight **Social-Emotional Development** · Formation of close bonds with responsive and affectionate caregivers · Use of words to name needs and desires · Playing side by side with peers but also interacting at times · Increasing awareness of ownership and boundaries of self ("Me!" "Mine!") · Developing sense of power and will ("No!")	· Considerable diversity exists in age when, and in manner in which, babies develop motor skills. · Self-feeding and self-help skills emerge later when families encourage children to rely on others for meeting basic needs. · Children's temperaments and physical abilities affect their exploration of the environment. · In unsafe environments families may limit children's exploration. · Some young children learn two or three languages, especially when knowing more than one language is valued by caregivers. · Ability to pretend is displayed early by some children and later by others. · Nonverbal communication varies with culture. For instance, a child may be discouraged from making eye contact with an elder as a sign of respect. · Children who have few experiences with peers may appear tentative, detached, or aggressive. · Infants and toddlers who spend time in multiage settings interact differently than do those accustomed to same-age groups. · Some children are encouraged by families to share possessions, and others are encouraged to respect individual rights of property.	· Provide a safe, appropriate, sensory-rich environment so infants can move, explore surroundings, and handle objects. · Hold infants gently, and care for their physical needs in an attentive manner. · Learn and respond sensitively to each infant's manner of approaching or resisting new people, objects, and events. · Encourage but do not rush infants to learn motor skills, such as walking. · Learn what each family wants for its children, and try to provide culturally sensitive care. · Recognize that children's early images of themselves are influenced by unconscious messages from adults (e.g., "I enjoy holding you" or "I'm sad and unable to attend to your needs"). · Speak to infants regularly to enrich their language development. · Communicate regularly with families about infants' daily activities, including how much and what they eat and drink, how well they sleep, and what their moods are during the day.
Early Childhood (2–6 Years) 	**Physical Development** · Increasing abilities in such motor skills as running and skipping, throwing a ball, building block towers, and using scissors · Increasing competence in basic self-care and personal hygiene **Cognitive Development** · Dramatic play and fantasy with peers · Ability to draw simple figures · Some knowledge of colors, letters, and numbers · Recounting of familiar stories and events **Social-Emotional Development** · Developing understanding of gender · Emerging abilities to defer immediate gratification, share toys, and take turns · Modest appreciation that other people have their own desires, beliefs, and knowledge · Some demonstration of sympathy for people in distress	· Children master coordinated physical skills (e.g., skipping) at different ages. · Individual differences in fine motor proficiency and gross motor agility are substantial. · Some children enter kindergarten having had few social experiences with age-mates; others have been in group child care since infancy. · Family and cultural backgrounds influence the kinds of skills that children have mastered by the time they begin school. · Some children have had a lot of experience listening to storybooks, but others have been read to only rarely. · Many children at this age have difficulty following rules, standing quietly in line, and waiting for their turns.	· Provide sensory-rich materials that encourage exploration (e.g., water table, sandbox, textured toys). · Arrange a variety of activities (e.g., assembling puzzles, coloring, building with blocks, dancing) that permit children to exercise fine motor and gross motor skills. · Encourage children to engage in cooperative and fantasy play by providing props and open play areas. · Read to children regularly to promote vocabulary and preliteracy skills. · Give children frequent opportunities to play, interact with peers, and make choices. · Communicate expectations for behavior so that children learn to follow the rules of group settings. · Communicate regularly with families about children's academic and social progress.

Developmental Trends (continued)

Age	What You Might Observe	Diversity	Implications
Middle Childhood (6–10 Years) 	**Physical Development** · Ability to ride a bicycle · Successful imitation of complex physical movements · Participation in organized sports **Cognitive Development** · Development of basic skills in reading, writing, mathematics, and other academic subject areas · Ability to reason logically about concrete objects and events in the immediate environment **Social-Emotional Development** · Increasing awareness of how one's own abilities compare with those of peers · Desire for time with age-mates, especially friends of the same gender · Increasing responsibility in household chores · Adherence to rules in games · Understanding of basic moral principles (e.g., fairness and equity)	· Children begin to compare their academic and physical performance to that of others, and children who perceive they are doing poorly may have less motivation to achieve. · Many children are unable to sit quietly for long periods. · Individual differences are evident in children's performance in academic areas. · Children differ in temperament and sociability; some are outgoing, whereas others are more reserved and shy. · A few children may show unacceptable levels of aggression toward others.	· Tailor instructional methods (e.g., cooperative groups, individualized assignments, choices in activities) and materials to meet diversity in children's talents, background knowledge, and interests. · Address deficiencies in basic skills (e.g., in reading, writing, and math) before they develop into serious delays. · Provide moderately challenging tasks that encourage children to learn new skills, perform well, and seek additional challenges. · Provide the guidance necessary to help children interact more successfully with peers (e.g., by suggesting ways to resolve conflicts and finding a "buddy" for a newcomer to a school or club). · Prohibit bullying and enforce codes of conduct.
Early Adolescence (10–14 Years) 	**Physical Development** · Onset of puberty · Significant growth spurt **Cognitive Development** · Emerging capacity to think and reason about abstract ideas · Preliminary exposure to advanced academic content in specific subject areas **Social-Emotional Development** · Continued (and perhaps greater) interest in peer relationships · Emerging sexual interest in the opposite gender or same gender, depending on orientation · Challenges to parents, teachers, and other authorities regarding rules and boundaries · Occasional moodiness	· Young adolescents exhibit considerable variability in the age at which they begin puberty. · Academic problems often become more pronounced during adolescence; students who encounter frequent failure become less engaged in school activities. · Adolescents seek out peers whose values are compatible with their own and who will give them recognition and status. · Some young adolescents begin to engage in deviant and risky activities (e.g., unprotected sex, cigarette smoking, use of drugs and alcohol).	· Suggest and demonstrate effective study strategies as adolescents begin to tackle difficult subject matter. · Give struggling adolescents the extra academic support they need to be successful. · Provide a regular time and place where young adolescents can seek guidance and advice about academic or social matters (e.g., offer your classroom or office as a place where students can occasionally eat lunch). · Provide opportunities for adolescents to contribute to decision making in clubs and recreation centers. · Hold adolescents accountable for their actions, and impose appropriate consequences when they break rules.
Late Adolescence (14–18 Years) 	**Physical Development** · Achievement of sexual maturity and adult height · For some teens, development of a regular exercise program · Development of specific eating habits (e.g., becoming a vegetarian, consuming junk food) **Cognitive Development** · In-depth study of certain academic subject areas · Consideration of career tracks and job prospects **Social-Emotional Development** · Dating · Increasing independence (e.g., driving a car, making choices for free time) · Frequent questioning of existing rules and societal norms	· Some adolescents make poor choices regarding the peers with whom they associate. · Older adolescents aspire to widely differing educational and career tracks (e.g., some aspire to college, others anticipate securing employment immediately after high school, and still others make no plans for life after high school). · Some teens participate in extracurricular activities; those who do are more likely to stay in school until graduation. · Some teens become sexually active, and some become parents. · Teenagers' neighborhoods and communities offer differing opportunities and temptations.	· Communicate caring and respect for all adolescents. · Allow choices in academic subjects and assignments, but hold adolescents to high standards for performance. · Provide the guidance and assistance that low-achieving students may need to be more successful. · Help adolescents explore higher education opportunities and a variety of career paths. · Encourage involvement in extracurricular activities. · Arrange opportunities for adolescents to make a difference in their communities through volunteer work and service learning projects.

MyEducationLab

Practice identifying developmentally appropriate practices for children by completing a Building Teaching Skills and Dispositions section in Chapter 1 of MyEducationLab.

illustrations of educators guiding young people of various ages and responding to the unique needs of each youngster. The first of these, "Engaging in Developmentally Appropriate Practice with Infants, Children, and Adolescents," appears below. You can also build your capacity to meet the needs of individual children at a particular age level with a Building Teaching Skills and Dispositions exercise in MyEducationLab.

Development and Practice

Engaging in Developmentally Appropriate Practice with Infants, Children, and Adolescents

Infancy

- **Set up a safe and stimulating environment for exploration.**

  A caregiver in an infant center designs her environment so infants can safely crawl, walk, and climb both inside and on the playground. A quiet corner is reserved for small infants not yet able to move around. Various materials and toys are carefully arranged to be in reach and invite use. Duplicates of heavily used toys are available.

- **Arrange clean and quiet areas for meeting physical needs.**

  A teacher in an early intervention program sets up his environment so that he can help toddlers meet their physical needs in a hygienic and quiet area. He talks to children during caregiving routines such as feeding, diapering, and toileting, explaining what's happening and praising children when they take small steps toward self-care.

- **Provide culturally sensitive care, and support families' home languages.**

  A family child care provider who is bilingual in Spanish and English uses both languages with toddlers in her care. She has cloth and cardboard books in both languages (some of the books are homemade), as well as recordings of songs and stories.

Early Childhood

- **Provide reassurance to children who have difficulty separating from their families.**

  A child care provider establishes a routine for the morning. After children say goodbye to their parents, they stand at the window with him, watch their parents walk to their cars, and then find an activity to join.

- **Create a classroom environment that permits children to explore their physical and cultural world.**

  A preschool teacher makes several "stations" available to children during free-choice time. The stations include a water table and areas for playing with blocks, completing puzzles, doing arts and crafts, engaging in dramatic play, and listening to audio recordings of books.

- **Introduce children to the world of literature.**

  A preschool teacher reads to the children at least once each day. She chooses books with entertaining stories and vivid illustrations that readily capture the children's attention, interest, and imagination.

Middle Childhood

- **Encourage family members to become active participants in their children's activities.**

  A religious educator invites children's parents and other family members to contribute in some small way to one of the classes. Different parents assist with musical performances, bake cookies, and give hands-on help during lessons.

- **Ensure that all students acquire basic academic skills.**

  A second-grade teacher individualizes reading instruction for her students based on their current knowledge and skills. She works on mastery of letter identification and letter-sound correspondence with some, reading of simple stories with others, and selection of appropriate books with a few students who are already reading independently. She makes sure that all children have regular opportunities to listen to stories in small groups and on audiotape.

- **Give children the guidance they need to establish and maintain positive relationships with their peers.**

  When two children are quarreling, their teacher asks them to generate a few suggestions from which they can eventually choose to settle the dispute.

Early Adolescence

- **Design a curriculum that is challenging and motivating and that incorporates knowledge and skills from several content areas.**

  A middle school teacher designs a unit on "war and conflict," integrating writing skills and knowledge of social studies. He encourages students to bring in newspaper clippings about current events and to write about political debates.

- **Assign every young adolescent an adviser who looks after the adolescent's welfare.**

  During homeroom with her advisees, a seventh-grade teacher personally makes sure that each student is keeping up with assignments. She also encourages her advisees to talk with her informally about their academic and social concerns.

- **Show sensitivity to youngsters who are undergoing the physical changes of puberty.**

  A sports coach makes sure that adolescents have privacy when they dress and shower after team practice.

Late Adolescence

- **Expect students to meet high standards for achievement, but give them the support and guidance they need to meet those standards.**

  An English composition teacher describes and then posts the various steps involved in writing—planning, drafting, writing, editing, and revising—and asks his students to use these steps for their essays. He then monitors his students' work, giving feedback and suggestions as necessary and making sure that students execute each step in a way that enhances the quality of their writing.

- **Encourage adolescents to give back to their communities.**

  A high school requires all students to participate in 50 hours of volunteer work or service learning in their town.

- **Educate adolescents about the academic requirements of jobs and colleges.**

  A high school guidance counselor posts vacant positions in the area, listing the work experience and educational requirements for each.

Applying Knowledge of Child Development in the Classroom and Community

In later chapters we pinpoint specific strategies that you can use in your work with children. Here we offer four general strategies that will help you get started in nurturing children's potential for positive growth:

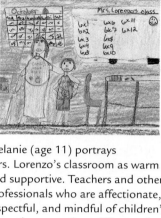

Melanie (age 11) portrays Mrs. Lorenzo's classroom as warm and supportive. Teachers and other professionals who are affectionate, respectful, and mindful of children's strengths can make a difference in children's lives.

- *Look for and capitalize on children's strengths.* Individual children have different strengths, depending on their genes, present environment, and past experiences. Age is also a factor in a child's strengths. For instance, an infant who carefully observes patterns of light may, at later ages, proceed to become a determined explorer in the sand, an industrious builder of blocks, a leader among middle school classmates and, eventually, an insightful critic of society's traditional ways of doing things.

It is not always easy for adults to see children's strengths because adults are inclined to evaluate children according to their own standards of maturity. Sometimes children make life difficult for adults, as Tonya initially did in our introductory case study. Children who struggle or act out may provoke adults to dwell on children's limitations. With extra effort, a change in tactics, and a solid faith in children's capacity for positive growth, educators can determine what children are able to accomplish and help them build on these resources.

- *Recognize that children's immaturity serves a purpose.* Human beings take longer to reach physical maturity than do members of any other species. Such a lengthy childhood allows children to learn what they need to know to become effective participants in adult society—from survival skills to the basic patterns, beliefs, and tools of their culture (Gould, 1977; Leakey, 1994).

When we compare children's abilities to our own, children inevitably come up short. For example, we might describe preschoolers as being self-centered and limited in the ability to think beyond immediate circumstances. Yet focusing on the personal relevance of new information is actually a reasonable way to make sense of it, particularly for a small child with restricted world knowledge. From a developmental perspective, the "immaturities" youngsters display often serve a purpose and promote development over the long run (Bjorklund & Ellis, 2005; Bjorklund & Green, 1992; Bruner, 1972).

- *Meet diverse needs.* To some degree, almost all children follow similar developmental pathways, but exceptions are everywhere, sometimes as a product of different cultures and environments and sometimes as a result of variability in genetic makeup. Regardless of their origin, children's differences require thoughtful accommodation. For example, children can learn a lot from one another's traditions, beliefs, and behaviors. However, children do not always notice the strengths of peers who come from backgrounds different from their own. Helping them avoid stereotypical thinking and cope with discrimination, racism, prejudice, and oppression are important agendas for teachers and other school professionals (García Coll et al., 1996). In addition, some children have personal experiences—perhaps growing up in poverty or losing a family member to death or incarceration—that present them with unusual challenges. These experiences, as well, necessitate sensitivity and practical measures. Finally, perceptive adults routinely encounter variations in young people's temperaments and talents. Groups of youngsters never fit a single developmental mold, and adults need to plan activities that respect culture, group differences, and individual needs (Dahlberg, Moss, & Pence, 1999).

Teachers can more effectively meet the needs of children when they learn about children's backgrounds, cultures, and families. Art by Belinda, age 12.

- *Nudge children toward advanced thinking and behaving.* To some extent, adults must *meet children where the children are,* at their current level of functioning. But to promote development, adults must also introduce tasks of increasing complexity. A school counselor, for instance, may work with a shy child to set specific goals that will promote her effective interaction with peers. One such goal

Find guidance through professional organizations such as the National Association for the Education of Young Children and academic journals such as *Child Development*. Cover of *Teaching Young Children* reprinted with permission from the National Association for the Education of Young Children. Cover of *Child Development* reprinted with permission from Blackwell Publishing.

might be to stand close to a small group of children and make a point of saying something complimentary or relevant to their conversation. Initially, children may need occasional reminders and words of praise for such behaviors, but eventually they will initiate these behaviors on their own, without any prodding from adults.

Strengthening the Commitment

A commitment to developmentally appropriate practice isn't something that can be applied automatically or that necessarily lasts forever. Teachers and other practitioners must continually discern the group-based characteristics and individual needs of young people. Furthermore, researchers continue to advance the frontiers of knowledge about child development. Therefore, educators can—and must—continue to learn more about youngsters' needs. Following are three useful things you can do:

• ***Continue to take courses in child development.*** Additional course work is one sure way of keeping up to date on (a) the latest theoretical perspectives and research results on child and adolescent development and (b) their practical implications for work with young people. Such course work has been shown to enhance professional effectiveness with children (Darling-Hammond, 1995; Darling-Hammond & Bransford, 2005).

• ***Find colleagues who share your concerns about children.*** New teachers sometimes feel overwhelmed with pressures to achieve countless school district objectives, and they may temporarily lose sight of the developmental perspectives they had previously gained in college. Working together, teachers can remind one another to focus on children's needs by selecting age-appropriate curricular programs and designing physical settings suitable for the children with whom they work (Early et al., 2007).

• ***Obtain new perspectives from colleagues.*** Many professional organizations hold regular meetings at which you can hear researchers and practitioners exchange ideas. Such meetings enable everyone to learn about the latest research findings and theoretical advances in development and discover new methods for supporting youngsters. Professional organizations also publish journals and magazines with new research findings and standards for instruction, care, and guidance of young people.

Throughout this chapter we have maintained that children's developmental paths depend significantly on the guidance of teachers and other caring adults. As you will discover throughout this book, you can do much to help children navigate their individual developmental journeys. You can definitely make a difference in children's lives.

 Summary

The Field of Child Development

The field of child development examines how human beings change from the times of conception and prenatal development, throughout infancy and childhood, and on into adolescence. Each child's developmental journey is guided by three factors: nature, nurture, and the child's own activity. Developmental theorists typically focus on the progression of children in three domains—physical, cognitive, and social-emotional—and look at how a variety of environmental contexts affect children's developmental course.

Basic Issues in Development

Developmental theorists wrestle with three basic issues related to children's development. First, they wonder how much development is influenced by nature (heredity) and how much by nurture (environment). Second, they speculate about the extent to which developmental paths are universal (true for everyone) or diverse (unique to individuals). And third, they debate about whether developmental changes can be characterized as qualitative (involving major transformations) or quantitative (reflecting gradual trends). Clearly, development is influenced by nature *and* nurture, some aspects of development are universal and others reflect diversity, and the course of development is characterized by both qualitative and quantitative change.

Theories of Child Development

Developmentalists have proposed a wide variety of explanations as to how and why children and adolescents change over time. These explanations can be categorized into seven general theoretical frameworks: biological, behaviorist and social learning, psychodynamic, cognitive-developmental, cognitive process, sociocultural, and developmental systems perspectives. These perspectives often focus on different domains of development and may place greater or lesser importance on nature versus nurture, universality versus diversity, and qualitative versus quantitative change.

Developmental Periods

Infancy (birth to 2 years) is a remarkable time of rapid growth and emergence of basic human traits, including emotional bonds with other people, language, and increasing motor mobility. Early childhood (2–6 years) is a time of imaginative play, rapid language development, advances in gross motor and fine motor skills, and expansion of social skills. During middle childhood (6–10 years), children tackle in earnest the tasks that they will need to participate effectively in adult society; they also develop friendships and internalize many of society's rules and prohibitions. In early adoles-

cence (10–14 years), youngsters are preoccupied with the physical changes of puberty and sensitive about how they appear to others; at the same time, they are thinking in increasingly abstract and logical ways. Late adolescence (14–18 years) is a period of intensive interaction with peers and greater independence from adults. Although many older adolescents make wise choices, others engage in risky and potentially dangerous behaviors.

Commitment to Developmentally Appropriate Practice

Effective care of youngsters is based on an understanding of universal developmental pathways and respect for individual differences. As a future educator, you can identify and capitalize on individual children's strengths and nudge children toward increasing responsibility. Through ongoing education, conversations with colleagues, and participation in professional organizations, you can keep up to date on advancements in child development and maintain an optimistic outlook on your ability to help children.

Applying Concepts in Child Development

The exercises in this section will help you build your skills in using knowledge of child development in your work with children.

Case Study

Latisha

Read the case and then answer the questions that follow it.

Latisha, who is 13 years old, lives in a housing project in an inner-city neighborhood in Chicago. An adult asks her to describe her life and family, her hopes and fears, and her plans for the future. She responds as follows:

> My mother works at the hospital, serving food. She's worked there for 11 years, but she's been moved to different departments. I don't know what my dad does because he don't live with me. My mother's boyfriend lives with us. He's like my step father.
>
> In my spare time I just like be at home, look at TV, or clean up, or do my homework, or play basketball, or talk on the phone. My three wishes would be to have a younger brother and sister, a car of my own, and not get killed before I'm 20 years old.
>
> I be afraid of guns and rats. My mother she has a gun, her boyfriend has one for protection. I have shot one before and it's like a scary feeling. My uncle taught me. He took us in the country and he had targets we had to like shoot at. He showed us how to load and cock it and pull the trigger. When I pulled the trigger at first I feel happy because I learned how to shoot a gun, but afterward I didn't like it too much because I don't want to accidentally shoot nobody. I wouldn't want to shoot nobody. But it's good that I know how to shoot one just in case something happened and I have to use it.
>
> Where I live it's a quiet neighborhood. If the gangs don't bother me or threaten me, or do anything to my family, I'm OK. If somebody say hi to me, I'll say hi to them as long as they don't threaten me. . . . I got two cousins who are in gangs. One is in jail because he killed somebody. My other cousin, he stayed cool. He ain't around. He don't be over there with the gang bangers. He mostly over on the west side with his grandfather, so I don't hardly see him. . . . I got friends in gangs. Some of them seven, eight years old that's too young to be in a gang. . . . They be gang banging because they have no one to turn to . . . . If a girl join a gang it's worser than if a boy join a gang because to be a girl you should have more sense.

> A boy they want to be hanging on to their friends. Their friends say gangs are cool, so they join.
>
> The school I go to now is more funner than the school I just came from. We switch classes and we have 40 minutes for lunch. The Board of Education say that we can't wear gym shoes no more. They say it distracts other people from learning, it's because of the shoe strings and gang colors.
>
> My teachers are good except two. My music and art teacher she's old and it seems like she shouldn't be there teaching. It seem like she should be retired and be at home, or traveling or something like that. And my history teacher, yuk! He's a stubborn old goat. He's stubborn with everybody.
>
> When I finish school I want to be a doctor. At first I wanted to be a lawyer, but after I went to the hospital I said now I want to help people, and cure people, so I decided to be a doctor. (J. Williams & Williamson, 1992, pp. 11–12)[a]

- In what ways do we see the contexts of family, school, neighborhood, and culture affecting Latisha's development?
- Based on your own experiences growing up, what aspects of Latisha's development would you guess are probably universal? What aspects reflect diversity?
- What clues do we have that Latisha's teachers can almost certainly have a positive impact on her long-term development and success?

Once you have answered these questions, compare your responses with those presented in Appendix A.

[a]From "'I Wouldn't Want to Shoot Nobody': The Out-of-School Curriculum as Described by Urban Students," by J. Williams and K. Williamson, 1992, *Action in Teacher Education, 14*(2), pp. 11–12. Adapted with permission of Association of Teacher Educators.

Interpreting Children's Artifacts and Reflections

Consider chapter concepts as you analyze the following artifact created by a child.

James's Changes, Big and Small

Twelve-year-old James wrote about the combination of gradual changes and more dramatic overhauls he experienced in his life as he adjusted to his seventh-grade year of middle school. His essay is shown at right and retyped below, with punctuation and spelling errors intact. As you read his reflections, decide which of his changes reflect a series of incremental, *quantitative changes,* and which other changes seem to be entirely new experiences, *or qualitative changes,* for James.

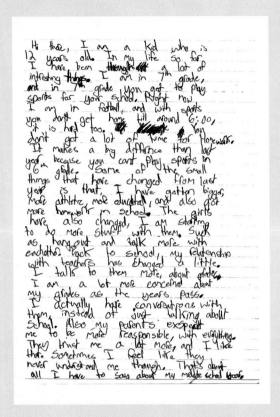

> Hi there, I am a kid who is 12 years old. In my life so far I have been through a lot of intresting things. I am in 7th grade, and in 7th grade you get to play sports for your school. Right now I am in football, and with sports you don't get home til around 6:00, it is hard too. You don't get a lot of time for Homework. It makes a big difference than last year because you can't play sports in 6th grade. Some of the small things that have changed from last year is that, I have gotten bigger, more athletic, more educated, and also got more homework in school. The girls have also changed, I am starting to do more stuff with them. Such as hang out and talk more with each other. Back to school, my relationship with teachers has changed a little. I talk to them more, about grades. I am a lot more concerned about my grades as the years pass. I actually have conversations with them, instead of just talking about school. Also my parents exspect me to be more responsible, with everything. They trust me a lot more, and I like that. Sometimes I feel like they never understand me though. That about all I have to say about my middle school year.

Once you have analyzed the artifact, compare your ideas with those presented in Appendix B. For further practice in analyzing children's artifacts and reflections, go to the Activities and Applications section in Chapter 1 of MyEducationLab.

Developmental Trends Exercise

In this chapter you learned the value of identifying children's strengths. In the section "Applying Knowledge of Child Development in the Classroom and Community," you read that these strengths provide the foundation for future growth. The following table describes five experiences by youngsters that reflect one or more underlying developmental strengths. For each experience, the table identifies youngsters' developmental strengths, an implication for building on these strengths, or both. Notice that some of the table cells have been left empty to give you a chance to make your own notes. Go to the Activities and Applications section in Chapter 1 of MyEducationLab to apply what you've learned about children's developmental strengths as you fill in the empty cells in the table.

Identifying Developmental Strengths in Youngsters

Age	Youngsters' Experiences	Developmental Concepts *Identifying Developmental Strengths*	Implications *Building on Developmental Strengths*
Infancy **(Birth–2 Years)**	An 8-month-old baby, Marita, has an ear infection and fever. She is in distress and cries often, reaching out for caregivers.	Marita is communicating her distress, having learned that caregivers can comfort her when she is hurt, tired, or scared. The baby's developmental strengths are her *expectation that others will help her* and her *ability to communicate her distress.*	
Early Childhood **(2–6 Years)**	A 3-year-old child, Sydney, asks questions constantly. Sydney wants to know why the sky is blue, why leaves are green, why a doll is broken, and why it is time for a nap.	Sydney has an insatiable and healthy curiosity. The child has also learned that he can engage adults in conversations by asking a series of questions. Sydney's developmental strengths are a *desire for new knowledge* and the possession of *rudimentary conversation skills.*	Answer the child's questions when you can, tell him politely when you are *not* able to answer his questions, and read him books and arrange other educational experiences that address his most pressing interests.

Developmental Trends Exercise (continued)

Age	Youngsters' Experiences	Developmental Concepts *Identifying Developmental Strengths*	Implications *Building on Developmental Strengths*
Middle Childhood (6–10 Years)	Several 9-year-old boys and girls are playing football at recess. The game appears to be fun, but it is punctuated with arguments over whose turn it is to play particular positions and whether or not there has been a touchdown, the ball is in or out, or a tackle has been too rough.		Tell the children that their football game looks like fun and that they seem to be working out their differences. Make sure that no one is bullying other children, and intervene if necessary.
Early Adolescence (10–14 Years)	Between classes, middle school students talk in the hallways, pass notes, and laugh. Boys and girls congregate in separate groups, eye one another, and seem to be self-conscious.	These young adolescents are learning to relate to one another in entirely new ways. Their developmental strengths are the *enthusiasm with which they approach peer relationships* and the *heightened interest they show in social networks*.	Permit free talk during passing times between classes, but ask one teacher or staff member to be nearby to intervene if necessary (e.g., if youngsters are inclined to harass one another). Be a receptive listener to young adolescents who feel slighted or ridiculed by peers.
Late Adolescence (14–18 Years)	A group of high school students believes that school is "dumb" and that classes are boring. The students see their teachers as hypocritical and out of touch. They have some specific thoughts on how rules and classes should be changed. They decide to write a letter to the newspaper and demand that either the school be changed or they be allowed to graduate early.	These adolescents are questioning the way schools are designed. Their developmental strengths are an *ability to see how the world could be different* and their *idealism* that school could be improved dramatically.	

Key Concepts

child development (p. 4)
physical development (p. 5)
cognitive development (p. 5)
social-emotional development (p. 5)
context (p. 5)
nature (p. 5)
nurture (p. 5)

temperament (p. 6)
maturation (p. 6)
sensitive period (p. 7)
universality (p. 8)
diversity (p. 8)
qualitative change (p. 9)
quantitative change (p. 9)
stage (p. 9)

stage theory (p. 9)
theory (p. 11)
biological theory (p. 11)
behaviorism (p. 12)
social learning theory (p. 12)
psychodynamic theory (p. 13)
cognitive-developmental theory (p. 13)

cognitive process theory (p. 14)
sociocultural theory (p. 15)
developmental systems theory (p. 15)
developmentally appropriate practice (p. 23)

MyEducationLab

Now go to Chapter 1 of MyEducationLab at www.myeducationlab.com, where you can:

·   View instructional objectives for the chapter.
·   Take a quiz to test your mastery of chapter objectives. Detailed feedback is provided to explain why your responses are correct or incorrect.
·   Deepen your understanding of particular concepts and principles with Review, Practice, and Enrichment exercises.

·   Complete Activities and Applications exercises that give you additional experience in interpreting artifacts, increase your understanding of how research contributes to knowledge about chapter topics, and encourage you to apply what you have learned about children's development.
·   Apply what you have learned in the chapter to your work with children in Building Teaching Skills and Dispositions exercises.
·   Observe children and their unique contexts in Video Examples.

Using Research to Understand Children and Adolescents

Elementary School Principal Jack Reston had recently joined a committee in his district that was examining student absenteeism policies. Jack realized that data from children and families could inform the work of his committee. He decided to conduct research in his school:

I initiated my research project with a review of our school's attendance rate profile for the last 5 years. The profile showed little or no change in the attendance rate. This was a concern because I cross-referenced the attendance rate with the funds allocated for various attendance incentives designed to motivate students and could easily see that the dollars spent on incentives were not affecting the attendance rate. I sat at my desk and thought about all my current and past efforts. . . .

I began by asking three questions:

1. What student characteristics are associated with student absenteeism?
2. What are some longitudinal effects of student absenteeism?
3. What are some effective strategies to prevent student absenteeism?

I reviewed current studies, literature, local and national profiles, written surveys, and interviews. I found that absenteeism was highly associated with dropping out of school, academic failure, and delinquency. I learned what students and parents in our school believed about the relationship between school and absenteeism. I concluded that I really did not understand the belief systems of families at risk for poor attendance in school. I conducted a massive survey of students and parents within a four-day period of time. Surveys gathered data concerning such things as respectfulness of students, safety in school, conflict management, discipline, school rules, self-esteem, and academics. In addition, the survey gathered data on mobility rates, volunteerism, and levels of education in parents. The identity of the families surveyed was kept unknown. Instead, the surveys were coded as "at risk" or "not at risk" data. . . .

Student teachers from a nearby university and local educators with experience in action research interviewed selected students and parents. The interviews were conducted over the telephone or face-to-face. (Reston, 2007, pp. 141–142)[a]

In analyzing the responses, Jack learned that, by and large, at-risk students at his school were not motivated by such extrinsic rewards as drawings for prizes or certificates. He also learned that students did not perceive rules to be fair or effectively enforced by the school. In reflecting on these perceptions and the relatively low achievement of the at-risk students, Jack realized that he needed to change both school policies and his style of interacting with students:

This information led to major changes in our approach to improving attendance in our school. First, we stopped spending large sums of money for rewards and drawings. Although these are nice things for students, they are ineffective in dealing with the problem of poor attendance. Second, we recognized punitive measures were having little effect on attendance. This led us to the belief that students succeeding in school were more likely to attend school regularly.

We began a concentrated effort to improve the success of students at school both academically and emotionally. This included the use of student/parent/teacher/principal contracts, daily planners for students, individual conferences between the student and the principal every 14 days to review grades and behaviors, better assessments to locate students having academic problems, improved instructional techniques and alignment of curriculum, and more concentrated efforts to improve the self-esteem of students. . . .

Based on these findings, I worked with teachers and parents to develop quick responses that unite the student, parent, educator, and community in a preventive effort to minimize absenteeism. (Reston, 2007, p. 142)[a]

- What strategies did Jack follow to make sure his research was of high quality?

- What ethical practices did Jack use as he conducted his research?

[a]Excerpts from "Reflecting on Admission Criteria" by J. Reston. In *Action Research: A Guide for the Teacher Researcher* (3rd ed., pp. 141–142), by G. E. Mills, 2007, Upper Saddle River, NJ: Merrill/Prentice Hall. Reprinted with permission of the author.

Case Study:
Jack's Research

Outline:

Case Study: Jack's Research

Principles of Research

Analyzing Developmental Research

Gathering Data as an Educator

Summary

Applying Concepts in Child Development

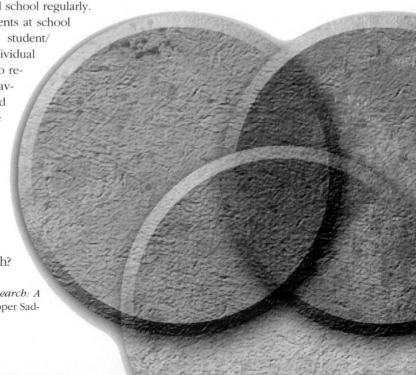

Research can be a useful way to improve educational services for children. For research to be truly helpful, it must be based on valid information and guided by ethical principles. Jack Reston enhanced the quality of his data by first examining other investigations into the issue and then gathering comprehensive survey and interview responses from both children and parents. He also followed ethical practices, by protecting the confidentiality of participants' individual responses and engaging all members of the community in a search for solutions. In the end Jack was able to make good on his promise, implementing new policies that supported children's academic abilities, coping skills, and interpersonal relationships at school.

How might researchers go about designing a research investigation that ethically examines children's developing sense of humor?

Principles of Research

To make a meaningful contribution to knowledge of child development, researchers must follow three basic principles. First and foremost, they must obey a strict ethical code. Second, they must follow the steps of the scientific method. Finally, they must select children and adolescents who can provide the desired information. We examine each of these principles in turn.

Ethical Protection of Children

A paramount concern for researchers is that they conduct research in an ethical manner; in particular, that they are honest and respectful of the rights of children (American Psychological Association, 2002; Office for Human Research Protections, 2007; Society for Research in Child Development, 2007). To protect children's rights, researchers follow these specific ethical standards:

- *Do no harm.* Researchers prioritize the welfare of children over their own desires for information. They avoid procedures that cause children stress, embarrassment, or pain.
- *Get approval from authorities.* Before collecting data from children, researchers obtain approval for their proposed study from authorities in research ethics at their university, school district, or other organization. In their proposals, researchers report the activities children will perform, any risks children might encounter, plans for reducing these risks to minimal levels, and measures for advising children and families about the procedures and their rights.
- *Obtain consent from participants and their families.* Also before collecting data, researchers obtain permission for participation. Researchers explain what the study entails in terms of time and procedures and ask both parents and children if the children are able and willing to take part in the research. If participant permission is unnecessary because researchers will not intrude on children's customary activities—for example, if they plan to observe children's spontaneous play at the park—researchers obtain the approval of appropriate institutional authorities ahead of time.
- *Preserve children's privacy.* Researchers usually describe group trends in their results. When researchers single out a particular child, they identify the child with a fictitious name and withhold other identifying information.
- *Be honest.* Children generally expect adults to be honest. Researchers do not exploit or undermine this assumption. Thus deception with children is almost always avoided.
- *Communicate openly.* After children provide information, researchers respond to any questions or concerns children or parents might have. When researchers write up their results, they often send families a brief description of their findings. Researchers also share the results with other investigators and, if appropriate, the public.

The Scientific Method

The **scientific method** is a powerful strategy for gaining knowledge because it requires researchers to think critically about the data they collect and the conclusions they draw. For developmental researchers, the scientific method commonly includes these general steps:

1. *Pose a question.* Researchers clearly state the question they want to answer. When they can make predictions about the outcomes of their study, they also state hypotheses.

scientific method
Multistep process of carefully defining and addressing a research question using critical thinking and analysis of the evidence.

2. *Design an investigation*. Once the question is clear, researchers must figure out what kinds of information will help answer the question and, if applicable, test hypotheses.
3. *Collect data*. Researchers recruit children and then gather information using carefully defined procedures.
4. *Analyze the data*. Researchers organize the data, categorize children's responses, look for themes, and, when appropriate, perform statistical tests. After making sense of the data, they draw conclusions relevant to the research question.
5. *Share the results*. Researchers write up the study's purpose, methods, results, and conclusions and present the paper at a conference, submit it to a journal, or both. Scientific peers evaluate the paper on its merits, identify any flawed arguments, and build on the ideas they find especially convincing. This give-and-take among scientists leads to scientific progress.

Research Participants

In most forms of developmental research, investigators wish to make fairly broad claims about children. In other words, investigators usually want to draw general conclusions about children of a certain age or background. To make their investigations manageable, however, they must limit their interest to a reasonable number of children. Thus researchers first define a population and then select a subgroup, or **sample,** of that population. For example, imagine that a team of developmental psychologists wants to know what older adolescents think about employment. Perhaps these scholars are interested in adolescents in public high schools in San Francisco, California. With the help of administrators in San Francisco schools, the researchers obtain a list of homeroom teachers and randomly select 10 percent of these teachers. Next, the researchers ask the selected teachers to distribute letters, consent forms, and surveys to students and parents. If the return rate for the materials is fairly high, the researchers can be reasonably confident that their *sample* of adolescents is representative of the larger *population* of adolescents in public schools in San Francisco.

Ideally, individuals in the sample reflect the characteristics of the population. Yet large, representative samples are not always possible. For example, many potential participants may decide not to join the study, or they may drop out before data collection is completed. The resulting sample may become so small that the results cannot be said to represent trends in the overall population. Furthermore, generalizing to a large population is simply not the goal for all kinds of research. Some developmental scholars study a child or small group of children intensively with the aim of portraying, with depth and insight, life as the child or children experience it. These researchers hope to analyze children's experiences in enough depth that they can draw accurate conclusions about the experiences of *these children*—not about children in general.

As you read research studies, you can look for information that the investigators have provided about their participants. One issue you may notice is that children from middle-income, European American backgrounds have been overrepresented in developmental research and that youngsters from ethnic and racial minority groups, language environments other than English-only families, and low-income communities have been underrepresented (e.g., Coll et al., 1996; McLoyd, Aikens, & Burton, 2006). Fortunately, many developmental researchers are now studying children from more diverse backgrounds and making extra efforts to document children's experiences in hard-to-find populations, such as migrant and homeless families. These outreach efforts are currently enriching our knowledge of diversity in the daily challenges children face and the core skills children learn in their families and communities (C. E. Snow & Kang, 2006; Spencer, 2006). In writing this book, we have made special efforts to include research that comes from diverse samples of children, and we encourage you to watch for information about children's backgrounds when you read research studies. When the backgrounds of research participants differ significantly from those of the children with whom you will be working, you will want to be cautious about accepting the researchers' conclusions and seek out investigations with more diverse samples of children.

Researchers adapt ethical standards, steps in scientific thinking, and procedures for recruiting participants to fit their own research questions. Usually they make good choices, implementing sound methods that adequately answer their questions. Occasionally, though, researchers collect information haphazardly or draw unwarranted interpretations from their

sample
The specific participants in a research study; their performance is often assumed to indicate how a larger population of individuals would perform.

data. Because investigations do vary in quality, it is important to analyze reports critically rather than take conclusions at face value. In the next section we examine developmental research in greater detail.

Analyzing Developmental Research

High-quality developmental research offers you a world of trustworthy knowledge about child development. To interpret developmental research sensibly, you need to become familiar with common data collection techniques and research designs.

Data Collection Techniques

Researchers rely on four major techniques for collecting information: self-reports, tests and other assessment tasks, physiological measures, and observations of behavior. Each of these four techniques offers a unique window into the minds and habits of children and adolescents.

Self-reports. Researchers often ask children to explain their beliefs, attitudes, hopes, and frustrations. In fact, some of the most informative research data comes in the form of children's and adolescents' own statements about themselves—that is, in the form of **self-reports.** Self-reports take two primary forms, interviews and questionnaires.

During **interviews,** researchers ask questions to explore the reasoning of individual children in considerable depth. When interviewers succeed in making children feel safe and comfortable, they can learn a lot about how children think about things. In the "Research: Early Adolescence" video in MyEducationLab, you can listen as the interviewer gently but persistently asks 12-year-old Claudia a series of questions about why she grouped seashells precisely as she did. The interviewer begins the discussion in this way:

Interviewer:	All right. Why did you make the groups that you did?
Claudia:	Mm, some, they were the ones that looked the most alike.
Interviewer:	How did you decide which shells to put where?
Claudia:	Um, I looked at them, like, and how they looked on every side. And I put them with the ones that looked closest like each other.
Interviewer:	Okay. So what were you looking for when you were grouping them?
Claudia:	Um, details.

Up until this point, Claudia describes her reasoning in a fairly general way. After a series of questions and requests for information from the interviewer, Claudia elaborates:

Interviewer:	Why are those in a group?
Claudia:	Um, they looked kind of the same. Feel like they both, they have the little thing there. And they fold over like that and have a tip.
Interviewer:	Okay. What makes them different from the other ones?
Claudia:	They're longer kind of. And they're smoother than the other ones.
Interviewer:	Oh, okay. And then those ones at the far corner over there. Now tell me about those ones.
Claudia:	They were smaller than these, so I put them together. And they both pretty much, or all of 'em pretty much, had the same kind of thing.
Interviewer:	Like what?
Claudia:	Like, they all had the cone at the top. The kind of pocket area.

Developmental researchers use **questionnaires** when they need to gather responses from a large number of participants. When young people complete questionnaires, they typically read questions or statements on a paper-pencil inventory and choose from defined options that express feelings, attitudes, or actions. For example, in studies of adolescents' motivation, researchers have occasionally asked adolescents to indicate how much they agree with the statement that hard work and planning pay off in life and how true it is that they want to learn as much as possible in class or, alternatively, just want to avoid doing poorly in school. In examining questionnaire responses, researchers have learned that adolescents' motivational beliefs are related to the particular courses they select in high school and the levels of achievement they attain (Crosnoe & Huston, 2007; Witkow & Fuligni, 2007).

Seven-year-old Grace drew this picture of an apple tree. What kinds of interview questions might you ask Grace if you wanted to learn more about her understanding of apple trees?

MyEducationLab

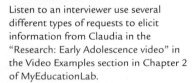

Listen to an interviewer use several different types of requests to elicit information from Claudia in the "Research: Early Adolescence video" in the Video Examples section in Chapter 2 of MyEducationLab.

self-report
Data collection technique whereby participants are asked to describe their own characteristics and performance.

interview
Data collection technique that obtains self-report data through face-to-face conversation.

questionnaire
Data collection technique that obtains self-report data through a paper-pencil inventory.

Both interviews and questionnaires have advantages. Valuable insights emerge from interviews in which researchers ask children to express their views, probe children's understandings in a thorough yet sensitive fashion, and confirm what children say with other types of data. Questionnaires offer the advantage of being an efficient way to determine group trends in youngsters' experiences. These self-report techniques have definite limitations, though. Interviews are time-consuming and highly dependent on an interviewer's skills. Questionnaires exceed many children's reading abilities and do not allow researchers to probe, nor do they allow children to express confusion or mixed feelings. In addition, when researchers are unfamiliar with children's typical ways of thinking, they may unintentionally create response options that are out of sync with children's actual ideas. Despite such difficulties, self-report techniques can give researchers vivid glimpses into the thoughts and actions of growing youngsters.

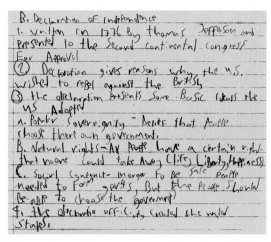

Fourteen-year-old Connor took these notes in his history class. How might you design an interview that examines Connor's understanding of the abstract concepts he recorded (e.g., "popular sovereignty" and "social contract")?

Tests and other assessment tasks. A **test** is an instrument designed to assess knowledge, abilities, or skills in a fairly consistent fashion from one individual to the next. Tests allow adults to draw inferences about children's internal processes—their learning, reasoning, and ideas. Some tests involve paper and pencil, whereas others do not, but all typically yield a result in the form of a number (e.g., a score on an intelligence test) or category (e.g., "alert" or "proficient").

In research studies, tests are frequently used to gauge the effectiveness of educational programs. For example, in an evaluation of an early intervention, infants from low-income families regularly completed tests of cognitive ability from ages 3 months to 12 years and again at age 21 (F. A. Campbell, Ramey, Pungello, Sparling, & Miller-Johnson, 2002). Test scores indicated that individuals who participated in a full-time high-quality child care program beginning as infants not only exhibited cognitive gains in the first few years of life but also had higher reading and math scores at age 21 compared to individuals who did not participate in the program. A second intervention, beginning at age 5 and lasting for 3 years, was less effective. Thus these tests were valuable in revealing that interventions may be most effective when initiated at a very young age.

Developmental scholars also measure children's abilities in ways that we would not necessarily think of as "tests." They make use of a variety of other **assessments,** such as asking children to perform certain tasks and then examining the understandings and skills revealed by the children's performance. For instance, researchers conducting separate investigations might record children's efficiency in navigating through a maze, their accuracy in detecting emotional expressions, or their understanding of commonly used verbal expressions. Some assessments involve spoken language—not the in-depth interviews described earlier but rather brief question-and-answer exchanges, such as the following assessment of 14-year-old Alicia's understanding of proverbs:

Interviewer:	What does it mean when someone says, "Better to light a candle than to curse the darkness"?
Alicia:	Well, it means, probably, that you're actually getting somewhere than just complaining about it and not doing anything about it.
Interviewer:	What does it mean when someone says, "An ant may well destroy a dam"?
Alicia:	I think it probably means that even though they're really small, they can still change things.

An advantage of tests and other assessment tasks is that they provide clues to children's thinking. From her responses, we know that Alicia can look beyond common expressions to determine their essential, underlying meanings. Assessments tell us only so much, however—we cannot tell *how* Alicia was able to decipher the proverbs. Had she previously encountered them, or did she apply strong reasoning skills on the spot? By themselves, single tests and assessments can rarely tell us how children acquired their ideas or how they might change their skills if given particular kinds of instruction. Accordingly, researchers sometimes administer assessments repeatedly over a period of time, perhaps before, during, and after instruction or some other intervention.

MyEducationLab

Observe this interview in the "Cognitive Development: Late Adolescence" video, located in the Video Examples section in Chapter 2 of MyEducationLab.

test
Instrument designed to assess knowledge, abilities, or skills in a consistent fashion across individuals.

assessment
Task that children complete and researchers use to make judgments of children's understandings and skills.

MyEducationLab

Watch an infant become accustomed to a toy in the "Habituation" video located in the Video Examples section in Chapter 2 of MyEducationLab.

Physiological measures.   To learn about children's physical development, researchers often turn to **physiological measures,** indications of such bodily conditions as heart rate, hormone levels, bone growth, brain activity, eye movements, body weight, and lung capacity. Physiological measures provide valuable information about children's health and physical growth.

In addition, physiological measures have enabled significant advances in our knowledge of infants' cognitive development. For example, researchers have learned a great deal about infants' attention, perception, and memory by exploiting infants' tendency to respond differently to familiar and unfamiliar stimuli. When infants are shown the same object or pattern repeatedly, they grow accustomed to it and lose interest (L. B. Cohen & Cashon, 2006). This tendency, called **habituation,** can be assessed through changes in heart rate, sucking, and eye movements. For example, in a study of visual perception, 4-month-old infants spent a decreasing amount of time visually focusing on a particular object (Granrud, 2006). After infants habituated to the object (presumably becoming bored with it), the researcher either changed the object's size or kept it constant, but in both cases moved the object closer. Infants were apt to look at an object of a different size with renewed interest, essentially treating it as something they hadn't seen before. Apparently, even 4-month-olds can distinguish the actual physical sizes of objects and the retinal images of those objects, presumably by using depth cues in the environment.

New medical technologies have also improved our understanding of brain development. We have learned of fascinating developmental patterns through animal research, analyses of brains of individuals who died during childhood, and new technologies that can be safely implemented with living children. An example of the last of these methods is magnetic resonance imaging (MRI), which measures the varying magnetic densities of different parts of the brain (Paus, 2005). One recent investigation examined MRI data on the brains of healthy individuals from age 7 to age 30 (Sowell, Delis, Stiles, & Jernigan, 2001). Compared to the children's brains, the adults' brains showed fewer but stronger connections in areas of the brain that support judgment, restraint, and the ability to plan for the future (Figure 2-1).

An advantage of physiological measures is that they give precise indications of how children's bodies and brains are functioning. A disadvantage is that the meaning of the data they yield is not always clear. For example, the fact that infants perceive differences among various perceptual stimuli does not necessarily indicate that they are consciously aware of these patterns or that they can act on them in any meaningful way. Another limitation is that many physiological tests cannot be administered very often because they cause discomfort (e.g., some brain-scan procedures can be quite noisy) or may be harmful if done too frequently (as is the case with X-rays).

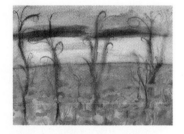

Ten-year-old Laura drew this picture of a field of poppies. How might you validly and reliably conduct observations to learn about Laura's techniques in planning, drawing, and coloring her pictures?

Observations.   Researchers conduct **observations** when they carefully watch the behavior of youngsters. Observations can offer rich portraits of children's lives, particularly when they take place over an extended time and are supplemented with interviews, tests, and other data.

Researchers who conduct observations generally keep a detailed record of significant events that take place in a particular setting, such as a neighborhood playground or family home. The following observation reveals interactions between a father and his 5-year-old daughter, Anna:

| 11:05 a.m. | Anna looks at her father, who is sitting on the couch reading the newspaper: "Wanna play Legos, Dad?" Dad says, "Sure" and puts down the paper and gets on the floor. Anna pushes a pile of Legos toward Dad and says, "Here. You can build the factory with the volcanoes." |
| 11:06 a.m. | Dad looks puzzled and says, "What factory?" Anna laughs and says, "The one where they make molten steel, silly!" Dad says "Oh, I forgot" and picks up a gray Lego and fits a red one to it. (Pellegrini, 1996, p. 22) |

physiological measure
Direct assessment of physical development or physiological functioning.

habituation
Changes in children's physiological responses to repeated displays of the same stimulus, reflecting loss of interest.

observation
Data collection technique whereby a researcher carefully observes and documents the behaviors of participants in a research study.

Although observers hope to describe events as faithfully as possible, they must make decisions about what to record and what to ignore. The observer who writes about Anna and her father may focus on the pair's negotiations over what to play and what to pretend. Other events, such as Anna dropping toys or her father scratching his head, would receive less attention.

MRI scan:
Cross-section

MRI scan:
Skull tissue
electronically
erased

MRI scan:
Surface of
the brain

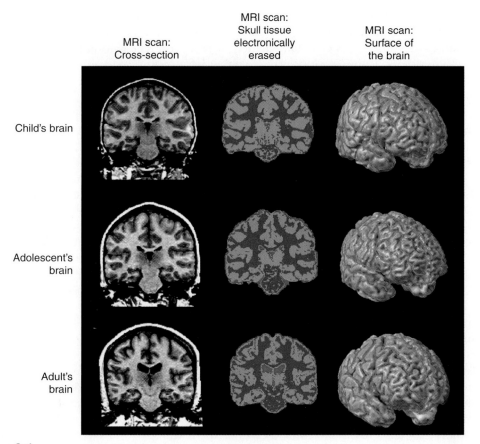

Child's brain

Adolescent's
brain

Adult's
brain

Figure 2-1

Images of three brains from magnetic resonance imaging (MRI): a child's brain (top row), an adolescent's brain (middle row), and an adult's brain (bottom row). Comparisons of the three brains in the middle column reveal how parts of the brain mature with age. The green reveals a decrease in the proportion of volume in the cortex—the wrinkled, caplike structure devoted to advanced psychological processes—that is made up of neurons ("gray matter"). This decrease may reflect increasing specialization in brain function in adults relative to children. The blue reveals an increase in the proportion of cells that insulate and protect neurons ("white matter"), which may reflect faster, more efficient processing. The red reveals increases in cerebrospinal fluid, which fills in the gaps around the brain, protecting and nourishing it; this fluid expands in volume when brain connections become more efficient and take up less space.

From E. R. Sowell, P. M. Thompson, D. Rex, D. Kornsand, K. D. Tessner, T. L. Jernigan, and A. W. Toga, "Mapping Sulcal Pattern Asymmetry and Local Cortical Surface Gray Matter Distribution *in vivo:* Maturation in the Perisylvian Cortices," 2002, *Cerebral Cortex, 12,* pp. 17–26. Reprinted by permission of Oxford University Press.

Researchers frequently use observations to document characteristics and behaviors (e.g., hairstyles, dress codes, bullying behaviors) that young people display in public settings. Observations are also helpful for studying actions that individuals may be unaware of or unable to articulate (e.g., the types of questions that teachers direct toward boys and girls) and behaviors that violate social rules (e.g., temper tantrums, petty thefts). Observations of what children look at and listen to likewise tell us a lot about children's interests. For example, by observing 7-month-old Madison in the "Emotional Development: Infancy" video in MyEducationLab, you can see Madison's interest in the visual properties of toys and books.

The strength of observations is their ability to tell us what children actually *do*—not simply what children *say* they do or what parents report about children's actions. Observations have their weaknesses, however. For one thing, the presence of an observer might actually change the behaviors under investigation. Children will sometimes be deterred from showing typical behaviors. They may misbehave or, alternatively, stay on task more than usual. Some young people become self-conscious or even anxious in the company of a stranger. To minimize these reactions, researchers often spend considerable time in a setting before they observe formally. That way, children grow accustomed to researchers and eventually carry on as they normally would.

MyEducationLab

Go to the "Emotional Development: Infancy" video in the Video Examples section in Chapter 2 of MyEducationLab and observe Madison's eye movements as she examines the visual properties of objects. What can you learn from Madison's eye movements?

Another weakness of observations is that researchers' expectations can influence their conclusions. For example, an observer who perceives children as hostile may categorize an interaction between two boys as "hitting," whereas an observer who perceives children as friendly may see the same scuffle as "energetic play." Researchers handle this problem by spending as much time as possible in the setting, carefully defining the events and behaviors they observe, and discussing their observations with other observers.

Accuracy in data collection.   Regardless of how researchers collect their data, they continually ask themselves how they know they are getting accurate information. In other words, researchers are concerned with **validity,** the extent to which their data collection methods actually assess what they want to assess. Most importantly, researchers must show that they are examining the essential parts of a well-defined domain. For instance, researchers who see mathematical skill as being comprised of both computational proficiencies (adding, subtracting, multiplying, dividing) and problem-solving abilities (making sense of situations by determining underlying mathematical patterns) must make a point to include *both* types of competencies in their assessments.

Researchers must also rule out the influence of other, irrelevant traits. For instance, do scores on a test of mathematical ability reflect children's knowledge of a particular culture—for instance, are there too many questions about American sports? Does a test of scientific reasoning assess children's desire to please the experimenter as much as it assesses finesse in thinking skills? Only when researchers can say no to such questions do they have some assurance that their methods are valid.

The validity of data is also enhanced when investigators reflect on the perspectives of research participants. Skilled researchers recognize that young people bring their own expectations and agendas to interactions with adults. Some participants (adolescents especially) may give responses to shock a researcher or in some other way undermine the research effort. Others may tell a researcher what they think the researcher wants to hear. Furthermore, children and adolescents may understand words and phrases differently than researchers do. Probing sensitively, searching for confirmation through a variety of sources, and reassuring children that they are not personally being evaluated are strategies researchers use to improve the validity of data.

Researchers must also ask whether their data collection techniques are yielding consistent, dependable results—in other words, whether their methods have **reliability.** Data are reliable when the same kind of result is obtained in a variety of circumstances. In general, reliability is lower when unwanted influences (usually temporary in nature) affect the results. Children and adolescents, like adults, inevitably perform differently on some occasions than on others; they may be more or less rested, attentive, cooperative, honest, or articulate. Their performance is also influenced by characteristics of the researcher (e.g., gender, educational background, ethnic origin, appearance) and conditions in the research setting (e.g., how quiet the room is, how instructions are worded, what kinds of incentives are given for participation).

Sometimes the assessment instrument itself influences the reliability of scores, as can occur when two different forms of a single assessment yield dissimilar conclusions about children. This could happen if one form is more difficult or if two researchers interpret the same data differently. When the researchers are making subjective judgments (e.g., about the sophistication of children's artistic skills), they must establish clear criteria or run the risk of making undependable judgments.

Reliability and validity are in fact related principles. Usually, measures that are *un*reliable cannot be valid. A technique that yields fluctuating scores would typically not be measuring anything well; rather, it would be picking up distractions, errors in a test, or other unwanted influences. However, reliability by itself does not *guarantee* validity. Even when children perform at consistent levels (a triumph of reliability), researchers can easily misinterpret the meaning of children's performance (a breakdown in validity). For example, a group of children with limited English skills may consistently perform at low levels on state mathematics tests when the instructions and problems are written in English, not because they do not understand math but because they cannot read in English. Thus, although reliability is an essential aspect of validity, by itself it does not *guarantee* validity.

In summary, a variety of factors can distort the validity of data (see Table 2-1). Researchers generally cannot rule out *all* threats to validity, but they can show that they have taken reasonable precautions to minimize distortions in the data.

validity
Extent to which a data collection technique actually assesses what the researcher intends for it to assess.

reliability
Extent to which a data collection technique yields consistent, dependable results—results that are only minimally affected by temporary and irrelevant influences.

Table 2-1   Potential Threats to Validity in Information Collected from Children and Adolescents

Source of Information	Possible Distortion	Example	Implication
Self-Reports (Interviews and Questionnaires)	Memory of research participants	In a study of children's informal family experiences related to science, a 9-year-old forgets about his family's frequent trips to the local natural history museum.	When soliciting information from children (perhaps about their life experiences or their understandings of particular concepts), begin with general questions and then ask specific follow-up questions to probe children's meanings.
	Interpretations by research participants	When asked if she has encountered any sexual harassment at her school, a teenager focuses only on unwanted physical contacts. She does not share the researcher's more comprehensive definition, which also includes verbal harassment.	When asking children and adolescents for their opinions and experiences, define your terms carefully.
	Defensiveness of research participants	In an anonymous survey, a young adolescent prefers not to admit that she has experimented with marijuana.	Respect children's right to privacy, but recognize that they may not always be honest with you about sensitive issues.
Tests and Other Assessment Tasks	Response style of research participants	Children rush through a test, responding quickly and not very carefully, so that they can have a longer recess.	Encourage children to work carefully and thoroughly on tests, and give them reasons and incentives for performing at their best.
	Cultural bias in test content	Some children taking a mathematics test have difficulty with two questions—one asking them to calculate the perimeter of a football field and another asking for the area of a baseball diamond—because they have little familiarity with these sports.	Carefully screen test content and eliminate any items that may either penalize or offend children from particular backgrounds.
	Participants' familiarity with test format	Some children in a third-grade class have never taken tests involving a matching-item format and so skip all items using this format.	Give children ample practice with the test formats you will be using.
Physiological Measures	Participants' attention to stimuli	In a study on infants' habituation, half of the babies tested are sleepy and do not attend to the objects shown to them.	When you want to draw conclusions about whether infants can make distinctions among stimuli, present them with tasks only when they are rested, fed, and alert.
	Participants' motivation	In a study of lung capacity of adolescents, participants are not motivated to perform at their best.	Establish rapport with participants, and encourage them to do their best on physical tasks.
	Instrumentation problems	A computer operator examining brain images fails to separate pictures of brain matter from those of surrounding tissues. The result is that the estimates of brain matter are confounded with the data on total brain volume.	Ensure that physiological data are produced according to the highest technical standards. Do not interpret information you are not adequately trained to analyze.
Observations	Bias of observers	In a study of gender differences in sharing behavior, an observer expects girls to share their possessions more often than boys and so is more apt to notice such actions in girls.	Think about your own biases about children and how those biases may color what you "see."
	Attention limitations of observers	In a study of nonverbal communication in older adolescents, a researcher misses a third of the smiles, gestures, winks, and other subtle communication behaviors that they display.	Keep in mind that you can take in only a limited amount of information in any given period of time; take this fact into account when planning how you will observe and categorize children's behaviors.
	Effects of the observer's presence	During a researcher's observations of an after-school science club, young adolescents are unusually quiet, businesslike, and on task.	Be alert to ways that children might change their behavior when they know that you are watching.

Source: Basic threats to validity in self-reports, tests, and observations identified by Hartmann & George, 1999.

Having carefully collected information from children, researchers must also consider the meaning of the data within the broader context of the study. To a large extent, the research design directs the interpretation of the data.

Research Designs

The *research design* translates the research question into the concrete details of a study. For example, the design specifies the procedures and schedule of data collection and strategies for analyzing the data. In child development research the design typically focuses on one of these themes: (a) the effects of new interventions on children, (b) the elements of children's development that occur in association with one another, (c) the aspects of children's behavior that change with time and those others that stay the same, or (d) the nature of children's everyday experiences.

Studies that identify causal effects of interventions.   In an **experimental study,** a researcher manipulates one aspect of the environment and measures its impact on children. Experiments typically involve an intervention, or *treatment*, of some sort. Participants are divided into two or more groups, with separate groups receiving different treatments or perhaps with one group (a **control group**) receiving either no treatment or a presumably ineffective one. Following the treatment(s), the researcher looks at the groups for differences in the children's behavior.

In a true experimental design, participants are assigned to groups on a *random* basis; they have essentially no choice in the treatment (or lack thereof) that they receive.[1] Random assignment increases the likelihood that any differences among the groups (perhaps differences in motivations or personalities of group members) are due to chance alone. With the exception of administering a particular treatment, the experimenter makes all conditions of the research experience identical or very similar for all of the groups. The researcher thus tries to ensure that the only major difference among the groups is the experimental treatment. Therefore, any differences in children's subsequent behaviors are almost certainly the *result* of treatment differences. As an example, in one classic experiment preschool-aged children (2½ to 5½ years old) who had been randomly assigned to observe an adult hitting and punching a Bobo doll (a 5-foot-tall inflated punching figure) were later more aggressive when they played independently than were children who had been randomly assigned to a condition without an aggressive adult role model (Bandura, Ross, & Ross, 1963).

In many situations experiments are impossible, impractical, or unethical. When random assignment is not a viable strategy, researchers may conduct a **quasi-experimental study,** in which they administer one or more experimental treatments but do not randomly assign participants to treatment and control groups (D. T. Campbell & Stanley, 1963). For example, a team of researchers might examine the effects of an after-school recreation program on aggressive behavior in middle school students. The researchers establish the program at one middle school and then enlist a second middle school to serve as a control group. Before starting the program, the researchers collect data to ensure that students at the two schools share certain characteristics (e.g., type of community and family income levels). The researchers cannot, however, make sure that the groups are similar in every respect. The possibility exists that some other variable (e.g., presence of gangs at one school but not the other) may account for any later difference in students' aggressive behavior.

Experiments are unique among research designs in the degree to which outside influences are controlled and therefore eliminated as possible explanations for the results obtained. For this reason, experiments are the method of choice when a researcher wants to identify possible cause-and-effect relationships. Another strength of experiments is that their rigorous procedures allow other researchers to replicate the conditions of the study. A common limitation, however, is that to ensure adequate control of procedures, researchers must sometimes conduct their interventions in artificial laboratory settings that are considerably different from conditions in the real world. Also, ethical and practical considerations make

MyEducationLab

Learn more about Bandura's classic experiment in the "Bandura's Experimental Research on Children's Aggression" video located in the Video Examples section in Chapter 2 of MyEducationLab.

experimental study
Research study in which a researcher manipulates one aspect of the environment (a treatment), controls other aspects of the environment, and assesses the treatment's effects on participants' behavior.

control group
Group of participants in a research study who do not receive the treatment under investigation; often used in an experimental study.

quasi-experimental study
Research study in which one or more experimental treatments are administered but in which random assignment to groups is not possible.

---

[1]Ethical considerations may lead researchers to give members of the control group an alternative treatment—something of value that will not compromise the experimental comparison. In other circumstances researchers make the experimental treatment available to children in the control group *after* the study has been completed.

Consider the following questions:

- What is the relationship between the regularity with which children are sad and depressed and the extent to which they are rejected by peers?
- How is children's tendency to be socially cooperative and productive associated with their rejection by peers?

These two questions ask about relationships between variables—between children's sadness and peer rejection and between productive social behaviors and peer rejection. The nature of such relationships is sometimes expressed in terms of a particular number—a statistic known as a *correlation coefficient.*

A correlation coefficient is a number between −1 and +1; most correlation coefficients are decimals (either positive or negative) somewhere between these two extremes. A correlation coefficient simultaneously tells us about the direction and strength of the relationship between two variables.

Direction of the relationship. The sign of the coefficient (+ or −) tells us whether the relationship is positive or negative. In a *positive correlation*, as one variable increases, the other variable also increases. In children, the emotional condition of being sad and depressed is positively related to rejection from peers (Peets, Hodges, Kikas, & Salmivalli, 2007). In a *negative correlation*, as one variable increases, the other variable decreases. The tendency of children to exhibit productive social behaviors (e.g., being kind and friendly to others) is negatively correlated with their rejection by peers (Peets et al., 2007).

Strength of the relationship. The size of the coefficient tells us how strong the relationship is. A number close to either +1 or −1 (e.g., +.89 or −.76) indicates a *strong correlation*: The two variables are closely related, so knowing the level of one variable allows us to predict the level of the other variable with considerable accuracy. A number close to 0 (e.g., +.15 or −.22) indicates a *weak correlation*: Knowing the level of one variable allows us to predict the level of the other variable, but we cannot predict with much accuracy. Coefficients in the middle range (e.g., those in the .40s and .50s, whether positive or negative) indicate a *moderate correlation*.

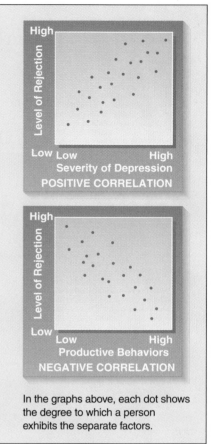

In the graphs above, each dot shows the degree to which a person exhibits the separate factors.

Figure 2-2

Correlation coefficients as statistical summaries of relationships.

it impossible to conduct true experiments related to some research questions, and when quasi-experiments are carried out instead, causal effects are not fully certain.

Studies that identify associations.   Some studies are aimed at uncovering patterns already present in children's lives. In an investigation examining associations, researchers collect information on one variable, such as the amount of time per week parents read to children, and see if it is related to another variable, such as the size of children's vocabulary. Associations often are examined with a statistic known as a **correlation,** which measures the extent to which two variables are related to each other. If a correlation exists, one variable changes when the other variable does, in a somewhat predictable fashion. The direction (positive or negative) and strength of a correlation are often summarized by a statistic known as the *correlation coefficient*, which we describe in Figure 2-2.

In a **correlational study,** investigators look for naturally occurring associations among existing characteristics, behaviors, or other variables. For example, in a study with 8- to 11-year-old children, Shavers (2000) found an association between children's exposure to community violence and children's aggression. Children who had seen a lot of violence in their neighborhoods tended to act aggressively themselves. Because these data are correlational in nature, they do not give definitive clues as to what factors might lead children who have been exposed to violence to become aggressive themselves. Although community violence might have provoked aggression in children, other conditions, such as parents' difficulty in supervising children, could have been the cause. Or perhaps a factor outside the family, such as high unemployment rates, triggered both community violence and aggresssion in children.

Correlational studies have the advantages of being relatively inexpensive to conduct and permitting the analysis of several relationships in a single investigation. One disadvantage, however, is that cause-and-effect relationships cannot be determined from correlational data alone. This is a serious limitation: Although correlational studies may demonstrate that an association exists between two or more variables, they can never tell us the specific factors that explain *why* it exists. In other words, *correlation does not necessarily indicate causation.*

correlation
Extent to which two variables are related to each other, such that when one variable increases, the other either increases or decreases in a somewhat predictable fashion.

correlational study
Research study that explores relationships among variables.

Studies that show developmental change and stability.   Some investigations, known as *developmental studies*, examine how children grow, change, or stay the same as they become older and have more experiences. One approach is a **cross-sectional study,** in which a researcher compares individuals at two or more age levels at the same point in time and assesses the same characteristic or behavior for each age-group. For example, in a study with first- and third-grade boys, Coie, Dodge, Terry, and Wright (1991) found that first graders were more likely to be targets of aggression than were third graders.

Another option for studying developmental stability and change is the **longitudinal study,** in which a researcher studies one group of children or adolescents over a lengthy period of time, often for several years and sometimes even for decades. Longitudinal studies allow us to see any changes in a characteristic when the same measurement is taken on repeated occasions. Longitudinal designs also allow us to examine the factors in children's early lives that forecast their later performance. An example of a longitudinal study is Eron's (1987) investigation into factors potentially related to aggressive behavior. Eron collected data at three points in time, first when the participants were in third grade, a second time 10 years later, and a third time 12 years after that. Factors evident when the participants were children, including a punitive style of discipline by their parents, children's preferences for watching violent television shows, and children's lack of a guilty conscience about hurting others, were predictive of their aggressiveness and criminal behavior 10 and 22 years later.

To strengthen inferences that can be made about change and stability in child development, some researchers have creatively modified developmental designs. To address questions about short-term learning, some researchers have tried *microgenetic methods*, which you might think of as brief but thorough longitudinal designs. Researchers implementing microgenetic methods may study children's actions and strategies while learning a new task over a few hours, days, or weeks (Siegler, 2006; Vygotsky, 1978). Other variations include a combination of cross-sectional and longitudinal designs. For instance, a *cohort-sequential design* replicates a longitudinal study with new *cohorts*—that is, with one or more additional groups of people born in certain subsequent years. To illustrate, Suhr (1999) conducted a cohort-sequential study to examine children's scores in mathematics, reading recognition, and reading comprehension. Scores were collected every 2 years for children who were born in 1980, 1981, 1982, and 1983. Suhr found that growth in skills was rapid between ages 5 and 10 but slowed down after age 10. Because the data included children from four different birth years, Suhr could be reasonably confident that the spurt of learning that occurred between 5 and 10 years was a reasonably accurate result and not an anomaly of one particular group.

The particular strengths and limitations of developmental studies depend largely on the features of the individual designs. Cross-sectional studies offer an efficient snapshot of how characteristics or behaviors probably change with age, but these age differences can be attributed to a variety of factors, including maturation, exposure to schooling experiences, and general changes in society. Longitudinal studies allow prediction of later characteristics based on earlier qualities but are expensive, time-consuming, and of questionable relevance to other populations of children. The hybrid designs that combine the features of cross-sectional and longitudinal designs have definite advantages, but they are extremely expensive to carry out and create demands for continued involvement in research that many potential research participants would rather avoid.

Studies that describe children's everyday experiences in natural contexts.   In a *naturalistic study*, a researcher examines children as they behave and interact in their families, peer groups, schools, clubs, and elsewhere. The researchers try to portray the views of the children themselves as they carry out their daily lives. Some of these studies, known as **ethnographies,** look at the everyday rules of behavior, beliefs, social structures, and other cultural patterns of an entire group of people—perhaps a community, classroom, or family. Researchers who conduct ethnographies typically spend many months and occasionally even a year or more collecting detailed notes in an ordinary setting, getting to know the people who congregate there and the meaning of their ways (Wolcott, 1999).

In another type of naturalistic investigation, a researcher conducts a **case study,** wherein a single person's or a small group's experiences are documented in depth over a period of time. (Research case studies are not to be confused with the case studies that begin and end the chapters in this book, which are more limited in scope.) Other naturalistic

cross-sectional study
Research study in which the performance of individuals at different ages is compared at a single point in time.

longitudinal study
Research study in which the performance of a single group of people is tracked over a period of time.

ethnography
Naturalistic research study in which investigators spend an extensive period of time documenting the cultural patterns of a group of people in the group's everyday settings.

case study
Naturalistic research study in which investigators document a single person's or a small group's experiences in depth over a period of time.

studies take the form of **grounded theory studies,** in which researchers typically collect in-depth data on a particular topic—often one related to people's experiences and perceptions related to a particular phenomenon—and use those data to develop a theory about that phenomenon (Corbin & Strauss, 2008). For example, a researcher might ask young children to describe and draw pictures of enjoyable playgrounds in an attempt to capture the general experience of play in children (Hyvönen & Kangas, 2007). Grounded theory studies are especially helpful when current theories about a phenomenon are either inadequate or nonexistent (Creswell, 2002).

The results of naturalistic studies tend to be more verbally descriptive and less reliant on statistical tests than are results presented for the three other designs we've examined. As an example, two researchers conducted interviews with 17 adolescent boys living in either a residential treatment center or a halfway home (V. A. Lopez & Emmer, 2002). Using a grounded theory approach, the researchers asked the boys about their violent crimes and identified two motives. In "vigilante crimes," the boys used physical aggression to avenge another person's actual or perceived wrongful act. For example, 16-year-old Tax used a vigilante motivation in trying to protect his cousin:

> We had went over there to go use the phone and I went to go use the restroom. And when I came out, they had beat him [cousin] down, and hit him with a brick in his head, and cracked his skull open. So I got into a fight with one of them. I hit him with a lock and broke his jaw. He had to get three stitches in his head. (V. A. Lopez & Emmer, 2002, p. 35)

In "honor crimes," the boys used violence to protect themselves or their gang. Seventeen-year-old Muppet gave this explanation for his participation in a drive-by gang shooting:

> Around my birthday me and a bunch of my cousins [fellow gang members] found out about B [name of rival gang] named A who was talking shit and had jumped one of my cousins so we found out where he [rival gang member] lived and we went by and shot up his trailer house. We don't like Bs [members of rival gang] to begin with. (V. A. Lopez & Emmer, 2002, p. 37)

A key strength of naturalistic studies is their sensitivity to children's own perspectives on everyday events and relationships. In the study we just examined, the young people viewed their aggressive acts as justifiable ways to preserve their own identities and solve conflicts. Such studies often make it possible to capture the complexities and subtle nuances of children's experiences in particular environments. Naturalistic studies have several limitations, however. They are difficult and time-consuming to carry out, usually require extensive data collection, and produce results that fail to disentangle causes and effects in children's lives.

In the description of research designs in this section, we included several studies focusing on one topic, children's aggression. Each of the designs contributed unique information regarding the aggression of youngsters. For instance, we learned that in some settings children exposed to aggressive models imitate the aggressive acts they have seen, that children's exposure to violence in the community is associated with children's own agression, that punitive child rearing by parents is associated with their children's aggressiveness later in life, and that violent youth see their aggressive acts as justified.

More generally, each of the four designs we've examined affords valuable insights into child development. Table 2-2 presents additional examples of the four designs, showing the kinds of data analyses researchers might use with each kind of study.

Becoming a Thoughtful Consumer of Research

As you read research studies, you will want to get in the habit of reading the methods, results, and conclusions critically. If you ask a few simple questions of investigations, you can begin to distinguish studies that are worthy of your consideration from those that are not.

As an illustration, imagine that at an elementary school faculty meeting, teachers and administrators want to improve children's ability to get along with peers and teachers. They use various terms to describe what they're talking about—the labels "character education" and "moral education" frequently pop up—but eventually decide that what they *most* want to do is increase the frequency of kind, respectful, and cooperative behaviors that children exhibit to one another and to school staff. A committee of teachers is appointed to study the matter in greater depth, and in particular to look at what research has to say about effective and

grounded theory study
Naturalistic research study in which investigators develop and elaborate new theories while comparing data (such as interview statements from participants) to the researchers' emerging interpretations.

Table 2-2   Examples of Data Analysis in Developmental Research Designs

Design	Illustration of Data Analysis	Explanation
Studies That Identify Causal Effects of Interventions	Forty-eight Canadian families with 5- to 10-year-old children participated in a study on sibling disputes. Half of the families were randomly assigned to a mediation training condition in which parents received coaching on helping children consider one another's perspectives during sibling conflicts; the remaining families received no training (J. Smith & Ross, 2007). Following are a few of the behaviors recorded during sibling disputes among the older children in the trained and untrained family groups:	The table compares the proportions of time participants in the trained and untrained groups, on average, engaged in particular behaviors when involved in a sibling conflict. These data suggest that children of parents trained in mediation spoke more calmly, explained themselves, and suggested solutions more often than did children of untrained parents. The groups did not differ in insults. Many other results from the full report are not included here, but overall, those children whose parents had participated in mediation training resolved conflicts more constructively than did children of untrained parents.

Proportions of Time Children Engaged in Behavior

Children's Behaviors	Families with Mediation Training	Families Without Mediation Training
Insult	.04	.05
Talk Calmly	.41	.06
Explain	.40	.19
Suggest Solutions	.45	.07

Design	Illustration of Data Analysis	Explanation
Studies That Identify Associations	One hundred and sixty-six Finnish children participated in a study on friendship during their first- and second-grade years (Laursen, Bukowski, Aunola, & Nurmi, 2007). Two groups of children were identified during first grade: those who had mutually close friendships and those who did not. Among the first-grade children who did *not* have close friends, there was a positive correlation between being physically aggressive and being socially isolated a year later (the correlation for this group was +.40). This association did not exist among children who had close friends in first grade (the correlation for this group was –.08).	A *correlation coefficient* is a number that measures the degree of association between two variables (see Figure 2-2). In this study there was a moderate positive association between being physically aggressive and later social isolation among first graders who did not have close friends. The graph below shows one example of a .40 correlation. Notice the slight general trend for increases in aggression to be associated with increases in later social isolation.

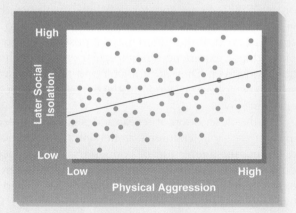

Example of a .40 correlation coefficient represented visually. Each dot shows the degree to which a person exhibits the two factors, aggression and later social isolation.

continued

ineffective programs. Meeting after school the following day and periodically during the next few weeks, the committee addresses the following questions:

• ***What is the purpose of analyzing existing research?*** The purpose of the committee's analysis is to inform the selection of an effective educational program that fosters respectful and cooperative behaviors in children. With the help of a reference librarian at a nearby university, the committee identifies promising electronic databases and keywords (e.g., *character education, moral education, prosocial behavior*) to use in its search. It soon finds articles examining three widely used programs: an Ethics Curriculum for Children (Leming, 2000), the Positive Action program (Flay & Allred, 2003), and the Caring School Community (Solomon, Watson, Delucchi, Schaps, & Battistich, 1988), as well as an Internet site that compares the effectiveness of these and other similar programs (Institute of Education

Table 2-2 Examples of Data Analysis in Developmental Research Designs (continued)

Design	Illustration of Data Analysis	Explanation
Studies That Show Developmental Change and Stability	A group of 1,329 13-year-old European American and African American adolescents completed a questionnaire about self-esteem. Efforts were made to recruit the adolescents to take the same self-esteem instrument at ages 15, 17, and 19; complete data were available for 567 of these individuals (Gutman & Eccles, 2007). In the graph below,[a] the developmental changes in self-esteem scores are plotted separately for European American girls and boys. 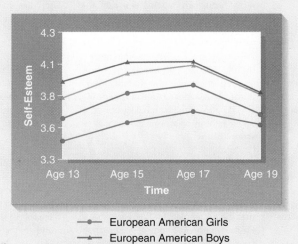	In a longitudinal study, a single group of children is studied over an extended time period. When the same measures are taken on multiple occasions, the scores can be tracked and a growth curve charted. In this study adolescents' self-reports of self-esteem increased between ages 13 and 17 and then decreased from 17 to 19. There were some variations present by gender and ethnicity. For example, at age 15, European American boys reported the highest self-esteem, followed by African American boys, African American girls and, lastly, European American girls.
Studies That Describe Children's Everyday Experiences in Natural Contexts	Nine 11- to 17-year-old adolescents from New York City participated in interviews about their experiences with having one or both parents being HIV positive (and in some cases having AIDS) (Woodring, Cancelli, Ponterotto, & Keitel, 2005). Following are excerpts from three adolescents' responses (Woodring et al., 2005): · Losing her, where am I to go? Where will I live? I'm only 16. I have nowhere, nothing. (p. 662) · I have to be strong for me and my sister 'cause I know I'm going to have to take on that responsibility and take care of my sister. (p. 663) · Really I always want to keep my grades up. I want to be good. I try to make her [Mom] happy. (p. 667)	In qualitative studies researchers often conduct in-depth interviews, through which children and adolescents can express their thoughts in their own words. The researchers then identify *themes* (ideas mentioned regularly) in interview responses. In this investigation several distinct themes were identified, including coping with loss, dealing with transitions, and adjusting to everyday demands of school. As was done in this study, actual statements from participants are usually included in naturalistic research reports to illustrate the themes.

[a]From Gutman, L. M., & Eccles, J. S. (2007). Stage-environment fit during adolescence: Trajectories of family relations and adolescent outcomes. *Developmental Psychology, 43*, 522–537. Adapted with permission from the American Psychological Association.

Sciences, 2006). The committee prints out the resources it has found and begins to read. It initially focuses on three articles that seem especially helpful, as shown in Table 2-3.

- ***Who participated in the investigations?*** The committee notes that all three investigations had fairly large samples. The studies drew from different parts of the country and recruited children from families with varying income levels and ethnic backgrounds. However, none of the samples is as diverse as the population at the committee's own school, which includes many children from various ethnic backgrounds and immigrant origins.

- ***What are the designs of the studies?*** Each of the studies used a quasi-experimental design. Because participants were not randomly assigned to treatment and control groups, the committee cannot know for sure whether any group differences in outcomes were due to the program content, to preexisting differences between the groups, or to some other factor.

Table 2-3 Analyzing Research on Program Effectiveness: The Case of "Character Education"

Purpose of the Analysis: *Finding a program that fosters kind, respectful, and cooperative behaviors in elementary school children*

Questions for the Analysis	Selected Programs for Review		
	Ethics Curriculum for Children (Leming, 2000)	Positive Action (Flay & Allred, 2003)	Caring School Community (Solomon et al., 1988)
What are the objectives of the research?	The researchers evaluated the Ethics Curriculum for Children, a program that aims to promote elements of "good character" using a read-aloud multicultural literature-based program. The program is organized around traits of courage, loyalty, justice, respect, hope, honesty, and love.	The researchers evaluated Positive Action, a program that aims to promote character development and social-emotional skills of children and adolescents and to reduce drug use, school suspension rates, and violence rates through classroom discussion, role playing, games, songs, and other structured activities.	The researchers evaluated the Caring School Community, a program that aims to foster productive social behaviors (e.g., cooperation) and a general sense of affection and respectfulness through structured classroom lessons, cross-age buddies, schoolwide initiatives, and activities at home.
Who participated in the investigation?	The Ethics Curriculum for Children has been used in more than 1,500 schools. In Leming's study, participants were 965 first- to sixth-grade students from predominantly European American and African American backgrounds in semirural areas of Pennsylvania and Illinois.	Positive Action has been used in more than 11,000 schools. In Flay and Allred's study, participants were students from European American, African American, and Hispanic American backgrounds in 36 elementary schools in a Southeastern school district.	The Caring School Community program has been implemented in more than 2,700 classrooms. In Solomon and colleagues' studies, participants were approximately 600 K–4 students from six elementary schools in a middle- to upper-middle income suburban community in Sam Ramon, California.
What is the design of the study?	A quasi-experimental design compared outcomes for children who participated in the ethics curriculum to outcomes of children in control-group classes that did not use this curriculum or another character education program.	A quasi-experimental design compared outcomes for children who participated in the Positive Action curriculum with children in schools in the same district that did not implement Positive Action. Positive Action and control-group schools served families with similar income levels.	A quasi-experimental design compared outcomes for children in three schools who participated in the Caring School Community with children in three other schools in the same district. The treatment and control-group schools served families with similar income levels.
What information is presented about the validity and reliability of the data?	Teachers completed a rating scale of each student's character-related behavior before and after the program. The items on the scale were internally consistent—that is, they all seemed to be assessing the same characteristic—which indicates high reliability and indirectly suggests adequate validity as well. However, teachers may have been biased in their observations of children, threatening the validity of the rating-scale scores.	The researchers obtained school records of disciplinary referrals, out-of-school suspensions, and extended absences. School officials typically follow strict guidelines in keeping records for disciplinary referrals and suspensions, but possibly school faculty members were biased in the students they did (and did not) refer for disciplinary action.	Outside observers were carefully trained in rating the children's behaviors and did not know which schools were and were not participating in the Caring School Community program. The researchers presented several forms of evidence to indicate good reliability and validity of the data. For example, observers' ratings of students' cooperative behaviors were positively correlated with teachers' ratings of students' behavior in small groups.
Is the study published in a reputable journal?	Yes. The study was published in *Journal of Moral Education*. The author and his colleagues have also published a few other reports on the curriculum.	Yes. The study was published in *American Journal of Health Behavior*. The authors have published extensively on this program.	Yes. The study was published in *American Educational Research Journal*. Numerous other investigations on the program have been published in reputable journals.
Do the analyses suggest significant results in areas of concern for your own purposes?	No. The results focusing on behavior change are difficult to interpret. In grades 1–3, participants in the Ethics Curriculum showed *less* desirable behavior than did children in the control-group classes. (As the researcher points out, teachers in the experimental-group classes may have had higher expectations for their students; their lower ratings may have reflected their disappointment at not seeing dramatic changes.) In grades 4–6, participants in the program did exhibit better behavior than those in the control group.	Not primarily in the areas of concern for the committee. Students in the Positive Action schools had lower rates of violence and suspensions but not absenteeism than students in the control-group schools. The focus of the study was on rates of violence and suspension (which decreased following the curriculum) and on absenteeism (which did not decrease). However, the authors did not specifically indicate improvements in behaviors of concern to this analysis (e.g., respectfulness, cooperation).	Yes. Compared to students without exposure to this program, students in the Caring School Community exhibited higher levels of spontaneous helping behaviors and supportive and friendly behaviors. No differences were found in an additional measure of helping behaviors.
Overall, does the program meet the needs of the school?	No. The program has merits, but the evidence is not strong for an increase in helpful and cooperative behaviors in children.	Maybe. The program appears to decrease students' violence but does not dramatically increase helpful and cooperative behaviors.	Yes. The program appears to increase students' helpful, cooperative behaviors in school settings.

Note: Given that the goal of the analysis is to find a program that fosters cooperative and helpful behaviors of children at elementary school, instruments and results that targeted helping behaviors and productive conduct of elementary children are included in the table, and reports about other outcomes (e.g., knowledge, attitudes, values, and achievement) and data from other age-groups are not included.

- *What information is presented about the validity and reliability of the data?*[2] The strength of the data varied across the three studies. For example, the evaluation of the Ethics Curriculum for Children depended on teacher ratings of students' behaviors; in making their ratings, the teachers may have been affected by observer bias, seeing what they *expected* to see in various students. The evaluation of Positive Action involved school records related to disciplinary referrals, suspensions, and absentee rates. Absenteeism can be recorded accurately, but teachers' and administrators' judgments of which students warranted disciplinary action could have been influenced by personal biases toward or against particular students. The investigators examining the Caring School Community program appeared to have been especially thoughtful about the quality of their data, making sure that observers did not know which children were participants in the program.

- *Are the studies published in reputable journals?* All three of the articles were published in reputable journals. The *Journal of Moral Education, American Journal of Health Behavior*, and *American Educational Research Journal* all scrutinize manuscripts, publishing only those that, in the eyes of several expert reviewers, use sound research methods.

- *Do the analyses suggest significant results in areas of concern?* As shown in Table 2-3, results were not consistently favorable in the Ethics Curriculum for Children study. Results were generally favorable for the Positive Action and Caring School Community programs. Furthermore, the committee finds additional support for the Positive Action and Caring School Community programs in the other resources it examines (Battistich, 2003; Institute of Education Sciences, 2006). After considerable thought, the committee decides that the outcomes for the Positive Action program are only tangentially related to the goals of fostering cooperative and helping behaviors and that the Caring School Community yielded results that most closely align with its own goals for a curriculum.

After completing its analysis, the committee recommends the Caring School Community to the school faculty (see the final row in Table 2-3). In doing so, the committee cites the program's favorable outcomes in fostering children's helping and cooperative behaviors, the high validity and reliability of the data, and an extensive set of studies available on the program's effects. The committee members express some concern that the children who participated in the research studies were not as diverse as the children in their own school, but other teachers suggest they might address this problem themselves by learning more about the different helping and cooperative behaviors used by children from various backgrounds (McMahon, Wernsman, & Parnes, 2006).

As you read research articles and reports, you can ask yourself questions similar to the ones the committee addressed. You will probably find that it takes some practice to adapt your analysis to the particular data collection techniques and designs present in individual investigations. For example, when reading ethnographic reports, you would look for information about the details of people's ordinary activities and should not expect to find sophisticated statistics or large sample sizes. When examining cross-sectional studies, you would want the investigators to consider several possible explanations (maturation, increasing experience, etc.) for any differences in children's abilities across distinct age groups and not take any particular explanation for granted. With experience, you will gradually gain expertise that will help you distinguish dependable information about child development from sources you cannot trust.

Now that you have a general understanding of the basic principles, methods, and uses of research, you can practice reading developmental research reports with a critical eye. You are also ready to reflect on the things children do, say, and write.

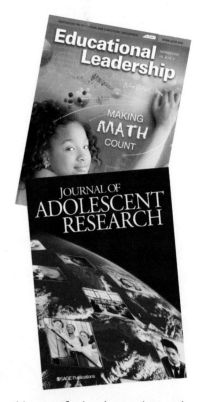

Many professional magazines and journals are available to help you learn more about the development of children and adolescents.
Cover from *Educational Leadership*, 65(3). November 2007. Copyright © 2007 by the Association for Supervision and Curriculum Development. Reprinted with permission. Learn more about ASCD at www.ascd.org.
Cover from *Journal of Adolescent Leadership*, 23(2), March 2008. Copyright © 2008 by Sage Publications. Reprinted with permission.

Gathering Data as an Educator

As you have seen, academic researchers work diligently to collect information about children and adolescents in ways that are ethical, sensitive, valid, and reliable. Teachers and other school professionals do the same, although their strategies are somewhat different.

---

[2]Researchers who conduct naturalistic investigations often use other terms besides validity and reliability to describe the quality of their data. For example, researchers might suggest that they have tried to produce *trustworthy* or *credible* results by spending a long time observing children, asking the children for their interpretations of the research conclusions, and corroborating their results with several distinct kinds of data.

Increasing the Accuracy of Conclusions About Children

As an educator or other professional working with children, you can use some of the same methods of data collection used by academic researchers. Unlike researchers, however, you will usually not have the luxury of controlled conditions for collecting information. Your primary motivations, of course, will be to effectively teach and in other ways nurture young people.

Because you will likely have a busy classroom of children or another occupation that poses many demands on your attention, you must take extra care to think critically about the information you collect. We recommend these tactics:

• ***Continually question the validity and reliability of the information you collect.*** Validity and reliability are and must be ongoing concerns not only for researchers but also for teachers and other practitioners. Educators must be appropriately cautious when interpreting data they have gathered about children.

As educators gain experience with children and adolescents, they become better able to draw inferences about youngsters' perspectives on life. They must remember, however, that no single behavior or statement is likely to be a completely trustworthy reflection of a young person's understandings and values.

• ***Form multiple hypotheses.*** In your efforts to observe children and adolescents, never be content with a single interpretation, no matter how obvious that explanation might seem to you. Always consider multiple possible reasons for the behaviors you observe, and resist the temptation to settle on one of them as "correct" until you've had a chance to eliminate other possibilities. In this regard, teachers and some other practitioners actually have an advantage over professional researchers. Whereas researchers often see children for only brief periods, practitioners can deepen their understanding of children's needs as new information becomes available.

• ***Use multiple sources of information.*** Because no single source of data ever has "perfect" validity and reliability, teachers and other school personnel try to use many sources of information to understand and draw conclusions about children's development. Three kinds of data collection are commonly used by educators: observing children's behavior, listening to children's statements, and interpreting the products of children's work. We now offer additional suggestions for increasing the accuracy of inferences about children's behaviors, statements, and work products.

Observing Children

If you carefully watch children and adolescents in classrooms, community clubs, and other settings, you can learn a lot about their interests, values, and abilities. Here are some suggestions to enhance your observation skills:

Teachers can learn a lot from watching children's facial expressions, postures, and other nonverbal behaviors. These two girls appear to be enjoying their time together on the computer.

• ***Observe how children respond to the demands of particular settings.*** Teachers and other practitioners often watch children move among various settings, such as the classroom, cafeteria, and playground. As you observe children and adolescents in particular settings, ask yourself what they are doing, why they might be behaving as they are, how they might be interpreting events, and how the setting may be affecting their behavior. When you are able to gather observations across multiple settings, you can gain deeper insights into the abilities and needs of individual children. For example, a child who appears uninhibited and happy on the playground but fearful and tense in the classroom may need additional help academically or another kind of assistance from adults.

• ***Observe youngsters' nonverbal behaviors.*** Careful observation of children's postures, actions, and emotional expressions can provide important information about their preferences and abilities. For example, an infant caregiver may learn that one 18-month-old toddler slows down, pulls at his ear, and seeks comfort when he's sleepy, whereas another child of the same age speeds up, squirms, and becomes irritable when ready for a nap. During an interview with a teenage boy, a school counselor might notice that he seems withdrawn and despondent. In response, the counselor inquires sympathetically about how things are going for him at home and school.

• ***Consider children's developmental states.*** When you sense an unmet need, analyze the situation using your knowledge of child development. Your emerging familiarity with typical characteristics of different age-groups can help you target your observations of children. Often, by noticing recurrent themes in children's actions and statements, you can get a sense of their thoughts and feelings. Observation Guidelines tables throughout the book can assist you in identifying particular developmental abilities in children and adolescents. The first of these, "Learning from Children and Adolescents," suggests some general things to look for in your work with young people.

• **_Separate direct observations from inferences._** To learn to observe well, you need to begin to distinguish what you actually see from what you think it means. It is probably

Observation Guidelines

Learning from Children and Adolescents

Characteristic	Look For	Example	Implication
What Children Do	· Exploration of the environment through manipulation of objects, focused attention, and attempts to make sense of events in conversations with other people (may indicate inquisitiveness for certain kinds of information) · Preferred activities during free time (may show children's foremost desires and interests) · Interest in people, including initiating interactions as well as responding to others' social gestures (may indicate comfort levels in social situations) · Quiet periods of self-absorption (may indicate either thoughtful self-reflection or sadness) · Facial expressions (reflecting enjoyment, excitement, sadness, confusion, anger, or frustration) · Tenseness of limbs (might indicate either intense concentration or excessive anxiety) · Slouching in seat (might indicate fatigue, boredom, or resistance to an activity)	Whenever his teacher engages the class in a discussion of controversial issues, James participates eagerly. When she goes over the previous night's homework, however, he crosses his arms, slouches low in his seat, pulls his hat low over his eyes, and says nothing.	Provide a safe environment with interesting and attractive objects for active exploration. Make changes to the environment based on the preferred activities of children who inhabit it. Use children's body language as a rough gauge of interest, and modify activities that do not appear to be engaging children's attention and interest. Speak individually and confidentially with children who often show signs of sadness or anger.
What Children Say	· Verbal expressions of likes and dislikes · Thoughtful and insightful questions about the topic at hand (indicates high task engagement and motivation) · Questions that have already been answered (might indicate either inattentiveness or lack of understanding) · Complaints about the difficulty of an assignment (might indicate low motivation, lack of ability or confidence, or an overloaded schedule of academic and social obligations)	In a whining tone, Danielle asks, "Do we really have to include _three_ arguments in our persuasive essays? I've been thinking really hard and can only come up with one!"	Read between the lines in the questions children ask and the comments they make. Consider what their questions and comments might indicate about their existing knowledge, skills, motivation, and self-confidence.
What Children Produce in Assessments and Artifacts	· Careful and thorough work (indicates high motivation) · Unusual and creative ideas, artwork, or constructions (indicates high motivation and a willingness to take risks) · Numerous sloppy errors (might indicate that a child did an assignment hurriedly, has poor proofreading skills, or has a learning disability)	When Martin's social studies teacher gives several options for how students might illustrate the idea of _democracy_, Martin creates a large poster of colorful, cartoonlike characters engaging in such activities as voting, free speech, and making new laws.	When looking at and evaluating children's work, don't focus exclusively on "right" and "wrong" answers. Examine a variety of artifacts when drawing inferences about children's abilities and interests.

never possible to be entirely objective, but you can make some headway in tempering your own reactions to events. One strategy that may help you is to keep separate records of what you see and how you make sense of the experience. Here are some notes from a student teacher, Ana, who recorded her observations in a "Notetaking" column and her interpretations in a "Notemaking" one:

Notetaking	Notemaking
A child is working at the computer. There are fourteen students working at their desks. Six students are working with another teacher (aide) in the back of the room. It is an English reading/writing group she is working with—speaking only in English. I see a mother working with one child only and she is helping the student with something in English. There is a baby in a carriage nearby the mother. I hear classical music playing very lightly. I can only hear the music every once in a while when the classroom is really quiet. I stand up and move around the room to see what the children at their desks are working on. They are writing scary stories. The baby makes a funny noise with her lips and everyone in the class laughs and stares for a few seconds, even the teacher. . . .	The class seems to be really self-directed. . . . I am not used to seeing students split up into different groups for Spanish and English readers because in my class they are Spanish readers, but it is really good for me to see this because it happens in a lot of upper grade settings, and I will be working in an upper grade bilingual setting next placement. I really like the idea of putting on music during work times. I know that when I hear classical music it really helps me to relax and calm down, as well as focus. I think that it has the same effect on the students in this class. I'm noticing more and more that I really cherish the laughter in a classroom when it comes from a sincere topic or source. It is also nice to see the students *and* the *teacher* laughing. . . . (C. Frank, 1999, pp. 11–12)[3]

Trying to notice the nuances in children's activities without jumping to conclusions can help you become a more perceptive observer. By distinguishing what you see from what it might mean, you can also learn about your own expectations and priorities as a teacher, as Ana might have done when rereading her "Notemaking" comments.

- *Try out different kinds of observations.* The kinds of observations you conduct will depend on what you hope to gain from watching and listening to children. *Running records* are narrative summaries of a child's activities during a single period of time (Nicolson & Shipstead, 2002). Running records provide teachers and other professionals with opportunities to focus on a particular child and draw conclusions about the child's emerging developmental abilities. In Figure 2-3 you can see an excerpt from a running record prepared by a language specialist who was observing a child with a hearing impairment. After carefully scrutinizing the running record, the language specialist concluded that Taki understood some aspects of spoken language when she followed directions. However, Taki needed help when completing the Listening Lotto game. These kinds of conclusions can offer professionals good ideas about next steps. Possibly, the language specialist realized she might need to look further into Taki's hearing ability.

Anecdotal records are descriptions of brief incidents observed by teachers and other professionals (Nicolson & Shipstead, 2002). An anecdotal record is typically made when an adult notices a child take an action or make a statement that is developmentally significant. For example, anecdotal records are sometimes made of children's accomplishments, physical milestones, social interaction patterns, ways of thinking, and concerns. Anecdotal records tend to be much briefer than running records, and they may be written up later in the day. Teachers can accumulate notes about children, use the notes to help identify individual needs, and share them with family members during conferences, informal conversations, and meetings. Figure 2-4 shows teacher-prepared anecdotal records for three young children.

Teachers sometimes use *checklists* and *rating scales* when they wish to evaluate the degree to which children's behaviors reflect specific criteria. Checklists allow observers to note whether a child's actions or work products reflect specific standards. For example, Figure 2-5 on page 54 shows a checklist a debate teacher might use to evaluate a student's oral presentation. Rating scales are similar to checklists, but these ask observers not simply whether a child shows a particular behavior but rather how *often* or *consistently* the child shows the be-

---

[3]From *Ethnographic Eyes: A Teacher's Guide to Classroom Observation* (pp. 11–12), by Carolyn Frank, 1999, Portsmouth, NH: Heinemann. Copyright 1999 by Carolyn Frank. Reprinted with permission.

Center/Age level: Center for Speech and Language/3- to 6-Year-Olds

Date:	7/17	Time:	10:20–10:26 AM
Observer:	Naoki	Child/Age:	Taki/5;1
		Teacher:	Camille

	Comments
Taki is seated on the floor with Kyle (4;8) and Camille, the teacher, in a corner of the classroom; both children have their backs to the center of the room. Taki sits with her right leg tucked under her bottom and her left leg bent with her foot flat on the floor. The Listening Lotto card is in front of her on the floor, and she holds a bunch of red plastic markers in her right hand. Camille begins the tape.	10:20
The first sound is of a baby crying. Taki looks up at Camille, who says, "What's that?" Taki looks at Kyle, who has already placed his marker on the crying baby. Camille says, "That's a baby crying," and points to the picture on Taki's card. Taki places the marker with her left hand as the next sound, beating drums, begins.	No intro of game. Hearing aid working.
Taki looks at Kyle as the drumming continues. Camille points to the picture of the drums on Taki's card, and Taki places her marker.	Understands process.
The next sound is of a toilet flushing. Taki looks at Kyle and points to the drums. Kyle says, "Good, Taki. We heard drums banging." Taki smiles. Camille says, "Do you hear the toilet flushing?" as she points to the correct picture. Taki places her marker and repositions herself to sit cross-legged. She continues to hold the markers in her right hand and place them with her left. . . .	10:22 Kyle supportive of Taki.

Conclusions: Taki's receptive language was on display when she followed the teacher's directions in Listening Lotto (put markers on the appropriate spots), but she did not demonstrate success on her own. Her fine motor control was in evidence as she adeptly handled small markers.

Figure 2-3

Running record for Taki during Listening Lotto. Note that developmentalists often list a child's age in both years and additional months, separating the two numbers by a semicolon. For instance, Taki's age of 5 years and 1 month is indicated as "5;1."
From *Through the Looking Glass: Observations in the Early Childhood Classroom* (3rd ed., pp. 118–119), by S. Nicolson and S. G. Shipstead, 2002, Upper Saddle River, New Jersey: Merrill/Prentice Hall. Copyright 2002 by Pearson Education. Reprinted with permission.

10/5 Tatiana (2;0):	While sitting on the floor in the art area peeling the wrappers off crayons, she looked up as the caregiver grew near and said, "I making the crayons all naked."
1/15 Maggie (4;8):	I listened as Maggie chattered on and on while the two of us cleaned up the block area. Finally I winked and said, "It all sounds like baloney to me." Maggie quickly asked, "What's baloney?" I replied, "It's a word that means you made all that up!" She thought for a few seconds and said, "No, it's salami!"
2/24 Matthew (7;4):	While discussing *In a Dark, Dark Room and Other Scary Stories* by Alvin Schwartz, Matthew thoughtfully shared, "Do you know what kind of scary things I like best? Things that are halfway between real and imaginary." I started to ask, "I wonder what . . ." Matthew quickly replied, "Examples would be aliens, shadows, and dreams coming true." (Nicolson & Shipstead, 2002, p. 139)

Figure 2-4

Anecdotal records for young children.
From *Through the Looking Glass: Observations in the Early Childhood Classroom* (3rd ed., p. 139), by S. Nicolson and S. G. Shipstead, 2002, Upper Saddle River, New Jersey: Merrill/Prentice Hall. Copyright 2002 by Pearson Education. Reprinted with permission.

havior. Using the rating scale in Figure 2-6, a teacher can indicate how often a child shows particular behaviors relating to being on task during independent seatwork (Pellegrini, 1996).

One means of recording observations is not necessarily better than another. Instead, each observational system has a distinct purpose. As you gain experience in observing youngsters, you are likely to see how your own understanding of individual children grows when you use several observational methods and supplement them by listening to what children say.

Directions: On the space in front of each item, place a plus sign (+) if performance is satisfactory; place a minus sign (−) if the performance is unsatisfactory.

_____ 1. States the topic at the beginning of the report.

_____ 2. Speaks clearly and loudly enough to be heard.

_____ 3. Uses language appropriate for the report.

_____ 4. Uses correct grammar.

_____ 5. Speaks at a satisfactory rate.

_____ 6. Looks at the class members when speaking.

_____ 7. Uses natural movements and appears relaxed.

_____ 8. Presents the material in an organized manner.

_____ 9. Holds the interest of the class.

Figure 2-5

Checklist for evaluating an oral presentation.

From *Writing Instructional Objectives for Teaching and Assessment* (7th ed., pp. 82–83), by Norman E. Gronlund, 2004, Upper Saddle River, NJ: Merrill/Prentice Hall. Copyright 2004 by Pearson Education. Reprinted with permission.

Directions: For each item, indicate how frequently the child shows this type of behavior during seatwork by circling the appropriate description.

1. Settles quietly during beginning of task.

   Never   Seldom   Sometimes   Frequently   Always

2. Shows strong interest in completing task.

   Never   Seldom   Sometimes   Frequently   Always

3. Concentrates on task despite difficulties and interruptions.

   Never   Seldom   Sometimes   Frequently   Always

4. Works through task from beginning until end.

   Never   Seldom   Sometimes   Frequently   Always

Figure 2-6

Rating scale of a child's concentration during seatwork.

Copyright © 1996. From *Observing Children in Their Natural Worlds: A Methodological Primer*, by A. D. Pellegrini. Reproduced by permission of Routledge, Inc., a division of Informa plc.

Listening to Children

From a young age, children are motivated to tell adults what makes them happy, relieved, or satisfied, on the one hand, and distressed, angry, or sad, on the other. It is up to adults to set aside the time, put youngsters at ease, and let them speak their minds. Here's how you can gain access to children's perspectives:

• ***Let children know you care.*** The surest way into a child's heart is, of course, to express affection sincerely and consistently. When you have earned a child's trust, the child is more likely to articulate what's on his or her mind.

• ***Develop your interviewing skills.*** Too often, conversations between adults and children are short, ask-a-question-and-get-an-answer exchanges. Lengthier dialogues, perhaps with an individual child or a small group of children, can be far more informative. To find out what young people believe, adults must not only encourage them to talk but also follow up with probing questions and frequent reassurances that these ideas and opinions are important (Pramling, 1996).

Getting children to talk takes experience, but there are a few things you can do (D. Fisher & Frey, 2007; Graue & Walsh, 1998). For instance, try a combination of open-ended questions ("How was your day?") and close-ended questions ("Did you watch TV when you went home from school?"). Also, include some general requests for information that are not in question form ("Tell me more about that"). Try not to ask a long series of questions, or your probing may seem like an inquisition. Make sure you pause after asking a question to give children plenty of time to formulate their thoughts, and communicate that you really care about what they have to say. Sometimes it is appropriate to ask children how *other children* view life; this can be an effective way to help them feel safe in speaking their minds. For example, rather than asking children how they feel about achievement tests, ask them how *other children* feel ("How did kids at your school feel last week when they took the state achievement test?").

When talking with children, always consider factors that affect how they respond. Certainly the relationship between adult and child is significant, but so are other variables, including ethnicity and gender (Holmes, 1998; Veale, 2006). A child's age is also influential. Many younger children become confused with abstract terms, and some adolescents may hide their true feelings.

• ***Listen openly and intently to children's experiences.*** Unless adults listen to young people, they cannot fully understand young people's experiences. Sometimes children see the world in the same way as adults, but at other times they have vastly different viewpoints. For example, in a study with sixth graders in the Philadelphia public schools (B. L. Wilson & Corbett, 2001), young adolescents appeared to share many priorities and goals with adults. The students stated that they wanted teachers to push them to complete assignments (even when they resisted), to maintain order (even when they misbehaved), and to ensure they understood material (even when they struggled). Despite their apparent desire to succeed, these youngsters were unaware of what it took to do well when subjects became difficult, and they were naive about skills needed for success in college. From these results, we realize that teachers need to be persistent in explaining concepts, teaching study skills, and preparing adolescents for the reality of college.

- ***Develop classroom routines that allow students to express their understandings.*** Classroom teachers can establish classroom procedures that allow children to share their understandings (D. Fisher & Frey, 2007). For example, some teachers use the Think–Pair–Share discussion strategy, in which teachers stop midway through a lesson, ask children to think about a particular question or issue, have children form pairs to discuss their responses, and finally ask children to share their ideas with the rest of the class (Lyman, 1981). Other teachers use the Whip Around technique, a structured activity at the end of a lesson: They pose a question, ask children to write their responses on a piece of paper, and then "whip around" the group asking children to give their responses orally (D. Fisher & Frey, 2007). From such responses teachers can gain a sense of what children have learned and what information needs to be reviewed the following day. These techniques can be effective forms of self-expression for children, provided that teachers communicate that everyone is encouraged to participate and no one will be ridiculed for what he or she says.

Interpreting Assessments and Artifacts

In addition to observing and listening to gain a sense of how children think, you can also examine their assignments and the many other products they create—artwork, scribbled notes to friends, and so forth. To learn from children's performance on tests and from their artifacts, you might follow these recommendations:

- ***When evaluating children's responses to your own assessments, use explicit scoring criteria.*** You are most likely to be accurate in the judgments you make about children's understandings and performance when you use carefully designed evaluation criteria. If you have shared the criteria with children ahead of time (and we encourage you to do so), children will be able to guide their learning toward clear standards and will better understand your feedback (Stiggins, 2007).

- ***Keep in mind both the advantages and limitations of paper-pencil tests.*** Paper-pencil tests are often an efficient way of determining what children have and have not learned. Furthermore, a well-designed test can reveal a great deal about children's thinking processes. However, appraisals of children that rely exclusively on test scores often paint a lopsided picture of their abilities. For instance, children who have limited reading and writing skills (perhaps because they have a learning disability or have only recently begun to learn English) are likely to perform poorly. Furthermore, paper-pencil tests, by their very nature, cannot provide certain kinds of information. For instance, they tell us little if anything about children's self-confidence, motor skills, ability to work well with others, or expertise at using equipment.

- ***Interpret standardized tests cautiously.*** No single assessment has perfect validity and reliability, and as a result, major decisions about children, such as whether they are promoted to the next grade or allowed to graduate from high school, should *never* be made on the basis of a single test score (American Educational Research Association, 2000).

- ***Remember that validity and reliability apply to all assessments.*** Never overinterpret any single product a child has created. For example, imagine that a 6-year-old draws a self-portrait with a frowning face, as Teresa's son once did. The boy's teacher concluded that he was unhappy and had low self-esteem, but nothing could have been further from the truth: The child was (and continues to be) a generally happy, self-confident individual.

Perhaps on that single occasion he was simply having a bad day or did not like the teacher who asked him to draw the picture.

• *Watch for cultural bias in assessments.* Children often interpret test questions differently than do adult examiners, particularly when the children come from different cultural backgrounds. As an example, one team of researchers examined the science test responses of a culturally and linguistically diverse group of elementary children (Luykx et al., 2007). Many of the children misinterpreted questions because of their cultural and language backgrounds. For instance, several of the Spanish-speaking children confused the abbreviations of *F* and *C* (intended to stand for Fahrenheit and Celsius) with the Spanish words *frío* and *caliente*, and a few Haitian children misconstrued an item that asked how long they would be able to play between 4 p.m. and a 6 p.m. dinner, probably because they typically would have had their own main meal (which they called "dinner") earlier in the day. This assessment seems to have been unfairly biased against children who did not speak English or had different everyday experiences than the other children.

In general, an assessment is tainted with **cultural bias** when it offends or unfairly penalizes some individuals because of their ethnicity, gender, socioeconomic status, or cultural background. When examining children's responses yourself, you can consider how children's apparent errors may arise because of a language difference or distinct cultural perspective. If you suspect a cultural bias, you will need to obtain additional information from children before drawing any firm conclusions about their abilities.

• *Assess environments to determine the extent to which they support children's well-being.* Some assessment strategies identify the strengths, priorities, and limitations of families, classrooms, and other settings. For example, in our opening case study, Jack Reston learned that his school was not meeting the needs of all children as well as he hoped. In addition, assessment strategies are vital to prevention programs and other community services. For instance, a community team planning a program to prevent substance abuse could examine conditions in the community that possibly encourage students to use and abuse illicit street drugs (U.S. Department of Health and Human Services, 2007c). Assessment data might document the particular risks faced by members of the community and any factors that protect against these risks, the presence of any existing prevention programs, and gaps between existing resources and needs that would ideally be addressed by the new program.

Promising tactics for gathering information from children include compiling information from multiple sources, reflecting on the advantages and disadvantages of each particular piece of data, and drawing conclusions from comprehensive bodies of data. You can practice your growing observation skills of what children do, say, and create in the classroom by completing this chapter's Building Teaching Skills and Dispositions exercise in MyEducationLab.

Conducting Action Research

To understand and address challenges in meeting children's needs, teachers can conduct systematic studies of children's experiences in school, with the goal of seeking more effective services for them. In our introductory case study, Jack Reston conducted research in order to evaluate and improve absenteeism policies at his school. Such locally focused research, known as **action research,** takes numerous forms, perhaps assessing the effectiveness of a new teaching technique, gathering information about adolescents' opinions on a schoolwide issue, or conducting an in-depth case study of a particular child (Cochran-Smith & Lytle, 1993; G. E. Mills, 2007).

Action research employs the following steps (G. E. Mills, 2007):

1. *Identify an area of focus.* The teacher-researcher begins with a problem and gathers preliminary information that might shed light on the problem. Usually this involves perusing the research literature for investigations of related problems and perhaps also surfing the Internet or conducting informal interviews of colleagues or students. He or she then identifies one or more research questions and develops a research plan (data collection tech-

---

MyEducationLab

Gain practice in analyzing how children can interpret assessments in unanticipated ways by completing an Understanding Research exercise in Chapter 2's Activities and Applications section in MyEducationLab.

MyEducationLab

Practice making inferences about what children do, say, and create in the classroom by completing a Building Teaching Skills and Dispositions exercise in Chapter 2 of MyEducationLab.

---

cultural bias
Extent to which an assessment offends or unfairly penalizes some individuals because of their ethnicity or cultural background, gender, or socioeconomic status.

action research
Systematic study of an issue or problem by a teacher or other practitioner, with the goal of bringing about more productive outcomes for children.

niques, necessary resources, schedule, etc.) for answering those questions. At this point, the teacher seeks guidance from supervisors and experts in research ethics and considers how he or she might eventually improve the situation being addressed in the research.

2. *Collect data.* The teacher-researcher collects data relevant to the research questions. Such data might be obtained from questionnaires, interviews, observations, achievement tests, children's journals or portfolios, or existing records (e.g., school attendance patterns, rates of referral for discipline problems, hours spent by volunteers on school projects). Many times the teacher-researcher uses two or more of these sources in order to address research questions from various angles.

3. *Analyze and interpret the data.* The teacher-researcher looks for patterns in the data. Sometimes the analysis involves computing particular statistics (e.g., percentages, averages, correlation coefficients). At other times it involves an in-depth, nonnumerical inspection of the data. In either case, the teacher-researcher relates the patterns observed to the original research questions.

4. *Develop an action plan.* The final step distinguishes teachers' research from the more traditional research studies we described earlier: The teacher-researcher uses the information collected to identify a new practical strategy—for instance, to change instructional techniques, counseling practices, home visiting schedules, or school policies.

A good example of research by a teacher is a case study conducted by Michele Sims (1993). Initially concerned with why middle school students of average intelligence struggle to comprehend classroom material, Sims began to focus on one of her students, a quiet boy named Ricardo. She talked with Ricardo, had conversations with other teachers and with university faculty, wrote her ideas in her journal, and made notes of Ricardo's work. The more she learned, the better she understood who Ricardo was as an individual and how she could better foster his development. She also became increasingly aware of how often she and her fellow teachers overlooked the needs of quiet students:

> We made assumptions that the quiet students weren't in as much need. My colleague phrased it well when she said, "In our minds we'd say to ourselves—'that child will be all right until we get back to him.'" But we both wanted desperately for these children to do more than just survive. (Sims, 1993, p. 288)

Action research serves many positive functions. It can solve problems, broaden perspectives on adults' relationships with children, foster a community spirit among adults who are jointly caring for children, and make schools and communities more humane (Noffke, 1997). For individual teachers, conducting research is also a good way to improve their abilities to grasp and meet the needs of youngsters. The Development and Practice feature "Getting a Flavor for Conducting Research as a Teacher" suggests some initial steps you can take.

Development and Practice

Getting a Flavor for Conducting Research as a Teacher

- **Keep a journal of your observations and reflections.**

  A high school English teacher keeps a daily log of students' comments and insights about the novels they are reading.

- **Talk with your colleagues about what you are observing and hypothesizing.**

  A school counselor notices that girls in a school club are excited about their participation. She asks colleagues for their ideas about why the girls are so interested.

- **Encourage children and families to contribute to your inquiry.**

  A teacher in an infant room hears parents complain that their employers do not grant them time off to care for their children when sick. She asks three parents who have been most vocal to help her look into federal and corporate policies regarding family leave.

- **Collect information and write about children you seem unable to reach.**

  A middle school teacher keeps a journal of her observations of students who sit in the back of the room and appear to be mentally "tuned out." After a few weeks, she begins to form hypotheses about strategies that might capture the interest and attention of these students.

- **Conduct informal research on topics on which children or families can help.**

  A career counselor examines his community's employment rates and enlists the help of adolescents to survey local businesses about possible needs that youngsters could meet in after-school jobs.

Ethical Guidelines for Teacher-Researchers

Regardless of how you collect data from or about children, you must protect children's well-being. We recommend that you learn as much as possible at college about your legal and ethical responsibilities as a school professional. In addition, we offer the following guidelines:

- ***Keep your supervisor informed of your research initiatives.*** You and your principal (or other supervisor) are ultimately responsible for your actions with children. Furthermore, supervisors are knowledgeable about policies in your school, district, and community that relate to research. Your supervisor can advise you as to whether you should obtain districtwide approval and written parent permission and will probably ask you questions about your plans to present the results at conferences. When you eventually collect your data, school leaders can give you a fresh set of eyes when it comes to interpreting the information and can advise you about the implications for any changes in practice that might be worth trying.

- ***Be tentative in your conclusions.*** Never put too much weight on any single piece of information. Instead, collect a variety of data sources—such as writing samples, test scores, projects, informal observations of behavior—and look for general trends. Even then, be cautious in the conclusions you draw, and consider multiple hypotheses to explain the patterns you see. Finally, when sharing your perceptions of children's talents and abilities with parents, acknowledge that these are your *interpretations*, based on the data you have available, rather than irrefutable facts.

- ***Administer and interpret tests or research instruments only if you have adequate training.*** Many instruments, especially psychological assessments, physiological measures, and standardized achievement tests, must be administered and interpreted by individuals trained in their use. In untrained hands they can yield results that are highly suspect and, in some cases, potentially harmful.

- ***Be sensitive to children's perspectives.*** Children are apt to notice any unusual attention you give them. For instance, when Michele Sims was collecting data about Ricardo, she made the following observation:

  > I'm making a conscious effort to collect as much of Ricardo's work as possible. It's difficult. I think this shift in the kind of attention I'm paying to him has him somewhat rattled. I sense he has mixed feelings about this. He seems to enjoy the conversations we have, but when it comes to collecting his work, he may feel that he's being put under a microscope. Maybe he's become quite accustomed to a type of invisibility. (Sims, 1993, p. 285)

When data collection makes children feel so self-conscious that their performance is impaired, a teacher-researcher must seriously consider whether the value of the information collected outweighs possible detrimental effects.

- ***Maintain confidentiality.*** It may be appropriate for teachers to share results of their research with colleagues. Some also make their findings known to an audience beyond the walls of their institution; for instance, they may make presentations at conferences or write journal articles describing what they have learned. However, you must never broadcast research findings in ways that violate children's anonymity. Teachers must likewise protect their data sources from examination by onlookers. For example, it would be unwise to leave a notebook containing running records or completed checklists on a table where other children and adults would have access to them.

Knowledge about children comes from a variety of sources—not only from research but also from one's own intuition, conversations with other teachers, and children's classroom assignments, behaviors, and verbal statements. None of these sources is adequate in and of itself. Each becomes more powerful and effective when complemented by other approaches. Effective teachers and other practitioners draw from as many resources as possible when deciding how best to meet the needs of children.

Summary

Principles of Research

Research with children needs to be guided by strong ethical standards, the scientific method, and access to children and adolescents who can supply needed information. The manner in which researchers integrate these principles into their investigations depends largely on the kinds of methods they use.

Analyzing Developmental Research

Developmental researchers use various methods for collecting data, including interviews and questionnaires, tests and other assessment tasks, physiological measures, and observations. Regardless of the method, the data should be accurate measures of the characteristics or behaviors being studied (a matter of *validity*) and should be only minimally influenced by tempo- rary, irrelevant factors (a matter of *reliability*). Developmental researchers also use a research design that matches their question. Designs differ in the extent to which they allow researchers to draw conclusions about cause-and-effect relationships, find associations among two or more variables, trace age trends over time, and observe children and adolescents in natural environments. To make the most of developmental studies, you must judge whether the conclusions are warranted and applicable to your own work with young people.

Gathering Data as an Educator

Teachers and caregivers often gather data about children and adolescents. Educators can learn a great deal from their everyday observations of youngsters, conversations with them, and assessments of the products they create.

Applying Concepts in Child Development

The exercises in this section will help you build your ability to infuse knowledge of child development into your work with children.

Case Study

The Study Skills Class

Read the case and then answer the questions that follow it.

As a last-minute teaching assignment, Deborah South took on a study skills class of 20 low-achieving and seemingly unmotivated eighth graders. Later she described a problem she encountered and her attempt to understand the problem through action research (South, 2007):

> My task was to somehow take these students and miraculously make them motivated, achieving students. I was trained in a study skills program before the term started and thought that I was prepared. . . .
>
> Within a week, I sensed we were in trouble. My 20 students often showed up with no supplies. Their behavior was atrocious. They called each other names, threw various items around the room, and walked around the classroom when they felt like it. . . .
>
> Given this situation, I decided to do some reading about how other teachers motivate unmotivated students and to formulate some ideas about the variables that contribute to a student's success in school. Variables I investigated included adult approval, peer influence, and success in such subjects as math, science, language arts, and social studies, as well as self-esteem and students' views of their academic abilities.
>
> I collected the majority of the data through surveys, interviews, and report card/attendance records in an effort to answer the following questions:
>
> · How does attendance affect student performance?
> · How are students influenced by their friends in completing school-work?
> · How do adults (parents, teachers) affect the success of students?
> · What levels of self-esteem do these students have?
>
> As a result of this investigation, I learned many things. For example, for this group of students attendance does not appear to be a factor—with the exception of one student, their school attendance was regular. Not surprisingly, peer groups did affect student performance. Seventy-three percent of my students reported that their friends never encouraged doing homework or putting any effort into homework.
>
> Another surprising result was the lack of impact of a teacher's approval on student achievement. Ninety-four percent of my students indicated that they never or seldom do their homework to receive teacher approval. Alternatively, 57 percent indicated that they often or always do their homework so that their families will be proud of them.
>
> One of the most interesting findings of this study was the realization that most of my students misbehave out of frustration at their own lack of abilities. They are not being obnoxious to gain attention, but to divert attention from the fact that they do not know how to complete the assigned work.
>
> When I looked at report cards and compared grades over three quarters, I noticed a trend. Between the first and second quarter, student performance had increased. That is, most students were doing better than they had during the first quarter. Between the second and third quarters, however, grades dropped dramatically. I tried to determine why that drop would occur, and the only common experience shared by these 20 students was the fact that they had been moved into my class at the beginning of the third quarter.
>
> When I presented my project to the action research class during our end-of-term "celebration," I was convinced that the "cause" of the students' unmotivated behavior was my teaching . . . . This conclusion, however, was not readily accepted by my critical friends and colleagues . . . . who urged me to consider other interpretations of the data. (pp. 1–2)[a]

[a]From "What Motivates Unmotivated Students?" by D. South. In *Action Research: A Guide for the Teacher Researcher* (3rd ed., pp. 1–2), by G. E. Mills, 2007, Upper Saddle River, NJ: Merrill/Prentice Hall. Reprinted with permission of the author.

· What methods did Deborah use to collect her data? What were the potential strengths and limitations of each method?
· Deborah tentatively concluded that her own teaching led to the dramatic drop in grades from the second quarter to the third. Is her conclusion justified? Why or why not?

Once you have answered these questions, compare your responses with those presented in Appendix A.

Interpreting Children's Artifacts and Reflections

Consider chapter concepts as you analyze the following artifact created by a child.

I Went to Davis's House

The note at right was written by 9-year-old Alex. He left it on the kitchen counter for his parents when they were out for a walk. As you examine it, consider what Alex understands about the mechanics of English and what additional evidence you would like to obtain from Alex.

Once you have analyzed the artifact, compare your ideas with those presented in Appendix B. For further practice in analyzing children's artifacts and reflections, go to the Activities and Applications section in Chapter 2 of MyEducationLab.

> I went
> to davis's
> house
> Alex

Developmental Trends Exercise

In this chapter you learned that a variety of factors affect the accuracy of conclusions about children. The following table describes information collected about the experiences of five youngsters. For each of these experiences, the table identifies factors that affect interpretations about the information, offers an implication for drawing accurate conclusions from the information, or both. Go to the Activities and Applications section in Chapter 2 of MyEducationLab to apply what you've learned about research on children as you fill in the empty cells in the table.

Drawing Reasonable Conclusions About Children and Adolescents

Age	A Youngster's Experience	Developmental Concepts *Considering the Accuracy of Information*	Implications *Drawing Reasonable Conclusions*
Infancy (Birth–2 Years)	An 18-month old baby, Harriet, is drowsy when an unfamiliar adult tries to examine her recognition of common household words, such as *ball*. The girl fails to point to particular objects when the adult asks her to do so.	The fact that Harriet is not alert, the task is somewhat artificial, and the adult is a stranger raises questions about *the task's validity as an indication of the child's verbal ability.*	
Early Childhood (2–6 Years)	Four-year-old Seth takes a children's picture book, points at each page, and tells the teacher what each page says.		The researcher realizes that more observations are needed to determine whether Seth can read. It may also be helpful to talk with the boy about his interests and abilities in reading.

Development Trends Exercise (continued)

Age	A Youngster's Experience	Developmental Concepts _Considering the Accuracy of Information_	Implications _Drawing Reasonable Conclusions_
Middle Childhood (6–10 Years)	A teacher is conducting action research on her students' performance in mathematics. One 9-year-old boy, Ryan, turns in a blank paper each time the class does math worksheets. Ryan has recently moved from another state, and the teacher does not yet know what Ryan's skills are. He is very quiet.	The teacher examines each child's written work, talking with children individually about their interests in math and watching them as they perform mathematical operations. The teacher appreciates that she is just getting to know Ryan and that there are many reasons why he might not be completing the math problems. The inference that Ryan is not able to do the work may not be _valid_.	The teacher cannot draw firm conclusions about Ryan's mathematical skills. There are countless reasons why he might not be doing well on the worksheets—perhaps he has not yet been exposed to multiplication, feels anxious about math, or is bored with the task. Alternatively, he might be shy and worried about being in the new classroom. The teacher realizes that she needs more information before she can draw any conclusions about Ryan's abilities.
Early Adolescence (10–14 Years)	Twelve-year-old Mary completes a survey related to sexual harassment at school. In her responses to some items, Mary reports that she has been touched inappropriately while walking down the school hall and has been the recipient of unwanted comments about her physical appearance. On other items, Mary responds that she has not been a victim of sexual harassment.	The researcher notices that Mary's responses are not consistent (that is, not _reliable_) and therefore may not be _valid_. It is possible that Mary interprets some of the items differently than the researchers do or perhaps she completed the survey while distracted or unmotivated to give her honest responses.	The researcher determines that it will be necessary to look at all students' responses before drawing conclusions about sexual harassment at school. The researcher may choose to implement other surveys or follow up with informal interviews among a few of the students.
Late Adolescence (14–18 Years)	Seventeen-year-old Melinda has had a brain scan. Her scan seems to show that some brain areas, especially those areas devoted to planning ahead and using good judgment, are less mature than those in typical adult brains.	Adolescent brains are undergoing continuous refinement as they change with maturational processes and experience. The results of a single brain scan should not be taken too seriously, however. Any single result _cannot_ be assumed to be completely _valid_ or _reliable_.	

Key Concepts

scientific method (p. 34)
sample (p. 35)
self-report (p. 36)
interview (p. 36)
questionnaire (p. 36)
test (p. 37)

assessment (p. 37)
physiological measure (p. 38)
habituation (p. 38)
observation (p. 38)
validity (p. 40)
reliability (p. 40)

experimental study (p. 42)
control group (p. 42)
quasi-experimental study (p. 42)
correlation (p. 43)
correlational study (p. 43)
cross-sectional study (p. 44)

longitudinal study (p. 44)
ethnography (p. 44)
case study (p. 44)
grounded theory study (p. 45)
cultural bias (p. 56)
action research (p. 56)

MyEducationLab

Now go to Chapter 2 of MyEducationLab at www.myeducationlab.com, where you can:

· View instructional objectives for the chapter.
· Take a quiz to test your mastery of chapter objectives. Detailed feedback is provided to explain why your responses are correct or incorrect.
· Deepen your understanding of particular concepts and principles with Review, Practice, and Enrichment exercises.

· Complete Activities and Applications exercises that give you additional experience in interpreting artifacts, increase your understanding of how research contributes to knowledge about chapter topics, and encourage you to apply what you have learned about children's development.
· Apply what you have learned in the chapter to your work with children in Building Teaching Skills and Dispositions exercises.
· Observe children and their unique contexts in Video Examples.

chapter 3

Family, Culture, and Community

Cedric Lavar Jennings is a senior at Ballou High School, an inner-city school in Washington, D.C. Throughout his school career his grades have been exemplary, and he has recently learned that he has been accepted at Brown University for the following year.

Cedric and his mother, Barbara, have been a family of two since Cedric's birth and are very close. They live in a lower-income neighborhood, where crack cocaine dealers regularly do business and gunshots are frequent background noise at night. Despite such an environment, Cedric has flourished, in large part because of his mother's support. Not only is he a high achiever, but he is also a very likable young man with a strong moral code.

One night, Barbara and Cedric attend the Parent-Teacher-Student Association meeting at Ballou. After the meeting they go to Cedric's homeroom, where the homeroom teacher is handing out first-semester grade reports. Cedric is appalled to discover a B on his grade sheet. In *A Hope in the Unseen,* Suskind (1998) reports what happens next:

> "I got a B in physics! I can't believe it."
>
> He begins ranting about the cheating in his class, about how he thinks a lot of other kids cheated. . . . Barbara remembers that he mentioned something about this a week ago—but she dismissed the whole matter.
>
> Squeezed into a school desk next to him, she wants to tell Cedric that it doesn't matter. None of it. Some small hubbub about cheating and grades is meaningless now that he's been admitted to Brown, the top college acceptance of any Ballou student in years.
>
> But, of course, he knows all that, too. And the more dismissive her look, the more rabid he becomes. Then she gets it: it's about her watching over him, defending him, always being there. ". . . I mean, what are *we* going to do?!" he shouts at the end of his furious soliloquy about what's right and fair and just.
>
> She's up. "Well, Lavar [she usually calls him by his middle name], we'll just have to go have a word with that teacher." A second later, they're stomping together through the halls, headed for the physics classroom of an unsuspecting Mr. Momen. They find that he is alone. He turns and offers greetings as they enter, but Cedric launches right in—the whole diatribe, offered with added verve from his rehearsal with his mom.
>
> Mr. Momen, a wry, sometimes sarcastic man in his mid-forties, mournfully shakes his head, a helmet of gray-flecked hair. "Cedric, you got a B for the marking period," he says in precise, accented English. "The test for you is irrefutable. The curve says yours is a B, and that, for you, is a B for the marking period. So, okay. That's it, yes?"
>
> "But kids are cheating! You leave the room and they open the book. Lots of them. You don't know what goes on. You shouldn't leave the room, that's when it starts. It ends up that I get penalized 'cause I won't cheat."
>
> "Cedric, stop. I can't, myself, accuse all of them of cheating," says Mr. Momen, shrugging.
>
> Barbara watches the give-and-take, realizing that the teacher has artfully shoved Cedric into a rhetorical corner by placing her son's single voice against the silent majority—his word against theirs.
>
> Years of practice at this have taught her much: choose your words meticulously and then let them rumble up from some deep furnace of conviction. "My son doesn't lie," she says, like an oracle, "not about something like this."
>
> The silent majority vanishes. She stands, straight and motionless, a block of granite. Momen looks back at her, eye to eye. Soon, the silence becomes unbearable. He's forced to move. "I guess he could take a retest I make for him," he says haltingly. "It will be a hard test, though, that I will make for you, Cedric."
>
> "Fine," says Barbara, closing the deal. "Thank you, Mr. Momen. We can go now," she says. Once they're in the hallway, she whispers to Cedric, "You *will* be getting an A on that test, Lavar. You understand?" She doesn't expect an answer.
>
> After a week of ferocious study, Cedric does get his A on the special test—scoring 100—and an A for the marking period. He brings home the paper and lays it on the dining room table, like a prize, a trophy.

Case Study:
Cedric and Barbara Jennings

Outline:

Case Study: Cedric and Barbara Jennings

Cradles of Child Development

Family Structures

Family Processes

Children in a Diverse Society

Summary

Applying Concepts in Child Development

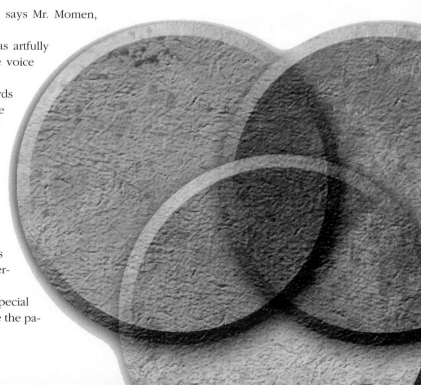

Barbara looks at it for a moment. "On the next stop, you know you'll be on your own. I won't be there to come to the rescue," she says, feeling as though a clause of their partnership has expired.

"Well, then," he says a little tersely, tapping the paper once with his index finger, "I guess this paper is sort of your diploma." (pp. 113–115)[a]

- Why did Cedric assume his mother would help him at school?

- What qualities did Cedric learn from his mother?

[a]From *A Hope in the Unseen,* by Ron Suskind, copyright © 1998 by Ron Suskind. Used by permission of Broadway Books, a division of Random House, Inc.

As a child, Cedric had found his mother to be a loving caregiver. Barbara had tended to his needs, staying within earshot and coming to his aid when he called her. Having grown accustomed to his mother's faithful care, Cedric could now safely assume she would back him up when he asked for her help. Like Cedric, most children can depend on their family for love and reassurance, food and shelter, and oversight and guidance. As you might expect, the family's care has profound effects on children. For example, the family helps children develop a sense of who they are and how they should act in society. From Barbara, Cedric had learned to work hard, act with integrity, and confront injustice. Having benefited from his mother's support, Cedric could now enter society as a productive young man.

Cradles of Child Development

A happy and healthy childhood depends on a loving relationship with families, regular exposure to the traditions of a culture, and participation in a responsive community. Let's look more closely at these three contexts and their primary contributions to children's development.

Family

Parents and other family members play a major role in children's socialization.

A **family** consists of two or more people who live together and are related by such enduring factors as birth, marriage, adoption, or long-term mutual commitment. Families with children usually have one or two adults (most often the parents) who serve as heads of the family and care for the children for many years. The heads of the family have authority over children and are responsible for children's welfare.

Every child needs at least one adult devoted to his or her health, education, and welfare (Bronfenbrenner, 2001). Typically, the adults in a child's family have the necessary dedication to meet the child's many needs. Caring for children ideally begins before birth, when prospective parents take protective measures to increase their chances of having a healthy pregnancy. After birth, sensitive hands-on care makes it possible for infants to form close bonds with parents, explore the world, and develop harmonious relationships with people outside the family (Ainsworth, 1963, 1973; Bowlby, 1969/1982; Morelli & Rothbaum, 2007). As youngsters grow, families continue to feed and clothe them and attend to their basic needs. But just as importantly, family members are key figures in the **socialization** of children. That is, by encouraging certain behaviors and beliefs (and *dis*couraging others), parents and other heads of family help children act and think in ways their society deems appropriate and responsible. For instance, they teach and model proper ways of behaving in various situations, reward particular behaviors and punish others, and arrange for children to gain certain kinds of experiences and steer them clear of less productive ones (Grusec & Davidov, 2007; Maccoby, 2007; Rogoff et al., 2007).

family
Two or more people who live together and are related by such enduring factors as birth, marriage, adoption, or long-term mutual commitment.

socialization
Systematic efforts by other people and institutions to prepare youngsters to act in ways deemed by society to be appropriate and responsible.

Culture

Culture refers to the characteristic *behaviors* and *beliefs* of a long-standing social group. Cultural behaviors include the everyday routines that families and children carry out as they maintain households, work and play, use tools, and relate to one another. Cultural behaviors also include a group's periodic rituals, such as worshipping and celebrating holidays.

The effects of culture can be observed by comparing the customs of people in distinct groups or separate regions. For instance, different cultural groups exhibit variations in meal practices (what, how, and with whom they eat), division of responsibility in families (who obtains food, prepares dinner, and disciplines the children), and social practices (how and with whom children play, how marital partners are selected). Cultural groups also use different communication styles. For example, in some cultures children are expected to take a turn in adults' conversations, and in other cultures children are shooed to the sidelines of adults' discussions (M. Cole, 2006; Rogoff, 2003).

Belief systems, although not as obvious as behaviors, are an equally important part of a group's cultural heritage. Core beliefs vary among different societies. For example, **individualistic cultures** encourage independence, self-assertion, competition, and expression of personal needs (Kağitçibaşi, 2007; Markus & Hamedani, 2007; Oyserman & Lee, 2007; Triandis, 2007). Many families from the United States and Western Europe raise their children in an individualistic manner. Core ideas in **collectivistic cultures** are that people should be obedient to and dependent on authority figures, honorable and cooperative, and invested in accomplishments of groups rather than personal achievements. Many families in Asia, Africa, and South America raise their children in a collectivistic manner.

The two bookends of culture—behaviors and beliefs—are closely related. Common behavioral practices are grounded in beliefs about what is true, healthy, appropriate, and rational (Kitayama, Duffy, & Uchida, 2007). Adults within a culture, therefore, can justify their typical ways of raising children by asserting familiar values. As one example, consider how families defend their sleeping practices. Many European American parents have their children sleep alone in their own rooms or beds, and they explain that the practice ensures nighttime privacy for adults and fosters independence in children. Other parents, particularly those in certain Asian cultures, sleep beside their children and say that co-sleeping arrangements foster intimacy and solidarity among family members (Shweder et al., 1998).

Ultimately, by growing up in a culture, children experience human life as predictable and meaningful. Culture also adds an intellectual dimension to life by exposing children to the accumulated wisdom, advanced discoveries, and creative works of society.

Community

A child's **community** includes the local neighborhood and the surrounding area. It gives the child and family a bridge to the outside world, supplying playmates and outlets for children's recreation. Particularly when they are young, children tend to make friends with other youngsters who play with them in the neighborhood or join them at a local school, sports team, or other nearby institution. As they grow older, youngsters generally decide how to spend their spare time based on opportunities that are reasonably close by and affordable. You can see how important recreational opportunities are to youngsters by listening to 14-year-old Brendan in the "Neighborhood: Early Adolescence" video in MyEducationLab. Here's how Brendan describes his neighborhood:

> There's a lot of people. Nice people. And there's fun stuff to do around here. . . . We play football or sports in the backyards, and we have playgrounds and a basketball court.

Communities also affect children indirectly in that they fortify parents with social networks and services. For example, parents may have their own friends who occasionally step in to supervise children's activities, model and offer advice on effective parenting strategies, and provide the emotional support that parents need, especially in times of trouble (Bronfenbrenner, 2005; Cochran & Niego, 2002; C. J. Patterson & Hastings, 2007). Many institutions within the community—health clinics, social service agencies, homeless shelters, houses of worship, and so on—also back up families' efforts to keep children on productive pathways.

culture
Behaviors and belief systems that characterize a long-standing social group and provide a framework for how group members decide what is normal and appropriate.

individualistic culture
Cultural group that encourages independence, self-assertion, competition, and expression of personal needs.

collectivistic culture
Cultural group that encourages obedience to and dependence on authority figures and being honorable, cooperative, and invested in group accomplishments.

community
The neighborhood in which a child and his or her family live and the surrounding vicinity.

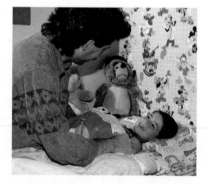

Cultures differ in their practices and beliefs related to children's sleeping.

MyEducationLab

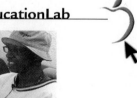

Go to the Video Examples section in Chapter 3 of MyEducationLab to watch the "Neighborhood: Early Adolescence" video and listen to Brendan talk about recreational opportunities.

Finally, communities tell children what society wants them to become as adults. The activities in which local adults engage—whether productive employment and community volunteerism, on the one hand, or drug trafficking and gang affiliation, on the other—convey to youngsters what behaviors are expected. For example, when most adults in a neighborhood have stable, well-paying jobs, children are more likely to stay in school and aspire to similar types of employment (Jencks & Mayer, 1990). Adults in the community who are friendly to neighborhood children can be especially influential role models when children's own parents are punitive and hostile or when children and their families face economic hardships (Silk, Sessa, Morris, Steinberg, & Avenevoli, 2004; M. A. Zimmerman, Bingenheimer, & Notaro, 2002). In the "Neighborhood: Late Adolescence" video in MyEducationLab, 15-year-old Robin is impressed by friendly gestures from her neighbors:

> Next door there is these two, this old couple. They're really, really nice . . . we went over to their house for a Christmas party one time. The entire neighborhood came.

We might expect that Robin will show similar friendly behaviors to her own neighbors when she becomes an adult. In contrast, when neighbors partake in criminal activities, prey on youth, and allow youngsters to get into trouble, children are at increased risk for exhibiting such negative behaviors as bullying their peers, destroying others' property, cheating and telling lies, and being disobedient at school (Eamon & Mulder, 2005).

Considering Children's Origins in the Classroom

Children enter school having been shaped by formative experiences in their family, culture, and community. In the best of circumstances, these contexts have been fountains of nurture: The family has cared for children, the culture has given meaning to children's lives, and the community has provided children with external social contacts and decent living conditions. With optimal support, children can typically reach their potential, becoming physically healthy, exercising their natural talents, and evolving into responsible citizens, as Cedric did in our opening case study. The Basic Developmental Issues table "Considering Family, Culture, and Community" provides examples of the many favorable ways in which nature and nurture, universality and diversity, and qualitative and quantitative change are manifested in the family, culture, and community.

Yet the best of circumstances do not always prevail. Accordingly, teachers can learn about the skills and understandings that individual children have acquired from their surroundings and address any major adversities children have encountered. Following are three fundamental ways to accommodate children's experiences in their family, community, and culture:

As children gain increasing mobility with age, their neighborhoods expand, as shown in these drawings by (top) Marsalis, age 7½, and (bottom) James, age 13. Marsalis stays very close to home, but James can easily travel a mile or more on his bicycle.

- ***Learn about children's complex social lives.*** To understand individual children, we need to consider how their specific environmental experiences affect their outlook on life. For example, imagine a boy who spends little time with his parents due to their long work hours but receives ample and loving attention from his grandmother. The boy is achieving at high levels in school yet feels apprehensive when he is praised for his accomplishments in front of classmates. He enjoys rich immigrant traditions at home, but these customs seem alien to many of his classmates. By learning about this child's family, his teacher is apt to invite not only his parents but also his grandmother to school meetings, to speak privately with the boy about his schoolwork rather than doing so in front of peers, and to include some of his family's immigrant customs in classroom activities.

Bronfenbrenner's bioecological model of human development, which you learned about in Chapter 1, offers a useful framework for thinking about children's participation in multilayered social systems (see Figure 1-2 in Chapter 1). The family is, of course, the preeminent social system, typically loving the child and providing opportunities to learn fundamental skills (Bronfenbrenner, 1979, 2005; Bronfenbrenner & Morris, 2006). Children are also affected by friends and other adults with

Basic Developmental Issues

Considering Family, Culture, and Community

Issue	Family	Culture	Community
Nature and Nurture	As agents of nature, parents give their children genes for basic human traits and for their own individual characteristics (such as dispositions to be physically healthy or frail). As agents of nurture, families typically care for children, serve as role models, engage children in affectionate relationships, and encourage children's participation in routine activities.	The general capacity for culture has evolved over millions of years and is inscribed in the human genetic code. For example, children's desire to learn from others probably has a genetic basis. In the daily lives of children and families, cultural traditions and beliefs nurture children in that they give meaning, purpose, and predictability to interpersonal relationships, activities, tool use, and communication systems.	Human beings are a social species with a natural inclination to congregate in communities. When a community contains friendly neighbors, decent housing, accessible playmates, safe playgrounds, and reasonably stable and well-paying jobs for heads of family, it is an especially nurturing context for children's development.
Universality and Diversity	Children universally need one or more adults to advocate enthusiastically and steadfastly for their welfare, and families usually serve in this manner. Families differ considerably in their structures (that is, membership) and styles of expressing affection and authority.	Children need (and almost always have) opportunities to participate in meaningful cultural activities. Cultural diversity occurs in beliefs (such as whether or not children are perceived to be capable of reasoning at a young age) and behaviors (such as how men and women each contribute to household maintenance).	Communities universally create a link to the outside world for children and families. Communities vary in population density, other geographical features, and degree of support for children and families.
Qualitative and Quantitative Change	Some changes in family roles occur in a trendlike, quantitative fashion, such as when children gradually become more responsible for their own behavior. For example, children may slowly learn the steps in preparing a meal (e.g., washing the vegetables, buttering the bread, and grilling the meat). Some changes facilitate entirely new ways of thinking and behaving (a qualitative transformation), as when an 8-year-old boy is asked to look after his 4-year-old sister for the first time.	Some cultures view development in terms of abrupt qualitative changes; for instance, certain rituals signify passage from childhood to adulthood and may be accompanied by an immediate and major change in young people's roles in the community. Other cultures view development as a series of small, gradual steps; for instance, children are gradually given more independence.	Children's experiences in communities show a few qualitative changes. For example, getting a driver's license or part-time job can shift youngsters' behaviors in fairly dramatic ways—the youngsters can suddenly make many choices about pastimes and purchases. Many changes are probably incremental in form, such as children gradually learning about a city's neighborhoods as they venture farther from home during walks and bicycle rides.

whom they have regular contact and by society's practices (e.g., parents' employers provide various salary levels, health care plans, and family leave policies that affect children's standard of living and general welfare; Conger & Dogan, 2007). Usually children can move easily from one social group to the next, but occasionally children become distressed when key individuals in their lives fail to get along or place incompatible demands on them. For example, imagine an adolescent girl whose parents dislike her friends, leading her to feel torn by conflicting loyalties (e.g., A. C. Fletcher, Hunter, & Eanes, 2006). Teachers can comfort children who articulate such concerns and also watch for nonverbal signs of distress, such as being withdrawn or acting out, which may indicate children's difficulty in adapting to pressures in the environment. Perhaps even more importantly, teachers themselves can invest in good relationships with children. In some cases teachers' affectionate care and children's close friendships at school can compensate for poor relationships at home (Criss, Pettit, Bates, Dodge, & Lapp, 1992; Crosnoe & Elder, 2004).

• *Help children cope effectively with adverse circumstances, and capitalize on their assets.* In a theoretical extension to Bronfenbrenner's model, psychologist Margaret Beale Spencer has examined *risk factors* in children's environments that increase children's vulnerability to problematic outcomes (e.g., dropping out of school, being incarcerated, becoming an adolescent parent) and the *protective factors* that offset these risks (Spencer, 2006). Examples of risk factors include economic poverty, unstable family conditions, restrictive gender stereotypes, racial discrimination, and underfunded schools. Examples of protective factors include being intelligent, physically attractive, or a member of a high-status social group, and having well-educated parents and a compassionate and involved extended family. Teachers should look at *every* child as having a unique profile of risks that may require services, resources, or instruction, as well as assets that can set the stage for new growth. For example, a teacher may approach a girl who frequently ridicules peers with the suggestion that together they brainstorm solutions for expressing anger productively. Having gotten to know the girl personally, the teacher may realize that the girl is self-reflective and able to address her own social problems if given some guidance.

• *Appeal to children's initiative.* Rarely do children submit passively to pressures from other people or institutions. Instead, children invariably pursue their own goals, enlisting cooperation from other people, learning new skills, and adapting the environment to better meet their needs (Bronfenbrenner & Morris, 2006; Spencer, 2006). For example, in the context of their families, children may ask for help (as Cedric did in our introductory case study), compete for attention, resist discipline, and attempt to negotiate rules (Kuczynski & Parkin, 2007). This sense of initiative is a valuable resource that can be cultivated at school. For instance, teachers and counselors can encourage youngsters to learn skills (e.g., presenting themselves professionally during a job interview) that will help them achieve their goals (e.g., getting a part-time job). Educators can also ask children to help address problems themselves at school and in the community. For instance, a teacher might ask children who complain about a dirty playground to recommend tactics that will discourage littering and foster everyone's pride in the school environment (Howard, 2007).

One important course of action for learning about a child's background is finding out who is in the child's family. We turn to this topic now.

Family Structures

A child's **family structure** refers to the makeup of the family—the people who live with the child in a family home, including any other children residing there and the adult or adults who care for the child and any siblings. Consider these statistics compiled on family structures of American children:

- 67 percent live with two parents.
- 23 percent live with their mother only.
- 5 percent live with their father only.
- 5 percent live without a parent in their household and instead reside in some other living arrangement, such as with grandparents, other relatives, or foster parents (Federal Interagency Forum on Child and Family Statistics, 2007).

More than one in four children grow up in a family headed by a single parent.

Keep in mind that some children's circumstances defy such cut-and-dried categories. Many children are in the process of adjusting to one or more family changes, perhaps the addition of a new stepparent, the marriage of their previously unmarried parents, or the coming or going of a parent's unmarried (*cohabiting*) partner in the family home. Alternatively, some children live with one parent yet stay in contact with their second parent, in accordance with custody agreements or informal arrangements.

Many people in Western society have strong opinions about the kinds of families that are most suitable for raising children. But, in fact, children eagerly soak up affection from sensitive, considerate family members, often with little concern for how their family's makeup compares to society's stereotypes of proper family structures. You can develop an appreciation for the benefits that children of various ages derive from their families by completing

family structure
In a family with children, the family's makeup; specifically, the children in a family home and the adults who live with and care for the children.

this chapter's Building Teaching Skills and Dispositions exercise in MyEducationLab. You should also know that different family structures afford somewhat distinct benefits and challenges for children, and these characteristics merit thoughtful consideration by educators. In the sections that follow, we look at children's experiences in particular types of families and the strategies that practitioners can use to work effectively with a broad range of families.

MyEducationLab

Go to Chapter 3's Building Teaching Skills and Dispositions section in MyEducationLab to complete the exercise and develop a deeper understanding of how children gain vital support from their families.

Mothers and Fathers

When a mother and father are present in the home, children tend to form close bonds with both parents (M. E. Lamb, Chuang, & Cabrera, 2005). Being nurtured by two people is certainly advantageous for children—it gives them two loving role models and magnifies the affection they receive.

Being in a two-parent family also exposes children to two distinct styles of parenting. Mothers typically spend more time providing physical care (e.g., feeding, bathing, scheduling doctors' appointments), watching over the children, and displaying affection (e.g., kisses, hugs, smiles) toward children (Belsky, Gilstrap, & Rovine, 1984; Craig, 2006; Parke & Buriel, 2006). As children grow, relationships with mothers tend to be more intimate than those with fathers, and mothers are more likely to encourage children to open up about personal matters (Harach & Kuczynski, 2005; Smetana, Metzger, Gettman, & Campione-Barr, 2006).

In contrast, fathers in many cultures are more physically playful with children than are mothers, and they help children get along with people outside the family (Craig, 2006; Engle & Breaux, 1998; M. E. Lamb et al., 2005; Parke & Buriel, 2006). Nevertheless, fathers are not simply playmates; most fathers spend substantial amounts of time caring for their children and are quite competent in feeding, bathing, and in other ways nurturing children (M. E. Lamb, Frodi, Hwang, Frodi, & Steinberg, 1982; Mackey, 2001). In many societies fathers become more involved as children grow older, especially in disciplining and modeling subtle masculine qualities, such as being a dependable source of financial support for one's family (Engle & Breaux, 1998; Munroe & Munroe, 1992). Furthermore, fathers often play an important role in fostering adolescents' confidence by regularly communicating the expectation that youngsters are capable of competent, self-reliant behavior (Parke & Buriel, 2006).

Children become increasingly aware of such differences between their mothers and fathers and act strategically to benefit from these differences. For example, children often approach mothers with problems about friends, emotional difficulties, and concerns about family rules; in contrast, children seek out fathers as companions for one-on-one time outside the home (Kuczynski & Parkin, 2007).

A 5-year-old boy drew this picture of his traditional two-parent family: *(clockwise, from right)* his father, himself, his mother, and his older brother. Also included are the family goldfish and the family's house and driveway.

Children are also affected by their parents' relationship. A man and woman have much to work out on a daily basis as an intimate couple and as **coparents,** partners in raising their children (Schoppe-Sullivan, Mangelsdorf, Frosch, & McHale, 2004). Many parents air their differences constructively and search for solutions that are mutually beneficial, giving children valuable lessons in cooperation and conflict resolution (J. P. McHale & Rasmussen, 1998). Children gain in another way when their parents have good relationships: Happily married parents are inclined to shower affection on their children (M. Dube, Julien, Lebeau, & Gagnon, 2000; Ward & Spitze, 1998).

In comparison, the lessons some other children receive are less favorable. For instance, some children frequently overhear parents' heated arguments. Such loud and bitter exchanges are poor models for dealing with conflict. Arguments also put parents in a foul mood, which can quickly spill over into tense, harsh, and inconsistent interactions with children (S. G. O'Leary & Vidair, 2005). Marital conflict is associated with assorted problems in youngsters, including physical aggression, depression, anxiety, and difficulties in personal relationships (Feinberg, Kan, & Hetherington, 2007; Frosch, Mangelsdorf, & McHale, 2000; L. F. Katz & Low, 2004; Sarrazin & Cyr, 2007).

Largely because of troubled marriages, children who begin life in two-parent families do not necessarily remain in that situation. We look now at how children fare during and following the divorce of parents.

coparents
The two (or more) parents who share responsibility for rearing their children.

Divorcing Parents

Once an infrequent occurrence, divorce is now fairly commonplace. In the United States approximately one in five first marriages ends in divorce or separation within 5 years of the wedding; one-third of first marriages are disrupted within 10 years (Bramlett & Mosher, 2002). At any given time, approximately 13 percent of children in the United States are living with a parent who is divorced or separated from his or her spouse (U.S. Census Bureau, 2007b).

For children, the divorce of parents is not a single event but instead a series of occurrences, each one requiring adjustment. Ongoing marital friction often precedes a divorce (Sarrazin & Cyr, 2007). Recall that exposure to heated conflict is difficult for children to deal with, so even before the divorce, the children may struggle. Nevertheless, children do not typically see their parents' divorce as inevitable or desirable, especially when their parents have previously reassured them that they have been trying to work out their differences (Wallerstein & Kelly, 1980). Thus news of a divorce can be a crushing blow for children. Moreover, at the time of the announcement, parents may not be able to offer children adequate comfort, burdened as they are with their own distress (Kaslow, 2000).

As the divorce is being finalized, the coparents must decide where the children will live and how decisions about the children's education and welfare will be made. Family educators and other professionals in the courts can ease the stresses of the uncertainty and the strains of the decision-making process. Parents who enter mediation are more likely to settle custody issues without going to trial, and parents who participate in divorce education programs are more attentive to children's needs, more willing to give their children access to the nonresident parent, and less inclined to involve children in parental disputes than are parents who do not attend such programs (J. B. Kelly, 2007).

Regardless of how the divorce is settled, the months after it are difficult for many children and parents (Hetherington, Cox, & Cox, 1978). Custodial parents often experience strain in completing all the tasks involved in maintaining an organized household, including shopping, cooking, cleaning, paying bills, and monitoring children's activities and homework (Wallerstein & Kelly, 1980). Financial setbacks can complicate everyone's adjustment. Parents who previously owned a house may have to sell it, and so, on top of everything else, children must move to new (and inevitably smaller) quarters and lose proximity to close friends and neighbors. Between one-quarter and one-half of children move with their custodial parent at least once within 2 years of their parents' separation (J. B. Kelly, 2007).

As the coparents begin to establish separate households, children learn how their parents will get along (or not) and what role each parent will now play with them. One parent may withdraw from the children and eventually invest, both emotionally and financially, in a new life and perhaps a new family. Thus one unfortunate consequence of some divorces is that children lose contact with one of their parents, more often their father (J. B. Kelly, 2007). However, this trend is by no means universal. Many fathers actively seek joint custody arrangements after a divorce (R. A. Thompson, 1994b). Continued contact between fathers and children is facilitated by fathers continuing to live nearby and remaining committed to their parenting role, as well as by mothers and fathers going through mediation during custody deliberations (Emery, Laumann-Billings, Waldron, Sbarra, & Dillon, 2001; R. W. Leite & McKenry, 2002). Sometimes noncustodial fathers redefine their roles with children, perhaps becoming fun-loving companions (e.g., taking regular trips to the movies, amusement parks) rather than nurturers and disciplinarians (Asmussen & Larson, 1991).

Every family experiencing divorce is unique, but some general factors appear to affect children's response to the change. Divorce can be especially overwhelming for young children, who may erroneously believe that their own naughty behavior caused the family's breakup (Fausel, 1986; Wallerstein, 1984). Older children and adolescents usually find their parents' divorce quite painful, yet most cope reasonably well with the change, at least over the long run, and especially if they have easygoing temperaments and age-appropriate social skills (Forehand et al., 1991; Hetherington, Bridges, & Insabella, 1998). Even so, some evidence suggests that parents' divorce can be disruptive for children and adolescents for a period of years and sometimes decades (Conway, Christensen, & Herlihy, 2003; Hetherington et al., 1998; Wallerstein, Lewis, & Blakeslee, 2001).

Children's favorable adjustment to divorce is facilitated by several factors. Coparents and other adults can help children by maintaining affectionate relationships with them, holding firm and consistent expectations for their behavior, willingly listening to their concerns, and encouraging them to keep up contact with friends, nonresident parents, and other family members (Hetherington & Clingempeel, 1992; J. Kelly & Emery, 2003; J. B. Kelly, 2007; Pedro-Carroll, 2005). Children who have good coping skills before the divorce are more likely to adjust favorably to it; effective coping skills allow children to accept the finality of the divorce, not blame themselves, and remain hopeful about the future (Pedro-Carroll, 2005). And, of course, children are likely to flourish when coparents establish reasonably productive relationships with one another, agree on expectations and disciplinary measures, and keep a lid on their own disputes (Hetherington et al., 1978; J. B. Kelly, 2007). In a few cases divorce is actually beneficial for children's development, for instance when children become shielded from high levels of parental conflict or are removed from contact with an abusive parent (Sarrazin & Cyr, 2007).

Single Parents

All families are unique, but as a group families headed by one parent are especially diverse in their backgrounds. Most single parents are divorced or have never been married, but a few are widowed, separated, or have a spouse who is only temporarily absent (U.S. Census Bureau, 2007b). Approximately 8 in 10 single parents are women, but an increasing number are men, given that more single men are adopting children and higher numbers of divorced fathers are receiving custody of their children (C. J. Patterson & Hastings, 2007; U.S. Census Bureau, 2007b). Single parents also differ by age and income. For example, young single mothers tend to have limited financial resources and often live in undesirable housing arrangements, but older unmarried mothers are generally well educated and able to provide adequate food, shelter, and opportunities for their children (C. J. Patterson & Hastings, 2007).

Single parents carry out the tasks of parenting with the realization that much responsibility falls on their shoulders. This realization often leads single parents to see their children's needs as a top priority. Perhaps because of this clear focus, many single-parent families cope well, particularly if they have a reasonable standard of living and the support of a stable network of family and friends (C. J. Patterson & Hastings, 2007). In fact, the simpler structure of single-parent families provides some advantages: Children may be shielded from intense conflict between parents, observe strong coping skills in their custodial parent, and enjoy the intimacy of a small family. Consider what Cedric Jennings (from our introductory case study) wrote in his application to Brown University:

> [B]eing a black male in a single parent home is sometimes tough without that male figure to help in the growing process. But I thank God for my loving mother. I even see some of my peers that have a mother and father, but are heading in the wrong direction. Some of them are into drug-dealing and others try to be "cool" by not doing good in school and not going to classes. But my mother has instilled so many positive values in me it would be hard to even try to get on the wrong track. (Suskind, 1998, p. 107)[1]

Single-parent families do experience unique challenges, though. Single parents, mothers and fathers alike, often express reservations about their ability to "do it all"—juggle children, home, and work responsibilities (R. A. Thompson, 1994b). Unless they have the support of extended family members, neighbors, or friends, single parents may have difficulty coping when they are tired, sick, or emotionally taxed, and they may be unable to offer children the rich range of roles, activities, and relationships that seem to maximize positive developmental outcomes (Garbarino & Abramowitz, 1992; Weintraub, Horvath, & Gringlas, 2002). Fortunately, many single parents are well aware of their personal limitations, and so they reach out to others for assistance.

Parents and Stepparents

Many divorced parents eventually remarry. When they do, they and their children become members of a **stepfamily,** a family in which an original parent-and-children family structure

---

[1]From *A Hope in the Unseen,* by Ron Suskind, copyright © 1998 by Ron Suskind. Used by permission of Broadway Books, a division of Random House, Inc.

stepfamily
Family created when one parent-child(ren) family combines with another parent figure and any children in his or her custody.

MOM is WOW

She is great at hide-and-seek
She takes me to look at an antique
I get to see her three times a week

MOM is WOW

She helped teach me multiplication
She encourages my imagination
She is involved when it comes to participation

MOM is WOW

She's a great stepmom, I guarantee
She lets us watch Disney TV
She is an important part of the family tree

MOM is WOW

No matter what, she is never late
If I have a question, she will demonstrate
When it comes to stepmoms, she's great

MOM is WOW

Figure 3-1

In her fourth-grade class, 9½-year-old Shea wrote a Mother's Day poem for her stepmother. Shea's teacher provided the "Mom is wow" structure for students to follow.

expands to include a new parent figure and any children in his or her custody.[2] Approximately 1 out of 10 children in two-parent families live with a biological or adoptive parent and a stepparent (Federal Interagency Forum on Child and Family Statistics, 2007).

As is true for all family structures, children in stepfamilies experience benefits and challenges. A new adult may bring additional income to the family and can help with household duties. Children can forge relationships with a new parent figure and, possibly, with new brothers and sisters. Yet children may feel that they must now share a parent's time and affection with the new spouse. They may believe, too, that the new stepparent is interfering with a possible reunion of the divorced parents and that by showing affection to the stepparent, they are betraying the nonresident parent (Berger, 2000; Bigner, 2006).

For a stepfamily to blend successfully, it must establish its own identity and traditions. Having entered the marriage with habits of their own, the man and woman must jointly decide how to spend money, divide household chores, prepare and serve meals, and celebrate holidays. The couple must also develop productive ways of expressing and resolving conflicts and determining rules and disciplinary techniques. And, whereas a couple without children can initially focus on one another, the newly married parent and stepparent must attend to the needs of the children as well as their own relationship (Berger, 2000). Qualities that characterize healthy stepfamilies include flexibility, respect, patience, good communication, a sense of humor, and commitment to the marriage (Michaels, 2006).

Most children in stepfamilies eventually adjust reasonably well to their new family situation (Berger, 2000; Hetherington et al., 1998). Relationships between stepparents and children are not always as affectionate as those between biological parents and children, and stepparents may have greater difficulty disciplining children (Furstenberg, Nord, Peterson, & Zill, 1983; Hetherington et al., 1999). Yet in many (probably most) instances, stepparents soon become important parts of children's lives. Figure 3-1 is a Mother's Day poem by 9½-year-old Shea for her stepmother Ann, who at the time had been a family member for about 3 years. It reveals clearly the close relationship that had developed between Shea and Ann.

Children are usually better able to establish a close relationship when their parent is careful not to portray the stepparent as a replacement for the noncustodial parent (Michaels, 2006). Spared from this pressure, children often develop loving relationships with stepparents, as 24-year-old Katy suggests in her description of her feelings for her stepmother, who married her father when Katy was 8 years old:

> My mother is really, when I'm home, a mom to me, she feels like the mom I've always known. But Alice, my stepmother, when she does things like that it feels real special. It's almost more special because it comes from a love that she has for me as a person. 'Cause my parents love me since I was born, but my stepmother has grown to love me. Not just as part of my father but for who I am. It's special; it's different. (Crohn, 2006, p. 127)

Extended Family

Many children have strong ties with relatives, including grandparents, aunts, uncles, and others. In some cases extended family members are primary caregivers of children, and in other circumstances adult relatives live with the children's parents or occasionally look after the children when the parents are busy.

Many children enjoy especially close relationships with their grandparents. In the United States, 8 percent of all children live with at least one grandparent (Bernstein, 2003). Grandparents often become primary guardians when a child's parents are young and economically poor, neglectful, imprisoned, or incapacitated by illness or substance abuse, or when a parent dies (L. M. Burton, 1992; C. J. Patterson & Hastings, 2007). Custodial grandparents sometimes worry that they do not have adequate energy and financial resources to raise a second

[2]Stepfamilies are also known as *reconstitued families* or *blended families*.

generation of children, yet their mature outlook and extensive parenting skills often lead them to be more competent caregivers than the noncustodial parents (C. B. Cox, 2000). For example, grandmothers are generally less punitive and more responsive to children's needs than teen mothers are, and children cared for by grandmothers typically have more economic stability, show greater self-reliance, and are better able to avoid such risky behaviors as drug abuse and vandalism (Chase-Lansdale, Brooks-Gunn, & Zamsky, 1994; R. D. Taylor & Roberts, 1995).

In some families, other extended family members assume central roles in the lives of children (A. O. Harrison, Wilson, Pine, Chan, & Buriel, 1990; Stack & Burton, 1993). In U.S. society, aunts, uncles, and cousins may step forward to raise children when they are the only viable caregivers. And in some other areas of the world, male members of the extended family, such as uncles, regularly serve as primary father figures for children (Engle & Breaux, 1998).

Adoptive Parents

Two or 3 out of every 100 children in the United States are adopted (U.S. Census Bureau, 2004). Adoption is probably most often a positive event for children, who can form ties with loving parents. It can also be a blessing for adoptive parents and siblings, who find themselves— sometimes overnight—with a new child in the family. In Figure 3-2, 7-year-old Connor conveys his excitement on becoming a big brother to 8-month-old Alex.

The last few decades have seen several changes in adoption practices. One growing practice is *open adoption,* in which the birth mother (perhaps in consultation with the birth father) chooses the adopting family with help from an agency. Adoptive families often gain access to medical records through open adoption, and adopted children may have a chance to meet their birth parents. Another trend is *international adoption,* through which orphaned or relinquished children living in one country are adopted by families in another country. More than 10 percent of U.S. adopted children are foreign born (U.S. Census Bureau, 2004). In another trend, many adoption agencies have become increasingly flexible in evaluating potential adoptive parents; the result is a growing number who are single, older, gay, lesbian, or from lower-income groups (Bigner, 2006). The adoption of increasing numbers of older children is an additional trend.

Although adopted children are at slightly greater risk for emotional, behavioral, and academic problems compared to children reared by biological parents, most adopted children thrive in the new family and grow up to be well-adjusted individuals (Freeark, 2006; Palacios & Sánchez-Sandoval, 2005). Adopted children seem to cope best when family members talk openly about the adoption yet provide the same love and nurturance that they would offer any biological offspring (Bigner, 2006; Brodzinsky, 2006).

Occasionally children adopted at an older age have physical or mental disabilities or may require special services due to preexisting conditions or poor care earlier in life (Rutter, 2005; Rycus, Freundlich, Hughes, Keefer, & Oakes, 2006). In extreme cases children may have been previously abused or neglected or had several different placements before being adopted, and these children sometimes find it difficult to form secure relationships with new family members (Rycus et al., 2006). Professional intervention can be helpful (and is sometimes critical) for adoptive families when children's past unstable family life now leads them to resist forming close bonds with new family members.

Foster Care

In *foster care,* children are placed with families through a legal but temporary arrangement. Tragically, parents' neglect and maltreatment of children and personal substance abuse are common reasons for children's placement in foster care (Bigner, 2006; Connell-Carrick, 2007).

The challenges of being foster parents can be enormous. Foster parents must build a trusting relationship with a child who might have been abused, may currently feel unloved, and may experience an emotional or behavioral difficulty (M. E. Cox, Orme, & Rhoades, 2003; Orme & Buehler, 2001). Foster parents must also deal with numerous social

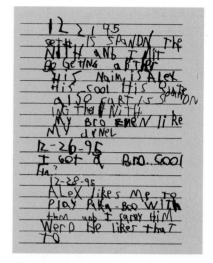

Figure 3-2

In his journal, 7-year-old Connor communicates his excitement about becoming a big brother. Eight-month-old Alex is placed in Connor's family on December 20, and in the first journal entry the following day, Connor hopes that Alex will become his brother (when the court finalizes the adoption). Right away, Connor finds the baby to be both cool and cute. After a few days (December 28 entry), Connor is aware of some of Alex's likes, such as playing peekaboo and being carried by him. (In his journal, Connor also talks about his friends spending the night.)

International adoptions have become increasingly common. Many adoptive parents encourage their children to learn about their native culture as well as the culture of their adoptive family.

service agencies, and they generally receive minimal financial support. Fortunately, many prospective caregivers are drawn to become foster parents because they themselves grew up in foster care or have a special interest in caring for children who have survived difficult family circumstances (Barber & Delfabbro, 2004).

The majority of U.S. children in foster care are reunited with their families within a year (U.S. Department of Health and Human Services, 2007a). However, some children in foster care are eventually adopted, on average at about 6 or 7 years of age, often by their foster parents and sometimes by other adults who are eager to adopt older children (U.S. Department of Health and Human Services, 2007a). Unfortunately, because of heavy caseloads in agencies, crowded court dockets, and the general preferences of adoptive parents for newborn infants, foster children may be shuffled among numerous temporary arrangements before being placed into permanent homes (McKenzie, 1993). Such a transitory existence is particularly detrimental when children have already faced challenges—perhaps neglect, abuse, abandonment, or early exposure to drugs or HIV.

Despite the odds, many children in foster care have good outcomes, doing well in school and forming healthy relationships with peers (Kufeldt, Simard, & Vachon, 2003). Teachers can support children in foster care by helping them settle into peer group settings and addressing any problems they may experience in learning. For example, children in foster care have a higher-than-average rate of disabilities and often require special educational services. In addition, teachers can help youngsters cope with disrupted ties to families and any daily challenges they face in the foster care system. Without such sensitivity from teachers, children in foster care may feel that school is just one more setting where they do not belong. One youngster in foster care expressed his concern that people at school did not understand his experiences:

> Like, at my school, they don't understand why I leave early for a court hearing, and having all the meetings and appointments are time consuming. Living in a normal home without foster care, you don't have to worry about other people besides your parents taking responsibility for you, like your caseworker, or worrying about what your judge is gonna think about what you did. I mean you don't have 50 million other people looking down at you. (Geenen & Powers, 2007, p. 1095)

Other Heads of Family

Our discussion of family structures has not been exhaustive; some children experience variations on these configurations or live in other family arrangements altogether. For instance, a growing number of children live with *gay* or *lesbian parents*. Almost 800,000 U.S. households have same-sex adult partners, and 33 percent of women and 22 percent of men with same-sex partners are raising one or more children in their home (T. Simmons & O'Connell, 2003; U.S. Census Bureau, 2007a). Children who have gay or lesbian parents are as intelligent and well adjusted as other children, and most grow up to be heterosexual adults (Golombok et al., 2003; C. J. Patterson, 2006; Wainright, Russell, & Patterson, 2004). Children of homosexual parents may notice that their parents are stigmatized by society, but these children usually cope with this prejudice without too much difficulty (C. J. Patterson, 2006).

An increasing number of heterosexual couples have children together and do not marry. Compared to married parents, *cohabiting parents* tend to be (on average) younger, less educated, and less financially stable; somewhat less satisfied with their relationships; and less warm and attentive to their children (Aronson & Huston, 2004; C. J. Patterson & Hastings, 2007). Children of cohabiting couples tend to achieve lower grades in school and exhibit more behavior problems, but these effects may diminish when cohabiting couples have good social support and access to adequate financial resources (C. J. Patterson & Hastings, 2007). Of course, countless cohabiting parents offer their children secure and loving homes and raise well-adjusted children.

Adolescent parents often need and receive support from government and social agencies. Although many adolescent parents are sensitive and reliable caregivers, some single adolescent mothers experience a lot of stress and lack awareness of children's emotional, cognitive, and social needs (Borkowski et al., 2002). Teenage parents who are anxious and simultaneously hold unrealistic ideas about child development can become inattentive, inconsistent, and overly critical with their children. The unhappy result is that their children face risks for developmental delays. For example, a number of children of adolescent mothers show delayed language development and lower-than-average academic achievement (Borkowski et al., 2002). Nonetheless, many adolescent parents are competent caregivers, and practitioners can better the odds for these young mothers and their children when they effectively educate and support the teens and provide developmentally appropriate care for the children. For example, teachers can address any academic weaknesses adolescent mothers have, encourage regular school attendance, and appeal to the new mothers' desire to be good role models for their own children (Zachry, 2005). Ally, a young mother who had struggled in school, reveals her newfound commitment to school:

> I came back to school for my son. I don't want him to grow up . . . and have to wake him up every morning, fighting every morning to go to school, and for him to say to me, why should I finish if you didn't finish? That would really hurt me . . . I want him to see me . . . and for him to be like, my mom did it—you know, it was hard for her even though she dropped out a few times but she still went on and she did it, no matter how hard it was. (Zachry, 2005, p. 13)

Accommodating Diverse Family Structures

Most teachers and other school professionals place a high value on being inclusive and respectful of children and their families. Following are some specific tactics educators can use to support children and their varied families:

- ***When organizing activities, make them flexible enough to be relevant to a wide range of family circumstances.*** School assignments and extracurricular activities sometimes involve one or more family members. In high school biology classes, students may be asked to trace the occurrence of physical traits (e.g., brown hair and blond hair) in several generations of their family. Such tasks, though well intentioned, may exclude youngsters whose family structures don't fit the traditional mold. With a little creativity, teachers can easily broaden activities so that they accommodate diverse family structures. For instance, the biology teacher can be more inclusive by presenting data on several generations of a hypothetical biological family and asking all class members to analyze the data. As another example, recall the Mother's Day poem Shea wrote to her stepmother (Figure 3-1). Shea's teacher gave her enough time to write two poems, one for her mother and one for her stepmother.

- ***Encourage acceptance of diverse family structures.*** Occasionally children tease classmates from nontraditional families. For instance, some children of gay or lesbian parents may be ridiculed because of their parents' sexual orientation, and adopted children sometimes hear other children question the motives of birth parents or the closeness of children's bonds with adoptive parents (Gartrell, Deck, Rodas, Peyser, & Banks, 2005; Hare, 1994). At the preschool and elementary levels, teachers can counteract such attitudes by reading stories about children in a variety of family structures and expressing the view that loving families are formed in many ways. In the secondary grades adolescents tend to be more informed and accepting about diverse family structures; nevertheless, teachers should keep an ear open for, and emphatically discourage, any derogatory comments about other youngsters' family circumstances.

Model, discuss, and encourage acceptance of all family structures.

- ***Include fathers and other heads of family.*** When children live in two-parent families, people outside the family often direct communication about children to mothers alone. Educators can try to equalize communications to mothers and fathers when both are present in the home. By doing so, they can validate the incredibly influential roles that mothers and fathers alike play in children's lives. It is also important to acknowledge the presence of other heads of family, such as grandparents serving as guardians. And whenever possible, extended family members should be welcome at school open houses, plays, and concerts.

- ***Be supportive when children undergo a major family transition.*** Many events, including divorce, remarriage, departure of a parent's nonmarital partner, death of a family member, or movement from one foster family to another, can change a child's family life dramatically. In each case one or more old relationships may end, and new relationships may begin. During family transitions children may also move to new residences and, as a result, lose important contacts (Adam, 2004). Adjustment to major family transitions takes time, and practitioners should be prepared to offer long-term support. For example, teachers and counselors can help children identify and express their feelings, understand that they are not being abandoned and did not cause their parents' divorce, distinguish events in the family that they can and cannot control, and find strengths in themselves that have sustained them during family transitions (Pedro-Carroll, 2005).

● ***Remain patient while children are figuring out how to adjust to new family structures.*** Youngsters may find that they must learn to adapt to moving back and forth between two houses and following two sets of rules. Consider 16-year-old Selina's articulation of the tensions that arise when she prepares to change households:

> It gets to about five o'clock on Sunday and I get like a really awful feeling and then . . . aah, packing up again . . . I don't complain about it. That's just the way it is. There's no *point* complaining about it, nothing's going to change. . . . [But] usually on a Sunday around that time . . . we're upset because we're having to move and everyone's tempers . . . you know, you get quite irritable. . . . (Smart, Neale, & Wade, 2001, p. 128)

In such circumstances teachers can express sympathy for the child's frustration but also encourage the child to come up with a plan for keeping track of belongings (including homework) during moves between houses.

● ***Let children say what they want to say; don't pry.*** Children often prefer to keep family matters to themselves. They may feel that teachers and counselors are inappropriately interested in their personal lives (Smart et al., 2001). It is desirable, therefore, for adults to offer reassurance without being too inquisitive. When children do bring up family problems, help them consider options for dealing with the problems and protect their privacy when possible.

● ***Reach out to students who are living in foster care.*** Children in foster care may be emotionally overburdened and have trouble asking for assistance. Furthermore, they may have profound academic and social needs and may sometimes engage in behaviors that upset even experienced professionals. Nevertheless, children in foster care almost invariably benefit when adults articulate clear and consistent expectations and offer ongoing personal support. Teachers and other school personnel can also offer practical help with homework and assignments when children miss school because they are attending court hearings or moving between residences.

How heads of family treat one another and their children affects the skills and dispositions that children develop. In fact, family *processes* overshadow family *structures* in the power of their effects on children. Let's turn to the research on the nature and consequences of relationships within the family.

Family Processes

As you are learning, the family is a social system made up of two or more members who are bound by affection, commitment, and ongoing communication. Parents and children regularly interact as they care for one another, maintain the household, and work and play. In this section we examine *family processes*—the frequent interchanges that family members have with one another. We focus on influences within families, including the effects of families on children and those of children on families. We also examine risk factors for families and offer suggestions on how to establish productive working relationships with families.

Families' Influences on Children

As powerful agents of socialization, parents and other heads of family implement at least three influential practices: using distinctive approaches to caregiving that blend affection with discipline; encouraging children to participate in everyday routines; and providing children with resources and experiences related to the parents' own employment.

Parenting styles.   The foundation of parenting is love. Parents generally communicate affection by responding sensitively to children's gestures, giving them emotional support, and celebrating their accomplishments. Warm, responsive parenting strengthens close attachments between parents and children, as we will explore further in Chapter 11.

A second vital element of parenting is discipline. Children have strong wills of their own but generally lack foresight and self-restraint. Parents must help children curb their impulses, anticipate the outcomes of their actions, follow rules, and make amends for wrongdoings. Parents have numerous options for disciplining children, including reasoning, scolding, temporarily withdrawing affection, removing privileges, imposing additional restrictions and, occasionally, spanking children (Maccoby, 2007). Ideally, a reasonable balance between love and appropriate discipline fosters children's cognitive skills and **self-regulation,** the ability to direct and control personal actions and emotions (Eisenberg, Smith, Sadovsky, & Spinrad, 2004; Laible & Thompson, 2007; Maccoby, 2007).

Most parents throughout the world manage to find acceptable, balanced ways to show love and wield authority (R. H. Bradley, Corwyn, McAdoo, & Coll, 2001; Rohner & Rohner, 1981; Scarr, 1992). However, parents vary in the specific ways in which they tend to express affection and implement discipline; that is, they develop characteristic **parenting styles.** Research on parenting styles was pioneered in the 1960s by American psychologist Diana Baumrind and has been subsequently refined by Baumrind and numerous other developmental scholars (Baumrind, 1967, 1971, 1980, 1989, 1991). Whereas Baumrind's original work depicted parents as selecting one from a limited number of fairly stable ways of nurturing and controlling children, contemporary research indicates that parents' methods are varied, dynamic, and embedded in context.

Considerable evidence with U.S. families indicates that a style of parenting that blends warmth with some degree of control is associated with mature, competent, independent, and considerate behavior in children (Dornbusch, Ritter, Leiderman, Roberts, & Fraleigh, 1987; Gonzalez & Wolters, 2006; Hetherington & Clingempeel, 1992; Lamborn, Mounts, Steinberg, & Dornbusch, 1991; Steinberg, Elmen, & Mounts, 1989). Parents who use this approach, called an **authoritative parenting style,** are affectionate and responsive, ask children to show age-appropriate behavior, give reasons for why certain standards of behavior are necessary, consider children's perspectives, and include children in decision making.

In a second, very different approach, known as the **authoritarian parenting style,** parents exert strong control and demand immediate compliance while offering little affection, few reasons for requests ("Clean your room because I told you to—and I mean *now!*"), and hardly any chances for negotiation. Like authoritative parenting, authoritarian parenting reflects efforts to direct children's behavior, but authori*tative* parents guide children with warmth and flexibility, whereas authori*tarian* parents are less affectionate and more rigid. Children of consistently authoritarian parents tend to be withdrawn, mistrusting, and unhappy; they are apt to have low self-esteem, little self-reliance, and poor social skills; and they have a greater-than-average tendency to act aggressively toward others (Coopersmith, 1967; Lamborn et al., 1991; Simons, Whitbeck, Conger, & Conger, 1991).

Nevertheless, research yields mixed results regarding the long-term effects of authoritative versus authoritarian parenting (Baumrind, 1982; Deater-Deckard, Dodge, Bates, & Pettit, 1996; D. Rowe, Vazsonyi, & Flannery, 1994; Steinberg, Lamborn, Darling, Mounts, & Dornbusch, 1994). One likely reason is that some parents—especially those in certain cultural and ethnic groups—productively combine elements of the two styles. For example, many Asian American families make high demands for obedience and discourage negotiation over rules (and so appear "authoritarian"), but they do so within the context of a close, supportive parent-child relationship (Chao, 1994, 2000). In some families such a style is bolstered by principles of Confucianism, which teach children that parents are right and that obedience and emotional restraint are essential for family harmony (Chao, 1994). In fact, some Chinese American children may feel disappointed when their parents fail to use an involved, directive style, which they see as an expression of love. Moreover, the children of very controlling Asian American parents often do quite well in school (Chao, 1994; Dornbusch et al., 1987).

In general, authoritarian parenting is more common in families from collectivistic cultures, not only in East Asian but also in Middle Eastern societies (Chao, 2000; Dwairy et al., 2006; Kağitçibaşi, 2007; Rudy & Grusec, 2006). In collectivistic cultures strict control and demands for full and immediate compliance are associated with parental warmth and acceptance—not rejection—and seem to help children adjust well in their society. In contrast, many families from the United States and Western Europe raise their children in an individualistic manner.

self-regulation
Process of directing and controlling one's personal actions and emotions.

parenting style
General pattern of behaviors that a parent uses to nurture and discipline his or her children.

authoritative parenting style
Parenting style characterized by emotional warmth, high expectations and standards for behavior, consistent enforcement of rules, explanations regarding the reasons behind these rules, and the inclusion of children in decision making.

authoritarian parenting style
Parenting style characterized by strict expectations for behavior and rigid rules that children are expected to obey without question.

Parents find many ways to express affection and guide their children.

Authoritative parenting fits well in an individualistic culture because it fosters children's autonomy. Individualistic parents who do not temper firm control with flexibility tend to be aloof or rejecting, potentially undermining children's adjustment.

Other aspects of families' lives may make the authori*tative* style ineffective or difficult to implement. When families live in dangerous neighborhoods, for example, parents may better serve children by being sternly directive, particularly if parents communicate the consequences of disregarding strict rules (Hale-Benson, 1986; McLoyd, 1998b). In other circumstances parents are strict not because they are consciously preparing children to survive in hazardous environments, but rather because economic hardship and other family stresses provoke them to be short tempered with children (Bronfenbrenner, Alvarez, & Henderson, 1984; L. F. Katz & Gottman, 1991; Russell & Russell, 1994).

In some cases parents exert *little control* over children, and children generally suffer from this lack of direction. For example, parents who use a **permissive parenting style** appear to care about their children, but they relinquish important decisions to children (even fairly young ones)—allowing them to decide, for example, when to go to bed, what chores (if any) to do around the house, and what curfews to abide by ("Fine. Just ignore what I say!"). Children in such families are typically immature, impulsive, demanding and dependent on parents, and, not surprisingly, disobedient when parents ask them to do something they do not want to do. These children also tend to have difficulty in school, to be aggressive with peers, and to engage in delinquent acts as adolescents (Lamborn et al., 1991; Pulkkinen, 1982).

A few parents are not only permissive but also indifferent to their children. When using an **uninvolved parenting style,** parents make few demands and respond to children in an uncaring and rejecting manner. Children of uninvolved parents frequently exhibit serious difficulties in many areas, including problems with school achievement, emotional control, tolerance for frustration, and delinquency (Lamborn et al., 1991; Simons, Robertson, & Downs, 1989).

The actual effects of these and other styles of parenting depend partly on children's interpretations of parents' intentions. Children see parents' discipline as being legitimate (if not always welcome) to the degree that parents have previously been involved, affectionate caregivers. Through a variety of tactics, which differ among cultural groups, parents demonstrate their concern to children and usually convince the children that they as parents are imposing restrictions for children's own good. As a result, children usually accept parents' authority, even though they may sporadically (and sometimes recurrently) haggle with parents (Hoffman, 1994). What seems especially important to children is that their parents have built a relationship with them that is respectful, polite, and responsive (Grusec & Davidov, 2007; Maccoby, 2007; Martinez & Forgatch, 2001). In contrast, when parents use harsh discipline and come across as demeaning, cruel, or hostile, children may comply with parents' demands only if the parents are physically present, and when later alone, children may feel resentful and choose to disregard parents' instructions.

The apparently significant impact of parenting styles raises the question of how parents develop particular strategies in the first place. A variety of experiences seem important, including how parents themselves were raised, which cultural patterns they have observed, and whether parents are overwhelmed by stressful conditions in their lives (Bornstein, 2006a). In addition, children's own characteristics influence parents' disciplinary techniques. For example, parents are more likely to reason with characteristically compliant children, whereas parents regularly use harsh discipline with chronically irritable and combative children (K. E. Anderson, Lytton, & Romney, 1986; Bornstein, 2006a). Situational factors, especially parents' current goals and the kinds of misbehavior children exhibit, also affect parents' strategies with children (Grusec & Davidov, 2007). Finally, parents' disciplinary techniques and gestures of affection are sometimes influenced by instruction they receive from educators and other professionals (D. Gross et al., 2003).

The big picture that emerges from research on parenting is, once again, that families are complex systems. Children are affected by parents' discipline, but children also influence parents' strategies. In fact, parents with more than one child may use different strategies depending on individual children's behaviors. In addition, parents' interactions with children are based on methods that can change in tone and technique from one event to the next, depending on

permissive parenting style
Parenting style characterized by emotional warmth but few expectations or standards for children's behavior.

uninvolved parenting style
Parenting style characterized by a lack of emotional support and a lack of standards regarding appropriate behavior.

everyone's mood and ongoing activities. Although parenting styles are not fully stable qualities, parents' disciplinary techniques and children's levels of compliance (or resistance) often evolve into intertwined habits for family members (Bornstein, 2006a; Kochanska & Aksan, 1995; Maccoby, 2007). For example, a mother may regularly respond to her son's minor transgressions (perhaps raiding the cookie jar, reading her mail) by raising her eyebrows, putting her hands on her hips, smiling, and asking, "*What* are you doing?" Her familiar good-natured question triggers her son's sheepish smile and reply, "Nothing, Mommy, nothing!"

Children naturally carry lessons about authority from home to school. Teachers can help children adjust to unfamiliar methods of discipline by communicating how and why the classroom is governed as it is. School and classroom newsletters can occasionally address the topic of discipline for parents, explaining how teachers use discipline at school. As we will see shortly, teachers must also take special measures with children who have been exposed to harmful styles of parenting.

Daily activities and preparation for school.   Parents informally teach children essential skills during shared activities. **Guided participation,** in which a child engages in everyday adult tasks and routines, typically with considerable direction and supervision, is an important way in which parents support children's learning. In a (typically) nurturing manner, parents allow children to participate with them in many activities, such as cooking and eating, completing errands, and going to places of worship. With parental guidance, children are motivated to participate in these routines and take on increasing levels of responsibility (Gauvain & Perez, 2007; Rogoff, 2003).

Children learn a lot from participating in routine activities with parents.

Parents also influence children through the experiences they arrange for children outside the home. Especially when children are young, parents organize such activities as playdates at friends' houses and other outings (Gauvain, 2001). Through such repeated activities, parents often encourage children to look ahead and plan for the future. When children are young, parents may ask them what they will do later in the day or what they might need ("It looks like it might rain. Did you pack a jacket?"). As they grow older, parents may help youngsters think through new and complex tasks ("When the interviewer asks you about your job experience, it would be good to tell him about your volunteer work in the scouts.").

Some of the activities parents arrange, both inside and outside the home, affect children's academic learning and expectations about school. For instance, parents informally teach children the purposes and patterns of language and expose children to books, art, music, computer technology, and scientific and mathematical thinking (Eccles, 2007; Hess & Holloway, 1984; Scott-Jones, 1991). When children enter school, their families comment on various aspects of schooling—how to behave, what goals to strive for, how hard to try, and so on. These informal teaching activities probably affect children's cognitive skills as well as their motivation to achieve (Eccles, 2007). Increasingly, parents also influence children by selecting a school from among many choices, including public, private, or charter schools; home schooling arrangements; or schools that embody particular cultural values, such as African-centered education (Madhubuti & Madhubuti, 1994).

Families play another important role through their involvement (or lack of involvement) in children's schooling. At home, many heads of family discuss school activities with children, assist with homework, and praise children or give feedback about in-class projects. At school, heads of family may volunteer in the classroom, participate in parent advisory groups, join fund-raising initiatives, confer with teachers about children's classroom progress, and so forth. Students whose parents are involved in school activities achieve at higher levels than do students whose parents are not involved, perhaps because the former parents convey high value for education, communicate effectively with teachers, and gain insights into the kinds of help children need at home (C. E. Cooper & Crosnoe, 2007; Eccles, 2007). Yet not every family finds it easy to become involved in children's education. Well-educated and affluent parents sometimes find it easier to offer the kinds of enriched academic experiences at home that prepare children for school and may also feel more comfortable about volunteering at school (Magnuson, 2007). As we will soon suggest, many teachers are successful in fostering the involvement of families from varied backgrounds (C. E. Cooper & Crosnoe, 2007).

guided participation
Active engagement in adult activities, typically with considerable direction and structure from an adult or other more advanced individual; children are given increasing responsibility and independence as they gain experience and proficiency.

Parents' employment.   Most parents, both married and single, are employed either inside or outside the home (U.S. Census Bureau, 2007c, 2007d). By being employed, heads of family earn income to meet children's basic needs for food, clothing, and shelter. When income is plentiful, families can also give children access to books and academic supplies, travel, home computers, diverse recreational activities, and so forth.

Parents' employment is developmentally influential in a second way: It occupies parents' time and so creates the need for other adults to supervise children's activities. When children are young, working parents usually choose one of the following arrangements for children's care: looking after the children themselves while in the workplace; placing children with relatives, particularly grandparents; enrolling children in an organized facility, such as a child care center or preschool; or employing a nonrelative to provide care in the child's or provider's home (J. O. Johnson, 2005). When children reach middle childhood and early adolescence, employed parents tend to rely primarily on schools to care for youngsters during the day. They may also have children participate in enrichment activities (e.g., classes in music, art, or computer skills) and sports programs or arrange for supervision by other family members (e.g., a grandparent or older sibling).

Some children come home to an empty house or apartment after school and tend to their own needs until their parents finish work.

Almost one in five school-aged children of employed parents care for themselves after school (J. O. Johnson, 2005). Children's frequent self-care is a concern because children are typically less able than adults to anticipate and avoid dangerous situations (for example, a child may answer the front door without first looking through the peephole). Children are less inclined than adults to think about long-term consequences of their choices (for example, a hungry child might grab a bag of potato chips rather than make a sandwich). Older children generally understand how to care for themselves but may face increased risk of sexual activity and physical aggression (L. Harris et al., 2007; Lord & Mahoney, 2007). Nevertheless, many children in self-care do well: They check in with parents by phone, make nutritious snacks, do chores, and begin their homework (M. E. Lamb & Ahnert, 2006). Self-care arrangements appear more effective when parents explain safety procedures, convey expectations for behavior when home alone, and monitor children's activities by phone (Galambos & Maggs, 1991; Steinberg, 1986).

Parents' employment also influences children's development by transmitting certain values about work and social roles. Employed parents can serve as role models by showing they are responsible citizens who contribute to the greater good of society. In addition, parents transmit to children defined ideas and practices that they have acquired in their jobs (Conger & Dogan, 2007; Kohn, 1977). Middle-income jobs often require extensive consultation with others, and people employed in such positions typically have a fair amount of autonomy. Lower-income jobs more often emphasize close adherence to rules, such as coming to work on time and sticking to strict routines. Parents in both income groups seem to prepare their children to fit into jobs with income levels similar to their own, with middle-income parents valuing self-direction in their children and lower-income parents preferring conformity to authority.

Work can interfere with effective parenting, however, especially when parents must work excessively long hours, receive no health care, or work in dangerous jobs (Conger & Dogan, 2007; Crouter & Bumpus, 2001). Jobs that do not permit parents to take off time to give birth, adopt children, or care for sick children also can adversely affect parents and children (R. Feldman, Sussman, & Zigler, 2004; Kamerman, 2000).

Children's Influences on Families

As you have learned, while children are under parents' regular guidance and control, they are also busily expressing their own wants and needs, often quite emphatically (recall Cedric's outraged response to his B in physics: ". . . what are *we* going to do?!"). Through their requests, demands, and actions, children influence parents and siblings.

Children's effects on parents.   Socialization of children involves *reciprocal influences,* whereby children and their parents simultaneously affect one another's behaviors and together create the environment in which they all live. Parents largely set the tone, but children contribute immensely to family dynamics.

We have already seen how children's own behaviors affect parents' disciplinary techniques. But in fact, reciprocal influences are evident in parent-child interactions from the very beginning (R. Q. Bell, 1988). Babies demand comfort by crying, but they also coo, chatter, lure their parents into contact in a most disarming manner, and in other ways communicate that parents are important people in their lives. A father intent on sweeping the kitchen floor, for example, may find it hard to resist the antics of his 6-month-old daughter who wriggles, chatters, and smiles at him.

Reciprocal influences continue as children grow. For example, preschoolers and parents play games that require both parties to take turns and imitate one another (Kohlberg, 1969). During middle childhood and adolescence, youngsters and their parents take cues from each other's actions. In Figure 3-3, 10-year-old Samuel thanks his mother for teaching him how to behave. Realizing that his mother's underlying motive is to help him, Samuel is likely to listen to her requests in the future. She, in turn, is likely to respond with gratitude to his gestures of appreciation. During adolescence, youngsters may bring home their enthusiasm for new hobbies, interests, and technologies. For instance, when Jeanne's son Alex was a high school senior, he encouraged her to take an art history class with him, and their increased appreciation for diverse art forms led to many mother-son conversations.

Reciprocal influences also occur during the family's exchanges of emotions. When parents do their part to establish a warm climate for the family, children usually reciprocate with affectionate gestures. The note in Figure 3-4, in which 6-year-old Alex offers comfort to his father on the day that Dad's own father (Alex's grandfather) has died, illustrates a child's affectionate response. In contrast, when parents establish a negative climate, children may learn to accuse and ridicule their parents. Some family members intensify demands as they interact, as shown in this interchange:

Figure 3-3

Ten-year-old Samuel thanks his mother for all she has taught him.

Mother:	I told you to clean your room. This is a *disaster*.
Daughter:	Get outta *my* room!
Mother:	[raises her voice] You clean up that mess or you're grounded! [stamps her foot]
Daughter:	Hah! You can't make me!
Mother:	For a month! [shouting now]
Daughter:	You stink! [stomps out of her room and marches to the front door]
Mother:	For two months! [shouting louder]
Daughter:	As if you'd notice I was gone! [slams door]

During this exchange, things go from bad to worse: The daughter is blatantly disobedient, the mother intensifies her demands, and both mother and daughter become angrier. Such exchanges are common in some troubled families (Cavell, Hymel, Malcolm, & Seay, 2007; G. R. Patterson & Reid, 1970). When patterns of negative interaction become habitual, it is difficult for family members to learn new ways of responding to one another. However, both parents and children can grow and change, often in response to intensive counseling and other interventions.

Various aspects of children's temperaments and natural abilities may be partly responsible for the routine exchanges that families develop. For example, in a study with 6-month-old infants, easily frustrated infants tended to provoke mothers' intrusive behavior and discourage their physical stimulation (Calkins, Hungerford, & Dedmon, 2004). The same principle seems to apply with children's intellectual abilities (T. G. O'Connor, 2006; Scarr, 1992). For example, a father with an extensive vocabulary and advanced verbal reasoning may genetically endow his daughter with similar talents. As her verbal skills blossom, the young girl may ask her parents to read to her, explain the meanings of challenging words, and discuss complex ideas. On the surface, the parents promote their daughter's verbal abilities through their actions. But the daughter also influences her parents, instigating and shaping her own opportunities for learning.

Some of children's influences on the family are environmental in origin: Children educate parents about what they have learned at school and in the community. A good example comes from the field of political socialization. In a series of studies, children whose classrooms participated in "Kids Voting USA," a program in citizenship education for students

Figure 3-4

Six-year-old Alex wrote this sympathy card to his father the day Alex's grandfather (his father's father) died. Children reciprocate the affection their parents give them; this includes offering comfort when they see their parents are distressed.

from kindergarten through grade 12, were compared with children whose classrooms did not participate (M. McDevitt, 2005; M. McDevitt & Kiousis, 2007). Not only did the children in the citizenship program learn more about political issues and practices, they also apparently brought their excitement about politics home. Parents of participating children began to pay more attention to the news, talked more often about politics, and formed stronger opinions about candidates and political issues. By discussing political issues with their children, parents in turn helped the children clarify emerging political ideas. Interest seems to have "trickled up" from children to parents, with parents in turn becoming more purposeful in their conversations about politics.

Siblings' responses to one another.   Children have an impact not only on their parents but also on any siblings present in the family. Approximately 80 percent of children in the United States and in Europe live in a household with at least one sibling (Dunn, 2007; Kreider & Fields, 2005).

Sibling relationships are characterized by familiarity and emotion. During early and middle childhood, children spend more time with siblings than with parents or children outside the family (Dunn, 2007; S. M. McHale & Crouter, 1996). As they interact, siblings express emotions that range from joy and full-bellied laughter to outright anger. The relationships that evolve among siblings are often quite close, but they occasionally are a source of stress (Dunn, 2007).

Siblings serve many purposes for children. First and foremost, the presence of brothers and sisters creates the possibility that close sibling relationships will supplement parent-child bonds (Dunn, 2007). Other functions of siblings depend on the relative ages of children. In mainstream Western society, older siblings often look after young children when parents do brief errands. In many other societies, older children are the primary caregivers for younger brothers and sisters for a significant part of the day (Parke & Buriel, 2006; Weisner & Gallimore, 1977). Older siblings also serve as role models, tutors, and playmates for younger children.

Sibling rivalry is often a fact of life in families with multiple children. Children regularly compete for limited resources, including parents' attention, and occasionally become downright combative over seemingly trivial issues (such as who gets to select first from a full plate of freshly baked cookies: "*Lemme* go first!" "No, it's *my* turn!"). Competition among siblings probably has some benefits, including creating a motivation to learn new skills so as to keep up with or outsmart siblings. However, resentment may brew if one child feels slighted by a parent who appears to favor another (G. H. Brody, Stoneman, & McCoy, 1994; Dunn, 2007).

Within a single family, individual children may encounter quite different child-rearing strategies (Dunn, 2007). For example, the intellectual and social experiences of children depend partly on their *birth order*—that is, on whether children were born first, second, or somewhere later down the line. Older siblings tend to have a slight advantage academically, perhaps because of the exclusive time they had with their parents before any brothers or sisters came along, and also possibly because they themselves benefit from teaching younger siblings (G. H. Brody, 2004; Chiu, 2007; Zajonc & Mullally, 1997). Younger siblings show greater skill in interacting with peers, possibly as a result of negotiating with older siblings and learning how to outmaneuver them and gain favor with parents (Dunn, 1984; N. Miller & Maruyama, 1976).

Despite their importance for many children, siblings are by no means essential for healthy development. *Only children*—children without brothers or sisters—are often stereotyped as lonely, spoiled, and egotistical, but research findings on their adjustment are favorable (S. Newman, 2001). On average, only children perform well in school and enjoy particularly close relationships with their parents (Falbo, 1992; Falbo & Polit, 1986).

If children do have siblings, teachers can often take advantage of their close-knit relationships, especially when children face a loss or challenge. For instance, in times of family crisis (e.g., the death of a grandparent or a parent's imprisonment), children may appreciate contact with siblings, perhaps on the playground, in the lunchroom, or in the nurse's office. Educators can also show their sensitivity to the importance of siblings during schoolwide events. For example, many schools welcome the entire family during back-to-school nights, and school personnel might make durable toys and child-friendly snacks available for younger siblings. During parent-teacher conferences, teachers should avoid making comparisons between students and their siblings. And when making classroom placements, teachers and other school personnel can listen respectfully to families' perspectives on siblings' needs. For

My brother helps me play football.

Children learn many things from their brothers and sisters. Art by Alex, age 10.

instance, some parents of twins favor keeping them together in the classroom, especially in the early grades and if the children have had little experience being separated (Preedy, 1999; N. L. Segal & Russell, 1992; Tinglof, 2007). At the same time, teachers will have their own experiences with siblings and can share these with parents, for example, as when a teacher notices that twins become disruptive when together in the classroom.

Risk Factors in Families

As you have seen, "good" families—those that foster children's physical, cognitive, and social-emotional development—come in a wide variety of packages, and they use many, probably countless, distinct styles. In sometimes strikingly different ways, a multitude of psychologically healthy families adequately meet children's basic needs.

Unfortunately, not all families provide optimal environments for children. **Child maltreatment** is the most serious outcome of an unhealthy family environment. Maltreatment takes four major forms (English, 1998; Whipple, 2006). *Neglect* occurs when caregivers fail to provide food, clothing, shelter, health care, or affection and do not adequately supervise children's activities (the *uninvolved* parents we described earlier would be considered neglectful if they were truly disengaged from their children). Caregivers engage in *physical abuse* when they intentionally cause physical harm to children, perhaps by kicking, biting, shaking, or punching them. If spanking causes serious bruises or other injuries, it, too, is considered physical abuse. Caregivers engage in *sexual abuse* when they seek sexual gratification from children through such acts as genital contact or pornographic photography. Caregivers engage in *emotional abuse* when they consistently ignore, isolate, reject, denigrate, or terrorize children or when they corrupt children by encouraging them to engage in substance abuse or criminal activity. Sadly, some parents and other caregivers submit children to more than one form of abuse, as one woman's recollection illustrates:

> My father used to do the weirdest things to me. I hate him. He was in the navy, back in the war and stuff like that. I guess he picked up weird things like that. He used to put me in the corner and put a bag over my head and every time he'd walk by he'd kick me—just like a dog. My mom told me once he put a tick on my stomach and let the tick suck my blood. Things like that—really gross, things that a father would never do to their (sic) daughter. He'd stick toothpicks up my fingernails until it would bleed. [Did he sexually abuse you, too?] Oh, yeah. When I was six. Had to get me to the hospital. I had twenty stitches. I just can't talk about it. (Belenky, Clinchy, Goldberger, & Tarule, 1986, p. 159)

Dear Diary,
 Father was home early from the bar. He was really drunk this time. I was just sitting down reading a book when he started hitting me. My mom tried to help me but it was no use. Finnaly went to a corner when he fainted. After that mom and I left for Aunt Mary. Maybe we'll be safe there.

Like the father described in this child's diary entry, many family members who are abusive suffer from serious psychological problems.

Tragically, children can suffer long-term consequences from being neglected or assaulted by family members (Ayoub, 2006; Whipple, 2006). Children who have been maltreated are at risk for becoming aggressive, withdrawn, and depressed, for viewing themselves negatively, and for developing maladaptive ways of coping and interacting with other people. Children who have been maltreated are also at risk for physical problems and even death.

The occurrence of child maltreatment seems to be related to characteristics of both the adult perpetrator and the child victim. Adults who maltreat children usually suffer from serious psychological problems, such as depression and anxiety, and substance abuse problems (Ayoub, 2006; Whipple, 2006). Many have little contact with family or friends, are economically disadvantaged, move around a lot, were maltreated themselves as children, have large families to care for, and believe that physical punishment is appropriate and justified by their cultural or religious beliefs. Some abusive parents are quite naive about children's development and become angry when children fail to fulfill unrealistic expectations. Children most likely to be maltreated are those who are very young (premature infants are especially at risk), have disabilities, or are irritable and not easily soothed (Ayoub, 2006; Whipple, 2006).

Educators and others working with children and adolescents must, by law, contact proper authorities (e.g., the school principal or Child Protective Services) when they suspect child abuse or neglect. Two helpful resources are the National Child Abuse Hotline (1-800-4-A-CHILD®, or 1-800-422-4453) and the Internet Web site for Childhelp USA® at www.childhelpusa.org.

child maltreatment
Adverse treatment of a child in the form of neglect, physical abuse, sexual abuse, or emotional abuse.

Observation Guidelines

Identifying Family Conditions

Characteristic	Look For	Example	Implication
Family Structure	· Single versus multiple caregivers · Presence or absence of siblings · Extended family members living in the home · Nonrelatives living in the home · Children's relationships with other family members	Alexis's chronic kidney disease causes periodic bouts of fatigue and irritability. During flare-ups, she finds comfort in being with her older sister at recess and lunch. Alexis's teachers have observed the girls' close relationship and provide opportunities for them to be together when Alexis is feeling poorly.	Accept all heads of family as valued, legitimate caregivers of children. Include extended family members (especially those who appear to be regular caregivers) at school functions. Give youngsters time to be with siblings in times of personal or family crisis.
Cultural Background	· Language(s) spoken at home · Children's loyalty to and sense of responsibility for other family members · Children's attitudes toward cooperation and competition · Children's and parents' communication styles (whether they make eye contact, ask a lot of questions, are open about their concerns, etc.)	Carlos is very reserved in class. He follows instructions and shows that he wants to do well in school. However, he rarely seeks his teacher's help. Instead, he often asks his cousin (a classmate) for assistance.	Remember that most children and parents value academic achievement, despite what their behaviors may make you think. Adapt instructional styles to children's preferred ways of interacting and communicating. Consider how families' cultural knowledge and skills might enrich the classroom.
Family Livelihood	· Presence of a family business (e.g., farm, cottage industry) that requires children's involvement · Children in self-care for several hours after school · Older children and adolescents with part-time jobs (e.g., grocery store work, paper routes) · Parental unemployment	April completes several chores on the family farm before going to school each morning. She keeps records of the weight and health of three calves born last year. She constructs charts to show their progress as a project for her seventh-grade science class.	Take young people's outside work commitments into account when assigning homework. For example, give students at least 2 days to complete short assignments and at least a week for longer ones.

continued

When a concern is expressed to Child Protective Services, the authorities may be able to verify the maltreatment and provide the family with counseling, parent education, housing assistance, substance abuse treatment, home visits, and referrals for other services. About one-fifth of child victims are placed in foster care after an investigation of child maltreatment (U.S. Department of Health and Human Services, 2007b). Unfortunately, reports to Child Protective Services do not always lead to immediate services for maltreated children or their families. Sometimes authorities cannot find sufficient evidence to substantiate suspicions, and at other times high caseloads prevent authorities from giving prompt assistance (Larner, Stevenson, & Behrman, 1998; Wolock, Sherman, Feldman, & Metzger, 2001).

As they wait for intervention, maltreated children desperately need stable, caring relationships with adults outside the family. Sadly, many maltreated children have acquired negative social behaviors that elicit rejection from other adults, and possibly for this reason maltreated children are at risk for developing low-quality relationships with teachers (Pianta, Hamre, & Stuhlman, 2003). Teachers can try to avoid being provoked and instead make special efforts to address children's reactions to maltreatment (e.g., inattentiveness, disruptive behavior, or withdrawal from activities). When an investigation is under way, continued sensitivity from teachers is essential, because children now must adjust to changes in family structure (e.g., a child might be placed with a foster family) or family climate (e.g., a mother might become depressed when she learns she could lose custody of her children).

Forming Partnerships with Families

Parents and teachers have much in common. They both take on tough (but gratifying) responsibilities that demand long hours, an unwavering devotion to children, and flexible methods. Of course, parents and teachers occasionally find themselves on opposite sides of the

Observation Guidelines (continued)

Characteristic	Look For	Example	Implication
Parenting Styles	· Parents' warmth or coldness toward their children · Parents' expectations for their children's behavior and performance · Parents' willingness to discuss issues and negotiate solutions with their children · Possible effects of children's temperaments on parents' disciplinary styles · Children's interpretations of parents' motives in disciplinary practices · Cultural values, such as honoring one's elders, that give meaning to parents' disciplinary customs · Dangers and opportunities in the community that influence the use and effects of a given parenting style	At a parent-teacher conference, Julia's parents express their exasperation about trying to get Julia to do her homework: "We've tried everything—reasoning with her, giving ultimatums, offering extra privileges for good grades, punishing her for bad grades—but nothing seems to work. She'd rather hang out with her friends every night."	Acknowledge that most parents have their children's best interests at heart and use disciplinary methods they have seen others use. Recognize that parents often adapt their parenting styles to children's temperaments. With all children, communicate high expectations, show sensitivity to children's needs, and give reasons for your requests.
Disruptive Influences	· Change in family membership (e.g., as a result of death, divorce, remarriage, or cohabitation) · Change of residence · Physical or mental illness in parents or other family members · Parental alcoholism or substance abuse · Economic poverty · Long-term stress in the family	Justin has had trouble concentrating since his parents' divorce, and he no longer shows much enthusiasm for class activities.	Show compassion for children undergoing a significant family transition. Listen patiently if children want to talk. Realize that some families may quickly return to healthy functioning, but others may be in turmoil for lengthy periods. Seek the assistance of a counselor when children have unusual difficulty.
Maltreatment	· Frequent injuries, usually attributed to "accidents" · Age-inappropriate sexual knowledge or behavior · Extreme withdrawal, anxiety, or depression · Excessive aggression and hostile behaviors · Untreated medical or dental needs · Chronic hunger · Poor hygiene and grooming · Lack of warm clothing in cold weather	Johnny often has bruises on his arms and legs, which his mother says are the result of a "blood problem." He recently broke his collarbone, and soon after that he had a black eye. "I fell down the stairs," he explained but refused to say more.	Immediately report possible signs of child maltreatment to a school counselor or principal. Contact Child Protective Services for advice about additional courses of action that should be followed.

table, as initially happened in our introductory case. When teachers and families ultimately communicate effectively (Barbara and Mr. Momen eventually did, with help from Cedric), they are likely to magnify their positive effects on children. Ideally, then, teachers and parents (and other heads of family) become partners that collaborate in support of children's learning. We offer the following recommendations on forming constructive partnerships with families:

● ***Get to know who is in children's families.*** As you have learned, families come in many forms and are equally diverse in their styles of parenting. Thus an important first step is to determine who the guardians are and whether other family members care for children on a daily basis. The Observation Guidelines table "Identifying Family Conditions" lists characteristics of families that teachers can take into consideration when working with children and families.

● ***Communicate with each of the children's primary caregivers.*** When two parents are actively involved in a child's life—whether they live in the same household or not—teachers should try to get to know both parents and show respect for the role that each plays

Adolescent Development

Eleven . . . is a time of breaking up, of discord and discomfort. Gone is the bland complaisance of the typical ten-year-old. Eleven is a time of loosening up, of snapping old bonds, of trial and error as the young child tests the limits of what authority will and will not permit.

Louise Bates Ames, Ph.D.
Your Ten- to Fourteen-Year-Old
Gesell Institute of Human Development

To understand your adolescent, you need to consider . . .
 . . . the child's basic individuality.
 . . . what is expected of anyone of his or her particular age level.
 . . . what environment your child finds himself or herself in.

Eleven-year-olds can be . . .
  egocentric,
  energetic,
  always "loving" or "hating";

   as well as . . .
      not as cooperative or accepting as in the past
      more angry than in the past
      inattentive
      hungry all the time
      more interested in the clothes they wear
       (but not in cleaning them!)
      uncertain
      more apt to cry
      fearful
      rebellious
      very interested and involved in family activities

Figure 3-5

Teachers can be valuable sources of information about child and adolescent development. In this flier for parents, middle school teacher Erin Miguel describes several common characteristics of young adolescents.
Reprinted with permission of Erin Miguel, Jones Middle School, Columbus, Ohio.

When you suspect you have views that conflict with those of a child's parents or guardians, share your perspectives about the child's needs and ask family members to do the same.

in the child's development. All too often, fathers, grandparents, and other primary caregivers are left out of the picture.

● ***When first meeting with parents and other heads of family, take active steps to establish rapport.*** Most parents want to be heard rather than just "talked at," yet some may be reluctant to voice their perspectives without some encouragement, and some parents are actually anxious, uncertain, or distrustful (Hoover-Dempsey & Sandler, 1997). Educators can look for signs of discomfort, use friendly body language, comment optimistically about children's abilities, display a sense of humor, and treat parents as authorities who can help them learn about children's needs. Educators can also encourage input by asking specific questions (e.g., "What does Kira like to do in her free time?") and assuring parents that they should feel free to call whenever they have questions or concerns.

● ***Reassure parents about the age-related challenges youngsters face.*** For example, parents may worry about separating from their babies at the child care center; handling oppositional behaviors of young children; supporting the acquisition of indispensable academic skills during middle childhood; and helping young adolescents cope with mixed feelings about puberty. You can find a list of parents' concerns and ways teachers might address them in the Developmental Trends table "The Family's Concerns for Children of Different Ages." Teachers can also play an enormously helpful role in casting children's developmental abilities in a positive light, as you can see in a middle school teacher's handout for parents in Figure 3-5.

● ***Step into their shoes.*** Families sometimes live very different lives than those of the professionals who work with them. By talking with community leaders, reading the research about local cultures, and listening sympathetically to parents, educators can learn a lot about families' lives. For example, by seeking information about homeless families who reside in temporary shelters, teachers would learn about the many efforts these parents make to protect their children from harmful people in their environment (Torquati, 2002). With such insights, teachers can advise parents about the school's procedures for ensuring a safe, stimulating environment for children.

● ***Remember that most parents view their children's behavior as a reflection of their own competence.*** Parents typically feel proud when their children are successful in school and get along well with friends. In contrast, parents may respond to their children's academic failures or behavior problems with embarrassment, shame, anger, or denial. Teachers are more likely to have productive discussions with parents if they avoid placing blame and instead propose that students, parents, and teachers work as a team to identify solutions.

● ***Be alert for possible cultural differences.*** When conferring with parents about children's problematic classroom behaviors, educators should keep in mind that people from different cultural groups usually have distinct ideas about how children should be disciplined. For example, many Chinese American parents believe that Western schools are too lenient in correcting inappropriate behavior (Hidalgo, Siu, Bright, Swap, & Epstein, 1995; Kağitçibaşi, 2007). In some Native American and Asian cultures, a child's misbehaviors may be seen as bringing shame on the family or community; thus a

Developmental Trends

The Family's Concerns for Children of Different Ages

Age	Topics	Diversity	Implications
Infancy (Birth–2 Years) 	**Physical Development** · Ensuring infants' basic safety by structuring the environment so they cannot put themselves in danger (e.g., by tumbling down stairs, swallowing cleaning supplies) · Meeting infants' physical needs (e.g., feeding on a baby's schedule, diapering, and easing baby into a sleep schedule that conforms to adults' patterns) · Giving proper nutrition to match physiological needs and pace of growth **Cognitive Development** · Talking with infants and responding enthusiastically to their smiles and babbling · Encouraging infants to take turns in conversations and simple games · Providing appropriate sensory stimulation **Social-Emotional Development** · Watching for infants' preferences and abiding by these (for example, after noticing that an infant enjoys watching trucks, selecting picture books with trucks to share with the child) · Arranging for consistent, stable, responsive caregivers to whom children can become emotionally attached · Affirming infants' feelings so that they begin to understand emotions · Responding with reasonable promptness to infants' cries so that they learn that they can rely on parents	· Some parents may promote independence in infants by encouraging them to try self-help actions, such as picking up bits of food and feeding themselves; others may prefer to do these things for infants. · Nap time may depend on parents' beliefs about how much sleep children need and the proper way to help them fall asleep. · Parents may differ in how much they talk with infants. Some may verbalize frequently; others may soothe infants and focus on nonverbal gestures. · Families differ in beliefs about out-of-home care. Some parents resist commercial child care and will leave infants only for brief periods with familiar relatives. Other parents are comfortable with employed caregivers. · Concerns of parents depend partly on the temperament and health status of infants. When infants are difficult to soothe or are sick, parents may be quite concerned.	· Complete daily records of infants' physical care so parents are aware of how their infants' needs were met and the kind of day they had. · Talk with parents about the developmental milestones you notice in infants. For example, tell parents when you see a new tooth breaking through the gums. · Post a chart of typical developmental milestones (e.g., rolling over, sitting up, uttering a first word) so that parents can think about what their infants might be presently learning. Select a chart that emphasizes the wide variation in ages at which infants normally attain developmental milestones. · Ask parents to share their concerns about their infants, and offer appropriate reassurance.
Early Childhood (2–6 Years)	**Physical Development** · Ensuring children's basic safety (e.g., protecting them from street traffic and household chemicals) · Helping children with self-care routines (e.g., dressing, brushing teeth, bathing) · Finding appropriate outlets for physical energy **Cognitive Development** · Answering children's seemingly incessant questions · Channeling curiosity into constructive activities · Reading stories and in other ways promoting a foundation for literacy · Preparing for transition to formal schooling **Social-Emotional Development** · Curbing temper tantrums · Promoting sharing among siblings and peers · Addressing conflicts and aggressive behavior · Forming relationships with new caregivers in child care and preschool	· Some parents, worrying about their children's safety, are exceptionally reluctant to leave them in the care of others. · Low-income families have little or no discretionary income with which to purchase books and other supplies for cognitive enrichment. · Some kindergartners and first graders have had little or no prior experiences with other children; for instance, they may be only children or may not have previously attended child care or preschool. · Some parents (especially those from higher-income, professional backgrounds) may give children too many intellectually challenging activities and too few chances to relax or play.	· Suggest possible approaches to teaching young children about self-care habits, social skills, and impulse control. · Keep parents regularly informed about their children's progress in both academic and social skills. · Provide books and other stimulating materials that parents can check out and use at home. · When highly educated parents seem overly concerned about accelerating their children's cognitive development, suggest literature that encourages a balance between stimulation and relaxation.

continued

Developmental Trends (continued)

Age	Topics	Diversity	Implications
Middle Childhood (6–10 Years) 	**Physical Development** · Fostering healthy eating habits · Using safety equipment (e.g., seat belts in the car, helmets for cycling or skateboarding) · Establishing exercise routines and limiting television and electronic games **Cognitive Development** · Helping children acquire habits and expectations that will aid them in their academic work · Promoting mastery of basic academic skills · Enhancing children's education through family involvement and outings **Social-Emotional Development** · Giving children increasing independence and responsibility (e.g., for waking up on time, doing homework) · Monitoring interactions with siblings, playmates · Instilling moral values (e.g., honesty, fairness)	· Some parents may be overly stressed from work responsibilities. · Some neighborhoods have few if any playgrounds or other places where children can safely play. · Children's special talents and interests influence their choices of activities outside the home. · Some children look after themselves for long periods after school, and they may or may not use this time wisely.	· Obtain and distribute literature about safety measures from local police, fire departments, and pediatricians' offices. · Provide resource materials (perhaps through a parent library in the classroom) that parents can use to assist their children with academic subject matter. · Encourage parents' involvement in school activities and parent-teacher groups. · Suggest facilities and programs in the community (e.g., youth soccer leagues, scout organizations) that provide free or inexpensive opportunities for after-school recreation and skill development.
Early Adolescence (10–14 Years)	**Physical Development** · Recognizing and dealing with early stages of puberty · Encouraging physical fitness · Affording basic clothing during periods of rapid growth **Cognitive Development** · Supporting school-based changes in expectations for academic performance · Identifying appropriate mechanisms for developing young adolescents' talents and interests **Social-Emotional Development** · Showing sensitivity to self-consciousness about appearance · Accommodating requests for more leisure time with peers · Dealing with increased conflict as adolescents seek greater autonomy	· Children differ markedly in the age at which they begin puberty. · Some youngsters may have little access to safe and well-equipped recreational facilities. · Some parents may have considerable difficulty allowing their children greater independence. · Overt parent-teenager conflicts are rare in some cultures, especially in those that cultivate respect for elders (e.g., many Asian cultures). · Various peer groups encourage behaviors that may or may not be productive.	· Identify and inform parents about age-appropriate athletic and social programs in the community. · Collaborate with other teachers to establish a homework hotline through which students can get ongoing support and guidance for home assignments. · Share with parents your impressions about reasonable expectations for independence and responsibility in young adolescents.
Late Adolescence (14–18 Years)	**Physical Development** · Keeping track of teenagers' whereabouts · Encouraging high school students to maintain realistic schedules that allow adequate sleep · Worrying about risky driving · Concern about possible alcohol and drug use **Cognitive Development** · Encouraging youth to persist with increasingly challenging academic subject matter · Understanding adolescents' expanding capacity for logical, systematic thinking · Educating adolescents about employment prospects and college requirements **Social-Emotional Development** · Worrying about the loss of parental control over teenagers' social activities · Finding a reasonable balance between supervision and independence · Monitoring adolescents' part-time jobs	· Alcohol and drugs are readily available in most communities, but their use is more frequent and socially acceptable in some neighborhoods and peer groups than in others. · Some parents refuse to believe that their children may be engaged in serious health-compromising behaviors, even when faced with the evidence. · Families differ in their knowledge of, and experiences with, higher education; some are unable to counsel their children about options in postsecondary education. · Parents differ in the extent to which they encourage teenagers' part-time employment.	· Suggest ways in which adolescents can maintain regular contact with their families when they are away from home for lengthy periods (e.g., by making regular phone calls home). · Provide information about possible careers and educational opportunities after high school; include numerous options, including part-time and full-time vocational programs, community colleges, and 4-year colleges and universities.

Sources: W. A. Collins, 1990; Maccoby, 1984; Montemayor, 1982; Mortimer, Shanahan, & Ryu, 1994; Paikoff & Brooks-Gunn, 1991; Pipher, 1994; Warton & Goodnow, 1991; Youniss, 1983.

common disciplinary strategy is to ignore or ostracize the child for an extended period of time (Pang, 1995; Salend & Taylor, 1993). As educators talk with family members who have different cultural views, they can listen with an open mind and try to find common ground they can use to support children.

● *Reflect on and curb your biases.* Teachers and other practitioners are occasionally influenced by stereotypes of certain cultural or socioeconomic groups. For example, some caregivers in child care settings have negative views of low-income parents (Holloway, Fuller, Rambaud, & Eggers-Péirola, 1997). Practitioners can increase their effectiveness with families from diverse backgrounds by reflecting on their own assumptions about particular groups and looking for the unique qualities and characteristics—and especially the *strengths*—that each child and parent is apt to have.

● *Strive to build positive relationships with families of all ethnic backgrounds.* Children and parents from ethnic minority groups are less likely to enjoy supportive relationships with teachers than are children and parents from European American backgrounds (J. Hughes & Kwok, 2007). Poor relationships are likely to occur when teachers are unaware of families' cultural perspectives and uncomfortable with their communication styles (J. Hughes & Kwok, 2007). Knowing that good parent-teacher and teacher-child relationships are beneficial for *all* children, teachers can make extra efforts to reach out to families with backgrounds different from their own.

● *Encourage families to get involved in their children's education.* Parents and other family members are more likely to become involved in children's education when they believe that (a) their involvement is important, (b) they can exert a positive influence on their children's educational achievement, and (c) school personnel want their involvement (R. M. Clark, 1983; Hoover-Dempsey & Sandler, 1997; Lareau, 1989). Thus many teachers encourage families to help children with academic objectives, giving examples of family involvement that are likely to foster children's achievement (Pomerantz, Moorman, & Litwack, 2007). For example, when Teresa's son Alex was in fourth grade, he brought home a weekly newsletter from school. Every issue contained the same reminder that children should read nightly for 20 minutes (and by implication, that parents should verify that this reading took place). With older students, teachers may use slightly different tactics, ones that cultivate family involvement but play down the directive role of parents. For example, Teresa recalls that when her son Connor was in middle school, she and her husband received a booklet containing tearsheets with suggestions on how parents might contribute to school activities (such as driving on field trips, volunteering in the classroom, and bringing in treats for special events); it was easy to go through the booklet, choose a few activities, and send the sheets back to school.

Parents and guardians can support their children's education by participating in school activities, as these mothers are doing by helping out at a school-sponsored carnival.

● *Address barriers to involvement.* Although most parents and other primary caregivers want what is best for their children, many do not participate in school meetings and other activities. Some parents have exhausting work schedules, lack adequate child care, or have difficulty communicating in English. Still others may believe that it is inappropriate to bother teachers with questions about their children's progress. And some parents are actively involved when their children are in elementary school but increasingly withdraw as their children move to middle and secondary levels (J. L. Epstein, 1996; Finders & Lewis, 1994; Roderick & Camburn, 1999). A few parents avoid school because of their own painful memories. One father put it this way:

> They expect me to go to school so they can tell me my kid is stupid or crazy. They've been telling me that for three years, so why should I go and hear it again? They don't do anything. They just tell me my kid is bad.
> See, I've been there. I know. And it scares me. They called me a boy in trouble but I was a troubled boy. Nobody helped me because they liked it when I didn't show up. If I was gone for the semester, fine with them. I dropped out nine times. They wanted me gone. (Finders & Lewis, 1994, p. 51)

Certainly, it is not easy to override parents' deep-seated reservations about schools, but teachers can communicate their genuine desire to visit with parents at school or have them become involved in some other way. And when parents fail to take them up on this offer, teachers can

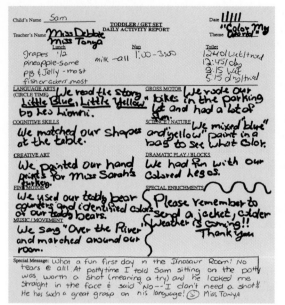

Figure 3-6

A structured daily activity form completed for 2½-year-old Sam. Parents often appreciate information about what their children did and learned during the day.

recognize the beneficial roles that parents play at home, such as limiting children's television and encouraging children's reading (J. S. Lee & Bowen, 2006).

• **Ask family members about talents they would be willing to share.** Many family members have special abilities (such as woodworking, calligraphy, storytelling) that they would happily demonstrate at school. Likewise, some parents are bilingual, and they might step forward to translate school materials for other parents who speak little English (Finders & Lewis, 1994). To benefit from these talents, you may wish to ask families at the beginning of the year about their interests in sharing particular kinds of expertise with the school.

• **Use a variety of communication formats.** Families appreciate hearing about children's accomplishments, and they deserve to know about behaviors that consistently interfere with children's learning and adjustment. Likewise, teachers can learn a lot about a child's needs from talking with family members. Here are a few helpful forms of communication:

- *Meetings.* In most schools parent-teacher-student conferences are scheduled one or more times a year. These meetings are an excellent forum for celebrating children's successes and identifying areas that need additional attention. For example, at one conference it may be mutually agreed that the teacher will find new assignments that better match the child's needs, the child will begin keeping track of due dates for homework, and the family will reserve a quiet place at home for the child to do homework uninterrupted.

- *Written communications.* Educators can use structured forms to let parents know what their children are doing. Prepared forms that specify activities and leave space for individual comments can be helpful. In Figure 3-6 teachers describe 2½-year-old Sam's first day in the toddler room, including information about their program and how Sam fared. More formal newsletters communicate school- and community-wide events, resources, and policies.

  - *Telephone conversations.* Telephone calls are useful when issues require immediate attention. For example, teachers might call parents to express concern when a student's behavior deteriorates unexpectedly. But they might also call to express their excitement about an important step forward. Parents, too, should feel free to call teachers. Keep in mind that many parents are at work during the school day; hence it is often helpful for teachers to take calls at home during the early evening hours.

  - *E-mail and Web sites.* Increasingly, educators find that they can maintain regular contact with parents electronically—for instance, by sending e-mail messages and creating Web pages that list events and assignments. In Figure 3-7 you can see an e-mail message sent by a school counselor to parents. Notice that the counselor not only advises parents of a problem but asks for their help in encouraging proper behavior. Such electronic communication, of course, can be used only when parents have easy access to computer technology and the Internet.

  - *Parent discussion groups.* In some instances teachers, counselors, and principals may want to assemble a group of parents to discuss mutual concerns. For example, school leaders might want to use a discussion group as a sounding board for evaluating possible school improvement plans.

• **Accommodate language and literacy differences.** When a child's parents speak a language other than English, educators often try to include in conversations someone who can converse fluently with the parents in their native tongue (and ideally, someone whom the parents trust). Educators should also have newsletters and other written messages translated whenever it is reasonable to do so.

Hello!

How much money would it take for you to agree to go back to your 7th grade year of school? You couldn't pay me enough!!!

Disrespect and thoughtless comments to peers seem to be on the upswing in the 7th grade at [our school]. Today we had a town meeting, and I had one of my serious chats with the class about the importance of treating others properly. I strongly encouraged students to step back and evaluate their own behavior. I asked them to think about whether their parents would be proud of how they treat others. I also asked if they personally were proud of how they treat others.

I think most of you know me well enough by now to know that I have a low tolerance for people who treat others poorly. If your child is having trouble with peers, please encourage him or her to talk with me. If s/he is struggling with taking that first step, I hope you would take the time to call me to discuss it. Unless I'm aware of concerns, I can't work on making things better.

It takes a village.

Nancy

Figure 3-7

Professionals who work with families can sometimes stay in touch by electronic mail. In this e-mail message a counselor alerts parents to the social climate at school.
Courtesy of Nancy S. Rapport.

- ***Inform parents of services available to them.*** Families in distress often appreciate hearing about agencies that offer supportive services. For example, families who have been found to be seriously maltreating their children may be at risk for having their children placed in foster care. In such cases, teachers and other professionals must protect children, but often they can advise parents about potentially helpful services, such as parent education and outlets for family recreation (Staudt, 2001).

- ***When appropriate, visit families in their homes.*** Home visits are a widely used way of supporting parents' efforts at home, especially with young children (Gomby, Culross, & Behrman, 1999). Home visiting programs typically focus on educating parents about children's needs and preventing such problems as neglect or abuse. To make home visits maximally effective, educators can present themselves as friendly and nonjudgmental, make an effort to establish rapport with parents and other family members, and offer practical suggestions for helping children to learn. One educator considers home visits a vital first step in communicating with migrant families:

> At the beginning of the school year, [personnel from the school] went house by house in their whole zone. . . . Everybody—the counselors, the librarian, the clerks, the paraprofessionals—went to visit families. Everybody's home was visited at least once by somebody in the school in a positive fashion. OK? They told [parents] *"Mire Señora, queremos que sepa que en la escuela nos importa su hija o hijo y queremos saber dónde vive y si le podemos ayudar en algo, estamos para servirle.* [Look, Miss, we want you to know that we care about your daughter or son and we want to know where you live and if we can help you in any way, we are here to serve you.]" And we began to get parents who said, "They care to come out here on an afternoon, when it's hot, you know, and visit? They really care about us!" (G. R. López, Scribner, & Mahitivanichcha, 2001, p. 264)

None of the strategies just described will, in and of itself, guarantee a successful working relationship with parents and other heads of families. Meetings with parents occur somewhat infrequently. Written communication is ineffective with parents who have limited literacy skills. Some families do not want to be visited at home. And, of course, not everyone has a telephone, let alone e-mail. Despite difficulties with staying in touch, effective teachers and other practitioners do their best to form productive partnerships with families (e.g., see the Development and Practice feature "Making Schools Family Friendly").

Development and Practice

Making Schools Family Friendly

- **Help children and their families feel that they are valued members of the school.**

  A caregiver of toddlers provides storage boxes ("cubbies") for each child. On the outside the child's name is posted, and photographs of the child and his or her family are displayed. Children regularly point to their parents and other family members throughout the day.

- **Recognize the significance of families in children's lives.**

  A music teacher asks students to bring in the lyrics from their favorite family songs. She posts the words of the songs on a bulletin board labeled "My Family and Me."

- **Acknowledge the strengths of families' varying backgrounds.**

  When planning a lesson on the history of farming in Colorado, a middle school social studies teacher asks families if they could bring in any farm tools (or photographs of tools) that they use while planting and harvesting crops.

- **Use a variety of formats to communicate with parents.**

  A fourth-grade teacher works with the children in his class to produce a monthly newsletter for parents. Two versions of the newsletter are created, one in English and one in Spanish.

- **Tell parents about children's many strengths, even when communicating information about shortcomings.**

  A school counselor talks on the phone with the parents of a student. She describes several areas in which the student has made considerable progress but also asks for advice about strategies that might help him stay on task and be more agreeable with peers.

- **Be sensitive to parents' concerns about their children.**

  A school counselor talks with worried parents of a 16-year-old girl who has begun smoking and possibly experimenting with drugs. Thinking about the girl's interest in photography, the counselor tells the parents about the school's after-school photography club, with hopes that the companionship of more academically oriented peers might get the student back on the right track.

- **Encourage all parents and guardians to get involved in school activities.**

  A high school principal sends home a book of "coupons" printed with assorted activities that parents and other family members might do to help the school (e.g., tutoring in the classroom, baking goodies for a school open house, serving on the parent advisory group). She accompanies the book with a letter expressing her hope that all parents will return at least one coupon that commits them to a particular activity.

Children in a Diverse Society

Increasingly diverse populations of children attend school, creating an opportunity—and a responsibility—for teachers to adjust their methods for the betterment of all children. In this section we focus on the range of experiences children have as members of defined social groups and as residents of particular kinds of communities. We begin with an analysis of ethnicity and other aspects of children's backgrounds and then proceed to give recommendations for meeting the needs of children from diverse backgrounds. Next we examine communities that children live in, the specific challenges children face when their families live in economic poverty, and strategies for helping children address these challenges.

Children's Experiences in Diverse Groups

As a result of immigration patterns during the past several centuries, the United States and many other nations have become highly diverse. In the United States today, about 1 in 5 children live with at least one foreign-born parent (Federal Interagency Forum on Child and Family Statistics, 2007). In addition, approximately 1 in 5 children speak a language other than English at home, and 1 in 20 have limited mastery of English (Federal Interagency Forum on Child and Family Statistics, 2007). Some children who are learning English also have encountered significant gaps in their school enrollment due to such factors as their family's recent immigration and changes in parents' employment. For example, roughly 10 to 15 percent of English language learners in urban school districts have had interrupted formal schooling (DeCapua, Smathers, & Tang, 2007; Walsh, 1999). Furthermore, as you can see in Table 3-1, the numbers of children in various "ethnic minority" groups (that is, children from Asian American, African American, Hispanic American, and Native American backgrounds) are increasing at proportionally higher rates than the number of children from European American backgrounds. Let's look further at the experiences of children from diverse backgrounds.

Ethnicity.   Ethnicity has a powerful influence on children and their families. A child's **ethnicity** indicates his or her affiliation with a group of individuals who share certain values, beliefs, behaviors, and, often, a common cultural history and heritage. An ethnic group may be comprised of people of the same race, national origin, or religious background.

Culture, ethnicity, and society are overlapping but distinct concepts. Often a single society (such as citizens of the United States) may be comprised of several ethnic groups. And one ethnic group can be composed of individuals from numerous cultural groups. For example, people who are *Hispanic* tend to be Spanish- or Portuguese-speaking (or descended from individuals who spoke these languages), and they may originate from one of several very different regions (Spain, Portugal, Mexico, Central and South American countries, Spanish-speaking Caribbean nations); as a result, Hispanics share a few common values but have many distinct cultural practices (C. B. Fisher, Jackson, & Villarruel, 1998; García & Jensen, 2007). The implication of this heterogeneity is that knowing a child comes from a Hispanic

Table 3-1   Percentages of U.S. Children in Ethnic Groups

Ethnicity	Estimates for Year			Projections for Year	
	1980	1990	2000	2010	2020
White	74	69	61	56	53
Black	15	15	16	15	15
Hispanic	9	12	17	21	24
Asian	2	3	4	4	5
American Indian/Alaska Native; multiple race; or any other race	1	1	4	5	6

ethnicity
Membership in a group of people with a common cultural heritage and shared values, beliefs, and behaviors.

Note: Figures are for U.S. children 17 years and under. Accumulated percentages may not equal 100 due to rounding error. Data from 2000 and after are not fully comparable to data from previous years due to changes in census categories.

Source: Federal Interagency Forum on Child and Family Statistics, 2007.

American background gives only a rough idea as to what his or her cultural practices and beliefs might be.

Ethnicity also overlaps, to some degree, with race. In some ethnic groups, members may come from a single race, but this is not always the case. In general, *ethnicity* has a stronger association with cultural dimensions, and *race* connotes physical similarities such as skin color or eye shape (Coles, 2006). A child's race, often apparent to others, can be an especially strong factor in how he or she is treated and whether the child encounters discrimination or favoritism.

Today many children are *multiethnic,* claiming ancestry from more than a single ethnic group. For instance, a child whose mother has African American and Native American heritages and whose father immigrated from England may be exposed to a variety of family traditions (E. W. King, 1999). Multiethnic children may affiliate with two or more ethnic groups and selectively carry out particular traditions depending on the context (e.g., eating contemporary American foods in restaurants and traditional Vietnamese dishes at family gatherings). Multiethnic children often undergo a lengthy developmental process in deciding how to blend or preserve their multiple heritages (Northrup & Bean, 2007; also see Chapter 12).

Membership in a particular racial or ethnic group is not always a good indication of children's cultural beliefs.

Ethnicity and socialization.   Families play a major role in imparting ethnic beliefs and practices. For instance, in some ethnic groups, including those found in many Hispanic, Native American, and Asian communities, obligation to family is especially important. Children raised in these cultures are likely to feel responsibility for their family's well-being and a strong sense of loyalty to other family members—reflecting the *collectivistic* values we spoke of earlier in the chapter (Franklin, 2007; García, 1994; Karenga & Karenga, 2007; Parke & Buriel, 2006). For example, Chinese families who immigrate to the United States typically strive to instill in their children honor of family, respect for elders, and eagerness to achieve academically (Chao, 2000).

In Western societies most families from diverse cultural and ethnic backgrounds instill in their children the importance of getting a good education (Immerwahr, 2004). Yet families from different ethnic groups may hold varying views on how likely it is their children will succeed academically, how satisfied they are with various levels of achievement, and the extent to which children's achievements derive from natural ability or hard work (Eccles, 2007). For example, European and American parents are more likely than Japanese parents to overestimate their children's abilities and underestimate their children's difficulties. And whereas European American parents tend to see academic ability as partly the result of genetic endowment, many Asian American parents transmit the belief that high academic achievement is mainly the outcome of effort and persistence (Crystal & Stevenson, 1991; Hess, Chang, & McDevitt, 1987). Families from various cultural groups may also communicate different ideas about why children should do well in school, how academic achievement relates to other domains of life, and which methods of instruction are most effective. For instance, in many Hispanic cultures, being well educated does not refer solely to having a good formal education; it also means being successful in social situations and showing respect to others (Okagaki & Sternberg, 1993; Parke & Buriel, 2006).

Gender and diversity.   Most cultures socialize girls and boys somewhat differently. For instance, many parents in the United States encourage daughters to engage in stereotypically feminine behaviors (e.g., playing with dolls, helping other people) and freely express emotions. Meanwhile, they are apt to encourage sons to undertake stereotypically masculine activities (e.g., playing with blocks, engaging in rough-and-tumble play) and hide feelings that convey weakness, such as fear and sadness (Lippa, 2002; Ruble, Martin, & Berenbaum, 2006). Parents also tend to assign household chores based on traditional male and female roles. For example, they may ask their daughters to wash dishes and clean the house and their sons to mow the lawn and take out the garbage (S. M. McHale, Bartko, Crouter, & Perry-Jenkins, 1990; Ruble et al., 2006). Furthermore, parents hold different expectations about the potential accomplishments of sons and daughters. For instance, parents are more likely to enroll sons in competitive sports leagues and programs for gifted students, expect science to be easier for sons, and more fully explain scientific concepts to sons than daughters (Crowley, Callanan, Tenenbaum, & Allen, 2001; Eccles, Wigfield, & Schiefele, 1998; Tenenbaum & Leaper, 2003).

Group and individual differences exist in how families socialize children to become men and women. Most cultural groups make clear distinctions between what "men do" and what "women do" and prepare children to act according to gender-typical roles. For example, Japanese parents encourage daughters to be obedient and dutiful and sons to be independent and responsible (Rindfuss, Liao, & Tsuya, 1992). Many older girls and women in Asian Indian and Muslim cultures wear veils to protect their modesty and adhere to religious customs (Coles, 2006). Yet some ethnic groups permit boys and girls to act similarly. For instance, many African American mothers and fathers raise their children in a family climate where household duties are shared equally by men and women, and sons and daughters alike are encouraged to become powerful and helpful people (Coles, 2006; P. T. Reid, 1985).

Immigration and social change. Cultural and ethnic differences become salient when people move from one environment to another—for instance, when they immigrate to a new country. When different cultural groups exist in the same region, the two groups interact and learn about one another. As people participate in the customs and take on the values of a new culture, **acculturation** occurs. Acculturation takes four different forms:

- **Assimilation.** Some people totally embrace the values and customs of the new culture, giving up their original cultural identity in the process. Assimilation is typically a gradual process that occurs over several generations and under conditions in which immigrants feel accepted by the host society[3] (Delgado-Gaitan, 1994; Kağitçibaşi, 2007).
- **Selective adoption.** Immigrants may acquire some customs of the new culture while also retaining other customs from their homeland. For instance, families may begin to celebrate some of the holidays of their new culture while continuing to observe other holidays from their country of origin. Children are likely to adopt new customs when their parents encourage them to embrace their new society's customs and when their community accepts them as valued participants (Kağitçibaşi, 2007).
- **Rejection.** Sometimes people move to a new culture without taking on any of their new community's cultural practices. Complete rejection of a new culture may occur when individuals have little need to interact with people in that culture or when the new society segregates immigrants to isolated regions (Kağitçibaşi, 2007).
- **Bicultural orientation.** Some people retain their original culture yet also acquire beliefs and master practices of their new culture, and they readily adjust behaviors to fit the particular contexts in which they find themselves (Hong, Morris, Chiu, & Benet-Martínez, 2000). A bicultural orientation is promoted when the new society is tolerant of diversity (Kağitçibaşi, 2007).

In previous decades total assimilation was considered by many people in the United States to be the optimal situation for immigrants and, more generally, members of ethnic minority groups. The route to success was presumed to entail blending into a "melting pot" in which people of different backgrounds became increasingly similar. More recently, however, researchers have discovered that when young immigrants give up their family's cultural traditions, they are at greater risk for developing serious conflicts with their parents and engaging in dangerous behaviors, such as using alcohol and drugs, having unprotected sex, and engaging in criminal activities (C. B. Fisher et al., 1998; Hwang, 2006; Ying & Han, 2007).

Increasingly, the idea that the United States is a melting pot is giving way to the idea that the country can be more productively thought of as a "mosaic" of cultural and ethnic pieces that all legitimately contribute to the greater good of society (C. B. Fisher et al., 1998). Consistent with this view, many immigrant children adjust most successfully when they learn certain aspects of their new culture while also retaining aspects of their original culture—that is, when they show a pattern of either *selective adoption* or *bicultural orientation*. Nevertheless, not every child of immigrants feels welcome in the new society, and in conditions of rampant discrimination, the child may cope more effectively by preserving the family's original cultural practices and staying clear of cruel and insensitive treatment from the host society (Kağitçibaşi, 2007).

acculturation
Process of taking on the customs and values of a new culture.

assimilation
Form of acculturation in which a person totally embraces a culture, abandoning a previous culture in the process.

selective adoption
Form of acculturation in which a person assumes some customs of a new culture while also retaining some customs of a previous culture.

rejection
Form of acculturation in which a person fails to learn or accept any customs and values from a new cultural environment.

bicultural orientation
Form of acculturation in which a person is familiar with two cultures and selectively draws from the values and traditions of one or both cultures depending on the context.

---

[3]As you'll learn in Chapter 6, *assimilation* has a different meaning in Piaget's theory of cognitive development. The terms *cultural assimilation* and *cognitive assimilation* are two distinct concepts.

Challenges faced by children from minority backgrounds. When children come from cultural backgrounds different from mainstream culture, they must not only tackle basic developmental tasks (such as mastering language and learning about the physical world) but also face other challenges as well. For example, to the extent that children from diverse cultural backgrounds follow customs very different from those of people in the dominant cultural groups, misunderstandings on both sides can result. To illustrate, in some ethnic minority groups in the United States, parents rarely engage children in the question-answer sessions ("What does a doggie say?" "Wuff!" "That's right! A dog says, 'Ruff, ruff!'") seen in many European American homes and in most American classrooms (Losey, 1995; Rogoff, 2003). Unaccustomed to this communication pattern, a child may be puzzled when questioned in this way. Meanwhile, teachers and caregivers unfamiliar with a child's cultural background may think something is wrong when the child doesn't respond to seemingly "simple" questions.

Children often adjust well when they remain knowledgeable about their ethnic heritage and also master customs of mainstream society.

Another challenge many ethnic minority children and families face is *discrimination,* inequitable treatment as a result of their group membership. For instance, children from ethnic and racial minority groups might encounter racist insults from peers, rude treatment from storeowners, and low academic expectations from teachers (G. H. Brody et al., 2006). Furthermore, their parents are apt to get less information about home mortgages (even when income and credit history are good) and may encounter discrimination in job interviews, sometimes because of overt racist beliefs and at other times because of employers' subtle psychological biases (M. A. Turner et al., 2002; J. C. Ziegert & Hanges, 2005). Due in part to such discrimination, ethnic minority families are more likely than European American families to live in undesirable neighborhoods and to lack sufficient income to purchase books, magazines, and computers.

Because of discrimination, racism, and segregation, children and families from ethnic minority backgrounds must develop coping strategies that allow them to adjust effectively under adverse circumstances (García Coll et al., 1996; McAdoo & Martin, 2005; Varela et al., 2004). One coping strategy is to develop a strong **ethnic identity,** an awareness of being a member of a particular group and the commitment to adopting certain values and behaviors characteristic of the group. Youngsters develop a sense of ethnic identity out of the array of messages they receive from families, peers, community, and the media. For instance, they may hear tales of ancestors' struggles and victories in a discriminatory setting, and they may see media portrayals of their ethnic group in particular roles—perhaps as leaders and trailblazers for humane causes or, alternatively, as violent and deviant troublemakers (C. B. Fisher et al., 1998; Spencer, 2006). Eventually, many youngsters form a coherent set of beliefs about their cultural group, take pride in their cultural traditions, and reject demeaning messages from other people (Luster, 1992; Ogbu, 1994; Phinney, 1990; Spencer, Noll, Stoltzfus, & Harpalani, 2001).

A second important coping strategy is to take advantage of confidence-building strategies that are present in some form in every culture. As an illustration, many African American families cultivate positive personal qualities, such as deep religious convictions and commitments to extended family members, which sustain children in difficult environmental conditions, including high unemployment and poverty (Coles, 2006; McCreary, Slavin, & Berry, 1996). As another illustration, many children in Hispanic families benefit from their parents' strong work ethic and high educational aspirations for them (García & Jensen, 2007).

School performance. Despite the challenges they face, many children and adolescents from diverse cultural and ethnic backgrounds manage to hold their own in the classroom. On average, children of immigrant families perform as well academically as native-born children of similar income backgrounds, and they stay in school longer. Many children of Asian families and those of highly educated parents are especially successful (Aldous, 2006; Davenport et al., 1998; Flynn, 1991; Fuligni, 1998). Not all ethnic groups enjoy academic success, however. African American, Native American, and Hispanic American children have, on average, historically performed at somewhat lower levels on achievement tests and in the classroom compared to peers of European American and Asian American descent (Chatterji, 2006; L. S. Miller, 1995). Furthermore, students in these three groups are more likely to be

ethnic identity
Awareness of being a member of a particular ethnic or cultural group and willingness to adopt certain values and behaviors characteristic of that group.

identified as having special educational needs and to drop out prior to graduation (Federal Interagency Forum on Child and Family Statistics, 2007; Portes, 1996).

The lower school achievement of members of some ethnic minority groups occurs because of several factors, including environmental stresses associated with economic hardship, limited access to good schools and educational opportunities, failures of schools to recognize children's cultural strengths, low expectations from some teachers, and (in the case of recent immigrants from non–English-speaking countries) language barriers (Chatterji, 2006; Holliday, 1985; McLoyd, 1998b; Stevenson, Chen, & Uttal, 1990; Villegas & Lucas, 2002).

Creating supportive environments for children from diverse groups.   With the growing diversity in our population, teachers can expect that, regardless of the community in which they work, they will have the opportunity to work with youngsters from diverse ethnic groups. You can see some illustrations of adults nurturing the strengths of youngsters from culturally and linguistically diverse backgrounds in the Development and Practice feature "Accommodating Children from Culturally and Linguistically Diverse Backgrounds." Here are some related strategies for helping children achieve academic and social success:

● ***Reflect on your own cultural beliefs.*** All professionals make assumptions that come from the cultural environments—mainstream or not—in which they grew up. Like all human beings, teachers generally see their own customs as normal and sensible, particularly if they belong to a dominant culture (P. J. Miller & Goodnow, 1995). You can become sensitized to this tendency by comparing your attitudes and practices with those of other cultures and reflecting on how every culture's ideas and routines have developed in large part because of

Development and Practice

Accommodating Children from Culturally and Linguistically Diverse Backgrounds

• **Think about how cultural beliefs and practices serve adaptive functions for children.**

A third-grade teacher notices that few of the children are willing to answer her questions about common pets, even though it is clear from her individual conversations with them that they have pets and know the answers. She discovers that bringing attention to oneself is not appropriate in the children's culture and so modifies her style to allow for group responses.

• **Build on children's background experiences.**

A teacher asks her class of inner-city African American children to translate a poem written in a local dialect by an African American scholar. She puts words to the poem on an overhead transparency and asks children to translate each line into Standard English. In doing so, she cultivates a sense of pride about knowing two language systems (Ladson-Billings, 1994).

• **Use materials that represent all ethnic groups in a positive and competent light.**

A history teacher peruses a history textbook to make sure that it portrays all ethnic groups in a nonstereotypical manner. He supplements the text with readings that highlight important roles played by members of various ethnic groups throughout history.

• **Establish connections with local communities.**

A high school teacher encourages adolescents to take part in community service projects. The students may choose from a wide range of possibilities, including neighborhood cleanups, story time with preschoolers at the library, and volunteer work at a food bank or soup kitchen.

• **Provide opportunities for children of different backgrounds to get to know one another better.**

To promote awareness of and involvement in community issues, a teacher engages his class in a large-scale public service project. He forms small groups that will work on different aspects of the project, such as collecting data about public opinions, identifying relevant community agencies, and contacting local officials who might be willing to speak to the class. The teacher is careful to form groups that are each comprised of children from various neighborhoods and ethnic groups.

• **Expose youngsters to successful models from various ethnic backgrounds.**

A high school teacher invites several successful professionals from minority groups to speak with her class about their careers. When some youngsters seem interested in particular career paths, she arranges for them to spend time with these professionals in their workplaces.

• **Be neutral, inclusive, and respectful regarding children's religious practices.**

A preschool teacher encourages children in her class to bring in artifacts that show how they celebrate holidays during the winter months. Children bring in decorations and religious symbols related to Christmas, Ramadan, Kwanzaa, Hanukkah, and the winter solstice. The teacher passes around the materials and explains that children in her class celebrate many different holidays.

• **Orient recent immigrants to the culture of mainstream society and to the school's expectations and events.**

A high school offers a Newcomer Program for recent immigrants, teaching incoming students about practices in American society and advising students about the school's calendar, extracurricular activities, and sponsored social events (National Clearinghouse for English Language Acquisition, 2006).

specific pressures and opportunities in earlier periods in history (Howard, 2007). To heighten your awareness of cultural origins, you might read historical biographies of prominent figures in various cultures, study anthropologists' reports of different communities, and reflect on your past reactions to unfamiliar groups (e.g., when tutoring children from immigrant families, volunteering in homeless shelters, or visiting another country) (C. F. Meyer & Rhoades, 2006).

• *Accept that what you do (and don't do) can perpetuate inequities.* Although very few professionals intentionally discriminate against young people based on their ethnicity or skin color (Howard, 2007; Sleeter & Grant, 1999), their actions sometimes perpetuate group differences. For instance, some teachers rarely modify or individualize instruction for students with diverse needs; instead, they present instruction in a take-it-or-leave-it manner. Clearly, teaching children from diverse backgrounds requires more than giving lip service to cultural diversity; it requires a genuine commitment to modifying interactions with children so they can achieve their full academic potential (Bakari, 2000).

• *Recognize the diversity that exists within social groups.* It is human nature to see cultural groups as simple, uniform entities. The reality is that any given group (e.g., children who are Native Americans or those whose families emigrated to the United States) is usually quite heterogeneous. For example, immigrant parents hold beliefs about education that vary depending on their country of origin and their own personal experiences—some might be seasonal migrant workers and others diplomats, foreign-born university students, or political asylum seekers (Kağitçibaşi, 2007). Similarly, the manner in which immigrant children learn English in the United States varies according to ethnicity and cultural origin (Leventhal, Xue, & Brooks-Gunn, 2006). And, of course, children within a given group have varied interests, skills, and views that transcend their group's general patterns. Teachers can get to know children as individuals by asking them about their hopes for the future, preferences for spending free time, responsibilities at home, and prior experiences with academic subjects (Villegas & Lucas, 2007).

• *Make an effort to accommodate the practices and values of children's cultures.* Practitioners increase their effectiveness with youngsters by tailoring their practices to children's cultural backgrounds (Howard, 2007; Pérez, 1998; Villegas & Lucas, 2002, 2007). Being careful not to stereotype children, teachers can occasionally use instructional strategies that are sufficiently flexible that they allow children to use some of their cultural strengths and traditions. For example, a teacher may include some assignments that permit children to work either alone or with others. The Observation Guidelines table "Identifying Cultural Practices and Beliefs" on page 98 lists some values and styles of approaching tasks that teachers and other school personnel can accommodate.

• *Include numerous cultural perspectives in curricula and instructional strategies.* As societies become the multicultural mosaic we spoke of earlier, it is essential that schools reflect this diversity. In **culturally responsive teaching,** teachers use their knowledge of children's cultural backgrounds and individual characteristics as they select curricula and instructional strategies (Howard, 2007; Villegas & Lucas, 2002, 2007). For example, in a classroom with a few children from immigrant families, a teacher might examine immigration during a social studies unit and invite immigrant parents to come to class and discuss their experiences in moving from one society to another. In addition, teachers can enrich the curriculum by addressing the perspectives and contributions of people from more than one culture. Following are examples of what teachers might do:

- In history, look at wars and other major events from diverse perspectives (e.g., the Spanish perspective of the Spanish-American War and Native American groups' views of pioneers' westward migration in North America).
- In social studies, examine discrimination and oppression.
- In literature, present the work of minority authors and poets.
- In art, consider creations and techniques by artists from around the world.
- In music, teach songs from many cultures and nations.

Adults naturally make assumptions based on the cultural environment in which they grew up. They should be aware of this tendency and accept that others' cultural viewpoints are also valid.

MyEducationLab

Gain practice in analyzing differences between and within immigrant groups by completing an Understanding Research exercise in Chapter 3's Activities and Applications section in MyEducationLab.

culturally responsive teaching
A teacher's use of particular instructional strategies based on knowledge of children's cultural backgrounds and individual characteristics.

Observation Guidelines

Identifying Cultural Practices and Beliefs

Characteristic	Look For	Example	Implication
Individualism	· Independence, assertiveness, and self-reliance · Eagerness to pursue individual assignments and tasks · Willingness to compete against others · Pride in one's own accomplishments	When given the choice of doing a project either by herself or with a partner, Melissa decides to work alone. She is thrilled when she earns a third-place ribbon in a statewide competition.	Provide time for independent work, and accommodate children's individual achievement levels. Give feedback about personal accomplishments in private rather than in front of peers.
Collectivism	· Willingness to depend on others · Emphasis on group accomplishments over individual achievements · Preference for cooperative rather than competitive tasks · Concern about bringing honor to one's family · Strong sense of loyalty to other family members	Tsusha is a talented and hard-working seventh grader. She is conscientious about bringing home her graded work assignments to show her parents, but she appears uncomfortable when praised in front of classmates.	Stress group progress and achievement more than individual successes. Make frequent use of cooperative learning activities.
Behavior Toward Authority Figures	· Looking down in the presence of an authority figure (common in some Native American, African American, Mexican American, and Puerto Rican children) vs. looking an authority figure in the eye (common in some children of European American descent) · Observing an adult quietly (an expectation in some Native American and some Hispanic groups) vs. asking questions when one doesn't understand (common in some European American groups)	A Native American child named Jimmy never says a word to his teacher. He looks frightened when his teacher looks him in the eye and greets him each morning. One day, the teacher looks in another direction and says, "Hello, Jimmy" as he enters the classroom. "Why hello Miss Jacobs," he responds enthusiastically (Gilliland, 1988, p. 26).	Recognize that different cultures show respect for authority figures in different ways; don't misinterpret lack of eye contact or nonresponse as an indication of disinterest or disrespect.
Valued Activities	· Hopes for high achievement in traditional academic areas (common in many cultural groups in Western countries) · Personal values for school achievement but lack of confidence in performing academically in some ethnic minority students · Expectations for excellence in culture-specific activities, such as art or dance (often seen in traditional Native American and Polynesian communities)	Clarence is obviously a very bright young man, but he shows considerable ambivalence about his ability to achieve in his high school classes. He often earns high marks in papers he write, but he rarely participates in class discussions and does not seem to show his knowledge on tests.	Show how academic subjects relate to children's lives. Acknowledge youngsters' achievement in nonacademic as well as academic pursuits. Continually communicate confidence in the potential achievement of youngsters and encourage hard work and good study habits.
Conceptions of Time	· Concern for punctuality and acknowledgment of deadlines for assignments (common for some students of European descent) · Lack of concern for specific times and schedules (observed in some Hispanic and Native American communities)	Lucy and her parents are diligent about going to parent-teacher conferences, but they often arrive well after their scheduled time.	Encourage punctuality as a way of enhancing children's long-term success in mainstream Western society. At the same time, recognize that not all children are especially concerned about clock time. Be flexible when parents seem to disregard strict schedules.

Sources: Banks & Banks, 1995; Basso, 1984; García, 1994; Garrison, 1989; Gilliland, 1988; C. A. Grant & Gomez, 2001; Heath, 1983; Irujo, 1988; Kağitçibaşi, 2007; Kirschenbaum, 1989; Losey, 1995; McAlpine & Taylor, 1993; L. S. Miller, 1995; Ogbu, 1994; Oyserman & Lee, 2007; N. Reid, 1989; Shweder et al., 1998; Spencer, 2006; Tharp, 1994; Torres-Guzmán, 1998; Trawick-Smith, 2003; Triandis, 2007.

- In physical education, teach games or folk dances from other countries and cultures. (Asai, 1993; Boutte & McCormick, 1992; K. Freedman, 2001; Koza, 2001; NCSS Task Force on Ethnic Studies Curriculum Guidelines, 1992; Pang, 1995; Sleeter & Grant, 1999).

Teachers should adjust their culturally responsive strategies to the age range of their students. For example, during middle childhood, children can learn about the tangible customs and livelihoods of different cultures. One example of a lesson in diversity is represented in Figure 3-8. In this artwork, 9-year-old Dana shows her understanding of different sources of light in two very different settings, that of a large, modern city and that of the Masai, a cattle-herding tribe of east Africa. As children grow older, they become increasingly able to learn details about different people's perspectives and circumstances. Figure 3-9 shows 13-year-old Carol's notes on the distinct perspectives of different groups discussed in her American history class. In previous lessons Carol learned about lasting contributions Native Americans have made to government, art, language, food, and sports in the United States. Here, Carol focuses on the "New Arrivals" who came to the New World in the 1600s, writing about the separate experiences of men and women, and of European settlers, African settlers, and enslaved Africans.

Figure 3-8

Nine-year-old Dana learned about how different people use natural and artificial light. Art by Dana.

- ***Address gaps in children's understandings.*** When children have missed a lot of school or previously studied in culturally *un*responsive schools, they almost inevitably lack basic skills. Teachers can help children by addressing academic areas in which children have delays. Confidence in children's potential is key, as a fifth-grade teacher at one school discovered when she considered the implications of culturally responsive teaching for a Hispanic student learning English:

> [The student] ". . . couldn't put two sentences together, let alone write the five-paragraph essay that is required to pass our 5th grade assessment." The teacher's first reaction was to ask, "How was this student allowed to slip by all these years without learning anything beyond 2nd grade writing skills?" When the teacher launched her [Culturally Responsive Teaching] project, however, her perspective became more proactive. She realized that she couldn't just deliver the 5th grade curriculum—she had to meet this student where he was. She built a personal connection with the student, learned about his family culture and interests (a fascination with monkeys was a major access point), and used this relationship to reinforce his academic development. The student responded to her high expectations and passed his 5th grade writing assessment. (Howard, 2007, p. 20)

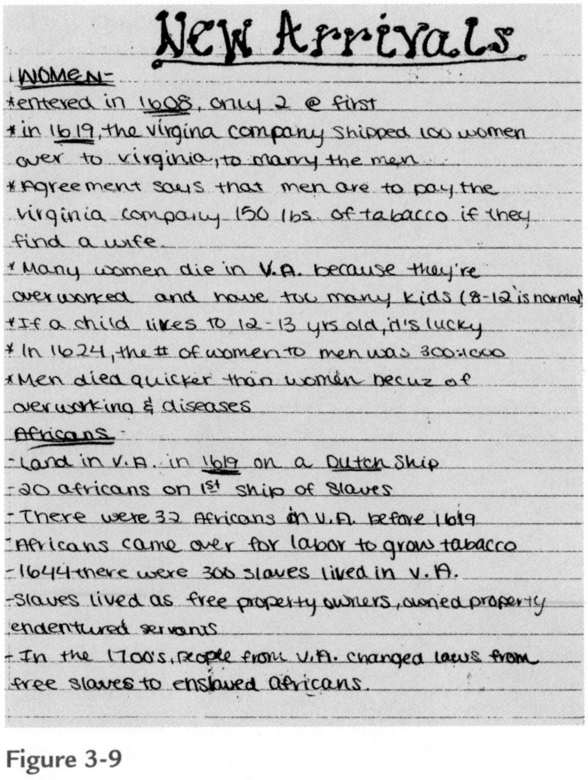

- ***Foster respect for diverse cultures and ethnic groups.*** When talking about diverse cultural practices, teachers can emphasize the merits of particular traditions. Teachers can also select materials that represent cultural groups in a positive and competent light—for instance, by choosing books and movies that portray people of varying ethnic backgrounds as legitimate participants in society rather than as exotic "curiosities" who live in a separate world. Educators should also avoid (or at least comment critically on) materials that portray members of minority groups in an overly simplistic, romanticized, exaggerated, or otherwise stereotypical fashion (Banks, 1994; Boutte & McCormick, 1992; Pang, 1995).

- ***Create opportunities for children from diverse backgrounds to interact.*** When youngsters have positive interactions with people from backgrounds other than their own, they gain further respect for different cultures. In schools in which children come from several distinct backgrounds, teachers and school counselors might promote friendships among students from different groups by using cooperative learning activities, teaching simple phrases in other students' native languages, and encouraging schoolwide participation in extracurricular activities. In

Figure 3-9

Thirteen-year-old Carol took these notes in her American history class. Throughout the unit, her teacher made a point of discussing the perspectives of different groups. Carol's notes show that she learned about the hardships faced by men and women in the New World in the 1600s; she also learned about European settlers, African settlers, and enslaved Africans.

culturally homogeneous schools, professionals might take youngsters beyond school boundaries—perhaps engaging them in community service projects or arranging a visit to a culturally inclusive center for the arts.

- **Recognize that children may follow practices from two or more cultures.** Earlier we introduced the idea that immigrant children often adjust well when they hold onto their family's cultural beliefs and practices rather than fully replacing these beliefs and practices with those favored by the dominant society. Teachers often find that children are selective in the customs they absorb from their new communities. The same principle holds for multiethnic children: Children raised by parents from different ethnic cultures are likely to value traditions from both sides of the family.

- **When cultural conflicts occur, find constructive ways to address them.** Occasionally, children and families follow cultural practices that are contradictory—at least on the surface—to those adhered to in the classroom. When this happens, it is a good idea to learn more about these practices. Investing such an effort can better help practitioners understand why children act as they do and what accommodations might be made ("OK, avoiding certain foods shows their religious devotion; I can certainly offer other snack choices").

Showing respect for diverse cultural perspectives does not necessarily mean that "anything goes" or that there are no moral judgments to be made. No one, for example, needs to embrace a cultural practice in which some people's basic human rights are blatantly violated. Showing respect does mean, however, that adults and children must try to understand another cultural group's behaviors within the entirety of that culture's beliefs and traditions (M. N. Cohen, 1998).

- **Confront inequities.** As you have learned, children and families from ethnic minority backgrounds and immigrant groups often face discrimination. Living in substandard housing and dealing with ignorant remarks about their ethnicity is frustrating for children and family members, and teachers can take the stand that inequities will *not* be tolerated at school. To profess its commitment to fairness and justice, one school district displays a statement of "Equity Vision":

> Roseville Area Schools is committed to ensuring an equitable and respectful educational experience for every student, family, and staff member, regardless of race, gender, sexual orientation, socioeconomic status, ability, home or first language, religion, national origin, or age. (Howard, 2007, p. 20)

Of course, children and families want to see good words backed up with good deeds. Teachers and principals must confront any policies that inadvertently favor one group or another (e.g., assigning inexperienced teachers to work with students who need the most help, having low expectations for students from ethnic minority backgrounds, and preferentially treating subgroups of students when selecting recipients for awards) (Villegas & Lucas, 2007).

Community Resources

As a bridge to the outside world, a community offers social and material resources that sustain children and their families. Here we examine the nature of the community and the impact of family income on children's lives. In a subsequent section, we offer specific recommendations for working with children from low-income families.

Type of community. Communities vary in their population density and geographical features, such as climate, natural resources, and predominant cultures. These and other features of the community pervade the lives of families and affect the development of children. For instance, children who live in large cities often have ready access to ongoing events and resources related to music, art, drama, science, sports, and diverse cultures. Experiencing cultural events firsthand can be exciting and motivating for children. In Figure 3-10, 6-year-old Lee displays his enthusiasm for an art museum he visited in a large city.

Not every child in a big city can take advantage of its splendors, however. Some families can afford to live in nicely maintained houses, enroll their children in well-staffed schools, and take their children to museums, concerts, and sports events. Others cannot. Forced to live in unsafe neighborhoods, economically poor families and their children regularly encounter

Figure 3-10

Six-year-old Lee created this drawing after visiting an art museum. In it, he represents some of the themes he perceived in the museum's paintings, including warfare, religion, and community.

such problems as drugs, violence, crime, and racial segregation (D. S. Massey & Denton, 1993; Schaefer-McDaniel, 2007). Disadvantaged families often must send their children to dilapidated schools with records of low student achievement and limited success in recruiting and retaining highly qualified teachers (Dichele & Gordon, 2007; Jacob, 2007).

Families living in rural settings, particularly farming communities, often foster a cooperative spirit and strong work ethic in children (García, 1994). Many farm families structure chores so that all family members contribute to the family's economic livelihood. Furthermore, farm families periodically help others in the community with seasonal projects, such as harvesting crops. In addition, parents from these backgrounds are often actively involved in their children's education (Provasnik et al., 2007). A downside of rural environments is that many students must travel many miles to attend school each day and cannot participate in extracurricular activities (North Central Regional Educational Laboratory, 2008). Some rural schools must spend such a high proportion of available funds on transportation services that insufficient resources remain to invest in computers, Internet access, and other basic supplies and services (Provasnik et al., 2007).

On average, families in suburban communities have higher incomes than those who live in inner cities or rural areas, and their schools are often of higher quality. Children and their families often have easy access to the educational and cultural resources of the big city, and nearly everyone has a bit of backyard and privacy. As a result of these and other advantages, more high school students from suburban cities attend college than do students from big cities or rural areas (National Center for Education Statistics, 2007). However, economic resources are not equally distributed in suburban communities, not all young people have an optimistic outlook about their chances for future success, and students in suburban schools are as likely as their counterparts in large cities to engage in risky behaviors such as drinking alcohol and using illegal drugs (Gaines, 1991; Greene & Forster, 2004).

Family income. A child's experience in a community is strongly affected by the family's personal and financial resources. This idea is captured in the notion of the family's **socioeconomic status (SES),** its standing in the community based on such variables as family income level, the prestige of parents' jobs, and parents' levels of education. A family's socioeconomic status—whether high-SES, middle-SES, or low-SES—gives us a sense of how much flexibility family members have with regard to where they live and what they buy, how much influence they have in political decision making, what educational opportunities they can offer children, and so on.

In many respects, family income is only a modest contributor to children's development. After all, it is the family's guidance and relationships that directly affect children; material resources are of secondary importance. Evidence of this developmental prioritization comes from children of affluent families: Despite attending good schools and living in safe neighborhoods, these children are at risk for emotional problems and substance abuse if parents put excessive pressure on them or are not involved in their day-to-day activities (Luthar & Latendresse, 2005). However, it is equally important to recognize that at the other end of the financial spectrum, economically poor families sometimes have so little in physical comfort and financial security that their ability to nurture may be compromised (G. W. Evans & Kim, 2007; Hoover-Dempsey & Sandler, 1997; McLoyd, 1998b). We now examine the hardships faced by children from economically disadvantaged families.

Children living in economic poverty. Approximately 17 percent of U.S. children live in poverty (Federal Interagency Forum on Child and Family Statistics, 2007). Children and adolescents living in poverty face serious challenges. Typical problems include these:

- ***Poor nutrition and health care.*** Some children are poorly fed and have little access to adequate health care; as a result, they may suffer from malnutrition and other chronic health problems.

- ***Inadequate housing and material goods.*** Many children live in tight quarters, perhaps sharing one or two rooms with several other family members. Some children have no place to live at all, except, perhaps, the family car or a homeless shelter. Some children from homeless families are reluctant to come to school because they lack bathing facilities and presentable clothing. And even the most basic school supplies may be beyond their reach.

socioeconomic status (SES)
One's general standing in an economically stratified society, encompassing family income, type of job, and education level.

- ***Toxic environment.*** Compared to their economically advantaged peers, children in poor families are more likely to be exposed to factory pollution, toxic waste dumps, allergens that trigger asthma, and excessive noise.

- ***Gaps in background knowledge.*** Teachers typically assume that children have had certain kinds of experiences before they begin school—for instance, that they have been read to, have seen many kinds of animals at farms or zoos, and have had ample opportunities to explore their physical environment. However, some children who live in extreme poverty may miss out on such foundational experiences. At home, poor children are, on average, less often spoken to and receive less overall cognitive stimulation than do children from economically advantaged families.

- ***Increased probability of disabling conditions.*** Children who live in poverty are more likely to have physical, mental, or social-emotional disabilities.

- ***Emotional stress.*** Children function less effectively when under stress, and many poor children and their families live in chronically stressful conditions, constantly worrying about where their next meal is coming from or how long the landlord will wait before evicting them for not paying the rent. Experiencing chronic emotional stresses, low-income parents may lose their patience with children and become punitive and insensitive. In addition, children from low-income families are more likely to be subjected to maltreatment by parents or other adults and to encounter violent crimes in their neighborhoods.

Children and adolescents in low-income neighborhoods may have fewer choices for recreation than their economically advantaged peers.

- ***Lower quality schools.*** Schools in low-income neighborhoods and communities are often poorly funded and equipped, and they have high teacher turnover rates. Furthermore, some teachers at these schools have lower expectations for students—and offer a less demanding curriculum, assign less homework, and set lower standards for performance—than teachers of middle-SES students.

- ***Public misconceptions.*** People from economically advantaged backgrounds often have mixed feelings about low-SES families: They may feel pity yet simultaneously believe that poor people are responsible for their misfortunes, perhaps because of laziness, promiscuity, or overdependence on social welfare programs (Berliner, 2006; G. W. Evans, 2004; G. W. Evans & Kim, 2007; Gershoff, Aber, & Raver, 2005; Linver, Brooks-Gunn, & Kohen, 2002; McLoyd, 1998a, 1998b; Murnane, 2007; Parke et al., 2004; Pawlas, 1994; Portes, 1996; Sidel, 1996).

Obviously, poverty creates serious threats to children's welfare. Some children and adolescents find the challenges of poverty so overwhelming that they engage in behaviors—dropping out of school, abusing drugs and alcohol, participating in criminal activities—that create further problems. However, many other children and adolescents from poor families do well despite the adversities they face: They arc relatively hardy as they confront life's hardships (Kim-Cohen, Moffitt, Caspi, & Taylor, 2004). These youngsters show **resilience,** an ability to thrive despite adverse environmental conditions. For instance, almost half of low-income high school graduates subsequently enroll in college (National Center for Education Statistics, 2003). Let's examine strategies educators use to nurture this resilience in low-income youngsters.

Working with Children from Low-Income Families

Adults who want to "make a difference" in children's lives are especially likely to do so in schools and other institutions serving low-SES populations. But to be effective, teachers and other adults must be committed to their jobs, think creatively about how they can make the most of limited resources, and show a contagious enthusiasm for learning (L. W. Anderson & Pellicer, 1998; Ogden & Germinario, 1988). Experts offer these recommendations for working with children from low-income families:

- ***Invest in children's strengths.*** When teachers concentrate on youngsters' weaknesses, youngsters become easily discouraged and may soon resign themselves to the idea

resilience
Ability of some youngsters (often enhanced with environmental support) to thrive despite adverse environmental conditions.

that their efforts are in vain. In contrast, focusing on what's *right* with children can generate in both adults and children optimism, enthusiasm, and a definite commitment to learning. For example, many children of poor immigrant families have two parents at home to support them; are physically healthy; and have extended families who are concerned about their welfare, have a cohesive community on which to draw, and are committed to working hard (Shields & Behrman, 2004). If children work part time to help their families make ends meet, they may have a good understanding of the working world. If they are children of single, working parents, they may know far more than peers about cooking, cleaning, and taking care of younger siblings (Whiting & Edwards, 1988).

- *Foster a sense of community.* Children from low-income backgrounds may appreciate teachers' efforts to build a **sense of community**—a collection of shared beliefs that the group (e.g., a class or school) has shared goals, respects one another's efforts, and believes that everyone makes an important contribution (L. W. Anderson & Pellicer, 1998; Downey, 2000; M. Watson & Battistich, 2006). For example, teachers can assign chores on a rotating basis, use cooperative learning activities, involve children and adolescents in cross-grade tutoring, and encourage everyone's participation in extracurricular activities (Downey, 2000). Because youngsters often feel more connected to their community when, in some small way, they give something back, educators can also sponsor community service projects. For example, members of a school might conduct a neighborhood cleanup, volunteer in a nursing home, serve as readers at the local library, or raise funds to benefit community causes (Ladson-Billings, 1994). In Figure 3-11 you can see a mural painted by teenagers as part of the city of Boston's Mural Crew.

- *Convey clear and consistent expectations for children's behavior.* For all children, and especially for those who have had more than their share of life's challenges, knowing what's expected is important. Hence adults need to describe their expectations in clear, concrete terms (Downey, 2000). For instance, when finishing lunch in the cafeteria, children might be asked explicitly to "empty the napkins and leftovers into the trash bin, put the trays and dishes on the counter, and go quietly outside." When working in cooperative groups, young people might be reminded, "Everyone needs to participate in the discussions and contribute to the group project."

Figure 3-11

The Mural Crew program of the Boston Youth Clean-up Corps (BYCC) enlists groups of teenagers to beautify the city with public works of art, such as this one, *A Saturday Afternoon in Jamaica Plain.*
Artists: Antonio, Gabe, Awurama, Agapito, Nikia, Alyssa, and Jon. Supervising artists: Heidi Schork and Teig Grennan.

sense of community
In a classroom or school, a collection of widely shared beliefs that students, teachers, and other staff have common goals, support one another's efforts, and make important contributions to everyone's success.

● ***Show relevance of academic skills to children's lives and needs.*** Finding personal relevance in classroom activities and subject matter is important for any child, but it may be especially critical for children from low-SES backgrounds (L. W. Anderson & Pellicer, 1998; Lee-Pearce, Plowman, & Touchstone, 1998). Helping children see how they can use skills in their everyday lives makes learning meaningful as well as motivating.

● ***Introduce children to key institutions in their community.*** When children have not had the opportunity to see institutions in their society, they can often learn a lot from brief visits. For instance, teachers sometimes take their classes on field trips to a zoo, museum, post office, fire station, and so forth, and thereby create new knowledge for children to build on in academic lessons. When field trips are too expensive or logistically impossible, an alternative is to bring the community to children—for instance, by having a representative of the local zoo bring some of the zoo's smaller residents to the children to observe or by asking a police officer to describe the many public services that the police department provides.

● ***Communicate high expectations for children's success.*** Some children from low-SES backgrounds do not expect much of their own academic skills. Typically, these children have lower aspirations for higher education and possible careers (M. S. Knapp & Woolverton, 1995; S. M. Taylor, 1994). Yet teachers can communicate a can-do attitude, encourage students to challenge themselves, and provide support to help students reach their goals. Offering help sessions for challenging classroom material, finding low-cost academic enrichment programs available during the summer, and helping adolescents fill out applications for college scholarships are just a few examples of such support.

● ***Give homeless children school supplies and help them ease into new communities.*** Educators who work with children of homeless families can help them adjust to their new settings. For example, teachers, principals, and school counselors might pair homeless children with classmates who can explain school procedures and introduce them to peers; provide a notebook, clipboard, or other portable "desk" on which children can do their homework at the shelter; find adult or teenage volunteers to tutor them at the shelter; ask civic organizations to donate school supplies; meet with parents at the shelter rather than at school; and share copies of homework assignments, school calendars, and newsletters with shelter officials (Pawlas, 1994).

Virtually all children face challenges of one kind or another—perhaps stressful family dynamics, a mismatch between home and school cultures, or extremely limited economic resources. Yet virtually all children, too, want to be successful in school and in the world at large. By building on youngsters' strengths, being optimistic about their potential for future growth, and giving them the academic and social-emotional support they need, teachers and other practitioners can, without doubt, help them make significant progress in their developmental journeys.

Summary

Cradles of Child Development

Family, culture, and community provide essential foundations for child development. These three contexts teach children who they are as human beings, how they should relate to others, and what they can aspire to become as adults. Educators can help children by considering the lessons children learn in their complex environments and the interactive effects the three contexts have on children's behavior and well-being.

Family Structures

Families come in many forms, including two-parent families, single-parent families, stepfamilies, adoptive families, foster families, extended families, and numerous other types. Many youngsters experience one or more changes in family structure (e.g., as a result of divorce, remarriage, or death of a parent) at some point during their childhood or adolescence. Individual family structures present unique benefits and challenges for children, but ultimately the quality of family relationships exceeds family structure in developmental significance. Teachers can be inclusive of families by recognizing the existence of many structures and encouraging families of all kinds to support their children's academic progress.

Family Processes

Parents influence children's development through the relationships they build with children, the activities they include children in, and their manner of showing affection and disciplining children. In addition, parents may affect children's development through their employment outside the home; for instance, some children of working parents care for themselves during after-school hours. Children influence their families, in turn, by virtue of their temperaments, interests, and abilities. Children also influence one another as siblings, but having a sibling is not vital to normal, healthy development.

Most families provide safe and nurturing environments for children. However, some families maltreat children, either by neglecting them or by subjecting them to physical, sexual, or emotional abuse. Such maltreatment can have negative long-term effects on children's development.

Effective partnerships between educators and families rest squarely on good communication. Teachers can use several methods of communication (e.g., parent-teacher-student conferences, newsletters, the telephone), and they can en-courage parents to become actively involved in their children's education.

Children in a Diverse Society

Children and families are profoundly affected by their experiences in ethnic, cultural, and immigrant groups. To a large extent, children's ethnicity affects their values, actions, and styles of communicating. Boys and girls are socialized somewhat differently, depending on their ethnicity and the particular beliefs of their families. Children also are influenced by their community's character and by the incomes of their families. Educators can build on children's experiences in the community and importantly, help economically disadvantaged children by providing support, resources, and acknowledgment of children's personal strengths.

Applying Concepts in Child Development

The exercises in this section will help you consider the implications of children's experiences with families, cultures, and communities for your work.

Case Study

Four-Year-Old Sons

Read the case and then answer the questions that follow it.

A common behavior displayed by preschoolers is asking a lot of *why* questions. Consider how two mothers of 4-year-old boys interpret their sons' incessant questioning. Elizabeth describes her son Charles as

> . . . mouthing off; just always mouthing off. Whenever I say anything to him, he asks me "Why?" Like I say we're going to the store and he says "Why?" Or I tell him "Don't touch the bug 'cuz it's dead" and he says "Why?" Like he's just trying to get me mad by never listening to me. He never accepts what I say. He mouths off all the time instead of believing me. It's like he just wants to tease me. You know, he tests me. (Belenky, Bond, & Weinstock, 1997, pp. 129–130)

In contrast, Joyce describes her son Peter this way:

> Well, you know, he's got such an active mind, always going; like he's never satisfied with just appearances—he's always trying to figure out how things tick, why they do. So if I ask him to do something or tell him to do something, he's always asking why. He really wants to understand what's

the goal—what's the purpose—how come? He's really trying to piece the world all together . . . and understand it all. It's wonderful. Or if I say, "We're going to the store," he wants to know why. He's real interested in figuring out how one thing leads to another. It's great, because sometimes he helps me realize that I haven't really thought through why I'm saying what I am. And so we do think it through. (Belenky et al., 1997, p. 130)

- How do the two mothers interpret their sons' questions differently? How might their interpretations help us to predict their disciplinary styles?
- How might Elizabeth and Joyce have developed their particular parenting styles?
- What kinds of educational opportunities might these mothers create at home for their children? What might teachers do to encourage each mother's involvement at school?

Once you have answered these questions, compare your responses with those presented in Appendix A.

Interpreting Children's Artifacts and Reflections

Consider chapter concepts as you analyze the following reflections from adolescents.

In My Neighborhood

Nicole Schaefer-McDaniel interviewed young adolescents living in New York City about their perceptions of their neighborhoods. As you read excerpts from the interviews, consider aspects of the neighborhoods that may have supported the adolescents' development and other aspects that may have presented challenges. You will see that some of the youngsters are quoted more than once.

John, age 11:   [The park] is always peaceful and not a lot of noise. It always quiet and no trouble happening here. (Schaefer-McDaniel, 2007, p. 422)[a]

Melanie, age 13:   It's [the park] big and enough for everybody and they got card tables that what we do basically is play cards and it's right next to like if we were playing in the house, we walk right down the block [to the park] . . . there's a whole lot of stuff to do and it's like you don't have to walk far. (p. 423)

[a] From Nicole Schaefer-McDaniel, *Journal of Adolescent Research*, 22(4), 413–436. Copyright © 2007 by SAGE Publications, Inc. Reprinted by permission of SAGE Publications.

Latisha, age 11:	It [the neighborhood] is good 'cause there's good parts around there and there's restaurants and that's the best part about my neighborhood . . . food . . . and [hair] salons. (p. 424)
Tyrone, age 11:	The entire avenue . . . there's a lot of violence there especially when there's a block party . . . some people comes with guns. (p. 425)
Latisha, age 11:	It's [the neighborhood] good 'cause . . . the cops are always around there just in case something happens. (p. 425)
Romel, age 12:	We have real protection and cops . . . and like because like right next to our school is like three [police] stations and up there . . . there's nothing . . . so anything goes wrong you got police right here. (p. 426)
Mike, age 11:	. . . 'cause my mother thinks it's too dangerous around there . . . so I either go to backyard in school or sometime I go [to

	another nearby school yard] . . . this block is dangerous . . . this one is dangerous . . . so I don't really like these blocks . . . I'd rather stay on my block. (p. 426)
Melanie, age 13:	A lot of men out there and they always like fighting . . . and I don't like to walk past places in the night where there's a whole bunch of men. (p. 427)
John, age 11:	You can see a lot of trash . . . a lot . . . people just throw them trash bags. (p. 427)
Latisha, age 11:	What I hate the most is around here a lot of buildings get burned and some of the buildings they have a fire and the building burns down. (p. 428)

Once you have analyzed the children's reflections, compare your ideas with those presented in Appendix B. For further practice in analyzing children's artifacts and reflections, go to the Activities and Applications section in Chapter 3 of MyEducationLab.

Developmental Trends Exercise

In this chapter you learned that children and adolescents are strongly influenced by the family, culture, and community in which they grow. The following table describes family experiences of five children and adolescents. For each experience, the table identifies a family's conditions, an implication for working with families, or both. Go to the Activities and Applications section in Chapter 3 of MyEducationLab to apply what you've learned about families as you fill in the empty cells in the table.

Working Effectively with Families

Age	A Youngster's Experience	Developmental Concepts *Identifying Family Conditions*	Implications *Working Effectively with Families*
Infancy (Birth–2 Years)	Eight-month-old Yves sits in his high chair at the child care center. Yves is hungry but cries rather than feeding himself the diced peaches and turkey on his tray. His caregiver, Mrs. Phillipe, talks with Yves's mother and learns that during mealtimes at home, the mother holds Yves and places soft, tiny bits of food directly into his mouth.	Little Yves encounters different feeding customs at home and at the child care center. These different practices may be rooted in dissimilar cultural beliefs about desirable qualities in social groups (e.g., for being close to one another or showing independence) and in cultural behaviors in caring for infants (e.g., encouraging infants to relax as caregivers tend to them or, in contrast, fostering their self-care).	
Early Childhood (2–6 Years)	Tawaia is the fourth and youngest child in the Hume family. At 4 years, Tawaia seems to her teacher, Ms. Brookhart, to be socially perceptive. Ms. Brookhart notices Tawaia's ability to charm her friends into sharing their toys with her. Ms. Brookhart also observes that Tawaia can hold her ground during verbal tussles with other children, occasionally selecting insults that aptly push other children's hot buttons.		Show sensitivity to the bonds that children have with siblings, allowing them to comfort one another during times of family loss. Try not to compare children to their siblings, though, and also do not assume that children without siblings are lonely or spoiled.
Middle Childhood (6–10 Years)	Nine-year-old Michael is the only child of his single mother, Ms. Clementine. Michael seems to be mature for his age, particularly in the chores he does around the house, including making dinner twice a week when his mother is at work. Michael feels protective toward his mother, whom he knows to be hard working and devoted to him.	Children in single-parent families often have close relationships with their parents. Michael enjoys a close bond with his mother, and he also seems to have been coached by her in making constructive use of his time alone, when he looks after himself in the late afternoon while his mother is still at work.	

Developmental Trends Exercise (continued)

Age	A Youngster's Experience	Developmental Concepts *Identifying Family Conditions*	Implications *Working Effectively with Families*
Early Adolescence (10–14 Years) 	Mr. Drake, a middle school math teacher, holds an advising meeting with one of his students, Janice, and her parents, Mr. and Mrs. Lee. During the conference, Janice answers questions for the family, and Mr. and Mrs. Lee quietly smile and nod their heads. Later Mr. Drake notices that Mr. and Mrs. Lee fail to take him up on his suggestion that they participate in one of the school's many parent-staffed events.	Mr. and Mrs. Lee may hold different cultural beliefs from Mr. Drake about the appropriate roles of parents in children's academic learning. Janice's parents are respectful of Mr. Drake but may not feel it is appropriate for them to ask questions of him during meetings. Furthermore, they may be more inclined to help Janice with her homework than to become involved at school events.	Invite families to participate as they can in school activities, but also make certain to acknowledge the important roles that families play in supporting children's academic learning at home.
Late Adolescence (14–18 Years)	Mr. Vogel notices that one of his students, Christy, has suddenly become quiet and withdrawn during homeroom period. He talks with her privately and learns that her parents have recently told her they are getting a divorce. Christy explains that her parents have been arguing constantly during the last year, and she finds the divorce to be traumatic.	Changes in family structure can be unsettling for children and adolescents for months and sometimes longer. Some adolescents may adjust to parents' divorce easily, but most adolescents need time to sort through the changes, make sense of their parents' conflicts, and regroup under new custody arrangements.	Listen sensitively when children inform you that they are troubled by a family disruption. Help children sort through the practical issues that inevitably arise when children face a change in living arrangements or find that they must move back and forth between their parents' houses.

Key Concepts

family (p. 64)
socialization (p. 64)
culture (p. 65)
individualistic culture (p. 65)
collectivistic culture (p. 65)
community (p. 65)
family structure (p. 68)
coparents (p. 69)

stepfamily (p. 71)
self-regulation (p. 77)
parenting style (p. 77)
authoritative parenting style (p. 77)
authoritarian parenting style (p. 77)
permissive parenting style (p. 78)

uninvolved parenting style (p. 78)
guided participation (p. 79)
child maltreatment (p. 83)
ethnicity (p. 92)
acculturation (p. 94)
assimilation (p. 94)
selective adoption (p. 94)
rejection (p. 94)

bicultural orientation (p. 94)
ethnic identity (p. 95)
culturally responsive teaching (p. 97)
socioeconomic status (SES) (p. 101)
resilience (p. 102)
sense of community (p. 103)

MyEducationLab

Now go to Chapter 3 of MyEducationLab at www.myeducationlab.com, where you can:

- View instructional objectives for the chapter.
- Take a quiz to test your mastery of chapter objectives. Detailed feedback is provided to explain why your responses are correct or incorrect.
- Deepen your understanding of particular concepts and principles with Review, Practice, and Enrichment exercises.

- Complete Activities and Applications exercises that give you additional experience in interpreting artifacts, increase your understanding of how research contributes to knowledge about chapter topics, and encourage you to apply what you have learned about children's development.
- Apply what you have learned in the chapter to your work with children in Building Teaching Skills and Dispositions exercises.
- Observe children and their unique contexts in Video Examples.

Biological
Beginnings

Laurie and Tom had hoped for a natural childbirth with their first child, but during her labor, Laurie had lost confidence and complied with her doctor's advice that she take medications to strengthen contractions and diminish the pain (Bailes & Jackson, 2000). The outcome was joyous—a healthy son, Evan—but for a long time afterwards, the new parents regretted that Laurie had felt compelled to take somewhat risky and possibly unnecessary medications.

When Laurie and Tom learned they were expecting their second child, they planned once again for a natural childbirth, this time more deliberately. Laurie saw a doctor and had regular checkups with her nurse-midwife, ate well for herself and her baby-to-be, and asked for reassurance. Gradually a specific plan for the birth emerged. Laurie would deliver the baby at home with help from Tom and the midwife. The doctor would meet them at the hospital (a 5-minute drive from Laurie and Tom's house) if medical intervention proved necessary. Laurie's mother would look after Evan and support the laboring parents.

With a definite plan in place, Laurie relaxed during her pregnancy. Baby-to-be grew quietly. Laurie and Tom prepared the nursery for the new baby and helped Evan anticipate changes to his family. And they waited.

One evening close to her due date, Laurie went to sleep as usual but woke at 2 a.m. with clear fluid leaking from her body. Her membranes had broken. Labor was imminent! She called her midwife, who asked her to take her temperature and try to go back to sleep. Her temperature was normal, and Laurie slept a little. She woke at 6:30 a.m. and fed Evan. Two hours later, the midwife arrived and evaluated Laurie's condition and the baby's heart rate. Everyone was ready.

Productive contractions had not yet begun, however. The midwife reminded Laurie that her doctor wanted to become involved if labor had not started within 12 hours after her membranes had broken. Laurie became concerned. She, Tom, and the midwife put their heads together.

> The three of them jointly formulated a plan to encourage labor to start and to monitor maternal and fetal well-being. Laurie would walk, do nipple stimulation, rest, eat, and increase her fluid intake. She would also check her pulse and temperature every 3–4 hours. The midwife asked them to call every 2 hours or so, and planned to visit again at 2 PM. There were few contractions, but Laurie was confident that her body would labor before time ran out.[a] (p. 541)

Yet Laurie had not experienced regular contractions when the midwife returned at 2 p.m. Tests performed by the midwife suggested that Laurie and the baby were fine. The midwife telephoned the doctor, who decided he would be willing to wait to intervene until the next morning as long as Laurie consented to take antibiotics in the meantime. Laurie agreed to take the antibiotics so as to prevent infection.

Laurie and Tom tried traditional methods of triggering labor such as stimulating her nipples. No contractions occurred. The midwife went home, and Laurie and Tom took a nap and then ate dinner. Finally, contractions began in earnest. The midwife returned, only to find contractions slowing down. Laurie worried that her labor would stall, as it had with her first baby. The midwife reassured Laurie but decided to give the couple their privacy and went home. During a later phone call, the midwife suggested that Laurie and Tom go for a brisk walk. When they returned, contractions intensified. The baby was coming!

> By 3 AM, contractions were sharper still and required more attention. The midwife suggested that Laurie and Tom get into the shower together to aid relaxation; and they did so for almost an hour. After the shower and the 4 AM dose of antibiotics, they were able to settle down and do some of the special things they had planned for labor. Tom had prepared Laurie's favorite omelet seasoned with herbs he had grown for her in the kitchen windowbox. She nibbled on the omelet between contractions. Tom quietly read scriptures to her as he did every evening. When the work of labor

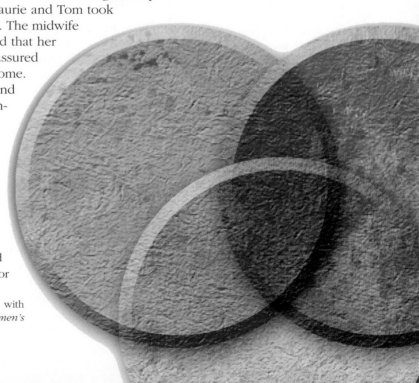

Case Study:
Birthing the Baby

Outline:

Case Study:
Birthing the Baby

Genetic Foundations
of Child Development

Prenatal Development

Birth of the Baby

Summary

Applying Concepts in Child
Development

[a]Excerpts from Shared Responsibility in Home Birth Practice: Collaborating with Clients, by Alice Bailes and Marsha E. Jackson in *Journal of Midwifery and Women's Health,* 2000, *45*(6), 537–543.

became even more intense, Laurie asked Tom to stop reading, turn off the lights, and massage her back. She and Tom labored together in the dark alone. The midwife came in periodically to check FHTs [fetal heart tones] and to make sure that all was well.

By 5:30 AM, daylight began to come through the bedroom windows, renewing Laurie's energy. Grandma and Evan were still sleeping when Laurie told Tom and the midwife that it was time to push. Tom asked the midwife to invite Grandma in for the birth. Laurie's birth plan specified that she wanted to give birth in an upright position. The midwife and Tom assisted Laurie into a supported standing position for second stage. During pushing, the FHTs were checked about every 5 minutes and Laurie smiled between contractions knowing that the home birth was proceeding as planned. At 6:03 AM, Laurie and Tom were thrilled when . . . their healthy 8 pound 4 ounce baby girl arrived.

Evan woke at his usual time to find a new baby sister in his parents' bed. He climbed into the bed, eager to hold the new baby.[a] (pp. 541–542)

- What major changes did Laurie and Tom's baby-to-be undergo during her earliest developments?

- What factors contributed to a healthy beginning for Laurie and Tom's baby?

While Laurie and Tom were planning their childbirth, their baby-to-be was growing quietly and changing constantly. During the 9 months of her prenatal development, their future child was transformed from a single cell, charged with a unique genetic makeup, into a fully formed baby, ready to live, to learn, and, ultimately, to love. Laurie and Tom's baby had a healthy beginning because Laurie ate well, tried to relax, sought social support, and obtained medical care. Of course, natural biological processes were also an essential part of the baby's growth. In this chapter we show that prenatal growth and childbirth are extraordinary symphonies of developmental processes, each orchestrated by both genes (nature) and the environment (nurture). We find that there are many things prospective parents and supportive professionals can do to give children healthy beginnings.

Genetic Foundations of Child Development

Like Laurie and Tom's children, every child has a unique profile of hereditary instructions that support his or her life, growth, human traits, and individuality. These guidelines are contained in a child's **genes,** the basic units of heredity.

Structure of Genes

The structure of human genes is sufficiently intricate that it carries all the necessary instructions for forming a body, bit by bit. Each gene tells the body to create one or more proteins under particular conditions or to regulate other genes (Brett, Pospisil, Valcárcel, Reich, & Bork, 2002). Proteins produced by genes create life-sustaining reactions that, with adequate nutrition and a favorable environment, ultimately culminate in the physical characteristics of a growing child. For example, some proteins guide the production of new cells with particular properties (e.g., elastic skin cells or message-sending brain cells). Other proteins tell the body to increase in size, fight infection, repair damage, carry chemical signals throughout the body, activate or inhibit other genes, and so forth.

The 25,000 or so genes that exist in the human body are laid out in an orderly way on rod-like structures called **chromosomes** (International Human Genome Sequencing Consortium, 2004; Watson et al., 2004). Chromosomes are organized into 23 distinct pairs that are easily seen with a high-powered microscope (Figure 4-1). These 46 chromosomes reside in the center of virtually every cell in the body. One chromosome of each pair is inherited from the mother, the other from the father.

Genes are made up of deoxyribonucleic acid, or **DNA.** A DNA molecule is structured like a ladder that has been twisted many times into a spiral staircase (see Figure 4-2). Pairs of chemical substances comprise steps on the staircase, and a gene is comprised of a series of these steps. Location on the staircase helps scientists determine the identity of particular genes. Side by side with genes on the DNA ladder are other steps that tell genes when they

gene
Basic unit of heredity in a living cell; genes are made up of DNA and contained on chromosomes.

chromosome
Rodlike structure that resides in the nucleus of every cell of the body and contains genes that guide growth and development; each chromosome is made up of DNA and other biological instructions.

DNA
A spiral-staircase–shaped molecule that guides the production of proteins needed by the body for growth and development; short for *deoxyribonucleic acid.*

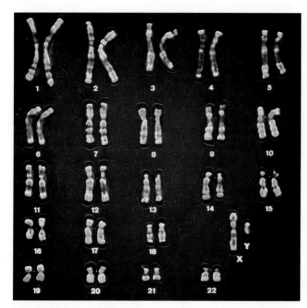

Figure 4-1

Photograph of human chromosomes that have been extracted from a human cell, colored, magnified, and arranged in order of size.
CNRI/Science Photo Library/Photo Researchers, Inc.

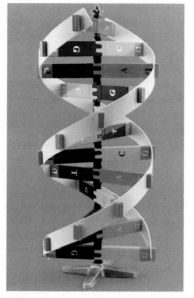

Figure 4-2

A DNA molecule is structured like a ladder that has been twisted into a spiral staircase.
Courtesy FBI

should turn on and off and still other steps whose functions are still a mystery. The hierarchical relationships among the body, its cells, chromosomes, genes, and DNA molecules are represented in Figure 4-3.

Operation of Genes

The vast majority of genes are identical for all children (National Human Genome Research Institute, 2003; Venter et al., 2001). Among these universal genes are those that make it possible for children to develop basic human abilities, such as communicating with language, walking and running, and forming social relationships. Unless children have extremely serious genetic defects or grow up in an especially deprived or abusive environment, they all develop basic human capacities. The remaining (small) proportion of genes varies among children. Genes that vary predispose individual children to be relatively tall or short, heavy or thin, active or sedentary, eager to learn new things or content to rely on existing knowledge, emotionally agreeable or combative, and healthy or vulnerable to disease. Remarkably, universal and individual genes blend together in their effects, such that a given child develops a distinctive appearance, laughter, running stride, and the like.

In one respect, genes are the start of a long chain of events (see Figure 4-4). Genes directly affect the operations of individual cells; single cells grow together in communities that become organs, brain circuits, and other systems of the body; and these physiological systems influence the child's behavior, relationships, and learning. Thus genes are powerful, but they are *not* simple recipes or blueprints for traits. Rather, the proteins that originate from genetic instructions are released into the child's cells, and their effects depend partly (largely, in some cases) on the child's health and activity. To illustrate, an 8-year-old boy genetically predisposed to asthma may rarely have respiratory flare-ups because his family gives him proper medical care and shields him from dogs and cats, his personal triggers for wheezing and coughing.

In another respect, the causal chain operates in reverse, with the child's experiences affecting genetic expression (look again at Figure 4-4). That is, the environment provides opportunities for learning and exposure to nutrition and toxins; these experiences affect brain and body; and the health and operations of bodily systems activate (or suppress) particular genes. For example, a 12-year-old girl who grows up in a weight-conscious, appearance-obsessed family might develop an eating disorder that undermines her health and delays the activation of genes that would, under conditions of adequate nutrition, direct her progress through puberty.

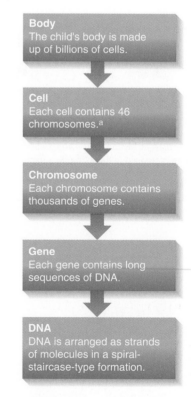

Body
The child's body is made up of billions of cells.

Cell
Each cell contains 46 chromosomes.[a]

Chromosome
Each chromosome contains thousands of genes.

Gene
Each gene contains long sequences of DNA.

DNA
DNA is arranged as strands of molecules in a spiral-staircase-type formation.

[a] Reproductive cells, with their 23 chromosomes, are exceptions.

Figure 4-3

Genetic structures in the body are organized hierarchically.

Figure 4-4

Genes and environment interact through ripples of changes in the child's brain and body. Genes directly affect cells and indirectly influence other systems in the body and contact with the environment. The environment directly affects the child's experience; experience, in turn, influences the child's brain and body and indirectly affects the operation of cells and expression of genes. Particular direct and indirect effects are transformed over time, as new genes come into play and as the child's activity, experience, nutrition, relationships, and exposure to toxins also change.
Sources: Gottlieb, 1992; T. D. Johnston & Edwards, 2002.

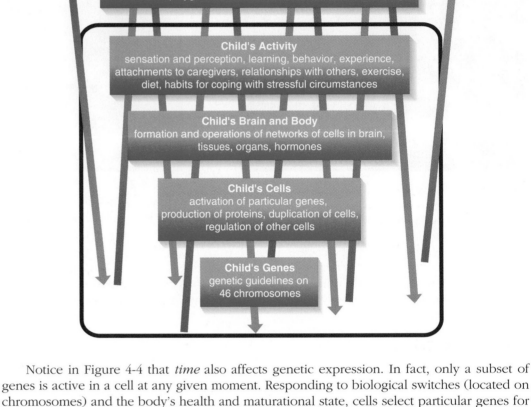

MyEducationLab

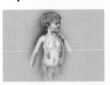

Go to the Video Examples section in Chapter 4 of MyEducationLab to watch an animated video depicting the effects of hormones on children's growing bodies.

Notice in Figure 4-4 that *time* also affects genetic expression. In fact, only a subset of genes is active in a cell at any given moment. Responding to biological switches (located on chromosomes) and the body's health and maturational state, cells select particular genes for activation. Other genes remain dormant until it is their turn to be called into action. This fact helps explain the order of maturational changes in physical appearance and motor skills. To illustrate, a child is born with genes for sexual maturation but the body waits to trigger these hormones until the beginning of adolescence. It also explains why some diseases and mental health conditions seem to appear out of nowhere: Genes that make people vulnerable to some conditions remain silent until maturational states and environmental circumstances elicit their effects.

In summary, genes do their work as part of a complex system of physical processes. Soon we will tell more about how genes contribute to a child's individual traits, but first we need to explain how a child acquires his or her genetic makeup in the first place.

Formation of Reproductive Cells

As we have said, normal human cells contain 46 chromosomes. There is an important exception: Male and female reproductive cells, called **gametes,** have only 23 chromosomes each—half of each chromosome pair. Gametes, which take the form of *sperm* in men and *ova* in women, are created by a process of cell division called **meiosis** (see Figure 4-5).

Meiosis.   During meiosis, nature forms new reproductive cells so that a child has some genetic characteristics from both parents as well as some novel features. Meiosis begins when the 46 chromosomes within a male or female *germ cell* (a precursor to a gamete) pair up into 23 matched sets. The germ cell then duplicates each chromosome, and pairs of chromosomes line up side by side. Next, segments of genetic material are exchanged between each pair. This *crossing-over* of genetic material shuffles genes between paired chromosomes and produces new hereditary combinations that do not exist in either parent's chromosomes.

gamete
Reproductive cell that, in humans, contains 23 chromosomes rather than the 46 chromosomes present in other cells in the body; a male gamete (sperm) and a female gamete (ovum) join at conception.

meiosis
The process of cell division and reproduction by which gametes are formed.

General Process of Meiosis

Each germ cell has 46 chromosomes. Chromosomes begin to move together and pair up into 23 matched sets in the germ cells.

Sperm in Men

Production of sperm begins for boys at puberty. During an initial phase, germ cells (precursors to sperm) are formed. *Only one pair from the 23 pairs of chromosomes is shown here.*

Ova in Women

Production of ova begins for girls during prenatal development. During an initial phase, germ cells (precursors to ova) are formed. *Only one pair from the 23 pairs of chromosomes is shown here.*

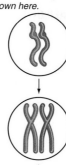

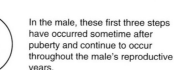

Each chromosome replicates (duplicates) itself. Notice that the single strands in the previous step have doubled in this step.

Crossing-over occurs: Pairs of duplicated chromosomes temporarily unite and exchange segments of chromosomes. This shuffling of genes between paired chromosomes—known as *crossing-over*—ensures unique combinations of genes that differ from those of both the mother and the father.

In the male, these first three steps have occurred sometime after puberty and continue to occur throughout the male's reproductive years.

In the female, these first three steps have occurred during prenatal development. At the completion of crossing-over, germ cells will rest until puberty.

The pairs of doubled chromosomes separate and the cell divides, forming two new cells, each containing 23 double-structured chromosomes. Chromosomes randomly join with others in one of the two new cells. This process is called the *first meiotic division*. It further ensures genetic individuality.

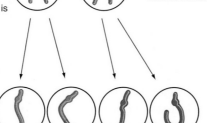

Two cells are formed, each with 23 double chromosomes.

Meiosis resumes during puberty. With each ovulation, the germ cell will complete the first meiotic division producing two cells, each with 23 double chromosomes. One cell receives the majority of cell material and becomes viable. The other cell may reproduce but neither it nor its progeny will be a viable gamete.

The second meiotic division takes place. The cell divides in two and the double-structured chromosomes are separated. Chromosomes are now single-structured: the new cell now has one chromosome from each pair, and a total of 23 chromosomes. Resulting cells are now gametes that mature and become ready to unite at conception.

There are now four male gametes (sperm).

Only one potentially viable ovum, which has 23 chromosomes, remains. This step of the second meiotic division occurs only if the ovum is fertilized with a sperm.

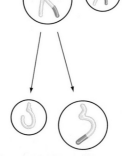

During conception, the sperm enters the ovum.

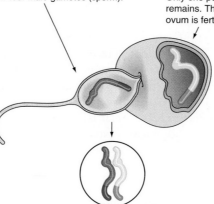

The two sets of 23 chromosomes, one from the father and one from the mother, unite to form a zygote.

Figure 4-5

Reproductive cells. Meiosis is the multistep process of forming gametes, cells that join in reproduction to form a new organism. During conception, the sperm enters the ovum and the two sets of 23 chromosomes are fused to form a zygote. The new offspring has some characteristics from both parents as well as some new chromosome structures not present in either parent.
Sources: K. L. Moore & Persaud, 2008; Sadler, 2006.

After crossing-over takes place, the pairs of duplicated chromosomes separate and the cell divides into two new germ cells with half from each pair. Chance determines which of the duplicated chromosomes from each of the 23 pairs moves to one or the other of the two new cells. This phase thus provides a second route to genetic individuality. During this first cell division, one of the two new female germ cells gets the bulk of the cell matter and is strong and healthy—that is, it is viable—whereas the second, smaller cell disintegrates. Both new male germ cells are viable.

A second cell division takes place, and the duplicated chromosomes separate. Each new cell receives one of the duplicate chromosomes from each pair. The resulting male germ cells are ready to mature and become male gametes (sperm). The female germ cell undergoes this second division only after being fertilized by a sperm. When the female cell divides, once again, only one of the two new cells, a female gamete (an ovum), is viable. The process of meiosis thus produces one ovum and four sperm.[1]

The process of meiosis ensures that some traits are preserved across generations and other entirely new traits are created. Children share some features with both of their parents because they inherit half of their chromosomes from each parent. Children are unlike their parents (and siblings) in other respects because parts of chromosomes change slightly during meiosis; the chromosome structures that children inherit are *not* exact duplicates of parents' chromosomes.[2] Furthermore, a single gene transmitted from parent to child (and shared by both) may operate differently in the two family members because other genes (not shared by both) may intensify or weaken that gene's effects.

Gender.   When one sperm and one ovum unite at conception, the 23 chromosomes from each parent come together and form a new being (the **zygote**) with 46 chromosomes. The 23rd chromosome pair determines the gender of the individual: Two *X chromosomes* (one each from the mother and father) produce a female, and a combination of an *X chromosome* and a *Y chromosome* (from the mother and father, respectively) produces a male. If you look at the photograph of human chromosomes in Figure 4-1, you can see the XY pair near the bottom right corner, which makes this individual a male.

How twins are created.   Occasionally, a zygote splits into two separate cell clusters, resulting in two offspring instead of one. *Identical,* or **monozygotic twins,** come from the same fertilized egg and so have the same genes. At other times, two ova simultaneously unite with two sperm cells, again resulting in two offspring. These **dizygotic twins,** also known as *fraternal* twins, are as similar to one another as ordinary siblings. They share some genetic traits but not others.

Because monozygotic and dizygotic twins differ in the degree to which they share genes, researchers have studied them extensively. Twin studies permit rough estimates of the relative effects of heredity and environment on human characteristics. In many cases monozygotic twins are quite similar to one another in terms of how easily they learn new concepts, how helpful and cooperative they are, and how aggressive they are with others, whereas dizygotic twins are less similar (Caspi et al., 2004; Knafo & Plomin, 2006; Plomin & Spinath, 2004). Even so, "identical" twins are not identical in all psychological characteristics or even in their physical features—an indication that environment, experience, children's own choices, and even random factors also affect development throughout life.

Genetic Basis of Individual Traits

So far, you have learned that children have both uniform genes (that make them resemble one another in their human abilities) and variable genes (that contribute to their individuality). Uniform human genes, carried by all parents, are transmitted to every child. Genes that

These monozygotic twins share the same genetic instructions. Identical twins are usually quite similar in physical appearance and share many psychological characteristics, such as being particularly intelligent or gregarious. However, despite their many similarities, identical twins make their own choices, experience some different environments, form some separate friendships, and, as a result, develop into two distinctly unique individuals.

zygote
Cell formed when a male sperm joins with a female ovum; with healthy genes and nurturing conditions in the uterus, it may develop into a fetus and be born as a live infant.

monozygotic twins
Twins that began as a single zygote and so share the same genetic makeup.

dizygotic twins
Twins that began as two separate zygotes and so are as genetically similar as two siblings conceived and born at different times.

[1]Sperm are produced continuously throughout a male's reproductive years. During sexual intercourse, between 200 and 600 million sperm are deposited in the woman's vagina (K. L. Moore & Persaud, 2008). In girls, up to 2 million germ cells are present at birth. Many subsequently decay, and only about 40,000 remain at the beginning of adolescence. About 400 ova will be released during ovulation over the woman's lifetime (K. L. Moore & Persaud, 2008).
[2]In any given parent, each event of meiosis begins with the exact same chromosomes from that parent. The process of meiosis tweaks the structure of chromosomes slightly; no two meiotic events change chromosomes in precisely the same way.

vary among children are transmitted through systematic patterns of inheritance as well as through less common mechanisms and by biological errors during meiosis and other cell divisions. Let's look more closely at how children receive traits that contribute to their individuality.

Common mechanisms of genetic transmission.   When the two sets of 23 chromosomes combine into matched pairs during conception, the corresponding genes inherited from each parent pair up. Each gene pair includes two forms of the protein-coding instructions—two **alleles**—related to a particular physical characteristic. Sometimes the two genes in an allele pair give the same instructions ("Have dark hair!" "Have dark hair!"). At other times they give very different instructions ("Have dark hair!" "Have blond hair!"). When two genes give different instructions, one gene is often more influential than its counterpart. A **dominant gene** manifests its characteristic, in a sense overriding the instructions of a **recessive gene** with which it is paired. A recessive gene influences growth and development primarily when its partner is also recessive. For example, genes for dark hair are dominant and those for blond hair are recessive. Thus a child with a dark hair gene and a blond hair gene will have dark hair, as will a child with two dark hair genes. Only when two blond hair genes are paired together will a child have blond hair.

However, when two genes of an allele pair "disagree," one gene doesn't always dominate completely. Sometimes one gene simply has a stronger influence than others, a phenomenon known as **codominance.** *Sickle cell disease,* a blood disease, is an example. The disease develops in its full-blown form only when a person has two (recessive) alleles for it. Nevertheless, when an individual has one recessive allele for sickle cell disease and one "healthy" allele, he or she may experience temporary, mild symptoms when short of oxygen; occasionally develop more serious health problems; and have greater-than-average resistance to malaria (Information Center for Sickle Cell and Thalassemic Disorders, 2002; Kark, 2000).

In reality, the influence of genes is often even more complex. Many physical traits and most psychological ones are dependent on multiple genes rather than on a single pair of alleles. In **polygenic inheritance,** many separate genes each exert some influence on the expression of a trait. Height, skin color, and vulnerability to certain illnesses, including some kinds of diabetes, epilepsy, and cancer, are all determined by several genes that each contribute small effects (Dibbens, Heron, & Mulley, 2007; J. M. Tanner, 1990). Of course, complex traits affected by polygenic inheritance are also affected by nutrition, activity, and other environmental influences.

Problems in genetic instructions.   Sometimes problems occur in the genetic instructions that children receive (see Table 4-1). There are two primary types of genetic disorders, chromosome abnormalities and single-gene defects. A child with a *chromosome abnormality* may have an extra chromosome, a missing chromosome, or a wrongly formed chromosome. Because each chromosome holds thousands of genes, a child with a chromosomal abnormality tends to have many affected genes, and the result can be major physical problems and mental retardation. Chromosomal abnormalities occur when chromosomes divide unevenly during meiosis. They can also occur after meiosis, when the zygote's cells divide unevenly, leaving the growing zygote with some cells with normal chromosomes and others with abnormal chromosomes. Chromosomal abnormalities may be caused by a variety of factors, including parents' exposure to viruses, radiation, and drugs.

Chromosome abnormalities occur in 4 percent of births (Hellings & Burns, 2004). One such abnormality, an extra 21st chromosome or an extra piece of one, causes *Down syndrome.* Children with Down syndrome typically show delays in mental growth and are susceptible to heart defects and other health problems. Apparently, the extra 21st chromosome causes biochemical changes that redirect brain development. The severity of disabilities caused by Down syndrome and many other chromosomal abnormalities varies considerably from one child to the next.

alleles
Genes located at the same point on corresponding (paired) chromosomes and related to the same physical characteristic.

dominant gene
Gene that overrides any competing instructions in an allele pair.

recessive gene
Gene that influences growth and development primarily when the other gene in the allele pair is identical to it.

codominance
Situation in which the two genes of an allele pair, although not identical, both have some influence on a characteristic.

polygenic inheritance
Situation in which many genes combine in their influence on a particular characteristic.

Positive attitudes of educators, advocacy by parents, and federal legislation have improved educational services and opportunities for many children with chromosomal abnormalities, genetic defects, and other disabilities.

MyEducationLab

Watch a video about the special medical needs of children with Down syndrome in the Video Examples section in Chapter 4 of MyEducationLab.

Table 4-1 Common Chromosomal and Genetic Disorders in Children

Disorder	Incidence	Characteristics[a]	Implications for Care
Chromosome Abnormalities. Children with chromosome abnormalities are born with an irregular number of chromosomes (more than or fewer than 46) or with one or more chromosomes that have irregular structures (deletions from or duplications to parts of an individual chromosome, or with a part of one chromosome moved to another location).			
Down syndrome	1 per 700–1,000 births	Children with Down syndrome have one extra chromosome. Physical characteristics include distinctively shaped eyes, a protruding tongue, thick lips, flat nose, short neck, wide gaps between toes, short fingers, specific health problems, and risks for heart problems and hearing loss. Mental retardation can range from mild to severe. Children often have good visual discrimination skills and may be better at understanding verbal language than producing it.	Provide explicit instruction in any delayed skills (e.g., in language). Address health issues such as heart problems and potential feeding difficulties.
Klinefelter syndrome	1 per 500–1,000 boys	Only boys have Klinefelter syndrome; they have one Y chromosome and two X chromosomes. Diagnosis may not occur until adolescence, when testes fail to enlarge. Affected boys tend to have long legs, to grow modest breast tissue, and to remain sterile. They tend to show lower than average verbal ability and some speech and language delays.	Offer an enriched verbal environment. Medical treatment may be given to support development of male sexual characteristics.
Turner syndrome	1 per 2,500–5,000 girls	Only girls have Turner syndrome; they have one X chromosome and are missing the second sex chromosome. Affected girls have broad chests, webbed necks, short stature, and specific health problems. They do not show normal sexual development. They may show normal verbal ability but lower-than-average ability in processing visual and spatial information.	Provide instruction and support related to visual and spatial processing. Hormone therapy helps with bone growth and development of female characteristics.
Prader-Willi syndrome	1 per 10,000–25,000 births	A deletion of a gene segment on chromosome 15 is inherited from the father. Children with this syndrome tend to become obese and show mental retardation; they also have small hands and feet and are short in stature. They may develop maladaptive behaviors such as throwing frequent temper tantrums and picking at their own skin. Beginning at ages 1–6 years, children may eat excessively, hoard food, and eat unappealing substances.	Create developmentally appropriate plans to help children regulate eating, decrease inappropriate behaviors, and increase acceptable emotional expression. Seek medical care as necessary.
Angelman syndrome	1 per 10,000–30,000 births	A deletion of a gene segment on chromosome 15 is inherited from the mother. Children with this syndrome show mental retardation, a small head, seizures, and jerky movements. They have unusual, recurrent bouts of laughter not associated with happiness.	Provide appropriate educational support suited to children's skills and developmental levels. Seek medical care as necessary.
Single-Gene Defects. Children with single-gene defects have a problem on a dominant gene (an error on one of the 22 paired chromosomes, that is, on any chromosome except X or Y), a recessive defect on both chromosomes in one of the 22 matched pairs, a problem in a recessive gene on the X chromosome (boys), or a problem in a gene on both X chromosomes (girls).[b]			
Neurofibromatosis	Mild form occurs in 1 per 2,500–4,000 births; severe form occurs in 1 per 40,000–50,000 births	Children with this dominant-gene defect develop benign and malignant tumors in the central nervous system. The condition may be caused by an error in a gene that would normally suppress tumor growth. Learning disabilities are somewhat common and mental retardation occurs occasionally. Most individuals experience only minor symptoms, such as having colored and elevated spots on their skin.	Address learning disabilities; offer adaptive services to children with mental retardation. Tumors may need to be removed or treated. Surgery or braces may be needed if the spine becomes twisted.

[a]This table describes typical symptoms for children with particular chromosomal and genetic problems. Children's actual level of functioning depends on the medical treatments they receive; their experiences with families, teachers, other caregivers, and other children; and their health and other genes they might possess. New medical treatments and educational interventions are constantly being tested, and many will increase quality of life for these children.

[b]X-linked defects based on a single dominant gene also occur but are rare. For example, children who receive the gene for hypophosphatemia on the X chromosome produce low levels of phosphate and, as a result, have soft bones that are easily deformed.

Table 4-1   Common Chromosomal and Genetic Disorders in Children (continued)

Disorder	Incidence	Characteristics[a]	Implications for Care
Huntington disease (HD)	3–7 per 100,000 births	Children with this dominant-gene defect develop a progressive disorder of the central nervous system. Signs typically appear by age 35 to 45, though age of first symptoms has varied between 2 and 85 years. HD may be caused by the production of a protein that destroys brain cells. Early signs include irritability, clumsiness, depression, and forgetfulness. Eventually, loss of control over movements of arms, legs, torso, or facial muscles occurs, speech becomes slurred, and severe mental disturbances arise.	Remove sharp edges from the physical environment. When memory deteriorates, provide visual instructions about daily tasks. Medication may be given to alleviate movement problems and depression.
Phenylketonuria (PKU)	1 per 15,000 births, with rates highest in people of Celtic origin (e.g., from Ireland and Scotland)	Children with this recessive-gene defect are at risk for developing mental retardation, eczema, seizures, and motor and behavioral problems such as aggression, self-mutilation, and impulsiveness. When children have both recessive genes for PKU, their livers cannot produce an enzyme that breaks down phenylalanine (an amino acid); this substance accumulates and becomes toxic to the brain.	Provide educational materials to enhance planning and memory skills and compensate for limitations. When phenylalanine is restricted from their diet, children develop much more normally, and mental retardation is avoided. Subtle problems may still result (e.g., awkward pencil grip and learning disabilities).
Sickle cell disease	1 per 500–600 children of African (black) descent; rates are also elevated in people of Mediterranean descent	Children with this recessive-gene defect develop problems with blood circulation. The disease causes red blood cells to grow rigid, and passage of blood through small blood vessels causes pain. Children may experience many serious conditions, including stroke, infection, tissue damage, and fatigue. Symptoms become obvious during the first or second year of life.	Be alert to medical crises, such as strokes. Offer comfort to children who are tired or in pain. Treatments include blood transfusions, medication for pain and infections, and other medicines to reduce frequency of medical crises.
Cystic fibrosis (CF)	1 per 3,300 children from European American backgrounds and 1 per 9,500 children from Hispanic American backgrounds	Children with this recessive-gene defect have glands that produce large amounts of abnormally thick, sticky mucus, which creates serious problems for breathing and digestion. CF is usually noticed in infancy due to persistent coughing, wheezing, pneumonia, and big appetite with little weight gain. Many individuals with CF now live well into their 40s.	Be aware of symptoms that require medical care. The condition is often treated with physical therapy, medication, and bronchial drainage.
Tay-Sachs disease	1 per 2,500–3,600 children among Ashkenazi Jews (of Eastern European ancestry)	Children with this recessive-gene defect develop a fatal, degenerative condition of the central nervous system. They lack an enzyme required to break down a fatty substance in brain cells. At about 6 months of age, children slow down in development, lose vision, display an abnormal startle response, and go into convulsions. Other functions are gradually lost, and children become mentally retarded, cannot move, and die by age 3 or 4.	Offer love and attention as you would to other children. Be alert to new accommodations that may be needed in the environment, such as stabilizing and securing the surroundings when children lose sight. There is no known cure or treatment.
Thalassemia (Cooley's anemia)	1 in 800–2,500 individuals of Greek or Italian descent in the United States; rates are lower in other groups	Children with this recessive-gene develop a disease of blood cells in which oxygen is not transmitted effectively. They become pale, fatigued, and irritable within their first 2 years of life. Individuals with serious forms of the condition may develop feeding problems, diarrhea, and enlargement of the spleen and heart, infections, and unusual facial features and bone structures. Young people severely impaired by this condition sometimes die by early adulthood.	Help children cope with their health problems. Treatment may include blood transfusions, antibiotics, and occasionally bone marrow transplants.
Duchenne muscular dystrophy	1 per 3,000–4,000 boys	Only boys acquire this X-linked recessive-gene defect, which causes a progressive muscular weakness because of a gene's failure to produce an essential protein needed by muscle cells. Between ages 2 and 5, affected boys begin to stumble and walk on their toes or with another unusual gait. They may lose the ability to walk between ages 8 and 14 and may later die from respiratory and cardiac problems.	Watch for respiratory infections and heart problems. Treatments include physical therapy, orthopedic devices, surgery, and medications to reduce muscle stiffness.

Sources: Blachford, 2002; Burns, Brady, Dunn, & Starr, 2000; Cody & Kamphaus, 1999; Dykens & Cassidy, 1999; Massimini, 2000; K. L. Moore & Persaud, 2008; Nilsson & Bradford, 1999; M. P. Powell & Schulte, 1999; J. T. Smith, 1999; Waisbren, 1999; Wynbrandt & Ludman, 2000.

A second type of genetic disorder occurs when a child inherits a *single-gene defect* from one or both parents. Resulting physical problems tend to be more specific and subtle than those caused by chromosomal abnormalities. Nonetheless, some single-gene defects are quite serious. The usual pattern of inheritance is that children who inherit a dominant-gene defect show the problem. Those who inherit a recessive-gene defect show the problem only if both genes in the allele pair are defective (transmission is slightly different in X-chromosome-linked defects).

Some genetic problems do not fit neatly into the categories of chromosomal abnormality or single-gene defect. For instance, some conditions may be mild or severe depending on the particular sequence of chemical compounds on a gene. An example is *Fragile X syndrome,* which results from a genetic defect on the X chromosome. When this defect is small and limited, people who carry the problem gene are able to produce some of a particular protein needed by the body, and as a result they may show no symptoms or only mild learning disabilities. But the defect can intensify as it is passed from one generation to the next and lead to Fragile X syndrome (Narayanan & Warren, 2006). Children with Fragile X syndrome develop severe learning disabilities, emotional problems, and mental retardation. Their physical characteristics include prominent ears, long faces, double-jointed thumbs, and flat feet, and they typically possess other health conditions, such as being prone to sinus and ear infections (Hagerman & Lampe, 1999; Narayanan & Warren, 2006). In addition, these children tend to be socially anxious, sensitive to touch and noise, and inclined to avoid eye contact and to repeat certain activities over and over again (e.g., spinning objects, waving their arms, saying the same phrase); in other words, they show symptoms of an autism spectrum disorder (described on p. 142 and in Chapter 12). The problems of girls with Fragile X are generally less serious than comparable symptoms in boys because girls have a second X chromosome that usually is healthy enough to produce some of the missing protein. Boys, on the other hand, have a Y chromosome that is unable to produce the needed protein.

Other physical problems can occur when several genes act together to make a developing fetus vulnerable to poor nutrition, trauma, and other adverse conditions. *Spina bifida* (in which the spinal cord is malformed) and *cleft palate* (in which a split develops in the roof of the mouth) are examples of such conditions, which tend to run in some families but do not follow simple patterns of genetic transmission. It appears that affected children have genes that make them susceptible to particular environmental threats, such as their mother's vitamin deficiency or illness, during their prenatal development (K. L. Moore & Persaud, 2008).

All children require individualized care, but those with chromosomal abnormalities, single-gene defects, and other genetic conditions and birth defects may need interventions tailored to their specific conditions. In several places in this book, you will find recommendations for supporting the learning of children with disabilities. Because these children ultimately are in most respects similar to (rather than different from) children without such problems, it also makes sense for teachers to draw on their understanding of how typical developmental progressions are fostered.

The Awakening of Genes

Earlier we explained that only some genes are active in cells at any particular time. As a result, some genes have an almost immediate influence on the development of physical characteristics, but many others don't manifest themselves until later in *maturation,* when provoked to do so by hormones and other factors. For example, body length at birth is determined largely by prenatal conditions in the mother's uterus and is only minimally influenced by heredity. By 18 months of age, however, we see a definite correlation between children's heights and the heights of their parents, presumably because genetic factors have begun to exert their influence (J. M. Tanner, 1990).

Some emerging characteristics are tightly controlled by genetic instructions, a phenomenon known as **canalization** (Waddington, 1957). For instance, basic motor skills are highly canalized: Crawling, sitting, and walking appear under a wide range of circumstances and almost invariably appear without training or encouragement. Only extremely unusual environmental conditions can stifle them, such as when a young child exposed to heavy doses of a toxic substance (e.g., lead paint) is seriously delayed in mastering basic motor and psychological skills (Gottlieb, 1991, 1992). Spared from such toxic substances and allowed to move freely for even small amounts of time, children invariably develop indispensable motor skills.

MyEducationLab

Watch a video about a couple's experience raising a child with spina bifida in the Video Examples section in Chapter 4 of MyEducationLab.

canalization
Tight genetic control of a particular aspect of development.

Many skills are *not* canalized, however. Most of the abilities that children acquire at school—reading, writing, mathematical problem solving, and so on—are modified by experiences children have both in and out of the classroom. Social skills also rely on environmental support. For example, deciphering other people's intentions, learning to anticipate others' actions, and taking turns during conversation are competencies that are refined with social experience.

Another developmental factor in genetic expression is the operation of *sensitive periods*. In Chapter 1 we explained that a sensitive period is an age range, dictated by heredity, during which certain environmental experiences are especially important for normal development. During a sensitive period, the child is biologically ready to make a substantial leap forward in the maturation of structures of the brain or body, and particular experiences are needed to direct this growth.

Sensitive periods are observed in some aspects of perceptual abilities, language acquisition, and the formation of close bonds with caregivers. For example, as you'll learn in Chapter 9, children are especially sensitive to language input during infancy and early childhood. With regular opportunities for participation in conversations, young children easily learn one or more languages. Children deprived of language during early childhood require considerable intervention if they are to learn a first language later in life. Sensitive periods also play a role in the effects of harmful substances. That is, some environmental substances may be highly detrimental at one phase of development, yet exert little or no effect at other phases. Later in this chapter you will learn that prenatal development includes sensitive periods for the formation of limbs, organs, facial structures, and brain connections.

In other areas, such as learning to read and engage in productive social relationships, there is no single restricted time frame for learning. Children who have had inadequate experiences or instruction in these areas can frequently make up later for lost time in the early years. However, educators should not simply wait for children who lag behind peers to catch up in fundamental academic and social skills. Such competencies build cumulatively over time, and without appropriate intervention, delayed children may easily fall further behind and come to see themselves as incapable.

The Blending of Heredity and Environment

Numerous environmental and personal factors influence genetic expression. These include nutrition, illness, medication, stressful events, temperature, exposure to light, intensity of stimulation, opportunities for physical activity, and styles of caregiving. For example, parents who are reasonably relaxed, attentive, and affectionate help their infants and young children remain calm and poised to learn about the world. These engaged and confident parents appear to influence children's habitual responses to stress, having the specific effect of activating a gene in their children that inhibits stress responses (Diorio & Meaney, 2007; Kaffman & Meaney, 2007).

Some aspects of *temperament,* such as fearfulness, have a genetic basis but are also influenced by the environment. Although this boy is hesitant about separating from his mother in the morning, she has worked out a daily transition that calms his fears.

As you are finding out, complex psychological traits, such as personality characteristics and intellectual talents, are the outcomes of numerous genes (nature) and environmental experiences (nurture). For instance, there appear to be genetic origins to becoming particularly cheerful, outgoing, moody, anxious, or aggressive, and to becoming sedentary and cautious or physically active and a risk taker—all reflecting the various *temperaments* we spoke of in Chapter 1 (Rothbart, Posner & Kieras, 2006; A. C. Wood, Saudino, Rogers, Asherson, & Kuntsi, 2007; M. U. Zuckerman, 2007). Yet these traits are clearly influenced as well by the environment (Plomin, Owen, & McGuffin, 1994). We're not born wild or shy; instead, we're born with certain tendencies that our environments may or may not encourage.

There are at least three mechanisms by which the child's genetic makeup affects his or her experiences in particular environments (Reiss, 2005; Scarr, 1992, 1993; Scarr & McCartney, 1983). A *passive gene-environment relation* occurs when parents' genetic tendencies correlate with the kind of setting in which they raise their children. Especially when their children are young, parents select environments based on their own preferences and genetic tendencies. For example, a father with a strong imagination and a love of drama may take his son to theater performances. The father's interest in dramatic expression may have some genetic basis, and the child may share this genetically based talent. Thus the boy's genes correlate with his environment, but the association is considered passive because the boy is not determining the environment—his father is. In an *evocative gene-environment relation,* children's own characteristics elicit specific kinds of reactions from the environment. For example, a calm and compliant child may have a soothing effect on caregivers, who respond with warmth. Finally, an *active gene-environment relation* occurs when children have particular talents that influence environments made accessible to them. For instance, an athletic youngster may join a baseball team, organize neighborhood games, request sports equipment from parents, and in other ways create occasions for practicing athletic skills.

It should be increasingly clear to you that genes do not direct appearance, behavior, or even cell functioning in any simple, predetermined fashion. Genes operate in concert with one another; are affected by nutrition, stress, and other environmental agents; and are activated by hormones and physiological events. Furthermore, individual genes may be influential at particular points in development, suddenly bringing out characteristics that seem to come "from nowhere." In general, a child's genes provide rough guidelines that may be either stretched or compressed, depending on the influence of other genes and the child's health, schooling, interpersonal relationships, and environmental resources.

Some young people have genetically based temperaments that make them somewhat prone to withdraw from social contact, act impulsively, or respond aggressively to conflict. Adults can help these young people learn social skills for forming healthy relationships.

Acknowledging Nature and Nurture in Children's Lives

Genetic influence may seem like a very abstract topic compared to the world of real children in schools and community settings. Nevertheless, anyone working closely with children and adolescents must understand the power of heredity. At the same time, recognition that the environment also guides human development should inspire everyone's optimism about children's potential for positive growth. With these points in mind, we offer the following recommendations:

• ***Expect and make allowances for individual differences.*** Teachers and other practitioners who value a multitude of physical characteristics, personality types, and talents can put youngsters at ease. Children who are tall and short, chubby and thin, coordinated and clumsy, shy and outgoing, and calm and irritable all have a rightful place in the hearts of adults who teach and nurture them.

• ***Remember that environmental factors influence virtually every aspect of development.*** Children's development is *not* simply an outgrowth of biology. Even when children have inherited the potential for certain talents, temperaments, and deficits, their paths can be steered one way or another by environmental factors—physical experiences, social interactions, school instruction, and so on. For instance, children who are genetically predisposed to be irritable, distractible, or aggressive can, with guidance, learn more adaptive and socially productive ways of responding (e.g., DeVault, Krug, & Fake, 1996; Reiss, 2005; T. R. Robinson, Smith, Miller, & Brownell, 1999). And children who have significant biology-based disabilities can, with systematic instruction tailored to their individual needs, make dramatic gains in their intellectual and social development. You can see an example of such instruction in the Building Teaching Skills and Dispositions exercise in Chapter 4 of MyEducationLab.

MyEducationLab

Go to the Building Teaching Skills and Dispositions section in Chapter 4 of MyEducationLab to see how a teacher might nurture the talents of children with disabilities.

• ***Intervene when children struggle.*** There is an extended window of time for learning many things, but we cannot leave it to chance that delayed children will catch up on their own. Basic intellectual, social, and emotional skills affect many aspects of life, making it important to offer extra guidance when children's progress is unusually slow. Furthermore, without appropriate intervention, children who straggle far behind peers may come to doubt their capability for future learning, leading to even more serious problems, such as dropping out of school.

• ***Be mindful of your own reactions to children's challenging temperaments.*** Children who are genetically inclined to be somewhat irritable and combative commonly elicit impatient reactions from adults. For example, a harsh, punitive parenting style by adoptive parents appears to be associated with aggressive behavior in the children's birth parents, presumably because some adoptive children, acting aggressively in part due to inherited temperaments, provoke their adoptive parents to act impatiently (Ge et al., 1996; T. G. O'Connor, Deater-

Deckard, Fulker, Rutter, & Plomin, 1998). Although most of the research on children's temperamental effects is conducted with parents, the same tendency may occur to a lesser extent with teachers, who also interact with children regularly. Thus, teachers and other professionals can endeavor to remain calm while they teach oppositional children to cope effectively with frustration, anger, and disappointment (Keogh, 2003).

• ***Encourage children to make growth-promoting choices.*** Especially as they grow older, youngsters actively seek experiences compatible with their natural tendencies. Adults can help them find activities and resources that allow them to cultivate their talents and remediate their weaknesses. For instance, a socially outgoing boy with an excessive amount of energy and little self-control may be inclined to interrupt adults and peers. His teachers may need to remind him to hold his tongue and give others a chance to speak. They might also encourage the boy to join the drama club, a sports team, or other groups in which he can exercise leadership skills while increasing his self-control.

From a biological standpoint, the child is a complex, coordinated system with interacting parts and processes—notably, genes, body, environment, and the child's initiative and activity. This system originates before birth, during the prenatal period.

Prenatal Development

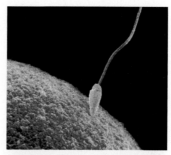
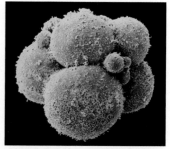

During **prenatal development,** the period of growth between conception and birth, a simple, single cell changes into a complex human being. During this remarkable developmental journey, the new being undergoes a series of changes, takes nourishment from the mother, and grows in an environment especially suited to its emerging yet fragile capabilities.

Phases of Prenatal Growth

During its prenatal growth, the developing baby-to-be must accomplish a wide range of tasks, including growing new cells, moving through the mother's body, settling into an interior wall of the mother's uterus, taking in nutrition and expelling wastes, forming and refining basic body structures, and activating rudimentary learning abilities. Prenatal development is divided into three phases: the periods of the *zygote, embryo,* and *fetus.*

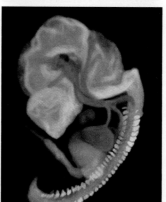

Development of the zygote.   During the middle of a woman's menstrual cycle, an *ovum* (female gamete) emerges from one of her two *ovaries* (see Figure 4-6). Several protective cells surround the ovum. The ovum enters the adjacent *fallopian tube,* a narrow and curved pipe that connects the ovary to the uterus. The ovum is guided toward the uterus by fringelike cell structures in the fallopian tube. When a man ejaculates during sexual intercourse, he releases millions of sperm into the woman's vagina, but only about 200 will find their way into the uterus and move toward the fallopian tube (K. L. Moore & Persaud, 2008). As the ovum is gently ushered down

Human prenatal development begins at conception (top left) and then progresses through the periods of the zygote (top right), embryo (bottom left), and fetus (bottom right).

the fallopian tube, sperm swim first slowly up the vagina and then more rapidly as they enter the uterus and proceed up the fallopian tube. When a conception takes place, a single sperm attaches to and eventually enters the ovum. The ovum cooperates by rearranging its exterior layers so that no other sperm can enter. The ovum and the sperm then combine their chromosomes, and the zygote, a new being, is formed.

The zygote creates new cells as it travels through the fallopian tube and toward the uterus. In a process called **mitosis,** the zygote duplicates its cells such that all of these new cells share its original 46 chromosomes. During mitosis, the spiral staircase of DNA straightens itself up and splits down the middle, and each half re-creates the original structure. After two exact copies of each chromosome have been formed, one copy from each pair moves to opposite sides of the

prenatal development
Growth that takes place between conception and birth.

mitosis
The process of cell duplication by which chromosomes are preserved and a human being or other biological organism can grow.

Figure 4-6

Development of the zygote.
Based on K. L. Moore, Persaud, & Shiota, 2000.

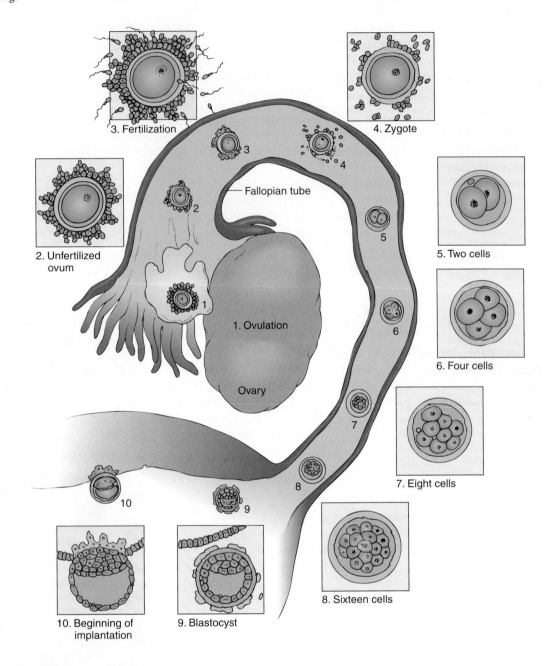

1. Ovulation
2. Unfertilized ovum
3. Fertilization
4. Zygote
5. Two cells
6. Four cells
7. Eight cells
8. Sixteen cells
9. Blastocyst
10. Beginning of implantation

Fallopian tube
Ovary

cell, the cell gradually splits, and two new cells are formed. This process of mitosis continues throughout the life span and permits both growth and replacement of cells.

In the zygote, mitosis takes place in the following manner. The first cell divides into two cells; these two cells divide to make four cells; four divide into eight; and by the time the zygote has 16 cells, it is entering the uterus (see Figure 4-6). These cells align themselves as the exterior lining of a sphere (see the *blastocyst* in Figure 4-6). Now about a week old, the zygote attaches itself to the wall of the uterus. The zygote separates into two parts: One is a tiny being that will develop further into an embryo, and the other becomes the *placenta,* the spongy structure in the uterus that provides nourishment. Cells begin to specialize and merge with other similar cells to form distinct structures, such as the nervous system and brain. The implanted zygote releases hormones, telling the ovaries that a conception has occurred and that menstruation should be prevented. In 2 short weeks, the new being has initiated growth, taken a journey, and found a hospitable home.

Development of the embryo.   The period of the **embryo** extends from 2 through 8 weeks after conception. Tasks of the embryonic period are to instigate life-support systems and form basic bodily structures. The placenta becomes larger, stronger, and more refined as it goes about its job of supplying food, liquid, and oxygen; removing wastes; and secreting

embryo
During prenatal weeks 2 through 8, the developing being that is in the process of forming major body structures and organs.

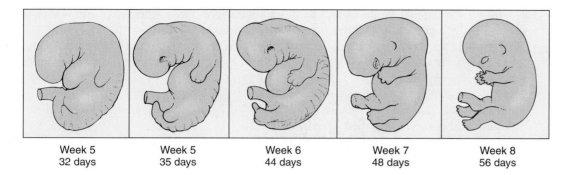

Figure 4-7

Development of the embryo.
Based on K. L. Moore et al., 2000.

Week 5	Week 5	Week 6	Week 7	Week 8
32 days	35 days	44 days	48 days	56 days

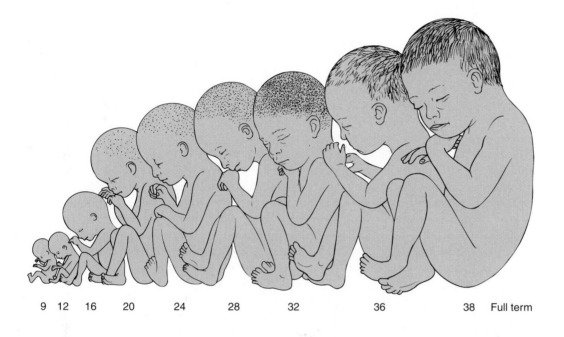

9 12 16   20   24   28   32   36   38   Full term

Figure 4-8

Development of the fetus.
Based on K. L. Moore & Persaud, 2008.

hormones that sustain the pregnancy. An *umbilical cord* forms and connects the embryo to the placenta.

The embryo itself undergoes rapid structural changes and increases in size. During prenatal development, growth tends to occur from top to bottom (head first, feet last) and from inside to outside (torso before limbs, arms and legs before hands and feet). Consistent with these trends, the head and heart are among the first structures to develop (see Figure 4-7). The growth of the neural tube that will give rise to the brain and spinal cord is well under way early in the embryonic period. Neurons—the cells that form connections in and to the brain—emerge and move to their proper places. Buds of limbs begin to develop, and by the eighth week, fingers and toes are recognizably distinct as separate digits. Also during this phase, internal organs appear and begin to develop.

Development of the fetus.   The period of the **fetus** lasts from week 9 until birth. During this period, the developing being grows rapidly, receiving finishing touches that will permit life outside the womb (see Figure 4-8). The many organs and structures that were initiated earlier are now expanded, and they become coordinated with other systems in the body. The fetus's body is elaborated through a series of specific changes:

- *Third month*. The head is large in comparison to the rest of the body but now slows down in rate of growth. The eyes move to their proper places, and the fetus becomes increasingly human looking. The external genitalia grow. The fetus begins to show reflexes and muscular movement, but shifts in position are small and not yet felt by the mother.

fetus
During prenatal week 9 until birth, the developing being that is growing in size and weight and in sensory abilities, brain structures, and organs needed for survival.

- *Fourth month.* The fetus grows rapidly in length (height). Weight increases slowly. Hair grows on the head and eyebrows. Eye movements occur.
- *Fifth month.* The fetus continues to grow rapidly in length. Fine hair covers the body, and a greasy substance protects the fetus's delicate skin. The mother can usually feel the fetus's movement by now.
- *Sixth month.* The fetus has red, wrinkled skin and a body that is lean but gaining weight. Fingernails are present. The respiratory system and central nervous system are still developing and coordinating their operations.
- *Seventh month.* Eyes open and eyelashes are present. Toenails grow. The body begins to fill out. The brain has developed sufficiently to support breathing.
- *Eighth month.* Skin is pink and smooth. Fat grows under the skin. The testes (in males) descend. (K. L. Moore & Persaud, 2008; Sadler, 2006)

During the final months of prenatal development, the fetus is refining its basic body structures and also gaining weight, slowly at first and more steadily as birth approaches. On average, the fetus at 6 months weighs approximately 1 pound, 13 ounces; at 7 months, 2 pounds, 14 ounces; and at 8 months, 4 pounds, 10 ounces (K. L. Moore & Persaud, 2008). Birth weights vary, of course, but on average, the newborn infant weighs 7 pounds, 8 ounces. These last few weeks of weight gain increase the chances of an infant's survival after birth. In fact, infants rarely survive when they are born before they have progressed through at least 5½ half months of prenatal development or weigh less than 1 pound, 2 ounces. (We examine the health and treatment of early and small infants later in this chapter.)

The brain also expands and matures during the final weeks and months of prenatal growth. Structurally, the outer layers of the brain (those closest to the skull) bunch up and form folds and creases, creating a staggering number of potential circuits for transmitting information. Functionally, the fetus's brain is being prepared to carry out vital reflexes, such as sucking, swallowing, and looking away from bright lights. In the weeks before birth, the fetus's brain also activates circuits for sensing stimulation, including sounds and visual patterns. In one study, pregnant mothers who were a few days before their deliveries were randomly assigned to one of two treatments, music-exposure and non-music-exposure conditions (James, Spencer, & Stepsis, 2002). Both groups of mothers had earphones placed on their abdomens. In the music-exposure condition, a single song, "Little Brown Jug," was played repeatedly over a 4-hour period. In the non-music-exposure group, no sound was emitted from the earphones. Compared to fetuses not exposed to the music, fetuses exposed to the song showed more fluctuations in their heart rates, indicating that, in some primitive way, they were attending to the music. Remarkably, the researchers also found evidence that the infants retained their memory of the music. After birth, both the music-exposed and nonexposed fetuses (now infants) listened for a half hour as the "Little Brown Jug" played repeatedly in their earphones. Compared to the infants who had not previously been exposed to this music, infants who were exposed prior to birth were more likely to stay awake longer and to fluctuate in heart rate during the hour after music exposure.

In another investigation, fetuses learned to recognize some flavors, presumably because substances from the mother's diet are transmitted into the womb's fluid and swallowed by the fetus (Mennella, Jagnow, & Beauchamp, 2001). Studies such as these suggest that rudimentary abilities to learn and remember simple patterns are present before birth. As you will see in later chapters, these initial learning abilities continue to evolve in important ways over the course of childhood and adolescence.

In summary, the formation of a human life is the outcome of countless changes. The body grows step by step, carefully managed by nature, constantly drawing from nurture. In spectacular feats of coordination, new cells extend body parts so that these structures become increasingly defined—for example, simple paddles turn into elongated arms, arms add hands, and eventually hands add fingers. Prenatal development and genetic expression show a wonderful balance between nature and nurture, universality and diversity, and qualitative and quantitative change, as you can see in the Basic Developmental Issues table "Biological Beginnings" on the following page.

Basic Developmental Issues

Biological Beginnings

Issue	Genetic Foundations	Prenatal Development
Nature and Nurture	Nature forms gametes (sperm and ovum) and fuses them to form a future child with a genetic makeup that becomes a permanent, influential agent of change for the child. Nurture is evident in environmental effects on the parents' chromosomes, as can occur when radiation and illness create errors in reproductive cells. During and after prenatal development, nature and nurture work in concert: Genes do their work in the context of the offspring's physiology, nutrition, and experience.	Nature and nurture are closely intertwined during the baby-to-be's prenatal development. The effects of nature are evident in predictable, ordered changes to body structures and in the formation and operation of supporting physical structures, such as the placenta, that make growth possible. The effects of nurture are seen with nutrition, protection from harmful substances, and the mother's stress management.
Universality and Diversity	The vast majority of children are born with 46 chromosomes. Most genes take the form of uniform instructions for necessary proteins to build human bodies and brains. Some genes vary systematically across children and permit individual differences in height, weight, physical appearance, motor skills, intellectual abilities, and temperament. Errors in chromosomes and genes are another source of diversity.	In healthy prenatal beings, there is considerable universality in the sequence of changes. The small being proceeds through phases of the zygote, embryo, and fetus, and ultimately is born after approximately 9 months. Diversity occurs because of variations in mothers' health, exposure to harmful substances, genetic vulnerabilities of the fetus, and the efficiency with which physical structures in the womb sustain life.
Qualitative and Quantitative Change	Qualitative changes are made possible by the careful sequence with which particular genes are triggered into action. At appropriate times, selected genes are activated and create qualitative changes in the child's body, such as growth in particular areas of the body and the transformations of puberty. When genes direct the body to mature and grow larger, they also permit quantitative changes, such as increases in height and weight.	The future baby undergoes a series of predictable qualitative transformations: The zygote moves through the fallopian tubes, grows new cells, and burrows into the inside wall of the uterus; the embryo creates many new cells, which form the basic organs and structures of the body; and the fetus builds and refines these preliminary structures, activating physiological processes needed for survival. Quantitative changes are present in the rapid production of new cells, particularly in the brain and body prior to birth.

Medical Care

Prospective parents invariably hope for healthy children. To enhance their chances of giving birth to strong, well-formed infants, prospective mothers can seek medical care before getting pregnant. When they do become pregnant, women can shield their developing offspring from harmful substances and obtain ongoing medical care.

Preparing for pregnancy. A woman can increase her chances of having a healthy infant by caring for herself *before* becoming pregnant. Physicians and nurses advised of a woman's wish for a child may suggest that she watch her diet, take approved vitamin supplements, exercise moderately, and avoid alcohol and drugs. They may also ask her about her prescriptions and over-the-counter medicines, because some can be harmful to fetuses. For example, the antianxiety drug diazepam (Valium) increases the chances the offspring will develop a cleft lip, and the acne medication isotretinoin (Accutane) in some cases appears to cause serious malformations in offspring (M. R. Davidson, London, & Ladewig, 2008; Sadler, 2006). Obviously, these and other potentially dangerous substances are not recommended for women who are pregnant or likely to conceive. Medical personnel may also address particular health problems that can be activated or complicated by pregnancy, such as hypertension or diabetes. Finally, a physician or nurse may discuss any concerns that the woman has about her age. Pregnant women under age 17 sometimes have poor nutrition and give birth to infants with low birth weight. Advanced age in mothers and fathers (35 or older for mothers, 40 or older for fathers) is associated with slightly elevated risks for genetic problems, and older mothers are at minor risk for complications during the pregnancy and giving birth to a baby with physical malformations (M. R. Davidson et al., 2008).

Yet the responsibility for avoiding toxic substances must not rest entirely on mothers-to-be. Prospective fathers, too, should take precautions in the days, weeks, and months before conceiving a child. Evidence is growing that men's exposure to mercury, lead, alcohol, cigarettes, and other substances is associated with miscarriage (spontaneous loss of the offspring), low birth weight, and birth defects in their offspring (Sadler, 2006).

A man and woman concerned about conceiving a child with significant birth defects may consult a genetic counselor. Prospective parents are most likely to work with a genetic counselor when they have had several miscarriages, have given birth to a child with a genetic defect or chromosomal abnormality, or are aware of family history of a genetic disorder, mental retardation, or birth defects (Meyerstein, 2001). The genetic counselor examines the family's medical records, other pertinent records, and information the couple provides about the health of siblings, parents, and other biological relatives. Diagnostic tests may be conducted, including an analysis of the potential parents' chromosomes. Genetic counselors inform the couple of medical facts, inheritance patterns, estimated risks for having a child with a birth defect or disorder, ways to deal with risks, and health-care and reproductive options. Counselors may recommend that prenatal diagnostic tests be conducted during a pregnancy. Genetic counselors also provide supportive counseling and make appropriate referrals to mental health professionals.

To protect their children, pregnant women can eat healthfully, see their doctor, reduce their stress, and avoid potentially harmful substances, such as alcohol and cigarettes.

Avoiding harmful substances. During prenatal development, some babies-to-be are unfortunately exposed to potentially harmful substances, or **teratogens.** Examples of teratogens include many prescription and nonprescription drugs; alcohol; infectious agents such as rubella, syphilis, and human immunodeficiency virus (HIV); and dangerous environmental chemicals, such as lead and polychlorinated biphenyls (K. L. Moore & Persaud, 2008).

Prenatal development includes a series of *sensitive periods* for forming physical structures. These physical structures are most vulnerable to teratogens when the structures are first emerging, growing speedily, and laying the foundation on which more refined extensions must build. Thus the timing of exposure to teratogens partly determines their impact on the developing being (see Figure 4-9). For example, a newly formed *zygote* has not yet begun to form separate body parts and tends not to sustain structural defects when exposed to teratogens. Occasionally, exposure to teratogens can cause death of the zygote, but more often a few cells will die or become damaged, and these cells will be replaced with healthy cells (K. L. Moore & Persaud, 2008). During the *embryonic period,* however, damage can be serious. The principal structures of the body, including the limbs and the internal organs, are formed during the period of the embryo, and exposure to drugs, alcohol, and other teratogens can cause major structural problems. For example, limbs are particularly sensitive to harm 24 to 36 days after conception (K. L. Moore & Persaud, 2008). Keep in mind that during this early, critical phase of the pregnancy, women may not yet know they are pregnant. Finally, growth during the *fetal period* is less susceptible to serious structural damage, although there are some exceptions: Notably, the brain continues to grow until (and after) birth and, as a result, the fetus's brain can be damaged late in pregnancy.

The genetic makeup of both mother and baby moderates the effects of teratogens. For example, phenytoin (Dilantin) is an anticonvulsant medication prescribed for some people who have epilepsy. Between 5 and 10 percent of children exposed to phenytoin as embryos develop a small brain, mental retardation, wide spaces between eyes, a short nose, and other distinctive facial features (K. L. Moore & Persaud, 2008). About a third of exposed embryos show minor congenital problems, and half are unaffected. Presumably, genetic factors are partly responsible for these different outcomes.

The amount of teratogen exposure is also important: The greater the exposure, the more severe and widespread the effects. Clearly, women who are pregnant must exercise caution

teratogen
Potentially harmful substance that can cause damaging effects during prenatal development.

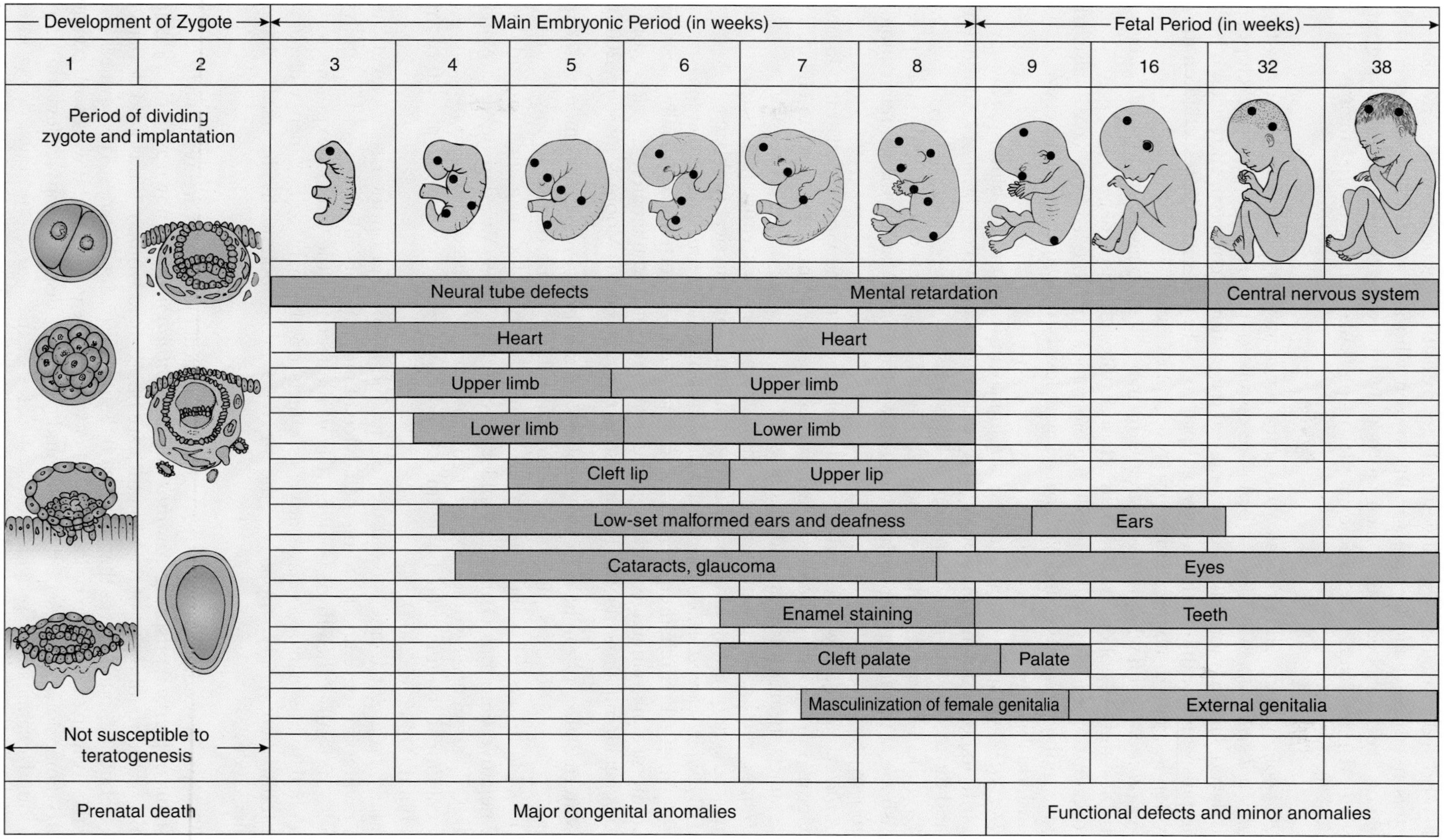

Figure 4-9

Sensitive periods in prenatal development. The effects of teratogens depend in part on timing of exposure. Black dots indicate sites that are growing rapidly and are particularly susceptible to damage from teratogens. Purple rows indicate highly sensitive periods for physical structures. Green rows indicate less sensitive periods for structures.

Adapted from *Before We Are Born: Essentials of Embryology and Birth Defects*, 7th edition, by K. L. Moore & T. V. N. Persaud, p. 313, copyright © 2008, with permission from Elsevier.

in the food and substances they ingest and the toxins they encounter in the environment. In fact, this need for caution extends to all women who are sexually active and capable of becoming pregnant, because women are not always aware that they are carrying rapidly growing offspring. Here are some examples of particular teratogens and their potential effects on offspring:

- *Alcohol.* Women who drink alcohol during pregnancy can give birth to infants with *fetal alcohol syndrome.* Cells in the brain are disrupted, physical and motor development is delayed, facial abnormalities occur, mental retardation is common, and children become impulsive and exhibit other behavioral problems. In less severe cases, children may develop learning disabilities or minor physical problems.
- *Nicotine.* Women who smoke cigarettes are more likely to give birth to small, lightweight babies and (less often) to lose their offspring through miscarriage.
- *Cocaine.* Women using cocaine during pregnancy are more likely to have a miscarriage; give birth prematurely; and have babies with low birth weight, small head size, lethargy, and irritability.
- *Heroin.* Pregnant women who use heroin may miscarry or give birth prematurely. After birth, exposed infants may be irritable, suffer respiratory complications, and even die, and those who survive may have a small head size.
- *Organic mercury.* Pregnant women who ingest high levels of mercury from diets rich in fish are at risk for giving birth to children with abnormal brains, mental retardation, and motor problems.
- *Rubella.* Pregnant women who become infected with the virus rubella (also known as German or three-day measles) early in their pregnancy may give birth to children with cataracts, heart problems, and deafness.
- *Herpes simplex.* Pregnant women with the herpes simplex virus are at risk for having a miscarriage or giving birth prematurely to infants with physical problems.
- *HIV infection and AIDS.* Pregnant women with the HIV virus are at risk for passing on the virus to their children, and children who become infected may initially show delays in motor skills, language, and cognitive development, and ultimately develop more serious health impairments. (M. R. Davidson et al., 2008; K. L. Moore & Persaud, 2008)

Maternal anxiety can also create problems for the fetus. Pregnant women who experience high levels of stress place their infants at risk for being born with low birth weight and irritable dispositions and, later in life, with difficulty in focusing attention and dealing with negative emotions (Huizink, Mulder, & Buitelaar, 2004; Van den Bergh & Marcoen, 2004). Of course, most women experience some level of stress during their pregnancy, and mild emotional strain is probably harmless and may even help stimulate growth of the fetus's brain (DiPietro, 2004).

Many pregnant women avoid teratogens and keep a lid on their stress levels, using their own good sense and heeding the advice of medical personnel, concerned family and friends, and public health campaigns. Given the fact that the father's exposure to environmental toxins can also have adverse effects on the baby-to-be, men will also undoubtedly increasingly appreciate the need to avoid potentially harmful substances (Sadler, 2006).

Implementing medical procedures.   Several medical procedures are available to check on the status of prenatal offspring. An *ultrasound examination* (also known as ultrasonography) has become a routine part of the obstetric care of pregnant women. Ultrasound devices emit high-frequency sound waves that bounce off tissues of varying densities. The device is passed over the woman's abdomen or inserted in her vagina. The echoes to the waves are converted to two-dimensional images of the fetus, and these are displayed on a television monitor. Ultrasound examinations provide good estimates of the age of the fetus, detect multiple fetuses, and reveal some major abnormalities (London, Ladewig, Ball, & Bindler, 2007; K. L. Moore & Persaud, 2008). Ultrasounds are also used as anatomical guides during the implementation of other prenatal tests. Finally, ultrasound examinations confirm the reality of the pregnancy for expectant parents, as you can see in the following exercise.

Interpreting Children's Artifacts and Reflections

My Baby Is Real!

One of the first artifacts of childhood is often available before birth: images of fetuses produced during ultrasound examinations. As you read the following reflections of six parents, identify their feelings about these images and any apprehension they had about the results of the examination.

1. Yes, when (she) got pregnant I didn't really understand it. But after we had the ultrasound I did. . . . It was the most exciting thing I have done as far as the baby is concerned. It was more exciting than when I heard that we were going to have a baby. (a father; Ekelin, Crang-Svalenius, & Dykes, 2004, p. 337)[a]
2. That you can see so much! Awesome. Small, small fingers and everything looked perfect. And just everything works. There is a little heart beating and you can see so much even if the baby is only 18 cm (long). That there actually is something so almost completely developed it just has to grow. That such good technology exists—it's unbelievable . . . they can see so much. (a mother; p. 339)
3. And it became so very alive and I felt very close to the baby. Yes, it felt like a fine moment, it was a very philosophic . . . emotional moment . . . it felt very good. (a father; p. 339)
4. This is definitely one of the top ten on the list of fantastic memories in my life I think. I really believe that. It is really completely fantastic. It's really a big thing I think. (a father; p. 340)
5. . . . all I can say is that even if there should be some fault, if an arm or leg was missing I would never for my life be able to take it away. And even if it had Down's syndrome or something like that I would never manage to have an abortion. Never in my life. (a mother; p. 339)

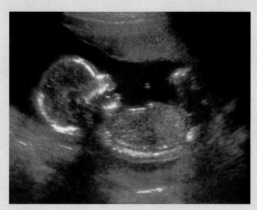

Seeing an ultrasound image of their developing baby can be a memorable experience for expectant parents.

6. I hadn't thought much about it. But it was there a little, little bit. We know a couple whose first child had spina bifida so they chose not to have that baby. So there is that possibility but it feels very far away for some reason. It won't affect us. The power of life makes one just believe that everything will be fine. (a father; p. 338)

[a]Excerpts reprinted from *Midwifery, 20*, M. Ekelin, E. Crang-Svalenius, & A. K. Dykes, "A Qualitative Study of Mothers' and Fathers' Experiences of Routine Ultrasound Examination in Sweden," pp. 335–344, copyright © 2004, with permission from Elsevier.

Ultrasound examinations provoked many strong feelings in the prospective parents quoted in the exercise. Several parents (quotes 1–4) expressed an overriding sense of joy upon receiving confirmation that their offspring were well formed and recognizably human. Two parents (quotes 5 and 6) were somewhat apprehensive as they contemplated the problems their children potentially could face. If the ultrasound had uncovered physical problems, the medical staff would likely have advised parents about diagnostic medical tests.

Several prenatal diagnostic techniques are generally implemented only with high-risk pregnancies. *Chorionic villus sampling* (CVS) is an invasive diagnostic procedure performed sometime between 10 and 12 weeks after conception (London et al., 2007). A needle is inserted into the woman's abdomen, or a tube is guided through her cervix (see the left side of Figure 4-10), and tiny amounts of chorionic villi (blood vessels that grow on the membrane surrounding the developing embryo or fetus) are collected. Abnormalities detected by CVS include chromosomal abnormalities, X-chromosome-linked disorders such as Tay-Sachs disease, and some diseases of the blood, such as sickle cell disease. Test results are typically available within a few days. The procedure entails a small risk for damage to an arm or leg of the embryo or fetus, and miscarriage is possible but unlikely (Sadler, 2006).

Amniocentesis is an invasive diagnostic procedure performed sometime between 13 and 18 weeks after conception (K. L. Moore et al., 2000). A needle is inserted into the woman's abdomen to draw a small amount of fluid from the uterus (see the right side of Figure 4-10). The fluid is analyzed for high concentrations of a fetal protein, which are present when fetuses have *neural tube defects* and some abdominal problems (Sadler, 2006). Fetal cells floating in the amniotic fluid are also analyzed for possible chromosomal abnormalities. Other problems detected by amniocentesis are biochemical defects, prenatal infections, and blood diseases. Results from cell cultures usually take 2 to 4 weeks to analyze. Risks associated with amniocentesis are trauma to the fetus, infection, and miscarriage (fetal loss rates are 1 percent; Sadler, 2006).

Figure 4-10

Prenatal diagnostic methods. In both chorionic villus sampling (A) and amniocentesis (B), an ultrasound procedure guides the test.

Based on K. L. Moore et al., 2000.

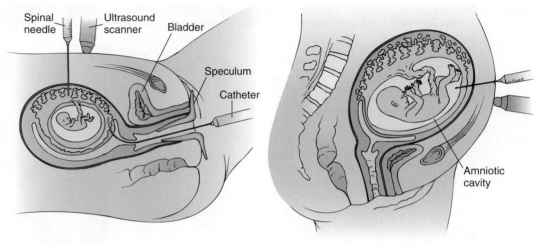

A. Chorionic villus sampling with a 7-week-old embryo

B. Amniocentesis with a 13-week-old fetus

Other tests are performed occasionally. For example, the mother's blood can be tested for the presence of fetal cells. Normally, not many fetal cells cross the placenta into the mother's circulation, but some do, and the mother's blood can be tested for high rates of fetal protein, which might indicate a neural tube defect in the fetus. In consultation with the mother, a physician may also use a *fetoscope,* an instrument with a tiny camera and light, to examine the fetus for defective limbs or other deformities. Corrective surgery is performed in rare circumstances.

When couples learn that their offspring has a chromosomal abnormality or other serious defect, they may be shocked initially and subsequently seek support from counselors, medical personnel, and family and friends (Lalor & Begley, 2006). Depending on their values and circumstances, some couples choose to terminate the pregnancy, concerned that they will not be able to care adequately for a child with special needs. Other couples want practical tips and emotional support in preparing for the birth of a child with a disability, believing in the fetus's right to life and their ability to be caring parents for the child.

Supporting Parents, Protecting Babies

If you have the opportunity to work with prospective parents, you can educate them about prenatal development and their future child's need for protection. Here are some specific tactics to take:

- *Encourage women to review their health before becoming pregnant.* Women who are planning a pregnancy or capable of becoming pregnant should consult their physician. In particular, women who take over-the-counter or prescription medications need to talk with their doctor about risks for a pregnancy and alternative ways of managing chronic conditions.

- *Remind sexually active women and men to take care of themselves.* Women may be several weeks along (or longer) in a pregnancy before they become aware of it. Consequently, women who might be pregnant should watch their diet, restrict their exposure to teratogens such as alcohol, and avoid x-rays. Men may need to be advised that they, too, can put their future children at risk by exposing themselves to harmful substances.

- *Urge pregnant women to seek medical care.* Nurses and other medical personnel will examine risks, reassure prospective mothers, and treat ongoing medical conditions safely. Under the guidance of a doctor, pregnant women often follow an exercise program. Getting regular exercise can help pregnant women keep up their stamina, prepare for birth, and ease stress. Pregnant women should also be encouraged to follow a diet that supports their own health as well as the nutritional needs of their fetus. Getting adequate rest is another important goal for pregnant women, even though doing so is not always possible, especially when they have other children, jobs, and ongoing household responsibilities.

- *Use well-researched strategies when trying to reach women who are at risk for late or no prenatal care.* Some pregnant women who are immigrants or adolescents, mentally ill, or inclined to abuse illegal substances are reluctant to seek medical care (P. A. Doyle et al., 2006). Yet prenatal care is necessary for all women in order to detect and treat problematic conditions in both mothers and offspring. For example, pregnant women with HIV can be treated with antiretroviral therapy, helping to control the infection and in many cases preventing transmission of the virus to their offspring. In addition, public health personnel can seek the advice of pregnant women in the local community for guidance about how best to convince *other* expectant mothers to get appropriate medical and nutritional care. Effective recruitment strategies can take a variety of forms, including toll-free hotline numbers, radio spots, and posters in various public locations (P. A. Doyle et al, 2006).

- *Advise pregnant women from low-income backgrounds about nutritional resources.* Like all expectant mothers, pregnant women who are economically disadvantaged benefit from a healthful diet. Yet low-income women may not be aware of free nutritious food in their community. For example, the federal Special Supplemental Nutrition Program for Women, Infants, and Children (WIC) offers supplemental foods with nutrients that are often lacking in the diets of low-income populations (e.g., protein, iron, calcium, and vitamins A and C), yet are vital for healthy prenatal development (U.S. Department of Agriculture Food and Nutrition Service, 2008).

- *Urge pregnant women to stay clear of teratogens.* Smokers can be encouraged to reduce the number of cigarettes they smoke or, better yet, to quit smoking altogether. For example, 20-year-old Veronica, first-time mother and smoker since the age of 13, was concerned that her smoking would harm her baby and decided to phase out cigarette smoking one cigarette at a time, until the fourth month of her pregnancy, when she quit altogether and commented, "I have done what I can, now the rest is up to God" (Nichter et al., 2007, p. 754). Expectant women who drink alcohol or take drugs need to be confronted with the dreadful and permanent damage these substances can cause in children. Obviously, pregnant women who are physiologically dependent on alcohol or drugs need immediate professional help.

- *Encourage pregnant women to relax.* Women who seem particularly anxious during pregnancy may benefit from help in dealing with stress. They can try relaxation techniques and consult with medical personnel or mental health professionals.

- *Ask pregnant women to speak their minds.* Many pregnant women have experiences they want to share. For example, they may have concerns about possible birth defects or simply want to communicate excitement, for instance, when they first feel the fetus stir within them. Many women appreciate sympathetic listeners who let them talk about their changing and sometimes conflicting feelings.

- *Ask fathers to talk about their experiences.* Many fathers are mystified with the physical changes their partners undergo during pregnancy. Some fathers feel excluded during pregnancy—although they had an obvious hand in creating the new being, they may believe they are not needed for further development. In reality, fathers can play an enormously important role in supporting expectant mothers. And many prospective fathers gain just as much as mothers from having a sensitive listener with whom to share their worries and hopes related to the baby.

- *Advise new parents about appropriate care when children have been exposed to teratogens.* Sadly, the brains and bodies of some children are impaired due to prenatal exposure to drugs, alcohol, infection, and other teratogens. Some of these effects are lasting, but even so, affected children certainly benefit from responsive, predictable, and developmentally appropriate care. For example, many children who have been exposed to cocaine and other serious teratogens develop good language, communication, and interpersonal skills when they receive high-quality care (J. V. Brown, Bakeman, Coles, Platzman, & Lynch, 2004). Special educational services may likewise enhance the academic and social skills of teratogen-exposed children.

● *Intervene when mothers continue to use drugs and alcohol after the birth.* For their own sake and that of their children, women who continue to abuse substances after their babies are born need professional treatment. Many of these mothers also need guidance with parenting skills (J. V. Brown et al., 2004; M. R. Davidson et al., 2008). Community counselors and family educators can advise families about helpful programs in their area.

Unlike many other developmental accomplishments, such as learning to talk, walk, and ride a bicycle, most aspects of prenatal development cannot be observed directly. Nonetheless, scientific evidence provides accurate benchmarks as to what is happening to the baby-to-be during the various phases of growth. In addition, as the pregnancy proceeds, there are some observable changes in mothers and fetuses. The Developmental Trends table "Prenatal Development" provides a useful synopsis of key prenatal developments and observable signs of growth.

After many months of pregnancy, most prospective parents are eager to meet their son or daughter, face-to-face. It is time for birth.

Developmental Trends

Prenatal Development

Phase of Prenatal Growth	What You Might Observe	Diversity	Implications
Zygote (Conception to 2 Weeks After)	· The zygote begins to develop at conception, after the fusing of sperm and ovum. The being's first cell divides into two cells, two divide into four, four divide into eight, and so forth. The zygote is a ball of cells as it travels down the fallopian tube and into the uterus. · No signs of pregnancy are noticeable to the prospective mother.	· Couples vary in their chances of conceiving a child. · Some children are conceived with the assistance of reproductive technologies. · A large number of zygotes perish because errors in chromosomes cause them to be seriously malformed and unable to grow. · Hormonal factors in the woman can also cause loss of zygotes.	· Encourage prospective parents to plan for a pregnancy by first taking stock of their health, talking with a physician, and, if they have concerns about potential genetic problems in their children, seeing a genetic counselor. · Persuade prospective parents to follow a physician's recommendations regarding appropriate uses of prescription medications, over-the-counter drugs, and vitamins. · Persuade sexually active women to avoid alcohol and drugs.
Embryo (2 Through 8 Weeks After Conception)	· Body parts and organs are being formed as the embryo rapidly develops. At the end of the period, the little being shows a head structure and limbs that are recognizably human. · The prospective mother may notice that her menstrual period is late. She may experience early signs of pregnancy, such as nausea, fatigue, a sense of abdominal swelling, and tender breasts.	· The embryo is especially susceptible to damage from harmful substances. The extent of harm done to the embryo by teratogens will depend on the timing and duration of exposure, the amount of the dose, and the biological vulnerability of the embryo. · Miscarriage is fairly common during this period.	· Encourage a prospective mother to see a physician if she believes she might be pregnant. · Encourage pregnant women to shield themselves from potentially harmful substances. Educate prospective mothers and fathers about the impact of teratogens on the developing embryo.
Fetus (9 Weeks After Conception Until Birth)	· Organs and body parts continue to grow and mature. · The mother can feel the fetus moving, lightly at first and actively over time. · The mother's abdomen swells, and the mother gains weight.	· Many pregnant women feel strong and healthy during the final months of pregnancy, but some continue to experience nausea and fatigue. · Fetuses vary in many respects, including their movements, growth rates and birth weights, and readiness for survival at birth.	· Advise pregnant women to follow the advice of their physician regarding diet and exercise. · Listen to prospective mothers and fathers talk about their hopes, fears, and expectations related to the baby. · Continue to advocate for abstinence from alcohol and drugs; discourage cigarette smoking. · Encourage pregnant women to manage their stress levels. · Tell pregnant women about prepared childbirth classes in their area.

Source: K. L. Moore & Persaud, 2008.

Birth of the Baby

The events leading up to and culminating in a human childbirth provoke a range of feelings in parents—excitement, fear, pain, fatigue, and joy, to name a few. These events are managed best when families prepare ahead of time, take advantage of adequate medical care, and hold reasonable expectations about the baby's abilities and needs.

Preparation for Birth

Although some anxiety is common, parents are highly individual in their feelings about pregnancy and birth. For example, a first-time mother may be eager to have her baby but anxious about the financial expenses that go along with raising a child. A couple may be worried about the birth, having previously suffered several miscarriages. Another couple with a strained relationship may have mixed feelings about raising a child together. Such feelings, along with lack of confidence in controlling pain, may influence the actual birth experience (Soet, Brack, & DiIorio, 2003). Excessive levels of stress make for an unpleasant experience for parents and can prolong the early stages of labor, raise the mother's blood pressure, and decrease oxygen to the baby. Parents can reduce their anxiety by seeking out information, getting organized for the baby, and preparing other children in their family for the new arrival.

Health-care providers and family educators can give useful information and reassurance to parents during the pregnancy. For example, they may teach relaxation techniques; offer tips for posture, movement, and exercise; and persuade women to eliminate potentially risky behaviors, such as drinking alcohol and smoking cigarettes. *Prepared childbirth classes* also are potentially helpful. These programs emphasize the natural aspects of birth and the woman's control over the process. They typically include the following elements:

- Information about changes in, and nutritional needs of, the prospective baby
- Preparation for the baby's arrival, including arrangements for the baby at home and decisions about breast or bottle feeding
- Relaxation and breathing techniques that encourage the mother to stay focused, manage pain, reduce fear, and use muscles effectively during the various phases of the labor
- Support from a spouse, partner, friend, or family member who coaches the mother throughout labor and delivery, reminds her to use the breathing techniques she has learned, massages her, and otherwise encourages her
- Education about the physiology and mechanics of delivery, types of positions during delivery, and pain medications and other medical interventions used with some women (M. R. Davidson et al., 2008; Dick-Read, 1944; Lamaze, 1958)

The pregnant woman and her partner, if she has one, may also prepare for birth by deciding where it will occur and who will attend to it. Hospitals offer the latest technology, well-trained medical staff, arrangements for insurance coverage, and pain medication, but they have disadvantages. As occurred with Laurie and Tom in our introductory case study, some parents perceive hospitals as instituting unnecessary and invasive treatments and as creating an impersonal climate that separates rather than unites family members during a momentous occasion. Community birth centers are homelike, inexpensive, and welcoming of extended contact with the newborn; however, they are less appropriate for women with high-risk deliveries, those who need emergency care, and those whose insurance does not cover costs. Home settings offer families a familiar and comforting environment, allow family members to participate, are inexpensive, and give extended contact with the newborn. They have disadvantages similar to those of community birth centers and in many cases offer no pain medication, few emergency procedures, and minimal access to trained birth attendants (Sherwen, Scoloveno, & Weingarten, 1999). Hospitals have responded to concerns about their lack of family orientation by creating birthing rooms that are attractive, comfortable, and large enough to accommodate several family members. In North America, physicians most often deliver babies, but other common attendants include certified nurse midwives, certified midwives who are not nurses, and lay midwives without formal training (Sherwen et al., 1999).

In addition to and sometimes instead of seeking conventional medical treatment, many women avail themselves of nontraditional therapies during pregnancy and childbirth

(M. R. Davidson et al., 2008). For example, some women obtain *acupuncture,* a treatment of traditional Chinese medicine in which thin stainless steel needles stimulate precise locations on the body so as to relieve pain and promote wellness. Other women choose *biofeedback,* a method for controlling muscle tension and other basic physiological reactions, or *self-hypnosis,* a self-induced state of relaxation and receptivity to suggestions about reducing pain and anxiety. Many women derive enhanced well-being from *prayer,* during which they address (silently or vocally) the divine being of their faith, or from *meditation,* a quiet transcendent state when the mind is still, peaceful, and uncluttered. Other common complementary and alternative therapies include *massage therapy,* relaxing manipulation of the body's soft tissues to reduce tension and promote comfort, and *hatha yoga,* an Eastern practice of gentle exercises and breathing techniques. Overall, nontraditional therapies offer the advantages of being relatively low in cost, emphasizing wellness, and being noninvasive (M. R. Davidson et al., 2008). Unfortunately, however, some women pass up lifesaving medical treatments in favor of alternative therapies that have undocumented effects.

The Birth Process

Amazingly, medical researchers are still not able to pinpoint the cascade of changes necessary to trigger the uterine contractions that begin a woman's labor (M. R. Davidson et al., 2008). Presently, medical researchers believe that a combination of factors precipitates labor, including hormonal changes in the mother's body and maturation of the fetus's body.

Typically, the mother's uterus begins preparations for birth 38 to 40 weeks into the pregnancy. Here is the incredible sequence of events that constitutes the birth process:

- As the pregnancy advances, the mother experiences *Braxton Hicks contractions.* These irregular contractions exercise the mother's uterine muscles without causing the cervix to open.
- In most cases (95%), the baby settles in a head-downward position, which facilitates its passage through the birth canal. When babies are in breech position (positioned to come out buttocks or legs first) or in a sideways position (a shoulder would likely come out first), the mother is monitored closely and often undergoes a cesarean delivery.
- A few events may occur in the days immediately before labor begins. The mother may experience a descent of the baby into the pelvis, feel a rush of energy, lose 1 to 4 pounds as her hormonal balance changes, and notice vaginal secretions. Sleep is difficult at this time. Accordingly, health providers may help mothers use relaxation techniques and reassure them that sleep disturbances prior to labor do not usually interfere with its progression.
- In the *first stage of labor,* the mother experiences regular uterine contractions that widen the cervix opening (see Figure 4-11, picture A). These contractions last until the cervix is dilated to about 10 centimeters (approximately 4 inches). Mothers experience pain, especially in their pelvis and back. This first stage typically takes about 12 to 16 hours for mothers who are having their first baby and 6 to 8 hours for mothers who have previously delivered one or more babies. Medical personnel keep track of the cervix opening and monitor the fetal heartbeat. They may offer the mother pain medication and encourage her to walk around. At the beginning of the first stage of labor, contractions are spaced widely apart (e.g., every 15 to 30 minutes) and mild to moderate in intensity. When the cervix dilates to 3 centimeters, an "active" phase begins and lasts until full dilation. Contractions become stronger and longer (they last 30 to 60 seconds) and occur every 2 to 3 minutes.
- In the *second stage of labor,* the cervix is fully dilated, the baby proceeds down the birth canal, and the child is born (see Figure 4-11, pictures B, C, and D). This stage may take about half an hour, but in first pregnancies it often lasts up to 2 hours. Contractions come often and hard. They appear every other minute and last for a minute at a time. Mothers must push hard to help move the baby down and out. Medical personnel continue to watch the fetal heartbeat. The doctor may use forceps or call for a cesarean delivery if uterine contractions slow down or the baby does not move quickly enough. Too fast is not good either, however, because the pressure might tear mother's tissues or the baby's head. Thus, the doctor or midwife may place a hand on the part of the baby coming out and ease out the baby methodically. Medical personnel may also help rotate the baby's head so that it can get past the mother's pelvic bones. As the head comes out, the doctor or midwife checks to make sure the umbilical cord is not wrapped around the head, and if it is, the cord is

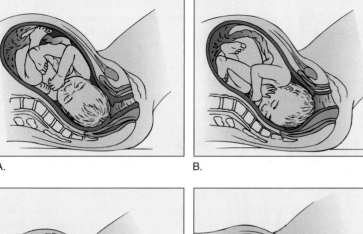
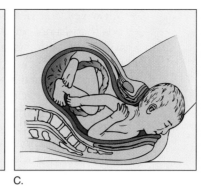

A.   B.   C.

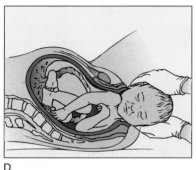
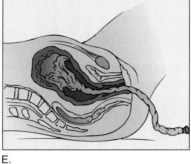

D.   E.

Figure 4-11

Stages of a normal birth. In the first stage of labor, the mother's cervix dilates (A). After numerous contractions the cervix opens completely, the baby's head moves down the vagina, and the second stage of labor begins (B). The second stage continues with the mother pushing with each contraction, the baby moving down the vagina, and the baby's head appearing (C). Gradually, the shoulders and rest of the body emerge (D). The third stage of labor is the delivery of the placenta (E).

Based on Demarest & Charon, 1996.

moved. The nose and mouth are cleansed of fluids. The mother continues to push to release the baby's shoulders and the rest of the body. The baby is gently wiped dry, and after the blood has drained from the umbilical cord into the baby's body, the cord is clamped and cut. The baby is born! The baby is placed on the mother, and the father or other coach may take a turn holding him or her. Oftentimes the baby is alert and looks around the room—a stunning and memorable event for parents and other family members.

- In the *third stage of labor,* the placenta and fetal membranes (collectively known as the *afterbirth*) are expelled by the uterus (see Figure 4-11, picture E). Usually, this process happens naturally and without assistance, although medical personnel must watch to make sure it happens. The mother is checked to see if lacerations have occurred or if medical treatment is needed.

- In the *fourth stage of labor,* 1 to 4 hours after birth, the mother's body begins to readjust after its considerable exertion. Having lost some blood, the mother may experience a slight decrease in blood pressure, shake and feel chilled, and want to eat and drink water (M. R. Davidson et al., 2008; Demarest & Charon, 1996; Sherwen et al., 1999).

Medical Interventions

Medical personnel, midwives, and the mother's partner can do many things to comfort the mother as she goes through labor and delivery. Following are some examples of interventions that are typical in many Western societies (M. R. Davidson et al., 2008; Enkin et al., 2000; Sherwen et al., 1999):

- Physicians may *induce labor*—that is, start it artificially—with medications (e.g., Pitocin). Candidates for an induced labor include women past their due dates and those with diabetes or pregnancy-induced hypertension.

MyEducationLab

To observe the final moments of a normal birth and the extensive testing of the newborn that takes places immediately after birth, go to the Video Examples section in Chapter 4 of MyEducationLab.

Many parents feel an overwhelming sense of joy when their baby arrives.

- Midwives, coaches, and medical staff may help relieve the mother's pain by using methods that do not require medication. For example, some mothers are assisted by a warm whirlpool bath, visual images of the cervix opening, music, hypnosis, biofeedback, and massage.
- Physicians sometimes offer *analgesics,* medicines that reduce pain without loss of consciousness. Medications injected into the mother's spine (such as *epidural analgesia*) are an especially common method for labor relief. Generally, these medications are not offered early in labor, because they may slow progress, but also not too late, because physicians want the medicine to be metabolized (used and broken down in the body) by mother and baby prior to birth. Some analgesic medications can increase the need for other medical interventions, such as use of forceps and cesarean deliveries, and they may reduce breathing in the newborn.
- Physicians may offer *anesthetics* to women in active labor if extreme pressure must be applied (such as occurs in the use of forceps) or when a cesarean delivery must be performed. Anesthetics cause loss of sensation and in some cases also lead to loss of consciousness.
- Women sometimes take *opioids* (also known as narcotics), medicines that reduce the sensation of pain by changing the way it is perceived by the brain. Opioids have several disadvantages, including limited effectiveness in reducing pain, occasional side effects such as nausea and drowsiness, and tendency to adversely affect the baby's breathing and breastfeeding.
- During a *cesarean delivery,* the baby is removed surgically from an incision made in the mother's abdomen and uterine wall. Almost 30 percent of babies born in the United States are delivered through cesarean surgery, a rate that many people suggest is higher than it should be (Centers for Disease Control and Prevention, 2005d). Cesarean deliveries are performed when the physician believes the safety of the mother, child, or both is at stake. Examples of conditions that might lead to a cesarean delivery are fetal distress, health problems of the mother, failure to progress in labor, infections in the birth canal, and the presence of multiple babies.

Regardless of the specific medical treatments expectant mothers receive, mothers and their families invariably appreciate consideration of their individual needs and preferences. Nurses, midwives, and other attendants can be compassionate caregivers whose sympathetic reassurance helps women to cope with the pain and loss of control that accompanies the birthing process. Women by and large also appreciate the presence and support of their husbands, other partners, friends, or close family members during labor and delivery (S. Price, Noseworthy, & Thornton, 2007).

In addition, many medical personnel do their best to accommodate women's cultural practices related to birth. For example, some Hispanic women prefer to stay at home during early stages of labor, and when they do arrive at the hospital, they want their partners to remain at their side (Spector, 2004). Many Muslim women may be distressed when male doctors and nurses see them uncovered; thus medical personnel might take measures to ensure that these women are covered and accompanied by husbands during examinations (M. R. Davidson et al., 2008). Some Korean women remain silent during labor and delivery, and attendants must be alert to the fact that labor may be progressing without the women's vocalizations. Women from some cultural groups (e.g., some Native Americans and the Hmong from Laos) may ask to take the placenta home for burial in the ground because of their religious beliefs, and many attendants now honor this request (M. R. Davidson et al., 2008; Fadiman, 1997).

Babies at risk. Some babies are born before they are able to cope with the demands of life outside the womb. Two categories of babies require special care:

- ***Babies born early.*** The **premature infant** is born before the end of 37 weeks after conception (Sherwen et al., 1999). Premature labor may be triggered by several factors, including infection, presence of twins or triplets, abnormalities in the fetus, death of the fetus, abnormalities in the mother's uterus or cervix, and serious disease in the mother. Extremely early babies (born after only 32 or fewer weeks of prenatal growth) face serious risk factors, including higher than typical rates of death during infancy. Immediately after birth, premature infants are also at risk for health problems, including breathing problems, anemia, brain hemorrhages, feeding problems, and temperature instability.

MyEducationLab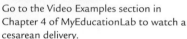

Go to the Video Examples section in Chapter 4 of MyEducationLab to watch a cesarean delivery.

MyEducationLab

Find out how mothers who have just given birth express their gratitude toward husbands and other companions at the birth by completing an Understanding Research exercise in Chapter 4's Activities and Applications section in MyEducationLab.

premature infant
Infant born early (before 37 weeks of prenatal growth) and sometimes with serious medical problems.

• ***Babies born small for date.*** Some infants are small and light given the amount of time they have had to develop in the mother's uterus. These babies are at risk for many problems, including neurological deficiencies, structural problems with body parts, breathing difficulties, vision problems, and other serious health problems (Sadler, 2006). These children may have chromosomal abnormalities, been exposed to infections or harmful substances, or received inadequate nutrition during their prenatal development.

Developmental care for babies at risk. Babies born especially early or small may not have the physical maturity to breathe independently, regulate their body's changes in temperature, or suck adequately to meet nutritional needs. Despite these challenges, babies can often survive with access to life-sustaining devices and medicines. Physicians and nurses also strive to create a therapeutic atmosphere that is nurturing and developmentally appropriate. The following guidelines are recommended for those who care for a fragile infant:

- Reduce the infant's exposure to light and noise.
- Regulate the amount of handling of the infant by medical staff.
- Position the baby to increase circulation.
- Encourage parents to participate in the care of the infant.
- Inform parents about the infant's needs.
- Arrange activities such as diapering and changing clothes so that interruptions to sleep and rest are minimized.
- Encourage parents to cuddle with the infant and carry him or her often and for long periods.
- Swaddle the baby in a blanket or with arms bent and hands placed near the mouth to permit sucking on fingers or hands.
- Massage the baby.
- Educate parents about caring for the child as he or she grows older. (Als et al., 1994; T. Field, 2001; Sherwen et al., 1999)

When fragile babies become strong enough to leave the hospital and go home with their families, they may need continued specialized treatments. Their families, as well, may benefit from support because these babies often show a lot of distress and are not easily soothed. If parents of premature and other health-impaired infants learn to fulfill infants' needs confidently and tenderly, however, these infants are likely to calm down and develop healthy habits for responding to distress (J. M. Young, Howell, & Hauser-Cram, 2005). Furthermore, fragile infants who repeatedly relax in the arms of their caregivers will have the chance to participate in nurturing interactions, form close bonds with caregivers, and gain needed mental energy for exploring the environment.

As with all children, the developmental journeys of premature and sick newborn infants are typically *not* destined to be rocky ones (Bronfenbrenner, 2005). In fact, many premature and small infants go on to catch up with peers in their motor, intellectual, and communication skills, particularly when families, educators, and other professionals meet their special needs (Sheffield, Stromswold, & Molnar, 2005). Others have intellectual delays or persisting medical problems, such as visual problems or asthma, and these children benefit from appropriate medical care, hope and advocacy from families, and educational services that help them progress academically and socially. As they grow older, these children may also require continued services, such as speech therapy and other individualized educational interventions (Sheffield et al., 2005). Without sensitive care and, if needed, effective intervention, some premature and low-birth-weight infants continue to be physically distressed and face later problems in coping with negative emotions and in learning at school (Nomura, Fifer, & Brooks-Gunn, 2005; Shenkin, Starr, & Deary, 2004).

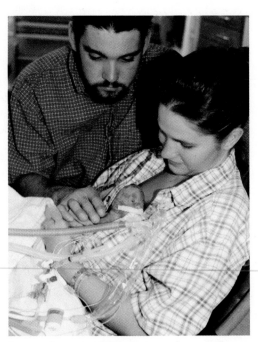

Responsive care of all infants, and especially fragile infants, entails careful consideration of their physical, social-emotional, and intellectual needs.

Responsive care of fragile and healthy infants alike entails careful consideration of infants' physical, social-emotional, and intellectual needs. In our final section in this chapter, we relay some ideas for helping caregivers identify and meet the psychological needs of these wondrous little people.

Development and Practice

Showing Sensitivity to the Needs of Newborn Infants

- **Carefully observe the sensory abilities of newborn infants.**

  A pediatric nurse watches a newborn infant scanning her parents' faces. The nurse explains to parents that infants have only limited visual acuity at birth, but they can see some shapes and patterns, are especially attracted to human faces, and develop better vision in their first few months.

- **Observe the physiological states of newborn infants.**

  A family educator talks with parents about their newborn infants, commenting that infants commonly sleep for long periods but usually have brief periods each day when they are receptive to gentle interaction.

- **Notice the kinds of stimuli that attract infants' attention.**

  A mother watches her newborn infant while he is awake and alert. She notices that her son intently observes her face and certain other stimuli, such as the edges of the bassinet.

- **Encourage parents to articulate their growing awareness of infants' preferences for being soothed.**

  A pediatrician asks a new mother how she is getting along with her baby. When the mother reports that the baby cries a lot, the doctor

  asks her about the kinds of attention the baby finds most comforting. The doctor also explains that most infants find it soothing to be held tenderly, but some infants also calm down while riding in a car or stroller. The doctor suggests that the mother keep informal records of the infant's fussy times and the kinds of care that eventually prove soothing.

- **Model sensitive care for new parents.**

  A family educator shows a new father how to hold the baby, change her diaper, and interact quietly and sensitively with her.

- **Offer appropriate care to fragile infants.**

  A hospital offers lifesaving care to fragile infants and attends to their sensory abilities and psychological needs by reducing light, noise, and unnecessary medical procedures, and massaging the infants a few times each day.

Enhancing Parents' Sensitivity to Newborn Infants

To give infants a healthy start on life, parents and other caregivers must recognize infants' abilities, interests, and styles of self-expression. Family educators and other professionals can support infants indirectly—yet powerfully—when they teach family members how to observe their infants closely and respond sympathetically to infants' individual needs. To get a sense of how you might enhance caregivers' awareness of infant needs, examine the illustrations in the Development and Practice feature "Showing Sensitivity to the Needs of Newborn Infants." Also consider these recommendations:

> • ***Reassure new mothers that they will be able to find the necessary energy and insight to take good care of their baby.*** Many new mothers return home from the hospital feeling tired, sore, and overwhelmed by the demands of an infant, as reflected in these comments:

- "I guess I expected that our lives would change dramatically the moment we walked in the door with him . . . which they did!"
- "It's hard, and sometimes I don't want the responsibility."
- "I felt very much like I didn't know what to do!"
- "Some people are giving too much advice."
- [The pain was] ". . . more than expected." (George, 2005, pp. 253–254)

These observations reveal the need for a series of adjustments by new mothers. Although many mothers may want information about infants and their care, they are best able to act on this information when they have caught up on their rest and feel supported by friends, family, and health-care professionals.

> • ***Share what you know about infants' sensory and perceptual abilities.*** Infants learn a lot about the world from their sensory and perceptual abilities. **Sensation** refers to the infant's detection of a stimulus; for example, a newborn baby may sense a father's stroking movements on her hand. Infants (and adults, for that matter) sense many things that they don't necessarily focus on or think about. When infants do attend to and interpret a sensation, **perception** takes place, such as when the baby, now 6 months old, watches a moving image and perceives it to be his father.

At birth, many newborn infants look intently at the faces of parents and others, giving people the impression that infants are learning from the beginning of life. In fact, they are.

sensation
Physiological detection of stimuli in the environment.

perception
Interpretation of stimuli that the body has sensed.

What newborn infants actually *perceive* cannot be determined with certainty, but researchers have established that newborn infants are able to *sense* basic patterns and associations. The majority of infants can see well-defined contrasts and shapes, such as large black-and-white designs on checkerboards, but it takes time for the various parts of the eye to work efficiently and to connect with brain structures necessary for making sense of visual stimuli. During the first year of life, vision improves dramatically. Infants can see best from a distance of about 6 to 12 inches, develop a preference for looking at faces, and are increasingly able to explore the visual properties of objects (Courage & Adams, 1990; D. L. Mayer & Dobson, 1982; van Hof-van Duin & Mohn, 1986). The sense of hearing is actually more advanced at birth than is vision. Recall that late in prenatal development, fetuses begin to hear and recognize repeated vocal and musical patterns. Typically developing infants are also born with the ability to experience touch, taste, and smell. Sensory and perceptual abilities continue to develop, and these abilities will, of course, make critical contributions to infants' subsequent learning about the world.

- ● *Point out the physiological states of newborn infants.* Unless they have previously had a child or been around newborn infants, parents may be surprised at how their infants act, how long they sleep, and how they respond to stimuli. Family educators and medical personnel can educate parents by explaining the nature of infants' **states of arousal,** the physiological conditions of sleepiness and wakefulness that infants experience throughout the day. Infant practitioners can also point out infants' **reflexes,** their automatic motor responses to stimuli. One example of a reflex is an infant blinking his eyes when his father moves him close to a bright light. Take a look at the Observation Guidelines table "Indicators of Health in Newborn Infants" on page 140 for the kinds of physical conditions you might explain to parents.

- ● *Encourage families to watch infants' responses to particular stimuli.* Infants give off clues about what they like and dislike, find interesting, and experience as pleasant or painful. However, it may take a while for caregivers to decipher infants' signals and the circumstances that elicit them. When infants are drowsy, asleep, or agitated, they tend not to show curiosity. When they are rested, comfortable, and awake, they may scan the visual environment, intently study the properties of objects, such as a mobile over the crib, and smile at familiar vocalizations from a parent. By observing the textures, tastes, sounds, and visual properties that attract infants' sustained attention, parents and other caregivers can guess about the concepts that infants are identifying. For instance, perhaps they are learning that the blanket feels soft, the juice tastes sweet, the melody is pleasing, and the rubber duck is attractive.

- ● *Ask families about the kinds of stimulation that infants find soothing.* Babies have distinct preferences for how they like to be comforted. For example, different babies may relax to varying sensations—listening to the rumble of the clothes dryer, nursing at Mother's breast, sleeping on Father's chest, or going for a ride in the car. Mothers and fathers who have not yet found the antidote to their infants' fussy periods may be grateful for suggestions from practitioners about a range of soothing techniques.

- ● *Model sensitive interactions with infants.* Not all caregivers are naturally inclined to interact in a gentle, reassuring manner with infants. Practitioners can show parents and other caregivers how to slow their pace, hold the baby gently but firmly, speak quietly, and watch for signs that the baby is ready to interact (e.g., the baby looks into caregivers' faces) or is distressed by the interaction (e.g., the baby looks away).

- ● *Show parents how to care for the baby.* First-time parents may appreciate some hands-on tips for administering to the physical needs of a new baby. Unless they have seen a baby being bathed, nursed, fed a bottle, diapered, or carried, new parents may not know how to perform these caretaking functions.

- ● *Offer early and continued support to parents of fragile infants.* Infants who are at risk for one reason or another—for example, those who are premature or have serious disabilities—can require unusually high vigilance from parents. Infants might cry often,

state of arousal
Physiological condition of sleepiness or wakefulness.

reflex
Automatic motor response to a particular kind of stimulus.

MyEducationLab

Go to the Video Examples section in Chapter 4 of MyEducationLab to watch a nurse shows a new mother how to hold her baby while breastfeeding.

Observation Guidelines

Indicators of Health in Newborn Infants

Characteristic	Look For	Example	Implication
Adjustment After Birth	· First breaths are taken within a half minute after birth (the doctor may suction fluid from the mouth and throat). · Attempts to nurse at the breast or suck on the nipple of a bottle occur within a few hours after birth (the baby may lose a few ounces of weight during the first few days). · First urination and bowel movements occur within first 2 days. · Head may be elongated after birth but gradually regains round appearance; skin may be scratched and contain discolored spots that disappear within a few days.	Immediately after birth, Trinisha begins crying. Her head is misshapen and she has some blotchy spots on her skin. Her mother places Trinisha on her chest, and the baby quiets down, opens her eyes, and scans the room.	Before birth, encourage parents to arrange for appropriate medical care for their newborn babies. After birth, reassure parents about the appearance of newborn infants.
States of Arousal	*Quiet sleep:* The infant lies still with closed eyelids and relaxed facial muscles. · *Active sleep:* Although the infant is sleeping, eyes may open and shut and move from side to side, facial expressions change and include grimaces, and breathing is irregular. · *Drowsiness:* The infant's eyelids may open and close without focus, and breathing is regular and rapid. · *Quiet alert:* The infant is awake, calm, happy, and engaged with the world. · *Active waking:* The infant wriggles and shows bursts of vigorous movements, breathing is irregular and skin is flushed, and the infant may moan or grunt. · *Crying:* The infant cries and thrashes, the face is flushed and distressed.	In the first few days after birth, baby Kyle spends most of his time sleeping. Some of his sleep appears peaceful, and at times he appears to be dreaming. When Kyle is awake, he sometimes looks intently at people and objects close to him. At other times he appears agitated, and these episodes tend to escalate into loud and persistent crying.	Help parents notice the distinct states of arousal that infants experience. Encourage them to develop a sensitive style of responding to infants' distress. Help parents recognize when infants are in the quiet, alert state, advising them that this is a good time to interact calmly with babies.
Reflexes	· *Rooting:* When touched near the corner of the mouth, the infant turns toward the stimulus, as if in search of breast or bottle. · *Sucking:* When a nipple or finger touches the infant's mouth, he or she begins to suck it. · *Grasping:* The infant grasps onto a finger or other small object placed in his or her hand. · *Moro reflex:* When startled, the infant stretches arms outward and then brings them together as in a hugging, embracing motion. · *Babinski reflex:* When the inner side of the infant's foot is rubbed from heel to toe, the infant's big toe moves upward and the other toes fan inward toward the bottom of the foot. · *Stepping:* When the baby is held upright under the arms with feet dangling and touching a hard surface, the legs take rhythmic steps. · *Tonic neck reflex:* If the infant is lying on his or her back and the head is moved toward one side, the arm on that side extends out and away from the body, and the other side is flexed close to the head with clenched fist (resembling a fencing position).	Little Josefina lies on her back on a blanket as her mother washes the dishes. When her mother accidentally drops and breaks a dish, Josefina appears alarmed, extends her arms, and seems to be grasping for something in midair.	Gently demonstrate infants' reflexes to family members. Family members, including the baby's siblings, may begin to use the grasping reflex as a way to interact with the baby. Explain that reflexes show that infants' brains and bodies are operating as they should.

Sources: C. W. Snow & McGaha, 2003; Wolff, 1966.

be difficult to console, or need an intensive course of treatment. Some infants with health problems may be sluggish and seek out little interaction from their parents. In such cases family members may have practical questions about optimal care for their children, and they may also benefit from counseling and other services.

Summary

Genetic Foundations of Child Development

All children have a set of genetic instructions that influence their characteristics at birth and the many physical features that emerge as they grow. Most of the genes that children inherit are ones they share with other children, giving them a common human heritage. Other genes contribute to children's individuality by disposing them to look and act in certain unique ways. Genes exert their effects on children through complex and interactive processes in cells and bodily systems; the effects of genes are mediated by children's health, other physiological processes, and children's experiences in particular environments. Teachers and other professionals can show that they value children's individual genetic profiles, such as their unique combinations of temperaments, physical features, and exceptional talents. Practitioners can also express their confidence that, whatever children's natural abilities, children have the potential to achieve high personal and academic standards.

Prenatal Development

At conception, the new being inherits a unique genetic makeup and begins the lifelong process of growing, changing, and interacting in and with the environment. Development begins at conception, when the *zygote,* a one-celled being, divides multiple times and becomes a ball of cells that burrows into the uterus. From weeks 2 through 8 after conception, the *embryo* grows rapidly, forming structures needed to sustain future growth and developing rudimentary organs and body parts. Between week 9 and birth, the *fetus* continues to grow quickly, now putting the finishing touches on the body and brain and becoming sufficiently heavy and strong to live in the outside world. Professionals can support healthy prenatal growth by informing prospective parents (and all sexually active women) about the damaging effects of teratogens to unborn children; the need to evaluate their health and medical regimens before a pregnancy; and the value of stress reduction, a healthful diet, appropriate exercise, and ongoing medical care during pregnancy.

Birth of the Baby

The birth of the baby is an exciting event for parents, who can ease their anxiety by preparing for childbirth. Birth is a multi-stage process that is often helped along by family members and professionals in the medical community, such as doctors, nurses, and midwives. The health and medical needs of newborn infants depend on their birth weight, size, prior exposure to teratogens, and genetic vulnerabilities. Family educators and other professionals can help parents develop realistic expectations about their newborn infants and respond sensitively to their physical and psychological needs.

Applying Concepts in Child Development

The exercises in this section will help you build your ability to use your knowledge of children's beginnings in your work with families and their offspring.

Case Study

Understanding Adam

Read the case and then answer the questions that follow it.

Michael Dorris adopted Adam at age 3. As a small child, Adam was sweet and affectionate but delayed in size and prone to seizures. Michael noticed intellectual delays but believed that Adam would catch up over time. When Adam was 5, Michael took a new job and enrolled his son in a child care center. Michael hoped that Adam's teachers would be able to teach Adam basic skills, such as using the toilet and tying his shoes, that so far had exceeded Adam's grasp.

In the excerpt that follows, Michael is beginning to come to grips with the full impact of Adam's disabilities:

> Every morning and late afternoon, as I drove him to and from his school, I talked a steady stream, pointing out interesting sights, asking about his activities, recounting tales of my adventures at work. At its midpoint our route traversed a railroad track, and this was the only thing on Adam's mind. He had noticed it shortly after we moved to the area and identified it with "The Little Engine That Could."
>
> "Choo choo train!" he sang the first time we rumbled over it, and I, delighted at this recognition, chimed in.

> "Choo choo!"
>
> That night, on the way home, he watched for the crossing and when it came in sight, he said, "Choo choo." He did the same the next morning and the next evening, and the next and the next. For the two years he attended his day care, he never once failed to chime it, but he rarely said anything else. I would be talking to him about all the positive features of dry pants—the trips we could take without diaper bags, the luxury of rash-free skin, the approval and celebration of children and adults alike—and in the middle of it he'd say "choo choo" and cut me off. I could be close to the punch line of a story—"Who's been sleeping in my bed and is *still in it?*"
>
> "Choo choo."
>
> At such times I might reply with an attitude that was annoyed and frustrated, or, alternatively cajoling and happy.
>
> "Choo choo," my five-year-old son would obstinately rejoin.
>
> . . . Adam always crossed those tracks in the same way, as if he had never done so before. . . . It was as if he were hanging from the rung of a ladder by his hands and refused to go forward, preferring to dangle in one spot until he dropped. He had grasped a single connection in the universe that resonated to him, and it was enough, it was sufficient, it obscured from his view everything behind it.

. . . [T]here was never more than a single, solitary thing on Adam's mind at any one time. Ideas did not compete for his attention; he was loyal, sticking with a fascination until he wore it out. . . .

. . . For years I assumed I was fighting the effects of his medication, battering the barriers of his late start, scaling self-protective walls erected against the neglect he experienced as an infant. It was not until the following summer, when Adam was still five years old, that I began to have an inkling that my real adversary was the lingering ghost of Adam's biological mother, already dead . . . of acute alcohol poisoning. (Dorris, 1989, pp. 43–45)[a]

· Adam was eventually diagnosed with *fetal alcohol syndrome (FAS)*. What characteristics do children with FAS have?

· What conditions lead to FAS? In other words, how was it that Adam came to develop FAS?
· Adam eventually learned many practical skills, such as how to read and hold down a simple job. What kinds of support would Adam have needed to achieve a good quality of life?

Once you have answered these questions, compare your responses with those presented in Appendix A.

[a]From *The Broken Cord,* by Michael Dorris, copyright 1989 by Michael Dorris. Used by permission of HarperCollins Publishers, Inc., New York.

Interpreting Children's Artifacts and Reflections

Consider chapter concepts as you analyze the following artifact created by a child.

Horses by Nadia

Autism spectrum disorders are a group of related disabilities in communicating and acquiring basic social and cognitive skills (Centers for Disease Control and Prevention, 2007a; National Institute of Mental Health, 2008a). The most severe of the autism spectrum conditions is commonly known as *autism*. Children with autism typically have difficulty in learning to speak and comprehend language. They also generally withdraw from eye contact and other social interaction; do not understand social gestures or participate in pretend games; tend to repeat particular actions incessantly (e.g., repeatedly turning the pages of a book); resist changes in routine; and exhibit unusual reactions to sensory experiences (e.g., they may shudder at the sensation of being draped with silk yet not react with pain after running into a wall). Autism appears to be caused by both genetics and such environmental factors as exposure to teratogens (Arndt, Stodgell, & Rodier, 2005; Freitag, 2007).

Nadia, an English child of Ukrainian immigrants, was identified as being autistic at age 6 (Selfe, 1977). By age 3, Nadia had spoken only 10 words, and she uttered these few words rarely. Her language did not progress much further in the following years, and she found it especially difficult to learn abstract and superordinate concepts (e.g., "furniture") (Selfe, 1995). Nadia was also clumsy, showed no concern for physical danger, and displayed regular temper tantrums. Yet like a small minority of other children with autism (Treffert & Wallace, 2002; Winner, 2000), Nadia was an exceptionally talented artist. After noticing her unusual artistic ability, Nadia's parents and a psychologist gave her paper and pens. Nadia drew several times a week, reproducing pictures she had studied days before in children's books, newspapers, or other printed material. Nadia's drawings were realistic but also creative representations of images she had seen—she occasionally reversed the orientation, changed

the size, or constructed a composite of several images. As you examine two of her drawings, shown below, consider these questions:

· Nadia was not able to describe her art in any depth using words. How might *nature* have played a role in Nadia's artistic ability and her language delay?
· Horses were Nadia's favorite topic. How might *nurture* have played a role in Nadia's interest in horses?

Once you have analyzed Nadia's artifacts, compare your ideas with those presented in Appendix B. For further practice in analyzing children's artifacts and reflections, go to the Activities and Applications section in Chapter 4 of MyEducationLab.

Artwork by Nadia. Horse; age 3½ years (left). Horse and rider; age 5½ years (right). Originally published in Selfe, Lorna (1977). *Nadia: A Case of Extraordinary Drawing Ability in an Autistic Child.* London: Academic Press. Used with permission of Lorna Selfe.

Developmental Trends Exercise

In this chapter you learned that children's biological beginnings are important determinants of their long-term abilities and health. The following table describes factors that affect the health of babies-to-be and newborn infants. For each of these health circumstances, the table identifies a factor that affects an offspring's health, offers an implication for supporting offspring and families, or both. Go to the Activities and Applications section in Chapter 4 of MyEducationLab to apply what you've learned about children's biological beginnings as you fill in the empty cells in the table.

Promoting Healthy Beginnings for Children and Their Families

Period of Development	The Experiences of Children and Families	Developmental Concepts *Identifying Factors That Affect Children's Beginnings*	Implications *Helping Families Give Offspring Healthy Beginnings*
Prior to Conception	Kuri and Taro want to have a child. They go to the doctor to discuss their desire to plan for a healthy pregnancy.	The *health of any children conceived by a couple* depends on several factors, including the mother's health prior to the pregnancy and her diet, actions, stress levels, and exposure to teratogens during the pregnancy. Increasingly, the father's health is also being recognized as an important factor. The health of children's genes is mostly beyond their parents' control, although some parents may choose to terminate a pregnancy when diagnostic prenatal tests reveal a serious problem.	Encourage prospective parents to talk with their doctor before conception and to make the necessary adjustments to their lifestyle. For example, a woman will want to find out whether any medicines she takes can affect the health of her offspring. Couples concerned about possible birth defects may choose to see a genetic counselor.
During the First Few Weeks of Pregnancy	A pregnant woman, Antoinette, does not know she is pregnant and continues to drink large amounts of alcohol and smoke a pack of cigarettes each day. Antoinette contracts a cold virus and takes over-the-counter medicines.		Encourage women who are sexually active and able to conceive children to shield themselves from teratogens as a matter of course.
From 9 Weeks After Conception Until Birth	A pregnant woman, Larissa, is highly anxious about giving birth to a child because she does not have a job or supportive partner. Late in her pregnancy, Larissa and her mother go to prepared childbirth courses at their local community college.	*Excessive stress* can be harmful to both the mother and her unborn child. *Preparation for childbirth* can reassure parents about the birth process and help them express their preferences for the birth, including who will be present and how they might respond to various possible scenarios.	
At Birth	Annie and Alberto give birth to a premature baby, Riley, 6 weeks early. He weighs only 4 pounds, 2 ounces. Riley receives intensive medical care and is strong enough to go home with his parents 2 weeks later.		Offer appropriate and nurturing care to babies at risk. Address the medical needs of fragile infants, and help parents care for infants in a responsive manner. As premature infants grow, provide them with services, intervention, and educational experiences that help them flourish.

Key Concepts

gene (p. 110)	monozygotic twins (p. 114)	polygenic inheritance (p. 115)	teratogen (p. 126)
chromosome (p. 110)	dizygotic twins (p. 114)	canalization (p. 118)	premature infant (p. 136)
DNA (p. 110)	alleles (p. 115)	prenatal development (p. 121)	sensation (p. 138)
gamete (p. 112)	dominant gene (p. 115)	mitosis (p. 121)	perception (p. 138)
meiosis (p. 112)	recessive gene (p. 115)	embryo (p. 122)	state of arousal (p. 139)
zygote (p. 114)	codominance (p. 115)	fetus (p. 123)	reflex (p. 139)

MyEducationLab

Now go to Chapter 4 of MyEducationLab at www.myeducationlab.com, where you can:

- View instructional objectives for the chapter.
- Take a quiz to test your mastery of chapter objectives. Detailed feedback is provided to explain why your responses are correct or incorrect.
- Deepen your understanding of particular concepts and principles with Review, Practice, and Enrichment exercises.

- Complete Activities and Applications exercises that give you additional experience in interpreting artifacts, increase your understanding of how research contributes to knowledge about chapter topics, and encourage you to apply what you have learned about children's development.
- Apply what you have learned in the chapter to your work with children in Building Teaching Skills and Dispositions exercises.
- Observe children and their unique contexts in Video Examples.

chapter

5

Physical Development

Two brothers, Tom (age 13) and Phillip (age 15), are talking with psychologist William Pollack about the impact of organized sports on their lives:

"There used to be nothing to do around here," Tom told me [Dr. Pollack], referring to the small, economically depressed town where he and his brother live.

"There was like just one bowling alley, and it was closed on weekends. We had nothing to do, especially during the summer," Phillip agreed.

"Not quite a year ago," Tom explained, "three of our best friends died of an OD."

Indeed, the autumn before, three teenage boys in the same sleepy town had all drunk themselves into oblivion and then overdosed on a lethal cocktail of various barbiturates. Sure, the town had always had its problems—high unemployment, poorly funded schools, and many broken families. But this was different. Three boys, the oldest only sixteen, were gone forever.

The mood in the town was sullen the summer following the deaths, and Tom and Phillip were resolved to change things. "We went to the mayor and to the priest at our church, and we asked if we could set up a regular sports program for kids around here," Phillip explained.

"A softball league," Tom added.

"What a great idea," I told the boys.

"Yeah. At first we were just ten guys," said Tom.

"But then, like, everybody wanted to sign up—girls too," explained Phillip. "Now there are too many kids who want to play. More than a hundred. But the state government offered to help with some money and coaches."

"So it is making a difference, to have this new league?" I asked the boys.

"Hell, yeah," Phillip replied. "Now, we've got a schedule. We've got something to do."

"I'm not sure I'd be here anymore if it wasn't for the league," added Tom. "For a long time I couldn't deal with things. Now I've got a place to go." (Pollack, 1998, p. 274)[a]

- What kinds of physical changes would Tom and Phillip have experienced before and during the summer when they decided to set up a baseball league?

- How did the sports league affect the well-being of these two brothers and other youngsters in the community?

[a]From REAL BOYS by William Pollack, copyright © 1998 by William Pollack. Used by permission of Random House, Inc.

Case Study:
The Softball League

Outline:

Case Study: The Softball League

Principles of Physical Development

The Brain and Its Development

Physical Development During Childhood

Physical Well-Being

Special Physical Needs

Summary

Applying Concepts in Child Development

Organized sports can allow children and adolescents to exercise, improve physical skills, and make productive use of leisure time. Art by Eric, age 12.

As children develop, they undergo numerous physical changes. They grow taller and stronger. They learn to crawl, walk, and run. They become increasingly proficient at using writing utensils and handling other small objects. Tom and Phillip, the two adolescent boys in the introductory case study, would have previously gone through many of these physical changes and were presently facing challenges associated with adolescence, such as making good choices for their free time. Fortunately, Tom and Phillip dealt with their increasing independence productively by arranging for a sports league. The result was that Tom, Phillip, and other youngsters were able to practice athletic skills, forge friendships, and have fun. Like Tom and Phillip, children can do a variety of things to stay healthy, and adults can find numerous ways to help them. In this chapter we examine age-related changes in physical development and the implications of children's activities and adults' support for children's physical well-being.

Principles of Physical Development

A child's physical development is the outcome of countless orderly changes. As you learned in Chapter 4, genes assert their instructions within cells, telling bodies to complete one critical change after another until individuals have adult bodies and are ready (physically, at least) to have children of their own. Nurture, of course, is present every step of the way. Let's look at the remarkable principles of growth that characterize physical development.

• *Different parts of the body mature at their own rates.* Genes tell certain parts of the body to grow during distinct time periods. Early in development heads are proportionally closer to adult size than are torsos, which are more advanced than arms and legs. In the upper limbs, the hand approaches adult size sooner than the forearm does; the forearm approaches adult size sooner than the upper arm does. Likewise in the lower limbs, the foot is more advanced than the calf, which is more advanced than the thigh. Figure 5-1 illustrates how relative body proportions change throughout childhood and adolescence.

Internally, separate systems grow at different rates as well (J. M. Tanner, 1990). For instance, the lymphoid system (e.g., tonsils, adenoids, lymph nodes, and the lining of the small intestines) grows rapidly throughout childhood and then slows in adolescence. This system helps children resist infection, which is particularly important during the early and middle childhood years when children are exposed to many contagious illnesses for the first time. In contrast, reproductive organs expand slowly until adolescence, when a substantial burst of growth occurs.

The outcome of separate systems growing at distinct rates is that the body as a whole increases in size, albeit somewhat unevenly in its parts. Typical growth curves for height and weight reveal rapid increases during the first 2 years, slow but steady growth during early and middle childhood, an explosive spurt during adolescence, and a leveling off to mature levels by early adulthood (Canessa, 2007; Hamill et al., 1979). Patterns of growth are similar for boys and girls, although girls tend to have their adolescent growth spurts about a year and a half earlier, and boys, on average, end up a bit taller and heavier.

• *Functioning becomes increasingly differentiated.* As you learned in Chapter 4, every cell in the body (with the exception of sperm and ova) contains the same genetic instructions. But as cells grow, they take on specific functions, some aiding with digestion, others transporting oxygen, still others transmitting information to various places in the body, and so on. Thus individual cells "listen" to only a subset of the many instructions they have available. This progressive shift from having the *potential* to become many things to manifesting a specific working process or form is known as **differentiation.**

Figure 5-1

Physical development during childhood and adolescence. Children grow taller and heavier as they develop, and the characteristics and relative proportions of their bodies change as well.
Based on Diagram Group, 1983.

6 mo.   2 yrs.   5 yrs.   8 yrs.   11 yrs.   14 yrs.   16 yrs.

6 mo.   2 yrs.   5 yrs.   8 yrs.   11 yrs.   14 yrs.   16 yrs.

MyEducationLab

Observe developmental differentiation in hand grips by comparing three children holding writing utensils: Corwin in "Literacy: Infancy," Zoe in "Neighborhood: Early Childhood," and Elena in "Neighborhood: Middle Childhood." (Find Video Examples in Chapter 5 of MyEducationLab.)

differentiation
A gradual transition from general to more specific functioning over the course of development.

Development of a boy at ages 1, 5, 9, 13, and 17. Notice the gradual, systematic changes: The boy grows taller, his face becomes more angular, his trunk becomes long, and his hair color darkens. The boy is wearing the same T-shirt in all five photos.

Differentiation characterizes other aspects of physical development as well. For instance, during prenatal development, the arms first protrude as simple buds from the torso, but then become longer, sprout globular hands, and eventually differentiate into fingers. Motor skills, too, become increasingly differentiated: They first appear as global, unsteady actions but gradually evolve into precise, controlled motions. You can see a clear developmental progression toward fine motor control by comparing the writing-implement grips of 16-month-old Corwin, 4-year-old Zoe, and 9-year-old Elena in three videos in MyEducationLab.

- *Functioning becomes increasingly integrated.* As cells and body parts differentiate, they must also work together. Their increasingly coordinated efforts are known as **integration** (J. M. Tanner, 1990). As examples, the various parts of the eye coordinate their mechanical movements to permit vision; separate areas of the brain form connections that allow exchanges between thoughts and feelings; and fingers become longer and more adept at synchronizing movements for handling small objects (see Figure 5-2).

- *Each child follows a unique growth curve.* Children's bodies appear to pursue predetermined heights—perhaps not as specific as 4′9″ or 6′2″, but definite ballpark targets for height, nonetheless. Growth curves are especially evident when things go temporarily awry in children's lives. Circumstances such as a serious illness or poor nutrition may briefly halt height increases. But when health and adequate nutrition are restored, children grow rapidly. Before you know it, they're back on track—back to where we might have expected them to be, given their original rate of growth. Exceptions to this self-correcting tendency occur when severe malnutrition is present very early in life or extends over a lengthy time period. For instance, children who are seriously undernourished during the prenatal phase tend not to catch up completely, and they are at risk for later mental and behavioral deficiencies, motor difficulties, and brain damage (Chavez, Martinez, & Soberanes, 1995; Rees, Harding, & Inder, 2006; Roseboom, de Rooij, & Painter, 2006).

- *Physical development is characterized by both quantitative and qualitative changes.* Quantitative changes are perhaps most obvious. Children continually eat, of course, and in most cases gain weight on an incremental basis. Motor skills, which may seem to the casual observer to appear overnight, are also generally the result of numerous gradual advancements. For instance, a child may slowly improve in dexterity as she ties her shoes and gains practice at pulling the laces. Yet qualitative changes in motor skills occur as well. To illustrate, Figure 5-3 shows how both walking and throwing a ball change stylistically over time. During their initial attempts at walking, toddlers must concentrate on balance and upright posture, and they take short steps, make flat-footed contact with toes turned outward, and flex their knees as their feet contact the ground (Gallahue & Ozmun, 1998). A few years later, they increase their stride, make heel-toe contact, swing their arms a bit, lift themselves vertically as they proceed, and show increased pelvic tilt. The mature pattern of walking, achieved between ages 4 and 7, is characterized by a reflexive arm swing, a narrow base of support, a relaxed and long stride, minimal vertical lift, and a decisive heel-toe contact.

- *Children's bodies function as dynamic, changing systems.* The specific systems in the body change over time, as do the relationships among them, and children's own activity is an important part of overall functioning. To illustrate, infants apply considerable effort

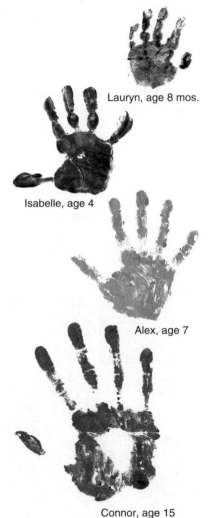

Lauryn, age 8 mos.

Isabelle, age 4

Alex, age 7

Connor, age 15

Figure 5-2

As children develop, their body parts become increasingly *differentiated* as well as progressively *integrated*. For example, the separate fingers on a child's hand start out rather similar looking but become increasingly distinct and better able to coordinate their movements. These handprints are shown at 25% of actual size.

integration
An increasing coordination of body parts over the course of development.

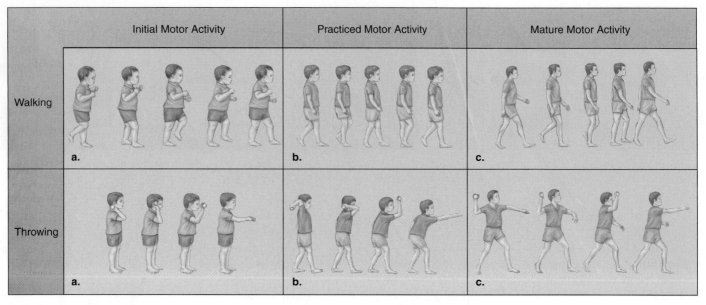

	Initial Motor Activity	Practiced Motor Activity	Mature Motor Activity
Walking	a.	b.	c.
Throwing	a.	b.	c.

Figure 5-3

Developmental sequences showing qualitative change in walking and overhand throwing. In *walking*, children tend to progress from (a) difficulty maintaining balance and using short steps with flat-footed contact, to (b) a smoother pattern, where arms are lower and heel-toe contact occurs, to (c) a relaxed gait, with reflexive arm swing. In *overhand throwing*, the trend is from (a) stationary feet and action mainly from the elbow, to (b) ball held behind head, arm swung forward and high over shoulder, and a definite shift forward with body weight, to (c) movement of foot on same side as throwing arm; definite rotation through hips, legs, spine, and shoulders; and a step with foot opposite to the throwing arm as weight is shifted. Based on Gallahue & Ozmun, 1998.

MyEducationLab

Observe Madison reaching for objects in the "Emotional Development: Infancy" video. (Find Video Examples in Chapter 5 of MyEducationLab.)

in learning to coordinate the various muscles needed for reaching for objects with their arms and hands. Having moved their limbs spontaneously during the prenatal period and immediately after birth, infants gradually gain experience with movement and by 3½ to 4 months after birth, they begin to reach for objects, first shakily and then more smoothly (Thelen & Smith, 2006). After some small improvements, though, infants often exhibit *declines* in speed, directness, and smoothness in reaching, as if they must figure out how to integrate changes in muscle tone or deal with some other new factor. By 12 months, however, most infants can reach easily and quickly. You can see 7-month-old Madison adeptly reach for objects and transfer objects from one hand to the other in the "Emotional Development: Infancy" video in MyEducationLab.

Children actively use their new motor abilities to help them accomplish desired goals and in the process offset their personal limitations. For example, infants who make large and vigorous movements spontaneously in their first few months of life must learn to control such movements before they can successfully reach for objects. In contrast, infants who generate few and slow movements in their first few months have a different set of problems to solve: They must learn to apply muscle tone while extending arms forward and holding them stiffly. Thus the act of reaching, like so many universal accomplishments, shows dramatic individual differences in pathways to proficiency.

● ***Children's health is affected by their involvement in a multilayered environment.*** As you learned in Chapter 1, Bronfenbrenner's (2005) *bioecological model* offers a useful framework for understanding the interrelated environmental systems in which children live. Applied to children's physical development, the bioecological model clarifies the numerous settings that directly and indirectly impinge on children's health-related decisions and habits (H. W. Gardiner & Kosmitzki, 2008; Kazak, 2006). Children's experiences within their families are especially important to their health. For example, from their countless experiences at home, many children learn to like particular foods and dislike others, cope with stress or let anxious feelings escalate, and follow an active or sedentary lifestyle. Parents' jobs indirectly affect children's health by providing the family with helpful resources, including food, medical insurance, and housing in a toxin-free environment (Y. R. Harris & Graham, 2007; C. F. Moore, 2005). Outside the family, peers offer supplementary influences, for instance by providing companionship at recreation centers. At school, teachers and other personnel often arrange for physical activity and see to it that children have access to reasonably healthful lunches and snacks. External societal forces, particularly the media and community, also affect children's physical development. For instance, youngsters may head to the gym or basketball court in the hope of emulating the lean bodies of famous athletes, or alternatively take illicit drugs after seeing neighbors do the same. In addition, local governments may or may not effectively enforce laws regarding use of cigarettes and alcohol, and community groups may provide access to effective or ineffective health services for youth (Steinberg, 2007).

As you have seen, general principles of physical development come to life in individual children as a result of a variety of factors, including heredity, family, community, and personal activity. We now turn to more specific aspects of physical development, beginning with the brain, the most complex system of the body.

The Brain and Its Development

The brain is an extraordinary organ that regulates the activities of other systems in the body, senses information in the environment, and guides the child's movement. The child's brain also permits advanced human abilities: It forms associations between environmental stimuli and mental concepts, fills everyday experience with emotional meaning, translates thoughts and feelings into words and behaviors, and determines actions needed to achieve desired outcomes.

Altogether, the brain has approximately 100 billion **neurons,** cells that transmit information to other cells (Naegele & Lombroso, 2001; R. W. Williams & Herrup, 1988). Each neuron has numerous **dendrites** that react to chemicals released by other neurons, as well as a long, armlike **axon** that sends information on to additional neurons (Figure 5-4). The dendrites and axons of various neurons come very close to one another at junctions called **synapses.** When any particular neuron is stimulated by a sufficient amount of chemicals from one or more of its neighbors, it either "fires," generating an electrical impulse that triggers the release of its own chemicals (culminating in the stimulation and subsequent firing of nearby neurons), or it is inhibited from firing. Neurons fire or are inhibited from firing depending on the amount and types of chemicals that neighbors send their way.

Most of the brain's hundreds of millions of neurons have thousands of synapses, so obviously a great deal of cross-communication occurs (R. F. Thompson, 1975; Wickens, 2005).

neuron
Cell that transmits information to other cells; also called nerve cell.

dendrite
Branchlike part of a neuron that receives information from other neurons.

axon
Armlike part of a neuron that sends information to other neurons.

synapse
Junction between two neurons.

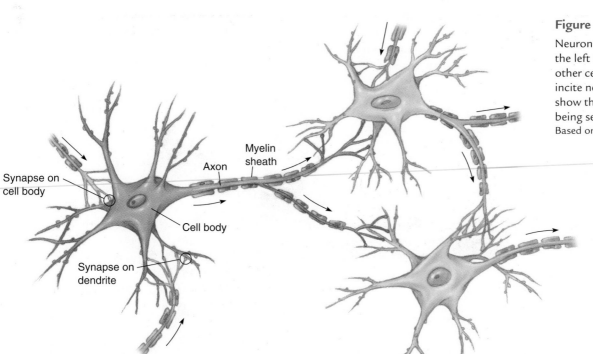

Synapse on cell body

Axon

Myelin sheath

Cell body

Synapse on dendrite

Figure 5-4

Neurons in the brain. The neuron on the left is receiving information from other cells. Next, it will fire and incite neurons at right to fire. Arrows show the direction of messages being sent.
Based on N. R. Carlson (2007).

glial cell
Cell in the brain or other part of the nervous system that provides structural or functional support for one or more neurons.

hindbrain
Part of the brain controlling the basic physiological processes that sustain survival.

midbrain
Part of the brain that coordinates communication between the hindbrain and forebrain.

forebrain
Part of the brain responsible for complex thinking, emotions, and motivation.

cortex
Part of the forebrain that enables conscious thinking processes, including executive functions.

executive functions
Purposeful and goal-directed intellectual processes (e.g., planning, decision making) made possible by higher brain structures.

Furthermore, some groups of neurons grow and work together as "communities" that specialize in certain functions. Following the principle that there is strength in numbers, these communities, called *circuits,* are laid out in side-by-side wires that reach out to other groups of neurons. The outcome is that important processes of the brain (such as feeling emotions, paying attention, and learning new ideas) are supported by robust structures.

Neurons are assisted by other kinds of brain cells, called **glial cells.** Glial cells outnumber neurons by about 10 to 1 and give neurons structural support and protection. Glial cells also produce chemicals that neurons need to function properly, repair injured neurons, and dispose of seriously damaged neurons (N. R. Carlson, 2007; Wickens, 2005).

Structures and Functions

The brain is organized into three main parts: the hindbrain, the midbrain, and the forebrain (Figure 5-5). Each of these parts is organized further into specialized systems with identifiable functions:

- The **hindbrain** controls basic physiological processes that sustain survival, including breathing, blood pressure, sleep, arousal, balance, and movement (thank your hindbrain for your slow, methodical breathing as you sleep blissfully at night).
- The **midbrain** connects the hindbrain to the forebrain and acts as a kind of relay station between the two; for instance, it sends messages to the forebrain about priorities for attention ("Hello! Alarm clock ringing! Hello! Alarm clock ringing!").
- The **forebrain** produces complex thinking, emotional responses, and the driving forces of motivation ("It's 6:00 a.m.? Ugh! I can sleep another 10 minutes if I skip breakfast!").

The *forebrain* is of special relevance to educators and other practitioners because it allows children to learn and develop distinct abilities and personalities. The forebrain contains the **cortex,** a wrinkled cap that rests on the midbrain and hindbrain. The cortex is where interpreting, reasoning, communicating, planning, decision making, and other purposeful, conscious thinking processes (collectively known as **executive functions**) take place. The cortex is also the seat of many personality traits, such as being enthusiastic and sociable or quiet and introverted, and of habitual ways of responding to physical events and novel information. For example, a 10-year-old girl's cortex would control the way she snuggles up to her father on the sofa in the evening, her exuberant style in social groups, her understanding of how to read, and, of course, much more.

Physiologically, the cortex is extremely convoluted. Bundles of neurons repeatedly fold in on themselves. This physical complexity permits a huge capacity for storing information as well as for transmitting information throughout the brain. Consistent with the principle of differentiation, various parts of the cortex develop specific functions, which we now examine.

Areas of specialization within the cortex. The cortex consists of regions (called *lobes*) that specialize in particular functions, such as decision making and planning (front),

Figure 5-5

Structure of the human brain. The human brain is an enormously complex and intricate structure with three main parts: the hindbrain, midbrain, and forebrain.
Based on N. R. Carlson (2007).

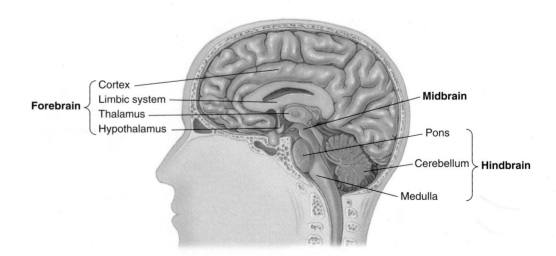

understanding and production of language (sides), and visual processing (rear). In addition, the cortex is divided into two halves, or *hemispheres*. The **left hemisphere** controls the right side of the body, and the **right hemisphere** manages the left side. In most people the left hemisphere dominates in *analysis,* breaking up information into its constituent parts and extracting order in a sequence of events (N. R. Carlson, 2007; Wickens, 2005). Talking, understanding speech, reading, writing, mathematical problem solving, and computer programming are all beneficiaries of left-hemisphere processing. It is usually the right hemisphere that excels in *synthesis,* pulling together information (especially nonlinguistic information) into a coherent whole. The right hemisphere therefore usually dominates when we attempt to recognize faces, detect geometrical patterns, and read body language. It is also key to appreciation of musical melodies, humor, and emotions.

The specializations of the two hemispheres are ensured by the physical layout of neural circuits. The left hemisphere has neurological connections to fewer regions of the brain than does the right; this layout permits the application of rules in specific, structured domains, such as language and mathematics. The left hemisphere does its work close to home, so to speak. The right hemisphere is more amply connected with distant areas in the brain, permitting associations with all kinds of thinking and feeling (Goldberg & Costa, 1981; Semrud-Clikeman & Hynd, 1991; Teeter & Semrud-Clikeman, 1997).

Although these particular layouts (i.e., left focusing on analysis, right on synthesis) apply to most people, left-handed individuals often have reversed patterns, with the right hemisphere dominant in analysis and the left hemisphere more involved in synthesis (Toga & Thompson, 2003). Yet other individuals (particularly those who use both hands equally well) often blend psychological functions within hemispheres (Sheehan & Smith, 1986).

Despite their separate specialties, the two hemispheres are in constant communication, trading information through a thick bundle of connecting neurons. Therefore, no single mental activity is exclusively the domain of one hemisphere or the other (N. R. Carlson, 2007). Both hemispheres almost always work together. For example, the right hemisphere may process a complex emotion, such as the mixed feelings people experience at a high school graduation, while the left hemisphere searches for the right words to communicate these feelings.

Supplementing the numerous circuits existing *within* the cortex are connections *between* the cortex and other parts of the brain. As an illustration, basic, "energizing" activities that reside partly in areas of the brain outside the cortex (e.g., certain aspects of attention, emotion, and motivation) regularly interact with more reflective, "intellectual" processes that take place in the cortex. For example, children who feel alert and happy may readily grasp a classroom lesson, but children who are sad, angry, or distracted may not. Yet, especially as they get older, children can use thinking processes to control their emotions to some degree. For instance, a boy who initially feels anxious during a challenging lesson may convince himself that he has the ability to understand the material and needs to take a deep breath and complete the assignment.

Malformations in the brain.   In some cases, people's brains have unusual circuits or missing or distorted structures, malformations that can interfere with learning and behavior. For example, too many or too few cells may form, or the connections among cells may be laid out in unusual ways (C. A. Nelson, Thomas, & de Haan, 2006). Such neurological conditions may affect children's abilities to pay attention, learn efficiently, control impulses, deal with negative emotions, and so forth.

Some neurological disorders are not obvious at birth, or even in the first few years of life. For example, **schizophrenia,** a serious psychiatric disorder that affects 1 in 100 people, often does not surface until adolescence or adulthood (N. R. Carlson, 2007). Individuals with schizophrenia display such symptoms as thought disorders (e.g., irrational ideas and disorganized thinking), hallucinations (e.g., "hearing" nonexistent voices), delusions (e.g., worrying that "everyone is out to get me"), and social withdrawal (e.g., avoiding eye contact or conversation with others). Such symptoms appear to result, at least in part, from structural abnormalities or overactive synapses in certain parts of the brain (Wickens, 2005).

What factors cause serious malformations in brain development? Errors in genetic instructions can trigger problems in brain chemistry and architecture, leading to learning difficulties. Other neurological abnormalities may be due to a mother's drug or alcohol use, illness, or stress during pregnancy. For example, prenatal exposure to rubella (German measles) can

left hemisphere
Left side of the cortex; largely responsible for sequential reasoning and analysis, especially in right-handed people.

right hemisphere
Right side of the cortex; largely responsible for simultaneous processing and synthesis, especially in right-handed people.

schizophrenia
A psychiatric condition characterized by irrational ideas and disorganized thinking.

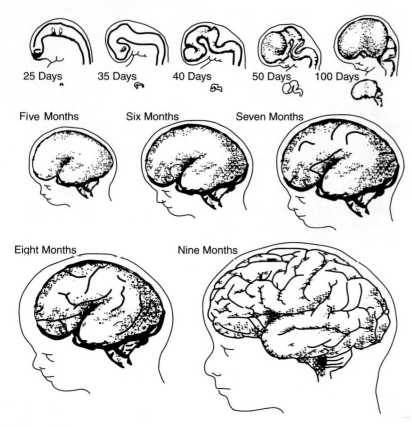

25 Days   35 Days   40 Days   50 Days   100 Days

Five Months   Six Months   Seven Months

Eight Months   Nine Months

Figure 5-6

Changes in the human brain during prenatal development. During the first few months, the basic structures appear (in the top row of drawings, the relative size of the brains has been increased to show detail of the structures). During the middle months of prenatal development, these structures become more distinct. During the final weeks prior to birth, the cortex folds in and out of itself, preparing the fetus for learning as a baby.

From "The Development of the Brain" by W. Maxwell Cowan, 1979, *Scientific American, 241,* p. 106. Illustration copyright 1979 by Tom Prentiss. Reproduced by permission.

reduce the number of neurons formed, lead to small brains, and ultimately produce mental retardation (C. A. Nelson et al., 2006). In cases of schizophrenia, a variety of factors, including genes, viral infections and malnutrition during prenatal development, childbirth complications, and stressful environments during childhood, may share responsibility (N. R. Carlson, 2007; E. Walker & Tessner, 2008).

Developmental Changes in the Brain

The magnificent intricacy of the human brain is made possible by a lengthy process in which its parts are formed, refined, and interconnected. In fact, nature and nurture sculpt the brain throughout the child's prenatal development, infancy, childhood years, and adolescence.

Prenatal development. During prenatal development, the brain's most basic parts are formed. The brain begins as a tiny tube approximately 25 days after conception. This seemingly simple tube grows longer in places and folds inward to form pockets, as illustrated in Figure 5-6 (Cowan, 1979; Rayport, 1992). Three bulges can be recognized early on; these bulges become the forebrain, midbrain, and hindbrain. Soon the brain takes on more complex features, with the forebrain cleaving down the middle and beginning to specialize into its distinct left and right hemispheres (Stephan, Fink, & Marshall, 2007).

Before the brain can develop any further, it must first become a factory for neurons. Beginning the fifth week, neurons reproduce in the inner portion of the tube. This production peaks between the third and fourth prenatal months, when a hundred thousand new neurons are generated *each minute* (C. A. Nelson et al., 2006). The vast majority of neurons that will ever be used by a person are formed during the first 7 months of prenatal development (Rakic, 1995).

Newly formed neurons move, or *migrate,* to specific brain locations where they will do their work. Some young neurons push old cells outward, creating brain structures underneath the cortex. Others actively seek out their destination, climbing up pole like glial cells and ultimately giving rise to the cortex. Once in place, neurons send out axons in efforts to connect with one another. Groups of axons grow together as teams, reaching toward other groups of neurons (their targets) that attract them by secreting certain chemicals. As axons get close to their targets, they generate branches that become synapses with the target cells. The target cells do their part as well, forming small receptors with their dendrites.

Only about half of neurons ultimately make contact with other cells. Those that make contact survive; the others die. Nature's tendency to overproduce neurons and eliminate those that fail to connect ensures that the brain invests in workable connections (M. Diamond & Hopson, 1998; P. R. Huttenlocher, 1990).

Infancy and early childhood. Beginning at birth, the infant's brain has two important tasks: (a) ensuring survival outside the womb and (b) learning about people, things, language, sensations, emotions, and events. Coming from healthy prenatal environments, most newborns are well prepared to breathe, suck, swallow, cry, and form simple associations. With survival taken care of, the brain forms countless new connections (synapses) among neurons, a phenomenon called **synaptogenesis.** Neurons sprout large numbers of dendrites that stretch in different directions, reaching out toward neighboring neurons. (In Figure 5-7 you can see the rapid development of dendrites in areas of the cortex that support vision.) In the first few years of life, so many new synapses appear that their

synaptogenesis
A universal process in brain development whereby many new synapses appear in the first few years of life.

Newborn   1-Month-Old   3-Month-Old   6-Month-Old

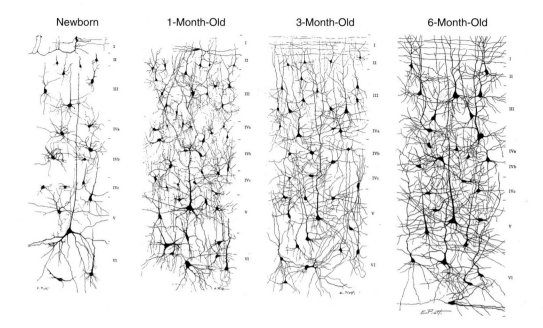

Figure 5-7

Drawings of the cellular structure of an infant's visual cortex. Comparison of these drawings at four different ages reveals the rapid and extensive growth of dendrites during infancy. Drawings were based on Golgi stain preparations from Conel (1939–1975).

Reprinted by permission of the publisher from *The Postnatal Development of the Human Cerebral Cortex*, Vols. I–VIII, by Jesse LeRoy Conel, Cambridge, MA: Harvard University Press, Copyright © 1939, 1975 by the President and Fellows of Harvard College.

number far exceeds adult levels (C. A. Nelson et al., 2006). Then, following this fantastic proliferation of synapses, frequently used connections become stronger, and connections not often used wither away in a process known as **synaptic pruning.** Particular regions of the brain take their turns growing and shedding synapses over a period of many years (P. R. Huttenlocher, 1990; C. A. Nelson et al., 2006).

Why do children's brains create a great many synapses, only to eliminate a sizable proportion of them later on? In the case of synapses, more is not necessarily better (Bruer & Greenough, 2001; Byrnes, 2001). Psychologists speculate that by generating more synapses than will ever be needed, human beings have the potential to adapt to a wide variety of conditions and circumstances. As children encounter certain regularities in their environment, some synapses are a nuisance because they are irrelevant to children's actual experiences in that setting. Synaptic pruning, then, may be Mother Nature's way of making the brain more efficient.

Early brain development is also marked by **myelination,** a process in which glial cells grow around the axons of neurons to form a fatty coating *(myelin)* that insulates axons and enables them to conduct electrical charges more quickly. Just as synaptic proliferation and pruning proceed through areas of the brain in a particular order, myelination also occurs in a predictable sequence (Yakovlev & Lecours, 1967). It actually begins during the prenatal period, coating neurons involved in basic survival skills. In infancy it occurs with neurons that activate sensory abilities, followed by those involved in motor skills later in childhood, and eventually (well into adolescence) with those responsible for complex thinking processes and judgment (M. Diamond & Hopson, 1998; C. A. Nelson et al., 2006).

The trends we've just described—synaptogenesis, synaptic pruning, and myelination—are all driven largely by heredity. Yet nature also allows *nurture* to influence the formation of brain structures. As children observe basic properties in visual stimuli, spoken language, and bodily sensations, their brains convert these observations into circuits that essentially obligate the brain to process later incoming information as if it were following similar patterns. This tendency of the brain to convert early patterns into circuits that support and constrain future learning has been described as a process of making *neural commitments* (Kuhl, 2007; Kuhl, Conboy, Padden, Nelson, & Pruitt, 2005). For example, when infants regularly hear certain sounds in their language (e.g., the sound *ba* in English), they seem to form neural commitments for these sounds, enabling them to recognize the sounds in full-blown words (e.g., *ba*ll). Such neural commitments almost certainly help young children learn the language they hear around them but may later *limit* their ability to learn a second language that uses somewhat different sounds. (You will learn more about language development in Chapter 9.)

From a neurological perspective, the connections that are formed during infancy and early childhood become the foundation of many later abilities. For example, in the first months of life, neurological circuits permit basic skills in visually scanning objects, recognizing faces, and

synaptic pruning
A universal process in brain development whereby many previously formed synapses wither away, especially if they have not been used frequently.

myelination
The growth of a fatty sheath around neurons that allows them to transmit messages more quickly.

MyEducationLab

Observe 7-month-old Madison using her emerging perceptual skills to learn about the properties of a toy in the "Emotional Development: Infancy" video. (Find Video Examples in Chapter 5 of MyEducationLab.)

distinguishing novel and familiar stimuli (M. H. Johnson, 1999). When these rudimentary abilities begin to emerge, they are rather reflex-like. A 2-month-old baby may visually track a ball as it travels through the air but does not really *think* about what he or she is seeing. With maturation and experience, infants think about their perceptions and use them to guide behavior. In the "Emotional Development: Infancy" video in MyEducationLab, you can observe 7-month-old Madison intently studying the properties of a blue toy. There is nothing mechanical about the way Madison is handling the toy—she definitely gives the impression of actively thinking about the visual properties of objects. More generally, children increasingly reflect on experiences that they previously responded to automatically or with little analysis.

Middle childhood.   During the elementary school years, the two hemispheres become increasingly distinct (Sowell et al., 2002). In addition, the brain continues to nurture groups of neurons that are used regularly. Synaptic pruning of weak connections becomes a major force of change during childhood. Yet even as unused synapses are being pruned back, new ones continue to be formed during learning, especially in the cortex (National Research Council, 1999; C. A. Nelson et al., 2006). In addition, the process of myelination continues, protecting neurons and speeding up transmission of messages (Yakovlev & Lecours, 1967).

This neurological pattern of solidifying useful neurological circuits allows for the rapid and sustained learning of children. Children become knowledgeable about whatever strikes their fancy—comic books, dance movements, cake decorating, or hunting strategies. Likewise, they learn much about the habits and motives of people in their lives; this knowledge helps them fit comfortably into family and peer groups. Children also become fluent in their native tongue, flexibly and expertly using sophisticated words and grammatical structures.

One other outcome of neurological changes in childhood is that children become capable of handling multiple mental tasks simultaneously. For example, they can keep a growing number of ideas in mind at once. You can see this capacity being tapped in the "Memory: Early Childhood" video clip in MyEducationLab. In the clip 6-year-old Brent listens to 12 words and tries to recall them. (He is able to recall 6 words.) A year or so earlier he probably would have recalled fewer words, and in a few more years, he likely will recall more. Yet in part because their brain circuits are still under construction, children in the elementary grades have limited ability to plan realistically for the future. Despite good intentions, they cannot easily sustain commitments to goals, especially when other events and motives intervene. For example, they occasionally forget things when they leave home in the morning. In addition, their emotions are being processed at lower levels of the brain because the cortex is not yet fully developed. Thus it takes many years of neurological maturation (and encouragement from caregivers) before youngsters are able to express their feelings in a manner that is both genuine and culturally appropriate.

MyEducationLab

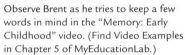

Observe Brent as he tries to keep a few words in mind in the "Memory: Early Childhood" video. (Find Video Examples in Chapter 5 of MyEducationLab.)

Adolescence.   The cortex continues to change in important ways during adolescence (Casey, Giedd, & Thomas, 2000; Sowell et al., 2001). For instance, myelination continues in parts of the brain used in sophisticated thought processes, such as planning ahead and controlling impulses (Benes, 2001; Bruer, 1999; Luna & Sweeney, 2004). Such developments allow youngsters to imagine the future and work toward long-term goals. Adolescents see the world in new ways, looking beyond its surface elements and detecting abstract principles. In the following Interpreting Children's Artifacts and Reflections exercise, you can see how one adolescent reflects on her expanding intellectual abilities.

Interpreting Children's Artifacts and Reflections

I Can See Clearly Now, My Brain Is Connected

As you read 16-year-old Sarah's self-reflection, think about the potential role that neurological development might play in her new intellectual abilities. What kinds of complex connections was Sarah able to make for the first time?

I remember walking by a building and I looked at its "For Rent" sign and, for the first time, I had all these weird thoughts.... I didn't just

think of it as a building, but I thought, gee, someone had to paint that sign and someone had to make that building—probably there were dozens of people who worked on the building to get it there. And, to me, it was the first time that I really realized what a big world it was and that it has a lot of people in it and I began to think: Where do I fit in? (Strauch, 2003, pp. 110–111)

In her observations of the building, Sarah saw not only its material qualities but also its ties to society and herself personally. Sarah's ability to probe beneath the surface of things required her to hold and compare several ideas in mind simultaneously: an image of the building, the efforts of construction workers, and implications for her place in society. This capacity grows steadily over childhood and culminates in abstract thinking in adolescence. However, at the same time that adolescents' brains unleash these high-brow abilities, they also incite new interests and a taste for risk and adventure (Steinberg, 2007; Strauch, 2003). Fortunately, continued development in the front part of the cortex eventually helps most adolescents envision the effects their actions might have for them, giving them the motivation to curtail seriously dangerous behaviors (V. F. Reyna & Farley, 2006).

Continued maturation of the cortex also helps adolescents reflect on their own and others' feelings. That is, adolescents become increasingly able to analyze emotions at higher levels of the brain, rather than responding to emotions spontaneously and nonreflectively, as they did in childhood (Killgore, Oki, & Yurgelun-Todd, 2001). Because these analytical abilities take some time to mature and also depend on experience, adolescents may be thoughtful one moment and rash the next. In the "Emotional Development: Late Adolescence" video in MyEducationLab, you can listen to 15-year-old Greg describe both impulsive reactions to anger and more controlled responses:

Interviewer:	What are some things kids do when they're angry?
Greg:	Hit lockers at school. They just get mad. . . .
Interviewer:	Okay.
Greg:	And they don't want you to be around 'em. They just are not pleasant to be around.
Interviewer:	Okay. What are some things that kids can do to calm themselves down?
Greg:	I don't know. Usually give it a night, 'cause they, if they're mad they usually don't get unmad by the end of the day.

While bouncing back and forth between an expanding intellect and a drive toward risk taking, adolescents are also benefiting from some changes that have been under way for years. For example, neurological pathways that support motor skills and speech reach an adult-like form during late childhood and adolescence (Paus et al., 1999). Also, circuits connecting language centers within the cortex continue to grow during adolescence, although at a slower rate than they did earlier (P. M. Thompson et al., 2000).

These and other neurological changes clearly show that teenagers' brains are works in progress. In fact, the brain evolves in systematic ways into the adult years (Sowell, Thompson, Holmes, Jernigan, & Toga, 1999). For example, myelination in the front region of the cortex, where planning, executive functions, and other complex cognitive processes occur, continues well beyond puberty (Giedd et al., 1999; Kolb & Fantie, 1989; C. A. Nelson et al., 2006). As a result of these numerous long-term changes, adults' brains are more efficient than children's brains are, both in terms of their connections (through synapses) and insulation (through myelination). You can see the effects of myelination and the process of synaptic pruning in the brain scans in Figure 5-8.

We summarize key neurological changes during developmental periods in Table 5-1, where we also suggest implications for educators who work with youngsters in particular age-groups. Some general applications from research on brain development are also discussed in the following section.

Applications of Research on Brain Development

Many teachers are interested in the flurry of studies that are currently being conducted on children's neurological development (E. Jensen, 2005). Yet we must be cautious in the applications we derive, because research into children's neurological functioning is still rather new and several steps removed from classroom practice (K. W. Fischer et al., 2007). No one knows, for example, exactly what it means when an area of the brain increases in size or activity during a particular developmental period: Are such changes the result of maturational developments or the outcome of repeated practice—or both? How much experience is needed to activate new circuits? To what degree can weak circuits be strengthened with instruction? Because so many questions persist, it makes sense to derive educational applications from

MyEducationLab

Listen to Greg describe both impulsive and controlled reactions to anger in the "Emotional Development: Late Adolescence" video. (Find Video Examples in Chapter 5 of MyEducationLab.)

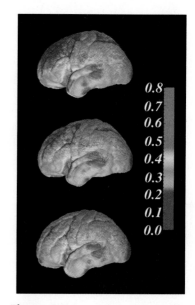

Figure 5-8

The images show the average proportion of neurons (gray matter) in the left hemisphere in brains of children (top), adolescents (middle), and adults (bottom). Warm colors (red and yellow) show high proportions of gray matter, and cool colors (blue and green) show low proportions. The decreased amount of red and yellow (neurons) in the adult's brain compared to the child's brain reflects a developmental decline in the proportion of cortex devoted solely to neurons. With development and increasing myelination, unused neurons die out, and active neurons become stronger and more efficient. From "Mapping Sulcal Pattern Asymmetry and Local Cortical Surface Gray Matter Distribution *in vivo*: Maturation in the Perisylvian Cortices," by E. R. Sowell, P. M. Thompson, D. Rex, D. Kornsand, K. D. Tessner, T. L. Jernigan, and A. W. Toga, 2002, *Cerebral Cortex, 12*, pp. 17–26. Reprinted by permission of Oxford University Press.

Table 5-1   Developmental Changes in the Brain

Developmental Period	Distinctive Neurological Changes	Implications
Prenatal Development	*The brain's basic parts are constructed:* · The primary structures of the brain emerge within the first few months of prenatal growth. · Neurons, the building blocks of the brain, are formed. They migrate to the places where they will do their work. · The cortex becomes convoluted, and the brain prepares circuits for reflexes and rudimentary learning processes.	· Encourage pregnant women to obtain adequate nutrition; to protect themselves from toxins, drugs, alcohol, injury, and excessive stress; and to obtain prenatal care from a physician. · Educate adolescents (especially adolescent girls and boys likely to conceive) about health threats to unborn children.
Infancy	*The brain activates circuits for reflexes, other basic physiological processes, and learning about the world:* · Many new connections form among neurons. Dendrites grow and expand their reach and complexity, initially in brain areas that support basic biological functions and later in areas that enable learning. · During the first year of life, synapses grow in density, especially in areas of the brain devoted to vision and hearing. · Synaptic pruning begins in certain areas. · Myelination occurs during infancy and continues throughout childhood, adolescence, and early adulthood.	· Provide infants with the nutrition they need to build healthy bodies and brains. · Offer infants stimulating environments that include rich visual patterns and human voices, but don't overdo it. Infants are hungry to explore the world, but they need to learn in their own ways, on their own timetable. · Carefully observe infants' reactions to stimuli to determine their preferences. Comment on the properties of objects, such as stripes and bright colors, that attract their attention. · Talk frequently to infants. They are able to learn a lot about language even when they are still unable to talk themselves. · Form stable and affectionate relationships with infants—their brains are as busy forming emotional circuits as they are learning to perceive objects, physical events, and properties of language.

continued

those neurological findings that are backed up with psychological research on children's learning. Here are some recommendations that integrate what we know about brain development with research on other aspects of child development:

• ***Be optimistic that children can continue to learn throughout childhood and adolescence.*** Some educators exaggerate the need for stimulating the brains of infants and forget that people learn throughout life. Certainly early stimulation *is* necessary for normal development of some functions, notably visual processing and depth perception. For instance, cats, monkeys, and people who have reduced or abnormal visual stimulation in their first few months sometimes develop lifelong difficulties with visual perception, apparently as a result of irreversible neurological change. On the other hand, a wide range of experiences provides sufficient stimulation for normal development in these visual areas of the brain (Bruer, 1999; Greenough, Black, & Wallace, 1987).

Virtually no evidence exists to indicate that structured stimulation must occur during early development for areas of the brain that support such culture-specific intellectual pursuits as learning in reading, mathematics, and music (Bruer, 1999; Greenough et al., 1987). On the contrary, we know from countless studies, as well as from our own everyday observations, that human beings continue to learn new information and skills quite successfully throughout the life span (Kolb, Gibb, & Robinson, 2003; C. A. Nelson et al., 2006). Thus you can have an important impact *throughout* the childhood and adolescent years if you offer such "brain-friendly" experiences as properly designed instruction, exposure to rich cultural contexts (e.g., visits to museums, libraries, and the like), and constructive social relationships. Early years are learning years, but so are later ones.

• ***Give young children many opportunities to learn spontaneously.*** In their everyday experiences, children learn a great deal about the physical world, social relationships,

Table 5-1   Developmental Changes in the Brain (continued)

Childhood	*The brain strengthens frequently used neurological circuits and allows underutilized connections to shrivel:*	· Take advantage of children's growing awareness of patterns in their environment. For example, ask children to think about changing seasons, tidal movements, and holidays.

Childhood

The brain strengthens frequently used neurological circuits and allows underutilized connections to shrivel:

- Synaptic pruning occurs in waves throughout distinct parts of the brain.
- The front part of the cortex (closest to the forehead), which is used for learning new information, controlling behavior, and planning ahead, undergoes synaptic pruning throughout childhood and adolescence and into adulthood.
- Myelination continues to protect neurons and speed up the transmission of signals.
- The two hemispheres of the brain take on increasingly distinct responsibilities.
- Although synapses are pruned during childhood, adolescence, and adulthood, new synapses continue to be formed, reflecting learning through experience.

· Take advantage of children's growing awareness of patterns in their environment. For example, ask children to think about changing seasons, tidal movements, and holidays.
· Encourage children to gain proficiency in more than one language.
· Informally expose children to advanced cultural and aesthetic systems, such as music, poetry, and geometric patterns.

Adolescence

The brain ignites new interests and passions, expands intellectual abilities, and fortifies emotional skills and long-term planning:

- Having begun in childhood, synaptic pruning in the front part of the cortex continues, allowing improvements in memory and attention.
- Myelination protects neurons and speeds up firing of neurons, especially in the front of the cortex, where planning and other complex cognitive processes occur.
- The cortex matures, helping adolescents integrate information from different sensory systems and engage in planning, decision making, and complex thinking processes.
- The brain strengthens the ability of higher centers of the brain to analyze and regulate emotions.
- New interests and passions (e.g., artistic pursuits, interests in politics, fascinations with sports) emerge.
- The two hemispheres of the brain continue to become specialized for different purposes.
- Circuits that support motor and speech functions continue to mature during late childhood and adolescence.

· Acknowledge the positive features of adolescents' newfound interests and passions.
· Ask adolescents to think about the future consequences of their actions.
· Protect adolescents from harm by steering them away from potentially risky events.

· Encourage adolescents to use their developing ability to think abstractly. For example, adolescents can systematically test hypotheses in science, contemplate the complex motivations of characters in literature, and envision multiple causes of political conflict in history classes.
· Provide opportunities for adolescents to participate in physical activity and, when they show an interest, to seek advanced training.
· Encourage adolescents to attend to the emotional expressions, experiences, and plights of other people.

Sources: N. R. Carlson, 2007; Casey et al., 2000; Cowan, 1979; M. Diamond & Hopson, 1998; P. R. Huttenlocher, 1990; M. H. Johnson, 1999; Killgore et al., 2001; National Research Council, 1999; C. A. Nelson et al., 2006; Paus et al., 1999; Rakic, 1995; V. F. Reyna & Farley, 2006; Sowell et al., 2001, 2002; Steinberg, 2007; P. M. Thompson et al., 2000; Yakovlev & Lecours, 1967.

language, and practices of their culture. If you watch a young child playing quietly in the sandbox or building a tower of blocks in a preschool, you are observing imaginative learning at work. For children, opportunities for play and informal experimentation are often just as advantageous as, and sometimes even more beneficial than, teacher-directed instruction (Bornstein, 2006b; Göncü & Gaskins, 2006; C. L. Smith, 2006).

In fact, because some neurological changes do not take place until middle childhood or later, youngsters may not even be able to benefit from certain kinds of educational experiences until middle childhood at the earliest. Sustaining attention on a single topic and inhibiting inappropriate actions are capacities that improve with experience but also depend on brain development. Accordingly, some expectations may be quite reasonable for older children yet unreasonable for younger ones (Elkind, 2007).

• ***Accommodate the needs of children with neurological delays and disabilities.*** Individualizing instruction is especially important for children who have neurological conditions that hinder their learning in certain domains. For example, children who have difficulty distinguishing among the various sounds of speech may have brain circuits that are not sufficiently formed to permit this activity. Intensive training in speech processing seems helpful to these children, presumably because of its effects on brain pathways (Simos et al., 2007). Similarly, children who have difficulty performing basic numerical operations occasionally have brain circuits that fail to exchange mathematical information easily, but these children are often receptive to intervention (Posner & Rothbart, 2007).

• ***Provide extra guidance to children who have had early exposure to drugs and alcohol.*** As you read in Chapter 4, some children who were exposed to alcohol, cocaine, and other drugs during their prenatal development have minor or more serious brain damage. As a result, these youngsters may need assistance in understanding abstract ideas, inhibiting inappropriate responses (such as impulsively hitting bothersome peers), and applying rules to multiple settings (e.g., "keep your hands to yourself" applies to the lunchroom and playground as well as to the classroom). Ultimately, adults must remember that, with proper guidance and instruction, many children of parents who abuse alcohol and drugs can lead productive and fulfilling lives. One 17-year-old girl with fetal alcohol syndrome expressed this idea eloquently:

> There are two things I want you to know: Do not call me a victim, and do not tell me what I cannot do. Help me to find a way to do it. (Lutke, 1997, p. 188)

• ***Coach young children in expressing their emotions productively.*** In Chapter 3 you learned that children typically learn many essential skills for *self-regulation,* the ability to direct and control one's personal actions and emotions, in the context of their families. Yet not all children receive adequate encouragement at home to behave appropriately in group settings or express their emotions in ways that are both culturally appropriate and personally satisfying, and occasionally children are born with neurological circuits that predispose them to be tense or combative (Eisenberg, 2006). By the time children enter school, there are marked individual differences in children's self-regulatory abilities. Some children begin school able to deal productively with disappointment, whereas others cannot easily restrain themselves when frustrated (Blair, 2002). Children who lack self-regulatory skills need the same loving, sensitive care as do other children, as well as extra guidance in expressing their emotions productively. (You will learn about emotional self-regulation in Chapter 11.)

• ***Give youngsters many opportunities to plan ahead.*** Long-term planning and self-control do not appear on the scene—or in the brain—fully formed. To help youngsters develop such critical executive functions as planning and goal setting, you can encourage young people to use a calendar or appointment book, help set agendas for class meetings, keep track of homework assignments, and determine steps needed to meet graduation requirements (Meltzer, Pollica, & Barzillai, 2007). (You will learn more about behavioral self-regulation in Chapter 13.)

• ***Help children who have been neglected or abused to form warm, trusting, and stable relationships.*** First relationships leave impressions on children's brains (Insel, 2000; Siegel, 2001). That is, children develop expectations, tentatively written into their neurological circuits, regarding how relationships unfold (e.g., whether caregivers are affectionate or rejecting), how emotions progress (e.g., whether anger defuses or explodes into a turbulent outburst), and how they should judge themselves (e.g., whether they are intrinsically worthy people or not). With faith in children's resilience, responsive adults can help ill-treated children learn new ways of relating to others. (You will learn about children's attachments and other aspects of their emotional development in Chapter 11.)

• ***Consider the connections that exist among cognitive processes, emotional experiences, and bodily sensations.*** Although we as adults may think about intellectual objectives for children without regard for children's social-emotional and physical needs, the reality is that in children's brains, these domains continually intermingle. Thus children's thoughts regularly trigger emotions, which in turn play out as sensations in the body (Immordino-Yang & Damasio, 2007). For example, as a group of children listen to a teacher's description about a recent famine, they may become visibly distressed—their fists clench, bodies fidget, and facial expressions become drawn. The teacher might talk about her own feelings, advise the children about the productive responses officials are taking in response to the tragedy, and perhaps solicit the children's ideas about how they, too, could play a role in addressing the problem.

• ***Shield adolescents from risk.*** Although adolescents develop increasingly efficient intellectual abilities, their powers of restraint are not yet fully mature. For example, adolescents are generally able to appraise the risks of potentially dangerous behaviors (e.g., drinking and driving, having unprotected sex), but they may temporarily lose good judgment in the heat of the moment, especially when they're with peers (V. F. Reyna & Farley, 2006; Steinberg, 2007). Thus efforts to educate adolescents about the possible consequences of risk-taking behaviors tend to be only modestly effective unless paired with mechanisms that limit adolescents' access to health-compromising and hazardous activities. For instance, adults can educate adolescents about problems with underage drinking but also make it not only illegal but also expensive and inconvenient for teens to obtain alcoholic beverages.

Physical Development During Childhood

As you have seen, systematic changes take place in physical size, bodily proportions, and neurological structures throughout childhood and adolescence. With these changes come new opportunities to practice motor skills, develop healthy habits, engage in physical activity, and relate to peers in unprecedented ways. We describe developmental periods in more detail in the next few pages.

Infancy (Birth–Age 2)

Infancy is an impressive period of rapid growth and development. However, even at birth, infants display remarkable reflexes. Before the umbilical cord is cut, the first reflex, *breathing,* begins, providing oxygen and removing carbon dioxide. Breathing and a few other reflexes begin in infancy and operate throughout life. Other reflexes, such as automatically grasping small objects placed in hands and responding to loud noises by flaring out arms and legs, last only a few months. Reflexes are evidence of normal neurological development, and their absence in early infancy is a matter of concern to physicians (Touwen, 1974).

As infants grow older, they add motor skills to their physical repertoire. Motor skills at first appear slowly, then more rapidly. In the first 12 to 18 months, infants learn to hold up their heads, roll over, reach for objects, sit, crawl, and walk. In the second year, they walk with increasing balance and coordination and can manipulate small objects with their hands. In the "Cognitive Development: Infancy" video in MyEducationLab, you can observe 16-month-old Corwin walking confidently and competently. Corwin holds his arms high to maintain balance, but he is also agile enough to walk quickly and stay upright while reaching down into a bag.

Motor skills emerge in a particular order, following *cephalocaudal* and *proximodistal* trends (Robbins, Brody, Hogan, Jackson, & Green, 1928). The **cephalocaudal trend** refers to the vertical order of emerging skills, proceeding from the head downward. Infants first learn to control their heads, then shoulders and trunk, and later their legs. The **proximodistal trend** refers to the inside-to-outside pattern in which growth progresses outward from the spine. Infants, for example, first learn to control their arms, then their hands, and finally, their fingers. As you learned in the earlier discussion of infants' reaching behaviors, these general motor trends coexist with sizable individual differences in styles and pathways to proficiency.

Because infants cannot use words to communicate physical needs, practitioners must seek information from families about their babies' sleeping, eating, drinking, diapering, and comforting preferences and habits. We offer ideas of what to look for in the Observation Guidelines table "Assessing Physical Development in Infancy."

Early Childhood (Ages 2–6)

Visit a local playground and you are likely to see preschool children engaged in nonstop physical activity. Physical movement is a hallmark of early childhood, and dramatic changes occur in both gross motor skills and fine motor skills. **Gross motor skills** (e.g., running, hopping, tumbling, climbing, and swinging) permit large movement through and within the environment.

MyEducationLab

Observe Corwin walk with good balance in the "Cognitive Development: Infancy" video. (Find Video Examples in Chapter 5 of MyEducationLab.)

cephalocaudal trend
Vertical ordering of motor skills and physical development; order is head first to feet last.

proximodistal trend
Inside-outside ordering of motor skills and physical development; order is inside first and outside last.

gross motor skills
Large movements of the body that permit locomotion through and within the environment.

Observation Guidelines

Assessing Physical Development in Infancy

Characteristic	Look For	Example	Implication
Eating Habits	· Ability to express hunger to adults · Developing ability to suck, chew, and swallow · Ability to enjoy and digest food without abdominal upset · Cultural and individual differences in how families feed infants	Wendy Sue is a listless eater who doesn't seem as interested in food as other infants in her child care program. The caregiver tells her supervisor she is worried, and the two decide to talk with the parents. It is possible that professional intervention might be needed.	To understand an infant's health, talk with parents and families. Ask the parents what they believe is appropriate care of children.
Mobility	· Developing ability to coordinate looking and touching · Growing ability to move toward objects · Temperamental factors that might affect exploration · Physical challenges that might affect exploration, including hearing and visual impairments · Temporary declines in exploration on occasion, such as when first separating from parents	Due to neurological damage at birth, Daniel's left arm and leg are less strong than those on his right side. His new child care teacher notices that he is reluctant to move around in the center. During a home visit, the teacher finds that Daniel's movements are somewhat lopsided, but he crawls around energetically. The teacher realizes that Daniel needs to feel secure at the center before he can freely explore there.	Set up the environment so infants will find it safe, predictable, attractive, and interesting. Help individual children find challenges and opportunities that match their abilities.
Resting Patterns	· Methods babies use to put themselves to sleep · Families' expectations for sleeping arrangements · Difficulties in falling asleep · Evidence that families understand risk factors for sudden infant death syndrome (SIDS)	Angie cries a lot when falling asleep, in part because she is used to sleeping on her stomach. Her teacher explains to her parents that he places babies on their backs in order to reduce the risk of SIDS. He rubs Angie's head to soothe her and help her adjust to her new sleeping position.	Talk to parents about risk factors for SIDS (see the upcoming section on "Rest and Sleep"). Explain why babies should be placed on their backs when they are falling asleep.
Health Issues	· Possible symptoms of infections, such as unusual behavior, irritability, fever, and respiratory difficulty · Suspicious injuries and unusual behaviors that may indicate abuse · Possible symptoms of prenatal drug exposure, including difficulty sleeping, extreme sensitivity, and irritability · Physical disabilities requiring accommodation	A child care teacher enjoys having Michael, age 18 months, in her care. Michael has cerebral palsy, making it difficult for him to scoot around. His teacher encourages him to move toward objects, but she also brings things to him to examine and play with. When he has a fever, she calls his mother or father, as she would for any child.	Remain alert to signs of illness and infection in children. Contact family members when infants have a fever or show other unusual physical symptoms.

Fine motor skills (e.g., drawing, writing, cutting with scissors, and manipulating small objects) involve more limited, controlled, and precise movements, primarily with the hands.

During the preschool years, children typically learn such culture-specific motor skills as riding a tricycle and throwing and catching a ball. Motor skills become smoother and better coordinated over time as a result of practice, longer arms and legs, and genetically guided increases in muscular control. Optimism and persistence in motor tasks play a role as well. For instance, when Teresa's son Alex was 4, he repeatedly asked his parents to throw him a softball as he stood poised with his bat. Not at all deterred by an abysmal batting average (about 0.05), Alex would frequently exclaim, "I almost got it!" His efforts paid off, as he gradually did learn to track the ball visually and coordinate his swing with the ball's path.

A lot of chatter, fantasy, and sheer joy accompany gross motor movements in early childhood. Often young children infuse pretend roles into their physical play. For example, they may become superheroes and villains, cowboys and cowgirls, astronauts and aliens. You can

fine motor skills
Small, precise movements of particular parts of the body, especially the hands.

observe creative and cooperative interactions between two 4-year-old children, Acadia and Cody, as they play on climbing equipment in the "Physical Activity: Early Childhood" video in MyEducationLab. The children practice a variety of gross motor skills (running, climbing, throwing a ball), all in the name of play.

Young children also make major strides in fine motor skills. Children begin to dress and undress themselves and eat with utensils. Some children develop an interest in building blocks, putting small pieces of puzzles together, or stringing beads. Other children spend considerable time drawing and cutting (see Figure 5-9), and they may form their own creative shapes (e.g., by combining circles and lines to represent human beings), represent objects from the real world, and mimic adults' cursive writing with wavy lines or connected loops (Braswell & Callanan, 2003; R. Kellogg, 1967).

We often find large individual differences in young children's fine motor skills. Some children, such as those born with certain chromosomal conditions (e.g., Turner syndrome; see Table 4-1) and those exposed to alcohol during prenatal development, tend to show delays in fine motor skills (Connor, Sampson, Streissguth, Bookstein, & Barr, 2006; Milne et al., 2006; Starke, Wikland, & Möller, 2003). Some evidence also indicates that certain fine motor activities (e.g., cursive handwriting) may be easier for girls than boys (M. R. Cohen, 1997). Fortunately, explicit instruction and practice can help children improve fine motor skills, although some differences in dexterity often persist (Bruni, 1998; Case-Smith, 1996; Maraj & Bonertz, 2007).

Middle Childhood (Ages 6–10)

Over the course of middle childhood, youngsters typically show slow but steady gains in height and weight. Their bodies grow larger without altering the basic structures. As a result, proportions of separate body parts change less than in infancy or early childhood. With these slow, continuous gains come a few losses: Children lose their 20 primary ("baby") teeth one by one, replacing them with permanent teeth that at first appear oversized in the small mouths of 6-, 7-, and 8-year-olds. Girls mature somewhat more quickly than do boys, erupting permanent teeth sooner and progressing toward skeletal maturity earlier.

In middle childhood, children build on their emerging physical capabilities. Many gross motor skills, once awkward, are now executed smoothly. Whereas preschoolers may run for the sheer joy of it, elementary school children put running to use in organized games and sports. They intensify their speed and coordination in running, kicking, catching, and dribbling. Becoming proficient in athletic skills can be gratifying for children. As you can see in Figure 5-10, when 6-year-old Alex was asked by his teacher to identify five things he liked to do, he chose five athletic activities. You can also observe the pleasure that 9-year-old Kyle and 10-year-old Curtis experience as they practice basketball skills in the "Physical Activity: Middle Childhood" video in MyEducationLab.

Children within this age range also improve further in fine motor skills. Their drawings, supported by physiological maturation and cognitive advances, are more detailed, and their handwriting becomes smaller, smoother, and more consistent (see Chapter 10). They also begin to tackle such fine motor activities as sewing, model building, and arts and crafts projects.

As children progress through middle childhood, they become increasingly sensitive about their physical appearance. Consider this fourth grader's self-critical viewpoint:

> I am the ugliest girl I know. My hair is not straight enough, and it doesn't even have the dignity to be curly. My teeth are crooked from sucking my thumb and from a wet-bathing-suit-and-a-slide accident. My clothes are hand-me-downs, my skin is a greenish color that other people call "tan" to be polite, and I don't say the right words, or say them in the right way. I'm smart enough to notice that I'm not smart enough; not so short, but not tall enough; and definitely, definitely too skinny. (Marissa Arillo, in Oldfather & West, 1999, p. 60)

For many children, self-consciousness increases as they get close to puberty. And it is not only the children themselves who notice their physical appearance: Other people do as well. In fact, people generally respond more favorably to children they perceive to be physically attractive. In a variety of cultures, physical attractiveness is correlated with, and probably a

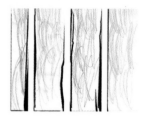

Figure 5-9

Isabelle, age 3½, traced shapes and wrote her name in the artwork on the left. Learning to spell her name, Isabelle included two *E*s and two *L*s. In the artwork on the right, she practiced her cutting, attempting to follow the black lines, and correcting her work in the third rectangle from the left, showing her desire to meet a standard of straightness.

Figure 5-10

When asked to choose five things he liked to do, 6-year-old Alex identified five athletic activities: kicking, running, swimming, skating, and boating.

puberty
Physiological changes that occur during adolescence and lead to reproductive maturation.

growth spurt
Rapid increase in height and weight during puberty.

menarche
First menstrual period in an adolescent female.

spermarche
First ejaculation in an adolescent male.

causal factor in, self-esteem (Chu, 2000; Dohnt & Tiggemann, 2006b; Harter, 1999). Thus, although many children exaggerate their own physical flaws, the reality is that appearance is influential in social relationships, and it does affect how children feel about themselves.

In the Development and Practice feature "Accommodating the Physical Needs of Infants and Children," we give examples of strategies for meeting individual and group needs for physical care, creating a hazard-free environment, and integrating physical activity into the curriculum.

Early Adolescence (Ages 10–14)

The most obvious aspect of physical change in early adolescence is the onset of **puberty.** Ushered in by a cascade of hormones, puberty involves a series of biological changes that lead to reproductive maturity. It is marked not only by the maturation of sex-specific characteristics but also by a **growth spurt,** a rapid increase in height and weight. The release of hormones has other physiological repercussions as well, such as increases in bone density, facial oil production (often manifested as acne), and sweat gland activity (Styne, 2003).

Girls typically progress through puberty before boys do. Puberty begins in girls sometime between ages 8 and 13 (on average, at age 10). It starts with a growth spurt, "budding" of the breasts, and the emergence of pubic hair. Whereas such changes are typically gradual, the onset of menstruation, **menarche,** is an abrupt event that can be either positive or frightening, depending on a girl's awareness and preparation. The first menstrual period tends to occur rather late in puberty, usually between 9 and 15 years of age. Nature apparently delays menstruation, and with it the possibility of conception, until girls are physically strong and close to their adult height and therefore physiologically better able to have a successful pregnancy.

For boys, puberty starts between 9 and 14 years (on average, at 11½ years), when the testes enlarge and the scrotum changes in texture and color. A year or so later, the penis grows larger and pubic hair appears; the growth spurt begins soon after. At about 13 to 14 years, boys have their first ejaculation experience, **spermarche,** often while sleeping. Boys seem to receive less information from parents about this milestone than girls do about menstruation, and little is known about boys' feelings about it. Later developments include growth of facial hair, deepening of the voice, and eventually the attainment of adult height. (The course of puberty for both boys and girls is depicted in Figure 5-11.)

In addition to the obvious sexual differences, boys and girls become increasingly distinct in other ways. Boys end up on average being taller than girls. Boys have a longer period of steady prepubescent growth, and they grow a bit more than girls do during their adolescent growth spurt. With the onset of puberty, boys also gain considerably more muscle mass than girls, courtesy of the male hormone *testosterone.*

Accompanying the physical changes of puberty are changes in adolescents' cognitive capacities, social relationships, and feelings about themselves (Brooks-Gunn, 1989; Brooks-Gunn & Paikoff, 1992). Continuing development of the cortex allows more complex thought, as we have seen, and hormonal fluctuations and additional changes in the brain affect emotions. Adolescents' rapidly changing physical characteristics can be a source of either excitement or dismay. For instance, Anne Frank looked positively on puberty, as this entry in her diary shows:

> I think what is happening to me is so wonderful, and not only what can be seen on my body, but all that is taking place inside. I never discuss myself or any of these things with anybody; that is why I have to talk to myself about them.
>
> Each time I have a period—and that has only been three times—I have the feeling that in spite of all the pain, unpleasantness, and nastiness, I have a sweet secret, and that is why, although it is nothing but a nuisance to me in a way, I always long for the time that I shall feel that secret within me again. (A. Frank, 1967, p. 146)

Others are not at all happy with their changing bodies. In *Reviving Ophelia,* therapist Mary Pipher (1994) describes ninth-grader Cayenne's perspective:

> She hated her looks. She thought her hair was too bright, her hips and thighs too flabby. She tried to lose weight but couldn't. She dyed her hair, but it turned a weird purple color and dried out. She felt almost every girl was prettier. She said, "Let's face it. I'm a dog." (p. 32)[1]

[1]From REVIVING OPHELIA by Mary Pipher, Ph.D., copyright © 1994 by Mary Pipher, Ph.D. Used by permission of G. P. Putnam's Sons, a division of Penguin Group (USA) Inc.

Development and Practice

Accommodating the Physical Needs of Infants and Children

- **Meet the physical needs of individual infants rather than expecting all infants to conform to a universal and inflexible schedule.**

  A caregiver in an infant program keeps a schedule of times infants usually receive their bottles and naps. That way, she can plan her day to rotate among individual infants, giving each as much attention as possible.

- **View meeting the physical needs of infants as part of the overall curriculum for their care and education.**

  An infant-toddler caregiver understands the importance of meeting physical needs in ways that establish and deepen relationships with each child. She uses one-to-one activities such as diaper changing and bottle feeding as occasions to interact.

- **Make sure the classroom is free of sharp edges, peeling paint, and other environmental hazards to which young children may be particularly vulnerable.**

  After new carpet is installed in his classroom, a preschool teacher notices that several children complain of stomachaches and headaches. He suspects that the recently applied carpet adhesive may be to blame and, with the approval of the preschool's director, asks an outside consultant to evaluate the situation. Meanwhile, he conducts most of the day's activities outdoors or in other rooms.

- **Provide frequent opportunities for children to engage in physical activity.**

  A preschool teacher schedules "Music and Marching" for midmorning, "Outdoor Time" before lunch, and a nature walk to collect leaves for an art project after nap time.

- **Plan activities that will help children develop their fine motor skills.**

  An after-school caregiver invites children to make mosaics that depict different kinds of vehicles. The children glue a variety of small objects (e.g., beads, sequins, beans, colored rice) onto line drawings of cars, trains, boats, airplanes, bicycles, and so on.

- **Design physical activities so that students with widely differing skill levels can successfully participate.**

  During a unit on tennis, a physical education teacher has children practice the forehand stroke using tennis rackets. First, she asks them to practice bouncing and then hitting the ball against the wall of the gymnasium. If some students master these basic skills, she asks them to see how many times in succession they can hit the ball against the wall. When they reach five successive hits, she tells them to vary the height of the ball from waist high to shoulder high (Logsdon, Alleman, Straits, Belka, & Clark, 1997).

- **Integrate physical activity into academic lessons.**

  When teaching about molecules and temperature, a fifth-grade teacher asks children to stand in a cluster in an open area of the classroom. To show children how molecules behave when something is cold, she asks them to stay close together and move around just a little bit. To show them how molecules behave when something is hot, she asks them to spread farther apart and move more actively.

- **Give children time to rest.**

  After a kindergarten class has been playing outside, their teacher offers a snack of apple slices, crackers, and milk. Once they have cleaned up their milk cartons and napkins, the children gather around him on the floor while he reads them a story.

- **Respect children's growing ability to care for their own bodies.**

  In an after-school program, a teacher allows the children to go to the restroom whenever they need to. He teaches children to hang a clothespin with their name on an "out rope" when they leave the room and then remove the pin when they return.

IN GIRLS
Initial elevation of breasts and beginning of growth spurt (typically between 8 and 13 years; on average, at 10 years)
Appearance of pubic hair (sometimes occurs before elevation of breasts)
Increase in size and structure of uterus, vagina, labia, and clitoris
Further development of breasts
Peak of growth spurt
Menarche, or onset of menstrual cycle (typically between 9 and 15 years)
Completion of height gain (about 2 years after menarche) and attainment of adult height
Completion of breast development and pubic hair growth

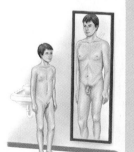

IN BOYS
Enlargement of the testes and changes in texture and color of scrotum (typically between 9 and 14 years; on average, at 11$\frac{1}{2}$ years)
Increase in penis size and appearance of pubic hair
Beginning of growth spurt (on average, at 12$\frac{1}{2}$ years)
Spermarche, or first ejaculation
Peak of growth spurt, accompanied by more rapid penis growth
Appearance of facial hair
Deepening voice, as size of larynx and length of vocal cords increase
Completion of penis growth
Completion of height gain and attainment of adult height
Completion of pubic hair growth

Figure 5-11

Maturational sequences of puberty.

During the adolescent growth spurt, appetites increase considerably. ZITS. © Zits Partnership. King Features Syndicate.

Puberty also seems to loosen restraints on problem behaviors. For example, the onset of puberty is associated with increased aggression; alcohol, drug, and cigarette use; and experimentation with such behaviors as lying, shoplifting, and burglary (Cota-Robles & Neiss, 1999; Crews, He, & Hodge, 2007; Martino, Ellickson, Klein, McCaffrey, & Edelen, 2008). As we suggested earlier in this chapter, adolescents' risk taking may be based partly in new brain circuits. Having a teenage brain, it seems, encourages young people to try new things, be daredevils, and affiliate with like-minded peers.

Age of onset of puberty is another significant aspect of adolescents' adjustment. Genetic factors have by far the strongest influence on the specific age at which youngsters go through puberty, but nurture also plays an important role (Mustanski, Viken, Kaprio, Pulkkinen, & Rose, 2004). In general, there has been a steady trend toward earlier puberty in industrialized nations during the last hundred years, with better nutrition and more calories probably being the primary reasons for the trend (de Muinck Keizer-Schrama & Mul, 2001; Ellis, 2004). Individual experiences are also influential. For example, family conflict seems to accelerate puberty in girls, possibly because of its effects on stress hormones, whereas low-income family environments delay maturation, perhaps because of their links to inadequate nutrition (Ellis, 2004; Hulanicka, Gronkiewicz, & Koniarek, 2001). Less information is available about personal factors associated with the maturational timing of boys.

Extremely early or late maturation can be a serious concern for adolescents and their families. Researchers have focused primarily on the potential vulnerabilities of early-maturing girls. Early-maturing girls become heavier and more curvaceous at younger ages, are often dissatisfied with their bodies, and may be swept into new social networks with older adolescents (Ge et al., 2003). Early-maturing girls are more likely to be unhappy and at risk for developing eating disorders, precocious sexual behaviors, and other problem behaviors than are later-maturing girls (Dick, Rose, Viken, & Kapriro, 2000; Ge, Conger, & Elder, 2001; C. D. Hayes & Hofferth, 1987; Weisner & Ittel, 2002). Early-maturing boys also face temptations and undergo stressful change during puberty, but their difficulties seem to be relatively short lived (Ge et al., 2003).

Youngsters who mature late often experience their own stresses. Compared to early-maturing boys, late-maturing boys tend to be less athletically inclined, more preoccupied with their muscle mass, less popular with peers, and underrepresented in leadership positions at school (R. T. Gross & Duke, 1980; H. F. Jones, 1949; Lindfors et al., 2007; McCabe & Ricciardelli, 2004; Simmons & Blyth, 1987). On the plus side, late-maturing boys are less likely to engage in risk-taking behaviors such as smoking, drinking, and delinquent activities (P. D. Duncan, Ritter, Dornbusch, Gross, & Carlsmith, 1985; Susman et al., 1985). Late-maturing girls generally show fewer health risks than early-maturing girls but may experience distinct vulnerabilities, including a concern with body image (McCabe & Ricciardelli, 2004).

The rapid physical changes of puberty are accompanied by new intellectual abilities and social relationships.

Development and Practice

Accommodating the Physical Needs of Adolescents

- **Show understanding of the self-conscious feelings that youngsters have about their changing bodies.**

  A middle school basketball coach gives students plenty of time to change clothes before and after practice. He also makes sure that all showers have curtains to ensure everyone's privacy.

- **Keep in mind that menstruation can begin at unexpected times.**

  An eighth-grade girl comes into class obviously upset, and her best friend approaches their teacher to explain that the two of them need to go to the nurse's office right away. The teacher realizes what has probably just happened and immediately gives them permission to go.

- **Make sure adolescents understand what sexual harassment is, and do not tolerate it when it occurs.**

  A high school includes a sexual harassment policy in its student handbook, and homeroom teachers explain the policy very early

in the school year. When a student unthinkingly violates the policy by teasing a classmate about her "big rack," his teacher takes him aside and privately explains that his comment not only constitutes sexual harassment (and so violates school policy) but also makes the girl feel unnecessarily embarrassed. The boy admits that he spoke without thinking and, after class, tells the girl he's sorry.

- **Be sensitive to adolescents' feelings about early or late maturation.**

  A middle school's health curriculum clearly describes the typical sequence of biological changes that accompanies puberty. It also stresses that the timing of these changes varies widely from one person to the next and that being "normal" takes many forms.

The timing of puberty does not necessarily establish lifelong patterns, however. Many adolescents learn constructive lessons from the trials and tribulations of their teenage years. The ability of adolescents to adjust positively to puberty depends to a large degree on their culture, parents, and school setting (Blyth, Simmons, & Zakin, 1985; J. P. Hill, Holmbeck, Marlow, Green, & Lynch, 1985; A. C. Peterson & Taylor, 1980; Stattin & Magnusson, 1989). In some cultures puberty is joyously welcomed by formal celebrations, such as the bar mitzvahs and bat mitzvahs for 13-year-olds of the Jewish faith and *quinceañeras* for 15-year-old girls in Mexican and Mexican American communities.

School personnel can help youngsters adjust by giving advance warning about physiological changes and reassuring youngsters that considerable variations in timing are well within the "normal" range. In the Development and Practice feature "Accommodating the Physical Needs of Adolescents," we give additional examples of strategies for accommodating both the changes of puberty and the diversity that exists among young adolescents.

Late Adolescence (Ages 14–18)

At about age 15 for girls and age 17 for boys, the growth spurt ends, and in the later teenage years, most adolescents reach sexual maturity. (However, because of individual differences, especially among boys, some teens show few signs of puberty until the high school years.) With sexual maturation comes increasing interest in sexual activity, including hugging, kissing, and, for many teens, more intimate contact as well (DeLamater & MacCorquodale, 1979). Later in this chapter, we will consider health risks associated with unprotected sexual contact among peers.

As you have learned, the brain continues to refine its pathways during adolescence, permitting more thoughtful control of emotions and more deliberate reflection about possible consequences of various behaviors. Nevertheless, many older adolescents continue to engage in behaviors that could undermine their long-term physical health—for instance, abusing alcohol and drugs and not wearing a seat belt while riding in an automobile (B. J. Guthrie, Caldwell, & Hunter, 1997; Wallander, Eggert, & Gilbert, 2004). Table 5-2 presents risky behaviors commonly seen in high school students.

The Developmental Trends table "Physical Development at Different Age Levels" summarizes the key characteristics of each age-group and provides implications for teachers and other professionals. In the next section we examine the practices that contribute to good health and, conversely, the choices that undermine it.

Physical Well-Being

With age, children and adolescents become more aware of "good health" (Figure 5-12). But they don't always make decisions that are best for their health. In the following sections, we

Table 5-2   Percentage of U.S. Students Grades 9–12 Who Reported Engaging in Risky Behaviors

Risky Behavior	Girls	Boys
Substance Use		
Alcohol (in last 30 days)	42.8	43.8
Cigarettes (in last 30 days)	23.0	22.9
Marijuana (in last 30 days)	18.2	22.1
Cocaine (in last 30 days)	2.8	4.0
Inhalants (in lifetime)	13.5	11.3
Heroin (in lifetime)	1.4	3.3
Methamphetamine (in lifetime)	6.0	6.3
Ecstasy (MDMA; in lifetime)	5.3	7.2
Hallucinogenic drugs (e.g., LSD, PCP angel dust; in lifetime)	6.8	10.2
Illegal steroids (in lifetime)	3.2	4.8
Sexual Behaviors		
Had sexual intercourse (in lifetime)	45.7	47.9
Sexually active (had intercourse in past 3 months)	34.6	33.3
No condom use during last intercourse (among sexually active adolescents)	44.1	30.0
Alcohol or drug use at last sexual intercourse (among sexually active adolescents)	19.0	27.6
Had four or more sexual partners (in lifetime)	12.0	16.5
Behaviors That Contribute to Unintentional Injuries		
Rarely or never wore seat belts in car	7.8	12.5
Bicycle riding without helmets (among those who rode bicycle in last 12 months)	79.9	86.1
Rode with a driver who had been drinking alcohol (in last 30 days)	29.6	27.2
Drove car after drinking alcohol (in last 30 days)	8.1	11.7

Source: Centers for Disease Control and Prevention, 2006.

Figure 5-12

As children grow older, they become more knowledgeable about what "good health" entails. Grace (age 11) drew this rendition of healthy and unhealthy people.
Modeled after Mayall, Bendelow, Barker, Storey, & Veltman, 1996.

consider issues related to health and well-being, including eating habits, physical activity, rest and sleep, and health-compromising behaviors. We also identify strategies that adults can use to encourage young people to develop healthful lifestyles.

Eating Habits

Children's nutrition affects all aspects of their physical well-being, including their energy level, growth, and ability to concentrate. Given the importance of nutrition, an essential question is, How do children learn to eat well?

Good eating habits start at birth. Breastfeeding is the preferred method of feeding infants because breast milk is rich in needed vitamins, provides infants with antibodies against illnesses, and is easier to digest than infant formulas (American Academy of Pediatrics [AAP], 2005; London et al., 2007). Breast milk also gives the developing brain the nutrients it needs to form protective myelinating layers around neurons (London et al., 2007). Of course, some mothers cannot easily breastfeed, others do not want to, and still others (e.g., mothers who carry the human immunodeficiency virus or are undergoing certain medical treatments) cannot do so safely, because it is possible to pass on infections and medications in breast milk. As an alternative, many families select one of the iron-fortified formulas that have been derived from the proteins of cow's milk or soybeans and commercially prepared to match infants' digestive abilities and needs for calories, vitamins, and minerals. Other specialty formulas are available for infants with food allergies and intolerances. Professional caregivers generally try to support families' preferences but also suggest medically proven strategies, such as introducing nutritious soft cereals and fruits at around 4 to 6 months of age and avoiding hard foods that infants cannot easily chew and swallow.

Developmental Trends

Physical Development at Different Age Levels

Age	What You Might Observe	Diversity	Implications
Infancy (Birth–2 Years) 	· Emergence of reflexes · Rapid growth and change in proportions of body parts · Increasing ability to move around, first by squirming; then rolling, crawling, creeping, or scooting; finally by walking · Increasing ability to coordinate small muscles of hands and eyes · Increasing self-help skills in such areas as feeding, dressing, washing, toileting, and grooming	· Children vary in timing and quality of gross motor skills (e.g., rolling over, crawling, and sitting up) depending on genetic and cultural factors. · Fine motor skills and eye–hand coordination may appear earlier or later depending on genetic makeup and encouragement from caregivers. · Self-help skills appear earlier when encouraged, but virtually all children learn them eventually, and sooner is not necessarily better.	· Celebrate each child's unique growth patterns, but watch for unusual patterns or differences that may require accommodation or intervention. · Provide a choice of appropriate indoor and outdoor experiences to help children practice their developing motor skills. · Don't push infants to reach milestones. Allow them to experience each phase of physical development thoroughly. · Be aware of serious developmental delays that call for professional intervention.
Early Childhood (2–6 Years)	· Loss of rounded, babyish appearance, with arms and legs lengthening and taking on more mature proportions · Boundless physical energy for new gross motor skills, such as running, hopping, tumbling, climbing, and swinging · Acquisition of fine motor skills, such as functional pencil grip and use of scissors · Transition away from afternoon nap, which may initially be marked by periods of fussiness in the afternoon	· Children differ considerably in the ages at which they master various motor skills. · Boys are more physically active than girls, but girls are healthier overall; these differences continue throughout childhood and adolescence. · Some home environments (e.g., small apartments, as well as larger houses in which parents restrict movement) limit the degree to which children can engage in vigorous physical activity; others may present hazardous environmental conditions (e.g., lead paint, toxic fumes). · Children with mental retardation may have delayed motor skills.	· Provide frequent opportunities to play outside or (in inclement weather) in a gymnasium or other large indoor space. · Intersperse vigorous physical exercise with rest and quiet time. · Encourage fine motor skills through puzzles, blocks, doll houses, and arts and crafts. · Choose activities that accommodate diversity in gross and fine motor skills.
Middle Childhood (6–10 Years)	· Steady gains in height and weight · Loss and replacement of primary teeth · Refinement and consolidation of gross motor skills and integration of such skills into structured play activities · Participation in organized sports · Increasing fluency in fine motor skills, such as handwriting and drawing	· Variations in weight and height are prominent at any single grade level. · Children begin to show specific athletic talents and interests. · Gender differences appear in children's preferences for various sports and physical activities. · Some neighborhoods do not have playgrounds or other safe play areas that foster gross motor skills. · Some children have delays in fine motor skills (e.g., their handwriting may be unusually uneven and irregular) as a result of neurological conditions or lack of opportunity to practice fine motor tasks. · Some children spend much of their non-school time in sedentary activities, such as watching television or playing video games.	· Integrate physical movement into academic activities. · Provide daily opportunities for children to engage in self-organized play activities. · Teach children the basics of various sports and physical games, and encourage them to participate in organized sports programs. · Encourage practice of fine motor skills, but don't penalize children whose fine motor precision is delayed.
Early Adolescence (10–14 Years) 	· Periods of rapid growth · Beginnings of puberty · Self-consciousness about physical changes · Some risk-taking behavior	· Onset of puberty may vary over a span of several years; puberty occurs earlier for girls than for boys. · Leisure activities may or may not include regular exercise. · Young teens differ considerably in strength and physical endurance, as well as in their specific talents for sports. Noticeable gender differences occur, with boys being faster, stronger, and more confident about their physical abilities than girls. · Peer groups may or may not encourage risky behavior.	· Be a role model by showing a commitment to physical fitness and good eating habits. · Provide privacy for changing clothes and showering during physical education classes. · Explain what sexual harassment is, and do not tolerate it, whether it appears in the form of jokes, teasing, or physical contact. · Encourage after-school clubs and leisure activities that help teenagers spend their time constructively. · Explain to adolescents that risky behaviors can cause them real harm.

continued

Developmental Trends (continued)

Age	What You Might Observe	Diversity	Implications
Late Adolescence (14–18 Years)	· In girls, completion of growth spurt and attainment of mature height · In boys, ongoing increases in stature · Ravenous appetites · Increasing sexual activity · Some serious risky behaviors (e.g., drinking alcohol, taking illegal drugs, engaging in unprotected sexual contact, driving under the influence of drugs or alcohol), due in part to greater independence and acquisition of driver's licenses	· Gender differences in physical abilities increase; boys are more active in organized sports programs. · Some teens begin to limit risky behaviors and make better decisions. · Eating disorders may appear, especially in girls. · Adolescents are less likely than younger children to get regular medical care. · Adolescents differ in their exposure to risky substances (e.g., drug use is more prevalent in some neighborhoods than others).	· Make sure that adolescents know "the facts of life" about sexual intercourse and conception. · Encourage abstinence when adolescents are not sexually active. · When adolescents are sexually active and committed to remaining so, encourage them to use protective measures and to restrict the number of partners. · Encourage young people to form goals for the future (e.g., going to college, developing athletic skills) that motivate productive actions. · Reduce adolescents' exposure to potentially risky situations. · Develop and enforce policies related to sexual harassment.

Sources: Bredekamp & Copple, 1997; Gallahue & Ozmun, 1998; V. F. Reyna & Farley, 2006; Steinberg, 2007; J. M. Tanner, 1990.

Families and caregivers continue to play an important role in children's diets as children grow and eat foods prepared for them. Unfortunately, some children are poorly fed, occasionally because parents have few financial resources; are homeless, physically or mentally ill; or simply limited in access to appropriate nutrition. Even in more fortunate financial circumstances, parents may rush to work in the morning and neglect to feed either themselves or their children. When children are underfed or given only nonnutritious foods, the outcomes can be quite serious. For example, half of children in developing countries and more than 1 in 20 children under age 5 in the United States have anemia (iron deficiency), a condition that can cause developmental delays and behavioral disturbances (Killip, Bennett, & Chambers, 2007; S. P. Walker et al., 2007).

As children begin to make more decisions on their own, their nutrition sometimes deteriorates. For instance, in a large-scale study of American children, 27 percent of children ages 2 to 6 had a good diet, but only 5 percent of adolescents ages 13 to 18 did (Federal Interagency Forum on Child and Family Statistics, 2007). Many children become less inclined to eat breakfast as they get older, and this practice may result in difficulty concentrating in school (Centers for Disease Control and Prevention [CDC], 2005c). Furthermore, the particular foods youngsters choose to eat may lack essential nutrients. In general, adolescents eat far too much "bad" stuff, such as high-fat and high-sodium foods, and far too little "good" stuff, such as fruits, vegetables, and whole grains. In fact, only about 20 percent of young people eat enough fruits and vegetables, and just 40 percent of children 2 to 17 years old meet the U.S. Department of Agriculture's recommendations for fiber (found in fruits, vegetables, whole grains, and beans and peas) (CDC, 2004, 2005c).

Part of the problem is that children don't understand how eating habits relate to health. At age 5, children know that some foods (e.g., fruits, vegetables, milk) are good for them but have no idea why (Carey, 1985). Even by ages 9 to 11, however, the vast majority of children still have not learned that the body breaks food down into the essential nutrients it needs to grow and thrive (Carey, 1985). Such ignorance can continue well into adolescence. For example, Jeanne's son Jeff, at 17, frequently boasted that he could get through an entire day on a few donuts and several cans of cola.

As young people gain increasing independence from adults, they gain more control over what they do and do not eat. Unfortunately, many adolescents choose relatively nonnutritious meals that are high in fat and sodium.

Overweight youth. A staggering number of children have become overweight during the last few decades. Currently, 18 percent of U.S. youngsters between 6 and 17 years old are overweight (Federal Interagency Forum on Child and Family Statistics, 2007). For many overweight children, their problems with eating and inactivity begin in early childhood. Amazingly, as many as 13 percent of American children 2 to 5 years old are overweight (CDC, 2007b).

Some children are very overweight. **Obesity,** the condition of being seriously overweight, is now considered a global health epidemic by the World Health Organization (2000). Children are considered obese if their body weight exceeds their "ideal" weight (a figure that takes into account their age, gender, height, and body build) by 20 percent or more (Rallison, 1986). Some obese children outgrow their baby fat, but others do not. Approximately 40 percent of obese 7-year-olds are obese as adults, and 70 percent of obese 10- to 13-year-olds become obese adults (L. H. Epstein, Wing, & Valoski, 1985). Childhood obesity is a concern because it may lead to serious health risks in adulthood, including diabetes, high blood pressure, high cholesterol, asthma, arthritis, and poor health status (CDC, 2005c; Jelalian, Wember, Bungeroth, & Birmaher, 2007). It has social consequences as well. Peers may torment obese youngsters, calling them names and excluding them from enjoyable social activities.

For some obese children, their weight problems have a genetic basis, but environmental factors, such as family eating patterns and restricted exercise, play a role in many cases (H. Thomas, 2006). Fortunately, interventions in health care clinics, including dietary counseling, calorie restriction combined with increases in physical activity, and behavioral techniques (e.g., setting specific goals, monitoring progress toward goals, and recognizing and rewarding progress), are often effective.

Increasingly, educators are realizing that schools are another important setting for addressing children's potential weight problems. Many educators are taking a hard look at cafeteria menus and replacing the high-fat and high-sugar snacks and drinks in school vending machines with more nutritious items (Budd & Volpe, 2006; CDC, 2005b; Lumeng, 2006). Other appropriate goals for schools include ensuring that students obtain adequate amounts of physical activity, decreasing time spent in sedentary activities (e.g., sitting for hours at a time without getting up during lessons), and tracking annual assessments of students' weight and height (Budd & Volpe, 2006; Lumeng, 2006). Some school programs have asked students to keep track of their own fat intake, soft drink consumption, and physical activity (Haerens et al., 2006). Such record keeping, when coupled with motivational techniques, can have desirable effects on youngsters' weight and health.

Eating disorders.   Whereas some young people eat too much, others eat too little and develop eating disorders that seriously threaten their health. People with **anorexia nervosa** eat little, if anything. In contrast, people with **bulimia** eat voraciously, especially fattening foods, and then purge their bodies by taking laxatives or forcing themselves to vomit. Unfortunately, extreme weight control methods, such as not eating, taking diet pills, vomiting, and taking laxatives, are fairly widespread among adolescents (CDC, 2004). In one national study among U.S. high school students, about 8 percent of the girls and 3 percent of the boys had vomited or taken laxatives during the past month in order to lose weight.

Individuals with eating disorders often have a distorted body image (believing they are "fat" even when they appear grossly thin to others), and they may exercise compulsively to lose additional weight. In addition to jeopardizing physical health, eating disorders tend to slow down the bodily changes associated with puberty (London et al., 2007). The malnutrition that accompanies anorexia in particular can cause heart failure; tragically, anorexia is also associated with higher-than-usual rates of suicide attempts (U.S. Department of Health and Human Services [USDHHS], 2000).

Many experts believe that society's obsession with thinness is partly to blame for anorexia nervosa and bulimia (Ahern & Hetherington, 2006). It is fashionable for girls and women in particular to be slender; thin is "in." Psychological factors, some of which may be partly inherited, may also come into play. Individuals with eating disorders are sometimes lonely, depressed, and anxious, and some have experienced child abuse or have problems with substance abuse (USDHHS, 2000).

Anorexia nervosa and bulimia are not easily corrected simply by encouraging individuals to change their eating habits. Young people with these conditions frequently require intensive and long-term intervention by medical and psychological specialists (Linscheid & Fleming, 1995). Educators should be alert to common symptoms such as increasing thinness, complaints of being "too fat," and a lack of energy. When they suspect an eating disorder,

obesity
Condition in which a person weighs at least 20 percent more than his or her optimal weight for good health.

anorexia nervosa
Eating disorder in which a person eats little or nothing for weeks or months and seriously jeopardizes health.

bulimia
Eating disorder in which a person, in an attempt to be thin, eats a large amount of food and then purposefully purges it from the body by vomiting or taking laxatives.

MyEducationLab

Find out how schools can have beneficial effects on students' eating habits and levels of physical activity by completing an Understanding Research exercise in Chapter 5's Activities and Applications section in MyEducationLab.

MyEducationLab

Go to the Video Examples section in Chapter 5 of MyEducationLab to watch a video of a young woman describing her experience with anorexia.

they should consult with a counselor, a school psychologist, or principal. Fortunately, many young people with eating disorders do respond favorably to treatment.

Promoting good eating habits. We end this section with thoughts about what teachers and other practitioners can do to foster good nutrition and eating habits:

- *Provide between-meal snacks when children are hungry.* Children need periodic snacks as well as regular meals. Crackers, healthy cookies, and fruit slices can invigorate active children. Nutritious snacks are particularly important for children who are growing rapidly and for those who receive inadequate meals at home. In providing snacks, educators must be aware of food allergies, family food preferences, and possible limitations in chewing and swallowing hard substances.

- *Offer healthful foods at school.* Teachers and other school personnel can advocate for healthful foods and drinks on the cafeteria line and in the vending machines at school (Budd & Volpe, 2006; Lumeng, 2006). When children are permitted to bring snacks, teachers can send home written recommendations for children and their families (e.g., carrot sticks, pretzels, and granola bars). As a fourth grader, Teresa's son Alex was advised that chocolate (a culinary passion for him) was *not* a good idea for a midmorning snack. He began to bring other snacks instead, such as granola bars (and, as you might suspect, he was happy to find granola bars sprinkled with chocolate chips).

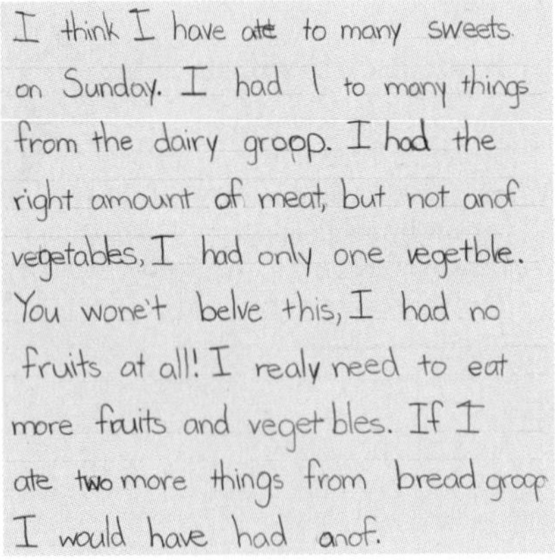

I think I have ate to many sweets on Sunday. I had 1 to many things from the dairy groop. I had the right amount of meat, but not anof vegetables. I had only one vegetble. You wone't belve this, I had no fruits at all! I realy need to eat more fruits and vegetbles. If I ate two more things from bread groop I would have had anof.

Figure 5-13

Charlotte (age 8) reflects on her eating habits over the weekend.

- *Regularly review the basics of good nutrition, and ask children to set goals for improving their eating habits.* Well-planned, school-based programs can be effective in changing children's eating habits and reducing their fat, sodium, and cholesterol intake. Such programs are more likely to be successful when they ask youngsters to set specific goals (e.g., reducing consumption of salty snacks), encourage them to chart their progress toward these goals, show them that they can stick with new eating patterns, and take cultural practices into account (Schinke, Moncher, & Singer, 1994; H. Thomas, 2006; D. K. Wilson, Nicholson, & Krishnarmoorthy, 1998).

A reasonable first step is to introduce children to basic food groups and ask them to evaluate their own diets based on recommended servings for each group. Figure 5-13 shows a third grader's analysis of her eating habits over the weekend.

- *Make referrals when you suspect children have eating disorders.* If you suspect a youngster has an eating disorder, you will want to contact the principal or another authority figure immediately. Youngsters with eating disorders urgently need medical intervention. Even with such care, they may have trouble concentrating at school and need services from school counselors or psychologists. Underlying problems with depression and anxiety are unlikely to be resolved overnight and will require your continued consideration.

- *Educate everyone about good and bad diets.* Teachers and other professionals can take the glamour out of being excessively thin by educating children about eating disorders. For instance, Teresa's son Connor first learned about anorexia nervosa when his third-grade teachers talked about eating disorders as part of a unit on the human body.

- *Follow up when you suspect serious nutritional problems.* Malnutrition can occur as a result of many factors. When low family income is the cause, practitioners can help families obtain free or reduced-cost lunches at school. When parental neglect or mental illness is possibly involved, teachers may need to report their suspicions to principals, counselors, or school nurses to find the best approach for protecting vulnerable children.

- *Convey respect for the feelings of children and adolescents.* Children and adolescents who struggle with obesity or eating disorders are certainly as distressed as their peers—and often even more so—when others make unflattering comments about their appearance. Adults can insist that classrooms, child care centers, and after-school programs are "no-tease zones" regarding weight and other physical conditions.

In addition, children who are eligible for free lunches at school may be embarrassed about their limited financial circumstances. In response, educators can minimize the extent to which these children feel that they stand out. For instance, a considerate staff member at one school took subsidized lunches and placed them in students' own lunch boxes, enabling children to avoid a potential stigma when eating with classmates from higher-income families (Mayall et al., 1996).

Physical Activity

Infants and toddlers are highly motivated to master new physical skills. As they wiggle, squirm, reach, and grasp, they exercise physical skills and also learn a lot about the world. For young children, physical activity is so enjoyable—and increasingly controllable—that they become even more active during the preschool years. Activity level then decreases in middle childhood and adolescence, sometimes by as much as 50 percent (D. W. Campbell, Eaton, McKeen, & Mitsutake, 1999; Rowland, 1990).

Infants are highly motivated to master new physical skills and explore their environment.

Children continue to need physical activity as they grow. Unfortunately, children are not always given sufficient outlets to move. One of the problems is that adults like children to remain still and quiet, particularly in groups, whereas many children prefer more rambunctious and boisterous activities. For example, a common quality of physical activity in early and middle childhood is **rough-and-tumble play,** or good-natured mock "fighting" (Bjorklund & Brown, 1998; A. P. Humphreys & Smith, 1987; Pellegrini, 2006). Children often derive considerable pleasure from it, find it a healthy release from intellectually demanding tasks, and defend it to adults as just "playing" or "messing around." Yet in schools and child care centers, rough play is rarely considered acceptable. Thus educators face the challenge of protecting children while allowing them to run, shout, and be exuberant. Many educators handle this dilemma sensibly by arranging for a safe playground and reasonable rules that reduce the chances of injury.

Another deterrent to physical activity is the perception that outdoor play takes time away from academic lessons. Yet before educators reduce or eliminate recess, they should consider that children are unable to sit and concentrate for long stretches of time without taking regular breaks for active play and interaction (Pellegrini & Bjorklund, 1997; Pellegrini & Bohn, 2005). Being able to move on the playground not only fosters a general sense of well-being but can actually help children focus their attention on academic learning. In many schools, children are also given a chance to move around within the classroom between and sometimes during lessons. Having a chance to get up, if only for a few moments, can help some children prepare their learning materials and settle into a learning task, as you can see in the Building Teaching Skills and Dispositions exercise in MyEducationLab.

MyEducationLab

Go to the Building Teaching Skills and Dispositions section in Chapter 5 of MyEducationLab to learn how some teachers arrange lessons that allow children to make productive use of fine motor skills and physical movement during a lesson.

Children can also frequently get needed exercise in physical education classes, yet unfortunately, at many schools, opportunities for physical activity are quite limited in physical education classes. Children spend much of their time listening and watching demonstrations and waiting in line for a turn to try a new skill. Elementary students spend less than 10 percent of physical education class time in moderate or vigorous physical activity, and middle school students spend only 17 percent of class time in such activity (Simons-Morton, Taylor, Snider, & Huang, 1993; Simons-Morton, Taylor, Snider, Huang, & Fulton, 1994).

As youngsters reach adolescence, exercise can help them maintain physical fitness and cope effectively with life's frustrations and stresses (J. D. Brown & Siegel, 1988). However, school tasks become increasingly sedentary in middle school and high school, and so adolescents are most likely to find opportunities for vigorous activity *outside* of school walls (Pate, Long, & Heath, 1994). Many do not get the exercise they need. For instance, in a recent national survey with high school students, only 55 percent of girls and 70 percent of boys participated in vigorous exercise that made them sweat or breathe hard (CDC, 2004).

Organized sports and individual athletic activities.   In this chapter's opening case study, Tom and Phillip established a softball league that became a valuable outlet for exercise. Organized sports offer the means for maintaining and enhancing physical strength, endurance, and agility. Sports can also promote social development by fostering communication, cooperation, and leadership skills. Particularly when parents and coaches encourage children to focus on trying hard and working together as a team, children often derive a great deal of enjoyment from sports and come to see themselves as reasonably competent athletes (Ullrich-French & Smith, 2006).

Organized sports can have a downside when adults promote unhealthy competition, put excessive pressure on children to perform well, and encourage athletically talented children

rough-and-tumble play
Playful physical "fighting" common in early and middle childhood.

MyEducationLab

Go to the Video Examples section in Chapter 5 of MyEducationLab to watch a video about youngsters' participation in risky sports (e.g., ski racing, rock climbing, and wakeboarding) and the kinds of guidance nurses may offer about protective measures youth can take.

at the expense of their less gifted teammates. Well-meaning parents and coaches can bolster children's athletic skills, but they can also rob children of their intrinsic enjoyment of sports and cause them to overexercise and become injured (R. E. Smith & Smoll, 1997). And as we authors have personally witnessed, some parents are extremely critical of their children's athletic performance on the sidelines of public games.

Some children do not like team sports but nevertheless want to exercise. A few are drawn to such individual athletic activities as running, skateboarding, snowboarding, and mountain biking. Although not part of teams, youngsters who engage in individual sports often spend time with peers while participating in these activities. Individual athletic activities have the advantages of requiring initiative and at least moderate levels of exercise. However, some individual sports (e.g., hang gliding, wakeboarding) incur risk for injury and are not always well supervised.

Encouraging physical activity.   Physical activity is an essential part of every child's day. Here are some specific strategies educators can follow to promote physical activity:

• ***Be "pro-ACTIVE."***   Teachers can incorporate physical movement into many activities, particularly at the elementary school level. Regular breaks that include physical activity can actually increase children's attention to more sedentary, cognitively demanding tasks (Pellegrini & Bjorklund, 1997; Pellegrini & Bohn, 2005).

Regular recess and breaks for physical movement not only promote children's physical well-being but also lead to improved attention and concentration in more cognitively oriented activities. Art by Grace, age 11.

• ***Provide appropriate equipment and guidance so children can safely engage in physical activity.***   Open space, playground equipment, balls, and other athletic props encourage physical exercise. Equipment should be chosen carefully to allow children to experiment freely yet safely, ideally minimizing times when adults have to say no to certain activities (M. B. Bronson, 2000). Equipment and exercise facilities should also be properly designed to fit children's body sizes and abilities (Frost, Shin, & Jacobs, 1998).

Expectations should not exceed the developmental abilities of children. For example, swimming "lessons" for infants are not advisable because infants who paddle around independently can swallow a potentially fatal amount of water (AAP Committee on Sports Medicine and Fitness and Committee on Injury and Poison Prevention, 2000). Swimming lessons for babies can also create a false sense of security, leading families to believe erroneously that small children don't need supervision around water. Figure 5-14 shows a swim record given by an instructor to parents of a 3½-year-old child; notice that the expectations are realistic for many children of preschool age.

By the middle elementary years, children can organize many physical activities and games themselves. Coaches, teachers, recreation directors, and other practitioners usually need to tolerate some bickering as children fuss over rules and in other ways learn to get along. Even so, adults may occasionally need to intervene to minimize physical aggression, remind children to follow safety rules, and integrate children who do not readily join in.

• ***Make exercise an enjoyable activity.***   By the time they reach high school, many young people have had unpleasant experiences with physical exercise and, as a result, associate exercise with discomfort, failure, embarrassment, competitiveness, boredom, injury, or regimentation (Rowland, 1990). Furthermore, many adolescents do not see physical exercise as a regular part of the daily lives of their parents or other family members.

Youngsters are more likely to engage in a physical activity if they enjoy it and find it reasonably challenging (W. C. Taylor, Beech, & Cummings, 1998). They may have intrinsic interest in developing particular skills (e.g., in karate), take pleasure in physical self-expression (e.g., through dance), or appreciate the camaraderie they gain from team sports and other group activities.

• ***Plan physical activities with diversity in mind.***   Not everyone can be a quarterback, and not everyone likes football. In fact, probably only a minority of youngsters find pleasure in competitive sports. But nearly all children and adolescents can find enjoyment in physical activity of some form. Offering a range of activities, from dance to volleyball, and modifying them for children with special needs can maximize the number of students who participate. For example, a child who is unusually short might look to such activities as soccer, cycling, or gymnastics that do not require exceptional height (Rudlin, 1993). Similarly, a girl in a wheelchair might go up to bat in a softball game and then have a classmate run the bases for her.

- ● ***Focus on self-improvement rather than on comparison with peers.*** Focusing on one's own improvement is, for most children, far more motivating than focusing on how well one's performance stacks up against that of peers. Dwelling too much on comparison with others may lead children and adolescents to believe that physical ability is largely a matter of "natural talent," when in fact most physical skills depend on considerable practice (Ames, 1984; Proctor & Dutta, 1995).

One obvious way to promote self-improvement is to teach skills in progression, from simple to complex (Gallahue & Ozmun, 1998). For example, a preschool teacher might ask children to hop on one foot as they pretend to be the "hippity hop bunny." Once they have mastered that skill, the teacher can demonstrate more complex skills, such as galloping and skipping. Carefully sequenced lessons give children feelings of success and make physical activities enjoyable. Even in competitive sports, the emphasis should be more on how well children have "played the game"—on whether they worked well together, treated members of the opposing team with respect, and were all-around good sports—than on whether they won or lost.

Another tactic is to ask children to chart their progress on particular athletic skills and exercises (CDC, 2002). In the following exercise, see how one teenage boy kept track of three activities over a 5-day period.

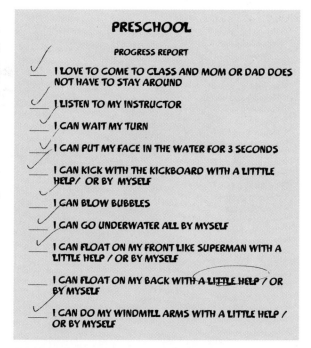

Figure 5-14

Progress report for a 3½-year-old girl in a preschool swimming class. Standards appear developmentally appropriate for this age level. Depending on a child's cultural experiences and individual temperament, the first standard, not wanting parents poolside, might be a difficult one to meet.

Interpreting Children's Artifacts and Reflections

How Many Can I Do Today?

Fifteen-year-old Connor kept a record of his performance on three activities: sit-ups, push-ups, and up-downs. As you examine his record, look for evidence that these activities were challenging for him. How did Connor's performance change as he adjusted to the new exercise routine?

Your Name: Connor   Your Age: 15   Adult Supervising: MOM

Record of Physical Activity

	Activity 1: Sit ups		Activity 2: Push ups		Activity 3: up-downs	
Day 1-5: Exercise	How many did you do?	How did it feel?	How many did you do?	How did it feel?	How many did you do?	How did it feel?
1	37	Good	26	Hard to keep Back Straight.	21	Hard to keep Balance
2	22	Stomach Sore from yesterday. Sore	30	Easy	25	Harder
3	26	Stomach is Better ok	22	Sore	23	Sore
4	15	Hurt really Bad!	20	Sore	25	Hard
5	30	tried to beat #1 But to Sore to	31	Beat It	25	use a lot of Energy
Day 6: Reflect	What parts of your body did you use? Stomach muscles!		What parts of your body did you use? Upper Body.		What parts of your body did you use? A full body work out	
	What did you do to prevent injury? Stopped when It hurt.		What did you do to prevent injury? Tried to keep Balance		What did you do to prevent injury? Stopped when I needed to	

Record of 15-year-old Connor's physical activity

Form adapted from *Planning for Physical Activity* (a BAM! Body and Mind Teacher's Corner resource) by the CDC, Fall 2002. Retrieved January 19, 2003, from http://www.bam.gov/teachers/activities/planning.htm.

Connor was trying out new exercises, and his performance showed it. Notice the drop in sit-ups between the first and second days. Connor complained that his stomach muscles hurt after his first attempts and only gradually recovered. He also reported enjoying the challenge of trying to beat his own records. The activities seem to be appropriate because he stopped when the exercises began to hurt, and an adult supervised his efforts.

Adults can help adolescents see how enjoyable and worthwhile exercise can be.

• ***Make sure that children don't overdo it.*** Becoming excessively involved in exercise can create medical problems for children. The soft and spongy parts of bones in growing children are susceptible to injury from repeated use, and especially from excessive weight-bearing forces (R. H. Gross, 2004; Micheli, 1995). Weight-training machines are almost always designed for larger adult-sized bodies, exacerbating children's chances for injury. Overuse injuries are also seen in distance running, competitive swimming, and gymnastics (Gallahue & Ozmun, 1998). Furthermore, excessive concern about being successful in athletics can lead youngsters to make health-compromising choices (taking steroids, gaining or losing weight too quickly, etc.). Medical experts recommend that children be discouraged from concentrating solely on one sport before adolescence, that they never be asked to "work through" stress fractures, and that they receive regular care from a physician who can monitor the possible health effects (e.g., delays in sexual maturation) of intensive training (AAP Committee on Sports Medicine and Fitness, 2000).

Rest and Sleep

Resting and sleeping are essential to growth and health. Sleep actually helps young people grow, because growth hormones are released at higher rates as children snooze. In addition to promoting growth, sleep may help the brain maintain normal functioning and promote its development (N. R. Carlson, 2007).

Infancy.   Newborn babies spend a long time sleeping—16 to 18 hours a day according to some estimates (Wolff, 1966). Gradually, infants develop wake/sleep cycles that correspond to adults' day/night cycles (St. James-Roberts & Plewis, 1996). They begin to sleep through the night when they are ready to, depending in part on sleeping arrangements and other factors. Teresa recalls that her sons as infants were oblivious to a pediatrician's guideline that they should be able to sleep through the night by 10 weeks of age and 10 pounds in weight. Infants' sleeping habits are affected not only by individual differences but also by varying cultural practices, suggesting that there is no single "best" way to put babies to sleep (Shweder et al., 1998).

Although there may be no best way, there is definitely one *wrong* way to put babies to sleep. Medical experts advise caregivers *not* to place babies on their stomachs for sleeping. This position puts babies at risk for **sudden infant death syndrome (SIDS),** a death that occurs (usually during sleep) without an apparent medical cause. SIDS is a leading cause of death among infants from 1 month through 1 year in age (AAP Task Force on Infant Sleep Position and Sudden Infant Death Syndrome, 2000). During the period that SIDS is most common (between 2 and 4 months), infants' brains are developing circuits that control arousal, breathing, heart rate, and other basic physiological functions. Small delays in neurological development may prove fatal if infants are under stress, for example, if they have a respiratory infection (F. M. Sullivan & Barlow, 2001). Perhaps infants who die suddenly do not wake when breathing becomes difficult, or they may be unable to clear their throats, a reflex known to be less active when infants sleep on their stomachs. It is quite possible that there are multiple causes of SIDS.

Infant caregivers must be well aware of current recommendations not only for reducing the risk of SIDS but for preventing suffocation more generally. These include placing babies on their backs (face up) to sleep, refraining from smoking nearby, keeping babies at a comfortable temperature, using a firm mattress, and avoiding soft surfaces and loose bedding (AAP Task Force on Infant Sleep Position and Sudden Infant Death Syndrome, 2000).

Early childhood through adolescence.   Time spent sleeping decreases steadily over the course of childhood and adolescence. Two-year-olds typically need 12 hours of sleep, 3- to 5-year-olds need 11 hours, 10- to 13-year-olds need 10 hours, and 14- to 18-year-olds need 8½ hours (Roffwarg, Muzio, & Dement, 1966). These figures, of course, are averages. The number of hours of sleep children of a particular age need to feel rested varies greatly.

MyEducationLab

To learn more about measures to reduce the risk of sudden infant death syndrome (SIDS), watch a video on the topic in the Video Examples section in Chapter 5 of MyEducationLab.

sudden infant death syndrome (SIDS) Death of an infant in the first year of life, typically during sleep, that cannot be explained by a thorough medical examination; the risk of SIDS is highest between 2 and 4 months.

Occasional sleep problems are normal occurrences in childhood. Nightmares are common between ages 3 and 6, and children may ask adults to help them battle the demons of the night that seem so real. Pronounced sleep disturbances (e.g., waking repeatedly during the night) may be due to serious health problems, excessive stress, use of street drugs, or side effects from prescribed medications. For instance, repeated nightmares are especially common among children who have been victims of abuse or other traumatic incidents (Durand, 1998; Vignau et al., 1997). Also, children with certain disabilities (e.g., cerebral palsy, severe visual impairment, autism, attention-deficit hyperactivity disorder) often have difficulty sleeping (Durand, 1998).

Our own experience tells us that adolescents are less likely than younger children to get sufficient sleep. Although they require less sleep than they did in their earlier years, adolescents are still growing rapidly, and their bodies need considerable time to rest (Mitru, Millrood, & Mateika, 2002). However, out-of-school obligations—extracurricular activities, part-time jobs, social engagements, and homework assignments—may keep teenagers up until the wee hours of the morning. In some cases adolescents make up for lost sleep at school. It's not uncommon for high school teachers (and college professors as well) to find students napping during class time—a practice hardly conducive to classroom learning!

When children and adolescents get insufficient sleep, they are likely to become irritable and have difficulty with changes in routine. Depending on their age, sleep-deprived youngsters may become aggressive and depressed, have trouble concentrating, perform at low levels academically, and engage in high-risk behaviors (Dahl & Lewin, 2002; Durand, 1998; Sadeh, Gruber, & Raviv, 2002). Of course, youngsters who are staying up late and finding it hard to sleep may experience a good deal of stress independent of their sleeping problems, and lack of sleep is probably only one factor in their adjustment problems.

Accommodating children's needs for rest and sleep.   Educators often have youngsters in their classrooms who do not sleep easily and soundly, including some who are truly sleep deprived. With this in mind, we offer the following suggestions:

• ***When appropriate, provide time for sleep during the day.***   Infants and toddlers *must* sleep during the day. It is common practice, and most certainly good practice, to include an afternoon nap time in the schedule of preschoolers who attend child care or school in the afternoon. A few older children and adolescents—for instance, youngsters with brain injuries or other chronic health conditions—may need an hour or two of sleep as well, perhaps on a couch in the school nurse's office (Ormrod & McGuire, 2007).

• ***Include time for rest in the daily schedule.***   Young children typically give up their afternoon nap sometime between ages 2 and 5, but for quite some time after that, they need to recharge their batteries with quiet and restful activities (e.g., listening to stories or music) in the afternoon. Children at any age level learn most effectively when they take an occasional, restful break from intense activity.

• ***Watch for children who appear sleepy, irritable, or distractible.***   Teachers and other practitioners can speak tactfully with family members when they think chronic fatigue is causing children to have trouble concentrating, maintaining reasonably good spirits, and resisting aggressive impulses.

• ***Encourage youngsters to make steady progress on assignments so they don't wait to start a lengthy one the night before it is due.***   At the high school level, adolescents may have several hours of homework each night. Add to this workload extracurricular events, social activities, family commitments, and part-time jobs, and you have adolescents who are seriously overstretched. When an out-of-school task is lengthy and complex, such as a major project or a research paper might be, teachers can encourage regular progress by giving interim deadlines for various *parts* of the project.

• ***Recognize that sleep problems can be a sign of illness or emotional stress.***   Words of acknowledgment and kindness ("You look tired today, Darragh. Did you sleep all right last night?") may give children permission to share their troubles and, as a result, take the first step toward resolving them.

Basic Developmental Issues

Physical Development

Issue	Physical Growth	Motor Skills	Physical Health and Activity
Nature and Nurture	Genetic instructions specify the particular changes that occur as bodies grow larger, and they also provide individual targets for mature height and weight. Yet normal progressions depend on healthful environments and experiences, such as adequate nutrition, movement, stimulation, affection, and protection from toxic substances.	Nature sets firm boundaries as to the motor skills a child can execute at any age range. For instance, a 6-month-old cannot run and a 10-year-old cannot clear 15 feet in the standing high jump. However, organized sports programs and other opportunities for regular exercise allow children to expand and refine their developing motor skills.	Nature influences children's activity level (e.g., 3-year-olds tend to be more physically active than 17-year-olds) and susceptibility to infection and illness. Nurture affects children's daily activities. For example, children learn many habits related to eating and exercising from their parents and others in their community.
Universality and Diversity	Children tend to show similar sequences in physical development (e.g., in the emergence of sexual characteristics associated with puberty) across a wide range of environments and cultures. However, the rate of development differs considerably from one child to the next, with differences being partly the result of genetic diversity and partly the result of personal choices and cultural variations in food, exercise, and so on.	Motor skills often develop in the same, universal sequence. For example, children can, on average, pick up crumbs at age 1, scribble with a crayon at age 2, and build a tower 10 blocks high at age 4 (Sheridan, 1975). Diversity is present in the specific ages at which children master motor skills, due in part to genetic differences and in part to variations in environmental support.	All children and adolescents need good nutrition, plenty of rest, and a moderate amount of physical activity to be healthy. Huge variation is present in the activity levels and eating habits of youngsters. In addition, children differ in their susceptibility to illness.
Qualitative and Quantitative Change	Many physical advancements are the result of a series of quantitative physiological changes (e.g., gradual increases in physical strength and dexterity). Qualitative changes are revealed in the new physical characteristics that emerge with puberty.	As a general rule, children must practice motor skills for a long time before they can execute them easily and gracefully, and a series of quantitative improvements allow more complex skills to emerge. Some motor skills, such as walking and throwing a ball, also change qualitatively with maturity and practice.	During the middle childhood years, children gradually gain control over what they eat and how they spend their leisure time (a quantitative change). Reorganization in thinking about safety and danger sometimes occurs in adolescence. Young people may shift from a preoccupation with safety to a thrill-seeking mind-set (a qualitative change).

As you have seen, the advances that occur in physical development take many forms and depend on several distinct factors, including maturational processes, adequate nutrition, physical activity, and sleep. In the Basic Developmental Issues table "Physical Development," we summarize how physical development shows nature and nurture, universality and diversity, and qualitative and quantitative change. Because good health comes not only from acquiring health-promoting habits but also from avoiding negative substances, we now focus on the important topic of health-compromising behaviors.

Health-Compromising Behaviors

Especially as they grow older and gain increasing independence from adult supervision, children and adolescents face many choices about how to spend their leisure time. They sometimes make decisions that undermine their health and physical well-being. Here we look at three health-compromising behaviors: cigarette smoking, alcohol and drug use, and unsafe sexual activity.

Cigarette smoking.   An alarming percentage of young people smoke cigarettes (see Table 5-2). European American teens are at most risk (almost one-third of these teens smoke or use some other form of tobacco), although many adolescents from other ethnic groups also smoke (CDC, 2004). Unfortunately, teens often continue to use tobacco when they become adults.

Because the health risks are so well publicized, it is difficult for many adults to understand why adolescents choose to smoke. Undoubtedly, "image" is a factor. Teens may smoke cigarettes to look older, rebel, and affiliate with certain peer groups. Advertising plays a role as well. The majority of teen smokers choose from only a few cigarette brands, perhaps because of the youthful, fun-loving images that certain tobacco companies cultivate in the media. Regardless of the reasons adolescents begin smoking, those who continue to smoke may develop health problems that they might otherwise avoid.

Alcohol and drug use.   Alcohol and drugs are among the most serious threats to physical health that adolescents face today. Occasionally a single episode with a particular drug leads to permanent brain damage or even death. (Recall the tragic event in our introductory case study of three boys dying after an attempt to get "high.") Losing judgment under the influence of alcohol and drugs, adolescents may put themselves at risk in other ways, such as engaging in unprotected sexual activity. Those who are intravenous drug users may share needles, putting themselves at risk of contracting the human immunodeficiency virus (HIV) (described later in the chapter) and other diseases (Thiede, Romero, Bordelon, Hagan, & Murrill, 2001). Figure 5-15 lists substances used by some adolescents.

Given the hazards of alcohol and drugs, why do some adolescents frequently use them? A variety of factors appear responsible. In general, adolescence is a time of trying new and sometimes bold experiences. For some, it's a matter of curiosity: After hearing about alcohol and drugs, not only from their peers but also from adults and the media, teens may simply want to experience the effects firsthand. For others, it's a way to seek self-definition (Who

Alcohol depresses the central nervous system and impairs coordination, perception, speech, and decision making; for instance, heavy drinkers may talk incoherently and walk with a staggered gait. Teens who drink excessively are more likely to have car accidents and commit rape.

Methylene dioxymethamphetamine (*MDMA*, or "ecstasy") gives its users a sense of euphoria and exuberance, sensory enhancements and distortions, and feelings of being at peace with the world and emotionally close to others (it is sometimes called the "hug drug"). However, the sense of euphoria often leads its users to ignore bodily distress signals, such as muscle cramping and dehydration; more serious effects include convulsions, impaired heart function, and occasionally death. It is often available at dance clubs ("raves"), where its effects are intensified by music and flashing lights.

Inhalants are attractive to many adolescents because they cause an immediate "high" and are readily available in the form of such household substances as glue, paint thinner, aerosol paint cans, and nail polish remover. These very dangerous substances can cause brain damage and death.

Marijuana delays reaction time, modifies perception, and instills a mild feeling of euphoria, but it can also heighten fears and anxieties. Teens who smoke marijuana may have red eyes, dry mouths, mood changes, loss of interest in former friends and hobbies, and impaired driving.

Methamphetamine ("speed") is a stimulant that gives users a sense of energy, alertness, confidence, and well-being. Overdoses are possible, addiction frequently occurs, and changes to the brain and heart may occur. People who use speed regularly combat psychiatric problems, such as believing that "everyone is out to get me."

Cocaine (including *crack*, a particularly potent form) overstimulates neurons in the brain and gives users a brief sense of intense euphoria; it can also cause tremors, convulsions, vomiting, respiratory problems, and heart failure. Cocaine users may be energetic, talkative, argumentative, and boastful; long-time users may appear anxious and depressed. Crack users are prone to violence and crime.

Lysergic acid diethylamide (LSD) is a psychedelic drug that gives its users the sensation of being on an exotic journey, or "trip." It is usually swallowed as a chemical on a piece of paper or as a drop of liquid placed on the tongue. It can impair judgment, provoke anxiety, trigger underlying mental problems and, in the case of "bad trips," cause serious distress.

Prescription medications are used by a growing number of adolescents because of their physical effects on the body. Prescription painkillers, such as OxyContin and Vicodin, are potentially addictive narcotics that reduce sensations of discomfort and increase feelings of pleasure and well-being. Anabolic steroids are another type of medication for which there is an illicit market among teenagers. Some adolescents use nonprescribed doses of steroids to increase muscle development, but they also inadvertently experience unwanted side effects and serious health problems.

Sources: G. R. Adams, Gullotta, & Markstrom-Adams, 1994; Atwater, 1996; DanceSafe, 2000a, 2000b; S. S. Feldman & Wood, 1994; L. D. Johnston, O'Malley, Bachman, & Schulenberg, 2007; Kulberg, 1986; National Institute on Drug Abuse, 2008; Neinstein, 2004; L. Smith, 1994; J. M. Taylor, 1994.

Figure 5-15

Effects and symptoms of adolescent substance abuse.

shall I be? How does it feel to be a certain kind of me?), leading to experimentation with a variety of new roles and behaviors, including drug use (Durkin, 1995; Shedler & Block, 1990).

Adult behaviors, too, influence substance abuse. Many adolescents who use drugs or alcohol have parents who have done little to promote adolescents' self-confidence, willingness to abide by society's rules, or ability to stay focused on long-term goals in the presence of immediate, conflicting interests (Botvin & Scheier, 1997; Jessor & Jessor, 1977). Furthermore, drug and alcohol use is more typical when people in the local community are relatively tolerant of such behavior (Poresky, Daniels, Mukerjee, & Gunnell, 1999).

Peer group norms and behaviors are yet another factor affecting substance abuse (J. A. Epstein, Botvin, Diaz, Toth, & Schinke, 1995; B. M. Segal & Stewart, 1996). To a great extent, use of alcohol and drugs is a social activity (Durkin, 1995), and teenagers may partake simply as a means of "fitting in." In other cases, teens inclined to violate laws may actively seek out peer groups similarly disposed to get in trouble (A. M. Ryan, 2000).

Regardless of their initial reasons for trying alcohol and drugs, youngsters' continued use often creates serious problems for them. If these substances give adolescents pleasure, satisfy a desire for thrills, alleviate anxieties, or deaden feelings of pain and depression, they may begin to use the substances regularly. Unfortunately, some users eventually develop an **addiction** to, or biological and psychological dependence on, drugs or alcohol. They grow physiologically accustomed to using the substance and need increasing quantities to produce a desired effect. If they try to stop, addicts experience intense cravings and severe physiological and psychological reactions (Hussong, Chassin, & Hicks, 1999; National Institute on Drug Abuse, 2008). Teenagers who are impulsive and disruptive, perform poorly in school, find little value in education, and have family members with mental illness or substance-abuse problems are especially at risk for becoming dependent on alcohol and drugs (Chassin et al., 2004; Kassel, Weinstein, Skitch, Veilleux, & Mermelstein, 2005).

Unsafe sexual activity. Teenagers get mixed messages about the acceptability of sexual activity. Social and religious norms often advocate abstinence, yet television and films depict alluring sexual behavior. Peers may urge participation in sexual activity, and teens themselves experience sexual desires. Schools usually do little to help teens sort out these messages and feelings. Although schools often include information about male and female anatomy, procreation, and birth in their health or biology curricula, they rarely offer much guidance about how to make sense of one's emerging sexuality or how to behave in romantic relationships.

Many teenagers do become sexually active. On average, about 4 or 5 in every 10 high school students in the United States reports having had sexual intercourse (CDC, 2006; see Table 5-2). In many cases sexual activity is carried out in a high-risk fashion. For example, 1 in 4 sexually active teenagers report having used no contraception during his or her first experience of intercourse (Abma, Martinez, Mosher, & Dawson, 2004). More than 1 in 10 high school students have had four or more sexual partners (CDC, 2006). From the perspective of physical health, early sexual activity is problematic because it can lead to sexually transmitted infections, pregnancy, or both.

Sexually transmitted infections. Sexually transmitted infections (STIs) vary in their severity. Syphilis, gonorrhea, and chlamydia can be treated with antibiotics, but teens do not always seek prompt medical help when they develop symptoms. Without treatment, serious problems can occur, including infertility and sterility, heart problems, and birth defects in future offspring. Genital herpes has no known cure, but medication can make its symptoms less severe.

Undoubtedly the most life-threatening STI is acquired immune deficiency syndrome (AIDS), a medical condition in which the immune system is weakened, permitting severe infections, pneumonias, and cancers to invade the body. AIDS is caused by HIV, which can be transmitted through the exchange of body fluids (e.g., blood and semen) during just a single contact. Half of all new HIV infections in the United States occur in young people between 13 and 24 years of age (Futterman, Chabon, & Hoffman, 2000). Sexual transmission is the primary means of HIV transmission during adolescence (AAP Committee on Pediatric AIDS and Committee on Adolescence, 2001).

The only good news about AIDS is that it has spurred public awareness campaigns that have led some groups to use safer sex practices, such as less intimate contact with new ac-

addiction
Physical and psychological dependence on a substance, such that increasing quantities must be taken to produce the desired effect and withdrawal produces adverse physiological and psychological effects.

quaintances and more frequent use of latex condoms (Catania et al., 1992; J. A. Kelly, 1995). Safe sexual practices are not universal, however. Many adolescents believe that their partner is "safe" and that only members of "high-risk groups" can spread HIV (Amirkhanian, Tiunov, & Kelly, 2001; J. D. Fisher & Fisher, 1992; J. A. Kelly, Murphy, Sikkema, & Kalichman, 1993; S. M. Moore & Rosenthal, 1991; L. S. Wagner, Carlin, Cauce, & Tenner, 2001).

Pregnancy. Pregnancy is a somewhat common occurrence among teens having unprotected sex. In the United States approximately 8 out of every 100 teenage girls between 15 and 19 years become pregnant each year (National Campaign to Prevent Teen Pregnancy, 2005). Many of these pregnancies end in miscarriage or abortion, but others, of course, go to full term. The current birthrate for American adolescent girls ages 15 to 19 is 4 births per 100 girls (Federal Interagency Forum on Child and Family Statistics, 2007). Most girls who become teenage mothers are from low-income families headed by single parents with low levels of education, believe that they have few if any educational or career options, and believe their baby will supply emotional closeness they don't find in other relationships (Coley & Chase-Lansdale, 1998).

As you read in Chapter 4, when young mothers have not fully matured physically, and especially when they do not have access to adequate nutrition and health care, they are at greater risk for medical complications during pregnancy and delivery. Problems arise after delivery as well. On average, teenage mothers have more health problems, are less likely to complete school or keep a steady job, and live in greater economic poverty than do other adolescent girls (Coley & Chase-Lansdale, 1998; Upchurch & McCarthy, 1990; U.S. Department of Education, 2005).

Addressing health-compromising behaviors.

Schools and community organizations can do a great deal to address behaviors that put children and adolescents at physical risk. We offer a few thoughts on appropriate support:

- ***Provide healthy options for free time.*** Children and adolescents are less likely to engage in health-compromising behaviors when they have better things to do with their time. For instance, in our opening case study, a softball league afforded a productive form of recreation. Community leaders can advocate for after-school youth centers, community athletic leagues, and public service programs for young people. As an example, the *First Choice* program, which has been implemented at more than 80 sites in the United States, is targeted at students who are at risk of dropping out of school or getting in serious trouble with the law (Collingwood, 1997; PE 4 Life, n.d.). The program focuses on fitness and prevention of drug use and violence. Elements that appear to contribute to its success include physical activity classes, a peer fitness leadership training program, parent support training, and coordination with mental health agencies and recreational facilities.

- ***Ask adolescents to keep their long-term goals continually in mind.*** Youngsters need personally relevant reasons to stay away from illegal substances and to make wise choices about sexual activity. Having firm long-term goals and optimism about the future can help them resist negative peer and media pressure.

- ***Prevent problems.*** It is much easier to teach children and adolescents to resist cigarettes, alcohol, and drugs than it is to treat dependence on these substances. One important approach is to establish a "no tolerance" policy on school grounds, in after-school programs, and in community centers. Youngsters are less likely to smoke, drink, or take drugs if they think they might be caught (Voelkl & Frone, 2000). On the other hand, scare tactics, simple lessons about the detrimental effects of tobacco and drugs, and attempts to enhance self-esteem are relatively ineffective. What seem to work better are programs that strive to change *behaviors* of children and adolescents. Such programs might ask young people to make a public commitment to stay clean and sober, teach them how to resist temptation, and give them strategies for solving social problems and coping with anxiety (Botvin & Scheier, 1997; Forgey, Schinke, & Cole, 1997).

- ***Implement programs that have demonstrated success with the population of young people with whom you work.*** Obviously, the kinds of programs educators can implement are determined largely by their particular

Children and adolescents are less likely to engage in health-compromising behaviors when they have constructive alternatives for their leisure time.

___

Student's Pledge

As a participant in the _____ High School Athletic Program, I agree to abide by all training rules regarding the use of alcohol, tobacco, and other drugs. Chemical dependency is a progressive but treatable disease, characterized by continued drinking or other drug use in spite of recurring problems resulting from that use. Therefore, I accept and pledge to abide by the training rules listed in the athletic handbook and others established by my coach.

To demonstrate my support, I pledge to:

1. Support my fellow students by setting an example and abstaining from the use of alcohol, tobacco, and other drugs.

2. Not enable my fellow students who use these substances. I will not cover up for them or lie for them if any rules are broken. I will hold my teammates responsible and accountable for their actions.

3. Seek information and assistance in dealing with my own or my fellow students' problems.

4. Be honest and open with my parents about my feelings, needs, and problems.

5. Be honest and open with my coach and other school personnel when the best interests of my fellow students are being jeopardized.

Student _____ Date _____

PARENTS: We ask that you co-sign this pledge to show your support.

___

Sample Letter from Coach to Parent about a Drug or Alcohol Violation

Dear Parent:

Your daughter _____ has violated the _____ High School extra-curricular activities code of conduct. She voluntarily came forward on Thursday afternoon and admitted her violation of the code, specifically, drinking alcohol. The code is attached.

We respect her honesty and integrity and hope you do as well. Admitting a mistake such as this is very difficult for her. Not only does she have to deal with authorities such as us, she must face you, her parents, as well as her peers—which is probably the most difficult. We understand that no one is perfect and that people do make mistakes. Our code, and the resulting consequences of violating the code, is a nationally recognized model and is designed to encourage this type of self-reporting where the student can seek help and shelter from guilt without harsh initial penalties. She has admitted to making a mistake and is willing to work to alleviate the negative effects of the mistake.

As you can see in the enclosed code, we require that your daughter complete 10 hours of drug and alcohol in-service education and counseling. In addition, she must sit out 10 practice days of competition. She is still part of the team and must attend practices and competition; she is just not allowed to compete or participate in games for 10 days.

We hope you understand and support our effort to provide a healthy athletic program for the students. If you have any questions, please call either one of us at the high school.

Sincerely,

___

Figure 5-16

Team Up drug prevention materials from high school athletic coaches.

From *Team Up: A Drug Prevention Manual for High School Athletic Coaches,* by the U.S. Drug Enforcement Administration, 2002, Washington, DC: U.S. Department of Justice Drug Enforcement Administration.

professional duties and the needs of youngsters with whom they work. One effective drug prevention program was developed by coaches and other staff members in the Forest Hills School District in Cincinnati, Ohio (see Figure 5-16). This comprehensive program enlists participation by school coaches, principals, other school staff, team captains, parents, and the adolescents themselves (U.S. Drug Enforcement Administration, 2002). Coaches speak openly and often with athletes about substance use. Peer pressure is also used to discourage alcohol and drug use. When athletes do break the rules, they are given defined consequences, but in a way that communicates hope that they will try harder next time.

• ***Encourage adolescents to protect themselves.*** Approaches to preventing adolescent pregnancy and transmission of STIs among adolescents are somewhat controversial. Many parents, for example, object to schools' advocacy of the use of condoms and other forms of "safe sex." (And, of course, at the present time condom use is no guarantee of protection against either infection or pregnancy.) Evidence suggests, however, that having condoms available in schools moderately increases condom use for those students who are already sexually active (and so may offer some protection against HIV infection) and does not necessarily increase rates of sexual activity (Alan Guttmacher Institute, 2001). Use of condoms among sexually active adolescents is far from universal, in part because of interpersonal factors (e.g., reluctance to use a condom or to ask that a partner use one) and situational factors (e.g., impaired judgment due to alcohol or drugs) (Manderson, Tye, & Rajanayagam, 1997). Programs that encourage sexual abstinence are a less-controversial alternative and can be effective in the short run, although such programs appear to be relatively ineffective over the long run (Dreweke & Wind, 2007).

Overall, it appears that messages to adolescents need to be tailored to the current risks they face (CDC, 2005a). For example, adolescents who have not yet been sexually intimate can be encouraged to remain abstinent. Those who are currently sexually active may benefit from advice to use protective measures and limit numbers of partners.

• ***Encourage adolescents with infections to abstain from sex or to use precautions.*** Sadly, many adolescents already are infected with HIV or other STIs. Obviously, they need medical treatment and care. They must also be encouraged to stop the spread of the infection. When infected adolescents remain sexually active, precautions are essential. Unfortunately, this is a message these youngsters are not always prepared to hear. For instance, although estimates vary, in the United States perhaps 40 to 70 percent of HIV-infected teenagers engage in unprotected sex (Belzer et al., 2001; D. A. Murphy et al., 2001).

The four areas we've discussed in this section—eating habits, physical activity, rest and sleep, and health-compromising behaviors—all have major effects on youngsters' physical development. In the Observation Guidelines table "Assessing Health Behaviors of Children

Observation Guidelines

Assessing Health Behaviors of Children and Adolescents

Characteristic	Look For	Example	Implication
Eating Habits	· Frequent consumption of junk food (candy, chips, carbonated beverages, etc.) · Unusual heaviness or thinness, especially if these characteristics become more pronounced over time · Lack of energy · Reluctance or inability to eat anything at lunchtime	Melissa is a good student, an avid runner, and a member of the student council. She is quite thin but wears baggy clothes that hide her figure, and she eats only a couple pieces of celery for lunch. Her teacher and principal suspect an eating disorder and meet with Melissa's parents to share their suspicion.	Observe what children eat and drink during the school day. Seek free or reduced-rate breakfasts and lunches for children from low-income families. Consult with specialists and parents when eating habits are seriously compromising children's health.
Physical Activity	· Improvements in speed, complexity, and agility of gross motor skills (e.g., running, skipping, jumping) · Restlessness, lethargy, or inattention during lengthy seatwork (possibly reflecting a need to have a physical break or to release pent-up energy) · Overexertion (increasing the risk of injury)	During a class field day, a fifth-grade teacher organizes a soccer game with her students. Before beginning the game, she asks them to run up and down the field, individually accelerating and decelerating while kicking the ball. She then has them practice kicking the ball in ways that allow them to evade another player. Only after such practice does she begin the game (Logsdon et al., 1997).	Incorporate regular physical activity into the daily schedule. Choose tasks and activities that are enjoyable and allow for variability in skill levels. Make sure youngsters have mastered necessary prerequisite skills before teaching more complex skills.
Rest and Sleep	· Listlessness and lack of energy · Inability to concentrate · Irritability and overreaction to frustration · Sleeping in class	A teacher in an all-day kindergarten notices that some of his students become cranky during the last half-hour or so of school, and so he typically reserves this time for storybook reading and other quiet activities.	Provide regular opportunities for rest. When a youngster seems unusually tired day after day, talk with him or her (and perhaps with parents) about how lack of sleep can affect attention and behavior. Jointly seek possible solutions to the problem.
Health-Compromising Behaviors	· The smell of cigarettes on clothing · Physiological symptoms of drug use (e.g., red eyes, dilated pupils, tremors, convulsions, respiratory problems) · Distortions in speech (e.g., slurred pronunciation, fast talking, incoherence) · Poor coordination · Impaired decision making · Mood changes (e.g., anxiety, depression) · Dramatic changes in behavior (e.g., unusual energy, loss of interest in friends) · Signs of sensory distortions or hallucinations · Rapid weight gain and a tendency to wear increasingly baggy clothes (in girls who may be pregnant)	A school counselor notices a dramatic change in James's personality. Whereas he used to be energetic and eager to engage in activities, he now begins to "zone out" during counseling sessions. He slumps in his chair, looking down or staring out the window. His limited speech is unintelligible. The counselor suspects drug use and asks him about his demeanor. James denies that anything is wrong, so the counselor confronts him directly about her suspicions, refers him to a drug treatment center, and consults with her supervisor about additional steps to take.	Educate children and adolescents about the dangers of substance abuse and unprotected sexual activity; teach behaviors that will enable youngsters to resist temptations, tailoring instruction to their cultural backgrounds. Enforce alcohol and drug policies on school grounds and in extracurricular activities. Encourage participation in enjoyable and productive leisure activities that will enable young people to interact with health-conscious peers. Consult with a counselor, psychologist, or social worker when you suspect that a youngster is pregnant or abusing drugs or alcohol.

and Adolescents," we identify characteristics and behaviors that bear on good and poor health. (Obviously, practitioners should not make inferences about health or provide treatment for which they are not trained.) We turn now to children who have special physical needs and the practices that can help these children achieve their full potential.

Special Physical Needs

Some children have long-term physical conditions that affect school performance, friendships, and leisure activities. Here we look at chronic illness, serious injuries, and physical disabilities in children and adolescents. We then identify strategies for accommodating these conditions.

Chronic Illness

All children get sick now and then, but some have ongoing, long-term illnesses as a result of genetic legacies (e.g., cystic fibrosis), environmentally contracted illnesses (e.g., AIDS), or an interaction between the two (e.g., some forms of asthma and cancer). These chronic conditions may cause children to experience noticeable limitations in strength, vitality, and alertness that occasionally affect their classroom performance (Turnbull, Turnbull, & Wehmeyer, 2007).

Teachers obviously are not doctors, but they may have occasion to notice how well children are caring for themselves. For instance, most children with diabetes can monitor blood sugar levels and take appropriate follow-up action. Yet children sometimes forget to take prescribed medication, and they are not always completely reliable in assessing their status. For example, children with asthma may not realize when they are having a severe reaction (Bearison, 1998). Accordingly, educators may need to keep an eye on children's symptoms, seek family help when conditions deteriorate, and obtain medical assistance in cases of emergency.

Teachers can also help children with chronic illnesses develop social skills and relationships. Some children who are ill feel so "different" that they are hesitant to approach peers (Turnbull et al., 2007). Furthermore, they may blame their physical condition (perhaps accurately, perhaps not) for any problems they have in social relationships (Kapp-Simon & Simon, 1991). As a result, they may become isolated, with few opportunities to develop interpersonal skills. Furthermore, absences from school are common among children with chronic illnesses because of hospitalization, doctor visits, and flare-ups of their condition.

Unfortunately, some healthy children actively avoid or reject peers who have serious illnesses. To some extent, such reactions reflect ignorance. Many children, young ones especially, have naive notions about illness. For instance, preschoolers may believe that people catch colds from the sun or get cancer by being in the same room as someone with cancer (Bibace & Walsh, 1981). As children get older, their conceptions of illness gradually become more complex, they grow more attuned to their own internal body cues, and they can differentiate among types of illness (Bearison, 1998).

Finally, teachers and other professionals may be able to help address the mental health needs of sick children. Some children with chronic illnesses are prone to anxiety and depression, and they may have trouble separating from their families when they arrive at school (Shapiro & Manz, 2004). Practitioners can offer sensitive support to especially sick children by giving them extra time to say goodbye to families in the morning and, when children seem especially sad or withdrawn, making appropriate referrals to counselors. The actual needs of youngsters with chronic illnesses vary significantly by developmental level, as do the accommodations that best address their needs, as you can see in the Developmental Trends table "Chronic Health Conditions in Children and Adolescents."

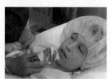

MyEducationLab

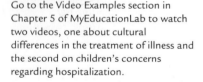

Go to the Video Examples section in Chapter 5 of MyEducationLab to watch two videos, one about cultural differences in the treatment of illness and the second on children's concerns regarding hospitalization.

Developmental Trends

Chronic Health Conditions in Children and Adolescents

Age	What You Might Observe	Diversity	Implications
Infancy (Birth–2 Years) 	· Irregular sleep and wake cycles · Trouble being soothed · Digestive problems · Breathing problems	· Some genetic conditions, such as cystic fibrosis, may be diagnosed during infancy. · Some infants initially show normal developmental advances, such as making eye contact, babbling, and smiling, and then slow down in their physical growth as illnesses progress.	· Provide emotional support to families when they struggle with the news that their children have a chronic or serious illness. · Determine the kinds of physical care that infants find comforting and soothing.
Early Childhood (2–6 Years) 	· Eating problems · Regular medication schedule · Some toileting problems · Greater susceptibility to many mild illnesses, such as the common cold · Belief that "being bad" is the cause of getting sick	· Some children may have special nutritional needs. · Some children may need to begin to take dietary supplements. · Children may fail to take prescribed medicines if their parents believe they are unnecessary or cannot afford to purchase them.	· Encourage children to adhere to diets advised by medical personnel. · Allow children to use the toilet whenever necessary. · Safeguard small children from environmental substances that exacerbate their symptoms (e.g., shield children with asthma from secondhand smoke).
Middle Childhood (6–10 Years) 	· Frequent teasing and inappropriately personal questions from other children · Periods of health followed by flare-ups of the condition · Some efforts by the child to manage symptoms at school (e.g., a child with asthma may monitor his or her lung function with a peak flow meter) · Greater than average number of absences from school	· A particular illness affects a child's ability to manage his or her health in distinct ways. · Absences from school vary depending on the child's illness, frequency of flare-ups, and the family's anxiety about the illness. · Some children are hospitalized occasionally or regularly. · Many children show some adverse reactions to particular treatments (e.g., becoming nervous or jittery after taking asthma medicine).	· Ask families for ideas about how you can support their child's physical well-being. · Advise family members of significant changes in their child's symptoms and health-management routines. · Insist that other children show understanding of children with chronic illnesses while also preserving sick children's right to privacy. · When children are absent due to hospitalizations, keep in touch through phone calls, e-mail, and notes from classmates. · Allow children (particularly those with diabetes) to eat nutritious snacks regularly throughout the school day.
Early Adolescence (10–14 Years) 	· Heightened concern about physical appearance · Some self-consciousness about being different due to illness · Growing knowledge of how to monitor health conditions · Transition from family care to self-care of chronic illnesses · Some feeling of being invincible to threats to health	· Some adolescents who were previously conscientious about their treatment regimens now become inconsistent in adhering to good medical routines. · Some adolescents with chronic health conditions may need accommodations at school or in particular classes, such as physical education. · Some adolescents may develop physical manifestations of their disease (e.g., adolescents with cystic fibrosis may develop enlarged and rounded fingertips). · Adolescents with diabetes may have an increase in symptoms when they are growing rapidly.	· Offer reassurance that all adolescents are valued members of the class and school. · Advise adolescents about the supportive services of school counselors. · Facilitate contact with classmates and teachers when adolescents are hospitalized or recuperating at home. · Talk privately with adolescents about seeing the school nurse as needed (e.g., to take inhaled medications).

continued

Developmental Trends (continued)

Chronic Health Conditions in Children and Adolescents

Age	What You Might Observe	Diversity	Implications
Late Adolescence (14–18 Years)	· Growing knowledge of the health condition and its optimal management · Some difficulties in physical education classes (e.g., breathing problems, fatigue, and weakness on hot days) · Some negative feelings when illness necessitates continued dependence on parents (e.g., being unable to obtain a driver's license because of a seizure disorder)	· Some adolescents who regularly miss school due to illness feel isolated and lonely when at school. · Some adolescents manage their health conditions effectively and make plans that realistically address their conditions. · Adolescents who engage in risky behaviors or follow chaotic lifestyles may fail to take prescribed medicines. · Adolescents with some serious health conditions are vulnerable to depression. · Some adolescents face declining health as well as the prospect of dying in early adulthood.	· At the beginning of the year, develop a plan for dealing with school absences and making up missed academic work. · Encourage adolescents to assume increasing responsibility for management and treatment of their condition. · Consult with a school counselor to learn appropriate ways to help an adolescent who is terminally ill.

Sources: Annett, 2004; Lemanek, 2004; Quittner, Modi, & Roux, 2004; Shapiro & Manz, 2004; R. A. Smith, Martin, & Wolters, 2004; Wallander et al., 2004; J. Williams, 2004; Young-Hyman, 2004.

Serious Injuries and Health Hazards

Injuries represent a major threat to children and adolescents. Every year, more young people die from accidental injuries than from cancer. In fact, for children and adolescents between 1 and 19 years of age, injuries are the leading cause of death (Deal, Gomby, Zippiroli, & Behrman, 2000). As children get older, their increasing independence makes them susceptible to certain kinds of injuries. In fact, injuries from firearms and motor vehicle crashes are the primary causes of death during the adolescent years (National Center for Health Statistics, 2005).

Although some injuries quickly heal, others have long-term effects that must be accommodated. For instance, each year in the United States approximately 475,000 infants, children, and adolescents sustain traumatic brain injuries from playground falls, bicycle mishaps, skiing accidents, and other traumatic events (Langlois, Rutland-Brown, & Thomas, 2004). Depending on location and severity, brain injuries can have temporary or lasting effects on physical functioning (e.g., seizures, headaches, poor motor coordination, fatigue) and psychological processes (e.g., impairments in perception, memory, concentration, language, decision making, or anger management). Thus assistance for children with brain injuries must be tailored to each individual's unique needs. For one child assistance may mean minimizing distractions in the classroom, for another it may mean allowing extra time to complete assignments, and for yet another it may mean adjusting expectations for performance, at least for the first few weeks or months (Turnbull et al., 2007).

Many childhood injuries are avoidable, of course, and schools can play a key role in educating children about preventive measures. Adults can teach children to use seat belts while riding in motor vehicles, wear helmets while biking and skating, and install smoke detectors at home (e.g., Klassen, MacKay, Moher, Walker, & Jones, 2000). Educators should also be aware of youngsters who are more vulnerable than others. For instance, children with Down syndrome are particularly susceptible to sprains and dislocations because of limited muscle tone and excessive mobility in their joints (P. L. Krebs, 1995).

Finally, educators can learn about hazardous substances that may be present in their community. For example, children can come into contact with lead in the dirt of play areas and in paint chips of older homes (Agency for Toxic Substances and Disease Registry, 1999). Depending on the amount of lead they ingest, children may develop blood anemia, kidney damage, colic, muscle weakness, and brain damage. Young children are affected more seriously by some toxic substances than are adults because children's brains and bodies are growing quickly (S. M. Kroger, Schettler, & Weiss, 2005). Some health problems may disappear if toxic substances are removed, but lasting declines in intelligence may result. Obviously, teachers and other professionals will want to do all they can to protect children from harmful substances in schools and community settings.

Physical Disabilities

Children with physical disabilities, such as cerebral palsy, muscular dystrophy, and blindness, have the same basic needs as other children, namely, a good diet, regular physical activity, and adequate rest and sleep. In addition, they may need specially adapted equipment (e.g., a wheelchair, a speech synthesizer, or a computer printer that produces Braille) and an environmental layout that permits safe movement.

Because physical activity and exercise are central to health, fitness, and mood, adults must find ways to adapt physical activities for children with special physical needs. Basically, such adaptation involves giving as much support as necessary to enable successful movement. For example, a teacher can assist students who have visual impairments by guiding their bodies into correct positions and inserting bells or other noisemakers inside playground balls (Poel, 2007).

Adults can help all children participate in physical activity to the fullest extent possible.

Promoting Physical Well-Being in All Children

Children with chronic illnesses, serious injuries, and physical disabilities often require individualized accommodations so they can achieve optimal health. Several general guidelines apply to *all* children but especially to those with special physical needs:

- ***Help every child participate in all activities to the fullest extent possible.*** In recent years children with special needs have increasingly joined their nondisabled peers in everyday school activities. In a practice called **inclusion,** children and adolescents with disabilities and other exceptional needs are educated within the general education classroom for all or part of the school day. Many educators have found that when they keep an open mind about what their students can accomplish, and especially when they think creatively about how they can adapt activities to the needs of individual students, almost all students can participate meaningfully in virtually all classroom activities (Logan, Alberto, Kana, & Waylor-Bowen, 1994; Salisbury, Evans, & Palombaro, 1997). For example, a workshop class can set up a buddy system so an adolescent with limited fine motor control can participate in wood carving.

- ***Seek guidance from parents or guardians and from specialized organizations.*** Parents and guardians often have helpful suggestions about adjustments that would enable their children to participate more fully in school and extracurricular activities. And professional organizations—most are easily found on the Internet—offer a wealth of ideas about adapting instruction and equipment for children with chronic physical conditions and disabilities. Two broadly focused organizations are the American Alliance for Health, Physical Education, Recreation and Dance and the National Consortium for Physical Education and Recreation for Individuals with Disabilities. Specific disabilities are the focus of other organizations, such as the American Athletic Association for the Deaf and the U.S. Association for Blind Athletes.

- ***Encourage children to monitor their health conditions.*** Children gradually learn to cope with the everyday demands of chronic health conditions, but they may need reminders to check on critical physiological states (e.g., to test blood glucose levels if diabetic), go to the nurse's office at appropriate times (e.g., to take medicines), and look after their recurring physical needs (e.g., to eat nutritious snacks and use the toilet regularly).

- ***Encourage children and their families to take protective measures.*** Caregivers and teachers can teach young children how to handle emergencies, such as how and under what circumstances to make an emergency phone call (M. C. Roberts, Brown, Boles, & Mashunkashey, 2004). In elementary school, teachers can explain (and enforce) safety rules for climbing and using slides. Schools can distribute safety brochures on topics such as seat belts, bicycle helmets, and fire and smoke safety. Child care directors can implement safety measures and periodically distribute tokens for pizza or movies when children arrive at the center buckled up in safety seats (M. C. Roberts et al., 2004).

inclusion
Practice of educating all students, including those with severe and multiple disabilities, in neighborhood schools and general education classrooms.

• ***Design environments to minimize injuries.*** Careful attention to equipment can reduce children's injuries (M. C. Roberts et al., 2004). For example, an infant caregiver can purchase cribs with slats close together to prevent babies' heads from getting stuck between them. The caregiver can also examine toys for choking hazards, set the temperature of water heaters below what would cause scalding, and confirm that the refrigerator door will not lock from the inside (M. C. Roberts et al., 2004). A principal can ensure that a playground has no sharp edges; that the ground's surface has soft; cushioning materials; and that smoke detectors in the school building are installed properly and regularly checked for working batteries.

• ***Know what to do in a health emergency.*** Some children have conditions that may occasionally result in life-threatening situations. For example, a child with diabetes may go into insulin shock, a child with asthma may have trouble breathing, or a child with epilepsy may have a seizure. When teachers learn that a child has a chronic health condition, they should consult with parents and school medical personnel to find out ahead of time how to respond to such emergencies.

• ***Educate peers about a disability.*** Peers are more likely to show kindness to a child with a physical or health impairment if they understand the nature of the disability. Peers should know, for example, that cancer cannot be spread through breathing the same air and that epileptic seizures, though frightening, are only temporary. Keep in mind, however, that a teacher should talk about a child's physical condition *only* if the child and his or her parents have given permission for the teacher to do so (Shapiro & Manz, 2004).

• ***Keep lines of communication open with children who are hospitalized or homebound.*** Sometimes children's physical conditions keep them out of school for lengthy periods of time. In such circumstances, children can often participate in classroom lessons, activities, and social events by telephone or computer hook-up. When they cannot, they may be especially appreciative of correspondence and photographs from classmates and other important people in their lives.

• ***Teach social skills to children who find themselves excluded from friendship groups.*** School absences and the stresses of a chronic condition (and occasional overprotection from parents) can put a strain on children's peer relationships. Teachers can keep an eye out for the inclusion of children with chronic illnesses, particularly when they reenter school after repeated or lengthy absences. Teachers can also coach children to try particular social skills, such as listening sympathetically, resolving conflicts, and gaining entry into an existing group of children (Kapp-Simon & Simon, 1991).

• ***Address any problems in learning that accompany children's illnesses.*** Depending on their health conditions and the medicines they take, children with chronic illnesses may develop learning disabilities, attention problems, and difficulty with learning in an organized and strategic manner (Shapiro & Manz, 2004). Teachers can address learning disabilities and teach children how to organize their work, set interim goals for complex assignments, and so forth.

• ***Use precautions when caring for children who are sick or injured.*** Educators can teach children basic safety precautions, such as sneezing into one's elbow, staying away from a friend's bloody knee, and washing hands after using the toilet. Adults also need to take precautions themselves. The use of appropriate barrier precautions for blood (e.g., latex gloves) is advisable when helping children who have skinned their knees or who have open wounds. Experts also direct caregivers to wash their hands after changing diapers and wiping noses (AAP Committee on Pediatric AIDS and Committee on Infectious Diseases, 1999).

Thoughtful attention to children's physical needs can enhance children's health, well-being, and ability to focus on their schoolwork. Such short-term effects pay dividends for future health, because good habits in childhood pave the way to healthy living later in life.

Summary

Principles of Physical Development

Different systems of the body grow at different rates. Over time, physiological functioning becomes both increasingly differentiated (e.g., different cells take on different roles) and increasingly integrated (e.g., different body parts work more closely together). Children's bodies seem to aim for certain targets in physical growth, even if growth is temporarily deterred by illness or inadequate nutrition. The body is a complex, dynamic system that grows and changes in a multilayered environmental setting.

The Brain and Its Development

The human brain is an intricate organ that regulates basic physiological functions (e.g., heart rate), sensations of pleasure and pain, motor skills and coordination, emotional responses, and intellectual processes. The brain consists of millions of interconnected circuits of neurons that make up the distinct parts of the brain. During prenatal development, neurons form and migrate to places where they will do their work. During infancy, the brain creates many connections among neurons; areas of the brain that support perceptual learning show particularly rapid growth. During early and middle childhood, the brain protects those connections that are used most often and lets the others die out; particular refinements also solidify language skills and complex learning processes. During adolescence, the brain enables new interests and passions and grows in areas that play key roles in forethought and judgment.

Physical Development During Childhood

Predictable changes in physical functioning occur during childhood and adolescence. During infancy, survival mechanisms, such as reflexes, are implemented, feeding moves from milk to a combination of milk and soft solids, and motor skills permit exploration. Early childhood is marked by vigorous physical activity and the acquisition of new motor skills. Middle childhood is a time of consolidation, when children's growth rate slows down and they put motor skills to purposeful use. Puberty marks the onset of adolescence and extends over several years' time. Adult height and sexual maturation are attained in late adolescence.

Physical Well-Being

Health depends on several factors, including eating habits, physical activity, and rest and sleep. Some children and adolescents show patterns of behavior (e.g., eating disorders, overreliance on sedentary activities, overcommitments that result in insufficient sleep) that may jeopardize their physical well-being. In adolescence, additional health-compromising behaviors may emerge as youths struggle with such temptations as cigarette smoking, alcohol, drugs, and unprotected sexual activity.

Special Physical Needs

Youngsters with chronic illness, serious injuries, and physical disabilities often benefit from modifications in instruction, equipment, and physical environment. Ultimately, educators should strive to make experiences as healthful and "normal" as possible for these children.

Applying Concepts in Child Development

The exercises in this section will help you increase your effectiveness in supporting children's physical development.

Case Study

Lucy

Read the case and then answer the questions that follow it.

In her early teenage years, Lucy had leukemia. After a long hospitalization, plus radiation and chemotherapy treatments that resulted in temporary hair loss, Lucy's disease finally went into remission. Eventually, Lucy was healthy enough to return to school, but her life at school was quite different from what it once had been. Her therapist, Mary Pipher (1994), explains:

It had been hard for her to return to school. Everyone was nice to Lucy, almost too nice, like she was a visitor from another planet, but she was left out of so many things. Her old friends had boyfriends and were involved in new activities. When she was in the hospital they would visit with flowers and magazines, but now that she was better, they didn't seem to know what to do with her.

Frank [her father] said, "Lucy's personality has changed. She's quieter. She used to clown around. Now she is more serious. In some ways she seems older; she's suffered more and seen other children suffer. In some ways she's younger; she's missed a lot."

Lucy had missed a great deal: ninth-grade graduation, the beginning of high school, parties, dating, sports, school activities and even puberty (the leukemia had delayed her periods and physical development). She had lots of catching up to do. She'd been so vulnerable that her parents were protective. They didn't want her to become tired, to eat junk food, to forget to take her medicines or to take any chances. Her immune system was weak and she could be in trouble with the slightest injury. Lucy, unlike most teens, didn't grimace at her parents' worries. She associated them with staying alive. (p. 84)[a]

· How did Lucy's illness affect her physical, social, and cognitive development?
· In some respects, Lucy probably developed more quickly than most students her age. What particular strengths might Lucy have had as a result of having combated a life-threatening illness?

· As a teacher working with this age-group, what strategies might you use to ease Lucy's return to school?

Once you have answered these questions, compare your responses with those presented in Appendix A.

[a]From REVIVING OPHELIA by Mary Pipher, Ph.D., copyright © 1994 by Mary Pipher, Ph.D. Used by permission of G. P. Putnam's Sons, a division of Penguin Group (USA) Inc.

Interpreting Children's Artifacts and Reflections

Consider chapter concepts as you analyze the following artifact from a child.

MyPyramid Worksheet by Alex

Twelve-year-old Alex is 4 feet, 11 inches tall and weighs 73 pounds. Alex is slender, athletically inclined, and reasonably attentive to his health. He is a rather picky eater, however, and has a decidedly sweet tooth. One Saturday morning, Alex agreed to record everything he ate and drank on that day (besides water) using an online form prepared by the U.S. Department of Agriculture. The form is customized to a person's age, height, and

weight (go to www.mypyramidtracker.gov). As you examine Alex's completed worksheet, consider these questions:

· What kinds of dietary goals are present on the worksheet? (Look under the fourth column.)
· Which of the dietary goals did Alex come closest to achieving?
· Which dietary goals did Alex fail to achieve?
· How did Alex fare in his physical activity?
· What insights did Alex have as he evaluated his diet and physical activity?

MyPyramid Worksheet by Alex, Age 12. From form published by U.S. Department of Agriculture (2008). *MyPyramid Plan*. Retrieved January 16, 2008 from *http://www.mypyramid.gov*

Once you have analyzed Alex's worksheet, compare your ideas with those presented in Appendix B. For further practice in analyzing children's artifacts and reflections, go to the Activities and Applications section in Chapter 5 of MyEducationLab.

Developmental Trends Exercise

In this chapter, you learned about many aspects of physical development in children and adolescents. The following table describes issues related to the physical well-being of youngsters at five different age levels. For each of these issues, the table identifies one or more concepts related to physical development, offers an implication for working with children of that age-group, or both. Go to the Activities and Applications section in Chapter 5 of MyEducationLab to apply what you've learned about brain development, typical physical changes, and factors affecting children's physical development as you fill in the empty cells in the table.

Supporting Physical Development

Age	A Youngster's Experience	Developmental Concepts — *Factors Affecting Physical Well-Being*	Implications — *Supporting Physical Well-Being*
Infancy (Birth–2 Years)	Thirteen-month old Naima appears to her caregiver to be a healthy, spirited child. The caregiver is surprised when Naima's parents point out that Naima occasionally seems to struggle in her motor development, as when she recently began to walk but then returned to crawling for a few weeks. They ask if something is wrong with Naima.	Naima is showing sequences of progress and typical regressions in her motor skills. Naima's progress and occasional regressions suggest a *dynamic system* at work. Children act on the world, discover that their bodies permit new skills, make preliminary progress in mastering these skills, and show occasional declines in proficiency as they figure out how to deal with one or more changing factors (e.g., increases in muscle tone).	Reassure parents that infants make substantial progress in motor skills over brief periods. Explain that some retreats are common and usually reflect the child's adjustment to a new factor, such as weight gain, a temporary illness, or a change in muscle tone. Of course, Naima's parents may be noticing something that is unusual about their daughter, and they will want to consult with their doctor if they are worried about her.
Early Childhood (2–6 Years)	In an orientation meeting for families at a child care center, one father asks how the center will help his 3-year-old son Jules develop a "strong brain." Jules's father brings in a newspaper article about the importance of providing enriching educational experiences for young children.		Reassure parents that you are eager to support children in all aspects of their development, including their brain development. Further explain that a well-rounded preschool environment with lots of hands-on experiences, opportunities for pretend play, stories and puzzles, stable relationships with teachers and peers, healthful snacks, and outdoor play will offer ample enrichment for children's growing brains.
Middle Childhood (6–10 Years)	Seven-year-old Roy is overweight. His doctor recently gave his mother a brochure on obesity in children. It seems that a range of factors contributes to Roy's obesity—his parents are both overweight, Roy has developed a preference for fatty foods, and he spends most of his free time at home watching television and playing video games. His parents ask Roy's teacher, Mr. McGinnis, how much exercise Roy gets at school and wonder if a lack of physical activity there is the problem. They also make a passing comment that it may simply be Roy's destiny to be a "big, chunky guy."	*Obesity* is a serious health risk in childhood. It predicts health problems in adulthood. Being obese as a child is predicted by familial weight problems, poor eating habits, and restricted physical activity. Because Roy is only 7 years old, he has a good chance of improving his weight level through adopting better eating habits and increasing his physical activity.	
Early Adolescence (10–14 Years)	Thirteen-year old Helen used to be known as the school "brainiac," but recently she has *not* been acting intelligently. In the last year, Helen has matured physically and now appears several years older than most of her peers. After her last class she has been drinking on school grounds with students from a local high school and stealing cosmetics from a local store.	It is common for young adolescents to engage in some *risky behaviors*. Helen may be an *early-maturing adolescent* who is imitating high-risk behaviors of older teenagers.	
Late Adolescence (14–18 Years)	Ms. Comstock thinks about the high school seniors she has in her literature courses. Her students appear to be attractive, bright young adults. But from private conversations with them, Ms. Comstock knows that these teenagers can be introspective and thoughtful one moment yet rash and impulsive the next. And although they certainly seem smart enough to stay on top of their homework assignments, they frequently fail to complete projects on time. For a second, she would love to see inside their brains. She wonders: Do they have the bodies of adults and the brains of children?	Brains continue to develop rapidly and systematically during adolescence and, in fact, into the adult years. *Brain development* during adolescence builds on the many changes of childhood. It refines the front part of the cortex, which supports planning, emotional control, reasoning, and judgment. It also enables new interests and a desire to experiment with risky behaviors.	Continue to communicate expectations to adolescents that they have the ability to act thoughtfully and appropriately, but also give them the scaffolding they need to be successful. For example, because it is difficult for them to keep long-term goals in mind, ask youngsters to turn in *parts* of assignments before handing in the final projects.

Key Concepts

differentiation (p. 146)
integration (p. 147)
neuron (p. 149)
dendrite (p. 149)
axon (p. 149)
synapse (p. 149)
glial cell (p. 150)
hindbrain (p. 150)
midbrain (p. 150)

forebrain (p. 150)
cortex (p. 150)
executive functions (p. 150)
left hemisphere (p. 151)
right hemisphere (p. 151)
schizophrenia (p. 151)
synaptogenesis (p. 152)
synaptic pruning (p. 153)
myelination (p. 153)

cephalocaudal trend (p. 159)
proximodistal trend (p. 159)
gross motor skills (p. 159)
fine motor skills (p. 160)
puberty (p. 162)
growth spurt (p. 162)
menarche (p. 162)
spermarche (p. 162)
obesity (p. 169)

anorexia nervosa (p. 169)
bulimia (p. 169)
rough-and-tumble play (p. 171)
sudden infant death syndrome
   (SIDS) (p. 174)
addiction (p. 178)
inclusion (p. 185)

MyEducationLab

Now go to Chapter 5 of MyEducationLab at www.myeducationlab.com, where you can:

· View instructional objectives for the chapter.
· Take a quiz to test your mastery of chapter objectives. Detailed feedback is provided to explain why your responses are correct or incorrect.
· Deepen your understanding of particular concepts and principles with Review, Practice, and Enrichment exercises.

· Complete Activities and Applications exercises that give you additional experience in interpreting artifacts, increase your understanding of how research contributes to knowledge about chapter topics, and encourage you to apply what you have learned about children's development.
· Apply what you have learned in the chapter to your work with children in Building Teaching Skills and Dispositions exercises.
· Observe children and their unique contexts in Video Examples.

chapter
6

Cognitive Development: Piaget and Vygotsky

Four-year-old Billy is fascinated by dinosaurs. He and his mother have read many children's books about dinosaurs, so he already has some knowledge about these creatures and the geological time periods in which they lived. As Billy and his mother visit a dinosaur exhibit at a natural history museum, they have the following conversation:

Mother: This is a real dinosaur rib bone. Where are your ribs? Where are your ribs? No that's your wrist. Very close.

Billy: Oh, yeah, right here.

Mother: Yeah, that's right. Here. Protecting your heart . . . and your lungs. And this was one from a dinosaur from the Jurassic period, also found from our country. In a place called Utah.

Mother: And this one . . . [Mother picks up a piece of fossilized dinosaur feces, known as *coprolite*] Oh! You're not . . . guess what that is. Look at it and guess what that is.

Billy: Um, what?

Mother: Guess. What's it look like?

Billy: His gum? What? Mom!

Mother: It's dinosaur poop.

Billy: Ooooo! (laughs)

Mother: That's real dinosaur poop.

Billy: I touched it! (laughs)

Mother: It's so old that it doesn't smell anymore. It turned to rock. It's not mushy like poop. It's like a rock. And that's from the Cretaceous period but we don't know what dinosaur made it. And this was also found in our country in Colorado. I think that's pretty funny.

Billy: What's this?

Mother: So this one . . . Oh, that's called . . . that's a stone that dinosaurs . . . remember in your animal book it says something about how sometimes chickens eat stones to help them digest—it helps them mush up their food in their tummy?

Billy: Yeah.

Mother: Well, dinosaurs ate stones to mush up their food in their tummy and this was one of the stones that they ate. They're so big, that to them this was a little stone. Right? And that also comes from Colorado.[a] (dialogue is from Crowley & Jacobs, 2002, p. 346; "Billy" is a pseudonym.)

- What knowledge does Billy currently have that can help him understand what he sees in the dinosaur exhibit?

- What does Mother do to help her son make better sense of the exhibit?

[a]Copyright © 2002 From *Learning Conversations in Museums* by Leinhardt, G., Crowley, K. & Knutson, K. Reproduced by permission of Routledge, Inc., a division of Informa plc.

Case Study: Museum Visit

Outline:

Case Study: Museum Visit

Piaget's Theory of Cognitive Development

Vygotsky's Theory of Cognitive Development

Comparing Piagetian and Vygotskian Perspectives

Summary

Applying Concepts in Child Development

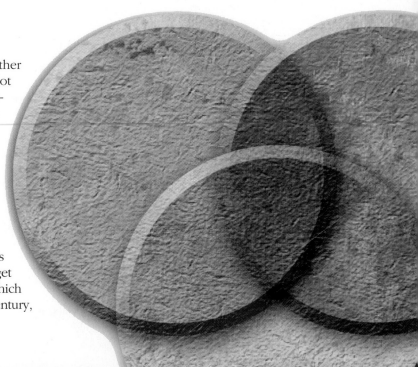

Thanks to the many books that 4-year-old Billy and his mother have previously read together, Billy appears to know a lot about dinosaurs and other animals. For instance, he is familiar with the words *Jurassic* and *Cretaceous,* and he knows that some animals have stones in their stomachs to aid digestion. Mother helps him connect what he is seeing to his prior knowledge—not only about geological periods and stomach stones but also about more commonplace concepts such as ribs and "poop." Yet Billy, like all children, is not simply a "sponge" who passively soaks up the information that his environment provides. Instead, his cognitive development is in large part the result of his *own active efforts* to make sense of his world.

As we begin our examination of cognitive development in this chapter, we consider the classic developmental theories of Jean Piaget and Lev Vygotsky, both of whom examined the active manner in which children learn. Formulated in the first few decades of the 20th century, these two theories have provided much of the foundation for our current understanding of how children's thinking changes with age. Between them, the two theories tell us a great deal about how children make sense of everyday events both on their own and in collaboration with adults and peers. As you will find out, the two theories also have much to say about how parents, teachers, and other adults can help children think and learn more effectively.

Piaget's Theory of Cognitive Development

Jean Piaget (1896–1980) was formally trained as a biologist. But he had an interest in philosophy as well and was especially curious about the nature of knowledge and how it changes with development. In the 1920s he began to observe the everyday actions of infants and children and to draw inferences about the thinking and reasoning that seemed to underlie their behavior. In his lab in Geneva, Switzerland, Piaget pioneered the **clinical method**, a procedure in which an adult presents a task or problem and asks a child a series of questions about it, tailoring later questions to the child's responses to previous ones. In one task, for example, an adult shows a child a box containing about a dozen wooden beads, two of which are white and the rest brown. The adult first shows the beads to a 6-year-old, whom we'll call "Brian."[1] The following discussion ensues:

Adult: Are there more wooden beads or more brown beads?
Brian: More brown ones, because there are two white ones.
Adult: Are the white ones made of wood?
Brian: Yes.
Adult: And the brown ones?
Brian: Yes.
Adult: Then are there more brown ones or more wooden ones?
Brian: More brown ones.
Adult: What color would a necklace made of the wooden beads be?
Brian: Brown and white. (Here [Brian] shows that he understands that all the beads are wooden.)
Adult: And what color would a necklace made with the brown beads be?
Brian: Brown.
Adult: Then which would be longer, the one made with the wooden beads or the one made with the brown beads?
Brian: The one with the brown beads.
Adult: Draw the necklaces for me.

Brian draws a series of black rings for the necklace of brown beads. He then draws a series of black rings plus two white rings for the necklace of wooden beads.

Adult: Good. Now which will be longer, the one with the brown beads or the one with the wooden beads?
Brian: The one with the brown beads. (dialogue from Piaget, 1952a, pp. 163–164)

Brian has difficulty with a question that, to us, seems quite simple. Even though all the beads are wooden and only some (albeit the majority) are brown, he concludes that there are more brown beads than wooden ones. In contrast, 8-year-old "Natalie" answers the question easily. Logically, she says, there must be more wooden beads than brown beads:

Adult: Are there more wooden beads or more brown beads?
Natalie: More wooden ones.
Adult: Why?
Natalie: Because the two white ones are made of wood as well.
Adult: Suppose we made two necklaces, one with all the wooden beads and one with all the brown ones. Which one would be longer?
Natalie: Well, the wooden ones and the brown ones are the same, and it would be longer with the wooden ones because there are two white ones as well. (dialogue from Piaget, 1952a, p. 176)

clinical method
Procedure in which an adult probes a child's reasoning about a task or problem, tailoring questions in light of what the child has previously said or done in the interview.

[1]Piaget identified children in his studies by abbreviations. We've substituted names throughout the text to allow for easier discussion.

Natalie exhibits **class inclusion,** the recognition that an object can belong both to a particular category and to one of its subcategories simultaneously.

Drawing from such interviews with preschoolers, school-age children, and adolescents, as well as from in-depth observations of the behaviors of infants and toddlers, Piaget developed a theory of cognitive development that has contributed a great deal to our understanding of how children and adolescents think and learn (e.g., Piaget, 1928, 1952b, 1959, 1985).

Key Ideas in Piaget's Theory

Central to Piaget's theory are the following principles:

- ***Children are active and motivated learners.*** In the opening case study, Billy seems quite eager to make sense of the fossils he sees in the natural history museum. Piaget proposed that children are naturally curious about their world and actively seek out information that can help them interpret and understand it (e.g., Piaget, 1952b). They often experiment with the objects they encounter, manipulating them and observing the effects of their actions. For example, we authors think back to the days when our children were in high chairs, experimenting with their food (pushing, squishing, dropping, and throwing it) as readily as they would eat it.

Many contemporary theorists share Piaget's view that much of a human being's motivation for learning and development comes from within. It appears that growing children are naturally inclined to try to make sense of the people, objects, and events around them (e.g., K. Fischer, 2005; K. Nelson, 1996a). You can see an example of such *intrinsic motivation* in the "Cognitive Development: Early Childhood" video in MyEducationLab, in which 2-year-old Maddie encounters an intriguing new object and actively manipulates it to discover some of its properties.

- ***Children organize what they learn from their experiences.*** Children don't just amass the things they learn into a collection of isolated facts. Instead, they pull their experiences together into an integrated view of how the world operates. For example, by observing that food, toys, and other objects always fall down (never up) when released, children begin to construct a basic understanding of gravity. As they interact with family pets, visit zoos, look at picture books, and so on, they develop an increasingly complex understanding of animals. Piaget depicted learning as a very *constructive* process: Children create (rather than simply absorb) their knowledge about the world.

In Piaget's terminology, the things that children learn and can do are organized as **schemes,** groups of similar actions or thoughts that are used repeatedly in response to the environment. Initially, children's schemes are largely behavioral in nature, but over time they become increasingly mental and, eventually, abstract (Inhelder & Piaget, 1958; Piaget, 1952b, 1954). For example, an infant may have a behavioral scheme for putting things in her mouth, a scheme that she uses in dealing with a variety of objects, including her thumb, toys, and blanket. A 7-year-old may have a mental but relatively concrete scheme for identifying snakes, one that includes their long, thin bodies, their lack of legs, and their slithery nature. As a 13-year-old, Jeanne's daughter Tina had her own opinion about what constitutes fashion, an abstract scheme that allowed her to classify various articles of clothing on display at the mall as being either "totally awesome" or "really stupid."

Piaget proposed that children use newly acquired schemes over and over in both familiar and novel situations. For example, in the "Cognitive Development: Infancy" video in MyEducationLab, you can observe 16-month-old Corwin repeatedly taking a toy out of a paper bag and then putting it back in. In the process of repeating their schemes, children refine them and begin to use them in combination. Eventually, they integrate schemes into larger systems of mental processes called **operations.** This integration allows them to think in increasingly sophisticated ways. For instance, 8-year-old Natalie's reasoning about the "beads" problem shows greater integration than 6-year-old Brian's: Although both children understand that some beads are both brown and wooden, only Natalie takes both characteristics into account simultaneously to conclude that there must be more wooden beads than brown beads. Brian apparently can consider only one characteristic at a time. As a result, he compares the brown beads only with the remaining wooden beads (the white ones) and so concludes that there are more brown ones than wooden ones.

class inclusion
Recognition that an object simultaneously belongs to a particular category and to one of its subcategories.

scheme
In Piaget's theory, an organized group of similar actions or thoughts that are used repeatedly in response to the environment.

operation
In Piaget's theory, an organized and integrated system of logical thought processes.

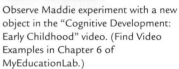

MyEducationLab

Observe Maddie experiment with a new object in the "Cognitive Development: Early Childhood" video. (Find Video Examples in Chapter 6 of MyEducationLab.)

MyEducationLab

Observe Corwin repeatedly using his "putting-in" and "taking-out" schemes in the "Cognitive Development: Infancy" video. (Find Video Examples in Chapter 6 of MyEducationLab.)

When children work together to construct a bird nest, they can apply knowledge and skills they have previously acquired (*assimilation*), but must also make adjustments that take into account the new materials the task involves (*accommodation*).

• ***Children adapt to their environment through the processes of assimilation and accommodation.*** According to Piaget, children's developing schemes allow them to adapt in ever more successful ways to their environment. Such adaptation occurs as a result of two complementary processes: assimilation and accommodation (e.g., Piaget, 1954). **Assimilation** entails responding (either physically or mentally) to an object or event in a way that is consistent with an existing scheme.[2] For example, an infant may assimilate a ball into her putting-things-in-the-mouth scheme, and a 7-year-old may quickly identify a new slithery object in the backyard as a snake.

Yet children must typically adjust their existing schemes at least a little bit in order to respond to a new object or event. Thus one of two forms of **accommodation** is likely to occur. Children will either modify an existing scheme to account for the new object or event or else form an entirely new scheme to deal with it. For example, an infant may have to open her mouth wider than usual to accommodate a large plastic ball or teddy bear's paw. The 7-year-old may find a long, slithery thing with a snakelike body that cannot possibly *be* a snake because it has four legs. After some research, he will develop a new scheme—*salamander*—for this creature.

Assimilation and accommodation work hand in hand as children develop knowledge and understanding of the world. Children interpret each new event within the context of their existing knowledge (assimilation) but at the same time modify their knowledge as a result of the new event (accommodation). For example, in the opening case study, Billy initially thinks that the piece of coprolite is a large wad of dinosaur gum—that is, he mistakenly assimilates the object into his "chewing gum" scheme. But with his mother's help, he creates a new scheme, "fossilized dinosaur poop," that more accurately accounts for what he is seeing. Later Mother helps Billy assimilate a large stone into a "stones-that-help-digestion" scheme he has previously acquired. In the process, however, he must also modify this scheme so that it applies to dinosaurs as well as to chickens.

• ***Interaction with the physical environment is critical for cognitive development.*** By exploring and manipulating the world around them—by conducting many little "experiments" with various objects and substances—children learn the nature of their physical world and continue to revise their existing schemes. The following anecdote from a preschool teacher illustrates this process:

> Tommy . . . had built a tower on a base of three regular blocks on end, with a round, flat piece of Masonite on top. Then on top of this were three more blocks and Masonite, supporting in turn a third story. . . . The tower was already taller than Tommy, and he had a piece of triangular Masonite in hand and was gently testing the tower's steadiness against his taps. Small taps and the tower would lean, settle, and become still. Again and again he varied the strength and place of the taps; watched, waited, tapped again, and finally—on purpose—did hit hard enough to topple the structure. Then the entire process of building the tower and testing it was repeated. (Hawkins, 1997, p. 200)

Likewise, as children and adolescents bounce, throw, hit, and catch balls in team sports, they undoubtedly continue to refine their understandings of such physical phenomena as force and inertia.

• ***Interaction with other people is equally critical.*** Piaget suggested that children learn a great deal from interacting with their fellow human beings. For example, as you will discover shortly, preschoolers can have difficulty seeing the world from anyone's perspective but their own. By conversing, exchanging ideas, and arguing with others, they gradually come to realize that different individuals see things differently and that their own view of the world is not necessarily a completely accurate or logical one. And older children and adolescents may begin to recognize logical inconsistencies in what they say and do when someone else points out these discrepancies.

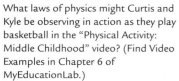
assimilation
In Piaget's theory, process of responding (either physically or mentally) to a new event in a way that is consistent with an existing scheme.

accommodation
Process of responding to a new event by either modifying an existing scheme or forming a new one.

---

[2]Note that Piaget's concept of *assimilation* is quite different from the process of *cultural assimilation* described in Chapter 3.

- ***The process of equilibration promotes increasingly complex forms of thought.*** Piaget proposed that children are sometimes in a state of **equilibrium:** They can comfortably address new situations using their existing schemes and operations. But equilibrium doesn't continue indefinitely. In their daily lives children regularly encounter circumstances for which their present knowledge and skills are inadequate. These circumstances create **disequilibrium,** a sort of mental "discomfort" that spurs children to try to make sense of and successfully deal with the situation at hand. By replacing or reorganizing certain schemes, children may be better able to address the situation, and so they can return to equilibrium. This process of moving from equilibrium to disequilibrium and back to equilibrium again is known as **equilibration** (e.g., Inhelder & Piaget, 1958). In some instances the end result is a better integrated, more inclusive, and more stable set of schemes and operations than children had previously. Thus, Piaget suggested, the equilibration process gradually leads to increasingly complex levels of thought and knowledge.

  Let's return to the example of Brian and his "beads" problem. The adult asks Brian to draw two necklaces, one made with brown and white beads and one made only with brown beads. The adult hopes that after Brian draws a brown-and-white necklace that is longer than an all-brown necklace, he will notice that his drawings are inconsistent with his statement that there are more brown beads than wooden ones. The inconsistency might lead Brian to experience disequilibrium, perhaps to the point where he would reevaluate his conclusion and realize that the number of all the brown beads plus two white ones *must* be greater than the number of brown beads alone. In this case, however, Brian seems to be oblivious to the inconsistency, remains in equilibrium, and therefore has no need to revise his thinking.

  Piaget was a bit vague about how the processes of assimilation, accommodation, and equilibration actually work (e.g., diSessa, 2006; Klahr, 1982). Nevertheless, contemporary developmentalists embrace the principles that children's new ideas are based on their earlier ones and that inconsistencies can sometimes spur children to develop more sophisticated understandings and abilities. Developmentally speaking, then, new and more advanced knowledge, skills, and cognitive processes don't just appear out of thin air.

- ***Children think in qualitatively different ways at different age levels.*** Piaget proposed that as a result of brain maturation, environmental experiences, and children's natural desire to make sense of and adapt to their world, cognitive abilities continue to undergo distinct, qualitative changes over the course of childhood and adolescence. He characterized youngsters' cognitive abilities as falling into four general stages of development (e.g., Piaget, 1971). The abilities at any one stage are constructed out of the accomplishments of any preceding stages. Thus, the four stages are *hierarchical*—each one depends on its predecessors—and so children progress through them in a particular order. To a considerable degree, they are also assumed to be *universal,* characterizing the cognitive development of children throughout the world.

  As you will discover later in the chapter, many psychologists question the notion that cognitive development is as stagelike as Piaget suggested. Nevertheless, Piaget's stages provide helpful insights into the nature of children's thinking at different age levels, and so we will look at the stages more closely.

Piaget's Stages of Cognitive Development

Piaget's four stages are summarized in Table 6-1. The ages of onset for all but the sensorimotor stage are *averages:* Some children show characteristics associated with a particular stage a bit earlier, others a bit later. Keep in mind, too, that many children are apt to be in *transition* from one stage to the next, displaying characteristics of two adjacent stages at the same time. Furthermore, children and adolescents don't always take advantage of their advanced cognitive abilities, and so they may show considerable variability in ways of thinking in their day-to-day activities (Chapman, 1988; Piaget, 1960b). Figure 6-1 depicts the transitional and flexible nature of children's progress through the stages.

Sensorimotor stage (beginning at birth).   Piaget believed that in the first month of life, infants' behaviors are little more than biologically built-in responses to particular stimuli—that

equilibrium
State of being able to address new events using existing schemes.

disequilibrium
State of being unable to address new events with existing schemes.

equilibration
Movement from equilibrium to disequilibrium and back to equilibrium; a process that promotes the development of increasingly complex forms of thought and knowledge.

Table 6-1   Examples of Acquisitions Associated with Each of Piaget's Four Stages

Stage	Age of Onset[a]	General Description	Examples of Acquisitions
Sensorimotor	Begins at birth	Schemes are based largely on behaviors and perceptions. Especially in the early part of the stage, children cannot think about things that are not immediately in front of them, and so they focus on what they are doing and seeing at the moment.	· *Trial-and-error experimentation:* Exploration and manipulation of objects to determine their properties · *Goal-directed behavior:* Intentional behavior to bring about a desired result · *Object permanence:* Realization that objects continue to exist even when removed from view · *Symbolic thought:* Representation of physical objects and events as mental entities *(symbols)*
Preoperational	Appears at about age 2	Thanks in part to their rapidly developing symbolic thinking abilities, children can now think and talk about things beyond their immediate experience. However, they do not yet reason in logical, adult-like ways.	· *Language:* Rapid expansion of vocabulary and grammatical structures · *Extensive pretend play:* Enactment of true-to-life or fanciful scenarios with plots and assigned roles (e.g., mommy, doctor, Superman) · *Intuitive thought:* Some logical thinking based on "hunches" and "intuition" rather than on conscious awareness of logical principles (especially after age 4)
Concrete Operations	Appears at about age 6 or 7	Adult-like logic appears but is limited to reasoning about concrete, real-life situations.	· *Distinction between one's own and others' perspectives:* Recognition that one's own thoughts and feelings may be different from those of others and do not necessarily reflect reality · *Class inclusion:* Ability to classify objects as belonging to two or more categories simultaneously · *Conservation:* Realization that amount stays the same if nothing is added or taken away, regardless of alterations in shape or arrangement
Formal Operations	Appears at about age 11 or 12	Logical reasoning processes are applied to abstract ideas as well as concrete objects and situations. Many capabilities essential for advanced reasoning in science and mathematics appear.	· *Reasoning about abstract, hypothetical, and contrary-to-fact ideas:* Ability to draw logical deductions about situations that have no basis in physical reality · *Separation and control of variables:* Ability to test hypotheses by manipulating one variable while holding other variables constant · *Proportional reasoning:* Conceptual understanding of fractions, percentages, decimals, and ratios · *Idealism:* Ability to envision alternatives to current social and political practices (sometimes with little regard for what is realistically possible in a given time frame)

[a]The ages presented for the preoperational, concrete operations, and formal operations stages are *averages:* For some children, characteristics associated with each stage appear a bit earlier; for others, they appear a bit later.

MyEducationLab

Observe exploratory and goal-directed behaviors in the "Emotional Development: Infancy" and "Cognitive Development: Infancy" videos. (Find Video Examples in Chapter 6 of MyEducationLab.)

goal-directed behavior
Intentional behavior aimed at bringing about an anticipated outcome.

object permanence
Realization that objects continue to exist even when they are out of sight.

symbolic thought
Ability to mentally represent and think about external objects and events.

is, they are *reflexes* (e.g., sucking on a nipple)—that help keep them alive. In the second month infants begin to exhibit voluntary behaviors that they repeat over and over, reflecting the development of perception- and behavior-based *sensorimotor schemes*. Initially, such behaviors focus almost exclusively on infants' own bodies (e.g., putting one's fist in one's mouth), but eventually they involve nearby objects as well. For much of the first year, Piaget suggested, infants' behaviors are largely spontaneous and unplanned. For example, 7-month-old Madison is clearly intrigued by a variety of toys that happen to be nearby her in the "Emotional Development: Infancy" video in MyEducationLab.

Late in the first year, after repeatedly observing that certain actions lead to certain consequences, infants gradually acquire knowledge of cause-and-effect relationships. At this point, they begin to engage in **goal-directed behavior:** They behave in ways that they know will bring about desired results. At about the same time, they acquire **object permanence,** an understanding that physical objects continue to exist even when they are out of sight. In the "Cognitive Development: Infancy" video in MyEducationLab, 16-month-old Corwin shows object permanence when he looks for a toy elephant that his mother repeatedly hides. His searches under a pillow are directed toward a particular goal: finding the elephant.

Piaget believed that for much of the sensorimotor period, children's thinking is restricted to objects in their immediate environment—that is, to the here and now. But in the latter half of the second year, young children develop **symbolic thought,** the ability to represent and think

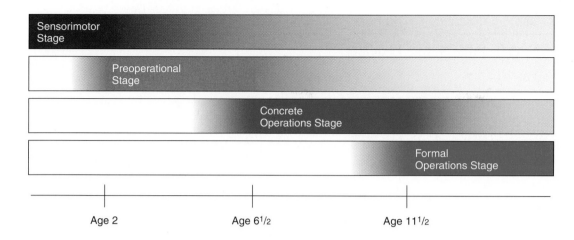

Figure 6-1

Children gain abilities associated with more advanced Piagetian stages slowly over time, and they don't necessarily leave behind the characteristics associated with previous stages.

about objects and events in terms of internal, mental entities, or *symbols* (Piaget, 1962). They may "experiment" with objects in their minds, first predicting what will happen if they do something to an object—say, if they give a toy car a hard push toward the edge of a tabletop—and then putting their plans into action. They may also recall and imitate behaviors they have seen other people exhibit—for instance, "talking" on a toy telephone or "driving" with a toy steering wheel.

The acquisitions of the sensorimotor stage are basic building blocks on which later cognitive development depends. The Observation Guidelines table "Assessing Cognitive Advancements in Infants and Toddlers" presents some of the behaviors you might look for as you work with infants and toddlers.

Preoperational stage (beginning at about age 2).   The ability to represent objects and events mentally (i.e., symbolic thought) gives children in the preoperational stage a more extensive worldview than they had during the sensorimotor stage. They can now recall past events and envision future ones that might be similar to their previous experiences. In addition, they begin to tie their experiences together into an increasingly complex understanding of the world.

Language skills virtually explode during the early part of the preoperational stage. The words in children's rapidly increasing vocabularies provide labels for newly developed mental schemes and serve as symbols that enable children to think about objects and events even when not directly in sight. Furthermore, language provides the basis for a new form of social interaction, verbal communication. Children can express their thoughts and receive information from other people in a way that was not possible during the sensorimotor stage.

The emergence of symbolic thought is reflected not only in rapidly expanding language skills but also in the changing nature of children's play. Preschoolers often engage in fantasy and make-believe, using realistic objects or reasonable substitutes to act out the behaviors of people they see around them. Piaget proposed that such pretend play enables children to practice using newly acquired symbolic schemes and familiarize themselves with the various roles they see others assume in society. This idea is illustrated in the following scenario, in which 5-year-olds Jeff and Scott construct and operate a "restaurant":

> In a corner of Jeff's basement, the boys make a dining area from several child-sized tables and chairs. They construct a restaurant "kitchen" with a toy sink and stove and stock it with plastic dishes and "food" items. They create menus for their restaurant, sometimes asking Jeff's mother how to spell certain words and sometimes using their knowledge of letter-sound relationships to guess how a particular word might be spelled.
>
> Jeff and Scott invite their parents to come to the new restaurant for lunch. The boys pretend to write their customers' meal orders on paper tablets and then scurry to the kitchen to assemble the requested lunch items. Eventually, they return to serve the meals (hamburgers, French fries, and cookies—all of them plastic—plus glasses of imaginary milk), which the adults "eat" and "drink" with gusto. After the young waiters return with the final bills, the parents pay for their "meals" with nickels and leave a few pennies on the tables as tips.

Observation Guidelines

Assessing Cognitive Advancements in Infants and Toddlers

Characteristic	Look For	Example	Implication
Repetition of Gratifying Actions	· Repetition of actions involving the child's own body · Repetition of actions on other objects · Evidence that the child repeats an action because he or she notices and enjoys it	Myra waves her arms, stops, and waves her arms again. She makes a sound and repeats it, as if she enjoys listening to her own voice.	Provide a variety of visual, auditory, and tactile stimuli; for instance, play "This little piggy" with an infant's toes, hang a mobile safely over the crib, and provide age-appropriate objects (e.g., rattles, plastic cups). Be patient and responsive when infants repeat seemingly "pointless" actions (e.g., dropping favorite objects).
Exploration of Objects	· Apparent curiosity about the effects that different behaviors have on objects · Use of multiple behaviors (feeling, poking, dropping, shaking, etc.) to explore an object's properties · Use of several sensory modalities (e.g., seeing, listening, feeling, tasting)	Paco reaches for his caregiver's large, shiny earring. The caregiver quickly removes the earring from her ear and holds its sharp end between her fingers while Paco manipulates the silver loop and multicolored glass beads that hang from it.	Provide objects that infants can explore using multiple senses, making sure the objects are free of dirt and toxic substances and are large enough to prevent swallowing.
Experimentation	· Creativity and flexibility in the behaviors the child uses to discover how things work · Specific problems that the child tackles and the approaches he or she uses to solve them	Jillian drags a step stool to her dresser so that she can reach the toys on top of it. One by one, she drops the toys, watching how each one lands and listening to the sound it makes on impact.	Childproof the environment so that experiments and problem-solving activities are safe. Provide objects that require a sequence of actions (e.g., stacking cups, building blocks, pull toys). Closely supervise toddlers' activities.
Imitation and Pretending	· Imitation of actions modeled by another person · Imitation of actions when the model is no longer present · Use of one object to stand for another	Darius holds a doll and sings to it in the same way his mother sings to him. He combs the doll's hair with a spoon and uses an empty plastic vitamin bottle to feed the doll.	Engage children in reciprocal, imitative games (e.g., peekaboo, hide-and-seek). Provide props that encourage pretend play (miniature shopping carts, plastic carpentry tools, dolls, etc.).

With the emergence of symbolic thought, young children are no longer restricted to the here and now and so can think and act far more flexibly than they did previously. At the same time, preoperational thinking has some definite limitations, especially when compared to the concrete operational thinking that emerges later. For example, Piaget described young children as exhibiting **egocentrism,** an inability to view situations from another person's perspective.[3] Preschoolers may play games together without ever checking to be sure that they are all playing according to the same rules. And they may say things without considering the perspective of the listener—for instance, leaving out critical details as they tell a story and giving a fragmented version that a listener cannot possibly understand. Here we see one reason why, in Piaget's view, social interaction is so important for development. Only by getting repeated feedback from other people can children learn that their thoughts and feelings are unique to them—that their own perception of the world is not always shared by others.

Preoperational thinking is also illogical (at least from an adult's point of view), especially during the preschool years. For example, recall 6-year-old Brian's insistence that there were

egocentrism
Inability of a child in Piaget's preoperational stage to view situations from another person's perspective.

[3]Consistent with common practice, we use the term *egocentrism* to refer to the egocentric thinking that characterizes preoperational thought. Piaget actually talked about different forms of egocentrism at *each* of the four stages of development. For instance, he described egocentrism in the formal operations stage as involving an inability to distinguish one's own logical conclusions from the perspectives of others and from constraints of the real world. Adolescents' unrealistic idealism about social issues is one manifestation of this formal operational egocentrism.

more brown beads than wooden beads, reflecting an inability to engage in class inclusion. Following is another example of the "logic" that characterizes preoperational thought:

> We show 4-year-old Lucy the three glasses at the top of Figure 6-2. Glasses A and B are identical in size and shape and contain an equal amount of water. We ask Lucy if the two glasses of water contain the same amount, and she replies confidently that they do. We then pour the water in Glass B into Glass C. We ask her if the two glasses of water (A and C) still have the same amount. "No," Lucy replies. She points to Glass A and says, "That glass has more because it's taller."

Piaget used this task to assess a logical thought process known as **conservation,** the recognition that an amount must stay the same if nothing is added or taken away, despite any changes in shape or arrangement. Lucy's response reveals that she is not yet capable of *conservation of liquid:* The differently shaped glasses lead her to believe that the actual amount of water has changed. Similarly, in a *conservation of number* task, a child engaging in preoperational thought might say that a row of five pennies spread far apart has more than a row of five pennies spaced close together, even though she has previously counted the pennies in both rows and found them to have the same number. Young children often confuse changes in appearance with changes in amount. Piaget suggested that such confusion is often seen in young children's reasoning because the preoperational stage depends more on perception than on logic.

Sometime around age 4 or 5, children show early signs of thinking more logically than they have previously. For example, they occasionally draw correct conclusions about class inclusion problems (e.g., the wooden beads problem) and conservation problems (e.g., the water glasses problem). But they base their reasoning on hunches and intuition rather than on any conscious awareness of underlying logical principles, and so they cannot yet explain *why* their conclusions are correct.

Concrete operations stage (beginning at about age 6 or 7). In the early primary grades, children become capable of thinking about and integrating various qualities and perspectives of an object or event. For example, children now know that other people may have perceptions and feelings different from their own. Accordingly, they realize that their own views may reflect personal opinion rather than reality, and so they may seek out external validation for their ideas ("What do you think?" "Did I get that problem right?").

Children in the concrete operations stage show many forms of logical thought, and they can readily explain their reasoning. For instance, they can easily classify objects into two categories simultaneously. (Recall 8-year-old Natalie's ease in solving and explaining the "beads" problem.) And they are capable of conservation: They readily understand that if nothing is added or taken away, an amount stays the same despite changes in shape or arrangement. For example, the second girl depicted in the "Conservation" video in MyEducationLab is quite confident that juice poured from a short, wide glass into a tall, thin glass hasn't changed in amount: "Just because this is skinny doesn't mean it's . . . this one is just wider, this one is skinnier, but they have the same amount of juice."

Children continue to develop their newly acquired logical thinking capabilities throughout the elementary school years. For instance, over time they become capable of dealing with increasingly complex conservation tasks. Some forms of conservation, such as conservation of liquid and conservation of number, appear at age 6 or 7. Other forms don't appear until later. Consider the task involving *conservation of weight* depicted in Figure 6-3. Using a balance scale, an adult shows a child that two balls of clay have the same weight. One ball is removed from the scale and smashed into a pancake shape. The child is then asked if the pancake weighs the same as the unsmashed ball or if the two pieces of clay weigh different amounts. Children typically do not achieve conservation of weight—that is, they don't realize that the flattened pancake weighs the same as the round ball—until age 9 or 10 (Piaget, 1950).

Although children displaying concrete operational thought show many signs of logical thinking, their cognitive development is not yet complete. For example, they have trouble understanding and reasoning about abstract or hypothetical ideas (hence the term *concrete* operations stage). In language, this weakness may be reflected in an inability to interpret the underlying, nonliteral meanings of proverbs. In mathematics, it may be reflected in confusion about such concepts as *pi* (π), *infinity*, and *negative number*. And in social studies, it

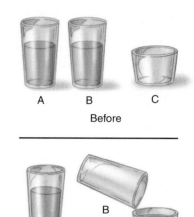

A   B   C
Before

B

A

C
After

Figure 6-2

Conservation of liquid: Do Glasses A and C contain the same amount of water after the water in Glass B is poured into Glass C?

MyEducationLab

See how children respond to various conservation tasks in the "Conservation" video. (Find Video Examples in Chapter 6 of MyEducationLab.)

conservation
Realization that if nothing is added or taken away, amount stays the same regardless of any alterations in shape or arrangement.

Figure 6-3

Conservation of weight: Balls A and B initially weigh the same. When Ball B is flattened into a pancake shape, how does its weight now compare with that of Ball A?

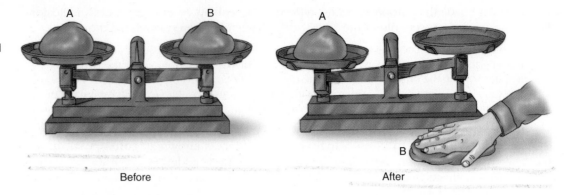

Before   After

MyEducationLab

Observe how 10-year-old Kent easily conserves number but has difficulty with abstract proverbs in the "Cognitive Development: Middle Childhood" video. Also, observe a developmental progression in reasoning about contrary-to-fact information in the "Thinking Logically About Contrary-to-Fact Premises" video. (Find Video Examples in Chapter 6 of MyEducationLab.)

may limit children's comprehension of such abstract notions as *democracy, communism,* and *human rights.*

Formal operations stage (beginning at about age 11 or 12).   Sometime around puberty, Piaget found, children become capable of thinking and reasoning about things that have little or no basis in physical reality. For instance, they can think logically about abstract concepts, hypothetical ideas, and statements that contradict what they know to be true in the real world. Also emerging are scientific reasoning abilities that enable children to identify cause-and-effect relationships in physical phenomena. As an example, consider the following task:

> An object suspended by a rope or string—a pendulum—swings indefinitely at a constant rate. Some pendulums swing back and forth very quickly, whereas others swing more slowly. Design an experiment that can help you determine what factor or factors affect a pendulum's oscillation rate.

To successfully tackle this problem, you must first *formulate hypotheses* about possible variables affecting a pendulum's swing. For instance, you might consider (a) the weight of the suspended object, (b) the length of the string that holds the object, (c) the force with which the object is pushed, and (d) the height from which the object is initially released. You must then *separate and control variables,* testing one factor at a time while holding all others constant. For instance, to test the hypothesis that weight makes a difference, you should try different weights while keeping constant the length of the string, the force with which you push each weight, and the height from which you release it. Similarly, if you hypothesize that the length of the string is critical, you should vary the length of the string while continuing to use the same weight and starting the pendulum in motion in the same manner. If you carefully separate and control variables, your observations should lead you to conclude that only *length* affects a pendulum's oscillation rate.

Once formal operational thinking appears, more advanced verbal and mathematical problem solving is also possible. For instance, adolescents become able to see beyond literal interpretations of such proverbs as "A rolling stone gathers no moss" and "An ant may well destroy a dam" to identify their underlying meanings. Adolescents become better able to understand such concepts as *negative number* and *infinity* because they can now comprehend how numbers can be below zero and how two parallel lines will never touch even if they go on forever. And they can understand the nature of proportions (e.g., fractions, ratios, decimals) and correctly use proportions when working on mathematical problems.

Because adolescents capable of formal operational reasoning can deal with hypothetical and contrary-to-fact ideas, they can envision how the world might be different from, and possibly better than, the way it actually is. Thus they may be idealistic about and devoted to social, political, religious, and ethical issues—global warming, world hunger, animal rights, and so on. Sometimes they offer recommendations for change that seem logical but aren't practical in today's world. For example, they may argue that racism would disappear overnight if people would just begin to "love one another," or they may propose that a nation can help bring about world peace by disbanding its armed forces and discarding all of its weapons. Piaget suggested that adolescent idealism reflects an inability to separate one's own logical abstractions from the perspectives of others and from practical considerations. Only through experience do adolescents eventually begin to temper their optimism with some realism about what is possible in a given time frame and with limited resources.

MyEducationLab

Observe 14-year-old Alicia interpret abstract proverbs in the "Cognitive Development: Late Adolescence" video. (Find Video Examples in Chapter 6 of MyEducationLab.)

Current Perspectives Related to Piaget's Theory

Piaget's theory has sparked a great deal of research about children's cognitive development. In general, this research supports Piaget's proposed *sequence* in which different abilities emerge (Flavell, 1996; Siegler & Richards, 1982). For example, children's early reasoning does depend more heavily on perception than on logic, and logical reasoning about concrete objects and events emerges before logical reasoning about abstract ideas (Flavell, Miller, & Miller, 2002; H. P. Ginsburg, Cannon, Eisenband, & Pappas, 2006). However, contemporary developmental researchers have found that many abilities appear considerably earlier or later than Piaget suggested and that often these abilities depend on particular experiences and cultural contexts.

Capabilities of different age-groups.   Using different research methods than those that were available to Piaget, present-day researchers have found that infants and preschoolers are apparently more competent than Piaget's descriptions of the sensorimotor and preoperational stages suggest. For instance, when Piaget studied the development of object permanence, he focused largely on whether infants looked and reached for an object that was covered up and so no longer in view. In contrast, contemporary researchers look at more subtle measures of object permanence, such as how long infants look at an object and how their heart rates change as they watch the object. These researchers have found, for example, that infants spend more time looking at an object that disappears in one spot and then immediately reappears in a very different spot—an event that apparently violates their basic understandings of how physical objects should behave. Such modern techniques reveal that infants show preliminary signs of object permanence as early as 2½ months old and continue to firm up this understanding over a period of many months (Baillargeon, 2004; L. B. Cohen & Cashon, 2006). Contemporary methods with preschoolers have taken a slightly different tact, with researchers making cognitive tasks and questions less artificial and laboratory-like, easing demands on children's memories, and so on. When tasks are modified in such ways, preschoolers are often quite capable of conservation and class inclusion (M. Donaldson, 1978; R. Gelman & Baillargeon, 1983; Rosser, 1994).

Piaget may have underestimated the capabilities of elementary school children as well. Many elementary students—and occasionally even 4-year-olds—show some ability to think abstractly and hypothetically about events that haven't been observed or have not yet occurred (Beck, Robinson, Carroll, & Apperly, 2006; S. Carey, 1985; Metz, 1995). Also, even first and second graders can understand simple ratios and proportions (e.g., fractions such as ½, ⅓, and ¼) if they can relate these concepts to everyday objects (Empson, 1999; Van Dooren, De Bock, Hessels, Janssens, & Verschaffel, 2005). And some older elementary school children can separate and control variables, especially when given hints about the importance of controlling all variables except the one they are testing (Danner & Day, 1977; Metz, 1995; Ruffman, Perner, Olson, & Doherty, 1993).

Yet Piaget probably *overestimated* what adolescents can do. Formal operational thinking processes emerge much more gradually than Piaget suggested, and even high school students don't use them as regularly as Piaget would have us believe (Flieller, 1999; Kuhn, Amsel, & O'Loughlin, 1988; Pascarella & Terenzini, 1991; Schauble, 1996). A related issue is whether formal operations is really the final stage of cognitive development, as Piaget suggested. Some theorists have proposed that many adults progress to a fifth, postformal stage in which they can envision multiple approaches to the same problem and recognize that each approach may be valid from a particular perspective (Commons, Richards, & Armon, 1984; Sinnott, 1998). Other theorists disagree, arguing that adult life simply poses different kinds of problems than the academically oriented ones that adolescents encounter at school (Schaie & Willis, 2000).

Effects of prior knowledge and experience.   Piaget acknowledged that as children gain new logical thinking skills, they may apply the skills in one content area but not necessarily in another (Chapman, 1988; Piaget, 1940). It is becoming increasingly apparent that for people of all ages, the ability to think logically in a particular situation depends on

Figure 6-4

What are some possible reasons why Herb is catching more fish than the others?
Based on Pulos & Linn, 1981.

background experiences relevant to the situation. Children as young as age 4 or 5 begin to show class inclusion and conservation after having practice with such tasks, especially if they can actively manipulate the task materials and discuss their reasoning with someone who already exhibits these logical abilities (D. Field, 1987; Halford & Andrews, 2006; Siegler & Svetina, 2006). Children ages 10 and 11 can solve logical problems involving hypothetical ideas if they are taught relevant problem-solving strategies, and they become increasingly able to separate and control variables when they have numerous experiences that require them to do so (Kuhn & Dean, 2005; S. Lee, 1985; Schauble, 1990). Junior high and high school students, and adults as well, often apply formal operational thought to topics about which they have a great deal of knowledge and yet think concretely about topics with which they are unfamiliar (Girotto & Light, 1993; M. C. Linn, Clement, Pulos, & Sullivan, 1989; Schliemann & Carraher, 1993).

As an illustration of how prior knowledge affects formal operational thinking, consider the fishing pond in Figure 6-4. In a study by Pulos and Linn (1981), 13-year-olds were shown a similar picture and told, "These four children go fishing every week, and one child, Herb, always catches the most fish. The other children wonder why." If you look at the picture, it is obvious that Herb is different from the three other children in several ways, including the bait he uses, the length of his fishing rod, and his location by the pond. Children who had fished frequently more effectively separated and controlled variables for this situation than they did for the pendulum problem described earlier, whereas the reverse was true for children without fishing experience. In the "Cognitive Development" videos for middle childhood and late adolescence in MyEducationLab, 10-year-old Kent and 14-year-old Alicia both consider the problem as they look at the picture in Figure 6-4. Notice how Kent, who appears to have some experience with fishing, considers several possible variables and remains open minded about the causal one. In contrast, Alicia, who is older but admittedly unfamiliar with fishing strategies, considers only two variables and immediately jumps to a conclusion about causation:

MyEducationLab

Observe how experience with fishing affects Kent's and Alicia's ability to identify variables in the "Cognitive Development" videos. (Find Video Examples in Chapter 6 of MyEducationLab.)

Kent: He has live . . . live worms, I think. Fish like live worms more, I guess 'cause they're live and they'd rather have that than the lures, plastic worms. . . . Because he might be more patient or that might be a good side of the place. Maybe since Bill has a boombox thing [referring to the radio], I don't think they would really like that because . . . and he doesn't really have anything that's extra. . . . But he's the standing one. I don't get that. But Bill, that could scare the fish away to Herb because he's closer. . . .

Alicia: Because of the spot he's standing in, probably. . . . I don't know anything about fishing. Oh, OK! He actually has live worms for bait. The other girl's using saltine crackers [she misreads *crickets*]. . . . She's using plastic worms, he's using lures, and she's using crackers and he's actually using live worms. So obviously the fish like the live worms the best.

One general factor that promotes more advanced reasoning is formal education. Going to school and the specific nature of one's schooling are associated with mastery of concrete operational and formal operational tasks (Artman & Cahan, 1993; Flieller, 1999; Rogoff, 2003). For instance, you may be happy to learn that taking college courses in a particular area (in child development, perhaps?) leads to improvements in formal reasoning skills related to that area (Lehman & Nisbett, 1990).

Effects of culture.   Research indicates that the course of cognitive development differs somewhat from one culture to another. For example, Mexican children whose families make pottery for a living seem to acquire conservation skills earlier than Piaget found to be true for Swiss children (Price-Williams, Gordon, & Ramirez, 1969). Apparently, creating pottery requires children to make frequent judgments about needed quantities of clay and water—judgments that must be fairly accurate regardless of the specific shape or form of the clay or water container. In other cultures, especially in some where children don't attend school, conservation may appear several years later than it does in Western cultures, and formal operational reasoning may never appear at all (M. Cole, 1990; Fahrmeier, 1978).

For some cultural groups, formal operational reasoning has little relevance to people's daily lives and activities (J. G. Miller, 1997). For instance, in some modern Asian societies, logical reasoning tends to be rooted in people's everyday, concrete realities. Adults in these cultures may find little purpose in applying rules of logic to artificial, contrary-to-fact situations and so don't always nurture such thinking in their schools or elsewhere (Norenzayan, Choi, & Peng, 2007).

Does cognitive development occur in stages?   In light of all the evidence, does it still make sense to talk about discrete stages of cognitive development? Even Piaget acknowledged that the characteristics of any particular stage don't necessarily hang together as a tight, inseparable set of abilities (Chapman, 1988; Piaget, 1940). Most contemporary developmental theorists now believe that cognitive development can more accurately be described in terms of gradual *trends*—for instance, a trend toward increasingly abstract thought—rather than discrete stages (e.g., Flavell, 1994; Kuhn & Franklin, 2006; Siegler & Alibali, 2005). They further suggest that Piaget's stages may better describe how children *can* think, rather than how they typically *do* think, and that the nature of cognitive development may be somewhat specific to different contexts, content areas, and cultures (Halford & Andrews, 2006; Klaczynski, 2001; Rogoff, 2003).

A perspective known as *information processing theory,* described in Chapter 7, characterizes general trends in cognitive processes we are likely to see as children develop. Yet some psychologists believe that, by entirely rejecting Piaget's notion of stages, we may be throwing the baby out with the bath water. These psychologists have combined some of Piaget's ideas with concepts from information processing theory to construct **neo-Piagetian theories** of how children's learning and reasoning capabilities change over time.

Key Ideas in Neo-Piagetian Theories

Neo-Piagetian theorists share Piaget's belief that children's developing skills and understandings change in distinct, qualitative ways over time. Unlike Piaget, however, they suggest that children's skills and understandings are fairly domain specific and tied to personal experiences in particular contexts. Following are several principles that are central to neo-Piagetian approaches:

- *Cognitive development is constrained by the maturation of information processing mechanisms in the brain.* Neo-Piagetian theorists have echoed Piaget's belief that cognitive development depends somewhat on brain maturation. One prominent neo-Piagetian, Robbie Case, has suggested that a mechanism in the brain known as **working memory** is especially important for cognitive development (e.g., Case, 1985, 1991). Working memory is that part of the human memory system in which people hold and actively think about new information. (For instance, you are using your working memory right now to make sense of what you're reading about cognitive development.) Children's working memory capacity increases with age, and so their ability to think about several things simultaneously increases as well. Neo-Piagetian theorists propose that children's limited working memory capacity at younger ages restricts their ability to acquire complex thinking and reasoning skills (Case & Okamoto, 1996; K. W. Fischer & Bidell, 1991; Lautrey, 1993). You'll learn more about the development of working memory in Chapter 7.

- *Children acquire new knowledge through both unintentional and intentional learning processes.* Many contemporary psychologists agree that children learn some things with little or no conscious awareness or effort. For example, consider this question about household pets: "On average, which are larger, cats or dogs?" Even if you've never intentionally thought about this issue, you can easily answer "Dogs" because of the many characteristics (including size) you've learned to associate with both species. Children unconsciously learn that many aspects of their world are characterized by consistent patterns and associations.

MyEducationLab

Learn more about the conservation skills in children of pottery-making communities by completing an Understanding Research exercise in Chapter 6's Activities and Applications section in MyEducationLab.

neo-Piagetian theory
Theoretical perspective that combines elements of Piaget's theory with more contemporary research findings and suggests that development in specific content domains is often stagelike in nature.

working memory
Component of memory that enables people to actively think about and process a small amount of information.

According to Robbie Case's neo-Piagetian perspective, children develop central conceptual structures in number, spatial relationships, and social thought (and perhaps in other areas as well). These structures affect children's reasoning and performance on a variety of relevant tasks.

Yet, especially as children's brains mature in the first year or two of life, they increasingly think actively and consciously about their experiences (see Chapter 5), and they begin to devote considerable mental attention to solving the little problems that come their way each day (Case & Okamoto, 1996; Pascual-Leone, 1970). As they do so, they draw on what they've learned (perhaps unconsciously) about common patterns in their environment, and they may simultaneously *strengthen* their knowledge of those patterns. Thus both the unintentional and intentional learning processes typically work hand in hand as children tackle day-to-day tasks and challenges and, in the process, enhance their knowledge about the world (Case, 1985; Case & Okamoto, 1996).

• *Children acquire cognitive structures that affect their thinking in particular content domains.* Neo-Piagetian theorists reject Piaget's proposal that children develop general-purpose systems of mental processes (operations) that they can apply to a broad range of tasks and content domains. Instead, they suggest, children acquire more specific systems of concepts and thinking skills that influence reasoning related to specific topics.

For example, Robbie Case has proposed that integrated networks of concepts and cognitive processes, called **central conceptual structures,** form the basis for much of children's thinking, reasoning, and learning in certain areas (Case, 1991; Case & Okamoto, 1996; Case, Okamoto, Henderson, & McKeough, 1993). A central conceptual structure related to *number* underlies children's ability to reason about and manipulate mathematical quantities. This structure reflects an integrated understanding of how such mathematical concepts as numbers, counting, addition, and subtraction are interrelated (see Chapter 10 for more details). A central conceptual structure related to *spatial relationships* underlies children's performance in such areas as drawing, construction and use of maps, replication of geometric patterns, and psychomotor activities (e.g., writing in cursive, hitting a ball with a racket). This structure enables children to align objects in space according to one or more reference points (e.g., the *x-* and *y*-axes used in graphing). And a central conceptual structure related to *social thought* underlies children's reasoning about interpersonal relationships, their knowledge of common patterns in human interaction, and their comprehension of short stories and other works of fiction. This structure includes children's general beliefs about human beings' thoughts, desires, and behaviors. Case has found evidence indicating that the three conceptual structures probably develop in a wide variety of cultural and educational contexts (Case & Okamoto, 1996).

• *Development in specific content domains can sometimes be characterized as a series of stages.* Although neo-Piagetian theorists reject Piaget's notion that a single series of stages characterizes cognitive development in general, they speculate that cognitive development in specific content domains often has a stagelike nature (e.g., Case, 1991; Case & Okamoto, 1996; K. W. Fischer & Immordino-Yang, 2006). Children's entry into a particular stage is marked by the acquisition of new abilities, which children practice and gradually master over time. Eventually, they integrate these abilities into more complex structures that mark

central conceptual structure
Integrated network of concepts and cognitive processes that forms the basis for much of one's thinking, reasoning, and learning in a specific content domain.

their transition into a subsequent stage. Thus, as is true in Piaget's theory, the stages are *hierarchical*, with each one being constructed out of abilities acquired in the preceding stage.

Even in a particular subject area, however, cognitive development is not necessarily a single series of stages through which children progress as if they were climbing rungs on a ladder. In some cases development might be better characterized as progression along "multiple strands" of skills that occasionally interconnect, consolidate, or separate in a weblike fashion (K. W. Fischer & Daley, 2007; K. W. Fischer & Immordino-Yang, 2006; K. W. Fischer, Knight, & Van Parys, 1993). From this perspective, children may acquire more advanced levels of competence in a particular area through any one of several pathways. For instance, as they become increasingly proficient in reading, children may gradually develop their word decoding skills, their comprehension skills, and so on—and they draw on all of these skills when reading a book. However, the rate at which each of the skills is mastered will vary from one child to the next.

Applying the Ideas of Piaget and His Followers

Piaget's theory and the subsequent research and theories it has inspired have numerous practical implications for educators and other professionals, as revealed in the following recommendations.

• ***Provide opportunities for children to experiment with physical objects and natural phenomena.*** Children of all ages can learn a great deal by exploring the physical world in a hands-on fashion (H. P. Ginsburg et al., 2006; Hutt, Tyler, Hutt, & Christopherson, 1989; B. Y. White & Frederiksen, 1998). In infancy this might involve having regular access to objects with visual and auditory appeal, such as mobiles, rattles, stacking cups, and pull toys. At the preschool level, it might involve playing with water, sand, wooden blocks, and age-appropriate manipulative toys. During the elementary school years, hands-on exploration might entail throwing and catching balls, working with clay and watercolor paints, and constructing Popsicle-stick structures. When children have significant physical disabilities that make such exploratory activities difficult, they should at least have regular opportunities to observe how various physical objects typically behave and interact (Bebko, Burke, Craven, & Sarlo, 1992).

Despite their increased capability for abstract thought, adolescents also benefit from opportunities to manipulate and experiment with concrete materials—perhaps equipment in a science lab, food and cooking utensils, or wood and woodworking tools. Such opportunities allow teens to discover laws of the natural world firsthand and to tie their newly emerging abstract ideas to the concrete physical world.

A potential downside, however, is that children and adolescents sometimes misinterpret what they observe, thereby either learning the wrong thing or confirming their existing misconceptions about the world (Hammer, 1997; Schauble, 1990; C. L. Smith, 2007). Consider the case of Barry, an 11th grader whose physics class was studying the idea that an object's mass and weight do *not*, in and of themselves, affect the speed at which the object falls. Students were asked to design and build an egg container that would keep an egg from breaking when dropped from a third-floor window. They were told that on the day of the egg drop, they would record the time it took for the eggs to reach the ground. Convinced that heavier objects fall faster and wanting his egg to fall as fast as possible, Barry added several nails to his egg's container. Yet when he dropped it, classmates timed its fall at 1.49 seconds, a time very similar to that for other students' lighter containers. He and his teacher had the following discussion about the result:

Teacher:	So what was your time?
Barry:	1.49. I think it should be faster.
Teacher:	Why?
Barry:	Because it weighed more than anybody else's and it dropped slower.
Teacher:	Oh really? And what do you attribute that to?
Barry:	That the people weren't timing real good. (C. Hynd, 1998, p. 34)

The Development and Practice feature "Facilitating Discovery Learning" presents and illustrates several recommendations for enhancing the effectiveness of discovery learning activities. Probably the most important suggestion in the feature is to *structure and guide* a

MyEducationLab

See examples of age-appropriate objects for exploration in the "Emotional Development: Infancy" video. (Find Video Examples in Chapter 6 of MyEducationLab.)

Development and Practice

Facilitating Discovery Learning

- **Make sure students have the necessary prior knowledge for discovering new ideas and principles.**

  A first-grade teacher asks students what they already know about air (e.g., people breathe it, wind is air that moves). After ascertaining that the students have some awareness that air has substance, she and her class conduct an experiment in which a glass containing a crumpled paper towel is turned upside-down and completely immersed in a bowl of water. The teacher eventually removes the glass from the water and asks students to explain why the paper towel didn't get wet. (You can see part of this lesson in the "Properties of Air" video in the Video Examples section in Chapter 6 of MyEducationLab.)

- **Show puzzling results to create disequilibrium.**

  A science teacher shows her class two glasses of water. In one glass an egg floats at the water's surface. In the other glass an egg rests on the bottom. The students give a simple and logical explanation for the difference: One egg has more air inside and so must be lighter. But then the teacher switches the eggs into opposite glasses. The egg that the students believe to be "heavier" now floats, and the "lighter" egg sinks to the bottom. The students are quite surprised and demand to know what is going on. (Ordinarily, water is less dense than an egg, so an egg placed in it will quickly sink. But in this demonstration, one glass contains salt water—a mixture denser than an egg and so capable of keeping it afloat.)

- **Structure and guide a discovery session so that students proceed logically toward discoveries you want them to make.**

  Many students in an eighth-grade science class believe that some very small things (e.g., a tiny piece of Styrofoam, a single lentil bean) are so light that they have no weight. Their teacher asks them to weigh a pile of 25 lentil beans on a balance scale, and the students discover that all of the beans together weigh approximately 1 gram. In the ensuing class discussion, the students agree that if 25 beans have weight, a single bean must also have weight. The teacher then asks them to use math to estimate how much a single bean weighs.

- **Help students relate their findings to concepts and principles in the academic discipline they are studying.**

  After students in a social studies class have collected data on average incomes and voting patterns in different counties within their state, their teacher asks, "How can we interpret these data using what we've learned about the relative wealth of members of the two major political parties?"

Sources: Bruner, 1966; de Jong & van Joolingen, 1998; N. Frederiksen, 1984; Hardy et al., 2006; D. T. Hickey, 1997; R. E. Mayer, 2004; Minstrell & Stimpson, 1996; E. L. Palmer, 1965 (egg example); C. L. Smith, 2007 (Styrofoam example); B. Y. White & Frederiksen, 1998, 2005.

---

discovery session to some extent. Occasionally children can learn from spontaneous explorations of their environment, for example, by experimenting with and discovering the properties of dry sand, wet sand, and water. By and large, however, they benefit more from carefully planned and structured activities that help them construct appropriate interpretations (Hardy, Jonen, Möller, & Stern, 2006; D. T. Hickey, 1997; B. Y. White & Frederiksen, 2005).

- ***Explore children's reasoning with problem-solving tasks and probing questions.*** By presenting a variety of Piagetian tasks involving either concrete or formal operational thinking skills and probing students' reasoning with a series of follow-up questions—that is, by using Piaget's clinical method—adults can gain valuable insights into how children and adolescents think about their world. The Observation Guidelines table "Assessing Piagetian Reasoning Processes in Children and Adolescents" lists some of the characteristics you might look for.

  In probing youngsters' reasoning, however, teachers and other practitioners need not stick to traditional Piagetian tasks. On the contrary, Piaget's clinical method is applicable to a wide variety of content domains and subject matter (e.g., diSessa, 2007). For example, in the "Research: Early Adolescence" video in MyEducationLab, you can hear an interviewer asking 12-year-old Claudia a series of questions to probe her reasoning during a categorization task (e.g., "How did you decide which shells to put where?" "What makes [those shells] different from the other ones?").

MyEducationLab

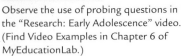

Observe the use of probing questions in the "Research: Early Adolescence" video. (Find Video Examples in Chapter 6 of MyEducationLab.)

- ***Keep Piaget's stages in mind when interpreting children's behavior and when planning activities, but don't take the stages too literally.*** Although Piaget's four stages are not always accurate descriptions of children's and adolescents' thinking capabilities, they do provide a rough idea of the reasoning processes you are apt to see at various age levels (Kuhn, 1997; Metz, 1997). For example, infant caregivers should remember that repetitive behaviors, even those that make a mess or cause inconvenience (dropping food, throwing toys), are one important means through which infants master basic motor skills and learn cause-and-effect relationships. Preschool teachers should not be surprised to hear young children arguing that the three pieces of a broken candy bar constitute more candy than a sim-

Observation Guidelines

Assessing Piagetian Reasoning Processes in Children and Adolescents

Characteristic	Look For	Example	Implication
Concrete Thought	· Heavy reliance on concrete manipulatives to understand concepts and principles · Difficulty understanding abstract ideas	Tobey solves arithmetic word problems more easily when he can draw pictures of them.	Use concrete objects and examples to illustrate abstract situations and problems.
Abstract Thought	· Ability to understand strictly verbal explanations of abstract concepts and principles · Ability to reason about hypothetical or contrary-to-fact situations	Elsa can imagine how two parallel lines might go on forever without ever coming together.	When working with adolescents, occasionally use verbal explanations (e.g., short lectures) to present information, but assess students' understanding frequently to make sure they understand.
Idealism	· Idealistic notions about how the world should be · Inability to take other people's needs and perspectives into account when offering ideas for change · Inability to adjust ideals in light of what can realistically be accomplished	Martin advocates a system of government in which all citizens contribute their earnings to a common "pool" and then withdraw money only as they need it.	Engage adolescents in discussions about challenging political and social issues.
Scientific Reasoning Skills	· Identifying multiple hypotheses for a particular phenomenon · Separation and control of variables	Serena proposes three possible explanations for a result she has obtained in her physics lab.	Have middle school and high school students design and conduct simple experiments. Include experiments about issues related to their backgrounds and interests.
Mathematical Reasoning Skills	· Understanding and using abstract mathematical symbols (e.g., π, the variable x in algebraic equations) · Understanding and using proportions in mathematical problem solving	Giorgio uses a 1:240 scale when drawing a floor plan of his school building.	Initially, introduce abstract mathematical concepts and tasks using simple examples (e.g., when introducing proportions, begin with fractions such as ⅓ and ¼). Progress to more complex examples only when youngsters appear ready to handle them.

ilar, unbroken bar (a belief that reflects lack of conservation). Elementary school teachers should recognize that their students may have trouble with proportions (e.g., fractions, decimals) and with such abstract concepts as *historical time* in history, and *negative number* and *pi* in mathematics (Barton & Levstik, 1996; Byrnes, 1996; Tourniaire & Pulos, 1985). And educators and other professionals who work with adolescents should expect to hear passionate arguments that reflect idealistic yet unrealistic notions about how society should operate.

Piaget's stages also provide guidance about strategies that are apt to be effective in teaching children at different age levels. For instance, given the abstract nature of historical time, elementary school teachers planning history lessons should probably talk only sparingly about specific dates before the recent past (Barton & Levstik, 1996). Also, especially in the elementary grades (and to a lesser degree in middle and high school), instructors should find ways to make abstract ideas more concrete for their students. As one simple example, a third-grade teacher, realizing that the abstract concept of *place value* might be a difficult one for 8- and 9-year-olds, showed her students how to depict two-digit numbers with blocks, using ten-block rows for the number in the tens column and single blocks for the number in the ones column. In Figure 6-5 one of her students, 8-year-old Noah, depicts the number 34 using this approach.

● ***Present situations and ideas that children cannot easily explain using their existing knowledge and beliefs.*** Events and information that conflict with youngsters' current understandings create disequilibrium that may motivate them to reevaluate and perhaps

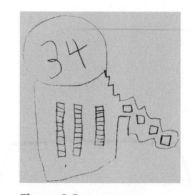

Figure 6-5

Noah's depiction of place value in the number 34.

modify what they "know" to be true (e.g., M. G. Hennessey, 2003; C. L. Smith, 2007). For instance, if they believe that "light objects float and heavy objects sink" or that "wood floats and metal sinks," an instructor might present a common counterexample: a metal battleship (floating, of course) that weighs many tons.

• *Use familiar content and tasks when asking children to reason in sophisticated ways.* Earlier we presented evidence to indicate that children and adolescents display more advanced reasoning skills when they work with topics they know well. With such evidence in mind, teachers and other practitioners might ask the young people they are working with to do the following:

• Conserve liquid within the context of a juice-sharing task.
• Separate and control variables within the context of a familiar activity (perhaps fishing, designing an effective paper airplane, or using various combinations of ingredients in baking cookies).
• Consider abstract ideas about subject matter that has already been studied in depth in a concrete fashion (e.g., introducing the concepts *inertia* and *momentum* to explain such everyday experiences as throwing a ball and driving quickly around a sharp curve).

• *Plan group activities in which young people share their beliefs and perspectives with one another.* As noted earlier, Piaget proposed that interaction with peers helps children realize that others often view the world very differently than they themselves do and that their own ideas are not always completely logical or accurate. Interactions with agemates that involve differences of opinion—situations that create **sociocognitive conflict**—can cause disequilibrium that may spur children to reevaluate their current perspectives.

Many contemporary psychologists share Piaget's belief in the value of sociocognitive conflict (e.g., De Lisi & Golbeck, 1999; P. K. Murphy & Alexander, 2008; C. L. Smith, 2007). They have offered several reasons why interactions with peers may help promote cognitive growth:

• Peers speak at a level that children can understand.
• Whereas children may accept an adult's ideas without argument, they are more willing to challenge and disagree with the ideas of their peers.
• When children hear competing views held by peers—individuals who presumably have knowledge and abilities similar to their own—they may be motivated to reconcile the contradictions. (Champagne & Bunce, 1991; Damon, 1984; Hatano & Inagaki, 1991)

When sharing their views with one another, however, children can also acquire misinformation (Good, McCaslin, & Reys, 1992). It is essential, then, that teachers monitor group discussions and correct any misconceptions or misinterpretations that youngsters may pass on to their peers.

Although children learn a great deal from their interactions with others, cognitive development is, in Piaget's theory, largely an individual enterprise: By assimilating and accommodating to new experiences, children develop increasingly advanced and integrated schemes over time. Thus Piaget's perspective depicts children as doing most of the mental "work" themselves. In contrast, Lev Vygotsky's theory places much of the responsibility for children's development on the adults in their society and culture. We turn to this theory now.

Vygotsky's Theory of Cognitive Development

Whereas Piaget had a background in biology, Russian psychologist Lev Vygotsky (1896–1934) had early training in law, history, philosophy, and literature. Vygotsky was deeply influenced by Karl Marx's proposal that changes in society over time have a significant impact on how people think and behave. And like Marx's colleague Friedrich Engels, Vygotsky saw much value in the use of *tools* for moving a society forward (M. Cole & Scribner, 1978). In Vygotsky's mind, however, some of these tools were *cognitive* entities—concepts, theories, problem-solving strategies, and so on—rather than actual physical objects.

Vygotsky believed that the adults in any society foster children's learning and development in an intentional and somewhat systematic manner. In particular, adults engage children in meaningful and challenging activities, show them how to use various physical and

sociocognitive conflict
Situation in which one encounters and has to wrestle with ideas and viewpoints different from one's own.

cognitive tools to facilitate their performance, and help them make sense of their experiences. Because Vygotsky emphasized the importance of adult instruction and guidance for promoting cognitive advancements—and more generally because he emphasized the influence of social and cultural factors in children's cognitive development—his perspective is known as a **sociocultural theory**.

With the assistance of his students, Vygotsky conducted numerous studies of children's thinking from the 1920s until his early death from tuberculosis in 1934. In his major writings, he typically described his findings only in general terms, saving the details for technical reports that he shared with the small number of research psychologists working in Russia at the time (Kozulin, 1986). But in his book *Thought and Language* he explained that his approach to studying children's cognitive development was radically different from that of Piaget and other psychologists of his era. Rather than determine the kinds of tasks children could successfully perform *on their own* (as Piaget did), he often examined the kinds of tasks children could complete *only with adult assistance*. For example, he described two hypothetical children who could, without help, do things that a typical 8-year-old might be able to do. He would give each of the children progressively more difficult tasks and offer some help, perhaps asking a leading question or suggesting a reasonable first step. With such assistance, both children could almost invariably tackle more difficult tasks than they could handle on their own. However, the *range* of tasks that the two children could complete with assistance might be quite different, with one child "stretching" his or her abilities to succeed at typical 12-year-old-level tasks and the other succeeding only with typical 9-year-old-level tasks (Vygotsky, 1934/1986, p. 187).

Western psychologists were largely unfamiliar with Vygotsky's work until the last few decades of the 20th century, when his major writings were translated from Russian into English (e.g., Vygotsky, 1934/1986, 1978, 1997). Although Vygotsky never had the chance to develop his theory fully, his views are clearly evident in many contemporary theorists' discussions of learning and development today. In fact, while Piaget's influence has been on the wane in recent years (Bjorklund, 1997), Vygotsky's influence has become increasingly prominent.

Key Ideas in Vygotsky's Theory

Vygotsky acknowledged that biological factors (e.g., brain maturation) play a role in development. Children bring certain characteristics and dispositions to the situations they encounter, and their responses to those situations vary accordingly. Furthermore, children's inherited traits affect their behavior, which in turn influences the particular experiences that children have (Vygotsky, 1997). However, Vygotsky's primary focus was on the role of nurture, and especially on the ways in which a child's social and cultural environments foster cognitive growth. Following are central ideas and concepts in Vygotsky's theory.

Providing labels for objects, such as the word *circle* for round things, is one way in which adults mediate children's interpretations of their environment.

- *Some cognitive processes are seen in a variety of species; others are unique to human beings.* Vygotsky distinguished between two kinds of mental processes, which he called *functions*. Many species exhibit *lower mental functions:* certain basic ways of learning and responding to the environment, such as discovering what foods to eat and how best to get from one location to another. But human beings are unique in their use of *higher mental functions:* deliberate, focused cognitive processes that enhance learning, memory, and logical reasoning. In Vygotsky's view, the potential for acquiring lower mental functions is biologically built in, but society and culture are critical for the development of higher mental functions.

- *Through both informal interactions and formal schooling, adults convey to children the ways in which their culture interprets the world.* In their interactions with children, adults share the *meanings* they attach to objects, events, and, more generally, human experience. As they do so, they actually *transform* the situations children encounter. This process of helping children make sense of their experiences in culturally appropriate ways is known as **mediation**. Meanings are conveyed through a variety of mechanisms—language, mathematical symbols, art, music, and so on. For example, in the "Museum Visit" case at the

sociocultural theory
Theoretical perspective that focuses on children's learning of tools, thinking processes, and communication systems through practice in meaningful tasks with other people.

mediation
In Vygotsky's theory, a process through which adults help children make culturally appropriate sense of their experiences, perhaps by attaching labels to objects or explaining the nature of certain phenomena.

cognitive tool
Concept, symbol, strategy, or other culturally constructed mechanism that helps people think more effectively.

self-talk
Talking to oneself as a way of guiding oneself through a task.

inner speech
"Talking" to oneself mentally rather than aloud as a way of guiding oneself through a task.

beginning of the chapter, Mother helps 4-year-old Billy make sense of several dinosaur artifacts. She points out how dinosaur ribs and human ribs serve the same function ("Protecting your heart . . . and your lungs"). She relates some of the artifacts to scientific concepts that Billy already knows (*Jurassic, Cretaceous*). And she substitutes everyday language ("dinosaur poop") for an unfamiliar scientific term *(coprolite)*.

Informal conversations are one common method by which adults pass along culturally appropriate ways of interpreting situations. But no less important in Vygotsky's eyes is formal education, where teachers systematically impart the ideas, concepts, and terminology used in various academic disciplines. Although Vygotsky, like Piaget, saw value in allowing children to make some discoveries themselves, he also saw value in having adults pass along the discoveries of previous generations (Vygotsky, 1934/1986).

Increasingly, contemporary developmental psychologists are recognizing the many ways in which culture shapes children's cognitive development. A society's culture ensures that each new generation benefits from the wisdom that preceding generations have accumulated. It guides children in certain directions by encouraging them to pay attention to particular stimuli (and not to others) and to engage in particular activities (and not in others). And it provides a lens through which children come to construct culturally appropriate interpretations of their experiences.

- ***Every culture passes along physical and cognitive tools that make daily living more effective and efficient.*** Not only do adults teach children specific ways of interpreting experience, but they also pass along specific tools that can help children tackle the various tasks and problems they are apt to face. Some tools, such as shovels, sewing machines, and computers, are physical objects. Others, such as writing systems, maps, and spreadsheets, are partly physical and partly symbolic. Still others, such as using rounding rules and mental arithmetic to estimate the cost of one's purchases at a store, may have little physical basis at all. In Vygotsky's view, acquiring tools that are partly or entirely symbolic or mental—**cognitive tools**—greatly enhances children's cognitive abilities.

Different cultures pass along different cognitive tools. Thus Vygotsky's theory leads us to expect greater diversity among children than Piaget's theory does. For instance, recall a point made earlier in the chapter: Children acquire conservation skills at a younger age if conservation of clay and water is important for their family's pottery business. Similarly, children are more likely to acquire map-reading skills if maps (perhaps of roads, subway systems, and shopping malls) are a prominent part of their community and family life (Liben & Myers, 2007). Children are more apt to have a keen sense of time if cultural activities are tightly regulated by clocks and calendars (K. Nelson, 1996a). And in the opening case study, Billy can relate museum exhibits to certain time periods—cognitive tools from the field of geology that can help him organize prehistoric artifacts—only because aspects of his culture (children's books, museums, etc.) have enabled him to acquire those organizational tools.

- ***Thought and language become increasingly interdependent in the first few years of life.*** One very important cognitive tool is language. For us as adults, thought and language are closely interconnected. We often think by using the specific words that our language provides. For example, when we think about household pets, our thoughts contain such words as *dog* and *cat*. In addition, we usually express our thoughts when we converse with others. In other words, we "speak our minds."

But Vygotsky proposed that thought and language are separate functions for infants and young toddlers. In these early years, thinking occurs independently of language, and when language appears, it is first used primarily as a means of communication rather than as a mechanism of thought. Sometime around age 2, thought and language become intertwined: Children begin to express their thoughts when they speak, and they begin to think in words (see Figure 6-6).

When thought and language first merge, children often talk to themselves, a phenomenon known as **self-talk** (you may also see the term *private speech*). Vygotsky suggested that self-talk serves an important function in cognitive development. By talking to themselves, children learn to guide and direct their own behaviors through difficult tasks and complex maneuvers in much the same way that adults have previously guided them. Self-talk eventually evolves into **inner speech,** in which children "talk" to themselves mentally rather than

In infancy, thought is nonverbal in nature, and language is used primarily as a means of communication.

THOUGHT LANGUAGE

At about 2 years of age, thought becomes verbal in nature, and language becomes a means of expressing thoughts.

With time, children begin to use *self-talk* to guide their own thoughts and behaviors.

Self-talk gradually evolves into *inner speech*, whereby children guide themselves silently (mentally) rather than aloud.

Figure 6-6

Vygotsky proposed that thought and language initially emerge as separate functions but eventually become intertwined.

aloud. They continue to direct themselves verbally through tasks and activities, but others can no longer see and hear them do it (Vygotsky, 1934/1986).

Recent research has supported Vygotsky's views regarding the progression and role of self-talk and inner speech. The frequency of children's audible self-talk decreases during the preschool and early elementary years, but this decrease is at first accompanied by an increase in whispered mumbling and silent lip movements, presumably reflecting a transition to inner speech (Bivens & Berk, 1990; R. E. Owens, 1996; Winsler & Naglieri, 2003). Furthermore, self-talk increases when children are performing more challenging tasks, at which they must exert considerable effort to be successful (Berk, 1994; Schimmoeller, 1998; Vygotsky, 1934/1986). As you probably know from your own experience, even adults occasionally talk to themselves when they face new challenges.

- **Complex mental processes begin as social activities and gradually evolve into internal mental activities that children can use independently.** Vygotsky proposed that complex thought processes, including the use of cognitive tools, have their roots in social interactions. As children discuss objects and events with adults and other knowledgeable individuals, they gradually incorporate into their own thinking the ways in which the people around them talk about and interpret the world, and they begin to use the words, concepts, symbols, and strategies that are typical for their culture.

The process through which social activities evolve into internal mental activities is called **internalization.** The progression from self-talk to inner speech just described illustrates this process: Over time, children gradually internalize adults' directions so that they are eventually giving *themselves* directions.

Not all mental processes emerge as children interact with adults, however. Some develop as children interact with peers. For example, children frequently argue with one another about a variety of matters—how best to carry out an activity, what games to play, who did what to whom, and so on. According to Vygotsky, childhood arguments help children discover that there are often several ways to view the same situation. Eventually, he suggested, children internalize the "arguing" process, developing the ability to look at a situation from several different angles *on their own.*

- **Children acquire their culture's tools in their own idiosyncratic manner.** Children do not necessarily internalize *exactly* what they see and hear in a social context. Rather, they often transform ideas, strategies, and other cognitive tools to make these tools uniquely their own. You may sometimes see the term **appropriation** used to refer to this process of internalizing but also adapting the ideas and strategies of one's culture for one's own use.

- **Children can perform more challenging tasks when assisted by more advanced and competent individuals.** Vygotsky distinguished between two kinds of abilities that children are apt to have at any particular point in their development. A child's *actual developmental level* is the upper limit of tasks that he or she can perform independently, without help from anyone else. A child's *level of potential development* is the upper limit of tasks that he or she can perform with the assistance of a more competent individual. To get a true sense of children's cognitive development, Vygotsky suggested, teachers should assess children's capabilities both when performing alone *and* when performing with assistance.

As noted earlier, Vygotsky found that children can typically do more difficult things in collaboration with adults than they can do on their own. For example, with the assistance of a parent or teacher, they may be able to read more complex prose than they are likely to read independently. They can play more difficult piano pieces when an adult helps them locate some of the notes on the keyboard or provides suggestions about what fingers to use. And notice how a student who cannot independently solve division problems with remainders begins to learn the correct procedure through an interaction with her teacher:

Teacher:	[writes 6)44 on the board] 44 divided by 6. What number times 6 is close to 44?
Child:	6.
Teacher:	What's 6 times 6? [writes 6]
Child:	36.
Teacher:	36. Can you get one that's any closer? [erasing the 6]
Child:	8.

internalization
In Vygotsky's theory, the gradual evolution of external, social activities into internal, mental activities.

appropriation
Gradual adoption of (and perhaps also adaptation of) other people's ways of thinking and behaving for one's own purposes.

Teacher: What's 6 times 8?
Child: 64 . . . 48.
Teacher: 48. Too big. Can you think of something . . .
Child: 6 times 7 is 42. (A. L. Pettito, 1985, p. 251)

MyEducationLab

Observe examples of children working within their zone of proximal development in the two "Zone of Proximal Development" videos. (Find Video Examples in Chapter 6 of MyEducationLab.)

● ***Challenging tasks promote maximum cognitive growth.*** The range of tasks that children cannot yet perform independently but *can* perform with the help and guidance of others is, in Vygotsky's terminology, the **zone of proximal development,** or **ZPD** (see Figure 6-7). A child's zone of proximal development includes learning and problem-solving abilities that are just beginning to emerge and develop.

Vygotsky proposed that children learn very little from performing tasks they can already do independently. Instead, they develop primarily by attempting tasks they can accomplish only in collaboration with a more competent individual—that is, when they attempt tasks within their zone of proximal development. In a nutshell, it is the challenges in life, not the easy successes, that promote cognitive development.

Whereas challenging tasks are beneficial, tasks that children cannot do even with considerable structure and assistance are of no benefit whatsoever (Vygotsky, 1987). (For example, it is probably pointless to ask a typical kindergartner to solve for x in an algebraic equation.) A child's ZPD therefore sets a limit on what he or she is cognitively capable of learning.

Naturally, any child's ZPD will change over time. As some tasks are mastered, other, more complex ones appear on the horizon to take their place. Furthermore, as we discovered earlier, children's ZPDs may vary considerably in "width." Whereas some children may, with assistance, be able to "reach" several years above their actual (independent) developmental level, others may be able to handle tasks that are only slightly more difficult than what they can currently do on their own.

● ***Play allows children to stretch themselves cognitively.*** Recall the scenario of Jeff and Scott playing "restaurant" presented earlier in the chapter. The two boys take on several adult roles (restaurant manager, server, cook) and practice a variety of adult-like behaviors: assembling the necessary materials for a restaurant, creating menus, keeping track of customers' orders, and tallying final bills. In real life such a scenario would, of course, be impossible. Very few 5-year-old children have the cooking, reading, writing, mathematical, or organizational skills necessary to run a restaurant. Yet the element of make-believe brings these tasks within the boys' reach (e.g., Lillard, 1993). In Vygotsky's words:

> In play a child always behaves beyond his average age, above his daily behavior; in play it is as though he were a head taller than himself. (Vygotsky, 1978, p. 102)

Many contemporary psychologists share Vygotsky's and Piaget's belief that play provides an arena in which youngsters can practice the skills they will need in later life. Not only does play promote social skills (e.g., cooperation and conflict resolution strategies), but it also helps children experiment with new combinations of objects, identify cause-and-effect rela-

zone of proximal development (ZPD) Range of tasks that one cannot yet perform independently but can perform with the help and guidance of others.

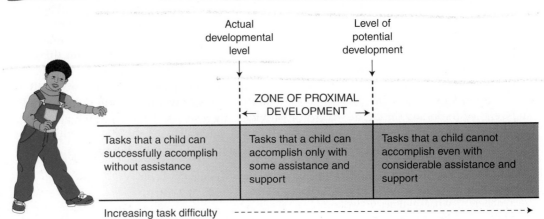

Figure 6-7

Tasks within a child's zone of proximal development are optimal for promoting cognitive advancements.

tionships, and learn more about other people's perspectives (Chafel, 1991; Lillard, 1998; Rubin, Fein, & Vandenberg, 1983; Zervigon-Hakes, 1984).

To some degree, play probably serves different purposes for different age-groups. For infants, one primary goal of play activities seems to be to discover what objects are like and can do, as well as what people can do to and *with* the objects. Through such discoveries, infants learn many basic properties of the physical world (Morris, 1977). Through more social games, such as peekaboo and pat-a-cake, infants practice imitation and acquire rudimentary skills in cooperation and turn-taking (Bruner & Sherwood, 1976; Flavell et al., 2002).

When play takes on an element of make-believe sometime around age 2, children begin to substitute one object for another and eventually perform behaviors involving imaginary objects—for instance, "eating" imaginary food with an imaginary fork (O'Reilly, 1995; Pederson, Rook-Green, & Elder, 1981). As Vygotsky suggested, such pretense probably helps children distinguish between objects and their symbolic representations and respond to internal representations (e.g., to the concept of *fork*) as much as to external objects (Bodrova & Leong, 1996; W. L. Haight, 1999; Karpov, 2003). When, in the preschool years, children expand their pretend play into elaborate scenarios—sometimes called **sociodramatic play**—they can also practice roles such as "parent," "teacher," or "server," and they learn how to behave in ways that conform to cultural standards and expectations. Furthermore, children engaging in sociodramatic play are apt to gain a greater appreciation of what other people might be thinking and feeling (Göncü, 1993; Karpov, 2003; Lillard, 1998).

As children reach school age, role-playing activities gradually diminish, and other forms of play take their place. For instance, elementary school children often spend time constructing things from cardboard boxes or Legos, playing cards and board games, and engaging in team sports. Many of these activities continue into adolescence. Although such forms of play do not mimic adult roles in as obvious a manner as "house" and "restaurant," they, too, serve a purpose. Especially in group games and sports, children must follow a specific set of rules. By adhering to restrictions on their behavior, children learn to plan ahead, think before they act, cooperate and compromise, solve problems, and engage in self-restraint—skills critical for successful participation in the adult world (Bornstein, Haynes, Pascual, Painter, & Galperin, 1999; Christie & Johnsen, 1983; Sutton-Smith, 1979).

Children's and adolescents' play activities are saturated with the practices and priorities of their particular culture. For example, consider Monopoly, a board game that is popular in some Western societies. By playing Monopoly, children learn about making money, buying and mortgaging real estate, paying rent and taxes, and making business decisions within a capitalistic society. Furthermore, they practice skills in mathematics (e.g., making change, calculating percentages) and business negotiation (e.g., selling and exchanging properties). Happily, children seem able to adapt the game to fit their own ability levels. For example, 14-year-olds use more complicated mathematical procedures when playing the game than 8-year-olds do (Guberman, Rahm, & Menk, 1998).

Play, then, is hardly a waste of time. Instead, it provides a valuable training ground for the adult world. Perhaps for this reason it is seen in children worldwide.

The game of Monopoly provides an opportunity to practice many skills important in Western societies, such as buying and mortgaging real estate, paying rent and taxes, and negotiating trades with other businesspeople.

Current Perspectives Related to Vygotsky's Theory

Vygotsky focused more on the processes through which children develop than on the abilities seen in children of particular ages. He did identify stages of development but portrayed them in only the most general terms. From our perspective, the stages are not terribly informative (we refer you to Vygotsky, 1997, pp. 214–216, if you would like to learn more about them). In addition, Vygotsky's descriptions of developmental processes were often imprecise and lacking in detail (Gauvain, 2001; Haenan, 1996; Wertsch, 1984). For these reasons, Vygotsky's theory has been more difficult for researchers to test and either verify or disprove than has Piaget's theory.

sociodramatic play
Play in which children take on specific roles and act out a scenario of imaginary events.

Despite such weaknesses, many contemporary theorists and practitioners have found Vygotsky's theory extremely insightful and helpful. Although they have taken Vygotsky's notions in many different directions, we can discuss much of their work within the context of several general ideas: social construction of meaning, scaffolding, participation in adult activities, and acquisition of teaching skills.

Social construction of meaning. Contemporary psychologists have elaborated on Vygotsky's proposal that adults help children attach meaning to the objects and events around them. They point out that an adult (e.g., a parent or teacher) often helps a child make better sense of the world through joint discussion of a phenomenon or event that the two of them have mutually experienced (Crowley & Jacobs, 2002; Eacott, 1999; Feuerstein, 1990). Such an interaction, sometimes called a **mediated learning experience,** encourages the child to think about the phenomenon or event in particular ways: to attach labels to it, recognize principles that underlie it, draw certain conclusions from it, and so on. In such a conversation, the adult must consider the prior knowledge and perspectives of the child and tailor the discussion accordingly, as Billy's mother does in the opening case study (Newson & Newson, 1975).

In addition to co-constructing meanings with adults, children often talk among themselves to derive meaning from their experiences. As we authors reflect back on our own childhood and adolescent years, we recall having numerous conversations with friends in our joint efforts to make sense of our world, perhaps within the context of identifying the optimal food and water conditions for raising tadpoles, deciding how best to carry out an assigned school project, or figuring out why certain teenage boys were so elusive.

School is one obvious place where children and adolescents can toss around ideas about a particular issue and perhaps reach consensus about how best to interpret and understand the topic in question. As an example of how members of a classroom might work together to construct meaning, let's look in on Ms. Lombard's fourth-grade class, which has been studying fractions. Ms. Lombard has never taught her students how to divide a number by a fraction. Nevertheless, she gives them the following problem, which can be solved by dividing 20 by ¾:

> Mom makes small apple tarts, using three-quarters of an apple for each small tart. She has 20 apples. How many small apple tarts can she make? (J. Hiebert et al., 1997, p. 118)

Ms. Lombard asks the students to work in small groups to figure out how they might solve the problem. One group of four girls—Jeanette, Liz, Kerri, and Nina—has been working on the problem for some time and so far has arrived at such answers as 15, 38, and 23. We join the girls midway through their discussion, when they've already agreed that they can use three-fourths of each apple to make a total of 20 tarts:

Jeanette:	In each apple there is a quarter left. In each apple there is a quarter left, so you've used, you've made twenty tarts already and you've got a quarter of twenty see—
Liz:	So you've got twenty quarters *left*.
Jeanette:	Yes, . . . and twenty quarters is equal to five apples, . . . so five apples divided by—
Liz:	Six, seven, eight.
Jeanette:	But three-quarters equals three.
Kerri:	But she can't make only three apple tarts!
Jeanette:	No, you've still got twenty.
Liz:	But you've got twenty quarters, if you've got twenty quarters you might be right.
Jeanette:	I'll show you.
Liz:	No, I've drawn them all here.
Kerri:	How many quarters have you got? Twenty?
Liz:	Yes, one quarter makes five apples and out of five apples she can make five tarts which will make that twenty-five tarts and then she will have, wait, one, two, three, four, five quarters, she'll have one, two, three, four, five quarters. . . .
Nina:	I've got a better . . .
Kerri:	Yes?
Liz:	Twenty-six quarters and a remainder of one quarter left. (J. Hiebert et al., 1997, p. 121)

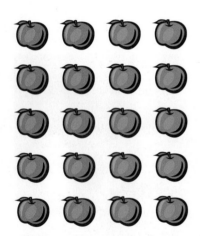

If you can make a single apple tart with ¾ of an apple, how many tarts can you make with 20 apples?

mediated learning experience
Discussion between an adult and a child in which the adult helps the child make sense of an event they have mutually experienced.

The discussion and occasional disagreements continue, and the girls eventually arrive at the correct answer: Mom can make 26 tarts and then will have half an apple left over.

Scaffolding.   Theorists have given considerable thought to the kinds of assistance that can help children successfully accomplish challenging tasks and activities. The term **scaffolding** is often used to describe the guidance or structure provided by more competent individuals to help children perform tasks in their ZPD. To understand this concept, think of the scaffolding used in the construction of a new building. The *scaffold* is an external structure that provides support for the workers (e.g., a place where they can stand) until the building itself is strong enough to support them. As the building gains substance and stability, the scaffold becomes less necessary and is gradually removed.

In much the same way, an adult guiding a child through a new task may initially provide a scaffold to support the child's early efforts. In the following example, notice how a mother helps her 4-year-old daughter Sadie assemble a toy from Duplo blocks (larger versions of Legos) by following a set of instructions:

Mother:	Now you need another one like this on the other side. Mmmmmm . . . there you go, just like that.
Sadie:	Then I need this one to go like this? Hold on, hold on. Let it go. There. Get that out. Oops!
Mother:	I'll hold it while you turn it. *(Watches Sadie work on toy.)* Now you make the end.
Sadie:	This one?
Mother:	No, look at the picture. Right here *(points to plan)*. That piece.
Sadie:	Like this?
Mother:	Yeah. (Gauvain, 2001, p. 32; reprinted with permission.)[4]

Scaffolding can take a variety of forms. Here are just a few of the many possibilities:

- Demonstrate the proper performance of the task in a way that children can easily imitate.
- Divide a complex task into several smaller, simpler tasks.
- Provide a structure or set of guidelines for how the task should be accomplished.
- Provide a calculator, computer software (word processing program, spreadsheet, etc.), or other technology that makes some aspects of the task easier.
- Ask questions that get children thinking in appropriate ways about the task.
- Keep children's attention focused on the relevant aspects of the task.
- Give frequent feedback about how children are progressing. (A. Collins, 2006; Gallimore & Tharp, 1990; Rogoff, 1990; D. Wood, Bruner, & Ross, 1976)

Depending on their particular knowledge and ability levels, different children at any single age or grade level may need different kinds of scaffolding to support their success (Lodewyk & Winne, 2005; Puntambekar & Hübscher, 2005; Rittle-Johnson & Koedinger, 2005). As children become more adept at performing a new task, their scaffolding is gradually phased out so that they eventually accomplish it entirely on their own.

In a Building Teaching Skills and Dispositions exercise in Chapter 6 of MyEducationLab, you can gain practice in applying the concepts *cognitive tool, zone of proximal development,* and *scaffolding* in both elementary and high school lessons.

Participation in adult activities.   Virtually all cultures allow—and in fact usually require—children to be involved in adult activities to some degree. Children's early experiences are often at the fringe of an activity. As children acquire greater competence, they gradually take a more central role in the activity until, eventually, they are full-fledged participants (S. Gaskins, 1999; Lave & Wenger, 1991; Rogoff et al., 2007).

In most cases children's early involvement in adult activities is scaffolded and supervised through what is sometimes known as **guided participation** (Rogoff, 2003). For example, when our own children were preschoolers, we authors often had them help us bake

[4]From *The Social Context of Cognitive Development* by M. Gauvain. Copyright © 2001 by Guilford Press. Reprinted with permission of The Guilford Press.

scaffolding
Support mechanism, provided by a more competent individual, that helps a child successfully perform a task within his or her zone of proximal development.

guided participation
Active engagement in adult activities, typically with considerable direction and structure from an adult or other more advanced individual; children are given increasing responsibility and independence as they gain experience and proficiency.

MyEducationLab

In the "Scaffolding" video, observe examples of how adults scaffold young children's efforts at assembling puzzles. (Find Video Examples in Chapter 6 of MyEducationLab.)

MyEducationLab

Go to the Building Teaching Skills and Dispositions section in Chapter 6 of MyEducationLab to apply the concepts *cognitive tool, zone of proximal development,* and *scaffolding* in two elementary and two high school lessons.

Virtually all cultural groups increasingly involve children in adult activities. For example, many communities in Rwanda have elevated traditional drum rhythms to a complex art form, and they encourage interested children to learn these rhythms and participate in public performances. Notice how the two boys at the end are closely observing the adults as the group performs for visitors.

cookies by asking them to measure, pour, and mix ingredients, but we stood close by and offered suggestions about how to get the measurements right, minimize spilling, and so on. Similarly, when taking our children to the office with us, we had them press the appropriate buttons in the elevator, check our mailboxes, open envelopes, or deliver documents to the department secretary, but we kept a close eye on what they were doing and provided guidance as necessary. In later years we gave them increasing responsibility and independence. By the time they were in high school, they were baking their own pastries, and they sometimes ran errands for us as we worked on our books and professional articles.

Parents are not the only ones who engage children in adult activities. Schools sometimes invite students to be members of faculty decision-making committees, and parent-teacher organizations ask students to help with school fund-raising efforts. Girl Scout troops introduce girls to salesmanship, accounting, and other adult business practices during annual cookie drives (Rogoff, 1995, 2003). Many local newspapers take on high school students as cub reporters, movie reviewers, and editorial writers, especially during the summer months.

In some instances adults work with children and adolescents in formal or informal **apprenticeships,** one-on-one relationships in which the adults teach the young people new skills, guide their initial efforts, and present increasingly difficult tasks as proficiency improves and the ZPD changes. Many cultures use apprenticeships as a way of gradually introducing children to particular skills and trades in the adult community—perhaps weaving, tailoring, or playing a musical instrument (D. J. Elliott, 1995; Lave & Wenger, 1991; Rogoff, 1990).

In apprenticeships, children learn not only the behaviors but also the language of a skill or trade (Lave & Wenger, 1991). For example, when master weavers teach apprentices their art, they might use such terms as *warp, weft, shuttle,* and *harness* to focus attention on a particular aspect of the process. Similarly, when teachers guide students through scientific experiments, they use words like *hypothesis, evidence,* and *theory* to help the students evaluate their procedures and results (Perkins, 1992). Furthermore, an apprenticeship can show children how adults typically think about a task or activity—a situation known as a **cognitive apprenticeship** (A. Collins, 2006; Rogoff, 1990; Roth & Bowen, 1995). For instance, an adult and child might work together to accomplish a challenging task or solve a difficult problem (perhaps sewing a patchwork quilt, solving a mathematical brainteaser, or collecting data samples in biology fieldwork). In the process of talking about various aspects of the task or problem, the adult and child together analyze the situation and develop the best approach to take, and the adult models effective ways of thinking about and mentally processing the situation.

From a Vygotskian perspective, gradual entry into adult activities increases the probability that children will engage in behaviors and thinking skills within their ZPD. It also helps children tie newly acquired skills and thinking abilities to the specific contexts in which they are apt to be useful later on (Carraher, Carraher, & Schliemann, 1985; A. Collins, 2006; Light & Butterworth, 1993).

In an apprenticeship, children learn both the skills and the language associated with a particular activity.

Acquisition of teaching skills.　As children learn new skills from more experienced members of their community, they may also learn how to teach those skills to someone else (Gauvain, 2001). With age and experience, they become increasingly adept at teaching others what they have learned. In a study in rural Mexico (Maynard, 2002), Mayan children were observed as they worked with younger siblings in such everyday activities as preparing food and washing clothes. The children's earliest form of "instruction" (perhaps around age 4 or 5) was simply to let a younger brother or sister join in and help. At age 6 or 7, children tended to be directive and controlling, giving commands and taking over if something wasn't done correctly. By the time they were 8, however, they were proficient teachers, using a combination of demonstrations, explanations, physical guidance, and feedback to scaffold their siblings' efforts.

For another example of how skillfully children can teach one another, let's return to the game of Monopoly. Four 8-year-old girls are playing the game while a researcher videotapes their interactions (Guberman et al., 1998). One girl, Carla, has limited math skills and little experience playing the game. On her first turn, she lands on Connecticut Avenue:

Nancy:　Do you want to buy it?
Carla:　Hmmmm . . . [There is a long pause and some unrelated discussion among the players.] How much is it again? Twelve hundred. . . .

apprenticeship
Mentorship in which a novice works intensively with an expert to learn how to accomplish complex tasks in a particular domain.

cognitive apprenticeship
Mentorship in which an expert and a novice work together on a challenging task and the expert suggests ways to think about the task.

Nancy: A hundred and twenty dollars.

Carla: A hundred and twenty [She starts to count her money] . . . a hundred [She is referring to a $10 bill]. . . .

Sarah: You give her one of these and one of these. [She holds up first a $100 bill and then a $20 bill of her own money.] (Guberman et al., 1998, p. 436; format adapted)

Notice how Nancy and Sarah scaffold Carla's initial purchase. Nancy asks her to consider buying the property and tells her the purchase price. When it is clear that Carla is having trouble counting out $120 (she thinks that a $10 bill is worth $100), Sarah gives her sufficient guidance that she can identify the needed bills by color alone. Later in the game, as Carla becomes more competent, the other girls reduce their support. For instance, at one point Carla lands on Virginia Avenue, with a purchase price of $160:

Carla hesitates making the payment, looking through her money. Eventually, she takes a $100 bill from her money and appears unsure how to continue.

Nancy: Just a fifty and a ten.

Carla gives a $50 bill and a $10 bill to the banker. (Guberman et al., 1998, p. 437; format adapted)

When children teach others, the "teachers" often benefit as much as the "students" (D. Fuchs, Fuchs, Mathes, & Simmons, 1997; Inglis & Biemiller, 1997; Webb & Palincsar, 1996). For instance, when youngsters study something with the expectation that they will be teaching it to someone else, they are more motivated to learn it, find it more interesting, and learn it more effectively (Benware & Deci, 1984; Semb, Ellis, & Araujo, 1993). Furthermore, when children who are relatively weak in a particular skill (compared to their age-mates) have the opportunity to guide younger children in that skill, they develop greater ability to guide themselves as well, presumably because they internalize the directions they have been giving someone else (Biemiller, Shany, Inglis, & Meichenbaum, 1998; D. R. Robinson, Schofield, & Steers-Wentzell, 2005).

Applying the Ideas of Vygotsky and His Followers

Vygotsky's work and the recent theoretical advances it has inspired have numerous implications for teaching and working with children and adolescents.

   • ***Help children acquire the basic cognitive tools of various activities and academic disciplines.*** Virtually every adult activity involves certain concepts and ways of thinking, and mastering them enables children to engage more successfully in the activity (Markus & Hamedani, 2007; K. Nelson, 1996a). For instance, children can become better musicians when they can read music and understand what *keys*, *chords*, and *thirds* are. They develop their carpentry skills when they know how to interpret blueprints and understand such terms as *plumb* and *right angle*. Furthermore, through such disciplines as science, mathematics, and social studies, our culture passes along key concepts (e.g., *molecule, negative number, democracy*), symbols (e.g., H_2O, π, x^3), and visual representations (e.g., graphs, maps) that can help growing children organize and interpret the physical and social worlds in which they live.

   • ***Use group learning activities to help children internalize cognitive strategies.*** Contemporary researchers have found that, as Vygotsky suggested, children often do internalize—and so eventually use independently—the complex thinking processes they first use in social interaction (e.g., Andriessen, 2006; P. K. Murphy, 2007). We find an example in **reciprocal teaching,** an approach to reading instruction that has had great success in enhancing children's reading comprehension skills (A. L. Brown & Palincsar, 1987; Palincsar & Brown, 1984, Palincsar & Herrenkohl, 1999). This approach is designed to foster four effective reading strategies:

   • *Summarizing:* Identifying the main ideas of a reading passage
   • *Questioning:* Asking oneself questions to check comprehension of ideas
   • *Clarifying:* Taking steps to better understand a confusing point
   • *Predicting:* Anticipating what points an author is apt to make in later sentences or paragraphs

reciprocal teaching
Approach to teaching reading comprehension in which students take turns asking teacher-like questions of their classmates.

A teacher and several students meet in a group to read a piece of text, occasionally stopping to discuss and process the text aloud. Initially, the teacher leads the discussion, asking questions about the text to promote summarizing, questioning, clarifying, and predicting. He or she gradually turns this "teaching" role over to different students, who for a short time take charge of the discussion and ask one another the same kinds of questions that their teacher has modeled. Eventually, the students can read and discuss a text almost independently of the teacher, working together to make sense of it and checking one another for comprehension and possible misunderstandings.

As an illustration, consider the following reciprocal teaching session for a group of six first graders reading a passage about snowshoe rabbits. In this particular case the teacher reads the text in small segments (at higher grade levels, the children themselves take turns reading). After each segment, the teacher pauses while the children discuss and make sense of the segment. As you read the dialogue, look for examples of summarizing, questioning, clarifying, and predicting (there is at least one instance of each).

> The children were reading about the snowshoe rabbit, and it was the 16th day of dialogue. The teacher had just read a segment of text describing the season in which baby rabbits are born and the ways in which the mother rabbit cares for her babies. A student named Kam is the dialogue leader.
>
> Kam: When was the babies born?
> Teacher: That's a good question to ask. Call on someone to answer that question.
> Kam: Robby? Milly?
> Milly: Summer.
> Teacher: What would happen if the babies were born in the winter? Let's think.
>
> Several children make a number of responses, including: "The baby would be very cold." "They would need food." "They don't have no fur when they are just born."
>
> Kam: I have another question. How does she get the babies safe?
> Kris: She hides them.
> Kam: That's right but something else. . . .
> Teacher: There is something very unusual about how she hides them that surprised me. I didn't know this.
> Travis: They are all in a different place.
> Teacher: Why do you think she does this?
> Milly: Probably because I heard another story, and when they're babies they usually eat each other or fight with each other.
> Teacher: That could be! And what about when that lynx comes?
>
> Several children comment that that would be the end of all the babies.
>
> Travis: If I was the mother, I would hide mine, I would keep them all together.
> Kris: If the babies are hidden and the mom wants to go and look at them, how can she remember where they are?
> Teacher: Good question. Because she does have to find them again. Why? What does she bring them?
> Milly: She needs to bring food. She probably leaves a twig or something.
> Teacher: Do you think she puts out a twig like we mark a trail?
>
> Several children disagree and suggest that she uses her sense of smell. One child, recalling that the snowshoe rabbit is not all white in the winter, suggests that the mother might be able to tell her babies apart by their coloring.
>
> Teacher: So we agree that the mother rabbit uses her senses to find her babies after she hides them. Kam, can you summarize for us now?
> Kam: The babies are born in the summer. . . .
> Teacher: The mother. . . .
> Kam: The mother hides the babies in different places.
> Teacher: And she visits them. . . .
> Kam: To bring them food.
> Travis: She keeps them safe.
> Teacher: Any predictions?
> Milly: What she teaches her babies . . . like how to hop.

Kris: They know how to hop already.
Teacher: Well, let's read and see.
(dialogue courtesy of A. S. Palincsar)

Notice how the teacher scaffolds the children's teaching strategies, in part by giving hints ("Kam, can you summarize for us now?") and in part by modeling effective questions ("What would happen if the babies were born in the winter?"). Notice, too, how the children support one another in their meaning-making efforts (Kris: "She hides them." Kam: "That's right but something else. . . .").

Reciprocal teaching has been used successfully with a wide variety of students, ranging from first graders to college students, to teach effective reading and listening comprehension skills. In many cases students become far more effective readers—sometimes even surpassing the achievement of their peers—and apply their new reading strategies when studying a wide variety of subject areas (Alfassi, 1998; A. L. Brown & Palincsar, 1987; Palincsar & Brown, 1984, 1989; Rosenshine & Meister, 1994).

• ***Present challenging tasks, and provide sufficient scaffolding to enable children to accomplish them successfully.*** To promote cognitive development, teachers and other adults must present some tasks and assignments that a child can perform successfully only with assistance—that is, tasks within the child's ZPD. Children at any single age level are likely to have different zones of proximal development and so may need different tasks and assignments. In other words, instruction is most effective when it is individually tailored to children's unique strengths and limitations (Horowitz, Darling-Hammond, & Bransford, 2005).

Children need some degree of support in tackling challenges, of course. Figure 6-8 shows a simple worksheet that scaffolds 4-year-old Hannah's early efforts to write the numerals 1 to 5. The Development and Practice feature "Scaffolding Children's Efforts at Challenging Tasks" presents several additional examples. One of the strategies listed in this feature—*teach children how to talk themselves through a complex new procedure*—makes use of Vygotsky's concept of *self-talk* to enable children to create their *own* scaffolding. Teaching children how to give themselves instructions and thereby guide themselves through a new task might proceed through five steps (Meichenbaum, 1977, 1985):

Figure 6-8

In this simple worksheet a preschool teacher scaffolds 4-year-old Hannah's efforts to write numerals.

1. *Cognitive modeling.* An adult model performs the desired task while verbalizing instructions that guide performance.
2. *Overt, external guidance.* The child performs the task while listening to the adult verbalize the instructions.
3. *Overt self-guidance.* The child repeats the instructions aloud *(self-talk)* while performing the task.
4. *Faded, overt self-guidance.* The child whispers the instructions while performing the task.
5. *Covert self-instruction.* The child silently thinks about the instructions *(inner speech)* while performing the task.

In this sequence of steps, depicted in Figure 6-9, the adult initially serves as a model both for the behavior itself and for the process of self-guidance. Responsibility for performing the task is soon turned over to the child. Eventually, responsibility for guiding the performance is turned over as well.

• ***Assess children's abilities under a variety of work conditions.*** To most effectively foster children's cognitive development, educators need to determine under what conditions the children are most likely to accomplish various tasks successfully. For instance, can children accomplish a task entirely on their own? If not, can they do it in collaboration with one or two peers? Can they do it if they have some adult guidance and support? By addressing such questions, teachers can get a better sense of the tasks that are in each child's ZPD (Calfee & Masuda, 1997; Haywood & Lidz, 2007; Horowitz et al., 2005). You'll see an example of this approach in the discussion of *dynamic assessment* in Chapter 8.

	TASK PERFORMANCE	**TASK INSTRUCTIONS**
Step 1	The adult performs the task, modeling it for the child.	The adult verbalizes instructions.
Step 2	The child performs the task.	The adult verbalizes instructions.
Step 3	The child performs the task.	The child repeats the instructions aloud.
Step 4	The child performs the task.	The child whispers the instructions.
Step 5	The child performs the task.	The child thinks silently about the instructions.

Figure 6-9

Five steps for teaching children to scaffold their own efforts through self-talk.

Development and Practice

Scaffolding Children's Efforts at Challenging Tasks

- **Ask questions that get children thinking in appropriate ways about a task.**

  As students in a high school science class begin to plan their experiments for an upcoming science fair, their teacher encourages them to separate and control variables by asking them to consider the following questions: *What do I think causes the phenomenon I am studying? What other possible variables might cause or influence it? How can I be sure that these variables are not influencing the results I obtain?*

- **Provide explicit guidance about how to accomplish a task, and give frequent feedback.**

  When an outdoor educator takes 12-year-olds on their first camping trip, he has the children work in pairs or threesomes to pitch their tents. Although he has previously shown the children how to pitch a tent, this is the first time they've actually done it themselves, and so he provides written instructions that they can follow. In addition, he circulates from campsite to campsite to check on each group's progress and provide assistance as necessary.

- **Provide a calculator, computer software (word processing program, spreadsheet, etc.), or other technology that makes some aspects of the task easier.**

  Children in a third-grade class have mastered basic addition, subtraction, and multiplication facts. They are now applying their knowledge of arithmetic to determine how much money they would need to purchase a number of recreational items from a mail-order catalog. Because the list of items is fairly lengthy and includes varying quantities of each item, their teacher gives them calculators to do the necessary multiplication and addition.

- **Teach children how to talk themselves through a complex new procedure.**

  A physical education teacher shows beginning tennis players how to use self-instructions to remember correct form when swinging the racket:

1. Say *ball* to remind yourself to look at the ball.
2. Say *bounce* to remind yourself to follow the ball with your eyes as it approaches you.
3. Say *hit* to remind yourself to focus on contacting the ball with the racket.
4. Say *ready* to get yourself into position for the next ball to come your way.

- **Divide a complex task into several smaller, simpler tasks, and perhaps ask children to tackle it in small groups.**

  A fourth-grade teacher has his students create a school newspaper that includes news articles, a schedule of upcoming events, a couple of political cartoons, and classified advertisements. Several students work together to create each feature, with different students assuming different roles (e.g., fact finder, writer, editor) and occasionally switching roles.

- **Gradually withdraw guidance as children become more proficient.**

  A preschool teacher has the 2- and 3-year-olds in her class take turns distributing the crackers, fruit, and napkins at snack time, and she asks all of them to bring their dishes and trash to the kitchen after they have finished eating. Initially, she must show the children how to carry the food so that it doesn't spill. She must also remind them to make sure that every child gets a serving and to clean up when they are done. As the year progresses, such explicit guidance and reminders are no longer necessary, although she must occasionally say, "I think two of you have forgotten to bring your cups to the kitchen. I'm missing the one with Big Bird on it and the one with Cookie Monster."

Sources: Gallimore & Tharp, 1990; Good et al., 1992; Lajoie & Derry, 1993; Lou et al., 1996; Meichenbaum, 1985; Rogoff, 1990; Rosenshine & Meister, 1992; R. J. Stevens & Slavin, 1995; D. Wood et al., 1976; S. G. Ziegler, 1987 (tennis example).

● ***Provide opportunities to engage in authentic activities.*** As we've already seen, children's participation in adult activities plays a critical role in their cognitive development. However, children spend much of their day at school, which is far removed from the working world of adults. A reasonable alternative is **authentic activities**—classroom tasks and projects that closely resemble typical adult activities. Following are examples:

- Writing an editorial
- Participating in a debate
- Designing an electrical circuit
- Conducting an experiment
- Creating and distributing a class newsletter
- Performing in a concert
- Planning a personal budget
- Conversing in a foreign language
- Constructing a museum display
- Developing a home page for the Internet

authentic activity
Instructional activity similar to one that a child might eventually encounter in the outside world.

By placing classroom activities in real-world contexts, teachers can often enhance students' mastery of classroom subject matter (Bereiter & Scardamalia, 2006; A. Collins, Brown, & Newman, 1989; De Corte, Greer, & Verschaffel, 1996). For example, students may show greater improvement in writing skills when they practice writing stories, essays, and letters to real people, rather than completing short, artificial writing exercises (E. H. Hiebert & Fisher, 1992). Likewise, they may gain a more complete understanding of how to use and interpret maps when they construct their own maps than when they engage in workbook exercises involving map interpretation (Gregg & Leinhardt, 1994a).

• ***Give children the chance to play.*** Many developmental theorists advocate including play into children's daily schedules, especially in the preschool and early elementary years (Chafel, 1991; Hirsh-Pasek, Hyson, & Rescorla, 1990; Van Hoorn, Nourot, Scales, & Alward, 1999). Following are several suggestions for promoting preschoolers' play (Frost, Shin, & Jacobs, 1998):

• Partition the classroom into small areas (e.g., a corner for blocks, a "housekeeping" area, an art table) that give children numerous options.
• Provide realistic toys (e.g., dolls, dress-up clothes, plastic dishes) that suggest certain activities and functions, as well as more versatile objects (e.g., Legos, wooden blocks, cardboard boxes) that allow children to engage in fantasy and imagination.
• Provide enough toys and equipment to minimize potential conflicts, but keep them limited enough in number that children must share and cooperate.

By observing children during play, teachers also can gain insights into the abilities and skills that individual children have acquired. Examples of things to look for are presented in the Observation Guidelines table "Observing the Cognitive Aspects of Young Children's Play."

MyEducationLab

Observe the variety of play areas for infants and young children in the "Environments" videos. (Find Video Examples in Chapter 6 of MyEducationLab.)

Observation Guidelines

Observing the Cognitive Aspects of Young Children's Play

Characteristic	Look For	Example	Implication
Exploratory Play with Objects	· Interest in exploring objects in the environment · Ability to manipulate objects · Use of multiple senses in exploratory play	When Tyler sees a new toy guitar among the toys in the playroom, he picks it up, inspects it on all sides, and begins to turn the crank (although not enough to elicit any musical notes). After Tyler leaves it to play with something else, Sarah picks it up. Rather than visually inspecting it, however, she sniffs it, then puts the crank in her mouth and begins to suck and chew on it.	Provide a wide variety of toys and other objects for infants and toddlers to explore and experiment with, making sure that all are safe, clean, and nontoxic. Recognize that children may use these things in creative ways (and not necessarily in the ways their manufacturers intended) and will move frequently from one object to another.
Group Play	· Extent to which children play with one another · Extent to which children in a group cooperate in their play activities	LaMarr and Matthew are playing with trucks in the sandbox, but each boy seems to be in his own little world.	Give children opportunities to play together, and provide toys that require a cooperative effort.
Use of Symbolic Thought and Imagination	· Extent to which children use one object to stand for another · Extent to which children incorporate imaginary objects into their play	Julia tells her friend she is going to the grocery store, then opens an imaginary car door, sits on a chair inside her "car," steers an imaginary steering wheel, and says, "Beep, beep" as she blows an imaginary horn.	When equipping a play area, include objects (e.g., wooden blocks, cardboard boxes) that children can use for a variety of purposes.
Role Taking	· Extent to which children display behaviors that reflect a particular role · Extent to which children use language (e.g., tone of voice, specific words and phrases) associated with a particular person or role · Extent to which children coordinate and act out multiple roles within the context of a complex play scenario	Mark and Alisa are playing doctor. Alisa brings her teddy bear to Mark's "office" and politely says, "Good morning, Doctor. My baby has a sore throat." Mark holds a Popsicle stick against the bear's mouth and instructs the "baby" to say "Aaahhh."	Provide toys and equipment associated with particular roles (e.g., toy medical kit, cooking utensils, play money).

Comparing Piagetian and Vygotskian Perspectives

Together, Piaget's and Vygotsky's theories and the research they've inspired give us a more complete picture of cognitive development than either theory provides alone. The Developmental Trends table "Thinking and Reasoning Skills at Different Age Levels" draws on elements of both perspectives to describe characteristics of children and adolescents in different age ranges.

Piaget's and Vygotsky's theories share common themes that continue to appear in more contemporary views of cognitive development. At the same time, they have important differences that have led modern researchers to probe more deeply into the mechanisms through which children's thinking processes develop.

Common Themes

If we look beyond the very different vocabulary Piaget and Vygotsky often used to describe the phenomena they observed, we notice four themes that their theories share: constructive processes, readiness, challenge, and the importance of social interaction.

Constructive processes in learning. Neither Piaget's nor Vygotsky's theory depicts cognitive development as a process of simply "absorbing" one's experiences. Rather, both theories portray the acquisition of new knowledge and skills as a very constructive process. In Piaget's view, children increasingly organize their thoughts as schemes and, later, as operations that they can apply to a wide variety of circumstances. In Vygotsky's view, children gradually internalize—in their own idiosyncratic ways—the interpretations and cognitive tools they first encounter and use in social contexts.

This perspective of children actively creating rather than passively absorbing knowledge is generally known as **constructivism.** Piaget's theory focuses largely on how children construct knowledge *on their own;* thus it is sometimes labeled **individual constructivism.** In contrast, the ideas of Vygotsky and his followers focus more on how children construct meanings in collaboration with adults and peers; thus they are sometimes collectively called **social constructivism.** Without doubt, children acquire increasingly sophisticated understandings and thinking processes through *both* their own individual efforts and joint meaning-making efforts with others (Salomon, 1993).

Readiness. Both Piaget and Vygotsky suggested that at any point in time a child is cognitively ready for some experiences but not for others. Both theorists acknowledged that brain maturation places some limits on what children can do at various points in development. But in addition, Piaget proposed, children can accommodate to new objects and events only when they can also assimilate the objects and events into existing schemes, and they can think logically about new problems only if they have constructed the relevant logical operations. Vygotsky, meanwhile, portrayed children's readiness for tasks as comprising an ever-changing zone of proximal development. As children master some skills and abilities, other, slightly more advanced ones emerge in immature forms that are ready for adult nurturance and support.

Teachers and other professionals who work with children must be very careful when considering the concept of *readiness,* however. Historically, some practitioners have assumed that biological maturation and background experiences (or the lack thereof) impose insurmountable limitations that prevent some children from being "ready" for a formal instructional setting such as kindergarten. In fact, all children are ready to learn *something.* The issue is not whether a child is ready, but what a child is ready for and how best to facilitate his or her cognitive development in both academic and nonacademic settings (Horowitz et al., 2005; Stipek, 2002; R. Watson, 1996).

Challenge. We see the importance of challenge most clearly in Vygotsky's concept of the zone of proximal development: Children benefit most from tasks that they can perform only with the assistance of more competent individuals. Yet challenge, albeit of a somewhat different sort, also lies at the heart of Piaget's theory: Children develop more sophisticated knowledge and thought processes only when they encounter phenomena they cannot adequately understand using their existing schemes—in other words, phenomena that create disequilibrium.

The idea that children construct rather than absorb knowledge has stood the test of time. This drawing reflects 6-year-old Laura's self-constructed conception of underwater ocean life. The air bubbles rising up from the fish and sea horse reveal her belief that sea creatures exhale in a manner similar to people.

constructivism
Theoretical perspective proposing that learners construct a body of knowledge and beliefs, rather than absorbing information exactly as it is received.

individual constructivism
Theoretical perspective that focuses on how people independently construct meaning from their experiences.

social constructivism
Theoretical perspective that focuses on people's collective efforts to impose meaning on the world.

Developmental Trends

Thinking and Reasoning Skills at Different Age Levels

Age	What You Might Observe	Diversity	Implications
Infancy (Birth–2 Years) 	· Physical exploration of the environment becoming increasingly complex, flexible, and intentional over time · Growing awareness of simple cause-and-effect relationships · Emergence of ability to represent the world mentally (e.g., as revealed in daily conversations and make-believe play)	· Temperamental differences (e.g., the extent to which infants are adventuresome vs. more timid and anxious) influence exploratory behavior. · Infants and toddlers who are emotionally attached to their caregivers are more willing to venture out and explore their environment (see Chapter 11). · In some cultures adults encourage infants to focus more on people than on the physical environment. When people rather than objects are the priority, children may be less inclined to touch and explore their physical surroundings.	· Set up a safe, age-appropriate environment for exploration. · Provide objects that stimulate different senses—for instance, things that babies can look at, listen to, feel, and smell. · Suggest age-appropriate toys and activities that parents can provide at home.
Early Childhood (2–6 Years) 	· Rapidly developing language skills · Reasoning that is, by adult standards, often illogical · Limited perspective-taking ability · Frequent self-talk · Sociodramatic play · Limited understanding of how adults typically interpret events	· Shyness may limit children's willingness to talk with adults and peers and to engage in cooperative sociodramatic play. · Adult-like logic is more common when children have accurate information about the world (e.g., about cause-and-effect relationships). · Children learn to interpret events in culture-specific ways.	· Provide numerous opportunities for children to interact with one another during play and other cooperative activities. · Introduce children to a variety of real-world situations and environments through picture books and field trips. · Talk with children about their experiences and possible interpretations.
Middle Childhood (6–10 Years) 	· Conservation, class inclusion, and other forms of adult-like logic · Limited ability to reason about abstract or hypothetical ideas · Emergence of group games and team sports that involve coordinating multiple perspectives · Ability to participate to some degree in many adult activities	· Development of logical thinking skills is affected by the importance of those skills in a child's culture. · Formal operational reasoning may occasionally appear for simple tasks and in familiar contexts, especially in 9- and 10-year-olds. · Regular involvement in adult activities is more common in some cultures than in others.	· Use concrete manipulatives and experiences to illustrate concepts and ideas. · Supplement verbal explanations with concrete examples, pictures, and hands-on activities. · Allow time for organized play activities. · Introduce children to various adult professions, and provide opportunities to practice authentic adult tasks.
Early Adolescence (10–14 Years)	· Increasing ability to reason about abstract ideas · Emerging scientific reasoning abilities (e.g., formulating and testing hypotheses, separating and controlling variables) · Increasing ability to reason about mathematical proportions · Some idealism about political and social issues, but often without taking real-world constraints into consideration · Increasing ability to engage in adult tasks	· Adolescents can think more abstractly when they have considerable knowledge about a topic. · Adolescents are more likely to separate and control variables for situations with which they are familiar. · Development of formal operational reasoning skills is affected by the importance of those skills in one's culture. · Adolescents' idealistic notions may reflect their religious, cultural, or socioeconomic backgrounds.	· Present abstract concepts and principles central to various academic disciplines, but tie them to concrete examples. · Have students engage in scientific investigations, focusing on familiar objects and phenomena. · Assign math problems that require use of simple fractions, ratios, or decimals. · While demonstrating how to do a new task, also talk about how to effectively *think* about the task.
Late Adolescence (14–18 Years) 	· Abstract thought and scientific reasoning skills becoming more prevalent, especially for topics about which adolescents have considerable knowledge · Idealistic notions tempered by more realistic considerations · Ability to perform many tasks in an adult-like manner	· Abstract thinking tends to be more common in some content areas (e.g., mathematics, science) than in others (e.g., history, geography). · Formal operational reasoning skills are less likely to appear in cultures that don't require those skills. · Teenagers' proficiency in particular adult tasks varies considerably from individual to individual and from task to task.	· Study particular academic disciplines in depth; introduce complex and abstract explanations and theories. · Encourage discussions about social, political, and ethical issues; elicit multiple perspectives regarding these issues. · Involve adolescents in activities that are similar or identical to the things they will eventually do as adults. · Explain how experts in a field think about the tasks they perform.

Importance of social interaction. In Piaget's eyes, the people in a child's life can present information and arguments that create disequilibrium and, as a result, can foster greater perspective taking or more logical thinking processes. For instance, when young children disagree with one another, they begin to realize that different people may have different yet equally valid viewpoints, and they gradually shed the egocentrism that characterizes preoperational thought.

In Vygotsky's view, social interactions provide the very foundation for thought processes: Children internalize the processes they use when they converse with others until, ultimately, they can use them independently. Furthermore, tasks within the ZPD can, by definition, be accomplished only when others assist in children's efforts.

Theoretical Differences

Following are four questions that capture key differences between Piaget's and Vygotsky's theories of cognitive development.

To what extent is language essential for cognitive development? According to Piaget, language provides verbal labels for many of the concepts and other schemes that children have already developed. It is also the primary means through which children interact with others and begin to incorporate multiple perspectives into their thinking. Yet in Piaget's view, much of cognitive development occurs independently of language.

For Vygotsky, however, language is absolutely critical for cognitive development. Children's thought processes are internalized versions of social interactions that are largely verbal in nature. Through two language-based phenomena—self-talk and inner speech—children begin to guide their own behaviors in ways that others have previously guided them. Furthermore, in their conversations with adults, children learn the meanings that their culture imposes on particular events and gradually begin to interpret the world in culture-specific ways.

The truth of the matter probably lies somewhere between Piaget's and Vygotsky's perspectives. Piaget clearly underestimated the importance of language: Children acquire more complex understandings of phenomena and events not only through their own interactions with the world but also (as Vygotsky suggested) by learning how others interpret those phenomena and events. On the other hand, Vygotsky may have overstated the case for language. Some concepts clearly emerge *before* children have verbal labels to attach to them (K. Fiedler, 2008; Halford & Andrews, 2006; L. M. Oakes & Rakison, 2003). Furthermore, verbal exchanges may be less important for cognitive development in some cultures than in others. For instance, adults in some rural communities in Guatemala and India place heavy emphasis on gestures and demonstrations, rather than on verbal instructions, to teach and guide children (Rogoff, Mistry, Göncü, & Mosier, 1993).

What kinds of experiences promote development? Piaget maintained that children's independent, self-motivated explorations of the physical world form the basis for many developing schemes, and children often construct these schemes with little guidance from others. In contrast, Vygotsky argued for activities that are facilitated and interpreted by more competent individuals. The distinction, then, is one of self-exploration versus guided exploration and instruction. Children almost certainly need both kinds of experiences: opportunities to manipulate and experiment with physical phenomena on their own and opportunities to draw on the wisdom of prior generations (Brainerd, 2003; Karpov & Haywood, 1998).

What kinds of social interactions are most valuable? Both theorists saw value in interacting with people of all ages. However, Piaget emphasized the benefits of interactions with peers (who could create conflict and disequilibrium), whereas Vygotsky placed greater importance on interactions with adults and other more advanced individuals (who could support children in challenging tasks and help them make appropriate interpretations).

Some contemporary theorists have proposed that interactions with peers and interactions with adults play different roles in children's cognitive development (Damon, 1984; Rogoff, 1991; Webb & Palincsar, 1996). When children's development requires that they abandon old perspectives in favor of new, more complex ones, the sociocognitive conflict that often occurs among age-mates (and the multiple perspectives that emerge from it) may be optimal for bringing about such change. But when children's development instead requires that they learn new skills, the thoughtful, patient guidance of a competent adult may be more beneficial (Gauvain, 2001; Radziszewska & Rogoff, 1991).

How influential is culture? Although Piaget eventually acknowledged that different cultural groups might foster different ways of thinking, he gave virtually no attention to culture as a prominent factor affecting the course of cognitive development (Chapman, 1988). In Vygotsky's view, however, culture is of paramount importance in determining the specific thinking skills that children acquire. Vygotsky was probably more on target here. Earlier in the chapter we presented evidence to indicate that children's reasoning skills do not necessarily appear at the same ages in different countries. In fact, some reasoning skills (especially those involving formal operational thought) may never appear at all unless a child's culture specifically cultivates them.

Teachers and other practitioners must keep in mind, however, that there isn't necessarily a single "best" or "right" way for a culture to promote cognitive development (Rogoff, 2003). Despite their diverse instructional practices, virtually all of the world's cultures have developed effective strategies for helping growing children acquire the knowledge and skills they will need to be successful participants in adult society.

In the Basic Developmental Issues table "Contrasting Piaget and Vygotsky," we compare the two perspectives in terms of our three general themes: nature and nurture, universality and diversity, and qualitative and quantitative change. Obviously, neither theorist was completely "right" or completely "wrong." Both offered groundbreaking insights into the nature of children's learning and thinking, and as you will discover in the next chapter, both have influenced more recent theories of cognitive development. In fact, Piaget's and Vygotsky's theories complement each other to some extent, with the former helping us understand how children often reason on their own and the latter providing ideas about how adults can help them reason more effectively.

Basic Developmental Issues

Contrasting Piaget and Vygotsky

Issue	Piaget	Vygotsky
Nature and Nurture	Piaget believed that biological maturation probably constrains the rate at which children acquire new thinking capabilities. However, his focus was on how interactions with both the physical environment (e.g., manipulation of concrete objects) and the social environment (e.g., discussions with peers) promote cognitive development.	Vygotsky acknowledged that children's inherited traits and talents affect the ways in which they deal with the environment and hence affect the experiences they have. But his theory primarily addresses the environmental conditions (e.g., engagement in challenging activities, guidance from more competent individuals, exposure to cultural interpretations) that influence cognitive growth.
Universality and Diversity	In Piaget's view, children make similar advancements in their logical reasoning capabilities despite the particular environment in which they grow up. Children differ in the ages at which they acquire new abilities, however.	From Vygotsky's perspective, the specific cognitive abilities that children acquire depend on the cultural contexts in which the children are raised and the specific activities in which they are asked and encouraged to engage.
Qualitative and Quantitative Change	Piaget proposed that children's logical reasoning skills progress through four qualitatively distinct stages. Any particular reasoning capability continues to improve in a gradual (quantitative) fashion throughout the stage in which it first appears.	Vygotsky acknowledged that children undergo qualitative changes in their thinking but did not elaborate on the nature of these changes. Much of his theory points to gradual and presumably quantitative improvements in skills. For instance, a child may initially find a particular task impossible, later be able to execute it with adult assistance, and eventually perform it independently.

Summary

Piaget's Theory

Piaget portrayed children as active and motivated learners who, through numerous interactions with their physical and social environments, construct an increasingly complex understanding of the world around them. He proposed that children's many cognitive acquisitions can be categorized as falling into four stages: (a) the sensorimotor stage, when cognitive functioning is based primarily on behaviors and perceptions; (b) the preoperational stage, when symbolic thought and language become prevalent, but reasoning is "illogical" by adult standards; (c) the concrete operations stage, when logical reasoning capabilities emerge but are limited to concrete objects and events; and (d) the formal operations stage, when thinking about abstract, hypothetical, and contrary-to-fact ideas becomes possible.

Developmental researchers have found that Piaget probably underestimated the capabilities of infants, preschoolers, and elementary school children and overestimated the capabilities of adolescents. Furthermore, children's reasoning on particular tasks depends somewhat on their prior knowledge, experience, and formal schooling relative to those tasks. Contemporary developmentalists doubt that cognitive development can really be characterized as a series of general stages that pervade children's thinking in diverse content domains. A few theorists, known as neo-Piagetians, propose that children acquire more specific systems of concepts and thinking skills relevant to particular domains and that these systems may sometimes change in a stagelike manner. Many others instead suggest that children exhibit more gradual trends in a variety of abilities. However, virtually all contemporary theorists acknowledge the value of Piaget's research methods, his portrayal of cognitive development as a constructive process, and the appearance of qualitative changes in cognitive development.

Vygotsky's Theory of Cognitive Development

Vygotsky suggested that human beings are different from other species in their acquisition of complex mental processes, which are largely the legacy of a social group's cultural heritage. In his view, adults promote children's cognitive development by sharing the meanings that their culture assigns to objects and events, introducing children to the many physical and cognitive tools that previous generations have created, and assisting children with challenging tasks. Social activities are often precursors to, and form the basis for, complex mental processes: Children initially use new skills in the course of interacting with adults or peers and slowly internalize these skills for their own, independent use. Often children first experiment with adult tasks and ways of thinking within the context of their early play activities.

Contemporary theorists have extended Vygotsky's theory in several directions. For instance, some suggest that adults can help children benefit from their experiences through joint construction of meanings, guided participation, and cognitive apprenticeships. Others recommend that adults engage children and adolescents in authentic, adult-like tasks, initially providing enough scaffolding that youngsters can accomplish those tasks successfully and gradually withdrawing it as proficiency increases. And most developmentalists believe that children's play activities prepare them for adult life by allowing them to practice a variety of adult-like behaviors and to develop skills in planning, cooperation, problem solving, and self-restraint.

Comparing Piagetian and Vygotskian Perspectives

Constructive processes, readiness, challenge, and social interaction are central to the theories of both Piaget and Vygotsky. However, the two perspectives differ on the role of language in cognitive development, the relative value of free exploration versus more structured and guided activities, the relative importance of interactions with peers versus adults, and the influence of culture.

Applying Concepts in Child Development

The exercises in this section will help you increase your effectiveness in applying Piaget's and Vygotsky's theories as you work with children and adolescents.

Case Study

Adolescent Scientists

Read the case and then answer the questions that follow it.

Scott Sowell has just introduced the concept of *pendulum* in his seventh-grade science class. When he asks his students to identify variables that might influence the frequency with which a pendulum swings, they suggest three possibilities: the amount of weight at the bottom, the length of the pendulum, and the "angle" from which the weight is initially dropped.

MyEducationLab

You can watch this lesson in the "Designing Experiments" video. (Find Video Examples in Chapter 6 of MyEducationLab.)

Mr. Sowell divides his students into small groups and gives each group a pendulum composed of a long string with a paper clip attached to the bottom (Figure A). He also provides extra paper clips that the students can use to increase the weight at the bottom. He gives his students the following assignment: *Design your own experiment. Think of a way to test how each one of these variables affects the frequency of swing. Then carry out your experiment.*

Jon, Marina, Paige, and Wensley are coming to grips with their task as Mr. Sowell approaches their table.

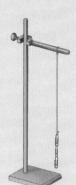

Figure A

Marina: We'll time the frequency as the seconds and the . . . um . . . what? [She looks questioningly at Mr. Sowell.]

Mr. S.:   The frequency is the number of swings within a certain time limit.

The group agrees to count the number of swings during a 15-second period. After Jon determines the current length of the string, Wensley positions the pendulum 25 degrees from vertical. When Jon says "Go" and starts a stopwatch, Wensley releases the pendulum. Marina counts the number of swings until, 15 seconds later, Jon says "Stop." Jon records the data from the first experiment: length = 49 cm, weight = 1 paper clip, angle = 25°, frequency = 22.

The group shortens the string and adds a second paper clip onto the bottom of the first clip. The students repeat their experiment and record their data: length = 36 cm, weight = 2 paper clips, angle = 45°, frequency = 25.

Wensley: What does the weight do to it?

Marina: We found out that the shorter it is and the heavier it is, the faster it goes.

Mr. Sowell joins the group and reviews its results from the first two tests.

Mr. S.:   What did you change between Test 1 and Test 2?

Marina: Number of paper clips.

Mr. S.:   OK, so you changed the weight. What else did you change?

Wensley: The length.

Marina: And the angle.

Mr. S.:   OK, so you changed all three between the two tests. So what caused the higher frequency?

Wensley: The length.

Marina: No, I think it was the weight.

Jon: I think the weight.

Paige: The length.

Mr. S.:   Why can't you look at your data and decide? [The students look at him blankly.] Take a look at the two tests.

The first one had one paper clip, and the second had two. The first test had one length, and the second test had a shorter length. Why can't you come to a conclusion by looking at the two frequencies?

Marina: All of the variables changed.

Mr. Sowell nods in agreement and then moves on to another group. The four students decide to change only the weight for the next test, so they add a third paper clip to the bottom of the second. Their pendulum now looks like Figure B. They continue to perform experiments but are careful to change only one variable at a time, or so they think. In reality, each time the group adds another paper clip, the pendulum grows longer. Mr. Sowell visits the students once again.

Figure B

Mr. S.:   One thing you're testing is length, right? And another thing is weight. Look at your system. Look at how you might be making a slight mistake with weight and length. [He takes two paper clips off and then puts one back on, hanging it, as the students have done, at the bottom of the first paper clip.]

Marina: It's heavier *and* longer.

Mr. S.:   Can you think of a way to redesign your experiments so that you're changing only weight? How can you do things differently so that your pendulum doesn't get longer when you add paper clips?

Jon: Hang the second paper clip from the bottom of the string instead of from the first paper clip.

When Mr. Sowell leaves, the students add another paper clip to the pendulum, making sure that the overall length of the pendulum stays the same. They perform another test and find that the pendulum's frequency is identical to what they obtained in the preceding test. Ignoring what she has just seen, Marina concludes, "So if it's heavier, the frequency is higher."

· In what ways does Mr. Sowell scaffold the students' efforts during the lab activity?
· With which one of Piaget's stages is the students' reasoning most consistent? Explain your choice.
· Use one or more of Piaget's ideas to explain why Marina persists in her belief that, despite evidence to the contrary, weight affects a pendulum's frequency.
· Drawing from current perspectives on Piaget's theory, identify a task for which the students might be better able to separate and control variables.

Once you have answered these questions, compare your responses with those presented in Appendix A.

Interpreting Children's Artifacts and Reflections

Consider chapter concepts as you analyze the following artifact created by a 14-year-old boy.

Fish in a Boat

Combining his pen-and-ink drawing skills and computer technology, 14-year-old Brady created this cartoon of fish rowing a boat upside-down at the water's surface. As you look at the cartoon, consider these questions:

· Brady used at least three physical tools in creating his cartoon: pen, paper, and a computer. Identify at least three *cognitive tools* that Brady also took advantage of in creating the cartoon.
· Identify a logical reasoning ability that creating this cartoon required. Also identify the Piagetian stage associated with this ability.

Once you have analyzed Brady's cartoon, compare your ideas with those presented in Appendix B. For further practice in analyzing children's artifacts and reflections, go to the Activities and Applications section in Chapter 6 of MyEducationLab.

START BAILING, HOWARD, WE'RE TAKING ON AIR FAST!

Developmental Trends Exercise

In this chapter you learned that challenging tasks and situations promote cognitive development. The following table describes experiences of five children and adolescents. For each of these experiences, the table identifies one or more developmental concepts related to challenge, offers an implication for working with children of that age-group, or both. Go to the Activities and Applications section in Chapter 6 of MyEducationLab to apply what you've learned about Piagetian and Vygotskian perspectives as you fill in the empty cells in the table.

Examining Challenges That Promote Cognitive Development

Age	A Youngster's Experience	Developmental Concepts *Identifying the Nature of the Challenge*	Implications *Facilitating Cognitive Growth*
Infancy (Birth–2 Years)	Eighteen-month-old Julia is becoming frustrated that the tower she's trying to build with wooden blocks keeps toppling over. Her caregiver sits on the floor beside her and helps her stack the blocks in such a way that the tower is more stable.	Building a block tower is in Julia's *zone of proximal development*: She can do it successfully only with assistance.	
Early Childhood (2–6 Years)	Four-year-old Jacob is trying to put together a simple picture puzzle. His progress is slow, but he persists. As he works, he continually makes comments such as, "Nope, doesn't fit," "Where's that green one?" and "Maybe if I turn it this way. . . ."	Jacob is engaging in *self-talk* as a way of guiding himself through a difficult task.	Encourage rather than discourage self-talk, because it enables children to guide themselves through difficult tasks without the assistance of others.

Age	A Youngster's Experience	Developmental Concepts *Identifying the Nature of the Challenge*	Implications *Facilitating Cognitive Growth*
Middle Childhood (6–10 Years)	"Metal always sinks, because metal is heavier than water," 9-year-old Rachel emphatically states. Her teacher shows her a postcard of a large cargo ship and says, "This ship is made almost entirely of metal. Why is it floating?" Rachel pauses, squinches her face, and thinks. "Wow, I don't know. Why *does* it float? That doesn't make sense!"		Present information that conflicts with what children currently believe as a way of helping them acquire more sophisticated understandings of the world.
Early Adolescence (10–14 Years)	As part of an assignment for his eighth-grade journalism class, 14-year-old Jamal shadows a local newspaper reporter for a day. The reporter gives Jamal a steno pad similar to the one she herself uses and encourages him to take notes as she interviews the mayor and police chief. Periodically she looks at Jamal's notes and offers suggestions on how he might improve them. At the end of the day, Jamal helps the reporter write a story for the paper using the notes they've both taken.	As a newcomer to the world of journalism, Jamal does not have the training he would need to write a newspaper story on his own. However, he can certainly contribute in meaningful ways to a story. The reporter is engaging Jamal in *guided participation* in an adult activity.	Engage children and adolescents in typical adult activities, for instance by introducing authentic activities in the classroom or by giving them opportunities to take on tasks in community agencies and businesses.
Late Adolescence (14–18 Years)	A high school social studies teacher in a wealthy school district presents some alarming statistics about the number of people living in poverty in the local community. When he asks his students to suggest some possible solutions to the situation, a heated debate ensues: "Some people are just lazy." "No they aren't! We just need to find them all jobs so they can earn a decent living." "Some people can't work because they have disabilities. How about if every rich family 'adopted' a poor family and helped it out?"	The students' diverse opinions about the problem reflect *sociocognitive conflict* that should promote disequilibrium and motivate the students to think about the matter more deeply. Yet some of the responses (e.g., finding jobs for everyone, asking rich families to "adopt" poorer ones) may be unrealistic, consistent with the *idealism* so typical of adolescence.	

Key Concepts

clinical method (p. 194)
class inclusion (p. 195)
scheme (p. 195)
operation (p. 195)
assimilation (p. 196)
accommodation (p. 196)
equilibrium (p. 197)
disequilibrium (p. 197)
equilibration (p. 197)
goal-directed behavior (p. 198)
object permanence (p. 198)

symbolic thought (p. 198)
egocentrism (p. 200)
conservation (p. 201)
neo-Piagetian theory (p. 205)
working memory (p. 205)
central conceptual structure
  (p. 206)
sociocognitive conflict (p. 210)
sociocultural theory (p. 211)
mediation (p. 211)
cognitive tool (p. 212)

self-talk (p. 212)
inner speech (p. 212)
internalization (p. 213)
appropriation (p. 213)
zone of proximal development
  (ZPD) (p. 214)
sociodramatic play (p. 215)
mediated learning experience
  (p. 216)
scaffolding (p. 217)
guided participation (p. 217)

apprenticeship (p. 218)
cognitive apprenticeship
  (p. 218)
reciprocal teaching (p. 219)
authentic activity (p. 222)
constructivism (p. 224)
individual constructivism
  (p. 224)
social constructivism
  (p. 224)

MyEducationLab

Now go to Chapter 6 of MyEducationLab at www.myeducationlab.com, where you can:

· View instructional objectives for the chapter.
· Take a quiz to test your mastery of chapter objectives. Detailed feedback is provided to explain why your responses are correct or incorrect.
· Deepen your understanding of particular concepts and principles with Review, Practice, and Enrichment exercises.

· Complete Activities and Applications exercises that give you additional experience in interpreting artifacts, increase your understanding of how research contributes to knowledge about chapter topics, and encourage you to apply what you have learned about children's development.
· Apply what you have learned in the chapter to your work with children in Building Teaching Skills and Dispositions exercises.
· Observe children and their unique contexts in Video Examples.

Cognitive Development: Cognitive Processes

Our colleague Dinah Jackson worked for many years in the Colorado public schools. At one point she asked students in grades 2 through 8 to write essays addressing the following question: *The land we live on has been here for a very long time, but the United States has been a country for only a little more than 200 years. How did the United States become a country?* Here are some of their responses:

Second grader:

2000 Days oh go George Washington gave us the Country To Live on.

Third grader:

The pilgrams came over in 17 hundred, when they came over they bilt houses. The Idiuns thout they were mean. Then they came friends, and tot them stuff. Then winter came, and dot died. Then some had babies. So thats how we got here.

Sixth grader:

The U.S.A. became a country by some of the British wanting to be under a different rule than of the kings. So, they sailed to the "new world" and became a new country. The only problem was that the kings from Britin still ruled the "new world". Then they had the revolutionary war. They bet Britin, and became an independent country.

Eighth grader:

We became a country through different processes. Technology around the world finally caught up with the British. There were boats to travel with, navigating tools, and the hearts of men had a desire to expand. Many men had gone on expeditions across the sea. A very famous journey was that of Christopher Columbus. He discovered this land that we live. More and more people poured in, expecting instant wealth, freedom, and a right to share their opinions. Some immigrants were satisfied, others were displeased. Problems in other countries forced people to move on to this New World, such as potato famins and no freedom of religions. Stories that drifted through people grew about this country. Stories of golden roads and free land coaxed other families who were living in the slums. Unfortunately, there were slums in America. The people helped this country grow in industry, cultures, religions, and government. Inventions and books were now better than the Europeans. Dime-novels were invented, and the young people could read about heroes of this time. May the curiosity and eagerness of the children continue

Case Study:

How the United States Became a Country

Outline:

Case Study: How the United States Became a Country

Basic Cognitive Processes

Metacognition and Cognitive Strategies

Adding a Sociocultural Element to Information Processing Theory

Children's Construction of Theories

Comparing and Critiquing Contemporary Approaches to Cognitive Development

Exceptionalities in Information Processing

Summary

Applying Concepts in Child Development

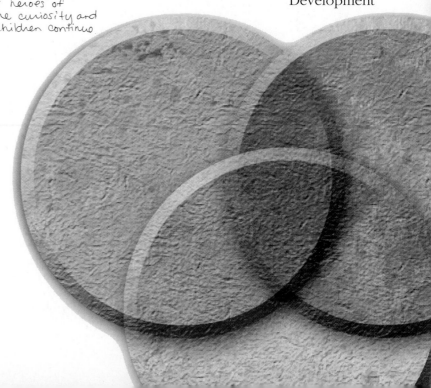

- What do the four compositions reveal about developmental changes in children's knowledge of written language?

- What do they reveal about developmental changes in children's knowledge of American history?

Certainly children know *more* as they get older, both about writing mechanics (spelling, punctuation, capitalization) and about American history. But if you look closely at what the children have written, changes in the *quality* of children's writing and knowledge of history are evident as well. For instance, whereas the third grader describes the nation's history as a list of seemingly unrelated facts, the sixth and eighth graders have pulled what they have learned into an integrated whole that "hangs together." In addition, the younger children's descriptions reflect very simplistic and concrete understandings (e.g., the country was a gift from George Washington, the Pilgrims came over and built houses). In contrast, the eighth grader uses abstract concepts (e.g., technological progress, freedom of religion, overly optimistic expectations for wealth) to explain immigration to the United States.

In the preceding chapter, we looked at two early theories of cognitive development, those of Jean Piaget and Lev Vygotsky. In this chapter our focus is on contemporary theories and research. As you will discover as you read the chapter, contemporary developmental psychologists often build on and extend Piaget's and Vygotsky's ideas in their explanations of how children and adolescents think and learn and in their recommendations for helping young people think and learn more effectively.

Basic Cognitive Processes

Do children become better able to pay attention as they grow older? Do they learn and remember things more effectively as they move through the elementary and secondary grades? In what ways does their knowledge change with age? Such questions reflect the approach of **information processing theory,** a theoretical perspective that addresses how human beings mentally acquire, interpret, and remember information and how such cognitive processes change over the course of development.

Information processing theory emerged in the late 1950s and early 1960s and has continued to evolve in the decades that have followed. Many early information processing theorists tried to draw parallels between how people think and how computers operate. As a result, computer terms are sometimes used to describe human thought processes. For example, information processing theory portrays people as *storing* (i.e., putting) information in memory and *retrieving* it from memory (i.e., finding it) when they need it at a later time.

Increasingly, however, researchers have found that people often think in distinctly non–computer-like ways. Unlike most computer programs, human beings actively pursue self-chosen goals and create new knowledge and understandings in somewhat idiosyncratic and unpredictable ways. Much of information processing theory now has a *constructivist* flavor similar to that of Piaget's theory. As an example, consider the second grader's explanation in the opening case study:

> 2000 Days oh go George Washington gave us the Country to Live on.

Almost certainly, no one has ever told her that the United States was a gift from George Washington. Instead, she uses something she has learned—that Washington was a key figure in the country's early history—to construct what is, to her, a logical explanation of her country's origin. Furthermore, not knowing how to spell *ago*, she uses two words she does know (*oh* and *go*) to construct a reasonable (albeit incorrect) spelling.

Key Ideas in Information Processing Theory

Figure 7-1 presents a model of what the human information processing system might look like. Although information processing theorists don't always agree about the specific mechanisms involved in learning and remembering information, many of them agree on several points.

- • *Input from the environment provides the raw material for learning and memory.* Human beings receive input from the environment through the senses (e.g., by seeing, hearing, or touching) and translate that raw input into more meaningful information. The first part of this process, detecting stimuli in the environment, is *sensation*. The second part, interpreting those stimuli, is *perception*.

information processing theory
Theoretical perspective that focuses on the specific ways in which people mentally acquire, interpret, and remember information and how such cognitive processes change over the course of development.

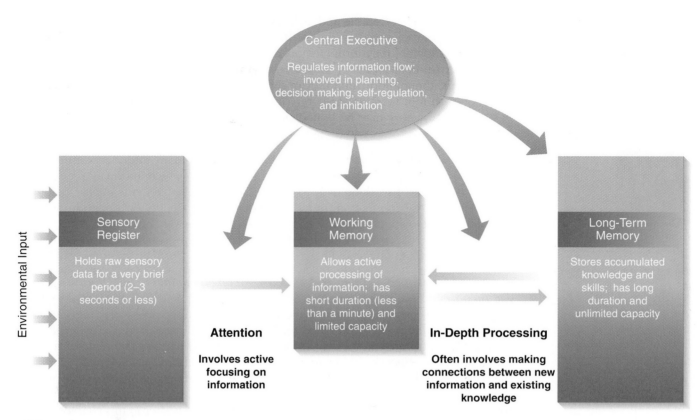

Figure 7-1

A model of the human information processing system.

Even the simplest interpretation (perception) of an environmental event takes time. Thus many theorists believe that human memory includes a mechanism that allows people to remember raw sensory data for a very short time (perhaps 2 to 3 seconds for auditory information and probably less than a second for visual information). This mechanism goes by a variety of names, but we'll refer to it as the **sensory register.**

• ***In addition to a sensory register, human memory includes two other storage mechanisms: working memory and long-term memory.*** In Chapter 6 we introduced the concept of **working memory,** that part of the human memory system in which people hold and actively think about new information. For instance, working memory is where children try to solve a problem or make sense of what they are reading. It can keep information for only a very short time (probably less than a minute), so it is sometimes called *short-term memory.*[1] Furthermore, working memory appears to have a limited capacity—only a small amount of "space" in which people can hold and think about events or ideas. As an illustration, try computing the following division problem in your head:

$$59\overline{)49{,}383}$$

Did you find yourself having trouble remembering some parts of the problem while you were dealing with other parts? Did you ever arrive at the correct answer of 837? Most people cannot solve a multistep division problem like this unless they can write it on paper. There simply isn't "room" in working memory to hold all the numbers in your head while simultaneously trying to solve the problem.

Long-term memory is the component that allows human beings to save the many things they've learned from their experiences. For instance, it might include such knowledge as where cookies can be found in the kitchen and how much 2 and 2 equal, as well as such

[1]In everyday language, people often use the term "short-term memory" to refer to memory that lasts for a few days or weeks. Notice how, in contrast, information processing theorists characterize short-term memory as lasting *less than a minute.*

sensory register
Component of memory that holds incoming information in an unanalyzed form for a very brief time (2–3 seconds or less).

working memory
Component of memory that enables people to actively think about and process a small amount of information.

long-term memory
Component of memory that holds knowledge and skills for a relatively long period of time.

skills as how to ride a bicycle and use a microscope. Things in long-term memory don't necessarily last forever, but they do last for a lengthy period, especially if they are used frequently. In addition, long-term memory appears to have an unlimited capacity, "holding" as
much information as a person could possibly need to save.

To think about information previously stored in long-term memory, people must retrieve
and reflect on it in working memory. Thus, although people's capacity to keep information
in long-term memory may be boundless, their ability to *think about* what they've stored is
limited to whatever they can hold in working memory at any one time.

● ***Attention is essential to the learning process.*** Many information processing theo-
rists suggest that attention is the primary process through which information moves from the
sensory register into working memory. Thus it plays a key role in the interpretation, storage,
and later recall of information. In the "Memory: Middle Childhood" video in MyEducation-
Lab, you can see what happens when a child isn't paying attention. Ten-year-old David remembers only 3 of the 12 words that the interviewer reads to him. He realizes that his lapse
in attention was the reason he did not recall more words: "My brain was turned off right now."

● ***A variety of cognitive processes are involved in moving information from working memory to long-term memory.*** Whereas attention is instrumental in moving information from the sensory register to working memory, more complex processes are needed if
people are to remember information for longer than a minute or so. Occasionally simply repeating information over and over (*rehearsing* it) is sufficient for its long-term storage. More
often, however, effective storage requires making connections between new information and
the concepts and ideas that already exist in long-term memory. For instance, people might use
their existing knowledge either to *organize* or expand (i.e., *elaborate*) on newly acquired information. We'll look at the development of such processes later in this chapter.

● ***People control how they process information.*** Some sort of cognitive "supervisor" is almost certainly necessary to ensure that a person's learning and memory processes
work effectively. This component, sometimes called the **central executive,** oversees the
flow of information throughout the memory system and is critical for planning, decision making, self-regulation, and inhibition of unproductive thoughts and behaviors (recall our discussion of *executive functions* in Chapter 5). Although the central executive is probably
closely connected to working memory, information processing theorists haven't yet pinned
down its exact nature.

● ***Cognitive development involves gradual changes in various components of the
information processing system.*** Many information processing theorists reject Piaget's notion of discrete developmental stages. Instead, they believe that children's cognitive processes
and abilities develop primarily through ongoing, gradual *trends*. In the following sections, we
look at developmental trends in various aspects of the human information processing system.

Sensation and Perception

Most sensory and perceptual development occurs in infancy. Researchers have reached the
following conclusions about infants' sensory and perceptual abilities.

● ***Some sensory and perceptual capabilities are present at birth. Others emerge
within the first few weeks or months of life.*** As you discovered in Chapter 4, even newborns can sense and discriminate among different sights, sounds, tastes, and smells (J. Atkinson, 1998; Bijeljac-Babic, Bertoncini, & Mehler, 1993; Flavell et al., 2002; Rosenstein & Oster,
1988; Winberg, 2005). And their ability to perceive—that is, to *interpret*—this sensory information appears quite early. For instance, newborns have some ability to determine the direction from which a sound is coming (Morrongiello, Fenwick, Hillier, & Chance, 1994).
Within the first week they seem to understand that objects maintain the same shape and size
even when the objects are rotated or moved farther away and, hence, *look* different (Slater,
Mattock, & Brown, 1990; Slater & Morison, 1985).

Many sensory and perceptual capabilities continue to improve during the first few
months—and in some cases the first year or two—of life (R. J. Adams, 1987; Ashmead, Davis,

central executive
Component of the human information
processing system that oversees the flow
of information throughout the system.

Whalen, & Odom, 1991; Aslin, 1993; Hillier, Hewitt, & Morrongiello, 1992). For example, at birth visual acuity is less than 20/600, but by 8 months of age it is around 20/80 (Courage & Adams, 1990). Young infants can nevertheless do a great deal with their limited eyesight. For instance, when they are only a few days old, they can recognize the contours of their mother's face and can detect and imitate facial expressions depicting happiness, sadness, and surprise (T. Field, Woodson, Greenberg, & Cohen, 1982; M. H. Johnson & de Haan, 2001; Walton, Bower, & Bower, 1992). However, visual perception is probably not fully developed until the preschool years, when the visual cortex—that part of the brain that handles complex visual information—becomes similar to that of an adult (T. L. Hickey & Peduzzi, 1987).

● ***Infants show consistent preferences for certain types of stimuli, especially social ones.*** As early as the first week of life, infants are drawn to new and interesting stimuli and events (Haith, 1990). They also show a distinct preference for social stimuli. For instance, within 3 days of birth, they recognize their mother's voice and will suck vigorously on a synthetic nipple if doing so turns on a recording of their mother speaking (DeCasper & Fifer, 1980). In the first month, they begin to show a preference for looking at faces over other objects, and by 4 months they also seem to prefer looking at human forms of movement (e.g., walking) over other movements (Bertenthal, 1993; Dannemiller & Stephens, 1988; Rakison, 2005). This early inclination to focus on social stimuli is, of course, highly beneficial: Infants must depend on others not only for their survival but also for learning language and other essential aspects of their culture.

● ***Perceptual development is the result of both biological maturation and experience.*** Both nature and nurture appear to be essential for perceptual development. We find an example of this principle in research on depth perception and fear of heights. To determine when infants acquire depth perception, researchers sometimes use a *visual cliff,* a large glass table with a patterned cloth immediately beneath the glass on one side and the same pattern on the floor under the other side (see Figure 7-2). In a classic early study (E. J. Gibson & Walk, 1960), infants ages 6 to 14 months were placed on a narrow platform between the "shallow" and "deep" sides of a visual cliff. Their mothers stood at one end of the table and actively coaxed them to crawl across the glass. Although most infants willingly crawled off the platform to the "shallow" side, very few ventured onto the "deep" side. By age 6 months, then, infants can apparently perceive depth and know that sharp drop-offs are potentially dangerous.

Figure 7-2

By refusing to crawl to the "deep" side of this glass-covered table (known as a *visual cliff*), infants show a fear of heights.

Certainly neurological maturation is involved in depth perception to some degree. Visual acuity must be sufficiently sharp and the brain must be sufficiently developed to enable infants to perceive edges, inclines, and the relative distances of objects. Some species that can walk almost immediately after birth (e.g., chicks, lambs, baby goats) show avoidance of the deep side of a visual cliff within the first day of life (E. J. Gibson & Walk, 1960), suggesting that an inborn fear of heights is fairly common in the animal kingdom. But learning also appears to be involved. Infants who have had experience with self-locomotion, either through crawling or using a walker, show greater fear of drop-offs than infants without such experience (Bertenthal, Campos, & Kermoian, 1994; J. J. Campos, Bertenthal, & Kermoian, 1992).

From an evolutionary perspective, it makes sense that both heredity and environment should play a role in perceptual development. Because perception of one's surroundings and emotional connections with caregivers are essential for survival, the human species has undoubtedly evolved some biologically built-in perceptual abilities and preferences (Rakison, 2005). At the same time, the specific environments to which humans must adapt vary from place to place, so the human brain has evolved to be responsive to local circumstances (J. J. Gibson, 1979; Greenough & Black, 1992; Thelen & Smith, 1998). Experiences that ensure optimal perceptual development are *not* those that involve intense, nonstop visual and auditory stimulation, however. Instead, they are ones that children with normal sensory abilities encounter in any reasonably nurturing environment (Bruer, 1999).

Attention

The development of attention is due, in part, to brain maturation, especially to the continuing development of the cortex in the first few years of life (Ridderinkhof & van der Molen, 1995; Ruff & Rothbart, 1996). The increasing involvement of the cortex in attention undoubtedly contributes to the following developmental trends.

MyEducationLab

Observe how Corwin's attention is drawn to a novel object in the "Cognitive Development: Infancy" video. (Find Video Examples in Chapter 7 of MyEducationLab.)

- ● ***Children's attention is affected by stimulus characteristics and, later, also by familiarity.*** In the "Cognitive Development: Infancy" video in MyEducationLab, 16-month-old Corwin is captivated by an unusual, multicolored toy he finds in a paper bag. Like all human beings, infants and toddlers quickly turn their attention to new, unusual, and perhaps intense stimuli—for instance, a flash of light, loud noise, or sudden movement (Bahrick, Gogate, & Ruiz, 2002; Snyder, 2007). Once they have gained some knowledge about their everyday world, familiarity comes into play as well. In particular, they are most likely to be drawn to objects and events that are moderately different, but not too different, from those they have previously experienced (McCall, Kennedy, & Applebaum, 1977; L. M. Oakes, Kannass, & Shaddy, 2002). This tendency to prefer novelty in moderation is consistent with Piaget's belief that children can accommodate to (and so benefit from) new stimuli only to the extent that they can also assimilate those stimuli into their existing schemes.

MyEducationLab

Observe Maddie's age-typical shifts in attention in the "Cognitive Development: Early Childhood" video. (Find Video Examples in Chapter 7 of MyEducationLab.)

- ● ***With age, distractibility decreases and sustained attention increases.*** Once they are captivated by an object or event, infants as young as 6 months are less distractible than they would be otherwise (Richards & Turner, 2001). How long young children can sustain their attention is partly a function of their temperament. Some toddlers can become quite engrossed in an activity when the task is self-chosen, intriguing, and free from interference by others. By and large, however, young children's attention moves quickly from one thing to another. Preschool and kindergarten children in free-play situations typically spend only a few minutes engaged in one activity before they move to another (Dempster & Corkill, 1999; Ruff & Lawson, 1990). Such distractibility isn't necessarily a bad thing, because it may draw children to other potentially valuable learning opportunities. But it requires adults to be flexible and patient when trying to keep young children's attention on any single task.

As children move through the elementary school years, they become better able to focus and sustain their attention on a particular task despite the presence of distracting stimuli (Higgins & Turnure, 1984; Lane & Pearson, 1982; Ruff & Lawson, 1990). For example, in one experimental study (Higgins & Turnure, 1984), children in three age-groups (preschool, second grade, and sixth grade) were given age-appropriate learning tasks in which they had to make a series of discriminations among similar stimuli. Some children worked on the tasks in a quiet room, others worked in a room with a little background noise, and still others worked with a great deal of background noise. Preschool and second-grade children performed most effectively under the quiet conditions and least effectively under the very noisy conditions. But the sixth graders performed just as well in a noisy room as in a quiet one. Apparently, the older children were able to ignore the noise, whereas the younger children were not.

- ● ***Attention becomes increasingly purposeful.*** By the time children are 3 or 4 months old, they show some ability to anticipate where an object of interest will soon appear and to focus their attention accordingly (Haith, Hazan, & Goodman, 1988). In the preschool years they begin to use attention specifically to help them learn and remember something, and their ability to use it effectively continues to improve during the elementary and middle school years (DeMarie-Dreblow & Miller, 1988; Hagen & Stanovich, 1977; P. Miller & Seier, 1994). Indeed, children's learning increasingly becomes a function of what they think they need to remember.

As an illustration of the purposeful nature of attention, imagine that you have the six cards shown in Figure 7-3 in front of you on a table. You are told to remember only the *colors* of the cards. Now the cards are flipped over, and you are asked where the green card is, where the purple card is, and so on. You are then asked to name the object that appeared on each card. Chances are, you will remember the colors far more accurately than the objects.

In one study (Maccoby & Hagen, 1965), children in grades 1 through 7 were asked to perform a series of tasks similar to the one just described. The older children remembered the background colors more accurately than the younger children did. Yet the older children were no better than younger ones at remembering the objects pictured on the cards.

In fact, the oldest group in the study remembered the *fewest* objects. These results suggest that older children are better at paying attention to and learning the things they need to know, but they are not necessarily better at learning information irrelevant to their goals.

Working Memory and the Central Executive

Working memory and the central executive (which, as noted earlier, are probably closely connected) are largely responsible for what children pay attention to, how they think about the information, and how well they remember it. Three developmental trends in working memory and the central executive enable children to handle increasingly complex cognitive tasks with age:

Figure 7-3

Imagine that you are told to remember the *colors* of each of these cards. After the cards are flipped over, do you think you would remember where each color appeared? Would you also remember what *object* appeared on each card, even though you were not asked to remember the objects?
Modeled after stimuli used by Maccoby & Hagen, 1965.

• ***Processing speed increases.*** As youngsters move through childhood and adolescence, they execute many cognitive processes more quickly and efficiently in working memory than they did in earlier years (Fry & Hale, 1996; R. V. Kail & Ferrer, 2007; Luna, Garver, Urban, Lazar, & Sweeney, 2004). Some of this increased speed and efficiency is undoubtedly due to the genetically driven *myelination* of neurons in the brain (see Chapter 5). Yet experience and practice are involved as well. By frequently practicing certain mental and physical tasks, children and adolescents develop **automatization** for these tasks. That is, they eventually become capable of performing the tasks very quickly and with little or no conscious effort. Once thoughts and actions become automatized, they take up very little "space" in working memory, enabling children to devote more working memory capacity to other, more challenging tasks and problems.

As an example of the benefits of automatization, consider how children's reading ability improves over time. When children first begin to read, they devote considerable mental effort to identifying the words on the page—for instance, figuring out what the letters f-r-i-e-n-d spell—and may recall little about the *meaning* of what they've read. But with increasing exposure to a variety of reading materials, word identification gradually becomes an automatized process, such that children immediately recognize most of the words they see. At this point, they can focus their efforts on understanding and remembering what they're reading.

The automatization process is one of the many ways in which Mother Nature ensures that children adapt to their particular social and cultural environments (Bjorklund & Green, 1992). Aside from a few built-in reflexes, children are born to be mentally flexible, with the potential to respond to their environments in a wide variety of ways. With experience and practice, they acquire the thinking processes and behaviors that their specific circumstances require, and they can execute those processes and behaviors with increasing efficiency and effectiveness.

• ***The capacity of working memory increases with age.*** One common way of measuring the capacity of working memory is to ask people to remember a sequence of unrelated items, perhaps a series of digits or several unrelated objects or words. Toddlers can remember more items than infants can, older children can remember more items than younger children can, and adolescents can remember even more. Much of this increase in working memory capacity is probably due to the fact that cognitive processes become faster and more efficient with age and so take up less "room." But the actual physical "space" of working memory may increase somewhat as well, presumably as a result of neurological changes (Fry & Hale, 1996; R. V. Kail, 2007; L. M. Oakes & Bauer, 2007).

• ***The central executive increasingly takes charge of cognitive processes.*** Thanks in large part to continuing maturation of the cortex, youngsters gain increasing control of their cognitive processes throughout childhood and adolescence (Kuhn, 2006; Luna et al., 2004; Zelazo, Müller, Frye, & Marcovitch, 2003). With such control comes a variety of new abilities. For instance, youngsters become better able to plan and direct their future actions and activities. They can better inhibit inappropriate thoughts and behaviors. And they can reflect on and think *about* their thinking, as we'll see in our discussion of *metacognition* later in the chapter. Keep in mind, however, that the central executive is still a "work in progress" even in adolescence and does not fully mature until adulthood.

automatization
Process of becoming able to respond quickly and efficiently while mentally processing or physically performing certain tasks.

infantile amnesia
General inability to recall events that have occurred in the early years of life.

knowledge base
One's knowledge about specific topics and the world in general.

Long-Term Memory

Some knowledge in long-term memory is virtually universal. For instance, most children around the globe soon learn that people typically have two legs but cats and dogs have four. Other knowledge, of course, depends on children's unique experiences and on the cultural contexts in which they grow up. For example, in the four children's compositions in the opening case study, we consistently see a European American perspective on the early days of the United States: The focus is on immigration and early European colonization. Were we to ask Native American children how the United States came into being, we might get very different perspectives, perhaps ones based on invasion or confiscation of property. Several developmental phenomena related to long-term memory enhance children's ability to understand and respond to their world.

● *The capacity to remember information in long-term memory appears very early and improves with age.* At birth, and apparently even *before* birth, children have some ability to learn from and remember their experiences (DeCasper & Spence, 1986; Kisilevsky et al., 2003). For example, as you learned in Chapter 4, newborn infants who had been exposed to the song "Little Brown Jug" while still in their mothers' wombs showed signs that they had heard and still remembered the song (James et al., 2002).

In infancy and the toddler years, the capacity for long-term memory manifests itself in a variety of ways. For instance, when a ribbon connected to a mobile is tied to a 2-month-old baby's foot, the baby easily learns that kicking makes the mobile move and remembers the connection over a period of several days—even longer if he or she is given an occasional reminder (Rovee-Collier, 1999). At age 6 months, infants can also recall and imitate actions they saw 24 hours earlier, and their memory for such actions increases in duration in the months that follow. By the time children reach their second birthday, they are able to retain a complex sequence of actions for a year or more (Bauer, DeBoer, & Lukowski, 2007). Such improvements in long-term memory ability are probably due, in large part, to brain maturation (Bauer, 2007; Hayne, 2007).

● *Children increasingly have conscious awareness of past events.* Despite the findings just described, children typically have little if any *conscious recall of things that happened during their first 2 years*—a phenomenon known as **infantile amnesia.** For much of the preschool period, recall of past events continues to be rather sketchy. The immaturity of certain brain structures in the early years may be partly responsible (Bauer, 2002; C. A. Nelson et al., 2006). Furthermore, early experiences may be stored in memory in a form that children cannot easily retrieve (Newcombe, Drummey, Fox, Lie, & Ottinger-Albergs, 2000; Richardson & Hayne, 2007).

When children gain proficiency in language, and particularly when people around them engage them in conversations about what they are experiencing, their conscious memory for past events improves dramatically (McGuigan & Salmon, 2004; C. A. Nelson & Fivush, 2004; K. Nelson, 1996b). It appears that talking about events enables children to store the events in a verbal (language-based) form, making the events easier to recall at a later time.

● *The amount of knowledge stored in long-term memory increases many times over.* This trend is an obvious one, and the four essays in the opening case study illustrate it clearly. Yet the obviousness of the trend does not diminish its importance in cognitive development. In particular, long-term memory provides the **knowledge base** from which children draw as they encounter, interpret, and respond to new events. As their knowledge base grows, children can interpret new events with greater sophistication and respond to them more effectively (Siegler & Alibali, 2005).

On average, older children and adults learn new information and skills more easily than do younger children. A key reason is that they have more existing knowledge that they can use to help them make sense of new information and experiences (Eacott, 1999; Halford, 1989; R. Kail, 1990). When the tables are turned—when young children know more about a particular topic than adults or older children do—the younger children are often the more effective learners (Chi,

Figure 7-4

Children who have had diverse experiences (museum trips, travel to historical sites, etc.) have a broad knowledge base on which to build when they study classroom subject matter.

Dear Diary,
Guess what!! We have all most made it to the west cost. I can't what to lye down on C.A. sand in a Calafona Beach. Hot and sunny, out like Floida.
The first place we went today was Bandelier National Monument. It is a Monument with lots of Hopi tribe houses. It is a place where a Hopie tribe has bilt a village that has been abandoned and is now a museum/monument.
Well, we where going on this tour through thes ancient adobe houses. Suddenly, the house we are standing in begins to shweek. We rush outside to find that a 7-8 year old child is swinging on the old wooden "poles" that help support the floor above, like manky bars. The kid reachis for the next pole and it crables in to dust.
It finally tured out to be all right. The mom was having a spazz about, we need to call 911, and, Does he need CPR? The tour guidem trying to calm her down and then came over to u. He Thanked us and bussed up out.
More to morrow
Amaryth

1978; Lindberg, 1991; W. Schneider, Korkel, & Weinert, 1989). For example, in one classic study, elementary and middle school children who were expert chess players could better remember where chess pieces were located on a chess board than could college-educated adults who were relative novices at chess (Chi, 1978).

Children vary considerably in the specific experiences they have, of course, and this diversity leads to the development of unique knowledge bases on which children build while learning new things. For example, in Figure 7-4, 10-year-old Amaryth describes a day when her family visited a national monument that was once a Hopi village. Travel opportunities such as this will undoubtedly enhance Amaryth's ability to learn about Native American civilizations in her history and social studies classes.

- *Children's knowledge about the world becomes increasingly integrated.* Children begin categorizing their experiences as early as 3 or 4 months of age (more about this point a bit later). Even so, much of what young children know about the world consists of separate, isolated categories and facts. In contrast, older children's knowledge includes many associations and interrelationships among concepts and ideas (Bjorklund, 1987). This developmental change is undoubtedly one reason that older children can think more logically and draw inferences more readily: They have a more cohesive understanding of the world around them.

As an example, let's return to the essays in the opening case study. Notice how the third grader presents a chronological list of events without any attempt at tying them together:

> The Idiuns thout they were mean. Then they came friends, and tot them stuff. Then winter came, and alot died. Then some had babies.

In contrast, the eighth grader frequently identifies or implies cause-and-effect relationships among events:

> More and more people poured in, expecting instant wealth, freedom, and a right to share their opinions. Some immigrants were satisfied, others were displeased. Problems in other countries forced people to move on to this New World, such as potato famins and no freedom of religions. Stories that drifted through people grew about this country. Stories of golden roads and free land coaxed other families who were living in the slums.

Another example of increasing integration is seen in children's knowledge of their local communities (Forbes, Ormrod, Bernardi, Taylor, & Jackson, 1999). In Figure 7-5 we present maps that three children drew of their hometown. The first grader's map includes only a few features of her town that she knows well (her house and school, nearby mountains) and distorts spatial relationships among the features. The third grader's map shows many features of his immediate neighborhood and their proximity to one another. The seventh grader's map encompasses numerous town landmarks and their relative locations on major streets. It also makes greater use of symbols—for instance, single lines for roads, squares for buildings, and distinctive letter *M*s to indicate McDonald's restaurants.

Children and adults alike sometimes organize their knowledge into schemas and scripts. **Schemas** (similar, but not identical, to Piaget's *schemes*) are tightly integrated sets of ideas about specific objects or situations. For example, you might have a schema for what a typical horse looks like (e.g., it's a certain height, and it has a mane and an elongated head) and a schema for what a typical office contains (it probably has a desk, bookshelves, and file cabinets). **Scripts** encompass knowledge about the predictable sequence of events related to particular activities. For example, you probably have a script related to how weddings typically proceed, and even many 3-year-olds can tell you what typically happens when you go to McDonald's for a meal (K. Nelson, 1997). Schemas and scripts help children make sense of their experiences and predict what is likely to happen in familiar contexts on future occasions.

Schemas and scripts increase in number and complexity as children grow older (Farrar & Goodman, 1992; Flavell et al., 2002). Like Piaget's sensorimotor schemes, children's earliest schemas and scripts tend to be behavioral and perceptual in nature. For instance, toddlers can act out typical scenarios (scripts) with toys long before they have the verbal skills to describe what they are doing (Bauer & Dow, 1994). As children get older, these mental structures presumably become less tied to physical actions and perceptual qualities.

schema
Tightly integrated set of ideas about a specific object or situation.
script
Schema that involves a predictable sequence of events related to a common activity.

As these children play "store," they show that they already have a well-developed script for what typically happens at the checkout counter.

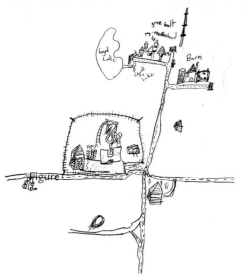

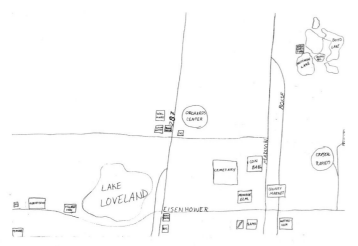

Figure 7-5

Three maps of Loveland, Colorado, drawn by a first grader (top), a third grader (middle), and a seventh grader (bottom).
Maps courtesy of Dinah Jackson.

Schemas and scripts often differ somewhat from one culture to another. Such cultural differences can influence the ease with which children understand and remember new information and events (Lipson, 1983; Pritchard, 1990; R. E. Reynolds, Taylor, Steffensen, Shirey, & Anderson, 1982). For example, in one study (R. E. Reynolds et al., 1982), eighth graders read a letter written by a young teenager, Sam, to his friend Joe. In it, Sam describes an incident in the school cafeteria earlier in the day:

> I got in line behind Bubba. As usual the line was moving pretty slow and we were all getting pretty restless. For a little action Bubba turned around and said, "Hey Sam! What you doin' man? You so ugly that when the doctor delivered you he slapped your face!" Everyone laughed, but they laughed even harder when I shot back, "Oh yeah? Well, you so ugly the doctor turned around and slapped your momma!" It got even wilder when Bubba said, "Well man, at least my daddy ain't no girl scout!" We really got into it then. After a while more people got involved— 4, 5, then 6. It was a riot! People helping out anyone who seemed to be getting the worst of the deal. (R. E. Reynolds et al., 1982, p. 358; italics omitted)

Many European American children incorrectly interpreted the incident as involving physical aggression, but African American children saw it for what it really was: a playful exchange of mock insults common among male youths in some African American communities.[2]

Thinking and Reasoning

From an information processing perspective, many developmental changes occur in basic thinking and reasoning processes. Here we look at three general developmental trends in thinking and reasoning. A bit later we'll examine changes in specific mental *strategies* that children use to learn and problem solve.

- ***Thought increasingly makes use of symbols.*** As you should recall from Chapter 6, Piaget proposed that infants' and toddlers' schemes are predominantly sensorimotor—that is, based on perceptions and behaviors. Near the end of the sensorimotor stage (at about 18 months, Piaget suggested), children begin to think in terms of **symbols,** mental entities (e.g., words) that do not necessarily reflect the perceptual and behavioral qualities of the objects or events they represent. Such symbolic thought enables children to infer characteristics they haven't directly observed. For example, when a 3-year-old who is familiar with common household pets hears her father use the word "cat," she might easily visualize a small animal that has pointy ears and whiskers, walks on four legs, and purrs.

  Piaget was probably correct in believing that sensorimotor representations of objects and events precede symbolic representations. However, the shift from one to the other is much more gradual than Piaget thought. Long before children reach school age, they begin to use such symbols as words, numbers, pictures, and miniature models to represent and think about real-life objects and events (DeLoache, Miller, & Rosengren, 1997; J. Huttenlocher, Newcombe, & Vasilyeva, 1999; K. Nelson, 1996a). Yet when children begin elementary school, they may initially have only limited success in dealing with the wide variety of symbols they encounter. For instance, elementary school teachers often use blocks and other concrete objects to represent numbers or mathematical operations, but not all kindergartners and first graders make the connection between the objects and the concepts they stand for (DeLoache et al., 1997; Uttal et al., 1998). Maps, too, are largely symbolic in nature, and children in the early grades often interpret them too literally, perhaps thinking that a road that is red on a map is actually painted red (Liben

symbol
Mental entity that represents an external object or event, typically without reflecting its perceptual and behavioral qualities.

[2]Such an exchange is sometimes called *playing the dozens* (see Chapter 9).

& Myers, 2007). As children grow older, their use of symbols to think, remember, and solve problems grows in frequency and sophistication. Eventually, their symbolic abilities allow them to transcend everyday realities, think about what could or should happen in the future, and develop abstract understandings about their physical and social worlds (Bandura, 2006; Tattersall, 2006).

- ***Logical thinking abilities improve with age.*** Although most information processing theorists reject Piaget's idea of discrete stages in logical thinking, they do agree that logical thinking improves—and often changes in qualitative ways—over time. Some logical thinking is evident even in infancy. Children as young as 6 months old can perceive a cause-and-effect relationship in a sequence of events. For instance, when 6-month-olds see one object hit another and watch the second object move immediately after the impact, they seem to understand that the first object has essentially "launched" the second one (L. B. Cohen & Cashon, 2006).

By preschool age, children can draw logical inferences from language-based information—for instance, they draw appropriate conclusions about events depicted in children's stories (M. Donaldson, 1978; R. Gelman & Baillargeon, 1983). However, preschoolers and elementary school children do not always draw *correct* inferences, and they have difficulty distinguishing between what *must* be true versus what *might* be true given the evidence before them (Galotti, Komatsu, & Voelz, 1997; Pillow, 2002).

The ability to reason logically improves markedly in adolescence. Yet even at this point, reasoning ability varies widely from one adolescent to another, and it is often influenced by personal motives and biases (Klaczynski, 2001; Kuhn, 2006; Kuhn & Franklin, 2006).

- ***Gestures sometimes foreshadow the emergence of more sophisticated thinking and reasoning.*** As children make the transition to more advanced forms of reasoning—perhaps about traditional Piagetian tasks or mathematical problems—they often show such reasoning in their gestures before they show it in their speech (Goldin-Meadow, 2006). The following scenario illustrates this trend:

> [A] 6-year-old child [is] attempting to justify her belief that the amount of water changed when it was poured from a tall, skinny glass into a short, wide dish. The child says, "It's different because this one's tall and that one's short," thus making it clear that she has focused on the heights of the two containers. However, in the very same utterance, the child indicates with her hand shaped like a C first the diameter of the glass and then, with a wider C, the larger diameter of the dish. The child speaks about the heights but has also noticed—not necessarily consciously—that the containers differ in width as well. (Goldin-Meadow, 1997, p. 13)

Gestures, like the 6-year-old's C-shaped hand gestures, appear to provide a way for children to "experiment" (cognitively) with new ideas. Gestures may also alleviate the strain on working memory as children first begin to wrestle with more complex ways of thinking (Goldin-Meadow, 2006; Goldin-Meadow, Nusbaum, Kelly, & Wagner, 2001).

Facilitating Basic Cognitive Processes

Our discussion of information processing theory thus far leads to several implications for working with children and adolescents.

- ***Provide a variety of sensory experiences for infants and young children.*** In the first few years of life, children learn many things about the physical world through direct contact—by looking, listening, feeling, tasting, and smelling. Thus infants, toddlers, and preschoolers should have a wide variety of toys and other objects to manipulate and play with, and their environment should be set up for safe movement and exploration. Children need enough options that they can identify activities and playthings that are within their current abilities yet also encourage cognitive growth. The Development and Practice feature "Providing Appropriate Stimulation for Infants" offers several suggestions for infant caregivers.

- ***Help children pay attention to things that are important for them to learn and remember.*** As we've seen, attention is a critical factor in learning. Yet many children, young ones especially, are easily drawn to extraneous sights and sounds that might distract them from planned activities. Even highly motivated high school students can't keep their minds

MyEducationLab

See examples of safe environments for infants and young children in the "Environments" videos in the Video Examples section in Chapter 7 of MyEducationLab.

Development and Practice

Providing Appropriate Stimulation for Infants

- **Give infants some choice and control in their sensory experiences.**

  A home child care provider offers a variety of simple toys and other objects for infants to explore and play with. She often places several items within reach, and she respects infants' occasional rejection and apparent dislike of certain items.

- **Be aware of the dangers of too much stimulation.**

  A teacher in an infant child care center realizes that the center is often busy and noisy. Knowing that too much stimulation can be unsettling, he monitors the sights, sounds, textures, and smells that are present at any one time. He tries to tone down the environment a bit when introducing a new stimulus for an infant to experience or explore.

- **Read cues.**

  A father helps a child care provider understand the signals his daughter typically gives. "She often turns away when she's had enough of something," he explains. "But at other times, she just acts sleepy. You know she's overstimulated if you put her in a quiet place and she perks up. If she's truly tired, then she quickly goes to sleep."

- **Avoid the "better baby" trap.**

  A child care provider recently attended a workshop on brain development, where several presenters misinterpreted the research, making a strong pitch for certain new products and claiming that the products are essential for maximizing intellectual growth. Fortunately, she knows enough about cognitive development to realize that children benefit equally from a wide variety of toys and that an intensive "sensory stimulation" approach is probably *not* in children's best interest.

- **Recognize that temperamental and cultural differences partly determine the optimal amount of stimulation for each child.**

  A teacher in a child care center has noticed that some of the toddlers in her group seem to respond to a good deal of sensory input by getting excited and animated, whereas others fuss, go to sleep, or in some other way indicate that they are experiencing information overload. Although she herself prefers a quiet, peaceful room, one of her coworkers enjoys lively salsa music and often plays it while the children are awake. The two teachers often compare notes about how different children respond to quiet versus more active environments.

on a single task indefinitely. Several strategies for helping children and adolescents focus their attention productively are presented in the Development and Practice feature "Getting and Keeping Children's Attention."

- ***Relate new information to children's existing knowledge.*** People of all ages learn new information more effectively when they can relate it to what they already know. Yet children and adolescents don't always make meaningful connections on their own. For instance, they may not realize that subtraction is simply the reverse of addition or that Shakespeare's *Romeo and Juliet* is in some ways similar to modern-day ethnic clashes in Europe, Asia, and North America. By pointing out such connections, adults can foster more effective learning and the development of a more integrated knowledge base (Ormrod, 2008b; J. J. White & Rumsey, 1994).

- ***Remember that children can think about only a small amount of information at any one time.*** Although working memory capacity increases somewhat during childhood and adolescence, young and old people alike can mentally manipulate only a very limited amount of material in their heads at once. Thus teachers and other adults who instruct children should pace any presentation of new information slowly enough that the children have time to "process" it all. They might also write complex directions or problems on a chalkboard or ask children to write them on paper. They should also teach more effective strategies for learning and solving problems (we'll say more about such strategies shortly).

- ***When determining what children know or are ready to learn, consider not only what they say but also what they do.*** Earlier we described a 6-year-old who said that a tall, thin glass had more water than a short, wide dish because of the height difference between the two containers. At the same time, she showed through her gestures that the tall container had a smaller diameter than the short one. Such discrepancies in what children say and do suggest a possible readiness for developing new ideas and logical reasoning skills—for instance, a readiness for acquiring conservation of liquid (Goldin-Meadow, 1997, 2006).

In some instances adults might assess children's current knowledge by asking them to draw rather than describe what they have learned. For example, Figure 7-6 shows 8-year-old Noah's knowledge of how a

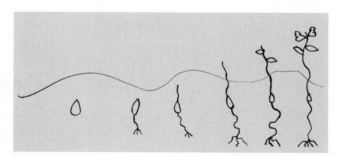

Figure 7-6

Noah's picture of how a seed becomes a plant.

Development and Practice

Getting and Keeping Children's Attention

- **Capture children's interest and attention with bright colors, intriguing sounds, and objects that invite manipulation and exploration.**

  A preschool teacher provides several musical instruments (e.g., a xylophone, toy guitar, and set of drums) for the children to play with. The teacher also allows the children to take turns composing simple songs on the classroom piano.

- **Minimize distractions, especially when working with young children.**

  A school psychologist is administering a battery of tests to a 7-year-old boy who is suspected of having a significant learning disability. Before the testing session, the psychologist puts away the kachina doll and Russian nesting dolls that decorate her office shelves. She also removes all of the testing materials from sight, putting items in front of the boy only as it is time to use them.

- **Present stimulating activities and lessons in which children *want* to pay attention.**

  In a unit on nutrition, a high school biology teacher has students determine the nutritional value of various menu items at a popular local fast-food restaurant.

- **Get children physically involved in tasks and lessons.**

  A middle school history teacher plans a special day late in the school year when all of his students will "go back in time" to the American Civil War. In preparation for the event, the students spend several weeks learning about the Battle of Gettysburg, researching typical dress and meals of the era, gathering appropriate clothing and equipment, and preparing snacks and lunches. On the day of the "battle," students assume various roles: Union and Confederate soldiers, government officials, journalists, merchants, housewives, doctors and nurses, and so on.

- **Incorporate a variety of activities into the daily schedule.**

  After explaining how to calculate the areas of squares and rectangles, a fourth-grade teacher has her students practice calculating areas in a series of increasingly challenging word problems. She then breaks the class into small cooperative groups. Each group is given a tape measure and calculator and asked to determine the area of the classroom floor, excluding those parts of the floor covered by several built-in cabinets that extend into the room. To complete the task, the students must divide the room into several smaller rectangles, compute the area of each rectangle separately, and add the subareas together.

- **Provide frequent breaks from sedentary activities.**

  To provide practice with the alphabet, a kindergarten teacher occasionally has students make letters with their bodies: one child standing with arms extended up and out to make a *Y*, two children bending over and joining hands to form an *M*, and so on.

---

seed becomes a plant. His picture clearly reflects his understanding that roots typically go down before a stalk grows up and that leaves gradually increase in size and number.

    ● ***Give children ongoing practice in using basic information and skills.*** Some information and skills are so fundamental that growing children must become able to retrieve and use them quickly and effortlessly. For instance, to write well, children should be able to form letters and words without having to stop and think about how to make an uppercase *G* or spell the word *friend.* And to solve mathematical word problems, they should have such number facts as "2 + 4 = 6" and "5 × 9 = 45" on the tips of their tongues.

    Ultimately, children can automatize basic information and skills only by using and practicing them repeatedly (J. C. Anderson, 1983; W. Schneider & Shiffrin, 1977). This is definitely *not* to say that teachers should fill each day with endless drill-and-practice exercises involving isolated facts and procedures. Automatization can occur just as readily when the basics are embedded in a variety of stimulating, challenging (and perhaps authentic) activities.

    The Developmental Trends table "Basic Information Processing Characteristics at Different Age Levels" summarizes the information processing capabilities of children and adolescents in various age-groups. We now focus on two manifestations of the *central executive:* metacognition and cognitive strategies.

Metacognition and Cognitive Strategies

As children grow older, they become more knowledgeable about their cognitive processes, and they increasingly take active control of these processes. Such knowledge and control of one's own mental processes is known as **metacognition,** and the specific mental processes in which they intentionally engage are known as **cognitive strategies.** In this section we look at development in five important aspects of metacognition: learning strategies, problem-solving strategies, metacognitive awareness, self-regulated learning, and epistemological beliefs.

metacognition
Knowledge and beliefs about one's own cognitive processes, as well as efforts to regulate those cognitive processes to maximize learning and memory.

cognitive strategy
Specific mental process that people intentionally use to acquire or manipulate information.

Developmental Trends

Basic Information Processing Characteristics at Different Age Levels

Age	What You Might Observe	Diversity	Implications
Infancy (Birth–2 Years) 	· Some ability to learn and remember evident from birth · Adult-like hearing acuity within hours after birth · Considerable improvement in visual acuity during the first year · Preference for moderately complex stimuli · Attention easily drawn to intense or novel stimuli · By 3 or 4 months of age, some ability to integrate information (e.g., acquisition of general concepts such as *dog* and *chair*)	· Attention spans are partly due to differences in temperament, but persistent inability to focus on any one object may signal a cognitive disability. · Exploration tendencies vary considerably: Some children may constantly seek new experiences, whereas others may be more comfortable with familiar objects.	· Change some toys and materials regularly to capture infants' interests and provide new experiences. · Provide objects that can be easily categorized (e.g., colored blocks, plastic farm animals). · Allow for differences in interest, attention span, and exploratory behavior; offer choices of toys and activities.
Early Childhood (2–6 Years) 	· Short attention span · Distractibility · Increasing conscious recall of past events · Some understanding and use of symbols · Limited knowledge base with which to interpret new experiences	· Pronounced disabilities in information processing (e.g., attention-deficit hyperactivity disorder, dyslexia) begin to reveal themselves in children's behaviors or academic performance. · Children's prior knowledge differs markedly depending on their cultural and socioeconomic backgrounds.	· Change activities often. · Keep unnecessary distractions to a minimum. · Provide a variety of experiences (field trips to the library, fire department, etc.) that enrich children's knowledge base. · Consult experts when learning delays or behavior problems might reflect a cognitive disability.
Middle Childhood (6–10 Years) 	· Increasing ability to attend to important stimuli and ignore irrelevant stimuli · Increasingly symbolic nature of thought and knowledge · Gradual automatization of many basic skills · Increasing exposure to environments beyond the home and family, leading to an expanding knowledge base · Knowledge of academic subject matter consisting largely of discrete, unintegrated facts, especially in science and social studies	· Many children with learning disabilities or attention-deficit hyperactivity disorder have short attention spans and are easily distracted. · Some children with learning disabilities have a smaller working memory capacity than their peers. · Mild cognitive disabilities may not become evident until the middle or upper elementary grades.	· Intersperse sedentary activities with physically more active ones to help children maintain attention. · Provide many opportunities to practice basic knowledge and skills (e.g., number facts, word recognition), often through authentic, motivating, and challenging tasks. · Begin to explore hierarchies, cause and effect, and other interrelationships among ideas in various disciplines.
Early Adolescence (10–14 Years) 	· Ability to attend to a single task for an hour or more · Basic skills in reading, writing, and mathematics (e.g., word identification, common word spellings, basic math facts) largely automatized · Growing (although not necessarily well integrated) knowledge base related to various topics and academic disciplines	· Many adolescents with information processing difficulties have trouble paying attention for a typical class period. · Many adolescents with sensory or physical disabilities (e.g., those who are blind or in a wheelchair) have less-than-average knowledge about some topics, due to fewer opportunities to explore the world around them.	· Provide variety in learning activities as a way of keeping young adolescents' attention. · Frequently point out how concepts and ideas are related to one another, both within and across content domains. · Provide extra guidance and support for those with diagnosed or suspected information processing difficulties.
Late Adolescence (14–18 Years)	· Ability to attend to a single task for lengthy periods · Extensive and somewhat integrated knowledge in some content domains	· High school students have choices in course selection, leading to differences in the extent of their knowledge base in various content areas. · Students' attention can vary considerably from one class to another, depending on their intrinsic interest in the subject matter at hand. (We'll look at developmental changes in intrinsic motivation in Chapter 13.)	· Occasionally give assignments that require adolescents to focus on a particular task for a long period. · Consistently encourage adolescents to think about the "hows" and "whys" of what they are learning. · Assess learning in ways that require adolescents to depict relationships among ideas.

Learning Strategies

Toddlers as young as 18 months show some conscious attempts to remember something. For example, when asked to remember where a Big Bird doll has been hidden in their home, they may stare or point at its location until they are able to go get it (DeLoache, Cassidy, & Brown, 1985). Yet overall, young children rarely make a point of trying to learn and remember something. For instance, 4- and 5-year-olds can remember a set of objects more successfully by playing with the objects than by intentionally trying to remember them (L. S. Newman, 1990).

As they progress through the elementary and secondary grades, children and adolescents develop *learning strategies*—techniques that they intentionally use to learn something—that help them remember information more effectively. Three that appear during the school years are rehearsal, organization, and elaboration.

Rehearsal. What do you do if you need to remember a telephone number for a few minutes? Do you repeat it to yourself over and over as a way of keeping it in your working memory until you can dial it? Such repetition of information as a way of remembering it is known as **rehearsal.**

Rehearsal is rare in preschoolers but increases in frequency and effectiveness throughout the elementary school years. By age 7 or 8, many children spontaneously rehearse individual pieces of information as a way of more easily remembering the information. By age 9 or 10, they become more strategic, combining several items into a single list as they rehearse. For example, if they hear the list "cat, dog, horse," they might say "cat" after the first item, "cat, dog" after the second, and "cat, dog, horse" after the third. Repeating list items in this cumulative manner helps children remember them more successfully, at least for a minute or so (Bjorklund & Coyle, 1995; Kunzinger, 1985; Lehmann & Hasselhorn, 2007). Yet rehearsal is a relatively *in*effective strategy for remembering information over the long run unless, in the process, children also try to make sense of the information by relating it to things they already know (Cermak & Craik, 1979).

Organization. Take a minute to study and remember the following 12 words, then cover them and try to recall as many as you can:

shirt	table	hat
carrot	bed	squash
pants	potato	stool
chair	shoe	bean

In what order did you remember the words? Did you recall them in their original order, or did you rearrange them somehow? If you are like most people, you grouped the words into three semantic categories—clothing, furniture, and vegetables—and recalled them category by category. In other words, you used **organization** to help you learn and remember the information.

As early as 3 or 4 months old, children begin to organize their experiences into categories (Quinn, 2002; Quinn & Bhatt, 2006). For instance, after seeing pictures of various dogs, they may gradually lose interest (reflecting the *habituation* we spoke of in Chapter 2), but their interest is apt to pick up again when, for a change, they see a picture of a cat. As infants approach their first birthday, some of their categories seem to be based on perceptual similarity (e.g., *balls* are round, *blocks* are cubes), but they also show emerging knowledge of more general, abstract categories (e.g., *vehicles, furniture*) (Horst, Oakes, & Madole, 2005; Mandler, 2007b; Pauen, 2002). By age 2, children may physically pick up objects and sort them by theme or function, perhaps using categories such as "things for the feet" or "kitchen things" (DeLoache & Todd, 1988; Fenson, Vella, & Kennedy, 1989; Mandler, Fivush, & Reznick, 1987).

As children move through the elementary, middle school, and secondary grades, they increasingly organize information to help learn it (Lucariello, Kyratzis, & Nelson, 1992; Nguyen & Murphy, 2003; Plumert, 1994; Pressley & Hilden, 2006). Their organizational patterns become more sophisticated, reflecting a variety of semantic, hierarchical, and often fairly abstract categories. They can also be more flexible in their organizational schemes. For

rehearsal
Attempt to learn and remember information by repeating it over and over.

organization
Process of identifying interrelationships among pieces of information as a way of learning them more effectively.

MyEducationLab

Notice Paul's ability to consider multiple organizational structures for sorting shells in the "Intelligence: Late Adolescence" video. (Find Video Examples in Chapter 7 of MyEducationLab.)

example, consider the alternatives that 17-year-old Paul identifies for organizing shells in the "Intelligence: Late Adolescence" video in MyEducationLab:

> Yeah, I could do them by color, smoothness. Some are rough, some got little jagged edges on them. Some are just smooth. And these big ones, they could do like patterns and stuff.

Elaboration.   If we authors tell you that we've both spent many years living in Colorado, you will probably conclude that we either live or have lived in or near the Rocky Mountains. In this situation you're not only learning the information we told you, you're also learning some information that you yourself supplied. This process of using your existing knowledge to embellish on new information is known as **elaboration.** Elaborating on new information typically facilitates learning and memory, sometimes quite dramatically.

Children begin to elaborate on their experiences in the preschool years (Fivush, Haden, & Adam, 1995). As a strategy that they *intentionally* use to help them learn, however, elaboration appears relatively late in development (usually around puberty) and gradually increases throughout the teenage years (W. Schneider & Pressley, 1989). Even in high school, it is primarily students with high academic achievement who use their existing knowledge to help them expand on and remember new information. Low achievers are much less likely to use elaboration when they study, and many students of all ability levels resort to rehearsal for difficult, hard-to-understand material (J. E. Barnett, 2001; Pressley, 1982). The following interview with 15-year-old "Beth," who earns mostly As in her classes but must work hard to get them, illustrates how infrequently some high school students elaborate on classroom subject matter:

Adult: Once you have some information that you think you need to know, what types of things do you do so that you will remember it?

Beth: I take notes . . . [pause].

Adult: Is that all you do?

Beth: Usually. Sometimes I make flash cards.

Adult: What types of things do you usually put on flash cards?

Beth: I put words I need to know. Like spelling words. I put dates and what happened then.

Adult: How would you normally study flash cards or your notes?

Beth: My notes, I read them over a few times. Flash cards I look at once and try to remember what's on the other side and what follows it. (interview courtesy of Evie Greene)

Notice how Beth emphasizes taking notes and studying flash cards, approaches that typically require little or no elaboration. In fact, the repetitive use of flash cards is really just a form of rehearsal.

Problem-Solving Strategies

By the time children are a year old, they have some ability to think about and solve problems. Imagine that an infant sees an attractive toy beyond her reach. One end of a string is attached to the toy, and its other end is attached to a cloth closer at hand. But between the cloth and the infant is a foam rubber barrier. The infant puts two and two together, realizing that to accomplish her goal (getting the toy), she has to do several things in sequence. She removes the barrier, pulls the cloth toward her, grabs the string, and reels in the toy (Willatts, 1990). This ability to break a problem into two or more subgoals and work toward each one in turn continues to develop during the preschool and elementary school years (e.g., Klahr & Robinson, 1981; Welsh, 1991).

The equipment: Balance and weights

The problem

Figure 7-7

A beam without weights balances on a fulcrum located at its center. After weights are hung from the beam in the manner shown here, will the beam continue to balance? If not, which side of the beam will drop?

elaboration

Process of using prior knowledge to embellish on new information and thereby learn it more effectively.

As children get older, their problem-solving strategies become increasingly mental rather than behavioral. Often their mental problem solving involves applying certain *rules* to a problem, with more complex and effective rules evolving over time. As an example, consider the balancing task depicted in Figure 7-7. The top half of the figure shows a metal beam balancing on a fulcrum at its midpoint. In the bottom half of the figure, we hold the beam steady while hanging 3- and 6-pound weights at particular locations (nine notches to the left of the fulcrum and four notches to the right, respectively). Will the beam continue to be balanced when we let go of it, or will one side fall?

Children acquire a series of increasingly complex rules to solve such a problem (Siegler, 1976, 1978). Initially (perhaps at age 5), they consider only the amount of weight on each side of the beam. Comparing 6 pounds to 3 pounds, they would predict that the right side of the beam will fall. Later (perhaps at age 9), they begin to consider distance as well as weight. They realize that weights located farther from the fulcrum have a greater effect, but their reasoning is not precise enough to ensure correct solutions. For the problem in Figure 7-7, they would merely guess at how greater distance compensates for greater weight. Eventually (perhaps in high school), they may develop a rule that reflects a multiplicative relationship between weight and distance:

> For the beam to balance, the product of weight and distance on one side must equal the product of weight and distance on the other side. In cases where the two products are unequal, the side with the larger product will fall.

Applying this rule to the problem in Figure 7-7, they would determine that the product on the left side ($3 \times 9 = 27$) is greater than the product on the right side ($6 \times 4 = 24$) and so would correctly predict that the left side will fall.

Strategy development as "overlapping waves."   Children tend to acquire new learning and problem-solving strategies gradually over time. Initially, they are likely to use a strategy infrequently and ineffectively. With time and practice, they become more adept at applying it efficiently, flexibly, and successfully to tackle challenging tasks (P. A. Alexander, Graham, & Harris, 1998; Siegler & Alibali, 2005).

By the time children reach elementary school, they may have several strategies to choose from when dealing with a particular learning or problem-solving task, and the specific strategy they use may vary from one occasion to another. Some strategies are apt to be developmentally more advanced than others, yet because children initially have trouble using the more advanced ones effectively, they may resort to less efficient but more dependable "backup" strategies. For example, even after children have learned their basic math facts ($2 + 4 = 6$, $9 - 7 = 2$, etc.), they sometimes resort to counting on their fingers to solve simple addition and subtraction problems. Eventually, however, children acquire sufficient proficiency with their new strategies that they can comfortably leave their less efficient ones behind (P. A. Alexander et al., 1998; Siegler & Alibali, 2005).

From an information processing perspective, then, development of strategies does not occur in discrete, one-step-at-a-time stages. Instead, each strategy develops slowly and increases in frequency and effectiveness over a lengthy period, perhaps over several months or years. Later it may gradually fade from the scene as a better strategy emerges to take its place. You might think of the rise and fall of various strategies as being similar to the *overlapping waves* depicted in Figure 7-8 (Siegler, 1996; Siegler & Alibali, 2005).

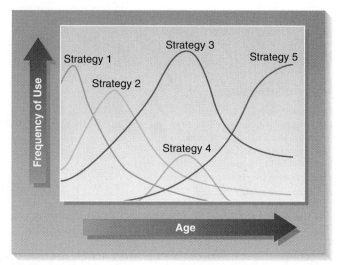

Figure 7-8

Strategic development as overlapping waves: Children gradually replace simple strategies with more advanced and effective ones. Here we see how five different strategies for dealing with the same task might change in frequency over time.
From *Children's Thinking* (4th ed., p. 98), by R. Siegler and M. W. Alibali, 2005, Upper Saddle River, NJ: Prentice Hall. Copyright 2005 by Prentice Hall. Adapted with permission of Prentice-Hall, Inc., Upper Saddle River, NJ.

Metacognitive Awareness

In addition to acquiring new learning and problem-solving strategies, children acquire increasingly sophisticated knowledge about the nature of thinking. This **metacognitive awareness** includes awareness of thought processes both in general and in oneself, an understanding of the limits of human memory, and knowledge of the relative effectiveness of various learning strategies.

Awareness of the existence of thought.   By the time children are 3 years old, they are aware of thinking as an entity in its own right (Flavell, Green, & Flavell, 1995). Their initial understanding of thought is quite simplistic, however. They are likely to say that a person is

metacognitive awareness
Extent to which one is able to reflect on the nature of one's own thinking processes.

"thinking" only when he or she is actively engaged in a challenging task and has a thoughtful or puzzled facial expression. They also view thinking and learning as relatively passive activities (e.g., the mind acquires and holds information but doesn't do much with it), rather than as the active, constructive processes they actually are (Flavell et al., 1995; Wellman, 1990).

Awareness of one's own thought processes. Young children have only a limited ability to look inward at their own thoughts and knowledge (Flavell, Green, & Flavell, 2000). Although many preschoolers have the words *know, remember,* and *forget* in their vocabularies, they don't fully grasp the nature of these mental phenomena in themselves. For instance, 3-year-olds use the term *forget* simply to mean "not knowing" something, regardless of whether they knew the information at an earlier time (Lyon & Flavell, 1994). And when 4- and 5-year-old children are taught a new piece of information, they may say that they've known it for quite some time (M. Taylor, Esbensen, & Bennett, 1994). The following interview, which a kindergarten teacher aide conducted with a bright 5-year-old whom we'll call "Ethan," illustrates the relatively superficial awareness that young children have of their own thought processes:

Aide:	When you learn a new song, like "The Horne Street School Song," how do you remember the words?
Ethan:	I just remember. I didn't know how to sing it for a while until I listened to the words enough to remember them.
Aide:	When I ask you during group time to "put on your thinking caps," what do I mean?
Ethan:	It means think. You think hard until you know what you are trying to think about. . . . I don't really know how you think, you just do. . . .
Aide:	How do you remember to give Mommy and Papa papers that we send home?
Ethan:	My good memory.
Aide:	Why do you have a good memory?
Ethan:	It's just good. It started when I turned three. I still had it when I was four, and now when I am five. (interview courtesy of Betsy Hopkins)

MyEducationLab

Go to the Building Teaching Skills and Dispositions exercise "Assessing Students' Metacognitive Awareness and Cognitive Strategies" in Chapter 7 of MyEducationLab to observe developmental trends in metacognition.

During the elementary and secondary school years, children and adolescents become better able to reflect on their own thought processes and increasingly aware of the nature of their thinking and learning (Wellman & Hickling, 1994). You can observe this developmental progression firsthand by completing a Building Teaching Skills and Dispositions exercise in Chapter 7 of MyEducationLab.

Understanding of memory limitations. Young children tend to be overly optimistic about how much they can remember. As they grow older and encounter a wide variety of learning tasks, they discover that some things are more difficult to learn than others (Flavell et al., 2002; B. L. Schwartz & Perfect, 2002). They also begin to realize that their memories are not perfect and that they cannot possibly remember everything they see or hear. For example, in one study (Flavell, Friedrichs, & Hoyt, 1970), preschoolers and elementary school children were shown pictures of 1 to 10 objects and asked to predict how many objects they could remember for a short time period. The average predictions of each of four age-groups and the average number of objects the children actually remembered were as follows:

Age-Group	Predicted Number	Actual Number
Preschool	7.2	3.5
Kindergarten	8.0	3.6
Grade 2	6.0	4.4
Grade 4	6.1	5.5

Notice that children in all four age-groups predicted that they would remember more objects than they actually did. But the older children were more realistic about the limitations of their memories.

Young children's overly optimistic assessment of their memory capabilities may actually be beneficial for their cognitive development. In particular, it may give them the necessary confidence to try new and difficult learning tasks—challenges that, from Vygotsky's perspective, promote cognitive growth (Bjorklund & Green, 1992).

Knowledge about effective learning and memory strategies.   Imagine that it's winter and you live in a cold climate. Just before you go to bed, some friends ask you to go ice skating with them after class tomorrow. What might you do to be sure you will remember to take your ice skates to class with you? Older children typically generate more strategies than younger children for remembering to take a pair of skates to school. Yet even 5- and 6-year-olds can often identify one or more effective strategies—perhaps writing a note to themselves, recording a reminder on a tape recorder, or leaving their skates next to their school bag (Kreutzer, Leonard, & Flavell, 1975).

Not only do children acquire more effective learning strategies (e.g., organization, elaboration) as they grow older, but they also become increasingly aware of what strategies are effective in different situations (Lovett & Flavell, 1990; W. Schneider & Lockl, 2002; Short, Schatschneider, & Friebert, 1993). Consider the simple idea that when you don't learn something the first time you try, you need to study it again. This is a strategy that 8-year-olds use, but 6-year-olds do not (Masur, McIntyre, & Flavell, 1973). Similarly, 10th graders are more aware than 8th graders of the advantages of using elaboration to learn new information (H. S. Waters, 1982). Even so, many children and adolescents seem relatively uninformed about which learning strategies work most effectively in different situations (Kuhn, Garcia-Mila, Zohar, & Andersen, 1995; J. W. Thomas, 1993). The following interview with "Amy," a 16-year-old with a history of low school achievement, illustrates how metacognitively naive some adolescents are:

Adult:	What is learning?
Amy:	Something you do to get knowledge.
Adult:	What is knowledge?
Amy:	Any information that I don't know.
Adult:	What about the things you already know?
Amy:	That doesn't count.
Adult:	Doesn't count?
Amy:	As knowledge, because I already know it.
Adult:	How do you know when you have learned something?
Amy:	When I can repeat it, and it is the same as what the teacher said or what I read, and I can remember it forever or a really long time. (interview courtesy of Jennifer Glynn)

Notice how Amy thinks she has learned something when she can repeat what a teacher or textbook has told her. She says nothing about *understanding* classroom subject matter. And curiously, she thinks of knowledge as things she *doesn't* know.

Self-Regulated Learning

As children and adolescents gain awareness of their learning and memory processes, they become more capable of **self-regulated learning**—that is, they begin to control and direct their own learning. Self-regulated learning involves strategies such as these:

- Setting goals for a learning activity
- Planning an effective use of learning and study time
- Keeping attention on the subject matter to be learned, and motivating oneself to persist in learning it
- Identifying and using appropriate learning strategies
- Monitoring progress toward goals, evaluating the effectiveness of learning strategies, and adjusting goals or learning strategies as necessary
- Evaluating the final knowledge gained from the learning activity (Meltzer & Krishnan, 2007; Muis, 2007; B. J. Zimmerman & Schunk, 2004)

As you can see, self-regulated learning is a complex, multifaceted process. For example, effective learners use a variety of strategies to keep their minds on their work, perhaps engaging in encouraging self-talk ("Good job, you're making progress") or turning a study task into an enjoyable game (Wolters, 2003, p. 194).

One especially important aspect of self-regulated learning is **comprehension monitoring,** checking one's own understanding frequently while learning something new. Comprehension monitoring skills continue to improve throughout the school years, such that youngsters become increasingly aware of when they actually know something. Young children (e.g., those in the early elementary grades) often overestimate how much they know or

self-regulated learning
Directing and controlling one's own cognitive processes in order to learn successfully.

comprehension monitoring
Process of checking oneself to make sure one understands what is being studied.

Effective learners engage in self-regulated learning. For instance, they set goals for themselves, choose effective learning strategies, and monitor their learning progress.

understand (W. Schneider & Lockl, 2002). As a result, they don't study new material as much as they should, and they seldom ask questions when they receive incomplete or confusing information (Dufresne & Kobasigawa, 1989; Markman, 1977; T. M. McDevitt, Spivey, Sheehan, Lennon, & Story, 1990). Yet even adolescents sometimes have difficulty assessing their own knowledge accurately. For instance, they may overestimate how well they will perform on an exam (e.g., Hacker, Bol, Horgan, & Rakow, 2000).

In its "mature" form, then, self-regulated learning is virtually nonexistent in elementary school students, and even many secondary students have difficulty effectively regulating their own learning (M. B. Bronson, 2000; B. J. Zimmerman & Risemberg, 1997). For example, in a study at a middle school in inner-city Philadelphia (B. L. Wilson & Corbett, 2001), the vast majority of students planned to graduate from high school and attend college. Yet few of them had a good understanding of what it would take to do well in their classes, as this interview with one student reveals:

Adult:	Are you on track to meet your goals?
Student:	No. I need to study more.
Adult:	How do you know that?
Student:	I just know by some of my grades. [mostly Cs]
Adult:	Why do you think you will be more inclined to do it in high school?
Student:	I don't want to get let back. I want to go to college.
Adult:	What will you need to do to get better grades?
Student:	Just do more and more work. I can rest when the school year is over. (dialogue from B. L. Wilson & Corbett, 2001, p. 23)

Notice how simplistic the student's notion of studying is: "Just do more and more work." Nowhere in the conversation does the student mention effective learning and self-regulation strategies, such as setting goals, organizing and elaborating on classroom material, or monitoring progress.

Epistemological Beliefs

As someone who learns new things every day, you undoubtedly have ideas about what "knowledge" and "learning" are. Such ideas are collectively known as **epistemological beliefs.** Included in people's epistemological beliefs are their views about the stability, certainty, structure, and source of knowledge, as well as about the goals and speed of learning activities. As children and adolescents develop, many (though not all) of them change their beliefs about knowledge and learning. Typical changes are shown in Table 7-1. For example, most children in the elementary grades think that the absolute truth about any topic is "out there" somewhere, waiting to be discovered (Astington & Pelletier, 1996; Kuhn & Weinstock, 2002). As they reach adolescence, some begin to realize that knowledge is a subjective entity and that two or more perspectives on a topic may each have some merit (Schommer, 1994b; Schommer, Calvert, Gariglietti, & Bajaj, 1997). Eventually some realize that certain perspectives have more merit than others—that each must be evaluated on the basis of research evidence and logical arguments (Kuhn & Weinstock, 2002).

Additional changes may also occur in high school. For example, 12th graders are more likely than 9th graders to believe that knowledge consists of complex interrelationships (rather than discrete facts), that learning happens slowly (rather than quickly), and that learning can be enhanced by practice and better strategies (Schommer et al., 1997). Some high school students continue to have very superficial views of knowledge and learning, however. For instance, recall how 16-year-old Amy defined *learning* simply as "something you do to get knowledge" and *knowledge* as "any information that I don't know."

Some epistemological beliefs are specific to particular content domains (Buehl & Alexander, 2006; Muis, Bendixen, & Haerle, 2006). For example, adolescents may believe that knowledge in mathematics, the natural sciences, and history is pretty much a "sure thing," whereas knowledge in some social sciences (e.g., psychology) is more tentative (D. Estes, Chandler, Horvath, & Backus, 2003; Haenen, Schrijnemakers, & Stufkens, 2003; B. K. Hofer, 2000; Muis, 2007; Schommer, 1994b). And many adolescents think that learning in math and physics classes means memorizing procedures and formulas and finding single "right" answers to problems (Muis, 2004; Schoenfeld, 1988).

Youngsters' epistemological beliefs influence the ways in which they study and learn at school (B. K. Hofer & Pintrich, 2002; Purdie, Hattie, & Douglas, 1996; Schommer et al., 1997).

MyEducationLab

Learn more about developmental changes in high school students' epistemological beliefs by completing an Understanding Research exercise in Chapter 7's Activities and Applications section in MyEducationLab.

epistemological beliefs
Beliefs regarding the nature of knowledge and knowledge acquisition.

Table 7-1   Developmental Changes in Epistemological Beliefs

With Regard to . . .	Children Initially Believe That . . .	As They Develop, They May Eventually Begin to Realize That . . .
The stability and certainty of knowledge	Knowledge about a topic is a fixed, unchanging, absolute "truth" that need not be questioned.	Knowledge about a topic (even that of experts) is tentative and dynamic. It continues to evolve as ongoing research adds new insights and ideas. Multiple perspectives about an issue are possible, but each should be critically examined and evaluated on the basis of objective evidence and logical arguments.
The structure of knowledge	Knowledge is a collection of discrete, largely unrelated facts.	Knowledge is a set of complex and interrelated ideas.
The source of knowledge	Knowledge comes from outside the learner, perhaps from firsthand observation of the physical world or perhaps from a teacher or other authority figure.	Knowledge is derived and constructed by learners themselves.
The goal of a learning activity	Learning involves committing certain facts and procedures to memory.	Learning involves gaining deep understanding of complex concepts and their interrelationships.
The speed of learning	Knowledge is acquired quickly, and in an all-or-nothing fashion, or else not at all. As a result, people either know something or they don't.	Knowledge is acquired gradually over time. Thus people can have greater or lesser degrees of knowledge about a topic.

Sources: Astington & Pelletier, 1996; B. K. Hofer & Pintrich, 1997, 2002; Kuhn & Franklin, 2006; Kuhn & Park, 2005; Kuhn & Weinstock, 2002; M. C. Linn, Songer, & Eylon, 1996; Muis, 2007; Perkins & Ritchhart, 2004; Schommer, 1994a, 1994b; Schommer et al., 1997.

When students believe that knowledge consists of discrete facts that are indisputably right or wrong, that one either has that knowledge or doesn't, and that learning happens quickly if at all, they may focus on rote memorization of the subject matter and easily give up if they find themselves struggling to understand it. In contrast, when students believe that knowledge is a complex body of information that is learned gradually with time and effort, they are apt to use a wide variety of learning strategies, and they persist until they've made sense of what they're studying (D. L. Butler & Winne, 1995; Kardash & Howell, 1996; Schommer, 1994b). Not surprisingly, then, students with more advanced epistemological beliefs achieve at higher levels in the classroom (B. K. Hofer & Pintrich, 1997; Schommer, 1994a).

More advanced levels of achievement may, in turn, bring about more advanced views about knowledge and learning (Schommer, 1994b; Strike & Posner, 1992). The more that students get beyond the "basics" and explore a discipline in depth—whether it is science, mathematics, history, or some other content domain—the more they discover that learning involves acquiring an integrated and cohesive set of ideas, that even experts don't know everything about a topic, and that truly complete and accurate "knowledge" of how the world operates may ultimately be an unattainable goal.

We speculate, however, that less sophisticated epistemological beliefs may have some benefits for young children. Children may initially be more motivated to learn about a topic if they think there are absolute, unchanging facts (and sometimes there are!) that they can easily learn and remember. And it is often very efficient to rely on parents, teachers, and the library as authoritative sources for desired information.

Cultural Diversity in Metacognition

Children's metacognitive beliefs and strategies are, in part, the result of the particular social and cultural environments in which they grow up. For instance, researchers have observed some consistent cultural differences in views about the nature of knowledge and learning. From the perspective of mainstream Western culture, the acquisition of knowledge is largely for one's personal benefit: People learn in order to understand the world and acquire new skills and abilities. But for many people in China, learning also has moral and social dimensions: It enables an individual to become increasingly virtuous and honorable and to contribute in significant ways to the betterment of society. From a traditional East Asian perspective, true learning is not a quick-and-easy process. Rather, it comes only with a great deal of diligence, concentration, and perseverance (Dahlin & Watkins, 2000; H. Grant & Dweck, 2001; J. Li & Fischer, 2004).

Cultural differences have also been observed in children's willingness to critically evaluate the knowledge and beliefs that adults pass along to them. Some cultures place high value on respecting one's elders or certain religious teachings. In doing so they may foster the epistemological belief that "truth" is a cut-and-dried entity that is best gained from authority figures (Kuhn, Daniels, & Krishnan, 2003; Qian & Pan, 2002). In addition, a cultural emphasis on maintaining group harmony may discourage children from discussing and critiquing diverse perspectives on a controversial topic (Kağitçibaşi, 2007; Kuhn & Park, 2005).

Consistent with a belief that learning requires diligence and perseverance, many East Asian parents and teachers encourage frequent use of rehearsal and rote memorization as learning strategies (Dahlin & Watkins, 2000; D. Y. F. Ho, 1994; Purdie & Hattie, 1996). Rehearsal and memorization are also common in cultures that value committing oral histories or verbatim passages of sacred text to memory (MacDonald, Uesiliana, & Hayne, 2000; Rogoff et al., 2007; Q. Wang & Ross, 2007). In contrast, many schools in mainstream Western societies ask students to focus on making sense of classroom material rather than memorizing it word for word. Even so, Western schools typically do insist that students learn certain things (e.g., word spellings, multiplication tables) by heart (Q. Wang & Ross, 2007).

This is not to say that school is the primary context in which youngsters acquire *all* learning strategies. For instance, in African cultures that have a strong tradition of oral storytelling, children have better strategies for remembering orally transmitted stories than American children (E. F. Dube, 1982). And in one study (Kearins, 1981), unschooled children in Australian aborigine communities more effectively remembered the spatial arrangements of objects than children who attended Australian schools. The aborigine children lived in a harsh desert environment with little rainfall, so their families moved frequently from place to place in search of new food sources. With each move, the children had to quickly learn the spatial arrangements of subtle landmarks in the local vicinity in order to find their way home from any direction.

The Developmental Trends table "Cognitive Strategies and Metacognitive Understandings at Different Age Levels" summarizes developmental changes in children's cognitive strategies and metacognitive understandings, as well as some of the metacognitive diversity you are likely to see in any age-group.

Promoting Metacognitive and Strategic Development

Most sophisticated cognitive processes involve metacognition; hence, metacognitive development is central to cognitive development. Children are more likely to acquire and use effective strategies when they are aware of the various strategies they use and monitor how well each one helps them reach their goals (Kuhn, 2001b). Following are several suggestions for fostering the development of metacognition and cognitive strategies.

• **_Engage children in discussions about the mind._** As we've seen, even preschoolers have some awareness of the mind and its activities. Adults probably enhance this awareness by regularly referring to mental activities in day-to-day conversations—for example, by asking children to put on their "thinking caps" or describing someone's mind as "wandering" (Wellman & Hickling, 1994).

As children become more introspective in the elementary and secondary school years, they become better able to reflect on and describe the kinds of things they do (mentally) as they study and learn. At earlier points in the chapter, we've presented interviews in which children describe their views about thinking, learning, and studying. Such interviews can often shed light on young people's study strategies and epistemological beliefs. They can be especially helpful when youngsters are having trouble mastering new knowledge and skills.

• **_Model and teach effective cognitive strategies._** Adults can often foster more effective problem-solving strategies by modeling them for children. For instance, infants as young as 10 months can overcome obstacles to obtain an attractive toy if an adult shows them how to do it (Z. Chen, Sanchez, & Campbell, 1997; Want & Harris, 2001). Engaging television programs in which young children are encouraged to join on-screen characters in solving various problems (e.g., as is done in Nickelodeon's *Blue's Clues* and Public Broadcasting Service's *Super Why!*) also help young children acquire new problem-solving strategies (e.g., D. R. Anderson et al., 2000; Crawley, Anderson, Wilder, Williams, & Santomero, 1999).

Learning strategies, too, can clearly be modeled and taught. For instance, 4- and 5-year-olds can be taught to organize objects into categories as a way of helping them remember the objects (Carr & Schneider, 1991; Lange & Pierce, 1992). As children encounter increasingly challenging learning tasks at school and elsewhere, simple categorization alone is, of course,

Developmental Trends

Cognitive Strategies and Metacognitive Understandings at Different Age Levels

Age	What You Might Observe	Diversity	Implications
Infancy (Birth–2 Years)	· Use of one object to obtain another (in the second year) · Emerging ability to plan a sequence of actions to accomplish a goal (appearing sometime around age 1) · General absence of intentional learning strategies; however, toddlers may look or point at a location to remember where a desired object is hidden · Little awareness and knowledge of thought processes (may have some awareness that other people have intentions, however; see Chapter 12)	· Emergence of early problem-solving strategies is somewhat dependent on opportunities to experiment with physical objects. · Willingness to engage in trial-and-error problem solving and other exploratory behavior is partly a function of temperamental differences and physical abilities.	· Model tool use and other simple problem-solving strategies. · Pose simple problems for infants and toddlers to solve (e.g., place desired objects slightly out of reach), but monitor children's reactions to make sure they are not unnecessarily frustrated in their efforts to solve problems.
Early Childhood (2–6 Years)	· Some rehearsal beginning in the preschool years, but with little effect on learning and memory · Occasional use of organization with concrete objects · Some ability to learn simple strategies modeled by others · Awareness of thought in oneself and others, albeit in a simplistic form; limited ability to reflect on the specific *nature* of one's own thought processes · Belief that learning is a relatively passive activity · Overestimation of how much information one can typically remember	· Children's awareness of the mind and mental events depends partly on the extent to which adults talk with them about thinking processes. · Many young children with autism have little conscious awareness of the existence of thought, especially in other people (see Chapter 12).	· Talk often about thinking processes (e.g., "I *wonder* if . . . ," "Do you *remember* when . . . ?"). · Model strategies for simple memory tasks (e.g., pinning permission slips on jackets to remind children to get their parents' signatures).
Middle Childhood (6–10 Years)	· Use of rehearsal as the predominant intentional learning strategy · Gradual increase in organization as an intentional, conscious learning strategy · Emerging ability to reflect on the nature of one's own thought processes · Frequent overestimation of one's own memory capabilities · Little if any self-regulated learning · Belief that true knowledge about a topic is "out there" somewhere and can often be gained from authority figures	· Chinese and Japanese children rely more heavily on rehearsal than their peers in Western schools; this difference continues into adolescence. · Children with cognitive disabilities are less likely to organize material as they learn it. · A few high-achieving children are capable of sustained self-regulated learning, especially in the upper elementary grades.	· Encourage children to repeat and practice the things they need to learn. · To encourage organization as a learning strategy, ask children to study information that is easy to categorize. · Ask children to engage in simple, self-regulated learning tasks; give them suggestions about how to accomplish the tasks successfully.
Early Adolescence (10–14 Years)	· Emergence of elaboration as an intentional learning strategy · Few and relatively ineffective study strategies (e.g., poor note-taking skills, little if any comprehension monitoring) · Increasing flexibility in the use of learning strategies · Emerging ability to regulate one's own learning · Belief that knowledge about a topic consists of a collection of discrete facts · Recognition that diverse perspectives may all have some merit, but without a critical evaluation of each perspective	· Adolescents differ considerably in their use of effective learning strategies. · Some adolescents, including many with cognitive disabilities, have few strategies for engaging effectively in self-regulated learning.	· Ask questions that encourage adolescents to elaborate on new information. · Teach and model effective strategies within the context of various subject areas. · Assign homework and other tasks that require independent learning; provide sufficient structure to guide students' efforts. · Give adolescents frequent opportunities to assess their own learning.

continued

Developmental Trends (continued)

Age	What You Might Observe	Diversity	Implications
Late Adolescence (14–18 Years) 	· Increase in elaboration · Growing awareness of which cognitive strategies are most effective in different situations · Increasing self-regulatory learning strategies (e.g., comprehension monitoring) · Increasing realization that knowledge involves understanding interrelationships among ideas · Emerging ability and willingness to critically evaluate conflicting perspectives on an issue (in some students)	· High-achieving teenagers are most likely to use sophisticated learning strategies (e.g., elaboration); low-achieving ones typically resort to simpler, less effective strategies (e.g., rehearsal). · Many teenagers with cognitive disabilities have insufficient reading skills to learn successfully from typical high school textbooks; furthermore, their study skills tend to be unsophisticated and relatively ineffective. · Willingness to reflect on and critically evaluate others' ideas is, in part, a function of adolescents' cultural and religious upbringings.	· Continue to teach and model effective learning strategies both in and out of school. · Assign more complex independent learning tasks, giving the necessary structure and guidance for those who are not yet self-regulating learners. · Present various subject areas as dynamic entities that continue to evolve with new discoveries and theories. · Teach specific criteria (e.g., research evidence, logical consistency) by which to evaluate diverse perspectives.

MyEducationLab

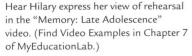

Hear Hilary express her view of rehearsal in the "Memory: Late Adolescence" video. (Find Video Examples in Chapter 7 of MyEducationLab.)

not enough. By the time they reach high school, students will need to learn—and often must be explicitly taught—strategies such as elaboration, comprehension monitoring, goal setting, note taking, and time management. Ideally, such instruction should be integrated into lessons about academic topics, rather than in a separate course or unit (Hattie, Biggs, & Purdie, 1996; Meltzer et al., 2007; Pressley, El-Dinary, Marks, Brown, & Stein, 1992). Once adolescents become proficient in advanced strategies, they are apt to find these strategies more rewarding than simple rehearsal. In the "Memory: Late Adolescence" video in MyEducationLab, 16-year-old Hilary describes her feelings about rehearsal this way:

> Just felt like I was trying to memorize for a test or something. . . . Sometimes it's kind of boring or repetitious, [just] going over it.

Small-group learning and problem-solving activities, especially when structured to encourage effective cognitive processes, can also promote more sophisticated strategies (e.g., A. King, 1999; Palincsar & Herrenkohl, 1999). One approach is to teach children how to ask one another thought-provoking questions about the material they are studying. The following exchange shows two fifth graders using such questions as they study material about tide pools and tidal zones:

Janelle:	What do you think would happen if there weren't certain zones for certain animals in the tide pools?
Katie:	They would all be, like, mixed up—and all the predators would kill all the animals that shouldn't be there and then they just wouldn't survive. 'Cause the food chain wouldn't work—'cause the top of the chain would eat all the others and there would be no place for the bottom ones to hide and be protected. And nothing left for them to eat.
Janelle:	O.K. But what about the ones that had camouflage to hide them? (A. King, 1999, p. 95)

Notice how Janelle's questions don't ask Katie to repeat what she has already learned. Instead, Katie must use what she's learned to speculate and draw inferences; in other words, she must engage in elaboration. Questioning like Janelle's appears to promote both better recall of facts and increased integration of ideas, undoubtedly because it encourages more sophisticated learning strategies (Kahl & Woloshyn, 1994; A. King, 1999; E. Wood et al., 1999).

Why are collaborative learning and problem-solving activities so beneficial? For one thing, group members scaffold one another's efforts, providing assistance on difficult tasks and monitoring one another's progress toward a particular goal. Second, group members must describe and explain their strategies, thereby allowing others to observe and possibly model them. Third, in a Vygotskian fashion, group members may internalize their group-based strategies. For instance, when they engage in mutual question asking, they may eventually ask *themselves,* and then answer, equally challenging questions as they read and study.

One effective way of acquiring new learning strategies is to practice them first in a group situation.

• *Expect and encourage increasingly independent learning over time.* On average, self-regulating learners achieve at higher levels in the classroom than non–self-regulators (Blair & Razza, 2007; Duckworth & Seligman, 2005). But self-regulated learning is a complex endeavor that involves many abilities (goal setting, attention control, flexible use of cognitive strategies, comprehension monitoring, etc.) and takes many years to master. Throughout the elementary and secondary school years, teachers and other adults must encourage and scaffold it in age-appropriate ways. For instance, they might provide examples of questions that encourage elaboration (e.g., "Explain why ____," "What is a new example of ____ ?"). They might provide a general organizational framework that children can follow while taking notes. They might provide guidance about how to develop a good summary (e.g., "Identify or invent a topic sentence," "Find supporting information for each main idea"). Such scaffolding is most likely to be helpful when children are studying subject matter they find difficult to comprehend yet *can* comprehend if they apply appropriate strategies—in other words, when the subject matter is within their zone of proximal development. As children develop increasing proficiency with each self-regulating strategy, the scaffolds can gradually be removed (Meltzer & Krishnan, 2007; Pressley et al., 1992).

   • ***Provide opportunities for children to evaluate their own learning, and help them develop mechanisms for doing so effectively.*** As noted earlier, self-regulating learners monitor their progress throughout a learning task and then evaluate their ultimate success in mastering what they've been studying. Researchers have offered several recommendations for promoting self-monitoring and self-evaluation:

   • Teach children to ask themselves, and then answer, questions about the topic (Rosenshine, Meister, & Chapman, 1996).
   • Have children set specific goals for each learning session and then describe how they've met each one (M. Morgan, 1985).
   • Provide specific criteria that children can use to judge their performance (Winne, 1995b).
   • Encourage children to evaluate their performance realistically, and then reinforce them (e.g., with praise or extra-credit points) when their evaluations match an adult's evaluation or some other external standard (McCaslin & Good, 1996; Schraw, Potenza, & Nebelsick-Gullet, 1993; Zuckerman, 1994).
   • Have children compile portfolios that include samples of their work, along with a written reflection on the quality and significance of each sample (Paris & Ayres, 1994; N. E. Perry, 1998; Silver & Kenney, 1995).

By engaging in ongoing self-monitoring and self-evaluation of their performance, children should eventually develop appropriate standards for their performance and apply those standards regularly to their accomplishments—true hallmarks of a self-regulating learner.

   • ***Promote more sophisticated epistemological beliefs.*** If they are to achieve at high levels in the high school and college years, young people must become aware that knowledge is not merely a cut-and-dried set of facts and that effective learning is not simply a process of mindlessly repeating those facts over and over. One way to foster more advanced epistemological beliefs is to talk specifically about the nature of knowledge and learning—for example, to describe learning as an active, ongoing process of making connections among ideas (Schommer, 1994b). But probably an even more effective approach is to provide experiences that lead children and adolescents to discover for themselves that knowledge is dynamic rather than static, that multiple perspectives on an issue may all have some validity, and that successful learning sometimes occurs only through effort and persistence. For example, teachers might give their students complex problems that have no clear-cut right or wrong answers, have students read conflicting accounts and interpretations of historical events, or ask students to compare several different explanations of a particular scientific phenomenon (Britt, Rouet, Georgi, & Perfetti, 1994; Leinhardt, 1994; M. C. Linn et al., 1996; Schommer, 1994b).

   In addition, discussions about controversial topics (e.g., various interpretations of a classic work of literature) can help children gain an increased understanding that there is not always a simple "right" answer to a question or issue (Kuhn, Shaw, & Felton, 1997; C. L. Smith, Maclin, Houghton, & Hennessey, 2000). Furthermore, by wrestling and struggling as a group with difficult subject matter, children may begin to understand that one's knowledge about a topic is likely to evolve and improve gradually over time. And when children have opportunities to formulate questions and problems, discuss and critique one another's explanations and analyses, and compare and evaluate potential solutions, they gain practice in these all-important skills (P. Bell & Linn, 2002; Kuhn & Weinstock, 2002; Muis et al., 2006).

MyEducationLab

Observe 8-year-old Keenan's self-evaluation of her work in the "Portfolio" video. (Find Video Examples in Chapter 7 of MyEducationLab.)

Adding a Sociocultural Element to Information Processing Theory

Earlier in the chapter we noted that children show a preference for social stimuli (e.g., human faces, their mother's voice) very early in life. Human beings appear to be predisposed to respond to and learn from others beginning on day one. For example, despite their poor eyesight, infants show preliminary signs of mimicking other people's facial expressions (e.g., by opening their mouths or sticking out their tongues) within the first hour after birth (Kugiumutzakis, 1999). Such early imitative behaviors are undoubtedly automatic and reflexive. In fact, babies appear to be hardwired for imitation to some degree. Evidence is emerging that some primate species, including human beings, have certain neurons that fire either when they perform a particular action themselves *or* when they watch another person perform it (Arbib, 2005; Iacoboni & Woods, 1999). Such neurons, known as *mirror neurons,* might explain why infants can imitate others so early in life: Some of the same neurons are involved when they watch another person's behavior and when they engage in the behavior themselves.

With the distinctly social nature of human beings in mind, some theorists have suggested that a combination of information processing and sociocultural perspectives (such as those of Vygotsky and his followers) provides a better explanation of how cognitive development occurs than either perspective can provide alone. In particular, information processing theory may tell us a great deal about *what* changes over time, and sociocultural views (notions about internalization, mediated learning experiences, guided participation, etc.) may help us explain *how* those changes occur (Gauvain, 2001; Hobson, 2004; Mareschal et al., 2007). Here we look at three aspects of this blend of information processing theory and sociocultural theory: intersubjectivity, social construction of memory, and collaborative use of cognitive strategies.

Intersubjectivity

For two people to interact and communicate, they must have shared understandings on which to build. For instance, each member of the pair should have some awareness of what the other person sees, knows, thinks, and feels. Such mutual understanding is known as **intersubjectivity.** The beginnings of intersubjectivity are seen at about 2 months of age, when infants and their caregivers focus on and interact with each other, making eye contact, exchanging smiles, taking turns vocalizing, and so on (Adamson & McArthur, 1995; Kingstone, Smilek, Ristic, Friesen, & Eastwood, 2003).

Sometime around 9 or 10 months of age, intersubjectivity becomes more complex, taking the form of **joint attention.** At this point, an infant and caregiver can focus on a single object, with both members of the pair monitoring the *other's* attention to the object and coordinating their behaviors toward the object (Adamson & McArthur, 1995; Carpenter, Nagell, & Tomasello, 1998; Trevarthen & Hubley, 1978). You can see joint attention in action as 16-month-old Corwin and his mother read a book together in the "Literacy: Infancy" video in MyEducationLab.

Early in the second year, infants also begin to show **social referencing,** looking at someone else for clues about how to respond to or feel about a particular object or event (Feinman, 1992; Klinnert, Emde, Butterfield, & Campos, 1986). Children are most likely to engage in social referencing when they encounter a new and uncertain situation. For example, in one study (Klinnert, 1984), 1- and 1½-year-old infants were shown three new toys to which their mothers had been instructed to respond with a happy, fearful, or neutral expression. Upon seeing each new toy, most infants looked at their mother and chose actions consistent with her response. They typically moved toward the toy if Mom showed pleasure, but moved away from it if she showed fear.

As information processing theorists tell us, attention is critical to learning and cognitive development. As we bring the sociocultural perspective into the picture, we see that awareness of a *partner's* attention is critical as well (Gauvain, 2001; Mundy & Newell, 2007). For instance, when an adult uses a word that a toddler has never heard before, the toddler will often look immediately at the speaker's face and follow the speaker's line of vision to the object being referenced. In this way, children probably learn many object labels (D. A. Baldwin, 2000). In general, a child can learn from a person with more experience only if both people are focusing on the same thing and *know* that they are sharing their focus. Because intersubjectivity is so criti-

MyEducationLab

Observe joint attention in the "Literacy: Infancy" video. (Find Video Examples in Chapter 7 of MyEducationLab.)

intersubjectivity
Awareness of shared perceptions and understandings that provide the foundation for social interaction.

joint attention
Phenomenon in which two people (e.g., a child and caregiver) simultaneously focus on the same object or event, monitor each other's attention, and coordinate their responses.

social referencing
Looking at someone else (e.g., a caregiver) for clues about how to respond to a particular object or event.

cal for children's ability to learn from more experienced members of their community, it appears to be a universal phenomenon across cultures (Adamson & Bakeman, 1991).

Social Construction of Memory

In Chapter 6 we explained how adults often help children construct meaning from events (see "Social Construction of Meaning," p. 216). An adult can also help a child reconstruct events that the two of them have previously experienced and stored in their respective long-term memories. Almost as soon as children are old enough to talk, their parents begin to engage them in conversations about past events (Fivush, Haden, & Reese, 1996; Gauvain, 2001; Ratner, 1984). Initially, the parents do most of the work, reminiscing, asking questions, prompting recall, and so on, but by the time children are 3, they, too, are active participants in the conversations (Fivush et al., 1996).

Discussions about past events have several benefits (Fivush, Haden, & Reese, 2006; Gauvain, 2001). First, as noted in the earlier discussion of infantile amnesia, children are more likely to remember the experiences they talk about. Second, because adults focus on certain aspects of events and not others, children learn what things are important to remember. Third, because adults are apt to interpret events in particular ways (e.g., finding some things amusing and others distasteful), children acquire perspectives and values appropriate for their culture. For example, when European American mothers recall past events with their 3-year-olds, they often refer to the thoughts and feelings of the participants. In contrast, Asian mothers are more likely to talk about social norms and expectations, such as what someone *should* have done instead. Such differences are consistent with the priorities and values of these cultures (Bauer, 2006; Mullen & Yi, 1995; Q. Wang & Ross, 2007).

Talking about events occasionally has a downside, however, especially for young children (Brainerd & Reyna, 2005; Ghetti & Alexander, 2004; Leichtman & Ceci, 1995). Imagine that a man identified as "Sam Stone" briefly visits a preschool classroom. He comments on the story the teacher is reading to the children, strolls around the perimeter of the room, waves good-bye, and leaves. Later an adult asks, "When Sam Stone got that bear dirty, did he do it on purpose or was it an accident?" and "Was Sam Stone happy or sad that he got the bear dirty?" When asked such questions, children may recall that Sam soiled a teddy bear, even though he never touched a stuffed animal during his visit (Leichtman & Ceci, 1995, p. 571). Such susceptibility to leading questions is more common in 3- and 4-year-olds than in 5- and 6-year-olds. Older children are less likely to be swayed by the power of suggestion (Leichtman & Ceci, 1995).

When asking children to describe a past event, adults must be careful not to ask leading questions that may influence what children "remember."

When teachers and other professionals ask young children to describe events they have witnessed—say, a fight on the playground or a possible theft in the classroom—they should be careful to ask questions that do not communicate any foregone conclusions about what children may have experienced or witnessed. For instance, one might simply say, "Tell me what happened as best as you can remember it." Furthermore, adults should, whenever possible, seek additional evidence that might either corroborate or cast doubt on young children's recollections.

Collaborative Use of Cognitive Strategies

Earlier in the chapter we mentioned that children acquire more sophisticated cognitive strategies when adults model and teach those strategies. A sociocultural perspective suggests that adults should go a step further, engaging children in activities that require collaborative use of particular strategies. Through joint discussion and use of strategies—typically with considerable adult guidance and scaffolding at first—children gradually internalize those strategies and begin using them independently (Freund, 1990; Gauvain, 2001). The following example illustrates such internalization:

> Ben, age 4, shuffles into the family room with a jar of pennies that he has been saving. He announces to his mother that he wants to count them to see how much money he has. With mother looking on, Ben dumps the coins on the coffeetable and begins to count the pennies, one by one. All is going well until he counts some pennies a second time. Mother interrupts and suggests that he put the pennies in rows so that he doesn't count any twice. Ben agrees to do this, but he aligns his rows poorly. Mother shows him how to straighten them by making a few sample rows herself. She also tells him that it is important to put 10 coins in each row and

no more. They finish building the rows together and then they count the pennies: there are 47. A few days later Ben tells his mother that his father gave him some more pennies so he needs to count them again. Mother looks on as Ben dumps the pennies on the coffeetable and begins, on his own, to set up rows of 10.[3] (Gauvain, 2001, p. 140)

Strategies associated with self-regulated learning, too, may have their roots in social interaction. At first, other people (e.g., parents, teachers) might help children through a particular learning task by setting goals for the activity, keeping children's attention focused on the task, monitoring learning progress, and so on. Developmentally speaking, a reasonable bridge between other-regulated learning and self-regulated learning is **co-regulated learning,** in which an adult and one or more children share responsibility for directing the various aspects of the learning process (McCaslin & Good, 1996; Meltzer & Krishnan, 2007). For instance, the adult and children might mutually agree on the specific goals of a learning endeavor, or the adult might describe the criteria that indicate successful learning and then have children evaluate their own performance in light of those criteria. Initially, the adult might provide considerable scaffolding for the children's learning efforts. The scaffolding can gradually be removed as children become more effectively self-regulating.

Enhancing Information Processing Through Social Interaction

In this and the preceding chapter, we've identified numerous implications of the information processing and sociocultural perspectives. Following are additional implications that emerge when we consider both perspectives simultaneously:

• *Regularly engage infants in social exchanges.* In the early months, social interaction with infants may simply involve making eye contact, smiling and talking, extending a finger to be grabbed, and so on. Later it is more likely to involve jointly looking at, manipulating, experimenting with, and talking about objects. Such activities, simple though they may be, foster the mutual awareness (intersubjectivity) so essential for later information sharing and perspective taking (Hobson, 2004; K. Nelson, 2005).

• *Talk with children about their experiences.* Children begin to talk about their experiences almost as soon as they begin to speak, and by age 2 they do it fairly often (van den Broek, Bauer, & Bourg, 1997). Adults should join in: Talking with children about joint experiences not only enhances children's memories of what they are seeing and doing but also helps children interpret their experiences in culturally appropriate ways (Fivush et al., 2006; Leichtman, Pillemer, Wang, Koreishi, & Han, 2000).

• *Involve children and adolescents in joint activities that require new strategies.* Information processing theorists point out that a good deal of cognitive development involves the acquisition of increasingly effective and efficient cognitive strategies. Vygotsky suggested that children often internalize the processes they first use in a social context and that they are most likely to benefit from challenging tasks when they have the guidance and support of more experienced individuals. Taken together, the two perspectives highlight the importance of having adults work closely with youngsters to scaffold the use and eventual mastery of sophisticated approaches to learning and problem solving (McCaslin & Good, 1996; Meltzer & Krishnan, 2007).

Children's Construction of Theories

Piaget, Vygotsky, and contemporary information processing and sociocultural theorists have all suggested that children *construct* their own understandings of their physical and social worlds. Some developmental psychologists suggest that children gradually combine these self-constructed understandings into integrated belief systems, or *theories,* about particular topics. This approach to cognitive development is known as **theory theory.** No, you're not seeing double here. Although the term *theory theory* may seem rather odd, to us it suggests that many psychologists, dry as their academic writings might sometimes be, do indeed have a sense of humor.

co-regulated learning
Process through which an adult and child share responsibility for directing various aspects of the child's learning.

theory theory
Theoretical perspective proposing that children construct increasingly integrated and complex understandings of physical and mental phenomena.

[3]From *The Social Context of Cognitive Development* by M. Guavain. Copyright © 2001 by Guilford Press. Reprinted with permission of The Guilford Press.

Children's theories about the world begin to emerge quite early in life. As an illustration, by 5 or 6 months of age, children appear to have some understanding that human beings and other animals are different from inanimate objects—for instance, that living and nonliving entities move in distinctly different ways (L. B. Cohen & Cashon, 2006; Mandler, 2007b). As children grow older, they increasingly understand that the *insides* of living creatures are as important as, and perhaps more important than, outside appearance (S. A. Gelman, 2003). Even though they have not yet learned about genetics, DNA, and the like, they realize that biological entities are defined primarily by their origins and internal properties. For example, consider the following problem:

> These fruits are red and shiny, and they're used to make pies and cider, and everybody calls these things apples. But some scientists . . . looked way deep inside them with microscopes and found out these weren't like most apples. These things had the inside parts of pears. They had all the cells of pears and everything like that, and when they looked to see where they came from they found that these came off of pear trees. And, when the seeds from this fruit were planted, pear trees grew. So what are these: apples or pears? (Keil, 1989, pp. 305–306)

Children as young as 8 or 9 typically say that the fruits are pears, not apples. Here is one child's explanation:

Child: Because the seeds, when you plant the seeds a pear tree would grow, and if it were an apple, an apple tree would grow. They've got the insides of a pear and an apple wouldn't have the insides of a pear if it wasn't a pear.
Adult: Then how come it looks like this?
Child: It's been sitting out for a long time and it turned red. (dialogue from Keil, 1989, p. 171)

In contrast, children understand that nonliving, human-made objects are largely defined by their functions, not their internal makeup (Greif, Kemler Nelson, Keil, & Gutierrez, 2006; Keil, 1989). For instance, if bowling balls are reshaped into objects that hold liquid for drinking, children conclude that these objects are cups rather than bowling balls. One child explained such a conclusion this way:

Child: They're used for the same purpose as cups and they look like cups and you can drink from them and you can't bowl with them, they're definitely cups!
Adult: Can they still be cups if they're made out of the same stuff as bowling balls?
Child: Yeah . . . and if you could melt down a glass and make it into a bowling ball without breaking it to bits, it would still be a bowling ball and not a cup. (dialogue from Keil, 1989, p. 174)

It appears that within the first 3 years of life, children begin to form theories about the physical world, the biological world, the social world, and the nature of thinking (Geary, 2005; Wellman, Cross, & Watson, 2001; Wellman & Gelman, 1998). As they grow older, they expand on and refine their theories, integrating many of the facts, concepts, and beliefs they acquire and identifying numerous interrelationships among ideas (J. A. Dixon & Kelley, 2007; Keil, 1994; Wellman & Gelman, 1998). We now explore children's theories of the physical world as an example. We will explore their theories about other people's thoughts, feelings, and actions—collectively known as *theory of mind*—in Chapter 12.

Children's Theories of the Physical World

Young infants are amazingly knowledgeable about the physical world. For example, by age 3 or 4 months, they show signs of surprise when one solid object passes directly through another one, when an object seems to be suspended in midair, or when an object appears to move immediately from one place to another without traveling across the intervening space to get there (Baillargeon, 1994; Newcombe, Sluzenski, & Huttenlocher, 2005; Spelke, Breinlinger, Macomber, & Jacobson, 1992). Such findings suggest that young infants know that objects (a) are substantive entities with definite boundaries, (b) fall unless something holds them up, and (c) move in a continuous manner across space. These findings also suggest to some theorists that infants have some basic knowledge about the physical world that is biologically built-in and present at birth (Baillargeon, 2008; Flavell et al., 2002; Spelke, 2000).

The idea that some knowledge and inclinations might be biologically preprogrammed is known as **nativism.**[4] Built-in knowledge about the world would have an evolutionary advantage, of course—it would give infants a head start in learning about their environment—and evidence for it has been observed in other species as well (S. A. Gelman & Kalish, 2006; Spelke, 2000). Nevertheless, the extent to which the human brain is hardwired with certain knowledge, or at least with built-in predispositions to acquire that knowledge very early and easily, is, at present, an unresolved issue (M. Cole & Hatano, 2007; K. Nelson, 2005; Rakison, 2005).

Whatever their origins may be, children's early conceptions of objects provide a foundation for constructing an integrated and increasingly elaborate theory of the physical world. But especially in the preschool and early elementary years, children's theories develop with little or no direct instruction from adults and so often include naive beliefs and misconceptions about how the world operates. Consider the following conversation with a 7-year-old whom we'll call "Rob":

Children's early theories often include naive beliefs and misconceptions about the world. When 4-year-old Isabelle is asked "How were lakes made?" she offers an unlikely—but in her mind quite plausible—explanation: "You get a bucket and you fill it up with water. You get lots and lots of buckets." She illustrates her theory with the picture shown here.

Adult:	How were the mountains made?
Rob:	Some dirt was taken from outside and it was put on the mountain and then mountains were made with it.
Adult:	Who did that?
Rob:	It takes a lot of men to make mountains, there must have been at least four. They gave them the dirt and then they made themselves all alone. [*sic*]
Adult:	But if they wanted to make another mountain?
Rob:	They pull one mountain down and then they could make a prettier one. (dialogue from Piaget, 1929, p. 348; format adapted)

The belief that people play a significant role in influencing physical phenomena (e.g., forming mountains, making clouds move, causing hurricanes) is common in the preschool and early elementary years, and some cultures actually promote it (O. Lee, 1999; Piaget, 1960a). Young children may also believe that natural objects and phenomena have a particular purpose. For instance, they may believe that pointy rocks exist so that animals can scratch themselves when they have an itch (Kelemen, 1999, 2004; Piaget, 1929). Another widely held misconception is that the sun revolves around the earth—that at night, it "goes" to the other side of the world (Vosniadou & Brewer, 1987).

Some misconceptions persist well into adolescence. For example, many high school and college students believe that an object continues to move only if a force continues to act on it and that an object dropped from a moving train or airplane will fall straight down (diSessa, 1996; diSessa, Gillespie, & Esterly, 2004; McCloskey, 1983). In reality, of course, an object continues to move at the same speed in a particular direction unless a force acts to *change* its speed or direction (reflecting the law of inertia), and an object dropped from a moving train or plane not only falls but also continues to move forward (reflecting the laws of gravity and inertia).

Several factors probably contribute to inaccuracies in children's theories about the world (D. B. Clark, 2006; E. M. Evans, 2001; Glynn, Yeany, & Britton, 1991b). Sometimes misconceptions result from how things appear to be. For example, from our perspective here on earth, the sun looks as if it moves around the earth, rather than vice versa. Sometimes misconceptions are encouraged by common expressions in language (e.g., the sun "rises" and "sets"). Various cultural mechanisms—fairy tales, television shows, local folklore, occasionally even textbooks—may also play a role. For example, after cartoon "bad guys" run off the edge of a cliff, they usually remain suspended in air until they realize that there's nothing solid holding them up, and at that point they fall straight down.

Earlier in the chapter you learned that, in general, children's growing knowledge base about the world helps them make sense of and learn new information. But when children's "knowledge" is inaccurate, it often has a counterproductive effect, in that *children's erroneous beliefs about a topic interfere with their understanding of new information related to the topic* (P. K. Murphy & Mason, 2006; Vosniadou, 2003). For example, consider the fact that many children in the early elementary grades believe that the earth is flat rather than round. When adults tell them the earth is actually round, they may interpret that information within the context of what they already "know" and hence think of the earth as being *both* flat and round—in other words, shaped like a pancake (Vosniadou, 1994).

nativism
Theoretical perspective proposing that some knowledge is biologically built-in and available at birth or soon thereafter.

[4]As you will discover in Chapter 9, nativism also figures prominently in some theories of language development.

Facilitating Children's Theory Construction

Theory theory yields several practical implications for parents, teachers, and other adults who work with young people.

- ***Encourage and answer children's why and how questions.*** Young children ask many *why* and *how* questions: "Why is the sky blue?" "How does a telephone call know which house to go to?" Such questions often pop up within the context of shared activities with adults (Callanan & Oakes, 1992, p. 214). Although some adults find them bothersome, children's queries typically reflect their genuine desire to make sense of their world and to enhance their theories about what causes what and why things are the way they are (Chouinard, 2007; Elkind, 1987; Kemler Nelson, Egan, & Holt, 2004).

- ***When teaching a new topic, determine what children already know and believe about it.*** Adults can more successfully address children's misconceptions when they know what those misconceptions are (P. K. Murphy & Alexander, 2008). For example, when beginning a new curriculum unit, teachers should probably assess students' existing beliefs about the topic, perhaps simply by asking a few informal questions that probe what students know and *mis*know.

- ***When children have misconceptions about a topic, work actively to help them acquire more accurate understandings.*** Even as children encounter more accurate and adult-like perspectives about the world, their existing misconceptions do not necessarily disappear. In fact, because early "knowledge" influences the interpretation of subsequent experiences, misconceptions are often quite resistant to change even in the face of blatantly contradictory information (Kuhn, 2001b; P. K. Murphy & Mason, 2006). Thus, teachers and other adults must make a concerted effort to help youngsters revise their early, inaccurate theories to incorporate more accurate and productive worldviews. In other words, they must help youngsters undergo **conceptual change.** Theorists and researchers have offered several strategies for promoting conceptual change:

  - Ask questions that challenge children's current beliefs.
  - Present phenomena that children cannot adequately explain within their existing perspectives—in other words, create *disequilibrium.*
  - Engage children in discussions of the pros and cons of various explanations of observed phenomena.
  - Explicitly point out what the differences between children's beliefs and "reality" are.
  - Show how the scientifically accepted explanation of an event or phenomenon makes more sense than any alternative explanation children themselves can offer.
  - Have children study a topic for an extended period so that accurate explanations are thoroughly understood rather than learned in a superficial, rote manner. (D. B. Clark, 2006; P. K. Murphy & Alexander, 2008; P. K. Murphy & Mason, 2006; C. L. Smith, 2007)

Comparing and Critiquing Contemporary Approaches to Cognitive Development

The Basic Developmental Issues table "Contrasting Contemporary Theories of Cognitive Development" compares information processing theory and theory theory with respect to nature and nurture, universality and diversity, and qualitative and quantitative changes. Both theories have extended our understanding of cognitive development far beyond Piaget's and Vygotsky's early ideas. Information processing theory has made significant inroads into the question of how human beings mentally process and learn new information and how cognitive processes change over the course of childhood and adolescence. Theory theory helps us understand why children's naive beliefs (e.g., "The world is flat") may persist even in the face of contradictory evidence. Together such approaches lead us to conclude that cognitive development involves more gradual changes and that the evolution of children's reasoning capabilities is more domain specific than Piaget suggested.

In their present forms, however, both the information processing and theory theory perspectives have limitations. Theory theory offers only vague descriptions of the nature,

conceptual change
Revision of one's knowledge and understanding of a topic in response to new information about the topic.

structure, and origins of children's self-constructed theories (K. Nelson, 1996a; Siegler & Alibali, 2005). Information processing theory is more precise, but its precision may not provide a completely accurate description of how human memory works. For instance, human beings seem to learn and remember many things that they don't consciously pay attention to and think about in working memory (Frensch & Rünger, 2003). Furthermore, mounting research evidence indicates that working memory and long-term memory are closely interconnected and possibly overlapping entities, rather than the two distinctly separate components depicted in Figure 7-1 (Kirschner, Sweller, & Clark, 2006; Ormrod, 2008b).

Perhaps the biggest challenge for today's developmental psychologists is to explain exactly how and why cognitive development occurs (Gauvain, 2001; Siegler & Alibali, 2005). Theorists have made some progress on this front, to be sure. For instance, children appear to have an innate need to adapt to their environment, and they almost certainly acquire more complex strategies as adults nurture such strategies. But we do not yet have a detailed understanding of how various aspects of heredity and environment work in concert to transform newborn infants into cognitively sophisticated adults. To arrive at such an understanding, psychologists must pull together the concepts and research findings of multiple theoretical perspectives—for instance, by integrating elements of information processing theory and sociocultural theory in the ways we did earlier.

Although we do not yet have a complete picture of cognitive development, existing theories and research findings tell us a great deal about what to look for in children's development and how to work effectively with various age-groups (see the Observation Guidelines table "Assessing Cognitive Processing and Metacognition"). What we have learned about cognitive development can also help us identify children who may be having difficulties in processing certain kinds of information, as we shall see now.

Basic Developmental Issues

Contrasting Contemporary Theories of Cognitive Development

Issue	Information Processing Theory	Theory Theory
Nature and Nurture	Nature endows children with certain brain mechanisms that enable them to direct their attention to particular stimuli, to actively deliberate about an event or task at hand, and to retain acquired knowledge and skills for lengthy periods. Furthermore, information processing difficulties (e.g., learning disabilities, attention-deficit hyperactivity disorder) often have biological origins. Nevertheless, the focus is primarily on environmental factors: in particular, on how environmental input is interpreted, stored, integrated, and remembered and on how formal instruction can best facilitate learning and cognitive development.	Rudimentary understandings of the physical world—or at least predispositions to divide up and interpret the world in particular ways—seem to be in place within the first few weeks or months after birth and may possibly be biologically built-in. As children observe and interact with their physical and social environments, they construct increasingly elaborate and integrated understandings and beliefs about various physical, social, and mental phenomena.
Universality and Diversity	The components of the information processing system (e.g., working memory, long-term memory, central executive) are universal. However, some children use their information processing capabilities more effectively than others. Children's prior knowledge and their mastery of various cognitive strategies influence the degree to which they can learn new information and skills effectively.	Any biologically built-in knowledge and predispositions are universal across cultures. However, informal experiences, formal schooling, and community practices and beliefs—things that are apt to differ from one culture to the next—lead children to embellish on their initial understandings in somewhat culture-specific ways.
Qualitative and Quantitative Change	Over the course of development, children and adolescents acquire a variety of new cognitive strategies that are qualitatively different from earlier ones. Each strategy evolves gradually over a lengthy period and becomes increasingly efficient and effective—a trend that reflects quantitative change.	As children gain more information about their world, they may add to their theories in a quantitative manner. Under certain conditions, however, new and compelling experiences spur children to overhaul their theories in a way that reflects qualitative change.

Assessing Cognitive Processing and Metacognition

Characteristic	Look For	Example	Implication
Intersubjectivity	· Reciprocal interaction with caregivers · Attempts to coordinate one's own actions toward an object with the actions of another person · Social referencing (i.e., responding to an object or event based on how an adult responds to it)	A teacher at a child care center is obviously frightened when a large dog appears just outside the fenced-in play yard, and she yells at the dog to go away. Fifteen-month-old Owen observes her reaction and begins to cry.	Regularly engage infants in affectionate and playful interactions (smiles, coos, etc.). Remember that your own actions and reactions toward objects and events will communicate messages about the value, appeal, and safety of those objects and events.
Attention	· Sustained attention to human beings and inanimate objects · Ability to stay on task for an age-appropriate period · On-task behavior when distracting stimuli are present	During after-lunch story time, a second-grade teacher has been reading Roald Dahl's *Charlie and the Chocolate Factory*. Most of the children are quiet and attentive the entire time, but Ben fidgets and squirms, and soon he finds a new form of entertainment: making silly faces at nearby classmates.	Monitor children's ability to pay attention in an age-appropriate fashion. If children have exceptional difficulty staying on task, minimize distractions, teach them strategies for focusing their attention more effectively, and give them opportunities to release pent-up energy appropriately.
Automatization of Basic Skills	· Retrieval of simple facts in a rapid, effortless fashion · Ability to use simple problem-solving strategies quickly and efficiently	Elena easily solves the problem $\frac{6}{12} = \frac{?}{36}$ because she realizes almost immediately that $\frac{6}{12}$ is the same as $\frac{1}{2}$.	Give children numerous opportunities to use and practice essential facts and skills; do so within the context of interesting and motivating activities.
Learning Strategies	· Use of rehearsal in the elementary grades · Use of more integrative strategies (e.g., organization, elaboration) in the secondary grades · Flexible use of strategies for different learning tasks	Terri studies each new concept in her high school physics class by repeating the textbook definition aloud three or four times. Later she can barely remember the definitions she has studied, and she is unable to apply the concepts when trying to solve physics problems.	Show struggling learners that their difficulties may be due to ineffective strategies, and teach them strategies that can help them learn more successfully.
Self-Regulated Learning Capabilities	· Initiative in identifying and seeking out needed information · Intentional efforts to keep attention focused on an assigned task · Effective planning and time management · Realistic appraisal of what has and has not been learned	At wrestling practice one day, John tells his coach that he has just read several articles about the pros and cons of using steroids to increase muscle mass. "I'm a little confused about why most experts advise against them," he says. "Can you help me understand their logic?"	When youngsters fail to complete independent assignments in a timely or thorough manner, provide more structure for subsequent tasks. Gradually remove the structure over time as they become better able to regulate their own learning and performance.
Beliefs About Knowledge and Learning	· Optimism that knowledge and skills improve when one focuses on understanding (rather than memorization) and persists in the face of temporary obstacles to learning · Attempts to master interrelationships among ideas (e.g., cause and effect, similarities and differences) · Eagerness to compare and critique various perspectives and theories	Several middle school students are studying for a test on westward migration in North America during the 1800s. Some students focus on cause-and-effect relationships among events. Others make a list of facts from the textbook and study them in a piecemeal fashion.	Convey the message that mastering any single domain is an ongoing, lifelong enterprise that requires effort and persistence. Especially when working with adolescents, communicate that knowledge about a topic includes an understanding of how various concepts and ideas are interrelated. Also communicate that competing perspectives each may have some merit but must be critically evaluated on the basis of evidence and logic.

Exceptionalities in Information Processing

All children learn and process information in a somewhat unique, idiosyncratic manner. But the information processing capabilities of some children are different enough that they require the use of specially adapted instructional practices and materials. Here we consider two kinds of exceptionalities in information processing: learning disabilities and attention-deficit hyperactivity disorder.

Learning Disabilities

A **learning disability** is a significant difficulty in one or more specific cognitive processes that cannot be attributed to a sensory impairment, general mental retardation, an emotional or behavioral disorder, or lack of instruction. The difficulty interferes with academic achievement to such a degree that special educational services are warranted (J. M. Fletcher, Lyon, Fuchs, & Barnes, 2007; National Joint Committee on Learning Disabilities, 1994). Many learning disabilities appear to have an inherited biological basis. For instance, some children with learning disabilities have minor abnormalities in certain brain structures, and others seem especially vulnerable to "interference" from brain signals irrelevant to the task at hand (Dempster & Corkill, 1999; Kovas, Haworth, Dale, & Plomin, 2007; Manis, 1996).

Children with learning disabilities are a diverse group, with a wide variety of talents, ability levels, and personalities. For instance, some children easily gain proficiency in mathematics but have exceptional difficulty with reading (see the discussion of *dyslexia* in Chapter 10), whereas others show the reverse pattern. Yet many children with learning disabilities do seem to have certain characteristics in common. They are apt to have trouble with executive functions—focusing their attention, self-regulating their learning, inhibiting inappropriate thoughts and behaviors, and so on (Meltzer, 2007). They may have few effective learning and problem-solving strategies at their disposal and so take a rather "passive" approach to learning tasks—for instance, mindlessly staring at a textbook instead of actively thinking about what the words mean (Brownell, Mellard, & Deshler, 1993; Meltzer & Krishnan, 2007). Some of them appear to have less working memory capacity than their age-mates, making it difficult to engage in several cognitive processes simultaneously (J. A. Stein & Krishnan, 2007; Swanson & Jerman, 2006). They may also suffer from low self-esteem and emotional problems, due at least partly to frustration about their repeated academic failures (Horowitz et al., 2005; MacMaster, Donovan, & MacIntyre, 2002).

As students reach the secondary school grades, the school curriculum becomes increasingly challenging, textbooks are written in more sophisticated language, and teachers expect greater independence and self-regulated learning. Unless they have considerable scaffolding to help them study and learn, students with learning disabilities become increasingly frustrated and discouraged. Perhaps for this reason, adolescents with learning disabilities are often among those students most at risk for dropping out of school (Barga, 1996).

Attention-Deficit Hyperactivity Disorder

Children with **attention-deficit hyperactivity disorder (ADHD)** have either or both of the following characteristics (American Psychiatric Association, 1994; Barkley, 1998):

- *Inattention*. Children may be easily distracted by either external stimuli or their own thoughts. They may daydream, have trouble listening to and following directions, or give up easily when working on difficult tasks.
- *Hyperactivity and impulsivity*. Children may seem to have an excess amount of energy. They may be fidgety, move around at inappropriate times, talk excessively, or have difficulty working or playing quietly. They may also show such impulsive behaviors as blurting out answers, interrupting others, making careless mistakes, and acting without thinking about potential consequences of their behavior.

A deficit in executive functions, and more specifically in the inhibition of inappropriate thoughts and actions, may be at the heart of ADHD (Barkley, 1998; Denckla, 2007). In some cases it may be the result of specific brain abnormalities, but in others it may reflect a delay

Children with learning disabilities typically have less effective learning and memory skills than their classmates and therefore may need extra structure and guidance to help them study effectively.

learning disability
Significant deficit in one or more cognitive processes, to the point where special educational services are required.

attention-deficit hyperactivity disorder (ADHD)
Disability characterized by inattention, by hyperactivity and impulsive behavior, or by all of these characteristics.

in normal neurological maturation processes (Gatzke-Kopp & Beauchaine, 2007; Sabbagh, Xu, Carlson, Moses, & Lee, 2006; P. Shaw et al., 2007).

In addition to inattentiveness, hyperactivity, and impulsivity, children identified as having ADHD may have difficulties with cognitive processing, academic achievement, interpersonal skills, or classroom behavior (Barkley, 1998; S. Goldstein & Rider, 2006). In adolescence, hyperactivity diminishes, and attention span and impulse control improve (E. L. Hart, Lahey, Loeber, Applegate, & Frick, 1995). Even so, adolescents with ADHD have greater difficulty than their peers in successfully meeting the challenges of the teenage years—the physical changes of puberty, more complex classroom assignments, increasing demands for independent and responsible behavior, and so on. And they are more prone to tobacco and alcohol use, traffic accidents, and dropping out of school (Barkley, 1998; S. Goldstein & Rider, 2006; Whalen, Jamner, Henker, Delfino, & Lozano, 2002).

Working with Children Who Have Information Processing Difficulties

Children with either a learning disability or ADHD are apt to be more different than they are similar. Hence teachers and other practitioners who work with them must consider the unique needs of each child. Yet several general suggestions are applicable to many children with information processing difficulties.

- ***Examine children's work for clues about specific processing difficulties.*** Writing samples, math homework, and other academic work can be a rich source of information about cognitive deficits that may hinder children's ability to learn and master classroom subject matter. For example, a child who solves a subtraction problem this way:

$$\begin{array}{r} 85 \\ -29 \\ \hline 64 \end{array}$$

may be applying an inappropriate rule ("Always subtract the smaller number from the larger one") to subtraction. A child who reads the sentence *I drove the car* as *I drove the cat* may be having trouble using context clues in reading words and sentences. The following exercise, "Pumpkin and Bat," can give you a taste of what error analysis might involve.

Interpreting Children's Artifacts and Reflections

Pumpkin and Bat

A few days before Halloween, Nathan, age 7, created and illustrated the writing sample shown here. Writing in small print, his first-grade teacher clarified what he intended to say: "I drew this pumpkin" and "A bat." As you look at Nathan's work, identify one or more patterns of errors in his word spellings, and speculate about cognitive processing difficulties that such errors might reflect.

With the exception of the *L* in the first line, Nathan correctly captured some of the sounds in the words he was trying to spell. For example, he acknowledged the *d* in *drew*, the *s* in *this*, and the *b* and *t* in *bat*. But he omitted several other consonants, as well as all of the vowel sounds except for the initial *I*. We might suspect that Nathan has difficulty hearing all the distinct sounds in spoken words and matching them with the letters he sees in written words. Such difficulties are common in young elementary school students who have significant reading disabilities (see Chapter 10).

- ***Help children keep their attention on the task at hand.*** Many children with information processing difficulties are easily distracted. Thus adults who work with them should minimize the presence of other stimuli likely to compete for their attention, perhaps by finding a quiet room for tasks requiring considerable concentration or by pulling down window shades when appealing alternatives lurk outside. Many children also benefit from specific training in attention-focusing strategies, such as keeping one's eyes directed toward a speaker or moving to a new location if the current one presents too many distracting sights and sounds (Buchoff, 1990).

- *Teach strategies for controlling hyperactivity and impulsivity.* All children, but especially those with information processing difficulties, need regular opportunities to release pent-up energy, perhaps in the form of recess, sports, or hands-on activities (Panksepp, 1998; Pellegrini & Bohn, 2005). In addition, after a period of high activity, adults might give children a "settling-in" time that allows them to calm down gradually (Pellegrini & Horvat, 1995). As an example, when children return from lunch, many elementary teachers begin the afternoon by reading a chapter from a high-interest storybook.

Teaching children to use self-talk can help them resist the tendency to respond too quickly and impulsively to situations and problems. For example, notice how one formerly impulsive child learned to talk himself through matching tasks in which he needed to find two identical pictures among several very similar ones:

> I have to remember to go slowly to get it right. Look carefully at this one, now look at these carefully. Is this one different? Yes, it has an extra leaf. Good, I can eliminate this one. Now, let's look at this one. I think it's this one, but let me first check the others. Good, I'm going slow and carefully. Okay, I think it's this one. (Meichenbaum & Goodman, 1971, p. 121)

- *Provide extra scaffolding for studying, doing homework, and completing other learning tasks.* Children with information processing difficulties often need considerable support for learning tasks, especially those they complete on their own. Such support might take a variety of forms: structured note-taking forms, handouts that list major ideas, memory tricks for remembering particular tidbits of information, teacher-supervised after-school homework programs, and so on (T. Bryan, Burstein, & Bryan, 2001; Cosden, Morrison, Albanese, & Macias, 2001; Meltzer, 2007).

- *Teach social skills.* Some children with learning disabilities have difficulty processing social information, and some with ADHD behave so impulsively that they alienate their peers. These children stand to benefit from specific training in social skills, which can enhance their interpersonal effectiveness (C. E. Cunningham & Cunningham, 1998; J. A. Stein & Krishnan, 2007). Chapters 12, 14, and 15 identify a variety of strategies for promoting effective interaction with others.

Children with learning disabilities and ADHD are hardly the only ones who are apt to have trouble processing and learning information. As a general rule, *children and adolescents process information less effectively than adults do*. In fact, even adults may have trouble using effective learning skills when they first tackle a new and unfamiliar subject (Ormrod, 2008b). Gaining the knowledge and metacognitive skills that enable effective learning and memory is ultimately a lifelong process.

Summary

Basic Cognitive Processes

Information processing theory focuses on how children acquire, interpret, and remember information and on how these cognitive processes change over the course of development. Information processing theorists propose that cognitive capabilities improve gradually with age and experience. Infants have many sensory and perceptual capabilities at birth or soon thereafter. In general, however, children are less efficient learners than adults are. For instance, they have shorter attention spans, a smaller working memory capacity, and a smaller and less integrated knowledge base to which they can relate new information and events.

Metacognition and Cognitive Strategies

The term *metacognition* encompasses both the knowledge that people have about their own cognitive processes and their intentional use of certain cognitive processes to facilitate learning and memory. Children's metacognitive knowledge and cognitive strategies improve throughout the school years. For instance, children become more proficient in such learning strategies as rehearsal, organization, and elaboration, and they acquire increasingly powerful and effective ways of solving problems. With age, they become more aware of the nature of thinking, learning, and knowledge, and they develop strategies for regulating their own learning.

Adding a Sociocultural Element to Information Processing Theory

Information processing theory can tell us a great deal about what abilities change over time, and sociocultural views can help us explain how those changes occur. Combining elements of both perspectives, then, can give us a more complete picture of cognitive development than we might get from either one alone. For example, children learn what to pay attention to in part by watching what other people pay attention to. And adults can help children become more effective, self-regulating learners by giving them control of a learning activity in a gradual, step-by-step manner.

Children's Construction of Theories

Some theorists propose that children gradually construct integrated belief systems (theories) about the physical world, the biological world, the social world, and mental events. Such theories are not always accurate, however. For instance, children's theories about the physical world may include erroneous beliefs about the solar system and laws of motion. To the extent that children's theories include misconceptions, they may interfere with children's ability to acquire more sophisticated understandings.

Comparing and Critiquing Contemporary Approaches to Cognitive Development

Contemporary theories (e.g., information processing theory, theory theory) have added considerably to Piaget's and Vygotsky's early notions of children's thinking and knowledge-building processes. Taken together, various theoretical perspectives give us a more complete picture of cognitive development than any single perspective can give us alone.

Exceptionalities in Information Processing

The information processing capabilities of some children (e.g., those with learning disabilities and those with attention-deficit hyperactivity disorder) are different enough that they require the use of specially adapted instructional practices and materials. Although children with such disabilities have diverse abilities and needs, all of them benefit from explicit instruction in effective cognitive strategies and teacher scaffolding for completing learning tasks.

Applying Concepts in Child Development

The exercises in this section will help you apply contemporary theories of cognitive development as you work with children and adolescents.

Case Study

The Library Project

Read the case and then answer the questions that follow it.

In the final year of her teacher education program, Jessica Jensen is a teacher intern in four eighth-grade social studies classes. She has recently assigned a month-long group project that involves considerable library research. Midway through the project, Jessica writes the following entry in her journal:

> Within each group, one student is studying culture of the region, one has religion, one has economy, and one government. The point is for the students to become "experts" on their topic in their region. There are a lot of requirements to this assignment. I'm collecting things as we go along because I think a project this long will be difficult for them to organize. . . .
>
> So we spent all week in the library. I collected a minimum of two pages of notes yesterday, which will be a small part of their grade. The one thing that surprised me in our work in the library was their lack of skills. They had such difficulty researching, finding the information they needed, deciding what was important, and organizing and taking notes. As they worked, I walked around helping and was shocked. The librarian had already gotten out all of the appropriate resources. Even after they had the books in front of them, most did not know what to do. For instance, if they were assigned "economy," most looked in the index for that particular word. If they didn't find it, they gave up on the book. After realizing this, I

had to start the next day with a brief lesson on researching and cross-referencing. I explained how they could look up *commerce, imports, exports,* and how these would all help them. I was also shocked at how poor their note-taking skills were. I saw a few kids copying paragraphs word for word. Almost none of them understood that notes don't need to be in full sentences. So, it was a long week at the library.

> Next week is devoted to group work and time to help them work on their rough drafts. With the difficulty they had researching, I can imagine the problems that will arise out of turning their notes into papers. (journal entry courtesy of Jessica Jensen)

- Initially, the intern realizes that her students will need some structure to complete the project successfully. In what ways do she and the librarian structure the assignment for the students?
- What specific strategies do the students use as they engage in their library research? In what ways are their strategies less effective than an adult's might be?
- How does the students' prior knowledge (or lack thereof) influence the effectiveness of their strategies?

Once you have answered these questions, compare your responses with those presented in Appendix A.

Interpreting Children's Artifacts and Reflections

Consider chapter concepts as you analyze the following interview with 9-year-old Aletha, a fourth grader:

Interview with Aletha

Adult: What is paying attention?

Aletha: What they are talking about is interesting and it's fun. Before we learn about anything new, my teacher asks us questions [about the new topic] and nobody knows the answers. When we are done, she asks us questions and you know all the answers. It's cool! To learn new things you have to pay attention. If you don't, then you won't know what's going on. If you are talking with your friends or fiddling, you are not paying attention, so the teacher will call on you and you won't know the answer. If you are not listening, then you are not paying attention. When it's interesting, I'm really paying attention. It's hard if you're not interested, but that's not how it works. You have to pay attention.

Adult: How do you pay attention if it's not interesting?

Aletha: I think of questions in my head and I have to pay attention to see if the teacher answers my questions before I want the answers. Then I have something to say when the teacher calls on me.

Adult: Can you do other things when you pay attention?

Aletha: Some things. You can't read a book because it's hard to do both. Sometimes in science we watch movies and we are allowed to keep notes because we have a test on the movie later. I write the stuff down so I can memorize it. That was easy [to take notes], but it's hard because I had to write while I was listening.

Adult: Is paying attention just listening?

Aletha: Not necessarily. You can listen and not have a clue. But if you don't listen, you obviously won't get it. (interview courtesy of a former student who wishes to remain anonymous)

· What beliefs does Aletha have about the nature of human learning and memory?
· What evidence do you see to indicate that Aletha is taking steps toward becoming a self-regulating learner?

Once you have answered these questions, compare your ideas with those presented in Appendix B. For further practice in analyzing children's artifacts and reflections, go to the Activities and Applications section in Chapter 7 of MyEducationLab.

Developmental Trends Exercise

In this chapter you've learned about a variety of cognitive and metacognitive processes that influence children's and adolescents' ability to interpret and respond effectively to their environment. The following table describes behaviors that youngsters at five different age levels exhibit. For each of these behaviors, the table identifies one or more relevant cognitive or metacognitive processes, offers an implication for working with children of that age-group, or both. Go to the Activities and Applications section in Chapter 7 of MyEducationLab to apply what you've learned about contemporary theories of cognitive development as you fill in the empty cells in the table.

Identifying Children's Cognitive Processes

Age	A Youngster's Experience	Developmental Concepts *Identifying Cognitive Processes*	Implications *Promoting Effective Processes*
Infancy **(Birth–2 Years)**	One Monday morning, 13-month-old Miguel meets his child care provider's new kitten for the first time. Miguel isn't sure what to make of this creature. When he sees that his caregiver is happily petting the kitten, he smiles and reaches out to touch the kitten's head.	Miguel is engaging in *social referencing*, checking to see how a trusted adult reacts to the new kitten and then responding in a similar way. Social referencing is an aspect of *intersubjectivity*, in which participants in a social situation have some awareness of what one another is looking at, thinking, or feeling.	As you introduce infants to new people, animals, and objects, model appropriate ways of interacting with and responding to them.
Early Childhood **(2–6 Years)**	A kindergarten teacher is reading Mercer Mayer's *What Do You Do with a Kangaroo?* to his class. As he often does during story time, he picks up a globe and points to the spot where the story takes place—in this case, Australia. "Most kangaroos live here in Australia," he says. "How come they don't fall off the world?" 5-year-old Andrea asks.		Listen carefully to children's comments for clues regarding their beliefs about their physical and social worlds. With age-appropriate explanations, nudge them toward more accurate understandings.

Developmental Trends Exercise (continued)

Age	A Youngster's Experience	Developmental Concepts *Identifying Cognitive Processes*	Implications *Promoting Effective Processes*
Middle Childhood (6–10 Years)	Although 10-year-old Kendall seems quite capable of doing typical fifth-grade work, he rarely stays on task for more than a few minutes during the school day. He is especially distractible during small-group activities and on other occasions when class activities are fairly noisy. He tends to remember very little of the material that is presented during such times.	*Attention* is critical for getting information into working memory and then (with further processing) into long-term memory. Distractibility is common for children in the preschool and early elementary years, but it is unusual for a boy as old as Kendall. Quite possibly Kendall has an undiagnosed *learning disability* or *attention-deficit hyperactivity disorder*.	
Early Adolescence (10–14 Years)	When Faith was in elementary school, she was a conscientious student who earned mostly As and Bs. Now, as a 13-year-old seventh grader, she often forgets to do her homework—sometimes she doesn't even know what her homework assignments are—and her grades have slipped to Cs and Ds. "I need to get my grades up," she tells the school counselor, "because I want to go to college. Next year I promise to work harder."	Faith apparently has not acquired many *self-regulated learning* skills: setting goals, planning study time, and so on. Such skills become increasingly important as students move through the grade levels and are expected to work more independently.	When students show a decline in academic achievement in middle school or junior high, assume that lack of self-regulation skills, rather than lack of motivation, is the culprit. But don't expect students to acquire self-regulated learning skills on their own. Instead, actively *teach* goal setting, self-motivation strategies, comprehension monitoring, and so on.
Late Adolescence (14–18 Years)	After failing the first exam in his Advanced Placement biology class, 17-year-old John tells his science teacher, "I've never done so poorly on a test before, and I studied really hard for it. I repeated everything over and over until I knew it cold!" The teacher looks at John's notebook for the class and responds, "I think I see what the problem is. Your class notes are nothing more than facts and definitions. But my test asked you to apply what you've learned to real-life situations and problems. Let me suggest some new ways to study...."		Especially at the high school level, encourage students to organize and make sense of information, rather than simply to repeat it verbatim. Help them discover that true mastery of a topic involves understanding how concepts and ideas relate to one another and to real-world situations and problems.

Key Concepts

information processing theory (p. 234)
sensory register (p. 235)
working memory (p. 235)
long-term memory (p. 235)
central executive (p. 236)
automatization (p. 239)
infantile amnesia (p. 240)

knowledge base (p. 240)
schema (p. 241)
script (p. 241)
symbol (p. 242)
metacognition (p. 245)
cognitive strategy (p. 245)
rehearsal (p. 247)
organization (p. 247)

elaboration (p. 248)
metacognitive awareness (p. 249)
self-regulated learning (p. 251)
comprehension monitoring (p. 251)
epistemological beliefs (p. 252)
intersubjectivity (p. 258)
joint attention (p. 258)

social referencing (p. 258)
co-regulated learning (p. 260)
theory theory (p. 260)
nativism (p. 262)
conceptual change (p. 263)
learning disability (p. 266)
attention-deficit hyperactivity disorder (ADHD) (p. 266)

MyEducationLab

Now go to Chapter 7 of MyEducationLab at www.myeducationlab.com, where you can:

· View instructional objectives for the chapter.
· Take a quiz to test your mastery of chapter objectives. Detailed feedback is provided to explain why your responses are correct or incorrect.
· Deepen your understanding of particular concepts and principles with Review, Practice, and Enrichment exercises.

· Complete Activities and Applications exercises that give you additional experience in interpreting artifacts, increase your understanding of how research contributes to knowledge about chapter topics, and encourage you to apply what you have learned about children's development.
· Apply what you have learned in the chapter to your work with children in Building Teaching Skills and Dispositions exercises.
· Observe children and their unique contexts in Video Examples.

Intelligence

Seventeen-year-old Gina has always been an enthusiastic and self-motivated learner. As a toddler, she talked early and often. As a 4-year-old, she asked her mother to identify a few words in a reading primer her aunt had given her, used the words to deduce many letter-sound relationships, and then deciphered additional words on her own. By the time she reached kindergarten, she was reading first- and second-grade-level storybooks.

In elementary school Gina consistently achieved straight As on her report cards until finally, in sixth grade, she broke the pattern by getting a B in history. Since then, she has earned a few more Bs, but As continue to dominate her record. Her performance has been highest in her advanced math courses, where she easily grasps the abstract concepts and principles that many of her classmates find difficult to understand.

Gina has other talents as well. She won her high school's creative writing contest 2 years in a row. She has landed challenging roles in her school's drama productions. And as the president of the National Honor Society during her senior year, she has masterfully coordinated a schoolwide peer-tutoring program to assist struggling students.

Gina's teachers describe her as a "bright" young woman. Her friends affectionately call her a "brainiac." Test results in her school file bear out their assessments: An intelligence test that she took in junior high school yielded a score of 140, and this year she performed at the 99th percentile on college aptitude tests.

This is not to say that Gina is strong in every arena. She shows little artistic ability in her paintings or clay sculptures. Her piano playing is mediocre despite 5 years of weekly lessons. In athletic events she has little stamina, strength, or flexibility. She is shy and unsure of herself at social events. And she hasn't earned an A in history since fifth grade, in large part because her idea of how best to learn history involves simply memorizing people, places, and dates.

- What evidence is there that Gina is intelligent?

- In which abilities does Gina exhibit her strongest talents?

- In which abilities is Gina somewhat less advanced?

Every child is intelligent to a certain degree. Some children are exceptionally intelligent, able to learn effectively in a variety of situations. Gina's performance reflects such consistency: She has earned high marks throughout her school career, and she achieves at high levels in many areas. Yet intelligence is not a set-in-concrete characteristic that youngsters either do or don't have. Gina has definite talents as well as a few areas that are challenging for her. Among her definite assets are academic areas that rely on advanced verbal skills and mathematical reasoning. Similarly, she excels at dramatic self-expression and has good organizational skills. Gina does not show the same extraordinary potential in history, art, music, athletics, or social situations, yet it seems likely that Gina might be able to develop these competencies further if she puts her mind to it and is assisted in her efforts. Not every child has Gina's exceptional intelligence, but every child is poised to make the most of his or her unique abilities if given appropriate support at home, school, and in the community.

Defining Intelligence

Theorists define and conceptualize intelligence in a variety of ways, but most agree that it has several distinctive qualities:

It is *adaptive,* such that it can be used flexibly to respond to a variety of situations and problems.

It involves *learning ability:* People who are intelligent in particular domains learn new information and behaviors more quickly and easily than people who are less intelligent in those domains.

Case Study:

Gina

Outline:

Case Study: Gina

Defining Intelligence

Theoretical Perspectives of Intelligence

Measuring Intelligence

Effects of Heredity and Environment on Intelligence

Developmental Trends in IQ Scores

Group Differences in Intelligence

Critique of Current Perspectives on Intelligence

Implications of Theories and Research on Intelligence

Exceptionalities in Intelligence

Summary

Applying Concepts in Child Development

• It involves the *use of prior knowledge* to analyze and understand new situations effectively.
• It involves the complex interaction and coordination of *many different mental processes.*
• It is *culture specific.* What is "intelligent" behavior in one culture is not necessarily intelligent behavior in another culture. (Greenfield, 1998; Laboratory of Comparative Human Cognition, 1982; J. Li, 2004; Neisser et al., 1996; Sternberg, 2007)

With these qualities in mind, we offer one possible (but intentionally broad) definition of **intelligence:** the ability to apply past knowledge and experiences flexibly to accomplish challenging new tasks.

Children apply their intellectual abilities in a wide variety of academic and social contexts. Because intelligence is adaptive, it helps children survive and thrive in their particular culture. For example, in mainstream Western culture, strong verbal skills help children succeed in society and are typically encouraged. But not all cultures value chattiness. In some cultures, talking a lot is interpreted as a sign of immaturity or low intelligence (Crago, 1988; Minami & McCabe, 1996; Sternberg, 2003a). One researcher working at an Inuit school in northern Quebec asked a teacher about a boy whose language seemed unusually advanced for his age-group. The teacher replied:

> "Do you think he might have a learning problem? Some of these children who don't have such high intelligence have trouble stopping themselves. They don't know when to stop talking." (Crago, 1988, p. 219)

In North America and western Europe, intelligence is largely thought of as an ability that influences children's academic achievement and adults' professional success. Such a view is hardly universal. Many people in African and Asian cultures think of intelligence as extending beyond academic abilities to include social skills—maintaining harmonious interpersonal relationships, showing respect for one's elders, working effectively together to accomplish challenging tasks, and so on (Keller, 2003; J. Li, 2004; Sternberg, 2007). In Buddhist, Confucian, and Taoist societies in China, Taiwan, and elsewhere, intelligence also involves acquiring strong moral values and making meaningful contributions to society (J. Li, 2004; Sternberg, 2007).

Theoretical Perspectives of Intelligence

Some psychologists have suggested that intelligence is a single, general ability that people "have" to varying degrees. Historically, considerable evidence has supported this idea (McGrew, Flanagan, Zeith, & Vanderwood, 1997; Neisser et al., 1996). Although different measures of intelligence yield somewhat different results, they virtually all correlate with one another: Individuals who score high on one measure tend to score high on others as well. Even tests with two different kinds of content (e.g., a verbal test assessing knowledge of vocabulary and a nonverbal test assessing ability to analyze geometric designs) tend to correlate with one another (Carroll, 1992; W. Johnson, te Nijenhuis, & Bouchard, 2007; Spearman, 1904).

Yet the correlations among various intelligence measures are sometimes only moderate ones. Children who get the highest scores on one test do not always get the highest scores on another test. For instance, youngsters who demonstrate exceptional ability in some areas of the school curriculum may exhibit only average performance in others (recall Gina's high performance in reading and math but average performance in art and music). Therefore, not all psychologists believe that intelligence is a single entity that people "have" in varying amounts. Instead, some argue, people can be more or less intelligent in different situations and on different kinds of tasks. In this section we present five theoretical perspectives on the single-entity versus multiple-abilities nature of intelligence.

Spearman's g

In the early 1900s, British psychologist Charles Spearman (1863–1945) proposed that intelligence comprises both (a) a single, pervasive reasoning ability (a *general factor*) that is used on a wide variety of tasks and (b) a number of narrow abilities *(specific factors)* involved in executing particular tasks (Spearman, 1904, 1927). From Spearman's perspective, children's performance on any given task depends both on the general factor and on any specific factors that the task involves. For example, measures of various language skills (vocabulary, word recognition, reading comprehension, etc.) are all highly correlated, presumably because they all reflect both general

intelligence
Ability to apply past knowledge and experiences flexibly to accomplish challenging new tasks.

intelligence and the same specific factor: verbal ability. A measure of language skills will correlate to a lesser extent with a measure of mathematical problem solving, because the two measures are apt to tap into somewhat different specific abilities.

Many contemporary psychologists have seen sufficient evidence in the positive correlations among diverse intellectual abilities to believe that a general factor in intelligence does exist (e.g., N. Brody, 2006; Kovas et al., 2007). This factor is often known simply as Spearman's **g.** Some theorists suspect that the ability to process information quickly may be at the core of g, because substantial correlations have been found between children's IQ scores and measures of information processing speed, such as fast reaction times to familiar stimuli (Danthiir, Roberts, Schulze, & Wilhelm, 2005; Deary, 2003; Fry & Hale, 1996). Infants' mental processing helps illustrate this relationship. You may recall from Chapter 2 that infants tend to *habituate,* or lose interest in stimuli that are repeatedly presented to them, but they show renewed interest when a novel stimulus is presented. Children who, as infants, habituate quickly to the "same old thing" tend to have substantially higher IQ scores in childhood and adolescence (Kašek, 2004). These youngsters perk up again when they encounter something new and different, and they benefit from efficient processing as they later learn new concepts and language.

Not all psychologists agree that a g factor exists, however. Some suggest that the evidence for a single general factor in intelligence can be either strong or weak depending on the specific abilities measured and on the statistical methods used to analyze the data (Neisser, 1998a; Sternberg, 2003b; Sternberg & Grigorenko, 2000). Others argue that a predominance of test items reflecting the perspectives of a limited number of societies—the mainstream cultures of Europe and North America—is responsible for the appearance of a single factor emerging in statistical analyses (Gardner, 2006). A few psychologists point out that evidence of the complex circuitry of the human brain (see Chapter 5) makes one general factor a misleading oversimplification of intellectual functioning (Horn & Masunaga, 2000). Finally, still other psychologists recognize that even if g exists, it is sometimes more constructive for practitioners to focus on children's specific talents and limitations (McGrew, 2005). For example, it can be quite helpful for a teacher to learn that a child has trouble identifying sounds and matching them with letters, skills that can then be taught. In contrast, knowing a child's most recent IQ score provides virtually no information about specific instructional strategies that might benefit the child.

Cattell-Horn-Carroll Theory of Cognitive Abilities

The Cattell-Horn-Carroll theory of cognitive abilities is a blend of views that were originally inspired by the work of Raymond Cattell (1905–1998), a British psychologist who worked in the United States. Extending the ideas of Spearman, Cattell (1963, 1987) found evidence for two distinctly different components of general intelligence. First, Cattell proposed, children differ in **fluid intelligence,** their ability to acquire knowledge quickly and adapt to new situations effectively. Second, they differ in **crystallized intelligence,** the knowledge and skills they have accumulated from their experiences, schooling, and culture. These two components may be more or less relevant to different kinds of tasks. Fluid intelligence relates more to novel tasks, especially those that require rapid decision making and are largely nonverbal in nature. Crystallized intelligence is more important for familiar tasks, especially those that are heavily dependent on language and prior knowledge.

According to Cattell, fluid intelligence is largely the result of inherited biological factors, whereas crystallized intelligence depends on both fluid intelligence and experience and so is influenced by both heredity and environment (Cattell, 1980, 1987). Fluid intelligence peaks in late adolescence and begins to decline gradually in adulthood. In contrast, crystallized intelligence continues to increase throughout childhood, adolescence, and most of adulthood (Cattell, 1963).

Cattell's research spawned numerous studies. Psychologists John Horn and John Carroll examined numerous individuals' test scores and realized that Cattell's distinction between fluid and crystallized abilities needed further differentiation. Eventually other scholars joined the effort, and a new integrative framework emerged, the Cattell-Horn-Carroll (CHC) theory of cognitive abilities (P. L. Ackerman & Lohman, 2006; Carroll, 1993, 2003; Horn, 2008; McGrew, 2005). In the CHC theory, intelligence has three layers, or *strata*. At the top layer (Stratum III) is general intelligence, or g. Emerging out of g are 10 broad abilities (in Stratum II), including *fluid intelligence*

Spearman's concept of g reflects the idea that intelligence may involve a general ability to think and reason about a wide variety of tasks.

g
General factor in intelligence that influences performance in a wide variety of tasks and content domains.

fluid intelligence
Ability to acquire knowledge quickly and thereby adapt effectively to new situations.

crystallized intelligence
Knowledge and skills accumulated from one's prior experience, schooling, and culture.

Figure 8-1

Cattell-Horn-Carroll model
of human abilities.
Abilities based on McGrew (2005).

Stratum III: General Intelligence *g*

Stratum II: Broad Abilities

Stratum I: Examples of Narrow Abilities

Reading/Writing — Recognizing words and comprehending text while reading

Auditory Processing — Identifying speech sounds in short-term memory

Decision/Reaction Time — Making rapid choices as to whether a series of side-by-side lines are of equal or different lengths

Cognitive Processing Speed — Copying familiar words or numbers at a rapid pace

Crystallized Intelligence — Understanding spoken words, sentences, and longer statements

Fluid Reasoning — Inferring the underlying properties of events and materials

Short-Term Memory — Attending to and recalling a series of numbers in the same order in which they were presented

Long-Term Storage & Retrieval — Recalling verbal items that are paired in memory, such as states with their capital cities

Visual-Spatial Abilities — Rotating a spatial form mentally and determining whether it matches another visual form

Quantitative Knowledge — Achieving in mathematics courses

and *crystallized intelligence,* the two abilities originally identified by Cattell. The other eight broad abilities are:

- *Quantitative knowledge* (applying knowledge about mathematical operations)
- *Reading/writing* (performing complex literacy skills)
- *Long-term storage and retrieval* (putting information into memory and remembering it)
- *Short-term memory* (attending to and remembering a small number of items for a short time)[1]
- *Visual-spatial abilities* (generating visual images and identifying patterns in an incomplete visual display)
- *Auditory processing* (analyzing and synthesizing sound elements and auditory patterns)
- *Cognitive processing speed* (performing easy and familiar tasks efficiently)
- *Decision/reaction speed* (making decisions quickly about simple stimuli).[2]

From out of these broad abilities, 70 to 100 very specific abilities (Stratum I) are differentiated—reading speed, mechanical knowledge, visual memory, and so on (see Figure 8-1). A considerable amount of data supports the CHC model. For example, numerous studies validate its assumptions about the multidimensional and hierarchical structure of intelligence, and the model is also generally consistent with research on the brain, developmental changes in children's intelligence, and evidence for hereditary and environmental factors in intelligence (McGrew, 2005). In addition, many school psychologists suggest that the CHC model can productively guide services for individual children who achieve at exceptionally advanced or delayed levels in academic areas or for those who are advanced in some areas and delayed in other subjects (Bergeron & Floyd, 2006; Fiorello & Primerano, 2005; Floyd, Bergeron, & Alfonso, 2006; Volker, Lopata, & Cook-Cottone, 2006). For example, when one teacher noticed that a sixth-grade girl appeared to be having trouble with short-term memory and basic reading skills, she consulted with a school psychologist (Fiorello & Primerano, 2005). Applying the comprehensive CHC model, the psychologist administered a battery of tests and found that most of the girl's abilities were strong (e.g., she had good language skills, vocabulary, long-term memory, and knowledge of letter-sound relationships), but she had difficulty remembering a sequence of spoken words (i.e., a problem with short-term [working] memory for auditory information). The psychologist recommended that the girl receive drills in spelling and letter-sound combinations so that these skills would eventually require little of her limited memory capacity. Other recommendations included allowing her to use a tape recorder during class, encouraging her to obtain notes from the teacher and a friend, and making available books on tape so she could review the information as many times as she needed to master it.

A disadvantage of the CHC model is that it is still evolving and obviously very complex, making its implications occasionally unclear. In addition, although it has been informed by numerous kinds of data, it is based primarily on existing intelligence tests and

[1]This component reflects the limited capacity of working memory, described in Chapters 6 and 7.
[2]An additional seven abilities (e.g., general knowledge, kinesthetic abilities, general cognitive speed) are currently under investigation for possible inclusion as broad abilities in the middle stratum (McGrew, 2005).

might be enhanced with additional data about human abilities, particularly perspectives from children's performance in non-Western cultures and nontraditional academic settings.

Gardner's Multiple Intelligences

American psychologist Howard Gardner (1995, 2003) concedes that a general factor may exist in intelligence, but he questions its usefulness in explaining people's performance in particular situations. In his view, children and adults have at least eight distinctly different abilities, or *multiple intelligences,* which are described and illustrated in Table 8-1. Gardner suggests that there may also be a ninth, "existential" intelligence dedicated to philosophical and spiritual issues (e.g., Who are we? Why do we die?). However, evidence for it is weaker than that for the other intelligences (Gardner, 1999, 2003), and so it is not included in the table.

Gardner presents some evidence to support the existence of multiple intelligences. For instance, he describes people who are quite skilled in one area (perhaps in composing music) and yet have seemingly average abilities in the other areas. He also points out that people who suffer brain damage sometimes lose abilities that are restricted primarily to one intelligence. One person might show deficits primarily in language, whereas another might have difficulty with tasks that require spatial reasoning. Thus, whereas Spearman's theory and the Cattell-Horn-Carroll model are based heavily (although not exclusively) on traditional test scores, Gardner and his colleagues argue that other kinds of data (e.g., studies of people with exceptional talents, studies of people with brain injuries) *must* be seriously considered to get a good picture of human beings' abilities (Gardner & Moran, 2006).

Furthermore, Gardner believes that the multiple intelligences may take somewhat different forms in different cultures, depending on how each culture shapes and molds the raw talents of its growing children. For example, in Western culture, spatial intelligence might be

Table 8-1   Gardner's Multiple Intelligences

Type of Intelligence[a]	Examples of Relevant Behaviors
Linguistic Intelligence Ability to use language effectively	· Making persuasive arguments · Writing poetry · Identifying subtle nuances in word meanings
Logical-Mathematical Intelligence Ability to reason logically, especially in mathematics and science	· Solving mathematical problems quickly · Generating mathematical proofs · Formulating and testing hypotheses about observed phenomena[b]
Spatial Intelligence Ability to notice details of what one sees and to imagine and manipulate visual objects in one's mind	· Conjuring up mental images · Drawing a visual likeness of an object · Making fine discriminations among very similar objects
Musical Intelligence Ability to create, comprehend, and appreciate music	· Playing a musical instrument · Composing a musical work · Showing a keen awareness of the underlying structure of music
Bodily-Kinesthetic Intelligence Ability to use one's body skillfully	· Dancing · Playing basketball · Performing pantomime
Interpersonal Intelligence Ability to notice subtle aspects of other people's behaviors	· Correctly perceiving another's mood · Detecting another's underlying intentions and desires · Using knowledge of others to influence their thoughts and behaviors
Intrapersonal Intelligence Awareness of one's own feelings, motives, and desires	· Identifying subtle differences in one's experiences of such similar emotions as sadness and regret · Identifying the motives guiding one's own behavior · Using self-knowledge to relate more effectively with others
Naturalist Intelligence Ability to recognize patterns in nature and differences among natural objects and life-forms	· Identifying members of particular plant or animal species · Classifying natural forms (e.g., rocks, types of mountains) · Applying one's knowledge of nature in such activities as farming, landscaping, or animal training

[a]Gardner has also suggested the possibility of an existential intelligence dedicated to philosophical and spiritual issues, but he acknowledges that evidence is weaker for it than for the eight intelligences described here.

[b]This example may remind you of Piaget's theory of cognitive development. Many of the stage-relevant characteristics that Piaget described fall within the realm of logical-mathematical intelligence.

Sources: Gardner, 1983, 1993, 1999, 2000a; Gardner & Hatch, 1990.

In Gardner's theory of multiple intelligences, the ability to draw lifelike renditions of three-dimensional objects falls in the domain of spatial intelligence. Art by Oscar, seventh grade (top), and Daniela, eighth grade (bottom).

reflected in painting, sculpture, or geometry. But among the Gikwe bushmen of the Kalahari Desert, it might be reflected in the ability to recognize and remember many specific locations over a large area (perhaps over several hundred square miles), identifying each location by the rocks, bushes, and other landmarks found there (Gardner, 1983).

Gardner's perspective offers the possibility that the great majority of children are intelligent in one way or another. Many educators have wholeheartedly embraced such an optimistic view of human potential and propose that all students can successfully master classroom subject matter when instructional methods capitalize on each student's intellectual strengths (e.g., L. Campbell, Campbell, & Dickinson, 1998; M. Kornhaber, Fierros, & Veenema, 2004). In psychological circles, however, reviews of Gardner's theory are mixed. Some psychologists do not believe that Gardner's evidence is sufficiently compelling to support the notion of eight or nine distinctly different abilities (N. Brody, 2006; A. R. Jensen, 2007; Sternberg, 2003a). Others agree that people may have a variety of relatively independent abilities but argue for intelligences other than the ones Gardner has described (e.g., Horn & Noll, 1997; Sternberg et al., 2000). Still others reject the idea that abilities in specific domains, such as in music or bodily movement, are really "intelligence" per se (Bracken, McCallum, & Shaughnessy, 1999; Sattler, 2001).

Sternberg's Triarchic Theory

In speculating about the nature of intelligence, American psychologist Robert Sternberg has made a number of distinctions that involve *threes* of something—hence the term *triarchic*. For one thing, he suggests that people may be more or less intelligent in three different domains (Sternberg, 1998, 2004, 2005; Sternberg et al., 2000). *Analytical intelligence* involves making sense of, analyzing, contrasting, and evaluating the kinds of information and problems often seen in academic settings and on intelligence tests. *Creative intelligence* involves imagination, invention, and synthesis of ideas within the context of new situations. *Practical intelligence* involves applying knowledge and skills effectively to manage and respond to everyday problems and social situations.

In addition, Sternberg proposes that intelligent behavior involves an interplay of three factors, all of which vary from one occasion to the next: (a) the environmental *context* in which the behavior occurs, (b) the way in which one's prior *experiences* are brought to bear on a particular task, and (c) the *cognitive processes* required by the task (Sternberg, 1985, 1997, 2003a). These three factors are summarized in Figure 8-2.

Role of environmental context. As noted earlier, intelligence involves adaptation. In Sternberg's view such adaptation might take one of three forms: (a) modifying a response to deal successfully with specific environmental conditions, (b) modifying the environment to better fit one's own strengths and needs, or (c) selecting an alternative environment more conducive to success. Furthermore, behavior may be more or less intelligent in different cultural contexts. For example, learning to read is an adaptive response in some cultures yet largely irrelevant to others.

Sternberg has identified three general skills that are especially adaptive in Western culture. One is *practical problem-solving ability,* such as

Figure 8-2

In Sternberg's triarchic model of intelligence, three different factors influence intelligent behavior.

the ability to identify exactly what the problem is in a particular situation, reason logically about the problem, and generate a multitude of possible problem solutions. A second skill is *verbal ability,* such as the ability to speak and write clearly, develop and use a large vocabulary, and understand and learn from what one reads. A third is *social competence,* such as the ability to relate effectively to other human beings, be sensitive to others' needs and wishes, and provide leadership.

Role of prior experience.   Intelligent behavior sometimes involves the ability to deal successfully with a brand-new situation. At other times, it involves the ability to deal with familiar situations rapidly and efficiently. In both cases, a child's prior experiences play a critical role. When children encounter a new task or problem, they must draw on past experience and consider the kinds of responses that have been effective in similar circumstances. When they deal with more familiar tasks, basic skills must be well practiced so that the necessary processes can be completed quickly and effortlessly.

Role of cognitive processes.   In addition to considering how context and prior experience affect behavior, we must also consider how a child thinks about (mentally processes) a particular task or situation. Sternberg suggests that numerous cognitive processes are involved in intelligent behavior: interpreting a new situation in productive ways, sustaining concentration on a task, separating important information from irrelevant details, identifying possible problem-solving strategies, finding relationships among seemingly different ideas, making effective use of external feedback, and so on. Some of these processes facilitate *knowledge acquisition* relevant to a task at hand, others are directly involved in the actual *performance* of the task, and still others comprise *metacognition* that oversees the entire endeavor (Sternberg, 2004). Different cognitive processes are likely to be relevant to different situations, and so a child may behave more or less "intelligently" depending on the specific cognitive processes needed at the time.

To date, research neither supports nor refutes the notion that intelligence has the various triarchic components that Sternberg describes. Certain aspects of Sternberg's theory (e.g., how various factors work together, what specific roles metacognition plays) are described in such general terms that they are difficult to test empirically (Sattler, 2001; Siegler & Alibali, 2005). The empirical evidence that does exist does not yet make a clear case that the practical abilities identified in Sternberg's theory are really different from general intelligence (N. Brody, 2006; L. Gottfredson, 2003). Sternberg himself acknowledges that most of the research supporting his theory has been conducted with relatively small samples and by his own research team (Sternberg, 2003b, 2005), rather than with large samples by outsiders who might be more objective or critical. Nevertheless, Sternberg's perspective helps us understand intelligence in terms of the specific cognitive processes that may underlie it. Furthermore, it reminds us that a child's ability to behave intelligently may vary considerably, depending on the particular context and specific knowledge and skills that a task requires. Some theorists believe that context makes all the difference in the world—a belief that is clearly evident in the concept of distributed intelligence.

Distributed Intelligence

Implicit in our discussion so far has been the assumption that intelligent behavior is something that children and adolescents engage in with little if any help from external resources. But some psychologists point out that youngsters are far more likely to behave intelligently when they have the support of their physical, social, and cultural environments (A. Bennett et al., 2007; Pea, 1993; Perkins, 1995; Sternberg, Grigorenko, & Bridglall, 2007). For example, it's easier for many adolescents to solve for x in the equation

$$\frac{7}{25} = \frac{x}{375}$$

if they have pencil and paper, or perhaps even a calculator, with which to work out the problem. And they are more likely to write a convincing persuasive essay if they brainstorm their ideas with peers before beginning to compose their notes.

The concept of distributed intelligence reminds us that children and adolescents often perform more intelligently when they work with others to tackle problems; employ charts, equations, and other symbolic tools to represent and transform information; and use computers to organize and manipulate data.

This idea that intelligent behavior depends on physical, social, and cultural support mechanisms is sometimes referred to as **distributed intelligence.** Children and adolescents can "distribute" their thinking (and therefore think more intelligently) in at least three ways (Pea, 1993; Perkins, 1992, 1995). First, they can use physical objects, especially technology (e.g., calculators, computers), to handle and manipulate large amounts of information. Second, they can work with others to explore ideas and solve problems. Third, they can represent and think about the situations they encounter using the various symbolic tools their culture provides—for instance, the words, diagrams, charts, mathematical equations, and so on that help them simplify or make better sense of complex topics and problems.

The framework of distributed intelligence has considerable appeal to many educators who recognize that *all* children—not just those who are advantaged with "smart" genes or those whose families foster their academic skills at home—deserve to have their abilities nurtured at school (Barab & Plucker, 2002; Hoerr, 2003). The framework appeals to other educators because its core ideas are frequently validated in research: Children often develop more advanced skills when working together, using new technologies, and tackling significant, realistic learning problems (G. Fischer & Konomi, 2007; Greeno, 2007). Theorists have only begun to explore the implications of a "distributed" view of intelligence, however. Much work remains to be done, both in identifying the specific ways in which the environment can support intelligent behavior and in determining how great an effect such support is likely to have.

The five perspectives just presented provide widely diverging views of human intelligence. Their differences with respect to the three themes—nature and nurture, universality and diversity, and qualitative and quantitative change—are presented in the Basic Developmental Issues table "Contrasting Theories of Intelligence."

Measuring Intelligence

Although psychologists have not been able to agree on what intelligence is, they have been trying to measure it for more than a century. In the early 1900s, school officials in France asked the psychologist Alfred Binet (1857–1911) to develop a way of identifying students who would have exceptional difficulty in regular classrooms and would therefore be in need of special educational services. To accomplish the task, Binet devised a test that measured general knowledge, vocabulary, perception, memory, and abstract thought. He found that students who performed poorly on his test tended to perform poorly in the classroom as well. Binet's test was the earliest version of what we now call an **intelligence test.** Today intelligence tests are widely used to assess children's cognitive functioning and predict academic achievement, especially when a child may possibly have special educational needs.

Tests of General Intelligence

Most intelligence tests in use today have been developed to do the same thing that Alfred Binet's first test was intended to do: identify people with special needs. In many cases, intelligence tests are used as part of a diagnostic battery of tests to determine why certain children are showing developmental delays or academic difficulties and whether they require special interventions or educational services. In other instances, intelligence tests are used to identify children with exceptionally high ability who are probably not being challenged by the regular school curriculum and may require more in-depth instruction or advanced classwork to nurture their cognitive growth.

Intelligence tests typically include a wide variety of questions and problems for children to tackle. By and large, the focus is not on what children have specifically been taught at school, but rather on what they have learned and deduced from their general, everyday experiences.

Examples of general intelligence tests.   To give you a feel for the nature of general intelligence tests, we briefly describe three of them.[3]

distributed intelligence
Thinking facilitated by physical objects and technology, social support, and concepts and symbols of one's culture.

intelligence test
General measure of current cognitive functioning, used primarily to predict academic achievement over the short run.

[3]You can find descriptions of several widely used standardized tests at www.ctb.com (for CTB and McGraw-Hill), www.riverpub.com (for Riverside Publishing), and www.harcourt.com (for Harcourt Assessment and Psychological Corporation).

Contrasting Theories of Intelligence

Issue	Spearman's General Factor (g)	Cattell-Horn-Carroll Theory of Cognitive Abilities	Gardner's Multiple Intelligences	Sternberg's Triarchic Theory	Distributed Intelligence
Nature and Nurture	Spearman did not specifically address the issue of nature versus nurture. Subsequent researchers have found evidence that g is probably influenced by both heredity and environment.	Proponents of the Cattell-Horn-Carroll model claim that some aspects of intelligence, such as fluid intelligence, are strongly determined by inherited factors. Other abilities, including crystallized intelligence, are influenced by both heredity and environmental experiences.	Gardner believes that heredity provides some basis for individual differences in the various intelligences. However, culture influences the form that each intelligence takes, and formal schooling influences the extent to which each intelligence flourishes.	Sternberg emphasizes the roles of environmental context (e.g., culture) and prior experience in intelligent behavior. Thus his focus is on nurture.	Environmental support mechanisms (physical tools, social interaction, and the symbolic representations of one's culture) influence a person's ability to behave intelligently.
Universality and Diversity	Spearman assumed that the existence of g is universal across cultures. However, people vary both in their general intellectual ability and in more specific abilities.	Substantial evidence exists that the multidimensional structure of abilities is universal. Individual children differ in levels of general intelligence, broad abilities, and specific abilities.	According to Gardner, the various intelligences are products of human evolution and so are seen worldwide. However, any particular intelligence will manifest itself differently in different environments and cultures.	The three factors that influence intelligent behavior (context, experience, cognitive processes) are universal. Different cultures may value and require different skills, however, so intelligence may take particular forms in each culture.	The physical, social, and symbolic support mechanisms at one's disposal vary widely from situation to situation and from one cultural group to another.
Qualitative and Quantitative Change	Spearman derived his theory from various tests of cognitive abilities. Implicit in such tests is the assumption that abilities change quantitatively over time.	Some evidence indicates a quantitative increase in fluid analytical abilities in childhood and adolescence and a gradual decline in adulthood (Cattell, 1963). Other evidence indicates that abilities change somewhat in a qualitative manner. For example, intelligence may be seen in 2-month-olds' responsiveness to the environment, in 8-month-olds' imitation of others' actions, and in 2-year-olds' labeling of objects (Tusing & Ford, 2004).	Growth in each intelligence has both quantitative and qualitative elements. For example, in logical-mathematical intelligence, children gain skills in increments (quantitatively) but also acquire new (and qualitatively different) abilities.	The effects of relevant prior experiences, more automatized knowledge and skills, and more efficient cognitive processes involve quantitative change. The acquisition of new strategies over time involves qualitative change.	Some contexts enhance intelligence quantitatively (e.g., children might remember more from a book when they not only read it but also can listen to an audiotape of the book). Other contexts enhance intelligence qualitatively (e.g., children are more likely to elaborate on a book's content when they are taught how to ask one another thought-provoking questions about the material; see Chapter 7).

Wechsler Intelligence Scale for Children. One widely used intelligence test is the fourth edition of the *Wechsler Intelligence Scale for Children,* or *WISC-IV* (Wechsler, 2003), designed for children and adolescents ages 6 to 16. The WISC-IV consists of 15 subtests, with various subtest scores being combined to obtain composite scores in Verbal Comprehension, Perceptual Reasoning, Working Memory, and Processing Speed. Many of the subtest scores are also combined to determine a total score, known as a Full Scale IQ. Examples of items like those on the WISC-IV are presented in Figure 8-3.

Stanford-Binet Intelligence Scales. A second commonly used instrument is the fifth edition of the *Stanford-Binet Intelligence Scales* (Roid, 2003; Thorndike, Hagen, & Sattler, 1986). The Stanford-Binet can be used with children as young as 2, adolescents, and adults. The individual being assessed is asked to perform a wide variety of tasks, some involving verbal material and responses (e.g., defining vocabulary words, finding logical inconsistencies in a story, or interpreting proverbs) and others involving concrete objects or pictures (e.g., remembering a sequence of objects, copying geometric figures, or identifying absurdities in pictures). The Stanford-Binet yields an overall IQ score, and its most recent edition (Roid, 2003) also yields Verbal and Nonverbal IQs, plus more specific scores in Fluid Reasoning, Knowledge, Working Memory, Visual-Spatial Processing, and Quantitative Reasoning.

Universal Nonverbal Intelligence Test. The WISC-IV and Stanford-Binet depend heavily on language: Even when tasks involve reasoning about strictly nonverbal, visual material, the child

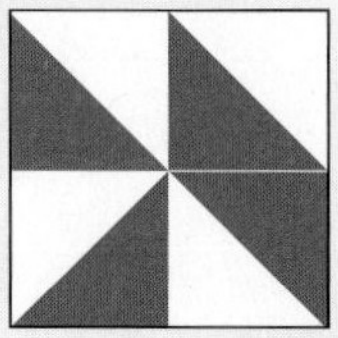

Figure 8-3

Items similar to those found on the *Wechsler Intelligence Scale for Children*®—Fourth Edition. Copyright © 2003 by Harcourt Assessment, Inc. Reproduced by permission. All rights reserved.

Following are descriptions of 6 of the 15 subtests on the WISC-IV, along with items similar to those included in the subtests.

Similarities
This subtest is designed to assess a child's verbal reasoning and concept formation.

- In what way are a lion and a tiger alike?
- In what way are an hour and a week alike?
- In what way are a circle and a triangle alike?

Comprehension
This subtest is designed to assess a child's understanding of general principles and social situations.

- What should you do if you see someone forget his book when he leaves a restaurant?
- What is the advantage of keeping money in a bank?
- Why is copper often used in electrical wires?

Information
This subtest is designed to assess a child's general knowledge about a broad range of topics.

- How many wings does a bird have?
- What is steam made of?
- What is pepper?

Letter-Number Sequencing
This subtest is designed to assess a child's working memory capacity. In each item, a letter-number sequence is presented, and the child is asked to

repeat first the numbers (in numerical order) and then the letters (in alphabetical order).

- Q-3 [Response: 3-Q]
- M-3-P-6 [Response: 3-6-M-P]
- 5-J-4-A-1-S [Response: 1-4-5-A-J-S]

Arithmetic
This subtest is designed to assess a child's ability to solve orally presented arithmetic problems within a certain time limit, tapping into both working memory capacity and knowledge of arithmetic.

- Sam had three pieces of candy and Joe gave him four more. How many pieces of candy did Sam have altogether?
- Three women divided eighteen golf balls equally among themselves. How many golf balls did each person receive?
- If two buttons cost $.15, what will be the cost of a dozen buttons?

Block Design
This subtest is designed to assess a child's ability to analyze and reproduce geometric designs, thus tapping into visual-spatial ability. The child looks at a series of designs, such as the one below, and is asked to re-create them using blocks that are solid red on two sides, solid white on two sides, and diagonally red and white on the remaining two sides.

is usually given verbal instructions about how to complete them. In contrast, some measures of intelligence involve no language whatsoever. An example is the *Universal Nonverbal Intelligence Test,* or *UNIT* (Bracken & McCallum, 1998; McCallum & Bracken, 2005). Designed for children and adolescents ages 5 to 17, the UNIT consists of six subtests involving memory or reasoning regarding visual stimuli (see Figure 8-4). Its content (e.g., people, mice,

Symbolic Memory is primarily a measure of short-term visual memory and complex sequential memory for meaningful material. The task is to view a sequence of universal symbols for 5 seconds and then re-create it from memory using the Symbolic Memory Cards.

Spatial Memory is primarily a measure of short-term visual memory for abstract material. The task is to view a pattern of green and/or black dots on a 3 × 3- or 4 × 4-cell grid for 5 seconds and then re-create the pattern from memory using green and black chips on a blank Response Grid.

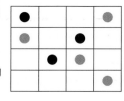

Object Memory is primarily a measure of short-term recognition and recall of meaningful symbolic material. The examinee is presented a randomly arranged pictorial array of common objects for 5 seconds, after which the stimulus page is removed, and a second pictorial array is presented containing all of the previously presented objects and additional objects to serve as foils. The task requires the examinee to identify objects presented in the first pictorial array by placing a response chip on the appropriate pictures.

Cube Design is primarily a measure of visual-spatial reasoning. The task requires the examinee to use two-colored cubes to construct a three-dimensional design that matches a stimulus picture.

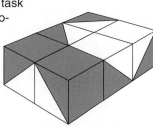

Analogic Reasoning is primarily a measure of symbolic reasoning. The task requires the examinee to complete matrix analogies that employ both common objects and novel geometric designs by pointing to one of four multiple choice options.

Mazes is primarily a measure of reasoning and planful behavior. The examinee uses paper and pencil to navigate and exit mazes by tracing a path from the center starting point of each maze to the correct exit, without making incorrect decisions en route. A series of increasingly complex mazes is presented.

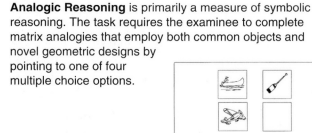

Figure 8-4

Items similar to those on the Universal Nonverbal Intelligence Test (UNIT).

cheese) was chosen from objects and symbols presumed to be universal across all industrialized cultures. Instructions are given entirely through gestures, pantomime, and modeling, and the child responds by either pointing or manipulating objects.

Nonverbal tests such as the UNIT are especially useful for children who have hearing impairments or language-related learning disabilities, as well as for children for whom English is a second language. For instance, children who are deaf and children who have been raised speaking a language other than English perform better on the UNIT than on more traditional language-based intelligence tests (Krivitski, McIntosh, Rothlisberg, & Finch, 2004; Maller, 2000; McCallum, 1999).

IQ scores. In the early 20th century, some psychologists began to calculate scores for intelligence tests by comparing a child's *mental age* (referring to the age-group of students whose performance was most similar to the child's performance) with his or her chronological age (W. Stern, 1912; Terman, 1916). The mathematical formula involved division, and so the resulting score was called an *intelligence quotient,* or **IQ score.**[4] Even though we still use the term *IQ,* intelligence test scores are no longer based on the old formula. Instead, they are determined by comparing a person's performance on the test with the performance of others in the same age-group. Scores near 100 indicate average performance: People with a score of 100 have performed better than half of their age-mates on the test and not as well as the other half. Scores well below 100 indicate below-average performance on the test, and scores well above 100 indicate above-average performance.

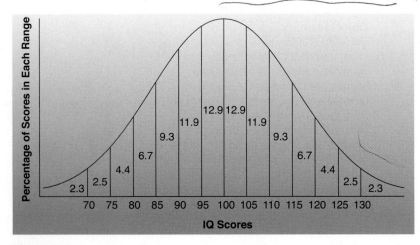

Figure 8-5

Percentage of IQ scores in different ranges.

Figure 8-5 shows the percentage of people getting scores at different points along the scale (e.g., 12.9% get scores between 100 and 105). Notice how the curve is high in the middle and low at both ends. This shape tells us that many more people obtain scores close to 100 than scores very much higher or lower than 100. For example, if we add up the percentages in different parts of Figure 8-5, we find that approximately two-thirds (68%) of individuals in any particular age-group score within 15 points of 100 (i.e., between 85 and 115). In contrast, only 2 percent score as low as 70, and only 2 percent score as high as 130.[5]

Figure 8-5 does not include scores below 70 or above 130. Such scores are possible but relatively rare. For instance, Gina, in the opening case study, once obtained a score of 140 on an intelligence test. A score of 140 is equivalent to a percentile rank of 99.4. In other words, only 6 people out of every 1,000 would earn a score as high as or higher than Gina's.

Validity and reliability of general intelligence tests. In Chapter 2 we introduced the concepts of validity and reliability. In general, the *validity* of an intelligence test is the extent to which it actually measures intelligence. The *reliability* of an intelligence test is the extent to which it yields consistent, dependable scores.

Researchers take a variety of approaches in their efforts to determine the validity of intelligence tests. For instance, they look for evidence that older children perform better on the test items than younger children—a result consistent with the assumption that children think more intelligently with age. Children's *IQ scores* do not necessarily increase with age, however, because these scores are based on peer comparisons rather than on improvement over

IQ score

Score on an intelligence test, determined by comparing one's performance with the performance of same-age peers.

[4]Alfred Binet himself objected to the use of intelligence quotients, believing that his tests were too imprecise to warrant such scores. Lewis Terman, an American psychologist, was largely responsible for popularizing the term *IQ* (Montagu, 1999a).

[5]This symmetrical and predictable distribution of scores happens by design rather than by chance. If you have some knowledge of descriptive statistics, you probably recognize Figure 8-5 as a normal distribution. IQ scores are based on a normal distribution with a mean of 100 and, for most tests, a standard deviation of 15.

time. As an example of age differences in performance on test questions, observe how three children define the word *freedom* in the "Intelligence" videos for middle childhood, early adolescence, and late adolescence in MyEducationLab:

Kate (age 8):   You want to be free. Or you want to play something . . . and you got caught and they have to keep you like in jail or something like in a game and you want to get free.

Ryan (age 13):   It means that you can, like, do stuff that you want.

Paul (age 17):   Basically something that everyone has these days or should have. It's the right to be able to make your own decisions and choose for yourself what you want to do or want to be.

Notice how, with age, the responses get increasingly abstract and complex. Kate limits her definition to a specific behavior, getting out of "jail" in a game. Ryan defines the term more abstractly and broadly, implying that it has relevance to a wide variety of situations. Paul offers an abstract definition as well, but his is more specific and precise than Ryan's.

Researchers also examine the validity of intelligence tests by determining how closely IQ scores correlate with school achievement and other indicators of intelligence. Many research studies indicate that traditional measures of general intelligence, such as the WISC-IV and the Stanford-Binet, have considerable validity in this respect. On average, children and adolescents who earn higher scores on these tests have higher academic achievement and complete more years of education than their lower-scoring peers (N. Brody, 1997; Gustafsson & Undheim, 1996; P. E. Williams, Weiss, & Rolfhus, 2003a). To a lesser extent, IQ scores also predict later performance in the adult workplace (Sattler, 2001; Sternberg, 1996). We have less information about the UNIT, because it has only recently arrived on the scene, but emerging evidence indicates that it, too, has some validity as a measure of intelligence (Farrell & Phelps, 2000; Fives & Flanagan, 2002; Krivitski et al., 2004; McCallum & Bracken, 1997, 2005; E. L. Young & Assing, 2000).

To determine the reliability of intelligence tests, researchers look at various indications of consistency, especially the extent to which the same test yields similar scores on two different occasions, the extent to which different subtests within a particular test yield similar results for a particular child, and the extent to which two different examiners score a child's performance in the same way. Children's scores on the WISC-IV, Stanford-Binet, and UNIT are highly reliable in these respects (Anastasi & Urbina, 1997; Sattler, 2001; P. E. Williams, Weiss, & Rolfhus, 2003b; E. L. Young & Assing, 2000).

Specific Ability Tests

Whenever we summarize a child's performance with a single IQ score, as we often do with general intelligence tests, we are to some extent buying into Spearman's concept of *g*. In contrast, **specific ability tests** have been developed to assess more narrowly focused cognitive abilities. Some of these tests, called *aptitude tests,* are designed to assess a person's potential to learn in particular content domains, such as mathematics or auto mechanics. Others focus on specific aspects of cognitive processing (e.g., memory for auditory information, ability to think and reason about spatial relationships) and are often used in identifying learning disabilities.

Specific ability tests have both strengths and limitations. They typically have high reliability and a reasonable degree of validity, at least in terms of how accurately they measure the specific abilities they're designed to assess (Anastasi & Urbina, 1997). Specific ability tests also have the advantage of providing reasonable clues as to how youngsters will later perform in particular contexts or professions. For example, in one study of intellectually talented adolescents, those who scored well on an aptitude test measuring spatial ability were especially likely to become engineers as adults (Shea, Lubinski, & Benbow, 2001). As a drawback, specific ability tests are typically designed to include only one or a few narrowly defined intellectual domains. For example, if a psychologist were to administer a single ability test rather than a more comprehensive intelligence instrument with well-defined subtests, it is possible that important clues to a child's talents and difficulties would be missed.

MyEducationLab

Notice how children's word definitions become increasingly sophisticated with age in the "Intelligence" videos for middle childhood, early adolescence, and late adolescence in the Video Examples section in Chapter 8 of MyEducationLab.

specific ability test
Test designed to assess a specific cognitive skill or the potential to learn and perform in a specific content domain.

Dynamic Assessment

The approaches described so far focus on what children can *currently* do with little or no assistance from anyone else. In contrast, **dynamic assessment** focuses on assessing children's ability to learn in new situations, usually with an adult's assistance (Feuerstein, 1979; Feuerstein, Feuerstein, & Gross, 1997; Haywood & Lidz, 2007; Tzuriel, 2000). Typically, dynamic assessment involves (a) identifying one or more tasks that children cannot initially do independently, (b) providing in-depth instruction and practice in behaviors and cognitive processes related to the task(s), and then (c) determining the extent to which each child has benefited from the instruction (Feuerstein, 1979, 1980; Lidz & Gindis, 2003; Tzuriel, 2000). Accordingly, dynamic assessment is sometimes called *assessment of learning potential*.

Dynamic assessment is consistent with several theoretical perspectives. As Sternberg has pointed out, intelligence involves adaptation to new situations (Sternberg, 1997, 2004). And as the concept of distributed intelligence reminds us, intelligent behavior is heavily context dependent. But Vygotsky's theory of cognitive development is probably most relevant here. As you learned in Chapter 6, Vygotsky proposed that we can get a more complete picture of children's cognitive development when we assess not only their *actual developmental level* (the upper limit of tasks they can successfully accomplish on their own), but also their *level of potential development* (the upper limit of tasks they can accomplish when they have the assistance of more competent individuals).

Dynamic assessment is a fairly new approach to assessing intelligence, so psychologists are only beginning to discover its strengths and weaknesses. On the plus side, it often yields more optimistic evaluations of children's abilities than traditional measures of intelligence and may be especially useful in assessing the abilities of children who have been raised outside of mainstream Western culture (Jeltova et al., 2007; Swanson & Lussier, 2001; Tzuriel, 2000). Furthermore, dynamic assessment can provide a wealth of qualitative information about children's experiences and approaches to learning and so may be helpful in guiding future instruction (Feuerstein, 1979; Hamers & Ruijssenaars, 1997; Moore-Brown, Huerta, Uranga-Hernandez, & Peña, 2006; Tzuriel, 2000). For example, in an intervention using dynamic assessments with children from culturally and linguistically diverse backgrounds, many of the children displayed competencies that were not evident on traditional intelligence tests (Moore-Brown et al., 2006). To illustrate, a boy named Justin was initially able to tell only a very simple story but after a brief period of instruction, he articulated complex ideas, expressed varied vocabulary, and used advanced grammar. In studying Justin's responses and records, his assessment team realized that his previous academic delays had probably been due to his frequent absences, tardiness, and weak educational foundation—not to limited intelligence. Accordingly, the team was optimistic that Justin could benefit a great deal from instruction designed to develop his missing academic skills.

Yet disadvantages of dynamic assessment are also emerging. Dynamic assessment often involves considerable training before it can be used appropriately, and it typically requires a great deal of time to administer (Anastasi & Urbina, 1997; Tzuriel, 2000). Furthermore, questions have been raised about how best to determine the validity and reliability of dynamic assessment instruments, and those instruments that have been evaluated have fared poorly in comparison to more traditional measures of intelligence (Swanson & Lussier, 2001; Tzuriel, 2000). Accordingly, when educators and psychologists use dynamic assessment to assess children's capabilities, they should do so cautiously and always within the context of other data. Generally, practitioners will find dynamic assessment to be of greater value in certain circumstances (e.g., determining what a child is capable of learning when appropriate help is available, major obstacles are removed, and second chances are given) and of less value in others (e.g., determining how much the child has learned and can now apply independently, and using test results to identify children possibly in need of special educational services) (Haywood & Lidz, 2007).

Assessing the Abilities of Infants and Young Children

If an adult is to assess a child's cognitive abilities accurately, the child must, of course, be a cooperative participant in the process—for instance, by staying alert, paying attention, and maintaining interest in the assessment tasks. Yet infants and young children are not always able to cooperate. Infants may be sleepy, fussy, or afraid of the stranger conducting the

dynamic assessment
Systematic examination of how a child's knowledge or reasoning may change as a result of learning a specific task or performing it with adult guidance.

assessment. Young children may have short attention spans, lose interest in the test questions and materials, or misinterpret instructions. Because of such factors, which can vary considerably from one occasion to the next, test scores for infants and young children are not always reliable (Anastasi & Urbina, 1997; L. Ford & Dahinten, 2005).

Nevertheless, teachers, child care providers, and other professionals sometimes need to monitor the cognitive development of infants and young children, perhaps to identify significant developmental delays that require intervention or perhaps to determine readiness for various kinds of educational experiences. Here we briefly describe the nature of tests available for infants, toddlers, and preschoolers.

Tests for infants and toddlers. Infants born in hospital settings are typically assessed as soon as they are born. At both 1 minute and 5 minutes after birth, a doctor or nurse evaluates their color, heart rate, reflexes, muscle tone, and breathing, giving each characteristic a rating between 0 and 2. A perfect score on this *Apgar Scale* is 10. A more in-depth assessment for young infants from birth until 2 months is the *Neonatal Behavioral Assessment Scale* (Brazelton Institute, 2008; Brazelton & Nugent, 1995). Often used to identify significant neurological abnormalities, it assesses alertness and attention, the quality of visual and auditory processing, and a variety of reflexes and behaviors.

Perhaps the most widely used test for older infants and toddlers is the second edition of the *Bayley Scales of Infant Development* (Bayley, 2005; L. Ford & Dahinten, 2005). Designed for children ages 1 month to 3½ years, it includes five scales. Three scales—for cognitive development (attention, memory, concept formation, etc.), language, and motor skills—are assessed through interactions with the child. Two additional scales—for social-emotional functioning and adaptive behavior—are assessed through parent questionnaires.

Tests of cognitive abilities for infants and toddlers might better be called *developmental assessments* than intelligence tests per se. They appear to assess current cognitive functioning reasonably well and can be helpful in identifying significant cognitive disabilities if used in combination with other information (Bradley-Johnson, 2001; Sattler, 2001). For example, when combined with observations of a child, interviews with parents, and medical records, developmental assessment results can help identify particular needs that can be addressed before they become serious problems. However, educators should keep in mind that measures of cognitive growth in the first few years of life are only modestly related to intelligence in later years (Fagan, Holland, & Wheeler, 2007; Hayslip, 1994; McCall, 1993). "Bright" babies do not necessarily become the brightest fourth graders, and toddlers who appear slow to learn may eventually catch up to, or even surpass, their peers (more about this point in the discussion of IQ stability later in the chapter).

In the "Intelligence: Infancy" video in MyEducationLab, you can observe 14-month-old Corwin stacking blocks and identifying pictures of various objects and animals. Such tasks are typical of developmental tests for toddlers. An examiner administering such a test might also rate Corwin on such characteristics as attention, engagement in the test activities, and emotional regulation.

Tests for preschoolers. As you've previously learned, the Stanford-Binet Intelligence Scales can be used for children as young as 2 years. Another commonly used test for young children is the third edition of the *Wechsler Preschool and Primary Scale of Intelligence,* or WPPSI-III (Wechsler, 2002). Suitable for children ages 2½ to 7, the WPPSI-III has 14 subtests, some similar to those on the WISC-IV and others (e.g., naming a pictured object) more appropriate for young children. In addition to an overall IQ, it yields a Verbal IQ (based on subtests that depend heavily on a child's language skills), a Performance IQ (based on subtests that require only minimal use of language), a score for General Language, and (for children ages 4 and older) a measure of Processing Speed.

As measures of intelligence for young children, both the Stanford-Binet and WPPSI-III correlate with other measures of intelligence and provide reasonable estimates of children's current cognitive functioning. In other words, their scores have some validity and reliability (Lichtenberger & Kaufman, 2003; McCallum, 1991; Sattler, 2001). Although young children's

MyEducationLab

Observe an Apgar Scale being performed on a newborn child in the video "An Apgar Assessment." (Find Video Examples in Chapter 8 of MyEducationLab.)

The Bayley Scales of Infant Development, designed for children ages 1 month to 3½ years, are sometimes used when significant developmental delays are suspected.

MyEducationLab

Observe tasks similar to those on infant tests of cognitive abilities in the "Intelligence: Infancy" video. (Find Video Examples in Chapter 8 of MyEducationLab.)

IQ scores correlate somewhat with their scores in later years, the correlations are modest at best—no doubt because many young children have high energy levels, short attention spans, and little interest in sitting still for more than a few minutes. Thus measures of IQ obtained in the preschool years should *not* be used to make predictions about children's academic performance over the long run (Bracken & Walker, 1997).

Other tests for preschoolers, known as *school readiness tests,* are designed to determine whether children have acquired cognitive skills (e.g., the ability to pay attention; to count and perform simple mathematical procedures; and to identify letters, colors, and shapes) that many kindergarten and first-grade teachers view as essential foundations for their curricula. Although widely used in school districts, such tests have come under fire in recent years, for two reasons. First, the scores they yield correlate only moderately at best with children's academic performance even a year or so later (G. J. Duncan et al., 2007; La Paro & Pianta, 2000; Stipek, 2002). Second, by age 5, most children are probably ready for some sort of structured educational program. Rather than determining whether children can adapt to a particular educational curriculum and environment, it is probably more beneficial to determine how the school curriculum and environment can be adapted to fit each child's particular needs (Lidz, 1991; Stipek, 2002).

As you can see, we must be careful about how we interpret and use the results of intelligence tests and other measures of cognitive abilities. As a general rule, and especially when test results are used to make decisions about young children, educators and other practitioners should use test scores only in combination with other information: observations of the children in a variety of settings, interviews with parents and teachers, and so on. Practitioners should also reserve judgment about the extent to which IQ scores reflect children's inherited abilities, on the one hand, or their environments and background experiences, on the other. In the next section we sift through the data concerning the relative effects of heredity and environment.

Effects of Heredity and Environment on Intelligence

As you are finding throughout this book, it is next to impossible to separate the relative influences of heredity and environment on human characteristics. People who have similar genetic makeups (e.g., brothers and sisters, parents and their children) typically live in similar environments as well. So when we see similarities in IQ among members of the same family, it is hard to know whether those similarities are due to genes or to the environments that family members share. Nevertheless, a significant body of research tells us that both heredity and environment affect intelligence.

Evidence for Hereditary Influences

Earlier we mentioned that measures of information processing speed correlate with IQ scores. Speed of processing depends on neurological efficiency and maturation, which are in large part genetically controlled. From this standpoint, then, we have some support for a hereditary basis for intelligence (Polderman et al., 2006). The fact that children with certain genetic defects (e.g., Down syndrome) have, on average, significantly lower IQ scores than their nondisabled peers (Keogh & MacMillan, 1996) provides further evidence of heredity's influence. But perhaps the most convincing evidence comes from twin studies and adoption studies.

Twin studies. Numerous studies have used monozygotic (identical) twins and dizygotic (fraternal) twins to get a sense of how strongly heredity affects IQ. Because monozygotic twins begin as a single fertilized egg, which then separates, their genetic makeups are virtually equivalent. In contrast, dizygotic twins are conceived as two separate fertilized eggs. They share about 50 percent of their genes, with the other 50 percent being unique to each twin. Most twins are raised together by the same parent(s) and in the same home, and so they share similar environments. Thus comparisons between the correlations of IQs in monozygotic and dizygotic twins can inform us about the impact of heredity on intelligence. For example, in one study, children were studied over several years to determine how their IQ scores correlated with siblings' scores (E. G. Bishop et al., 2003). If you take a look at the two columns for twins in Table 8-2, you will notice that the correlations for monozygotic twins are consistently higher

Table 8-2   Correlations Between IQs of Sibling Pairs Living Together

Age of Children[a]	Monozygotic Twins	Dizygotic Twins	Non-Twin Biological Siblings	Adopted Siblings
Age 1	.59	.40	.38	.07
Age 3	.77	.51	.37	.26
Age 7	.76	.40	.47	.04
Age 9	.80	.21	.40	.24

[a]Tests of ability were administered to the same children repeatedly over several years as part of a longitudinal study.
Source: E. G. Bishop et al., 2003.

than the correlations for dizygotic twins, non-twin siblings, and adopted siblings.[6] This pattern has been observed in many other investigations as well and indicates that intelligence has a sizable genetic basis. In fact, even when twins are raised separately (perhaps because they have been adopted and raised by different parents), they typically have similar IQ scores (Bouchard & McGue, 1981; W. Johnson, Bouchard, et al., 2007; Plomin & Petrill, 1997).

Adoption studies.   Another way to identify the effects of heredity is to compare adopted children with both their biological and adoptive parents. Adopted children tend to be similar to their biological parents in genetic makeup. Their environment, of course, more closely matches that of their adoptive parents. Researchers have found that adopted children's IQ scores are more highly correlated with their biological parents' IQs than with their adoptive parents' IQs. In other words, in a group of people who place their infants up for adoption, those with the highest IQs tend to have offspring who, despite being raised by other people, also have the highest IQs. Furthermore, the IQ correlations between adopted children and their biological parents become stronger, and those between the children and their adoptive parents become weaker, as the children grow older, especially during late adolescence (Bouchard, 1997; McGue, Bouchard, Iacono, & Lykken, 1993; Plomin, Fulker, Corley, & DeFries, 1997; Plomin & Petrill, 1997). (If you find this last research result puzzling, we'll offer an explanation shortly.)

Researchers also compare correlations among the IQs of adopted siblings with correlations among twins and nonadopted siblings (ordinary biological brothers and sisters). If you look again at Table 8-2, you can see that the IQ correlations for dizygotic twins and nonadopted siblings are higher than most of the correlations for adopted siblings. In other words, children who are genetically related resemble one another intellectually more than do children who are unrelated biologically.

Keep in mind that twin and adoption studies do not completely separate the effects of heredity and environment (W. A. Collins, Maccoby, Steinberg, Hetherington, & Bornstein, 2000; Wahlsten & Gottlieb, 1997). For example, an adopted child has shared a common environment for at least 9 months—the period of prenatal development—with his or her biological mother. Likewise, monozygotic twins who are separated at birth are often placed by adoption agencies in families that are similar in educational backgrounds and income levels. Furthermore, twin studies and adoption studies do not allow researchers to examine the ways in which heredity and environment might interact in their effects on measured intelligence. And interactive effects are often added to the "heredity" side of the scoreboard (W. A. Collins et al., 2000; Turkheimer, 2000). Despite such glitches, twin and adoption studies point convincingly to a genetic component in intelligence (Bouchard, 1997; N. Brody, 1992; E. Hunt, 1997; Neisser, 1998a; Petrill & Wilkerson, 2000).

This is not to say that children are predestined to have an intelligence level similar to that of their biological parents. Environment also makes an appreciable difference, as we shall now see.

Even when identical twins are raised by different families, they typically have similar IQ scores, indicating that intelligence has a biological component. However, twins raised in different homes are somewhat less similar than twins raised in the same home, indicating that environment affects intelligence as well.

[6]In our teaching experiences, we have found that some students erroneously interpret the higher correlations as indicating that identical twins have higher intelligence. This is, of course, not the case. The size of each correlation indicates the *strength of the relationship* between IQs, not the level of twins' intelligence per se.

Evidence for Environmental Influences

Numerous sources of evidence converge to indicate that environment has a significant impact on IQ scores. We find some of this evidence in twin and adoption studies. Investigations into the effects of nutrition, toxic substances, home environment, early intervention, and formal schooling provide additional support for the influence of environment. Also, a steady increase in performance on intelligence tests during the past several decades—known as the *Flynn effect*, to be discussed shortly—is probably at least partly attributable to environmental factors.

Twin studies and adoption studies revisited.   Twin studies also reveal evidence for environmental effects. Comparing across multiple separate investigations, researchers have found an average correlation of .85 for monozygotic twins reared together and an average correlation of .74 for monozygotic twins reared apart (Devlin, Daniels, & Roeder, 1997). In other words, twins raised in different homes have less similar IQs than twins raised in the same home. Adoption studies, too, indicate that intelligence is not determined entirely by heredity (Capron & Duyme, 1989; Devlin, Fienberg, Resnick, & Roeder, 1995; Waldman, Weinberg, & Scarr, 1994). For instance, in one study (Scarr & Weinberg, 1976), some children of low-income parents (with unknown IQs) were adopted by middle-class parents with IQs averaging 118 to 121. Other children remained with their biological parents. IQ averages of adopted children were 105, whereas IQ averages of nonadopted children were 90. Although the adopted children's IQ scores were, on average, lower than those of their adoptive parents, they were about 15 points higher than the scores for the children who were raised by their biological parents. Thus, in a range of comprehensive studies examining genetic contributions to intelligence, there is almost always some indication of an effect for the environment (e.g., Kovas et al., 2007).

Effects of early nutrition.   Severe malnutrition, either before birth or during the early years of life, can limit neurological development and have a long-term impact on cognitive development and intelligence (McDermott, Durkin, Schupf, & Stein, 2007; Ricciuti, 1993). Attention, memory, abstract reasoning, and general school achievement are all likely to suffer from inadequate nutrition. Children sometimes recover from short periods of poor nourishment (due, perhaps, to war or illness), but the adverse effects of long-term deprivation are more enduring (Sigman & Whaley, 1998).

Some research studies have examined the effects of providing medically approved food supplements and vitamins to infants and young children who would not otherwise have adequate nutrition. Such interventions are most likely to enhance the development of motor skills, but in some instances cognitive development is enhanced as well (Pollitt & Oh, 1994; Sigman & Whaley, 1998).

Effects of toxic substances.   A variety of toxic substances, or *teratogens,* in children's prenatal environments—for instance, alcohol, drugs, radiation, lead-based paint dust—affect neurological development and thus also affect children's later IQ scores (e.g., Dilworth-Bart & Moore, 2006; Michel, 1989; Ris, Dietrich, Succop, Berger, & Bornschein, 2004; Schuler, Nair, & Harrington, 2003; Streissguth, Barr, Sampson, & Bookstein, 1994). You may recall learning about *fetal alcohol syndrome* in Chapter 4. Children with fetal alcohol syndrome have mothers who consumed large amounts of alcohol during pregnancy; as a result these children show poor motor coordination, delayed language, and mental retardation. Exposure to toxic substances can also threaten intelligence during infancy and early childhood because children's brains are growing rapidly during the first few years of life and are especially vulnerable to harm.

Effects of home environment.   One likely explanation for the beneficial effects of adoption is that adoptive parents, who typically have adequate financial resources and high levels of education, can provide a more stimulating home environment than the biological parents might have been able to offer. Correlational studies indicate that stimulating home environments (e.g., those in which parents interact frequently with their children, make numerous learning and reading materials available, encourage the development of new skills, use complex sentence structures in conversation) are associated with higher IQ scores in children (R. H. Bradley & Caldwell, 1984; Tong, Baghurst, Vimpani, & McMichael, 2007). Furthermore, when two biologically *un*related children of the same age are raised by the same parents (typically because one or both children are adopted), the children's IQs tend to be more similar than we would expect by chance alone, a relationship that can be attributed primarily to the influence of a common home environment (N. L. Segal, 2000).

We find especially convincing evidence for the beneficial effects of stimulating home environments in an ongoing project in Romania (C. A. Nelson, 2005). As a result of previous government policies, most Romanian orphans were at one time raised in large institutions. After a change in government and the intervention of a team of developmental psychologists, some institutionalized infants (randomly selected) were placed with adults willing to serve as foster parents. (Sadly, the intervention team could not find foster families for all of the infants.) As researchers periodically assessed the children's physical and cognitive development, they found dramatic differences between the two groups. Despite adequate nutrition, children remaining in an institution throughout infancy and the preschool years had smaller head circumferences and less brain activity than the foster children. When intelligence was assessed, the institutionalized children had an average IQ of 64, which is on par for a person with mental retardation, whereas the foster children, on average, had IQs in the normal range.

Effects of early intervention.

When children live in impoverished or neglectful home environments, enriching preschool programs and other forms of early intervention can make an appreciable difference. For instance, high-quality child care and preschool programs (e.g., Head Start) frequently lead to short-term IQ gains and other cognitive and academic benefits (Bronfenbrenner, 1999; NICHD Early Child Care Research Network, 2002; Zigler, 2003). The effects of such programs don't continue indefinitely, however. Without follow-up interventions during the elementary school years, cognitive advantages (e.g., higher IQ scores and academic achievement) often diminish over time and in some cases disappear altogether (Brooks-Gunn, 2003; Farran, 2001).

We must not be disheartened by such results. Publicly funded preschool programs such as Head Start often enroll the most economically disadvantaged children in the community. To study the long-term effects of these programs, researchers sometimes have difficulty finding an appropriate control group. For instance, they may compare children who attended the programs with children who, though not attending preschool, grew up in more advantaged circumstances (Schnur, Brooks-Gunn, & Shipman, 1992). Therefore, it is difficult to detect the advantages of the intervention because the groups were not identical beforehand. Furthermore, early intervention often leads to long-term improvements in areas not reflected in IQ test scores. For instance, children who attend intensive, developmentally appropriate academic preschool programs are, later on, more likely to have high achievement motivation and self-esteem, less likely to exhibit serious behavior problems or need special education services, and more likely to graduate from high school and attend college (Kağitçibaşi, 2007; Ludwig & Phillips, 2007; McCall & Plemons, 2001; NICHD Early Child Care Research Network, 2006a).

Early intervention is most effective in fostering intellectual development when it is tailored to children's existing abilities and interests. But bombarding infants and small children with constant or intense stimulation is *not* effective. As you discovered in Chapter 6, children seem to have a natural desire to learn about their environment, and most eagerly explore their surroundings. But they can handle only so much information—and certainly only so much *new* information—at any one time. Furthermore, pushing young children into exceptionally challenging (perhaps age-*in*appropriate) activities can cause stress, depression, and, in some cases, physical harm (Elkind, 1987). Ultimately, a secure, supportive relationship with one or more caregivers or teachers is just as important as age-appropriate toys and activities (Loeb, Fuller, Kagan, & Carrol, 2004; NICHD Early Child Care Research Network, 2002).

Effects of formal schooling.

The very act of attending school leads to small increases in IQ. In Western societies, children who begin their educational careers early and attend school regularly have higher IQ scores than children who do not. When children must start school later than they would otherwise for reasons beyond their families' control, their IQs are at least 5 points lower for every year of delay. Furthermore, children's IQ scores decline slightly (usually only temporarily) over the course of the summer months, when children are not attending school. And other things being equal, children who drop out of school have lower

Research indicates that stimulating preschool experiences often increase IQ in economically disadvantaged children, at least over the short run.

IQ scores than children who remain in school, losing an average of almost 2 IQ points for every year of high school not completed (Ceci, 2003; Ceci & Williams, 1997).

The benefits of schooling for intellectual growth are seen in a wide variety of cultures. As Vygotsky pointed out, schooling provides a systematic means through which children can acquire many concepts and perspectives that previous generations have developed to tackle day-to-day tasks and problems effectively. In addition, participation in school generally encourages the acquisition of the advanced cognitive processes you read about in Chapter 7 (e.g., elaboration, organization, metacognition) (M. Cole, 2006; Nettelbeck & Wilson, 2005).

The Flynn effect.   The past few decades have seen a slow, steady increase in people's average performance on IQ tests throughout the industrialized world (Flynn, 1987, 2007; Neisser, 1998b). This trend is commonly known as the **Flynn effect.** A similar change has been observed in children's performance on traditional Piagetian tasks (Flieller, 1999). Conceivably some genetic factors may be having an impact here. For example, recent decreases in the numbers of children conceived by first cousins and other close relatives appear to have strengthened the overall intelligence of human beings (Mingroni, 2007). Yet most theorists believe that the Flynn effect is largely the result of changes in children's environments worldwide. Better nutrition, smaller family sizes, higher quality home environments, better schooling (for parents as well as children), and more enriching and informative stimulation (increased access to television, reading materials, etc.) are all possible contributing factors (Daley, Whaley, Sigman, Espinosa, & Neumann, 2003; Flynn, 2003; Neisser, 1998b).

How Nature and Nurture Interact in Their Influence on Intelligence

Clearly both nature and nurture influence intelligence. What is less clear is *how much* influence each of these factors has. A few theorists have tried to estimate nature's contribution (the *heritability* of IQ) from the correlations obtained in twin and adoption studies (e.g., Kovas et al., 2007; McGue et al., 1993; Plomin et al., 1997). But most psychologists now believe that it may ultimately be impossible to separate the relative effects of heredity and environment. They suggest that the two combine to influence children's cognitive development and measured IQ in ways that we can probably never disentangle (e.g., W. A. Collins et al., 2000; Rogoff, 2003; Turkheimer, Haley, Waldron, D'Onofrio, & Gottesman, 2003). Theorists have made the following general points about how nature and nurture interact as they affect intellectual development:

• *Heredity establishes a range rather than a precise figure.* Heredity does not dictate that a child will have a particular IQ score. Instead, it appears to set a range of abilities within which children will eventually fall, with the actual ability level each one achieves depending on his or her specific environmental experiences (Weinberg, 1989). Heredity may also affect how susceptible or resistant a child is to particular environmental influences (Rutter, 1997). For example, high-quality instruction may be more important for some children than for others. In the opening case study, Gina learned how to read before she attended school and with only minimal help from her mother. Yet other, equally intelligent children may learn to read *only* when they have systematic reading instruction tailored to their individual needs.

• *Genetic expression is influenced by environmental conditions.* As you learned in Chapter 4, genes are not entirely self-contained, independent "carriers" of developmental instructions. Rather, the particular instructions they transmit are influenced by the supportive or nonsupportive nature of children's environments. In an extremely impoverished environment—one with a lack of adequate nutrition and little if any stimulation—heredity may have little to say about the extent to which children develop intellectually. In an ideal environment—one in which nutrition, parenting practices, and educational opportunities are optimal and age-appropriate—heredity can have a significant influence on children's IQ scores (Ceci, 2003; Turkheimer, Haley, Waldron, D'Onofrio, & Gottesman, 2003).

Furthermore, intelligence is the result of many genes, each contributing a small amount to measured IQ (Sattler, 2001). These genes may "kick in" at different points in development, and their expression will be influenced by particular environmental conditions at those times.

Flynn effect
Gradual increase in intelligence test performance observed in many countries during the past several decades.

Thus we do not have a single heredity–environment interaction, but rather a number of heredity–environment interactions all contributing to intellectual growth (Simonton, 2001).

• ***Especially as they get older, children choose their environments and experiences.*** Children may actively seek out environmental conditions that match their inherited abilities—a phenomenon known as **niche-picking** (Flynn, 2003; Halpern & LaMay, 2000; Scarr & McCartney, 1983). For example, children who, genetically speaking, have exceptional quantitative reasoning ability may enroll in advanced mathematics courses, delight in tackling mathematical brainteasers, and in other ways nurture their own inherited talents. Children with average quantitative ability are less likely to take on such challenges and so have fewer opportunities to develop their mathematical skills. In such circumstances the relative effects of heredity and environment are difficult to tease apart.

Earlier we mentioned that the IQ correlations between adopted children and their biological parents become stronger over time. We now have a possible explanation for this finding. Children gain increasing independence as they get older. Especially as they reach adolescence, they spend less time in their home environments, and they make more of their own decisions about the kinds of opportunities to pursue—decisions undoubtedly based, in part, on their natural talents and tendencies (McGue et al., 1993; Petrill & Wilkerson, 2000). Similarly, correlations between the IQs of monozygotic twins increase in strength with age and presumably as twins become better able to act on the genetic tendencies they share (you can see an age-related increase in IQ correlations for monozygotic twins in Table 8-2) (Hoekstra, Bartels, & Boomsma, 2007).

You might think of intelligence as being the result of four factors (Gottlieb, 1991, 1992). *Genetic activity* affects *neural activity* (i.e., the operation of neurons in the brain), which in turn affects *behavior*, which in turn affects the *environment*. But influence moves in the opposite direction as well: The environment affects behavior, and these two (through stimulation, nutritional intake, physical activity, etc.) affect neural activity and genetic expression. The continuing interplay of genetics, neural activity, behavior, and environment is depicted in Figure 8-6.

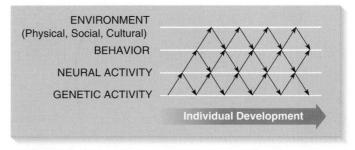

Figure 8-6

Bidirectional influences among genetic activity, neural activity, behavior, and environment.
From *Individual Development and Evolution: The Genesis of Novel Behavior* (p. 186), by G. Gottlieb, New York: Oxford University Press, Inc. Copyright © 1991 by Gilbert Gottlieb. Reprinted with permission.

Developmental Trends in IQ Scores

In one sense, children definitely become more "intelligent" as they develop: They know more, can think in more complex ways, and can solve problems more effectively. However, IQ scores are based not on how much children develop over time, but rather on how well children perform in comparison with their age-mates. By definition, the average IQ score for any age-group is 100. On average, then, IQ does not increase with age.

Nevertheless, IQ scores do change in two important ways over the course of development:

• ***IQ scores become increasingly stable.*** As noted previously, children's early performance on infant measures of cognitive development are not terribly predictive of their later intelligence. We've already encountered two reasons for the poor predictive powers of infant tests. First, infants' moods and priorities may be at odds with the demands of testing. Second, the various genes contributing to intelligence are activated at different times over the course of development. In addition, the types of items on intelligence tests for young children are often considerably different than items on tests for older children and adolescents. The Developmental Trends table "Intelligence at Different Age Levels" identifies some commonly used indicators of intelligence at various age levels, along with important considerations to keep in mind for each level.

As children progress through the school years, their IQ scores tend to hover within an increasingly narrow range. Although children continue to develop cognitively, each child's relative intelligence in comparison with peers changes less as time goes on (N. Brody, 1992; Neisser et al., 1996; Sattler, 2001). As an example, look once again at the chapter's opening case study. Gina obtained an IQ score of 140 (equivalent to the 99th percentile) in junior high school and performed at a similar level on college aptitude tests several years later.

niche-picking
Tendency to actively seek out environments that match one's inherited abilities.

Intelligence at Different Age Levels

Age	What You Might Observe	Diversity	Implications
Infancy (Birth–2 Years)	· Success on test items that involve early developmental accomplishments (e.g., recognition of previously seen objects, visual preferences, eye–hand coordination) · Distractibility and short attention span · Variability in performance from one assessment to the next · Performance dependent on examiner's ability to establish a positive relationship with the infant	· Temperamental differences (e.g., a tendency to be shy or cautious) affect infants' willingness to interact with the examiner and test materials. · Compared to full-term infants, infants born prematurely are less physically developed and more easily fatigued and so tend to obtain somewhat lower test scores. However, with good medical care and families' responsive involvement, many premature infants gradually develop into healthy, intelligent individuals. · Exposure to drugs or alcohol before birth may adversely affect test performance.	· Create a secure and comfortable examiner–child relationship before beginning an assessment. · Use results only to identify significant developmental delays requiring immediate intervention; refrain from making long-term predictions about intellectual growth. · Communicate honestly with parents about their child's test performance, while also describing the test's strengths and weaknesses as an assessment tool.
Early Childhood (2–6 Years)	· Success on test items that involve naming objects, stacking blocks, drawing circles and squares, remembering short lists, and following simple directions · Short attention span, influencing test performance · Variability in test scores from one occasion to the next	· Significant developmental delays in the early years may indicate mental retardation or other disabilities. · On average, children from lower-income families perform at lower levels on measures of cognitive development than children from middle-income families; however, enriching preschool experiences can narrow and occasionally eliminate the gap.	· Use IQ tests primarily to identify significant delays in cognitive development; follow up by seeking intervention programs for children with such delays. · Provide preschool experiences that foster children's language skills, knowledge of numbers and counting, and visual-spatial thinking.
Middle Childhood (6–10 Years)	· Success on test items that involve defining concrete words, remembering sentences and short sequences of digits, understanding concrete analogies, recognizing similarities among objects, and identifying absurdities in illogical statements · Some consistency in test scores from one occasion to the next · Noticeable differences among children in mastery of classroom subject matter	· For this age range, many intelligence tests become increasingly verbal in nature; thus proficiency with the English language can significantly affect test performance. · Children with learning disabilities may perform poorly on some parts of an intelligence test. · Children from some ethnic minority groups may perform poorly in situations where the examiner has not established rapport.	· Individualize instruction to match children's varying abilities to learn in particular content domains. · Do *not* assume that poor performance in some domains necessarily indicates limited ability to learn in other areas. · Take children's cultural and linguistic backgrounds into account when interpreting IQ scores.
Early Adolescence (10–14 Years)	· Success on test items that involve defining commonly used abstract words, drawing logical inferences from verbal descriptions, and identifying similarities between opposite concepts · Considerable individual differences in the ability to understand abstract material	· Some adolescents (especially those from certain ethnic minority groups) may not perceive high test performance as having personal benefits and so may not be motivated to perform at their best. · Some adolescents who are gifted may try to hide their talents; cultures that stress traditional male and female roles may actively discourage females from achieving at high levels.	· Expect considerable diversity in adolescents' ability to master abstract classroom material, and individualize instruction accordingly. · Make sure that school enrichment programs include students from ethnic minority groups; do not rely exclusively on IQ scores to identify students as gifted.
Late Adolescence (14–18 Years)	· Success on test items that involve defining infrequently encountered words, identifying differences between similar abstract words, interpreting proverbs, and breaking down complex geometric figures into their component parts · Relative stability in most adolescents' IQ scores · Increasing independence to seek out opportunities consistent with existing ability levels (niche-picking)	· Concerns about appearing "too smart" may continue into the high school years. · Some members of minority groups may underperform because their awareness of negative group stereotypes creates debilitating anxiety during a test (see the discussion of *stereotype threat* on p. 298).	· Provide challenging activities for teenagers who are gifted. · Encourage bright adolescents from lower-income families to pursue a college education, and help them with the logistics of college applications (e.g., applying for financial aid).

Sources: Bayley, 2005; Brooks-Gunn, 2003; Brooks-Gunn, Klebanov, & Duncan, 1996; Colombo, 1993; G. A. Davis & Rimm, 1998; S. I. Greenspan & Meisels, 1996; Luckasson et al., 2002; Mayes & Bornstein, 1997; McLoyd, 1998b; Ogbu, 1994; Steele, 1997; Terman & Merrill, 1972; A. Thomas & Chess, 1977; Thorndike et al., 1986; Wechsler, 2002, 2003.

Despite the increasing stability of IQ scores, we must remember that these scores simply reflect youngsters' performance on a particular test at a particular time. Some degree of change (sometimes as much as 10 to 20 points' worth, and occasionally even more) can reasonably be expected over the years. The longer the time interval between two administrations of an intelligence test, the greater the change in IQ we are likely to see, especially when young children are involved (B. S. Bloom, 1964; L. G. Humphreys, 1992; McCall, 1993; Sattler, 2001). IQ scores and other measures of cognitive ability are most likely to increase when children are highly motivated and independent learners and when they have ongoing exposure to stimulating activities, high-quality instruction, and a variety of reading materials (e.g., Echols, West, Stanovich, & Kehr, 1996; Sameroff, Seifer, Baldwin, & Baldwin, 1993; Schellenberg, 2004).

- ***IQ scores become increasingly accurate predictors of future academic achievement.*** As IQ scores become more stable with age, their usefulness in predicting classroom performance also increases. Yet educators should remember two things about the relationship between IQ and academic achievement. First, intelligence by itself does not *cause* achievement. Even though children with high IQs typically perform well in school, we cannot say conclusively that their high achievement is actually the result of their intelligence. Intelligence certainly plays an important role in school performance, but many other factors—motivation, quality of instruction, family resources and support, peer group norms, and so on—are also involved. Second, the relationship between IQ scores and achievement is an imperfect one, with many exceptions. For a variety of reasons, some children with high IQ scores do not perform well in the classroom. And other children achieve at higher levels than would be predicted from their IQ scores alone. Educators and other adults should never base their expectations for children's achievement solely on intelligence test scores.

Adults should never base their expectations for children's achievement solely on intelligence test scores. Many students achieve at higher levels than their IQ scores predict.

Group Differences in Intelligence

In this section we shift our focus from individual children to groups of children. Specifically, we now examine research findings related to possible gender, socioeconomic, ethnic, and racial differences in intelligence test performance. As we make this transition, we need to issue a warning: The same principles that we identified for differences among individual children do *not* fully generalize to differences among groups. Thus, although you have learned that differences in genes contribute to variations in children's intelligence, you *cannot* assume that any group differences are likewise based in heredity (Sternberg et al., 2007).

As you read the upcoming pages, please keep two additional ideas in mind. First, *there is a great deal of individual variability within any group.* We will describe how children of different groups perform on average, yet some children are very different from that "average" description. Second, *there is almost always a great deal of overlap between any two groups.* As an example, consider gender differences in verbal ability. Research studies often find that girls have slightly higher verbal performance than boys (Halpern, 2006; Spelke, 2005). Yet the difference is typically quite small, with a great deal of overlap between the two groups. Figure 8-7 shows the typical overlap between girls and boys on measures of verbal ability. Notice that many of the boys perform at higher levels than some of the girls, despite the average advantage for girls. Obviously, we could not use such data to make predictions about how particular girls and boys would perform in classrooms and other settings.

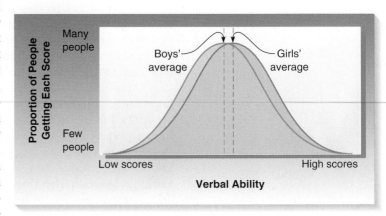

Figure 8-7

Typical "difference" between girls and boys in verbal ability.

Gender Differences

Apart from a greater frequency of mental retardation in boys than girls, there are rarely any significant gender differences in IQ scores (Halpern et al., 2007; Neisser et al., 1996). This finding is at least partly a function of how intelligence tests are developed: As a general rule, test constructors eliminate any test items on which one gender performs better than the other.

Average differences in more specific cognitive abilities are sometimes found but are usually small. Girls are often slightly better at such verbal tasks as reading and writing (Halpern, 2004, 2006; Hedges & Nowell, 1995; Maccoby & Jacklin, 1974). Especially after puberty, boys perform somewhat better on some tasks involving visual-spatial thinking (which require people to imagine two- or three-dimensional figures and mentally manipulate them), and adolescents with extremely high mathematical ability are more likely to be male than female (Benbow, Lubinski, Shea, & Eftekhari-Sanjani, 2000; Gallagher & Kaufman, 2005; Hegarty & Kozhevnikov, 1999). In verbal, visual-spatial, and mathematical domains, however, there is typically a great deal of overlap between the two genders.

Some gender differences in specific intellectual abilities may be partly due to hormonal differences or subtle anatomical differences in the brain (Halpern, 2004; Halpern & LaMay, 2000; O'Boyle & Gill, 1998). Environmental factors appear to play a role as well. In many cultures boys and girls have distinctly different experiences growing up. For instance, in mainstream Western cultures boys are more likely to have toys that require physical manipulation in space (building blocks, model airplanes, footballs, etc.), and such items can foster the development of visual-spatial skills. In contrast, girls are more likely to have dolls, housekeeping items (e.g., dishes, plastic food), and board games—items that are apt to encourage verbal communication with peers (Halpern, 1992; Leaper & Friedman, 2007). Researchers occasionally observe other patterns of gender differences in particular ethnic groups—for instance, Hispanic girls may demonstrate better visual-spatial ability than Hispanic boys—and such findings are almost certainly due to environment rather than heredity (Huston, 1983; Schratz, 1978).

In recent years, perhaps because of the push for more equitable educational opportunities, males and females have become increasingly similar in their abilities (Jacklin, 1989; Spelke, 2005). For all intents and purposes, educators should expect boys and girls to have similar potential in virtually all subject areas. Boys and girls don't always *believe* they have similar abilities, however, as you will discover in Chapter 12.

Socioeconomic Differences

Intelligence test scores are correlated with socioeconomic status (SES). On average, children from lower-SES families earn somewhat lower IQ scores, and they also perform at lower levels in school, than children from middle-SES families (Brooks-Gunn, 2003; Linver et al., 2002). Children who grow up in persistently impoverished conditions are at greatest risk for poor performance in these respects, but many children who endure only short-term poverty suffer to some degree (McLoyd, 1998b).

Several factors probably contribute to differences in IQ and school achievement among socioeconomic groups (Berliner, 2005; McLoyd, 1998b; L. S. Miller, 1995). Poor nutrition, lack of health care, and greater-than-average exposure to environmental toxins can impede neurological development. Parents who work long hours (especially single parents) may have little time to spend with their children and may be unable to find or afford high-quality child care (Marshall, 2004). Some parents with limited educational backgrounds may have little knowledge about how best to help children acquire academic skills (P. A. Edwards & Garcia, 1994; Portes, 1996). And a family without a dependable income must, in general, place higher priority on survival and physical well-being than on toys, books, and other materials that nurture children's cognitive growth. Once children begin school, they may lack the knowledge and skills (e.g., familiarity with letters and numbers) upon which more advanced learning depends. Their lower school attendance rates, due to health problems, family crises, and frequent changes of residence, further decrease their opportunities for acquiring the academic skills so critical for their school success.

In addition, teachers—especially those who have grown up in middle-SES families—often have lower academic expectations for children from lower-income homes. As a result, they may give these children less time and attention, fewer opportunities to learn, and less challenging assignments (K. Alexander, Entwisle, & Thompson, 1987; McLoyd, 1998b; Rosenthal, 1994). Without intending it, some teachers thus increase any socioeconomic differences in cognitive ability that already exist.

High-quality preschool programs can boost IQ scores (at least over the short run) and enhance school achievement, and the benefits seem to be greatest for children from low-SES families (e.g., Magnuson, Meyers, Ruhm, & Waldfogel, 2004). Programs that teach parents how to provide stimulating activities for, and interact effectively with, their growing children can also make a difference (F. A. Campbell & Ramey, 1994; Ceci, 2003). And when teachers have high expectations for students from lower-income backgrounds, the students are more likely to perform at high levels (Midgley, Feldlaufer, & Eccles, 1989; M. Phillips, 1997).

Ethnic and Racial Differences

Some measures of early cognitive functioning in infants reveal no differences among ethnic groups (Fagan & Singer, 1983). However, ethnic and racial differences in intelligence and more specific cognitive abilities appear in the preschool years and persist throughout childhood and adolescence. On average, Asian Americans and European Americans outperform African Americans and Hispanic Americans (N. Brody, 1992; McCallum, 1999; Neisser et al., 1996; Nisbett, 2005). In some studies Asian Americans score at the highest levels of all, outscoring European Americans by 1 to 5 IQ points (N. Brody, 1992; Flynn, 1991).

Speculations about the source of such differences have prompted considerable debate. In their 1994 book *The Bell Curve,* Richard Herrnstein and Charles Murray used three consistently observed group differences—European American families have higher incomes than African American families, children from upper- and middle-income families have higher IQ scores than children from lower-income families, and European American children have higher IQ scores than African American children—to conclude that European Americans have a genetic advantage over African Americans. As you might suspect, the book generated considerable controversy and a great deal of outrage.

Scholars have poked many holes in the logic used in *The Bell Curve* (Jacoby & Glauberman, 1995; Marks, 1995; Montagu, 1999b; Sternberg et al., 2007). They find numerous weaknesses in the research studies and statistical analyses upon which Herrnstein and Murray based their conclusions. Most of these studies were correlational rather than experimental studies and therefore, as you might recall from Chapter 2, are not clear evidence of causality. The critics also argue that any innate differences in intelligence have not had sufficient time to emerge in human evolution, nor does it seem logical that some groups would evolve to be less adaptive (i.e., less intelligent) than others. They point out, too, that the very concept of *race,* though widely used to categorize people in our society, has no simple basis in biology: It is virtually impossible to identify a person's "race" by analyzing his or her DNA.

In past years some theorists have suggested that cultural bias in intelligence tests explains ethnic and racial differences in IQ scores. Today, however, most theorists believe that the tests themselves are not the primary culprits and suggest that other environmentally based factors—perhaps including socioeconomic status, discrimination, motivation, and anxiety—are to blame. Let's look at each of these possible explanations.

Cultural bias. A test has **cultural bias** when one or more of its items either offend or unfairly penalize people of a particular ethnic background, gender, or socioeconomic status, to the point that the validity of the test results is affected. Certain characteristics of intelligence tests may lead some children to attain scores that underestimate their intelligence. For instance, many contemporary intelligence tests focus on abstract thinking and other cognitive processes important in industrialized Western societies but less relevant to other cultures (Greenfield et al., 2006; J. G. Miller, 1997; Ogbu, 1994). Lack of familiarity with a test's questions and tasks may also hamper children's performance (Heath, 1989; Neisser et al., 1996). Facility with the English language is a factor as well: Children for whom English is a second language perform relatively poorly on test items that are primarily verbal in nature (E. C. Lopez, 1997).

Despite such considerations, cultural bias does not appear to be the primary factor accounting for group differences in IQ. Publishers of intelligence tests routinely employ individuals from diverse backgrounds to ensure that test content is fair and appropriate for students of all races and ethnicities (R. L. Linn & Miller, 2005). When children's native language is English, English-based intelligence tests have similar reliability and validity (e.g., they predict future academic performance equally well) for different ethnic and racial groups (R. T. Brown, Reynolds, & Whitaker, 1999; Neisser et al., 1996; Sattler, 2001). Group

cultural bias
Extent to which an assessment instrument offends or unfairly penalizes some individuals because of their ethnicity, gender, or socioeconomic status.

differences are observed even when tests are intentionally designed to minimize culture-specific content, as is true for the nonverbal UNIT test described earlier (McCallum, 1999; Neisser, 1998a).

Socioeconomic status. One likely reason for the lower IQ scores of African American and Hispanic American children is that, on average, these children grow up in families and neighborhoods with lower incomes than do European American children (Brooks-Gunn et al., 1996; McLoyd, 1998b). As we've seen, socioeconomic status can affect the quality of prenatal and postnatal nutrition, availability of stimulating toys and books, quality of educational experiences, and a host of other environmental factors that influence intellectual development and test performance. Keep in mind, however, that children from low-income families have many strengths—perhaps creativity with common materials or greater familiarity with everyday household tasks—that their economically advantaged classmates may *not* have (Torrance, 1995).

Discriminatory practices. Even when different ethnic and racial groups have similar economic resources, systematic and long-term discrimination (e.g., exclusion from better schools and jobs, lower expectations for classroom performance) can limit minority children's opportunities for intellectual growth (Ogbu, 1994). Widespread discrimination may cause heredity to have an indirect effect on intelligence, in that inherited skin color or other physical characteristics (rather than inherited intellectual potential per se) elicit responses from society that affect intellectual development. Following is a helpful analogy:

> Consider a culture in which red-haired children are beaten over the head regularly, but all other children are treated well. . . . The effect of a red-hair gene on red hair is a "direct" genetic effect because the gene affects the color via an internal biochemical process. By contrast . . . the red-hair genes affect IQ *indirectly*. (N. Block, 1999, pp. 466–467, emphasis added)

In other words, although there may be a small difference in intelligence between racial groups, this is not because one group is genetically inferior but rather because society treats groups of children inequitably.

Motivation to do well on an intelligence test increases the IQ scores that children earn, especially on group-administered paper-pencil tests.

Motivation and anxiety. Many children try to perform at their best on intelligence tests (Flynn, 1991; Ogbu, 1994). But others, including some African American and Hispanic American youngsters, may have little motivation to do well. Some may give minimal answers (e.g., "I don't know") as a way of shortening a testing session that they find confusing and unsettling (Zigler & Finn-Stevenson, 1992). Some children may simply not see the point of answering questions that fail to match up with their own cultural perspectives on what intelligence is (Sternberg et al., 2007). Others may exhibit a phenomenon known as **stereotype threat:** They perform more poorly—unintentionally and perhaps as a result of excessive anxiety—if they believe that members of their group typically do not do well on particular kinds of tests (A. H. Jordan & Lovett, 2007; McKown & Weinstein, 2003; Steele, 1997).

Undoubtedly, the factors just described have different influences (and in some cases, no influence at all) on how individual children perform on an intelligence test. An encouraging trend is that the IQ scores and other measures of cognitive ability of various ethnic and racial groups have, in recent years, become increasingly similar. Such a trend can be attributed only to more equitable environmental conditions across society (Ceci, Rosenblum, & Kumpf, 1998; Dickens & Flynn, 2001; Huang & Hauser, 1998).

Critique of Current Perspectives on Intelligence

At present, the psychological study of intelligence is a virtual minefield of explosive issues: What is intelligence? How should we measure it? How much is it influenced by hereditary (and so presumably unchangeable) factors? Can enriching experiences significantly improve it? The answers to such questions have major implications for educational practice, political decision making, and social policy, but they have not yet been completely answered. In ad-

stereotype threat
Reduction in performance (often unintentional) as a result of a belief that one's group typically performs poorly.

dition, several fundamental concerns about contemporary research and practice related to intelligence and intelligence tests must be raised:

- ***Research has relied too heavily on traditional intelligence tests.*** Existing intelligence tests have been designed primarily to identify individuals who may require special interventions or educational services, and in this context they can be quite helpful. Yet researchers have used them in other ways as well—for instance, to make cross-group comparisons, draw conclusions about the relative effects of heredity and environment in intellectual development, and evaluate the effectiveness of preschool programs for low-income children—without due consideration of the appropriateness of IQ tests for such purposes. Traditional intelligence tests are probably too limited to help researchers completely answer broad theoretical questions about the origins and development of intelligence. As psychologist Robert Sternberg once put it, "there is more to intelligence than IQ" (1996, p. 15).

- ***IQ scores are too often interpreted out of context.*** Over the years, the use of intelligence tests has been quite controversial. In earlier decades (as recently as the 1970s), IQ scores were frequently used as the sole criterion for identifying children as having mental retardation. In part as a result of this practice, children from racial and ethnic minority groups were disproportionately represented in special education classes, where their potential for academic achievement was not always recognized or effectively nurtured.

Most clinical and school psychologists, counselors, and other specialists now have sufficient training in assessment to understand that a single IQ score should never warrant a diagnosis of "mental retardation" or any other condition. Decisions about special educational placement and services must always be based on multiple sources of information about a child. Yet many other people (including a few teachers) view IQ scores as permanent characteristics. For instance, we often hear remarks such as "She has an IQ of such-and-such" spoken in much the same matter-of-fact manner as someone might say "She has brown eyes."

For most children, IQ scores are reasonably accurate reflections of their current cognitive development and learning potential. But for some children, IQs may be poor summaries of what they can do at present or are likely to do in the future. Teachers and other professionals must be extremely careful not to put too much stock in any single intelligence score, especially when working with children from diverse backgrounds.

Some cultures nurture abilities that are not reflected in traditional intelligence tests.

- ***Assessment of intelligence focuses almost exclusively on skills valued in mainstream Western culture.*** The items found on traditional intelligence tests focus on cognitive skills (logical reasoning, abstract thought, etc.) that are valued primarily in middle-class North American, European, and Australian societies (Gardner, 2006; Sternberg et al., 2007). Such a bias enhances the tests' ability to predict students' school achievement because schools in these societies place heavy emphasis on the same set of skills.

Yet other cultural and socioeconomic groups nurture other abilities that may be equally beneficial for children's long-term academic and professional success. For example, cooperation is a valued skill in Mexican culture, and so Mexican American children often show exceptional skill in cooperating with peers (Abi-Nader, 1993; Mejía-Arauz, Rogoff, Dexter, & Najafi, 2007; Okagaki & Sternberg, 1993; Vasquez, 1990). In parts of Polynesia, intelligence might be reflected in art, music, or dance (N. Reid, 1989). Ultimately, we can gain a better understanding of children's intellectual abilities only when we broaden the ways in which we assess those abilities.

- ***Intelligence tests overlook dispositions and metacognitive strategies that are important contributors to intellectual functioning.*** Most descriptions and measures of intelligence focus on specific things that a child *can* do (abilities), with little consideration of what a child is *likely* to do (dispositions). Intelligence tests don't evaluate the extent to which children view a situation from multiple perspectives, examine data with a critical eye, regulate their own learning, and metacognitively reflect on their thoughts and actions. Nor do they assess children's self-discipline. Yet such qualities are often just as important as

MyEducationLab

Find out the extent to which measures of both self-discipline and intelligence are correlated with school achievement by completing an Understanding Research exercise in Chapter 8's Activities and Applications section in MyEducationLab.

intellectual ability in determining success in academic and real-world tasks (Duckworth & Seligman, 2005; Kuhn, 2001a; Perkins, 1995).

- ***Many theorists have placed higher priority on assessing current intelligence than on developing future intelligence.*** Implicit in the practice of intelligence testing is the assumption that intelligence is a relatively fixed, and perhaps largely inherited, ability. In our view, there has been entirely too much focus on sorting children and entirely too little on fostering their cognitive growth. Fortunately, some psychologists and educators are now calling for a shift in focus from the *assessment* of intelligence to the *development* of intelligence (A. Bennett et al., 2007; Boykin, 1994; Sternberg et al., 2000). As theorists and researchers gain a better understanding of the nature of intelligence and the environmental factors that promote it, schools can, we hope, shift to a more proactive approach, one in which all children are given the opportunities and resources they need to maximize their learning.

Implications of Theories and Research on Intelligence

Given existing knowledge about the nature and development of intelligence, as well as our concerns about shortcomings in the field, we offer the following suggestions to teachers and other practitioners who work with infants, children, and adolescents:

- ***Maintain a healthy skepticism about the accuracy of IQ scores.*** Intelligence tests can, in many cases, provide a general idea of children's current cognitive functioning. Yet IQ scores are rarely dead-on measures of what children can do. As we have seen, the scores of young children can vary considerably from one testing to the next and are not always accurate predictors of children's future academic success. Furthermore, the scores of children from diverse ethnic and linguistic groups are often affected by background experiences, motivation, and English proficiency. We cannot stress this point enough: IQ scores should *never* be used as the sole criterion in making diagnoses and decisions about children.

- ***Support early intervention programs in your community.*** Early intervention is especially important for infants and toddlers with developmental disabilities, as well as for those living in low-income neighborhoods or unstable family settings. Such intervention can take the form of regular checkups and nutritional support for pregnant women, stimulating infant care and preschool programs, or suggestions and materials for helping inexperienced parents nurture their children's cognitive growth at home. Intervention is most effective when it integrates a variety of services into a single support network and considers children's physical, social, and emotional needs as well as their cognitive development (Loeb et al., 2004; Shonkoff & Phillips, 2000). Ideally, then, teachers who work with young children at risk for academic difficulties should closely coordinate their efforts with health care professionals, social workers, and other professionals who are actively involved in nurturing children's development.

- ***Cultivate youngsters' intellectual abilities throughout the school years.*** Research evidence strongly supports the role that schools can play in fostering children's potential throughout their school years (A. Bennett et al., 2007; Sternberg et al., 2007). In particular, youngsters from economically disadvantaged families are positively affected when teachers foster their curiosity and explicitly teach advanced intellectual abilities. For example, teachers can help children fill any gaps in their knowledge, make sure they are familiar with basic mathematical concepts and reading processes, and scaffold their ability to apply what they learn to new contexts (A. Bennett et al., 2007).

- ***Be open-minded about the ways in which children might demonstrate intelligence.*** As we've seen, some psychologists believe that human intelligence isn't a single entity—that it is, instead, a collection of relatively separate abilities that children may have to varying degrees. Take Gardner's multiple-intelligences perspective as you try the following "Sunflower" exercise.

Interpreting Children's Artifacts and Reflections

Sunflower

To the right are 10-year-old Amaryth's drawings of a sunflower and an insect that she found on it. Identify one or more of Gardner's multiple intelligences that Amaryth put to use in creating the drawings. You may want to refer back to Table 8-1 (p. 277) as you do this exercise.

Amaryth certainly needed to rely on her naturalist intelligence to detect patterns in the sunflower's seeds. She also made good use of her spatial intelligence to measure the insect and various parts of the sunflower and then to magnify the objects as she sketched them (notice her references to "real size"). And to some degree she drew on her linguistic intelligence as she tried to capture in words the very nonverbal nature of what she was seeing. For example, notice how she used an analogy to describe the sunflower's stem ("very fuzzy like my arm").

To the extent that intelligence is culture dependent, intelligent behavior is likely to take different forms in children from different cultural backgrounds (Gardner, 1995; Neisser et al., 1996; Perkins, 1995; Sternberg, 1985). The Observation Guidelines table "Seeing Intelligence in Children's Daily Behavior" presents a variety of behaviors that may reflect higher intelligence than children's IQ scores reveal.

● *Capitalize on children's individual strengths and abilities when teaching new topics and skills.* Gardner's theory, in particular, encourages educators to use a variety of approaches in instruction, building on the diverse abilities that different children may have (Gardner, 1999, 2000b; M. Kornhaber et al., 2004). For instance, the following scenario illustrates how some children may learn more effectively when they can use their visual-spatial skills:

> In third grade, Jason loved to build with blocks, Legos, toothpicks, Popsicle sticks, anything that fit together. During a unit on ancient history, Jason built an object for every culture studied. He fashioned Babylonian ziggurats out of Legos, Egyptian pyramids with toothpicks and small marshmallows, the Great Wall of China from miniature clay bricks which he made, the Greek Parthenon from Styrofoam computer-packing, Roman bridges out of popsicle sticks and brads, and Mayan temples with molded plastic strips resurrected from an old science kit. While appearing apathetic during most classroom activities, Jason was highly animated during his building projects. History came alive for Jason when he could build the structures of each era and culture studied. (L. Campbell et al., 1998, p. 79)

● *Consider the specific cognitive abilities that classroom lessons require of children.* Teachers generally target specific intellectual skills when designing classroom lessons, as you can see in the Building Teaching Skills and Dispositions exercise in MyEducationLab. Some children will have difficulty with one or more abilities that are required by a lesson, such as visual-spatial abilities when doing geometry, auditory processing when learning to read, or short-term (working) memory when listening to lengthy instructions. When children struggle with one or more abilities, teachers may find it helpful to offer specific kinds of support until children have developed the necessary prerequisite skills. In addition, school psychologists and other specialists can offer useful advice to classroom teachers about helping children with various intellectual strengths and limitations succeed academically.

● *Promote more "intelligent" cognitive strategies.* Look back once again at the chapter's opening case study. Gina's relative weakness in history is due largely to her ineffective study strategies. In fact, teachers, parents, and other adults can promote more effective learning, studying, and problem solving—and in doing so can promote more intelligent behavior—by teaching children more sophisticated and effective cognitive and metacognitive strategies (Perkins, 1995; Perkins & Grotzer, 1997; Sternberg, 2002; also see Chapter 7).

● *Give children the support they need to think more intelligently.* The notion of distributed intelligence tells us that intelligent behavior should be relatively commonplace when children have the right physical tools, social groups, and symbolic systems with which

MyEducationLab

Go to Chapter 8's Building Teaching Skills and Dispositions section in MyEducationLab to learn how different classroom lessons require children to use distinct clusters of intellectual abilities.

Observation Guidelines

Seeing Intelligence in Children's Daily Behavior

Characteristic	Look For	Example	Implication
Oral Language Skills	· Sophisticated vocabulary · Colorful speech · Creative storytelling · Clever jokes and puns	Jerome entertains his friends with clever "Your momma's so fat . . ." jokes.	Look for unusual creativity or advanced language development in children's everyday speech.
Learning Ability	· Ability to learn new information quickly · Exceptional knowledge about a variety of topics · Ability to find relationships among diverse ideas · Excellent memory	Four-year-old Gina teaches herself to read using several reading primers she finds at home. Initially, her mother identifies a few words for her. From these words she deduces many letter-sound correspondences that enable her to decipher additional words.	Make note of situations in which children learn and comprehend new material more quickly than their peers. Look for creative analogies and interconnections.
Problem-Solving Skills	· Ability to solve challenging problems · Flexibility in applying previously learned strategies to new kinds of problems · Ability to improvise with commonplace objects and materials	A fourth-grade class plans to perform a skit during an upcoming open house. When the children puzzle about how to hang a sheet from the ceiling (to serve as a stage curtain), Jeff suggests that they turn their desks to face the side of the classroom rather than the front. This way, the sheet can be hung from a light fixture that runs the length of the room.	Present unusual tasks and problems for which children have no ready-made strategies.
Cognitive and Metacognitive Strategies	· Use of sophisticated learning strategies · Desire to understand rather than memorize · Effective comprehension monitoring	Shannon, a sixth grader, explains that she learned the countries on South America's west coast (Colombia, Ecuador, Peru, Chile) by creating the sentence "*Colin eats peas and chocolate*."	Ask children to describe how they think about the things they are trying to learn and remember.
Curiosity and Inquisitiveness	· Voracious appetite for knowledge · Tendency to ask a lot of questions · Intrinsic motivation to master challenging subject matter	Alfredo reads every book and article he can find about outer space. He has a particular interest in black holes.	Find out what children like to do in their free time.
Leadership and Social Skills	· Ability to persuade and motivate others · Exceptional sensitivity to other people's feelings and body language · Ability to mediate disagreements and help others reach reasonable compromises	As a high school student, Gina organizes and directs a schoolwide peer tutoring program.	Observe how children interact with their peers at play, in cooperative group work, and in extracurricular activities.

Sources: B. Clark, 1997; A. W. Gottfried, Gottfried, Bathurst, & Guerin, 1994; Lupart, 1995; Maker, 1993; Maker & Schiever, 1989; Perkins, 1995; Torrance, 1995; Turnbull et al., 2007; Winner, 1997.

to work (Barab & Plucker, 2002; Pea, 1993). Rather than asking the question "How intelligent are these children?" educators might instead ask themselves "How can I help these children think as intelligently as possible? What tools and social networks can I give them? What useful concepts and procedures can I teach them?"

Children and adolescents often differ considerably in the extent to which they display intelligent thinking and behavior. For the most part, educators can easily accommodate such variability within the context of normal instructional practices. In some cases, however, young learners have ability levels so different from those of age-mates that they require special educational services to help them reach their full potential. We turn now to exceptionalities in intelligence.

Exceptionalities in Intelligence

No matter how we define or measure intelligence, we find that some children and adolescents show exceptional talent and others show significant cognitive delays relative to their peers. The two ends of the intelligence continuum are commonly known as *giftedness* and *intellectual disability*.[7]

giftedness
Unusually high ability in one or more areas, to the point where children require special educational services to help them meet their full potential.

Children Who Are Gifted

Gina, described in the opening case study and revisited in the Observation Guidelines table, is an example of someone who is gifted (you may also see the term *gifted and talented*). In general, **giftedness** is unusually high ability or aptitude in one or more areas (e.g., math, science, creative writing, art, or music) to the point where special educational services are necessary to help a youngster meet his or her full potential (e.g., C. M. Ackerman & Fifield, 2005; Gromko, 2004; U.S. Department of Education, 1993). When we try to pin down giftedness more precisely, we find considerable disagreement about how to do so (K. R. Carter, 1991; Turnbull et al., 2007). Many school districts identify students as gifted primarily on the basis of general IQ scores, often using 125 or 130 as a minimum cutoff point. But some experts argue that IQ scores should not be the only criterion for selection into special services, and that such factors as creativity, motivation, and children's everyday accomplishments might also be considered. These less formal indicators may be especially useful for identifying talented children from diverse backgrounds who, perhaps because of a language barrier or weak academic preparation, are not as likely to score at exceptionally high levels on intelligence tests (Council for Exceptional Children, 1995; Louis, Subotnik, Breland, & Lewis, 2000; Renzulli & Reis, 1986; Sternberg & Zhang, 1995).

Children who are gifted are typically very different from one another in their particular strengths and talents, but as a group they tend to share certain characteristics. Typically, they process information more quickly and remember it more easily, have more advanced reasoning and metacognitive skills, and use more effective learning and problem-solving strategies (K. R. Carter & Ormrod, 1982; Steiner & Carr, 2003; Winner, 1997, 2000). Often they have an exceptional drive to learn, seek out new challenges, make their own discoveries, and master tasks with little instruction from others (D. A. Greenspan, Solomon, & Gardner, 2004; Winner, 2000). They tend to set extremely high standards for their performance, sometimes to the point of unrealistic perfectionism (W. D. Parker, 1997; Tsui & Mazzocco, 2007). Most have high self-esteem, good social skills, and above-average emotional adjustment, although a few extremely gifted children have social or emotional difficulties, such as being overly sensitive to criticism (Edmunds & Edmunds, 2005; A. W. Gottfried et al., 1994; Preuss & Dubow, 2004). In the following "Solar System" exercise, you can observe several qualities of giftedness firsthand.

Interpreting Children's Artifacts and Reflections

Solar System

As an assignment for one of Jeanne's classes, a graduate student conducted the following interview with her 7½-year-old daughter, whom we'll call "Mia." As you read the interview, look for characteristics that suggest exceptional intelligence.

Mom: What are you learning in science?
Mia: The solar system.
Mom: What are you learning about the solar system?
Mia: The planets.
Mom: What are you learning about the planets?
Mia: There are only eight planets.
Mom: How do you know that?
Mia: The teacher taught us a poem to help us remember.

Mom: What was the poem?
Mia: My Very Educated Mother Just Served Us Nine Pizzas.
Mom: What does that stand for?
Mia: Mercury, Venus, Earth, Mars, Jupiter, Saturn, Uranus, Neptune, Pluto. (She counts the planets on her fingers a couple of times.) Oops, there are nine planets, not eight. I made a mistake.
Mom: Anything else you want to share?
Mia: Yeah. Pluto is the farthest planet from the sun and the smallest planet. Earth and Mars are the only planets to have moons. Mars has two moons and the Earth has only one. . . . [Pluto] has the largest orbit around

continued

[7]In the United States, different states may establish somewhat different criteria for these two categories, especially with regard to determining eligibility for special educational services.

	the sun, and it was discovered in 1936, and it takes 284 years to go around the sun one time.	Mia:	Venus is the second planet away from the sun. It's always very cloudy there and really hot. It's the hottest planet.
Mom:	How do you know all that?		
Mia:	I picture outside space in my head and I can see all the planets outside in space, and I keep looking until I see Pluto.	Mom:	While you were talking with me, all these ideas came to your head. How did you remember all this information?
Mom:	How do you remember when Pluto was discovered and how long it takes for Pluto to go one time around the sun?	Mia:	I was thinking I was a spaceman and I just lifted off from Earth and crash-landed on Venus. I was dying there. So I recharged my ship and came back to Earth.
Mia:	I remember 1936 because I was born in 1996, that sounds a lot like 1936. To remember that it is 284 days [she previously said 284 *years*, so apparently misspeaks here[a]], I just hear the teacher saying it in my head and thinking that is a really long time.	Mom:	Why were you dying there?
		Mia:	All the clouds around Venus were trapping the heat in. It was very hot, so I wanted to leave. (interview courtesy of an anonymous student)
Mom:	Any other facts you want to share?		

[a]Pluto's orbit around the Sun actually takes 248 Earth years.

You undoubtedly noticed the sheer *quantity* of what Mia remembers about the solar system. Her knowledge is quite remarkable for a 7-year-old. You may also have picked up on her metacognitive skills: Mia can easily reflect on and describe her own thought processes. In addition, Mia seems to have made use of a relatively advanced learning strategy— elaboration—to remember facts about the planets. For instance, to remember that Venus is cloudy and hot, she imagined this scenario: "I was a spaceman and I just lifted off from Earth and crash-landed on Venus. . . . All the clouds around Venus were trapping the heat in. It was very hot, so I wanted to leave." Given Mia's obvious engagement with the subject matter during the lesson, we might guess that she is a highly motivated and self-regulating learner. All of these qualities—exceptional knowledge and memory, advanced metacognitive skills, effective learning strategies, high motivation, and self-regulated learning—are telltale signs of giftedness.

Giftedness may be partly an inherited characteristic. Some individuals who are gifted show unusual brain development, perhaps advanced development in the right hemisphere or greater involvement of both hemispheres in performing certain kinds of tasks (Winner, 2000). Environmental factors probably play a significant role as well (B. Clark, 1997; A. W. Gottfried et al., 1994; Shavinina & Ferrari, 2004). For instance, children who are gifted are more likely to be firstborn or only-born children and thus generally have more attention and stimulation from their parents than other children do. Children who are gifted also tend to have many opportunities to practice and enhance their abilities from a very early age, long before they have been identified as being gifted. And they are more likely to seek out enriching opportunities— an example of the *niche-picking* phenomenon described earlier.

As is true for Gina in the opening case study, a child's giftedness is often evident throughout childhood and adolescence. Some gifted children use unusually advanced language beginning in infancy, and others show signs of giftedness in early childhood, exhibiting intense curiosity and persistent interests (A. W. Gottfried et al., 1994; C. Harrison, 2004). Yet others are "late bloomers"; their talents become evident relatively late in the game, perhaps as environmental conditions bring such talents to fruition.

Fostering the development of children who are gifted. Gifted students tend to be among our schools' greatest underachievers. When required to progress at the same rate as their nongifted peers, they achieve at levels far short of their capabilities (K. R. Carter, 1991; J. J. Gallagher, 1991; Rogers, 2002). Drawing on Vygotsky's theory of cognitive development, we could say that children who are gifted are unlikely to be working within their zone of proximal development if they are limited to the same tasks assigned to their peers, diminishing their opportunities to develop more advanced cognitive skills (Lubinski & Bleske-Rechek, 2008). In the "Intrinsic Motivation: Middle Childhood" video in MyEducationLab, 9-year-old Elena reveals her desire for challenge in her description of PEAK, a program at her school for students who are gifted:

Adult: What do you like best about school?
Elena: I like PEAK. . . . It's for smart kids who have, like, good ideas for stuff you could do. And so they make it more challenging for you in school. So instead of third-grade math, you get fourth-grade math.

MyEducationLab

Observe Elena's desire for a challenging curriculum in the "Intrinsic Motivation: Middle Childhood" video. (Find Video Examples in Chapter 8 of MyEducationLab.)

Many students with special gifts and talents become bored or frustrated when their school experiences don't provide tasks and assignments that challenge them and help them develop their unique abilities (Feldhusen, 1989; Feldhusen, Van Winkle, & Ehle, 1996; Winner, 2000). They may lose interest in school tasks and put in only the minimum effort they need to get by in the classroom, as Geoff, a gifted 11th grader, reveals in the letter shown in Figure 8-8.

Yet some children and adolescents try to hide their exceptional talents. They may fear that peers will ridicule them for their high academic abilities and enthusiasm for academic topics, especially at the secondary school level (Covington, 1992; DeLisle, 1984; Stormont, Stebbins, & Holliday, 2001). Girls in particular are likely to hide their talents, especially if they have been raised in cultures that do not value high achievement in females (Covington, 1992; G. A. Davis & Rimm, 1998; Nichols & Ganschow, 1992). Gifted Asian Americans, partly because of their belief that learning requires hard work and continuing practice (see Chapter 7) and partly because of cultural traditions of conformity and respect for authority, may willingly comply when asked to perform unchallenging assignments (J. Li & Fischer, 2004; Maker & Schiever, 1989).

Several strategies for helping children and adolescents with exceptional abilities maximize their potential are presented and illustrated in the Development and Practice feature "Addressing the Unique Needs of Gifted Children and Adolescents."

Keep in mind that a child can be gifted and also have a disability. For example, some children with exceptional gifts and talents have learning disabilities, ADHD, autism, emotional disorders, or physical or sensory challenges (e.g., Hettinger & Knapp, 2001; S. Moran & Gardner, 2006). In such situations teachers and other practitioners must, when planning instruction, address the disabilities as well as the areas of giftedness. A few gifted children—for example, those with a limited English background or those who have specific learning disabilities—may even need some training in basic skills (Brown-Mizuno, 1990; C. R. Harris, 1991; Udall, 1989).

intellectual disability
Disability marked by significantly below-average general intelligence and deficits in adaptive behavior.

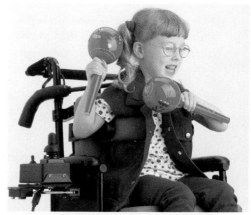

Some children who are gifted also have disabilities—possibly learning disabilities, emotional disorders, or physical challenges. This girl's teacher must take both her giftedness and her physical disability into account when planning instruction.

Children with Intellectual Disabilities

Up to this point in the book we've used the term *mental retardation* in reference to children with low general intelligence, because all of our readers are likely to be familiar with this term. Now that we are focusing specifically on the lower end of the intelligence continuum, we should point out that many advocates prefer the term *intellectual disability* because it has less of a social stigma (American Association on Intellectual and Developmental Disabilities, 2008). Children with an **intellectual disability** show developmental delays in most aspects of their academic and social

---

Dear Mr. P—— [the school principal]:

I have found in recent months that it is time for me to make the next step in my life. This step is graduation. I would like to graduate a year early in May, this year, with the class of 2002.

This is a step I have chosen as the best for me for several reasons. The first reason is that I would like to spend a semester studying abroad in Austria. I have chosen Austria because it is a country where German is spoken and this is the language I have been learning for four years....

I have also decided to graduate because several people have suggested that this is my best option, as they believe that I am at a maturity level that indicates I should move on. These people, among others, are primarily my parents, my advisor, and the school counselor. They suggest that I am ready to graduate, but perhaps not ready for college, which is why I've chosen to do a foreign exchange and give myself time to further mature and prepare for college.

Besides these reasons, I personally believe that I would have extreme difficulty attending school next year and succeeding.

I have been told that this same thing is seen every year, when seniors become tired of attending, as they lack the motivation to succeed. I am afraid that this would happen to me, but on a higher level, as I already feel that I am losing motivation. Attending school next year could mean dire consequences for my transcript, my G.P.A., and my life.

When speaking with [the school counselor], we decided that I need to finish an internship and one job shadow, and I will have the credits necessary to graduate by the end of the school year. I plan to set up several internships over a period of five days in five different fields of engineering, so I can get an idea of what each field is like....

I hope you understand my reasons for leaving and I am sure that you will support me in my decision to graduate early. It will be difficult to change in such a gigantic way, but it will be very beneficial for me in the end.

Sincerely,

Geoff A——

Figure 8-8

Many students who are gifted lose interest in school when not sufficiently challenged by classroom activities. Here are excerpts from a letter in which Geoff, an 11th grader, requests permission to graduate early. School officials found his rationale convincing and granted his request.

Development and Practice

Addressing the Unique Needs of Gifted Children and Adolescents

- **Individualize instruction in accordance with students' specific talents.**

  Two mathematically gifted junior high school students study calculus with a retired mathematician who volunteers her time three mornings a week. A classmate with exceptional reading skills is assigned classic works of literature appropriate to his reading level.

- **Form study groups of gifted students who have similar abilities and interests.**

  A music teacher provides semiweekly instruction and practice sessions for a quintet of musically talented 10- and 11-year-olds. As the group gains skill and camaraderie, it begins meeting daily, even though the teacher cannot always be there to give assistance.

- **Teach complex cognitive skills within the context of specific school topics rather than sparately from the standard school curriculum.**

  A teacher has an advanced science study group conduct a series of experiments related to a single topic. To promote critical thinking, she gives the students several questions they should ask themselves and then answer as they conduct the experiments.

- **Provide opportunities for independent study.**

  A second-grade teacher finds educational software through which a mathematically gifted 8-year-old can study decimals, exponents, square roots, and other concepts that she appears to be ready to master.

- **Encourage students to set high goals for themselves, but without expecting perfection.**

  A school counselor encourages a student from a low-income, single-parent family to consider going to a prestigious college. He also helps the student find sources of financial assistance for higher education.

- **Seek outside resources to help students develop their exceptional talents.**

  A high school student with a high aptitude for learning foreign languages takes a Russian course at a local university.

Sources: Ambrose, Allen, & Huntley, 1994; Feldhusen, 1989; Fiedler, Lange, & Winebrenner, 1993; Kulik & Kulik, 1997; Lupart, 1995; Milner & Ford, 2007; Moon, Feldhusen, & Dillon, 1994; W. D. Parker, 1997; Piirto, 1999; Spicker, 1992; Stanley, 1980; Turnbull et al., 2007; Winner, 2000.

---

functioning. Two characteristics must both be present in order for a child to be diagnosed with an intellectual disability or mental retardation (American Association on Intellectual and Developmental Disabilities, 2008):

- *Significantly below-average general intelligence.* Children with an intellectual disability perform poorly on traditional intelligence tests, with IQ scores being no higher than 65 or 70 (reflecting performance in the bottom 2 percent of the age-group). In addition, they learn slowly and perform quite poorly on school tasks in comparison with age-mates, and they show consistently poor achievement across virtually all academic subject areas.

- *Deficits in adaptive behavior.* Low intelligence test scores and poor academic performance are insufficient evidence to classify children as having an intellectual disability. An additional criterion is a deficit in **adaptive behavior,** which includes *practical intelligence* (management of the ordinary activities of daily living) and *social intelligence* (appropriate conduct in social situations). In these areas children and adolescents with an intellectual disability often exhibit behaviors typical of individuals much younger than themselves.

Children and adolescents with an intellectual disability show impairments in many aspects of information processing, including attention, working memory, executive functioning, learning strategies, and metacognition. They have trouble generalizing what they learn to new situations and often exhibit a sense of helplessness about their ability to learn new things (Borkowski & Burke, 1996; Butterfield & Ferretti, 1987; Dempster & Corkill, 1999; Seligman, 1975; Turnbull et al., 2007). Their play activities are the kinds that would ordinarily be observed in much younger children (F. P. Hughes, 1998; Malone, Stoneham, & Langone, 1995).

Intellectual disabilities are often caused by abnormal genetic conditions (e.g., Down syndrome). Sometimes an intellectual disability runs in families, such that many family members' abilities fall at the lower end of the normal distribution of intelligence (Kail, 1998). Yet heredity is not always to blame. Some instances of intellectual disabilities are due to noninherited biological causes, such as severe malnutrition or substance abuse during the mother's pregnancy (e.g., recall our earlier discussion of fetal alcohol syndrome), oxygen deprivation associated with a difficult birth, or environmental toxins (Keogh & MacMillan, 1996; McLoyd, 1998b; Streissguth et al., 1994; Vogel, 1997). Conditions in the home, such as parental neglect or an extremely impoverished and unstimulating home life, may also be at fault (Bat-

adaptive behavior
Behavior related to daily living skills and appropriate conduct in social situations.

Development and Practice

Maximizing the Development of Children and Adolescents with Intellectual Disabilities

- **Encourage infants to use the strengths they have, and offer opportunities and support for acquiring new knowledge and skills.**

  An 18-month-old who has intellectual and physical disabilities has recently begun attending an infant care center. His caregiver thinks creatively about how to help him interact with his physical environment. For example, she glues Popsicle sticks to the pages of cardboard books so that he can easily grab them and turn the pages. To help him feel secure in his infant chair, she puts skid-proof material on the seat of the chair and cushions at the sides to keep him upright.

- **Introduce new material at a slower pace, and provide many opportunities for practice.**

  A fourth-grade teacher gives a student only two new addition facts a week, primarily because any more than two seem to overwhelm him. Every day, the teacher has the student practice writing the new facts and review addition facts learned in previous weeks.

- **Explain tasks concretely and in very specific language.**

  An art teacher gives a student explicit training in the steps she needs to take at the end of each painting session: (1) Rinse the paintbrush at the sink, (2) put the brush and watercolor paints on the shelf in the back room, and (3) put the painting on the counter by the window to dry. Initially, the teacher needs to remind the student of every

step in the process. However, with time and practice, the student eventually carries out the process independently.

- **Give explicit guidance about how to study.**

  A teacher tells a student, "When you study a new spelling word, it helps if you repeat the letters out loud while you practice writing the word. Let's try it with house, the word you are learning this morning. Watch how I repeat the letters—H...O...U...S...E—as I write the word. Now you try doing what I just did."

- **Give feedback about specific behaviors rather than about general areas of performance.**

  A vocational educator tells a student, "You did a good job in wood shop this week. You followed the instructions correctly, and you put away the equipment when you were finished with it."

- **Encourage independence.**

  A life skills instructor shows a student how to use her calculator to figure out how much she needs to pay for lunch every day. The instructor also gives the student considerable practice in identifying the correct bills and coins to use when paying various amounts.

Sources: K. L. Fletcher & Bray, 1996; Patton, Blackbourn, & Fad, 1996; Perkins, 1995; Turnbull et al., 2007.

---

shaw & Shapiro, 1997; Feuerstein, 1979; M. M. Wagner, 1995). Undoubtedly as a result of such factors as malnutrition, ingestion of lead dust in old buildings, and other environmental hazards, children from poor, inner-city neighborhoods are overrepresented among school children identified as having intellectual disabilities (U.S. Department of Education, Office of Civil Rights, 1993).

Fostering the development of children with intellectual disabilities. The great majority of children and adolescents with intellectual disabilities attend school, and many of them are capable of mastering a wide variety of academic and vocational skills. The Development and Practice feature "Maximizing the Development of Children and Adolescents with Intellectual Disabilities" presents and illustrates several effective strategies.

Teachers and other adults must remember that children with intellectual disabilities have many strengths and that they are more likely to master new knowledge and skills when instruction builds on what they know and do well. In *Expecting Adam,* Martha Beck (1999) describes how her son Adam, who has Down syndrome, learned the alphabet. Soon after Adam turned 3, Beck and her husband began regular drills on alphabet letters, but they made little progress until they stumbled on a different instructional approach 3 years later:

[F]rom the time he started preschool at three, we kept running Adam through the alphabet, repeating the name of each letter, along with its major sound, thousands and thousands of times in the strained voices of tourists who believe they can overcome any language barrier by sheer volume.

It didn't work. When quizzed without prompting, Adam never recognized the letters on his own. By the time he was six I was ready to give up.

Then one day John [Adam's father] was holding up a plastic letter and making its sound, which happened to be "EEEEEEE," when Adam suddenly perked up and said, "Wizbef!" This is the way he pronounces his sister Elizabeth's name. . . . During that day, we discovered that Adam's learning capacity went way beyond anything we expected—as long as everything he learned related directly to someone he cared about. He had absolutely no interest in, for example, "E is for egg." But E for Elizabeth—now *that* was crucial information.

In the end we all learned the alphabet this way. The symbols we had been trying to link to abstract sounds ended up as a parade of personalities: Adam first, of course, and then Billy, Caleb, Diane, Elizabeth, Francine, Grandpa . . . As we figured out how he learned, the landscape of our son's mind began to reveal itself to us. Instead of a rationally constructed structure of empirical observations, logical conclusions, and arbitrary symbols, Adam's mental world seems to be more like a huge family reunion. It is a gathering of people, all linked by Adam's affection into a complex universe of relationships and characteristics. In this world, Adam learned as fast as anyone I know. Long before he could read or write even the most basic words (or so I thought), Adam came home to tell me, in his garbled tongue, about the new boy who had just moved into his class, and who had become Adam's friend. When I couldn't understand his pronunciation of the boy's name, Adam grabbed a pencil in his stubby, grubby little-boy fingers, and wrote "Miguel Fernando de la Hoya" on a piece of paper—a piece of paper, needless to say, which I intend to frame. (M. Beck, 1999, pp. 314–315)[8]

Adam's experience suggests that children with an intellectual disability may sometimes think in ways that are qualitatively different from other children. When classroom teachers and other practitioners trust in the potential of children with intellectual disabilities and accommodate the occasionally distinctive ways in which they learn, these children are most likely to thrive.

[8]From EXPECTING ADAM by Martha Beck, copyright © 1999 by Martha Beck. Used by permission of Crown Publishers, a division of Random House, Inc.

Summary

Characterizing Intelligence

Intelligence involves effective learning processes and adaptive behaviors and may manifest itself differently in different cultures. Some theorists believe that intelligence is a single entity (a general factor, or *g*) that influences children's learning and performance across a wide variety of tasks and subject areas. This belief is reflected in the widespread use of IQ scores as general estimates of academic ability. There is growing recognition that intelligence is somewhat hierarchical, with many specific abilities being distinct aspects of a few more general abilities. Other theorists (e.g., Gardner, Sternberg) propose that intelligence consists of a number of somewhat independent abilities and therefore cannot be accurately reflected in a single IQ score. There is also increasing evidence that children are more likely to behave "intelligently" when they have physical, social, and symbolic support systems to help them in their efforts.

Measuring Intelligence

Most intelligence tests have been developed primarily to identify individuals who have special needs (e.g., those who are gifted or have an intellectual disability). Contemporary intelligence tests include a variety of tasks designed to assess what people have learned and deduced from their everyday experiences. Performance on these tests is usually summarized by one or more IQ scores, which are determined by comparing an individual's performance with the performance of others of the same age. In some instances specific ability tests or dynamic assessments may be more useful for evaluating children's capabilities in specific areas or for predicting their ability to benefit from certain kinds of instruction. Tests for infants and young children are often helpful

in identifying those who have significant developmental delays. However, results of tests given to small children should not be used to make long-term predictions about cognitive development.

Influences of Heredity and Environment on Intelligence

Studies with twins and adopted children indicate that intelligence may be partly an inherited characteristic. But environmental conditions, including nutrition, toxic substances, home environment, enriching preschool programs, and formal schooling, can also have a significant impact on IQ scores. Heredity and environment interact in their influence, to the point where it may be virtually impossible to separate the relative effects of these two factors on individual children's intellectual development.

Developmental Trends and Group Differences

Performance on intelligence tests predicts school achievement to some degree, with IQ scores becoming increasingly stable and having greater predictive power as children grow older. Nevertheless, some children's IQ scores change considerably over time, especially during the early years.

On average, children from low-income families earn slightly lower IQ scores than children from middle-income families. Males and females perform similarly on general tests of intelligence, although modest gender differences are sometimes observed on measures of specific cognitive abilities. Average differences in IQ scores are frequently found among various ethnic and racial groups, with substantial evidence indicating that environmental factors are at the root of these differences.

Critique of Current Perspectives on Intelligence

Research on intelligence has relied heavily on traditional intelligence tests, which emphasize skills valued in mainstream Western culture and overlook dispositions and metacognitive strategies as important contributors to intellectual performance. Some theorists are now calling for a shift in focus from the assessment of intelligence to its development.

Implications of Theories and Research on Intelligence

Used within the context of other information, intelligence tests can often provide a general idea of children's current cognitive functioning. Yet educators and other practitioners should remain optimistic about every child's potential for intellectual growth. They should anticipate that different children will be intelligent in different ways and should capitalize on children's unique strengths and abilities to promote learning and achievement. And they should give children the social support and the physical and symbolic tools that can enhance intelligent thinking and performance.

Exceptionalities in Intelligence

Children and adolescents identified as being gifted show exceptional achievement or promise in one or more domains. Giftedness may reflect itself differently in different cultures, but in general, gifted individuals demonstrate rapid learning, advanced reasoning, and sophisticated cognitive strategies. In contrast, an intellectual disability is characterized by low general intellectual functioning and deficits in adaptive behavior. In individual children, either kind of exceptionality may have genetic roots, environmental causes, or both. Children with unusually high or low intelligence maximize their cognitive development when instruction is geared to their specific strengths and weaknesses.

Applying Concepts in Child Development

The exercises in this section will help you increase your effectiveness in nurturing children's intellectual abilities.

Case Study

Fresh Vegetables

Read the case and then answer the questions that follow it.

Twelve-year-old Steven had no known genetic or other organic problems but had been officially labeled as having mental retardation (an intellectual disability) based on his low scores on a series of intelligence tests. His prior schooling had been limited to just part of one year in a first-grade classroom in inner-city Chicago. His mother had kept him home after a bullet grazed his leg while he was walking to school one morning. Fearing for her son's safety, she would not let him outside the apartment after that, not even to play, and certainly not to walk the six blocks to the local elementary school.

When a truant officer finally appeared at the door one evening 5 years later, Steven and his mother quickly packed their bags and moved to a small town in northern Colorado. They found residence with Steven's aunt, who persuaded Steven to go back to school. After considering Steven's intelligence and achievement test scores, the school psychologist recommended that he attend a summer school class for students with special needs.

Steven's summer school teacher soon began to suspect that Steven's main problem might simply be a lack of the background experiences necessary for academic success. One incident in particular stands out in her mind. The class had been studying nutrition, and so she had asked her students to bring in some fresh vegetables to make a large salad for their morning snack. Steven brought in a can of green beans. When a classmate objected that the beans weren't fresh, Steven replied, "The hell they ain't! Me and Momma got them off the shelf this morning!"

If Steven didn't know what *fresh* meant, the teacher reasoned, then he might also be lacking many of the other facts and skills on which any academic curriculum is inevitably based. She and the teachers who followed her worked hard to help Steven make up for all those years in Chicago during which he had experienced and learned so little. By the time Steven reached high school, he was enrolling in regular classes and maintaining a 3.5 grade point average.

- Did Steven have mental retardation (an intellectual disability)? Why or why not?
- The school psychologist recommended that Steven be placed in a special class for students with special needs. Was such a class an appropriate placement for Steven? Why or why not?

Once you have answered these questions, compare your responses with those presented in Appendix A.

From Ormrod, Jeanne E., & Dinah McGuire, *Case Studies: Applying Educational Psychology,* 2e. Published by Merrill, an imprint of Pearson Education. © 2007 by Pearson Education. Adapted by permission of the publisher.

Interpreting Children's Artifacts and Reflections

Consider chapter concepts as you analyze the following artifact from a child.

Jermaine's Life

Jermaine has strong verbal skills and an active imagination (Hébert & Beardsley, 2001). An African American first-grade boy growing up in a rural community in Alabama, Jermaine has become inspired by the storytelling of his grandfather, and he receives ample encouragement from a few teachers at school who have noticed his remarkable talents. Yet Jermaine also faces some distinct hardships. His family is economically poor, and his single mother is frequently away from home. Jermaine and his older sister are expected to care for their brother and an elderly aunt.

Neighbors ostracize Jermaine and his sister as "odd" or "crazy" because their brother and aunt have disabilities and also because the family fails to worship at the local church, as is the custom in their community (Hébert & Beardsley, 2001, p. 92). And not every teacher likes Jermaine. One teacher who observed him on the school bus commented, "that boy is just too hard to handle," and the assistant principal has referred to him as "that bad little boy I have to keep an eye on" (Hébert & Beardsley, 2001, p. 93).

So far, Jermaine is managing to draw on his strengths and overcome his obstacles. Blending his natural talents with his personal life experiences, Jermaine has developed a keen sense of curiosity and a love of words. He likes to daydream at school and conjure up new worlds late at night as he gazes at the stars. Jermaine has decided to write about his life and fantasies in a book he calls "Jermaine's Life." As you read the following excerpt from "Jermaine's Life," remember that he wrote it in first grade, and consider these questions:

- Jermaine earns high scores in verbal abilities on standardized tests, distinguishes himself in literature arts, and is identified as gifted. How does the excerpt from Jermaine's book offer additional evidence of his talent in verbal abilities?
- What kinds of educational services might help Jermaine reach his full potential?

I was leaving Jermaine's world. I needed to go see my sister. It was soon to be her wedding. I wanted to stop her from marrying a jerk. I was riding my dragon through the hills. My dragon and I bumped into a gate. I wanted to show off my powers, so I burned

the gate down with my powerful triton. We walked to where the gate had been. Suddenly, thousands of dragons arrived. They were breathing fire and smoke. I looked around. I knew we had to get out of there. I saddled up my dragon, grabbed my triton, and tried to escape. One of the dragons fired at my bottom. One fried my hair until I was bald. Another tried to claw me. I spoke out in my kingly voice, "What is this NONSENSE?" A dragon said, "Who ARE you talking to?" "Who ARE YOU talking to? I am the most powerful king you will ever meet." "OH HO! Fried King for supper tonight!" All the dragons were happy to hear that. "Fried! No, not fried," I said. "I would taste better boiled. And if you are going to boil me, you'll need some water." The dragons turned and began to walk toward a pond several miles away. Dragons do not like to have water too close. It might put out their fire. It took them many hours to get to the pond. They walked so slowly because they were afraid. I turned south and went back to my world. I decided to never return. My dragon agreed with me. He was glad that none of the other dragons had noticed that he was toothless. (Hébert & Beardsley, 2001, p. 93)[a]

Once you have analyzed the excerpt from "Jermaine's Life," compare your ideas with those presented in Appendix B. For further practice in analyzing children's artifacts and reflections, go to the Activities and Applications section in Chapter 8 of MyEducationLab.

[a]Hébert, T. P., & Beardsley, T. M. (2001). Jermaine: A critical case study of a gifted black child living in rural poverty. *Gifted Child Quarterly*, 45, 85–103.

Developmental Trends Exercise

In this chapter you encountered five different perspectives on the nature of intelligence: Spearman's general factor (g) and specific factors, the Cattell-Horn-Carroll theory of cognitive abilities, Gardner's multiple intelligences, Sternberg's triarchic theory, and distributed intelligence. The following table presents descriptions of children and adolescents at each age level, one or more theoretical perspectives that some of the descriptions reflect, and potential educational implications. Go to the Activities and Applications section in Chapter 8 of MyEducationLab to apply what you've learned about intelligence as you fill in the empty cells in the table.

Using Various Theories of Intelligence to Understand Youngsters' Behaviors

Age	A Youngster's Experience	Developmental Concepts *Applying Theories of Intelligence to Patterns in Youngsters' Behaviors*	Implications *Helping Youngsters Reach Their Full Potential*
Infancy **(Birth–2 Years)**	When Meghan was born, features of her face, fingers, and toes made it clear that she has Down syndrome. Now almost 2, Meghan has just a few words in her speaking vocabulary, and she learns new things more slowly than her age-mates. She has only recently learned to walk and also shows delays in learning to feed and dress herself.		When children show delays in many different areas, identify a variety of interventions that can support their development in each domain. For example, when working with children with an intellectual disability, provide explicit instruction not only in cognitive and linguistic skills but also in adaptive behaviors.
Early Childhood **(2–6 Years)**	Five-year-old Robin has discovered many addition and subtraction facts on her own and is now insisting that her mother help her understand what multiplication is. Robin also enjoys taking apart small household gadgets (e.g., ballpoint pens, flashlights) to see how they work. Yet she is a physically awkward child who has had trouble learning such skills as tying shoes, and she seems at a loss about how to play with the other children in her kindergarten class.	Robin shows strengths and weaknesses consistent with Gardner's theory of *multiple intelligences*. In particular, she seems to be stronger in logical-mathematical intelligence than in bodily-kinesthetic intelligence and interpersonal intelligence.	Provide experiences that help children develop both their strong and weak areas. Use their strengths as a way of getting them actively engaged in activities in which they can also work on their weaknesses. For example, if a child is strong in math and science but weak in social skills, have the child practice social skills in a cooperative group project with one or two classmates who also have high logical-mathematical intelligence.

Developmental Trends Exercise (continued)

Age	A Youngster's Experience	Developmental Concepts *Applying Theories of Intelligence to Patterns in Youngsters' Behaviors*	Implications *Helping Youngsters Reach Their Full Potential*
Middle Childhood (6–10 Years)	When it comes to learning and remembering things about African American history, 9-year-old Tyrone is like a sponge, absorbing almost everything he reads. He explains his good memory this way: "When I'm reading something, I keep asking myself questions about it and then try to answer them. If I can't answer a question, I go back and read the stuff again."	Tyrone's ability to engage in comprehension monitoring and reflect on his thought processes is unusual for a 9-year-old (see Chapter 7). The role of specific cognitive and metacognitive processes in intelligence is most evident in the Cattell-Horn-Carroll theory of cognitive abilities and Sternberg's triarchic theory.	
Early Adolescence (10–14 Years)	For a science fair project, 13-year-old Jacquita interviews more than 100 students about their eating habits—how often they eat fresh fruits and vegetables, how often they go to fast-food restaurants, and so on. At first, Jacquita has difficulty organizing and making sense of her data. But after her teacher shows her how to use a computer spreadsheet, she easily summarizes her findings and creates several bar graphs for her science fair poster.		Give youngsters the physical and symbolic tools they need to think and act intelligently. For example, share with students the many symbolic systems that adults in Western societies use to collect, analyze, and interpret data (e.g., questionnaires, spreadsheets, statistical procedures) and teach students how to use calculators, computers, and other physical tools to make the use of symbolic systems easier and more efficient.
Late Adolescence (14–18 Years)	Mark is quite motivated to do well in his high school classes. Class material doesn't always come easily to him, but he studies hard and so gains a firm grasp of the subject matter. He is especially knowledgeable about current events, as he spends much of his leisure time reading the local newspaper and such news magazines as *Time* and *The Economist*.	The Cattell-Horn-Carroll theory is relevant here. It appears that Mark has average or above-average, but not exceptional, *fluid intelligence*. However, he has accumulated considerable knowledge (especially about current events), reflecting high *crystallized intelligence*.	Help children and adolescents acquire an in-depth and well-integrated knowledge base about topics that will be especially useful in adult life. For example, teach classroom subject matter in ways that promote true understanding and integration of ideas, rather than mindless memorization of discrete facts.

Key Concepts

intelligence (p. 274)
g (p. 275)
fluid intelligence (p. 275)
crystallized intelligence (p. 275)

distributed intelligence (p. 280)
intelligence test (p. 280)
IQ score (p. 284)
specific ability test (p. 285)

dynamic assessment (p. 286)
Flynn effect (p. 292)
niche-picking (p. 293)
cultural bias (p. 297)

stereotype threat (p. 298)
giftedness (p. 303)
intellectual disability (p. 305)
adaptive behavior (p. 306)

MyEducationLab

Now go to Chapter 8 of MyEducationLab at www.myeducationlab.com, where you can:

- View instructional objectives for the chapter.
- Take a quiz to test your mastery of chapter objectives. Detailed feedback is provided to explain why your responses are correct or incorrect.
- Deepen your understanding of particular concepts and principles with Review, Practice, and Enrichment exercises.

- Complete Activities and Applications exercises that give you additional experience in interpreting artifacts, increase your understanding of how research contributes to knowledge about chapter topics, and encourage you to apply what you have learned about children's development.
- Apply what you have learned in the chapter to your work with children in Building Teaching Skills and Dispositions exercises.
- Observe children and their unique contexts in Video Examples.

chapter
9

Language Development

As a young boy growing up in rural Vermont, Mario had the good fortune to learn two languages. At home, his parents spoke Spanish almost exclusively, in part because they wanted to pass their cultural heritage along to their son. Most of Mario's early exposure to English was in the English-speaking child care centers and preschools he attended off and on from the time he was 2 years old.

When Mario was 5, his dominant language was Spanish, but he was proficient in English as well. After his first 2 months in kindergarten, his teacher wrote the following in a report to Mario's parents:

> [Mario is] extremely sociable. He gets along fine with all the children, and enjoys school. He is quite vocal. He does not seem at all conscious of his speech. His slight accent has had no effect on his relations with the others. Whenever I ask the class a question, he is always one of the ones with his hand up.
>
> His greatest problem seems to be in the give and take of conversation. Since he always has something to say, he often finds it difficult to wait his turn when others are talking. When he talks, there are moments when you can see his little mind thinking through language—for he sometimes has to stop to recall a certain word in English which he might not have at his finger tips. (Fantini, 1985, p. 28)

The "slight accent" in Mario's English led a speech therapist to recommend speech therapy, which Mario's parents declined. In fact, all traces of an accent disappeared from Mario's speech by age 8, and his third-grade teacher was quite surprised to learn that he spoke a language other than English at home.

Standardized tests administered over the years attested to Mario's proficiency in English. Before he began kindergarten, his score on a standardized English vocabulary test was at the 29th percentile, reflecting performance that, though a little on the low side, was well within an average range. Later, when he took the California Achievement Test in the fourth, sixth, and eighth grades, he obtained scores at the 80th percentile or higher (and mostly above the 90th percentile) on the reading, writing, and spelling subtests. When Mario spent a semester of fifth grade at a Spanish-speaking school in Bolivia, he earned high marks in Spanish as well, with grades of 5 on a 7-point scale in reading, writing, and language usage.

As Mario grew older, his vocabulary and written language skills developed more rapidly in English than in Spanish, in large part because most of his school instruction was in English. His father described the situation this way:

> [B]y about fifth grade (age ten), he had entered into realms of experience for which he had no counterpart in Spanish. A clear example was an attempt to prepare for a fifth grade test on the topic of "The Industrial Revolution in England and France." It soon became clear that it was an impossibility to try to constrain the child to review materials read and discussed at school—in English—through Spanish. With this incident, [use of English at home] became a fairly well established procedure when discussing other school topics, including science, mathematics, and the like. (Fantini, 1985, p. 73)[a]

- Throughout much of his childhood and adolescence, Mario needed to use different languages in different contexts. Did the distinctly different linguistic environments in Mario's everyday life adversely affect his language development?

[a]Excerpts from *Language Acquisition of a Bilingual Child: A Sociolinguistic Perspective*, by A. E. Fantini, 1985. Clevedon, England: Multilingual Matters. (Available from the SIT Bookstore, School for International Training, Kipling Road, Brattleboro, VT 05302.) Reprinted with permission.

Case Study:
Mario

Outline:

Case Study: Mario

Theoretical Perspectives of Language Development

Trends in Language Development

Development of a Second Language

Diversity in Language Development

Exceptionalities in Language Development

Summary

Applying Concepts in Child Development

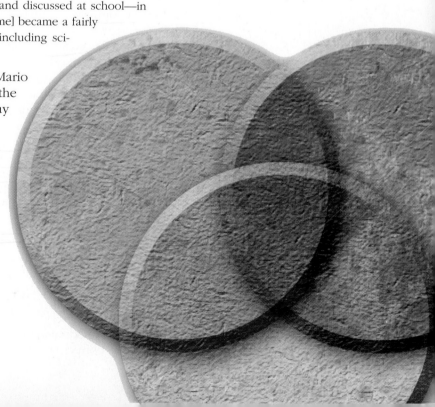

Acquiring the language of one's culture is an extremely complex and challenging undertaking. To understand and use a language effectively, children must master four basic components of the language. First, they must master **phonology:** They must know how words sound and be able to produce the sequence of sounds that make up any given word. Second, they must master **semantics,** the meanings of a large number of words. Third, they must have a good command of **syntax,** rules for how words can legitimately be combined to form understandable phrases and sentences. Finally, children must master the **pragmatics** of language, the use of social conventions and speaking strategies that enable effective communication with others.

Mastering these four components of language is a remarkable achievement for any child. For children like Mario who acquire more than one language, the task is even more challenging. Given the multifaceted nature of human language, it is not surprising that Mario needed some extra time to acquire basic skills in both English and Spanish. At age 5, he had minor difficulties with English phonology (the kindergarten teacher mentioned a "slight accent"), semantics (his score on a vocabulary test was a tad on the low side), and pragmatics (especially turn taking). Over the long run, however, Mario's bilingual upbringing clearly did *not* hinder his language development. The accent in his English disappeared by age 8, and test scores in the fourth and fifth grades were well above average.

In this chapter we often revisit Mario as we explore the multifaceted nature of human language and its development over childhood and adolescence. We begin our discussion by looking at several theoretical perspectives on how children acquire their first language—that is, their **native language.**

Theoretical Perspectives of Language Development

By age 3 or 4, most children have acquired sufficient proficiency in language that they are able to carry on productive conversations with the people around them. How they accomplish this monumental task in such a short time is one of the great mysteries of child development.

Theorists have offered numerous explanations for how children learn their native language. Here we describe early theories based on modeling and reinforcement plus four more contemporary perspectives: nativism, information processing theory, sociocultural theory, and functionalism.

Early Theories: Modeling and Reinforcement

Some early theorists suggested that language development is largely the result of modeling—that children simply imitate the speech of others. Observation and imitation of others are certainly involved in language development to some degree (e.g., Arbib, 2005). Infants occasionally imitate the specific sounds and general sound patterns that parents and other caregivers make (M. H. Goldstein & Schwade, 2008; Tronick, Cohn, & Shea, 1986). And older children sometimes pick up other people's words and expressions. For instance, when Mario began attending an English-speaking preschool, he came home using such expressions as "Shut up!" and "Don't do dat!" which he had apparently acquired by listening to his classmates (Fantini, 1985, p. 97).

The behaviorist B. F. Skinner (1957) suggested that *reinforcement* also plays a role, in that parents and other adults in a child's environment praise or in some other way reward increasingly complex language use. In Skinner's view, when infants make a variety of speech sounds in a seemingly random fashion, adults respond favorably to—and so encourage children to repeat—only those sounds used in the local language. As children grow older, Skinner proposed, adults begin to reinforce the use of single words, then the use of multiword combinations, and eventually only word combinations that are, from an adult's perspective, grammatically correct.

As complete explanations of how children acquire language, however, these early theories have not held up under the scrutiny of research. The speech of young children includes many phrases (e.g., "Allgone milk") that people around them neither say nor reinforce (N. Chomsky, 1959; Cook & Newson, 1996; D. Lightfoot, 1999). Moreover, parents usually reinforce their children's statements based on what is factually accurate rather than what is grammatically correct (R. Brown & Hanlon, 1970; O'Grady, 1997). Even in the elementary and

phonology
The sound system of a language; how words sound and are produced.

semantics
The meanings of words and word combinations.

syntax
Rules consistently used to put words together into sentences.

pragmatics
Conventions and strategies used in effective and socially acceptable verbal interactions.

native language
The first language a child learns.

secondary school years, the great majority of grammatical errors in children's speech go uncorrected (Bohannon, MacWhinney, & Snow, 1990). And children may continue to produce grammatically incorrect sentences despite feedback that the sentences need revision, as the following dialogue illustrates:

Child: Nobody don't like me.
Mother: No, say "nobody likes me."
Child: Nobody don't like me.

[Eight repetitions of this dialogue]

Mother: No, now listen carefully; say "nobody likes me."
Child: Oh! Nobody don't likes me. (McNeill, 1966, p. 68)

Clearly, then, neither modeling nor reinforcement sufficiently explains how children eventually acquire an adult-like form of their native language.

Although parents and other adults certainly model and reinforce children's early efforts at speech, modeling and reinforcement alone do not adequately account for language development.

Nativism

In an approach known as **nativism,** some theorists have turned to biology to explain language development.[1] One early pioneer, Noam Chomsky (1965, 1976, 2006), proposed that growing children have a biologically built-in mechanism—a **language acquisition device**—that enables them to learn many complex aspects of language in a very short time. This mechanism provides certain "prewired" knowledge and skills that make the task of learning language much simpler than it would be if children had to start from scratch.

Many psychologists share Chomsky's belief that human beings, though certainly not born knowing any particular language, nevertheless inherit some predispositions that assist them in acquiring linguistic knowledge and skills. Beginning at a very early age, infants can detect subtle differences among very similar speech sounds. They can divide a steady stream of sound into small segments (e.g., syllables) and identify common patterns in what they hear. They seem to have a few built-in concepts (e.g., colors such as red, pink, and yellow) that predispose them to categorize their experiences in certain ways. And possibly they also have a *Universal Grammar,* a set of parameters that predispose them to form certain kinds of grammatical structures but not others (N. Chomsky, 2006; Gopnik, 1997; D. Lightfoot, 1999; O'Grady, 1997).

Several lines of research converge to support the belief that language has roots in biology. First, children from diverse cultural and linguistic backgrounds tend to reach milestones in language development at similar ages. Virtually all children, even those who are congenitally deaf and have never heard a human voice, begin to produce speechlike syllables at about 6 or 7 months of age on average (Kuhl & Meltzoff, 1997; J. L. Locke, 1993). In general, children who have regular exposure to a particular language—either spoken or manually signed—make similar progress in producing meaningful words and stringing them together into appropriate, interpretable sequences (Crago, Allen, & Hough-Eyamie, 1997; L. A. Pettito, 1997; Snedeker, Geren, & Shafto, 2007).

A second body of evidence comes from brain research (Aitchison, 1996; J. L. Locke, 1993; Strozer, 1994). For most people, the left hemisphere of the cortex dominates in speech and language comprehension. Two specific regions of the left cortex of the brain seem to specialize in language functions (see Figure 9-1). *Broca's area,* located near the forehead, plays a key role in producing speech. *Wernicke's area*, behind the left ear, is heavily involved in understanding speech. But remember a point made in Chapter 5: No single mental activity—language included—is exclusively the domain of one hemisphere or the other. The right hemisphere is actively involved in sifting through multiple possible meanings of an ambiguous statement, perceiving humor and sarcasm, and using manual languages such as American Sign Language (Beeman & Chiarello, 1998; Neville & Bavelier, 2001; Ornstein, 1997). In addition, the right hemisphere dominates in language activities for a sizable

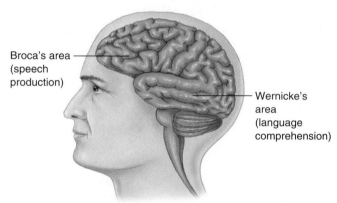

Broca's area (speech production)

Wernicke's area (language comprehension)

Figure 9-1

Primary language specialization centers in the brain.

nativism
Theoretical perspective proposing that some knowledge is biologically built-in and available at birth or soon thereafter.

language acquisition device
Biologically built-in mechanism hypothesized to facilitate language learning.

[1]You have also seen the influence of nativism in the discussion of *theory theory* in Chapter 7.

number of left-handers, as well as for children who incur serious injuries in their left hemispheres before age 1 (Kolb & Whishaw, 1996; Ornstein, 1997; Stiles & Thal, 1993).

Additional evidence for the nativist view comes from the finding that there appear to be *sensitive periods* in certain aspects of language development (Bortfeld & Whitehurst, 2001; Bruer, 1999; J. L. Locke, 1993). Children who have little or no exposure to *any* language in the early years often have trouble acquiring language later on, even with intensive language instruction (Curtiss, 1977; Newport, 1990). And acquiring phonological and syntactic skills in a second language is usually easier if the process begins in childhood or early adolescence instead of late adolescence or adulthood. Youngsters typically learn how to pronounce a second language flawlessly only if they study it before midadolescence or, even better, in the preschool or early elementary years, as Mario did (Bialystok, 1994a; Collier, 1989; Flege, Munro, & MacKay, 1995; Jia & Aaronson, 2003). They may also have an easier time mastering complex aspects of a second language's syntax when they are immersed in the language within the first 5 to 10 years of life (Bialystok, 1994a, 1994b; J. S. Johnson & Newport, 1989). From a nativist perspective, the predictable timing of such sensitive periods suggests the influence of genetically driven maturational processes.

Despite such findings, researchers have yet to obtain clear evidence that human beings do, in fact, inherit a specific neurological mechanism—Chomsky's hypothesized *language acquisition device*—that is dedicated solely to learning language. Even if research eventually confirms the existence of such a mechanism, questions would remain about the cognitive and motivational processes that enable children worldwide to acquire the language of their cultural group (Pinker, 1987). The theoretical perspectives that follow better address these processes.

Information Processing Theory

Information processing theorists focus on the specific cognitive processes that children use as they acquire language. From an information processing perspective, one essential ingredient in language learning is attention (M. Harris, 1992; Pruden, Hirsh-Pasek, Golinkoff, & Hennon, 2006). Infants pay attention to human speech and speech-related events from a very early age. Within a few days after birth, they show a preference for human voices over other sounds, can distinguish between familiar and unfamiliar voices, and in some instances expend considerable effort to hear a familiar one (DeCasper & Fifer, 1980; Fifer & Moon, 1995; J. L. Locke, 1993). Infants are also more likely to look at speakers who use the short, simple, rhythmic language that adults frequently use when talking to young children (R. P. Cooper & Aslin, 1990; Fernald, 1992; P. S. Kaplan, Goldstein, Huckeby, & Cooper, 1995). Adults seem to know (perhaps unconsciously) that attention is critical for language learning. For instance, when talking with young children, they are apt to point to the people or objects under discussion and make sure that the children are looking in the appropriate direction (M. Harris, 1992).

Reasoning is another critical player in language development (M. Atkinson, 1992; H. S. Cairns, 1996; Cromer, 1993). For instance, young children seem to form hypotheses about the meanings of words based on the context in which the words are used. In one study (T. K. Au & Glusman, 1990), researchers showed preschoolers an unfamiliar animal and consistently called it a *mido*. Later they presented a collection of odd-looking animals (including some midos) and asked the children to find a *theri* in the set (see Figure 9-2). Although the children had no information to guide their selection, they always chose an animal other than a mido. Apparently, they deduced that because the midos already had a name, a theri had to be a different kind of animal.

Working memory, too, is a factor in children's acquisition and use of language (M. A. Bell, Wolfe, & Adkins, 2007). Effective communication involves knowledge not only about spoken language but also about appropriate eye contact, gestures, and tone of voice (T. M. McDevitt & Ford, 1987). Given the limited capacity of working memory, a simple conversation might potentially involve coordinating so many skills that any meaningful ex-

Even in the first few weeks of life, most infants enjoy listening to the human voice, and they will expend considerable effort to hear a familiar one.

This is a *mido*.

Which one of these is a *theri*?

Figure 9-2

Children are more likely to attach new words to objects for which they don't already have labels. In this situation, a child is likely to choose either the purple crocodile-like creature or the yellow dinosaur-like creature as being a *theri*. After T. K. Au & Glusman, 1990.

change of information would be impossible. But fortunately, children soon *automatize* many aspects of language (e.g., word pronunciations, simple syntax, retrieval of common word meanings), freeing up working memory capacity for more complex language tasks.

Some theorists suggest that automatization of basic language skills in infancy and early childhood partly involves making *neural commitments* to particular aspects of language. In other words, the brain gradually dedicates particular brain circuits to particular linguistic tasks—recognizing certain sounds, producing those sounds, and so on (see the section "Developmental Changes in the Brain" in Chapter 5). Information processing theorists use the concept of automatization to make a counterargument to nativists' claim that sensitive periods in second-language learning reflect biologically built-in time frames. In particular, they propose that gaining proficiency in the sounds and other structural elements of one's native language early in life can enhance automatization in the use of that language, but only at the expense of learning a second, quite different language (Kuhl, 2004; Mareschal et al., 2007; Merzenich, 2001). Perhaps, then, what appear to be predetermined "best" times for learning particular aspects of language are simply the result of the brain's tendency to adapt fairly quickly to its particular linguistic environment.

Sociocultural Theory

Whereas information processing theorists consider the cognitive processes involved in acquiring and using language, sociocultural theorists look more at how social interactions foster language development. From this perspective children are *socialized* to use language (Ochs, 2002; Ochs & Schieffelin, 1995). Such **language socialization** involves both explicit instruction about language (e.g., parents may insist that children say "please" and "thank you") and more indirect means of communicating appropriate linguistic behaviors (e.g., parents may model turn taking and other cultural conventions of social interaction). Furthermore, social interactions provide a means through which children *internalize* language. Consistent with Vygotsky's theory of cognitive development, children use words first in their interactions with others, and then, through the process of internalization, gradually incorporate these words into their everyday thought processes (Hobson, 2004; K. Nelson, 1996a).

From a sociocultural perspective, a process critical for language acquisition is *intersubjectivity*, a concept we introduced in Chapter 7. In particular, if children are to learn new words in their interactions with others, they must share with their conversation partners a mutual awareness of what each of them is looking at or thinking about (D. A. Baldwin, 2000; Mundy & Newell, 2007; Tomasello, 1999). Not only do adults gain children's attention by pointing at certain objects and speaking in a high-pitched, singsongy manner, but children, too, contribute to a state of mutual attention by observing where adults are looking. By considering both the direction of an adult's gaze and the content of his or her speech, a child can often infer the meanings of new words. As an illustration, imagine that a father and his 3-year-old daughter are shopping at the local supermarket. "Oh good," the father exclaims, "a carambola. I love carambolas!" If the daughter has never heard the word *carambola* before, she will likely look at her father's face and then follow his gaze to the object in question (in this case, a yellow-green, star-shaped fruit). But she is apt to do this only if she realizes that her father is probably looking at the object he is talking about.

As early as the second year, and quite possibly before that, children use what they know or can surmise about other people's thoughts to assist them in learning word meanings (Golinkoff & Hirsh-Pasek, 2006; Mundy & Newell, 2007; Tomasello, 1999). For example, in one study (D. A. Baldwin, 1993), 18-month-olds were looking at one new toy while an adult looked at another. When the adult exclaimed, "A modi!" the children typically turned their attention to see what the adult was looking at. A short time later, when the children were asked to get the modi, they were most likely to choose the toy the adult had been looking at, even though they themselves had been looking at something different when they first heard the word.

Functionalism

Another important question involves motivation: Why do children *want* to learn the language of their society? Some psychologists argue that over the course of evolution, human beings

language socialization
Direct and indirect means through which other people teach children the language and verbal behaviors deemed to be appropriate in their culture.

developed language skills in large part because language serves several useful functions—hence the term **functionalism**—for the species. Language helps children acquire knowledge, establish productive interpersonal relationships, control their own behavior, and influence the behavior of others (L. Bloom & Tinker, 2001; Budwig, 1995; Ganea, Shutts, Spelke, & DeLoache, 2007; Pinker, 1997). From a very early age, children seem to be aware of the power of language in controlling the actions of others and, in the process, helping them satisfy their own needs and desires. For instance, when Mario attended preschool as a 3-year-old, he quickly learned such expressions as "No do dat no more!" and "Get auto here!" (Fantini, 1985, pp. 97–98). We can reasonably guess that such language enabled Mario to control his classmates' behaviors in ways that more gentle speech might not have.

Functionalists point out that language development is closely intertwined with—and, in fact, is critical for—development in other domains (L. Bloom & Tinker, 2001; Langacker, 1986). For instance, as you discovered in Chapter 6, language enhances cognitive development in several ways: by providing symbols with which children can mentally represent and remember events, allowing children to exchange information and perspectives with others, and enabling children to internalize processes they first use in their social interactions. Language is essential for social and moral development as well. Through conversations and conflicts with adults and peers, children learn socially acceptable ways of behaving toward others and, in most cases, eventually establish a set of principles that guide their moral decision making (see Chapters 12 and 14).

Language is so important for the human species that children seem to have the ability not only to learn it but also to *create* it. We find an example in a study of children attending a school for the deaf in Nicaragua (Senghas & Coppola, 2001). Before coming to the school, the children had little or no exposure to sign language, and teachers at the school focused primarily on teaching them how to lip-read and speak Spanish. Although many of the children made little progress in Spanish, they became increasingly adept at communicating with one another through a variety of hand gestures, and they consistently passed this sign language along to newcomers. Over a period of 20 years, the children's language became more systematic and complex, with a variety of syntactic rules taking shape. Many of the innovations originated with children ages 10 or younger—a finding that lends further support to the idea that young minds are especially proficient in acquiring language.

Critiquing Theories of Language Development

The Basic Developmental Issues table "Contrasting Contemporary Theories of Language Development" summarizes how nativism, information processing theory, sociocultural theory, and functionalism differ with respect to the broad themes of nature and nurture, universality and diversity, and qualitative and quantitative change. Another important difference among various theoretical perspectives is one of focus: Nativism focuses largely on syntactic development, information processing and sociocultural theories look more closely at semantic development (with sociocultural theories also considering pragmatic skills), and functionalism considers how motivation fits into the overall picture. Therefore, theorists often shift from one perspective to another or combine elements of two or more perspectives, depending on the particular aspect of language development they are discussing.

A key source of controversy remains, however. Most nativists propose that children inherit a mechanism whose sole function is to facilitate the acquisition of language, whereas other theorists (especially those who take an information processing or functionalist approach) believe that language development arises out of more general cognitive abilities that promote learning across a wide variety of domains. Research evidence points to language-specific learning mechanisms for at least *some* aspects of language acquisition (Maratsos, 1998; D. L. Mills & Sheehan, 2007; Siegler & Alibali, 2005; Trout, 2003). Children of all cultures learn language very quickly, and they acquire complex syntactic structures (e.g., "John told me that he had gone shopping") that enhance their ability to express subtle nuances in meaning even when those structures aren't really necessary for communicating their thoughts and needs to others. In addition, children with very low general intelligence show marked differences in language development depending on their particular disability (Bellugi et al., 2007; N. G. S. Harris, Bellugi, Bates, Jones, & Rossen, 1997; Tager-Flusberg & Skwerer, 2007). Let's compare children who have Down syndrome with children who have *Williams syndrome*, a genetic disorder characterized by distinctive facial fea-

functionalism
Theoretical perspective of language development that emphasizes the purposes language serves for human beings.

Basic Developmental Issues

Contrasting Contemporary Theories of Language Development

Issue	Nativism	Information Processing Theory	Sociocultural Theory	Functionalism
Nature and Nurture	By and large, children develop language only when they are exposed to it; thus, environmental input is essential. But children also appear to rely on one or more biological mechanisms that provide predetermined "knowledge" about the nature of language and possibly also provide skills that help them decipher linguistic input.	Most information processing theorists assume that language learning involves a complex interplay between inherited inclinations and abilities, on the one hand, and experiences that facilitate effective language learning (e.g., attention-getting actions by parents, frequent practice in using words), on the other.	Sociocultural theorists don't necessarily discount the role of heredity, but they focus on the social contexts that promote development and on the cultural legacy (e.g., culture-specific interpretations of words and phrases) that a society passes along from one generation to the next.	As their needs and desires become increasingly ambitious and complex, children propel their own language development through their efforts to communicate more effectively. Their needs and desires are probably the result of both heredity and environment.
Universality and Diversity	Although human languages differ in many respects, most have certain things in common (e.g., most include both nouns and verbs). Furthermore, children in different language communities reach milestones in language development at similar ages. Diversity exists primarily in the specific phonological, semantic, syntactic, and pragmatic features of various languages.	Information processing mechanisms that affect language acquisition (e.g., attention, automatization) are universally relevant across cultures. Children's unique language experiences, which differ among and within cultures, lead both to differences in the language(s) that children speak and to differences in children's knowledge of a particular language (e.g., the precise meanings they assign to specific words).	Some mechanisms that promote language development (e.g., intersubjectivity) may be universal across cultures. At the same time, different societies cultivate many culture-specific linguistic practices.	The drive to understand and be understood by others is universal. Different cultural groups may be more responsive to, and so nurture, certain ways of communicating more than others.
Qualitative and Quantitative Change	Children often acquire specific syntactic structures in a predictable sequence, with noticeable, stagelike changes in linguistic constructions occurring after each new acquisition (e.g., see the discussion of question formation in the upcoming section "Syntactic Development").	Many changes in language development—for instance, children's ever-enlarging vocabularies, ongoing refinement of word meanings, increasing automatization in pronunciation and other skills, and expanding working memory capacities (enabling production of longer and more complex sentences)—come about in a trendlike, quantitative fashion.	The nature of adult–child relationships that nurture language development may change both quantitatively and qualitatively over time. For example, qualitative change occurs in the development of intersubjectivity. Initially intersubjectivity involves only an interaction between an adult and a child. Later it involves a mutual focus on, as well as shared understandings of, an object (see Chapter 7).	With development, children's needs and desires change in both quality and intensity. (For example, whereas a 2-year-old might simply be interested in getting "more cookie" sometime within the next few minutes, a 15-year-old might ask, "When I'm old enough to drive, can I have my own car if I earn the money for it?") Thus both qualitative changes (e.g., use of new grammatical structures, such as dependent clauses) and quantitative changes (e.g., increasing sentence length) are to be expected.

tures, poor muscle tone, and abnormalities in the circulatory system. Children with both conditions typically have low measured IQ scores (often between 50 and 70), putting them in the bottom 2 percent of their peer group. Yet children with Down syndrome usually have delayed language development (consistent with their cognitive development), whereas children with Williams syndrome often have such good language skills that they are initially perceived as having normal intellectual abilities. A difference in language skills between two groups makes sense only if a language-specific mechanism guides language development somewhat independently of other aspects of cognitive development.

Other theoretical issues related to language development also remain unanswered. Following are two unresolved issues that have potential implications for teachers, caregivers, and other practitioners:

MyEducationLab

Notice how Corwin has greater facility in understanding words (receptive language) than in pronouncing them (expressive language) in the "Intelligence: Infancy" video. (Find Video Examples in Chapter 9 of MyEducationLab.)

• ***Which comes first, language comprehension or language production?*** Psychologists studying language development frequently make a distinction between receptive and expressive language skills. <u>Receptive language is the ability to understand what one hears and reads.</u> In other words, it involves language *comprehension*. In contrast, **expressive language** <u>is the ability to communicate effectively</u> either orally or on paper. In other words, it involves language *production*.

It would be quite reasonable to assume that receptive language skills must precede expressive language skills—that children must understand what words and sentences mean before using them in speech and writing. Yet many theorists don't believe the relationship between receptive and expressive language is so clear-cut (R. E. Owens, 2008). Children sometimes use words and expressions whose meanings they don't completely understand. Teresa recalls a 3-year-old preschooler who talked about the "accoutrements" in her purse, presumably after hearing others use the word in a similar context. Although the girl used the word appropriately in this situation, she did not understand all of its connotations. That is, her production exceeded her comprehension. Ultimately, receptive and expressive language skills probably develop hand in hand, with language comprehension facilitating language production and language production also enhancing language comprehension.

MyEducationLab

Hear examples of infant-directed speech in the infancy clips of the "Cognitive Development," "Intelligence," and "Literacy" videos. (Find Video Examples in Chapter 9 of MyEducationLab.)

• ***What role does infant-directed speech play in language development?*** Earlier we mentioned that infants seem to prefer the short, simple, rhythmic speech that adults often use when they talk to young children. Such **infant-directed speech** (also called *motherese* or *caregiver speech*) is different from normal adult speech in several ways (Kuhl & Meltzoff, 1997; Littlewood, 1984). It is spoken more slowly and distinctly and at a higher pitch. It is somewhat repetitive, uses a limited vocabulary, and consists of sentences with few words and simple grammatical structures. It includes exaggerated shifts in tone that help convey a speaker's message. And it is generally concerned with objects and events that take place in close temporal and physical proximity to the child.

Adults often use infant-directed speech when they converse with young children, adjusting its specific characteristics to the age of the listener (Rondal, 1985). Logically, such speech should facilitate language development, because its clear pauses between words, simple vocabulary and syntax, exaggerated intonations, and frequent repetition should make it easier for children to decipher what they hear. The problem with this hypothesis is that infant-directed speech is not a universal phenomenon. Adults in some cultures do not think of young children as suitable conversation partners and so speak to them rarely if at all. Despite these circumstances, the children successfully acquire the language of their community (Heath, 1983; Ochs & Schieffelin, 1995; O'Grady, 1997).

If infant-directed speech isn't essential for language development, what, then, is its purpose? One possibility is that it is one effective way in which adults can enhance their ability to communicate effectively with young children (O'Grady, 1997). Many parents interact frequently with their infants and toddlers and undoubtedly want to be understood. Infant-directed speech may also be part of parents' and other adults' attempts to establish and maintain affectionate relationships with children (Trainor, Austin, & Desjardins, 2000).

receptive language
Ability to understand the language one hears or reads.

expressive language
Ability to communicate effectively through speaking and writing.

infant-directed speech
<u>Short, simple, high-pitched speech often used when talking to young children.</u>

Trends in Language Development

Children's first form of communication is crying. Soon thereafter, they also begin to communicate by smiling and cooing and, a bit later, by pointing and gesturing (e.g., Goldin-Meadow,

2006; Tomasello, Carpenter, & Liszkowski, 2007). On average, they begin using a few recognizable words sometime around their first birthday, and they are putting these words together before their second birthday. During the preschool years, their vocabulary grows considerably, and their sentences become longer. By the time they enroll in elementary school, at age 5 or 6, they use language that seems adult-like in many respects. Yet throughout the elementary and secondary school years, children and adolescents learn thousands of new words, and they become capable of comprehending and producing increasingly complex sentences. They also continue to develop skills for conversing appropriately with others, and they acquire a better understanding of the nature of language. In the following sections, we explore numerous aspects of language development over the course of infancy, childhood, and adolescence.

Semantic Development

As you learned in Chapter 7, infants begin categorizing objects as early as 3 or 4 months of age. An important next step is to attach labels—words—to those categories. Young children appear to understand the meanings of some words as early as 8 months of age, and they typically say their first word at about 12 months (Fenson et al., 1994; M. Harris, 1992; O'Grady, 1997; Tincoff & Jusczyk, 1999). By the time children are 18 months old, many have 50 words in their expressive vocabularies (O'Grady, 1997). There is considerable variability from child to child, however. For example, Mario did not say his first word until he was 16 months old, and by his second birthday he was using only 21 words (Fantini, 1985).

At some point during the end of the second year or beginning of the third year, a virtual explosion in speaking vocabulary occurs, with children learning 30 to 50 words a month and, later, as many as 20 new words each day (M. Harris, 1992; O'Grady, 1997). In the preschool years, children also begin to organize their knowledge of various words into general categories (e.g., *juice, cereal,* and *morning* are all related to *breakfast*), hierarchies (e.g., *dogs* and *cats* are both *animals*), and other interword relationships (S. A. Gelman & Kalish, 2006; M. Harris, 1992).

At 6 years of age, children's semantic knowledge typically includes 8,000 to 14,000 words, of which they use about 2,600 in their own speech (Carey, 1978). By the sixth grade, their receptive vocabulary includes, on average, 50,000 words. By high school, it includes approximately 80,000 words (G. A. Miller & Gildea, 1987; Nippold, 1988; R. E. Owens, 2008). Thus children learn several thousand new words each year and so, on average, must learn numerous new words *every day* (Nagy, Herman, & Anderson, 1985).

The dramatic increase in the number of words that children can use and understand is the most obvious aspect of semantic development. Yet several other principles also characterize semantic development, as we see now.

- **Children initially focus on lexical words; grammatical words come a bit later.** All languages have two main categories of words (Shi & Werker, 2001). **Lexical words** have some connection, either concrete or abstract, to objects or events in people's physical, social, and psychological worlds. They include nouns (e.g., *horse, freedom*), verbs (e.g., *swim, think*), adjectives (e.g., *handsome, ambiguous*), and adverbs (e.g., *quickly, intentionally*). **Grammatical words** (also known as *function words*) have little meaning by themselves but affect the meanings of other words or the interrelationships among words or phrases. They include articles (e.g., *a, the*), auxiliary verbs (e.g., the *have* in *I have swum*), prepositions (e.g., *before, after*), and conjunctions (e.g., *however, unless*). By the time children are 6 months old, they can distinguish between lexical words and grammatical words and show a distinct preference for lexical words (Bornstein & Cote, 2004; Shi & Werker, 2001).

- **Over time, children continue to refine their understandings of lexical words.** Children's initial understandings of lexical words are often fuzzy: Children have a general idea of what certain words mean but define them imprecisely and may use them incorrectly. One common error is **underextension,** in which children attach overly restricted meanings to words, leaving out some situations to which the words apply. For example, Jeanne once asked her son Jeff, then 6, to tell her what an *animal* is. He gave this definition:

> It has a head, tail, feet, paws, eyes, nose, ears, lots of hair.

Like Jeff, young elementary school children often restrict their meaning of *animal* primarily to nonhuman mammals, such as dogs and horses, and insist that fish, birds, insects, and

lexical word
Word that in some way represents an aspect of one's physical, social, or psychological world.

grammatical word
Nonlexical word that affects the meanings of other words or the interrelationships among words in a sentence.

underextension
Overly restricted meaning for a word, excluding some situations to which the word applies.

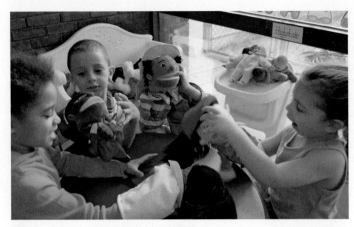

Preschoolers are, in many respects, quite proficient in using their native language. Yet they still have much to learn; for instance, they may exhibit underextension or overextension in their initial understandings of words.

people are *not* animals (Carey, 1985; Saltz, 1971). Another frequent error is **overextension:** Words are given meanings that are too broad and so are applied to inappropriate situations. For example, a child might say "I'm *barefoot* all over!" or "I'll get up so early that it will still be *late*" (Chukovsky, 1968, p. 3; italics added).

In addition to underextending and overextending word meanings, children sometimes confuse the meanings of similar words. The following conversation illustrates 5-year-old Christine's confusion between *ask* and *tell:*

Adult:	Ask Eric his last name. [Eric Handel is a classmate of Christine's.]
Christine:	Handel.
Adult:	Ask Eric this doll's name.
Christine:	I don't know.
Adult:	Ask Eric what time it is.
Christine:	I don't know how to tell time.
Adult:	Tell Eric what class is in the library.
Christine:	Kindergarten.
Adult:	Ask Eric who his teacher is.
Christine:	Miss Turner. (dialogue from C. S. Chomsky, 1969, p. 55; format adapted)

In a similar manner, young children often confuse comparative words, sometimes interpreting *less* as "more" or thinking that *shorter* means "longer" (R. E. Owens, 2008; Palermo, 1974).

• ***Children have difficulty with grammatical words throughout the elementary and middle school years.*** Children's mastery of a particular grammatical word typically evolves slowly over a period of several years. For instance, although 3-year-olds can distinguish between the articles *a* and *the*, children as old as 9 are occasionally confused about when to use each one (R. E. Owens, 2008; Reich, 1986). Children in the upper elementary and middle school grades have trouble with many conjunctions, such as *but, although, yet, however,* and *unless* (E. W. Katz & Brent, 1968; Nippold, 1988; R. E. Owens, 2008). As an illustration, consider the following two pairs of sentences:

Jimmie went to school, but he felt sick.
Jimmie went to school, but he felt fine.

The meal was good, although the pie was bad.
The meal was good, although the pie was good.

Even 12-year-olds have trouble identifying the correct sentence in pairs like these, reflecting only a vague understanding of the connectives *but* and *although* (E. W. Katz & Brent, 1968). (The first sentence is correct in both cases.)

• ***Understanding of abstract words emerges later than understanding of concrete words.*** As you learned in Chapter 6, children become increasingly able to think abstractly as they grow older, and this trend is reflected in their semantic development (e.g., Anglin, 1977; Quinn, 2007). Young children in particular are apt to define words (even fairly abstract ones) in terms of the obvious, concrete aspects of their world. For example, when Jeanne's son Jeff was 4, he defined *summer* as the time of year when school is out and it's hot outside. By the time he was 12, he knew that scientists define summer in terms of the earth's tilt relative to the sun—a much more abstract notion.

How children learn word meanings.   To learn the meanings of words, children must first divide the continuous stream of speech they hear into its individual word "pieces." Doing so is not as easy as you might think: Even in the simplified infant-directed speech described earlier, one word flows quickly into the next, without pause (Jusczyk, 1997). Despite such nonstop verbal action, infants begin to identify the specific words in speech by 7 or 8 months of age (Aslin, Saffran, & Newport, 1998; Bortfeld, Morgan, Golinkoff, & Rathbun, 2005). Exactly how they do it remains a mystery, but they probably rely on numerous clues, including the

overextension
Overly broad meaning for a word, such that it is used in situations to which it doesn't apply.

characteristic rhythm, stress patterns, and consistencies in word sequences they hear in their native language (Estes, Evans, Alibali, & Saffran, 2007; Jusczyk, 2002).

Once children have identified the specific words in the speech they hear around them, how do they zero in on the meanings of those words? In some cases adults provide direct instruction at home and at school, perhaps by labeling objects or by asking questions ("Where is the _____?") while looking at picture books with children (Dunham, Dunham, & Curwin, 1993; Raikes et al., 2006; Sénéchal, Thomas, & Monker, 1995). More often, however, caregivers, teachers, and other individuals don't explicitly identify what they are referring to when they use new words. As a result, youngsters must learn many words by inferring their meaning from the contexts in which the words are used (Akhtar, Jipson, & Callanan, 2001; Pinker, 1987; Waxman, 1990). Infants and young toddlers sometimes need numerous repetitions of a particular word before they understand and use it (Peters, 1983; Pruden et al., 2006; Woodward, Markman, & Fitzsimmons, 1994). But by the time children are 2 or 3, they can often infer a word's general meaning after only one exposure—a process known as **fast mapping** (Carey & Bartlett, 1978; Heibeck & Markman, 1987; Pinker, 1982).

Young children seem to use a number of general "rules" to fast-map word meanings. Following are some examples:

- If I see several objects and know labels for all of them except one, a new word is probably the name of the unlabeled object. (Recall the research study involving the words *mido* and *theri* described earlier.)
- If someone uses a word while pointing to a particular object, the word probably refers to the *whole* object rather than to just a part of it.
- Generally speaking, when a word is used to refer to a particular object or action, it refers to *similar* objects or actions as well.
- If a word is preceded by an article (e.g., "This is a *ball*"), it refers to a category of objects. If it has no article in front of it (e.g., "This is *Tobey*"), it is the name of a *particular* object (i.e., it is a proper noun). (T. K. Au & Glusman, 1990; Choi & McDonough, 2007; S. A. Gelman & Raman, 2003; S. A. Gelman & Taylor, 1984; Golinkoff, Hirsh-Pasek, Bailey, & Wenger, 1992; Jaswal & Markman, 2001; Markman, 1989)

As children get older, they continue to refine their understandings of words through repeated encounters with the words in different contexts and sometimes through explicit instruction and feedback (Carey & Bartlett, 1978). As an example, consider how three children in the same family once defined the word *plant:*

Andrew (age 7):   Something that people plant in a garden or somewhere.
Amaryth (age 10):   A growing thing that's sometimes beautiful.
Anthony (age 13):   A life-form that uses sunlight and carbon dioxide to live.

Notice how Andrew's definition is quite concrete and limited (apparently) to contexts in which his parents and other people might have used the word. Amaryth's definition is more general, in that it includes a characteristic of all plants: growth. Only Anthony's definition includes characteristics that a biologist might identify. Presumably Anthony had acquired this understanding of the word *plant* in one of his science classes at school.

Fostering semantic development.   Researchers have identified several strategies that teachers, parents, and other caregivers can use to help children learn word meanings:

- ***Talk regularly to, with, and around infants and toddlers.***   Even when young children do not yet talk themselves, they learn a great deal from hearing their native language. Initially, they learn its basic characteristics, such as its typical rhythms and stress patterns and the specific sounds (phonemes) that it does and does not include. Later, as they begin to mentally "divide" others' speech into individual words, they also begin to draw inferences about what some of those words mean. Although the simple sentences and attention-grabbing tones of parents may initially attract infants into conversation, over the long run it is the richness of other people's language—a wide variety of words, complex syntactic structures, and so on—that facilitates children's vocabulary development (B. Hart & Risley, 1995; Hoff & Naigles, 2002; Pan, Rowe, Singer, & Snow, 2005).

Children are more likely to learn words that they hear frequently—a principle that programs such as *Sesame Street* effectively use to promote language development (Rice, Huston, Truglio, & Wright, 1990).

fast mapping
Inferring a word's general meaning after a single exposure.

Children acquire more accurate understandings of words when they see concrete examples.

- **Give definitions.** By the time children are school age, they often learn words more easily when they are told specifically what the words mean—in other words, when they are given definitions (Tennyson & Cocchiarella, 1986). Definitions are especially helpful when the essential characteristics of a concept are abstract or otherwise not obvious. Children can usually learn what a *circle* is and what *red* means even without definitions, because roundness and redness are characteristics that are easily noticed. But the important characteristics of such concepts as *polygon* and *fragile* are more subtle, and for words like these, definitions can be very helpful.

- **Provide examples and nonexamples.** Children often acquire a more accurate understanding of a word when they are shown several examples (Barringer & Gholson, 1979; Tennyson & Cocchiarella, 1986). Ideally, such examples should be as different from one another as possible so that they illustrate a word's entire range. To illustrate, if adults limit their examples of *animal* to dogs, cats, cows, and horses, children will understandably draw the conclusion that all animals have four legs and fur (a case of underextension). If, instead, adults also present goldfish, robins, beetles, earthworms, and people as examples of *animal*, children are apt to realize that animals can differ considerably in physical appearance.

In addition to having examples, children benefit from having nonexamples of a word, especially those that are "near misses" (Winston, 1973). For instance, to learn what a *salamander* is, a child might be shown several salamanders and such similar animals as a snake and a lizard and told that the latter two critters are "not salamanders." By presenting nonexamples, including the near misses, adults minimize the extent to which children are likely to overextend their use of words.

- **Give feedback when children use words incorrectly.** Misconceptions about word meanings sometimes reveal themselves in children's speech and writing. Astute teachers and caregivers listen closely not only to what children say but also to how they say it, and they also look at how children use words in their writing. For instance, a preschooler might mistakenly refer to a rhinoceros as a "hippo," an elementary school student might deny that a square is a rectangle, and a high school student might use the term *atom* when she is really talking about molecules. In such situations adults should gently correct the misconceptions, perhaps by saying something along these lines: "A lot of people get hippos and rhinoceroses confused, because both of them are large and gray. This animal has a large horn on its nose, so it's a rhinoceros. Let's find a picture of a hippo and see how the two animals are different."

What dose worrisome meen?
What is and dose prevaricate mean?
Sobriquct?

Regular reading promotes vocabulary development. On this page of her fifth-grade journal, 10-year-old Amaryth has jotted down unknown words in a book she is reading.

- **Encourage children to read as much as possible.** Avid readers learn many more new words and so have larger vocabularies than do children who read infrequently (Fukkink & de Glopper, 1998; Stanovich, 2000; Swanborn & de Glopper, 1999). And when an adult reads storybooks to young children, the children are more likely to develop their vocabularies if the adult occasionally stops to ask about or explain potentially unfamiliar words (Brabham & Lynch-Brown, 2002).

Syntactic Development

Which one of the following sentences is grammatically correct?

- Growing children need nutritious food and lots of exercise.
- Experience students find to be many junior high school an unsettling.

You undoubtedly realized that the first sentence is grammatically correct and the second is not. But *how* were you able to tell the difference? Can you describe the specific grammatical rules you used to make your decisions?

Rules of syntax—the rules we use to combine words into meaningful sentences—are incredibly complex (e.g., N. Chomsky, 2006). Much of our knowledge about syntax is in an unconscious form. Although we can produce acceptable sentences and can readily understand the sentences of others, we cannot always put our finger on exactly what it is we know about language that allows us to do these things.

Despite the complex and elusive nature of syntactic rules, children seem to pick up on them rather quickly. By the time children reach school age, they have mastered many of the basics of sentence construction (McNeill, 1970; Reich, 1986). Even so, they are apt to show gaps in their syntactic knowledge throughout the elementary school years and, to a lesser extent, in the secondary school years as well. Following are noteworthy aspects of syntactic development over the course of childhood and adolescence.

- **Some syntax appears in children's earliest word combinations.** Initially, children use only single words to express their thoughts. For instance, at 18 months, Teresa's son Connor would simply say "mo" if he wanted more of whatever he was eating or playing with at the time. And like many toddlers, he would stretch out his arms and plead "Up!" when he wanted to be carried or cuddled. Developmentalists sometimes use the word **holophrase** to refer to such one-word "sentences."

Yet even when children are using only holophrases themselves, they show some awareness of the syntax in the speech they hear around them (Gertner, Fisher, & Eisengart, 2006; Kedar, Casasola, & Lust, 2006). And as they begin to combine words into two-word "sentences" in the latter half of their second year, simple syntactic rules seem to guide their constructions (R. Brown, 1973; H. S. Cairns, 1996; O'Grady, 1997). For example, their two-word combinations might reflect description ("Pillow dirty"), location ("Baby table"), or possession ("Adam hat") (R. Brown, 1973, p. 141). Children's early multiple-word sentences, known as **telegraphic speech,** include lexical words (rather than grammatical words) almost exclusively. By using such words, children maximize the meaning their short sentences convey—they get "the most bang for the buck"—just as many adolescents and adults do when they send text messages (and as adults used to do when they sent telegrams via the *telegraph*).

As children's sentences increase in length, they also increase in syntactic complexity—for instance, by including a subject, verb, and object (e.g., "I ride horsie") or describing both an action and a location ("Put truck window," "Adam put it box") (R. Brown, 1973, p. 205). And sometime before age 3 children begin to include grammatical words—*the, and, because,* and so on—in their sentences (O'Grady, 1997; R. E. Owens, 2008).

- **Young children rely heavily on word order when interpreting sentences.** By the time they are 1½, children have some understanding that, at least in English, word order affects meaning (Gertner et al., 2006; Hirsh-Pasek & Golinkoff, 1996). For instance, they know that "Big Bird is washing Cookie Monster" means something different from "Cookie Monster is washing Big Bird." Yet young children are sometimes misled by the order in which words appear (O'Grady, 1997). For instance, many preschoolers seem to apply a general rule that a pronoun refers to the noun that immediately precedes it. Consider the sentence "John said that Peter washed him." Many 4-year-olds think that *him* refers to *Peter* and so conclude that Peter washed himself. Similarly, kindergartners are apt to have trouble with the sentence "Because she was tired, Mommy was sleeping" because no noun appears before *she*.

- **Children's questions increasingly incorporate multiple syntactic rules.** In some languages it's very easy to ask questions. In Chinese, for instance, a person can change a statement into a question simply by adding *ma* to the end of the sentence. In English, however, asking questions is more complicated. At a minimum, it requires switching the order of the subject and verb ("Are you hungry?"). When past tense is involved, asking a question requires putting the auxiliary verb but *not* the main verb first ("Have you eaten yet?"). And when something other than a yes or no answer is called for, a question word (e.g., *who, what, where, how*) must also appear at the beginning ("What did you eat?").

English-speaking children seem to master these question-asking rules one step at a time. Initially, their questions may be nothing more than telegraphic sentences with a rise in pitch at the end (e.g., "Kitty go home?") (R. Brown, 1973, p. 141). At about age 2½, they attach question words to the beginning, and sometime in their third year, they add an auxiliary verb such as *is* or *does*. However, preschoolers often neglect one or more of the rules for asking questions. For instance, they may ask "What you want?" (forgetting to add the auxiliary verb) or "What you will do?" (forgetting to put the auxiliary verb before the subject) (de Villiers, 1995, pp. 516, 518).

holophrase
A single word used to express a complete thought; commonly observed in children's earliest speech.

telegraphic speech
Short, grammatically incomplete sentences that include lexical (rather than grammatical) words almost exclusively; common in toddlers.

Preschoolers are known for their many *why* and *how* questions. With age, their questions reflect an increasing ability to integrate multiple syntactic rules.

But by the time they are 5, most English-speaking children have mastered the correct syntax for questions (de Villiers, 1995).

> • ***Children tend to learn general rules for word endings before they learn the many exceptions.*** Knowledge of syntax includes knowledge about when to use word endings (suffixes) such as *-s*, *-er*, and *-ed*. When children first learn the rules for using suffixes (e.g., *-s* indicates plural, *-er* indicates a comparison, and *-ed* indicates past tense), they often apply these rules indiscriminately, without regard for exceptions. Thus a child might say "I have two *foots*," "Chocolate is *gooder* than vanilla," or "I *goed* to Grandma's house." This phenomenon, known as **overregularization,** is especially common during the preschool and early elementary years. It gradually diminishes as children master the irregular forms of various words: The plural of *foot* is *feet*, the comparative form of *good* is *better*, the past tense of *go* is *went*, and so on (Cazden, 1968; G. F. Marcus, 1996; Siegler, 1994).

Yet most high school students (and many adults as well) haven't completely mastered the irregularities of the English language (G. F. Marcus, 1996). For instance, throughout his high school years, Jeanne's son Jeff consistently said "I have *broughten* . . ." despite Jeanne's frequent reminders that he should say "I have *brought*. . . ."

> • ***The ability to comprehend passive sentences evolves gradually during the preschool and elementary school years.*** In a passive sentence, the subject of the sentence is the recipient, rather than the agent, of the action that the verb conveys. Passive sentences frequently confuse young children, who may incorrectly attribute the action to the subject. Consider these two sentences:

> The boy is pushed by the girl.
> The cup is washed by the girl.

Preschoolers are more likely to be confused by the first sentence—that is, to think that the boy is the one doing the pushing—than by the second sentence (Karmiloff-Smith, 1979). The first sentence has two possible "actors," but the second sentence has only one: Both boys and girls can push someone else, but cups can't wash girls. Complete mastery of passive sentences doesn't appear until the late elementary school years (O'Grady, 1997; Sudhalter & Braine, 1985).

> • ***Children can be confused by sentences with multiple clauses.*** At about age 4 children begin to produce simple subordinate clauses, such as those that follow and modify nouns (e.g., "This is the toy *that I want*") (R. E. Owens, 2008, p. 295). Yet throughout the elementary school years children struggle to understand certain kinds of multiple-clause sentences. Sentences with one clause embedded in the middle of another clause seem to be especially difficult, particularly if the noun tying the clauses together has a different function in each clause. Consider the sentence "The dog *that was chased by the boy* is angry" (R. E. Owens, 2008, p. 346). The dog is the subject of the main clause ("The dog . . . is angry") but is the recipient of the action in the embedded clause (". . . [dog] was chased by the boy"). Seventh graders easily understand such sentences, but younger children overrely on word order to interpret them and so may conclude that the boy, rather than the dog, is angry (R. E. Owens, 2008).

> • ***Knowledge of syntactic rules continues to develop at the secondary level.*** In middle school and high school, adolescents learn more subtle aspects of syntax, such as subject–verb and noun–pronoun agreement, correct uses of *that* versus *which* to introduce subordinate clauses, functions of punctuation marks such as colons and semicolons, and so on. They rarely develop such knowledge on their own, however. Instead, most of their syntactic development probably occurs as the result of formal instruction, especially through courses in language arts, English composition, and foreign languages (e.g., Pence & Justice, 2008).

How children acquire syntactic knowledge. Even infants have some awareness of patterns in speech. For example, in one study (G. F. Marcus, Vijayan, Bandi Rao, & Vishton, 1999), 7-month-olds heard a series of "sentences" each comprised of three nonsense syllables (e.g., *ga, na, ti, li*). Infants in Group 1 consistently heard them in a predictable "ABA" pattern (e.g., "Ga ti ga," "Li na li"), whereas infants in Group 2 consistently heard them in an "ABB" pattern (e.g., "Ga ti ti," "Li na na"). After losing interest in these sentences (reflecting

overregularization
Use of a syntactic rule in situations where an exception to the rule applies.

the *habituation* we spoke of in Chapter 2), they heard another series of "sentences" with new nonsense syllables. Some of these sentences followed the ABA pattern (e.g., "Wo fe wo"), whereas others followed the ABB pattern (e.g., "Wo fe fe"). The infants paid greater attention when listening to the pattern that was new for them, showing that the pattern they had heard before was "the same old thing," even though new sounds were involved.

Such sensitivity to patterns is undoubtedly essential for syntactic development. Some theorists suggest that acquiring syntax involves discovering the probabilities with which various word combinations appear in sentences (MacWhinney & Chang, 1995; Saffran, 2003; Sirois, Buckingham, & Shultz, 2000). For example, children may notice that *the* is usually followed by names of things or by "describing" words (e.g., they might hear "the dog," "the picnic," or "the pretty hat"). In contrast, *the* is rarely followed by words that identify specific actions (e.g., they never hear "the do" or "the went"). In addition, children may engage in **semantic bootstrapping,** using word meanings as a basis for forming syntactic categories (Bates & MacWhinney, 1987; S. A. Gelman & Kalish, 2006; Pinker, 1984, 1987). For instance, they may notice that labels for people and concrete objects always serve particular functions in sentences, that action words serve other functions, that spatial-relationship and direction words serve still others, and so on. Through this process they may gradually acquire an intuitive understanding of nouns, verbs, prepositions, and other parts of speech—an understanding that allows them to use various kinds of words appropriately in sentences.

Although theorists do not yet have a clear understanding of how children acquire syntactic rules, most agree that syntactic development is largely a constructive and unconscious process, especially in the early years (Aitchison, 1996; H. S. Cairns, 1996; Karmiloff-Smith, 1993). Young children typically receive little if any direct instruction about how to form sentences. Instead, they apparently develop their own set of syntactic rules through their observations of certain regularities in other people's speech. They may occasionally misapply the rules (as is seen in overregularization), but with time and practice they become adept at using most rules appropriately.

Formal language arts instruction brings some syntactic knowledge to a conscious level. Beginning in the upper elementary and middle school grades, children often learn to identify the various parts of a sentence (e.g., subject, direct object, prepositional phrase, subordinate clause) about which they acquired intuitive knowledge years earlier. They also study various verb tenses (e.g., present, past, present progressive) even though they have been using these tenses in their everyday speech for quite some time.

Fostering syntactic development.   Especially as they are learning the more complex and subtle aspects of syntax, children and adolescents often benefit from ongoing instruction and practice in various syntactic structures. Following are several examples of how caregivers and teachers can promote youngsters' syntactic development.

• ***Expand on young children's telegraphic speech.***   When young children speak in telegraphic sentences, caregivers can engage in **expansion** by repeating the sentences in a more mature form. For example, when a toddler says, "Doggy eat," mother might respond by saying, "Yes, the doggy is eating his dinner." Expansion gives children gentle feedback about the incompleteness of their own utterances and possibly encourages them to use more complex syntactic forms (Morgan, Bonamo, & Travis, 1995; Scherer & Olswang, 1984; Strapp & Federico, 2000).

• ***Teach irregular forms of verbs and comparative adjectives.***   Children do not always hear the irregular forms of verbs and adjectives in everyday speech (R. E. Owens, 2008). For example, their young playmates may talk about what's *badder* or *worser*, and many adults confuse the past tenses of the verbs *lay* and *lie* (which are *laid* and *lay*, respectively). Some formal instruction in irregular forms may therefore be the only way that children discover which terms are correct and which are not.

• ***Describe various sentence structures, and give children considerable practice in their use.***   Having children examine and practice common syntactic structures (active and

Especially in adolescence and adulthood, many advances in language development probably occur as a result of formal instruction.

semantic bootstrapping
Using knowledge of word meanings to derive knowledge about syntactic categories and structures.

expansion
Repetition of a child's short utterances in more complete and grammatically correct forms.

passive voice, independent and dependent clauses, etc.) has at least two benefits. First, children should be better able to vary their sentence structure as they write—a strategy associated with more sophisticated writing (Byrnes, 1996; Spivey, 1997). Second, learning the labels for such structures (e.g., *passive voice*) in English should help them acquire analogous structures in other languages they study at a later time.

• *Provide ample opportunities for children to express their ideas in relatively formal contexts, and give feedback about appropriate syntax.* In typical everyday conversation, adults and children alike often use incomplete sentences and are lax in their adherence to grammatical rules (Cook & Newson, 1996; D. Lightfoot, 1999). But what's common in casual speech is often frowned on in writing and public speaking. In formal and public situations (e.g., a letter to the editor of a local newspaper or a presentation to a large group), correct grammar is, in many people's minds, an indication that the writer or speaker is educated and is therefore someone to take seriously (Purcell-Gates, 1995; H. L. Smith, 1998).

Development of Listening Skills

As you might guess, children's ability to understand what they hear is closely related to their semantic and syntactic development. The development of listening skills is characterized by several additional trends as well.

• *In the first year, infants learn to focus primarily on sounds important in their native language.* The basic elements of spoken language—all the consonants and vowels a language includes—are collectively known as **phonemes.** Phonemes are the smallest units of speech that indicate differences in meaning in a particular language. For instance, the word *bite* has three phonemes: a "buh" sound, an "eye" sound, and a "tuh" sound. If we change any one of these sounds—for instance, if we change *b* to *f (fight)*, long *i* to long *a (bait)*, or *t* to *k (bike)*—we get a new word with a different meaning.

Beginning on day one, infants can discriminate among a wide variety of phonemes, including many that they don't hear in the speech around them (Aldridge, Stillman, & Bower, 2001; Jusczyk, 1995; Werker & Lalonde, 1988). Before long, they show a noticeable preference for sounds and words they hear frequently. For instance, 5-month-olds pay more attention to their own names than to other, similar-sounding words (Mandel, Jusczyk, & Pisoni, 1995). When infants reach 8 or 9 months, they also seem to prefer listening to the sounds and rhythms of their native language (Jusczyk & Aslin, 1995; Saffran, Aslin, & Newport, 1996). For instance, Mario showed an early preference for Spanish rather than English (Fantini, 1985).

This early tuning-in to a particular language gradually alters what infants "hear" and "don't hear" in speech. By the time children are a year old, they primarily hear the differences that are important in their own languages (Jusczyk, 1997; Werker & Tees, 1999). For example, 1-year-old infants in English-speaking countries continue to hear the difference between the "L" and "R" sounds, a distinction critical for making such discriminations as *lap* versus *rap* and *lice* versus *rice*. In contrast, Japanese children gradually lose the ability to tell the difference, presumably because the Japanese language treats the two sounds as a single phoneme. Similarly, babies in English-speaking societies lose the ability to distinguish among various "S" sounds that comprise two or more different phonemes in certain other languages.

As you can see, the first year of life is an important one for learning which differences among speech sounds are essential for understanding one's native language. Yet children continue to fine-tune their discriminative powers throughout early and middle childhood. For instance, they may have some difficulty distinguishing between words that differ by only one phoneme until they are 5 years old (Gerken, 1994; Rayner, Foorman, Perfetti, Pesetsky, & Seidenberg, 2001). Furthermore, they may continue to hear some sound differences not important in their own language until they are 8 to 10 years old (Siegler & Alibali, 2005).

• *Young children rely more heavily on context than older children, but youngsters of all ages take context into account.* Children do not necessarily need to focus on every sound, or even every word, when they listen to what other people say. For instance, 18-month-olds often know from the context which word a speaker is going to say after hearing only the first two phonemes (Fernald, Swingley, & Pinto, 2001). Furthermore, using various contextual clues, children often realize that what a speaker says is different from what the

phonemes
Smallest units of a spoken language that
signify differences in meaning.

speaker actually means (M. Donaldson, 1978; Flavell et al., 2002; Paul, 1990). For example, kindergartners may correctly conclude that a teacher who asks "Whose jacket do I see lying on the floor?" is actually requesting the jacket's owner to pick it up and put it where it belongs.

Sometimes young children are *too* dependent on context for determining the meaning of language, to the point where they don't listen carefully enough to understand a spoken message accurately. They may instead "hear" what they think the speaker means based on their beliefs about the speaker's intentions. As an example, look at the cows and horses in Figure 9-3. *Are there more cows or more black horses?* There are four cows but only three black horses, so obviously there are more cows. Yet if you ask 6-year-olds this question, they are apt to tell you that there are more black horses. In probing the children's reasoning, it becomes clear that most of them interpret the question as a request to compare only the *black* cows with the black horses. For example, one child defended his incorrect answer by saying, "There's more black horses 'cos there's only two black cows" (Donaldson, 1978, p. 44).[2]

Older children and adolescents consider the context in a somewhat different way, in that they compare a message to the reality of the situation. Such a comparison enables them to detect sarcasm—to realize that the speaker actually means the exact opposite of what he or she is saying (Capelli, Nakagawa, & Madden, 1990). For instance, they understand that someone who says "Oh, that's just *great!*" in the face of dire circumstances doesn't think the situation is "great" at all.

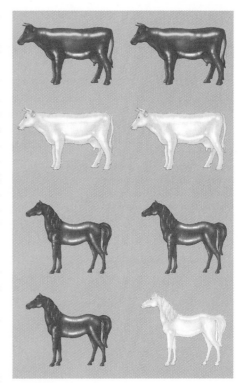

Figure 9-3

Are there more cows or more black horses?

● ***Young children have an overly simplistic view of what "good listening" is.*** Children in the early elementary grades believe they are good listeners if they simply sit quietly without interrupting the person speaking. Older children (e.g., 10- and 11-year-olds) are more likely to recognize that good listening also requires an understanding of what is being said (T. M. McDevitt et al., 1990). And in adolescence, many youngsters begin to realize that being a *socially effective* listener also involves listening to others in an open-minded, nonjudgmental, and empathic manner (Imhof, 2001).

● ***Elementary school children do not always know what to do when they don't understand what they hear.*** In a series of studies (T. M. McDevitt, 1990; T. M. McDevitt et al., 1990), children in grades 1, 3, and 5 were given the following dilemma:

> This is a story about a girl named Mary. Mary is at school listening to her teacher, Ms. Brown. Ms. Brown explains how to use a new computer that she just got for their classroom. She tells the children in the classroom how to use the computer. Mary doesn't understand the teacher's directions. She's confused. What should Mary do? (T. M. McDevitt, 1990, p. 570)

Some children responded that Mary should ask the teacher for further explanation. But others said that Mary should either listen more carefully or seek clarification of the procedure from other children. Many children, younger ones especially, believe it is inappropriate to ask a teacher for help, perhaps because they have previously been discouraged from asking questions in school or at home (Marchand & Skinner, 2007; T. M. McDevitt, 1990). Cultural background plays a role here as well. Many children growing up in Asian and Mexican American communities are reluctant to ask questions because they've been taught that initiating a conversation with an adult is disrespectful (Delgado-Gaitan, 1994; C. A. Grant & Gomez, 2001).

● ***Older children and adolescents become increasingly able to find multiple meanings in messages.*** As children move into the middle and secondary grades, they become aware that some messages are ambiguous and have two or more possible meanings (Bearison & Levey, 1977; Nippold, 1988; R. E. Owens, 2008). They also become better able to understand and explain **figurative speech,** speech that communicates meaning beyond a literal interpretation of its words. For instance, they understand that idioms should not be taken at face value—that a person who "hits the roof" doesn't really hit the roof and that someone who is "tied up" isn't necessarily bound with rope. In addition, they become

---

[2]This task might remind you of Piaget's *class inclusion* problems (e.g., see the *beads* problem near the beginning of Chapter 6). Piaget interpreted children's responses from the perspective of logical reasoning processes, but here we see a different factor at work: Children's inferences about a speaker's intentions overshadow their attention to the question's literal meaning.

figurative speech
Speech that communicates meaning beyond a literal interpretation of its words.

MyEducationLab

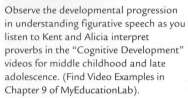

Observe the developmental progression in understanding figurative speech as you listen to Kent and Alicia interpret proverbs in the "Cognitive Development" videos for middle childhood and late adolescence. (Find Video Examples in Chapter 9 of MyEducationLab).

increasingly adept at interpreting similes and metaphors (e.g., "Her hands are like ice," "That man is the Rock of Gibraltar"). And in the late elementary years, they begin to draw generalizations from proverbs such as "Look before you leap" and "Don't put the cart before the horse." In the "Cognitive Development" videos for middle childhood and late adolescence in MyEducationLab, you can observe how children's ability to understand proverbs improves with age. For example, whereas 10-year-old Kent seems baffled by the old adage "A rolling stone gathers no moss," 14-year-old Alicia offers a reasonable explanation: "Maybe when you go through things too fast, you don't collect anything from it." Adolescents' ability to interpret proverbs in a generalized, abstract fashion continues to develop throughout the secondary school years (R. E. Owens, 2008).

Although children's ability to understand figurative language depends to some degree on their cognitive maturity, it may also depend on how much they have been exposed to such language. Many inner-city African American communities make heavy use of figurative language, such as similes, metaphors, and hyperbole (intentional exaggeration), in their day-to-day conversations, jokes, and stories (Hale-Benson, 1986; Ortony, Turner, & Larson-Shapiro, 1985; H. L. Smith, 1998). The following anecdote illustrates this point:

> I once asked my mother, upon her arrival from church, "Mom, was it a good sermon?" To which she replied, "Son, by the time the minister finished preaching, the men were crying and the women had passed out on the floor." (H. L. Smith, 1998, p. 202)

With such a rich oral tradition, it is not surprising that many inner-city African American youth are especially advanced in their ability to comprehend figurative language (Ortony et al., 1985).

Cognitive factors influencing the development of listening comprehension. Not only does children's ability to understand what they hear depend on their knowledge of word meanings and syntax, but it also depends on their general knowledge about the world. For instance, children can better understand a peer's description of a newly purchased Volkswagen Beetle if they have a schema for Volkswagen Beetles. They can better understand a friend's story about a trip to a fast-food restaurant if they have a script for what such visits typically entail. Children's schemas, scripts, and other knowledge about the world enable them to draw inferences from the things they hear, thus filling gaps in the information actually presented.[3]

In addition, children's ability to understand and remember what they hear is limited to what they can reasonably hold in working memory at a single time (Anthony, Lonigan, & Dyer, 1996; L. French & Brown, 1977). When information exceeds their working memory capacity, it will, as a common expression puts it, "go in one ear and out the other." Because young children tend to have less working memory capacity than older children and adults, they will be especially limited in their ability to understand and remember what others tell them. Preschoolers, for instance, often have trouble remembering and following directions with multiple steps (L. French & Brown, 1977).

Children's general cognitive abilities play a role as well. Interpreting messages in nonliteral ways requires abstract thinking and an ability to draw analogies across diverse situations (Winner, 1988). Given what we know about the development of abstract thought, it is hardly surprising that children have difficulty understanding metaphors and proverbs in the preschool and early elementary years.

Promoting listening comprehension. Parents, teachers, caregivers, and others who work with toddlers, preschoolers, and students in the primary grades must take into account the limited listening comprehension skills that young children are likely to have (see the Development and Practice feature "Promoting Listening Skills in Young Children"). Following are three more general suggestions for adults who work with children and adolescents at all age levels.

• ***Take children's semantic and syntactic development into account when speaking to them, and check frequently to be sure they understand.*** Using vocabulary and syntactic structures appropriate to the age-group is, of course, essential if adults want chil-

---

[3]To refresh your memory about *schemas* and *scripts*, reread the section "Long-Term Memory" in Chapter 7.

Development and Practice

Promoting Listening Skills in Young Children

- **Present only small amounts of information at one time.**

  A preschool teacher helps the 3- and 4-year-olds in her class make "counting books" to take home. She has previously prepared nine sheets of paper (each with a different number from 1 to 9) for each child. She has also assembled a variety of objects that the children can paste on the pages to depict the numbers (two buttons for the "2" page, five pieces of macaroni for the "5" page, etc.). As she engages the children in the project, she describes only one or two steps of the process at a time.

- **Expect children to listen attentively only for short periods.**

  A kindergarten teacher has learned that most of his students can listen quietly to a storybook for no more than 10 or 15 minutes at a stretch, and he plans his daily schedule accordingly.

- **Discuss the components of good listening.**

  A first-grade teacher explains to her students that "good listening" involves more than just sitting quietly, that it also involves paying attention and trying to understand what the speaker is saying. Later, after a police officer has visited her class to discuss bicycle safety, she asks the children to repeat some of the safety precautions the officer mentioned.

- **Discuss courses of action that children should take when they don't understand a speaker.**

  A second-grade teacher encourages his students to ask questions whenever they don't understand something he tells them in class.

---

dren to understand their messages. Furthermore, rather than assuming that their messages have been understood, adults should in some way assess children's understandings, perhaps by asking questions, having children restate ideas in their own words, or having them demonstrate what they've learned through actions or pictures (Jalongo, 2008).

- ***Adjust the length of verbal presentations to the attention span of the age-group, and avoid information overload.*** As information processing theory tells us, people of all ages can understand a message only when they are paying attention, and they can handle only a limited amount of information at a time. Given such limitations, children and adolescents alike often benefit from hearing something more than once (e.g., Wasik, Karweit, Burns, & Brodsky, 1998).

- ***Encourage critical listening.*** Sometime around age 3 to 6, children begin to realize that what people say is not necessarily what is true (e.g., Koenig, Clément, & Harris, 2004; K. Lee, Cameron, Doucette, & Talwar, 2002). Yet throughout the elementary and secondary school years, children and adolescents sometimes have difficulty separating fact from fiction in the messages they hear. Children who are taught not to believe everything they hear are more likely to evaluate messages for errors, falsehoods, and ambiguities. For example, when children are reminded that television commercials are designed to persuade them to buy something, they are less likely to be influenced by the commercials (Calvert, 2008; Halpern, 1998; D. F. Roberts, Christenson, Gibson, Mooser, & Goldberg, 1980).

Development of Speaking Skills

As children become more adept at understanding what other people say, they also become more adept at expressing their own thoughts, ideas, and wishes. Following are several trends that characterize the development of speech and other means of communication in infancy, childhood, and adolescence.

- ***In the first year of life, children become increasingly proficient in making speech sounds, and they increasingly specialize in the phonemes of their native language.*** Between 1 and 2 months of age, infants typically begin **cooing,** making vowel sounds in an almost "singing" manner (e.g., "aaaaaaa," "ooooooo"). Sometime around 6 months, they begin **babbling,** combining consonant and vowel sounds into syllables that they repeat over and over (e.g., "mamamamama," "doodoodoo") without apparent meaning. With time, babbling becomes increasingly speechlike in nature, as infants combine different syllables into language-like utterances. Also with time, infants gradually drop the sounds they don't hear in the speech around them (J. L. Locke, 1993). In essence, infants first babble in a universal "language" that includes a wide variety of phonemes but later babble only in their native tongue.

cooing
Making and repeating vowel sounds (e.g., "oooooo"); common in early infancy.

babbling
Repeating certain consonant-vowel syllables over and over (e.g., "mamamama"); common in the latter half of the first year.

MyEducationLab

Observe one girl's effective use of gestures in the "Conversation with a Five-Year-Old" video. (Find Video Examples in Chapter 9 of MyEducationLab.)

• ***Infants and young children sometimes use gestures to communicate.*** As early as age 1, some children try to communicate through actions rather than words. An infant might put his fingers in his mouth to indicate that he wants something to eat. A toddler might wrinkle her nose and sniff as a way of "talking" about flowers. To some degree, the use of such gestures seems to pave the way for later language development (Goodwyn & Acredolo, 1998; Goodwyn, Acredolo, & Brown, 2000; Volterra, Caselli, Capirci, & Pizzuto, 2005).[4] Youngsters don't entirely abandon gestures as they gain proficiency in spoken language, however. As you almost certainly know from your own experience, facial expressions and hand motions can often enhance people's verbal messages.

• ***Pronunciation continues to improve in the early elementary years.*** As we've discovered, children say their first word sometime around their first birthday, and by age 2 or so most children talk a great deal. Yet children typically do not master all the phonemes of the English language until they are about 8 years old (Hulit & Howard, 2006; R. E. Owens, 2008). During the preschool years, they are likely to have difficulty pronouncing *r* and *th* (they might say "wabbit" instead of "rabbit" and "dat" instead of "that"). Most children have acquired these sounds by the time they are 6, but at this age they may still have trouble with such consonant blends as *spl* and *thr* (R. E. Owens, 2008; Pence & Justice, 2008).

Recall the kindergarten teacher's reference to Mario's "slight accent." Mario mastered Spanish pronunciation by age 3. A few months later, he could produce many of the additional phonemes required for English. Nevertheless, Spanish sounds occasionally crept into Mario's English for several years thereafter (Fantini, 1985).

As children grow older, they become better able to carry on lengthy conversations about a single topic.

• ***As children grow older, their conversations with others increase in length and depth.*** Early conversations tend to be short. Most young children are quite willing and able to introduce new topics into a conversation, but they have difficulty maintaining a sustained interchange about any single topic (Brinton & Fujiki, 1984; K. Nelson, 1996a). As they grow older, they can carry on lengthier discussions about a single issue or event. And in adolescence, the content of their conversations gradually becomes more abstract (R. E. Owens, 2008).

• ***Children become increasingly able to adapt their speech to the characteristics of their listeners.*** As early as age 3, preschoolers use simpler language with toddlers than they do with adults and peers (T. M. McDevitt & Ford, 1987; Shatz & Gelman, 1973). Yet preschoolers and elementary school children don't always take their listeners' visual perspectives and prior knowledge into account and so may provide insufficient information for listeners to understand what they are saying (Glucksberg & Krauss, 1967; T. M. McDevitt & Ford, 1987). For instance, a child might ask "What's this?" without regard for whether the listener can see the object in question. To some extent, such speech may reflect the *egocentrism* that Piaget described (see Chapter 6). However, it may also be the result of young children's lack of proficiency in precisely describing the objects and events they are currently experiencing or have previously witnessed (T. M. McDevitt & Ford, 1987).

As children grow older, they become increasingly able to take other people's knowledge and perspectives into account and so are better able to make their meanings clear (D. Matthews, Lieven, & Tomasello, 2007; Sonnenschein, 1988). They also become better able to read the subtle nonverbal signals (e.g., the puzzled brows, the lengthy silences) that indicate others' confusion about their messages (T. M. McDevitt & Ford, 1987).

• ***Over time, children become more skillful at narratives.*** Beginning in the preschool years, children can tell a story, or **narrative**—an account of a sequence of events, either real or fictional, that are logically interconnected (McKeough, 1995; Sutton-Smith, 1986). Young children's narratives are usually quite short, as illustrated by one 5-year-old's account of what she did at her preschool earlier in the day:

> My class and me went outside to play. And we played in the sprinkler and we played on the toys and we made soap.

By age 5 or 6, many children can create a narrative that reflects a reasonable sequence of events and includes simple cause-and-effect relationships between characters' mental states

narrative
Verbal account of a temporal sequence of logically interconnected events; a story.

[4]Gestures also play a role in young children's reasoning (see Chapter 7).

and behaviors (Kemper, 1984; McKeough, 1995; Nicolopoulou & Richner, 2007). Narratives become increasingly complex during the elementary years. Definite plot lines begin to emerge, and descriptions of people's thoughts, motives, and emotions become increasingly sophisticated (Bauer, 2006; Kemper, 1984; R. E. Owens, 2008).

The nature of children's narratives varies somewhat from culture to culture. For example, in some African American communities, narratives may include several events that, on the surface, seem unrelated yet all contribute to a single underlying message—perhaps providing strategies for helping a baby brother (Hale-Benson, 1986; Trawick-Smith, 2003). Children from some backgrounds may have little or no experience with certain kinds of narratives before beginning school (Heath, 1986). For example, in some lower-socioeconomic communities in the southern United States, children have numerous opportunities to talk collaboratively about events in which both they and their listeners have participated, but they are rarely asked to recount events that they *alone* have experienced (Heath, 1986).

MyEducationLab

Observe the development of narratives in three videos in the Video Examples section in Chapter 9 of MyEducationLab: "Conversation with a Five-Year-Old," "A Seven-Year-Old's Nonfictional Narrative," and "A Thirteen-Year-Old's Fictional Narrative."

• ***Creative and figurative expressions emerge during the elementary years and continue into adolescence.*** Many children enjoying "playing" with language in some way (Nippold, 1988; R. E. Owens, 2008). For instance, good friends might converse in "pig Latin" in which any initial consonants are moved to the ends of words, and a long-*a* sound is added to each word. (As an illustration, the sentence *This sentence is written in pig Latin* would be "Is-thay entence-say is-ay itten-wray in-ay ig-pay atin-lay.") Children also take delight in jokes and riddles that play on the multiple meanings of words or similar-sounding phrases ("How much do pirates pay for their earrings?" "A buccaneer").

Creative word play is especially common in many African American communities (e.g., Smitherman, 2007). It sometimes takes the form of **playing the dozens,** playful teasing of one another through exaggerated insults—for example, "Your mama's so fat she's got to sleep in the Grand Canyon" (Goodwin, 2006, p. 232).[5] Exaggeration (hyperbole) is evident in African American narratives as well. In the following exchange, 12-year-old Terry and his neighbor Tony begin with a kernel of truth (a cat fight in the neighborhood) and then let their imaginations run wild:

Terry:	Didja hear 'bout Aunt Bess' cat las' night?
Tony:	No, what 'bout dat ol' cat?
Terry:	Dat cat get in a fight.
Tony:	A fight?
Terry:	Yeah, it kilt a dog.
Tony:	Ain't no cat can kill no dog.
Terry:	Dis cat, he kilt a big dog, dat ol' German shepherd stay down by ol' man Oak's place.
Tony:	What'd you do?
Terry:	Me? I kilt a horse.
Tony:	You ain't kilt no horse, (pause) more'n likely a mouse. Where?
Terry:	On Main Street. Yesterday.
Tony:	And you kilt one, for sure?
Terry:	Yea, me 'n dat ol' cat, we built a big fire, stirred it aroun', threw oil in it, got it goin' good, and I rod [*sic*] dat horse right in.
Tony:	Ya did?
Terry:	Yup.
Tony:	I know, it took a while to git de cat outta de fire, 'bout (pause) maybe a week or so, 'n Mr. Rowe [who owns a bicycle shop on Main Street] give us a bicycle, 'n we ride de horse, 'n my friend, Steve, he ride de horse, too, 'n we come back and foun' dat ol' cat done kilt dat big dog.
Terry:	Why?
Tony:	'Cause dat cat say "Wow, I'm de greates', ain't no dog kin git me," (pause) like ain't no fire gonna git *me* (pause) 'n my horse (pause) 'n my bicycle. (Heath, 1983, pp. 183–184; reprinted with the permission of Cambridge University Press)

• ***Adolescents sometimes use their own teen lingo in conversing with peers.*** Many adolescents express themselves in ways that are unique to their age-group, or perhaps

playing the dozens
Friendly, playful exchange of insults, common in some African American communities; also called *joaning* or *sounding.*

---

[5]You can find other examples of playing the dozens in the story about Sam and Bubba on p. 242 of Chapter 7.

School provides an excellent context in which children and adolescents can develop their speaking skills.

to a small group of friends. For example, over the years, teenagers have used a variety of adjectives—*cool, boss, radical, wicked awesome*, and so on—to describe something they really like. At age 16, Jeanne's son Alex insisted on addressing everyone (including his mother) as "Dude." Such expressions help adolescents establish themselves as belonging to a particular peer group in much the same way that their clothing and hairstyles do (J. R. Harris, 1995).

How children develop speaking skills.   Children's increasing proficiency in oral language is the result of many things: better muscular control of the lips and tongue, more semantic and syntactic knowledge, growing awareness of what listeners are apt to know and believe, acquisition of abstract reasoning ability, and so on. But to a considerable degree, the development of speaking skills also comes from practice, practice, practice.

Sometimes preschoolers' conversational partners are adults, who typically take the lead in discussions. In their interactions with peers, however, children can converse more as equal partners. Furthermore, when children assume the roles of "mommy," "teacher," "doctor," or "storekeeper" in play activities, they can experiment with the variety of linguistic styles and jargon that they associate with such roles (Christie & Johnsen, 1983; K. Nelson, 1986).

During the elementary and secondary school years, experience almost certainly continues to play a key role in the development of speaking skills. Such experience comes in the forms of both structured activities (e.g., oral presentations at school) and unstructured interactions (e.g., conversations with friends). For instance, the prevalence of word play and figurative language in inner-city African American communities is probably largely responsible for the especially creative speech of the children who grow up in these communities (Ortony et al., 1985; H. L. Smith, 1998; Smitherman, 2007).

Promoting speaking skills.   To help children and adolescents develop their speaking skills, teachers and other adults should, of course, give them many and varied opportunities to speak in both structured and unstructured contexts. The following strategies can also be beneficial:

MyEducationLab

Observe Corwin's turn-taking ability in the "Cognitive Development," "Intelligence," and "Literacy" videos for infancy in the Video Examples section in Chapter 9 of MyEducationLab.

• ***Regularly engage infants in "conversation."***   In the "Cognitive Development," "Intelligence," and "Literacy" videos for infancy in MyEducationLab, you can observe several "conversations" that 16-month-old Corwin has with his mother. Although Corwin says few words distinctly enough to be understood, he knows how to take turns in the dialogue and understands enough of what his mother says to respond appropriately to her questions.

As early as 3 or 4 months of age, most infants readily participate in verbal interactions with adults. Even at this point they have some knowledge of turn taking: They may quietly listen when an adult speaks to them and vocalize when the adult stops (Ginsburg & Kilbourne, 1988). Young infants also tend to mimic the intonations (e.g., changes in pitch and stress) that a caregiver uses (Masataka, 1992). When a caregiver mimics *their* vocalizations, infants' speechlike sounds increase in frequency (K. Bloom, Russell, & Wassenberg, 1987). It appears, then, that experience with verbal interaction has benefits even for children who do not yet understand much of what they hear.

Another effective strategy is to teach infants gestures they can use to communicate their wishes. For instance, caregivers might teach babies signs for *more* and *please* (see Figure 9-4). Infants as young as 6 months old can successfully learn a few hand signs to communicate with caregivers (Goodwyn et al., 2000; R. H. Thompson, Cotnoir-Bichelman, McKerchar, Tate, & Dancho, 2007; R. H. Thompson, McKerchar, & Dancho, 2004).

• ***Let children know when their message is difficult to understand.***   People of all ages occasionally have trouble communicating their thoughts clearly to others. Young children may have particular difficulty because of their limited ability to consider the knowledge and perspectives of their listeners. Asking questions or expressing confusion when children describe events and ideas ambiguously or incompletely should gradually help them express their thoughts more precisely and take into account what their listeners do and do not know (e.g., D. Matthews, Lieven, & Tomasello, 2007).

• ***Ask children to recall real events and speculate about fictional ones.***   Adults often pose questions that encourage children to respond in narrative form. For instance, a teacher might ask, "What did you do this weekend?" or say "Make up a story about what

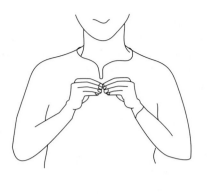

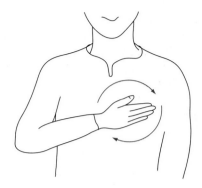

"More"

"Please"

Place your fingertips together in front of your chest, as if adding something to the top of a pile.

Hold your hand close to your heart with palm facing toward your chest, and move it clockwise (from an observer's viewpoint) to indicate pleasure.

Figure 9-4

Children as young as 6 months can be taught to communicate through simple gestures. Examples of useful gestures are the signs for *more* and *please* in American Sign Language.

might happen if someone brought a cow to show-and-tell." Giving children opportunities to narrate events, either actual incidents or fictional creations, provides a context in which they can practice speaking for sustained periods and build on the rich oral traditions of many cultural groups (Hale-Benson, 1986; Hemphill & Snow, 1996; McCarty & Watahomigie, 1998).

Storytelling ability can be enhanced by specific training and practice (McKeough, 1995; J. R. Price, Roberts, & Jackson, 2006). Consider how 6-year-old Leanne's ability to tell a story improved over a 2-month period as a result of specific instruction in how to conceptualize and tell stories:

Before instruction:
A girl—and a boy—and a kind old horse. They got mad at each other. That the end. (McKeough, 1995, p. 170)

After instruction:
Once upon a time there was a girl. She was playing with her toys and—um—she asked her mom if she could go outside—to play in the snow. But her mom said no. And then she was very sad. And—and she had to play. So she she [sic] asked her mom if she could go outside and she said yes. She jumped in the snow and she was having fun and she had an idea and she jumped in the snow and she felt happy. (McKeough, 1995, p. 170)

• ***Encourage creativity in oral language.*** Linguistic creativity can be expressed in many ways, including through stories, poems, songs, rap, jokes, and puns. Such forms of language not only encourage creative language use but also help children identify parallels between seemingly dissimilar objects or events. Recognizing commonalities enables children to construct similes, metaphors, and other analogies. Hyperbole can be encouraged as well, as long as children realize that they are intentionally stretching the truth. For the assignment shown in Figure 9-5, 6-year-old Morris was instructed to write a fact and then a "tall sentence" in which he should fantasize or exaggerate.

In addition, the playful use of language can help children discover general characteristics of language, as an incident in Mario's childhood illustrates:

Seven-year-old Mario tells his parents a joke that he has heard at school earlier in the day. He relates the joke in English: "What did the bird say when his cage got broken?" His parents have no idea what the bird said, so he tells them, "Cheap, cheap!"

Mario's parents find the joke amusing, so he later translates it for the family's Spanish-speaking nanny: "*¿Qué dijo el pájaro cuando se le rompió la jaula?*" He follows up with the bird's answer: "*Barato, barato.*" Mario is surprised to discover that the nanny finds no humor in the joke. He knows that he has somehow failed to convey the point of the joke but cannot figure out where he went wrong. (Fantini, 1985, p. 72)[6]

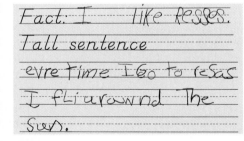

Figure 9-5

Morris (age 6) shows that he knows the difference between a fact ("I like recess") and a "tall sentence" ("Every time I go to recess I fly around the sun").

[6]From *Language Acquisition of a Bilingual Child: A Sociolinguistic Perspective*, by A. E. Fantini, 1985, Clevedon, England: Multilingual Matters. (Available from the SIT Bookstore, School for International Training, Kipling Road, Brattleboro, VT 06302.) Reprinted with permission.

sociolinguistic behaviors
Social conventions (often culture specific) that govern appropriate verbal interaction.

The joke, of course, gets lost in translation. The Spanish word *barato* means "cheap" but has no resemblance to the sound that a bird makes. Only several years later did Mario understand that humor that depends on wordplay does not always translate from one language to another (Fantini, 1985). His eventual understanding of this principle was an aspect of his growing *metalinguistic awareness*, a topic we examine shortly.

Development of Pragmatics

The pragmatic aspects of language include verbal and nonverbal strategies for communicating effectively with others. Strategies for initiating conversations, changing the subject, telling stories, and arguing persuasively are all forms of pragmatic knowledge. Also falling within the domain of pragmatics are **sociolinguistic behaviors**—behaviors that are considered polite and socially acceptable in verbal interactions in one's particular culture.

Most children begin to acquire pragmatic skills (e.g., prefacing a request with "please" and responding politely to other people's questions) long before they reach school age. Preschoolers also learn that certain ways that they might speak to their peers ("Shut up!" "Get auto here!") are unacceptable when talking to adults (J. B. Bryant, 2001). Children continue to refine their knowledge of pragmatics throughout the preschool years and elementary grades (Garvey & Berninger, 1981; R. E. Owens, 2008; Warren-Leubecker & Bohannon, 1989). Our own observations indicate that this process continues into the middle and high school years as well. However, children from different cultures often learn different social conventions, particularly in matters of etiquette, as you will see now.

Cultural differences in sociolinguistic behaviors. Cultural differences in sociolinguistic behaviors sometimes lead to misunderstandings in cross-cultural interactions. For example, some Native American communities believe it unnecessary to say hello or good-bye (Sisk, 1989). When children from these communities fail to extend greetings, an adult may erroneously conclude that they are being rude. And in some Native American and Asian cultures, children learn to display steady, neutral facial expressions even when they experience strong feelings inside (Camras, Chen, Bakeman, Norris, & Cain, 2006; D. Montgomery, 1989). An adult from a different cultural background might easily misinterpret a child's lack of facial expression as a sign of boredom or disinterest.

Following are additional cultural differences that may lead to misunderstandings in classrooms and other group settings. These differences are summarized in the Observation Guidelines table "Identifying Cultural Differences in Sociolinguistic Conventions."

Talking versus being silent. Relatively speaking, mainstream Western culture is a chatty one. People often say things to one another even when they have very little to communicate, making small talk as a way of maintaining interpersonal relationships and filling awkward silences (Irujo, 1988; Trawick-Smith, 2003). In some African American communities as well, people speak frequently and often with a great deal of energy and enthusiasm (Gay, 2006; Lein, 1975).

In certain other cultures, however, silence is golden. Brazilians and Peruvians often greet their guests silently, Arabs stop talking to indicate a desire for privacy, and many Native American communities value silence in general (Basso, 1972; Menyuk & Menyuk, 1988; Trawick-Smith, 2003). And as noted in Chapter 8, some cultures interpret talking a lot as a sign of immaturity or low intelligence.

Interacting with adults. In many European American families, children feel they can speak freely when they have comments or questions. Yet in many Hispanic, Native American, and Southeast Asian cultures and in some African American communities, children learn very early that they should engage in conversation with adults only when their participation has been directly solicited. In such cultures, speaking directly and assertively to adults is seen as rude, perhaps even rebellious (Banks & Banks, 1995; Delgado-Gaitan, 1994; C. A. Grant & Gomez, 2001). For example, in some parts of Mexico and in the Yup'ik culture of Alaska, children are expected to learn primarily by close, quiet observation of adults. Accordingly, these children rarely ask questions or otherwise interrupt what adults are doing (García, 1994; Gutiérrez & Rogoff, 2003).

Making eye contact. Among many people from European American backgrounds, looking someone in the eye is a way of indicating that they are trying to communicate or are listen-

MyEducationLab

Observe many pragmatic skills (e.g., maintaining eye contact, making polite requests) in the "Conversation with a Five-Year-Old" video. (Find Video Examples in Chapter 9 of MyEducationLab.)

Observation Guidelines

Identifying Cultural Differences in Sociolinguistic Conventions

Characteristic	Look For	Example	Implication
Talkativeness	· Frequent talking, even about trivial matters, *or* · Silence unless something important needs to be said	When Muhammed abruptly stops talking to his peers and turns to read his book, the other children think his action is rude.	Don't interpret a child's sudden or lengthy silence as necessarily reflecting apathy or intentional rudeness.
Style of Interacting with Adults	· Willingness to initiate conversations with adults, *or* · Speaking to adults only when spoken to	Elena is exceptionally quiet in class, and she answers questions only when her teacher directs them specifically at her. At lunch and on the playground, however, she readily talks and laughs with her friends.	Keep in mind that some children won't tell you when they're confused. If you think they may not understand, take them aside and ask specific questions to assess what they have learned. Provide additional instruction to address any gaps in understanding.
Eye Contact	· Looking others in the eye when speaking or listening to them, *or* · Looking down or away in the presence of adults	Herman always looks at his feet when an adult speaks to him.	Don't assume that children aren't paying attention just because they don't look you in the eye.
Personal Space	· Standing quite close to a conversation partner, perhaps touching that person frequently, *or* · Keeping distance between oneself and others when talking with them	Michelle is noticeably uncomfortable when other people touch her.	Give children some personal space during one-on-one interactions. In addition, to facilitate cross-cultural interactions, teach children that what constitutes personal space differs from culture to culture.
Responses to Questions	· Answering questions readily, *or* · Failing to answer very easy questions	Leah never responds to "What is this?" questions, even when she knows the answers.	Be aware that some children are not accustomed to answering the types of questions that many Western adults ask during instruction. Respect children's privacy when they are reluctant to answer personal questions.
Wait Time	· Waiting several seconds before answering questions, *or* · Not waiting at all, and perhaps even interrupting others	Mario often interrupts his classmates during class discussions.	When addressing a question to an entire group, give children several seconds to think before calling on one child for an answer. When some children interrupt regularly, communicate a procedure (e.g., hand raising and waiting to be called on) to ensure that everyone has a chance to be heard.

ing intently. But in many African American, Hispanic, and Native American cultures, a child who looks an adult in the eye is showing disrespect. Children in such cultures are taught to look down in the presence of adults (Torres-Guzmán, 1998; Trawick-Smith, 2003). The following anecdote shows how accommodation to this culturally learned behavior can make a difference:

> A teacher [described a Native American] student who would never say a word, nor even answer when she greeted him. Then one day when he came in she looked in the other direction and said, "Hello, Jimmy." He answered enthusiastically, "Why hello Miss Jacobs." She found that he would always talk if she looked at a book or at the wall, but when she looked at him, he appeared frightened. (Gilliland, 1988, p. 26)

Maintaining personal space. In some cultures, such as in some African American and Hispanic communities, people stand close together when they talk and may touch one another frequently (Hale-Benson, 1986; Slonim, 1991; Sue, 1990). In contrast, European Americans and Japanese Americans tend to keep a fair distance from one another—they maintain some **personal space**—especially if they don't know one another very well (Irujo, 1988; Trawick-Smith, 2003). Adults who work regularly with children must be sensitive to the personal space that children from various cultural backgrounds need in order to feel comfortable in interactions with others.

Responding to questions. A common interaction pattern in many Western classrooms is the **IRE cycle:** A teacher *initiates* an interaction by asking a question, a student *responds* to the question, and the teacher *evaluates* the response (Mehan, 1979). Similar interactions are frequently found in parent–child interactions in middle-income European American homes. For example, parents might ask their toddlers such questions as "Where's your nose?" and "What does a cow say?" and praise them for correct answers. But children from some backgrounds are unfamiliar with such question-and-answer sessions when they first come to school. Such is the case for some children raised in lower-income homes, as well as for some children raised in Mexican American, Native American, and Hawaiian communities (Losey, 1995; Rogoff, 2003).

Furthermore, different cultural groups teach children to answer different kinds of questions. European American parents frequently ask their children questions that they themselves know the answers to. Parents from certain other cultures rarely ask such questions (Crago, Annahatak, & Ningiuruvik, 1993; Heath, 1989; Rogoff & Morelli, 1989). For instance, parents in some African American communities in the southeastern United States are more likely to ask questions involving comparisons and analogies. Rather than asking "What's that?" they may instead ask "What's that *like?*" (Heath, 1980). Also, children in these communities are specifically taught *not* to answer questions that strangers ask about personal and home life (e.g., "What's your name?" "Where do you live?"). Teachers' comments about these children reflect a lack of understanding about the culture from which the children come:

> "I would almost think some of them have a hearing problem; it is as though they don't hear me ask a question. I get blank stares to my questions. Yet when I am making statements or telling stories which interest them, they always seem to hear me."

> "The simplest questions are the ones they can't answer in the classroom; yet on the playground, they can explain a rule for a ballgame or describe a particular kind of bait with no problem. Therefore, I know they can't be as dumb as they seem in my class." (Heath, 1980, pp. 107–108)

Meanwhile, parents describe the confusion their children are experiencing:

> "My kid, he too scared to talk, 'cause nobody play by the rules he know. At home I can't shut him up."

> "Miss Davis, she complain 'bout Ned not answerin' back. He says she asks dumb questions she already know about." (Heath, 1980, p. 107)

Waiting and interrupting. Teachers frequently ask their students questions and then wait for an answer. But exactly how long do they wait? The typical **wait time** for many teachers is a second or even less, at which point they either answer a question themselves or call on another student (M. B. Rowe, 1974, 1987). Yet people from some cultures leave lengthy pauses before responding as a way of indicating respect, as this statement by a Northern Cheyenne illustrates:

> Even if I had a quick answer to your question, I would never answer immediately. That would be saying that your question was not worth thinking about. (Gilliland, 1988, p. 27)

For some cultural groups, then, children are more likely to participate in class and answer questions when given several seconds to respond (C. A. Grant & Gomez, 2001; Mohatt & Erickson, 1981; Tharp, 1989).

In contrast, children from certain other backgrounds may interrupt adults or peers who haven't finished speaking—an action that some of their teachers might interpret as rudeness. In some African American, Puerto Rican, and Jewish families, however, family discourse often consists of several people talking at once. In fact, people who wait for their turn might find themselves excluded from the discussion altogether (Condon & Yousef, 1975; Farber, Mindel, & Lazerwitz, 1988; Hale-Benson, 1986; Slonim, 1991). And in some Hawaiian communities, an interruption is taken as a sign of personal involvement in the conversation (Tharp, 1989).

personal space
A child's personally and culturally preferred distance from other people during social interaction.

IRE cycle
Adult–child interaction pattern marked by adult *initiation*, child *response*, and adult *evaluation;* in Western cultures, such a pattern is often seen in instructional settings.

wait time
The length of time a teacher pauses, after either asking a question or hearing a student's comment, before saying something.

How sociolinguistic behaviors develop. As we've seen, even young infants exhibit turn taking in their "conversations" with others, in that they tend to remain quiet when an adult is talking. This tendency may be essential to language development (J. L. Locke, 1993) and therefore may reflect a biological predisposition. By and large, however, conversational etiquette and other sociolinguistic conventions are probably the result of language socialization in children's local cultural groups (Ochs, 2002; Rogoff, 2003).

Sometimes adults explicitly teach sociolinguistic behaviors. Mario once explained to his parents how his kindergarten teacher encouraged students to take turns when speaking in class (we present an English translation of Mario's Spanish):

> [A]t school, I have to raise my hand . . . and then wait a long, long time. And then the teacher says: "Now you can speak, Mario," and she makes the other children shut up, and she says, "Mario's speaking now." (Fantini, 1985, p. 83)[7]

Children also learn many conventions through imitating the behaviors of others—perhaps mimicking the way their parents answer the telephone, greet people on the street, and converse with friends and relatives. In addition, the feedback youngsters receive from others (sometimes blatant, sometimes more subtle) may encourage them to behave in certain ways and not others. For instance, most young children eventually learn that they get along better with their peers if they ask for something nicely ("May I please have that?") rather than make demands ("Gimme dat!"). And older children and adolescents may discover that when they stand too close to others, their conversational partners act uneasy and perhaps back up to create a more comfortable distance.

Taking sociolinguistic differences into account. When the sociolinguistic behaviors expected at home differ significantly from those expected at school and in other group settings, a sense of confusion, or **culture shock,** can result. Such culture shock can interfere with children's adjustment to the group setting and, ultimately, with their behavior and achievement as well (Banks & Banks, 1995; Phalet, Andriessen, & Lens, 2004; Phelan, Yu, & Davidson, 1994). Adults further compound the problem when, interpreting children's behaviors as being unacceptable or otherwise "odd," they jump too quickly to the conclusion that certain youngsters are unable or unwilling to make productive contributions to the group (Bowman, 1989; Hilliard & Vaughn-Scott, 1982).

Clearly, teachers and other practitioners must educate themselves about the diverse sociolinguistic patterns they are likely to encounter in day-to-day interactions with children. Furthermore, they must keep children's varying conversational styles in mind as they design group lessons and activities. For example, teachers might vary the questions they ask in class to include those that different students are accustomed to answering at home. And they should allow sufficient wait time for all students to think about and respond to questions.

Some children lack pragmatic skills desirable in *any* culture. For example, we authors have known children and adolescents who seemed so insistent on dominating a conversation that no one else could contribute to the discussion. When youngsters haven't mastered basic conventions of conversational etiquette, they may have trouble establishing and maintaining productive relationships with adults and peers. In such cases educators can provide guided practice in missing skills. If difficulties persist despite ongoing efforts to address them, children should be evaluated by a speech-language pathologist, school psychologist, or other appropriate specialist.

Teachers interact with students more effectively when they take sociolinguistic differences into account. For example, in some cultures, looking an adult in the eye is a sign of respect. In other cultures, it is interpreted as *dis*respect.

Development of Metalinguistic Awareness

Children's **metalinguistic awareness** is their conscious understanding of the nature and functions of language. For instance, it includes awareness that speech is comprised of smaller units (words, phonemes, etc.), that printed words have one-to-one correspondences to spoken words, and that language is an entity separate from its meaning. It also includes the

culture shock
Sense of confusion that occurs when one encounters an environment with expectations for behavior very different from those in one's home environment.

metalinguistic awareness
Extent to which one consciously understands and thinks about the nature and functions of language.

[7]See footnote 6 on p. 335.

ability to distinguish between what a person says and what he or she actually means (Yaden & Templeton, 1986).

In the late preschool or early elementary school years, children become consciously aware that words are the basic units of language, that spoken words are comprised of phonemes, and that different phonemes tend to be associated with different letters or letter combinations (Lonigan, Burgess, Anthony, & Barker, 1998; T. A. Roberts, 2005; Tunmer, Pratt, & Herriman, 1984). As they move into the upper elementary and middle school grades, they also begin to recognize and label the component parts of speech, at least partly as a result of formal instruction about nouns, verbs, and so on (e.g., Sipe, 2006; Vavra, 1987). More sophisticated aspects of metalinguistic awareness, such as recognizing and interpreting phrases and sentences with multiple meanings, continue to develop throughout adolescence (Nippold & Taylor, 1995; R. E Owens, 2008).

The Developmental Trends table "Language Skills at Different Age Levels" summarizes characteristics you are likely to see in children's linguistic knowledge and skills at various age levels.

How children develop metalinguistic awareness.   Theoretical accounts of metalinguistic development focus almost exclusively on the effects of experience. One factor that probably promotes metalinguistic awareness is "playing" with language through rhymes, chants, jokes, puns, and so on. For example, rhymes help children discover the relationships between sounds and letters. Jokes and puns help children discover that words and phrases can have more than one meaning (Bradley & Bryant, 1991; Cazden, 1976; Christie & Johnsen, 1983).

Children's early experiences with books also promote metalinguistic awareness (Yaden & Templeton, 1986). The very process of reading to children helps them realize that printed language is related to spoken language. In addition, some children's books playfully address the nature of language. An example is *Amelia Bedelia Goes Camping* (Parish & Sweat, 2003), one in a series of books featuring a rather obtuse maid who takes everything her employers say quite literally. For instance, when they tell Amelia it's time to "hit the road," she hits the road with a stick—a response that our own children found quite amusing.

Formal language instruction further fosters metalinguistic awareness. By exploring parts of speech, various sentence structures, and the like, children and adolescents gain a better grasp of the underlying structure of language. By reading and analyzing poetry and classic literature, they discover a variety of mechanisms (similes, metaphors, symbolism, etc.) that a writer might use to convey multiple layers of meanings.

Finally, research consistently indicates that knowledge of two or more languages (bilingualism) promotes greater metalinguistic awareness (X. Chen et al., 2004; Diaz & Klingler,

Developmental Trends

Language Skills at Different Age Levels

Age	What You Might Observe	Diversity	Implications
Infancy (Birth–2 Years) 	· Interest in listening to the human voice and in exchanging vocalizations with adults · Repetition of vowel sounds (cooing) at age 1–2 months and consonant-vowel syllables (babbling) at about 6 months · Understanding of some common words at about 8 months · Use of single words at about 12 months · Use of two-word combinations at about 18 months · Rapid increase in vocabulary in the second year	· In the latter half of the first year, babbling increasingly reflects phonemes of the native language. · Temperament may influence the development of expressive language; more cautious children may wait a bit before beginning to speak. · Chronic ear infections can interfere with early language development. · Infants with severe hearing impairments orally babble, but the quality of their babbling changes little over time. They may also "babble" manually if their caregivers regularly use sign language to communicate with them.	· Engage young infants in "conversations," using simplified and animated speech (i.e., infant-directed speech) and responding when they vocalize. · Label and describe the objects and events children observe. · Teach simple hand signs that preverbal infants can use to communicate. · Ask simple questions (e.g., "Is your diaper wet?" "What does a cow say?"). · Repeat and expand on children's early "sentences" (e.g., follow "Kitty eat" with "Yes, the kitty is eating").

Developmental Trends (continued)

Age	Topics	Diversity	Implications
Early Childhood (2–6 Years)	· Rapid advances in vocabulary and syntax · Incomplete understandings of many simple words (e.g., underextension, overextension, confusion between simple comparatives such as *more* vs. *less*) · Overregularization (e.g., *foots, gooder, goed*) · Overdependence on word order and context (instead of syntax) when interpreting messages · Superficial understanding of what "good listening" is · Difficulty pronouncing some phonemes and blends (e.g., *r, th, spl*) · Increasing ability to construct narratives	· Children raised in bilingual environments may show slight delays in language development, but any delays are short lived and usually not a cause for concern. · Major language impairments (e.g., abnormal syntactic constructions) reveal themselves in the preschool years.	· Read age-appropriate storybooks as a way of enhancing vocabulary. · Give tactful corrective feedback when children's use of words indicates inaccurate understandings. · Work on simple listening skills (e.g., sitting quietly, paying attention). · Ask follow-up questions to make sure that children accurately understand important messages. · Ask children to construct narratives about recent events (e.g., "Tell me about your camping trip last weekend").
Middle Childhood (6–10 Years)	· Increasing understanding of temporal words (e.g., *before, after*) and comparatives (e.g., *bigger, as big as*) · Incomplete knowledge of irregular word forms · Literal interpretation of messages (especially before age 9) · Pronunciation mastered by age 8 · Consideration of a listener's knowledge and perspective when speaking · Sustained conversations about concrete topics · Construction of narratives with plots and cause-and-effect relationships · Linguistic creativity and wordplay (e.g., rhymes, word games)	· Some minor language impairments (e.g., persistent articulation problems) become evident and can be addressed by specialists. · African Americans often show advanced ability to use figurative language (e.g., metaphor, hyperbole). · Bilingual children are apt to show advanced metalinguistic awareness.	· Teach irregular word forms (e.g., the superlative form of *bad* is *worst*, the past tense of *bring* is *brought*). · Use group discussions as a way to explore academic subject matter. · Have children develop short stories that they present orally or in writing. · Encourage jokes and rhymes that capitalize on double meanings and homonyms (sound-alike words). · When articulation problems are evident in the upper elementary grades, consult with a speech-language pathologist.
Early Adolescence (10–14 Years)	· Increasing awareness of the terminology used in various academic disciplines · Ability to understand complex, multiple-clause sentences · Emerging ability to look beyond literal interpretations; comprehension of simple proverbs · Emerging ability to carry on lengthy conversations about abstract topics · Significant growth in metalinguistic awareness	· Frequent readers tend to have larger vocabularies. · Girls are more likely than boys to converse about intimate and confidential matters. · African American teens may bandy insults back and forth in a playful manner. · Adolescents may prefer to use their native *dialects* even if they have mastered *Standard English* (see discussion in upcoming "Ethnic Differences" section).	· Begin to use the terminology used by experts in various academic disciplines (e.g., *simile* in language arts, *theory* in science). · Use classroom debates to explore controversial issues. · Present proverbs and ask children to consider possible underlying meanings. · Explore the nature of words and language as entities in and of themselves.
Late Adolescence (14–18 Years)	· Acquisition of many terms related to specific academic disciplines · Subtle refinements in grammar, mostly as a result of formal instruction · Mastery of a wide variety of connectives (e.g., *although, however, nevertheless*) · General ability to understand figurative language (e.g., metaphors, proverbs, hyperbole)	· Boys are apt to communicate their thoughts in a direct and straightforward manner; girls are more likely to be indirect and tactful. · A preference for one's native dialect over Standard English continues into the high school years.	· Consistently use the terminology associated with various academic disciplines. · Distinguish between similar abstract words (e.g., *weather* vs. *climate, velocity* vs. *acceleration*). · Explore complex syntactic structures (e.g., multiple embedded clauses). · Consider the underlying meanings and messages in poetry and fiction. · When teenagers have a native dialect other than Standard English, encourage them to use it in informal conversations and creative writing; encourage Standard English for more formal situations.

Sources: C. Baker, 1993; Bruer, 1999; Bruner, 1983; N. Chomsky, 1972; Eilers & Oller, 1994; Elias & Broerse, 1996; Fantini, 1985; Fenson et al., 1994; Fifer & Moon, 1995; Goodwyn et al., 2000; Hale-Benson, 1986; Imhof, 2001; J. L. Locke, 1993; T. M. McDevitt, 1990; K. Nelson, 1973; Nicolopoulou & Richner, 2007; O'Grady, 1997; Ortony et al., 1985; R. E. Owens, 2008; Pence & Justice, 2008; L. A. Pettito, 1997; H. L. Smith, 1998; R. H. Thompson et al., 2007.

1991; Moran & Hakuta, 1995). By the time Mario was 5, he showed considerable awareness of the nature of language:

> Mario was well aware that things were called in one of several possible ways, that the same story could be retold in another language (he was capable of doing this himself), and he knew that thoughts were convertible or translatable through other forms of expression. . . . He knew that a [language] could be varied so as to make it sound funny or to render its messages less transparent, such as in Pig Spanish. . . .
>
> [As Mario grew older,] he became increasingly analytical about the medium which so many take for granted as their sole form of expression. He demonstrated interest, for example, in the multiple meaning of some words ("'right' means three things"); and in peculiar usages ("Why do you call the car 'she'?"); as well as intuitions about the origins of words ("'soufflé' sounds French"). (Fantini, 1985, pp. 53–54)[8]

Promoting metalinguistic development.   Factors that promote metalinguistic awareness—language play, reading experiences, formal instruction, and bilingualism—have several implications for teaching and working with children.

• *Explore multiple meanings through ambiguities, jokes, riddles, and the like.* Having fun with language can be educational as well as entertaining. For example, teachers and parents might ask children to identify the double meanings of such sentences as *He is drawing a gun* and *This restaurant even serves crabs* (Wiig, Gilbert, & Christian, 1978). Jokes and riddles provide another vehicle for exploring multiple meanings (Shultz, 1974; Shultz & Horibe, 1974):

> Call me a cab.
> Okay, you're a cab.

> Tell me how long cows should be milked.
> They should be milked the same as short ones, of course.

• *Read literature that plays on the nature of language.* One of our favorites is *The Phantom Tollbooth* (Juster, 1961), which has considerable fun with word meanings and common expressions. In one scene the main character (Milo) asks for a square meal and is served (you guessed it) a plate "heaped high with steaming squares of all sizes and colors." Among the all-time classics in English wordplay are Lewis Carroll's *Alice's Adventures in Wonderland* and *Through the Looking Glass*. These books are packed with whimsical uses of double word meanings, homonyms, and idioms, as the following excerpt from *Through the Looking Glass* illustrates:

> "But what could [a tree] do, if any danger came?" Alice asked.
> "It could bark," said the Rose.
> "It says, 'Boughwough!'" cried a Daisy. "That's why its branches are called boughs."

• *Encourage children to learn a second language.* Promoting metalinguistic awareness is just one of several benefits of learning a second language. In the next section we look more closely at second-language learning and bilingualism.

Development of a Second Language

As the adult workplace becomes increasingly international in scope, there is greater need than ever before for children to learn one or more languages in addition to their native tongue. Here we address three issues related to the development of a second language: the optimal timing for second-language learning, the nature of bilingualism, and approaches to teaching a second language.

The Timing of Second-Language Learning

As you discovered in our discussion of nativism and information processing theory early in the chapter, the brain seems to adapt to its particular environment—including its *linguistic* environment—fairly early in development. Clearly, however, the human brain is quite capa-

---

[8]See footnote 6 on p. 335.

ble of learning *two* or more languages rather than just one (e.g., Kuhl, 2004). When, like Mario, human beings are regularly exposed to two languages within the first few years of life, the same language-specific areas of the brain appear to handle both languages (K. H. Kim, Relkin, Lee, & Hirsch, 1997). When people learn a second language quite a bit later, perhaps in early adulthood, the brain devotes noticeably distinct neural structures to it, especially in the area of the cortex known as Broca's area (K. H. Kim et al., 1997). Regardless of the timing, learning two languages instead of one results in greater brain development in areas related to language (Mechelli et al., 2004).

As noted earlier, exposure to a second language in the first few years of life may be especially important for acquiring flawless pronunciation and the complex syntactic structures of that second language. Early exposure to a second language seems to be most advantageous if the second language is very different from the first. For example, a native English speaker benefits more from an early start in Japanese or Arabic than from an early start in, say, Spanish or German (Bialystok, 1994a; Strozer, 1994). However, any advantage young children may have because of neurological flexibility may be counterbalanced by the greater cognitive maturity, world knowledge, and metalinguistic sophistication on which adolescents and adults can build as they study a new language (Bialystok, 1994b; Collier, 1989; Long, 1995). Furthermore, people can learn the vocabulary of a particular language at virtually any age (Bruer, 1999). Thus people of all ages can acquire proficiency in a second language. Given research findings to date, there appears to be no definitive "best" time to begin (e.g., Kuhl et al., 2005; G. Stevens, 2004).

Throughout the school years, children and adolescents have considerable potential for mastering a new language.

Although there may be no hard-and-fast sensitive period for acquiring a second language, getting an early start on second-language instruction certainly has benefits (T. H. Cunningham & Graham, 2000; Diaz, 1983; A. Doyle, 1982; A. M. Padilla, 2006; Reich, 1986). Learning a second language leads, on average, to higher achievement in reading, vocabulary, and grammar. Furthermore, it sensitizes youngsters to the international and multicultural nature of the world in which they live. Children who learn a second language during the elementary school years express more positive attitudes toward people who speak that language, and they are more likely to enroll in foreign language classes in high school. And in classrooms in which children speak only one of two different languages (perhaps some speaking only English and others speaking only Spanish), instruction in the second language promotes cross-communication and peer interaction.

Bilingualism

Bilingualism is the ability to speak two languages fluently. Bilingual individuals can easily switch from one language to the other, and they readily distinguish the contexts in which they should use each one. At least half of the world's children are bilingual or multilingual, typically because they've been exposed to two or more languages regularly and from an early age (Hoff-Ginsburg, 1997). At one time many psychologists believed that bilingual environments were detrimental to children's linguistic and cognitive development, but results from recent research have generally been quite favorable. Children raised in bilingual environments from birth or soon thereafter sometimes show initial delays in language development, but by elementary school they have caught up to their monolingual peers and easily keep the two languages separate (C. Baker, 1993; Bialystok, 2001; Fennell, Byers-Heinlein, & Werker, 2007). And when they are truly fluent in both languages, they tend to perform better in situations requiring advanced cognitive functioning—for instance, on intelligence tests and on tasks requiring creativity (Bialystok & Senman, 2004; Diaz & Klingler, 1991; García, 1994; Moran & Hakuta, 1995).

Being bilingual may also have cultural and personal advantages. In many Native American groups, the ancestral language is important for conducting local business and communicating oral history and cultural traditions, yet adults in those groups realize that mastery of spoken and written English is essential for children's long-term success (McCarty & Watahomigie, 1998). Although Puerto Rican children will have more educational and professional opportunities if they know English, they often speak Spanish at home and with peers, partly as a way of showing respect to their elders and partly as a way of maintaining a sense of

bilingualism
Knowing and speaking two languages fluently.

English language learner (ELL)
School-age child who is not fully fluent in English because his or her family speaks a language other than English at home.

immersion
Approach to second-language instruction in which students hear and speak the second language almost exclusively in the classroom.

bilingual education
Approach to second-language instruction in which students are instructed in academic subject areas in their native language while simultaneously being taught to speak, read, and write in the second language.

cultural identity (Nieto, 1995; Torres-Guzmán, 1998). A statement by Marisol, a high school student, illustrates the latter point:

> I'm proud of [being Puerto Rican]. I guess I speak Spanish whenever I can. . . . I used to have a lot of problems with one of my teachers 'cause she didn't want us to talk Spanish in class and I thought that was like an insult to us, you know? (Nieto, 1995, p. 127)

And in some cases, being bilingual is the only way children can maintain personal relationships with important people in their lives. For instance, some children are bilingual in English and American Sign Language as a way of communicating effectively with one parent who can hear and another who is deaf (L. A. Pettito, 1997).

Teaching a Second Language

Most children in Western, English-speaking countries are exposed to only one language before they reach school age. That single language may or may not be English. For instance, in the United States, several million children are members of families who speak a language other than English at home (D. Meyer, Madden, & McGrath, 2005; National Association of Bilingual Education, 1993; Pérez, 1998). Many of these children have little exposure to English before they begin school. School-age children who are fluent in their native language but not in English are often referred to as **English language learners (ELLs).** More than 5% of the public school population in the United States has limited proficiency in English, and the number increases every year (Federal Interagency Forum on Child and Family Statistics, 2007; D. Meyer et al., 2005; U.S. Department of Education, 1993). To the extent that elementary and secondary school students have only limited proficiency in English, they are apt to have trouble with schoolwork in an English-based classroom (A. M. Padilla, 2006; Slavin & Cheung, 2005; Valdés, Bunch, Snow, & Lee, 2005). In the Building Teaching Skills and Dispositions exercise in MyEducationLab, you can discover some of the challenges that English language learners and their teachers are likely to face at school.

Just as very young children typically learn their native language through informal daily exposure, so, too, can they learn two languages simultaneously if (like Mario) they have frequent, ongoing exposure to both languages. But when children begin to learn a second language at an older age, perhaps in the elementary grades or even later, they often learn it more quickly if their language-learning experiences are fairly structured (Strozer, 1994). Yet teaching a foreign language for one 45-minute period a day (as is typically done in high schools) hardly promotes mastery. Two more intensive approaches, immersion and bilingual education, can be quite effective, with each being useful in somewhat different situations.

To keep our discussion simple, let's assume that students are living in an English-speaking country. If these students are native English speakers, total **immersion** in the second language—hearing and speaking it almost exclusively in the classroom during the school day—appears to be the more effective approach. Alternatively, some schools have had success with *dual-immersion* programs, in which some topics are taught exclusively in English and others are taught exclusively in the second language. For native English speakers, immersion in the second language for part or all of the school day helps students acquire proficiency in the language fairly quickly, and any adverse effects on achievement in other academic areas appear to be short lived (Collier, 1992; T. H. Cunningham & Graham, 2000; Genesee, 1985; A. M. Padilla, 2006).

In contrast, English language learners who live in an English-speaking country typically fare better in **bilingual education,** in which they receive intensive instruction in English while studying other academic subject areas in their native language (McBrien, 2005b; Snow, 1990; Willig, 1985; Wright, Taylor, & Macarthur, 2000). The optimal bilingual education program proceeds through a gradual phase-in of instruction in English, perhaps in a sequence such as the following:

1. Students join native English speakers for classes in subject areas that do not depend too heavily on language skills (e.g., art, music, physical education). They study other subject areas in their native language and also begin classes in English as a Second Language (ESL).
2. Once students have acquired some English proficiency, instruction in English begins for one or two additional subject areas (perhaps for math and science).
3. When it is clear that students can learn successfully in English in the subject areas identified in step 2, they join their English-speaking classmates in regular classes in these subjects.

4. Eventually students are sufficiently proficient in English to join the mainstream in all subject areas, and they may no longer require their ESL classes (Krashen, 1996; A. M. Padilla, 2006; Valdés et al., 2005).

Ideally, the transition from instruction in a student's native language to instruction in English occurs very gradually over a period of several years. Simple knowledge of basic conversational English is not enough for success in an English-only curriculum (A. M. Padilla, 2006). Ultimately, students must have sufficient mastery of English vocabulary and grammar that they can readily understand and learn from English-based textbooks and lectures, and such mastery takes considerable time to achieve—often 5 to 7 years' worth (Cummins, 1981, 1984, 2000).

Why is immersion better for some students whereas bilingual education is better for others? Remember, language is an important foundation for cognitive development: It provides symbols for mentally representing the world, enables children to exchange ideas with others, helps them internalize sophisticated cognitive strategies, and so on. Native English speakers who live in an English-speaking country but are immersed in a different language at school still have many opportunities—at home, with their friends, and in the local community—to continue using and developing their English. In contrast, non-native English speakers may have few opportunities outside of their homes to use their native language. If they are taught exclusively in English, they may very well lose proficiency in their native language before developing adequate proficiency in English—a phenomenon known as **subtractive bilingualism**—and their cognitive development will suffer in the process. Because bilingual education is designed to foster growth in *both* English and a child's native language, it is apt to promote cognitive as well as linguistic growth (McBrien, 2005b; Pérez, 1998; Tse, 2001; Winsler, Díaz, Espinosa, & Rodriguez, 1999).

The Development and Practice feature "Working with English Language Learners" offers several suggestions for accommodating language differences in elementary and secondary school classrooms.

subtractive bilingualism
Phenomenon in which immersion in a new-language environment leads to deficits in one's native language.

MyEducationLab

Learn more about subtractive bilingualism, as well as the benefits of bilingual education, by completing an Understanding Research exercise in Chapter 9's Activities and Applications section in MyEducationLab.

Development and Practice

Working with English Language Learners

· **Teach early reading skills in a student's native language.**

When working with students whose families have recently immigrated from Mexico, a first-grade teacher teaches basic letter-sound relationships and word decoding skills in Spanish (e.g., showing how the printed word *dos* can be broken up into the sounds "duh," "o," and "sss").

· **If you don't speak a student's native language yourself, recruit and train parents, community volunteers, or other students to assist in providing instruction in that language.**

A boy in a kindergarten class has grown up speaking Hmong, a language spoken in some Asian immigrant communities in the United States. His teacher recruits a fourth grader who can read an English picture book to the boy and translate it into Hmong. At one point the teacher points to a lily pad on a page of the book and asks the fourth grader to describe a lily pad in Hmong, because the younger child has never seen lily pads in his own environment. (You can see this example in action in the "Reading a Picture Book to a Hmong Student" video in Chapter 9's Video Examples section of MyEducationLab.)

· **When using English to communicate, speak more slowly than you might otherwise, and clearly enunciate each word.**

A third-grade teacher is careful that he always says "going to" rather than "gonna" and "want to" rather than "wanna."

· **Use visual aids to supplement verbal explanations.**

A high school history teacher uses photographs she's downloaded from the Internet to illustrate a short lecture on ancient Egypt.

· **During small-group learning activities, encourage same-language students to communicate with one another in their native language.**

When a science teacher breaks students into cooperative groups to study the effects of weight, length, and amount of push on a pendulum's oscillation rate, she puts three native Chinese speakers into a single group. She suggests that they can talk in either English or Chinese as they do their experiments.

· **Have students work in pairs to make sense of textbook material.**

As two middle school students read a section of their geography textbook, one reads aloud while the other listens and takes notes. They frequently stop to talk about what's been read, and then they switch roles.

· **Have students, read, write, and report about their native countries.**

A middle school social studies teacher has students conduct research on a country from which they or their ancestors have immigrated. The students create posters to display what they've learned, and they proudly talk about their posters at an "International Day" that students from other classes attend.

Sources: Strategies are based on research and recommendations by Comeau, Cormier, Grandmaison, & Lacroix, 1999; Espinosa, 2007; García, 1995; Herrell & Jordan, 2004; Igoa, 1995; Krashen, 1996; McClelland, 2001; McClelland, Fiez, & McCandless, 2002; A. M. Padilla, 2006; Slavin & Cheung, 2005; Valdés et al., 2005.

Diversity in Language Development

As is true in other developmental domains, children in any single cultural group vary in the ages at which they achieve milestones (e.g., babbling, saying first words) in language development. For example, shy or reserved children may begin to speak somewhat later than more outgoing ones (K. Nelson, 1973). In addition to such individual differences, researchers have observed group differences related to children's gender, socioeconomic status, and ethnicity.

Gender Differences

As infants and toddlers, girls are, on average, more verbally active than boys. Girls also begin to speak about a month earlier, form longer sentences sooner, and have a larger vocabulary (Halpern & LaMay, 2000; Reznick & Goldfield, 1992; Van Hulle, Goldsmith, & Lemery, 2004). Once they reach the school years, girls outperform boys on tests of verbal ability (see Chapter 8). This gender difference in verbal ability is quite small, however, with considerable overlap between the two groups (see Figure 8-7 in Chapter 8).

Qualitative gender differences exist as well, for children and adults alike. On average, males, who see themselves as information providers, speak more directly and bluntly. In contrast, females, who seek to establish and deepen relationships through their conversations, are more likely to be indirect, tactful, and polite (R. E. Owens, 2008; Tannen, 1990).

Socioeconomic Differences

As mentioned in the earlier discussion of nativism, children from diverse backgrounds tend to reach language milestones at similar ages. However, children from higher-income homes tend to have larger vocabularies (B. Hart & Risley, 1995; Hoff, 2003; Wasik & Bond, 2001). This difference appears to be at least partly due to the quantity and quality of language that mothers use with their children. Although mothers from all income levels tend to interact frequently with their children, on average mothers from higher-SES families talk with their babies more, ask more questions, elaborate more on topics, and, in general, expose their children to a greater variety of words (B. Hart & Risley, 1995, 1999; Hoff, 2003).

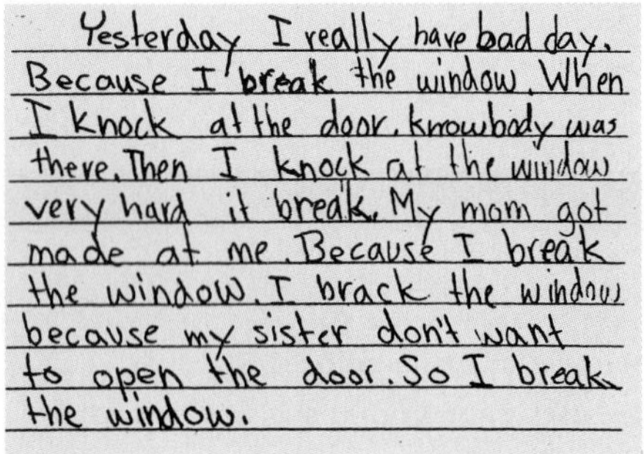

Ethnic Differences

As you've already learned, sociolinguistic conventions, use of figurative language, and narrative styles often differ from one ethnic group to another. In addition, children from different ethnic and cultural groups may use a form of English different from the **Standard English** typically considered acceptable at school. More specifically, they may speak in a **dialect,** a form of English (or, more generally, a form of any language) that includes some unique pronunciations and syntactic structures. Dialects tend to be associated either with particular geographical regions or with particular ethnic and cultural groups. An example is shown in Figure 9-6. In this narrative, an English-speaking fifth grader living in the Northern Mariana Islands of the Pacific Ocean mixes present and past tenses in his description of a past event, much as he is apt to do in his everyday speech.

Perhaps the most widely studied ethnic dialect is **African American English** (also known as *Black English Vernacular* or *Ebonics*). This dialect, which is actually a group of similar dialects, is used in many African American communities throughout the United States and is characterized by certain unique pronunciations, idioms, and grammatical constructions. For example:

- The *th* sound at the beginning of a word is often pronounced as *d* (e.g., *that* is pronounced "dat").
- The *ng* sound at the end of a word is typically pronounced as *n* (e.g., *bringing* is pronounced "bringin").
- The *-ed* ending on past-tense verbs is often dropped (e.g., "We walk to the park last night").
- The present- and past-tense forms of the verb *to be* are consistently *is* and *was,* even if the subject of the sentence is the pronoun *I* or a plural noun or pronoun (e.g., "I is runnin'," "They was runnin'").

> Yesterday I really have bad day. Because I break the window. When I knock at the door, knowbody was there. Then I knock at the window very hard it break. My mom got made at me. Because I break the window. I brack the window because my sister don't want to open the door. So I break the window.

Figure 9-6

A local dialect is evident in this writing sample from a fifth grader who lives in the Northern Mariana Islands of the Pacific Ocean.
Writing sample courtesy of the Commonwealth of the Northern Mariana Islands Public School System and of the Pacific Resources for Education and Learning (PREL).

Standard English
Form of English generally considered acceptable in school (as reflected in textbooks, grammar instruction, etc.) and in the media.

dialect
Form of a language characteristic of a particular geographic region or ethnic group.

African American English
Dialect of some African American communities that includes pronunciations, idioms, and grammatical constructions different from those of Standard English.

- The verb *is* is often dropped in simple descriptive sentences (e.g., "He a handsome man").
- The word *be* is used to indicate a constant or frequently occurring characteristic (e.g., "He be talking" describes someone who talks much of the time). (Hulit & Howard, 2006, pp. 345–346)

If you look back at Terry and Tony's discussion of a cat fight (p. 333), you should notice some of these characteristics in their speech.

At one time many researchers believed that an African American dialect represented a less complex form of speech than Standard English. They therefore urged educators to teach students to speak "properly" as quickly as possible. But psychologists now realize that African American dialects are, in fact, very complex languages with their own predictable idioms and grammatical rules and that these dialects promote communication and complex thought as readily as Standard English (Alim & Baugh, 2007; Fairchild & Edwards-Evans, 1990; Hulit & Howard, 2006).

Many children and adolescents view their native dialect as an integral part of their cultural identity (McAlpine, 1992; Ogbu, 2003; Tatum, 1997). Furthermore, when a local dialect is the language most preferred by residents of a community, it is often the most effective means through which youngsters can communicate in daily interactions. However, many people in mainstream Western culture associate higher social status with people who speak Standard English, and they perceive speakers of other dialects in a lesser light (DeBose, 2007; Purcell-Gates, 1995; H. L. Smith, 1998). In addition, children who have proficiency in Standard English have an easier time learning to read (Charity, Scarborough, & Griffin, 2004; T. A. Roberts, 2005). For such reasons, most experts recommend that all youngsters acquire proficiency in Standard English (e.g., Craft, 1984; DeBose, 2007; Ogbu, 1999).

Ultimately, children and adolescents function most effectively when they can use both their local dialect and Standard English in appropriate settings. For example, although teachers may wish to encourage Standard English in most written work or in formal oral presentations, they might find other dialects quite appropriate in creative writing or informal classroom discussions (DeBose, 2007; Ogbu, 1999, 2003; Warren & McCloskey, 1993). One teacher of African American children has made the point this way:

> I don't want them to be ashamed of what they know but I also want them to know and be comfortable with what school and the rest of the society require. When I put it in the context of "translation" they get excited. They see it is possible to go from one to the other. It's not that they are not familiar with Standard English. . . . They hear Standard English all the time on TV. It's certainly what I use in the classroom. But there is rarely any connection made between the way they speak and Standard English. I think that when they can see the connections and know that they can make the shifts, they become better at both. They're bilingual! (Ladson-Billings, 1994, p. 84)

Exceptionalities in Language Development

Language delays are often seen in children with general intellectual disabilities or severe forms of autism (we discuss autism spectrum disorders in Chapter 12). Here we describe language difficulties for two additional groups of children: those with specific language impairments and those with sensory impairments.

Specific Language Impairments

Some children seem to develop normally in all respects except for language. Children with **specific language impairments** have delays or abnormalities in spoken language or in language comprehension that significantly interfere with their performance at school and elsewhere. Such impairments may involve problems in one or more of the following:

- Receptive language (e.g., inability to distinguish among different phonemes, difficulty understanding or remembering directions)
- Articulation (e.g., mispronunciations or omissions of certain speech sounds)
- Fluency (e.g., stuttering, an atypical rhythm in speech)
- Syntax (e.g., abnormal syntactic patterns, incorrect word order)
- Semantics (e.g., infrequent use of grammatical words, such as prepositions and conjunctions; frequent use of words with imprecise meanings, such as *thing* or *that;* difficulty interpreting words that have two or more meanings)

specific language impairment
Disability characterized by abnormalities in producing or understanding spoken language, to the point where special educational services are required.

- Pragmatics (e.g., talking for long periods without letting others speak) (American Speech-Language-Hearing Association, 1993; Hulit & Howard, 2006; Joanisse, 2007)

Specific language impairments are also suspected when children don't demonstrate age-appropriate language. However, speech patterns that reflect a regional or ethnic dialect and those that are due to a bilingual background do *not* fall within the realm of specific language impairments. (Recall the speech therapist who inappropriately recommended that Mario have speech therapy.)

In comparison with their nondisabled peers, children with specific language impairments have greater difficulty perceiving and mentally processing particular aspects of spoken language—perhaps the quality, pitch, duration, or intensity of specific sounds in speech (Corriveau, Pasquini, & Goswami, 2007; P. R. Hill, Hogben, & Bishop, 2005; J. W. Montgomery & Windsor, 2007). Some of these children have problems with reading and writing as well (Catts, Adlof, Hogan, & Weismer, 2005; J. R. Johnston, 1997; Tallal, 2003). Personal and social problems may also emerge. Some youngsters feel so self-conscious about their language disability that they are reluctant to speak to peers (Patton et al., 1996). And if they sound "odd" or are difficult to understand, they may suffer the ridicule of thoughtless classmates and have difficulty making friends (Durkin & Conti-Ramsden, 2007; LaBlance, Steckol, & Smith, 1994; Rice, Hadley, & Alexander, 1993).

In some cases specific language impairments are inherited (D. V. M. Bishop, 2006; Spinath, Price, Dale, & Plomin, 2004). In other instances they are associated with specific brain abnormalities (J. L. Locke, 1993). But often the exact cause of an impairment is unknown (T. F. Campbell et al., 2003; Hulit & Howard, 2006; P. P. Wang & Baron, 1997).

Although trained specialists typically work with children who have impaired language skills, parents, teachers, and other adults can also facilitate the language development of these youngsters. Several recommendations are presented in the Development and Practice feature "Working with Children Who Have Specific Language Impairments."

Development and Practice

Working with Children Who Have Specific Language Impairments

- **Be on the lookout for children who exhibit significant delays or other language problems unusual for their age-group.**

  A preschool teacher consults with a speech-language pathologist about a 4-year-old girl who communicates only by pointing and gesturing. "She's certainly not shy," the teacher explains. "She often tries to get other children's attention by poking them, and she loves to sit on my lap during story time."

- **Encourage children to speak.**

  An 11-year-old has trouble pronouncing the s sound (e.g., he says "thpethial" for *special*) and is meeting regularly with a speech therapist to address the problem. Nevertheless, his fifth-grade teacher encourages him to speak in class, especially in small-group settings. When he does so, she models acceptance of his disability, and if a classmate makes fun of his speech, she discreetly takes the classmate aside and explains that all children have strengths and weaknesses and that everyone in her class deserves respect and support.

- **Listen patiently.**

  A high school student often stutters when she speaks and may sometimes struggle for several seconds midway through a sentence

  to pronounce a particular word. Her teachers know that she is able to complete her thoughts if they give her time.

- **Ask for clarification when a message is unclear.**

  An 8-year-old boy often says "this" or "that thing there" when referring to objects in the classroom. Suspecting that he may have an undiagnosed language disability, his third-grade teacher refers him to a school psychologist for evaluation, but she also asks him to call objects by their names.

- **Provide guidance about how to talk effectively with others.**

  A middle school student often dominates conversations in small-group discussions, rambling on at such length that her classmates have trouble getting a word in edgewise. Her teacher meets with her during lunch one day to remind her of the importance of letting everyone participate. Together they identify a strategy that will help her keep her comments to a reasonable period: Whenever she starts to speak, she will look at the second hand on her watch and be sure to yield the floor after a maximum of 30 seconds.

Sources: L. Bloom & Lahey, 1978; Patton et al., 1996; Turnbull et al., 2007.

Sensory Impairments and Language Development

Children with severe visual impairments (e.g., blindness) typically have normal syntactic development but are apt to have more limited vocabularies than their sighted agemates (M. Harris, 1992). Because they cannot always see the objects and events around them, they simply don't have as many opportunities to make connections between words and their meanings (M. B. Rowe, 1978; Hobson, 2004).

Children with hearing impairments (e.g., deafness) are at risk for delays in both syntactic and semantic development, especially if an impairment was present at birth or emerged early in life (M. Harris, 1992). Furthermore, children who have been completely deaf from birth or soon thereafter typically need special training to develop proficiency in speaking. Yet these children are apt to show normal language development in *sign language* if family members and others use it as the primary means of communicating with them (M. Harris, 1992; Newport, 1990; L. A. Pettito, 1997). Deaf infants who are regularly exposed to sign language often begin to "babble" with their hands at 7 to 10 months. They are apt to sign their first word at around 18 to 22 months, with multiword phrases following soon thereafter. Like hearing children, children who use sign language appear to construct rules that guide their language use, and they gradually expand on and refine these rules over time (Goldin-Meadow & Mylander, 1993; L. A. Pettito, 1997).

Happy Mother's Day!

Children with hearing loss can interact more effectively with classmates who know sign language. Here, Marianne, a hearing child, has created a Mother's Day card using the sign for "I love you."

A case study of BoMee (Wilcox, 1994) illustrates just how much is possible when parents provide a linguistically rich environment through sign language. BoMee was born in Korea 8 weeks prematurely. Although she could hear at birth, early illnesses or medications apparently caused profound hearing loss early in life. At age 2½, BoMee was adopted by American parents, who communicated with her regularly in sign language. Within a few weeks after BoMee's arrival, they also began to sign their self-talk as a way of "thinking aloud." For instance, BoMee's mother might sign "What goes next in this recipe?" or "Where are my shoes?" Within a week, BoMee began signing her own self-talk, such as "Where my shoes are?" Soon self-talk was a regular feature in BoMee's problem-solving activities. On one occasion, BoMee was trying to put a dress on her doll, but the dress was too small. She signed to herself:

> Hmmm, wrong me. This dress fit here? Think not. Hmmm. For other doll here. (Translation: *Hmmm, I'm wrong. Does this dress go on this doll? I don't think so. Hmmm. It goes on this other doll.*) (Wilcox, 1994, p. 119)

BoMee showed other normal linguistic behaviors as well. She simplified her language when she signed to her baby brother. And just as hearing children typically read aloud in the early stages of reading, BoMee signed "out loud" when she began to read.

Like Mario, BoMee may have had an advantage in the development of metalinguistic awareness. She was exposed to both English-based signs and American Sign Language (which have somewhat different vocabularies and syntactic structures) and quickly became bilingual in her knowledge of the two language systems. She understood very early that some people talked and others used sign language. Furthermore, shortly after her third birthday, she appropriately signed "This Little Piggy" in two different ways—in English-based signs and in American Sign Language—to people who understood only one of the two languages. Clearly, then, children with hearing loss can have very normal cognitive and linguistic development when their language environment is appropriate for them.

Children who have sensory impairments typically work with specialists to develop strategies for living successfully in a world of sighted, hearing people. Yet teachers, parents, and other adults can also help these children in many ways. Examples are presented in the Development and Practice feature "Working with Children Who Have Hearing Impairments."

Mastery of the basic underpinnings of language (i.e., semantics and syntax) and proficiency in the receptive and expressive aspects of spoken language (i.e., listening and speaking) are, of course, important in their own right. But they also provide the foundation for receptive and expressive skills in written language. We turn to development of reading, writing, and other academic domains in the next chapter.

Development and Practice

Working with Children Who Have Hearing Impairments

- **Intervene as early as possible to address correctable hearing impairments.**

  Among the children in a preschool class for low-income children is a 3-year-old boy who is deaf. His mother expresses interest in a cochlear implant but cannot afford one. The boy's teacher and an audiologist who consults at the school locate a charitable organization that will pay for the cost of surgery. With the implant, the boy begins to hear the language around him, and both his receptive and expressive language rapidly develop.

- **Communicate messages through multiple modalities.**

  A 15-year-old who is deaf has a student-specific aide who accompanies her to all of her classes and manually translates the content of teachers' lectures and explanations. Even so, her teachers make sure that they communicate as much as possible through sight as

well as sound. For example, they write important points on the chalkboard and illustrate key ideas with pictures and other graphics.

- **Learn elements of American Sign Language and finger spelling, and teach them to children's peers.**

  A teacher in a combined first- and second-grade class has several students who are deaf, and so she both speaks and signs to her class as she presents new information and describes assignments. All of her students know enough American Sign Language to converse easily with one another. (The teacher and students are depicted in the two "Language" videos in the Video Examples section in Chapter 9 of MyEducationLab.)

Sources: Bruer, 1999; Newport, 1990; Svirsky, Robbins, Kirk, Pisoni, & Miyamoto, 2000.

Summary

Theoretical Perspectives of Language Development

Although modeling, reinforcement, and feedback almost certainly play some role in language development, early theories based on such processes could not adequately account for the fact that most children acquire a very complex language system in a very short period, and with only limited guidance from adults. Several more recent theoretical perspectives have emerged, each focusing on somewhat different aspects of language development. *Nativists* propose that young children have certain "prewired" knowledge and skills that facilitate language acquisition. *Information processing theorists* apply general principles of cognition (e.g., the importance of attention, the process of automatization) to explain how some aspects of language may develop. *Sociocultural theorists* emphasize the role that social interactions play in language learning. *Functionalists* propose that children develop language primarily because it enhances their effectiveness in social groups and increases their ability to satisfy their own needs. Many theorists draw from elements of two or more of these perspectives when explaining how language develops. Nevertheless, some areas of incompatibility among the theories (e.g., whether children inherit some neurologically based language "preprogramming") remain unresolved.

Trends in Language Development

Children and adolescents continue to develop their linguistic knowledge and skills throughout infancy, childhood, and adolescence. For instance, school-age children add several thousand new words to their vocabulary each year. Over time, they rely less on word order and more on syntax to interpret other people's messages, and they can comprehend and produce sentences with increasingly complex syntactic structures.

Their conversations with others increase in length, they become better able to adapt the content of their speech to the characteristics of their listeners, and they become more aware of the unspoken social conventions that govern verbal interactions in their culture. They also acquire a growing understanding of the nature of language as an entity in and of itself.

Development of a Second Language

Research findings are mixed with regard to the "best" time to learn a second language. Nevertheless, research consistently indicates that knowing two or more languages enhances achievement in reading and other language arts, promotes greater metalinguistic awareness, and fosters multicultural sensitivity. An *immersion* approach to teaching a second language is effective only when children have ample opportunity to continue developing their native language outside of school. In other situations, *bilingual education*, in which youngsters study academic topics in their native language and receive separate instruction in spoken and written English, yields more favorable results.

Diversity and Exceptionalities in Language Development

Subtle qualitative differences have been observed in the conversational styles of males and females. Children from higher-SES backgrounds tend to have larger vocabularies, probably because they are likely to be exposed to a wider variety of words. Different ethnic groups may show differences in sociolinguistic behaviors, storytelling traditions, use of figurative language, and dialects.

Some children have disabilities that affect their language development. Specific language impairments include abnormalities in receptive or expressive language that significantly interfere with children's performance and accomplishments in and out of school. Children with hearing impairments and, to a lesser extent, those with visual impairments may have more limited language proficiency because of reduced exposure to language or reduced awareness of the meaningful contexts in which it is used.

Applying Concepts in Child Development

The exercises in this section will help you increase your ability to apply what you've learned about language development as you work with children and adolescents.

Case Study

Boarding School

Read the case and then answer the questions that follow it.

Some parts of Alaska are so sparsely settled that building local high schools makes little economic sense. So in certain Native American communities, older students are sent to boarding school for their high school education. A high priority for boarding school teachers is to help students master Standard English. With this information in mind, consider the following incident:

> Many of the students at the school spoke English with a native dialect and seemed unable to utter certain essential sounds in the English language. A new group of speech teachers was sent in to correct the problem. The teachers worked consistently with the students in an attempt to improve speech patterns and intonation, but found that their efforts were in vain.
>
> One night, the boys in the dormitory were seeming to have too much fun, and peals of laughter were rolling out from under the door. An investigating counselor approached cautiously and listened quietly outside the door to see if he could discover the source of the laughter. From behind the door he heard a voice, speaking in perfect English, giving instructions to the rest of the crowd. The others were finding the situation very amusing. When the counselor entered the room he found that one of the students was speaking. "Joseph," he said, "You've been cured! Your English is perfect." "No," said Joseph returning to his familiar dialect, "I was just doing an imitation of you." "But if you can speak in Standard English, why don't you do it all of the time?" the counselor queried. "I can," responded Joseph, "but it sounds funny, and I feel dumb doing it." (Garrison, 1989, p. 121)

- Why might Joseph prefer his native dialect to Standard English?
- Is Joseph bilingual? Why or why not?
- The counselor told Joseph that he had "been cured." What beliefs about Joseph's native dialect does this statement reflect?
- Is it important for Joseph and his classmates to master Standard English? Why or why not? What implications does your answer have for classroom instruction?

Once you have answered these questions, compare your responses with those presented in Appendix A.

Interpreting Children's Artifacts and Reflections

Consider chapter concepts as you analyze the following artifact created by an 8-year-old.

Figure of Speech

In response to an assignment in his third-grade class, 8-year-old Jeff drew his interpretation of the common expression *Your eyes are bigger than your stomach*. As you look at Jeff's drawing, consider these questions:

- What aspects of language has Jeff mastered?
- What aspect of language has he apparently *not* yet mastered?
- Is Jeff's performance on this assignment usual or unusual for his age?

Once you have analyzed Jeff's drawing, compare your ideas with those presented in Appendix B. For further practice in analyzing children's artifacts and reflections, go to the Activities and Applications section in Chapter 9 of MyEducationLab.

Developmental Trends Exercise

In this chapter you discovered a variety of ways in which receptive language and expressive language change as children grow older. The following table describes the language-related behaviors of children and adolescents in five different age ranges. For each youngster, the table indicates whether the behavior is typical or unusual for the age-group, suggests developmentally appropriate responses to the behavior, or both. Go to the Activities and Applications section in Chapter 9 of MyEducationLab to apply what you've learned about language development as you fill in the empty cells in the table.

Assessing Developmental Progress in Language

Age	A Youngster's Experience	Developmental Concepts *Recognizing Typical and Unusual Behaviors for the Age-Group*	Implications *Facilitating Acquisition of Language Skills*
Infancy **(Birth–2 Years)**	When a caregiver at a child care center exclaims, "Your daddy's here!" 10-month-old Midori looks eagerly in the direction of the door. But despite Midori's apparent understanding of the word *Daddy*, she does not yet say his name, not even a reasonable approximation such as "Dada." Sometimes she says "dadadadada," but with little regard for whether her father is present.	This behavior is typical for the age-group. Although children can understand some words as early as 8 months, on average they don't say their first word until sometime around their first birthday. Midori's repetition of the syllable *da*, apparently without reference to anything in her environment, is an instance of *babbling*.	Regularly engage infants in "conversations" in which they can practice vocalizing, taking turns, maintaining eye contact, and using other basic language skills. Simplify your language somewhat (e.g., use *infant-directed speech*), but use a variety of words in appropriate contexts.
Early Childhood **(2–6 Years)**	Twenty kindergartners sit quietly and politely as the school principal describes the procedure they should follow during a fire drill. After the principal leaves the room, however, many of them are unable to describe the procedure she has spoken about.	This behavior is typical for the age-group. Young children often think that being a "good listener" simply means sitting still and being quiet. They do not necessarily realize that listening also involves understanding and remembering what the speaker says.	
Middle Childhood **(6–10 Years)**	Seven-year-old Arthur's sentences are rarely more than two or three words long.	Such speech is unusual for the age-group. Children typically begin putting two words together sometime around age 2, and their sentences become increasingly long after that. By school age, their sentences are adult-like in many respects.	
Early Adolescence **(10–14 Years)**	In an oral report in his seventh-grade history class, 14-year-old Roy says such things as "John Wesley Powell looked for *gooder* boats to use" and "He *goed* down the Grand Canyon in a canoe."	These errors are unusual for the age-group. Adding *-er* to irregular adjectives and *-ed* to irregular verbs are examples of *overregularization*. Overregularization of such common words as *good* and *go* is often seen in the early elementary years but is rare in adolescence.	When children's syntax and word usage are unusual, consider whether a local dialect or family communication patterns might be the cause. Encourage Standard English in formal situations, but allow the dialect in everyday conversation with family and friends. If dialect differences cannot account for what you observe, consult with a specialist about appropriate interventions.

Developmental Trends Exercise (continued)

Age	A Youngster's Experience	Developmental Concepts *Recognizing Typical and Unusual Behaviors for the Age-Group*	Implications *Facilitating Acquisition of Language Skills*
Late Adolescence (14–18 Years)	When talking to members of a high school soccer team just before the first game of the season, a coach says, "Remember, ladies, a chain is only as strong as its weakest link." The girls nod in agreement and vow that they will all try to play their best.		Use a variety of common expressions when talking with adolescents, but check to be sure that your listeners can see beyond the surface meanings to understand your underlying messages.

Key Concepts

phonology (p. 314)
semantics (p. 314)
syntax (p. 314)
pragmatics (p. 314)
native language (p. 314)
nativism (p. 315)
language acquisition device (p. 315)
language socialization (p. 317)
functionalism (p. 318)
receptive language (p. 320)
expressive language (p. 320)

infant-directed speech (p. 320)
lexical word (p. 321)
grammatical word (p. 321)
underextension (p. 321)
overextension (p. 322)
fast mapping (p. 323)
holophrase (p. 325)
telegraphic speech (p. 325)
overregularization (p. 326)
semantic bootstrapping (p. 327)
expansion (p. 327)
phonemes (p. 328)

figurative speech (p. 329)
cooing (p. 331)
babbling (p. 331)
narrative (p. 332)
playing the dozens (p. 333)
sociolinguistic behaviors (p. 336)
personal space (p. 338)
IRE cycle (p. 338)
wait time (p. 338)
culture shock (p. 339)
metalinguistic awareness (p. 339)

bilingualism (p. 343)
English language learner (ELL) (p. 344)
immersion (p. 344)
bilingual education (p. 344)
subtractive bilingualism (p. 345)
Standard English (p. 346)
dialect (p. 346)
African American English (p. 346)
specific language impairment (p. 347)

MyEducationLab

Now go to Chapter 9 of MyEducationLab at www.myeducationlab.com, where you can:

· View instructional objectives for the chapter.
· Take a quiz to test your mastery of chapter objectives. Detailed feedback is provided to explain why your responses are correct or incorrect.
· Deepen your understanding of particular concepts and principles with Review, Practice, and Enrichment exercises.

· Complete Activities and Applications exercises that give you additional experience in interpreting artifacts, increase your understanding of how research contributes to knowledge about chapter topics, and encourage you to apply what you have learned about children's development.
· Apply what you have learned in the chapter to your work with children in Building Teaching Skills and Dispositions exercises.
· Observe children and their unique contexts in Video Examples.

Development in the Academic Domains

Phyllis Jones and her son Benjamin lived in a low-income, inner-city, African American neighborhood. Here is their story:

[Phyllis Jones] finished high school and two years of college, and regrets that she did not go farther. She wishes she had "listened to her grandmother" who was "always pushing" her to study; instead, "I did enough just to get by." She is deeply concerned about her son's education, and determined that he will go farther than she did. She is particularly concerned about his learning to read, noting that "without reading, you can't do anything," and that "readers are leaders—I want Benjamin to read and read and read. . . ."

Mrs. Jones decided that the only way to be certain that Benjamin would learn to read was to teach him herself. She began buying books for him when he was an infant, and she asked friends and relatives to give him books as Christmas and birthday presents. Before he turned 3, she bought him a set of phonics tapes and workbooks, which she used to conduct regular lessons, helping Benjamin learn to recognize the forms and sounds of letters, combinations of letters, and eventually entire words. She also gave him lessons in letter formation, handwriting, and spelling. When Benjamin was 3, he began attending a Head Start program, while his mother continued to teach him at home. She tried to make these activities "fun for Benjamin." She was pleased with his interest in reading and writing, and sometimes frustrated that he did not learn as quickly as she wanted him to.

Benjamin sometimes pretended to read magazines, newspapers, and books. His mother was gratified by his enthusiasm, commenting on his "reading" of *The Gingerbread Man*, "you can hear the laughter and joy in his voice." But she also told Benjamin he was "not really reading." On one occasion, she pointed to the print in the book Benjamin was pretending to read and said "these are what you read. Someday you will learn to read." Another time she commented, "Benjamin thinks he can read. What he'll do is recite some words from a story and exclaim with great joy 'I can read! I can read!' I explained to him that he isn't reading. Reading is looking at a book and saying the words that are written there. But I say one day he will read—soon, just like Tony [an older friend of Benjamin's]." By the time Benjamin was 4, his mother noted that he knew "all of his alphabet by sight. Praise God!"

When Benjamin turned 4, Mrs. Jones began taking him to a reading program at the storefront church she attended. This program was designed for older children, but she thought he would "pick up something." She also continued to work on reading and writing at home, using index cards to make a card game to teach Benjamin how to write his name. When he was about 4½, Benjamin began sounding out words that he noticed around him, such as "off" and "on." His mother commented, "now he wants to know what everything spells and wants to guess at some of them. He asked me on the bus if E-M-E-R-G-E-N-C-Y spelled 'emergency'." On another occasion, when she picked Benjamin up at Head Start, "he said, 'Guess what we did today? I'll give you a hint—it begins with J. Then he said the word was J-E-M, which was supposed to be 'gym'." His mother was delighted with his interest in reading: "Hurrah! I hope it carries through the rest of his life." By the end of his second year in Head Start, when he had just turned 5, Benjamin could read a number of simple words by sounding them out and had a small sight vocabulary. His mother took great pride in these achievements: "Hallelujah! He can read!" (McLane & McNamee, 1990, pp. 103–105)[a]

- Certainly the books, workbooks, and audiotapes that Phyllis Jones provided for Benjamin helped him gain many fundamental reading skills. What other things did she *also* do that probably promoted Benjamin's reading development?

[a]Reprinted by permission of the publisher from *Early Literacy* by Joan Brooks McLane and Gillian Dowley McNamee, pp. 103–105, Cambridge, MA: Harvard University Press. Copyright © 1990 by Joan Brooks McLane and Gillian Dowley McNamee.

Case Study:
Phyllis and Benjamin Jones

Case Study: Phyllis and Benjamin Jones

Reading Development

Writing Development

Mathematics Development

Science Development

Development in Other Academic Domains

Using Content Area Standards to Guide Instruction

Summary

Applying Concepts in Child Development

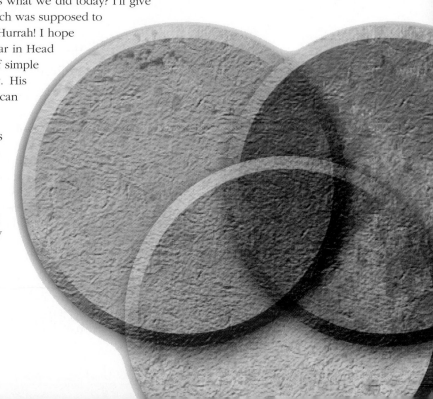

n both her words and her actions, Phyllis Jones consistently communicated that reading is a useful, enjoyable, and ultimately very *important* activity. She also communicated that reading involves translating specific written symbols into the words and meanings of spoken language. And she conveyed optimism that Benjamin would eventually be able to make sense of those written symbols—"soon, just like Tony." Through such messages and through the many books and workbooks she provided, Phyllis immersed Benjamin in a literacy-rich environment—a context that clearly nurtured his early literacy skills.

Phyllis Jones knew how important reading and writing are for success in the adult world, and so she provided a solid foundation on which Benjamin's reading and writing development could build. Like Phyllis, many parents in industrialized countries share with their children basic elements of reading, writing, arithmetic, geography, music, and so on. For instance, they may teach their children letters and numbers, show them globes and road maps, and sing or play music for them. Such academically rich home environments get children off to a good start in acquiring the knowledge and skills they will need as socially and professionally productive adults (e.g., Liben & Myers, 2007; Serpell, Baker, & Sonnenschein, 2005).

By the time children reach age 5 or 6, schools take over much of the responsibility for passing along the rich cultural heritage of modern-day societies. In this chapter we look at how knowledge and skills in a variety of academic disciplines develop over the course of childhood and adolescence. We also identity strategies for promoting children's development in various academic domains.

Reading Development

Children's literacy skills—their skills in reading and writing—obviously build on their knowledge of spoken language. The thousands of words and innumerable grammatical structures that children master in speech are basic elements of written language as well. However, written language differs from spoken language in important ways. To learn to read and write, children must learn the relationships between how words sound and are produced in speech, on the one hand, and how they look and are written on paper, on the other. Children must also master nuances of the written symbol system that have no counterparts in spoken language, such as punctuation marks and appropriate uses of upper- and lowercase letters (Coker, 2007; Liberman, 1998; Paris & Cunningham, 1996).

Reading is a complex, multifaceted process that continues to develop throughout childhood and adolescence. In the upcoming sections, we look at children's acquisition of basic knowledge about written language (emergent literacy) and then examine the development of several critical aspects of reading.

Emergent Literacy

Through early exposure to reading and writing, young children learn many things about written language. For instance, they learn the following:

- Print has meaning and conveys information.
- Different kinds of printed matter (storybooks, newspapers, grocery lists, greeting cards, etc.) serve different purposes.
- Spoken language is represented in a consistent way in written language (e.g., specific alphabet letters are associated with specific sounds, words are always spelled the same way).
- Written language includes some predictable elements and conventions (e.g., fairy tales often begin with "Once upon a time," and in English, writing proceeds from left to right and from the top of the page to the bottom) (Paris & Cunningham, 1996; Pérez, 1998; Serpell et al., 2005; Treiman, Cohen, Mulqueeny, Kessler, & Schechtman, 2007; Weiss & Hagen, 1988).

emergent literacy
Knowledge and skills that lay a foundation for reading and writing; typically develops in the preschool years from early experiences with written language.

Such basic knowledge about written language, which lays a foundation for reading and writing development, is known as **emergent literacy**.

Parents and other adults promote emergent literacy in numerous ways (McLane & McNamee, 1990; Stephenson, Parrila, Georgiou, & Kirby, 2008; Teale, 1978). They provide easy access to reading and writing materials. They model reading and writing behavior. They take children on frequent trips to the library. They talk about the things they've read and written. They demonstrate that reading and writing are useful and enjoyable activities. But perhaps most importantly, they read to children regularly (L. Baker, Scher, & Mackler, 1997; Serpell et al., 2005). Reading to children is especially valuable when parents and other caregivers talk with children about what they are reading together (Panofsky, 1994; Whitehurst et al., 1994). By doing so, adults engage children in the *social construction of meaning* we discussed in Chapter 6.

Children who are read to frequently during the preschool years learn to read more easily once they reach elementary school (Sénéchal & LeFevre, 2002; Whitehurst et al., 1994). Associating literacy activities with pleasure may be especially important. Children who enjoy their early reading experiences are more likely to read frequently on their own later on (L. Baker et al., 1997). Thus authentic literacy activities (e.g., reading children's stories) are often more beneficial for young children than activities involving drill and practice of isolated skills (Serpell et al., 2005).

By observing young children as they interact with books and writing implements, teachers and caregivers can infer a great deal about what children have learned about the nature of written language. For instance, children may pretend to read storybooks and associate certain letters with certain sounds, as Benjamin Jones did in the opening case study. The Observation Guidelines table "Assessing Emergent Literacy in Young Children" offers several ideas about what to look for.

Letter Recognition and Phonological Awareness

Before Benjamin Jones was 3, his mother Phyllis began teaching him the letters of the alphabet. Knowing letters and the sounds that each one represents is an obvious prerequisite for learning to read (M. Harris & Giannouli, 1999; Scarborough, 2001). But in addition, children are more successful readers when they have **phonological awareness**—when they can hear the distinct sounds that make up words (Boscardin, Muthén, Francis, & Baker, 2008; Stanovich, 2000). Phonological awareness includes abilities such as these:

- Hearing the specific syllables within words (e.g., hearing "can" and "dee" as separate parts of *candy*)
- Dividing words into discrete word sounds or *phonemes* (e.g., hearing the sounds "guh," "ay," and "tuh" in *gate*)[1]
- Blending separate phonemes into meaningful words (e.g., recognizing that, when put together, the sounds "wuh," "eye," and "duh" make *wide*)
- Identifying words that rhyme (e.g., realizing that *cat* and *hat* end with the same sounds).

Phonological awareness develops gradually during the preschool and early elementary years (Barron, 1998; Goswami, 1999, 2007; Lonigan, Burgess, Anthony, & Barker, 1998). Most children can detect the syllables within words by age 4, well before they begin school and start learning to read. Soon after, perhaps around age 5, they begin to realize that many syllables can be divided into two parts: an *onset* (one or more consonants that precede the vowel sound) and a *rime* (the vowel sound and any consonants that follow it). By the time they are 6 or 7, many children can identify the individual phonemes in spoken words. This last ability seems to emerge hand in hand with learning to read (Anthony & Francis, 2005; Goswami, 1999; M. Harris & Giannouli, 1999).

Researchers have consistently found letter recognition and phonological awareness to be important factors affecting children's reading ability, especially when they are first beginning to read (e.g., Anthony & Francis, 2005; Chow, McBride-Chang, & Burgess, 2005; Kirby, Parrila, & Pfeiffer, 2003; Scarborough, 2001). Phyllis Jones helped Benjamin acquire phonological awareness with the help of phonics workbooks and audiotapes. Yet parents and teachers can often cultivate phonological awareness just as effectively within the context of lively, enjoyable listening, reading, and spelling activities (Muter, 1998). The Development and Practice feature "Promoting Phonological Awareness and Letter Recognition in Young Children" on page 359 presents several useful strategies.

[1]This aspect of phonological awareness is sometimes called *phonemic* awareness.

phonological awareness
Ability to hear the distinct sounds of which spoken words are comprised.

Observation Guidelines

Assessing Emergent Literacy in Young Children

Characteristics	Look For	Example	Implication
Attitudes Toward Books	· Frequent manipulation and perusal of books · Interest and attentiveness when adults read storybooks · Eagerness to talk about stories that are read	Martina often mentions the Berenstain Bears books that her father reads to her at home.	Devote a regular time to storybook reading, choose books with colorful pictures and imaginative story lines, and occasionally stop to discuss and interpret characters and events in a story. Make regular trips to the library.
Behaviors with Books	· Correct handling of books (e.g., holding them right-side up, turning pages in the appropriate direction) · Pretend reading · Use of picture content to construct a logical sequence of events when pretending to read · Asking "What does this say?" about particular sections of text	Rusty doesn't seem to know what to do with the books in his preschool classroom. He opens them haphazardly and apparently sees nothing wrong with ripping out pages.	If children have had only limited experience with books, occasionally read one-on-one with them. Let them hold the books and turn the pages. Ask them to make predictions about what might happen next in a story.
Letter and Word Recognition	· Recognition of product names when they appear in logos and other familiar contexts · Correct identification of some alphabet letters · Recognition of own name in print	Katherine sees a take-out bag from a local fast-food restaurant and correctly deduces that it says "Burger King."	Prominently label any coat hooks, storage boxes, and other items that belong to individual children. Write children's names in large letters on paper and encourage them to trace or copy the letters. When children are ready, ask them to put their first name (or first initial) on their artwork.
Writing Behaviors	· Production of letter-like shapes · Writing in a left-to-right sequence · Ability to write some letters correctly or almost correctly · Ability to write own name	Hank can write his name, but he frequently reverses the N and sometimes leaves it out altogether.	Give children numerous opportunities to experiment with writing implements (paper, crayons, markers, pencils, etc.) in both structured tasks and unstructured situations. Guide letter and word formation when children show an interest.
Knowledge About the Nature and Purposes of Written Language	· Awareness that specific words are always spelled in the same way · Correct identification of telephone books, calendars, and other reference materials · Pseudowriting for particular purposes	When Shakira and Lucie pretend to grocery shop, they write several lines of squiggles on a piece of paper. They say that this is a list of items they need to get at the store.	Encourage play activities that involve pretend writing (e.g., writing and delivering "letters" to friends or classmates). Let children see you engaging in a wide variety of reading and writing activities.

Sources: Some ideas and examples from Dickinson, Wolf, & Stotsky, 1993; Hawkins, 1997; McLane & McNamee, 1990; Paris, Morrison, & Miller, 2006; D. W. Rowe & Harste, 1986; Serpell et al., 2005; Share & Gur, 1999; Sulzby, 1985; Treiman et al., 2007.

Word Recognition

At age 4, Benjamin could sound out some of the printed words he encountered. Most 4-year-olds don't have as much knowledge of letter-sound relationships as Benjamin did, but they can correctly identify certain words that appear in familiar contexts. For example, many preschoolers correctly identify the word *stop* when it appears on a red, octagonal sign beside the road. They can "read" the word *Cheerios* on a cereal box. They know that a word at a fast-food restaurant is *McDonald's* when the *M* takes the form of the well-known golden arches (Ehri, 1994; Juel, 1991; Share & Gur, 1999).

Sometime around age 5, children begin to look more closely at words. Initially, they are apt to focus on one or two visually distinctive features, perhaps seeing the "tail" hanging down at the end of *dog* or the two "ears" sticking up in the middle of *rabbit*. Soon after, they begin to use some of a word's letters for phonetic clues about what the word must

Development and Practice

Promoting Phonological Awareness and Letter Recognition in Young Children

⏱ **Read alphabet books that use colorful pictures, amusing poems, or entertaining stories to teach letters and letter sounds.**

A preschool teacher shares *Alphabet Adventure* (Wood & Wood, 2001) with her group of 4-year-olds. The children eagerly follow along as the main character, "Little i," looks for her lost dot, and they delight in finding various letters on each page.

⏱ **Have children think of words that rhyme.**

A kindergarten teacher challenges his students to think of at least five words that rhyme with *break*.

· **Ask children to identify words that begin (or end) with a particular sound or group of sounds.**

A first-grade teacher says, "Listen to the 'str' sound at the beginning of *string*. What are some other words that begin with 'str'?"

· **Say several words and ask children which one begins (or ends) in a different sound.**

A second-grade teacher asks, "Listen carefully to these four words: *end, dent, bend,* and *mend*. Which one ends in a different sound than the others? Listen to them again before you decide: *end, dent, bend,* and *mend*."

· **Show pictures of several objects and ask children to choose the one that begins (or ends) with a different sound from the others.**

A kindergarten teacher shows his class pictures of a dog, a door, a wagon, and a dragon. "Three of these things start with the same sound. Which one starts with a *different* sound?"

⏱ **Have children practice writing alphabet letters on paper and representing letters in other ways.**

A first-grade teacher has children make letters with their bodies. For example, one child stands with his arms outstretched like a *Y*, and two others bend over and clasp hands to form an *M*.

---

be. For example, they might read *box* by looking at the *b* and *x* but ignoring the *o* (Ehri, 1991, 1994).

Once children have mastered letter-sound relationships, they rely heavily on these relationships as they read (Ehri, 1991, 1994; Farrington-Flint & Wood, 2007). Doing so allows them to identify such simple words as *cat, bed, Dick,* and *Jane*. However, they have difficulty when they encounter words that violate general pronunciation rules. For instance, using the rule that *ea* is pronounced "ee" (as in *meat* and *treat*), they might read *head* as "heed" or *sweater* as "sweeter."

By the middle elementary grades, most children have a reasonable **sight vocabulary**: They can recognize a sizable number of words immediately and with little effort. That is, a good deal of word recognition has become *automatized*. When they encounter words that aren't in their sight vocabulary, they draw on letter-sound relationships, familiar prefixes and root words, common spelling patterns, and context clues to decipher the words (Ehri & Robbins, 1992; Kuo & Anderson, 2006; Nagy, Berninger, Abbott, Vaughan, & Vermeulen, 2003).

Reading Comprehension

In its most basic form, reading comprehension involves understanding the words and sentences on the page. But for advanced readers, it also means going *beyond* the page to identify main ideas, make inferences and predictions, detect an author's assumptions and biases, and so on (Perfetti, 1985). Thus reading comprehension is a very *constructive* process: Readers combine what they see on the printed page with their existing knowledge and beliefs—both about the world at large and about the nature of written language—to derive meaning from text (Cromley & Azevedo, 2007; Gaskins, Satlow, & Pressley, 2007; C. A. Weaver & Kintsch, 1991).

Several general trends characterize the development of reading comprehension in childhood and adolescence:

· ***Children's growing knowledge base facilitates better reading comprehension.*** As children grow older, they become better able to understand what they read, in part because they know more regarding the topics about which they are reading (Rayner et al., 2001). In fact, children's reading comprehension ability at *any* age is influenced by topic knowledge (Cromley & Azevedo, 2007; Gaskins et al., 2007; Lipson, 1983). For example, when second graders read about spiders, those who already know a lot about spiders

Young readers often rely heavily on context clues to help them identify words. As they learn various letter-sound relationships, they become increasingly proficient at sounding out new words. With time and practice, they develop a sizable sight vocabulary and can recognize many words quickly and easily.

sight vocabulary
Words that a child can immediately recognize while reading.

remember more and draw inferences more easily than peers who know less about the topic (Pearson, Hansen, & Gordon, 1979).

• **_Children become familiar with common structures in fictional and nonfictional texts._** Most 5- and 6-year-olds can distinguish between books that tell stories and books that provide information (S. L. Field, Labbo, & Ash, 1999). As children get older, they also learn how various kinds of text are typically organized, and such knowledge helps them make better sense of what they read. For instance, they gradually acquire a **story schema** that represents the typical components of fictional narratives (main characters, plot, problem resolution, etc.) and use this schema to impose a coherent structure on a short story or novel (Graesser, Golding, & Long, 1991; N. L. Stein, 1982; Zwaan, Langston, & Graesser, 1995). With age, they also begin to use common structures in nonfiction to enhance their comprehension. For instance, when reading a textbook, they may rely on headings and subheadings to help them identify key ideas and organize what they are studying (Byrnes, 1996; Gaskins et al., 2007).

By the time they reach high school, many adolescents no longer take everything they read at face value. Instead, they begin to read text with a critical eye.

• **_Children become increasingly able to draw inferences from what they read._** The ability to draw inferences seems to be a key factor in children's reading comprehension (Cromley & Azevedo, 2007). Especially as children reach the upper elementary grades, they become more adept at drawing inferences and, hence, more effectively learn new information from what they read (Chall, 1996; Paris & Upton, 1976; Pressley & Harris, 2006). At this point, however, they tend to take the things they read at face value, make little attempt to evaluate the quality of ideas, and often don't notice obvious contradictions (Chall, 1996; Markman, 1979; Walczyk, Marsiglia, Johns, & Bryan, 2004). As youngsters reach adolescence and move into the secondary grades, they read written material with a more critical eye (Chall, 1996). They begin to recognize that different authors sometimes present different viewpoints on a single issue. They also become more aware of the subtle aspects of fiction, such as the underlying themes and symbolism of a novel.

Metacognition in Reading

As you learned in Chapter 7, the term _metacognition_ encompasses children's knowledge and beliefs about their own cognitive processes, as well as their efforts to control these processes in order to learn more effectively. Some aspects of metacognition are specific to particular skill areas and academic domains.

As children learn to read, one of the first aspects of metacognition to emerge is an awareness that reading involves more than identifying the words on a page—that it involves making _sense_ of text. Such an awareness probably depends, in part, on how adults portray the process of reading to young children. For instance, when a researcher asked a first grader named Marissa if something she had just read made sense to her, she responded, "What I read never makes sense. The teacher just gives us books so we can practice reading words—they don't have to make sense" (Gaskins et al., 2007, pp. 196–197).

Successful readers obviously _do_ realize that reading is largely a process of sense-making (Gaskins et al., 2007). As children gain more experience with reading, and especially with reading textbooks and other informational text, they also develop a variety of strategies for comprehending written material. For instance, adolescents can more easily identify main ideas than elementary school children can (van den Broek, Lynch, Naslund, Ievers-Landis, & Verduin, 2003). High school students are more likely to monitor their comprehension as they read and also to backtrack (i.e., reread) when they don't understand something the first time, than are children in the upper elementary and middle school grades (Garner, 1987; Gaskins et al., 2007; Hacker, 1995). Not all adolescents use effective metacognitive reading strategies, however, and those who engage in little metacognition often have considerable difficulty understanding and remembering what they read (Alvermann & Moore, 1991; Cromley & Azevedo, 2007; Hacker, 1995).

With proper instruction and support, children and adolescents can learn to use effective metacognitive strategies and improve their reading comprehension as a result. One useful approach is _reciprocal teaching_, described in Chapter 6. The Development and Practice feature "Promoting Effective Reading Comprehension Strategies" presents additional suggestions.

story schema
Knowledge of the typical elements and sequence of a narrative.

Development and Practice

Promoting Effective Reading Comprehension Strategies

- **Teach reading comprehension skills in all subject areas.**

  When a life skills instructor tells his students to read a section of their first aid manual, he also suggests several strategies they might use to help them remember what they read. For example, as students begin each section, they should use the heading to ask a question they think the section will address. At the end of the section, they should stop and consider whether their question was answered.

- **Model effective reading strategies.**

  A girl in a seventh-grade history class reads aloud a passage describing how, during Columbus's first voyage across the Atlantic, many members of the crew wanted to turn around and return to Spain. Her teacher says, "Let's think of some reasons why the crew might have wanted to go home." One student responds, "Some of them might have been homesick." Another suggests, "Maybe they thought they'd never find their way back if they went too far."

- **Encourage children to relate what they are reading to things they already know about the topic.**

  Children in a third-grade classroom are each reading several books on a particular topic (e.g., dinosaurs, insects, outer space). Before they begin reading a book, their teacher asks them to write answers to three questions: (a) What do you already know about your topic? (b) What do you hope to learn about your topic? and (c) Do you think what you learn in your books will change what you already know about your topic?

- **Ask children to identify key elements of the stories they read.**

  A fourth-grade teacher instructs his students to ask themselves five questions as they read stories: (a) Who is the main character? (b) Where and when did the story take place? (c) What did the main characters do? (d) How did the story end? and (e) How did the main character feel?

- **Suggest that children create mental images that capture what they are reading.**

  When a high school English class reads Nathaniel Hawthorne's *The Scarlet Letter*, the teacher suggests that students try to envision what the two main characters, Arthur Dimmesdale and Hester Prynne, might look like. She then asks several students to describe their mental images. (You can see this example in action in the "Scarlet Letter" video in Chapter 10's Video Examples section of MyEducationLab.)

- **Scaffold children's early efforts to use complex strategies.**

  A middle school science teacher asks her students to write summaries of short textbook passages. She gives them four rules to use as they develop their summaries: (a) Identify the most important ideas, (b) delete trivial details, (c) eliminate redundant information, and (d) identify relationships among the main ideas.

Sources: Gambrell & Bales, 1986; Gaskins et al., 2007; Pressley et al., 1994; Rinehart, Stahl, & Erickson, 1986; Short & Ryan, 1984; H. Thompson & Carr, 1995.

In general, as young people move through the elementary and secondary grades, they read with greater fluency and flexibility and become able to read increasingly complex and challenging material. The Developmental Trends table "Reading at Different Age Levels" traces the development of reading over the course of childhood and adolescence.

Diversity in Reading Development

To some extent, development of literacy skills occurs in tandem with overall intellectual development. Many (but not all) children who are later identified as intellectually gifted begin to read earlier than their peers, and some read frequently and voraciously (Piirto, 1999; Turnbull et al., 2007). Children with general intellectual disabilities (e.g., mental retardation) learn to read more slowly than their age-mates, and they acquire fewer effective reading strategies. In some instances they may develop excellent word identification skills yet understand little or nothing of what they read (Cossu, 1999).

Children with visual or hearing impairments may be at a disadvantage when learning to read, in part because their general language development may be delayed (see Chapter 9). In addition, children who are visually impaired cannot see the printed page when caregivers read to them in the early years, and so they know less about the conventions of written language (the left-to-right progression of words, the use of punctuation, etc.) when they begin school (Tompkins & McGee, 1986). Children with hearing impairments who have learned a manual language (e.g., American Sign Language) rather than spoken language cannot take advantage of letter-sound relationships and may have limited knowledge of the idioms and other irregularities of day-to-day speech (J. F. Andrews & Mason, 1986; Chall, 1996). Many graduating high school students who are deaf read at only a fourth- or fifth-grade level (Chall, 1996).

Some children with learning disabilities have considerable difficulty learning to read. In its extreme form, this difficulty is known as **dyslexia,** a disability that often has biological roots (Galaburda & Rosen, 2001; Shaywitz, Mody, & Shaywitz, 2006; Snowling, Gallagher, & Frith, 2003). Contrary to popular belief, dyslexia is typically *not* a problem of visual perception, such as reading words or letters backwards. Instead, many children with dyslexia have

dyslexia
Inability to master basic reading skills in a developmentally typical time frame despite normal reading instruction.

Developmental Trends

Reading at Different Age Levels

Age	What You Might Observe	Diversity	Implications
Infancy (Birth–2 Years) 	· Physical exploration of simple cloth and cardboard books · Increasing enjoyment of storybooks · More attention to pictures than to story lines · Attention to and enjoyment of rhythm and rhymes in spoken language	· Some toddlers may participate actively in storybook reading (e.g., by pointing to and labeling objects in pictures), whereas others may listen quietly while an adult reads.	· Read books with catchy rhythms and rhymes to capture and maintain attention. · During story time, label and talk about the pictures in books. Recognize that toddlers may not be able to sit still for an entire story.
Early Childhood (2–6 Years) 	· Attention focused largely on pictures rather than print during adult storybook reading (especially before age 6) · Incorporation of books and familiar story lines into play activities · Some knowledge of conventions of written language (e.g., left-to-right direction) by age 4 · Increasing knowledge of letters and letter-sound correspondences · Identification of a few words in well-known contexts (e.g., words on commercial products) · Use of a word's distinctive features (e.g., a single letter or overall shape) to read or misread it	· Children who have had little exposure to books and reading before starting school may have less knowledge about the nature of reading. Some cultures emphasize oral language more than written language. · When parents speak a language other than English, they may provide early literacy experiences in their native tongue; such experiences provide a good foundation for reading and writing in English. · Some children begin school knowing the alphabet and may have a small sight vocabulary as well. Others may need to start from scratch in learning letters and letter sounds.	· Read to young children using colorful books with high-interest content. · Teach letters of the alphabet through engaging, hands-on activities. · Teach letter-sound relationships through storybooks, games, rhymes, and enjoyable writing activities. · Encourage children to read words that can easily be identified from their contexts. · Encourage parents to read regularly to children and to make frequent visits to the local library.
Middle Childhood (6–10 Years) 	· Ability to hear individual phonemes within words · Increasing proficiency in identifying unfamiliar words · Growing sight-word vocabulary, leading to greater reading fluency · Beginning of silent reading (at age 7 or 8) · Increasing ability to draw inferences · Tendency to take things in print at face value, without critically evaluating the content or looking below the surface for underlying themes	· Children with deficits in phonological awareness have a more difficult time learning to read. · Children with hearing impairments may be slower to master letter-sound relationships. · On average, girls develop reading skills earlier than boys. · Children vary widely in their use of effective comprehension strategies.	· Explore "families" of words that are spelled similarly. · Assign well-written trade books (e.g., children's paperback novels) as soon as children are able to read and understand them. · Engage children in discussions about books. Focus on interpretation, inference drawing, and speculation. · For children who struggle with reading, explicitly teach phonological awareness and word identification skills, especially within the context of meaningful reading activities.
Early Adolescence (10–14 Years) 	· Automatized recognition of most common words · Ability to learn new information through reading · Emerging ability to go beyond the literal meaning of text · Emerging metacognitive processes that aid comprehension (e.g., comprehension monitoring, backtracking)	· Adolescents with deficits in phonological awareness continue to lag behind their peers in reading development. · Individuals who were poor readers in elementary school often continue to be poor readers in adolescence. · Some individuals (e.g., some with mental retardation) may have excellent word identification skills yet not understand what they read. · Individuals with sensory challenges may have less general world knowledge on which to build as they construct meaning from what they read.	· Assign age-appropriate reading materials in various academic areas; provide scaffolding (e.g., questions to answer) to guide youngsters' thinking and learning as they read. · Begin to explore classic works of poetry and fiction. · Use reciprocal teaching to promote poor readers' comprehension skills (see Chapter 6). · Seek the advice and assistance of specialists to help promote the reading skills of youngsters who lag far behind their peers.

Developmental Trends (continued)

Age	What You Might Observe	Diversity	Implications
Late Adolescence (14–18 Years)	· Automatized recognition of many abstract and discipline-specific words · Ability to consider multiple viewpoints about a single topic · Ability to critically evaluate what is read · More sophisticated metacognitive reading strategies	· Poor readers draw few if any inferences from what they read and use few if any effective metacognitive processes. · As classroom learning becomes more dependent on reading textbooks and other written materials, adolescents with reading disabilities may become increasingly frustrated in their attempts to achieve academic success. · Girls are more likely than boys to enroll in advanced literature classes.	· Expect that many teenagers can learn effectively from textbooks and other reading materials, but continue to scaffold reading assignments, especially for poor readers. · Encourage adolescents to draw inferences and make predictions from what they read. · Ask students to critically analyze classic works of poetry and fiction. · Modify reading materials and paper-pencil assessments for individuals with delayed reading development.

Sources: K. Cain & Oakhill, 1998; Chall, 1996; Dryden & Jefferson, 1994; Ehri, 1994; M. A. Evans & Saint-Aubin, 2005; Felton, 1998; M. Harris & Hatano, 1999; Hedges & Nowell, 1995; Hulme & Joshi, 1998; P. Johnston & Afflerbach, 1985; McBride-Chang & Treiman, 2003; McLane & McNamee, 1990; Nagy et al., 2003; Paris et al., 2006; R. E. Owens, 2008; Raikes et al., 2006; L. Reese, Garnier, Gallimore, & Goldenberg, 2000; T. A. Roberts, 2005; Serpell et al., 2005; Share & Gur, 1999; Trawick-Smith, 2003; Trelease, 1982; Treiman et al., 2007; Turnbull et al., 2007; Wigfield et al., 1996; Yaden & Templeton, 1986.

deficits in phonological awareness (Goswami, 2007; Swanson, Mink, & Bocian, 1999).[2] Others have deficits in the ability to identify visual stimuli quickly, which translates into difficulty automatizing connections between printed words and their meanings (Stanovich, 2000; Wimmer, Mayringer, & Landerl, 2000; Wolf & Bowers, 1999). Some children with reading disabilities may also have general information processing difficulties, such as a smaller working memory capacity or a tendency to process information at a slower-than-average rate (Wimmer, Landerl, & Frith, 1999; Wolf & Bowers, 1999).

We find further diversity in children's reading development as a function of their gender, socioeconomic status, ethnicity, and native language.

Gender differences. On average, girls read better than boys (Weaver-Hightower, 2003). And in the high school grades, girls are more likely than boys to enroll in advanced literature classes (Wigfield, Eccles, & Pintrich, 1996). Boys tend to have less interest in reading than girls do, in part because boys find fewer books at school that pique their curiosity and in part because many of them prefer more physically active pastimes (Freedman, 2003; Taylor & Lorimer, 2002–2003). A tenth grader named Devin expressed the latter reason this way: "Why should I want to read about doing things when I can actually *do* them?" (Newkirk, 2002, p. 54).

Socioeconomic differences. As the opening case study illustrates, many low-income parents regularly read to their children and in other ways foster literacy development (Jimerson, Egeland, & Teo, 1999; McLane & McNamee, 1990). Yet many others have little knowledge of how to promote emergent literacy through storybook readings and other reading activities. On average, then, children from lower-income families come to school with fewer literacy skills than children from middle- and upper-income families (Serpell et al., 2005). This socioeconomic disparity in reading ability not only persists, but in fact *increases*, over the course of the elementary and secondary school years (Chall, 1996; Jimerson et al., 1999; Portes, 1996). Thus as children from low-income families get older, they fall further and further behind their more economically advantaged peers.

Ethnic and cultural differences. Ethnic and cultural groups differ considerably in their emphasis on reading activities with young children. Some African American groups focus more on oral storytelling than on book reading (Trawick-Smith, 2003). Some Native American communities stress art, dance, and oral histories that carry on the group's cultural traditions (Trawick-Smith, 2003). Immigrant Hispanic parents often place higher priority on promoting their

---

[2]The writing sample in the "Pumpkin and Bat" exercise in Chapter 7 (p. 267) shows unusual difficulty with letter-sound relationships. Its author, 7-year-old Nathan, was diagnosed as having a reading disability.

Ethnic and cultural groups differ in the extent to which they regularly read to young children. Within any single group, however, some families engage in frequent book-reading activities, whereas other families spend very little time with books.

children's social and moral development (e.g., encouraging children to be helpful and cooperative, teaching them right from wrong) than on promoting early literacy skills (Gallimore & Goldenberg, 2001; Halgunseth, Ispa, & Rudy, 2006).

Even when young children have been regularly immersed in books, their cultural backgrounds influence their interpretations of what they read. As an example, Rosenna Bakari, a colleague of ours who specializes in African-centered education, describes an incident involving her 7-year-old daughter Nailah:

> [An event] that always stands out in my mind is a reading comprehension question that Nailah had in a workbook. The question asked why two brothers drew a line down the middle of a messy room to clean it. The answer was pretty obvious: The boys were dividing the room in half so that they could each clean their part. However, Nailah could not get to that answer no matter how I scaffolded her. When I told her the answer, she replied, "Why would they divide the room up? They should just both clean it together." I immediately realized that in her African-centered world, division rarely takes place. Most things in our house are communal. Each child is responsible for the other. So for her to get to that answer would have taken something beyond reasonable reading comprehension. She would have had to understand that there are people in the world who operate under different views about sharing and responsibility. That's a more difficult task for a seven-year-old. (R. Bakari, personal communication, 2002)

People from virtually all ethnic groups in Western society know that literacy is essential for children's eventual success in the adult world (Gallimore & Goldenberg, 2001; Pérez, 1998; Spera, 2005). Yet educators must be sensitive to what children's early language and literacy experiences have been and use them as the foundation for reading instruction. For example, children and adolescents from all backgrounds respond more favorably to literature and textbooks that reflect their own culture's ways of living and thinking (Gollnick & Chinn, 2002).

Cross-linguistic differences.   The more regular and predictable a language's letter-sound relationships are, the more easily children learn to read (Goswami, 2007; M. Harris & Hatano, 1999; Patel, Snowling, & de Jong, 2004). Languages differ considerably in the extent to which spelling precisely captures how words are pronounced. For instance, Spanish, Italian, German, Dutch, Turkish, and Swahili have highly regular and predictable spelling patterns, such that a word's spelling usually tells a reader exactly how the word is pronounced and its pronunciation tells a writer exactly how the word is spelled. English, French, and Danish are less regular, in that some sounds can be represented by two or more different letters or letter combinations. Some languages don't use an alphabet at all, so that predictable relationships between the forms of spoken and written language are few and far between. For instance, Chinese and Japanese are written as *characters* that represent entire syllables rather than individual phonemes.

Curiously, phonological awareness seems to be an important factor even in reading non-alphabetic languages such as Chinese and Japanese (Chow et al., 2005; McBride-Chang & Ho, 2000; J. C. Ziegler, Tan, Perry, & Montant, 2000). The underlying cause of this relationship has not been pinned down, but it may in some way be related to the fact that when people read, they mentally retrieve the sounds of written words as one way of connecting the words with their meanings (Rayner et al., 2001; J. C. Ziegler et al., 2000). Children in China, Taiwan, and Japan are often taught one or more alphabetic, phonetic systems for representing their language in writing before they are taught more traditional characters, and such training increases their phonological awareness (Goswami, 2007; Hanley, Tzeng, & Huang, 1999).

Promoting Reading Development

MyEducationLab

Go to Chapter 10's Building Teaching Skills and Dispositions section in MyEducationLab to observe and analyze strategies for teaching reading skills at different age levels.

Traditionally, reading is taught primarily in elementary school. Many teachers and other adults assume that middle school and high school students read well enough to learn successfully from textbooks and other printed materials. But as you have learned, this assumption is not always warranted. Even at the high school level, many adolescents have not yet mastered all of the skills involved in reading effectively. Furthermore, children who have trouble reading in elementary school often continue to be poor readers in the secondary grades (Felton, 1998; Shaywitz, 2004) and so may be in particular need of ongoing instruction and support in reading skills. We offer the following general strategies for promoting reading development throughout childhood and adolescence:

• **Help parents of young children acquire effective storybook reading skills.** In the "Literacy: Infancy" video in MyEducationLab, Corwin's mother enthusiastically engages her son in a discussion about the book they are looking at:

Mother:	Do you wanna see the cow? Would you like to read with Mama? You ready for the cow? Where is he? [turns the page] Huh! The cow says . . .
Corwin:	Mooo!
Mother:	What's that? [points to something in the book]
Corwin:	Boon.
Mother:	Balloon! We can count! One . . .
Corwin:	Two.
Mother:	Two! [reading book] This is my nose. Where's your nose?
Corwin:	[touches his nose]
Mother:	Nose! Where's your toes?
Corwin:	[grabs his toes]
Mother:	There's your toes!

Notice how Mother models enthusiasm for the book and uses its content to review object labels (*balloon, nose, toes*) and general world knowledge (numbers, what a cow says) with Corwin. Yet some parents have little awareness of how to read to young children, perhaps because they themselves were rarely read to when they were young. Such parents benefit from explicit instruction in strategies for reading to children—labeling and describing pictures, asking questions that encourage inferences and predictions, inviting children to make comments, and so on. When parents begin to use such strategies as they read to their children, their children acquire larger vocabularies, better knowledge of written language, and appreciation for literature (Edwards & Garcia, 1994; Gallimore & Goldenberg, 2001; H.-Z. Ho, Hinckley, Fox, Brown, & Dixon, 2001; Whitehurst et al., 1994).

• **Use meaningful and engaging activities to teach basic reading skills.** Explicit instruction in basic reading skills—relating letters to sounds, identifying simple words, finding main ideas, and so on—facilitates reading development, especially for poor readers (Ehri, Dreyer, Flugman, & Gross, 2007; Elbro & Petersen, 2004; Rayner et al., 2001). To become truly effective readers, children must automatize the most basic aspects of reading, including letter-sound relationships and recognition of common words (M. J. Adams, 1990; Ehri, Nunes, Stahl, & Willows, 2001; Stanovich, 2000). As you should recall from Chapter 7, automatization develops primarily through practice, practice, and more practice.

One approach, of course, is to provide drill-and-practice activities—workbook exercises, flash cards, and so on—that help children automatize specific reading skills (e.g., see Figure 10-1). Unfortunately, many children find such activities dull and boring (E. H. Hiebert & Raphael, 1996; J. C. Turner, 1995). Instruction in basic skills does not *have* to be dull and boring, however. With a little thought, teachers, parents, and other adults can develop enjoyable, meaningful activities to teach almost any basic reading skill. For instance, to promote phonological awareness in young children, adults might conduct a game of "Twenty Questions" (e.g., "I'm thinking of something in the room that begins with the letter *B*") or ask children to bring something from home that begins with the letter *T*. To foster greater automatization in word recognition, they might simply engage children in a variety of authentic reading activities (Ehri, 1998; Share, 1995).

Under no circumstances should teachers postpone teaching reading comprehension until basic skills are automatized. To do so would be to communicate the message that reading is a meaningless, tedious task, rather than a source of enlightenment and pleasure (Serpell et al., 2005). In an approach known as *whole language* instruction, some educators have suggested that virtually all basic literacy skills—knowledge of letter-sound relationships, root words, common spelling patterns, and so on—be taught within the context of reading children's books and other authentic written materials (e.g., K. S. Goodman, 1989; K. S. Goodman & Goodman, 1979; C. Weaver, 1990). Studies with kindergartners and first graders have found

MyEducationLab

Observe strategies Corwin's mother uses during picture book reading in the "Literacy: Infancy" video. (Find Video Examples in Chapter 10 of MyEducationLab.)

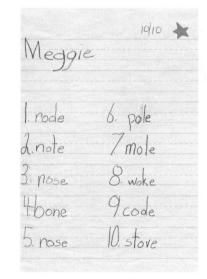

Figure 10-1

In this assignment, 7-year-old Meggie, a first grader, practices words with a long *o* sound and silent *e*. Instruction in specific letter-sound relationships and common spelling patterns helps children with both reading and spelling. However, too much focus on such drill and practice may lead children to conclude that reading and writing are meaningless, joyless activities.

that whole-language approaches are often quite effective in promoting emergent literacy—familiarity with the nature and purposes of books, pretend reading, and so on (Purcell-Gates, MyIntyre, & Freppon, 1995; Sacks & Mergendoller, 1997; Stahl & Miller, 1989). On the downside, however, letter-sound relationships and phonological awareness are often shortchanged in strictly whole-language instruction (Juel, 1998; Rayner et al., 2001; T. A. Roberts & Meiring, 2006). Thus, many theorists urge that teachers strike a balance between whole-language activities and basic-skills exercises, and in fact this is what many teachers do (Biemiller, 1994; Rayner et al., 2001; Xue & Meisels, 2004).

• ***Keep in mind that some literacy skills transfer from one language to another.***
Even in an English-speaking country, reading instruction doesn't necessarily need to begin in English. For example, English language learners often learn to read more quickly and successfully when they are initially taught to read in their native language (Slavin & Cheung, 2005). As they gain proficiency in English and begin to tackle English reading materials, they readily apply some of the knowledge they've acquired in one language—phonological awareness, vocabulary, and so on—to the other language (Bialystok, McBride-Chang, & Luk, 2005; C. P. Proctor, August, Carlo, & Snow, 2006).

• ***Identify and address reading problems early.*** If children initially struggle with reading, they are apt to read as little as possible and thereby limit their opportunities for practice, improvement, and automatization of basic skills. As a result, the gap between them and their peers widens over time (Stanovich, 2000). To minimize the damage, then, children should make up any reading deficits early in the game, ideally with explicit training in basic skills in first grade or even earlier. Children with early reading difficulties benefit from deliberate and intensive training in letter recognition, phonological awareness, word identification, and comprehension strategies (e.g., Ehri et al., 2007; Elbro & Petersen, 2004; Morris, Tyner, & Perney, 2000; W. Schneider, Roth, & Ennemoser, 2000; Vadasy, Sanders, & Peyton, 2006).

• ***Use high-interest works of fiction and nonfiction.*** Children and adolescents read more energetically and persistently, use more sophisticated metacognitive strategies, and remember more content when they are interested in what they are reading (R. C. Anderson, Shirey, Wilson, & Fielding, 1987; J. T. Guthrie et al., 1998, 2004). For example, in the "Literacy: Late Adolescence" video in MyEducationLab, 14-year-old Alicia describes the importance of being able to choose what she reads:

> I really don't like it when the reading is required. I can't read books if they're required. I just avoid reading them because they don't seem very interesting. And even after you read them, even though they might be interesting, they're not as interesting as if you picked them up by yourself.

As much as possible, then, teachers, parents, and other adults should choose reading materials that are likely to be relevant to young people's own lives and concerns, and they should give youngsters some choices about what to read.

• ***Conduct group discussions about stories and novels.*** Children and adolescents often construct meaning more effectively when they discuss what they read with peers. For instance, adults can form "book clubs" in which children lead small groups of peers in discussions about specific books (Alvermann, Young, Green, & Wisenbaker, 1999; McMahon, 1992; Rief & Heimburge, 2007). They can hold "grand conversations" about a particular work of literature, asking youngsters to share their responses to questions with no single right answers—perhaps questions related to interpretations or critiques of various aspects of a text (Eeds & Wells, 1989; E. H. Hiebert & Raphael, 1996). By tossing around possible interpretations of what they are reading, children often model effective reading and listening comprehension strategies for one another (R. C. Anderson et al., 2001).

• ***Have children use a variety of media to capture their interpretations of what they read.*** Group discussions are hardly the only mechanisms for fostering the interpretation of literature. Children might also perform skits to illustrate stories, write personal letters

MyEducationLab

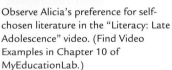

Observe Alicia's preference for self-chosen literature in the "Literacy: Late Adolescence" video. (Find Video Examples in Chapter 10 of MyEducationLab.)

We Wear the Mask
by Paul Laurence Dunbar

We wear the mask that grins and lies,
It hides our cheeks and shades our eyes,–
This debt we pay to human guile;
With torn and bleeding hearts we smile,
And mouth with myriad subtleties.

Why should the world be overwise,
In counting all our tears and sighs?
Nay, let them only see us, while
We wear the mask.

We smile, but, O great Christ, our cries
To thee from tortured souls arise.
We sing, but oh the clay is vile
Beneath our feet, and long the mile;
But let the world dream otherwise,
We wear the mask!

Figure 10-2

Interpreting poetry through art. Jeff's brightly colored painting is the cheerful face ("mask") that its African American owner presents in public. The black face is the flip side of the mask, as viewed by the person wearing it. Depicted in the holes of the mask are a lynching (left eye); a whipping (right eye); an African American woman and a white baby (nostrils), reflecting white owners' rape of slaves; and a slave ship with someone being thrown overboard (mouth).

that one character in a story might send to another character, or create works of art that illustrate the setting or characters of a novel or the underlying meaning of a poem. Figure 10-2 shows how 16-year-old Jeff illustrated Paul Laurence Dunbar's poem "We Wear the Mask" as an assignment for his American literature class.

- **_Encourage reading outside of school._** Reading beyond school walls—for instance, reading during the summer months—probably accounts for a significant portion of young people's growth in reading (D. P. Hayes & Grether, 1983; Stanovich, 2000). Providing books that children can take home to read or reread (perhaps accompanied by audiotapes) encourages outside reading and can significantly enhance reading comprehension skills (Koskinen et al., 2000). Visits to the local library can also encourage outside reading. In fact, when planning a library visit, teachers might extend an invitation for parents to accompany the group. In some cases such a visit may be the first time parents have ever been to a library (Heath, 1983).

Writing Development

Children begin attempting to write long before they reach school age, especially if they often see people around them writing. By 18 months of age—sometimes even earlier—many toddlers can hold a pencil or crayon and scribble enthusiastically (McLane & McNamee, 1990; Winner, 2006). Children's early efforts with pencil and paper are largely exploratory, reflecting experimentation with different kinds of marks on paper and other surfaces.

With the increasing motor coordination they acquire during the preschool years, children become better able to control their hand movements and can produce recognizable shapes. By age 4, their writing is clearly different from drawing (Graham & Weintraub, 1996; Sulzby, 1986). For instance, it may consist of wavy lines or connected loops that loosely resemble adults' cursive writing. Children's early writing—or more accurately, _pseudowriting_—often reveals considerable knowledge about written language, as the following exercise, "Pseudowriting Samples," illustrates.

MyEducationLab

Observe 16-month-old Corwin's early attempt at scribbling in the "Literacy: Infancy" video. (Find Video Examples in Chapter 10 of MyEducationLab.)

Interpreting Children's Artifacts and Reflections

Pseudowriting Samples

Three preschoolers created the artifacts you see here. After being asked to do some writing, 3½-year-old Cooper created the artifact on the left, saying that the slanted vertical strokes and curved horizontal line in the bottom left-hand corner were "*D*s" and "*R*," respectively. Four-year-old

Tommy wrote the "letter" in the middle and told his teacher it said, "Dear Mommy, from Tommy." Five-year-old Kathleen created the piece on the right without explaining its meaning. As you look at the artifacts, identify aspects of written language that each child has mastered.

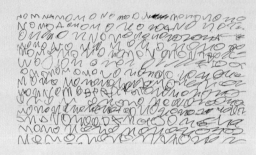

Cooper understands that writing involves making marks on paper and includes particular alphabet letters. The older two children have also learned that writing consistently proceeds horizontally across the page. (If we were to watch them writing, we could determine whether they also know that, in English, writing proceeds from left to right and from the top of the page to the bottom.) Tommy has apparently seen enough examples of cursive writing to know that letters are sometimes connected to one another. Kathleen's writing more closely resembles printing than cursive writing and includes actual letters. The letters *M*, *N*, and *O* are most common, but on closer inspection, you can also find *A, B, D, U,* and *V.*

By the time children are age 5, they frequently incorporate letters and letter-like forms in their pseudowriting (Graham & Weintraub, 1996). Some preschoolers don't yet realize that writing must take a particular form to have meaning, however, and even those who do are often unable to distinguish between true writing and meaningless marks on a page. For instance, children may scribble something and ask an adult, "What did I write?" (McLane & McNamee, 1990).

True writing is, of course, much more than simply putting letter-like forms on paper. To become skillful writers, growing children must not only master handwriting and spelling but also learn conventions of capitalization and punctuation, discover how to communicate thoughts clearly, and metacognitively regulate the entire writing effort. Unless some of these skills and processes are automatized, virtually any writing task exceeds the limits of a typical child's working memory capacity (e.g., Graham, 2006b).

Handwriting

During the elementary school years, children's handwriting gradually becomes smaller, smoother, and more regular (Graham & Weintraub, 1996). Little if any improvement in handwriting occurs after elementary school, and for some youngsters handwriting quality actually declines during adolescence (Graham & Weintraub, 1996). Some legibility may be lost because adolescents write more quickly than younger children. In fact, rapid, automatized handwriting (or, as an alternative, automatized keyboarding) is an important factor in effective writing (Berninger, 2004; Graham, Harris, & Fink, 2000; D. Jones & Christensen, 1999).

Spelling

As you might guess, phonological awareness is as important in spelling as it is in reading (P. Bryant, Nunes, & Aidinis, 1999; Holm, Farrier, & Dodd, 2007; Lennox & Siegel, 1998). Benjamin Jones showed phonological awareness when, as a 4-year-old, he captured both the "juh" and "mm" sounds in *gym* to spell "JEM."

Children learn the correct spellings of a few words (such as their names) almost as soon as they learn how to write letters of the alphabet. But in their early writing they tend to engage in considerable guesswork about how words are spelled, creating **invented spellings** that correctly capture certain sounds but may only vaguely resemble actual words (Treiman, 1998). Consider the invented spellings in this kindergartner's creation entitled "My Garden" (note that "HWS" is *house*):

THIS IS A HWS

THE SUN

WL SHIN

ND MI

GRDN

WL GRO (Hemphill & Snow, 1996, p. 192)

As children develop greater phonological awareness, their spellings increasingly represent most or all of the phonemes they hear (Gentry, 1982; Hemphill & Snow, 1996). Sometime around first or second grade, they also begin to incorporate common letter patterns (e.g., *-ight*, *-ound*, and *-ing* in English) into their spelling (P. Bryant et al., 1999; Critten, Pine, & Steffler, 2007; Nation & Hulme, 1998). All along, of course, they are learning more and more *correct* spellings, and eventually they automatize many of these spellings, retrieving them quickly and easily as they write (Rittle-Johnson & Siegler, 1999).

Syntax and Grammar

As children grow older, they use longer sentences and more varied sentence structures in their writing. By the time they are 12 or 13 years old, the syntactic structures they use in written work are considerably more complex than those they use in speech. With age, too, comes increasing automatization of punctuation and capitalization rules (Byrnes, 1996; Gillam & Johnston, 1992; Nippold, Ward-Lonergan, & Fanning, 2005; Ravid & Zilberbuch, 2003).

Composition Skills

When preschool children engage in early writing activities at home, they often do so with a particular purpose in mind, such as labeling a possession or writing a letter to a grandparent. Only when children enter kindergarten or first grade do most of them begin to write for writing's sake. Children's earliest compositions are usually narratives, such as recollections of personal experiences or short, fictional stories (Hemphill & Snow, 1996). Expository writing (e.g., research reports, persuasive essays) arrives on the scene considerably later (R. E. Owens, 2008), possibly because teachers typically don't ask for such writing until the upper elementary grades.

The nature and quality of children's and adolescents' compositions change in many ways throughout the elementary and secondary school years, as reflected in the following trends:

- ***Children develop their topics in greater depth as they grow older.*** When children of various ages are asked to write about a particular topic, older ones tend to include more ideas than younger ones do (Donovan, 1999; Scardamalia & Bereiter, 1986). Such growth continues throughout the school years. For instance, when writing persuasive essays, high school students include more arguments than elementary and middle school students do, and 12th graders include more arguments than 9th graders (Knudson, 1992; McCann, 1989).

- ***Children increasingly take their audience into account when they write.*** In our discussion of language development in the preceding chapter, we mentioned that children become increasingly able to adapt their speech to the characteristics of their listeners. The same is true for writing: With age and experience, children become better able to envision the audience to whom they are writing and tailor their text accordingly (Graham, 2006b; Knudson, 1992; Perfetti & McCutchen, 1987).

- ***With age comes a growing ability to write a cohesive composition.*** In the elementary grades, children use few if any devices to tie their compositions together. For

invented spelling
A child's early, self-constructed word spelling, which may reflect only some of the word's phonemes.

We became a country by way of common sense. The inhabitants on American soil thought it rather silly and ridiculus to be loyal to, follow rules and pay taxes to a ruler who has never seen where they live. King George III had never set foot (as far as I know) on American soil, but he got taxes and other things from those who lived here. When America decied to unit and dishonnor past laws and rules, England got angry. There was a war. When we won, drew up rules, and accepted states America was born.

In a more poetic sense, we became a country because of who lived here and what they did. They actions of heros, heroines, leaders, followers and everyday people made America famous, an ideal place to live. The different cultures and lifestyles made America unique and unlike any other place in the world. If you think about it, it's like visiting the worlds at Epcot in Florida. You can go from country to country without leaving home.

Figure 10-3

In her account of how the United States became a country, an eighth grader tries to help the reader understand what she is saying—an approach known as *knowledge transforming*. (We've kept her spelling errors intact.)

instance, they may write a story by beginning with "Once upon a time," listing a sequence of events that lead only loosely to one another, and then ending with "They lived happily ever after" (McLane & McNamee, 1990). Their nonfiction, too, may be little more than a list of facts or events. Older children, and especially adolescents, are more capable of analyzing and synthesizing their thoughts as they write, and so they compose more cohesive, integrated texts (McCutchen, 1987; R. E. Owens, 2008; Spivey, 1997).

• *Especially in adolescence, a knowledge-telling approach gradually evolves into a knowledge-transforming approach.* Young writers often compose a narrative or essay simply by writing down ideas in the order in which the ideas come to mind. Such an approach is known as **knowledge telling** (Bereiter & Scardamalia, 1987; Graham, Harris, & Olinghouse, 2007; McCutchen, 1996). But with age, experience, greater automatization of basic writing skills, and an increasing ability to take the characteristics of potential readers into account, some adolescents (and a few younger children as well) begin to think of writing as a process of helping potential readers *understand* what they're saying. This approach, known as **knowledge transforming,** is illustrated by an eighth grader's response to the question *How did the United States become a country?*, shown in Figure 10-3.

Metacognition in Writing

Good writers think about a topic ahead of time and carefully plan how they are going to write about it. They also critically evaluate their work, looking not only for grammatical and spelling errors but also for omissions, ambiguities, logical flaws, and contradictions (Graham, 2006b). Such editing skills emerge slowly and are incomplete even by the end of adolescence, in large part because youngsters' metacognitive capabilities are still developing. Children and adolescents alike have considerable difficulty identifying problems in their own writing, particularly those related to clarity and cohesiveness (Beal, 1996; Berninger, Fuller, & Whitaker, 1996; Fitzgerald, 1987). Because they have trouble reading their own writing as another person might read it, they are apt to think they are expressing themselves more clearly than they really are (Bartlett, 1982; Beal, 1996). As a result, they often don't revise their work unless a teacher or other adult specifically urges them to do so. When they *do* rewrite, they tend to make only small, superficial changes (Beal, 1996; C. A. Cameron, Hunt, & Linton, 1996; Francis & McCutchen, 1994). More critical self-evaluation and self-editing, if it develops at all, is apt to come later, perhaps in college writing classes.

The Developmental Trends table "Writing at Different Age Levels" identifies changes in writing seen during infancy and the preschool, elementary school, and secondary school years.

Diversity in Writing Development

As is true for reading development, writing development tends to be correlated with general intelligence. Some children who are gifted exhibit extraordinary writing talent. In contrast, most children with general intellectual disabilities (e.g., mental retardation) and some children with specific learning disabilities have problems in handwriting, spelling, and expressing themselves coherently on paper (J. M. Fletcher, Lyon, Fuchs, & Barnes, 2007; Turnbull et al., 2007).

Children with writing disabilities typically focus their writing efforts more on addressing mechanical issues (spelling, grammar, etc.) than on communicating clearly (Graham, Schwartz, & MacArthur, 1993). The quality of their writing improves considerably when the mechanical aspects of writing are minimized (e.g., when they can dictate their stories and other compositions) and when they are given specific steps to follow as they write (Hallenbeck, 1996; MacArthur & Graham, 1987; Sawyer, Graham, & Harris, 1992).

knowledge telling
Writing down ideas in whatever order they come to mind, with little regard for communicating the ideas effectively.

knowledge transforming
Writing about ideas in such a way as to intentionally help the reader understand them.

Writing at Different Age Levels

Age	What You Might Observe	Diversity	Implications
Infancy (Birth–2 Years)	· Development of eye–hand coordination, including the *pincer grasp*, through which infants use thumb and forefinger to pick up and hold objects · Appearance of scribbling at 18 to 24 months · Interest in mimicking "writing"; experimentation with writing implements	· Individual differences appear in the development of fine motor skills. · Infants can imitate only what they see, so those who never see anyone writing are unlikely to mimic writing or understand that some objects are used for writing.	· Allow toddlers to manipulate small objects that do not present choking hazards. · Have a variety of tools available for supervised scribbling and coloring (e.g., fat crayons or washable, nontoxic markers). · Tape writing paper to the table or floor to permit easier writing.
Early Childhood (2–6 Years)	· Increasing muscular control in writing and drawing · Pseudowriting (e.g., wavy lines, connected loops) in preschool play activities · Ability to write own name (perhaps at age 4) · Ability to write most letters of the alphabet (at age 4 or later) · Invented spellings (at ages 5 to 6)	· Some cultures place greater emphasis on writing than others. · Some children have little exposure to written materials at home and so have less knowledge of letters. · Children with visual impairments have less awareness of print conventions (left-to-right progression, use of punctuation, etc.).	· Make writing implements (pencils, markers, paper) easily accessible. · Give children opportunities to write their names and a few other meaningful words. · Have children act out stories they have orally composed.
Middle Childhood (6–10 Years)	· Gradual increase in smoothness of handwriting; gradual decrease in handwriting size · Increasing use of letter-sound relationships and common letter patterns when spelling words · Predominance of narratives in writing · Difficulty identifying problems (especially problems of clarity) in own writing	· Better readers tend to be better writers, presumably because general language ability provides a foundation for both reading and writing. · Children with deficits in phonological awareness have a more difficult time learning to spell. · Girls show higher achievement in writing and spelling beginning in the elementary years. · Children with dyslexia often have poor handwriting skills.	· Engage children in authentic writing activities (e.g., writing letters to relatives, creating a newsletter). · Provide regular practice in spelling, grammar, and punctuation (often within authentic activities). · Explore various ways in which particular phonemes and phoneme combinations are spelled in the English language. · Introduce expository forms of writing (e.g., descriptions, lab reports). · Build opportunities for editing into the schedule; provide criteria with which children can self-evaluate and revise their writing.
Early Adolescence (10–14 Years)	· Automatized spelling of most common words · Increasing use of expository forms of writing · Use of longer and more complex syntactic structures · Tendency not to edit and revise very much unless strongly encouraged to do so	· Some older children and adolescents (e.g., those with learning disabilities) may have exceptional difficulty with spelling and sentence structure. · Some adolescents write often in their spare time (e.g., keeping diaries, writing notes to friends), whereas others write only when required to do so at school.	· Provide continuing instruction in spelling, punctuation, and grammar. · Introduce persuasive and argumentative forms of writing. · Suggest a specific audience for whom to write. · Give feedback on first drafts, including guidance on how to improve clarity and cohesiveness. · Encourage adolescents to use local dialects in creative writing projects.
Late Adolescence (14–18 Years)	· Ability to write about a particular topic in depth · More organized and cohesive essays · Increasing tendency to knowledge-transform rather than knowledge-tell · More revisions than at younger ages, but with a focus on superficial rather than substantive problems	· Individuals with learning disabilities may focus largely on mechanics (spelling, use of correct grammar, etc.) while writing, perhaps because such skills are not yet automatized. · Individuals from some cultural backgrounds (e.g., those from some East Asian countries) may be reluctant to put their thoughts on paper unless they are certain that their thinking is correct.	· Assign and scaffold lengthy writing projects. · Teach specific strategies for organizing and synthesizing ideas. · Show examples of effective writing (e.g., writing that illustrates knowledge transforming). · For teens who have language-based learning disabilities, downplay the importance of correct spelling and grammar when evaluating written work; teach strategies for overcoming or compensating for weaknesses.

Sources: Beal, 1996; Berninger et al., 1996; Byrnes, 1996; Cameron et al., 1996; Dickinson et al., 1993; Dien, 1998; J. M. Fletcher, 2007; Gentry, 1982; Glaser & Brunstein, 2007; Graham, 2006b; Graham et al., 2007; Graham & Perin, 2007; Graham & Weintraub, 1996; Halpern, 2006; M. Harris & Hatano, 1999; Hedges & Nowell, 1995; Hemphill & Snow, 1996; Kellogg, 1967; MacArthur & Graham, 1987; McLane & McNamee, 1990; R. E. Owens, 2008; Rittle-Johnson & Siegler, 1999; Robin, Berthier, & Clifton, 1996; Rochat & Bullinger, 1994; Rochat & Goubet, 1995; Shanahan & Tierney, 1990; Smitherman, 1994; Spivey, 1997; Trawick-Smith, 2003; Yaden & Templeton, 1986.

Figure 10-4

Once infants are old enough to sit up on their own, they can begin to explore the properties of paper and paint, as 5-month-old Lauryn did in this early finger painting. Such activities should be closely supervised, of course, and only nontoxic substances used.

MyEducationLab

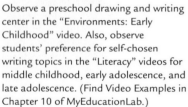

Observe a preschool drawing and writing center in the "Environments: Early Childhood" video. Also, observe students' preference for self-chosen writing topics in the "Literacy" videos for middle childhood, early adolescence, and late adolescence. (Find Video Examples in Chapter 10 of MyEducationLab.)

Group differences in writing. Gender differences in writing are often found: Girls tend to write and spell somewhat better than boys (Halpern, 2006; Weaver-Hightower, 2003). Girls are also more confident than boys about their writing abilities, even when no differences in the actual writing performance of the two groups exist (Pajares & Valiante, 1999).

Researchers have observed a few cultural differences that are apt to influence children's writing development. Some cultural groups rely more on other forms of visual representation than on traditional paper-pencil writing. For instance, the Yup'ik peoples of northern Canada frequently engage in *storyknifing*, in which they carve symbols and pictures in the mud while simultaneously telling tales about the family's or community's history (deMarrais, Nelson, & Baker, 1994). And those cultures that do rely heavily on writing may vary considerably in their writing practices. For instance, Vietnamese children are often reluctant to commit their ideas to paper unless they're confident that their ideas are correct and will not be misinterpreted (Dien, 1998).

Promoting Writing Development

As we have seen, writing skills continue to develop over the course of childhood and adolescence and, often, in adulthood as well. Accordingly, promoting writing development must be a long-term effort (Graham, 2006b). Psychologists and experienced educators have offered several suggestions for facilitating children's and adolescents' writing development.

• ***Provide tools for drawing and writing as soon as children are old enough to use them.*** Quite early in life, children can begin to explore—and so discover what they can do with—drawing, writing, and painting tools (e.g., see Figure 10-4). As fine motor skills, cognitive abilities, and knowledge of written symbols continue to improve during the preschool years, children will become increasingly able to produce recognizable shapes and letters.

• ***Present authentic writing tasks, and offer choices about writing topics.*** Youngsters write more frequently, and in a more organized and communicative (e.g., knowledge-transforming) manner, when they can write for a "real" audience (not just for their teacher) and when they're interested in their topic (Benton, 1997; Graham, 2006b; McCourt, 2005). For example, when one high school English teacher noticed that several very capable students weren't completing assigned writing tasks, he began asking students to write about their personal experiences and share their work with others on the Internet. The students suddenly began writing regularly, presumably because they could write for a real audience and could now choose what they wrote about (Garner, 1998).

In some instances teachers might ask parents or other family members to coauthor students' essays or short books, perhaps about family histories, favorite songs, or "Words of Advice from Our Parents" (McCaleb, 1994, p. 175). These compositions might also include drawings or family photographs. Such joint writing efforts between students and their families often lead to improved school–home communication and may be especially useful as a way of showing appreciation of children's diverse cultural backgrounds (McCaleb, 1994).

• ***Scaffold children's writing efforts.*** Such scaffolding can take a variety of forms, including the following:

- Ask children with limited writing skills to dictate rather than write their stories.
- Ask children to set specific goals for their writing, and help them organize their thoughts before beginning to write.
- Help children brainstorm ideas for communicating effectively (e.g., by using examples, analogies, and similes; see Figure 10-5).
- Provide an explicit structure for children to follow as they write (e.g., for a persuasive essay, ask students to include a main argument, supporting arguments, and rebuttals to possible counterarguments).
- Suggest that children initially focus on communicating clearly and postpone attention to writing mechanics (e.g., spelling, punctuation) until later drafts.
- Provide specific questions that children should ask themselves as they critique their writing (e.g., "Are the ideas logically organized?").

- Ask children to collaborate on writing projects, or to read and respond to one another's work.
- Encourage use of word processing programs.
  (Benton, 1997; Glaser & Brunstein, 2007; Graham et al., 2007; Graham & Perin, 2007; K. R. Harris & Graham, 1992; McLane & McNamee, 1990; Page-Voth & Graham, 1999; Sitko, 1998; Sperling, 1996)

- ***Include writing assignments in all areas of the curriculum.*** Writing shouldn't be a skill that only elementary teachers and secondary English teachers teach. In fact, writing takes different forms in different disciplines. Writing fiction is very different from writing a science lab report, which in turn is very different from writing an analysis of historical documents. Ideally, all teachers should teach writing to some degree. Particularly at the secondary level, they should teach the writing skills specific to their own academic disciplines (De La Paz, 2005; Newell, Koukis, & Boster, 2007; Sperling, 1996).

Mathematics Development

Mathematics is actually a cluster of domains—arithmetic, algebra, geometry, statistics, and so on—that use somewhat different methods for representing and solving quantitative problems. Much of our focus here will be on the development of knowledge and skills that are central to all of these domains, including counting, basic concepts and procedures, and metacognition.

Number Sense and Counting

By 5 or 6 months of age, infants have some awareness of quantity. Although they certainly aren't counting at this age, they do seem to notice the difference between a set of two objects and a set of three objects, as well as the difference between a set of 16 dots and a set of 32 dots (Canfield & Smith, 1996; Wynn, 1995; Xu & Spelke, 2000). As they approach their first birthday, they also show some understanding of *more* versus *less*. For example, 11-month-olds notice the difference between sequences of pictures that reflect increases versus decreases in quantity (Brannon, 2002).

Except for small groupings (e.g., sets of two or three objects), infants' awareness of quantity is fairly imprecise. The ability to count may be necessary to distinguish between similar quantities—say, between sets of seven versus eight objects (Geary, 2006; Lipton & Spelke, 2005; Siegler & Robinson, 1982). Many children in Western cultures begin counting before their third birthday, and many 3- and 4-year-olds can correctly count to 10 (Geary, 2006; H. P. Ginsburg et al., 2006). Five-year-olds can often count far beyond 10 (perhaps to 50), although they may get confused about the order of such numbers as 70, 80, and 90 (Fuson & Hall, 1983). As children work with two- and three-digit written numbers in the elementary grades, they increasingly master the correct sequence of numbers well into the hundreds and beyond (Case & Okamoto, 1996).

When children first begin to count, they don't necessarily do so in a way that accurately determines amount (Geary, 2006; Wynn, 1990). For example, they may say two successive numbers (e.g., ". . . three, four . . .") while pointing to a single object and so count it twice. Or, instead, they may point to two successive objects while saying only one number. But by the time they are 4 or 5, most children have mastered several basic principles of counting, including the following:

- *One-one principle.* Each object in the set being counted must be assigned one and only one number word. In other words, you say "one" while pointing to one object, "two" while pointing to another object, and so on until every object has been counted exactly once.
- *Cardinal principle.* The last number word counted indicates the number of objects in the set. In other words, if you count up to five when counting objects, then there are five objects in the set.
- *Order-irrelevance principle.* A set of objects has the same number regardless of the order in which individual objects are counted. (Gallistel & Gelman, 1992; R. Gelman & Gallistel, 1978; Griffin, Case, & Capodilupo, 1995)

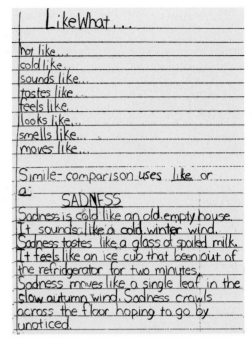

Figure 10-5

After her class brainstorms the kinds of similes a writer might use, 11-year-old Charlotte practices using similes in a description of sadness.

Initially children apply these principles primarily to small number sets (e.g., of 10 objects or fewer), but within a few years they can apply the principles to larger sets as well. As they do so, their ability to recognize that quantity stays the same regardless of changes in arrangement also improves (Geary, 2006). This ability reflects the *conservation of number* of which we spoke in Chapter 6.

Mathematical Concepts and Principles

In addition to building on a basic understanding of numbers, mathematical reasoning requires an understanding of many other concepts and principles. An especially critical one in the early elementary grades is the *part–whole principle*, the idea that any single number can be broken into two or more smaller numbers (e.g., 7 can be broken into 1, 2, and 4) and that any two or more numbers can be combined to form a larger number. This principle is probably central to children's understanding of addition and subtraction (Baroody, Tiilikainen, & Tai, 2006; Sophian & Vong, 1995).

Another important concept in mathematical reasoning is the idea of *proportion*, as reflected in fractions, ratios, and decimals. As you should recall from Chapter 6, Piaget suggested that children become capable of proportional reasoning when they enter the formal operations stage, sometime around age 11 or 12. But in fact, proportional reasoning emerges very gradually over the course of childhood and adolescence. As early as 6 months of age, infants show some intuitive awareness of different proportions—for instance, by habituating to visual displays reflecting a 2-to-1 ratio between two kinds of objects but then showing renewed interest when a 4-to-1 ratio is presented (McCrink & Wynn, 2007). By the early elementary grades children can understand simple, specific fractions (e.g., ½, ⅓) if they can relate these fractions to everyday objects (Empson, 1999; Van Dooren et al., 2005). Yet they are apt to continue to struggle with more complex fractions and other proportions until well into adolescence (Byrnes, 1996; Geary, 2006; Van Dooren et al., 2005). Part of the problem seems to be that they misapply their knowledge of whole numbers (Ni & Zhou, 2005). For example, because 4 is greater than 3, they are apt to conclude that ¼ is greater than ⅓. And because 256 is greater than 7, they are apt to think that 0.256 must be greater than 0.7.

Middle school and high school math classes increasingly focus on abstract concepts, such as *pi* (π), *irrational number*, and *variable*. Mathematical principles, such as *the product of two negative numbers is a positive number* and *the angles of a triangle always have a total of 180°*, also become increasingly abstract. Because such concepts and principles tend to be far removed from the concrete realities with which children and adolescents are familiar, formal instruction about them is usually necessary (Byrnes, 1996; De Corte et al., 1996; Geary, 1994).

Basic Arithmetic Operations

Two of the most basic mathematical operations are, of course, addition and subtraction. Infants seem to have a preliminary understanding of these processes well before their first birthday (McCrink & Wynn, 2004; Wynn, 1992). For example, imagine that two Mickey Mouse dolls are placed on a table in front of you. An experimenter lowers a screen to block your view of the dolls, and then you watch the experimenter take one of the dolls from behind the screen and put it away. You assume that only one doll remains on the table, but as the screen is raised, you still see *two* dolls there. Even 5-month-olds seem to be surprised by this outcome, indicating an awareness that something isn't as it should be.

By age 2½ or 3, children clearly understand that adding objects to a set increases quantity and subtracting objects from a set decreases quantity (J. Huttenlocher, Jordan, & Levine, 1994). By age 3 or 4, many begin to apply their knowledge of counting to simple addition and subtraction problems, typically using procedures they develop on their own (Bermejo, 1996; H. P. Ginsburg et al., 2006; Siegler & Jenkins, 1989). One early strategy is to use fingers to represent the objects in question. Consider the problem *If I have 2 apples and you give me 3 more apples, how many apples do I have altogether?* A child might put up two fingers and then three more fingers and count all the fingers to reach the solution, "5 apples." Somewhat later, children may begin to use a *min* strategy, in which they start with the larger of the two numbers (for the apple problem, they would start with 3) and then add on, one by one, the smaller number (e.g., counting "three apples . . . then four, five . . . five apples altogether") (Siegler & Jenkins, 1989). They might do something similar for subtraction, starting with the original number of objects and then counting down the number of objects removed: "Five . . . then four, three . . . three apples left." Still later, of course, children learn and retrieve many basic addition and subtraction facts (e.g., $2 + 3 = 5$, $5 - 3 = 2$) that allow them to by-pass the more cumbersome counting strategies.

By the early elementary years, children use a variety of strategies for solving simple addition and subtraction problems, including physically counting objects, counting on fingers, and retrieving addition and subtraction facts from memory. As they get older, they increasingly rely on memory and depend less on fingers and other objects (Ashcraft, 1982; Siegler & Jenkins, 1989). The changing frequency of various addition strategies over time reflects the *overlapping waves* idea presented in Chapter 7 (e.g., see Figure 7-8 on p. 249).

In North America, formal instruction in multiplication usually begins in second or third grade. Once again, children typically learn and use a mixture of strategies (Cooney & Ladd, 1992; Geary, 2006). When working with small numbers, they may simply use addition (e.g., solving "$3 \times 3 = ?$" by adding $3 + 3$ and then adding another 3 to the sum). Sometimes they count by twos, fives, or some other number (e.g., solving "$5 \times 4 = ?$" by counting "five, ten, fifteen, twenty"). Sometimes they apply certain rules, such as *anything times zero is zero* or *anything times 1 is itself*. Gradually, retrieval of basic multiplication facts replaces such strategies (Cooney, Swanson, & Ladd, 1988). Children often encounter simple division problems in the preschool years (e.g., when they must share food or toys with others), and even some 3-year-olds may use counting to divide quantities somewhat equitably (K. Miller, 1989). With formal instruction, children become more efficient and precise. As they tackle division problems, children often rely on their knowledge of other arithmetic facts, especially multiplication facts (e.g., if $5 \times 4 = 20$, then $20 \div 5 = 4$) (Geary, 1994).

When children encounter arithmetic problems involving two-digit or larger numbers, and especially when the problems involve "carrying" or "borrowing" across columns, they must also master the concept of *place value*. This idea that digits reflect different quantities depending on the column (whether they are in the ones column, tens column, and so on) is a fairly abstract one that many children have trouble with in the elementary grades (Fuson & Kwon, 1992; Geary, 2006). And if children don't understand place value, they are apt to make errors when they tackle problems that require carrying or borrowing (Geary, 1994). As examples, consider the addition and subtraction problem solutions presented in the following exercise, "Arithmetic Errors."

Long before receiving formal instruction in addition at school, young children often develop addition and multiplication strategies on their own by building on their finger-counting skills.

Interpreting Children's Artifacts and Reflections

Arithmetic Errors

For each of these problems, a child has correctly retrieved basic math facts but arrived at an incorrect solution. Identify the inappropriate strategy the child has used in each case.

$$\begin{array}{r} 26 \\ +47 \\ \hline 613 \end{array} \qquad \begin{array}{r} 603 \\ -305 \\ \hline 208 \end{array}$$

The child who solved the addition problem on the left simply put the sums of $6 + 7$ (13) and $2 + 4$ (6) side by side at the bottom. The child who solved the subtraction problem on the right apparently knew that borrowing was necessary to perform the subtraction in the ones column. Finding only a zero in the tens column, she instead borrowed "10" from the hundreds column. Thus, she subtracted $13 - 5$ in the ones column and $5 - 3$ in the hundreds column. Such mistakes are less common when children not only know *how* to carry and borrow but also know *why* carrying and borrowing make sense.

A possible central conceptual structure for number. Neo-Piagetian theorist Robbie Case and his colleagues (Case & Mueller, 2001; Case & Okamoto, 1996; Case et al., 1993; Griffin, Case, & Siegler, 1994) have suggested that during the preschool and elementary school years, children gradually develop a *central conceptual structure* that integrates much of what they know about numbers, counting, addition, subtraction, and place value.[3] In Case's view, 4-year-olds understand the difference between "a little" and "a lot" and recognize that adding objects leads to more of them and subtracting objects leads to fewer of them. Such knowledge might take the form depicted in the top half of Figure 10-6. Furthermore, many 4-year-olds can accurately count a small set of objects and conclude that the last number they count equals the total number of objects in the set (the cardinal principle). This process is depicted in the bottom half of Figure 10-6. Thus 4-year-olds can visually compare a group of 5 objects with a group of 6 objects and tell you that the latter group contains more objects, and they may also count accurately to either 5 or 6. Yet they cannot answer a question such as "Which is more, 5 or 6?" because the question involves knowledge of *both* more-versus-less and counting. It appears that they have not yet integrated their two understandings of number into a single conceptual framework.

By the time children are 6 years old, they can easily answer simple "Which is more?" questions. Case proposed that at the age of 6, the two structures in Figure 10-6 have become integrated into the more comprehensive structure depicted in Figure 10-7. As illustrated in the figure, children's knowledge and reasoning about numbers now include several key elements:

- Children understand and can say the verbal numbers "one," "two," "three," and so on.
- They recognize the written numerals 1, 2, 3, and so on.
- They have a systematic process for counting objects: They say each successive number as they touch each successive object in a group. Eventually, children count by mentally "tagging" (rather than physically touching) each object.

Figure 10-6

Hypothetical numerical structures at age 4.
From "The Role of Central Conceptual Structures in the Development of Children's Thought" by R. Case, Y. Okamoto, in collaboration with S. Griffin, A. McKeough, C. Bleiker, B. Henderson, & K. M. Stephenson, 1996, *Monographs of the Society for Research in Child Development*, 61(1, Serial No. 246), p. 6. Copyright 1996 by the Society for Research in Child Development. Adapted with permission from the Society for Research in Child Development.

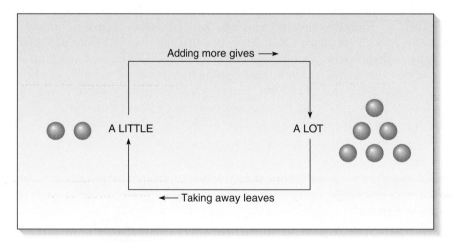

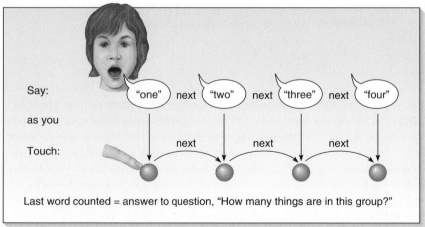

[3]See Chapter 6 for a more general discussion of *central conceptual structures* in neo-Piagetian theory.

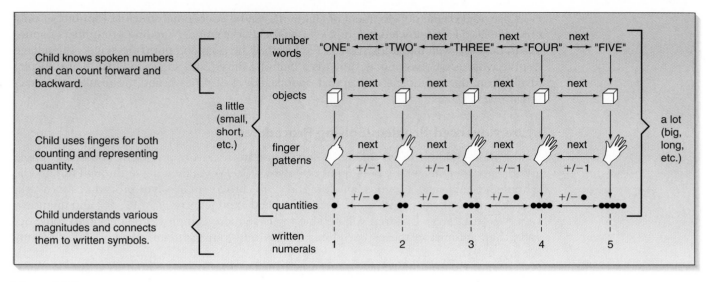

Figure 10-7

Hypothetical central conceptual structure at age 6.

Source: From "Differentiation, Integration, and Covariance Mapping as Fundamental Processes in Cognitive and Neurological Growth" by R. Case & M. P. Mueller, 2001, *Mechanisms of Cognitive Development: Behavioral and Neural Perspectives* (J. L. McClelland & R. S. Siegler, Eds.), p. 201. Mahwah, NJ: Erlbaum. Adapted with permission from Lawrence Erlbaum Associates.

- They also use their fingers for representing small quantities (e.g., 3 fingers equals 3 objects). Their use of fingers for both counting objects and representing quantities may be a key means through which they integrate the two processes into a single conceptual structure.
- They equate movement toward higher numbers with such concepts as "a lot," "more," and "bigger." Similarly, they equate movement toward lower numbers with such concepts as "a little," "less," and "smaller."
- They understand that movement from one number to the next is equivalent to either adding one unit to the set or subtracting one unit from it, depending on the direction of movement.
- They realize that any change in one dimension (e.g., from 3 to 4) must be accompanied by an equivalent change along other dimensions (e.g., from "three" to "four" and from ••• to ••••).

In essence, the more comprehensive conceptual structure at age 6 forms a mental "number line" that children can use to facilitate their understanding and execution of such processes as addition, subtraction, and comparisons of quantities.

At age 8, Case proposed, children have sufficiently mastered this central conceptual structure that they can begin using two number lines simultaneously to solve mathematical problems. For instance, they can now answer such questions as "Which number is bigger, 32 or 28?" and "Which number is closer to 25, 21 or 18?" Such questions require them to compare digits in both the ones column and tens column, with each comparison taking place along a separate number line. In addition, 8-year-olds presumably have a better understanding of operations that require transformations across columns, such as "carrying 1" to the tens column during addition or "borrowing 1" from the tens column during subtraction. Finally, at about age 10, children become capable of generalizing the relationships of two number lines to the entire number system. They now understand how the various columns (ones, tens, hundreds, etc.) relate to one another and can expertly move back and forth among the columns. They can also treat the answers to mathematical problems as mental entities in and of themselves and so can answer such questions as "Which number is bigger, the difference between 6 and 9 or the difference between 8 and 3?"

Case tracked the development of children's central conceptual structure for number only until age 10. He acknowledged, however, that children's understanding of numbers continues to develop well into adolescence. For instance, he pointed out that teenagers often have trouble with questions such as "What is a half of a third?" and suggested that their difficulty results from an incomplete conceptual understanding of division and the results (e.g., fractions) that it yields.

More Advanced Problem-Solving Procedures

By the time children reach middle school, most are relatively proficient in solving simple arithmetic problems with whole numbers (Byrnes, 1996). As they move through the middle school and high school grades, much of the math curriculum involves procedures for working with proportions, negative numbers, roots, and exponents (e.g., $\sqrt{18}$, 4^3), and unknown variables (e.g., x, y). Children will be able to tackle more complex problems if, to some degree, they automatize these procedures so that they can use them quickly and efficiently (Geary, 1994).

Ideally, children must also *make sense of* these procedures, rather than simply learning to apply them in a rote, meaningless fashion. In other words, children's understanding of mathematical procedures should be closely tied to their understanding of mathematical concepts and principles, in much the same way that their understanding of addition and subtraction is closely connected to their understanding of numbers and counting (Geary, 1994; Hecht, Close, & Santisi, 2003; Rittle-Johnson, Siegler, & Alibali, 2001). In the "Intrinsic Motivation: Early Adolescence" video in MyEducationLab, 12-year-old Claudia reveals such sense making: "You can explain it all." When children can*not* make sense of mathematical procedures—perhaps because they haven't yet mastered the abstract concepts on which the procedures are based or perhaps because no one has shown them why certain manipulations are mathematically logical—they are apt to use the procedures incorrectly and have trouble applying them to real-world problems (Byrnes, 1996; Geary, 2006).

Metacognition in Mathematics

Not only should children understand what they're doing when they tackle mathematical problems, but they should also plan, monitor, and evaluate their problem-solving efforts. Such metacognitive oversight might involve setting goals for a problem-solving task, monitoring the effectiveness of various problem-solving strategies, and carefully scrutinizing a final solution to determine whether it's a logical one (Cardelle-Elawar, 1992; L. S. Fuchs et al., 2003; H. P. Ginsburg et al., 2006). Only a child who metacognitively reflects on his or her problem-solving efforts will recognize that a sum of 613 is *not* a reasonable answer to the problem 26 + 47.

Many elementary and secondary school students do not actively reflect on what they're doing as they solve mathematical problems (Carr & Biddlecomb, 1998; Roditi & Steinberg, 2007). Furthermore, even in the high school grades, students are apt to have fairly naive epistemological beliefs about the nature of mathematics and mathematical problem solving.[4] The following misconceptions about math are common:

- Mathematics is a collection of meaningless procedures that must simply be memorized and recalled as needed.
- Math problems always have one and only one right answer.
- There is only one right way to solve any particular math problem.
- A person will either solve a problem within a few minutes or else not solve it at all. (De Corte, Op't Eynde, & Verschaffel, 2002; Muis, 2004; Schoenfeld, 1988, 1992)

Such beliefs are often counterproductive when youngsters encounter unusual and complex problems for which they have no ready-made, prescribed procedures. Yet some teachers seem to encourage these beliefs, perhaps by teaching math facts and problem-solving procedures as things to be memorized rather than truly understood (Muis, 2004; J. C. Turner et al., 1998).

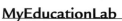

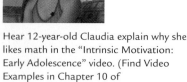

MyEducationLab

Hear 12-year-old Claudia explain why she likes math in the "Intrinsic Motivation: Early Adolescence" video. (Find Video Examples in Chapter 10 of MyEducationLab.)

---

[4]See Chapter 7 for a more general discussion of epistemological beliefs.

The Developmental Trends table "Mathematics at Different Age Levels" characterizes some of the mathematical knowledge and abilities commonly seen in infants, children, and adolescents.

Diversity in Mathematics Development

Virtually all children around the globe have a general awareness that objects and substances can vary in quantity and amount (Geary, 2006). But youngsters differ considerably in the extent to which they master mathematical concepts and procedures. Some children have learning disabilities that impede their ability to understand number concepts, automatize math facts, and solve simple math problems quickly—disabilities that in extreme form are known as **dyscalculia** (N. C. Jordan, Hanich, & Kaplan, 2003; A. J. Wilson & Dehaene,

dyscalculia
Inability to master basic numerical concepts and operations in a developmentally typical time frame despite normal instruction.

Developmental Trends

Mathematics at Different Age Levels

Age	What You Might Observe	Diversity	Implications
Infancy (Birth–2 Years)	· Some awareness that adding or subtracting something affects quantity (appearing at around 5 months) · Some ability to discriminate among different proportions (by 6 months) · Discrimination between sequences that show increases versus decreases in amount	· Some toddlers have familiarity with small-number words (e.g., *two*, *three*), usually because their parents often use the words in parent–child interactions. · Children with visual impairments may have fewer opportunities to make more-versus-less comparisons.	· Use small-number words (e.g., *two*, *three*) when talking with infants and toddlers if doing so makes sense within the context of everyday activities. · Provide age-appropriate toys that encourage children to focus on size or quantity (e.g., nesting cups, stacking blocks).
Early Childhood (2–6 Years)	· Clear understanding that adding objects results in an increase and removing objects results in a decrease (by age 2½ or 3) · Appearance of counting (at around age 3) · Increasing ability to count correctly (perhaps to 50 by age 5) · Emergence of self-constructed addition and subtraction strategies (e.g., counting objects or using fingers) · Some familiarity with division in everyday sharing tasks	· Chinese children learn to count at a younger age than children whose native language is English. The more "transparent" nature of Chinese number words is thought to be at least partly responsible for this difference. · At age 5, Chinese- and Japanese-speaking children have a better grasp of place value than English-speaking children (apparently because Chinese and Japanese number words make place value quite obvious). · On average, children from middle-income families begin counting at an earlier age than children from low-income families.	· Occasionally ask mathematical questions (e.g., "How many are there?" "Where's the triangle?") · In storybook reading sessions, occasionally read books that engage children in counting activities (e.g., *The Icky Bug Counting Book*, Pallotta & Masiello, 1992). · Use concrete manipulatives to help children learn counting and simple addition and subtraction.
Middle Childhood (6–10 Years)	· Increasing ability to count correctly into the hundreds and beyond · Acquisition of more efficient addition and subtraction strategies, including retrieval of number facts · Increasing mastery of multiplication and division strategies · Growing understanding of place value and its relevance to carrying and borrowing · Some understanding of simple fractions · Increasing ability to solve word problems	· Children vary considerably in the strategies they use at any given age level. For instance, some 8-year-olds have most basic math facts automatized, whereas others continue to rely heavily on fingers. · Children who speak certain Asian languages (e.g., Mandarin Chinese) master multidigit addition and subtraction at an earlier age than English-speaking children. · Some children begin to dislike math, typically because they have consistently been frustrated in their efforts to understand and master it.	· Help children understand the logic underlying basic mathematical procedures (e.g., show the relevance of the concept of *place value* to carrying and borrowing). · Provide frequent practice in basic arithmetic as a way of promoting automaticity. · Introduce number lines as a way of helping children understand how numbers relate to one another. · Have low-achieving fourth and fifth graders tutor first and second graders in basic math skills.

continued

Developmental Trends (continued)

Age	What You Might Observe	Diversity	Implications
Early Adolescence (10–14 Years)	· Increasing ability to understand abstract concepts (e.g., π, *variable*) · Increasing ability to understand and work with proportions · Naive epistemological beliefs about math (e.g., that it involves memorizing procedures without necessarily understanding them)	· Young adolescents who have not yet automatized basic arithmetic facts are apt to struggle when they encounter challenging math concepts and procedures. · Some adolescents tend to misapply their knowledge about whole numbers to problems involving fractions and decimals. · Young adolescents vary widely in their ability to understand and apply the abstract mathematical concepts that are typically introduced in the middle school grades.	· Conduct small-group activities in which students must devise and explain multiple approaches to solving a single problem. · Teach metacognitive strategies for solving problems (e.g., identify the goal to be achieved, break a complex problem into smaller steps, consider whether an obtained solution is reasonable).
Late Adolescence (14–18 Years)	· Increasing facility in working with abstract concepts and principles (e.g., *unknowns* such as *x* and *y*) · Difficulty translating word problems into algebraic expressions · Tendency for many teens to memorize and mindlessly apply mathematical procedures, rather than to reflect on and understand the procedures	· Individual differences in mathematical abilities increase in the high school years, due both to course "tracking" based on students' existing abilities and to the prevalence of elective math courses in high school. · On average, girls have less confidence about their ability to do math even when they achieve at the same level as boys.	· Ask teenagers to apply their math skills to real-life contexts and problems. · Allow teens to use calculators when performing complex mathematical operations (this strategy allows them to devote most of their working memory capacity to the overall problem-solving effort). · Minimize competition for grades and other rewards for math achievement (this strategy is especially important for girls).

Sources: Brannon, 2002; Byrne & Shavelson, 1986; Byrnes, 1996; Cardelle-Elawar, 1992; Carr & Biddlecomb, 1998; Case & Okamoto, 1996; Chipman, 2005; Cooney & Ladd, 1992; Cooney et al., 1988; Davenport et al., 1998; De Corte et al., 1996, 2002; Eccles, Freedman-Doan, Frome, Jacobs, & Yoon, 2000; Empson, 1999; Fuson & Hall, 1983; Fuson & Kwon, 1992; Gallistel & Gelman, 1992; Geary, 1994, 2006; H. P. Ginsburg et al., 2006; Greeno, Collins, & Resnick, 1996; Griffin et al., 1995; C. S. Ho & Fuson, 1998; J. Huttenlocher et al., 1994; Inglis & Biemiller, 1997; Klibanoff, Levine, Huttenlocher, Vasilyeva, & Hedges, 2006; McCrink & Wynn, 2004, 2007; K. Miller, 1989; K. F. Miller, Smith, Zhu, & Zhang, 1995; Schoenfeld, 1988, 1992; Siegler & Jenkins, 1989; Van Dooren et al., 2005; Wynn, 1990, 1992, 1995; Xu & Spelke, 2000.

2007). Others have little exposure to numbers and counting at home and so come to school lacking knowledge in these fundamental areas (Griffin et al., 1995). In addition, researchers often find gender and ethnic differences in mathematics development.

Gender differences.   Average differences between boys and girls in mathematics development tend to be fairly small, with some researchers finding a slight advantage for one gender or the other depending on the age-group and task in question (A. M. Gallagher & Kaufman, 2005). However, boys show greater *variability* in math. More boys than girls have very high math ability, especially in high school, and more boys than girls have significant disabilities in math (Halpern et al., 2007; Hedges & Nowell, 1995; Penner, 2003).

The prevalence of adolescent males at the upper end of the math-ability continuum may be partly due to biology, and in particular to sex-related hormones (e.g., estrogen, testosterone) that differentially affect brain development before and after puberty (Halpern, 1992; Hegarty & Kozhevnikov, 1999; Lippa, 2002). One area in which these hormones may come into play is in the development of **visual-spatial ability,** the ability to imagine and mentally manipulate two- and three-dimensional figures (see Figure 10-8). On average, boys and men perform better than girls and women on measures of visual-spatial ability, which appears to give them an advantage in certain kinds of mathematical tasks (A. M. Gallagher & Kaufman, 2005; Halpern et al., 2007).

Yet environmental factors also play a role in gender differences in mathematics (A. M. Gallagher & Kaufman, 2005). For example, in many Western societies, mathematics has historically been viewed as a "male" domain more suitable for boys than for girls. Some parents and (unfortunately) some teachers pick up on this stereotype and more actively expect and encourage boys (rather than girls) to learn math (Bleeker & Jacobs, 2004; Halpern et al., 2007; Tiedemann, 2000). Perhaps partly as a result of such differential expectations and encour-

visual-spatial ability
Ability to imagine and mentally manipulate two- and three-dimensional figures.

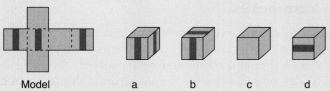

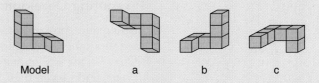

1. When the figure on the left is folded along the dotted lines, it becomes a three-dimensional object. Which one or more of the four figures on the right represent(s) how this object might appear from different perspectives?

Model   a   b   c   d

2. When the object on the left is rotated in three-dimensional space, it can look like one or more of the objects on the right. Which one(s)?

Model   a   b   c

Answer Key:
(1) Depending on the direction from which it is viewed, the object might look like either *a* or *d*.
(2) The object can be rotated to look like either *a* or *c*.

Figure 10-8

Examples of tasks requiring visual-spatial ability.
Source: Tasks modeled, respectively, after G. K. Bennett, Seashore, & Wesman, 1982; Shepard & Metzler, 1971.

agement, boys tend to express greater confidence about their math ability than girls do, even when actual achievement levels for both genders have been similar (Eccles et al., 2000; Vermeer, Boekaerts, & Seegers, 2000; Wigfield, Byrnes, & Eccles, 2006).

Ethnic and cultural differences.   One consistent research finding is that Asian and Asian American students achieve at higher levels in math than students from other North American cultural groups (J. Wang & Lin, 2005). Adult behaviors may partly account for this difference. Asian teachers provide more thorough explanations of mathematical concepts, focus classroom discussions more on making sense of problem-solving procedures, and assign more math homework than North American teachers do (Huntsinger, Jose, Larson, Krieg, & Shaligram, 2000; M. Perry, 2000; Schleppenbach, Perry, Miller, Sims, & Fang, 2007). And Asian parents are more likely to believe that math achievement comes from hard work (rather than being a "natural" talent) and so insist that children spend a good deal of their time at home on schoolwork (C. S. Ho & Fuson, 1998; Okagaki, 2001; J. Wang & Lin, 2005).

Many theorists speculate that the nature of number words in Asian languages (Chinese, Japanese, Korean) may also facilitate Asian children's mathematical development (Fuson & Kwon, 1992; K. F. Miller et al., 1995; Miura, Okamoto, Vlahovic-Stetic, Kim, & Han, 1999). In these languages the structure of the base-10 number system is clearly reflected in number words. For example, the word for 11 is literally "ten-one," the word for 12 is "ten-two," and the word for 21 is "two-ten-one." Furthermore, words for fractions reflect what a fraction *is.* For example, the word for ¼ is literally "of four parts, one." In contrast, English has many number words (e.g., *eleven, twelve, thirteen, twenty, thirty, one-half, one-fourth*) that "hide" the base-10 structure somewhat and don't reveal much information about the nature of proportions.

One thing that Asian languages and European languages have in common is a system for identifying virtually any possible number. But numbers and mathematics are cultural creations that are not universally shared across cultures. For example, the Pirahã society in a remote region of Brazil has three words for number that, roughly translated, mean *one or a very small amount, two or a slightly larger amount,* and *many.* People in Pirahã culture have difficulty distinguishing among similar quantities greater than three or four, apparently because counting has little usefulness in their day-to-day activities (Gordon, 2004).

The Oksapmin culture in Papua New Guinea provides another example of the culture-specific nature of mathematics. In the early 1980s Oksapmin people identified the numbers 1 through 29 using different body parts, progressing from the right hand and arm (1 was the right thumb) to the neck and head (14 was the nose) and then down the left arm (29 was the inside of the left forearm) (Saxe, 1981). Although such a system was certainly sufficient in Oksapmin culture at the time, it did not lend itself well to multiplication, division, or more complex mathematical procedures. As the Oksapmin people have become increasingly exposed to other cultures through schooling, trade, and the use of money, they have gained proficiency in using the base-10 number system and the more complex arithmetic operations it enables (Saxe & Esmonde, 2005).

Promoting Development in Mathematics

Mathematics probably causes more confusion and frustration for children and adolescents than any other academic subject. The hierarchical nature of the discipline may be partly to blame. To the extent that youngsters don't completely master math concepts and procedures at one grade level, they lack necessary prerequisites for learning math successfully in later grades. Yet developmental factors also figure prominently. When children have difficulty with abstract ideas, proportional thinking, and other developmental acquisitions on which mathematics depends, they are apt to struggle with mathematical reasoning and problem solving.

Without doubt, the most important factor affecting mathematics development is formal education (e.g., Case & Okamoto, 1996; H. P. Ginsburg, Posner, & Russell, 1981; Rittle-Johnson, 2006). We offer the following suggestions for teachers who work with children and adolescents on mathematical concepts and tasks:

- ***Teach numbers and counting in preschool and the primary grades.*** A basic understanding of numbers and counting forms the foundation for virtually every aspect of mathematics. When young children haven't acquired these basics at home, teachers can often make up the difference. Activities and games involving counting, comparing quantities, adding, and subtracting are apt to be beneficial (H. P. Ginsburg, Lee, & Boyd, 2008; Ramani & Siegler, 2008). For instance, regular practice in counting objects and comparing quantities (e.g., determining which of three groups of apples has the *most* apples) leads to improved performance not only in these tasks but in other quantitative tasks as well (Case & Okamoto, 1996; Griffin et al., 1995; Klibanoff et al., 2006).

- ***At all age levels, use manipulatives and visual displays to tie mathematical concepts and procedures to concrete reality.*** Concrete manipulatives (beans, blocks, Cuisinaire rods, toothpicks bundled in groups of 10 and 100, etc.) can often help children grasp the nature of addition, subtraction, place value, and fractions (Fujimura, 2001; Fuson & Briars, 1990; Greeno et al., 1996). Visual aids such as number lines and pictures of pizzas depicting various fractions can be helpful in the early elementary grades, and graphs and diagrams of geometric figures are useful for secondary students (Greeno et al., 1996; J. L. Schwartz, Yarushalmy, & Wilson, 1993). As noted in Chapter 6, children and adolescents alike benefit from concrete manipulatives and illustrations of abstract ideas.

- ***Encourage visual-spatial thinking.*** Although boys may have a biological advantage in visual-spatial thinking, structured experiences that *encourage* such thinking can help to reduce the gender gap (H. P. Ginsburg et al., 2008; Nuttall, Casey, & Pezaris, 2005; Sprafkin, Serbin, Denier, and Connor, 1983). In the preschool and early elementary grades, such experiences might involve building blocks, Legos, puzzles, simple graphs, and basic measurement tools. As children move into the middle elementary grades and beyond, visual-spatial tasks should also include ample work with complex graphs and three-dimensional geometry (H. P. Ginsburg et al., 2006; Nuttall et al., 2005; Sprafkin et al., 1983).

- ***As youngsters work on new and challenging mathematical problems, provide the physical and cognitive scaffolding they need to successfully solve the problems.*** Complex mathematical tasks and problems—those within a child's *zone of proximal development*—often put a strain on working memory and in other ways stretch children to their cognitive limits (Swanson, Jerman, & Zheng, 2008).[5] Fortunately, Western cultures have devised a variety of tools for easing the burden. For children in the early elementary grades, such tools may simply be pencil and paper for keeping track of quantities, calculations, and other information. Once children have mastered basic math facts and understand the logic behind arithmetic operations, they might use calculators or computers while working with large numbers or cumbersome data sets (Horowitz et al., 2005). Yet cognitive scaffolds are

---

[5]See Chapter 6 to refresh your memory about Vygotsky's concept of zone of proximal development.

valuable as well. For instance, a teacher might encourage students to brainstorm possible approaches to problems, model the use of new problem-solving strategies, and teach students various metacognitive strategies for monitoring and checking their progress (Calin-Jageman & Ratner, 2005; Rittle-Johnson & Koedinger, 2005; Roditi & Steinberg, 2007; Staples, 2007).

• ***Encourage children to invent, use, and defend their own strategies.*** As we've seen, young children often invent strategies (e.g., the *min* strategy) for adding and subtracting objects well before they have formal instruction in addition and subtraction. Rather than ignore strategies children have developed on their own, teachers should encourage those that seem to be effective. As children acquire more efficient strategies over time, they will gradually abandon their earlier ones (Geary, 1994; Siegler, 1989).

Also beneficial is specifically asking children to reflect on and explain in writing why they solved a problem as they did (Carr & Biddlecomb, 1998; Johanning, D'Agostino, Steele, & Shumow, 1999; Rittle-Johnson, 2006). As an example, Figure 10-9 shows 8-year-old Noah's explanation of how he solved the problem 354 − 298.

Strategy development doesn't have to be a solitary activity, however. Group discussions can often enhance children's mathematical understandings (Carr & Biddlecomb, 1998; Kline & Flowers, 1998; Lampert, Rittenhouse, & Crumbaugh, 1996). For instance, at the second-grade level, students might develop and justify their own strategies for adding two- and three-digit numbers (J. Hiebert & Wearne, 1996). At the high school level, they might work in groups to derive their own set of geometric theorems (Healy, 1993).

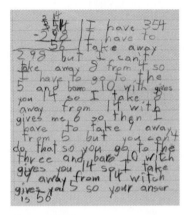

Figure 10-9

Noah's explanation of what he did when he solved the problem 354 − 298.

Science Development

As scientists observe physical and biological phenomena in nature, they use certain strategies (formulating and testing hypotheses, separating and controlling variables, etc.) to conduct systematic investigations, and they form theories to explain their findings. Development in science, then, involves both theory building and acquisition of scientific reasoning skills. It also involves advancements in epistemological beliefs about science.

Children's Theories About the Biological and Physical Worlds

In studying children's growing understandings of scientific phenomena, many developmental theorists take a *theory theory* approach, suggesting that children construct (rather than absorb) their knowledge and beliefs about physical and biological phenomena. Some theorists are also *nativists*, arguing that infants' brains are neurologically "preprogrammed" with some basic knowledge about their world, or at least with some preliminary dispositions to interpret events in certain ways.[6] For example, even young infants (i.e., those between 2 and 5 months old) seem to know that an object maintains its existence and shape as it moves, that two objects cannot occupy the same space at the same time, and that one object can influence another object only when the two come into contact (Baillargeon, 1994, 2004; Spelke, 1994). Researchers have not tested such understandings in newborns, however, partly because newborns' limited visual acuity would make it difficult to do so. Thus it is possible that young infants' early experiences, rather than biologically built-in preprogramming, are the source of their knowledge about physical objects.

One important step in early theory building is making a distinction between biological and nonbiological entities. By the time infants are 6 months old, most have some awareness that people and other animals move in ways that nonliving things do not (see Chapter 7). By age 3 or 4, children know that humans and other animals, but not nonliving objects, can move *themselves* and that living and nonliving entities "grow" in different ways (Jipson & Callanan, 2003; Massey & Gelman, 1988). At about age 4, children also realize that two living creatures in the same category, even if they look quite different, are apt to share many characteristics—for instance, that a blackbird has more in common with a flamingo (because both are birds) than it does with a bat (S. A. Gelman & Markman, 1986). By the middle elementary school years, children understand that both plants and animals are defined largely

[6]See Chapter 7 if you need a brief refresher about *theory theory* and *nativism*.

by their genetic heritage and internal makeup—for instance, that round, reddish fruits that come from pear trees must be pears rather than apples (again see Chapter 7).

Infants' early understandings of nonliving physical objects (e.g., the realization that two objects cannot occupy the same space at the same time) are consistent with classical principles of physics. As children get older and gain more experience with the physical world, they construct increasingly elaborate, but usually fairly concrete, theories about physical entities. Many school-age children view all physical phenomena either as actual substances (i.e., touchable "things" that have specific, although possibly changeable, locations) or as properties of those substances (Reiner, Slotta, Chi, & Resnick, 2000). This **substance schema** can be quite useful in explaining many everyday events (e.g., holding a ball, touching a hot stove). Yet children and adolescents tend to apply it inappropriately to such phenomena as light, heat, fire, and force, which in and of themselves have little or no substance (Reiner et al., 2000). For example, children are likely to think of *force* as something that a pitched ball "contains," rather than as the initial impetus for the ball's motion. And they are apt to think of *heat* as something that can "flow" from one object to another.

Another idea that children acquire quite early but eventually overapply is the concept of *gravity*. At 3 or 4 months of age, children have some understanding that objects fall down (never up) when there is nothing to support them (Baillargeon, 1994). This "downward" view of gravity works quite well on a small scale. But imagine the situation depicted in Figure 10-10. A rock is dropped at the equator, at the entrances to two tunnels that go through the earth. Tunnel A comes out at the equator on the opposite side of the earth. Tunnel B comes out at the South Pole. Into which tunnel will the rock fall? Many middle school students say that the rock will fall into Tunnel B, apparently thinking that gravity always pulls something "down." They respond in this way even if they have explicitly learned that gravity pulls objects toward the center of the earth (Pulos, 1997).

To some degree, children's not-quite-right theories undoubtedly reflect a limited ability to think about abstract ideas. Even though these theories don't always jibe with scientific explanations, they almost certainly reflect children's genuine desire to make sense of their experiences.

Scientific Reasoning Skills

As noted in Chapter 7, even in the first year of life children seem predisposed to identify cause-and-effect relationships in the world around them. But children's ability to think as scientists appears much later, and then only gradually. **Scientific reasoning** encompasses a number of cognitive processes, including planning an investigation, analyzing evidence, and drawing appropriate conclusions (Kuhn & Franklin, 2006). Taken together, such processes are often called the *scientific method*. Common to all of them is a conscious intention to acquire and evaluate new knowledge and explanations.

Planning and conducting a scientific investigation requires two abilities first introduced in Chapter 6: formulating hypotheses and then separating and controlling variables while testing those hypotheses. Such abilities emerge gradually over the course of middle childhood and adolescence. Formulating hypotheses depends on at least two things that change with age: (a) the ability to think about abstract and potentially contrary-to-fact ideas, and (b) a knowledge base that can help a person generate a *variety* of ideas. The ability to separate and control variables seems to depend partly on children's working memory capacity, which increases somewhat with age (Bullock & Ziegler, 1999). Elementary school children can often distinguish between experiments that do and do not control variables appropriately, yet they are apt to have trouble controlling variables in their *own* experiments—a task that requires them to keep track of several things simultaneously (Barchfeld, Sodian, Thoermer, & Bullock, 2005; Bullock & Ziegler, 1999; Metz, 2004).

Although adolescents are better able to separate and control variables than elementary school children, even they occasionally have difficulty doing so (Barchfeld et al., 2005; Kuhn et al., 1988). Furthermore, in their hypothesis testing, they tend to focus on and test hypotheses they think are correct and to ignore hypotheses that, in their minds, are *in*correct (Byrnes, 1996). Such *try-to-prove-what-I-already-believe* thinking reflects the *confirmation bias* we spoke of in Chapter 7.

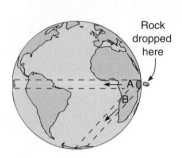

Figure 10-10

If a rock is dropped into a hole near the equator, into which of the two tunnels will it fall?

substance schema
General view of all physical phenomena as being either touchable substances or properties of those substances.

scientific reasoning
Cognitive processes central to conducting scientific research and interpreting findings appropriately.

Confirmation bias appears not only when adolescents test hypotheses but also when they analyze and interpret their data (Klaczynski, 2000; Kuhn et al., 1988; Schauble, 1990). In general, they tend to overlook results that conflict with their favorite hypotheses. And they often try to explain away unexpected results that they *cannot* ignore. For example, when students in a high school science lab observe results that contradict what they expected to happen, they might complain that "Our equipment isn't working right" or "I can never do science anyway" (Minstrell & Stimpson, 1996, p. 192). Even high school graduates and many college students are apt to think in such "unscientific" ways (Byrnes, 1996; Kuhn & Franklin, 2006).

Metacognition in Science

Ultimately, growing children must discover that science is, like other disciplines, a dynamic body of ideas that will continue to evolve over time as new data come in. They must also be able to reflect on and critically evaluate their own beliefs and theories. And, of course, they must be willing to change their views in the face of disconfirming evidence. Such understandings, abilities, and dispositions emerge only gradually over childhood and adolescence (Barchfeld et al., 2005; Elder, 2002; Kuhn & Pearsall, 2000). Giuliana, an eighth grader, reveals beliefs and attitudes about science that are fairly sophisticated for her age-group:

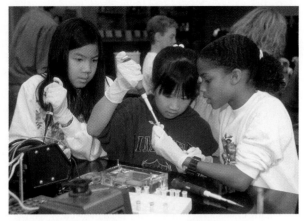

Although they are eager investigators, children and adolescents often have trouble evaluating the quality of their evidence.

> I think nothing is true. You can say about the Egyptians, for example, that once such and such was believed, but now there's another truth, we aren't sure of anything. We weren't there at the time of the Egyptians, and so we can only hypothesize about it. Historians rely on documents, studies, findings, but I really don't know how true it is what they say. We can say it's true now, but tomorrow another scientist may say "I've found another document that proves something else" and then we'll have two different things and we'll no longer know which is true and which is false. When the atom was discovered, it was considered the smallest particle, but now the quark's been discovered. What we believed before, now we don't believe anymore because the quark is smaller. Perhaps in fifty years' time an even smaller particle will turn up and then we'll be told that what we believed in before was false. It's really something to do with progress. (Mason, 2003, p. 223)

Youngsters' epistemological beliefs about the nature of science will undoubtedly affect the approaches they take (mentally) when they study science. For example, in the "Memory: Early Adolescence" video in MyEducationLab, 12-year-old Colin seems to view science largely as a collection of facts he needs to memorize. When asked what things are really hard to remember, he says this:

MyEducationLab

> I think long things like science and stuff where you have to remember a lot of stuff and stuff that really isn't . . . you really wouldn't want to remember it that much.

Students who believe that "knowing" science means understanding how various concepts and principles fit together and using those concepts and principles to explain everyday phenomena are going to study and learn more effectively than students who think that learning science means remembering isolated facts (M. C. Linn et al., 1996). And students who recognize that scientific theories will inevitably change over time are more likely to evaluate theories (including their own) with a critical eye (Bereiter, 1994; Kuhn, 1993, 2001a; M. C. Linn et al., 1996).

Observe Colin's epistemological beliefs about science in the "Memory: Early Adolescence" video. (Find Video Examples in Chapter 10 of MyEducationLab.)

The Developmental Trends table "Science at Different Age Levels" presents examples of scientific knowledge and reasoning you are apt to see in infancy, childhood, and adolescence.

Diversity in Science Development

For a variety of reasons, children and adolescents in any single age-group differ considerably in their science development. Youngsters with sensory impairments (e.g., blindness, hearing loss) may have fairly limited opportunities to observe certain scientific phenomena firsthand. For example, a child who is blind may be unaware that wood changes in size and color when it burns (M. B. Rowe, 1978). Another source of diversity is visual-spatial ability: Youngsters with strong visual-spatial skills should have an easier time imagining and understanding interrelationships

Science at Different Age Levels

Age	What You Might Observe	Diversity	Implications
Infancy (Birth–2 Years)	· Knowledge of a few basic principles of physics (e.g., two objects cannot occupy the same space at the same time) · Emerging awareness that humans and animals are fundamentally different from nonliving things · Increasing ability to infer cause-and-effect relationships	· Infants differ in the number and diversity of opportunities to explore interesting objects and surroundings. · Infants with sensory impairments (e.g., blindness, hearing loss) are more limited in the scientific phenomena they can observe.	· Put infants and toddlers in contexts in which they can safely explore and experiment with physical objects. · Let toddlers interact with small, gentle animals (e.g., rabbits, cocker spaniels) under your close supervision.
Early Childhood (2–6 Years)	· Increasing differentiation between living and nonliving things (e.g., they "grow" differently) · Increasing understanding that members of a biological category (e.g., *birds*) share many characteristics in common despite differences in appearance · Naive beliefs about the solar system (e.g., the earth is flat)	· Children in some cultures (e.g., Japanese children) are more likely to think of plants and nonliving objects as having "minds." · Children who grow up in inner-city environments may have little exposure to life cycles (e.g., calves being born, trees losing leaves in the fall and growing blossoms in the spring).	· Read simple nonfiction picture books that depict wild and domesticated animals. · Take children to zoos, farms, arboretums, and other sites where they can see a variety of animals and plants. · Talk with children about natural phenomena, pointing out the physical properties of objects (e.g., some objects float and others sink). · Engage children in simple hands-on investigations of natural phenomena.
Middle Childhood (6–10 Years)	· Intuitive understanding that biological entities are defined by their genetic heritage and internal makeup · Tendency to think of all physical phenomena as having physical and potentially touchable substance · Some ability to discriminate between valid and invalid tests of hypotheses	· Children differ considerably in their early exposure to scientific concepts (e.g., through family visits to natural history museums and access to age-appropriate science books). · Some children are apt to view supernatural forces (e.g., God, the devil, witchcraft) as being largely responsible for natural disasters or illness.	· Have children conduct simple experiments with familiar materials; for example, have them raise sunflowers with varying amounts of light and water. · Obtain computer programs that let students "explore" human anatomy or "dissect" small animals in a virtual "laboratory."
Early Adolescence (10–14 Years)	· Some ability to think abstractly about scientific phenomena and to separate and control variables · Formulation and testing of hypotheses influenced by existing beliefs (confirmation bias) · Some tendency to misapply scientific concepts (e.g., thinking that gravity pulls objects toward the South Pole)	· Especially in adolescence, boys tend to have more positive attitudes toward science than girls. Girls are more likely than boys to underestimate their science abilities. · Influences of religion on beliefs about natural phenomena (e.g., evolution) become especially noticeable in early adolescence.	· Have adolescents explore individual interests in science fair projects, scaffolding their efforts at forming hypotheses and controlling irrelevant variables. · Provide scientific explanations that are sufficiently concrete that young adolescents can understand and apply them.
Late Adolescence (14–18 Years)	· Increasing ability to understand abstract scientific concepts · Increasing ability to separate and control variables · Continuing confirmation bias in experimentation and interpretation of results · Increasing awareness that science is a dynamic and changing (rather than static) discipline	· On average, boys achieve at higher levels in science than girls, especially in the physical sciences; the gender gap in science achievement has decreased in recent years. · Boys are more likely than girls to aspire to careers in science. · Cultures that place high value on honoring authority figures tend to promote simplistic epistemological beliefs about science (e.g., a belief that scientific findings should not be questioned).	· Increasingly introduce abstract explanations for phenomena; for example, introduce the idea that heat results from molecules colliding at a certain rate. · To increase girls' interest and involvement in science, occasionally form same-gender groups in science labs and activities.

Sources: Baillargeon, 1994; Bandura et al., 2001; Barchfeld et al., 2005; Bullock & Ziegler, 1999; Cohen & Cashon, 2006; E. M. Evans, 2001; Flavell et al., 2002; S. A. Gelman & Markman, 1986; Halpern et al., 2007; Hatano & Inagaki, 1996; Jipson & Callanan, 2003; Keil, 1989; Klaczynski, 2000; Kuhn & Franklin, 2006; Leaper & Friedman, 2007; O. Lee, 1999; Lee-Pearce et al., 1998; Legare & Gelman, 2007; M. C. Linn & Muilenburg, 1996; Massey & Gelman, 1988; Metz, 2004; Nakazawa et al., 2001; Patrick et al., 2008; Pomerantz, Altermatt, & Saxon, 2002; Pulos, 1997; Qian & Pan, 2002; Reiner et al., 2000; M. B. Rowe, 1978; Schauble, 1990; Spelke, 1994; Tamburrini, 1982; Vosniadou, 1991; B. Y. White & Frederiksen, 1998; Wigfield et al., 1996.

among objects in space (L. Friedman, 1994; Halpern, 2006). For instance, children who can easily picture and manipulate objects in their minds can better grasp the idea that the moon revolves around the earth while the earth simultaneously revolves around the sun.

Gender differences. As is true for math, science has traditionally been regarded as a "male" domain (Eisenberg, Martin, & Fabes, 1996; Halpern et al., 2007). Perhaps for this reason, boys tend to like science more than girls do, and they are more likely than girls to aspire to careers in science (Bandura, Barbaranelli, Caprara, & Pastorelli, 2001). On average, girls get higher grades in science than boys do, but boys tend to come out slightly ahead on national science achievement tests, especially in the physical sciences (Halpern et al., 2007; Leaper & Friedman, 2007).

All-girl science classes with female teachers seem to enhance girls' achievement and aspirations in science (MacLean, Sasse, Keating, Stewart, & Miller, 1995; Shapka & Keating, 2003). Perhaps such classes convey the message that science is "for" females as much as it is for males. Of course, placing girls in a female-only environment is not the only way to inspire girls in science. Offering effective instruction, engaging activities, and ample encouragement about scientific careers are key elements of any science-friendly environment and may be especially important for girls (e.g., Burkam, Lee, & Smerdon, 1997; Patrick, Mantzicopoulos, & Samarapungavan, 2008).

Ethnic and cultural differences. Even if children do inherit some predispositions to interpret their natural environments in particular ways (as nativists suggest), their cultural environments shape many of their beliefs about the biological and physical worlds. For example, Japanese children are more likely than European American children to think of plants (e.g., a tree, a blade of grass) and certain nonliving objects as having some sort of "mind" that thinks (M. Cole & Hatano, 2007; Hatano & Inagaki, 1996). And cultural differences in schooling may influence youngsters' epistemological beliefs about the nature of science. For example, schools in China tend to encourage respect for authority figures and to downplay differences of opinion among experts. Possibly as a result, high school students in China are more likely than U.S. students to believe that science is simple rather than complex—that it involves discrete facts rather than interrelationships and unresolved issues (Qian & Pan, 2002).

Religion also comes into play when youngsters develop their theories about the world. For instance, in the elementary grades, some children are apt to think that supernatural forces (e.g., God, the devil, witchcraft) are largely responsible for illness or natural disasters (O. Lee, 1999; Legare & Gelman, 2007). And adolescents' acceptance or nonacceptance of Darwin's theory of evolution is closely connected to what their religion has taught them about how human beings and other living creatures came into being (E. M. Evans, 2001; Southerland & Sinatra, 2003).

Promoting Development in Science

In the first few years of life, children's science "education" is usually limited to informal experiences. At this point, perhaps the best strategy is simply to provide objects and experiences—building blocks, sand piles, field trips to farms and zoos, and so on—that help children acquire general knowledge on which more formal science instruction can later build.

Once children reach kindergarten or first grade, the curriculum typically includes some science topics. As we've seen, children's abstract and hypothetical reasoning capabilities and their ability to separate and control variables are fairly limited in the elementary grades. Thus, elementary school teachers tend to focus most science instruction on descriptions of natural phenomena rather than on explanations of why those phenomena occur (Byrnes, 1996). Yet even at the elementary level, it is probably counterproductive to portray science as primarily a collection of facts. By having students engage in simple scientific investigations almost from the very beginning of the science curriculum, teachers convey the message that science is an ongoing, dynamic process of unraveling the mysteries of our world (Kuhn, 2007).

Field trips to farms and zoos in the preschool and early elementary years can enrich children's knowledge about the animal kingdom.

At the middle school level, students' increasing ability to think about abstract ideas makes it possible to address some of the causal mechanisms that underlie natural phenomena. Even so, middle school teachers may not want to introduce ideas completely removed from students' everyday, concrete experiences (M. C. Linn et al., 1996; Reiner et al., 2000). For instance, when teaching eighth graders about heat, teachers may have better success if they talk about heat as something that "flows" from one object to another rather than as something that involves molecules moving and colliding with one another at a certain rate. Although the heat-flow model is, from a physical science perspective, not entirely accurate, students can effectively apply it to a wide variety of everyday situations—why a wooden spoon is safer than a metal one for stirring hot spaghetti sauce, why packing food in ice helps keep it cold, and so on (M. C. Linn & Muilenburg, 1996).

When students reach high school, they are more likely to have acquired the scientific knowledge and reasoning skills they need to begin thinking in truly abstract ways about natural phenomena (M. C. Linn et al., 1996). Nevertheless, teachers should continue to engage students in frequent hands-on science activities, not only through systematic laboratory experiments but also through informal, exploratory activities that relate scientific concepts and principles to everyday experiences. Secondary students in general, but especially females, are likely to achieve at higher levels when they have regular hands-on experiences with the phenomena they are studying (Burkam et al., 1997).

Several additional instructional strategies can be helpful for a wide variety of age groups:

Figure 10-11

In this pencil drawing, 9-year-old Corey depicts his perception of scientific "research" as something in which an adult tells him the steps to follow.

• *Engage students regularly in authentic scientific investigations.* Many school lab activities are little more than cookbook recipes: Students are given specific materials and instructions to follow step by step (see Figure 10-11). Such activities can certainly help make scientific phenomena more concrete for students. However, they are unlikely to encourage youngsters to engage in thinking processes (formulating and testing hypotheses, separating and controlling variables, and so on) that characterize true scientific reasoning (Keil & Silberstein, 1996; M. J. Padilla, 1991; J. Singer, Marx, Krajcik, & Chambers, 2000). So in addition, teachers should give students many opportunities to conduct investigations in which the procedures and outcomes are not necessarily predetermined. For instance, teachers might ask students to address such questions as "Does one fast-food restaurant provide more meat in a hamburger than others?" or "Is the local drinking water really safe to drink?" (M. J. Padilla, 1991; J. Singer et al., 2000).

Youngsters typically need some scaffolding for such activities, however. For instance, a teacher might do the following:

• Present situations in which only two or three variables need to be controlled.
• Ask students to identify several possible hypotheses about cause-and-effect relationships before beginning to experiment.
• Provide regular guidance, hints, and feedback regarding the need to control variables and evaluate observations objectively.
• Ask questions that encourage students to make predictions and critically analyze their observations (e.g., "What do you think will happen?" "What is your evidence?" "Do you see things that are inconsistent with what you predicted?").
(Byrnes, 1996; S. Carey, Evans, Honda, Jay, & Unger, 1989; Kuhn et al., 1988; Kuhn & Dean, 2005; Minstrell & Stimpson, 1996)

• *Provide age-appropriate explanations for physical and biological phenomena.* Although youngsters can discover a great deal through their own experimentation, they also need to learn the concepts, principles, and theories that scientists use to make sense of the world (Vygotsky, 1934/1986). Ideally, they should pull the things they learn into integrated, meaningful bodies of knowledge. Often teachers can make interrelationships concrete for students by presenting diagrams, flowcharts, or two- or three-dimensional models

(Glynn, Yeany, & Britton, 1991a; Schwarz & White, 2005). Also helpful is asking students themselves to organize what they're learning, as 9-year-old Trisha has done in her depiction of the water cycle in Figure 10-12.

• *Actively work to promote conceptual change.* Existing misconceptions probably interfere with children's and adolescents' development in science more than in any other academic discipline. Thanks to confirmation bias, youngsters are apt to seek out information that confirms, rather than contradicts, what they currently believe. Chapter 7 suggests several strategies for promoting conceptual change. Perhaps one of the most effective approaches is to give students opportunities to discuss competing perspectives within a classroom environment that communicates the message, "It's okay to make errors and change our minds" (Minstrell & Stimpson, 1996; C. L. Smith, 2007).

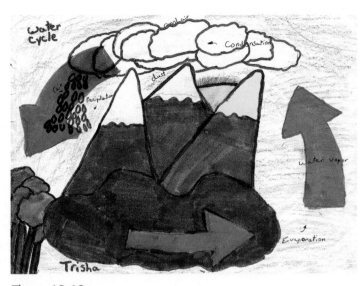

Figure 10-12

In this drawing of the water cycle, 9-year-old Trisha shows her understanding that various phenomena in nature are interrelated.

Development in Other Academic Domains

In their studies of children's development in academic subject areas, researchers have focused largely on reading, writing, mathematics, and science. Yet they have also learned a few things about children's development in history, geography, art, and music. We now look briefly at trends in each of these domains.

History

Children's first awareness of history typically involves their *own* history. Sometime between ages 2 and 4, children begin to construct an *autobiographical self:* They can recall past events in their own lives and begin to understand that they exist *in time*, with a past and a future as well as a present (see Chapter 12). As their improving language skills allow an increasing exchange of ideas with family members and playmates, they gradually expand their sense of history to include other people whom they know well.

Children's knowledge of history on a broader scale emerges largely as a result of formal instruction beginning in elementary school. In the elementary grades, children's understanding of history tends to be concrete and simplistic. For example, they may conceptualize the birth of the United States as resulting from a single, specific event (e.g., the Boston Tea Party) or as involving nothing more than constructing new buildings and towns (Ormrod, Jackson, Kirby, Davis, & Benson, 1999).

One source of difficulty for elementary school children is a limited ability to understand historical time. They might refer to events that happened "a long, long time ago" or "in the old days" but tell you that such events happened in 2005. And they tend to lump historical events into two general categories: those that happened very recently and those that happened many years ago. In Figure 10-13 we once again show you the first of four essays presented in the opening case study in Chapter 7. As a second grader, the essay's author obviously has little sense of how long a time span "2000 days" is. In the early grades, then, history instruction should probably focus on students' own personal histories and on events that have occurred locally and in the recent past (Byrnes, 1996).

At around age 10, children acquire some ability to put historical events in sequence and to attach them to particular time periods (Barton & Levstik, 1996). Accordingly, systematic history instruction usually begins in fourth or fifth grade. Yet when children first study the broader scope of history, they have little personal knowledge and experiences on which to build. They haven't lived in most of the time periods they study, nor have they seen most of the locations they learn about. What they *can* build on, however, is their knowledge of human beings. Children can better understand historical events when they discover that historical figures had particular goals, motives, and personalities—in other words, that people in history were,

MyEducationLab

Learn how children's understanding of historical time improves with age by completing an Understanding Research exercise in Chapter 10's Activities and Applications section in MyEducationLab.

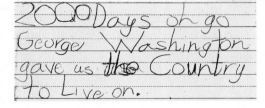

Figure 10-13

As shown in this response to the question *How did the United States become a country?*, second graders have only a limited ability to understand historical time.

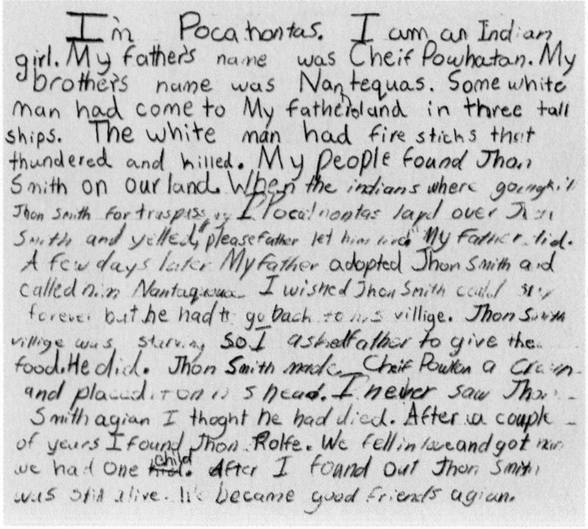

I'm Pocahontas. I am an Indian girl. My father's name was Cheif Powhatan. My brothers name was Nantequas. Some white man had come to My fatherland in three tall ships. The white man had fire sticks that thundered and killed. My people found Jhon Smith on our land. When the indians where going to kill Jhon Smith for traspassing I Pocahontas layd over Jhon Smith and yelled, please father let him live. My Father did. A few days later My Father adopted Jhon Smith and called him Nantaquaus. I wished Jhon Smith could stay forever but he had to go back to his village. Jhon Smith village was starving so I asked father to give them food. He did. Jhon Smith made Cheif Powhatan a crown and placed it on his head. I never saw Jhon Smith agian I thoght he had died. After a couple of years I found Jhon Rolfe. We fell in love and got married we had one child. After I found out Jhon Smith was still alive. We became good friends agian.

Figure 10-14

In this history assignment, 10-year-old Kaitlyn takes on the perspective of Pocahontas to describe events in the early 1600s.

in many respects, just ordinary folks (Brophy & VanSledright, 1997; Yeager et al., 1997). Figure 10-14 shows 10-year-old Kaitlyn's attempt to view events in the early 1600s as a Native American woman might have. Following are several additional strategies that can help children and adolescents gain a "human" understanding of history:

- Assign works of fiction that realistically depict people living in particular times and places.
- Role-play family discussions that focus on making decisions during critical times in history (e.g., deciding whether to send a teenage son off to war).
- Have "journalists" (two or three students) interview people (other students) who "participated" in various ways in a historical event. (Brophy & Alleman, 1996; Brophy & VanSledright, 1997)

Unfortunately, many history textbooks for elementary and secondary students describe historical events in a very one-sided, matter-of-fact way, communicating the message that "This is what happened" (Paxton, 1999; vanSledright & Limón, 2006; Wineburg, 1994). In reality, historians often don't know exactly how particular events unfolded. Instead, they construct a reasonable interpretation of events after looking at a variety of historical documents that provide varying perspectives of what transpired. The idea that history is often as much a matter of perspective and opinion as it is a matter of fact is a fairly abstract notion that students may not be able to fully comprehend until late adolescence (Byrnes, 1996; Seixas, 1996; Stahl & Shanahan, 2004). Even so, students can benefit from reading multiple accounts of events—including diaries, letters, newspaper articles, and so on—as early as fourth grade (Afflerbach, VanSledright, & Dromsky, 2003; Nokes, Dole, & Hacker, 2007; M. B. W. Wolfe & Goldman, 2005).

At its core, history is very much a socioculturally transmitted body of knowledge. Furthermore, different cultural groups are likely to put their own "spin" on historical events (Mosborg, 2002; Porat, 2004). For example, European American students tend to view U.S. history as being guided by principles of freedom and democracy, whereas African American students are more likely to view American history as being marked by racism and violation of human rights (T. Epstein, 2000). Such diverse impressions are almost certainly the result of how U.S. history has been explained both at home and at school. For instance, children's awareness of racism in American history depends to a considerable degree on the extent to which racist events and policies have been a focus of instruction in both textbooks and classroom lessons (J. M. Hughes, Bigler, & Levy, 2007; vanSledright & Limón, 2006).

Geography

The discipline of geography is concerned not only with where various natural features and cultural groups are located but also with why and how they got there. For instance, geographers study how rivers and mountain ranges end up where they do, why people are more likely to settle in some locations than in others, and how people in various locations make a living.

Unfortunately, many children and adolescents have an overly simplistic epistemological belief about geography as a discipline. Typically, they conceive of geography as being little more than the names and locations of various countries, capital cities, rivers, mountain ranges, and so on—perhaps, in part, because teachers often present geography this way (Bochenhauer, 1990; vanSledright & Limón, 2006). Even in the high school years, students rarely reflect on why various locations have the physical features they do or on how the economic and cultural practices of various social groups might be partly the result of their physical environment.

An essential cognitive tool in geography is, of course, the *map*. Central to geographical thinking is an understanding that maps depict the arrangement and characteristics of particular locations. By age 3 or 4, children have some ability to recognize relationships between simple graphics and the physical locations that the graphics represent (J. Huttenlocher et al., 1999; Peralta & Maita, 2007). During the next several years, children can increasingly use maps to identify locations in their immediate, familiar surroundings (Blades & Spencer, 1987; Davies & Uttal, 2007). However, their ability to use maps to navigate through *un*familiar territory remains fairly limited until adolescence at the earliest (Davies & Uttal, 2007; Liben, Kastens, & Stevenson, 2002).

When children in the early elementary grades look at larger-scale maps—perhaps those depicting a state or country—they tend to take what they see somewhat literally (Gardner, Torff, & Hatch, 1996; Liben & Downs, 1989b; Liben & Myers, 2007). For example, they may think that lines separating states and countries are actually painted on the earth or that an airport denoted by a picture of an airplane has only one plane. Young children also have trouble maintaining a sense of scale and proportion when interpreting maps. For instance, they might deny that a road could actually be a road because "it's not fat enough for two cars to go on" or insist that a mountain depicted on a three-dimensional relief map can't possibly be a mountain because "it's not high enough" (Liben & Downs, 1989b; Liben & Myers, 2007, p. 202). As children get older, and especially as they reach adolescence, they become more proficient in dealing with the symbolic and proportional nature of maps (Forbes et al., 1999; Liben & Myers, 2007).

Maps are a good example of the *cognitive tools* of which Vygotsky spoke (see Chapter 6). Accordingly, youngsters' facility with them depends in part on the sociocultural context in which they've been raised. Maps are commonplace in some cultures, nonexistent in others. Even in a "map-rich" society, children have varying degrees of experience with geography and maps. For instance, children whose families travel extensively tend to have greater appreciation of distance, more familiarity with diverse landscapes, and a better understanding of how maps are used (Liben & Myers, 2007; Trawick-Smith, 2003).

A major goal of any geography curriculum must be to foster an understanding of the symbolic nature of maps. Eventually youngsters must learn, too, that different maps are drawn to different scales, reflecting various proportions between graphic representation and reality (Liben & Downs, 1989b). One effective strategy is to ask children to create their *own* maps, perhaps of their neighborhood, town, or country (Enyedy, 2005; Forbes et al., 1999; Gregg & Leinhardt, 1994a). Teachers and other adults might also ask youngsters to look for patterns in what they see in maps and to speculate about why those patterns exist (Gregg & Leinhardt, 1994b; Liben & Downs, 1989a). For example, in the task presented in Figure 10-15, high school students must apply a basic geographic principle—that, historically, people who lived near large bodies of water had an easier time transporting goods to distant markets—in order to understand why Chicago had the prominence that it did. Ultimately, children and adolescents become more proficient geographers when they not only know *what is where* but also understand *why it is where it is.*

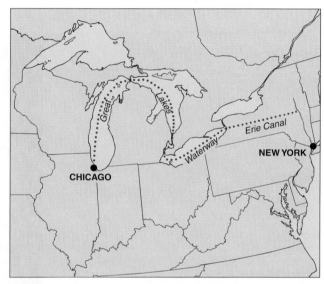

Why did Chicago become the major railroad center of the American Midwest in the middle of the 19th century?

Figure 10-15

By asking children to speculate about why things are located where they are, teachers can promote more sophisticated understandings of geography.

Art

As early as age 2, some children begin to represent their experiences on paper—for instance, by making a series of dots to mimic how an animal hops (J. Matthews, 1999; Winner, 2006). They also begin to experiment with geometric figures, especially lines and circles, as illustrated in Piece A in Figure 10-16. At age 3, their repertoire of shapes expands to include squares, rectangles, triangles, crosses, and Xs, and they soon begin combining such shapes to create pictures (Beaty, 1998; Golomb, 2004; Kellogg, 1967). Many of their early drawings are of people, which might initially consist of a circle (depicting either a head or a head plus body) with a few facial features (e.g., eyes, mouth) within it and four lines (two arms, two legs) extending from it. With age, preschoolers increasingly add features—perhaps hair, hands, fingers, and feet—to their human figures (see Piece B in Figure 10-16).

Sometime around age 4, children begin to combine drawings of several objects to create pictures of groups or nature scenes. Initially, they may scatter things haphazardly around the page, but eventually placement of objects on the page is somewhat consistent with everyday reality. For example, in the scene depicted in Piece C in Figure 10-16, grass appears at the bottom of the page, the tree appropriately grows up from the ground, and traditionally in-the-air things (bird, sun, clouds) are near the top. Notice how the sky (depicted by the blue at the very top) is restricted to a small space above everything else. The tendency to

Figure 10-16

Developmental progressions in children's art are clearly seen in these pieces by (A) Tina at age 2½, (B) Corey at age 5, (C) Corey at age 6, (D) Trisha at age 11, (E) Elizabeth at age 14, and (F) Joey at age 17.

(A)   (B)   (C)   (D)

(E)   (F)

depict sky as a separate entity at the top of the page is quite common in 5- and 6-year-olds (Golomb, 2004).

In the elementary grades, children become capable of producing a wide variety of shapes and contours, and their drawings and paintings become more detailed, realistic, and appropriately proportional (N. R. Smith et al., 1998; Winner, 2006). By the upper elementary grades, children represent depth in their drawings (Braine, Schauble, Kugelmass, & Winter, 1993). For example, in Piece D in Figure 10-16, 11-year-old Trisha has drawn the fence "behind" the house and barn, with the three hills "behind" one another and the fence. Notice how, in contrast to Piece C, the sky in Piece D fills up all of the unoccupied space.

Some children draw and paint very little once they reach adolescence, especially if art is not a regular part of the school curriculum, and so their artistic skills may progress very little beyond this point (S. Moran & Gardner, 2006; Winner, 2006). Those who continue to create art refine their abilities to show texture, depth, perspective, and spatial relationships (see Pieces E and F in Figure 10-16) (N. R. Smith et al., 1998; Willats, 1995). They may also try to convey mood and emotion by selectively using various shapes, hues, and intensities of color (N. R. Smith et al., 1998).

When a culture neither values nor encourages art, children's art skills evolve slowly if at all (Gordon, 2004; Trawick-Smith, 2003). But when drawing implements are readily available to children—as they are in many cultures—certain universals in artistic development appear in the preschool years (Case & Okamoto, 1996; Golomb, 2004; Kellogg, 1967). Young children worldwide draw their early "people" in much the same manner that 5-year-old Corey did in Piece B in Figure 10-16. Children from diverse industrialized cultures are also apt to draw houses as squares with smaller, internal squares depicting windows, doors, and perhaps chimneys (see Figure 10-17). And they begin to compose more complex pictures (such as that in Piece D in Figure 10-16) in the same sequence and at approximately the same ages regardless of their cultural background.

Other aspects of artistic development are more culture specific. For example, if children receive extensive instruction in artistic techniques, as many children do in Japan and China, their drawings are more elaborate, detailed, and true-to-life (Alland, 1983; Case & Okamoto, 1996). By the middle elementary grades, some children begin to mimic popular images in their local cultural environment, such as the drawings they see in comic books and children's magazines (B. Wilson, 1997; Winner, 2006).

Even with little instruction, however, some children appear to have a natural talent for art (Winner, 1996). For example, some children with autism spectrum disorders show exceptional proficiency and precision in their drawings at a very early age despite significant delays in their overall cognitive development (Treffert & Wallace, 2002). (As an example, look once again at young Nadia's drawings on p. 142 in Chapter 4.) One characteristic of autism we'll mention in Chapter 12—an unusual ability to focus on visual details—may very well be at the root of such talent. Children may be more inclined to capture the details in what they see when they have trouble *ignoring* those details (Grandin & Johnson, 2005).

Figure 10-17

Young children in a variety of industrialized cultures draw houses in much the same way that 4-year-old Kaitlyn did here.

Music

Human beings of all ages clearly enjoy music. For instance, 6-month-olds pay more attention to their mothers when Mother is singing (rather than talking) to them (Nakata & Trehub, 2004). Mother's lively songs help keep infants on an even keel, perking them up a bit if they seem low on energy but soothing them if they are overly aroused (Shenfield, Trehub, & Nakata, 2003). Even the way that most parents talk to their infants—a style known as *infant-directed speech*—has a singsongy quality to it, with considerable repetition and greater variation in pitch than is true in normal speech (see Chapter 9).

Just as young infants can hear subtle differences in spoken language that adults don't hear (again see Chapter 9), so, too, do they pick up on subtle changes in music that adults don't notice. For example, when a melody changes slightly (say, by a note or two within the same key), 8-month-olds are more likely than adults to notice the difference (Trainor & Trehub, 1992). But as youngsters grow older, and especially as they progress through the preschool and early elementary school years, they increasingly perceive patterns (melodies, keys, complex rhythms, etc.) rather than individual notes (Gromko & Poorman, 1998; Winner, 2006).

Children also gain considerable proficiency in singing during the early childhood years (Winner, 2006). At around age 2, they begin to repeat some of the song lyrics they hear. They soon add a rhythmic structure and up-and-down "melody" of sorts. By the time they are 5 or 6, most can sing a recognizable tune and keep it largely within the same key and meter. For most youngsters, further development in singing comes primarily from explicit voice training (Winner, 2006). Formal instruction is usually necessary for children to gain proficiency in playing a musical instrument as well (D. J. Elliott, 1995).

Another important aspect of musical development is **music literacy,** the ability to read and understand musical notation. As early as age 4, children can, when asked, invent ways to represent musical sounds with objects—for instance, using large, heavy objects to represent loud notes and smaller objects to represent softer notes (Gromko, 1996). At about the same age, they can also invent strategies for representing music on paper. For instance, they may make small circles or mountain "peaks" for high notes and make larger circles or "valleys" for lower pitches (Gromko, 1994, 1996, 1998). Standard musical notation is, of course,

music literacy
Ability to read and understand musical notation.

a cultural creation, and so children must be instructed in its interpretation. Youngsters' ability to read music can enhance their ability to hear and remember the subtle nuances of a musical piece (Gromko & Poorman, 1998).

Virtually all cultures have some form of music, and the types of music with which children grow up certainly affect their musical sensitivities and preferences (Hannon & Trehub, 2005; Werker & Tees, 1999; Winner, 2006). But within any single culture, children have varying abilities to hear and appreciate music. About 4 percent of children in any age-group have **amusia** (or tone deafness), an inability to detect the small changes in pitch that are common in melodies. Such youngsters show little or no improvement in their perception of musical tones despite instruction and practice, suggesting that the ability to hear music *as* music may have a biological basis (Gardner et al., 1996; Hyde & Peretz, 2004). In contrast, some children not only hear, but can also *remember,* subtle differences in pitch. Although most people can remember the relative pitches of notes in a melody, individuals with *absolute pitch* can also recall the *exact* pitch of a note they have repeatedly heard in, say, a popular song or soundtrack (Shellenberg & Trehub, 2003). Absolute pitch is more common in infants and preschoolers than in older children or adults, so possibly children lose this ability if everyday demands in their culture don't require it (Saffran & Griepentrog, 2001; Winner, 2006). For example, absolute pitch is more common in people who speak Asian languages such as Chinese and Vietnamese, in which spoken sounds have differing meanings depending on their pitch (D. Deutsch, Henthorn, & Dolson, 2004). It is also more common in children who begin music lessons before age 7 (Takeuchi & Hulse, 1993).

The ability to *produce* music seems to draw from both nature and nurture as well (D. J. Elliott, 1995; Treffert & Wallace, 2002). Some children with autism have exceptional instrumental talent. For example, after watching a movie on television one evening, 14-year-old Leslie Lemke sat down at the family piano and played Tchaikovsky's Piano Concerto No. 1, which had been a sound track for portions of the movie. He had never heard the concerto before that night, yet his rendition was flawless. Lemke is now a world-renowned pianist, even though he has autism and mental retardation, is blind, and has never had a piano lesson (Treffert & Wallace, 2002).

Some policy makers view art and music as luxuries that can easily be dropped from a school curriculum when budgets are tight. In reality, however, formal instruction in these domains appears to have distinct benefits for growing children. For instance, creating paintings or collages that capture certain events or moods can help children add descriptive words and other details to their short stories and poetry (Olshansky, 1995; Olshansky, O'Connor, & O'Byrne, 2006). Drawing illustrations of scientific phenomena or historical events can enhance children's understanding and memory of these phenomena and events (Edens & Potter, 2001; J. H. Davis, 2008). Entertaining others in a selective singing group enhances the self-esteem, resilience, and academic achievement of children who are otherwise at risk for school failure and dropping out (Jenlink, 1994). And instruction in both art and music can promote the development of certain cognitive processes and dispositions—including pattern recognition, sustained attention, executive control processes, and a willingness to take risks and "think outside the box"—that are potentially applicable to other academic domains as well (J. H. Davis, 2008; Schellenberg, 2006).

The Basic Developmental Issues table "Developmental Progressions in the Academic Domains" summarizes how our three general themes—nature and nurture, universality and diversity, and qualitative and quantitative change—play out in the various subject areas we've examined in this chapter.

Using Content Area Standards to Guide Instruction

Formal instruction in academic domains must, of course, take into account the knowledge and abilities that children and adolescents are likely to have at various ages. Within the past two or three decades, numerous discipline-specific professional groups have compiled comprehensive lists of topics and skills they believe to be appropriate for different grade levels.

amusia
Inability to detect the small changes in pitch that are common in melodies; an extreme form of tone deafness.

Basic Developmental Issues

Developmental Progressions in the Academic Domains

Issue	Reading and Writing	Math and Science	History and Geography	Art and Music
Nature and Nurture 	Although children appear to have a biological predisposition to learn spoken language (see Chapter 9), facility with *written* language is largely the result of exposure to printed materials. Nature can interfere with normal literacy development, however: Some children with biologically based disabilities have unusual difficulty learning to read and write.	Within the first few months of life, infants notice differences in quantity and appear to understand certain basic principles of physics (e.g., that no two objects can occupy the same space at the same time). Some theorists speculate that such early acquisitions reflect neurologically "preprogrammed" knowledge. By and large, however, children's knowledge of numbers and scientific phenomena develops through informal experiences and formal instruction.	The bodies of knowledge and cognitive tools that children acquire in history and geography are the result of nurture, as provided by both formal instruction in school and informal experiences within the family (trips to historical sites, use of maps on subway systems, etc.). However, maturational processes may partly determine the age at which children become able to think about historical time and understand the symbolic nature of maps.	Hereditary and maturational factors play some role in artistic and musical development. In the preschool years, children's ability to draw depends largely on maturation of fine motor skills. Furthermore, most children seem to have an inborn appreciation for music from birth. And some children show exceptional talent in art or music even without formal instruction. For the most part, however, development in art and music is the result of training and practice.
Universality and Diversity	Phonological awareness facilitates reading development even when written language is *not* based on how words are pronounced. However, children learn to read and write more easily when words have highly regular and predictable spelling patterns. Children's literacy development also depends on the extent to which their families and cultural groups model and encourage reading and writing.	Although children worldwide have some awareness of quantity and amount, their precision in measuring and comparing quantities depends on the number concepts and operations that their culture provides. Asian children seem to be especially adept in mathematics, in part because Asian languages make the structure of the base-10 number system quite obvious. Children's basic scientific knowledge (e.g., knowing that animals are fundamentally different from human-made objects) is similar worldwide, but their understandings of many natural phenomena (e.g., the origins of species) differ depending on their cultural and religious upbringings.	Because children's knowledge of history and geography is largely the product of the environment and culture in which they have been raised, universal acquisitions have not been identified. In industrialized societies, history is formally taught in school, and maps are widely used to aid navigation. In other cultures, however, children's knowledge of history comes from hearing stories from their elders, and people navigate largely by locating distinctive landmarks in the physical terrain.	Virtually all cultures have some form of art and music. Artistic styles and musical patterns differ considerably from culture to culture, however, and children's development in these areas varies accordingly. For instance, although preschoolers' drawings tend to be quite similar across cultures (e.g., early drawings of people may consist of circles with rudimentary facial features and four lines extending outward to represent limbs), by middle childhood their artwork begins to mimic the styles and images they see in their environment.

continued

Basic Developmental Issues (continued)

Issue	Reading and Writing	Math and Science	History and Geography	Art and Music
Qualitative and Quantitative Change	Reading and writing skills show many qualitative changes over time. For instance, children gradually shift their primary focus from word identification to comprehension (in reading), eventually switch from knowledge telling to knowledge transforming (in writing), and increasingly incorporate metacognitive processes in their literate activities (in both reading and writing). Literacy development is quantitative in the sense that children become able to recognize and spell more and more words each year, and basic reading and writing skills become increasingly automatized.	As children get older, they acquire more knowledge about mathematical and scientific concepts and principles—a progression that reflects quantitative change. In addition, they acquire more complex and sophisticated—and qualitatively different—ways of thinking about math and science. For example, elementary school children begin to rely on retrieval rather than counting objects or fingers as they solve addition and subtraction problems, and adolescents gain new reasoning skills (e.g., separating and controlling variables) in their scientific experimentation.	A good deal of development in history and geography is quantitative, in that children acquire more information about historical events and geographical locations. Qualitative changes are seen in how children *think* about history and geography. For example, with appropriate instruction children gradually begin to realize that knowledge of history is comprised not only of what *did* happen but also of varying perspectives of what *might have* happened. And as children gain proportional reasoning, they become better able to understand the various scales with which maps are constructed.	Many qualitative changes are seen in art and music development. For example, with growth and experience, children's drawings begin to address composition (e.g., creating an organized scene rather than a random collection of objects), perspective, and texture. And in the preschool years, their songs begin to reflect a consistent rhythm and key. Quantitative change is seen in such things as children's increasing knowledge of musical notation and increasing automaticity in playing a musical instrument.

Such lists, known as content area **standards,** are often used to guide instruction and assessment from kindergarten or first grade through high school. Table 10-1 lists Web sites at which you can find standards for a variety of academic domains.

In many countries, an additional source of guidance comes from standards created by state departments of education and other regional or local authorities. For instance, in the United States many states have *English language development (ELD)* standards for English language learners; you can find numerous examples using a search engine such as www.google.com or www.yahoo.com. Also, as a result of the *No Child Left Behind Act* of 2001, all 50 states now have standards for reading, mathematics, and science. Sometimes known simply as *NCLB*, this legislation mandates that school districts annually administer achievement tests in grades 3 through 8 to determine whether students are making "adequate yearly progress" in meeting state-determined standards. Schools that do not show progress are subject to sanctions and corrective actions (e.g., administrative restructuring, dismissal of faculty members), and students have the option of attending another public school at the school district's expense. Well intentioned as this legislation was, most research on its effects has not been favorable. For instance, because their livelihoods depend on their students' test scores, teachers spend more time on literacy, math, and science—and especially on basic topics and skills they think will be on the statewide tests—and less time on social studies, foreign language, the arts, and other disciplines (Pianta, Belsky, Houts, & Morrison, 2007; R. M. Thomas, 2005; Valli & Buese, 2007). And students who consistently perform poorly on the tests (many of whom come from low-income families) are likely to drop out of school rather than persist in academic endeavors that they perceive to be a lost cause (Hursh, 2007; R. Ryan, 2005; R. M. Thomas, 2005).

standards
In education, general statements regarding the knowledge and skills that students should gain and the characteristics that their accomplishments should reflect.

Table 10-1   Web Sites with Standards for Various Academic Disciplines

Academic Domain	Organization	Internet Address	Once You Get There . . .[a]
English and language arts	National Council of Teachers of English	www.ncte.org	Select *Standards* from the *Quick Links* menu.
Foreign language	American Council on the Teaching of Foreign Languages	www.actfl.org	Select *Standards for Foreign Language Learning* from the *Publications* menu.
Geography	National Council for Geographic Education	www.ncge.org	Select *Geography Standards* from the *Geography* menu.
Health, physical education, and dance	National Association for Sport and Physical Education	www.aahperd.org/naspe	Select *National Standards & Activity Guidelines* from the *Publications* menu.
History	National Center for History in the Schools	www.sscnet.ucla.edu/nchs	Click on *History Standards, Online Version.*
Mathematics	National Council of Teachers of Mathematics	www.nctm.org	Click on *Standards and Focal Points.*
Music	National Association for Music Education	www.menc.org	Click on *Resources* and then on *National Standards.*
Reading	International Reading Association	www.reading.org	Click on *Professional Standards* in the *Quick Links* box.
Science	National Academy of Sciences	www.nap.edu (site for National Academies Press, which publishes reports for several scientific organizations)	Click on *Education* (under *Topics*) and then on *Testing, Assessments, and Standards* (under *Subtopics*).
Visual arts	National Art Education Association	www.naea-reston.org	Click on *Publications* and then on *Publications List;* scroll to the two-column table below the list of titles.

[a]These steps worked for us when this book was in press in October 2008. Given the dynamic nature of many Web sites, you may find that you have to do something different when you get to the site in question.

Existing standards are certainly useful in helping teachers focus instruction on important educational goals in various academic domains. When teachers establish clear instructional goals and target instruction toward achieving those goals, all children, and especially those who struggle academically, are likely to make good progress (Hamre & Pianta, 2005). We worry, however, that many existing standards are based on topics and skills that are *typically taught* at various grade levels, rather than on developmental research regarding what youngsters can reasonably accomplish at different ages (e.g., vanSledright & Limón, 2006). We worry, too, that some lists of standards are so lengthy that teachers may provide only fragmented, superficial "coverage" of topics rather than designing lessons that foster elaboration, comprehension monitoring, and other effective cognitive and metacognitive processes (e.g., Schmidt, 2008; Valli & Buese, 2007).

Furthermore, if teachers rely exclusively on standards for particular academic domains, they are apt to neglect other, equally important domains, such as the development of general learning strategies, social skills, and emotional well-being. This is *not* to say that teachers must choose between strong academic standards and students' social-emotional growth. Effective teachers pursue both sets of objectives by integrating existing local, state, national, and international standards with other, nonacademic agendas. We turn to social-emotional aspects of children's development beginning in the next chapter.

Summary

Reading Development

When toddlers and preschoolers have multiple and varied experiences with reading and writing materials and activities, they learn a great deal about the nature of written language. For instance, they learn that spoken language is represented in consistent ways and that different kinds of printed materials serve different purposes. Such knowledge, known as *emergent literacy*, provides an important foundation for the reading and writing skills that children acquire once they begin school.

Skilled reading involves knowing letter-sound correspondences, recognizing letters and words quickly and automatically, constructing meaning from the words on the page, and metacognitively regulating the reading process. Phonological awareness (hearing the distinct sounds within spoken words), word identification skills, and the automatic recognition of many common words typically emerge in the early and middle elementary school years. Reading comprehension and metacognitive strategies continue to develop throughout childhood and adolescence.

Some children with sensory impairments or learning disabilities have more difficulty learning to read than their nondisabled peers. Researchers have also found gender, socioeconomic, ethnic, and cross-linguistic differences in reading development. Strategies for fostering reading development include teaching parents strategies for effective storybook reading, promoting children's phonological awareness, providing many opportunities to read authentic literature, and engaging children and adolescents in discussions about what they read.

Writing Development

To become skillful writers, children and adolescents not only must master handwriting and spelling but must also discover how to communicate their thoughts clearly; learn conventions of capitalization, punctuation, and syntax; and metacognitively regulate the entire writing effort. Handwriting is usually mastered in the elementary grades, but other aspects of writing continue to develop throughout the school years. For example, in the middle school and high school years, many youngsters gradually abandon a *knowledge-telling* approach to writing (in which they write ideas in whatever order the ideas come to mind) in favor of a *knowledge-transforming* approach (in which they conscientiously try to communicate their ideas to the reader). Self-evaluation and editing skills also improve somewhat during adolescence.

To a considerable degree, children's writing development is dependent on their general intellectual development, but some children have difficulty writing despite normal cognitive development in other areas. Gender and ethnic differences in writing development have also been observed. Teachers and other adults can promote writing development by introducing preschoolers to simple writing activities (e.g., making alpha-

bet letters, using pseudowriting in pretend play), assigning authentic writing tasks in the elementary and secondary grades, scaffolding youngsters' writing efforts, and requiring writing in all areas of the school curriculum.

Mathematics Development

Children have some awareness of quantity in the first year of life, but they learn to count only if their culture provides the cognitive tools (e.g., number words) that make counting possible. Often they create strategies for performing simple mathematical operations (e.g., adding and subtracting small numbers) on their own, but formal instruction is usually necessary for acquisition of complex concepts and procedures. For optimal mathematical development, children should truly understand (rather than simply memorize) mathematical procedures and learn that there is often more than one correct way to solve a problem.

Some children have learning disabilities that impede their ability to automatize math facts and solve simple math problems, and others have little exposure to numbers and counting before they begin school. Gender and cultural differences in mathematics have been observed as well. Concrete manipulatives and visual aids often facilitate children's mathematical development, especially in the preschool and elementary years. Also, once children have mastered and automatized basic facts and skills, tools that reduce the load on working memory (e.g., paper and pencil, calculators) can enhance their mathematical problem-solving abilities.

Science Development

Although children are possibly "prewired" with some basic knowledge of physics, by and large they acquire scientific knowledge through their informal experiences and formal instruction. As early as the preschool years, they begin to form theories (sometimes accurate, sometimes not) about categories of living creatures and cause-and-effect relationships in their physical world. Their ability to reason as scientists do (e.g., formulating and testing hypotheses, drawing conclusions from collected data) continues to improve in adolescence, but even many high school students have difficulty analyzing their data objectively.

Children's individual abilities (e.g., visual-spatial skills) and disabilities (e.g., blindness) affect their development in science, as do gender stereotypes and cultural beliefs. Authentic scientific investigations, age-appropriate explanations, and intentional efforts to bring about conceptual change can all enhance youngsters' scientific understandings and reasoning skills.

Development in Other Academic Domains

Such domains as history, geography, art, and music have received less attention in developmental research, but researchers are finding some trends in these areas. For instance, children in the early elementary grades are apt to have difficulty understanding the nature of historical time, and they may not appreciate that some historical "knowledge" is a matter of perspective rather than fact. Geographical reasoning requires understanding the symbolic and proportional nature of maps, which emerges gradually over the elementary and middle school years.

Art and music are found in virtually all cultures, but the specific forms that art and music take differ considerably from one society to another. Some universals are seen, to be sure—for instance, infants around the world seem to enjoy music, and children's early drawings of people are similar regardless of where they grow up—but advanced art and music abilities are largely dependent on instruction and practice.

Using Content Area Standards to Guide Instruction

Groups of subject-matter experts in various academic disciplines have developed content area standards describing topics believed to be appropriate for study at various grade levels. State departments of education and many local school districts have also created standards to guide instruction, especially in reading, writing, math, and science. Such standards provide useful guidance when teachers plan lessons for their own classrooms. Teachers must remember, however, that standards tend to be focused almost exclusively on academic achievement and neglect accomplishments in other areas (e.g., work habits, social skills, emotional well-being) that may be equally important for students' long-term development.

Applying Concepts in Child Development

The exercises in this section will help you increase your effectiveness in fostering children's and adolescents' development in various academic domains.

Case Study

Beating the Odds

Read the following case and then answer the questions at the end.

James A. Garfield Senior High School is located in a low-income neighborhood in East Los Angeles, California. In the 1980s, many of the students' parents were recent immigrants from Mexico, had limited formal education, and spoke little or no English. Garfield had a high dropout rate, in part because apathetic teachers and frequent campus violence (often between rival gangs) gave students little reason to stay in school.

Despite such circumstances, math teacher Jaime Escalante, himself an immigrant from Bolivia, was convinced that many Garfield students had the ability to achieve at high levels. To prove his point, he urged students in his calculus class to take the Advanced Placement (AP) calculus test, an instrument developed by the Educational Testing Service (ETS) to assess the extent to which students had achieved at a level equivalent to that in an introductory college calculus course. Scores on the test range from 1 to 5, with 3 being a "pass" and most colleges offering college credit for scores of 3, 4, and 5.

During the 1981–1982 school year, Mr. Escalante had 18 students (10 boys and 8 girls, all with Mexican heritage) in his calculus class. He required all class members (and their parents as well) to sign contracts in which they promised to attend class, pay attention, try hard, and do all assigned homework. Throughout the school year, teacher and students worked intensively, not only during class time, but also before school, after school, and on Saturdays. During study sessions, Mr. Escalante continually drilled students in basic calculus procedures, presented a wide variety of challenging problems to solve, and encouraged students to help one another. In the last few weeks before the AP test, most of the students devoted themselves almost exclusively to calculus, withdrawing from girlfriends, boyfriends, hobbies, and after-school jobs to prepare for the exam. (One student even took his textbook into the bathroom with him.) The class became a close-knit group, with teacher and classmates offering support and encouragement as needed.

Mr. Escalante often reminded his students of what their dedication might bring them: "You want to make your parents proud. You want to make your school proud. Think how good it will feel if you go to college and know you did the calculus AP. It isn't everybody who can do that" (Mathews, 1988, p. 14).

On May 19, the 18 students took the test under the supervision of the school counselor. Although they struggled with a few items, for the most part they were well prepared for the test and found it easier than they had expected. In fact, they performed at such high levels (and in some cases their answers were so similar) that ETS accused 12 of them of cheating. These students were vindicated when, on August 31 (this time under the watchful eye of ETS employees), they retook the test and all earned a score of 3 or higher.

At least 15 of the 18 students went on to college, many earned bachelor's degrees, and several attended graduate school. Mr. Escalante's 1981–1982 calculus class eventually produced teachers, accountants, medical technicians, and an aerospace engineer.[a]

- In what ways did nurture clearly play a role in the students' mathematical achievement? How might nature also have been involved?
- The calculus class consisted of 10 boys and 8 girls. Are these numbers consistent or inconsistent with research related to gender differences in mathematics?
- ETS employees based their suspicions about cheating partly on the similarity of answers they saw in students' responses. What other explanation for the similarity might there be?

Once you have answered these questions, compare your responses with those presented in Appendix A.

---

[a]Case based on Mathews, 1988; Menéndez, 1988.

Interpreting Children's Artifacts and Reflections

Draw on what you've learned about the development of reading and writing as you analyze the writing sample in this exercise.

The Pet Who Came to Dinner

Seven-year-old Justin wrote the story shown here. As you read it, consider these questions:

· What can you conclude about Justin's phonological awareness?
· What can you conclude about his knowledge of alphabet letters?
· What can you conclude about his knowledge of capitalization, punctuation, and grammar?
· What can you conclude about his ability to create a narrative?

Once you have analyzed Justin's story, compare your responses with those presented in Appendix B. For further practice in analyzing children's artifacts and reflections, go to the Activities and Applications section in Chapter 10 of MyEducationLab.

Developmental Trends Exercise

Development in various academic domains proceeds according to the same principles that characterize cognitive development in general. One key principle is that *early acquisitions provide a foundation on which later development can build*. The following table describes the behaviors of children and adolescents at five different age levels, identifies later knowledge and skills that might build on their behaviors, and offers implications for adults working with each age-group. Go to the Activities and Applications section in Chapter 10 of MyEducationLab to apply what you've learned about development in the academic domains as you fill in the empty cells in the table.

Identifying Building Blocks for Later Acquisitions in the Academic Domains

Age	A Youngster's Experience	Developmental Concepts *Identifying Knowledge and Skills on Which Later Acquisitions Can Build*	Implications *Helping Youngsters Acquire a Solid Foundation in the Academic Domain*
Infancy **(Birth–2 Years)**	As she sits in her highchair, 14-month-old Selena keeps throwing toys that have been placed on her tray. She seems upset when she no longer has the toys, yet as soon as her caregiver returns them to the tray, she throws them again.	By continually seeing objects move in particular directions (away from her and downward onto the floor), Selena is learning that certain actions lead to predictable results. Her observations in this and similar circumstances will provide a knowledge base to which she can later relate such concepts as *force*, *momentum*, and *gravity*.	
Early Childhood **(2–6 Years)**	As 5-year-old Rico builds a Lego house, he tells his teacher that he needs more red Legos. Seeing an opportunity for Rico to practice addition, the teacher says, "I see you have three red ones already. If I give you two more, how many red ones will you have altogether?" Rico counts three and then two more on his fingers and then happily responds, "Five!"		Encourage children to use any invented mathematical strategies that yield accurate results. Introduce children to more efficient strategies, and encourage automaticity for basic math facts, but allow children to use their previously acquired, more concrete strategies until they feel comfortable with the new ones.

Developmental Trends Exercise (continued)

Age	A Youngster's Experience	Developmental Concepts *Identifying Knowledge and Skills on Which Later Acquisitions Can Build*	Implications *Helping Youngsters Acquire a Solid Foundation in the Academic Domain*
Middle Childhood (6–10 Years)	Seven-year-old Leila's second-grade class is studying the *ight* "family" in spelling this week, so Leila is learning how to spell such words as *fight*, *tight*, and *bright*. In one assignment, Leila writes a short story she calls "The Bright Nightlight," in which she uses as many *ight* words as she can.	Through repeated practice, Leila is gradually automatizing the *ight* spelling pattern. By automatizing basic spelling and grammatical rules, Leila will be able to focus more effectively on (i.e., she can devote more working memory capacity to) composition skills and effective communication in her writing.	Provide a variety of activities in which children can automatize basic reading, writing, and math skills. Such activities are typically more effective when they are authentic and motivating in their own right.
Early Adolescence (10–14 Years)	A middle school history teacher asks students to "write a biography of a person in history as a real person who has both strengths and weaknesses." In a biography of Franklin Delano Roosevelt, 13-year-old Jesse describes Roosevelt's struggle with polio and determination to hide the severity of his disability when running for president.	By understanding that historical figures were in most respects just ordinary human beings (who were perhaps in extraordinary circumstances), Jesse will be able to apply his general knowledge of human thoughts, motives, and emotions to make sense of history—that is, to understand why historical events unfolded in particular ways.	Encourage youngsters to draw on what they know about human nature to understand why various historical figures acted as they did.
Late Adolescence (14–18 Years)	As her high school literature class discusses Carl Sandburg's poem "The Road and the End," 15-year-old Zia discovers that reasonable people may interpret the same information in distinctly different ways.	Zia may be able to apply her newly acquired understanding to other domains in addition to poetry. For instance, she can now more easily understand that scientists might formulate two or more different theories to explain a particular phenomenon. She may also realize that eye witnesses at an historical event might give divergent and possibly contradictory reports about what happened.	

Key Concepts

emergent literacy (p. 356)	dyslexia (p. 361)	dyscalculia (p. 379)	music literacy (p. 393)
phonological awareness (p. 357)	invented spelling (p. 369)	visual-spatial ability (p. 380)	amusia (p. 394)
sight vocabulary (p. 359)	knowledge telling (p. 370)	substance schema (p. 384)	standards (p. 396)
story schema (p. 360)	knowledge transforming (p. 370)	scientific reasoning (p. 384)	

MyEducationLab

Now go to Chapter 10 of MyEducationLab at www.myeducationlab.com, where you can:

· View instructional objectives for the chapter.
· Take a quiz to test your mastery of chapter objectives. Detailed feedback is provided to explain why your responses are correct or incorrect.
· Deepen your understanding of particular concepts and principles with Review, Practice, and Enrichment exercises.

· Complete Activities and Applications exercises that give you additional experience in interpreting artifacts, increase your understanding of how research contributes to knowledge about chapter topics, and encourage you to apply what you have learned about children's development.
· Apply what you have learned in the chapter to your work with children in Building Teaching Skills and Dispositions exercises.
· Observe children and their unique contexts in Video Examples.

chapter

11

Emotional
Development

Merv had experienced a difficult childhood growing up in an economically poor family in Hawaii. Her father had been an alcoholic, and her mother had been regularly upset and preoccupied with her own troubles. Neither parent took adequate care of Merv or her six brothers and sisters. Merv's parents frequently fought, and they often struck Merv and the other children. Food, shoes, clothing, and basic school supplies were scarce. And sadly, neighborhood parents considered Merv and her brothers and sisters to be unworthy playmates for their own children (Werner & Smith, 2001).

Remarkably, Merv beat the odds. By the time she reached her forties, Merv was a productive, well-adjusted woman who worked as a parent educator and had been married since age 16 to "a pretty neat guy . . . a schoolteacher" (Werner & Smith, 2001, pp. 100–101). Merv and her husband raised their seven children in a manner that was gentle and loving. Merv also remained close to her own brothers and sisters. She led a happy, fulfilled life.

What qualities were present in Merv's childhood that helped her ultimately become a well-adjusted, productive person? Merv credited four childhood experiences with making her strong. First of all, Merv learned to work hard:

> As children, we took care of the yard, the house, the clothes, each other, and the cars. We did everything. My father cooked when there was something to cook, and my mother simply coped. . . . When things got rough, I learned to dig in my heels and say, "How am I going to make this happen?" versus "This is too hard, I quit." (Werner & Smith, 2001, pp. 95–96)[a]

Second, Merv had "caring and supportive people" to guide and nurture her (Werner & Smith, 2001, p. 96). Merv thrived on the care she received from her grandmother Kahaunaele. During Merv's visits to Kahaunaele's house, Kahaunaele showered Merv with love, bathed the girl, and combed the tangles out of Merv's long hair. Having had one leg amputated years before, Kahaunaele had some discomfort when she moved around, yet she disregarded her own pain and inconvenience when it came to reassuring Merv. Here was one of Merv's poignant memories of Kahaunaele:

> I remember waking up at night with nightmares and crying, and being afraid, looking for someone to care for me. My vision, that I will never forget, is this woman [Kahaunaele] crawling on her hands and knees down the hall to come and make sure that I was okay. . . . Then, when I was all right and settled and feeling better, she would crawl back to her room. (p. 98)

Love from her grandmother was supplemented with kindness from several teachers and school staff. Merv's principal once said to her, "You are Hawaiian and you can be anything you choose to be" (p. 98). Merv was forever grateful for these words of encouragement.

Third, Merv received a good education. When she was 12 years old, she accepted an invitation to attend a prestigious school on another Hawaiian island. At the Kamehameha School, Merv was well cared for, and she progressed academically. However, at age 16, Merv became pregnant, married the father of her baby, and was expelled from school. Merv was soon allowed to return when a school counselor went "out on a major limb" for her, having realized that she was "not a bad student. She just made a mistake" (p. 100). Merv learned from the school that it is possible to make good choices in life:

> Going away to Kamehameha . . . helped me make some choices that I never knew I could. All around me in my neighborhood was alcoholism and abuse. . . . When I went away [to the school], I realized that it wasn't the way it had to be . . . I realized that I could make choices. (p. 100)

Finally, Merv learned to trust that there is goodness in the world. Merv saw hope as a vital quality for all young people, and noted that inspiration can be found in a variety of places:

> Somewhere, someplace down the line, somebody had taught me, "There is somebody greater than us who loves you." And that is my hope and my belief. Whatever that translates for you—a belief in God,

Case Study:

Merv

Outline:

Case Study: Merv

Erikson's Theory of Psychosocial Development

Attachment

Emotion

Temperament and Personality

Supporting Children and Adolescents with Emotional and Behavioral Problems

Summary

Applying Concepts in Child Development

a belief in a religion, a goal, a dream, something that we can hang on to. As adults, we need to give our young people hope and something to hang on to. As young people, we need to find our own. (Werner & Smith, 2001, p. 101)

- What basic need did Merv have that was initially unmet by her parents but was ultimately fulfilled by other people in her life?

- To what extent can teachers and other practitioners contribute to children's emotional development?

*Reprinted from *Journeys from Childhood to Midlife: Risk, Resilience, and Recovery*, by Emmy E. Werner and Ruth S. Smith. Copyright © 2001 by Cornell University. Used by permission of the publisher, Cornell University Press.

Every child needs to be loved. Merv's own parents neglected her, but fortunately several other people cherished her, tending to her need for affection. Her grandmother adored her, her brothers and sisters formed lasting bonds with her, and several of her teachers and other school staff educated and supported her as she grew. In this chapter you will find that warm, sensitive care is the mainstay of children's first relationships. When caregivers are kind and responsive, children begin to trust these caregivers and gain confidence in their own abilities. You will also learn that good relationships help children express their emotions productively and blossom into healthy, one-of-a-kind personalities. Finally, you will see that educators can contribute immensely to the emotional development of youngsters, as they did for Merv.

Erikson's Theory of Psychosocial Development

In the last few chapters, you learned that many changes take place in children's cognitive abilities—in their memory capacity, reasoning skills, language competencies, academic concepts, and so forth. Equally momentous transformations occur in the social-emotional domain. To give you an overview of these significant social-emotional changes, we begin with Erikson's theory of psychosocial development.

Lessons Learned from Life's Challenges

As you learned in Chapter 1, Erik Erikson (1902–1994) was a *psychodynamic theorist* who believed that people grow from life's challenges. In his own youth, Erikson struggled with who he was as a person. He often felt different than others, having been born to a single Danish mother in Germany during an era when two-parent families were the norm, and having peers who questioned his Jewish heritage because he had blond hair and blue eyes and did not resemble the Jewish people they knew (Crain, 2005). Erikson had little interest in school and failed to earn a college degree, yet he eventually became a well-known scholar of human development.

In his theory, Erikson suggested that people experience eight "crises," in the form of **psychosocial stages,** as they progress from birth to old age (Erikson, 1963, 1972). Each of the eight crises is a turning point, the resolution of which directs a person's future concerns. He called these eight levels *psychosocial* stages because the various challenges refer to qualitatively different concerns about oneself *(psycho-)* and relationships with other people *(-social)*. Erikson observed that when individuals constructively address these eight challenges, they gain lasting personal assets, but when their efforts fall short, they are apt to dwell on their social-emotional problems. As they move from stage to stage, people build on the assets and deficits they have previously acquired, occasionally revisiting unresolved crises during later personal experiences.

As they reflect on their life experiences, people navigate through each of the unfolding challenges. Let's look at the potential outcomes of the eight stages.

Trust versus mistrust (infancy).   According to Erikson, infants' primary developmental task is to learn whether or not they can trust other people. When caregivers can be depended on to feed a hungry stomach, change an uncomfortable diaper, and provide affection at

psychosocial stages
In Erikson's theory, eight periods of life that involve age-related challenges.

regular intervals, an infant learns *trust*—that others are dependable. When caregivers ignore the infant's needs, are inconsistent in their attention, or are abusive, the infant learns *mistrust*—that the world is an unpredictable and dangerous place.

Autonomy versus shame and doubt (toddler years). As toddlers gain better control of their muscles, they become capable of satisfying some of their own needs. Toddlers learn to feed, wash, and dress themselves, and to use the toilet. When parents and other caregivers encourage self-sufficient behavior, toddlers develop *autonomy,* a sense of being able to handle many problems on their own. But when caregivers demand too much too soon, refuse to let children perform tasks of which they are capable, or ridicule early attempts at self-sufficiency, children may instead develop *shame and doubt* about their inability to conduct themselves appropriately.

Developing a trusting relationship with a caregiver is the child's first social-emotional task.

Initiative versus guilt (preschool years). If all goes well, children spend their infancy and toddler years learning that the world is a good place, people love them, and they can make things happen. With a growing drive toward independence, preschoolers begin to have their own ideas about activities they want to pursue. For example, they may undertake simple art projects, make houses and roadways in the sandbox, or share fantasies about being superheroes with other children. When adults encourage such efforts, children develop *initiative,* an energetic motivation to undertake activities independently. When adults discourage such activities, children may instead develop *guilt* about acting inappropriately or having unacceptable feelings.

Industry versus inferiority (elementary school years). When they reach elementary school, children are expected to master many new skills, and they soon learn that they can gain recognition from adults through their academic assignments, athletic accomplishments, artistic performances, participation in community activities, and so on. When children complete projects and are praised for their accomplishments, they demonstrate *industry,* a pattern of working hard, gaining mastery in tool use, and persisting at lengthy tasks. But when children are ridiculed or punished for their efforts or when they find that they cannot meet adults' expectations, they may develop feelings of *inferiority* about their own abilities.

Children derive a sense of accomplishment from their success on concrete tasks.

Identity versus role confusion (adolescence). As they make the transition from childhood to adulthood, adolescents wrestle with questions of who they are and how they fit into the adult world. Values learned during childhood are now reassessed in light of a new sexual drive and the desire to be true to oneself. Initially, youth experience *role confusion*—mixed feelings about the specific ways in which they fit into society—and may experiment with a variety of actions and attitudes (e.g., affiliating with various peer groups, trying several distinct sports and hobbies, and learning about the views of different political groups). In Erikson's view, most adolescents eventually achieve a sense of *identity* regarding who they are and where their lives are headed.

Intimacy versus isolation (young adulthood). Once people have established their identities, they are ready to make commitments to one or more other individuals. They become capable of *intimacy*—that is, they form close, reciprocal relationships with others (e.g., through marriage or close friendships) and willingly make the sacrifices and compromises that such relationships require. When people cannot form intimate relationships (perhaps because of their reluctance or inability to forgo satisfaction of their own needs), a sense of *isolation* may result.

Generativity versus stagnation (middle age). During middle age, the primary developmental tasks are contributing to society and guiding future generations. When an individual makes a contribution, perhaps by raising a family or by working toward the betterment of society, a sense of *generativity,* or productivity, results. In contrast, an individual who is self-centered and unable or unwilling to help others develops a feeling of *stagnation*—dissatisfaction with lack of production.

Integrity versus despair (retirement years). According to Erikson, the final developmental task is a retrospective one. As individuals look back on their past experiences, they develop feelings of contentment and *integrity* if they believe they have led a happy, productive life. Alternatively, they may develop a sense of *despair* if they look back on a life of disappointments and unachieved goals.

For Erikson, successful progress through each stage is not an absolute accomplishment but rather a matter of degree. In other words, people advance at each stage when they develop *more* of the positive tendency and *less* of the negative tendency. Erikson believed that having modest deficits, balanced with adequate assets, helps people to act sensibly with the opportunities and threats they face in daily life. For example, a young boy who has learned to trust his parents may be somewhat hopeful when meeting a new teacher, yet having also known a few grouchy and short-tempered grown-ups, the boy might be cautious until he gets to know the teacher better. Because his optimism is tempered with restraint, the boy is ready to form healthy relationships. In contrast, with too much of a deficit (e.g., when uneasiness outweighs peace of mind), a tipping point is reached and a person becomes unhappy, isolated, and socially impaired.

Contemporary Perspectives on Erikson's Theory

Three strengths of Erikson's theory make it a compelling framework of human development. First, Erikson argued convincingly that important changes occur *throughout* the life span. Thanks in part to Erikson's theory, developmentalists now accept that catalysts for growth (e.g., a change in routine, an opportunity for a different kind of relationship, and new desires) surface at every age. Second, Erikson focused on truly significant social-emotional developments, including forming trusting relationships with other people and carving out one's identity. Finally, Erikson's stages reflect the idea that development is a dynamic synthesis of nature, nurture, and a person's own motivation to make sense of life (Côté, 2005; Lerner, 2002). Erikson's integrative model fits nicely with the contemporary view that developmental changes are complex blends of several interacting factors.

These contributions notwithstanding, Erikson's theory has some serious limitations. For one thing, Erikson's observations of the human condition were largely anecdotal and his conclusions rather vague (Crain, 2005). The systematic research findings that have accumulated since Erikson formulated his theory indicate that his stages are probably not completely accurate descriptions of what happens at each age period. For instance, Erikson believed that most people achieve a sense of identity by the end of adolescence. But as you will discover in Chapter 12, youth typically do not achieve a clear identity by late adolescence and instead solidify their personal commitments during the young adult years (Kroger, 2004). Also problematic is the fact that Erikson based his stages primarily on observations of *men* alone. Contemporary theorists find that contrary to Erikson's sequence, many women focus on intimacy at the same time as, and in some cases before, they dwell on their own identity (Josselson, 1988). Finally, Erikson may have underestimated just how differently various cultural groups think about particular assets and age levels. For example, many cultures intentionally discourage self-assertiveness *(autonomy)* in young children, sometimes as a way of protecting them from the very real dangers of their environments and at other times with the goal of deepening ties to family members (Kağitçibaşi, 2007; Morelli & Rothbaum, 2007; G. J. Powell, 1983). You can see a summary of the research on each of Erikson's stages in Table 11-1.

Despite the holes in Erikson's theory, this framework does offer a valuable perspective on human life. As we mentioned earlier, Erikson's framework has several strong points, and it offers the additional advantage to educators of inspiring optimism about young people's potential for growth. Most educators agree with Erikson that youngsters can usually find the inner strength they need to transform life's challenges into such worthwhile assets as a healthy self-confidence, a commitment to productive social values, and a solid work ethic. Although Erikson failed to provide detailed information about how to cultivate social-emotional skills and attributes in youngsters, other developmental scholars have taken up this cause, and we summarize their research in the remainder of this book. The developmental focus of Erikson's first stage, a trusting relationship with caregivers, has been thoroughly examined by researchers, and we look at this topic now.

Table 11-1   Developmental Research Related to Erikson's Stages

Stage	Age	Research
Trust vs. Mistrust	Birth to 1 year	Developmental investigations support Erikson's assertion that learning to trust others is a fundamental need for infants (Ainsworth, Blehar, Waters, & Wall, 1978; Bowlby, 1988). However, whereas Erikson indicated that infancy was a critical time for having a first trusting relationship, recent research indicates that children often get second chances. For example, when children receive unresponsive care during early infancy, their first attachments are likely to be insecure, but if their later care is warm and sensitive, the children may develop trusting relationships.
Autonomy vs. Shame and Doubt	1 to 3 years	Evidence supports Erikson's conclusion that toddlers have a strong will to practice emerging skills without restriction. For example, toddlers are motivated to handle objects, walk on their own, and explore a home's forbidden areas. Yet not every culture agrees with Erikson that autonomy is a virtue: Some groups see young children's drive for independence as an immature impulse that must be tempered (Kağitçibaşi, 2007; Morelli & Rothbaum, 2007; G. J. Powell, 1983).
Initiative vs. Guilt	3 to 5 years	Erikson aptly portrayed preschool-aged children as radiating a sense of purpose. Research confirms that young children show initiative in imaginative play, enthusiastic conversations, and effortful engagement with toys. With his attention on shame, doubt, and guilt in young children, Erikson also paved the way for contemporary research on these emotions. For example, developmental studies indicate that young children tend to feel distressed when they break a rule or fail to live up to a standard (Kagan, 1984; Kochanska, 1993).
Industry vs. Inferiority	6 to 10 years	Erikson saw middle childhood as a period for completing demanding tasks proficiently and confidently. Cross-cultural research indicates that adults routinely assign chores to children in this age range, reflecting widespread agreement that elementary school–aged children can act responsibly. Research also indicates that children compare their own abilities to those of peers, paying special attention to their relative proficiency in domains that they personally value, and they may lose confidence if they see themselves coming up short relative to others (Harter, 2006).
Identity vs. Role Confusion	10 to 20 years	Erikson's focus on identity has spawned a lot of research. Studies generally confirm Erikson's assertion that young people actively engage in soul searching related to who they are, what they believe in, and where they are going (Marcia, 1980, 1988). The tendency to wrestle with identity issues extends for a longer period than Erikson proposed, however. Researchers have also suggested that for girls and women, a focus on intimacy (the next stage in Erikson's model) may occur simultaneously with or precede the focus on identity (Josselson, 1988).
Intimacy vs. Isolation	Young adulthood	Research evidence confirms that taking part in intimate relationships is a typical concern of the young adult years. However, some critics suggest that being closely connected with others is a human quality that transcends any single time period (Gilligan, 1982). Furthermore, the early adult years are more complex than is captured in Erikson's primary focus on intimacy. For example, young adults frequently attend additionally to identity concerns, career prospects, and, in many cases, family matters, including the rearing of their own children.
Generativity vs. Stagnation	Middle age	During middle age, most adults organize their lives such that they contribute to the betterment of society, as Erikson proposed. One common critique of Erikson's theory is that he believed that men were primarily concerned with their careers and women with parenting their children. Yet in mainstream Western culture today, both career and family are serious concerns for men and women alike (B. E. Peterson & Stewart, 1996).
Integrity vs. Despair	Retirement years	Looking back on one's life is an important task for many older adults, and Erikson was on the mark in this regard (R. N. Butler, 1963; Haight, 1992). However, older adults tackle many other developmental tasks, including finding ways to cope with losses and make the best of their later years (Baltes, 1997). In other words, many older adults live in the present as well as the past.

Attachment

Human beings of all ages seem to have a fundamental need to feel socially connected to, and loved and respected by, other people. In other words, they have a **need for relatedness** (Deci & Moller, 2005; Park, Crocker, & Vohs, 2006). Across the life span, this need is fulfilled with social bonds of various types, including friendships, romantic ties, marital partnerships, and family relationships.

The child's first bond, called an **attachment,** is an enduring emotional tie that unites the child to one or more caregivers and has far-reaching effects on the child's development (Ainsworth, 1973). In the past few decades, the dominant theoretical perspective on caregiver–infant relationships has been **ethological attachment theory,** a perspective originally suggested by British psychiatrist John Bowlby (1907–1990) and later fleshed out by Canadian American psychologist Mary Ainsworth (1913–1999) (Ainsworth, 1963, 1973; Ainsworth, Blehar, Waters, & Wall, 1978; Bowlby, 1951, 1958).

Ethological attachment theory suggests that the human capacity for close relationships evolved over millions of years of human history. Attachment theorists speculate that severe

need for relatedness
Fundamental need to feel socially connected to, and loved and respected by, other people.

attachment
An enduring emotional tie uniting one person to another.

ethological attachment theory
Theoretical perspective that emphasizes the benefits to children derived from close bonds with caregivers, particularly protection from harm and a secure base from which to explore the environment.

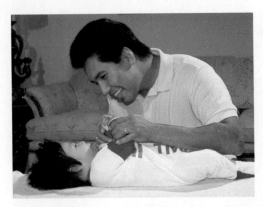

The attachments that infants form with parents and other primary caregivers provide a foundation for later relationships.

environmental conditions in our ancestors' past made it necessary for small children to stay close and attentive to their parents. Obviously, parents also had to be inclined to nurture and protect their children. These mutually close ties helped children to survive their infancy and develop the motivation to imitate parents' hunting, gathering of crops, use of tools, and interactions with others. This capacity for attachment, then, was presumably passed down from generation to generation.

In today's world, attachments can be seen in infants' crying, clinging, and crawling toward parents and other caregivers when distressed. Under less stressful conditions, infants show affection with snuggles, smiles, and cooing. However, what develops in infants is not simply a collection of discrete behaviors, such as crying and smiling, but also an underlying system of relating to parents. This system has two important elements. First, infants learn to use their parents as a *safe haven*. Infants depend on parents for protection from harm and for soothing comfort when feelings of hunger, fatigue, or fear escalate to unmanageable levels. Second, infants use parents as a *secure base*. Infants relax in the presence of their parents and go crawling about here and there, glancing back now and then for reassuring looks from Mom and Dad.

Developmental Course of Children's Attachments

In the process of forming attachments, infants learn a lot about other people and themselves. For example, a baby slowly develops expectations about shared routines ("When Grandma says, 'Peekaboo,' I hide my eyes and we both laugh"), beliefs about other people's trustworthiness ("Mommy takes care of me"), emotional connections ("I love my Daddy"), and a sense of self ("People love me; I am lovable"). To end up with this coherent system of expectations, infants must mature, develop cognitively, and gain considerable social experience.

Birth to 2 months. From birth, infants use social signals (e.g., watching other people and crying) that elicit care from others. Infants initially treat adults in an equal opportunity fashion, allowing anyone with the right touch to comfort them (Schaffer, 1996). Nevertheless, the foundations of individualized attachments are being formed, and infants begin to recognize familiar people through their faces, voices, smells, and characteristic behaviors.

Two to 6 months. From the second to the sixth months after birth, infants begin to learn that they cannot count on just anyone for affection and attention, but instead must turn to the few special people who regularly care for them. By the third month, infants recognize and smile selectively at people they know best (Camras, Malatesta, & Izard, 1991; Lavelli & Fogel, 2005). During this period, infants continue to depend on adults to carry most of the burden for initiating and maintaining a social exchange (Saarni, Campos, Camras, & Witherington, 2006). For example, caregivers notice when a baby is alert and calm, use this occasion to extend a friendly greeting, and wait for the baby to make a simple response that they treat as the baby's turn in the interaction. With experience, infants learn the rhythms of interaction and eagerly anticipate playful exchanges with caregivers, such as counting toes or singing during a diaper change. Toward the end of this period, infants continue to accept comfort from unfamiliar adults, although nature is about to put the breaks on their open-mindedness and approachability.

Seven months to 2 years. At about 7 months, infants show full-fledged attachments to one person or a small number of people, including, perhaps, a mother, father, grandparent, employed caregiver, or some combination of these and other individuals. Attachments can be seen when infants reach out to be picked up by familiar caregivers; protest when separated from them; and wriggle, coo, and show unmistakable looks of recognition when adored caregivers walk into the room.

During this period, infants also begin to show intense fears. Just as infants are learning to crawl and are motivated to explore, nature activates a useful fear of the unknown. As you might guess, the preferred antidote to scary things is direct contact with familiar caregivers. When puzzling phenomena appear out of nowhere, such as a barking dog (woof!) or a jack-in-the-box's loud, unexpected effect (pop!), infants demand reassurance (now!).

Adults unknown to the baby likewise now trigger fearful reactions. In the latter half of the first year of life and well into the second year, an unfamiliar adult often incites fear—

stranger anxiety—in infants (Mangelsdorf, Shapiro, & Marzolf, 1995; R. A. Thompson, 2006). This fear often intensifies into a red-faced, tearful, arm-flapping demand for the safe haven of a familiar caregiver. Of course, not all strangers will provoke this kind of reaction, but it is common for infants to become wary of unfamiliar people at this time.

The latter part of infancy is not simply about fright and flight, however. Infants increasingly engage in pleasant interactions with caregivers, smiling, pointing, vocalizing, and sharing eye contact, and in the process becoming active partners in social exchanges (Mundy et al., 2007). Children also begin to take turns in a conversation, as you can see in 16-month-old Corwin's interchanges with his mother in the "Literacy: Infancy" video in MyEducationLab. Corwin's vocalizations are simple, but they serve nicely as contributions to the exchange.

Early childhood. Children begin to think about their attachments during the early childhood years. Typically, young children appreciate the loving care they receive from parents and other beloved caregivers and actively reciprocate with affectionate gestures of their own. For example, children often create "love notes" to their parents, as you can see in the following "I Love Mommy" exercise.

Interpreting Children's Artifacts and Reflections

I Love Mommy

Three-year-old Ivy and four-year-old Alex prepared these notes (at the left and right, respectively) for their mothers. As you examine the notes, consider what the two children are trying to communicate and the cultural symbols they use to represent their feelings.

These two notes communicate the children's simple, heartfelt affection for their moms. Ivy and Alex have chosen the same graphic device, a stacks of hearts, to represent the depth of their feelings for their mothers. Hearts are a common symbol of love in mainstream Western culture. Young children often choose other devices as well, such as drawing themselves holding hands with a loved one.

As they did in their infant days, young children continue to use familiar caregivers as a safe haven, particularly when they are sick, scared, or distressed. However, urgent protests over separations are fewer now, and stranger anxiety also has become less intense, possibly because children are finally convinced that their parents *will* return to get them at the end of the day, and in the meantime, warm, reliable teachers and relatives are protecting them (Main & Cassidy, 1988; Schaffer, 1996). Increasingly, children also find that peers can play a supportive role in their daily lives. Particularly when they have enjoyed affectionate relationships with parents, young children play happily with peers in parents' absence (Howes, 1999; C. Hughes & Dunn, 2007).

stranger anxiety
Fear of unfamiliar adults in the latter half of the first year and into the second year of life.

Attachments to family members continue to be important during middle childhood and adolescence.

Middle childhood and adolescence. During middle childhood and adolescence, youngsters increasingly view their relationships in terms of mutual responsibilities. Youngsters now expect parents to keep tabs on them, celebrate their successes, and be there when needed. Youngsters likewise are learning the need to shoulder some responsibility for their relationships, and they also gradually realize that relationships with family members will endure despite occasional conflicts (R. A. Thompson, 2006). Routine separations (such as going to school each day or to summer camp for a week) generally induce little of the anxiety associated with late-infancy separations, although a few elementary school children continue to be anxious before and during separations. However, when relationships with parents are seriously disrupted, perhaps because of divorce or death, some youngsters may become angry, aggressive, or physically ill, and they may withdraw from their customary activities (Pribilsky, 2001).

As they progress through adolescence, most youngsters remain attached to parents and siblings, but family relationships change. Many adolescents now prefer to receive their affection behind the scenes, and they also become increasingly close to friends and romantic partners (Mayseless, 2005; Nickerson & Nagle, 2005). At this age peers offer reassurance to one another when times are tough, providing a new kind of safe haven, one that permits equal participation. Adolescents do not usually renounce their ties to parents, but they do strengthen connections with peers and prepare (consciously or not) for their inevitable departure from the family nest.

The developmental course of attachments we have outlined is one that assumes a trusting relationship with parents and parental figures. As we now see, most caregivers earn the trust of children, but in unfortunate exceptions a few caregivers do not.

Individual Differences in Children's Attachments

If you look around at young children you know, you may notice variations in how they respond when afraid, hurt, or upset. Some children seek and find comfort in the reassuring arms of caregivers; some are clingy and fretful; and others want to be left alone, denying that anything is (ever) wrong.

To study such differences in the laboratory, Ainsworth created a mildly stressful situation for 1-year-old infants. First, a mother and her infant were brought to a playroom and left alone. A stranger (a research assistant) soon entered the room and attempted to play with the baby. After 3 minutes, the mother left the room, leaving the baby alone with the stranger. Subsequently, the mother returned and the stranger departed, leaving mother and baby together. Next, mother departed, and baby was alone; the stranger returned at this point. Finally, the mother returned and the stranger departed (Ainsworth et al., 1978). This sequence, commonly known as the *Strange Situation,* has become a classic research tool for assessing attachment in young children.

In the Strange Situation, attention is focused primarily on the child's behavior. Observers rate the child's attempts to seek contact with a caregiver, the physical proximity of the child to the caregiver, the child's resistance to or avoidance of the caregiver, and the child's level of distress. From such ratings, the child is given one of several classifications:

- Infants who exhibit **secure attachment** seem to use caregivers as a secure base. When caregivers are present, infants actively explore new toys and surroundings. When caregivers return after leaving the room, infants smile at or talk to them, move over to greet them, or in other ways seek proximity to them. In the "Strange Situation" video in MyEducationLab, you can see a securely attached infant's distress at his father's departure and relief at his father's return. About 60 percent of infants are classified as securely attached (R. A. Thompson, 2006).
- Infants who exhibit **insecure-avoidant attachment** seem oblivious to a caregiver's presence. They fail to greet the caregiver upon his or her return and may even look away. Instead, they go about their business independently, and they are somewhat superficial in their interactions with toys. About 15 percent of children participating in Strange Situation studies are classified as insecure-avoidant (R. A. Thompson, 2006).
- Infants who exhibit **insecure-resistant attachment** seem preoccupied with their caregivers, but they are not easily comforted during reunions. When caregivers return, these infants remain distressed and angry; they may rush to parents and other caregivers

MyEducationLab

Observe an infant's distress at his father's departure, followed by the infant's relaxation during his father's return, in the "Strange Situation" video. (Find Video Examples in Chapter 11 of MyEducationLab.)

secure attachment
Attachment classification in which children use attachment figures as a source of comfort in times of distress and as a secure base from which to explore.

insecure-avoidant attachment
Attachment classification in which children appear somewhat indifferent to attachment figures.

insecure-resistant attachment
Attachment classification in which children are preoccupied with their attachment figures but gain little comfort from them when distressed.

yet quickly struggle to be released. Insecure-resistant infants comprise about 10 percent of participants in Strange Situation studies (R. A. Thompson, 2006).

- More serious problems in attachment, which were not part of Ainsworth's original classification, have subsequently been identified. For example, a **disorganized and disoriented attachment** style has been documented (Main & Solomon, 1986, 1990). Infants in this group lack a coherent way of responding to stressful events. These infants may be calm and contented one minute yet, without provocation, become angry the next minute. They may interrupt their own actions midstream, for example, by crawling toward caregivers and then suddenly freezing with apprehension. In addition, a very few children show *no* attachment behaviors or exhibit other extremely serious problems, such as displaying fear of caregivers rather than being comforted by them. Such serious problems frequently call for intervention by trained professionals. Approximately 15 percent of children show a disorganized and disoriented attachment, no attachment, or another serious attachment problem (R. A. Thompson, 2006).

The Observation Guidelines table "Assessing Young Children's Attachment Security" summarizes how children with particular kinds of attachments might act. In observing children, teachers and caregivers should guard against taking any single response from a child too seriously; they should instead look for patterns of behavior over time. We turn now to how attachments originate, expand from a single person to multiple caregivers, and affect long-term adjustment.

Origins of Attachment Security

What factors lead to different patterns of attachment? Research has shown that the quality of the caregiver–child relationship, the cultural setting, and the child's own behavior each play a role.

Quality of caregiver–child relationship.   The relationship between a caregiver and child is the most powerful factor in attachment security. When caregivers are sensitive and responsive to young children, protect them, and provide for their needs, children are inclined to develop secure attachments to these caregivers (Nievar & Becker, 2008; R. A. Thompson, 2006). Caregivers who are sensitive and responsive show these qualities:

- *They consistently respond to infants' needs.* Caregivers establish routines for feeding, diapering, and holding infants. They do not run in response to every whimper, but they are faithfully available when infants are distressed and express genuine needs (M. Cassidy & Berlin, 1994; R. A. Thompson, Easterbrooks, & Padilla-Walker, 2003). Caregivers who fail to show this quality may be neglectful or available only occasionally; others are callous to infants' feelings.
- *They regularly express affection.* Caregivers dote on babies by caressing them, holding them gently, looking into their eyes, talking to them, and expressing tenderness and warmth. Caregivers who fail to show this quality may be withdrawn or even hostile and rejecting.
- *They permit babies to influence the pace and direction of their mutual interactions.* Caregivers let infants take the lead on occasion. They carefully note where infants are looking, notice their body posture, and recognize when infants want to interact (Isabella & Belsky, 1991; Nievar & Becker, 2008; D. N. Stern, 1977). Caregivers act in synchrony with infants, letting them take a turn in an interaction by smiling, moving their hands, or babbling. Caregivers who fail to show this quality may be overly intrusive, perhaps to the point that babies look away from them, cry, or try to go to sleep. Other caregivers may fail to notice or respond to infants' bids for affection—for example, they may ignore infants' attempts to make eye contact.

Cultural setting.   Cultural groups vary in their emphasis on an exclusive, uninterrupted relationship with mothers. For example, many Japanese infants become quite upset when their mothers leave the room and take a while to calm down when their mothers return (Miyake, Chen, & Campos, 1985; Takahashi, 1990). In Japan, infants' separation from mothers is not common, mother–child intimacy is fostered, and any necessary babysitting duties are typically assumed by close relatives (especially grandparents) rather than by strangers (Saarni

disorganized and disoriented attachment
Attachment classification in which children lack a single coherent way of responding to attachment figures.

Observation Guidelines

Assessing Young Children's Attachment Security

Characteristic	Look For	Example	Implication
Secure Attachment	· Active, intentional exploration of the environment in the presence of the caregiver · Protest at being separated from a caregiver; ability to be soothed when the caregiver returns · Initial wariness of strangers, with subsequent acceptance if reassured by the caregiver	Luis cries when his father drops him off at the child care center in the morning. After a few minutes, he settles down and crawls to a familiar and affectionate caregiver who is beginning to become an additional attachment figure for him.	It is natural for young children to resist separation from family members. Help them establish a routine of saying good-bye in the morning, and give them extra attention during this transition. Reassure parents and other family members by describing how their children go about settling down and the activities the children typically turn to when they relax.
Insecure-Avoidant Attachment	· Superficial exploration of the environment · Indifference to a caregiver's departure; failure to seek comfort upon the caregiver's return · Apparent discomfort around strangers, but without an active resistance to their overtures	Jennifer walks around her new child care center with a frown on her face. She parts easily with her mother and willingly explores her new environment, albeit without much enthusiasm. Jennifer glances up when her mother comes at the end of the day, but she doesn't seem overjoyed about her mother's return.	Independence from parents is often a sign of children's familiarity with child care or preschool settings. For children who seem at ease with separation, support them throughout the day. When children appear indifferent to family members, form your own affectionate relationships with these children, knowing that such relationships could become children's first secure bonds.
Insecure-Resistant Attachment	· Exceptional clinginess and anxiety with caregiver · Agitation and distress at the caregiver's departure; continued crying or fussing after the caregiver returns · Apparent fear of strangers; tendency to stay close to caregiver in new situation	Irene tightly clutches her mother as the two enter the preschool building, and she stays close by as her mother signs her in for the morning. She is extremely upset when her mother leaves and remains distressed for quite some time after her mother's return a few hours later.	If children appear anxious when they enter a new child care or preschool setting, give them extra time to part from their parents. Sometimes a "comfort" object from home (a teddy bear or blanket) can help. Be patient and reassuring as you interact with these children, knowing that they may eventually form a secure attachment to you.
Disorganized and Disoriented Attachment or Other Serious Attachment Problem	· Unpredictable emotional responses · Cautious approaches to familiar caregiver · By end of first year, failure to contact caregiver when distressed · Reckless exploration without use of caregiver as a secure base · Reversed roles, with excessive concern about caregiver · No signs of attachment to family members or other familiar caregivers, or fear of them · Indiscriminately friendly behavior with no preferential actions toward family members · Signs of overwhelming grief after the death of a primary caregiver	Myles seems lost at school. He arrives hungry, walks aimlessly for some time, and eventually sits to play with blocks. He is aggressive with his peers, and his teacher sees bruises on his arms.	Provide special attention to and closely monitor children who seem disorganized and disoriented in their attachment. Be on the lookout for signs of abuse, and be ready to seek advice from authorities. Remember that these children are *not* doomed to serious lifelong problems, but you must work hard to establish positive, trusting relationships with them.

Sources: Ainsworth et al., 1978; Greenberg, 1999; Main & Solomon, 1986, 1990; R. A. Thompson, 2006; Zeanah, 2000.

et al., 2006). In contrast, in Germany, many babies do not fret much when their mothers leave the room, nor do they move frantically toward mothers when they return (K. E. Grossmann, Grossmann, Huber, & Wartner, 1981; LeVine & Norman, 2008). These mothers regularly leave infants to do brief errands, and the infants seem to grow accustomed to getting along on their own, at least for brief periods of time.

Cultural groups also differ in how parents respond to infants' distress (Morelli & Rothbaum, 2007). For example, Gusii mothers of Kenya continually hold, comfort, and watch their infants, and their infants rarely cry (LeVine, 2004). Gusii mothers are alarmed when they watch videos of Western mothers allowing infants to cry, even for a few moments. In comparison, some Western mothers believe that they are cultivating self-reliance in infants when they allow infants to comfort themselves. Consider the experience of a German aunt who is caring for Karl, almost 2 years of age, while his parents are away on a 2-week vacation:

> "Oh, he's a good boy, but a bit fussy," his aunt says. . . . The aunt tells of how early he wakes up in the morning, at six o'clock, "but I'm not to take him out of bed, Sigrid (Karl's mother) said, he's to stay there until nine or he'll just get used to it and she won't have it; she's done that from when he was a baby." So Karl is kept in bed, he stays quiet, she doesn't know what he does, hears him move about in his bed, babbling to himself. (LeVine & Norman, 2008, p. 134)

Almost universally, parents respond to their children in a warm and engaging way, but the styles of expressing involvement differ considerably across cultures (P. M. Cole & Tan, 2007). Many parents (especially those living in North America and Western Europe) frequently and tenderly respond to their infants' cooing and babbling. Consider an affectionate interaction between a U.S. father and his 3-month-old daughter Toto after a family event (Reissland, 2006). In the following exchange, the father interacts good-naturedly with Toto, regularly waiting for, and then commenting on, her vocalizations:

Father:	5:30 p.m. Post-mortem on a party.
Toto:	Eh.
Father:	What was your reaction? What was your reaction? Did you like the food?
Toto:	Ah! Ahaa ah.
Father:	Yeah, that milk huh? It wasn't so bad, huh? And the guests—did you like the guests?
Toto:	Eh.
Father:	No, not so interesting.
Toto:	Eh! Ah ah.
Father:	What about the host and hostess?
Toto:	Aha aaaaah!
Father:	Yeah! Uncle Jim and Auntie Ann!
Toto:	Aaah!
Father:	Yeah, they're very nice.
Toto:	Ha! Ha! Ha! Oh.
Father:	Yeah; and did you enjoy yourself?
Toto:	Aha! Aaah! Aaah!
Father:	Yeah you had a good time. Well that's nice.
Toto:	Ah haa!
Father:	Well that's really nice.
Toto:	Heheh! Ahh! Hehh!
Father:	Did you think so as well? Yeah, I think so. Hmm? Yes?
Toto:	Hah! Aaaah! Ah!
Father:	You didn't cry at all and you were very polite!
	(dialogue from Reissland, 2006, p. 44)

From this exchange and other similar interactions, Toto is learning that her father can be trusted to be warm, reliable, and respectful of her efforts at communication. Yet many parents from other societies do not focus on infants' vocalizations and instead show their sensitivity through gentle touch and anticipation of infants' needs. Like Toto, infants in these other cultures learn that their parents can be trusted to love and care for them.

Variations in core beliefs appear to be at the root of cultural differences in attachment. For example, in *individualistic societies,* parents encourage children to become independent, competitive, and assertive about their personal desires (Kağitçibaşi, 2007; Markus & Hamedani, 2007; Oyserman & Lee, 2007; Triandis, 2007; also see Chapter 3). Many parents from Western societies cultivate an individualistic orientation. These parents show their sensitivity by closely observing infants' signals of interest and current emotional states, treating vocalizations and emotional expressions as valid gestures (as Toto's father did), and respecting infants' independent explorations of their surroundings (Morelli & Rothbaum, 2007). Thus, separations from parents are usually only mildly stressful, and infants develop the habit of exploring the properties of nearby objects on their own.

In contrast, in *collectivistic societies,* parents encourage children to be obedient and dependent, cooperative, respectful, and invested in the family's harmony (see Chapter 3). Many parents from collectivistic societies, such as those in many Hispanic and Asian cultures, show their sensitivity by maintaining physical closeness with infants, anticipating infants' experiences (e.g., being hungry or having a dirty diaper), and tending to these needs before infants cry or protest (Morelli & Rothbaum, 2007). Parents from collectivistic societies also tend to foster close, dependent relationships. Experiencing this kind of upbringing, many infants from collectivistic societies find separations stressful, prefer to remain in close contact with caregivers, and gradually learn to moderate their own demands in accordance with parents' goals and the needs of the family as a whole.

Children's activities and characteristics.   A third factor affecting the security of children's attachment is the children themselves. Children actively participate in their relationships with caregivers by making their needs known, relaxing when comforted, and reciprocating with affection.

The manner in which individual children go about forming relationships with caregivers depends somewhat on their particular abilities and dispositions. For example, through their unique ways of handling stress and relating to others, infants influence the manner in which caregivers respond to them. Whereas some fuss a lot when scared, others protest less adamantly. Infants who are exceptionally fearful and irritable are somewhat difficult to care for, whereas those who are even tempered and sociable invite positive interactions. Similarly, some fussy babies do not as readily notice that their parents are trying to comfort them and find it difficult to relax in parents' arms (R. A. Thompson, 2006). Despite these possible influences of infants' dispositions, most parents are generally able to be sensitive to a wide range of emotional styles in children. Overall, then, children's dispositions play only a small role in the types of attachments they form.

Similarly, for most children with disabilities, their special circumstances may play only a minor role in the security of their bonds to parents and other caregivers. Babies who are premature, show developmental delays, and are unusually fussy tend to develop secure attachments as long as their individual needs are met with patience and compassion (van IJzendoorn, Goldberg, Kroonenberg, & Frenkel, 1992). Likewise, many babies with chromosomal or genetic disorders or other disabilities form secure attachments with parents who provide responsive and attentive care (E. A. Carlson, Sampson, & Sroufe, 2003; D. Howe, 2006).

Multiple Attachments

Because women physically bear children and often do most of the feeding, bathing, and diapering, early research examined *mothers* as primary attachment figures (Ainsworth et al., 1978; Bowlby, 1969/1982). Increasingly, research has examined the significant roles that fathers, other caregivers, and siblings play as attachment figures.

When two parents are present in the home, infants may frequently show an initial preference for one parent and soon thereafter treat the second parent as an attachment figure. Both parents are likely to instill secure attachments when they sensitively respond to children's needs and are present in children's lives for an extended time (Howes, 1999; R. A. Thompson et al., 2003). Nevertheless, mothers and fathers sometimes go about expressing their warmth in slightly different ways. Mothers tend to be more hands-on in physically caring for infants, enthusiastic and happy while interacting with infants, and thoughtful about what their infants might be thinking, whereas fathers tend to engage infants in fun, physical play (M. E. Lamb & Lewis, 2004; Lundy, 2003; Malmberg et al., 2007). You can observe a father's playful style with his 7-month-old daughter in the "Emotional Development: Infancy" video in MyEducationLab.

Contemporary research on attachment examines the nurturing bonds that children form with other people in addition to parents. For example, children in Israeli kibbutzim spend considerable time in settings with adults who are not members of their families (van IJzendoorn, Sagi, & Lambermon, 1992). Children in numerous societies also grow strongly at-

MyEducationLab

Observe 7-month-old Madison and her father interact playfully and affectionately in the "Emotional Development: Infancy" video. (Find Video Examples in Chapter 11 of MyEducationLab.)

tached to siblings, developing bonds that often las a lifetime (M. Lewis, 2005). Such networks of nurturing adults and siblings have important benefits for children, who can rely on many trustworthy individuals for affectionate care and gain options for different kinds of support over time (C. B. Fisher et al., 1998; Howes, 1999). For instance, a 1-year-old crawls to Grandma when a stranger enters the family home; at 6, the same child now seeks advice from his older sister as he faces bullies on the playground; and at 14, the youngster has heart-to-heart talks with an uncle about career options.

Children also form attachments to employed caregivers and teachers in child care centers and classrooms. Secure attachments with these figures, as with parents, depend on responsive care, sustained relationships, and mutual emotional investment (Ahnert, Pinquart, & Lamb, 2006; Howes, 1999). Yet the specific qualities of relationships with caregivers and teachers change somewhat as children grow. During the preschool and elementary years, children often develop close bonds with teachers, thriving on teachers' affectionate care and gaining a sense of security in their presence (H. A. Davis, 2003; Pianta & Steinberg, 1992). In the middle school years, close relationships with teachers occur but are now less common because young adolescents spend only a small portion of time with any single teacher, are in classes with large groups of students, and may feel anonymous in the classroom. When young adolescents have supportive relationships with their teachers, they tend to enjoy school, feel competent, and achieve at high levels academically (H. A. Davis, 2003; Roeser, Eccles, & Sameroff, 2000; Roeser, Midgley, & Urdan, 1996). In high school, the obstacles to close relationships with teachers intensify. Adolescents often find relationships with teachers to be adversarial—it's "us" against "them"—possibly because many high school teachers view adolescents as rebellious, independent, and resistant to close relationships with teachers (H. A. Davis, 2003). Yet good relationships with teachers are possible and clearly beneficial for youth. High school students who have supportive relationships with teachers are more likely to be well adjusted and to complete high school than students without such relationships (Battin-Pearson et al., 2000; Cotterell, 1992).

Many infants form close bonds with their older siblings.

Attachment Security and Later Development

A secure attachment during infancy predicts later positive long-term outcomes in youngsters. In Western cultures, children who have been securely attached as infants tend to become relatively independent, empathic, socially competent preschoolers, especially in comparison with children who have been insecurely attached (Sroufe, 1983; Sroufe, Egeland, Carlson, & Collins, 2005; Vaughn, Egeland, Sroufe, & Waters, 1979). In middle childhood and adolescence, they tend to be self-confident, adjust easily to school environments, establish productive relationships with teachers and peers, do well at classroom tasks, and eventually graduate from high school (Lucas-Thompson & Clarke-Stewart, 2007; R. F. Marcus & Sanders-Reio, 2001; E. O'Connor & McCartney, 2006; Schneider, Atkinson, & Tardif, 2001; Urban, Carlson, Egeland, & Sroufe, 1991). In non-Western cultures, securely attached children may develop slightly different characteristics that are valued in their society. As you learned earlier in this chapter, caregivers in Japan encourage infants to rely on immediate family members. For Japanese children, close and affectionate relationships with caregivers foster dependence on caregivers' benevolence and a desire to act harmoniously with others (Morelli & Rothbaum, 2007).

How is it that early attachments affect children's later relationships and adjustment? Attachment theorists believe that a secure attachment sets the stage for later relationships and helps children form positive, self-fulfilling expectations about other people. As children gain experience with primary caregivers, they begin to form an understanding, or *mental representation,* of what relationships with other people are like (Bowlby, 1969/1982, 1973; R. M. Ryan, Stiller, & Lynch, 1994). Especially when they are young, children's understanding of "typical" relationships is largely unconscious but nevertheless influential in directing how they relate to other individuals, including teachers (Hofer, 2006; Maier, Bernier, Pekrun, Zimmermann, & Grossmann, 2004; R. M. Ryan et al., 1994). Secure children expect other people to be trustworthy, and they give second chances to those who initially let them down—expectations and actions that feed and sustain healthy interpersonal ties. In contrast, children with insecure attachments may form expectations of other people as untrustworthy (Main, 1995).

Although attachment theorists initially suggested that an infant's early attachments to primary caregivers (especially the mother) set the tone for *all* future relationships (e.g., Bowlby, 1973), more recent research has shown otherwise. As Merv's experience in the opening case study reveals, the kinds of bonds children form with their mothers do not firmly dictate the kinds of bonds they make with other caregivers. Children who have had an insecure attachment or other serious problem in relationships with parents often develop secure attachments to caregivers outside the family (R. A. Thompson, 2006).

Quality of parenting can also change over time, leading to changes in children's attachments. For example, in one investigation children whose parents were initially harsh and insensitive but later exhibited higher quality parenting were likely to develop increasingly productive social skills (NICHD Early Child Care Research Network, 2006b). The reverse trend also occurs. Children's secure bonds sometimes deteriorate due to stressful events. For instance, children who initially form secure attachments but later live through one or more traumatic events (perhaps parents get divorced, a family member dies or suffers a debilitating illness, or the children are physically or sexually abused by a family member) may have difficulty forming good relationships as adolescents or adults (M. Lewis, Feiring, & Rosenthal, 2000; Mikulincer & Shaver, 2007; E. Waters, Merrick, Treboux, Crowell, & Albersheim, 2000).

Furthermore, as youngsters grow older, their attachments to peers (perhaps to best friends and, eventually, to romantic partners) may be significantly different from those they have previously formed with parents (M. W. Baldwin, Keelan, Fehr, Enns, & Koh-Rangarajoo, 1996; La Guardia, Ryan, Couchman, & Deci, 2000). Apparently, growing children and adolescents supplement their initial mental representation of what interpersonal relationships are like with new understandings of how relationships can unfold (M. W. Baldwin et al., 1996). Eventually, these various mental representations become integrated as a part of the child's personality (R. A. Thompson, 2006). In other words, children may initially develop trust in a parent and later become trusting people themselves.

Implications of Attachment Research

As we have seen, infants' attachments provide the foundation for later relationships. This foundation can be rebuilt if it's shaky, and it must occasionally be bolstered if, despite a solid beginning, it later weakens in the face of adverse circumstances (R. A. Thompson, 2006). In essence, secure attachment is like a multivitamin: It increases the chances of, but does not guarantee, good health. Conversely, a child with an early insecure attachment may, with love and guidance, become a happy, productive adult. Drawing from attachment literature, we offer these recommendations for adults who work with children and adolescents:

Children often form secure attachments to caregivers who sensitively care for them over an extended time.

• *Care for young children in a warm and sensitive manner.* Although family members are usually the recipients of children's first attachments, young children often form close bonds with employed caregivers, especially those who are familiar and trustworthy. The Development and Practice feature "Offering Warm and Sensitive Care to Infants and Toddlers" illustrates such high-quality care.

• *Give children time to adjust to you.* It takes time for infants to form bonds with new caregivers, although the particular difficulties infants face may depend partly on the quality of their relationship with parents. For example, infants who are securely attached to parents usually need time to adjust to an unfamiliar caregiver's unique personality and style of responding to them. In the meantime, caregivers will need to offer lots of comfort when infants protest separations from parents. Infants who have not yet experienced sensitive care may feel anxious or withdrawn for an even longer period of time before they are able to conclude that a new adult can be trusted. While children are adjusting, practitioners can be affectionate, meet children's needs, empathize with their feelings, and celebrate their accomplishments. In fact, children without prior secure attachments to parents often benefit immensely when other caregivers act consistently and lovingly (Howes & Ritchie, 1998; NICHD Early Child Care Research Network, 1997).

• *Promote emotional bonds in children of all ages.* The need for close attachments does not end with infancy. Children stand to gain immensely by having high-quality relation-

Offering Warm and Sensitive Care to Infants and Toddlers

· **Meet infants' needs in a timely fashion.**

An infant program has one caregiver for every three infants so that no child has to be left unattended for very long. When it is impossible to tend immediately to the needs of individual children, the caregiver reassures children that their needs are important and that she will provide care as soon as possible.

· **Respond positively to newly developed abilities.**

Caregivers in one center celebrate milestones as they notice them, including new teeth, advances in crawling, first steps, and first words. They share their admiration with family members but are sensitive to the desire of parents and other family members to be among the first to witness the accomplishment: "Raj is getting ready to walk, isn't he!"

· **Be polite but matter-of-fact when referring to infants' bodies.**

The director of an infant program trains staff members to use neutral terms for body functions. For example, she asks a new teacher not to use the term "stinky baby," but instead to make a simple statement that an infant's diaper needs to be changed.

· **Set limits and redirect unacceptable behavior in a firm, but gentle way.**

The director of an infant-toddler program reminds teachers that their role is one of a *nurturer* who helps children learn self-control rather than an *authority figure* who doles out punishments. Concretely, he suggests, "Tell children what they *can* do instead of telling them what they *cannot* do. For example, you might say, 'Walk inside, please. Run outside.'"

· **Structure group infant care so that infants can form and maintain stable relationships with caregivers.**

An infant-toddler program is arranged into separate rooms so that each caregiver has a small number of infants with whom to form close relationships. Toddler teachers make a point to visit the infant room occasionally, so that they get to know children who will soon be moving to their room. In another center, caregivers arrange groups of children that stay together; as the infants outgrow the "Infant Room," for example, they "graduate" together to the "Toddler Room," and their caregiver goes with them.

ships with their teachers during the elementary, middle, and high school years. Generally, teachers and caregivers of infants, young children, and elementary school children find it easier to become acquainted with individual children than do practitioners working with adolescents. However, teachers of middle and high school students can also express their concern for individual students and get to know those adolescents they advise or see often (H. A. Davis, 2003). Adults can also foster ties among youngsters, giving them chances to become involved in clubs and sports teams, work together in projects, and so forth.

• ***Model affectionate caregiving for family members.*** Parents who had insecure relationships themselves tend to lack confidence in their parenting and in some instances obtain little pleasure from interacting with their children (Mikulincer & Shaver, 2007). One of the most effective tactics family educators can take with insensitive parents is to *show* them (in person or through videotapes) how eagerly infants devour affectionate gestures, especially during such routine games as playing peekaboo and sharing simple nursery rhymes (Bakermans-Kranenburg, van IJzendoorn, & Juffer, 2003). Caregivers and educators can demonstrate how to hold a baby tenderly and return the baby's smiles, vocalizations, and eye contact. They also can point out the signals infants give to indicate that they are not ready to play (e.g., averting a gaze) or have had enough (e.g., pouting).

• ***Encourage parents to watch their children's self-initiated actions.*** Practitioners can encourage parents to watch their children carefully and notice children's interests and preferences. Babies can learn a great deal by performing such simple activities as looking at their fingers, sucking on their toes, and listening to voices. When parents appreciate the significance of infants' spontaneous learning, they are more inclined to affirm and extend it ("Look at that mirror, Abigail! Is it shiny? Do you see yourself?").

• ***Encourage parents to think about how infants and children understand events.*** Parents do not always understand what makes their babies "tick" ("Why does Mike keep jumping out of his crib? Every time he does this, he gets hurt. What is he *thinking?*"). Professionals can casually share ideas about infants' motives, feelings, and understandings to help parents appreciate how babies might view the world ("Mike is one determined little guy, isn't he? He really wants to explore his environment!"). When parents reflect on how infants feel and construe events, attachments tend to be more secure (Koren-Karie, Oppenheim, Dolev, Sher, & Etzion-Carasso, 2002).

● ***Advise parents about the special needs of children with disabilities.*** Some parents feel so overwhelmed by the challenge of caring for a child with a disability that they find it difficult to identify their child's unique perspective. Teachers and caregivers can help parents recognize their child's distinctive ways of communicating and expressing emotions. For example, you might ask parents of a blind baby if the baby enjoys exploring their faces with her hands. Similarly, you could point out to parents of a child with Down syndrome that children with this condition sometimes express their discomfort in subtle, rather than insistent ways, and that these children often appreciate it when caregivers occasionally slow down during interactions and give them a chance to control the flow of the exchange (D. Howe, 2006).

● ***When parents divorce, help children remain attached to both parents.*** Many divorced parents share custody of children, making it likely that children will maintain attachments to both parents. Teachers can help by sending home duplicate copies of newsletters and correspondence to both parents' homes. Family educators and counselors can also talk with parents about ways in which children of different ages handle rotations between two households (J. B. Kelly & Lamb, 2000).

● ***Acknowledge and encourage multiple attachments.*** In the child care center and at school, children may talk about a variety of people in their lives (e.g., brothers and sisters, aunts and uncles, grandparents, and neighbors). Teachers and other practitioners can encourage children to invite some of these individuals to school events and orientation meetings. And as you will learn in Chapter 15, teachers can establish a productive social climate in the classroom that fosters youngsters' relationships with one another.

● ***Offer a range of services when children are placed with new families.*** When children are removed from families because of maltreatment or neglect, children frequently form healthy bonds with new caregivers (Chisholm, Carter, Ames, & Morison, 1995; Howes & Segal, 1993; Marcovitch et al., 1997). However, professionals who work with children and their new families should not leave this adjustment to chance. Instead, they can prepare new families to recognize and meet children's individual needs. For example, a foster family might be advised to expect temper tantrums from an 8-year-old child who has recently joined the family. With coaching, family members can learn to communicate their expectations for controlled behavior, follow through with agreed-on consequences when rules are violated, and persist in showing love even though the child has not yet learned to reciprocate the affection.

● ***Encourage sympathetic dispositions in children.*** Some children who have had few affectionate relationships develop poor social skills and so may, in many people's eyes, be difficult children to like. They may appear self-centered and unconcerned about others' distress; for example, they may hit a peer who has gotten hurt rather than offer sympathy (Volling, 2001). To help a child who seems uncaring, you can model appropriate reactions when someone is hurt, talk about the hurt person's feelings, and encourage the child to offer help and show sympathy.

● ***Be especially sensitive and consistent with children who show insecurity or other attachment problems.*** Children who have not yet developed secure attachments to parents may benefit from your extra efforts to keep social routines affectionate and consistent, especially insofar as they affect children's arrivals and departures. In addition, without prior history of a warm, mutually loving relationship, children may need repeated experiences with the pleasant give-and-take of social interaction (C. S. Cain, 2006; Mercer, 2006). Depending on the age of the child, you might sit quietly with the child in a relaxing activity, such as building blocks together or tossing a ball back and forth.

● ***Address the needs of both parents and infants when parents struggle with unmet emotional needs.*** When parents themselves are emotionally depressed, they may be unresponsive toward their infants, or even hostile and intrusive (Teti, Gelfand, Messinger, & Isabella, 1995). In turn, infants may become chronically sad and withdrawn. Professional intervention that helps parents resolve their emotional needs may be a necessary step before they are able to use an involved, affectionate parenting style (Benoit & Parker, 1994; Main, Kaplan, & Cassidy, 1985). During the period in which a parent receives mental health treat-

Regularly scheduled educational and recreational activities can help adolescents form new bonds with a variety of supportive adults and peers.

ment, the other parent or another family member may be able to pick up the slack and provide children with loving attention.

• ***Seek professional guidance when attachment problems are serious.*** Some attachment problems are so serious that families require the services of a counselor, psychologist, or social worker (C. S. Cain, 2006; Mercer, 2006). Thus it is important for practitioners to be alert for signs of deeply troubled infant–family relationships. You should definitely seek professional guidance when you suspect a serious problem—for instance, when a distressed child never seeks comfort from a familiar caregiver, shows fear of a family member, or displays some other highly unusual style of responding to family members (see indicators of serious attachment problems in the Observations Guidelines table "Assessing Young Children's Attachment Security" on p. 412).

In their relationships with attachment figures, children learn to express their pleasure, distress, and other feelings. Expressing emotions is an important development in its own right and the focus of the next section.

Emotion

Emotions (sometimes referred to as *affective states*) are the feelings, both physiological and psychological, that people have in response to events that are personally relevant to their needs and goals (Campos et al., 2004). Emotions energize thinking and acting in ways that are often adaptive to present circumstances (Goleman, 1995; Saarni et al., 2006). For example, *sadness* may lead a child to find comfort from others and reassess whether a goal is possible; *anger* may spur a child to try a new tactic or abandon an unrealistic goal; and *happiness* may prompt a child to share positive feelings with others and pursue a similar pleasurable experience in the future (Saarni et al., 2006). These and other emotions are described in the Observation Guidelines table "Assessing the Emotions of Children and Adolescents."

Developmental Changes in Emotions

The ways that youngsters express, understand, and cope with emotions change with age and experience. Emotional development is characterized by these specific trends:

• ***Infants begin life with a few basic emotions and gradually add new feelings.*** *Contentment, interest,* and *distress* are shown within the first 6 months of life (Emde, Gaensbauer, & Harmon, 1976; Hiatt, Campos, & Emde, 1979; Stenberg & Campos, 1990). Hungry babies most certainly feel pleasure when they begin to feed (M. Lewis, 2000). A small smile may occur when infants are relaxed, happy, or enchanted with animated people. Infants show interest by watching objects carefully, inspecting their own body parts, mouthing fingers and toes, and tilting their heads to listen closely to the fine points of speech and music. Newborns exposed to a loud and sudden noise express distress, usually by crying; they do the same when hunger and fatigue mount.

As they mature, infants add to their basic emotions. Simple distress can become true *anger* when infants' desires are obstructed: Daddy does not come immediately to pick baby up, and Mommy does not indulge baby's desire to press buttons on the DVD player. Infants show their anger vividly by crying, thrashing, and looking directly, with accusation, at caregivers. Infants tend to show *fear* during the second half of the first year. This new emotion is evident in the stranger anxiety we examined earlier as a sign of attachment. Animals and objects that move in unexpected ways also often scare infants.

• ***Infants respond to other people's emotions.*** A basic ability to detect emotions in others is present even in infancy (Caron, Caron, & MacLean, 1988; Haviland & Lelwica, 1987; G. M. Schwartz, Izard, & Ansul, 1985). This is illustrated by the **emotional contagion** of babies: When one starts crying, others soon join in (Eisenberg, 1992; Hatfield, Cacioppo, & Rapson, 1994; Saarni et al., 2006). And within the first few months of life, infants react to the emotional expressions of caregivers in meaningful ways. For example, by 4 months, infants sometimes look away when other people show sad expressions, intently study the faces of

emotion
Affective response to an event that is personally relevant to one's needs and goals.

emotional contagion
Tendency for infants to cry spontaneously when they hear other infants crying.

Assessing the Emotions of Children and Adolescents

Characteristic	Look For	Example	Implication
Happiness	· Smiles · Laughter · Spontaneity	Paul, age 17, chatters with his friends during his school's end-of-the-year athletic field day. He is happy about having schoolwork over and looks forward to his summer job and paychecks.	Happiness helps people enjoy life and seek similar pleasurable experiences. Help children and adolescents find appropriate outlets to express their joy, and celebrate with them. Encourage them to talk about things they are happy about.
Anger	· Frowns and angry expressions · Possible retaliation toward the source of anger	Aranya, age 14, is furious that she wasn't admitted into an elective course, whereas her two closest friends were. Aranya is angry with her teacher, who she thinks dislikes her.	Anger helps people deal with obstacles to their goals, often spurring them to try new tactics. Help youngsters express their anger appropriately and determine how they can redirect their energy toward reasonable solutions.
Fear	· Frightened expression · Withdrawal from circumstances · Physiological responses, such as sweating	Tony, age 2½, sits on his mat, eyes wide, body tense. He stares at a new poster of a clown in his preschool classroom. On this particular day, he becomes downright scared; he runs to his teacher and buries his head in her lap.	Fear occurs when people feel threatened and believe that their physical safety and psychological well-being are potentially at stake. Fear motivates people to flee, escape from harm, seek reassurance, and perhaps fight back. Help children articulate their fears. Offer reassurance.
Sadness	· Sad expression · Crying · Pouting · Being quiet · Possible withdrawal from a situation	Greta, age 15, sits quietly on a bench near her locker. With her head hung low, she rereads the letter from a cheerleading organization. She has not been admitted to a prestigious cheerleading summer camp.	People are sad when they realize they cannot attain a desired goal or when they experience a loss, such as a friend moving to a distant city. Sadness causes some people to reassess their goals. Reassure children, help them express their sadness, and encourage them to consider ways to deal with sad feelings.
Disgust	· Wrinkled nose · Remarks such as "Phew!" · Withdrawal from the source of displeasure	Norton, age 8, looks skeptically at the meal he has just purchased in the school cafeteria. He wrinkles his nose and averts his gaze from the "tuna melt" on his plate.	Disgust occurs when people encounter food, smells, and sights they find repulsive. Disgust is nature's way of getting people to be wary of something that is potentially troublesome or threatening to their health. Respect children's feeling of disgust, but also encourage them to reflect on why they might have this reaction.
Anxiety	· Frequent worrying · Excessive fidgeting, hand wringing, or nail biting · Avoidance of source of anxiety	Tanesha, age 16, has to give an oral presentation to her class. She has spent a lot of time preparing but is worried that, when she is standing all by herself in front of the group, she might get so nervous that she forgets everything she wants to say.	As long as it is not excessive, anxiety can spur people to take steps to avoid problems and achieve valued goals. Teach youngsters strategies that keep anxiety at a manageable level, as well as strategies that help them achieve their goals.
Shame	· Signs of embarrassment · Attempts to withdraw from a situation · Looking down and away from other people	Luke, age 9, is stunned. He's just had an accident, urinating on the floor. He had felt a bit antsy beforehand but wasn't aware that he needed to use the toilet. Now 20 pairs of eyes are glued on him.	When children feel ashamed, they are aware of other people's standards for behavior and know they are not meeting those standards. Shame motivates children to try harder. Shame works only when it comes from within; adults should never intentionally ridicule students. Help children redirect their behavior so they can meet their own standards.

Observation Guidelines (continued)

Characteristic	Look For	Example	Implication
Guilt	· Sad expression · Self-conscious demeanor · Possible concern for a person who has been harmed	A.J., age 12, regrets bad-mouthing his friend Pete to other classmates. A.J. sinks down low in his chair, feeling remorse for what he said behind Pete's back and for Pete's sadness.	Guilt occurs when people do something that violates their own standards. It leads people to right the wrong. More generally, it causes people to behave in socially appropriate ways that protect others from harm. Help children express their feelings and realize that they can behave differently next time.
Pride	· Happy expression · Desire to show off work and accomplishments to other people	Jacinda, age 5, is beaming. For the last 20 minutes, she's painstakingly pasted sequins, stars, and feathers onto a mask. Her final product is a colorful, delicately adorned creation. She is happy with her work, as is evident from her ear-to-ear grin.	People are proud when they earn others' respect and meet their own goals. Pride fosters continued commitment to behaving appropriately and achieving high standards. Pride motivates people to share their accomplishments with others. Encourage children to identify things that make them proud. Share in their joy when they accomplish something meaningful for them.

Source: Adaptive functions of emotions based on material in Saarni et al., 2006.

people who look angry, and initially attend to others' fearful expressions and then look away (Montague & Walker-Andrews, 2001). When caregivers violate infants' expectations for a particular emotional expression (perhaps by showing no smiles after a period of social play), infants also react. Between 3 and 9 months, they may respond to a parent's deadpan face by smiling, crying, looking away, and using self-soothing behaviors such as sucking their thumbs (G. A. Moore, Cohn, & Campbell, 2001; Striano & Berlin, 2004; Tronick, Als, Adamson, Wise, & Brazelton, 1978).

● **Children learn to guide their actions on the basis of other people's emotional expressions.** In the first year or two of life, children also show an inclination to monitor the emotions of others, particularly parents and trusted caregivers. As you learned in Chapter 7, infants show *social referencing* early in their second year: They watch their parents' faces, especially in the presence of a novel or puzzling phenomenon (Boccia & Campos, 1989; Saarni et al., 2006). For instance, a 2-year-old girl may glance at Mommy's face when a new babysitter enters the house. By determining whether Mommy is smiling or frowning, the little girl gains a sense of how to respond to the babysitter.

● **Children expand their repertoire of basic emotions to include self-conscious emotions.** Simple emotions such as fear, anger, and pleasure in infancy are joined by **self-conscious emotions** in early childhood. These are affective states that reflect awareness of social standards (M. Lewis, 1993, 1995; Saarni et al., 2006). Self-conscious emotions include guilt, shame, and pride. Teresa recalls early displays of guilt in both of her sons. As toddlers and preschoolers, the boys would often respond angrily when misbehavior resulted in their being sent to their room or having a privilege taken away. Occasionally they'd swat at her or stomp out of the room. However, they'd often return a while later, looking at her face for signs of sadness and affectionately rubbing her arm as they apologized.

● **Children increasingly reflect on emotions.** As early as age 2 or 3, children talk about emotions that they and others experience ("Daniel got mad and pushed me"), and they realize that emotions are connected to people's desires ("Kurt loves to go down the slide and was really mad when he didn't get a turn") (Bretherton, Fritz, Zahn-Waxler, & Ridgeway, 1986; Dunn, Bretherton, & Munn, 1987; Wellman, Harris, Banerjee, & Sinclair, 1995). By middle childhood, they realize that their interpretations of a situation determine how they feel about it and that other people may have different interpretations and, as a result, different feelings ("Arlene feels bad because she thinks I don't like her") (P. L. Harris, 1989). Children also learn to connect words for emotions (*happy, sad, angry,* etc.) with particular facial expressions and with conditions under which these emotions may be elicited. In the drawings

self-conscious emotion
Affective state that reflects awareness of a community's social standards (e.g., pride, guilt, shame).

Figure 11-1

Drawings of basic emotional expressions by Alex (age 5) and Connor (age 13).

Figure 11-2

Seven-year-old Miguel drew and commented on his efforts to express anger appropriately. He wrote, "I try not to hit and shout."

emotional regulation
Strategies to manage affective states.

in Figure 11-1, two boys, ages 5 and 13, both show considerable knowledge of how different emotions might be reflected in people's facial expressions.

By middle childhood, children begin to realize that emotional expressions do not always reflect people's true feelings (Saarni et al., 2006; Selman, 1980). For instance, a 9-year-old may observe his teacher's cheerful demeanor yet realize she just lost her brother to cancer and is probably sad inside. During the end of middle childhood and the beginning of adolescence, children also understand that they and other people can have ambivalent and conflicting feelings (S. K. Donaldson & Westerman, 1986; Harter & Whitesell, 1989; N. Stein, Trabasso, & Liwag, 2000). For instance, a 12-year-old girl may love her father but be angry with him for moving out of the house; she may like going to see him during custodial visits but not like the feelings of turmoil the visits evoke in her.

● **Children and adolescents gradually learn to regulate their emotions.** As you discovered in Chapter 3, children slowly learn to control various aspects of their behavior. One important aspect of *self-regulation* is **emotional regulation,** the management of affective states (Campos, Frankel, & Camras, 2004; R. A. Thompson, 1994a). Children gradually acquire a constellation of strategies that help them cope with their feelings and deal with stressful situations (E. M. Brenner & Salovey, 1997; Saarni et al., 2006).

As newborns, infants need help when they feel hungry, scared, or hurt. Most can count on caregivers to help them find relief. But soon infants also learn to soothe themselves to some extent: They may suck on a thumb, avert their gaze from a stranger, or crawl away from a scary toy (Mangelsdorf et al., 1995; R. A. Thompson et al., 2003). Of course, they continue to depend as well on caregivers to help them manage uncomfortable feelings. Without such support, infants may develop unhealthy emotional habits. For example, if parents habitually leave crying babies alone for extended periods, the babies may grow increasingly agitated when they cry, a pattern that makes it difficult later for parents to calm them down (Eisenberg, Cumberland, & Spinrad, 1988; R. A. Thompson et al., 2003).

As children grow, experience a range of emotionally significant events, and observe role models, they acquire more coping strategies (Saarni et al., 2006). They may observe their parents controlling anger physically yet expressing it verbally: "I'm angry that you promised to make dinner but didn't do it!" They may then use a similar strategy in dealing with peer conflicts: "You said you would meet me at four o'clock but you never showed up. Where were you?!" In Figure 11-2 you can see 7-year-old Miguel's drawing and comments about being angry. He wrote about trying to cope with his anger, indicating that he is learning to control his temper. Youngsters who appropriately express their emotions are those most likely to be popular with peers (Fabes et al., 1999; Macklem, 2008).

Children also become better able to appraise advantages and disadvantages of particular coping strategies. For instance, a 14-year-old may observe a best friend becoming entangled in a fight or an intoxicated older sister heading for her car with keys in hand; in such circumstances the teenager might quickly identify a range of possible solutions and consider the potential benefits and disadvantages of each one. Sometimes children's appraisals of emotionally charged events enable them to deal directly with a problem, for instance, by confronting a peer. At other times, when they cannot change the situation, they instead try to deal with their emotions. For example, a child might alleviate anxiety about an upcoming classroom test by reminding himself that he has done well in the past on such examinations.

Children of different ages tend to seek out different kinds of people when they need reassurance in times of sadness or anger. In general, younger children are more inclined to go to adults (especially parents, other family members, and teachers), whereas older children and adolescents are more likely to seek the support of peers (Rossman, 1992; R. A. Thompson et al., 2003; Valiente, Fabes, Eisenberg, & Spinrad, 2004).

A final component of emotional regulation is determining when to express emotions publicly. Children gradually learn to curb their emotional reactions in ways that are socially acceptable and help them maintain good relationships with others (P. M. Cole, 1986; Saarni et al., 2006). For example, many preschoolers understand that rules of politeness discourage them from revealing their true feelings when disappointed by a gift from a well-meaning relative, and many elementary school children and adolescents (boys especially) believe they should not show sadness. These various developmental trends in children's emotional regulation have implications for teachers and practitioners, as you can see in the Building Teaching Skills and Dispositions exercise in MyEducationLab.

- • *Concern for others' feelings is an important emotional response that develops with age, especially when encouraged by adults.* Empathy is the capacity to experience the same feelings as another person, who perhaps may be in pain or distress (Damon, 1988; Eisenberg, 1982; Hoffman, 1991). You can hear 14-year-old Brendan express empathic concern as he talks about caring for injured birds in the "Neighborhood: Early Adolescence" video in MyEducationLab. When asked by the interviewer how he would improve his neighborhood if he could, Brendan replies that he would clean up the trash and "take all the birds that can't fly into your houses and take care of 'em until they're nursed back to health." Young people tend to be especially inclined to exhibit such empathic responses when their parents have previously been warm and responsive to them (Zhou et al., 2002).

- • *The upper elementary and secondary years bring new anxieties and pressures.* As youngsters grow more independent, they may find their needs and desires conflicting with those of parents and other authority figures (Arnett, 1999; Shanahan, McHale, Osgood, & Crouter, 2007). Concerns about fitting in at school, making mistakes in front of others, completing homework, achieving good grades, and having an ideal body type intensify during adolescence (Bokhorst, Westenberg, Oosterlaan, & Heyne, 2008; Knauss, Paxton, & Alsaker, 2007; Phelan et al., 1994). Peers themselves can be a source of aggravation due to inevitable conflicts that arise in social groups. Occasionally, adolescents intentionally ridicule one another, and when this happens, adolescents targeted with insulting remarks may feel humiliated and angry (Elison & Harter, 2007). Many such factors come into play for even the most "normal" adolescents, but some have additional challenges, perhaps living in poverty, experiencing ongoing family conflict, being abused by a family member, or having a child of their own, which can tax their coping skills (Cicchetti & Toth, 1998; Gee & Rhodes, 2008; M. Rutter & Garmezy, 1983).

Not surprisingly, many (though by no means all) adolescents perceive their lives as being quite stressful, particularly in industrialized Western countries (Arnett, 1999; Landis et al., 2007; Masten, Neemann, & Andenas, 1994). Some adolescents believe that the problems they face exceed their capabilities to cope effectively, but most find the resources they need to confront pressures in their lives (Masten et al., 1994). Adolescents may turn to their peers for understanding, or they may turn to television, video games, and music for distraction from their troubles (Landis et al., 2007). They may also express their frustrations through poetry and art. For example, early in his senior year of high school, 17-year-old Jeff felt "locked in" by the combined pressures of a demanding course load, impending due dates for college applications, and his role as confidant for several troubled friends. Late one night, he put his schoolwork aside to create the picture shown in Figure 11-3. Because he had trouble drawing human figures, he combined two favorite things—a soft drink can and black-and-white cowhide—to represent himself. As you can see, a cage and gigantic boulder hold him in, and so he cannot join in as his peers (represented by other soft drink cans) frolic freely in the distance.

Group Differences in Emotions

All children progress developmentally in their expression and control of emotions. To some degree, their developmental pathways are influenced by group membership—by gender, family and culture, and socioeconomic status.

Gender differences.   On average, male and female babies are similar in emotional states; any gender differences are subtle and situation dependent (Eisenberg et al., 1996). After the age of 2, however, consistent gender differences emerge. For instance, boys show more anger

MyEducationLab _____

Go to Chapter 11's Building Teaching Skills and Dispositions exercise in MyEducationLab to learn more about how children of various ages regulate their emotions and the implications of these developmental trends for teachers and practitioners.

MyEducationLab _____

Listen to Brendan express empathic concern for injured birds in the "Neighborhood: Early Adolescence" video. (Find Video Examples in Chapter 11 of MyEducationLab.)

Despite gains in emotional regulation, adolescents can be emotionally volatile on occasion.

empathy
Capacity to experience the same feelings as another person, especially when the feeling is pain or distress.

Figure 11-3

Drawing himself as a cow-patterned soda can, 17-year-old Jeff dramatically depicts how the pressures in his life prevent him from doing the things he would like to do.

than girls beginning in the preschool years, and girls more often report feeling sad, fearful, and guilty beginning in the elementary grades (Eisenberg et al., 1996). Girls also respond more negatively to failures, to such an extent that their subsequent performance may suffer (Dweck, 2000). And some girls are inclined to dwell on their problems rather than taking action or distracting themselves, a ruminating style that is a risk factor for becoming depressed (J. S. Hyde, Mezulis, & Abramson, 2008; Nolen-Hoeksema, Morrow, & Fredrickson, 1993). Meanwhile, as early as elementary school, boys begin to put on a self-confident front when they feel vulnerable (Eisenberg et al., 1996; Ruble et al., 2006). This style, too, has it disadvantages, especially when boys feel pressured to live up to unrealistic standards of personal strength.

Biology may be a source of some gender differences in emotions; for instance, rising hormonal levels at puberty are associated with increases in moodiness and depression in girls, but with aggressiveness and rebelliousness in boys (Buchanan, Eccles, & Becker, 1992; Davila, 2008; Ruble et al., 2006). Yet differences in socialization also contribute to gender differences in emotional responding (Eisenberg et al., 1996; Ruble et al., 2006). For instance, parents are more likely to discourage overt anger in daughters than in sons (Birnbaum & Croll, 1984; Malatesta & Haviland, 1982). More generally, parents are apt to discourage sons from expressing emotions yet may encourage daughters to talk about their feelings (J. H. Block, 1979; Eisenberg et al., 1996). At school, many teachers prefer the compliant, agreeable nature that girls are more likely to exhibit, and they assertively discipline boys who have trouble sitting still and keeping their thoughts and feelings to themselves (R. E. Bennett, Gottesman, Rock, & Cerullo, 1993; Pianta, 2006; Pollack, 1998).

Obviously, both boys and girls have emotional needs. Being careful not to stereotype the sexes, concerned educators can watch for occasions when girls and boys use styles of emotional regulation that make matters worse for them. For example, adults can watch for times when girls are ruminating over problems and help these girls work through their feelings, actively tackle the problems, and get on with life. Similarly, when boys seem to be trying hard to brush off a significant personal loss, adults can acknowledge that the event is, in fact, likely to be upsetting but can be tackled with active coping skills.

Family and cultural differences. Earlier we suggested that some differences in children's attachment-related behaviors are the result of culturally defined ways of caring for babies. Cultural differences in socialization practices continue throughout childhood, resulting in noticeable differences in emotional responding. For instance, in China and Japan, many children are raised to be shy and restrained, whereas children in Western Europe and North America are encouraged to be active, assertive, and emotionally expressive (Camras et al., 2006; P. M. Cole & Tan, 2007).

In general, children in individualistic cultures are encouraged to express the full gamut of their emotions, including happiness, pride, frustration, and anger (Morelli & Rothbaum, 2007).

Families within a cultural group can differ markedly from one another in emotional expression.

In these cultures, it is considered healthy and appropriate to reveal one's innermost feelings. In contrast, collectivistic cultures discourage emotions that disrupt a group's harmony. Displays of frustration, anger, and pride are not encouraged because they reflect self-absorption. For example, Nepalese children show relatively little anger, probably because their culture views annoyance and irritation as obstacles to inner peace and social harmony (P. M. Cole & Tan, 2007).

Yet families within any single culture can differ markedly in how they socialize children's emotional expression. In one study with families in England, researchers listened to conversations among 3-year-old children, their mothers, and their older siblings; some children *never* mentioned emotions during an hour-long conversation at home, whereas one child mentioned emotions more than 27 times (Dunn, Brown, & Beardsall, 1991). On average, mothers were more likely to talk about feelings than were the children. When they occur, family "lessons" about emotions may help children to understand how emotions operate. For example, in another study 6-year-old American children explained complex emotions more effectively when their parents had previously talked with them about why people behave as they do (J. R. Brown & Dunn, 1996).

Socioeconomic differences. Children living in families that face ongoing economic hardships are at heightened risk for emotional and behavioral problems. For example, children whose families have persistently low incomes are more prone to anxiety, depression, and behavior problems (e.g., physical aggression) than are children from advantaged backgrounds (Tolani & Brooks-Gunn, 2006). Environmental factors are almost certainly the primary reason for this difference. Children living in impoverished circumstances have more than their share of reasons to feel sad, fearful, and angry. For instance, they may not know where their next meal is coming from, and they are more likely to encounter violence and drug addiction in their neighborhoods. Their parents have limited resources (and sometimes limited energy) to address children's needs (McLoyd et al., 2006). Furthermore, many children from low-income backgrounds, particularly those with histories of learning problems, have few positive interactions with teachers at school (R. M. Clark, 1983).

Obviously not every child who grows up in a low-income environment is emotionally burdened. Many children who face financial hardships receive stable, loving care from their immediate and extended families and in the process acquire good coping skills. For example, many children whose parents emigrated from Mexico to the United States with limited financial resources show fewer emotional and behavioral problems than do American-born children (Espinosa, 2007, 2008).

Nor are children from middle- and high-income backgrounds immune to stress. Some middle-income parents project their own aspirations onto their children, expecting children to follow unrealistic developmental timetables, such as cooperatively sharing toys with peers at 18 months or reading at 3 years. When children fail to meet these timetables, parents may become overly critical and controlling (Hyson, Hirsh-Pasek, Rescorla, Cone, & Martell-Boinske, 1991). As a result, children may worry about parental expectations, particularly when they think they are not measuring up (M. Levine, 2006).

Promoting Children's Emotional Development

Emotions are an important part of children's everyday lives, yet many adults are uneasy in dealing with them (Sylvester, 1995). We propose that educators can promote emotional development if they consider emotions as *competencies*—that is, as valuable skills that can improve over time. We offer these suggestions for promoting children's abilities in emotional expression:

- ***Help crying infants find comfort.*** Caregivers can do several things to help infants in distress. First, they can strive to give timely reassurance—not always immediately, as they may sometimes have other demands, but not so late that crying escalates into turbulent agitation. Second, caregivers can allow and encourage actions that infants use to reduce stress. Searching for a favorite blanket, putting a finger in the mouth, tugging at an ear with a gentle hand—these are positive signs that infants are learning to soothe themselves. Third, caregivers can consciously invite a baby to join them in a calm state—by showing baby a smiling face, holding baby close to the chest, and trying to breathe in a shared rhythm (Gonzalez-Mena, 2002). Fourth, caregivers can investigate why an infant might be crying and try to meet the unfilled need or remove the painful stimulus. Finally, caregivers should try to stay calm and not take it personally—infants sometimes cry despite the most sensitive care.

- ***Create an atmosphere of warmth, acceptance, and trust.*** Children and adolescents alike learn most effectively when they have positive emotions, for instance, when they feel secure, happy, or excited about an activity (Boekaerts, 1993; Isen, Daubman, & Gorgoglione, 1987; Linnenbrink & Pintrich, 2004; Oatley & Nundy, 1996). And they are more likely to confide in an adult about troublesome issues if they know that the adult will continue to respect them no matter what they may reveal about themselves in heart-to-heart conversations.

- ***Consider using a research-based curriculum for fostering emotional development.*** To have a significant impact on children's emotional expression, adults need systematic ways to educate children about their feelings (Raver, 2002). One illustration of a comprehensive emotional education program is the *Promoting Alternative Thinking Strategies (PATHS)* curriculum (Domitrovich, Cortes, & Greenberg, 2007; Greenberg, Kusché, Cook, & Quamma, 1995). Second- and third-grade children are taught that all feelings are okay, some feelings are comfortable and others uncomfortable, feelings can help children learn what to do in certain situations, and some ways of dealing with emotions are better than others. Children keep a record of their feelings and use a poster showing a traffic signal as a

What Hits Me

Feeling excitment bubble inside know something great is waiting to happen to you. Feeling scared or nervous, want to dive under the covers and go back to sleep even though it is 8:30 and it is almost time to go to school. Feeling sad because your parents got divorced and you dad just moved out of the house. Feeling scared and excited at same time because you have discovered something that's mysterious and you are ditermind to figur it out.

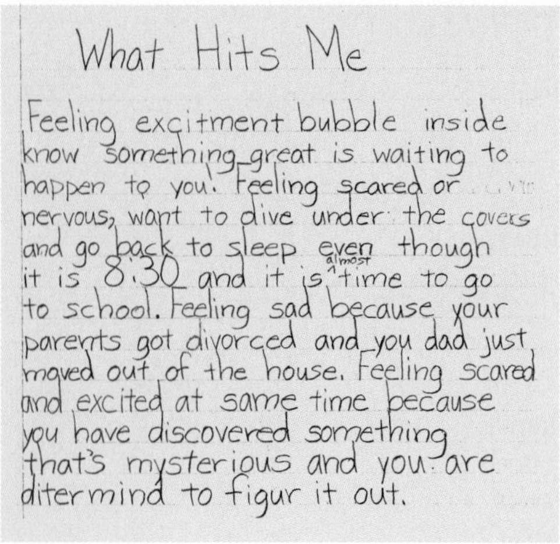

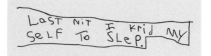

Figure 11-4

In this "What Hits Me" essay, 10-year-old Shea describes her experiences with various emotions.

guide to regulating their responses to feelings. Teachers encourage children to refer to the steps on a poster: to stop and calm down (red), to slow down and consider their options (yellow), and try a plan (green). This program has been shown to increase emotional understanding and decrease problem behaviors in children with diverse ability levels (M. T. Greenberg, Domitrovich, & Bumbarger, 2000; Riggs, Greenberg, Kusché, & Pentz, 2006).

• ***Offer age-appropriate outlets for emotional expression.*** When they are young, children can find safe outlets for emotional expression in play. Through fantasy play with peers, children often work out their fears and anger (Kohlberg & Fein, 1987; Riley, San Juan, Klinkner, & Ramminger, 2008). For older children, writing about feelings, perhaps in essays or journals shared only with a teacher or counselor, can provide a confidential outlet. In the essay in Figure 11-4, 10-year-old Shea describes her growing awareness of the various emotions she experiences. In the journal entry in Figure 11-5, 8-year-old Noah—ordinarily a happy, energetic student—reveals how upset he is about his parents' divorce.

• ***Discuss emotions experienced by characters in literature and history.*** Stories provide an occasion to talk about emotional states (Mar & Oakley, 2008). We have found in our own experience that children in the elementary grades are able to make appropriate inferences about characters' emotional states. For instance, in *Frog and Toad Are Friends* (Lobel, 1979), a book suitable for 4- to 8-year-olds, Frog waits impatiently to play with his hibernating friend, Toad, and plays a trick on him to get him up early. The story provides a forum for discussions about feelings that may arise between friends, such as anger at being teased or misled (Solomon, Watson, Battistich, Schaps, & Delucchi, 1992). Meanwhile, older children and adolescents might read firsthand accounts of historical events and talk about how people in various contexts have responded emotionally to hostilities and inequities.

LaST NiT I KriJ MY SeLF To SLeP.

Figure 11-5

In this journal entry, 8-year-old Noah reveals his sadness about his parents' recent divorce.

• ***Ask children to guess what emotions people may feel in particular scenarios.*** Children can practice analyzing situations and considering how those involved might feel. In Figure 11-6, you can see one situation that an elementary school counselor asks children to pretend they face. Adults can guide children to see that anger, fear, guilt, and other feelings are reasonable reactions to particular circumstances. In addition, they can ask children to think about how they might act when they have such uncomfortable feelings.

• ***Take cultural differences into account.*** Some cultures encourage open communication about feelings, whereas others actively discourage emotional expressiveness. Adults working with children from diverse cultures must continually be mindful of such differences when interpreting children's emotional expressions (or lack thereof).

• ***Help children keep anxiety at a manageable level.*** **Anxiety** is an emotional state characterized by worry and apprehension, often about future events with unknown outcomes. Children who are anxious may experience such physiological symptoms as muscle tension and headaches and have trouble concentrating.

Educators can do a variety of things to help keep anxiety at a manageable level. For instance, when teachers assign oral reports, they can encourage students to create index cards or other memory "crutches." Before giving an important test (such as the standardized tests that many school districts require), they can administer a practice test that gives students a general idea of what to expect. And, in general, they should communicate realistic expectations for classroom performance and provide the support students need to *meet* those expectations.

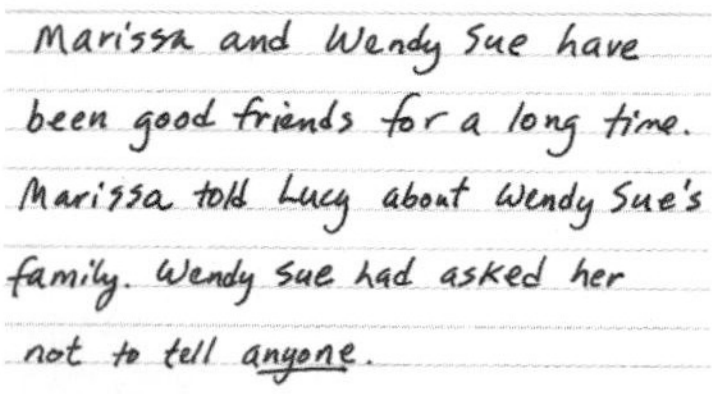

Marissa and Wendy Sue have been good friends for a long time. Marissa told Lucy about Wendy Sue's family. Wendy Sue had asked her not to tell anyone.

Figure 11-6

Counselors can ask children to pretend they are characters in particular situations, such as this one, and help them talk about how they might feel and respond.

Idea courtesy of Sally Tossey, Columbus, Ohio.

• ***Pay attention to your own emotions.*** Practitioners who work with children and families often find themselves frustrated by the people they serve (B. Davis, 2001). Teachers may become angry about seemingly rude children, apathetic parents, unrealistic external mandates, and inadequate resources for schools. Frustration and anger are natural emotions, but they must be handled with care. Exploding on the nearest bystander or retreating into personal despair are *not* good ideas; counting to 10 and finding another professional to talk with *can* be helpful in preserving one's mental health and gaining ideas about productive tactics for addressing difficult problems.

anxiety
Emotional state characterized by worry and apprehension.

● ***Model appropriate ways of dealing with negative emotions.*** Youngsters often struggle with how to deal with anger, fear, and sadness; they can benefit from seeing adults express these emotions appropriately (Delaney, 2006). Teresa vividly remembers how her fifth-grade teacher expressed anger: Rather than raising her voice, she lowered it to a whisper. The teacher's approach worked well: Students sensed her disappointment, responded with concern and guilt, and tried to make amends. Educators can enhance the benefits of modeling controlled, honest emotional reactions by offering an explanation: "I'm really angry now. Let's talk this out when we've both calmed down."

Adults can help relieve children's anxiety by talking through problems in a warm, supportive manner.

The Basic Developmental Issues table "Attachment and Emotional Development" shows how attachments and emotions draw from nature and nurture, show universality and diversity, and exhibit qualitative and quantitative change. As you have learned, nature furnishes children with inclinations to form attachments and express emotions, and nurture translates these abstract capacities into real-life relationships and abilities. In the next section of this chapter, we reveal how individual differences in emotional responding, first manifested during infancy as distinct temperaments, are slowly integrated into well-defined personalities.

Basic Developmental Issues

Attachment and Emotional Development

Issue	Attachment	Emotional Development
Nature and Nurture	Children are biologically predisposed to form close bonds with their parents and other primary caregivers, but they are more likely to form attachments to adults when they are treated in a sensitive and responsible fashion. Parents, in turn, are by nature predisposed to care for their offspring, but they learn specific ways of interacting with children from other family members and from the community and culture in which they live.	The full range of emotions is made possible by human genetic instructions; the brain is wired to experience anger, pleasure, fear, and so on. Genetic factors also affect individual differences in temperament (e.g., activity level, irritability, and ways of responding to new stimuli). Nurture affects ways in which emotions are expressed. Children learn to control expression of negative emotions by observing other people and practicing various ways of dealing with emotional experiences.
Universality and Diversity	The predisposition to form close social-emotional bonds is universal. Moreover, socially sensitive care is the common way to activate healthy attachments. However, not all children form secure attachments to their caregivers, and different environments place distinct demands on children. For example, being clingy and demanding may help infants who live in an environment with scarce resources. Similarly, being able to negotiate multiple relationships may enhance adjustment when numerous caregivers are present during the early years.	All children experience such basic emotions as happiness, sadness, anger, and fear. The tendency for emotional states to energize particular kinds of responses (e.g., fleeing in response to fear) is also universal. But substantial diversity is present in how children regulate their emotions (e.g., when trying to conceal their true feelings). Some children are more likely than others to respond to situations in a positive, upbeat fashion.
Qualitative and Quantitative Change	The development of attachments largely reflects quantitative change: Children gradually become more active as social partners, initiating conversations and other exchanges, taking turns to keep interactions going, and so on. Qualitative change occurs when young children, who have previously leapt into the arms of strangers, suddenly display stranger anxiety. During this phase, they are anxious around people they do not know and show a clear preference for attachment figures.	Children gradually gain knowledge and skills for assessing others' emotions. By watching facial expressions, listening to voice tones, and drawing inferences from behaviors, children learn how others express and control emotions. They also reflect on their own emotional states. However, the emergence of self-conscious emotions (pride, guilt, etc.) represents a qualitative change in development. As children become more aware of societal standards, they learn how to live up to these principles and may feel ashamed or guilty when they realize they don't meet expectations.

Temperament and Personality

Visit any group of children—perhaps at a local child care center, a school, or an after-school program—and you are bound to notice dramatic differences in individual children's energy, mood, spontaneity, and attention to academic tasks. Such variations reflect differences in children's *temperaments* and *personalities*.

Temperament and personality are related concepts. As noted in Chapter 1, *temperament* refers to a child's typical ways of responding to events and novel stimulation and of regulating impulses (J. Kagan & Fox, 2006; Rothbart & Bates, 2006). Individual differences in temperament are present even in infancy. For example, some infants are fussy and demanding; others are cheerful and easy to care for. Temperament has a genetic basis, as we shall see, but it also is very much affected by children's relationships and experiences.

As children grow older, they develop distinctive ways of behaving, thinking, and feeling. That is, they develop unique **personalities.** Temperament surely affects personality: A child who is timid relates to people and events differently than one who is socially confident. But personality includes more than temperament. Personality is affected by children's intellectual interests and the many habits they learn while growing up—for example, their traditions for fulfilling family obligations, strategies for dealing with stressful situations, styles of managing belongings, and preferences for spending leisure time.

Both temperament and personality help us understand how individual children respond to emotions, form relationships, and act within schools and other group settings. Temperament may be especially helpful to consider when children are infants and toddlers; personality may be more relevant as youngsters move through their childhood and adolescent years. Let's look more closely at both concepts and then consider their implications for educators.

Elements of Temperament and Personality

Temperament and personality are each made up of constellations of relatively independent dimensions. Individual children may have a lot, a little, or an in-between amount of each attribute.

Temperament.   Much of the initial work on temperament was done using parents' reports and researchers' observations of infants' typical behaviors. Parents and researchers judged the extent to which the infants exhibited such qualities as activity level and adaptability to change. In considering the dramatic individual differences that emerged out of this research, psychologists and educators realized that infants' temperaments partly determine the particular kinds of care that will be most effective. Infants rated as high or low on six dimensions are described in the Observation Guidelines table "Noticing Temperament in Infants and Toddlers."

More recent research has focused on the neurological basis of temperament. Psychologist Mary Rothbart and her colleagues suggest that particular temperaments emerge as children's brains develop distinctive capacities for responding to impulses and regulating attention, emotions, and activity (Rothbart, 2007; Rothbart & Bates, 2006). At birth, children react rather automatically to changes in stimuli by crying, thrashing their limbs, and looking away. But as they grow, children develop new ways to deal with sensations and environmental demands. For example, fear prompts children to be wary of potentially dangerous things, whereas a sense of initiative incites children to explore the world. Restraint emerges gradually, as children learn to direct their attention and actions flexibly, according to social rules and requirements and the likely consequences of possible decisions. These distinctive ways of responding to stimuli (reacting automatically, withdrawing out of fear, exploring with enthusiasm, and directing activity intentionally) are housed in different parts of the brain. As these various systems develop, they may be weak or strong, creating sizable individual differences in children's temperaments.

According to Rothbart and her colleagues, children may be low or high, or somewhere in between, on three dimensions of temperament (Rothbart, 2007; Rothbart & Bates, 2006):

- Children who score high on *extraversion/surgency* show high levels of optimistic anticipation, impulsivity, activity, and sensation seeking, and they smile and laugh often.

personality
Characteristic way a person behaves, thinks, and feels.

Noticing Temperament in Infants and Toddlers

Characteristic	Look For	Example	Implication
Activity Level	*High activity level:* · Squirms a lot · As infant, wiggles while getting diaper changed · As toddler, loves to run, climb, jump, and explore *Low activity level:* · Sits in high chair contentedly and watches the world go by · Sits quietly on own and plays with toys	Two-year-old Brenda is constantly on the move. Her caregiver finds he can more easily change her diaper if he cleans her bottom and then lets her stand, allowing her to help fasten the tabs on the new diaper.	For infants and toddlers with a *high activity level,* provide many opportunities for safe exploration of the environment, such as a safe obstacle course with a favorite toy at the end. Encourage children to dance to music. Incorporate movement into quiet activities; for example, while reading a book, encourage children to flip and touch the pages. For children with a *low activity level,* slow down to their pace and then invite more active play.
Sensitivity to Physical Input	*High sensitivity:* · Withdraws from bright lights · Cries when music is loud *Low sensitivity:* · Doesn't mind new stimulation · Doesn't pay much attention until stimulation is extreme	Angela reacts strongly to sudden changes, so her caregiver puts a new portable mobile in her lap and lets her get used to it before showing her how the mobile can be turned on to play music.	For *highly sensitive* children, keep the environment calm—dim the lights, play music quietly, and shield them from chaotic social events. For *less sensitive* children, watch for the kind of stimulation they crave. For example, if they like active social games, engage them in peekaboo or roll a ball on the floor and give them a turn.
Emotional Intensity	*High emotional intensity:* · Is fearful and cautious with new people and experiences · Shows dramatic displays of anger, sadness *Low emotional intensity:* · Is quiet and does not fuss much · Shows more interest when emotional exchanges are fairly intense	Habib is a very outgoing, passionate toddler. He laughs hard, cries hard, and has dramatic temper tantrums. His caregiver is patient with him and helps him verbalize his negative feelings when they seem to get out of control.	For children who are *emotionally intense,* empathize with their strong feelings, and suggest appropriate ways to express them ("I can see you're angry. Remember, don't bite. Say 'No!' instead."). Help children who are *less emotionally intense* to articulate their feelings ("You look sad, can you tell me how you're feeling?").
Sociability	*High sociability* · Smiles at new people · Enjoys playing in large groups · Is somewhat independent of caregivers *Low sociability* · Doesn't interact with new people unless it is clear they are friendly and in other ways safe · Prefers to play with just one other child · Stays close to familiar adult in new social situations	Tony is shy around other people, especially adults not in his immediate family. He would rather sit and play alone than join in an active group of toddlers climbing outside. His caregiver occasionally helps him join in on enjoyable interactions with other children.	For children who show *high sociability,* encourage this disposition. Also encourage them to sit and do quiet activities on their own. For children who show *low sociability,* let them warm up to new people slowly. For example, hold a child in your arms when meeting a new person; sit near the child when he or she ventures to play with an unfamiliar peer; and offer reassurance in new settings ("Let's go visit the preschool room and see what they do in there—they have an awesome slide").
Adaptability	*Ease with change:* · Has an easy time with transitions, such as moving inside after outdoor play · Notices changes in environment, such as new furniture, with interest but no concern *Difficulty with change:* · Resists new objects and experiences, such as new cups with unfamiliar lids · Acts out during transitions between activities · Is suspicious of new people	Thomas frets when going to bed at night. He acts out whenever the routine changes at school. When going somewhere new, he demands continual attention from a trusted adult. His caregiver gives him plenty of warning when a change in routine is expected and talks to him about novel events before they happen.	When children show *ease with change,* continue to make their world challenging, but also predictable. With children who have *difficulty with change,* establish routines so that children know what to expect from day to day, advise them when there is a departure from a regular routine ("Our nap time will be a little late today because we have a special visitor"), give them warning about a change ("When I turn off the light, it will be time to pick up toys"), and give choices when possible ("Would you prefer to build blocks or go to dramatic play?").

continued

Observation Guidelines (continued)

Characteristic	Look For	Example	Implication
Persistence	*High persistence:* · Can wait patiently while drink or bottle is being prepared · Shows tolerance for frustration *Low persistence:* · Wants comfort immediately · Gets frustrated easily	Rosemary shows no tolerance for frustration. When she is hungry, she wants her meal *now!* When completing puzzles, she *gets* angry when pieces don't fit immediately into the proper slots.	For *highly persistent* children, explain what you are doing to meet their needs ("I'm slicing up these apples for a healthy snack") and comment on their progress toward goals ("You are working hard on that puzzle!"). For children who show *little persistence,* offer comfort when they are frustrated ("May I sit with you while you do that?"), help them to consider other ways to reach their desired goal ("What if you turned the puzzle piece around like this?"), and encourage them to break up difficult tasks into smaller, more manageable parts.

Sources: Based on observational indicators of temperament and recommendations for dealing with them in Zero to Three: National Center for Infants, Toddlers, and Families, 2002. For basic distinctions in temperaments, see A. Thomas & Chess, 1977.

- Children who score high on *negative affectivity* tend to be shy and often fearful, frustrated, sad, uncomfortable, and not easily soothed.[1]
- Children who show high levels of *effortful control* are proficient in strategically focusing and shifting their attention. They effectively plan for the future, suppress inappropriate responses, and take pleasure in complex and novel stimuli.

These three temperamental dimensions are fairly stable, partly due to genetic factors. For example, identical twins reared in different homes often have similar temperaments (Henderson, 1982; Rothbart & Bates, 2006; Tellegren, Lykken, Bouchard, & Wilcox, 1988). Children's genetic makeup apparently affects their temperaments through its effects on brain structure and chemistry (J. Kagan & Fox, 2006; J. Kagan, Snidman, Vahn, & Towsley, 2007). That is, genes affect the density of synaptic connections in various parts of the brain and the concentrations of chemicals that make neurons fire or remain inactive (J. Kagan & Fox, 2006; see Chapter 5). For example, genetic factors seem to play roles in the amounts of specific chemicals released in the brain that trigger the feeling of irritability, sustain attention in the face of distraction, and provoke worrying (J. Kagan & Fox, 2006).

Children's temperaments may also remain somewhat stable because of persistent characteristics in children's environments, such as affectionate families or harsh neighborhoods, that consistently promote or undermine children's well-being, respectively. Yet environments can also interact with children's genetic tendencies. For example, children who are fearful and inhibited are more likely to overcome shyness when their parents expect them to act in a mature fashion rather than continually protecting them and when the children participate in child care rather than staying home all day with family (Arcus, 2001; Fox, Henderson, Rubin, Calkins, & Schmidt, 2001).

Environmental factors can also lead to subtle (and sometimes profound) changes in children's temperaments. Parents and other adults cultivate certain ways of responding that may alter how children's dispositional qualities are manifested. In other words, children's temperaments are the targets of socialization processes (Harwood, Miller, & Irizarry, 1995). For instance, Japanese parents do much to keep their babies pacified and quiet, in part out of regard for a cultural ideal of harmony and in part out of consideration for neighbors who live on the other sides of thin walls. Japanese mothers therefore talk infrequently, speak softly, and gently stroke their babies (Miyake, Campos, Kagan, & Bradshaw, 1986). In contrast, American mothers talk to infants often and in an expressive and evocative manner, perhaps in efforts to stimulate cognitive development and strengthen the caregiver–infant relationship (e.g., Trainor et al., 2000).

---

[1] Some recent research indicates that negative affectivity may actually be two separate dimensions, one related to fear and distress, and the other based in frustration, irritability, and anger (Rothbart & Bates, 2006).

Given moderate levels of stability in children's temperaments, teachers and other practitioners frequently notice the characteristic ways in which individual children handle themselves and require support. For example, a child high on *extraversion/surgency* may need help channeling energy into a few constructive outlets. A child high on *negative affectivity* may need quiet support in gradually joining a busy group. And a child low on *effort control* may need help focusing on classroom lessons.

Personality. Over time, a child integrates biologically based emotional tendencies with his or her experiences, relationships, and intellectual interests. The result is a distinctive and somewhat stable personality. For example, a child who is passionate about finding order in the material world may, as a 4-year-old, have an insatiable curiosity for dinosaurs; as an 8-year-old, be fascinated with space and aeronautics; as a 12-year-old, learn all he can about bridges and buildings; as a 16-year-old, become an expert in computers; and as a young man, prepare for a career in civil engineering.

This mother comforts her baby in a peaceful and soothing manner—an approach that may partly explain the baby's quiet and subdued mood.

Despite their relative stability, children's personalities can change slightly (and often temporarily) in response to the demands of particular situations. Thus a 12-year-old girl may be highly sociable (e.g., talking frequently, smiling at others, and befriending many peers) but find it difficult to make new friends when her family moves across the country and she encounters a new peer group with different customs and values. The demands of particular settings can likewise affect which aspects of complex personalities children reveal. For instance, a child may be spontaneous and cheerful on the playground but distracted and agitated in the classroom.

Recognizing that personality changes somewhat over time and across situations, psychologists have nevertheless found five dimensions of personality to be notably stable:

- *Extraversion* (extent to which one is socially outgoing)
- *Agreeableness* (extent to which one is warm and sympathetic)
- *Conscientiousness* (extent to which one is persistent and organized)
- *Neuroticism* (extent to which one is anxious and fearful)
- *Openness* (extent to which one is curious and imaginative)

These five dimensions were originally identified with adults, but they also characterize children to some degree (Caspi, 1998; Digman, 1989; John, 1990; John, Caspi, Robins, Moffitt, & Stouthamer-Loeber, 1994; McCrae, Costa, & Busch, 1986; Saarni et al., 2006). As with constancy in temperament, the stability of personality dimensions is due partly to genetics and partly to consistency in children's environments.

Helping Children Be Themselves

Teachers can plan lessons and activities that address the varied temperaments and personalities of youngsters in their care. Here are some specific suggestions:

- ***Identify the kinds of temperaments that you naturally prefer, as well as those that push your buttons.*** Many teachers prefer to work with children who are curious, happy to be at school, obedient, hard working, cooperative, intelligent, cautious, and efficient (Keogh, 2003; Wentzel, 2000). Teachers tend to find it less rewarding to work with children who are easily distracted, angry or irritable, disruptive, and exceptionally assertive. When teachers come to realize that they automatically (and often unconsciously) respond in certain ways to particular temperaments, they can take the first steps toward holding their biases in check.

- ***Adjust to young children's stylistic ways of responding to the world.*** Infant caregivers often look after active babies who love to crawl around their environment, sway to music, and squirm in their high chairs (A. Thomas & Chess, 1977; Zero to Three, 2002). To meet the needs of active infants, caregivers might permit them to explore and move often. In contrast, infants who show a lower activity level may sit contentedly and let the world come to them. Caregivers might sit quietly with them, talk softly about pictures in a book, and acknowledge their interests in toys.

- ***Consider children's temperaments when forming groups.*** Teachers can often help children who are shy or impulsive by pairing them with peers who might compensate for their limitations. For example, a first-grade teacher might plan a Halloween activity of making "dirt" cake, knowing she can count on one boy to be methodical in measuring cocoa and other ingredients. She could pair him with another boy who will attack the project enthusiastically but without restraint; together, they might make a good combination. Because there is never any guarantee that temperamentally dissimilar children will work effectively together, you also need to monitor the evolving dynamics of such groups once you form them.

- ***Allow children to apply their natural strengths, but also encourage them to try out new strategies for learning.*** Permitting children to choose from among a few specified options is an important way to respect children's individuality. For instance, children might be asked to report on a book they have read, choosing from an array of defined options, such as a written analysis, poster, or oral presentation. Yet children are naturally inclined to remain in their comfort zone, and they can benefit from occasional practice of their less developed talents. For example, a child who has trouble concentrating may be taught to use attention-focusing strategies, and a child who chooses books impulsively might be asked to prepare a checklist of desirable features and topics to refer to when selecting a new book at the library.

- ***Communicate your expectations about acceptable behaviors.*** When adults make expectations explicit and consistently enforce compliance, children with many kinds of temperaments and personalities thrive (Keogh, 2003). Children who are apprehensive about doing the right thing can be assured that they are indeed acting in an acceptable manner. Children who are inclined to act impulsively can be reminded of rules, consequences for misbehavior, and strategies they can use to keep track of their behaviors.

- ***Set up routines that youngsters can follow.*** Most children prefer a schedule that is somewhat predictable (H. A. Davis, 2003; Keogh, 2003). Children adjust to activities more easily when they know what to expect, for example, when they know that after they arrive at school in the morning, they are to place their backpacks and jackets in preassigned places, go straight to their desks, and begin writing a new entry in their class journals. Of course, some variation is inevitable and desirable, but familiar routines help everyone relax. Children also need to be advised of the procedural rules of a classroom, such as how to line up or disperse for lunch, and the circumstances under which they can sharpen their pencils, use the restroom, and ask for assistance.

- ***Help children cope with changes in routines.*** Children with some temperaments and personalities (for instance, those who are timid or irritable) may find alterations to routines particularly difficult (Keogh, 2003). To help these and other children, educators can tell youngsters ahead of time about anticipated modifications regarding school personnel, schedules, or rules. To illustrate, elementary school children can be introduced to a substitute teacher the week before their regular teacher departs for an extended family leave. Middle school adolescents can be shown the blueprints for a new auditorium before the existing structure is leveled, and high school students should receive a copy of a new code of conduct for their school before it is instituted. When changes *cannot* be anticipated ahead of time, children appreciate hearing as soon as possible about these alterations, especially those changes that may affect them personally.

- ***Physically arrange the classroom to minimize disruptions and noise.*** Defined pathways between desks and protected spaces in high-traffic areas can minimize tussles among children who are easily frustrated or lacking in social skills (K. Carter & Doyle, 2006; Emmer, Evertson, & Worsham, 2000). In addition, highly sensitive children may be overwhelmed by the chaos of the classroom and appreciate spending some time in a quieter setting. For example, children who are sensitive to sensory stimuli might occasionally be allowed to complete assignments in the school library.

- ***Make appropriate adjustments for children who show unusually high or low levels on one or more personality dimensions.*** Children with exceptional levels on particular personality dimensions stand out from other children. These children need to be accepted for who they are but also benefit from special accommodations that guide their learning, peer relationships, emotional expression, and motivation to follow rules. Let's consider how educators might adjust to some unusually high or low levels of the personality dimensions we introduced earlier:

- *Extraversion.* Extraverted children are active, assertive, emotionally expressive, talkative, enthusiastic, and socially outgoing. Extraverted children often appreciate opportunities to work on projects with peers. Teachers can also intersperse opportunities for physical movement around quiet activities to give these children needed exercise. Yet some exuberant children have trouble attending to learning activities and many need gentle reminders from teachers to stay focused (Rimm-Kaufman et al., 2002). Teachers might occasionally offer a public forum (such as a dramatic performance) for self-expression. In contrast, children who are shy may benefit from private conversations with teachers and friendly invitations from peers and playground supervisors to join in a game (Keogh, 2003).

- *Agreeableness.* Agreeable children are warm, responsive, generous, kind, sympathetic, and trusting. Children who are agreeable may be pleased when adults and other children notice and comment on their cooperative spirit. Children who are less prone to be agreeable and socially sensitive may benefit if teachers encourage them to compliment other children, share toys, offer comfort to others in distress, and voice opinions without putting people down. Extremely irritable children are at risk for developing behavior problems and sometimes learn to adjust more effectively when guided by school counselors or psychologists (Ehrler, Evans, & McGhee, 1999).

- *Conscientiousness.* Conscientious children are attentive, persistent in activities, organized, and responsible. Teachers can admire the persistence and organization shown by these children and point out how their style pays off in well-designed work products. Children who follow lower standards can be taught to set appropriate goals, resist counterproductive urges, and monitor their own progress toward goals (Muris, Meesters, & Rompelberg, 2006).

- *Neuroticism.* Neurotic children are anxious, fearful, lacking in confidence, and self-pitying. Children who are overly anxious and fearful may need support in dealing with negative feelings (Kwok, Hughes, & Luo, 2007). They also need encouragement to try challenging and potentially anxiety-arousing tasks they might otherwise avoid. Children who are relaxed and confident thrive when given continuous support from adults. No one is self-assured all the time, however, and adults can express extra support when normally confident children face momentous losses, personal failures, or traumatic events.

- *Openness.* Children who are open are curious, eager to explore their world, and imaginative. Children who are open intellectually are motivated to exercise their budding skills in many contexts. However, curious children are not always motivated to achieve in school and may need encouragement from teachers to tackle conventional academic assignments (Abe, 2005). Those who are less driven to explore art, literature, history, and the scientific world may need to be shown the intrigue and beauty of these and other fields.

- ***Recognize the complexity of children's personalities.*** The various dimensions of temperament and personality combine in a myriad of creative ways that can both delight and tax adults. For example, a teacher may have one child who is socially outgoing but a bit anxious and not terribly agreeable; another child who is self-confident and conscientious, but somewhat conforming and slow to exercise her imagination; another who worries constantly and craves approval from adults but is quietly curious and thoughtful; and many more other children, each with an individual profile. As you can see, every child has special needs when it comes to temperament and personality.

The Developmental Trends table "Emotional and Personal Development at Different Age Levels" encapsulates what you have learned about children's attachment, emotional qualities, and temperaments and personalities. By now it should be abundantly clear to you that children are well served when educators and other adults treat them sensitively and with appreciation for their individual qualities. Yet some children have such strong emotions that simply talking about feelings and modeling appropriate coping skills are not enough to ease their distress. In the final section, we turn to serious emotional problems that some youngsters have, as well as strategies that educators can use with these youngsters.

Emotional and Personal Development at Different Age Levels

Age	What You Might Observe	Diversity	Implications
Infancy (Birth–2 Years) 	· Attachment behaviors (seeking contact with caregiver when afraid, hurt, or hungry; being sufficiently relaxed in the presence of caregiver to explore the environment) · Distress at separation from caregiver · Increasing repertoire of ways to communicate feelings; crying and smiling gradually supplemented with laughter, hand gestures, and words · Beginning ability to soothe self by sucking thumb, hugging favorite blankets, pulling on ear, and so on	· Some children have multiple attachments and move easily from one caregiver to another, whereas other children may have a single close attachment and strongly protest separation from this person. · Some cultures encourage small children to express all their feelings, including anger and sadness. Other cultures place harmony above self-expression and discourage infants and toddlers from expressing certain feelings; instead, they teach restraint (Camras et al., 2006).	· Model productive emotional expressions, and remain calm when infants and toddlers cry and shout. · Be responsive and sensitive to the needs of infants—they are learning to trust you as you help them satisfy their needs. · Seek professional guidance when you encounter infants who appear to have serious attachment problems. · Take infants' separation distress seriously, and provide them with lots of reassurance. · Tell parents and other family members what you do to comfort their babies after they leave and how long it takes for the babies to settle down.
Early Childhood (2–6 Years) 	· Desire to be close to parents when afraid, hurt, or uncertain · Wide variety of emotions (e.g., happiness, sadness, fear, anger, disgust) · Familiarity with and use of labels for basic emotions · Emergence of self-conscious emotions (e.g., pride, guilt)	· Children vary in the number of close attachments they form, the extent to which they find reassurance in these attachment figures, and their responses to strangers. Some cling tightly to caregivers, others venture confidently to explore new environments and check out strangers. · Children vary in how they express their emotions. Some are very controlled, especially in masking anger and sadness. Others are more expressive.	· Realize that young children may initially be cautious or fearful in a new classroom or other group; they will become more confident as they begin to form attachments to their teachers. · Be patient in establishing relationships with young children; some may form attachments quickly, but others may take several weeks or months before trusting adults outside the home. · Teach appropriate ways of handling negative emotions. Encourage children to "use their words" rather than push or hit when angry.
Middle Childhood (6–10 Years) 	· Increasing number of bonds with people outside the family, including peers, teachers, and other adults · Increasing ability to regulate emotions	· Children are emotionally affected by major family disruptions (e.g., divorce of parents, death or illness of a family member). Changes in family membership may temporarily undermine children's security. · Some children have strong role models for emotional regulation (e.g., a parent may express negative feelings in productive ways).	· Incorporate discussions of emotional states into the curriculum; for example, address the feelings of characters in literature and history. · Model appropriate ways of expressing feelings. · Respect cultural differences in regulating emotions.
Early Adolescence (10–14 Years) 	· Frequent fluctuations in mood, partly as a result of hormonal changes and everyday stressful experiences · Careful regulation of emotions (e.g., hiding joy about a good grade in order to appear "cool" to peers)	· Individual adolescents differ in the extent to which they conform to typical gender roles in expressing emotions. · Some adolescents tend to internalize their stresses (e.g., experiencing depression or anxiety); others respond with overt behaviors (e.g., being violent, breaking the law).	· Be a supportive listener when young people want to share their anxieties. · Keep in mind that some moodiness is normal in the middle school grades. However, talk with parents or the school counselor about the emotional well-being of youngsters who seem especially troubled.
Late Adolescence (14–18 Years) 	· Seeking emotional intimacy with same-sex and opposite-sex peers · Continued attachments to parents, but with strong preferences for parental affection to be demonstrated in private rather than in public · Increasing ability to be comforted by peers when distressed	· For some adolescents, relationships with parents are full of conflict and offer little emotional support. · Some adolescents use drugs and alcohol to cope with negative emotions. · Some adolescents (girls especially) excessively ruminate over small setbacks and disappointments. · Some adolescents (boys especially) may hide their true feelings and project the impression that difficult experiences do not bother them.	· When adolescents are in minor conflicts with their parents, help them understand that most parents truly want the best for their children and behave accordingly (albeit sometimes punitively or coercively). · Refer youngsters to a school counselor when relationships with parents are extremely poor or the youngsters show signs of depression. · Ask adolescents to reflect on the emotional experiences of fictional characters and historical figures.

Supporting Children and Adolescents with Emotional and Behavioral Problems

Some children and adolescents have more than their share of negative emotional experiences, to the point where their quality of life and ability to tackle everyday problems are disrupted. These youngsters may have trouble handling intense emotions, showing emotions in culturally acceptable ways, coping with mixed emotions, or responding appropriately to other people's emotional displays. Other children find it difficult to follow everyday rules in families, schools, and society, and to act with consideration for others' feelings and welfare.

Common Emotional and Behavioral Disorders

Emotional and behavioral problems in youngsters are more common than many adults realize. Approximately 15 to 25 percent of children and adolescents in the United States are affected by a mental health problem (Tolani & Brooks-Gunn, 2006). We now look at depression, anxiety disorder, and conduct disorder and then formulate recommendations for working with youngsters who have ongoing emotional problems.

Depression.   People with **depression** feel exceptionally sad, discouraged, and hopeless; they may also feel restless, sluggish, helpless, worthless, or unusually guilty. Children and adolescents with depression may be unresponsive to caregivers, withdraw from social interactions with peers, report such physical complaints as headaches and stomach pain, and appear consistently sad and irritable (Oltmanns & Emery, 2007). Depressed children and adolescents may also have trouble concentrating, lose interest in their usual activities, have little appetite, and have difficulty sleeping (American Psychiatric Association, 1994). A variation of depression, *bipolar disorder,* occurs when individuals experience periods of extreme elation and hyperactivity as well as periods of deep depression.

The specific symptoms of depression vary somewhat from culture to culture. The American Psychiatric Association provides several examples of how depression might manifest itself in different cultures:

> Complaints of "nerves" and headaches (in Latino and Mediterranean cultures), of weakness, tiredness, or "imbalance" (in Chinese and Asian cultures), of problems of the "heart" (in Middle Eastern cultures), or of being "heartbroken" (among Hopi). (American Psychiatric Association, 1994, p. 324)

Many instances of depression and bipolar disorder probably have biological, and possibly genetic, roots (Cicchetti, Rogosch, & Toth, 1997; Griswold & Pessar, 2000). These conditions tend to run in families, are often foreshadowed by temperamental moodiness and insecure attachment, and may reflect chemical imbalances (Cicchetti et al., 1997; Griswold & Pessar, 2000; Oltmanns & Emery, 2007). Yet environmental factors also play a role in depression; for instance, the death of a loved one, mental illness or marital conflict in parents, child maltreatment, poverty, and inadequate schools may bring about or worsen depressive symptoms (Cicchetti et al., 1997; Oltmanns & Emery, 2007). When individuals succumb to extreme stress with a depressive episode, the event may alter their neurological chemistry, making it more likely that they will suffer another depressive episode in the future (Akiskal & McKinney, 1973; Antelman & Caggiula, 1977; Siever & Davis, 1985).

Depression rates in children vary by age and gender. Before adolescence, depression and bipolar disorder are rare. Their prevalence increases dramatically during adolescence. By the age of 19, approximately one in three girls and one in five boys has been seriously depressed one or more times (Oltmanns & Emery, 2007). Higher rates of depression may occur in girls beginning during adolescence because of hormone changes and the tendency of girls to continually ruminate on their problems (Nevid, Rathus, & Greene, 2006).

How might depression emerge in the life of a child? Let's consider Blake, a 5-year-old boy who's just entered kindergarten. His single mother suffers from depression and gives him little attention. She occasionally yields to his persistent demands but at other times vacillates between indifference and explosive anger. When Blake first comes to school, he clings anxiously to her. When she leaves, he is irritable and tired and has trouble focusing on activities and interacting with peers. He is not diagnosed with depression for another 10 years, when he now

depression
Emotional condition characterized by significant sadness, discouragement, hopelessness, and, in children, irritability.

shows classic symptoms—missing school, sleeping irregularly, abusing alcohol, and feeling sad much of the time. Blake exemplifies two of the vulnerability factors for depression: a possible genetic predisposition to negative emotions (possibly inherited from his mother) and an insecure attachment to his mother (the outcome of inconsistent and harsh parenting).

Youth with serious depression or bipolar disorder are at risk for considering or committing suicide. Suicide rates are low among 10- to 14-year-olds but increase eightfold among 15- to 24-year-olds (Nevid et al., 2006). Depressed individuals who contemplate suicide often believe that they face problems they cannot solve or have extreme emotional pain they wish to end (D. Miller, 1994; Nevid et al., 2006).

The overwhelming despair and high frequency of suicide that accompany depression make it a condition that educators must take seriously. Through their daily contact with youngsters, teachers have numerous opportunities to observe fluctuations in mood and performance and so may spot cases of possible depression in children. (Friends and family, though they may have closer ties to youngsters, may not comprehend or accept how serious the problem is.) Educators will want to offer emotional reassurance to young people who appear troubled, but they should consult with principals and counselors if they suspect severe depression or another serious emotional disturbance.

Anxiety disorder.   In its milder forms, anxiety is a common and very "normal" emotion. But some people, including some children and adolescents, worry excessively and find it difficult to control their worrisome thoughts and feelings; in other words, they have an **anxiety disorder** (American Psychiatric Association, 1994). Children with a *generalized anxiety disorder* tend to worry excessively about a wide variety of things, including their academic achievement, their performance in sports, and potential catastrophic events such as wars or hurricanes. Some individuals have more specific anxiety disorders, perhaps worrying excessively about gaining weight, having a serious illness, being away from family and home, feeling embarrassed in public, or being scared to go to school (Oltmanns & Emery, 2007).

Anxiety disorders tend to run in families (American Psychiatric Association, 1994; Last, Hersen, Kazdin, Francis, & Grubb, 1987). Family environment also seems to play a role in the onset of anxiety disorders. Preliminary data suggest that some anxious children have had insecure attachments to their parents and have been exposed to aloof and critical parenting (P. S. Moore, Whaley, & Sigman, 2004; Oltmanns & Emery, 2007).

Conduct disorder.   When children and adolescents display a chronic pattern of misbehavior and show little shame or guilt about their wrongdoings, they are sometimes identified as having a **conduct disorder.** Youngsters who display a conduct disorder ignore the rights of others in ways that are unusual for their age. Common symptoms include aggression toward people and animals (e.g., initiating physical fights, forcing someone into sexual activity, torturing animals), destruction of property (e.g., setting fires, painting graffiti), theft and deceitfulness (e.g., breaking into cars, lying about shoplifting so as not to be caught), and serious violations of rules (e.g., ignoring reasonable curfews, being truant from school) (American Psychiatric Association, 1994; Oltmanns & Emery, 2007). Approximately 2 to 6 percent of school-age youths could be classified as having a conduct disorder, with rates being three or four times higher for boys than for girls (Kazdin, 1997).

It is important to note that one or two antisocial acts do not necessarily indicate a serious conduct problem. Conduct disorders are more than a matter of "kids being kids" or "sowing wild oats." Instead, they represent deep-seated and persistent disregard for the rights and feelings of others. Youth with conduct disorders tend to see the world through conflict-colored glasses, for example, by always assuming that others have hostile intentions toward them (Dodge et al., 2003). In other words, they have the *hostile attributional bias* you will read about in Chapter 14.

Conduct disorder is manifested somewhat differently depending on youngsters' gender and age. Among young people with conduct disorder, boys are more likely to engage in theft and aggression; girls are apt to engage in sexual misbehavior. Conduct disorder is especially serious (and likely to foreshadow adjustment problems in the adult years) when it is manifested even before adolescence begins (Barrett, 2005). Youngsters who exhibit conduct disorders beginning in childhood are likely to have many problems in adulthood, including

anxiety disorder
Chronic emotional condition characterized by excessive, debilitating worry.

conduct disorder
Chronic emotional condition characterized by lack of concern for the rights of others.

antisocial and criminal behavior, frequent changes in employment, high divorce rates, little participation in families and community groups, and early death (Kazdin, 1997; Oltmanns & Emery, 2007). In contrast, conduct disorders that don't emerge until adolescence are often the result of affiliation with peers who engage in delinquent behavior; as these young people mature and find new social contacts, they tend to stop engaging in destructive acts.

As is true for the emotional disorders we've previously considered, biology may be *partly* to blame for conduct disorders. For instance, children and adolescents with conduct disorders may have difficulty inhibiting aggressive impulses, perhaps as a result of brain damage or other neurological abnormalities (Fishbein et al., 2006; Kazdin, 1997). Families may be influential as well: Conduct disorders are more common when children's parents provide little affection, are highly critical, and unpredictably administer harsh physical punishment (Blackson et al., 1999; G. R. Patterson, DeBaryshe, & Ramsey, 1989; Webster-Stratton & Hammond, 1999). Neighborhoods can also be a factor in conduct disorders, as when children witness violence in their communities and later become physically aggressive themselves (Shahinfar, Kupersmidt, & Matza, 2001). Tragically, some school environments contribute to the problem. Conduct disorders are more frequently observed in situations where teachers have low expectations for students, provide little encouragement or praise for schoolwork, and put little effort into planning lessons (Kazdin, 1997).

Supporting Youngsters with Emotional and Behavioral Problems

Effective programs for youngsters with emotional disorders are usually individualized. Without such adaptations, schools and other settings are difficult places for youths with serious emotional problems. As a telling statistic, fewer than half of students with serious emotional problems graduate from high school (L. M. Bullock & Gable, 2006; Reid, Gonzalez, Nordness, Trout, & Epstein, 2004). Teachers, psychologists, and special education professionals can collaboratively design support systems. In addition, educators can consider these strategies:

● ***Show an interest in the well-being of all children and adolescents.*** Many youngsters with emotional disorders have few positive and productive ties with individuals outside of school, and so their relationships with caring professionals may become all the more important. The many "little things" educators do each day, including greeting youngsters warmly, expressing concern when they seem worried, and lending a ready ear when they want to share their ideas or frustrations can make a world of difference (S. C. Diamond, 1991).

● ***Teach social skills.*** Many children and adolescents with emotional problems have difficulty maintaining friendships (Asher & Coie, 1990; Cartledge & Milburn, 1995; Macklem, 2008; Schonert-Reichl, 1993). You can support these youngsters by encouraging them to practice effective social skills, such as saying something friendly to a peer (Gillham, Reivich, Jaycox, & Seligman, 1995). We will offer additional recommendations for fostering children's social skills in Chapters 12, 14, and 15.

● ***Provide extra structure for youngsters who have high levels of anxiety.*** One especially effective strategy is to communicate expectations for performance in clear and concrete terms. Highly anxious youngsters perform better in well-structured environments, such as classrooms with explicit expectations for academic achievement and social behavior (Hembree, 1988; Stipek, 1993; Tobias, 1977). When they know what to expect and how they will be evaluated, these young people are more inclined to relax, enjoy themselves, and learn.

● ***Set reasonable limits for behavior.*** All children need to learn that aggression, destruction of property, and stealing are unacceptable. Establishing rules for appropriate behavior and imposing consequences (e.g., loss of privileges) for infractions provide the structure and guidance many children need to keep undesirable behaviors in check (Turnbull et al., 2007).

● ***Give children and adolescents a sense that they have some control.*** Some young people, especially those who consistently defy authority figures, often behave even less appropriately when people try to control them. With such youngsters, it is important that practitioners not get into power struggles, situations where only one person "wins" and the other inevitably loses (S. C. Diamond, 1991). Instead, adults might create situations in which children conform to expectations yet also know they have some control over what happens to them. For instance, students in a classroom can learn techniques for observing and monitoring their own actions, which you will learn more about in Chapter 13.

• **Advise parents about their children's needs.** Parents whose children have emotional and behavioral problems may appreciate advice on meeting children's emotional needs. Depending on the particular challenges that children face, parents may need guidance in establishing clear rules, recognizing children's good behaviors, and helping children to understand and regulate their emotions (Garland, Augustyn, & Stein, 2007).

• **Be alert for signs that a child or adolescent may be contemplating suicide.** Seriously depressed youngsters may not reach out for help when they believe that no one cares about them, think that they should be able to solve their problems on their own, or worry about their reputation if they were to disclose their mental anguish (Freedenthal & Stiffman, 2007). Fortunately, seriously depressed youngsters often give off signs (consciously or not) that they may be thinking about taking their own lives. Warning signs include the following (M. M. Jensen, 2005; Kerns & Lieberman, 1993; Spirito, Valeri, Boergers, & Donaldson, 2003):

Adults must always be alert for signs that a youngster is seriously depressed. If they suspect that a young person is contemplating suicide, they should seek trained help immediately.

- Signs of depression and helplessness
- Sudden withdrawal from social relationships (possibly after being rejected by peers or breaking up with a boyfriend or girlfriend)
- Disregard for personal appearance
- Serious health problems (e.g., a debilitating injury from an accident or a chronic condition resulting from an eating disorder)
- A dramatic personality change
- A sudden elevation in mood
- A preoccupation with death and morbid themes
- Serious problems at school, home, or in the community (e.g., expulsion from school, death of a friend, pregnancy, or arrest for illegal behavior)
- Overt or veiled threats (e.g., "I won't be around much longer")
- Actions that indicate "putting one's affairs in order" (e.g., giving away prized possessions)
- Substance abuse
- Preference for certain kinds of music (e.g., heavy metal rock music with morbid themes)
- Efforts to obtain suicidal means (e.g., medications, ropes, or guns)

Adults must watch out for these and other possible warning signs and take these behaviors seriously, particularly if they see more than one of the signs on the list. Educators should show genuine concern for potentially suicidal youngsters and seek trained help from a school psychologist or counselor *immediately* (McCoy, 1994; Spirito et al., 2003).

Receiving affectionate care from adults helps children from all backgrounds. As you have learned, effective practitioners build on the assets and address the limitations that individual children have in regulating emotions, forming relationships, and expressing their continually evolving personalities.

Summary

Erikson's Theory of Psychosocial Development

Erikson proposed that psychosocial characteristics emerge over the course of eight stages (the first beginning in infancy and the last occurring in old age). Erikson blazed many trails for later developmental scholars, yet the volumes of research inspired by his work have revealed that his theory does not accurately describe emotional development in some cultures, nor does it adequately account for the interplay of identity and intimacy, especially in females.

Attachment

Ideally, children's first attachments are close and enduring bonds between themselves and their caregivers. Sensitive and responsive attention is the necessary ingredient for the formation of secure attachments, but children also contribute by returning affection. Secure attachments in the early years lead to positive social-emotional outcomes later on. However, attachments manifest themselves somewhat differently in different cultures, and the nature of people's attachments can change over time.

Emotion

Emotions have adaptive functions for young people, helping them decide how to act. Children and adolescents become increasingly able to regulate their emotions in ways that are both socially acceptable and personally effective. Individual differences in emotional functioning are the result of both biology (e.g., temperament and gender-specific hormones) and environment (e.g., socialization by parents, peers, and culture). Dealing with youngsters' emotions is an important aspect of teaching and working with children and adolescents.

Temperament and Personality

Children are born with dispositions to respond to the world and express their emotions in certain ways. These constitutional inclinations, called temperaments, are also affected by experience and social relationships. As children grow, they integrate their temperamental dimensions with their intellectual interests, habits, and other experiences to acquire distinctive personalities. Teachers and other practitioners can help children enormously when they make accommodations for children's unique temperaments and personalities.

Supporting Children and Adolescents with Emotional and Behavioral Problems

Some youngsters face serious emotional and behavioral problems that require thoughtful accommodation from adults. Youngsters with depression, an anxiety disorder, or a conduct disorder often benefit from professional intervention. In addition, teachers and other adults can offer reassurance, communicate expectations for appropriate behavior, and address children's personal concerns, such as getting along with peers and needing to exert some control over everyday decisions.

Applying Concepts in Child Development

The exercises in this section will help you increase your effectiveness in nurturing children's emotional development.

Case Study

The Girly Shirt

Read the case and then answer the questions that follow it.

Eight-year-old Tim caused quite a disruption in class this morning. His teacher, Amy Fox, isn't quite sure why things got out of hand, and so she is meeting with Tim while the rest of the class is at lunch to learn what happened.

Ms. Fox:	Things got out of control in class this morning, didn't they, Tim?
Tim:	I guess they did.
Ms. Fox:	Tell me what happened.
Tim:	John and Steven were teasing me about my shirt. They really made me mad.
Ms. Fox:	They were teasing you about your shirt? What did they say?
Tim:	That it's too pink. That it's a "girly" color.
Ms. Fox:	Really? I don't think it's too "girly" at all. In fact, I rather like that color on you. But anyway, you say the boys teased you about it. What did you do then?
Tim:	I yelled at them. Then when you gave me that dirty look, they kept on laughing, and so I kept on yelling.

Ms. Fox: I see. John and Steven were certainly wrong to tease you about your clothes. I'll speak to them later. But right now I'm concerned about how you reacted to the situation. You were so loud that the class couldn't possibly continue with the lesson.

Tim: I know. I'm sorry.

Ms. Fox: I appreciate your apology, Tim. And I'd like to make sure that the next time someone hurts your feelings—maybe intentionally, maybe not—you don't blow up the way you did today. Let's come up with a plan for how you might keep your temper under better control.

- Considering what you have learned about trends in emotional development, is Tim's reaction typical for his age?
- What kind of plan might be effective in helping Tim control his anger?

Once you have answered these questions, compare your responses with those presented in Appendix A.

Interpreting Children's Artifacts and Reflections

Consider chapter concepts as you analyze the following artifact from an adolescent.

Paint Me Like I Am

Many young people express their innermost thoughts and feelings through poetry. WritersCorps, an organization that cultivates the literacy skills of youth from disadvantaged urban neighborhoods, has published the poems of numerous young people. Delia Garcia, an adolescent from San Francisco, California, wrote a poem, *Paint Me Like I Am*, which has been published by WritersCorps (2003). As you read Delia's poem, consider these questions:

- What kinds of emotions does Delia express in her poem?
- How might poetry help Delia cope with her complex feelings?

Paint Me Like I Am
Why don't you paint me
Like I am?
Paint me happy,
Laughing, running down a path of happiness
Paint me with a smile on my face.
Paint me with long wavy black hair
And my rosy cheeks.
Paint me with sunflowers, red and white roses.
Paint me with bears, rabbits and baby deer
In my arms, dancing around me.
Paint me somewhere wonderful
Somewhere where there's sunshine and
A light blue sky
With butterflies floating
Around that lovely sky.
Paint me without my sadness.

Paint me without my sorrow,
Paint me without my tears.
Paint me so my pain won't show.
Can you see the face telling you to paint me happy,
Paint me with my life, but most of all
Paint me free.
Delia Garcia[a]

(WritersCorps, 2003, p. 5)

Once you have analyzed the poem, compare your ideas with those presented in Appendix B. For further practice in analyzing children's artifacts and reflections, go to the Activities and Applications section in Chapter 11 of MyEducationLab.

[a]Reprinted with permission. WritersCorps (2003). *Paint Me Like I Am: Teen Poems from WritersCorps*. New York, NY: HarperTempest.

Developmental Trends Exercise

In this chapter you learned about core elements of children's social-emotional development: their first attachments to caregivers, their emotional expression, and their unique temperaments and personalities. The following table describes behaviors that youngsters at five different age levels exhibit. For each of these behaviors, the table identifies one or more relevant social-emotional qualities, offers an implication for working with children of that age-group, or both. Go to the Activities and Applications section in Chapter 11 of MyEducationLab to apply what you've learned about attachment, emotions, temperament, and personality as you fill in the empty cells in the table.

Nurturing Youngsters' Emotional Development

Age	A Youngster's Experience	Developmental Concepts *Identifying Emotional Qualities*	Implications *Nurturing Emotional Development*
Infancy **(Birth–2 Years)**	Edel is a healthy 1-year-old girl with Down syndrome. Her mother is going back to work and enrolls Edel in a child care center. During the first few weeks, when Edel is first dropped off in the morning, she clings to her mother and cries loudly as her mother leaves. When her mother returns in the afternoon, Edel is usually sitting quietly and mouthing and handling toys. Upon noticing her mother's arrival, Edel crawls to her, demands to be picked up, and snuggles into her mother's arms.		Be especially reassuring to infants when they first enter your care. Hold them gently, pamper them when they cry, and look after them with utmost sensitivity. Expect them to protest separations from parents, realizing that they eventually will form attachments to you.
Early Childhood **(2–6 Years)**	Mr. Bono notices that one of his preschool students, Phyllis, seems somewhat anxious at school. Phyllis appears timid and shy, and she stands on the fringes of group activities. She does not interact easily with other children and has no regular friends in the class. With a change in routine, such as missing story time because of a fire drill or having to stay inside during a bitter snow day, Phyllis is obviously upset.	As with all children, Phyllis has her own unique *temperament* and a budding *personality*. Depending on the particular constellation of temperamental or personality characteristics being considered, Phyllis might be described as emotionally intense, showing negative affectivity, or having an inclination toward neuroticism.	When children seem timid, shy, and nervous, offer them reassurance that everything is fine. Provide them with a well-structured learning environment, and when possible, give advance notice of changes in regular activities. When children have trouble making friends, help them ease into social groups.
Middle Childhood **(6–10 Years)**	A third-grade teacher returns children's graded mathematics assignments. Most children did well on the assignment, but two children, Brenda and Billy, had trouble keeping their attention on the task and so received low grades for their work. When Brenda receives her low grade, she cries and broods over the poor score for the remainder of the day. Billy, on the other hand, smiles when he gets the assignment back and says, "Oh well," but he later gets in trouble during recess for disruptive behavior.	Brenda and Billy seem to exhibit typical *gender differences in emotions*. Brenda responds negatively to her poor performance and ruminates about it all day. Billy seems to deny that there is a problem, but his disruptive behavior later in the day may be a sign that he is, in fact, trying to put on a self-confident front to mask his disappointment.	

Developmental Trends Exercise (continued)

Age	A Youngster's Experience	Developmental Concepts *Identifying Emotional Qualities*	Implications *Nurturing Emotional Development*
Early Adolescence (10–14 Years)	Thirteen-year-old Adam has confronted many hardships in his life, including his parents' divorce, economic poverty, and the death of a baby sister. Despite facing adversity, Adam is a reasonably happy and healthy young man. When he is sad or anxious, he makes a point to go for a ride on his bicycle and talk openly about his feelings with his parents and close friends. Sometimes when he feels particularly stressed, he goes to the movies with a friend or drops by the neighborhood youth center to play pool.	Adam seems reasonably well adjusted, perhaps due in part to the fact that he has learned a range of helpful techniques for *emotional regulation*.	Teach and encourage effective ways of regulating emotions. When adolescents are particularly troubled, remind them of the strategies that have helped them in the past, including expressing feelings to others, exercising, and distracting themselves with enjoyable activities.
Late Adolescence (14–18 Years)	Seventeen-year-old Nate recently broke up with his steady girlfriend. He appears despondent and tells his father and friends that he can't bear it anymore. He says he feels terrible, drinks alcohol excessively, and searches the Internet for Web sites about suicide.	Nate is showing some warning signs that he might be at risk for *suicide*. None of these indicators is definitive, but collectively they do suggest he is in serious trouble and needs immediate attention.	

Key Concepts

psychosocial stages (p. 404)
need for relatedness (p. 407)
attachment (p. 407)
ethological attachment theory
   (p. 407)
stranger anxiety (p. 409)

secure attachment
   (p. 410)
insecure-avoidant attachment
   (p. 410)
insecure-resistant attachment
   (p. 410)

disorganized and disoriented
   attachment (p. 411)
emotion (p. 419)
emotional contagion (p. 419)
self-conscious emotion (p. 421)
emotional regulation (p. 422)

empathy (p. 423)
anxiety (p. 426)
personality (p. 428)
depression (p. 435)
anxiety disorder (p. 436)
conduct disorder (p. 436)

MyEducationLab

Now go to Chapter 11 of MyEducationLab at www.myeducationlab.com, where you can:

· View instructional objectives for the chapter.
· Take a quiz to test your mastery of chapter objectives. Detailed feedback is provided to explain why your responses are correct or incorrect.
· Deepen your understanding of particular concepts and principles with Review, Practice, and Enrichment exercises.

· Complete Activities and Applications exercises that give you additional experience in interpreting artifacts, increase your understanding of how research contributes to knowledge about chapter topics, and encourage you to apply what you have learned about children's development.
· Apply what you have learned in the chapter to your work with children in Building Teaching Skills and Dispositions exercises.
· Observe children and their unique contexts in Video Examples.

Development of Self and Social Understandings

Angela Burgos teaches a class of fifth graders in Boston, Massachusetts. Most of her 21 students and their families are from Puerto Rico or the Dominican Republic. All of the children speak Spanish as their primary language and have been placed together in Angela's class to learn English and acquire basic academic skills.

Angela has strong convictions about her students' potential to achieve in school and make lifelong contributions in society. As she interacts with students, she communicates her faith in their abilities. When asked how she would describe success in her classroom, she replies:

> Well, success for me is when I see [an increase in] a student's self-confidence, self-esteem . . . and [see the student] become empowered, [when] he recognizes that no matter what obstacles he may encounter, he will still make a difference, and he will be somebody.[a] (Selman, 2003, p. 175)

Angela helps children develop positive self-perceptions by treating them with utmost respect, showing them how their personal experiences provide solid foundations for learning at school, and ensuring that they are academically successful.

To additionally prepare children for responsible roles in society, Angela helps acquaint children with the perspectives of other people. She finds literature to be an especially effective forum for enhancing children's social understandings. Recently the class has been reading the novel *Felita,* in which an 8-year-old Puerto Rican girl (Felita) narrates her experiences growing up in an economically poor neighborhood of New York City (Mohr, 1979). In the story, local buildings are dilapidated and schools are badly furnished, but Felita likes living there and enjoys her frequent interactions with her grandparents and best friend Gigi.

The children in Angela's class become upset when they learn that Felita's parents decide to move, giving Felita just one day to adjust to the change. Their discussion begins in this way:

Luis:	I think Felita was a little bit angry at her mom, because she didn't care about the move, but Felita did. She just kept on thinking about packing up things and going to the new neighborhood. That's why they brought it up, because Felita was sort of in a bad mood because she didn't want to move, but her mother didn't care about that.
Angela:	Okay. [*She points to Juanita, who has raised her hand.*]
Juanita:	I think her parents told her on the last day because if they told her more earlier she would have been more upset and done terrible stuff to not move away.
Angela:	She would have done terrible stuff not to move away—and in that sense, her parents were sort of protecting her from being hurt early and going through the process. Do you think that's fair for her to be—what do you think about her feelings? Being angry at her parents, or her mother? Who has a . . . [*points to Flora*] . . . yes?
Flora:	I think it's not fair because she doesn't know what it feels [like] . . . to Felita. She's just thinking by herself, her mother.
Angela:	So you don't think that Felita—I want to hear what you're saying—you agree with Felita? Is it okay for Felita to be angry?
Flora:	Yeah, because they didn't say—she doesn't feel what Felita feels about the neighborhood.
Angela:	Okay, so the parents are not taking Felita's feelings [about] her friends into consideration.

(dialogue from Selman, 2003, pp. 177–178)

The conversation continues with the other children taking Felita's side and concluding that Felita's parents were unfair and selfish. Some of the children describe occasions when they were angry with their own parents.

But of course there is another side to the story, and Angela asks the children to reconsider their conclusions. She suggests:

> Let's take the parents' point of view. . . . The parents are moving. Did they just decide one day, "Oh, it's time for us to move?" According to chapter 1, what did we find out? (Selman, 2003, p. 182)

Case Study:
Felita

Outline:

Case Study: Felita

Sense of Self

Social Cognition

Summary

Applying Concepts in Child Development

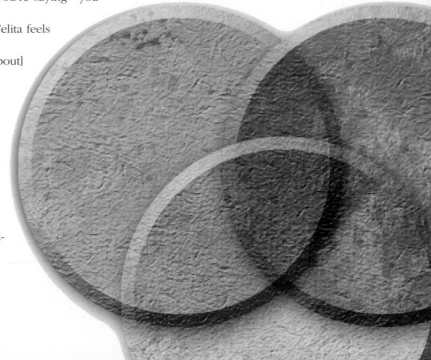

Angela writes down the children's answers on the chalkboard (e.g., "Bigger Apartment," "Better Neighborhood"; Selman, 2003, pp. 183–184). The children are now primed to reassess Felita's parents' motives:

Angela: So, the parents are looking out for whose best interests? Have they not taken the children into consideration?

Felipe: They did the decision by themselves.

Angela: Well, think about [*points to the list on the board*] bigger apartment, better neighborhood. We don't know what dangers are within their old neighborhood. A better future. Think about [that] as parents. Pretend you *are* parents. Does that mean that you're ignoring your children's feelings?

Class: No!

Angela: You're taking them into consideration. Think about your parents. What does that tell us here?

Luis: They want the best for their children.

Angela: That's right, and sometimes. . . .

Luis: Sometimes their parents, like they want to—sometimes parents give you something that you don't want because they love you. That's to help you.

Angela: Okay, they know you and they love you. What other reasons?

Rosario: Sometimes parents do mistakes, but they always want to get you with good stuff.

Angela: You might not understand it at the time, you might be angry, but then later on, it seems you're able to understand that mistake because you're looking at it from [another] point? . . . Right?

           (dialogue from Selman, 2003, p. 184)

- How did Angela foster favorable self-perceptions in children?

- When discussing the story, whose perspective did the children take initially?

- How did Angela help the children see that Felita's parents' also had a valid perspective?

[a]From Selman, Robert L. "To Connect: A Teacher's Pedagogical Vision and Her Empowerment of Students' Point of View." In *The Promotion of Social Awareness: Powerful Lessons from the Partnership of Developmental Theory and Classroom Practice.* © 2001 Russell Sage Foundation, 112 East 64th Street, New York, NY 10021. Reprinted with permission.

Children gradually develop understandings about themselves and other people. Angela helped her students view themselves in a favorable light through her many affirming responses to them. She treated the children respectfully, related academic concepts to their personal experiences, and showed them that they were capable students. Angela also guided the children's interpretations of other people. When reading the story *Felita,* the children readily embraced Felita's views and found it more difficult to see her parents' perspectives. Angela supported children's perspective taking with several tactics. She reminded the children of what they had read about Felita's parents; asked them to pretend that *they* were the parents in the story; and offered the interpretation that Felita's parents were, in fact, considering Felita's long-term needs. As a result, at least some of the children began to appreciate that Felita's parents (and perhaps their own parents as well) could be mistaken in their judgments of children's needs yet nevertheless be quite concerned about their children's well-being.

In this chapter, we examine children's developing sense of self and understandings of other people. We find that, like the children in Angela's class, youngsters can learn a great deal about both themselves and others from their own experiences and from the guidance of attentive adults.

Sense of Self

Children's knowledge, beliefs, judgments, and feelings about themselves are collectively known as a **sense of self.** Particular elements of a sense of self go by a variety of names, including self-concept, self-esteem, and self-worth. In general, one's *self-concept* addresses the question "Who am I?" It includes knowledge and beliefs about one's own characteristics, strengths, and weaknesses ("I get high grades in school," "My nose is a bit crooked"). The terms *self-esteem* and *self-worth* address the question "How good am I as a person?" They in-

sense of self
Knowledge, beliefs, judgments, and feelings about oneself as a person.

clude judgments and feelings about one's own value and worth (e.g., "I am proud of my academic record," "I hate my crooked nose!"). Children's perceptions of their personal qualities and their judgments about their value as human beings are closely related (Byrne, 2002; Harter, 2006; Pintrich & Schunk, 2002). For instance, children who focus largely on their negative features tend to believe they are unworthy people. Those who hold favorable impressions of their own characteristics tend to have high self-esteem. In this chapter, we examine self-concept and self-esteem together, often calling them self-perceptions but occasionally using the more specific terms when distinctions in the research merit their separation.

Effects of Children's Sense of Self

Children's sense of self serves several important functions (Harter, 2006). It helps children understand things that happen to them ("Other kids keep asking me to join their teams, so I must be good at sports"). It motivates them to engage in behaviors to which others might respond favorably ("If I'm nice to Russell, maybe he'll ask me to play with him"). It influences their reactions to events ("I'm upset that I'm not reading as well as my classmates"). It allows them to envision the various *future selves* they might become (see Figure 12-1). And once they begin to look seriously at a particular future self, it helps them make choices appropriate for their goals ("If I want to become a veterinarian, then I should take a biology class").

Perhaps most importantly, a sense of self helps a person find a comfortable niche in a complex world, one in which the individual feels capable, cared for, and respected. Many psychologists believe that human beings have a basic need to think of themselves as competent, likable, and worthy individuals—that is, to achieve and maintain a positive sense of self-worth (Covington, 1992; Park, Crocker, & Kiefer, 2007). To maintain a sense of self-worth, people use a variety of tactics, including affiliating with other individuals who are apt to treat them favorably and putting themselves in situations where they can be successful.

Most children do seem to focus more on what they do well than on what they do poorly, and so they are predisposed to think highly of themselves (K. Fischer, 2005; Harter, 2006; Jacobs, Lanza, Osgood, Eccles, & Wigfield, 2002). Often they downplay areas that give them trouble (e.g., "Math is dumb"). They may also explain their shortcomings in ways that enable them to maintain a positive sense of self. In the "Memory: Middle Childhood" video in MyEducationLab, you can see 10-year-old David give a healthy, upbeat spin on why he doesn't recall as many words as he expects to. He predicts that he might recall 12 out of 12 words but actually recalls only 3. Here is David's positive interpretation:

David:	Okay, shirt, carrot, bed. I'm sorry, I can't remember the rest of it. It's just, I don't know. My brain was turned off right now. I use it a lot during school hours so then I just like to relax. . . .
Interviewer:	What did you do to remember the ones that you remembered?
David:	Even though I said 12, I was just trying to challenge myself a little.

The need to protect one's self-worth is so strong that it sometimes leads children to create obstacles that give them an excuse for failing. In other words, youngsters occasionally do things that actually *undermine* their chances of success—a phenomenon known as **self-handicapping.** Self-handicapping takes a variety of forms, including the following:

- *Reducing effort:* Putting forth an obviously insufficient amount of effort to succeed
- *Setting unattainably high goals:* Working toward goals that even the most capable individuals couldn't achieve
- *Taking on too much:* Assuming so many responsibilities that no one could possibly accomplish them all
- *Procrastinating:* Putting off a task until success is virtually impossible
- *Cheating:* Presenting others' work as one's own
- *Using alcohol or drugs:* Taking substances that will inevitably reduce performance (E. M. Anderman, Griesinger, & Westerfield, 1998; Covington, 1992; D. Y. Ford, 1996; Riggs, 1992; Urdan, Ryan, Anderman, & Gheen, 2002; Waschbusch, Craig, Pelham, & King, 2007)

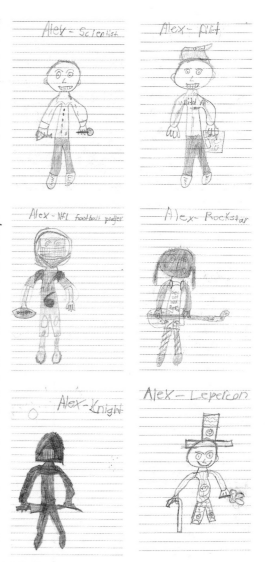

Figure 12-1

In these spontaneously created drawings, 10-year-old Alex envisions a variety of possible *future selves,* some realistic and others more fanciful.

MyEducationLab

Listen to David put a positive spin on why he didn't remember as many words as he had predicted in the "Memory: Middle Childhood" video. (Find Video Examples in Chapter 12 of MyEducationLab.)

self-handicapping
Action that undermines one's own success as a way of protecting self-worth during difficult tasks.

It might seem paradoxical that youngsters who want to be successful would actually try to undermine their own success. But if they believe they are unlikely to succeed no matter what they do—and especially if failure will reflect poorly on their intelligence and ability—they increase their chances of *justifying* the failure and thereby protecting their self-worth (Covington, 1992; Urdan et al., 2002). Self-handicapping is seen as early as elementary school and becomes increasingly common in the high school and college years (Urdan, 2004; Waschbusch et al., 2007; Wolters, 2003).

Regardless of precisely how children view their abilities, they tend to behave in ways that mirror their self-perceptions (Bong & Skaalvik, 2003; Caldwell, Rudolph, Troop-Gordon, & Kim, 2004; Valentine, DuBois, & Cooper, 2004). Those who see themselves as "good students" are more apt to pay attention in class, use effective learning strategies, and tackle challenging tasks and problems, whereas those who believe they are "poor students" are apt to misbehave in class, study infrequently, and avoid difficult subject matter. Children who see themselves as friendly and likable are apt to seek the company of classmates and perhaps run for student council, whereas those who believe they are disliked may keep to themselves or behave aggressively toward peers. As you might guess, children who routinely *under*estimate their ability avoid the many challenges that are apt to enhance their cognitive, social, and physical growth (Assor & Connell, 1992; D. Phillips & Zimmerman, 1990).

There are limits to the extent to which children's global self-perceptions affect their other psychological tendencies and actions, however. Children may view themselves as being generally worthy, competent individuals yet also believe they are *in*capable of taking on particular challenges, such as scaling a steep wall or giving a 5-minute presentation in class. To understand how children's beliefs about their potential achievement affect their performance in specific domains, psychologists examine children's *self-efficacy,* their beliefs that they are capable of executing particular behaviors or reaching certain goals. As you will learn in Chapter 13, children's self-efficacy strongly determines their willingness to pursue difficult tasks. Of course, children's general sense of self is vitally important as well, and we now examine the factors that influence it.

Factors Influencing Sense of Self

Just as children largely self-construct their understandings of the world around them (see Chapters 6 and 7), so, too, do they construct their understandings of who they are as people. To a considerable degree, they base their self-perceptions on their own past behaviors and performances (Damon, 1991; Marsh, Trautwein, Lüdtke, Köller, & Baumert, 2005). Thus children are more likely to believe they will succeed in school and later in college if they have been successful in their previous classes. Conversely, those children who struggle recurrently see their abilities as limited and their academic futures as bleak. A second grader named Tom, who had dyslexia, once described how he felt when struggling with reading in first grade:

> I falt like a losr. Like nobad likde me. I was afrad then kais wod tec me. Becacz I wased larning wale . . . I dan not whet to raed. I whoe whte to troe a book it my mom.
> *(I felt like a loser. Like nobody liked me. I was afraid that kids would tease me. Because I wasn't learning well . . . I did not want to read. I would want to throw a book at my mom.)* (N. F. Knapp, 2002, p. 74)

Through words and deeds, adults influence children's self-perceptions about their capability and worth.

Adults also influence children's sense of self, and in several ways. First, adults communicate messages about children's strengths, limitations, and overall worth through both words and deeds. Such lessons begin in infancy and extend throughout childhood and adolescence. When caregivers regularly give infants nurturance and affection, infants learn not only that their caregivers can be loving but also that they themselves are worthy of being loved (Bretherton, 1991). As children grow, parents enhance children's sense of self by treating children warmly and communicating expectations for mature behavior. Parents who accept children as they are—applauding children's abilities and taking *in*abilities in stride—are likely to have children with high self-esteem. Parents who punish children for things they cannot do, without also praising them for things done well, are apt to have children with low self-esteem (Harter, 1999, 2006). Adults outside the family are influential as well. Teachers foster a positive sense of self when they have high yet realistic expectations for children's performance and offer support to help children attain challenging goals (Dweck, 2000; M. J. Harris & Rosenthal, 1985).

Meanwhile, peers communicate information about children's social and athletic competence, perhaps by seeking out a child's companionship or ridiculing a child in front of others (Dweck, 2000; Harter, 2006). Peers contribute to children's sense of self in a second way as well: They provide information about what children "should" be able to do. How children evaluate themselves often depends on how their own performance compares to that of their peers (Guay, Boivin, & Hodges, 1999; Marsh & Hau, 2003). Children who see themselves achieving at higher levels than age-mates usually develop a more positive sense of self than those who, like Tom (the boy with dyslexia), consistently find themselves falling short.

Membership in one or more groups can also influence children's sense of self, especially in adolescence (Lave & Wenger, 1991; Spencer, 2006; Wigfield et al., 1996). In general, youngsters are more likely to have high self-esteem if they are members of a successful group (Phinney, 1989; Wigfield et al., 1996). If you think back to your own school years, perhaps you can recall taking pride in a regional championship earned by one of your school's athletic teams or feeling good about a community service project completed through an extracurricular club. Being a member of a particular ethnic group also affects a youngster's sense of self, as we discover later in this chapter in our analysis of ethnic identity.

So far our discussion has focused primarily on the effects of children's experiences—that is, the effects of environment—on their self-perceptions. Biology has an impact as well. Studies with twins and other siblings indicate a fairly substantial genetic basis for self-esteem (Neiss et al., 2005; Neiss, Sedikides, & Stevenson, 2006; Raevuori et al., 2007). Genes probably affect self-esteem indirectly through their effects on partially inherited characteristics (e.g., temperaments, physical skills, cognitive abilities, and physical and cognitive disabilities) that contribute to children's successes and failures in social, athletic, and academic pursuits. Physical appearance also makes a difference: Adults and peers alike respond more favorably to children who are physically attractive (e.g., Harter, 2006; Harter, Whitesell, & Junkin, 1998).

General Trends in Children's Sense of Self

Children's physical, cognitive, and social abilities change with age, and their perceptions of themselves shift accordingly. Researchers have observed the following developmental trends in sense of self:

• ***Children construct increasingly multifaceted understandings of who they are.*** Children in the early elementary grades tend to distinguish between two general aspects of themselves: how competent they are in daily activities and how much family and friends seem to like them. As they grow older, they make finer and finer discriminations (Davis-Kean & Sandler, 2001; Harter, 2006). In the upper elementary grades, they realize that they may be more or less advanced in their academic work, athletic activities, classroom behavior, likability among peers, and physical attractiveness. By adolescence, they also have self-perceptions about their ability to make friends, competence at adult-like work tasks, and romantic appeal. Each of these domains may have a greater or lesser influence on youngsters' overall sense of self. In general, youngsters have high self-esteem when they evaluate themselves as being strong in domains that are most important to them. For some, academic achievement may be the overriding factor, whereas for others popularity with peers may be more influential. For many children and adolescents around the world, physical attractiveness contributes heavily to overall self-esteem (D. Hart, 1988; Harter, 2006).

• ***As children grow older, their feelings of self-worth increasingly depend on peers' behaviors and opinions.*** In the early years, parents and other family members are key players in shaping children's sense of self. As children spend more time away from home, however, they become more aware of and concerned about what nonfamily members—and especially peers—think of them (Harter, 2006). Whereas parents often express approval for good behavior and high academic achievement, peers tend to favor children who are physically attractive, athletically skillful, and fun to be with. Peers do not entirely replace the influence of parents, however. Well into the adolescent years, youngsters' self-perceptions continue to be strongly affected by relationships with parents (Harter, 2006).

LUANN   **BY GREG EVANS**

Many adolescents encounter unrealistic self-evaluation criteria in magazines and other popular media.
LUANN: © GEC Inc./Dist. by United Feature Syndicate, Inc.

• *Most youngsters gradually internalize criteria that others use to evaluate their behavior and characteristics.* Just as Vygotsky proposed that children internalize many of the cognitive strategies they first use in social interactions, so, too, do psychologists specializing in the self suggest that children gradually internalize other people's ideas about desirable characteristics and behaviors (S. Burton & Mitchell, 2003; Harter, 2006). As youngsters acquire such criteria, their self-esteem is increasingly based on *self*-judgments rather than others' judgments. For example, a boy whose parents regularly praise him for his high grades is likely to begin judging *himself* by the grades he earns. You can see such internalization in an interview with 15-year-old Greg in the "Intrinsic Motivation: Late Adolescence" video in MyEducationLab:

Interviewer:	What are the things that make you want to do well in school?
Greg:	My parents. [*Both laugh.*]
Interviewer:	Okay.
Greg:	My parents mostly. . . . And myself . . . sometimes.
Interviewer:	Okay. How do your parents influence you wanting to do well in school?
Greg:	I don't know. They did well so they want me to. . . .
Interviewer:	You said that sometimes you also want to do well for you. Can you tell me more about that?
Greg:	'Cause, I mean, you feel better if you get all As than Cs or Fs.

Yet the standards that youngsters adopt are not always realistic or productive. For instance, a girl whose friends place a premium on fashion-magazine standards for thinness may think she is "fat" even when she is dangerously underweight—a misperception commonly seen in youngsters who have eating disorders (Attie, Brooks-Gunn, & Petersen, 1990; K. A. Peterson, Paulson, & Williams, 2007).

Despite the general trend toward greater dependence on self-evaluation, some youngsters remain heavily dependent on others' opinions well into adolescence. They may be so preoccupied with peer approval that they base their own sense of self-worth largely on what their peers think—or at least on what *they think* their peers think—of them (Dweck, 2000; Harter, 2006; Harter, Stocker, & Robinson, 1996). Teenagers who have such **contingent self-worth** are often on an emotional roller coaster, feeling elated one day and devastated the next, depending on how friends and classmates have recently treated them.

• *Youngsters gradually integrate their many self-perceptions into general abstractions of who they are.* Young children tend to define themselves in terms of specific, concrete, easily observable characteristics and behaviors. As they grow older, they begin to pull these characteristics and behaviors together into more general, abstract conceptions (D. Hart, 1988; Harter, 2006; Rosenberg, 1986). For examples of how children's self-perceptions change with age, try the following exercise, "Comparing Self-Descriptions."

MyEducationLab

Observe how Greg has internalized his parents' standards for academic performance in the "Intrinsic Motivation: Late Adolescence" video. (Find Video Examples in Chapter 12 of MyEducationLab.)

contingent self-worth
Overall sense of self that is highly dependent on others' opinions.

Comparing Self-Descriptions

When her children were younger, Jeanne once asked them to describe themselves. As you read their self-descriptions, identify one or more developmental trends in their responses.

Jeff (age 6):   I like animals. I like making things. I do good in school. I'm happy. Blue eyes. Yellow hair. Light skin.

Alex (age 9):   I have brown hair, brown eyes. I like wearing short-sleeved shirts. My hair is curly. I was adopted. I was born in Denver. I like all sorts of critters. The major sport I like is baseball. I do fairly well in school. I have a lizard, and I'm going to get a second one.

Tina (age 12):   I'm cool. I'm awesome. I'm way cool. I'm twelve. I'm boy crazy. I go to Brentwood Middle School. I'm popular with my fans. I play viola. My best friend is Lindsay. I have a gerbil named Taj. I'm adopted. I'm beautiful.

Notice how Jeff and Alex talked mostly about how they looked, how they behaved, and what they liked. In contrast, Tina described several abstract qualities—cool, awesome, boy crazy, popular, beautiful—that she had apparently derived from her many experiences over time. Notice, too, how both boys mentioned their performance in school. Tina focused more on social and physical qualities than on academic achievement (or, we might add, modesty). As we've seen, social acceptance and physical appearance are often high priorities in the minds of young adolescents.

• ***A sense of worth becomes more stable over time.*** Beginning in middle childhood and continuing into adolescence and beyond, self-esteem becomes fairly stable, such that those with positive self-perceptions tend to continue to see themselves in favorable terms (Robins & Trzesniewski, 2005). Conversely, children who think poorly of themselves in elementary school also tend to have low self-esteem in high school and adulthood. Several factors contribute to the increasing stability of self-perceptions:

- Children usually behave in ways consistent with what they believe about themselves, and their behaviors are apt to produce reactions from others that confirm their self-concepts.
- Children tend to seek out information that confirms what they already believe. Those with positive self-perceptions are more likely to seek out positive feedback, whereas some with negative self-perceptions may actually look for information about their weaknesses (S. Epstein & Morling, 1995; Swann, 1997).
- Children seldom put themselves in situations where they believe they won't succeed, thus minimizing the chances of discovering that they *can* succeed in a domain about which they've been pessimistic. For instance, if a middle school student believes he's a poor athlete and so refuses to go out for the baseball team, he may never learn that, in fact, he has the potential to become a good player.
- Many factors affecting self-esteem—inherited abilities and disabilities, parents' behaviors, physical attractiveness, and so on—remain relatively stable throughout childhood (O'Malley & Bachman, 1983; Raevuori et al., 2007).

This is *not* to say that once children acquire an unfavorable sense of self, they will always think poorly of themselves. Quite the contrary can be true, especially when circumstances change significantly (Harter, 2006; Marsh & Craven, 1997).

Changes in the Self over Childhood and Adolescence

The developmental trends just listed reflect gradual changes in sense of self over time. We now look at unique aspects of self-perceptions at five age levels: infancy, early childhood, middle childhood, early adolescence, and late adolescence.

Infancy (birth–age 2).   The first elements of children's sense of self appear in infancy. Through repeated physical experiences, babies discover that they have bodies that bring them discomfort (through hunger, fatigue, and injury) and pleasure (through feeding, sucking thumbs, and snuggling in the arms of caregivers) (R. A. Thompson, 2006). Children also form impressions of themselves as being lovable (or not) from the relationships they form with parents and caregivers. Infants who form secure attachments with caregivers develop positive self-perceptions, whereas infants who form insecure attachments do not (Harter, 2006; also see Chapter 11). Possibly, too, protests at being separated from caregivers reflect infants' emerging and uneasy insight that they exist separately from the people on whom they depend.

In the first year, infants' increasing ability to imitate other people's facial expressions also nourishes their early sense of self (Collie & Hayne, 1999; Meltzoff, 1990; R. A. Thompson, 2006). In order to mimic others (e.g., older brother opening his mouth wide), they must to some degree realize that they and the people they're looking at are separate entities. Late in the first year, activities involving joint attention come into play as well. When Mommy and baby examine a toy together, baby shifts her gaze between toy and Mommy's face. Baby begins to learn that she has a sense of "we-ness" with her mother but also is a being separate from Mommy (Emde & Buchsbaum, 1990).

In the second year, infants begin to recognize themselves in the mirror. In a clever study of self-recognition, babies 9 to 24 months were placed in front of a mirror (M. Lewis & Brooks-Gunn, 1979). Their mothers then wiped their faces, leaving a red mark on their noses. Older infants, especially those 15 months or older, touched their noses when they saw their reflections, as if they understood that the reflected images belonged to them.

Once young children develop a firm sense of themselves, they find it easier to share with others.

Early childhood (ages 2–6).   In early childhood, acquisition of language and other cognitive abilities makes further advancements possible. Once children begin to talk, their self-awareness becomes much more obvious. Children begin to refer to themselves by the pronouns *I* and *me,* and at ages 2 and 3 commonly exclaim "Mine!" during tussles with peers (L. Levine, 1983; M. Lewis & Brooks-Gunn, 1979; C. Moore, 2007). Learning about what is *mine* is a natural part of development and is probably a precursor to sharing. Young children also increasingly assert their competence and independence (e.g., by refusing assistance with putting on their jackets) and, as you learned in Chapter 11, they articulate their self-awareness by labeling emotions (e.g., "Happy me") (R. A. Thompson, 2006).

Another acquisition that depends on cognitive development is the **autobiographical self,** a mental "history" of important events in one's life. On average, children remember few if any events that occurred before age 3½, and their recall of events before age 2 is virtually nonexistent. Children's early recollections are usually sparse, fragmented snippets that don't hang together in any meaningful way. Memories for events become increasingly detailed and integrated during the preschool years, especially if children discuss their experiences with other people (Fivush & Nelson, 2004; M. L. Howe, 2003; R. A. Thompson, 2006). This ever-expanding personal history becomes an important part of how children conceptualize who they are as people (Bauer, 2006).

Initially, children see themselves largely in terms of obvious physical characteristics and simple psychological traits (Damon & Hart, 1988; Harter, 2006). (Recall that 6-year-old Jeff had "blue eyes" and was "happy.") As they learn from caregivers what things are "good" and "bad," they begin to apply these standards in evaluating themselves (Dweck, 2000; J. Kagan, 1981). Often they feel bad when they don't measure up. For instance, a 5-year-old boy may become quite frustrated when he discovers he can't spread peanut butter on bread as neatly as his father does.

By and large, however, most young children have positive self-concepts and high self-esteem. Often they believe that they are more capable than they really are and that they can easily overcome initial failures (Harter, 2006; Lockhart, Chang, & Story, 2002; Paris & Cunningham, 1996). Such optimism is perhaps due to their tendency to base self-assessments on their continuing improvements in "big boy" and "big girl" activities. Their overconfidence is probably beneficial for their development, in that it motivates them to try and persist at challenging tasks (Bjorklund & Green, 1992; Pintrich & Schunk, 2002).

Middle childhood (ages 6–10).   During middle childhood, children tend to see themselves in more complex physical and psychological terms. Consider the many domains 9-year-old Shea addresses in her *Song of Myself,* presented in Figure 12-2. Among other things, Shea describes herself as "kind, responsible, pretty, smart . . . a child of honesty."

Elementary school children are usually aware that they do some things well and other things poorly (Bouffard, Marcoux, Vezeau, & Bordeleau, 2003; Marsh & Craven, 1997; Wigfield, 1994). As they progress through the elementary school grades, they have many opportunities to compare themselves with others and become cognitively more able to *make* such compar-

autobiographical self
Mental "history" of important events in one's life.

isons. Most youngsters now receive some critical feedback from teachers and also observe some of their peers outshining them at least some of the time, and so their self-assessments typically decline from the overconfidence of the preschool years to levels that are more accurate (Harter, 2006; Marsh & Hau, 2003; Robins & Trzesniewski, 2005). Becoming more realistic about their talents and limitations probably helps children choose age-appropriate activities and work toward achievable goals (Baumeister, Campbell, Krueger, & Vohs, 2003; Harter, 2006). Generally, however—perhaps because they have so many domains to consider as they look for strengths—most children maintain reasonably positive self-esteem during the elementary school years (Bouffard et al., 2003; Wigfield & Eccles, 1994).

Early adolescence (ages 10–14).

A drop in self-esteem often occurs at about the time that youngsters move from elementary school to middle school or junior high school; this drop tends to be more pronounced for girls (Harter, 2006; Marsh, 1990b; Robins & Trzesniewski, 2005; Simmons & Blyth, 1987). The physiological changes of puberty may be one factor in the decline. Self-evaluations depend increasingly on beliefs about appearance and popularity, and boys and girls alike tend to think of themselves as being somewhat less attractive once they reach adolescence (Cornell et al., 1990; D. Hart, 1988; Harter et al., 1998). Changes in the school environment, such as disrupted friendships, more superficial teacher–student relationships, and more rigorous academic standards, probably also have a negative impact (Eccles & Midgley, 1989; Harter, 2006). (We will look more closely at youngsters' transitions to new school environments in Chapter 15.)

Also with early adolescence come two new phenomena that have implications for sense of self. First, youngsters become more cognitively able to reflect on how others see them (Harter, 1999). They may initially go to extremes in this respect, to the point where they think that in any social situation, everyone else's attention is focused squarely on them (Alberts, Elkind, & Ginsberg, 2007; Elkind, 1981a; Lapsley, 1993). This self-centered aspect of the young adolescent's sense of self is sometimes called the **imaginary audience.** Because they believe they are the center of attention, teenagers (girls especially) are often preoccupied with their physical appearance and can be quite self-critical. Many adolescents change the way they speak and act according to whom they are interacting with at the moment, thereby increasing the chances they will gain others' approval (Harter, 2006; Rosenberg, 1986). Yet young adolescents are generally not fully aware that they are acting somewhat inconsistently with different people.

Some adolescents become so worried about other people's opinions that they go overboard in trying to please others or alternatively become overly sensitive to others' remarks. For example, some adolescents become explosively angry when other people speak to them disrespectfully. Unfortunately, a few adolescents may also choose to respond to such humiliation with undue violence (Harter, 2006; Lowry, Sleet, Duncan, Powell, & Kolbe, 1995).

A second noteworthy phenomenon in early adolescence is the **personal fable.** Young teenagers often believe they are completely unlike anyone else (Aalsma, Lapsley, & Flannery, 2006; Elkind, 1981a; Lapsley, 1993). They are apt to think their own feelings are unique—that the people around them have never experienced such emotions. Hence they may insist that no one else, least of all parents and teachers, can possibly know how they feel. They may also believe that they have special powers and are invulnerable to harm.

Adults should keep in mind that modest levels of the personal fable and the imaginary audience appear to serve important functions in youngsters' developmental progress. The personal fable—in particular, the sense of invulnerability—may encourage young people to venture out into the world and try new things (Bjorklund & Green, 1992; Lapsley, 1993). The imaginary audience keeps youngsters "connected" to their larger social context. Because they continually attend to how others might judge their actions, they are more apt to behave in ways that their society will view favorably (Lapsley, 1993; R. M. Ryan & Kuczkowski, 1994). However, excessive concern about the self is associated with some risks. For example, having a strong personal fable is associated with depression in adolescents, possibly because it reflects a tendency to ruminate about one's own shortcomings (Aalsma et al., 2006). At some

Song of Myself

I am Shea
Above me are the bright colored leaves on the trees
Below me are seeds waiting to become flowers next spring
Before me are years to come full of new things to be learned
Behind me are memories I've forgotten
All around me are my friends lending me a helping hand
I see children having fun
I smell the sweet scent of flowers
I hear the birds talking to each other
I feel the fur of a helpless baby bunny
I move like wind as I run through the grass
I am old like the planets who have been here from the beginning
I am young like a seed waiting to sprout
I am the black of a panda's patches
I am the gold of the sun
I am the green of a cat's eye
I am the many colors of the sunset
I am a parrot, kangaroo, tiger, turtle
I am kind, responsible, pretty, smart
I think, plan, help, research
I give ideas to people that need them
I fear lightning
I believe that we all are equal
I remember my dreams
I dream of bad things as well as the good
I do not understand why some people pollute the Earth
I am Shea, a child of honesty
May I walk in peace

Figure 12-2

Shea's *Song of Myself.* Shea and her classmates were given "stems" to guide their writing (e.g., "Above me . . . ," "I feel . . . ," and "I am . . . ," "I dream . . .").

imaginary audience
Belief that one is the center of attention in any social situation.

personal fable
Belief held by many adolescents that they are unique beings invulnerable to normal risks and dangers.

A frequently observed phenomenon in early adolescence is the *personal fable:* Young teenagers often believe that they are so unique that no one else can possibly understand their thoughts and feelings.
ZITS © Zits Partnership, King Features Syndicate.

point, both the imaginary audience and personal fable apparently outlive their purposes for most teens, because these tendencies slowly fade away in late adolescence (Lapsley, 1993; Lapsley, Jackson, Rice, & Shadid, 1988).

Late adolescence (ages 14–18). As their worlds expand, teenagers have a greater variety of social experiences with people from diverse backgrounds. With their increasing ability to reflect on their own behaviors, they become consciously aware that they themselves take on different personalities when interacting with parents, teachers, friends, and romantic partners. Thus their sense of self may include multiple self-perceptions that they perceive to be somewhat contradictory (D. Hart, 1988; Harter, 2006; Wigfield et al., 1996). The contradictions can be a source of confusion, as one ninth grader revealed:

> I really don't understand how I can switch so fast from being cheerful with my friends, then coming home and feeling anxious, and then getting frustrated and sarcastic with my parents. Which one is the *real* me? (Harter, 1999, p. 67)

As high school students wrestle with the question *Who is the real me?,* they gradually broaden their sense of self to accommodate their variability (Harter, 2006). For instance, they may resolve their self-perceptions of being both "cheerful" and "depressed" by concluding that they are "moody," or they may explain their inconsistent behaviors in different situations by concluding that they are "flexible" or "open minded."

In the process of reconciling their "multiple selves," older adolescents make progress toward establishing a sense of **identity,** a self-constructed definition of who they are, what they find important, what they believe, and what they should do in life. You might recall from Erik Erikson's theory in Chapter 11 that a search for identity is a pivotal challenge for adolescents. Contemporary research indicates that before youngsters achieve a true sense of their adult identity, most need considerable time to explore career options, political views, religious convictions, and so on. One psychologist (Marcia, 1980, 1991) has observed four distinct patterns of behavior that may characterize an adolescent's search for identity:

- *Identity diffusion.* The adolescent has made no commitment to a particular career path or ideological belief system. Possibly there has been some haphazard experimentation with particular roles or beliefs, but the adolescent has not yet embarked on a serious exploration of issues related to self-definition.
- *Foreclosure.* The adolescent has made a commitment to an occupation and a particular set of beliefs. The choices have been made without much deliberation or exploration of other possibilities; rather, they have been based largely on what others (especially parents) have prescribed.
- *Moratorium.* The adolescent has no strong commitment to a particular career or set of beliefs but is actively exploring and considering a variety of professions and ideologies.
- *Identity achievement.* The adolescent has previously gone through a period of moratorium and emerged with a clear choice regarding occupation and commitment to political and religious beliefs.

identity
Self-constructed definition of who one is, what things one finds important, what one believes, and what goals one wants to accomplish in life.

Foreclosure—identity choice without prior exploration—rules out potentially more productive alternatives, and identity diffusion leaves young people without a clear sense of direction. Being in moratorium can be an uncomfortable experience for some adolescents, but it is often an important step in achieving a healthy identity (Berzonsky, 1988; Luyckx, Goossens, & Soenens, 2006; Marcia, 1988).

For most older high school students, then, the search for identity is hardly complete. Even so, their self-esteem has largely recuperated from the unsettling experiences of the middle school and early high school years (Harter, 2006). Several developmental advancements contribute to this rebound in sense of self. Most older adolescents have acquired the social skills they need to get along well with others. They have resolved many of the apparent inconsistencies in their self-perceptions and have considerable autonomy in choosing activities at which they are likely to be successful. And they increasingly judge themselves based on their *own* (rather than other people's) standards. You can see some of these factors at work in the essay presented in the following exercise, "Hermit Crab."

Interpreting Children's Artifacts and Reflections

Hermit Crab

As an assignment for one of her 11th-grade classes, 17-year-old "Kiley" (a pseudonym) wrote the essay shown here. As you read the essay, identify factors that seem to have contributed to Kiley's positive sense of self. (We have blanked out the name of Kiley's school but have left spelling and grammar errors intact.)

It was during high school that I discovered who I was. Freshman and sophomore year I was a hermit crab, slowly trying to change to a new shell. I was eager to make the process yet I was yearning for something to hold on to help ease the way. For me my path of stepping stones was the _____ High School music department.

When I walked into chorus my freshman year, I was petrified. I felt like I was involved in a cult of some sort. Everyone either seemed extremely friendly or in love with the music department. I have to admit that at first I thought that the music department was pretty lame. Everyday I would walk in and see everyone hugging their friends or people crying on each other's shoulders, what was this? Everyone seemed so dependent on each other. I had my thoughts of quitting; I didn't know a lot of people and wasn't excited at the thought of making friends with them either, but I stuck it out, singing has always been my passion and I wasn't about to never perform again. This is who I was, I wasn't about to let some crazy group of people intimidate me.

By the middle of my sophomore year I was a full time band geek; besides the fact that I wasn't even in the band. I finally let my walls cave in and let the music department be my second home. I loved it. I could come in during the middle of a bad school day and always find a friend, always have someone their for me. The seniors in the rest of the school always seemed so big, so intimidating, but when I walked through the doors of the music department everyone was equal; there were no judgments and everyone felt welcome.

The music department changed me. I am no longer shy or timid but I am me to the fullest extent of the word. I now have the ability to walk into a group of people and make friends instantly. The music department helped me realize that performing is my passion, it's what I love; it's who I am. I am now ready to go audition, to go out and show the world what I am made of. Throughout high school nothing else has made such a lasting impression on me, I am not going to sit back one day as a mother and tell my children about my freshman PE class; my only eventful memories are contained within the walls of the music department. . . .

The music department has given me the strength to move on. When I am nervous I know I can always think back to my _____ years, and the confidence that slowly grew with the help of loving arms. I may be unsure about the future but I am excited. I will always remember the friends I made, the confidence I earned, and the love I shared within the four years; or better yet the four solid walls of the _____ High School music department.

gender schema
Self-constructed body of beliefs about the traits and behaviors of males or females.

As she began high school, Kiley had electives in her class schedule, and this autonomy enabled her to sign up for a class (chorus) in which she could showcase one of her talents (singing). Kiley initially balked at the hugging and crying she saw in other students, considering such actions "dependent," but she eventually reinterpreted such behaviors as being supportive—and hence self-enhancing and confidence building. Furthermore, Kiley internalized some of her peers' standards for behavior, including the importance of being friendly and outgoing. In the music department, then, Kiley consistently received the positive messages so important for a healthy sense of self.

Even as older adolescents move rapidly toward independence, their attachments to family members, especially parents, continue to play a significant role in their sense of self. For instance, adolescents who have strong emotional bonds with parents tend to have higher self-esteem (Harter, 2006; Josselson, 1988; R. M. Ryan & Lynch, 1989). These well-adjusted adolescents receive adequate levels of affection and guidance from parents (Forthun, Montgomery, & Bell, 2006; Lapsley, 1993; R. M. Ryan & Lynch, 1989). Inasmuch as cultures vary in their expressions of warmth and control (see Chapter 3), youngsters around the world are exposed to a wide range of parenting styles that successfully promote a healthy sense of self (Harter, 2006). Yet some parenting styles (e.g., uninvolved parenting or rejecting authoritarian parenting) can cause adolescents to feel alienated from their parents and become susceptible to the opinions of others; that is, these adolescents are more likely to have the *contingent self-worth* described earlier (Forthun et al., 2006; Josselson, 1988; Marcia, 1988).

Diversity in Sense of Self

The various factors that influence sense of self—quality of relationships with parents and other caregivers, teacher and peer behaviors, inherited characteristics and abilities, and so on—all lead to considerable diversity among youngsters at any particular age level. Gender, culture, and ethnic background also contribute to variability in children's sense of self.

Gender differences.   From an early age, children show an interest in gender. By the end of the first year, infants can distinguish male and female faces, and by age 2½, most children know that they are a "boy" or a "girl" (Etaugh, Grinnell, & Etaugh, 1989; Lippa, 2002; C. L. Martin, Ruble, & Szbrybalo, 2002). By age 4 or 5, children understand that this state is permanent—that boys do not become girls if they grow their hair long and wear ribbons, and that girls do not become boys if they cut their hair short and wear boys' clothes (Bem, 1989; DeLisi & Gallagher, 1991; Ruble et al., 2007). As children become increasingly aware of the typical characteristics and behaviors of boys, girls, men, and women, they begin to pull their knowledge together into self-constructed understandings, or **gender schemas,** of "what males are like" and "what females are like." These gender schemas become part of their sense of self and provide guidance for how they themselves should behave—how they should dress, what toys they should play with, what interests and academic subject areas they should pursue, and so on (Bem, 1981; Ruble et al., 2006).

With the onset of puberty, being "male" or "female" takes on new meaning. Many youngsters show an upsurge in gender-specific interests beginning in adolescence (Galambos, Almeida, & Petersen, 1990; Harter, 2006; Ruble et al., 2006). For example, at age 13, Teresa's son Connor displayed a newfound interest in American football—definitely a rough, "manly" sport—and joined the middle school football team. To affirm their masculinity or femininity, many adolescents also begin to shy away from behaviors more closely associated with the opposite sex. In the "Emotional Development: Late Adolescence" video in MyEducationLab, 15-year-old Greg responds to the question "What are some things that kids do when they're sad?" by saying, "Cry . . . if you're a guy, you don't show it." And we authors both recall that, as adolescent girls, we had mixed feelings about mathematics. Although math was something we were good at, we thought of it as a "masculine" domain that would somehow make us look less feminine. (Fortunately, our interest rekindled in college, where we felt freer to "be ourselves" and not conform to sex-role stereotypes.) Even girls who have grown up in more recent and seemingly more open-minded decades tend to have less interest and confidence in subject areas that are traditionally masculine—for instance, mathematics, science, and sports (E. M. Evans, Schweingruber, & Stevenson, 2002; Leaper & Friedman, 2007; Wigfield et al., 1996).

Not only do behaviors and interests seem to differ by gender, but boys' and girls' overall sense of self-worth also differs. Beginning in the upper elementary or middle school grades,

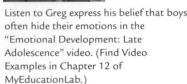

MyEducationLab

Listen to Greg express his belief that boys often hide their emotions in the "Emotional Development: Late Adolescence" video. (Find Video Examples in Chapter 12 of MyEducationLab.)

boys have a higher overall sense of self-worth than girls. This gender difference appears to be due to boys' tendency to *over*estimate their abilities and possibly also to girls' tendency to *under*estimate theirs (D. A. Cole, Martin, Peeke, Seroczynski, & Fier, 1999; Dweck, 2000; Harter, 2006). Girls also have more difficulty taking criticism and failure in stride (Dweck, 2000).

Additional gender differences exist in the specific areas of strength and weakness that youngsters perceive in themselves (J. H. Block, 1983; D. A. Cole et al., 2001; Harter, 2006). On average, boys see themselves as being better athletes, and they have greater self-confidence in their ability to control the world and solve problems. Girls are more apt to judge themselves as being well behaved in school and considerate in social relationships. Beginning in middle childhood, girls rate their physical appearance less favorably than boys do, and they are more preoccupied with how they look, reflecting the imaginary audience phenomenon described earlier (D. A. Cole et al., 2001; Harter, 2006). At school, both boys and girls tend to rate themselves higher in academic areas that are stereotypically "appropriate" for their gender (Eccles et al., 1998; Herbert & Stipek, 2005; Marsh, 1989). Especially in math and science—traditionally masculine domains—boys evaluate themselves more highly than girls do, even when no true differences in achievement exist (Eccles, 1989; Herbert & Stipek, 2005). Conversely, girls are generally more confident in reading and writing than are boys (Leaper & Friedman, 2007).

Of course, there are individual differences in how strictly children adhere to sex-role stereotypes. **Androgynous** youngsters show both feminine and masculine attributes. For instance, they might be nurturing with friends (a stereotypically feminine characteristic) yet assertive in classroom activities (a stereotypically masculine characteristic) (Bem, 1977). Children, adolescents, and adults who relax sex-role boundaries are more apt to pursue counterstereotypical interests and career paths (Harter, 2006; Liben & Bigler, 2002). These individuals also tend to be fairly well adjusted, perhaps because they have more choices in the standards by which they evaluate themselves and perhaps because others respond favorably to their wide range of accomplishments (Broderick & Korteland, 2004; Piche & Plante, 1991; D. E. Williams & D'Alessandro, 1994). Furthermore, contact with androgynous role models can help young people to effectively refine both their feminine and masculine qualities. Individuals with an emerging homosexual or bisexual orientation may view themselves somewhat differently than their same-sex peers and appreciate contact with nontraditional gender models (Carver, Egan, & Perry, 2004; see Chapter 15).

Heredity, environment, and self-socialization in gender differences.

Biology clearly has some influence on how boys and girls behave. The brain is permanently marked "male" or "female" by subtle differences in anatomy during prenatal development (Knickmeyer & Baron-Cohen, 2006; Ruble et al., 2006). At puberty, gender differences increase as rising hormones activate the progression of gender-related characteristics. In boys, for example, these rising hormones are associated with increased aggression—a stereotypically male characteristic (more about this point in Chapter 14).

The environment, too, plays a role by encouraging children to think about males and females in particular ways. Family, peers, and the broader community often reinforce children for "staying within bounds" and punish them (e.g., by ridicule or exclusion) when they violate accepted gender roles (Pipher, 1994; Ruble et al., 2006). For example, a boy who cries after breaking his arm may be called a "sissy," and a girl who excels in mathematics might be teased for being a "math geek." Other people also influence children's gender schemas through the typical roles they play in society (backhoe operators are almost always men), the preferences and priorities they express ("Wait! I have to put on my make-up!"), and the behaviors they model and encourage ("Why don't you gals go shopping while we guys watch the football game?") (Friedman, Leaper, & Bigler, 2007; Ruble et al., 2006; Tennenbaum & Leaper, 2002).

Yet by the time children reach elementary school, much of the pressure to act "appropriately" for their gender comes from within rather than from others (Bem, 1981; C. L. Martin, 2000; Ruble et al., 2006). This tendency for children and adolescents to conform to their own ideas about what behaviors are appropriate for girls and boys is known as **self-socialization.** For example, when teachers actively encourage children to engage in non–gender-stereotypical activities (boys playing with dolls, girls playing with toy cars, etc.), the children may comply for a short time, but they soon revert to their earlier, more gender-typical ways (Lippa, 2002).

As they gain social experience and develop cognitively, children gradually learn to apply more open-minded criteria for gender-appropriate behaviors (Ruble et al., 2006; Trautner, 1992).

androgyny
Tendency to have some characteristics that are stereotypically female (e.g., nurturance) and others that are stereotypically male (e.g., assertiveness).

self-socialization
Tendency to integrate personal observations and others' input into self-constructed standards for behavior and to choose actions consistent with those standards.

Especially in adolescence, much of the pressure to act "appropriately" for one's gender comes from within rather than from other people.

In other words, they soften previously rigid boundaries for the appearance and behaviors of boys and girls. Yet as we saw earlier, many adolescents temporarily embrace gender stereotypes once again, perhaps until they are comfortable with themselves as young men or women (Ruble et al., 2006). For instance, adolescents often begin looking at men and women in new ways, searching for masculine or feminine role models. Many adolescents expose themselves to images and advice related to gender roles in magazines and other media, as these teenage girls reveal in their discussions about particular magazines:

Sophie: I think that *More!* is for older girls really. Like the younger ones [comics and mags] where you've got, you've got ponies and stuff.
Naomi: And pictures of kittens.
Sophie: Yeah, there's *Girltalk* and *Chatterbox* and you go up and you get *Shout* and then you get *Sugar* and *Bliss* and then it's like *Just Seventeen, Nineteen,* and it's *More!* And then *Women's Own* and stuff like that, so you get the range.
(Nayak & Kehily, 2008, p. 135)

Some adolescents (particularly those from European American backgrounds) become preoccupied with images of slender, toned, and (for males) muscular bodies in the media. For girls and young women, extensive exposure to fitness and fashion magazines is associated with dissatisfaction with one's body and a strong desire to be thin (Dohnt & Tiggemann, 2006a; K. Harrison & Cantor, 1997; Tiggemann, 2003). As you learned in Chapter 5, such self-perceptions increase the probability of developing an eating disorder, and they also are linked to depression in girls (Harter, 2006).

Cultural differences.   Cultures tell children what they should think about, how they should relate to other people, and what it means to be a good person (see Chapter 3). These core lessons are integrated into children's sense of self (Morelli & Rothbaum, 2007).

Particular cultures differ in the extent to which they encourage children to attend to personal needs (those of the individual self) or other people's needs (those of the collective group). Some societies (e.g., in North America) place a lot of emphasis on the self. In *individualistic societies*, parents, teachers, and other adults encourage children to focus on their own wishes, motivations, and emotions (Markus & Hamedani, 2007; also see Chapters 3 and 11). Children are encouraged to become personally confident in their initiatives and have a strong sense of self-worth. In comparison, children in *collectivistic societies* place more emphasis on the group. Adults in these cultures encourage children to take pride in the accomplishments of their families and communities. Thus, for children in collectivistic societies, sense of self tends to include a strong sense of connection to family and community (Banks & Banks, 1995; A. O. Harrison et al., 1990; Markus & Kitayama, 1991). Children in these societies place special importance on being members of esteemed, honorable groups. Furthermore, children in collectivistic societies (e.g., in Southeast Asia) are more willing to acknowledge their weaknesses than is true for other groups. For these children, admitting personal limitations is a sign of humility (a desirable quality) rather than an indication of poor self-esteem (Brophy, 2004).

Thus, as a result of being socialized in a particular culture, children learn to think of themselves as having personal qualities or being in relationships with other people. For instance, a 6-year-old European American girl describes herself primarily in personal terms:

I am a wonderful and very smart person. A funny and hilarious person. A kind and caring person. A good-grade person who is going to go to Cornell [University]. A helpful and cooperative girl. (Q. Wang, 2006, p. 182)

In comparison, a Chinese boy of the same age mentions some of his own personal qualities but also emphasizes his ties to family:

I'm a human being. I'm a child. I like to play cards. I'm my mom and dad's child, my grandma and grandpa's grandson. I'm a hard-working good child. (Q. Wang, 2006, p. 182)

Children use their individual- or relationship-focused views of themselves to help remember events in their lives. For example, European American children are likely to mention their own preferences, opinions, and accomplishments when recalling events, whereas Chinese children are likely to mention incidents with other people, such as going to family parties (Q. Wang, 2006). Thus the content of autobiographical selves also varies somewhat by culture.

Ethnic differences. Children's self-perceptions are additionally influenced by their participation in one or more ethnic groups. By the time children reach kindergarten or first grade, some are quite aware that they belong to a different "group" than many of their age-mates. A variety of characteristics may make them stand out in a crowd, including their skin color, facial features, and language. By the beginning of elementary school, many children can accurately classify themselves as being African, Mexican, Laotian, and so on (Sheets, 1999). Parents and other family members may also give them labels (*black, Chinese,* and so on) that communicate that they are special in some important way. By early adolescence, youngsters actively consider how their life is affected by being a member of a particular ethnic group. By late adolescence, many youngsters achieve a strong **ethnic identity,** an awareness and pride in their ethnic heritage and willingness to adopt many of their ethnic group's behaviors (Phinney, 1989; Sheets & Hollins, 1999; also see Chapter 3).

When forming an ethnic identity, children attend closely to the tactics used by family members to foster loyalty to their group; they also listen to their family's explanations of the group's current status in society. For example, many African American parents speak with pride about their heritage, inform children about the valiant struggles of their ancestors, and teach children how to cope with racial prejudice (D. Hughes, 2003; Pahl & Way, 2006). In comparison, many Puerto Rican and Dominican families transmit cultural pride by posting flags, speaking Spanish, and celebrating the holidays of their native lands (French, Seidman, Allen, & Aber, 2006; Pahl & Way, 2006). Compared to Latino adolescents, African American adolescents spend more time exploring the implications of their ethnic identity, possibly because many African American children are acutely aware of discrimination and endeavor to replace negative stereotypes of African American people with more positive interpretations (Pahl & Way, 2006).

On average, children from ethnic minority backgrounds consider their ethnicity to be a more central feature of their self-concept than do children from majority backgrounds (Aboud, 1988; Ponterotto, Utsey, & Pedersen, 2006; K. L. Turner & Brown, 2007). For instance, European American children tend to see their ethnicity as the norm and don't feel a sense of urgency about learning more about their background. In contrast, children from other ethnicities see that they are different from peers and are motivated to learn about their origins. In addition, ethnic minority children sometimes develop more positive self-perceptions than do children from majority groups, possibly because they benefit from efforts by adults from underrepresented groups to portray their ethnic heritage in a positive light (H. Cooper & Dorr, 1995; Spencer & Markstrom-Adams, 1990; H. W. Stevenson et al., 1990; van Laar, 2000).

Yet not all the messages that ethnic minority children receive are positive ones. Children may be victims of prejudicial remarks. For example, Sozan, an adolescent girl whose family members were Kurdish refugees to the United States, regularly heard other students criticize her thick eyebrows and the scarf she wore out of respect for her religion, suggesting that she had a "unibrow" (i.e., one long eyebrow extending across her forehead) and was bald (McBrien, 2005a, p. 66). These were deeply hurtful comments, but Sozan, like many other ethnic minority youngsters, held onto her faith and customs. As you can see in her self-portrait in Figure 12-3, Sozan sees herself as a young Muslim woman, aware of opportunities in the United States (the building on the left is Harvard University) and possessing her own personal characteristics (being smart, clumsy, and interested in romance). Between the two figures, she originally wrote, "How I sometimes feel," drawing arrows pointing back and forth between the two images of herself, later crossing out these words and replacing them with "used to be as 5-year-old," during which time she had had the option of dressing in either casual Western clothing or traditional Islamic garb (McBrien, 2005a, p. 86).

Some children become deeply troubled by the impact of discrimination on their families and others who share their ethnic affiliation. In many cases, such distress leads ethnic minority children to view various ethnic groups as sharply divided and in competition for their loyalties. In a few communities, peers may accuse high-achieving minority youngsters of "acting white," a label that essentially means "you're not one of us" (Cross, Strauss, & Fhagen-Smith, 1999; Graham, 1997; Steinberg, 1996). In some cases youngsters' emerging ethnic identities lead them to reject the dominant group (Nasir & Saxe, 2003). Other ethnic minority children go through a period of rejecting their own ethnic group and identifying with the dominant ethnic group before embracing their ethnic heritage (Ponterotto et al., 2006).

MyEducationLab

Learn more about the process of forming an ethnic identity in different groups by completing an Understanding Research exercise in Chapter 12's Activities and Applications section in MyEducationLab.

Many children from minority groups incorporate a strong sense of ethnic identity into their sense of self.

ethinic identity
Awareness of being a member of a particular ethnic or cultural group and willingness to adopt certain values and behaviors characteristic of that group.

Figure 12-3

Sozan sees herself as a young Muslim woman who is committed to her cultural heritage but also wants to take advantage of the customs and opportunities in the United States.
Reproduced by permission. McBrien (2005a).

Obviously, children subjected to peer ridicule about their ethnicity need considerable support from adults (Rowley, Cooper, & Clinton, 2006). Many children develop a healthy ethnic identity when parents and other family members discuss the accomplishments of their ethnic group, involve children in ethnic holidays and celebrations, and prepare children for possible discrimination (Rowley et al., 2006). Teachers can help as well by developing partnerships with community youth organizations that are committed to the needs of ethnic minority youth. Teachers also can communicate supportive messages to youth: that all students are capable of significant accomplishments and the classroom will be an equitable environment in which similar opportunities are available to everyone (Barrow, Armstrong, Vargo, & Boothroyd, 2007; Rowley et al., 2006). And parents and teachers alike can listen patiently to the perspectives of those adolescents who initially adopt a fairly intense, inflexible, reactive, and perhaps hostile ethnic identity, before eventually settling into a more positive and open-minded one (Barrow et al., 2007; Cross et al., 1999).

Children who have more than one ethnic heritage, perhaps because of immigration or growing up in a *multiethnic* family, often undergo a lengthy period during which they explore their various heritages (see Chapter 3). Peers and adults outside the family may communicate their belief that one or more aspects of a particular ethnic heritage are somehow inferior or undesirable, causing confusion in some children who affiliate with two or more distinct ethnic groups (C. R. Cooper, Jackson, Azmitia, Lopez, & Dunbar, 1995; Kiang & Harter, 2005; Tatum, 1997). For an extended period of time, youngsters who are the beneficiaries of multiple cultural heritages may fluctuate back and forth between allegiances to one ethnic identity or another depending on their present circumstances (A. M. Lopez, 2003; Tatum, 1997; Yip & Fuligni, 2002). Consider Alice, who migrated from China to the United States at age 8. Although she gained fluency in English fairly quickly, for several years she had trouble reconciling the Chinese and American aspects of herself:

[A]t home my parents expect me to be not a traditional Chinese daughter . . . but they expect things because I was born in China and I am Chinese. And at school, that's a totally different story because you're expected to behave as an American. You know, you speak English in your school; all your friends speak English. You try to be as much of an American as you can. So I feel I'm caught somewhere in between. . . . I feel I can no longer be fully Chinese or fully American anymore. (Igoa, 1995, p. 85)

Sensitive adults can point out the advantages of having several distinct cultural heritages. Happily, many teens with multiethnic backgrounds ultimately emerge with a strong, often multifaceted, ethnic identity.

For the most part students with a positive ethnic identity (including those with a strong multiethnic identity) perform well academically (Chavous et al., 2003; Rowley, Cooper, & Clinton, 2006). Having a clear ethnic identity is also linked to high self-esteem, a willingness to help other people, and decreased use of violence (Arbona, Jackson, McCoy, & Blakely, 1999; Pegg & Plybon, 2005; Phinney, Cantu, & Kurtz, 1997; Umaña-Taylor & Alfaro, 2006). Furthermore, pride in one's ethnic heritage can serve as an emotional "buffer" against the insults and discrimination that children and adolescents from minority groups sometimes encounter. For example, in a study with Mexican-origin adolescents who reported high levels of discrimination, those who had a strong commitment to their ethnic identity had higher self-esteem than those with less commitment (Romero & Roberts, 2003). Other findings indicate that young people with a strong ethnic identity are less likely to use drugs and partake in other risky behaviors (Umaña-Taylor & Alfaro, 2006).

In their statements and actions, children reveal their emerging ethnic identity and other self-perceptions. In the Observations Guidelines table "Observing Indicators of Children's Self-Perceptions," you can see some of the ways that children manifest their thoughts and feelings about who they are and what they are becoming.

Spencer's model of identity development. As you have learned, children use their experiences and emerging cognitive abilities to construct a sense of self. Psychologist Margaret Beale Spencer (first introduced in Chapter 3) has created a developmental systems model that sums up these key ideas (see Figure 12-4). According to Spencer (2006), children encounter both risk factors (e.g., growing up in poverty and dealing with discrimination) and protective factors (e.g., being intelligent and having dedicated teachers). Many of these risks and protections are based in part on children's experiences in ethnic groups. For example, African American children often confront a society that sees them in predominantly negative ways, stigmatizing them for low academic achievement and dismissing their accomplishments. Yet many African American children have numerous advantages as well, such as strong extended family support and good coping skills (Barrow et al., 2007; Spencer, 2006). Conversely, European American children frequently achieve at high levels academically and enjoy certain privileges, such as absence of discrimination and adequate family income, but some European American youngsters acquire weak coping skills for dealing with anger, anxiety, and sadness, as indicated by relatively high suicide rates in this group (National Institute of Mental Health, 2008b; Spencer, 2006).

In Spencer's model, all children experience stressful circumstances to some degree. Yet how individual children respond to difficult events depends on their interpretations. For example, many children welcome the addition of a new father figure into the family home, especially when he shows concern for the children and adds needed income to the household. However, some children feel overwhelmed or even threatened by the presence of a new father figure, especially when they perceive him as displacing them in the family.

In response to environmental pressures, children develop an array of coping skills. In some cases, children develop adaptive personal abilities that foster their healthy development, but at other times children adopt maladaptive strategies that actually hinder their adjustment. For instance, one adolescent girl may respond to decreased attention from her parents (perhaps due to a parent's new job or a family crisis) by spending more time with grandparents and asking for help from her school adviser. A second girl may respond to the same circumstance by staying away from home, associating with deviant peers, and getting into trouble.

The quality of children's coping skills affects the kinds of identities they develop. Children may come to see themselves as effective or ineffective learners; as vital members of their families or as rejected children; and as a productive members of society or as individuals who resort to illegal activities. These and other possible identities may culminate in important developmental outcomes. For instance, an adolescent boy who sees himself as an academically talented student will likely try to get good grades and eventually earn a high school diploma. In contrast, a boy who sees himself as a renegade may drop out of school altogether.

Observation Guidelines

Observing Indicators of Children's Self-Perceptions

Characteristic	Look For	Example	Implication
Self-Concept	· Increased time spent looking in mirror and inspecting one's image (in infancy) · Verbal references to self (e.g., "I," "mine") (in infancy and early childhood) · Self-assessments of areas of proficiency and weakness (e.g., "I'm good at math but bad at reading") (in middle childhood and adolescence)	Fifteen-month old Sierra stands at the full-length mirror in her child care center. She looks up and down at her reflection, smiles, and, after noticing a scrape on her knee in the mirror, bends down to touch her knee and says "Ouch."	Express a genuine interest in the well-being of all youngsters. Encourage young children's emerging insights into their sense of self (e.g., "Look who's in the mirror!" and "I see you copying me! Can you make your hands do this?"). As children grow, compliment them on special accomplishments, extra effort on tasks, and unusual talents.
Self-Worth	· Comments on the self's inherent goodness or capability · Attempts to protect the self from threatening information (e.g., anger at hearing critical comments after a flawed high jump attempt) · Changes in mood depending on most recent treatment by peers (reflecting *contingent self-worth*)	After obtaining his graded math test, 13-year-old Emmett notices the low score written on the top, crumples up the paper, and throws it in the trash. The next time he has a math test, he does not study at all, even though he knows he's confused about the math concepts the class has been studying.	Encourage children to take disappointments in stride, suggesting that although they may not have done as well on particular tasks as they would have liked, with renewed effort, a change in tactics, and perhaps a little assistance, they have the ability to make sizable progress. Provide a range of activities and content domains so that everyone has a chance to excel in one or more domains.
Autobiographical Self	· Conversations with parents about past family events in which the child participated · Recollections about personally significant events or family celebrations	Five-year-old Jeremiah draws a picture of himself with his parents, two sisters, and the family dog in front of a farm. He explains that he and his family used to live in rural Idaho and then moved to the Oregon coast when his parents changed jobs.	Create assignments that ask children to reflect on their family origins and early experiences (e.g., have kindergarten children bring in photographs of themselves as preschoolers and talk about what they remember from that time). Ask older children to create self-portraits and write essays about memories of their early school years.
Gender Schema	· Insistence that boys must act one way and girls another (especially in early childhood) · Selection of stereotypically male toys (e.g., toy cars, blocks, action figures) by boys and traditionally female toys (e.g., dolls, board games) by girls · Heightened interest in same-sex role models in magazines and other media during adolescence	In her spare time, 13-year-old Janice likes to browse through her mother's fashion magazines, picking up tips on how to apply cosmetics. Her older brother Reggie reads his father's auto mechanics and hunting magazines.	Recognize that during various points in their development, many youngsters go overboard in trying to be exceptionally feminine or masculine. Accept that young people may go through phases of rigidly endorsing traditional gender roles, but also point out that both men and women have many opportunities in life and that few individuals of either gender can live up to unrealistic standards of physical attractiveness portrayed in the media.
Identity	· Early in the process of identity formation, varied levels of concern about the future, perhaps including: —Questions about jobs and lifestyles —Noncritical acceptance of career goals that parents have suggested —Expression of a desire to define personal lifelong goals for oneself · During late adolescence, more serious attempts to form an identity: —Active search for information about career options, political viewpoints, religious convictions, etc. —Occasional well-developed justifications for political and religious beliefs and future occupations	Mr. Decker asks the ninth graders in his advisee group to write a brief essay about the kinds of jobs they find personally appealing. Some of the students write about jobs their parents currently have, yet others write little, having apparently not given the issue much thought. A few of the students ask Mr. Decker if they can learn more about different jobs as part of their homeroom class.	Give children opportunities to examine and try out a variety of adult roles. With young children, rotate various props through a housekeeping area (e.g., dress-up clothes and equipment that might be found in a police station, gas station, or doctor's office) to foster children's imagination of themselves in different roles. With older children, ask parents to come to school to talk about their jobs. With adolescents, arrange internships in local businesses, community agencies, and other institutions.

Observation Guidelines (continued)

Characteristic	Look For	Example	Implication
Ethnic Identity	· Comments about being a member of a particular ethnic group · Growing preference for customs of one's own ethnic group (e.g., meal practices, holiday celebrations, tastes in music and art) · Frustration with discrimination toward one's ethnic group	Fourteen-year-old Diego is proud of his Latino heritage. He follows many of his parents' Mexican traditions, loves Mexican food, and regularly watches Spanish-speaking programs on television. Diego is angered by derogatory names for Hispanics used by a few students at his high school.	Foster ethnic pride by welcoming ethnic traditions at school. Encourage youngsters to write about their ethnic customs in class assignments, and infuse multicultural material into instruction. Also establish cooperative groups that cross ethnic lines and ensure that children from different ethnic groups take on equally responsible positions within groups. Adamantly discourage the use of ethnic slurs.

Spencer's model suggests that children develop multifaceted identities in contexts of support and challenge. In all ethnic groups, children face both risks and protective factors, but there are tremendous individual differences within groups in the outlooks on life that children develop. For example, one boy growing up in an impoverished environment may want to serve his community by becoming a doctor. He studies hard and goes on to college. His brother, in contrast, may see himself as a troublemaker, and he spends time with peers who shoplift and take drugs and is eventually incarcerated (Spencer, 2006). The developmental outcomes that youngsters attain, in turn, affect the new environments they inhabit as they grow. The effects in Spencer's model also operate in reverse, for example, with the identities that children develop in turn influencing how they cope with stressful life events (look again at Figure 12-4).

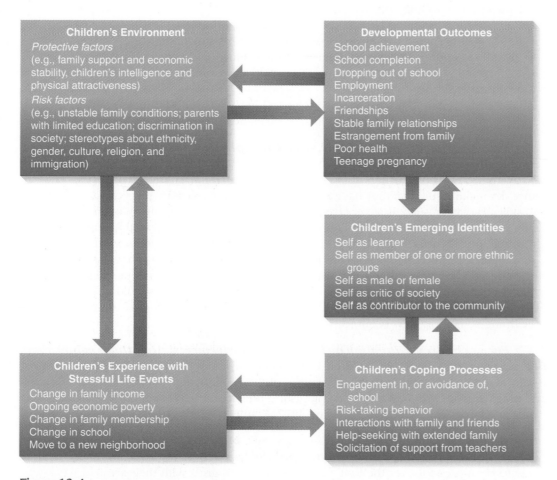

Figure 12-4

Factors influencing the identities and developmental outcomes of children from diverse backgrounds.
Adapted from Spencer, 2006.

Both common trends and considerable diversity exist in children's self-perceptions. The Developmental Trends table "Sense of Self at Different Age Levels" summarizes changes in self-perceptions and self-understandings across infancy, childhood, and adolescence, as well as some of the diversity you are likely to see.

Enhancing Children's Sense of Self

The interplay between self-esteem and behavior can create a vicious downward spiral: Poor self-esteem leads to less productive behavior, which leads to fewer successes, which perpetuates poor self-esteem. Yet simply telling youngsters that they are "good" or "smart" or "popular" is unlikely to make a dent in a poor sense of self (Damon, 1991; Marsh & Craven, 1997; Pajares, 1996). Such platitudes become meaningless when they contradict children's own observations.

The following strategies are far more likely to have a constructive impact on children's sense of self:

• ***Communicate a genuine interest in children's lives and well-being.*** As children observe how adults treat them and hear what adults say to them, they wonder, "What do these things mean about me?" Youngsters often interpret harsh words and thoughtless actions as indications that adults do not like them, possibly because they are not worthy of love. We urge all adults, but especially teachers, parents, and other caregivers, to think carefully about what they say and do to and with children, being sure that their words and actions consistently communicate care and respect. Messages of affection and high regard come in a variety of forms, including the following:

- Giving children a smile and warm greeting at the beginning of the day
- Complimenting children on a special talent, new skill, or exceptional effort
- Asking children to talk about important events in their lives (this strategy can also enhance their autobiographical selves)
- Being a good listener when children appear angry or upset
- Being well prepared for lessons and other activities with children
- Including children in decision making and in evaluations of their own performance
- Acknowledging that children can occasionally have an "off" day and not holding it against them
(L. H. Anderman, Patrick, Hruda, & Linnenbrink, 2002; Certo, Cauley, & Chafin, 2002; H. A. Davis, 2003; H. A. Davis, Schutz, & Chambless, 2001)

• ***Promote success on academic, social, and physical tasks.*** Experiences with success are powerful catalysts for the development of a positive sense of self (Damon, 1991; Marsh & Craven, 1997). Thus teachers should gear assignments to youngsters' capabilities—for instance, by making sure that they have already mastered any necessary prerequisite knowledge and skills. However, success at very easy activities is unlikely to have much of an impact. Mastering the significant challenges in life—earning the hard-won successes that come only with effort and persistence—brings more enduring and resilient self-perceptions (Dweck, 2000; Eisenberger, 1992; Winne, 1995a). Thus teachers and other practitioners are most likely to bolster youngsters' sense of self when they assign challenging tasks and provide the structure and support youngsters need to accomplish the tasks successfully. They should also help young people keep the little "failures" along the way in perspective: Mistakes are an inevitable part of learning something new (Clifford, 1990; Eccles & Wigfield, 1985).

• ***Focus children's attention on their own improvement rather than on how their peers perform.*** Youngsters are likely to be optimistic about their chances of future success if they see they are making regular progress—if they continually make gains through effort and practice. They are *un*likely to be optimistic if they focus their attention on how their age-mates are surpassing them (Deci & Ryan, 1992; Krampen, 1987; Stipek, 1996).

• ***Be honest about children's shortcomings, but also provide the guidance and support children need to deal with and possibly overcome them.*** Youngsters are more likely to be successful over the long run if they come to grips with their areas of weakness. If adults give only positive feedback—and especially if they provide inflated evaluations of

Developmental Trends

Sense of Self at Different Age Levels

Age	What You Might Observe	Diversity	Implications
Infancy (Birth–2 Years)	· Increasing awareness that one is separate from caregivers (in the first year) · Increasing recognition of self in mirror (in the second year) · Appearance of first-person pronouns, such as *I, me, mine* (late in the second year)	· The quality of child–caregiver relationships influences infants' beliefs that they are worthy of love. · The regularity with which adults comment on infants' images in a mirror and refer to infants' facial features (e.g., "We'd better wipe your runny nose") may affect infants' self-recognition.	· Communicate affection by cuddling and talking to infants and by attending to their physical needs in a timely and consistent manner. · Talk with infants and toddlers about their bodily features and possessions ("Where's your nose?" "Here's your teddy bear!").
Early Childhood (2–6 Years)	· Frequent use of *I, me,* and *mine,* especially at ages 2 and 3 · Emergence of an autobiographical self (beginning at age 3 or 4) · Concrete self-descriptions (e.g., "I'm a boy," "I'm pretty") · Overconfidence about what tasks can be accomplished	· Children whom others treat affectionately tend to develop a positive sense of self. Those who are rejected, ridiculed, or ignored have a harder time seeing themselves in positive terms. · Some children gain an emerging awareness that they belong to a particular racial or ethnic group (by age 5).	· Acknowledge children's possessions, but encourage sharing. · Engage children in joint retellings of recent events. · Don't disparage children's lofty ambitions ("I'm going to be president!"), but focus their efforts on accomplishable short-term goals.
Middle Childhood (6–10 Years)	· Increasing distinction among various aspects of oneself (e.g., among academic performance, athletic ability, and personal likability) · Increasing tendency to base sense of self on how one's own performance compares with that of peers · Increasing internalization of others' standards for performance (continues into adolescence) · Generally good self-esteem in most children	· Different children place greater or lesser importance on various domains (e.g., on academic performance vs. athletic prowess) in deriving their overall sense of self-worth. · In middle childhood, girls begin to evaluate their physical appearance less favorably than boys do.	· Praise children for their talents and accomplishments in numerous areas (e.g., in physical activities, social relationships, and specific academic subjects). · Help children find arenas in which they can be especially successful. · Teach hygiene and personal grooming habits that enhance children's physical attractiveness.
Early Adolescence (10–14 Years)	· Increasing tendency to define oneself in terms of abstract rather than concrete characteristics · Possible drop in self-esteem after the transition to middle school or junior high · Heightened sensitivity to what others think of oneself *(imaginary audience),* leading to a preoccupation with physical appearance · Belief in oneself as overly unique *(personal fable),* occasionally leading to a sense of invulnerability	· Drops in self-esteem, when sizable and not followed by a gradual rebound, can signal a problem. · On average, youngsters increasingly base their self-perceived strengths on gender stereotypes (e.g., boys see themselves as good in math, girls see themselves as good in reading) even when actual achievement levels are similar. · Members of ethnic groups vary in the extent to which their ethnic status plays a role in their core identity.	· When students are making the transition to middle school or junior high, be especially supportive and optimistic about their potential for success. · Be patient when adolescents show exceptional self-consciousness; give them strategies for presenting themselves well to others (e.g., how they might introduce themselves to unfamiliar peers).
Late Adolescence (14–18 Years)	· Decrease in the self-consciousness that was evident in early adolescence · Reflection about identity issues: Who am I? What do I believe? What course should my life take? · Reconciliation of many apparent contradictions in oneself	· Adolescents whose sense of self-worth continues to depend heavily on others' behaviors and opinions (those who have *contingent self-worth*) are more susceptible to mood swings and peer pressure. · Some adolescents willingly accept the professional goals and ideologies that their parents offer. Others engage in more soul-searching as they piece together their identity.	· Provide opportunities for adolescents to explore diverse belief systems and try on a variety of occupational "hats." · Be on the lookout for teens whose self-worth seems especially dependent on peers' opinions; help them discover areas of talent that can contribute to a more stable sense of self-worth.

children's performance—some children may be unaware of areas that need improvement (Dweck, 2000; T. D. Little, Oettingen, Stetsenko, & Baltes, 1995; Paris & Cunningham, 1996). And when adults praise children for successes on very *easy* tasks, children may conclude that they are not capable of handling anything more difficult (Pintrich & Schunk, 2002).

Realistically, then, adults must give children negative as well as positive feedback. When feedback must include information about children's shortcomings, the best approach is to give it within the context of high (yet achievable) expectations for future performance (Deci & Ryan, 1985; Pintrich & Schunk, 2002). Following are examples of how a teacher might put a positive spin on negative feedback:

- "You're generally a very kind person, but you hurt Jenny's feelings by making fun of her new outfit. Perhaps you can think of a good way to make her feel better."
- "In the first draft of your research paper, many of your paragraphs don't lead logically to the ones that follow. A few headings and transitional sentences would make a world of difference. Let's find a time to discuss how you might use these techniques to improve the flow of your paper."

When children have long-standing difficulties in certain domains, discovering that their failures are due to a previously undiagnosed disability, such as dyslexia or ADHD, sometimes helps repair some of the damage to self-esteem. Such a discovery helps children make sense of *why* they can't perform certain tasks as well as their peers. It can also spur children and their teachers to identify effective coping strategies. In the following reflection, one young adolescent boy reveals how, in coming to terms with his dyslexia, he's acquired a healthy sense of self despite his disability:

> Dyslexia is your brain's wired differently and there's brick walls for some things and you just have to work either around it or break it. I'm dyslexic at reading that means I need a little bit more help. If you have dyslexia the thing you have to find is how to get over the hump, the wall. Basically you either go around it and just don't read and get along in life without it or you break down the wall. (Zambo, 2003, p. 10)

In this photograph an adolescent girl and boy are working with children at a summer camp. Jobs and volunteer work can help adolescents enhance their sense of identity.

- ***Provide opportunities to explore a wide variety of activities and domains.*** Not all children and adolescents can achieve at superior levels in the classroom, nor can they all be superstars on the playing field. Youngsters are more likely to have a positive sense of self if they find an activity—perhaps singing, student government, or competitive jump-roping—in which they can shine (Harter, 1999). And by exploring many different fields and career options and beginning to zero in on a few possible career paths, young people take an important step toward forming a sense of their adult identity.

- ***Consider the unique needs of girls and boys.*** Many youngsters place little value on characteristics and abilities that they think are more "appropriate" for members of the opposite sex. In addition, they may place too much value on qualities they think they need to be "feminine" or "manly." Thus some teenage girls may strive for impossible standards of physical beauty. And some teenage boys may worry that they are maturing too slowly and lack the height and build of some of their classmates.

With these points in mind, teachers and other adults should probably use somewhat different tactics in nurturing the self-esteem of girls and boys. They might help girls identify realistic standards by which to judge their physical appearance. And given girls' tendency to react more negatively to failures, adults might encourage them to pat themselves on the back for their many successes, even those (and perhaps *especially* those) in traditionally male domains such as science and math. But boys, too, have special needs. Many boys are often brought up to believe they should be "tough" and hide any feelings of self-doubt or inadequacy. Adults may want to take special pains to acknowledge a boy's "softer" sides—for instance, his compassion and skill in interacting with small children.

● *Communicate respect for diverse ethnic and cultural backgrounds.* Although most educators today are aware of the need to respect the diversity in children's backgrounds, they do not always know how best to show such regard. An important first step, of course, is *understanding* various ethnic and cultural groups—their traditions, values, priorities, and so on (see Chapter 3). In addition to showing appreciation for children's native languages and dialects, educators can communicate respect for diverse groups through strategies such as these:

- Treat all children as full-fledged members of the classroom and community, rather than as exotic "curiosities" who live in a strange and separate world.
- Call children by their given names unless they specifically request otherwise (see Figure 12-5).
- Consistently look at historical and current events from diverse cultural perspectives—for instance, by considering American, European, African, and Arabic perspectives of recent events in the Middle East.
- Create situations in which youngsters from diverse backgrounds must collaborate to achieve success—for instance, through cooperative group activities or community service projects.

(Banks & Banks, 1995; Branch, 1999; Fantino & Colak, 2001; Howard, 2007; Ladson-Billings, 1994; Oskamp, 2000; Villegas & Lucas, 2007; Wong, 1993)

I had lots of friends back home, and I remember all of them, we used to play soccer together. I have also friends here now, well … mostly classmates.

School is OK but there is one thing that bothers me. My name is Mohammed, no other. Here, my teacher calls me Mo, because there are five other kids with the same name. My friends sometimes call me M J, which is not too bad, but I wish they will call me by my real name. I like what my grandma called me: "Mamet." I like how she used to say it. One thing makes me really mad. I have a pen pal called Rudy. He lives in Toronto. Once I showed his letter to my teacher and she said: "That is nice name." Now, all my friends call me Rudy. I hate it, because that's not me, that's not my name. My name is "MO-HA-MMED." Do you understand me?

Figure 12-5

For many children, their given name is an important part of their identity, as this reflection by a refugee child in Canada illustrates.

Excerpt from "Refugee Children in Canada: Searching for Identity," by A. M. Fantino and A. Colak, 2001, *Child Welfare, 80,* pp. 591–592, a publication of the Child Welfare League of America.

In their efforts to be sensitive to children's cultural background, some well-meaning practitioners make the mistake of thinking of children as belonging exclusively to a particular ethnic or cultural group. Yet in this age of increasing multiracial and multicultural intermingling, many youngsters cannot easily be pigeonholed. Teachers must keep in mind that some of their students are apt to have a blended ethnic or racial heritage, and many students from minority-group backgrounds want to be integral parts of both their local cultural groups and mainstream Western society (C. R. Cooper et al., 1995; A. M. Lopez, 2003; Root, 1999).

● *Give youngsters second chances to develop healthy self-perceptions.* Adolescents who struggle academically or have friendships with antisocial peers tend to see themselves as disconnected from school. These self-perceptions are not easily changed, but sometimes a new program or concerted efforts from a teacher can have a desirable effect. For example, in one instance a group of adolescents with learning disabilities were moved from one school (Piney Ridge), where they were failing, to another school in which teachers got to know them individually and encouraged their success (Youngblood & Spencer, 2002). With time the adolescents came to see themselves as capable academically and socially, as one boy explains:

Interviewer: What makes you. . . . Why do you think there's a difference between the
                student helping each other in this program and not helping each other at Piney?
Rashae: Because they're. . . . Well half of them over there criminal. They're like they just
                got out of jail or whatever. I mean, they just. . . . I think Piney Ridge like a school
                for bad kids.
Interviewer: So why do you think they're more likely to help you over here?
Rashae.   Because everybody over here nice. They don't think about just they self. Think
                about other people in the class. . . . Well we help one another in the class work or
                out of class.
                (dialogue from Youngblood & Spencer, 2002, p. 103)

● *Put self-esteem in its proper perspective.* The popular educational literature often overrates positive self-esteem as a target for intervention, sometimes to the point where it becomes the *only* target (Dweck, 2000). Certainly we want children and adolescents to feel good about themselves, but increasing evidence suggests that efforts to enhance self-esteem as *the* ultimate goal for children are ineffective, and for several reasons (Baumeister et al., 2003). First, children appreciate optimistic evaluations from adults but are more likely to be convinced of their capabilities when they see themselves surmounting challenges and fulfilling high standards of conduct. Thus, rather than telling children that they are smart and good, it makes more sense to create conditions where children achieve success. (You will learn several such specific strategies in Chapter 13.) Second, self-esteem seems to be closely linked to personal happiness and resilience yet, counter to society's expectations, it does *not* protect young people from numerous risks in life. Youngsters with high self-esteem do not avoid drugs, for example, any more than youngsters with low self-esteem (Baumeister et al., 2003). Hence, other developmental outcomes must receive equal billing by adults. Third, some children with an inflated sense of self are aggressive and callous to the feelings of others (Baumeister et al., 2003). Rather than simply being told about their own inherent goodness, these children need support in focusing on the needs of other people. Finally, and as you have learned, not every culture aspires to high self-esteem in its children, at least as self-esteem is typically conceptualized in Western cultures. Instead, some cultures socialize children to focus more on being humble and respectful of friends, family members, and adults in authority.

In addition to thinking about who they are and how they fit in society, youngsters also spend considerable time trying to make sense of other people. We look at social cognition now.

Social Cognition

As inherently social creatures, most children and adolescents spend much of their mental energy engaged in **social cognition,** speculating about what other people are thinking and feeling and then choosing their behaviors toward others accordingly. We begin with children's understanding of what other people think and proceed to examine biases in children's thinking that can lead to prejudice. We then consider the variations that exist in children's social-cognitive abilities and the many things adults can do to foster children's social cognition.

Understanding What Others Think

Just as children construct theories about their physical and biological worlds, so, too, do they construct theories about the psychological world. More specifically, they develop a **theory of mind** that eventually encompasses complex understandings of people's mental and emotional states—thoughts, beliefs, feelings, motives, intentions, and so on. Increasingly, children put these understandings to work in social interactions, stepping occasionally into others' shoes and looking at the world from others' perspectives. Such **social perspective taking** helps children make sense of actions that might otherwise be puzzling. Having a theory of mind and applying this theory by inferring others' people frames of mind in particular settings enable children interpret the behaviors of important people in their lives and, as a result, to interact with those individuals more effectively (Flavell, 2000; P. L. Harris, 2006; Selman, 2003). As you will see, an awareness of what others think changes considerably over the course of infancy, childhood, and adolescence.

Infancy (birth–age 2).   Infants quickly discover that, unlike inanimate objects, people are active, expressive, and responsive (Mandler, 2007a; Poulin-Dubois, Frenkiel-Fishman, Nayer, & Johnson, 2006). In the latter part of their first year, they also begin to realize that people have an "inner life" that objects do not. For instance, by about 9 or 10 months, infants show *intersubjectivity* (introduced in Chapter 7), an awareness that they share a focus of attention with a caregiver. At about the same time or shortly thereafter, they acquire some awareness of **intentionality.** That is, they know that other people behave in order to accomplish certain goals, and they begin to draw inferences about people's intentions from such actions as reaching for, pointing at, and gazing at objects (D. A. Baldwin, 2000; P. L. Harris, 2006; Kuhlmeier, Wynn, & Bloom, 2003; Woodward & Sommerville, 2000).

In the second year, infants become increasingly mindful of other people's mental states. For example, infants as young as 12 months engage in *social referencing* (also introduced in Chapter 7), the tendency to watch an adult respond to a new object or event and then act in a similar manner. At this point, then, they have some insights into other people's attentional focus and emotions (Moses, Baldwin, Rosicky, & Tidball, 2001). By 18 months, children clearly know that their own actions influence other people's emotions and behaviors. For instance, they are likely to offer an adult a food item to which the adult has previously reacted favorably, even though they themselves dislike that kind of food

social cognition
Process of thinking about how other people are likely to think, act, and react and choosing one's own interpersonal behaviors accordingly.

theory of mind
Awareness that people have an inner, psychological life (thoughts, beliefs, feelings, etc.).

social perspective taking
Imagining what someone else might be thinking or feeling.

intentionality
Engagement in an action congruent with one's purpose or goal.

(Repacholi & Gopnik, 1997).[1] Their early gestures to comfort others also suggest an attempt to consider others' perspectives (P. L. Harris, 2006) (we will examine helping behaviors in more detail in Chapter 14). In some cases, infants may even behave in ways that they know will annoy or upset someone else (Dunn & Munn, 1985; Flavell et al., 2002). For example, as a toddler, Jeanne's daughter Tina occasionally ran into the street and then looked tauntingly back at Mom as if to say, "Look at what I'm doing! I know this upsets you! Catch me if you can!"

Early childhood (ages 2–6).   In the preschool years, children become increasingly aware of people's mental states. Beginning at age 2 (sometimes even earlier), they spontaneously use words that refer to desires and emotions (e.g., *want, feel, sad*), and by age 3, "cognitive" words such as *think* and *know* appear in their speech (Astington & Pelletier, 1996; Bartsch & Wellman, 1995; Nixon, 2005). By the time children are 3, they also realize that the mind is distinct from the physical world—that thoughts, memories, and dreams are not physical entities (Baird & Astington, 2005; Wellman & Estes, 1986; Woolley, 1995).

In the third and fourth year, children develop an appreciation that other people have desires that differ from their own (P. L. Harris, 2006). Preschoolers are often eager to learn why people do the things they do, as this conversation between 2½-year-old Adam and his mother illustrates:

> Adam: Why she write dat name?
> Mother: Because she wanted to.
> Adam: Why she wanted to?
> Mother: Because she thought you'd like it.
> Adam: I don't want to like it.
>   (Wellman, Phillips, & Rodriguez, 2000, p. 908)

Inherent in Adam's question *Why she write dat name?* is an advancement in theory of mind: Preschoolers become increasingly aware of relationships between other people's desires and behaviors.

After gaining an appreciation that they and other people have desires, young children gradually gain an understanding of the nature of their own and other people's knowledge (P. L. Harris, 2006). Initially, preschoolers have trouble looking inward and describing their own thoughts. Furthermore, they may mistakenly assume that what *they* know is what other people know as well. Consider the following situation:

> Max puts a piece of chocolate in the kitchen cupboard and then goes out to play. While he is gone, his mother discovers the chocolate and moves it to a drawer. When Max returns later, where will he look for his chocolate? (based on Wimmer & Perner, 1983)

Max will look in the cupboard, of course, because that's where he thinks the chocolate is. However, 3-year-olds are quite certain he will look in the drawer, where the chocolate is actually located. Not until age 4 or 5 do children appreciate a *false belief:* They realize that circumstances may reasonably lead people to believe something different from what they themselves know to be true (Avis & Harris, 1991; Liu, Wellman, Tardif, & Sabbagh, 2008; Wellman et al., 2001; Wimmer & Perner, 1983).

Gradually, then, children develop an understanding of how people's perceptions, emotions, and desires influence their actions, and they become increasingly adept at inferring people's intentions and other mental states from behaviors and other events (Astington & Pelletier, 1996; Flavell, 2000; Wellman et al., 2000). For example, look at the two scenarios in Figure 12-6. *Which boy would like to swing?* Obviously the boy in the lower picture is the one who has an *intention* of using the swing. Most 5-year-olds correctly answer the question we've just asked you, but few 3-year-olds can (Astington, 1991).

Figure 12-6

Which boy would like to swing? Children who can correctly answer such questions can distinguish between intention and behavior.
Copyright © 1991 From "Intention in the Child's Theory of Mind" by J. W. Astington in *Children's Theories of Mind* (p. 168) by C. Moore & D. Frye. Reproduced by permission of Taylor and Francis Group, LLC, a division of Informa plc.

---

[1]In Chapter 6 we saw evidence that preschoolers are not as egocentric as Piaget said they were. Here we see evidence that even toddlers can occasionally take another person's perspective.

We were playing freeze tag one day at recess. Leslie got tagged and asked me to step on her shadow before anyone else. I stepped on Becca's shadow before I stepped on Leslie's and got mad. I told Leslie to stop being so selfish and bratty. She took it extremely personally and stormed off, told a teacher, and called her mom.

I later apologized and we became friends again. I invited her to my birthday and she came but I could tell she felt uncomfortable. So, I decided to do makeovers. I was playing around with lipsticks and accidentally messed up on Leslie's makeover, but laughed because I knew it could be fixed. She ran to see the "damage" in the mirror, started to cry, and called her mom and left.

From then on, I've never really understood her and we've never been close. We see eachother and say "hi" in the halls, but that's it.

Figure 12-7

In this reflective essay, 13-year-old Georgia expresses dismay that her friend Leslie misinterpreted several of her behaviors.

MyEducationLab

Observe advancements in children's awareness of subtle behavioral cues in the "Emotional Development" clips for middle childhood, early adolescence, and late adolescence in the Video Examples section in Chapter 12 of MyEducationLab.

recursive thinking
Thinking about what other people may be thinking about oneself, possibly through multiple iterations.

Middle childhood (ages 6–10). As children reach the elementary grades, they become capable of more sophisticated inferences about people's mental states. They realize that people's actions do not always reflect their true thoughts and feelings (Flavell et al., 2002; Gnepp, 1989; K. Lee et al., 2002). For example, a person may intentionally lie about a situation to mislead someone else, and another person who appears happy may actually be sad.

Middle childhood heralds more complex understandings of the nature of thinking as well. In particular, children understand that people *interpret* an event, rather than simply "recording" it, allowing for differences in perspectives among people (M. Chandler & Boyes, 1982; P. L. Harris, 2006). In the introductory case study, Angela nurtured children's emerging ability to consider multiple perspectives when she asked the children to consider not only Felita's view of the family's move but that of Felita's parents as well. At this age, children are also now apt to take people's preexisting expectations and biases into account when interpreting what people say and do (Pillow & Henrichon, 1996). In other words, children in the elementary grades increasingly realize that thinking and learning are active, constructive processes (Flavell et al., 1995; Wellman, 1990).

Finally, children now begin to recognize that people's thoughts and feelings are often closely intertwined. Thus different thoughts about a situation lead to different feelings about it (Flavell, Flavell, & Green, 2001; P. L. Harris, 1989). For example, a 9-year-old might say, "Arlene feels bad because she thinks I don't like her. I *do* like her, though."

Early adolescence (ages 10–14). As children move into early adolescence, they begin to appreciate that people can have mixed feelings about events and other individuals (S. K. Donaldson & Westerman, 1986; Flavell & Miller, 1998; Harter & Whitesell, 1989). And they realize that people may simultaneously have multiple, and possibly conflicting, intentions (M. J. Chandler, 1987). They also become increasingly thoughtful about the divergent perspectives that people may have about a single event. In the personal reflection presented in Figure 12-7, Georgia is puzzled by her former friend Leslie's misinterpretation of their relationship.

In adolescence, youngsters also become more observant of the subtle nuances of other people's behaviors—the drooping shoulders, raised eyebrows, and so on. You can see this advancement in the "Emotional Development" videos in MyEducationLab. In the "Middle Childhood" video, 10-year-old Daniel shows an understanding that people often (but not always) reveal their emotions in their facial expressions and body language. For example, they may smile when happy, frown when angry, or walk with drooping shoulders when sad. In the "Early Adolescence" and "Late Adolescence" videos, 13-year-old Crystal and 15-year-old Greg are sensitive to even more subtle cues. For example, people may get "hyper" or "won't stop talking" when they're happy, may "hide their face" or "don't talk" when sad, or "don't want you to be around them" when angry.

Courtesy of their expanding reasoning abilities, working memory capacity, and social awareness, young adolescents also begin to engage in **recursive thinking** (Abrams, Rutland, Cameron, & Ferrell, 2007; Oppenheimer, 1986; Perner & Wimmer, 1985). That is, they can think about what other people might be thinking about them and eventually can reflect on other people's thoughts about themselves through multiple iterations (e.g., "You think that I think that you think . . ."). This is not to say that adolescents (or adults, for that matter) always use this capacity. In fact, thinking only about one's own perspective, without regard for the perspectives of others, is a common phenomenon in the early adolescent years (recall our earlier discussion of the *imaginary audience*).

Late adolescence (ages 14–18). Older adolescents can draw on a rich knowledge base derived from numerous social experiences, and so they become ever more skillful at drawing inferences about people's psychological characteristics, intentions, and needs (Eisenberg, Carlo, Murphy, & Van Court, 1995; Paget, Kritt, & Bergemann, 1984). In addition, they are more attuned to the complex dynamics—not only thoughts, feelings, and present circumstances, but also past experiences—that influence behavior (Flanagan & Tucker, 1999; Selman, 1980; Tynes, 2007). And they realize that human beings are not always aware of why they act as they do (Selman, 2003). What we see emerging in the high school years, then, is a budding psychologist: an individual who can be quite astute in deciphering and explaining the motives and actions of others. Yet adults must remember that throughout childhood and adolescence, some youngsters are more perceptive than others, and the sophistication of social insights plays a significant role in youngsters' ability to interact effectively with other people (Astington & Pelletier, 1996).

As you have seen, it's a long road between infants' initial flickers of awareness that they and their caregivers have minds of their own to adolescents' far-reaching insights into how minds coordinate a broad array of mental states. In the Developmental Trends table "Social Cognition at Different Age Levels," you can see some of the primary social-cognitive accomplishments and common manifestations of diversity at each age level.

Factors Promoting Social Understandings

To some degree, development of a theory of mind and social perspective taking probably depend on brain maturation and the advancements in executive functioning that you read about in Chapters 4 and 7 (Andrews, Halford, Bunch, Bowden, & Jones, 2003; S.-J. Blakemore, 2007; Perner, Lang, & Kloo, 2002). Yet environmental factors are almost certainly involved as well. Discussions with adults about what people think, feel, want, and so on enhance children's awareness of thoughts and emotions as entities separate from physical reality (Jenkins, Turrell, Kogushi, Lollis, & Ross, 2003; Meins et al., 2003; Woolfe, Want, & Siegal, 2002). Parents who openly consider differing points of view during family discussions help children realize that multiple perspectives can legitimately exist (Astington & Pelletier, 1996; Taumoepeau & Ruffman, 2008). In the early years, sociodramatic play activities, in which children take on a variety of roles ("mommy," "doctor," etc.), can also help children imagine what people might think and feel in different contexts (Ashiabi, 2007; P. L. Harris, 1989; Lillard, 1998).

As you learned in this chapter, then, a sense of self and basic social understandings about other people both derive from nature *and* nurture. In the Basic Developmental Issues table "Comparing Sense of Self and Social Cognition," you can see other ways that the two characteristics reflect developmental dimensions.

Social-cognitive bias and prejudice.   Thinking about social situations can involve a lot of mental "work." Accordingly, people often take mental "shortcuts" to ease the load on working memory and make their dealings with others more efficient (L. A. Brenner, Koehler, Liberman, & Tversky, 1996; Tversky & Kahneman, 1990). Many of these shortcuts reflect **social-cognitive biases,** predispositions to interpret or respond to social situations in particular ways. For example, some children, but not others, tend to believe that a single action reflects a person's typical behavior and personality (Dweck, 2000; Karafantis & Levy, 2004).

Some social-cognitive biases are a minor nuisance; they lead to small distortions in thinking but don't cause grave harm. Others, however, have serious consequences. For instance, children occasionally jump to hasty conclusions about others based on group membership (e.g., gender, ethnicity, sexual orientation, religious affiliation). In other words, they respond on the basis of a **stereotype,** a rigid, simplistic, and erroneous characterization of a particular group. Often a stereotype encompasses a host of negative attributes (e.g., "stingy," "lazy," "promiscuous") and leads children to exhibit negative attitudes, feelings, and behaviors—that is, **prejudice**—toward the group in question.

The roots of stereotypes and prejudice lie in the natural tendency of human beings to categorize their experiences. In their first few years, children learn that people belong to different groups, such as boys and girls, and "blacks," and "whites," and many preschoolers can identify members of various ethnic groups (Aboud, 1988). As children are forming these social categories, they tend to favor their own group and expect less desirable characteristics and behaviors from members of other groups, especially if the different groups are in some form of conflict with one another (Aboud, 2005; Bigler & Liben, 2007; Black-Gutman & Hickson, 1996; Pfeifer, Brown, & Juvonen, 2007; Pitner, Astor, Benbenishty, Haj-Yahia, & Zeira, 2003).

On average, stereotypes and prejudice decrease as children move through the elementary grades (D. E. Carter, Detine-Carter, & Benson, 1995; F. H. Davidson, 1976; Pfeifer et al., 2007). This decline is probably due to children's increasing awareness of the limits of social categories.

social-cognitive bias
Mental shortcut in thinking about other people or social events.

stereotype
Rigid, simplistic, and erroneous characterization of a particular group.

prejudice
Display of negative attitudes, feelings, and behaviors toward particular individuals because of their membership in a specific group.

Social Cognition at Different Age Levels

Age	What You Might Observe	Diversity	Implications
Infancy (Birth–2 Years)	• Awareness of one's ability to share a focus of attention with caregiver *(intersubjectivity)* • Observation of other people's emotional reactions, followed by the child making a similar response *(social referencing)* • Emerging realization that other people have desires, goals, and intentions different from one's own	• Infants who receive inadequate care at home may be delayed in acquiring intersubjectivity and social referencing. • Infants who are autistic may avoid eye contact with caregivers.	• Get to know infants as individuals and the kinds of social interactions that each of them enjoys. • Use words such as *like, want,* and *think* regularly in descriptions of yourself and children. • Patiently explain why you must prohibit infants from pursuing tempting yet dangerous activities (thereby protecting them from harm as well as cultivating an awareness that your perspective differs from theirs).
Early Childhood (2–6 Years)	• Increasing use of "feeling" and "thinking" words (e.g., *want, sad, know*) • Growing realization that the mind does not always represent events accurately (e.g., that a person may have a false belief) • Growing ability to take others' perspectives	• Children whose parents talk frequently about thoughts and feelings tend to have a more advanced theory of mind. • Children with certain cognitive impairments (e.g., autism spectrum disorders) and those with reduced exposure to language as a result of hearing impairments tend to have a more limited theory of mind.	• Talk about various people's thoughts, feelings, perspectives, and needs. • Establish fun routines (e.g., tossing a ball, turning the pages of a book together) when individual children find it difficult to synchronize their behavior with others or tune into others' perspectives. • Recognize that selfish and territorial behaviors are common in early childhood, but encourage sharing.
Middle Childhood (6–10 Years)	• Recognition that people's actions do not always reflect their true thoughts and feelings • Growing realization that other people interpret (rather than simply remember) their experiences • Decrease in rigid stereotypes of particular groups of people (for most children)	• Children with certain disabilities (e.g., ADHD, autism, general intellectual disability) are more apt to have difficulty making accurate inferences about people's motives and intentions. • Children whose families or communities consistently promote unflattering images of particular groups may continue to have strong prejudices.	• Assist children in their attempts to discern the viewpoints of characters in stories and of public figures during historical events. • When addressing the experiences of a particular ethnic group (perhaps their literary accomplishments or struggles during historical events), make a point to expose children to individuals within the group who hold distinctly different perspectives.
Early Adolescence (10–14 Years)	• Recognition that people may have multiple and possibly conflicting feelings and motives • Emerging ability to think recursively about one's own and others' thoughts	• Some adolescents become so concerned about how other people see them that they succumb to peer pressure and take extreme measures to please other people. • Intellectual disabilities may hinder adolescents' abilities to consider multiple points of view.	• Conduct discussions that require adolescents to look at controversial issues from multiple perspectives. • Do not tolerate ethnic jokes or other remarks that show prejudice toward a particular group.
Late Adolescence (14–18 Years)	• Recognition that people are products of their environment and that past events and present circumstances influence personality and behavior • Use of a peer group as a forum for self-exploration and self-understanding • Increasing awareness that members of any single category of people (e.g., women, people with disabilities) can be very different from one another	• Most high school students use their social perspective-taking abilities constructively, but a few students use their knowledge of other people's psychological vulnerabilities to inflict harm on them. • Adolescents who are familiar with people from diverse cultures may find it relatively easy to infer the perspectives of individuals from different backgrounds.	• Talk about other people's complex (and sometimes conflicting) motives, perhaps while discussing contemporary issues, historical events, or works of fiction. • Assign autobiographies and other readings that depict individuals who have actively worked for the greater good of society, asking students to write about the motivations, beliefs, and ideas of these individuals.

Basic Developmental Issues

Comparing Sense of Self and Social Cognition

Issue	Sense of Self	Social Cognition
Nature and Nurture	Human beings appear to have an inborn need to think of themselves as competent, likable, and worthy individuals. A positive sense of self is fostered in environments wherein adults communicate messages about children's strengths and arrange for children to be successful, and in circumstances in which children interact with one another willingly and in a reasonably constructive manner.	The ability to consider other people's perspectives (their intentions, desires, thoughts, and so on) depends on having a normally maturing human brain. The capacities of theory of mind and social perspective taking are nurtured by social experiences with other people and, in particular, with exposure to different viewpoints.
Universality and Diversity	General developmental trends in self-perceptions are fairly universal. Most children first develop fairly simple views of the self and then increasingly see the self in complex terms. A second prevalent trend is for children to integrate their many discrete self-perceptions into general abstractions of their qualities as persons. Diversity emerges due to unique experiences in families and peer groups. Diversity is also reflected in the self-perceptions of boys and girls and children from different cultures and distinct ethnic groups.	Theory of mind appears to be a nearly universal capacity. A few children (e.g., some children with autism or serious intellectual disabilities) exhibit substantial delays in acquiring understandings of other people's desires, intentions, and thoughts and feelings. Diversity is present in the age at which children acquire specific elements of theory of mind. Children who have many opportunities to hear about other people's ideas, desires, and feelings tend to develop a theory of mind early. Children from different cultures also differ in the order with which they attain particular aspects of theory of mind and in how often they think about other people's perspectives.
Qualitative and Quantitative Change	Infants' basic awareness of themselves (e.g., arising from their experiences with bodily sensations and shared focus of attention with caregivers) is transformed qualitatively when children begin to speak and can exchange verbal information with others about thoughts and feelings. Other qualitative changes occur when adolescents fold their seemingly separate selves into unified abstract concepts that encompass complex psychological characteristics. Quantitative increases occur when children gradually increase their knowledge about things that they are good at and activities for which they lack proficiency.	A series of qualitative changes (e.g., the acquisition of *intersubjectivity* and *social referencing*) appear to set the stage for an emerging awareness that other people have their own (and potentially different) perspectives. Quantitative changes are evident in the increasingly sophisticated understandings that children have about other people's thoughts, intentions, desires, and feelings.

Many children gradually begin to realize that people who share membership in a category (e.g., "girls") are similar in some ways but very different in others. Yet other factors may work to maintain or strengthen stereotypes, and so some children show an increase in prejudice as they reach early adolescence (Black-Gutman & Hickson, 1996; Pfeifer et al., 2007). Parents may encourage prejudice through both words and actions—for instance, by telling ethnic jokes, restricting playmates to same-race peers, or enrolling their children in schools with as little racial and ethnic diversity as possible (Ashmore & DelBoca, 1976; Branch, 1999; McGlothlin & Killen, 2005). Popular images in television and other media—where males are often depicted as strong and aggressive, females appear to be weak and passive, and members of certain ethnic groups are consistently cast as unimportant characters or "bad guys"—may also have an impact (Corcoran & Parker, 2005; Huston et al., 1992; Maher, Herbst, Childs, & Finn, 2008; Signorielli & Lears, 1992; also see Chapter 15).

By adolescence and probably before, children who are victims of prejudice are well aware that others' treatment of them is discriminatory (Phinney & Tarver, 1988; R. D. Taylor, Casten, Flickinger, Roberts, & Fulmore, 1994). Over time they acquire a variety of strategies—seeking the support and companionship of other group members, forming a positive ethnic identity, and so on—for coping with prejudice and discrimination (Carranza, 2007; Swim &

Stangor, 1998). Even so, young people who are daily victims of prejudice are more likely than their peers to succumb to their distress by becoming ill or depressed (Allison, 1998; Tatum, 1997).

Diversity in Social Cognition

Both nurture and nature contribute to youngsters' growing abilities in social cognition. The effects of nurture sometimes reveal themselves in cultural and ethnic differences. The effects of nature are often evident in children with certain special needs.

Cultural and ethnic differences.   Children in a wide variety of cultures acquire a basic theory of mind, often at similar ages (Callaghan et al., 2005; P. L. Harris, 2006; Liu et al., 2008). Learning about other people's desires seems to be a fairly common initial acquisition, but cultures differ in subsequent accomplishments. For example, after grasping that other people are motivated to fulfill particular desires, Chinese children next develop an appreciation that people can be either knowledgeable or ignorant, whereas children in the United States and Australia next come to realize that different people may have varying beliefs (Wellman, Fang, Liu, Zhu, & Zhu, 2006).

Furthermore, *how much* children think about other people's thoughts and feelings depends, in part, on how much their culture encourages this process (Lillard, 1999). Some cultures frequently explain people's behaviors in terms of mental events, whereas others are more likely to focus on external circumstances. In the United States, children who live in urban areas often refer to people's psychological states when explaining good and bad behaviors (e.g., "He helped me catch bugs, because he and I like to catch bugs"). In contrast, children in rural areas are more likely to attribute people's behaviors to situational factors (e.g., "She helped me pick up my books, because if she didn't I would have missed the bus"). The latter approach is also common in many Southeast Asian cultures (Lillard, 1999; J. G. Miller, 1987).

Children with special needs.   Some children with disabilities seem to have a biological disadvantage in thinking about other people. Minor deficits in social cognition have been observed in many children with general intellectual disabilities. For example, children with Fragile X syndrome tend to perform at relatively low levels on theory of mind tasks (Cornish et al., 2005; P. Lewis et al., 2006). Other disabilities may hinder the development of social cognition indirectly by limiting children's experiences in certain areas. For instance, when children have significant hearing impairments beginning at birth or soon thereafter, they miss out on many discussions about "thinking," "feeling," "wanting," and the like, and so their theory of mind may develop more slowly (C. C. Peterson, 2002). Some children with ADHD find it difficult to take the perspective of other people, possibly in part because they may have fewer friends—and therefore fewer social experiences—as a result of their disruptive behaviors (Stormont, 2001).

One group of children with disabilities has an especially significant deficit in social cognition. Children with one of the **autism spectrum disorders** appear to have a distinctly difficult time thinking about themselves and other people. Common to these disorders are marked impairments in social cognition (e.g., self-awareness, perspective taking), social skills, and social interaction (Baron-Cohen, Tager-Flusberg, & Cohen, 1993; Hobson, Chidambi, Lee, & Meyer, 2006; C. C. Peterson, 2002). Although children with autism spectrum disorders tend to form close emotional attachments to their caregivers, they often prefer to be alone and have difficulty making friends (Hobson, 2004; Oppenheim, Koren-Karie, Dolev, & Yirmiya, 2008).

Aside from their similarities in social impairments, individuals with autism spectrum disorders differ considerably in the severity of their condition (hence the term *spectrum*). For instance, in *Asperger syndrome,* a fairly mild form, students have normal language skills and average or above-average intelligence. In severe cases, which are often referred to simply as *autism,* children have major delays in cognitive and linguistic development and exhibit certain bizarre behaviors—perhaps avoiding eye contact, constantly rocking or waving fingers, continually repeating what someone else has said, or showing unusual fascination with cer-

autism spectrum disorders
Disorders marked by impaired social cognition, social skills, and social interaction, as well as by repetitive behaviors; extreme forms are often associated with significant cognitive and linguistic delays and highly unusual behaviors.

tain objects (e.g., wristwatches) (American Psychiatric Association, 1994; Koegel, 1995; D. L. Williams, 2008). Underlying some of these behaviors may be an undersensitivity or oversensitivity to sensory stimulation (R. C. Sullivan, 1994; D. Williams, 1996). Temple Grandin, a woman who has gained international prominence as a designer of livestock facilities, recalls what it was like to be a child with autism:

> From as far back as I can remember, I always hated to be hugged. I wanted to experience the good feeling of being hugged, but it was just too overwhelming. It was like a great, all-engulfing tidal wave of stimulation, and I reacted like a wild animal. . . .
>
> When I was little, loud noises were also a problem, often feeling like a dentist's drill hitting a nerve. They actually caused pain. I was scared to death of balloons popping, because the sound was like an explosion in my ear. Minor noises that most people can tune out drove me to distraction. (Grandin, 1995, pp. 63, 67)

The vast majority of autism spectrum disorders are probably caused by abnormalities in the brain (Gillberg & Coleman, 1996; C. A. Nelson et al., 2006; Théoret et al., 2005). Increasing evidence indicates that autistic children undergo an unusual spurt in growth in the size of their brains during infancy and early childhood. Apparently, genetic instructions direct their brains to produce a high number of neurons that quickly crowd the growing brain and prevent strong connections from being formed between faraway regions (D. L. Williams, 2008). As a result, abilities that require coordination of different neurological functions, including language and social cognition, have insufficient neurological support to develop normally (Dyck, Piek, Hay, Smith, & Hallmayer, 2006).

Of course, children with autism spectrum disorders also exhibit numerous strengths. Many are able to resist distractions and become highly familiar with visual details in the objects and visual displays they study (Gernsbacher, Stevenson, Khandakar, & Goldsmith, 2008; Rondan & Deruelle, 2007). Occasionally, students with autism exhibit *savant syndrome,* in that they possess an extraordinary ability (e.g., exceptional artistic or musical talent) that is quite remarkable in contrast to other aspects of their mental functioning (Treffert & Wallace, 2002; Winner, 2000). One example of such a talent is the astonishing artistic ability that young Nadia revealed in her drawings of horses (see p. 142 in Chapter 4).

Many children with one of the autism spectrum disorders are in the general education classroom for all or part of the school day. Teachers can help these children feel secure by keeping the classroom layout and schedule fairly consistent. Capitalizing on children's strong visual-spatial skills, teachers can use objects, pictures, and photographs to convey ideas about academic topics (Hogdon, 1995; C. C. Peterson, 2002; Quill, 1995). In addressing children's social-cognitive limitations, teachers may vary their strategies partly depending on the age of the children. When working with young children, teachers can strive to establish one-on-one relationships with them, initially getting to know them by sitting beside them, expressing an interest in their activities with objects, and encouraging (but not demanding) give-and-take in interactions (Schreibman, 2008; Wieder, Greenspan, & Kalmanson, 2008). Teachers can also teach vocabulary for such internal mental processes as "thinking," "wishing," and "planning." And teachers can encourage pretend play that involves role-playing and can facilitate children's entry into peers' conversations (Schreibman, 2008).

As children with autism spectrum disorders grow older, they continue to need guidance in interpreting what other people are doing and how they can interact with peers. Teachers can advise older children with autism and Asperger syndrome about what to expect during upcoming social events, such as sitting with children from another classroom during a school play or holding hands with another child on a field trip. Teachers can also discourage actions that other youngsters find disturbing, such as repetitive behaviors, to reduce the chances that autistic children will be rejected by peers (Turnbull et al., 2007). Finally, some teachers set up buddy arrangements, in which a child without a serious disability is trained to interact with the child with autism and adjust to his or her needs, for example, by maintaining mutual attention with him or her and by commenting on ongoing activities (Kohler, Greteman, Raschke, & Highnam, 2007; Turnbull et al., 2007).

Teachers can often assist children with autism in interpreting social events and experiences.

When adults understand how children and adolescents think about and interpret social situations, they can better help youngsters interact effectively with peers.

MyEducationLab

Go to Chapter 12's Building Teaching Skills and Dispositions section in MyEducationLab to learn how adults can foster children's perspective taking during class discussions.

Fostering the Development of Social Cognition

The theories and research findings just reviewed have several implications for teachers and other adults who work with children and adolescents:

• *Talk about psychological phenomena and other people's perspectives in age-appropriate ways.* Adults frequently talk with children about thoughts and feelings, and together they may speculate about what other people (e.g., children's peers, figures in historical and current events, or fictional characters) might be thinking and feeling. Adults should, of course, try to gear such discussions to children's cognitive and linguistic capabilities. For instance, preschoolers understand such straightforward feelings as *sad, disappointed,* and *angry* (Saarni et al., 2006). Adolescents have sufficient cognitive and social reasoning capabilities to consider abstract and complex psychological qualities (e.g., being *passive aggressive* or having an inner *moral compass*) and to speculate about people's feelings in catastrophic circumstances, such as the atrocities committed in Bosnia and Rwanda in the name of "ethnic cleansing" in the 1990s or the devastation caused by Hurricane Katrina in 2005 (Yeager et al., 1997; Yilmaz, 2007).

• *Encourage children to look at situations from other people's perspectives.* Classrooms and other group situations provide many opportunities for children to look at the world as others do, and over time such opportunities enhance children's theory of mind and perspective-taking capabilities. You can see how teachers can foster children's perspective taking in the Building Teaching Skills and Dispositions exercise in MyEducationLab. The Development and Practice feature "Encouraging Social Perspective Taking" illustrates additional effective strategies.

• *Help children tune in to the nonverbal cues that can help them "read people's minds."* Some children (girls especially) readily pick up on the body language that reveals companions' thoughts and feelings (Bosacki, 2000; Deaux, 1984). Other children are less perceptive. The latter group can benefit from explicit instruction regarding signals they might look for—the furrowed brow that indicates confusion, the agitation that indicates frustration or impatience, the "silent treatment" that suggests anger, and so on (e.g., Beaumont & Sofronoff, 2008; Minskoff, 1980).

• *Intervene with children who face substantial delays in comprehending psychological concepts.* Children who are significantly delayed in their theory of mind may benefit from systematic exposure to psychological words (e.g., *wanting, thinking,* and *believing*). For example, let's consider Paula, a 9-year-old girl who had fetal alcohol syndrome. Paula was delayed in her cognitive and language development, had trouble interacting with other children,

Development and Practice

Encouraging Social Perspective Taking

• **Ask children to share their perceptions and interpretations with one another.**

A third-grade teacher finds several children arguing over why Serena tripped and fell during their game of tag. Meanwhile, Serena is crying. The teacher comforts Serena and then asks the children for their varying perspectives on what happened. He suggests that each of them may be partly right. He also urges them to be more careful when they play running games, as it is easy for children to bump one another accidentally during such activities.

• **Encourage children to speculate about characters' thoughts, emotions, and motives in works of literature.**

As a teacher in a child care center reads a story to a group of young children, she occasionally stops to ask questions about what the dif-

ferent characters might be thinking and feeling. For instance, while reading *The Berenstain Bears' Trouble with Pets* (Berenstain & Berenstain, 1990), she asks, "Why does the Bear family let Little Bird fly away?" and "How do you think Mama and Papa Bear feel when Lady makes a mess in the living room?"

• **Ask children to consider the perspectives of people they don't know.**

During a discussion of a recent earthquake in South America, an eighth-grade social studies teacher asks students to imagine how people must feel when they lose their home and possessions so quickly and don't know whether their loved ones are dead or alive.

and rarely used terms for her own or others' mental states (Timler, Olswang, & Coggins, 2005). An intervention was designed to foster Paula's awareness of how people in various settings experience events. Paula and two other children met with a speech-language specialist over several weeks and considered how characters in hypothetical scenarios might have thought about the events. After a few weeks, Paula regularly used mental state terms in her speech:

> "I *know* Marco didn't let me play soccer unless I gave him one dollar bill."
> "The teacher *thought* I was making this story up and I'm trying to get him in trouble because he told her a lie."
> "I *know* because I saw the toilet paper in the boy's hand."
> "She *knows* that we got the wrong pizza because we were arguing about where we wanted to go and we went to Dominoes."
> (Timler et al., 2005, p. 81)

● ***Actively work to break down stereotypes and prejudice.*** One effective strategy is to encourage children to see people as *individuals*—as human beings with their own unique strengths and weaknesses—rather than as members of particular groups (García, 1994; C. D. Lee & Slaughter-Defoe, 1995; Spencer & Markstrom-Adams, 1990). Even more effective is to increase interpersonal contacts among people from diverse groups (and ideally to create a sense that "we are all in this together"), perhaps through cooperative group activities, multischool community service projects, or pen pal relationships with children in distant locations (Devine, 1995; Koeppel & Mulrooney, 1992; Oskamp, 2000; Pfeifer et al., 2007).

Productive interactions with peers of diverse backgrounds and races help children discover that every individual has unique qualities.

In addition, adults should challenge any stereotypes and prejudicial attitudes they encounter in children's speech or actions. For example, if a teenager talks about "lazy migrant workers," a teacher might respond by saying, "I occasionally hear students express that view. I wonder where that stereotype came from. Migrant workers are often up before dawn and picking produce until dusk. And many of them take other demanding jobs when the growing season is over." Notice how the teacher confronts the "lazy migrant worker" stereotype tactfully and matter-of-factly and does not assume that the teen's remark has malicious intent. Youngsters often thoughtlessly repeat the prejudicial remarks of others. Playing on their interest to appear tolerant and open minded may be more effective than chastising them for attitudes they have not carefully thought through (Dovidio & Gaertner, 1999).

Knowing what other people are apt to be thinking and feeling certainly enhances youngsters' effectiveness in social interactions. But social cognition alone is not enough. Children and adolescents also need to know how best to direct their actions as they choose academic tasks, resolve moral dilemmas, and interact with peers. We turn to the development of these other important aspects of social development in the remaining chapters of the book.

 ## Summary

Sense of Self

Children's *sense of self* includes their beliefs about who they are as people (self-concept) and their judgments and feelings about their value and worth (self-esteem, self-worth). Most children tend to interpret events in ways that allow them to maintain a positive self-image. Realistic self-perceptions, or perhaps self-perceptions that are just slightly inflated, are optimal, in that they encourage children to set their sights on potentially achievable challenges.

To a considerable degree, children's sense of self is based on their own prior successes and failures. Yet other people also play a role, either by treating children in ways that communicate high or low regard, or (in the case of peers) by demonstrating the kinds of things children "should" be able to do at a certain age. Membership in various groups (e.g., athletic teams, ethnic groups) also has an impact, as do gender, physical appearance, disabilities, and other inherited characteristics.

With age, children construct increasingly complex and multifaceted understandings of who they are as people. In the early years, their self-perceptions are fairly simplistic, concrete, and categorical (e.g., "I have brown eyes," "I'm a boy"). But as they acquire the capacity for abstract thought, their self-descriptions increasingly include general, abstract qualities (e.g., "thoughtful," "dependable"). In adolescence they also begin to wrestle with who they ultimately want to become as human beings.

Social Cognition

As children grow older, they become more attuned to and interested in the mental lives of those around them. In the process of developing a *theory of mind*, they gradually learn that people have thoughts, feelings, and motives different from their own and that these thoughts, feelings, and motives can be complex and at times contradictory. They also become increasingly skilled in taking the perspectives of others. Unfortunately, youngsters' growing beliefs about other people may also include rigid stereotypes about certain groups, leading them to act toward members of those groups in prejudicial ways.

Classrooms and other group settings are important contexts in which children and adolescents develop increasing awareness of other people's needs and perspectives. Teachers and other adults can foster greater awareness and knowledge in numerous ways—for instance, by talking frequently about people's thoughts and feelings, exposing youngsters to multiple and equally legitimate perspectives about complex topics and events, and confronting inaccurate and counterproductive stereotypes.

Applying Concepts in Child Development

The exercises in this section will help you increase your effectiveness in nurturing children's self-perceptions and social understandings.

Case Study

Joachín's Dilemma

Read the case and then answer the questions that follow it.

Pedro Noguera reflects on the challenges that his son, Joachín, faced as an African American boy developing his identity:

> Joachín did extremely well throughout most of his early schooling. He was an excellent athlete (participating in soccer, basketball, and wrestling), played piano and percussion, and did very well in his classes. My wife and I never heard any complaints about him. In fact, we heard nothing but praise about his behavior from teachers, who referred to him as "courteous," "respectful," and "a leader among his peers." Then suddenly, in the tenth grade, Joachín's grades took a nosedive. He failed math and science, and for the first time he started getting into trouble at school. At home he was often angry and irritable for no apparent reason.
>
> My wife and I were left asking ourselves, "What's going on with our son? What's behind this sudden change in behavior?" Despite my disappointment and growing frustration, I tried not to allow Joachín's behavior to drive us apart. I started spending more time with him and started listening more intently to what he had to tell me about school and his friends. As I did, several things became clear to me. One was that all of the friends he had grown up with in our neighborhood in South Berkeley, California (one of the poorest areas of the city), were dropping out of school. These were mostly Black, working-class kids who didn't have a lot of support at home or at school and were experiencing academic failure. Even though Joachín came from a middle-class home with two supportive parents, most of his reference group—that is, the students he was closest to and identified with—did not.
>
> The other thing that was changing for Joachín was his sense of how he had to present himself when he was out on the streets and in school. As he grew older, Joachín felt the need to project the image of a tough and angry young Black man. He believed that in order to be respected he had to carry himself in a manner that was intimidating and even menacing. To behave differently—too nice, gentle, kind, or sincere—meant that he would be vulnerable and preyed upon. I learned that for Joachín, part of his new persona also involved placing less value on academics and greater emphasis on being cool and hanging out with the right people.
>
> By eleventh grade Joachín gradually started working out of these behaviors, and by twelfth grade he seemed to snap out of his angry state. He became closer to his family, his grades improved, he rejoined the soccer team, he resumed playing the piano, and he even started producing music. As I reflected on the two years of anger and self-destructiveness that he went through, I came to the conclusion that Joachín was trying desperately to figure out what it meant to be a young Black man. I realized that, like many Black male adolescents, Joachín was trapped by stereotypes, and they were pulling him down. During this difficult period it was very hard for me to help him through this process of identity formation. While he was in the midst of it the only thing I could do was talk to him, listen to him, and try to let him know what it was like for me when I went through adolescence.[a] (Noguera, 2003, pp. 19–20)

· What challenges did Joachín face in establishing his identity?
· What factors in Joachín's life ultimately helped him form a productive identity?

Once you have answered these questions, compare your responses with those presented in Appendix A.

[a]Excerpted from Pedro A. Noguera, "'Joaquín's Dilemma': Understanding the Link Between Racial Identity and School-Related Behaviors," in *Adolescents at School: Perspectives on Youth, Identity, and Education,* edited by Michael Sadowski (Cambridge, MA: Harvard Education Press, 2003), pp. 19–30. Copyright © by the President and Fellows of Harvard College. All rights reserved. For more information, please visit www.harvardeducationpress.org.

Interpreting Children's Artifacts and Reflections

Consider chapter concepts as you analyze the following artifact from an adolescent.

Two Histories

Rachel Stephanie Bolden-Kramer is an adolescent from San Francisco, California. In her poem, *Two Histories*, Rachel tells what it's like to have a dual ethnic heritage (WritersCorps, 2003). As you read Rachel's poem, consider these questions:

· How have other people responded to Rachel's ethnicity?
· How does Rachel show her commitment to a multiethnic identity?

Two Histories
Daddy wanted to name me Wilhemina after his mother.
You know you're supposed to name your baby after someone who's gone.
Not alive.
But then my mother protested.
I should carry her mother's name, Anne.
"Rachel" kept me from the arguments and sour family disputes.
But did it compromise or anger both sides?
And that's what I'm stuck with,
Every day
Every move
I'm a compromise
Light skin
But thick bone structure
Half 'n half Jewish girl who fights for BSU[a]

Latke and greens
The horah and the butterfly
Act White
Won't date Black men
Think she's better
Has good hair
Looks more Latina than half-breed
But that boy always called me mixed in such an ugly way
Some say, "Nigga get off the swing"
Others say, "You're really not like those other Black people"
And I get told it's better to pretend I'm White
But I got two histories in me
Both enslaved
And both warriors.
Rachel Stephanie Bolden-Kramer[b]

(WritersCorps, 2003, pp. 39–40)

Once you have analyzed the poem, compare your ideas with those presented in Appendix B. For further practice in analyzing children's artifacts and reflections, go to the Activities and Applications section in Chapter 12 of MyEducationLab.

[a]BSU refers to the Black Student Union.
[b]Reprinted with permission. WritersCorps (2003). *Paint Me Like I Am: Teen Poems from WritersCorps*. New York, NY: HarperTempest.

Developmental Trends Exercise

In this chapter you learned about how children think of themselves and other people. The following table presents five examples of youngsters' understandings of themselves or others. For each example, the table presents one or more relevant developmental principles, offers an implication for working with youngsters in that age-group, or both. Go to the Activities and Applications section in Chapter 12 of MyEducationLab to apply what you've learned about the self and social understandings as you fill in the empty cells in the table.

Determining How Children Think About Themselves and Others

Age	A Youngster's Experience	Developmental Concepts *Identifying Youngsters' Understandings of Self or Others*	Implications *Promoting Development in Sense of Self and Social Cognition*
Infancy (Birth–2 Years)	When 18-month-old Marvin sees his reflection in the mirror, he rubs his cheek to wipe off the lipstick his mother left when kissing him good-bye earlier in the day.	Marvin understands that he is a physical entity separate from the objects and people around him. Furthermore, he recognizes his image in the mirror, indicating that he has some awareness of his own appearance.	Help infants and toddlers learn about their physical selves not only by holding them in front of mirrors but also by showing them photographs of themselves and talking with them about various body parts ("Show me your nose!", "Did you fall and hurt your knee?").
Early Childhood (2–6 Years)	Arriving early at preschool one morning, 3-year-old Kesia helps her teacher reorganize the art supplies. At the teacher's instruction, she moves the colored markers from a bookshelf to the bottom drawer of a cabinet. Later she is quite surprised when her friend Darla looks for the markers on the shelf. "They're in the drawer, silly!" she exclaims.	Like Kesia, young preschoolers often mistakenly assume that other people know what they themselves know. Not until age 4 or 5 do children appreciate that others may have *false beliefs* based on prior learning experiences.	

continued

Developmental Trends Exercise (continued)

Age	A Youngster's Experience	**Developmental Concepts** _Identifying Youngsters' Understandings of Self or Others_	**Implications** _Promoting Development in Sense of Self and Social Cognition_
Middle Childhood (6–10 Years)	When asked to describe himself, Douglas replies that he is smart in math, dumb in reading, popular among his friends, mean to his younger brother, and helpful to his parents. He smiles and then sums it up, "Overall, I'm a pretty good guy!"	Douglas is aware that he has both strengths and weaknesses. He describes himself using psychological terms and has a generally positive sense of self.	Help children to be successful on a range of tasks and in numerous domains. When children struggle in particular areas, offer assistance and communicate your confidence that they will succeed if they change their tactics and persist when they begin to falter. Acknowledge their progress, particularly in areas of difficulty. Use psychological terms that are upbeat and affirming (e.g., being "persistent," "courageous," and "considerate").
Early Adolescence (10–14 Years)	Soon after beginning junior high school, 13-year-old Robert begins dressing like peers—for instance, by wearing oversized pants that hang low on his hips and balloon around his legs. And when he sees a few older boys secretly smoking cigarettes in a far corner of the schoolyard, he asks if he can "take a drag."		Expose youngsters to a wide variety of models of "acceptable" behavior, with particular emphasis on peers who maintain a "cool" image while engaging in healthful and productive activities.
Late Adolescence (14–18 Years)	As a 15-year-old, Rita is quite proud of her Puerto Rican heritage. She belittles certain extracurricular activities at her school, especially athletics and the National Honor Society, saying that they are "entirely too white" for her. Two years later, Rita is excelling in her science and math courses and plans to become a biologist. She learns about Puerto Rican women who have become skilled scientists and talks about following in their footsteps.	On the road to forming an _ethnic identity_, some adolescents may, like Rita, initially adopt a rigid, inflexible one that rejects the perceived values of other ethnic groups. Eventually, however, she becomes more open minded about behaviors that are acceptable for her. In general, youngsters with a strong ethnic identity have high self-esteem.	

Key Concepts

sense of self (p. 444)	personal fable (p. 451)	ethnic identity (p. 457)	recursive thinking (p. 468)
self-handicapping (p. 445)	identity (p. 452)	social cognition (p. 466)	social-cognitive bias (p. 469)
contingent self-worth (p. 448)	gender schema (p. 454)	theory of mind (p. 466)	stereotype (p. 469)
autobiographical self (p. 450)	androgyny (p. 455)	social perspective taking (p. 466)	prejudice (p. 469)
imaginary audience (p. 451)	self-socialization (p. 455)	intentionality (p. 466)	autism spectrum disorders (p. 472)

MyEducationLab

Now go to Chapter 12 of MyEducationLab at www.myeducationlab.com, where you can:

· View instructional objectives for the chapter.
· Take a quiz to test your mastery of chapter objectives. Detailed feedback is provided to explain why your responses are correct or incorrect.
· Deepen your understanding of particular concepts and principles with Review, Practice, and Enrichment exercises.

· Complete Activities and Applications exercises that give you additional experience in interpreting artifacts, increase your understanding of how research contributes to knowledge about chapter topics, and encourage you to apply what you have learned about children's development.
· Apply what you have learned in the chapter to your work with children in Building Teaching Skills and Dispositions exercises.
· Observe children and their unique contexts in Video Examples.

Development of
Motivation and
Self-Regulation

Janet Keany teaches a mathematics class for fifth and sixth graders who have a history of poor performance in math.[1] She has recently shown her class how concepts in geometry relate to aerodynamics, emphasizing that the size and shape of an object affect the ease with which it can fly. As a follow-up to the lesson, she asks her students to experiment with a variety of sizes and shapes of kites and then to design a kite using what they have learned.

The kite project lasts several days. A researcher observes the class throughout the project and interviews the children afterward. She finds that different children take very different approaches to the task and have widely varying perspectives about it. For instance, a girl named Sara approaches the task as a scientist might: She seems keenly interested in creating an aerodynamic kite design and realizes that doing so will take time and patience. She redesigns her kite three times to make it as aerodynamic as possible. After the project, she summarizes her results:

> . . . I wasn't completely successful, because I had a few problems. But I realized that most scientists, when they try experiments, well, they're not always right. . . . [I]f I can correct myself on [errors] then I don't really mind them that much. I mean, everybody learns from their mistakes. I know I do. . . . I think mistakes are actually good, to tell you the truth. . . .
>
> When I had my test flights, the shape flew really, really well, and I was going to stick with that shape. . . . I had no doubts because I knew that I could really do it; I knew I could put this together really well, 'cause I had a lot of confidence in myself. . . . (D. K. Meyer, Turner, & Spencer, 1997, pp. 511–512)

Unlike Sara, Amy sticks with a single kite design throughout the project even though she has trouble getting her kite to fly. Later, Amy tells the researcher:

> I knew from the start what shape I wanted. Once I had the materials it was very easy to make the kite. . . . [T]here wasn't enough wind for the kites to fly. (pp. 510, 513)

The researcher asks Amy how important the project was to her and whether she ever takes risks at school. She responds:

> I feel lazy because I don't like to make challenges for myself, to make goals. I just like to do it as I go along, not make goals or challenges. . . . I like to do well for [the teacher] and my parents, and myself, I guess. . . . [I]f it doesn't affect my grade, whether I do this or not, if I totally fail and do everything wrong, if it doesn't affect my grade, then I'll [take risks]. (pp. 510, 512)

Had her kite flown, how might Amy have explained it? Amy tells the researcher that it would probably have been "beginner's luck" (D. K. Meyer et al., 1994, 1997).

- What differences do you notice in how the two girls approach the kite-making activity?

- How might you characterize Sara's motivation for engaging in the activity? For whom does Amy say she wants to do well on the task?

- How does Sara explain her success? How does Amy explain her failure?

[1]Although the case is real, "Janet Keany" is a pseudonym.

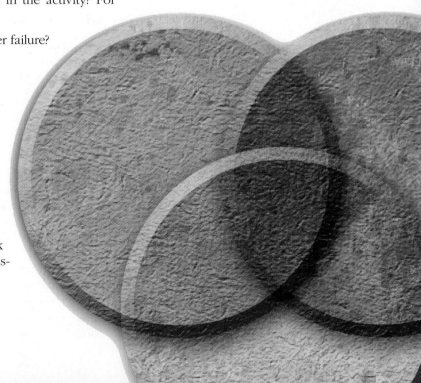

Case Study: Making Kites

Outline:

Case Study: Making Kites

Extrinsic and Intrinsic Motivation

Development of Goals

Development of Attributions

Diversity in Motivation

Motivating Children and Adolescents

Self-Regulation

Summary

Applying Concepts in Child Development

Sara is willing to experiment and make mistakes so that she can construct the best kite possible, whereas Amy prefers an easier, though less successful, course of action. Sara seems to find satisfaction in her accomplishments, whereas Amy seems to be more interested in pleasing her teacher and parents. Sara attributes her successful kite to her own effort and ability, whereas Amy concludes that her failure was due to poor weather conditions and suspects that any success on the task would have been a matter of luck. All of these differences illustrate aspects of motivation that we consider in this chapter.

Extrinsic and Intrinsic Motivation

In general, **motivation** energizes, directs, and sustains behavior: It gets people moving, points them in a particular direction, and keeps them going. We usually see motivation reflected in a certain amount of *personal investment* in particular activities, as exemplified by the time and effort that Sara put into creating her kite.

Virtually all children and adolescents are motivated in one way or another. One may express a keen interest in academic subject matter, seek out challenging course work, participate actively in classroom discussions, complete assignments diligently, and earn high grades. Another may be more concerned about social affairs, interacting with peers frequently, participating in numerous extracurricular activities, and chatting incessantly with friends on the phone or Internet. Still another may be focused on athletics, excelling in physical education classes, playing or watching sports most afternoons and weekends, and working out daily in hopes of making the varsity soccer team. And yet another, perhaps because of an undetected learning disability, poor social skills, or a seemingly uncoordinated body, may be interested primarily in *avoiding* academics, social situations, or athletic activities.

Sometimes youngsters have **extrinsic motivation:** They are motivated to either attain or avoid certain consequences in the outside world. For instance, they may complete a classroom assignment in order to get adult approval (as Amy did in the opening case), or they may lie about a misdeed in order to avoid being punished ("I didn't do it, *he* did!"). At other times youngsters have **intrinsic motivation:** They are motivated by factors within themselves or inherent in a task they are performing. For instance, they might read a book simply for the pleasure it brings, experiment with various kite shapes to find out which one flies best (as Sara did), or return a wallet to its owner as a way of being true to an internal moral code.

Both extrinsic and intrinsic motivation can spur children to acquire new knowledge and skills and engage in productive behaviors. But intrinsic motivation has numerous advantages over extrinsic motivation. Intrinsically motivated children are eager to learn classroom material, willingly tackle assigned tasks, use effective learning strategies, and are likely to achieve at high levels in school. In contrast, extrinsically motivated children may have to be enticed or prodded, are apt to study classroom topics only superficially, and are often interested in performing only easy tasks and meeting minimal classroom requirements (A. E. Gottfried, Fleming, & Gottfried, 2001; Reeve, 2006; Renninger, Hidi, & Krapp, 1992).

Children learn more effectively when they are intrinsically rather than extrinsically motivated.

Factors Affecting Extrinsic Motivation

Human beings of all ages usually behave in ways that bring desired results. In an early theory of learning known as *operant conditioning*, the behaviorist B. F. Skinner proposed that children learn and engage primarily in behaviors that lead to certain consequences, which he called **reinforcers** (e.g., Skinner, 1953, 1968). From Skinner's perspective, human behaviors are those that are currently being reinforced or have often been reinforced in the past. For instance, Miguel might practice the piano regularly if his parents continually praise him for his efforts. Brigita might throw frequent temper tantrums if she's learned that tantrums are the only way she can get special toys or privileges. Peter might misbehave in class if doing so gains him the attention of his teacher and classmates. The last of these examples illustrates an important point: Reinforcers are not always what we would typically think of as "rewards." The attention Peter gets for his misbehavior may seem unpleasant to others: Peter's teacher may scold him for acting out, or his classmates might shake their heads in disgust. But if Peter's misbehaviors increase as a result, then the attention is indeed a reinforcer.

In early infancy, children are largely concerned with **primary reinforcers,** which satisfy basic, built-in needs or desires. Some primary reinforcers, such as food and drinks, are essential for physiological well-being. Others, such as physical affection, cuddling, and smiles, are more social in nature. Human beings have probably evolved to appreciate these social reinforcers as a way of enhancing their connectedness to others and so, indirectly,

motivation
State that energizes, directs, and sustains behavior.

extrinsic motivation
Motivation provoked by the external consequences that certain behaviors bring.

intrinsic motivation
Motivation resulting from personal characteristics or from factors inherent in the task being performed.

reinforcer
Consequence of a response that leads to an increase in the frequency of that response.

primary reinforcer
Stimulus or event that satisfies a built-in biological need.

enhancing their chances of survival (Harlow & Zimmerman, 1959; Vollmer & Hackenberg, 2001; also see *ethological attachment theory* in Chapter 11).

Over time, children begin to associate certain other consequences with primary reinforcers. For example, a child might learn that praise from Mother often comes with a special candy treat or discover that a good grade frequently leads to a hug from Father. Through such associations, consequences such as praise, money, good grades, and attention (sometimes even attention in the form of a scolding) become reinforcing in their own right. That is, they become **secondary reinforcers.** Because secondary reinforcers are consequences that children *learn* to appreciate, the effectiveness of any one of them will differ considerably from one child to the next.

As children grow older, they become better able to **delay gratification:** They can forgo small, immediate reinforcers for the more substantial consequences their long-term efforts may bring down the road (e.g., Green, Fry, & Myerson, 1994; Rotenberg & Mayer, 1990; Vaughn, Kopp, & Krakow, 1984). For example, a 3-year-old is apt to choose a small toy she can have *now* over a larger and more attractive toy she cannot have until tomorrow. In contrast, an 8-year-old is usually willing to wait a day or two for a more appealing item. Many adolescents can delay gratification for weeks at a time. For instance, as a 16-year-old, Jeanne's son Jeff worked long hours stocking shelves at the local grocery store (hardly a rewarding activity!) to earn enough money to pay half the cost of a $400-a-night limousine for his high school prom. Some children and adolescents are better able to delay gratification than others, however, and those who have this ability are better able to resist temptation, carefully plan their future actions, and achieve at high levels at school (Bembenutty & Karabenick, 2004; Eigsti et al., 2006; Shoda, Mischel, & Peake, 1990).

In contrast to reinforcers, psychologists define **punishment** as a consequence that *decreases* the frequency of the response it follows.[2] Whereas children are likely to behave in ways that lead to reinforcement, they are *un*likely to behave in ways that lead to punishment. Punishment of undesirable responses (e.g., engaging in off-task behaviors during a lesson), especially when combined with reinforcement of more productive ones (e.g., sitting attentively during the lesson), can bring about lasting improvements in children's behavior (Landrum & Kauffman, 2006; Walters & Grusec, 1977). For example, when teachers and therapists work with children who have serious behavioral problems, they may award points (reinforcement) for appropriate behaviors and take away points (punishment) for misbehaviors. After a certain time interval (perhaps at the end of the day or week), children can exchange the points they've accumulated for small toys or privileges. Taking away previously earned points for unacceptable behavior (a strategy called *response cost*) can be quite effective in bringing about behavior change (Landrum & Kauffman, 2006; K. D. O'Leary & O'Leary, 1972). Many other forms of punishment are *not* effective, however, especially those that provide models of aggression, inflict physical or psychological harm, or involve suspension or expulsion from school (Brendgen, Wanner, Vitaro, Bukowski, & Tremblay, 2007; Hyman et al., 2004; Lansford et al., 2005; Skiba & Rausch, 2006).

As social learning theorists have pointed out, children's motivation is affected not only by the consequences they experience themselves but also by the consequences they see *other people* experience (e.g., Bandura, 1965, 1977). In other words, observed consequences may affect children vicariously. In **vicarious reinforcement,** a child who observes a peer being reinforced for doing something is likely to behave similarly. In **vicarious punishment,** a child who sees a peer being punished for a particular behavior is *un*likely to behave in that way. For example, by watching the consequences that their peers experience, children might learn that being elected to a student government office brings status and popularity, that acting out in class gets the teacher's attention, or that exhibiting unsportsmanlike conduct on the playing field results in being benched during the next game.

Factors Affecting Intrinsic Motivation

As the following principles reveal, some of the factors underlying intrinsic motivation are at work quite early in life, whereas others emerge over time as children learn more about themselves and their relationship with their environment.

[2]Be aware that the term *negative reinforcement* is *not* a synonym for punishment. Negative reinforcement increases rather than decreases the behavior it follows. You can learn more about negative reinforcement in a supplementary reading located in the Activities and Applications section in Chapter 13 of MyEducationLab.

secondary reinforcer
Stimulus or event that becomes reinforcing over time through its association with one or more other reinforcers.

delay of gratification
Forgoing small immediate rewards for larger ones at a future time.

punishment
Consequence of a response that leads to a decrease in the frequency of that response.

vicarious reinforcement
Phenomenon in which a child increases a certain response after seeing someone else reinforced for that response.

vicarious punishment
Phenomenon in which a child decreases a certain response after seeing someone else punished for that response.

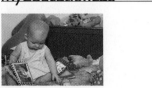
- *Children seem to have a natural predisposition to explore their environment.* Following in Jean Piaget's footsteps, many developmental theorists believe that children are naturally curious about their world and actively seek out information to help them make sense of it (e.g., Flum & Kaplan, 2006; Lieberman, 1993; Raine, Reynolds, & Venables, 2002). Even as infants, children are constantly experimenting to discover the properties of various objects and the outcomes of various actions. Later, as children gain proficiency in their native language, their seemingly incessant questions (e.g., "How do they make statues?" "Why does it rain sometimes?") are an additional means through which they try to satisfy their curiosity about the world around them (Callanan & Oakes, 1992, p. 218; Kemler Nelson et al., 2004).

- *Children strive for consistency in their understandings of the world.* Jean Piaget suggested that another key factor driving a child's learning and development is *disequilibrium*, an inconsistency between new information and what the child already believes to be true. According to Piaget, disequilibrium causes mental discomfort and spurs the child to integrate, reorganize, or in some cases replace existing schemes to accommodate to the new information (see Chapter 6). Like Piaget, many contemporary developmental theorists believe that beginning early in life, human beings have an innate need for consistency and coherence among the things they learn (e.g., M. B. Bronson, 2000; Egan, Santos, & Bloom, 2007; Sinatra & Pintrich, 2003).

- *Children tend to choose activities at which they think they can be successful.* Some psychologists propose that an important source of intrinsic motivation is an innate need to feel *competent*—to believe that one can deal effectively with one's environment (Deci & Ryan, 1992; Jacobs et al., 2002). A need for competence pushes children to acquire effective ways of dealing with various environmental circumstances. It may be one important reason why we human beings have, over the course of time, been able to adapt successfully to many different habitats (R. White, 1959).

As you learned in Chapter 12, children increasingly distinguish among various aspects of themselves, and they soon discover that they are good at some things and not so good at others. To maintain and enhance their sense of competence, children are apt to choose and persist at activities for which they have high **self-efficacy**—that is, activities at which they believe they can be successful (Bandura, 1982, 1997). For example, in the opening case study, Sara reveals a high sense of self-efficacy about building a kite: "I had no doubts because I knew that I could really do it; I knew I could put this together really well" (D. K. Meyer et al., 1997, p. 512).

Once youngsters have high self-efficacy for a task or activity, they eagerly seek out challenges that can further enhance their ability. In the "Intrinsic Motivation" videos for middle childhood and late adolescence in MyEducationLab, 9-year-old Elena and 15-year-old Greg both express their desire for challenge at school:

Interviewer:	What do you like best about school?
Elena:	I like PEAK [a program for students identified as gifted]. It's this thing where you go to this program. It's for smart kids who have, like, good ideas for stuff you could do. And so they make it more challenging for you in school. So instead of third-grade math, you get fourth-grade math.
Interviewer:	What do teachers do that encourage you to do well at school?
Greg:	[S]ome of them kind of make it a competition, like class rank and stuff. . . . And that makes you want to. . . . And the challenge. If it's a really hard class, then I . . . will usually try harder in harder classes.

When children have *low* self-efficacy for a particular activity or content domain, they may try to avoid it as much as possible. The following statements by students with reading disabilities reveal two common avoidance strategies, making excuses and blatantly refusing to perform assigned tasks:

When it comes time for reading I do everything under the sun I can to get out of it because it's my worst nightmare to read. I'll say I have to go to the bathroom or that I'm sick and I have to go to the nurse right now. My teacher doesn't know that I'll be walking around campus. She thinks I am going to the bathroom or whatever my lame excuse is. All I really want to do is get out of having to read. (Zambo & Brem, 2004, p. 5)

self-efficacy
Belief that one is capable of executing certain behaviors or reaching certain goals.

They (teachers) used to hand us all our homework on Mondays. One day my teacher handed me a stack about an inch thick and as I was walking out of class there was a big trash can right there and I'd, in front of everybody including the teacher, just drop it in the trash can and walk out. I did this because I couldn't read what she gave me. It was kind of a point that I wanted to get the teacher to realize. That while I'm doing it, inside it kind of like hurt because I really wanted to do it but I couldn't and just so it didn't look like I was goin' soft or anything like that I'd walk over to the trash and throw it in. (Zambo & Brem, 2004, p. 6)

• ***Children also prefer activities for which they have some autonomy.*** As early as 6 months of age, many infants become frustrated and angry when a device they've learned to operate by moving their arms suddenly stops playing music in response to their actions (M. W. Sullivan & Lewis, 2003). By 14 months, infants may actively resist parent requests that would prevent them from reaching their immediate goals (Dix, Stewart, Gershoff, & Day, 2007). And in general, children are more intrinsically motivated when they have a **sense of self-determination,** a belief that they have some choice and control regarding the things they do and the direction their lives take (Deci & Ryan, 1985, 1992; Ng, Kenney-Benson, & Pomerantz, 2004; Tsai, Kunter, Lüdtke, Trautwein, & Ryan, 2008). For instance, a child who thinks "I *want* to do this" or "I'd *like* to learn more about that" has a high sense of self-determination. In contrast, a child who thinks "I *must* do this" or "*My teacher wants* me to learn that" is thinking that someone or something else is directing the course of events. As an example, let's revisit 14-year-old Alicia's comment about required reading, to which we previously drew your attention in Chapter 10:

> I really don't like it when the reading's required. I can't read books if they're required. I just avoid reading them because they don't seem very interesting. And even after you read them, even though they might be interesting, they're not as interesting as if you picked them up by yourself.

Developmental trends in intrinsic motivation. The nature of youngsters' intrinsic motivation changes in several ways over the course of childhood and adolescence.

• ***As children grow older, their interests become increasingly stable.*** When we say that children have *interest* in a particular topic or activity, we mean that they find the topic or activity intriguing and rewarding in and of itself. Interest, then, is one form of intrinsic motivation. Psychologists distinguish between two general types of interest (e.g., Hidi, Renninger, & Krapp, 2004). **Situational interest** is evoked by something in the environment—something that is perhaps new, unusual, or surprising. In contrast, **personal interest** comes from within the child and is largely unrelated to immediate circumstances.

In infancy and early childhood, interests are mostly situational and short lived: Young children are readily attracted to novel, attention-getting stimuli and events for, say, a few seconds or minutes (e.g., Courage, Reynolds, & Richards, 2006). Sometimes these stimuli and events plant the seeds from which longer-term personal interests begin to grow (Hidi & Renninger, 2006). By the middle to upper elementary grades—sometimes even earlier—many children acquire personal interests that persist over a period of time and may ultimately become important parts of children's identities (J. M. Alexander, Johnson, Leibham, & Kelley, 2008; Hidi et al., 2004; K. E. Johnson, Alexander, Spencer, Leibham, & Neitzel, 2004). As an example of an enduring personal interest, look at Joey's drawings in Figure 13-1. Joey displayed an exceptional interest in art beginning at age 3. Throughout his childhood and adolescence, he had a strong interest in drawing the human form and, later, in fashion design. (Joey's self-portrait at age 17 appears in Figure 10-16 in Chapter 10.)

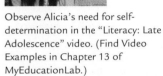
sense of self-determination
Belief that one has some choice and control regarding the future course of one's life.
situational interest
Interest evoked temporarily by something in the environment.
personal interest
Long-term, relatively stable interest in a particular topic or activity.

Age 8

Age 11

Age 17

Figure 13-1
In these drawings, Joey shows his long-term personal interest in drawing the human form.

• *Children and adolescents increasingly pursue activities that they perceive to be valuable for themselves.* A task or activity has **value** when children believe there are direct or indirect benefits in performing it (Dweck & Elliott, 1983; Feather, 1982; Wigfield & Eccles, 2000). Some activities are valued because they are associated with certain personal qualities. For example, a boy who wants to be smart and thinks that smart people do well in school will place a premium on academic success. Other activities have high value because they are seen as means to desired goals. For example, much as she disliked mathematics, Jeanne's daughter Tina struggled through math classes throughout high school because many colleges require 4 years of math. Still other activities are valued simply because they bring pleasure and enjoyment (Durik, Vida, & Eccles, 2006; Eccles & Wigfield, 1985; Eccles [Parsons], 1983).

In the elementary grades, children primarily choose activities that they perceive to be interesting and enjoyable. As they reach adolescence and proceed through the secondary grades, however, they increasingly choose activities that, in their minds at least, will be instrumental in helping them achieve their goals (Eccles et al., 1998; Okagaki, 2006; Wigfield, Tonks, & Eccles, 2004).

In contrast, children tend *not* to value activities that seem to require more effort than they're worth. For instance, a teenager who would ideally like to get straight As in school may begin to downplay the importance of As if she finds that they require forgoing much of her social life (e.g., Otis, Grouzet, & Pelletier, 2005). Children may also *de*value activities that they associate with frequent frustration and failure ("I don't see why I need to do these stupid geometry proofs!") and that may lessen their sense of competence (Wigfield & Eccles, 2000).

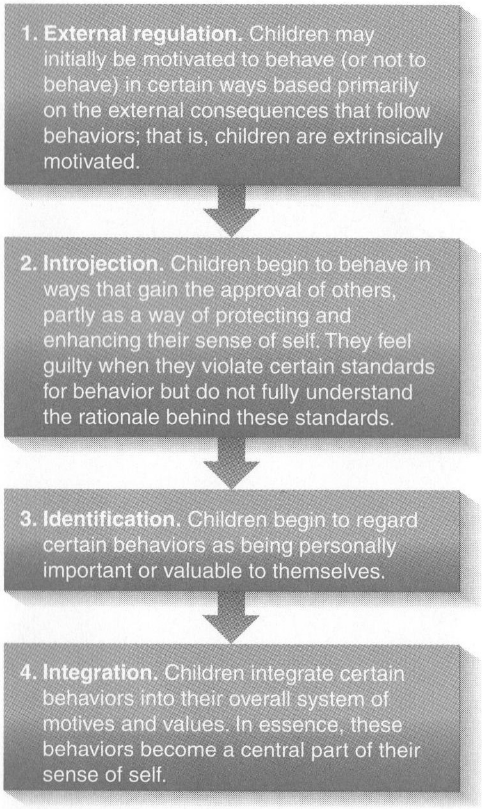

• *Over time, children internalize the motivation to engage in certain activities.* As children grow older, most begin to adopt some of the values and priorities of the people around them. Such **internalized motivation** typically develops gradually, perhaps in the sequence depicted in Figure 13-2 (Deci & Ryan, 1995). Initially, children may engage in some activities primarily because of the external consequences that result. For instance, students may do schoolwork to earn praise or avoid being punished for poor grades. With time other people's approval becomes increasingly important for children's sense of self. Eventually children internalize the "pressure" to perform certain activities and see these activities as important in their own right. Such internalization of values is most likely to occur if adults who espouse those values (parents, teachers, etc.) do the following:

• Engage in and thereby model valued activities themselves.
• Provide a warm, supportive, and somewhat structured environment for children.
• Offer enough autonomy in decision making that children have a sense of self-determination about their actions (Jacobs, Davis-Kean, Bleeker, Eccles, & Malanchuk, 2005; R. M. Ryan, Connell, & Grolnick, 1992; R. M. Ryan & Deci, 2000).

Some of our readers may think that internalized motivation is essentially the same as intrinsic motivation. Certainly internalized motivation is a *form* of intrinsic motivation, in that it comes from inside the child rather than from outside factors in the immediate, here-and-now environment. But in one important way it is quite different from other forms of intrinsic motivation. Intrinsic motivation that arises spontaneously within the child (e.g., curiosity about an intriguing object) can increase or decrease somewhat unpredictably. In contrast, because internalized motivation is a product of ongoing social and cultural factors and eventually becomes an integral part of children's sense of self—their beliefs about who they are as human beings—it remains fairly stable and dependable over time (Otis et al., 2005; Reeve, Deci, & Ryan, 2004; Walls & Little, 2005).

• *Intrinsic motivation for learning school subject matter declines during the school years.* Young children are often eager and excited to learn new things at school. But sometime between grades 3 and 9, children become less intrinsically motivated, and more *extrinsically* motivated, to learn classroom topics. Their intrinsic motivation may be especially low after they make the often anxiety-arousing transition from elementary school to a secondary-school format (Lepper, Corpus, & Iyengar, 2005; Otis et al., 2005; Wigfield et al., 2006). (Chapter 15 discusses this transition in more detail.)

1. External regulation. Children may initially be motivated to behave (or not to behave) in certain ways based primarily on the external consequences that follow behaviors; that is, children are extrinsically motivated.

2. Introjection. Children begin to behave in ways that gain the approval of others, partly as a way of protecting and enhancing their sense of self. They feel guilty when they violate certain standards for behavior but do not fully understand the rationale behind these standards.

3. Identification. Children begin to regard certain behaviors as being personally important or valuable to themselves.

4. Integration. Children integrate certain behaviors into their overall system of motives and values. In essence, these behaviors become a central part of their sense of self.

Figure 13-2

Possible sequence in which internalized motivation develops.
Based on Deci & Ryan, 1995.

value
Belief that a particular activity has direct or indirect benefits.

internalized motivation
Adoption of behaviors that others value, whether or not one's immediate environment reinforces those behaviors.

The decline in intrinsic motivation for academic subject matter is probably due to several factors. As children move through the grade levels, evidence mounts that they are not necessarily as competent as some of their peers, and they may shy away from activities for which they have low self-efficacy (Harter, 1992, 1996; Wigfield et al., 2006). Frequent reminders of the importance of good grades for promotion, graduation, and college admission may undermine their sense of self-determination (Deci & Ryan, 1992; Harter, Whitesell, & Kowalski, 1992). In addition, as youngsters grow older, they become more able to set and strive for long-term goals and begin to evaluate school subjects in terms of their relevance or *non*relevance to such goals, rather than in terms of intrinsic appeal (Otis et al., 2005). And they may grow increasingly bored and impatient with highly structured, repetitive activities (Battistich, Solomon, Kim, Watson, & Schaps, 1995; Larson, 2000). The following interview with a high school student named Alfredo illustrates this last point:

Adult: Do you think your classes are interesting?
Alfredo: Some of them are. But some of them are boring. You go to the same class every day and you just do the same type of work every day. Like biology, I like [the teacher of this] class. She's about the only one I like. And last year I had the same problem. The only class I liked last year was science. . . . We used to do different things every day . . . but like classes like Reading, you go inside, read a story with the same person every day. That's boring.
Adult: That's boring? So will you just not show up?
Alfredo: No, I'll go but I won't do nothing sometimes. (dialogue from Way, 1998, p. 198)

Despite the average downward trend in intrinsic motivation, some youngsters remain genuinely interested in academic subject matter throughout the school years, especially if they have internalized the importance of school learning (Otis et al., 2005; Walls & Little, 2005). Furthermore, virtually all children and adolescents have intrinsic motivation for *some* activities—perhaps for skateboarding, dance, or playing video games. The Observation Guidelines table "Recognizing Intrinsic Motivation in Children's Behaviors" lists characteristics and behaviors to look for.

Development of Goals

Many psychologists believe that human beings are purposeful by nature: People set goals for themselves and choose behaviors they think will help them achieve those goals (e.g., Dweck & Elliott, 1983; Locke & Latham, 2006; Shah, 2005). Some goals ("I want to finish reading my dinosaur book") are short term and transitory. Others ("I want to be a paleontologist") are long term and relatively enduring.

Short-term goals first emerge in infancy. As infants develop their motor skills (reaching, grabbing, crawling, etc.), they become increasingly capable of getting things they want, such as food on the high chair tray or Father's eyeglasses on a bedside table. Furthermore, they become increasingly capable of setting and working toward particular goals ("I want that toy, and I'm gonna get it!"). As you may recall from Chapter 6, Piaget proposed that infants begin to engage in such *goal-directed behavior* in the latter part of their first year. In fact, however, infants show signs of goal directedness well before this. For example, when one end of a string is attached to a 2-month-old baby's foot and the other end is attached to a mobile, at some point the baby realizes that foot motion makes the mobile move (Rovee-Collier, 1999). The infant begins to shake his or her foot more vigorously, apparently as a way to accomplish a particular goal: to gain an interesting visual display.

As children grow older, they increasingly adopt more broad-based, general goals and longer-term aspirations. Being happy and healthy, doing well in school, gaining popularity with peers, bringing honor to the family, having a rewarding career, and finding a long-term mate are just a few of the many possibilities (M. E. Ford, 1996; M. E. Ford & Smith, 2007; Schutz, 1994). Among these various goals are certain *core goals* that drive much of what youngsters do. For instance, those who attain high levels of academic achievement typically make classroom learning a high priority. Those who achieve at lower levels are often more concerned with maintaining social relationships (Wentzel & Wigfield, 1998; Wigfield et al., 1996). We look now at the nature of children's achievement and social goals, and also at their long-term future aspirations.

Observation Guidelines

Recognizing Intrinsic Motivation in Children's Behaviors

Characteristic	Look For	Example	Implication
Inquisitiveness	· Eagerness to explore and learn · Fascination with objects, other people, or both · Frequent and thoughtful questions · Lack of concern about external rewards for learning	Jamie often takes great interest in the new toys he finds in his preschool classroom. He is especially drawn to objects that come apart and can be reassembled in various ways.	Pique children's curiosity with puzzling situations, unusual phenomena, and opportunities to explore the physical world. Make sure their environment is safe for exploration.
High Self-Efficacy	· Obvious pleasure in mastering tasks · Eagerness to tackle challenging topics and activities · Willingness to take risks and make mistakes	Luana delights in trying to solve the brainteasers that her math teacher occasionally assigns for extra credit.	Give children the academic and social support they need to succeed at challenging tasks. Use evaluation procedures that encourage risk taking and allow for occasional mistakes.
Autonomy	· Pursuit of self-chosen activities · Willingness to engage in tasks that are only minimally structured	Mark, Reggie, and Cynthia form a rock band and practice together every chance they get. They actively seek out "gigs" both at school and in the community.	Provide opportunities for children to pursue self-chosen activities. Give them only as much structure as they need to be successful and achieve instructional goals.
Effective Learning Strategies	· Focus on making sense of subject matter, rather than on rote memorization of facts · Persistence in trying to solve difficult problems and understand complex ideas	At home, Lenesia reads an assigned chapter in her geography textbook. Despite reading the section on mountain formation several times, she is confused about how folded mountains form. The following day she asks her teacher to explain the process in a way she can better understand.	In both instruction and assessment activities, emphasize genuine understanding and integration of the subject matter, rather than rote memorization of isolated facts.
Long-Term Interests	· Consistent selection of a particular topic when choices are given · Frequent initiation of activities in a particular domain	Whenever his after-school group goes to the local library, Connor looks for books about military battleships and aircraft.	Relate instructional subject matter to children's interests and needs. Give them occasional choices regarding the topics they study and write about.
Priorities	· Consistent pursuit of certain activities over other alternatives · Apparent adoption of other people's values (e.g., a strong work ethic, the importance of maintaining a well-organized work space) as one's own (this characteristic reflects *internalized* motivation)	Audrey is clearly frustrated when unexpected events at home prevent her from doing a homework assignment as thoroughly as she'd like. "Even though I got an A," she says later, "I didn't do as well as I *could* have if I'd had more time."	Encourage activities that will be in youngsters' best interest over the long run. Do so in a warm, supportive environment in which youngsters have input into decision making.

Achievement Goals

Let's return once again to the opening case study. Sara is primarily concerned with constructing a kite that flies well, and she redesigns it three times to make it more aerodynamic. She doesn't mind the occasional stumbling blocks she encounters: "I mean everybody learns from their mistakes. I know I do" (D. K. Meyer et al., 1997, p. 511). In contrast, Amy sticks with her initial kite design, one that is easy to make but never gets off the ground. She says that she is primarily concerned with pleasing her teacher and parents, acknowledges that she rarely takes risks at school if a good grade is at stake, and then adds, "I feel lazy because I don't like to make challenges for myself, to make goals. I just like to . . . do it as I go along, not make goals or challenges" (p. 510).

mastery goal
Desire to acquire additional knowledge or master new skills (also known as a *learning goal*).

Both girls want to do well in school; that is, they both have *achievement goals*. However, their reasons for wanting to do well are quite different. Sara has a **mastery goal:** She wants to acquire new knowledge and skills related to kites and their construction, and to do so she must inevitably make a few mistakes. Amy has a **performance goal:** She wants to present herself as competent in the eyes of others and so tries to avoid mistakes if at all possible (e.g., Ames, 1992; Dweck & Elliott, 1983; Nicholls, 1984).[3]

Researchers have found it helpful to distinguish between two kinds of performance goals. In a **performance-approach goal,** the focus is on achieving positive outcomes, such as good grades, adult approval, or the respect of classmates. In a **performance-avoidance goal,** the focus is more on *avoiding undesirable* outcomes, such as exhibiting poor performance in public or being the subject of peer ridicule. Performance goals sometimes have an element of social comparison, in that children are concerned about how their accomplishments compare to those of their peers (Elliot & McGregor, 2000; Harackiewicz, Barron, Pintrich, Elliot, & Thrash, 2002).

In most instances, mastery goals are the optimal situation. To the extent that children and adolescents have mastery goals, they engage in the very activities that will help them learn: They pay attention at school, study in effective ways, and learn from their mistakes. Furthermore, they have a healthy perspective about learning, effort, and failure: They realize that learning is a process of trying hard and persevering even after temporary setbacks (E. M. Anderman & Maehr, 1994; Dweck & Elliott, 1983; Dweck, Mangels, & Good, 2004).

In contrast, children with performance goals—especially those with performance-*avoidance* goals—may be so concerned about how others evaluate them that they stay away from challenging tasks that would help them master new skills (Dweck, 1986; Urdan, 1997). Performance-*approach* goals are a mixed bag: They sometimes have very positive effects, spurring children on to achieve at high levels, especially in combination with mastery goals (Hidi & Harackiewicz, 2000; Linnenbrink, 2005). Yet by themselves, performance-approach goals may be less beneficial than mastery goals: To accomplish them, children may exert only the minimal effort required and use relatively superficial learning strategies such as rote memorization (Gabriele, 2007; Midgley, Kaplan, & Middleton, 2001). Performance-approach goals appear to be most detrimental when children are fairly young (e.g., in the elementary grades) and have low self-efficacy for classroom tasks (Hidi & Harackiewicz, 2000; A. Kaplan & Midgley, 1997; Midgley et al., 2001).

Mastery goals, performance-approach goals, and performance-avoidance goals are not necessarily mutually exclusive. On many occasions children may simultaneously have two kinds, or even all three (Covington & Müeller, 2001; Hidi & Harackiewicz, 2000; Meece & Holt, 1993). However, the relative prevalence of different achievement goals changes with age. Most young children seem to be primarily concerned with mastery goals. But by the time they reach second grade, they begin to show signs of having performance goals as well, and such goals become increasingly prevalent as they move into middle school and high school (Eccles & Midgley, 1989; Elliot & McGregor, 2000; Nicholls, Cobb, Yackel, Wood, & Wheatley, 1990). The greater emphasis on performance goals at older ages is probably due partly to youngsters' growing awareness of how their performance compares with that of peers and partly to an increasing focus on grades and other evaluations at the upper grade levels (Eccles et al., 1998; Nicholls et al., 1990).

As children get older, they become increasingly concerned with performance goals (such as impressing peers), sometimes at the expense of mastering school subject matter.

Social Goals

As you learned in Chapter 11, human beings seem to have a basic *need for relatedness*—that is, they want to feel socially connected with, and to secure the love and respect of, other people. For infants and toddlers, this need is reflected in early efforts to engage other people through crying, smiling, eye contact, and imitation, as well as in the close attachments they form with one or more caregivers (e.g., Striano, 2004). For many school-age children and adolescents, it may be reflected in the high priority they put on interacting with friends, sometimes at the expense of finishing chores, schoolwork, or other assigned tasks (W. Doyle, 1986; Wigfield, Eccles, Mac Iver, Reuman, & Midgley, 1991). In an interview in the "Intrinsic

performance goal
Desire to demonstrate high ability and make a good impression.

performance-approach goal
Desire to look good and receive favorable judgments from others.

performance-avoidance goal
Desire not to look bad or receive unfavorable judgments from others.

[3]You may sometimes see the term *learning goal* or *task involvement* instead of *mastery goal* and the term *ego involvement* instead of *performance goal* (e.g., Dweck & Elliott, 1983; Locke & Latham, 2006; Nicholls, 1984).

Motivation: Late Adolescence" video in MyEducationLab, 15-year-old Greg reveals the importance of social relationships in his life at school:

Interviewer:	What do you like best about school?
Greg:	Lunch.
Interviewer:	Lunch?
Greg:	All the social aspects. . . . Just friends and cliques. . . .

Like Greg, many high school students find the nonacademic aspects of school to be the most enjoyable and rewarding parts of the day (Certo et al., 2002; Otis et al., 2005).

Consistent with their need for relatedness, children and adolescents are apt to have a variety of **social goals,** perhaps including the following:

- Forming and maintaining friendly or intimate relationships with other people
- Gaining other people's approval
- Becoming part of a cohesive, mutually supportive group
- Achieving status and prestige within a peer group
- Meeting social obligations and keeping interpersonal commitments
- Assisting and supporting others, and ensuring their welfare
  (Berndt & Keefe, 1996; Dowson & McInerney, 2001; M. E. Ford, 1996; M. E. Ford & Smith, 2007; Hicks, 1997; Schutz, 1994)

Young people's social goals affect their behavior and performance in the classroom and other group settings. For instance, if they are seeking friendly relationships with peers or are concerned about others' welfare, they may eagerly engage in such activities as cooperative learning and peer tutoring (Dowson & McInerney, 2001). If they want to gain adults' attention and approval, they are apt to strive for good grades and in other ways shoot for performance goals (Hinkley, McInerney, & Marsh, 2001). A desire for peer approval can lead to a focus on performance goals as well, especially if youngsters are concerned about making a good impression (L. H. Anderman & Anderman, 1999). And if youngsters are seeking the approval of *low-achieving* peers, they may exert little effort in their studies (Berndt, 1992; B. B. Brown, 1993; Steinberg, 1996).

Future Aspirations

Children and adolescents often set long-term goals for themselves, in part by expanding their sense of self to envision possible *future selves* they might become (Harter, 1999; Oyserman & Markus, 1993; also see Chapter 12). For instance, they may hope to go to college, and they may want to get married, raise a family, or have a career in a certain field. Even young children set such goals for themselves but are apt to change their minds frequently—perhaps wanting to be a firefighter one week and professional basketball player the next. By middle to late adolescence, however, many (though by no means all) settle on a narrower range of careers and life paths they want to pursue (Marcia, 1980).

To a considerable degree, the long-term goals that adolescents set for themselves are related to their self-efficacy for being successful in various roles and careers (Bandura et al., 2001). Many are fairly optimistic. For instance, many teenagers in low-income, inner-city neighborhoods aspire to professional careers, perhaps in medicine, law, teaching, or computer science, even though few adults in their lives have had the education and support to pursue such careers themselves (Hemmings, 2004; B. L. Wilson & Corbett, 2001). Whether adolescents actually achieve their ambitious goals is, in part, the result of their ability to connect what they do *now* with their chances for being successful in the distant future (R. B. Miller & Brickman, 2004; Simons, Vansteenkiste, Lens, & Lacante, 2004).

Coordinating Multiple Goals

Most children and adolescents simultaneously have numerous and varied goals that they must juggle in one way or another. Sometimes they find activities that allow them to achieve several goals simultaneously. For instance, they might satisfy both achievement goals and social goals by forming a study group to prepare for an exam. But at other times they may believe they have to abandon one goal to satisfy another (Boekaerts, de Koning, & Vedder, 2006; McCaslin

social goal
Goal related to establishing or maintaining relationships with other people.

& Good, 1996; Phelan, Yu, & Davidson, 1994). For example, youngsters who want to do well in school may choose not to perform at their best so that they can maintain relationships with peers who don't value academic achievement. Students with mastery goals in particular subject areas may find that the multiple demands of school lead them to focus on performance goals (e.g., getting good grades) rather than studying the subject matter as thoroughly as they'd like. Brian, a junior high school student, expresses his ambivalence about striving for performance goals over mastery goals:

> I sit here and I say, "Hey, I did this assignment in five minutes and I still got an A+ on it." I still have a feeling that I could do better, and it was kind of cheap that I didn't do my best and I still got this A. . . . I think probably it might lower my standards eventually, which I'm not looking forward to at all. . . . I'll always know, though, that I have it in me. It's just that I won't express it that much. (S. Thomas & Oldfather, 1997, p. 119)

Teachers' instructional strategies and grading practices influence the extent to which their students have mastery goals at school and successfully juggle such goals with their social goals and performance goals (Midgley, 2002). For example, students are more likely to strive for mastery goals when assignments entice them to learn new skills (thus encouraging a focus on mastery), when they have occasional group projects (thus helping them also meet their social goals), and when evaluation criteria allow for risk taking and mistakes (thus helping them meet their performance goals). Students are unlikely to strive for mastery goals when assignments ask little of them (consider Brian's concern about low standards), when their teachers insist that they compete with one another for resources or high test scores, and when any single failure has a significant impact on final grades.

Development of Attributions

In the opening case study, Amy has not gotten her kite to fly. Even though she has put little effort into designing and constructing the kite, she chalks up her failure to insufficient wind and speculates that a successful kite would have been a matter of luck. In contrast, Sara, who has created a more aerodynamic kite, takes ownership of both her success ("I knew that I could really do it") and her little failures along the way ("I mean, everybody learns from their mistakes" [D. K. Meyer et al., 1997, pp. 511]).

The various explanations people have for their successes and failures—or in some cases for the successes and failures of others—are **attributions.** Children form a variety of attributions about the causes of events in their lives. They develop beliefs about why they do well or poorly on classroom assignments, why they are popular or have trouble making friends, why they are skilled athletes or total klutzes, and so on. They may attribute their successes and failures to such factors as aptitude or ability (how smart or proficient they are), effort (how hard they're trying), other people (how well an instructor teaches or how much other children like them), task difficulty (how easy or hard something is), luck, mood, illness, fatigue, or physical appearance. Such attributions differ from one another in three general ways (Weiner, 1986, 2000, 2004):

- *Internal versus external.* Children may attribute the causes of events to factors within themselves (*internal* things) or to factors outside themselves (*external* things). In the opening case study, Sara's attributions are clearly internal, whereas Amy's are mostly external.
- *Stable versus unstable.* Children may believe either that events are due to *stable* factors, which probably won't change much in the near future, or to *unstable* factors, which can vary from one occasion to the next. Sara attributes her success to her own, relatively stable ability ("I knew that I could really do it"). In contrast, Amy's explanations of "not enough wind" and "beginner's luck" are based on unstable factors that change unpredictably.
- *Controllable versus uncontrollable.* Children may attribute events to *controllable* factors, which they can influence and change, or to *uncontrollable* factors, which they cannot influence. Sara clearly sees herself in control of her success ("I knew I could put this together really well, 'cause I had a lot of confidence in myself"), whereas Amy of course has no control over bad weather conditions or a lucky break.

Children's attributions are self-constructed *interpretations* that don't always reflect reality. In general, children tend to attribute their successes to internal causes (e.g., high ability,

attribution
Belief about the cause of one's own or another person's success or failure.

"And remember, kids: If you play to the best of your ability and still lose the game, just blame it all on the umpire."

By blaming the umpire for a loss, children can more easily maintain a sense of competence. However, such external attributions are counterproductive when the true causes for success and failure are actually internal and within children's control.

MyEducationLab

Discover how an incremental versus an entity view affects adolescents' math achievement by completing an Understanding Research exercise in Chapters 13's Activities and Applications section in MyEducationLab.

incremental view (of ability)
Belief that ability can and does improve with effort and practice.

entity view (of ability)
Belief that ability is a "thing" that is relatively permanent and unchangeable.

hard work) and their failures to external causes (e.g., bad luck, other people's behaviors) (Marsh, 1990a; Whitley & Frieze, 1985). By patting themselves on the back for the things they do well and putting the blame elsewhere for poor performance, they can maintain a sense of competence (Clifford, 1990; Paris & Byrnes, 1989). Yet youngsters are most likely to be successful over the long run when they attribute successes and failures alike to *internal and controllable factors*—that is, to things they are doing or might do differently.

Researchers have observed several developmental trends in children's attributions:

- *Children increasingly distinguish among various attributions.* Up until age 5 or 6, children don't clearly discriminate among the possible causes of their successes and failures—effort, ability, luck, task difficulty, and so on (Eccles et al., 1998; Nicholls, 1990). Especially troublesome for young children is the distinction between effort and ability, which they gradually get a better handle on over time (Nicholls, 1990):

  - At about age 6, children begin to recognize that effort and ability are separate qualities. At this point they believe that people who try hardest are those who have the greatest ability and that effort is the primary determiner of successful outcomes.
  - At about age 9, they begin to understand that effort and ability can compensate for each other: People with less ability may have to exert greater effort to achieve the same outcomes as their more able peers.
  - By about age 13, children clearly differentiate between effort and ability. They realize that people differ both in their inherent ability to perform a task and in the amount of effort they exert. They also realize that a lack of ability sometimes precludes success no matter how much effort a person puts forth—that some people simply don't have what it takes to accomplish certain tasks.

- *Many children increasingly attribute their successes and failures to stable, uncontrollable characteristics rather than to effort.* Children have varying ideas of what *ability* is. Some have an **incremental view** of ability, thinking that they will almost certainly become proficient in an activity if they try hard and persevere. Others have an **entity view** of ability, believing that their capacity to perform various tasks is an inherited trait or is in some other way beyond their control (Dweck, 2000; Dweck & Leggett, 1988).

In the elementary grades, children tend to attribute their successes to effort and hard work, and so they are usually relatively optimistic about their chances for success and may work harder when they fail. By adolescence, however, they are apt to attribute success and failure more to a fairly stable ability that is beyond their control. To some degree, then, children move from an incremental view of ability in the elementary years to an entity view in adolescence (Dweck, 2000; Lockhart et al., 2002; Nicholls, 1990). Probably for this reason, adolescents are more discouraged by temporary setbacks than elementary school children are (Eccles & Wigfield, 1985; Pressley, Borkowski, & Schneider, 1987). And if they believe that their own low ability makes mastery of a topic or skill impossible, they may increasingly focus on performance goals (A. Kaplan, Middleton, Urdan, & Midgley, 2002).

Yet there are individual differences here: Some young people continue to hold an incremental view throughout high school. And others gradually discover the impact of hard work and effective learning strategies as they move through the high school grades (see the discussion of *epistemological beliefs* in Chapter 7). Adolescents who have an incremental view of ability are more likely to have mastery goals, seek out challenges to enhance their competence in various domains, persist in the face of difficulty, and achieve at high levels (Blackwell, Trzesniewski, & Dweck, 2007; Dweck & Leggett, 1988; Dweck et al., 2004).

- *As they get older, children and adolescents become more aware of the reactions that different attributions elicit.* Adults are often sympathetic and forgiving when children fail because of something beyond their control (illness, lack of ability, etc.) but frequently get angry when children fail simply because they didn't try very hard. By the time children reach fourth grade, most are aware of this fact and are apt to express attributions that elicit favorable reactions (Juvonen, 2000). For instance, a child who knows very well that she did poorly on a school assignment because she didn't put forth her best effort may distort the truth, telling her teacher that she doesn't "understand this stuff" or "wasn't feeling well."

Children also become more adept at tailoring their attributions for the ears of their peers. Generally speaking, fourth graders believe that their peers value diligence and hard work. Thus, they are likely to say that they did well on an assignment because they worked hard. In contrast, many eighth graders believe that their peers will disapprove of those who exert much effort on academic tasks. Thus, older students often convey the impression that they aren't working very hard—for instance, that they didn't study very much for an important exam (Howie, 2002; Juvonen, 2000).

• ***Children gradually develop predictable patterns of attributions and expectations for future performance.*** When young people have frequent success in new endeavors, they gain confidence that they can master a variety of tasks. They attribute their accomplishments to their own ability and effort and have an *I can do it* attitude known as a **mastery orientation.** Yet other youngsters, especially those who encounter a consistent string of failures, become increasingly pessimistic about their chances for future success. They develop an *I can't do it* attitude known as **learned helplessness.**

Even when children with a mastery orientation and those with learned helplessness initially have equal ability, those with a mastery orientation behave in ways that lead to higher achievement over the long run. In particular, they set ambitious goals, seek out new challenges, and persist in the face of obstacles. Children with learned helplessness behave quite differently. Because they underestimate their ability, they set goals they can easily accomplish, avoid challenges that might actually enhance their learning and development, and respond to failure in counterproductive ways (e.g., giving up quickly) that almost guarantee future failure (Dweck, 2000; Graham, 1989; C. Peterson, 1990; Seligman, 1991).

Occasionally preschoolers develop learned helplessness about a particular activity if they consistently fail at it, and they may conclude that they are "bad" children overall (Burhans & Dweck, 1995; Dweck, 2000). By age 5 or 6, a few children begin to show a general inclination toward learned helplessness that persists over time. Such children express little confidence about tackling challenging tasks and quickly abandon tasks at which they initially struggle (D. I. Ziegert, Kistner, Castro, & Robertson, 2001). By and large, however, children rarely exhibit extreme forms of learned helplessness before age 8, perhaps because they still believe that success is due largely to their own efforts (Eccles et al., 1998; Lockhart et al., 2002; Paris & Cunningham, 1996). Feelings of helplessness are more common in adolescence. For instance, some middle schoolers believe they have no control over things that happen to them and are at a loss for strategies that might get them on the road to success (Paris & Cunningham, 1996; C. Peterson, Maier, & Seligman, 1993).

Origins of Attributions

To some extent, children's attributions are the result of their previous success and failure experiences (Covington, 1987; Hong, Chiu, & Dweck, 1995). Those who usually succeed when they give a task their best shot are likely to believe that success is due to internal factors such as effort or high ability. Those who frequently fail despite considerable effort are likely to believe that success is due to something beyond their control—perhaps to a lack of genetic potential or to such external factors as luck or an adult's arbitrary and capricious judgments.

But children also pick up on other people's beliefs about why they have done well or poorly (Cimpian, Arce, Markman, & Dweck, 2007; Hareli & Weiner, 2002). Sometimes others' attributions are quite explicit, as the following statements illustrate:

• "That's wonderful. Your hard work has really paid off, hasn't it?" *(effort)*
• "You did it! You're so smart!" *(fairly stable ability)*
• "Hmmm, maybe this just isn't something you're good at." *(ability once again)*
• "Maybe you're just having a bad day." *(luck)*

A combination of observing chronic failure in oneself and hearing unflattering attributions from others can be devastating, as a journal entry by a high school student with an undiagnosed learning disability reveals:

> When I told one teacher in jr. high that I thought I had dyslexia, he told me that I was just lazy. Yeah, right! Me, lazy? I would end up with the same routine before every vocabulary test or

mastery orientation
General belief that one is capable of accomplishing challenging tasks, accompanied by an intent to master such tasks.

learned helplessness
General belief that one is incapable of accomplishing tasks and has little or no control of the environment.

important assignment. I would spend a week trying to memorize words that, no matter what I did, I couldn't spell right. On test days, I would turn in the test, and get an F. All I could do was hope that I'd do better on the next one.

It only got worse in high school, where there were more spelling and essay tests, with more complicated words that seemed too impossible to memorize. Finally, I just started to think, "Why should I even try? I am just going to end up with an 'F' anyway." It seems that an "F" was going to symbolize what I would end up in the future. (The Freedom Writers, 1999, p. 147)

In some instances adults communicate attributions indirectly rather than explicitly. For example, when adults criticize and express anger about children's poor performance, they imply that children have the ability to master the task and simply aren't trying hard enough. When they instead express pity, they imply that low ability is the reason for the failure (Graham, 1997; Pintrich & Schunk, 2002; Weiner, 1984). Adults communicate low ability, too, when they praise easy successes, provide unneeded assistance on easy tasks, or encourage children to abandon challenging ones (Hokoda & Fincham, 1995; Schunk & Pajares, 2004; Stipek, 1996). As children get older, they become increasingly attuned to such subtle messages (Barker & Graham, 1987).

Children's attributions inevitably influence the extent to which they are intrinsically or extrinsically motivated. Internal, controllable attributions should enhance children's sense of self-efficacy and sense of self-determination and therefore should increase their intrinsic motivation (Dweck, 2000; Weiner, 1986). When youngsters have little or no sense of control over their successes and failures or over their lives more generally, consistent use of extrinsic reinforcers (praise, special privileges, etc.) may sometimes be necessary to help them learn that their actions *do* affect the things that happen to them (J. Cameron, 2001).

Attributions, then, are an important source of diversity in youngsters, as indicated in the Basic Developmental Issues table "Contrasting Extrinsic and Intrinsic Motivation." We now look more closely at diversity in motivation.

Basic Developmental Issues

Contrasting Extrinsic and Intrinsic Motivation

Issue	Extrinsic Motivation	Intrinsic Motivation
Nature and Nurture	Primary reinforcers satisfy inborn and presumably inherited needs (e.g., hunger, thirst). Secondary reinforcers acquire their reinforcing effects through regular association with primary reinforcers in a child's environment.	Children appear to have a natural curiosity about their world. Their needs to feel competent and resolve apparent inconsistencies may also be inborn. Other factors that contribute to intrinsic motivation, such as self-efficacy, self-determination, interest-arousing situations, and internalized values depend largely on environmental conditions.
Universality and Diversity	By and large, primary reinforcers are universal around the world. Secondary reinforcers (e.g., praise) are *learned* reinforcers; thus, their effectiveness differs from child to child.	Innate sources of motivation, such as curiosity and the need for competence, are universal, as is the goal-directed nature of human behavior. Yet children have diverse interests, values, and goals. They also form different attributions for the things that happen to them, and such attributions influence their intrinsic motivation for particular activities.
Qualitative and Quantitative Change	Children increasingly learn to delay gratification, a trend that reflects quantitative change. Occasionally children respond differently to certain reinforcers than they have previously—a shift that reflects a qualitative change. For instance, a child who responds favorably to a teacher's praise in the elementary grades may later, as an adolescent, work hard to *avoid* teacher praise, perhaps for fear of being ridiculed as "teacher's pet."	Children shift from exclusively pursuing their own interests to internalizing some of the priorities and values of people around them, reflecting qualitative change. But for many youngsters, intrinsic motivation for learning academic subject matter declines over the school years, reflecting quantitative change.

Diversity in Motivation

Children and adolescents at any single age level can differ considerably in their responses to particular reinforcers (especially secondary reinforcers), as well as in their intrinsic motivation, long-term goals, and attributions. Such diversity is due largely to differences in young people's environments and past experiences.

Yet some diversity in motivation is due to biology. Sometimes biology has a direct impact on motivation. For example, temperamental differences influence children's inclinations either to be curious about and explore their surroundings or, in contrast, to cling to a caregiver for security (Keogh, 2003). And children with attention-deficit hyperactivity disorder (many of whom have poor impulse control) tend to have difficulty delaying gratification (Hoerger & Mace, 2006; Neef et al., 2005).

At other times biology's effects are indirect. This is the case, for instance, when disabilities limit what children can do. Many children with significant physical disabilities have little sense of self-determination because they must depend heavily on other people to help them meet their needs and achieve their goals (Sands & Wehmeyer, 1996). And children with cognitive disabilities (e.g., mental retardation or an undiagnosed learning disability) may show signs of learned helplessness about classroom tasks if their past efforts have repeatedly met with failure (Hersh, Stone, & Ford, 1996; B. Jacobsen, Lowery, & DuCette, 1986; Zambo & Brem, 2004).

Most diversity in children's motivation reflects idiosyncratic differences in children's environments and inherited characteristics. Yet some variation reflects common differences between males and females and among members of distinct cultural and ethnic groups.

Gender Differences

Researchers have observed gender differences in children's interests as early as age 4. On average, young boys are more likely to develop interests that involve acquiring considerable knowledge about a specific topic (e.g., about frogs, dinosaurs, or a particular sport) and to pursue this topic in depth. In contrast, young girls show more interest in creative activities such as drawing and painting (J. M. Alexander et al., 2008; K. E. Johnson et al., 2004). Furthermore, beginning in the elementary grades, boys and girls tend to find greater or lesser value in various academic domains depending, in part, on whether they view these domains as being stereotypically appropriate for their gender. Many children (but certainly not all of them) perceive some domains (e.g., writing, instrumental music) to be for girls and others (e.g., math, science) to be for boys (Eccles et al., 1998; Jacobs et al., 2005; Pajares & Valiante, 1999).

On average, girls are more concerned about doing well in school: They are more engaged in classroom activities, work more diligently on school assignments, and are more likely to graduate from high school (Duckworth & Seligman, 2006; Halpern, 1992, 2006; H. M. Marks, 2000; McCall, 1994). Furthermore, girls are currently more interested in getting a college education than boys are, and in many countries more females than males earn college degrees (Halpern et al., 2007; National Science Foundation, 2007).

Despite girls' eagerness to achieve academically, they tend to have less confidence about their abilities. When researchers compare girls and boys who have equal achievement levels, they find that girls have higher self-efficacy in gender-stereotypical "girl" domains (e.g., reading, the arts, social studies) and boys have higher self-efficacy in gender-stereotypical "boy" domains (Wigfield et al., 2006). In general, however, girls tend to underestimate their competence, whereas boys tend to overestimate it (D. A. Cole et al., 1999; Eccles et al., 1998; Pajares, 2005; also see Chapter 12). In addition, girls (especially many high-achieving girls) are more easily discouraged by failure than boys (Dweck, 1986, 2000). We can explain this difference, at least in part, by looking at gender differences in attributions. Some researchers have observed a tendency for boys to attribute their successes to a fairly stable ability and their failures to lack of effort, thus displaying the attitude that *I know I can do this if I work at it*. Girls tend to show the reverse pattern: They attribute their successes to effort and their failures to lack of ability, believing that *I don't know whether I can keep on doing it, because I'm not very good at this type of thing*. When encountering failure, then, boys are apt to have an incremental view of ability and girls are apt to have an entity view. Gender differences in attributions, which can appear even when youngsters' previous achievement levels have been equal, are most often observed in stereotypically male domains such as mathematics and sports (Dweck, 2000; Fennema, 1987; Stipek, 1984; Vermeer et al., 2000).

Historically, boys have had more ambitious career aspirations than girls (Deaux, 1984; Lueptow, 1984). In recent years, many girls—especially those in Western countries—have also begun to set their sights on challenging professions (Bandura et al., 2001; Lapan, Tucker, Kim, & Kosciulek, 2003). But even as traditional boundaries delineating "appropriate" professions for men and for women have begun to melt away, many adolescents limit themselves to gender-stereotypical careers (Lippa, 2002; Weisgram, Bigler, & Liben, 2007). Gender differences in career choices appear to be partly due to differences in self-efficacy for various academic domains (Bandura et al., 2001; Jacobs et al., 2002). Also, girls are more likely than boys to be attracted to people-helping professions (e.g., teaching, counseling) and to be concerned about balancing a career with family life (Chipman, 2005; Leaper & Friedman, 2007; Mahaffy & Ward, 2002).

Cultural and Ethnic Differences

Children and adolescents everywhere are naturally curious about their physical world and about the society in which they live. But some aspects of intrinsic motivation vary from culture to culture. For example, the amount and forms that autonomy and self-determination take differ considerably from group to group (d'Ailly, 2003; Rothbaum & Trommsdorff, 2007). Adults in some Native American communities give children far more independence and autonomy, and do so at an earlier age, than do many adults in mainstream American culture (Deyhle & LeCompte, 1999). In contrast, many African American parents give children *less* autonomy than the average American parent, apparently as a way of ensuring children's safety in potentially hostile environments (Hale-Benson, 1986; McLoyd, 1998b). And in some Asian cultures, young people often prefer that people they trust (parents, teachers, respected peers, etc.) make important choices for them (Hufton, Elliott, & Illushin, 2002; Iyengar & Lepper, 1999; Vansteenkiste, Zhou, Lens, & Soenens, 2005). Perhaps these children see trusted others as people who can make *wise* choices—choices that will ultimately lead to more harmonious interpersonal relationships and higher levels of learning and competence (Bao & Lam, 2008; Heine, 2007).

Children and adolescents from many ethnic and cultural groups place high value on getting a good education (Gallimore & Goldenberg, 2001; Okagaki, 2001; Phalet et al., 2004). But to some degree, different cultural groups seem to encourage different kinds of values related to school learning. For example, many Asian societies (e.g., many people in China, Japan, and Russia) emphasize learning for learning's sake: With knowledge comes personal growth, better understanding of the world, and greater potential to contribute to society. Important for these cultures, too, are hard work and persistence in academic studies, even if such studies are not intrinsically enjoyable (Hess & Azuma, 1991; Hufton et al., 2002; J. Li, 2006; J. Li & Fischer, 2004). Students from European American backgrounds are less likely to be diligent when classroom topics have little intrinsic appeal, but they often find value in academic subject matter that piques their curiosity and in assignments that require creativity, independent thinking, or critical analysis (Hess & Azuma, 1991; Kuhn & Park, 2005).

Youngsters from diverse cultural backgrounds may also define academic success differently and as a result may set different achievement goals. For instance, on average, Asian American students shoot for higher grades than students from other ethnic groups, in part because they believe their parents would be angry if they got grades lower than A– (Steinberg, 1996). Even so, Asian American students—and African American students as well—tend to focus more on mastery goals (i.e., on truly learning and understanding what they are studying) than European American students do (Freeman, Gutman, & Midgley, 2002; Qian & Pan, 2002; Shim & Ryan, 2006). And students raised in cultures that value group achievement over individual achievement (i.e., *collectivistic* cultures; see Chapter 3) tend to focus their mastery goals not on how much they alone can improve, but instead on how much they *and others* (perhaps classmates or siblings) can improve (A. Kaplan, 1998; J. Li, 2005).

Additional cultural differences are seen in the particular careers that youngsters shoot for and the particular activities that youngsters value. For instance, in China and Japan, children are encouraged to achieve and work in domains perceived to be especially important for the common good (e.g., science), rather than to pursue domains that are a good fit with their own talents and interests (Wigfield et al., 2004).

Finally, attributions for academic tasks and activities differ somewhat from culture to culture. For instance, students from Asian cultures are more likely to attribute classroom success and failure to unstable factors (e.g., effort, temporary situational conditions) than students brought up in Western cultures (J. Li & Fischer, 2004; Lillard, 1997; Weiner, 2004). Another common finding is a higher-than-average frequency of learned helplessness in children and adolescents of color (e.g., Graham, 1989; Holliday, 1985). Low teacher expectations and discriminatory practices in society at large may contribute to students' pessimism about their chances for success (Eccles et al., 1998; van Laar, 2000; Weiner, 2004). For instance, after consistently encountering racial prejudice in day-to-day activities, some students may begin to believe that because of the color of their skin, they have little chance of success no matter what they do.

The Developmental Trends table "Motivation at Different Age Levels" on pages 498–499 identifies motivational characteristics and examples of motivational diversity you are likely to see in different age-groups.

> **situated motivation**
> Phenomenon in which aspects of the immediate environment enhance motivation to learn particular things or behave in particular ways.

Motivating Children and Adolescents

A common misconception about motivation is that it is something children and adolescents "carry around" inside of them—for instance, that some students are consistently motivated to learn at school and others are not. It's certainly true that some sources of motivation *do* come from within. However, it's equally true that youngsters' immediate environments can have dramatic effects on their motivation to learn and achieve. Such environment-dependent motivation is known as **situated motivation** (Hickey & Granade, 2004; Paris & Turner, 1994). Yet simple pep talks ("I know you can do it if you try!") are not terribly helpful in motivating youngsters, especially for the long run (Brophy, 2004). Far more effective is providing scaffolding and guidance for challenging tasks, thereby enticing children to tackle those tasks largely for the pleasure and sense of competence they bring (Eccles, 2007; Hidi & Renninger, 2006; Lodewyk & Winne, 2005). The following strategies are also widely recommended:

• ***Focus on promoting intrinsic (rather than extrinsic) motivation.*** Externally imposed consequences—praise, money, good grades, and so on—often bring about desired changes in children's behavior. Such reinforcers have disadvantages, however. Although they provide a source of extrinsic motivation, they can undermine children's *intrinsic* motivation if children perceive them to be controlling, manipulative, or in some other way limiting their autonomy and sense of self-determination (Deci, Koestner, & Ryan, 2001; Vansteenkiste, Lens, & Deci, 2006). Furthermore, externally imposed reinforcers may communicate the message that assigned tasks are unpleasant chores (why else would a reinforcer be necessary?), rather than activities to be carried out and enjoyed for their own sake (Hennessey, 1995; Stipek, 1993).

Ideally, then, teachers, parents, and other adults should focus children's attention not on the external consequences of their efforts but on the internal pleasures (enjoyment, satisfaction, pride, etc.) that accompany certain tasks and activities. Adults can also increase children's intrinsic motivation for learning important topics and skills using strategies such as these:

• Communicating enthusiasm for a topic
• Piquing children's curiosity with new and intriguing objects and phenomena
• Incorporating fantasy, adventure, or suspense into activities
• Creating disequilibrium by presenting puzzling phenomena
• Getting children physically involved with a topic (e.g., through role playing or hands-on experimentation)
• Relating important skills and subject matter to children's interests and goals
• Offering choices when several alternatives will be equally effective in helping children acquire desired skills
• Identifying areas in which each child can be especially successful (Brophy, 2004; Patall, Cooper, & Wynn, 2008; Schraw, Flowerday, & Lehman, 2001)

You can see such factors at work in a Building Teaching Skills and Dispositions exercise in MyEducationLab.

MyEducationLab

Go to the Building Teaching Skills and Dispositions exercise "Identifying Strategies for Motivating Children and Adolescents" in Chapter 13 of MyEducationLab to hear youngsters of different ages describe things they find motivating.

Developmental Trends

Motivation at Different Age Levels

Age	What You Might Observe	Diversity	Implications
Infancy (Birth–2 Years) 	· Curiosity about objects and people · Enthusiasm for exploring the environment · Some goal-directed behavior as early as 3 months · Little or no need for praise, especially in the first year; greater appreciation of praise after age 1	· Temperament and culture influence children's willingness to explore and experiment with their physical environment. · Attachment security influences children's willingness to explore (see Chapter 11). · Children with significant disabilities may show less interest in physical exploration than their nondisabled peers.	· Create a predictable, affectionate environment in which children feel comfortable exploring and trying new things. · Provide new and unusual objects that pique children's curiosity. · Identify objects and events that can capture the interest of children with disabilities.
Early Childhood (2–6 Years) 	· Preference for small, immediate rewards over larger, delayed ones · Overconfidence about one's ability to perform new tasks · Rapidly changing, situation-dependent interests; emergence of stable interests in some children · Focus on obtaining the approval of adults more than that of peers · Focus on mastery (rather than performance) goals · Little understanding of the probable causes of successes and failures	· Differences in desire for social interaction are evident as early as age 3 or 4. · Children who begin school without basic knowledge of colors, shapes, letters, or numbers may see obvious differences between their own abilities and those of peers—differences that may set the stage for poor self-efficacy down the road if the missing knowledge is not soon addressed. · Learned helplessness in a particular domain occasionally appears as early as age 4 or 5, especially after a history of failure.	· Provide a wide variety of potentially interesting toys, storybooks, props for dramatic play, and other equipment. · Praise (or in some other way reinforce) desired behaviors as soon as they occur. · Provide the guidance and support children need in order to experience success more often than failure.
Middle Childhood (6–10 Years)	· Increasing ability to delay gratification · Increasing awareness of how one's own performance compares with that of peers; more realistic assessment of abilities · Increasing prevalence of performance goals · Increasing distinction between effort and ability as possible causes of success and failure; tendency to attribute successes to hard work	· As a result of low self-efficacy, children with a history of learning problems have less intrinsic motivation to learn academic subject matter. · Some very bright, talented girls may be reluctant to do their best because of concerns about appearing unfeminine or surpassing peers. · Children of color and children with disabilities are somewhat more likely to develop learned helplessness about their ability to achieve academic success.	· Communicate the message that with appropriate effort and support, virtually *all* children can master basic knowledge and skills in academic subject matter. · Focus children's attention on the progress they are making, rather than on how their performance compares to that of peers. · Stress the importance of learning for the intrinsic pleasure it brings; downplay the importance of grades and other external evaluations.

continued

• ***Enhance children's self-efficacy for mastering important knowledge and skills.*** One critical way to enhance children's self-efficacy in a particular domain is, of course, to help them achieve success in the domain—for instance, by tailoring instruction to their existing ability levels, scaffolding their efforts, and so on (Lodewyk & Winne, 2005; Valentine, Cooper, Bettencourt, & DuBois, 2002). Another effective approach is to show them *other people's* successes. When children see peers of similar age and ability successfully accomplish a task, they are more likely to believe that they, too, can accomplish it. In one study (Schunk & Hanson, 1985), elementary school children having trouble with subtraction were given 25 subtraction problems to complete. Children who had seen another student successfully complete the problems got an average of 19 correct, whereas those who saw a teacher complete the problems got only 13 correct, and those who saw no model at all solved only 8.

In certain circumstances, adult models can also enhance children's self-efficacy, especially if the adults have characteristics and backgrounds similar to children's own. For in-

Developmental Trends (continued)

Age	What You Might Observe	Diversity	Implications
Early Adolescence (10–14 Years)	· Increasing interest in social activities; increasing concern about gaining approval of peers · Declining sense of competence, often accompanying the transition to middle school or junior high · Decline in intrinsic motivation to learn school subject matter; increasing focus on performance goals · Increasing belief that skill is the result of stable factors (e.g., inherited ability) rather than effort and practice · Increasing motivation to learn and achieve in stereotypically gender-appropriate domains	· Girls have a stronger desire to interact frequently with peers. · Some adolescents believe that demonstrating high achievement can interfere with popularity. · Adolescents from some ethnic groups (e.g., those from many Asian cultures) continue to place high value on adult approval. · Some individuals develop a general sense of learned helplessness about achieving academic success.	· Evaluate adolescents on the basis of how well they are achieving instructional objectives, not on how well their performance compares with that of their classmates. · Assign cooperative group projects that allow adolescents to interact with one another, display their unique talents, and contribute to the success of the group. · When youngsters exhibit a pattern of failure, provide the support they need to begin achieving success in their endeavors.
Late Adolescence (14–18 Years)	· Ability to postpone immediate pleasures in order to gain long-term rewards · Increasing stability of interests and priorities · Increasing focus on the utilitarian value of activities · Tendency to attribute successes and failures more to ability than to effort · Some tentative decisions about career paths	· Girls work harder on school assignments and are more likely to graduate from high school than boys. · Adolescents from Asian cultures often attribute their successes and failures to effort rather than ability. · Many teens have career aspirations that are stereotypically gender appropriate.	· Point out the relevance of various academic content domains for adolescents' long-term goals. · Design assignments in which adolescents apply academic content to real-world adult tasks and problems. · Allow teens to pursue personal interests within the context of particular academic domains.

Sources: Bandura et al., 2001; L. A. Bell, 1989; Burhans & Dweck, 1995; H. Cooper & Dorr, 1995; Corpus, McClintic-Gilberg, & Hayenga, 2006; Deshler & Schumaker, 1988; Durkin, 1995; Dweck, 1986, 2000; Eccles & Midgley, 1989; Eccles et al., 1998; Fewell & Sandall, 1983; Graham, 1989; L. Green et al., 1994; Halpern, 1992, 2006; Harter, 1992, 1996; Jacobs et al., 2002; B. Jacobsen et al., 1986; K. E. Johnson et al., 2004; Juvonen, 2000; Leaper & Friedman, 2007; Lieberman, 1993; Lillard, 1997; Linder, 1993; Lockhart et al., 2002; Nicholls, 1990; Otis et al., 2005; Pajares & Valiante, 1999; Paris & Cunningham, 1996; Peak, 1993; C. Peterson, 1990; Portes, 1996; Rotenberg & Mayer, 1990; Rovee-Collier, 1999; Schultz & Switzky, 1990; Seligman, 1991; Vaughn et al., 1984; Wigfield, Byrnes, & Eccles, 2006; Wigfield et al., 1991; Ziegert et al., 2001.

stance, young people from ethnic minority groups benefit from observing successful minority adults, and youngsters with disabilities become more optimistic about their own futures when they meet adults successfully coping with and overcoming disabilities (Pang, 1995; L. E. Powers, Sowers, & Stevens, 1995).

● *Maintain children's sense of self-determination when describing rules and giving instructions.* Every group situation needs a few rules and procedures to ensure that children act appropriately and activities run smoothly. Furthermore, teachers and other adults must often impose guidelines and restrictions about how children carry out assigned tasks. And some students need considerable structure to keep them consistently engaged in productive activities (Emmer & Gerwels, 2006). The trick is to present rules, procedures, guidelines, restrictions, and structure without communicating an intention to *control* children's behavior and thereby undermining children's sense of self-determination. Instead, adults should present these things as *information*—for instance, as conditions that can help children accomplish important goals and objectives (Hagger, Chatzisarantis, Barkoukis, Wang, & Baranowski, 2005; Koestner, Ryan, Bernieri, & Holt, 1984; N. E. Perry, Turner, & Meyer, 2006). Following are examples:

● "We can make sure everyone has an equal chance to speak and be heard if we listen without interrupting and if we raise our hands when we want to contribute to the discussion."

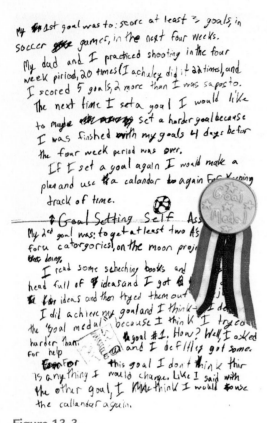

Figure 13-3

Children are often more motivated when they have specific goals to shoot for. Here 10-year-old Amaryth describes how she worked toward goals on the soccer field and in the classroom.

- "I'm giving you a particular format to follow when you do your math homework. If you use this format, it will be easier for me to figure out which concepts you understand and which ones you need more help with."

- "Let's remember that other children will be using the same paints and brushes later today, so we need to make sure everything we use now is still in tip-top shape when we're done. It's important, then, that we clean the brushes thoroughly when we're done painting."

- ***Encourage children to shoot for specific goals.*** Children often respond more favorably to goals they set for themselves than to goals others have set for them, possibly because self-chosen goals help them maintain a sense of self-determination (Lens, 2001; Wentzel, 1999). Yet many children and some adolescents have trouble conceptualizing a "future" that is abstract (e.g., getting a good education) and perhaps many years down the road (e.g., going to medical school) (Bandura, 1997; Husman & Freeman, 1999). They may initially respond more favorably to short-term, concrete goals—perhaps learning a certain number of math facts or irregular French verbs in a given week, getting the next belt in karate, or earning a merit badge in a scout troop (E. S. Alexander, 2006; Brophy, 2004; R. B. Miller & Brickman, 2004; Schunk & Rice, 1989). By setting and working for a series of short-term goals, youngsters get regular feedback about the progress they are making, acquire a greater sense of self-efficacy that they can master new skills, and achieve at higher levels (Kluger & DeNisi, 1998; Page-Voth & Graham, 1999; Schunk, 1996). In Figure 13-3, 10-year-old Amaryth describes goals she set for herself in athletics and academics, as well as how she worked to achieve her goals. Her teacher awarded her a Goal Medal for successfully meeting her goals.

As children reach adolescence, their increasing capacity for abstract thought allows many of them also to envision and work toward long-term goals (e.g., winning a spot on a varsity sports team or having a career in journalism). Yet perhaps as a result of low self-efficacy or limited financial resources, some of them set their sights quite low or in another way limit their future options. Teachers and other adults should not only encourage these young people to think ambitiously but also convince them that high goals are achievable. For instance, when encouraging girls to consider stereotypically masculine career paths, adults might provide examples of women who have led successful and happy lives in those careers. When encouraging teens from low-income families to think about going to college, adults might assist with filling out scholarship applications and scheduling appointments with college financial aid officers.

At the same time, it is essential that adolescents be realistic about the long-term goals toward which they strive. Doggedly pursuing unattainable career paths or other out-of-reach long-term goals is apt to undermine young people's physical and emotional well-being (G. E. Miller & Wrosch, 2007). In such instances the best course of action is to encourage youngsters to reconsider such goals and identify other options that might be reasonable substitutes (G. E. Miller & Wrosch, 2007).

- ***Encourage mastery goals as well as (ideally even more than) performance goals.*** To some degree, performance goals are inevitable in today's schools and in society at large. Children and adolescents will invariably look to their peers' performance as one criterion for evaluating their own performance, and many aspects of the adult world (gaining admission to college, seeking employment, working in private industry, etc.) are inherently competitive in nature. Yet adults do youngsters a disservice when they focus youngsters' attention on "looking good" and surpassing peers. When adults instead explain how certain knowledge and skills will be useful down the road, highlight ongoing progress, and acknowledge that effective learning requires exerting effort and making mistakes, they are emphasizing mastery goals that will enhance learning and achievement over the long run (Bong, 2001; Brophy, 2004; Urdan et al., 2002).

- ***Downplay the seriousness of failures.*** Children and adolescents are more apt to accept responsibility for their failures—and therefore to learn from them—if adults don't make a big deal of them (Katkovsky, Crandall, & Good, 1967; N. E. Perry & Winne, 2004). For instance, teachers might give students numerous opportunities to improve assignments and overall class grades (Ames, 1992). In some instances adults may also find it appropriate to focus children's attention on the *processes* they use to tackle assigned tasks and solve problems rather than on the final outcome of their efforts (Schunk & Swartz, 1993; Stipek & Kowalski, 1989). For example, a teacher may occasionally give an assignment with instructions like these:

> It doesn't matter at all how many you get right. In fact, these problems are kind of hard. I'm just interested in learning more about what [you] think about while [you're] working on problems like these. I want you to focus on the problem and just say out loud whatever you're thinking while you're working—whatever comes into your head. (Stipek & Kowalski, 1989, p. 387)

And under *no* circumstances should teachers insist that students display serious weaknesses—limited reading ability, poor math skills, and so on—in front of their classmates (Thorndike-Christ, 2008).

● ***Help youngsters meet their social goals.*** One of the reasons older children and adolescents focus so much on performance goals is that making a good impression will help them gain the respect and companionship of their peers. They encounter most of their peers at school and in other large-group situations and therefore will naturally make social goals a high priority in these settings (B. B. Brown, Eicher, & Petrie, 1986; Dowson & McInerney, 2001; Wentzel & Wigfield, 1998). The Development and Practice feature "Helping Children Meet Their Social Goals" suggests several ways in which educators can address youngsters' social needs within the context of academic instruction and other learning activities.

● ***Give encouraging messages about the causes of successes and failures.*** When commenting on children's successes, probably the best approach is to attribute their accomplishments partly to a relatively stable ability and partly to such controllable factors as effort and learning strategies (Schunk, 1990; Weiner, 1984). In this way, adults provide assurance

---

Development and Practice

Helping Children Meet Their Social Goals

· **Continually communicate the message that you like and respect the young people with whom you are working.**

A second-grade teacher tells a student that she saw his karate exhibition at the local mall over the weekend. "You were great!" she says. "How many years have you been studying karate?"

· **Plan learning tasks that involve social interaction.**

A sixth-grade social studies teacher incorporates classroom debates, small-group discussions, and cooperative learning tasks into each month's lesson plans.

· **Get youngsters involved in large projects in which they must all work toward the common good.**

The eighth graders at one middle school are sharply divided into "popular" and "unpopular" groups, and some students are routinely bullied or excluded from social interaction. The school music teacher suggests that a production of the musical *You're a Good Man, Charlie Brown* become a project for the entire class. All 92 eighth graders are either in the cast or working on costumes, scenery, or lighting. The sheer ambitiousness of the project and the fact that the class's efforts will eventually be on public display instill a cohesiveness and class spirit among the students, with formerly popular and unpopular students working collaboratively and respectfully with one another.

· **Teach strategies that enable youngsters to present themselves well to others.**

As fourth graders prepare for upcoming oral reports on their small-group science projects, their teacher offers suggestions for capturing their audience's interest. "You might present a puzzling question your classmates would really like to know the answer to," she says. "Or you might show them something that will surprise them. Hands-on activities are good, too. For example, perhaps you can think of a short, simple experiment they might conduct to arrive at the same conclusion *you* did."

· **Give praise in private when peers do not seem to value high achievement.**

A high school English teacher reads a particularly creative story written by a young man who, she knows, is quite concerned about maintaining his "cool" image. On the second page of his story (which the student's classmates are unlikely to see), she writes, "This is great work, Tony! I think it's good enough to enter into the state writing contest. Can we meet before or after school some day this week to talk more about the contest?"

· **Respect individual differences.**

A preschool teacher notices that some of his students have a greater need for social contact than others. Some children really seem to enjoy sociodramatic play activities, while others are more interested in manipulating and experimenting with physical objects. Although he interacts with all of the children regularly, he is careful not to interrupt when children are happily and productively engrossed in either interactive or solitary play activities.

Sources: M. E. Ford & Smith, 2007; Hamre & Pianta, 2005; Harter, 1999; Juvonen, 2000, 2006; Ormrod, 2008b; R. J. Stevens & Slavin, 1995; M. Thompson & Grace, 2001 (school play example); Wentzel & Wigfield, 1998; Wigfield et al., 1996.

that children are certainly capable of succeeding but remind them that continued success also requires work and perseverance. For example, a teacher might say:

- "You've done very well. Obviously you're good at this, and you've been trying very hard to get better."
- "Your project shows a lot of talent and a lot of hard work."

When identifying possible causes for failures, however, adults should focus primarily on effort and better strategies—attributions that are internal, unstable, and controllable—and they should usually give such feedback in private (Brophy, 2004; Cimpian et al., 2007; Dweck, 2000). Following are examples:

- "The more you practice, the better you will get."
- "Perhaps you need to study a little bit each night rather than waiting until the night before. And let's talk about how you might also study *differently* than you did last time."

When children's failures are consistently attributed to controllable factors such as lack of effort or ineffective strategies and when increased effort or new strategies do, in fact, produce success, children often work harder, persist longer in the face of failure, and seek help when they need it (Dweck & Elliott, 1983; Eccles & Wigfield, 1985; Graham, 1991; Robertson, 2000).

The most effective feedback—no matter whether it commends successes or identifies weaknesses—also maintains children's sense of self-determination. More specifically, it provides information about children's performance but doesn't convey a desire to control their behavior (Brophy, 2004; Burnett, 2001; Deci, 1992). For example, in complimenting a student who has written a good persuasive essay, a teacher might say, "Your arguments are well organized, easy to follow, and quite convincing" (emphasis on what the student has done well), rather than saying, "Good job in adhering to my guidelines and suggestions" (emphasis on following the teacher's instructions). And in admonishing students for off-task behavior during a cooperative learning activity, a teacher might ask, "Are you three going to have time to work on your project tonight if you don't finish it during class?" (emphasis on students' own time management concerns), rather than saying, "How many times do I have to remind this group to *get to work?*" (emphasis on keeping the students under control).

- ***Teach children to give themselves encouraging attribution messages as well.*** Numerous research studies have shown that children can be directly taught more productive attributions for their successes and failures, with higher achievement and more persistence in the face of failure often being the result (e.g., Berkeley, Mastropieri, & Scruggs, 2008; Dweck, 1975; Robertson, 2000). In these *attribution retraining* studies, children are asked to engage in a particular task (e.g., reading challenging text, solving arithmetic problems, constructing geometric puzzles), with occasional failures interspersed among more frequent successes. Within this context, one viable approach for changing attributions is for an adult to interpret each success in terms of high effort or good strategies and each failure in terms of insufficient effort or ineffective strategies. But even more effective is teaching children to explicitly attribute their *own* successes and failures to amount of effort or specific strategies (Berkeley et al., 2008; Dweck, 1975; J. W. Fowler & Peterson, 1981; Robertson, 2000).

Teachers must keep in mind that students' views of themselves and their abilities are not likely to change dramatically overnight (Hilt, 2005; Meece, 1994; Paris, 1990). Thus, efforts to help students acquire productive attributions must be an ongoing endeavor rather than a one-shot intervention.

- ***Use extrinsic reinforcers when necessary.*** Despite adults' best efforts, children sometimes have little interest in acquiring knowledge or skills critical for their later success in life. To encourage learning or desired behaviors in such situations, adults may have to provide extrinsic reinforcers—not only praise but perhaps also free time, grades, special privileges, or points toward a small prize. How can adults use such reinforcers without undermining children's intrinsic motivation? One effective strategy is to reinforce children not simply for doing something but for doing it *well*. Another is to communicate that an extrinsic reinforcer is merely a concrete acknowledgment of significant progress or achievement—an accomplishment about which

When used strategically over a short time period, extrinsic reinforcement can help children acquire foundational skills.

children should feel very proud (Brophy, 2004; J. Cameron, 2001). And especially when working with youngsters from cultures that place high priority on family or community ties, adults might point out the positive impact that children's actions have on other people (Abi-Nader, 1993; Dien, 1998; Suina & Smolkin, 1994). For example, a teacher might say, "Think how proud your family will be!" or "Everyone in school will appreciate the beautiful wall murals you all have painted in the hallway."

Whenever adults give reinforcement in a group situation, they should make sure that all children have a reasonable opportunity to earn it. For instance, they should be careful that in their attempts to improve the behavior of some children, they don't ignore other, equally deserving children. Furthermore, they should take into account the fact that a few children may have exceptional difficulty performing particular behaviors through no fault of their own. Consider the case of a young immigrant girl who had to adjust very quickly from a 10:00–5:00 school day in Vietnam to a 7:45–3:45 school day in the United States:

> [E]very week on Friday after school, the teacher would give little presents to kids that were good during the week. And if you were tardy, you wouldn't get a present. . . . I would never get one because I would always come to school late, and that hurt at first. I had a terrible time. I didn't look forward to going to school. (Igoa, 1995, p. 95)

When using concrete reinforcers, adults should help children delay gratification for longer and longer periods. For example, even 4- and 5-year-olds can learn to delay gratification for a few hours if their preschool teachers tell them that rewards for desired behaviors (e.g., sharing toys with other children) will be coming later in the day (S. A. Fowler & Baer, 1981). Teaching children effective waiting strategies—perhaps frequently reminding themselves, "If I wait a little longer, I will get a bigger cookie," or perhaps engaging in activities that get their minds off an upcoming reward—also enhances their ability to delay gratification (Binder, Dixon, & Ghezzi, 2000; Dixon & Cummings, 2001).

• **_Be especially attentive to the needs of students at risk._** **Students at risk** are students who have a high probability of failing to acquire the minimum academic skills necessary for success in the adult world. Many students at risk drop out before high school graduation, and many others graduate without basic skills in reading or mathematics (e.g., Boling & Evans, 2008; Laird, Kienzl, DeBell, & Chapman, 2007). Such individuals are often ill equipped to make productive contributions to their families, communities, or society at large.

Some students at risk have special educational needs, such as learning disabilities. Others have limited proficiency in English or in some other way have cultural backgrounds that don't mesh easily with the dominant culture at school. Still others may come from home environments in which academic success is neither supported nor encouraged (Barga, 1996; Payne, 2005; Phelan et al., 1994; Rumberger, 1995; Steinberg, Blinde, & Chan, 1984).

Children and adolescents at risk come from all socioeconomic levels, but youngsters of low-income, single-parent families are especially likely to leave school before high school graduation (Rumberger, 1995; Suh, Suh, & Houston, 2007). Boys are more likely to drop out than girls, and African Americans, Hispanic Americans, and Native Americans have higher dropout rates than other groups (L. S. Miller, 1995; Roderick & Camburn, 1999). Students at risk often have a long history of low academic achievement, ineffective learning strategies, poor relationships with teachers, and little emotional connectedness with their school (Belfiore & Hornyak, 1998; Christenson & Thurlow, 2004; V. E. Lee & Burkam, 2003; Suh et al., 2007).

Students at risk are a diverse group of individuals with a diverse set of needs and motives, but the motivational strategies we've listed in the preceding pages are critical for most of them. The Development and Practice feature "Encouraging and Supporting Students at Risk" offers additional suggestions. However, even the most motivated of youngsters will not succeed unless they also have some ability to direct and control their own actions and emotions. We turn to the development of such _self-regulation_ now.

Self-Regulation

As you've learned, children and adolescents have a greater sense of self-determination and are more intrinsically motivated when they can make choices about what they do and so can direct

student at risk
Student who has a high probability of failing to acquire the minimal academic skills necessary for success in the adult world.

Development and Practice

Encouraging and Supporting Students at Risk

- **Make the curriculum relevant to students' lives and needs.**

  In a unit on the physics of sound, a junior high school science teacher shows students how basic principles of sound reveal themselves in rock music. On one occasion the teacher brings in a guitar and explains why holding down a string at different points along the neck of the guitar creates different frequencies and thus different notes.

- **Use students' strengths to promote high self-efficacy in certain domains.**

  A low-income, inner-city elementary school forms a singing group (the "Jazz Cats") for which students must try out. The group performs at a variety of community events, and the students enjoy considerable visibility for their talent. Group members exhibit increased self-esteem, improvement in other school subjects, and greater teamwork and leadership skills.

- **Provide extra support for academic success.**

  At the beginning of class each day, a middle school teacher distributes a general outline that students can use to guide their note taking. She also writes two or three questions on the board that students should be able to answer at the end of the lesson.

- **Communicate optimism about students' chances for long-term personal and professional success.**

  A mathematics teacher at a low-income, inner-city high school recruits students to participate in an intensive math program. The teacher and students work on evenings, Saturdays, and vacations, and all of them later pass the Advanced Placement calculus exam (see the case study at the end of Chapter 10).

- **Show students that they are personally responsible for their successes.**

  A teacher says to a student, "Your essay about recent hate crimes in the community is very powerful. You've given the topic considerable thought, and you've clearly mastered some of the techniques of persuasive writing that we've talked about this semester. I'd like you to think seriously about submitting your essay to the local paper for its editorial page. Can we spend some time during lunch tomorrow fine-tuning the grammar and spelling?"

- **Get students involved in extracurricular activities.**

  A teacher encourages a student with a strong throwing arm to go out for the school baseball team and introduces the student to the baseball coach. The coach, in turn, expresses his enthusiasm for having the student join the team and asks several current team members to help him feel at home during team practices.

- **Involve students in school policy and management decisions.**

  At an inner-city high school, students and teachers hold regular "town meetings" to discuss issues of fairness and justice and establish rules for appropriate behavior. Meetings are democratic, with students and teachers alike having one vote apiece, and the will of the majority is binding.

Sources: Alderman, 1990; L. W. Anderson & Pellicer, 1998; Christenson & Thurlow, 2004; Cosden et al., 2001; Fredricks, Blumenfeld, & Paris, 2004; S. Goldstein & Brooks, 2006; Hamre & Pianta, 2005; A. Higgins, 1995 (town meetings example); Jenlink, 1994 (Jazz Cats example); Knapp, Turnbull, & Shields, 1990; Lee-Pearce et al., 1998; Milner, 2006.

the course of their lives to some degree. But making *wise* choices and directing oneself along productive paths require **self-regulation,** which includes capabilities such as the following:

- *Impulse control:* Resisting sudden urges to engage in forbidden or counterproductive behaviors
- *Emotional regulation:* Managing affective states so that they are productive and socially appropriate (see Chapter 11)
- *Self-socialization:* Forming beliefs about society's standards for behavior and voluntarily acting in accordance with those standards (see Chapter 12)
- *Goal setting:* Identifying and striving for valued, self-chosen goals
- *Delaying gratification:* Forgoing small, immediate rewards in anticipation of larger rewards at a later time
- *Self-motivation:* Creating conditions that make a task more engaging or rewarding
- *Self-regulated learning:* Directing and monitoring one's own attention and learning strategies in ways that promote effective cognitive processing (see Chapter 7)

As you discovered in Chapter 7, children who regulate their own learning and study habits are more academically successful than those who do not. Self-regulation is important in social relationships as well. Children who can control their emotional reactions and other behaviors in social contexts have better social skills and are more popular with peers than those who cannot (M. B. Bronson, 2000; Fabes et al., 1999; Patrick, 1997).

Developmental Trends in Self-Regulation

Many young children have considerable difficulty controlling their own behavior. Some parents in Western cultures complain about the "terrible twos," a period between the second and third birthdays when children are mobile enough to get into almost anything and make quite a fuss when they don't get their own way. Self-regulation requires several capabilities that are

self-regulation
Process of directing and controlling one's personal actions and emotions.

only beginning to emerge in young children. For instance, children must anticipate the consequences of various courses of action. They must also inhibit thoughts and behaviors that are unlikely to be productive. And they must have sufficient working memory capacity to think about what they want to do, how they might do it, and perhaps why they *shouldn't* do it. Such capabilities depend, in part, on neurological maturation in the early years (Biemiller et al., 1998; Blair, 2002; Dempster & Corkill, 1999; Rothbart, Sheese, & Posner, 2007).

As you've already learned in Chapters 5, 7, and 11, children become increasingly able to regulate their learning and emotional responses as they grow older. Researchers have identified three additional developmental trends in self-regulation:

• ***Children increasingly talk their way, and eventually think their way, through situations and tasks.*** The *self-talk* and *inner speech* that Vygotsky described seem to be key mechanisms through which children become able to regulate their behavior. As children acquire language skills, they begin to talk themselves through new challenges ("To tie my shoe, I need to put one lace over and then under the other; then I need to make a loop . . ."). Children gradually internalize their self-talk, first whispering to themselves and eventually just *mentally* telling themselves what they should do. Such external and internal self-talk help children self-regulate not only simple physical tasks such as tying shoes but also more complex skills such as resolving interpersonal conflicts and keeping one's mind productively focused during a classroom test (Berk, 1994; Biemiller et al., 1998; K. Carter & Doyle, 2006; Schutz & Davis, 2000).

• ***External rules and restrictions gradually become internalized.*** Children can comply with simple requests and restrictions by the time they are 12 to 18 months old (Kaler & Kopp, 1990; Kopp, 1982). As they become increasingly verbal, they begin to use self-talk to prevent themselves from engaging in prohibited behaviors even when caregivers are absent—for instance, saying "no" or "can't" to themselves as they begin to reach for an electric outlet (Kochanska, 1993). By age 3 or 4, many children are acquiring flexible strategies for regulating their own behavior in accordance with adult rules and prohibitions. For example, if they are asked to wait for a short time (e.g., 15 minutes), they might invent games or sing to themselves to pass the time more quickly (Mischel & Ebbesen, 1970). If a playmate has an enticing toy, they may turn away and engage in an alternative activity as a way of lessening the temptation to grab the toy (Kopp, 1982). Children who use such strategies are better able to resist temptations (Mischel, Shoda, & Rodriguez, 1989).

During the preschool, elementary, and secondary school years, children and adolescents increasingly take ownership of society's rules and regulations (Deci & Ryan, 1995; Kochanska, Coy, & Murray, 2001). Possibly this ownership proceeds through the process of internalization of motivation portrayed earlier in Figure 13-2 (Deci & Ryan, 1995). The first sign of internalization (the *introjection* phase) is evident when children feel some internal pressure (e.g., guilt) to comply with rules and regulations. Later (at the *identification* phase), children start to perceive rules and other desired behaviors to be important or valuable to them personally. This phase is evident in an interview with 9-year-old Elena in the "Neighborhood: Middle Childhood" video in MyEducationLab:

Interviewer:	Neighborhoods and cities have lots of different laws. Why do you think people make these laws?
Elena:	For example, they closed this road because a lot of children were playing around here and some people just came zipping right through fast and fast and not going to the speed limit.
Interviewer:	What would it be like if we didn't have laws?
Elena:	If we didn't have these laws, by the time I step out of the door probably I would have a broken leg.

Finally (at the *integration* phase), rules and regulations become an integral part of children's sense of self. At this point, a teenage girl might define herself as being "law abiding" or "concerned about others' welfare" and so strive to behave in ways consistent with her self-definition.

• ***Self-evaluation becomes more frequent.*** Infants and young toddlers do not seem to evaluate their own behavior, nor do they show much concern about how others evaluate it. In contrast, 2-year-olds often seek adults' approval for their actions (Stipek, Recchia, & Mc-Clintic, 1992). Sometime around age 3, children show the first signs of *self*-evaluation. For in-

MyEducationLab

Observe Elena's understanding of the usefulness of laws in the "Neighborhood: Middle Childhood" video. (Find Video Examples in Chapter 13 of MyEducationLab.)

Young Zoe has clearly internalized her parents' prohibitions against taking pens apart. Notice how she not only evaluates her own behavior but also punishes herself for it!

BABY BLUES © Baby Blues Partnership. KING FEATURES SYNDICATE.

stance, they look happy when they're successful and sad when they fail (Heckenhausen, 1984, 1987).

As children move through the preschool, elementary, and middle school years, they show a marked increase in self-judgment (M. B. Bronson, 2000; van Kraayenoord & Paris, 1997). Typically the criteria on which they base their self-evaluations are derived from feedback they have previously gotten from other people. Their parents have undoubtedly praised certain behaviors and criticized others, their teachers have given them frequent information about their academic performance, and their peers have often let them know in no uncertain terms about the effectiveness of their social skills. As their ability for self-reflection grows and they become increasingly concerned about others' perceptions, especially in adolescence, they look more closely at their own behavior and evaluate it in terms of how they think others will judge it (recall our discussion of the *imaginary audience* in Chapter 12).

Conditions That Foster Self-Regulation

To some extent children's ability to self-regulate their behavior is a function of biology. Self-regulation skills are examples of the *executive functions* we spoke of in Chapters 5 and 7. Accordingly, they are carried out primarily by the front part of the cortex, which continues to mature throughout childhood and adolescence (C. A. Nelson et al., 2006; Spear, 2007). Furthermore, individual differences in children's ability to resist impulses and delay gratification seem to depend partly on subtle brain differences that may be genetically determined (Birkas et al., 2006; Lakatos, Birkas, Nemoda, & Gervai, 2007).

Yet environmental factors—cultural norms, socialization practices, parents' expectations, and so on—also appear to play a role in the development of self-regulation abilities. For example, children and adolescents are more likely to become self-regulating when they have age-appropriate opportunities for independence (S. S. Feldman & Wentzel, 1990; I. W. Silverman & Ragusa, 1990; B. J. Zimmerman, 1998). Youngsters can best benefit from these opportunities if they are taught the skills they need to productively direct their own behaviors and overcome obstacles (Belfiore & Hornyak, 1998). Ideally, adults gradually release the apron strings, first providing considerable guidance but eventually giving only occasional suggestions and reminders as children show an ability to make good decisions (Mithaug & Mithaug, 2003; Stright, Neitzel, Sears, & Hoke-Sinex, 2001; B. J. Zimmerman, 2004). Such strategies may remind you of the *authoritative parenting style* described in Chapter 3. When parents, other caregivers, and teachers have warm and supportive relationships with children, set reasonable boundaries for behavior, and take everyone's needs into consideration, they create the conditions in which children learn to make appropriate choices and work toward productive goals (M. B. Bronson, 2000; Reeve, Bolt, & Cai, 1999; B. J. Zimmerman, 2004).

Adults promote self-regulation in another way as well: by modeling self-regulating behaviors (M. B. Bronson, 2000; B. J. Zimmerman, 2004). In a classic study (Bandura & Mischel, 1965), fourth and fifth graders watched adult models make a series of choices between small, immediate rewards and more valuable, delayed ones (e.g., plastic chess pieces available that day versus wooden ones that they could have in 2 weeks). Some children observed a model choosing the immediate rewards (e.g., saying, "Chess figures are chess figures. I can get much use out of the plastic ones right away," p. 701). Others observed a model choosing the delayed rewards (e.g., saying, "The wooden chess figures are of much better quality, more attractive, and will last longer. I'll wait two weeks for the better ones," p. 701). Immediately after they had observed the models, and also on a second occasion several weeks later, the children themselves were asked to choose between small, immediate rewards and larger, delayed ones (e.g., a small plastic ball now or a much larger one in 2 weeks). The children were more likely to delay gratification if they had seen the model do likewise.

Diversity in Self-Regulation

Probably as a result of subtle biological differences, children with impulsive temperaments as toddlers or preschoolers tend to have trouble inhibiting inappropriate behaviors in the elementary grades and adolescence (Eigsti et al., 2006; Eisenberg et al., 2004; M. Pfeifer, Goldsmith, Davidson, & Rickman, 2002). And children with some biology-based disabilities—for instance, children with brain injuries, learning disabilities, or mental illness—may have deficits in self-regulation (Hawley, 2005; Meltzer, 2007; Siegel, 1999).

But the environmental factors just identified also lead to considerable diversity in self-regulation. For example, some Asian cultural groups place a high priority on self-discipline and other aspects of self-regulation (P. M. Cole & Tamang, 2001; Morelli & Rothbaum, 2007; Zahn-Waxler, Friedman, Cole, Mizuta, & Hiruma, 1996). Even as toddlers, children are strongly encouraged to control their feelings, minimizing the "terrible twos" phenomenon mentioned earlier (D. Y. F. Ho, 1994). And preschoolers are expected to work diligently and persistently on assigned tasks. Consider the following scenario that took place one morning in Ms. Xiang and Ms. Wang's preschool class:

> The children are told to sit down at their desks. Once they are seated, the teachers distribute wooden parquetry blocks [blocks of various geometric shapes] to each child. The blocks come in a small box, which also contains pictures of several structures that can be made with them. Ms. Xiang says to the students:
>
>> "We all know how to build with blocks, right? Just pay attention to the picture of the building and build it. When we play games like this, we must use our minds, right? Once you are done, raise your hand and one of us will come by and check to make sure you've done it correctly. Begin. Do your best. Build according to order."
>
> The children begin to work in silence. Those who are working in a nonorderly way are corrected: a child whose box is placed askew on her desk has it placed squarely in the desk's upper right-hand corner by Ms. Xiang. After three minutes one little girl, who apparently knows the blueprints by heart, completes construction of a multistoried house. Raising her right arm in the air, she calls in a soft voice, "Teacher, I'm done." But the teachers do not hear her as they are busy helping less able builders. Finally, Ms. Xiang comes over and says to the little girl, "You're done already? Well, take it apart and build another." After ten minutes most of the children have completed their structures. The teachers come over to check their work. If a building has been constructed properly (that is, exactly as in the picture), the child is told to take it down piece by piece and then rebuild it. If the teacher spots an error, she tells the child to correct it. After fifteen minutes of building, tearing down, and rebuilding, some of the children grow a bit restive, squirming in their chairs and whispering to their deskmates. Ms. Wang says: "Keep still! There is no need to talk while you are working. Let's work quietly." After twenty minutes the children are told to put the blocks back in their boxes. A boy and a girl, today's monitors, collect the boxes of blocks and put them back neatly in a cupboard. The other children face the front, hands on their desks. (Tobin, Wu, & Davidson, 1989, pp. 76–78)

By the time children reach adolescence, virtually all societies require them to display considerable independence and self-control. At this point diversity in their self-regulation skills may become especially apparent. For instance, earlier in the chapter we mentioned that many adolescents from low socioeconomic backgrounds aspire to professional careers (medicine, law, etc.) that require high levels of education. Unfortunately, some of these youngsters lack the basic self-regulation skills they need for success in high school and college (Roderick & Camburn, 1999; B. L. Wilson & Corbett, 2001). Consider the case of Anna who, in her first semester of high school, earned mostly Ds and failed her science class. She explains her poor performance this way:

> In geography, "he said the reason why I got a lower grade is 'cause I missed one assignment and I had to do a report, and I forgot that one." In English, "I got a C . . . 'cause we were supposed to keep a journal, and I keep on forgetting it 'cause I don't have a locker. Well I do, but my locker partner she lets her cousins use it, and I lost my two books there. . . . I would forget to buy a notebook, and then I would have them on separate pieces of paper, and I would lose them." And, in biology, "the reason I failed was because I lost my folder . . . it had everything I needed, and I had to do it again, and, by the time I had to turn in the new folder, I did, but he said it was too late . . . 'cause I didn't have the folder, and the folder has everything, all the work. . . . That's why I got an F." (Roderick & Camburn, 1999, p. 305)

Students like Anna, who seem absentminded about school assignments or unable to focus their efforts on productive goals, often benefit considerably from interventions designed to help them acquire self-regulation skills.

Promoting Self-Regulation

Children and adolescents are more likely to engage in self-regulating behaviors when they are intrinsically motivated to accomplish certain goals or have internalized the importance of engaging in certain behaviors (M. B. Bronson, 2000; Otis et al., 2005). As you have learned, teachers and other adults can foster intrinsic motivation by creating conditions in which youngsters have high self-efficacy and can maintain their sense of self-determination. To promote the internalization of culturally valued activities and behaviors (academic achievement, reasonable self-restraint, etc.), they should provide a warm, supportive environment in which youngsters are given reasonable guidance about how to behave. With these points in mind, we offer the following recommendations for promoting self-regulation:

• ***Create an orderly and somewhat predictable environment.*** Children are in a better position to make wise choices and direct their activities appropriately when they have some structure to guide them, know what to expect in the hours and days ahead, and can reasonably anticipate that certain behaviors will yield certain outcomes (M. B. Bronson, 2000; Meltzer et al., 2007). Communicating general guidelines for behavior, establishing regular routines for completing tasks and assignments, identifying the locations of items that children may need during the day (glue, hole punches, dictionaries, etc.)—all of these strategies can help children work productively with only minimal adult supervision.

• ***Provide age-appropriate opportunities for choice and independence.*** Older children and adolescents need frequent opportunities to make their own decisions and direct their own activities. Independent assignments, computer-based instructional programs, group projects, homework, and the like often benefit these age-groups, especially when the activities are structured so that youngsters know how to proceed and understand the expectations for their performance (H. Cooper, Robinson, & Patall, 2006; Corno & Mandinach, 2004; B. J. Zimmerman, 1998). When youngsters make poor choices, adults should offer constructive feedback that will nurture, rather than dampen, their enthusiasm for independence on future occasions.

Although young children inevitably require some adult supervision to keep them safe, they, too, benefit from having some choice and independence (e.g., N. E. Perry, VandeKamp, Mercer, & Nordby, 2002). However, caregivers and teachers must anticipate and minimize problems that are likely to arise when children make their own decisions. For instance, preschool and kindergarten teachers might create a few rules for taking turns and sharing materials, designate certain areas of the classroom for messy activities (e.g., painting, working with clay), and put potentially dangerous objects out of reach (M. B. Bronson, 2000).

Children with mental and physical disabilities may especially need opportunities for independence, because adults often monitor their behavior and well-being fairly closely (Sands & Wehmeyer, 1996). Independent activities should, of course, be tailored to children's unique characteristics and abilities. For example, a teacher might ask a student with a significant intellectual disability to take the daily attendance sheet to the office but remind her that as soon as she has done so, she should return immediately to class (Patton et al., 1996). Or a teacher might give a student who is blind a chance to explore the classroom before other students have arrived, locating various objects in the classroom (wastebasket, pencil sharpener, etc.) and identifying distinctive sounds (e.g., the buzz of a wall clock) that will help the student get his bearings (J. W. Wood, 1998).

• ***Provide help and guidance when, but only when, children really need it.*** Being self-regulating doesn't necessarily always mean doing something independently. It also involves knowing when assistance is needed and seeking it out (Karabenick & Sharma, 1994). Adult assistance often provides the scaffolding that children need to succeed at new and challenging tasks. Accordingly, adults should welcome any reasonable requests for help or guidance and not convey the message that children are "dumb" or bothersome for asking (R. S. Newman & Schwager, 1992).

In some instances even adolescents may initially need considerable structure to get them on the road to independence. Recall Anna, the high school student who kept losing track of her class materials and assignments. For students like Anna, after-school homework programs are often effective (Belfiore & Hornyak, 1998; Eilam, 2001; S. D. Miller, Heafner, Massey, & Strahan, 2003). In one approach (Belfiore & Hornyak, 1998), students report to a particular classroom at the end of the regular school day, where they find their homework assignments on a shelf. They learn to use a checklist such as that depicted in Figure 13-4, checking off steps they have completed. They also learn to administer **self-reinforcement,** giving themselves a reward (e.g., allowing themselves to play a board game or spend time on a computer) whenever they have completed all the steps. In addition, they learn problem-solving strategies for difficulties they might encounter (e.g., asking a teacher for assistance when they can't find needed materials). Initially, a teacher monitors whether their checklists accurately reflect what they've accomplished, but eventually such monitoring is no longer necessary. And over time, as students acquire a sense of accomplishment about completing their homework each day, the self-imposed extrinsic reinforcers become less critical.

self-reinforcement
Self-imposed pleasurable consequence for a desired behavior.

STUDENT: _____ DATE: _____			
SUBJECT AREA: _____ GRADE: _____			
TEACHER: _____			
STEPS TO FOLLOW	**YES**	**NO**	**NOTES**
1. Did I turn in yesterday's homework?			
2. Did I write all homework assignments in my notebook?			
3. Is all homework in homework folder?			
4. Are all my materials to complete homework with me?			
5. BEGIN HOMEWORK?			
6. Are all homework papers completed?			
7. Did someone check homework to make sure it was completed?			
8. After checking, did I put all homework back in folder?			
9. Did I give this paper to teacher?			

Figure 13-4

Daily checklist for homework completion.
From "Operant Theory and Application to Self-Monitoring in Adolescents" by P. J. Belfiore and R. S. Hornyak, 1998. In *Self-Regulated Learning: From Teaching to Self-Reflective Practice* (p. 190), by D. H. Schunk & B. J. Zimmerman (Eds.), New York: Guilford Press. Copyright 1998 by Guilford Press. Reprinted with permission.

Sometimes, however, children ask for help when they really just want attention or companionship. For instance, if a 4-year-old asks for help on a puzzle, an astute preschool teacher might, after watching the child work at the puzzle, say, "I don't think you need help with this. But I can keep you company for a few minutes if you'd like" (M. B. Bronson, 2000).

• *To guide behavior, use suggestions and rationales rather than direct commands as much as possible.* Youngsters are more likely to internalize and follow guidelines for behavior when adults make suggestions about how to accomplish goals successfully and provide a rationale for why some behaviors are unacceptable (M. B. Bronson, 2000; Hoffman, 1975). Figure 13-5 shows how one fifth-grade teacher encourages self-regulation by using a handout that explains his expectations for behavior. The handout, distributed during

---

MY BROAD GOALS

• Plan and implement a balanced curriculum.

• Help students develop a repertoire of skills and styles of working (open-ended assignments/discrete assignments; collaboration/individual).

• Get students engaged in mental activity; emphasize learning and being a strategic thinker.

• Help students to be both organized and flexible, deal with a schedule, and set priorities for time and things done.

DISCIPLINE

Overarching Golden Rule
Treat others as you would like to be treated.

BASIC RULES

1. Be responsible for your own actions.
2. Use work time for school work; use recess time for play.
3. Appreciate other people; respect the rights of others.
4. Make your behavior appropriate for the situation.

I try to be fair and not play favorites. Everyone is valued and respected. I run the classroom to take care of everyone. The focus is on correcting the behaviors that need correcting so that we develop habit patterns of behavior that serve instructional goals.

My appeal: You've been taught at home for years how to behave. You have a good head—now use it.

Typical fifth-grade problems:

1. Cliques and excluding others—being angry at lunch, friends again after school. A problem especially with the girls.
2. Silliness and not setting boundaries for appropriate behavior, such as bringing recess into the classroom. A problem especially with the boys.
3. Too much undirected talk, talk across desks and across the room, especially during transition times.
4. Restroom problems—talking loudly in the hallways, messing around and loitering in the restrooms.
5. Whininess and sneakiness. Talk to me honestly and openly about problems.
6. "Romance" (going-with) talk or teasing. These are absolutely not allowed in the classroom.

Figure 13-5

A fifth-grade teacher's goals and expectations. In this handout, Michael Gee describes his expectations for students' behavior and encourages age-appropriate self-regulation.
Adapted with the permission of Michael Gee, Barrington Elementary School, Columbus, Ohio.

an open house at school, also gives parents important information about how the teacher conducts his classroom.

Consistent with what we have learned about cognitive development, younger children respond more favorably to suggestions that are concrete rather than abstract. For example, to avoid incidents of bumping and pushing in the cafeteria, teachers at one school asked students to imagine they had "magic bubbles" around them. The students could keep their bubbles from "popping" if they kept a safe distance between themselves and others. This simple strategy resulted in fewer behavior problems at lunchtime (Sullivan-DeCarlo, De-Falco, & Roberts, 1998).

• *Teach specific self-regulation skills.*   Children and adolescents become more self-regulating when they learn specific strategies for directing and evaluating their own behavior. Such strategies include the following:

- **Self-monitoring.** Children aren't always aware of how frequently they do something wrong or how infrequently they do something right. To help them focus on these things, adults can ask them to observe and record their own behavior. Such self-focused observation and record keeping often bring about significant improvements in children's academic and social behaviors (Mitchem & Young, 2001; J. R. Sullivan & Conoley, 2004; Webber, Scheuermann, McCall, & Coleman, 1993). Initially, however, some children may need assistance in monitoring their behavior accurately. For example, in a study with three chronically disruptive 9-year-olds, the children were initially reinforced when their self-ratings matched their *teachers'* ratings of their behavior. As the children became increasingly accurate, the teachers gradually phased out their feedback. For all three children, the frequency of disruptive behaviors decreased considerably, even after the children became the only ones monitoring their behavior (DuPaul & Hoff, 1998).
- **Self-instructions.** Sometimes children simply need a reminder about how to respond in particular situations. By teaching them specific ways of talking themselves through these situations, adults give them a means through which they remind *themselves* about appropriate actions, thereby helping them to control their own behavior. Such a strategy is often effective in helping children and adolescents with poor impulse control (Hains & Hains, 1988; Jutta, Jutta, & Karbach, 2008; Meichenbaum, 1985).
- **Self-motivation.** Children may also need strategies to keep themselves motivated during dull but important tasks. For example, they might consciously identify several reasons why completing an activity will help them over the long run. They might embellish a task in some way to make it more interesting. Or they might learn how to divide a lengthy task into a number of small pieces and then reinforce themselves after completing each one (Wolters, 2003).
- **Self-evaluation.** To become truly self-regulating, children must acquire appropriate criteria by which to judge their accomplishments. For instance, teachers might ask students to reflect on their improvement ("What can we do that we didn't do before?") or to complete self-assessment instruments that show them what to look for in their own performance (Paris & Ayres, 1994; N. E. Perry et al., 2002). At the secondary school level (and perhaps even sooner), young people might even play a role in identifying the criteria by which their performance might reasonably be evaluated.

The Development and Practice feature "Teaching Self-Regulation Skills" includes several illustrations of the strategies just described. Adults must, of course, monitor children's ability to use them and make adjustments accordingly. You can gain practice in promoting self-evaluation with respect to reading and writing by completing a second Building Teaching Skills and Dispositions exercise in Chapter 13 of MyEducationLab.

Many aspects of children's development are characterized by increasing self-regulation. Doing the right thing in the absence of adult supervision and choosing to help rather than hurt others are capacities that draw on self-regulatory abilities. In the next chapter, we turn to the important topic of moral development.

---

self-monitoring
Process of observing and recording one's own behavior.

self-instructions
Specific directions that one gives oneself while performing a complex behavior; a form of *self-talk.*

self-motivation
Intentionally using certain strategies to keep oneself on task during a dull but important activity.

self-evaluation
Judging one's own performance in accordance with predetermined criteria.

MyEducationLab

Go to the Building Teaching Skills and Dispositions exercise "Encouraging Self-Regulation" in Chapter 13 of MyEducationLab to enhance your ability to help children acquire self-regulation strategies in literacy.

Development and Practice

Teaching Self-Regulation Skills

- **Have children observe and record their own behavior.**

  When a student has trouble staying on task during class activities, her teacher asks her to stop and reflect on her behavior every 10 minutes (with the aid of an egg timer) and determine whether she has been on task during each interval. The student uses the checklist shown below to record her observations. Within a couple of weeks, the student's on-task behavior has noticeably improved.

  Self-Observation Record for _____ Karen _____

  Every ten minutes, put a mark to show how well you have been staying on task.

  +   means you were almost always on task
  1/2   means you were on task about half the time
  −   means you were hardly ever on task

9:00-9:10	9:10-9:20	9:20-9:30	9:30-9:40	9:40-9:50	9:50-10:00
+	+	−	+	1/2	−
10:00-10:10	10:10-10:20	10:20-10:30	10:30-10:40	10:40-10:50	10:50-11:00
1/2	−	recess		+	1/2
11:00-11:10	11:10-11:20	11:20-11:30	11:30-11:40	11:40-11:50	11:50-12:00

- **Teach children instructions they can give themselves as reminders of what they need to do.**

  A school counselor helps a fifth grader control his impulsive behavior on multiple-choice tests by having him mentally say to himself as he reads each question: "Read the entire question. Then look at each answer carefully and decide whether it is correct or incorrect. Then choose the answer that seems *most* correct."

- **Help children identify ways to embellish tedious tasks to make them more enjoyable and rewarding.**

  A third-grade teacher suggests that students practice writing the week's new spelling words at home every night. "That might not sound like much fun," she says, "but it's an important thing to do. Who can think of a way to make spelling practice more fun?" One student suggests cutting letters out of grocery store flyers and pasting them together to make the words. Another suggests trying to think of sentences that spell the words with first letters—for example, "*Eighty-nine overweight unicorns get hiccups*" spells *enough*.

- **Teach children to reinforce themselves for appropriate behavior.**

  A middle school teacher suggests that her students are more likely to develop regular study habits if they make a favorite activity—for example, shooting baskets or watching television—contingent on completing their homework first.

- **Encourage children to evaluate their own performance.**

  Early in baseball season, the coach of a boys' baseball team videotapes each boy as he practices batting, pitching, and fielding ground balls. The coach then models good form for each of these activities and lists several things the boys should look for as they watch themselves on tape.

Summary

Motivation

Motivation energizes, directs, and sustains behavior. It can be either extrinsic (evoked largely by the external consequences that certain behaviors will bring) or intrinsic (emanating from characteristics within a person or inherent in a task being performed). On average, children who are intrinsically motivated use more effective learning strategies and achieve at higher levels than those who are extrinsically motivated.

One key source of extrinsic motivation is the extent to which either primary reinforcers (things that satisfy built-in biological needs) or secondary reinforcers (things that have become reinforcing through frequent association with other reinforcing consequences) follow various behaviors. With age, children become increasingly able to forgo small, immediate rewards in favor of larger, delayed ones. An additional source of extrinsic motivation is punishment: Children tend to avoid behaviors that have previously led to unpleasant consequences either for themselves or for others.

Intrinsic motivation takes a variety of forms. Some forms, such as curiosity about intriguing events, a feeling of discomfort (disequilibrium) about apparent inconsistencies in the world, and general needs to feel competent and autonomous, may be universal. Others, such as personal interests, values, and self-chosen goals and aspirations, may be related to children's environmental circumstances and to their earlier successes with certain kinds of tasks. Most children gradually internalize some of the priorities and values of parents, teachers, and other influential adults in their lives, especially if the adults balance reasonable structure and guidance with some autonomy in decision making.

Among the important factors influencing children's motivation are the attributions children make regarding their successes and failures in particular activities. Children are most optimistic when they attribute both successes and failures to internal factors that they can control (e.g., amount of effort and use of good strategies). Ultimately, some children acquire a general *I can do it* attitude (a mastery orientation), whereas others acquire an *I can't do it even if I try* attitude (learned helplessness).

To some degree, children's intrinsic motivation to tackle particular tasks and pursue particular activities depends on factors that develop gradually over time (e.g., self-efficacy, sense of self-determination, a mastery orientation). Thus, children's motivation in any particular situation is not necessarily something they can turn "on" or "off" quickly and easily. However, children's current environments also affect their intrinsic motivation. Piquing youngsters' curiosity and interest, helping them be successful in their efforts to master new skills, enhancing their sense of autonomy, and encouraging them to set and strive for specific goals are just a few of the many things adults can do to enhance youngsters' motivation to engage in productive activities.

Self-Regulation

With age and experience, most children and adolescents become increasingly able to control and direct their own behavior and learning. They more effectively restrain their impulses and emotional reactions, gradually internalize adults' rules and restrictions, and begin to evaluate their own behavior using appropriate criteria. Yet even at the high school level, some youngsters don't regulate their own behaviors very effectively. Adults promote self-regulation through authoritative parenting and classroom management strategies, in which they establish definite guidelines for behavior while also attending to children's needs, listening to children's ideas and perspectives, and providing a reasonable rationale for requests and restrictions. Adults can also model self-regulating behaviors, give children age-appropriate opportunities for independence, and teach such specific skills as self-instructions, self-monitoring, and self-reinforcement.

Applying Concepts in Child Development

The exercises in this section will help you increase your effectiveness in enhancing children's and adolescents' motivation and self-regulation skills.

Case Study

Derrika

Read the case and then answer the questions that follow it.

In a study conducted in the Chicago public schools, Roderick and Camburn (1999) investigated the academic progress of students who had recently made the transition from relatively small elementary or middle schools to much larger high schools. Many students in their research sample experienced considerable difficulty making the transition from eighth to ninth grade, as the case of Derrika illustrates:

> Derrika liked to be challenged and felt her eighth-grade teachers cared and made her work. Derrika entered high school with plans to go to college and felt that her strong sense of self would get her through: "Nobody stops me from doing good because I really wanna go to college. . . . Nobody in my family's been to college . . . so I want to be the first person to go to college and finish."
>
> Derrika began having problems in eighth grade. Despite average achievement scores and previously high grades, she ended eighth grade with a C average and failed science. In high school, her performance deteriorated further. At the end of the first semester, Derrika received Fs in all her major subjects, had 20 absences, almost 33 class cuts for the last

two periods of the day, and had been suspended for a food fight. Derrika is vague in explaining her performance, except for biology, in which she admits, "I don't never get up on time." She feels that her elementary school teachers were better because, "If you don't want to learn, they are going to make you learn," while her current teachers think, "If you fail, you just fail. It ain't our fault. You're the one that's dumb." (Roderick & Camburn, 1999, p. 304)

- Given what you've learned about the development of self-regulation, how might you explain Derrika's sudden academic difficulties beginning in the eighth grade?
- To what factors did Derrika's elementary school teachers apparently attribute any academic failures she had? To what factors did her high school teachers attribute her failures?
- What strategies might a teacher, counselor, or other practitioner use to help Derrika get back on the road to academic success?

Once you have answered these questions, compare your responses with those presented in Appendix A.

Interpreting Children's Artifacts and Reflections

Consider what you've learned about self-regulation as you analyze the following essay written by an 11-year-old girl.

Tears of Pearls

When students in a sixth-grade class don't turn in homework assignments, a teacher intern insists that they write a 200-word essay explaining the missing homework and describing how they plan to be more diligent next time. In an essay shown on the next page, 11-year-old Andrea explains why she didn't turn in her analysis of the lyrics to the song

"Tears of Pearls," by the Australian singing duo Savage Garden. As you read the essay, consider these questions:

- What possible benefits might such an essay have?
- What evidence do you see that Andrea has developed some degree of self-regulation in her study habits?

Once you have analyzed Andrea's essay, compare your ideas with those presented in Appendix B. For further practice in analyzing children's artifacts and reflections, go to the Activities and Applications section in Chapter 13 of MyEducationLab.

---

200 word essay

I am very sorry this happened. I feel guilty that I forgot to pass the assignment Tears of Pearls in. Every time in social studies I will make sure I passed in <u>all</u> my assignments so that this will not happen again. I understand how hard it is for you to keep track of two classes work and I think it is a good idea you are doing this. I wish I wasn't so forgetful. Hopefully this will not happen to me again. Every night I will check my social studies folder to make sure the homework is complete. Now all I have to do is get it to school and put it in the pass in box. It was complete but I just forgot to pass it in. Every night I do my homework and my mom checks it and it goes in my back pack but sometimes I just forget to give it to you. I'm sorry. I really am. It is sometimes hard for us kids sometimes too. It is sometimes hard for us kids to be prepared but I guess that's just something we'll have to learn before middle school! Oh and sometimes we're packed with homework and the next day its hard to get it back together and into your and Mrs. Copeland's hands as soon as possible (A.S.A.P.). Like I said it's hard for you too and I can understand, but sometimes things (other) things are hard for us too. For the third time im really am sorry

sincerly,
Andrea

Developmental Trends Exercise

In this chapter you learned that motivation takes many forms and that virtually all children and adolescents are motivated in one way or another. The following table describes behaviors of youngsters at five different age levels. For each youngster, the table identifies motives that may be at work, offers suggestions for encouraging productive behavior, or both. Go to the Activities and Applications section in Chapter 13 of MyEducationLab to apply what you've learned about motivation as you fill in the empty cells in the table.

Observing Motivation in Youngsters' Behaviors

Age	A Youngster's Experience	Developmental Concepts *Identifying Motivational Phenomena*	Implications *Motivating Productive Behaviors*
Infancy **(Birth–2 Years)**	Now that she can easily crawl from place to place, 9-month-old Regina is into everything. Her child care provider once found her trying to insert a couple of house keys into an electrical outlet, and all of the cleaning supplies under the sink are a particular source of interest.		Make infants' and toddlers' environments safe for exploration. For example, put plastic plugs in electrical outlets and child-proof safety latches on cabinet doors.
Early Childhood **(2–6 Years)**	When her mother returns to work after a lengthy maternity leave, 3½-year-old Laura begins attending an all-day preschool. Laura's teachers find her behavior to be a challenge from the very first day. "She shows no patience or self-restraint," one teacher says. "When she wants something, she wants it *now*, and she'll throw a tantrum if she doesn't get it. If I immediately go to her, I can usually calm her down. But I never know when she might explode again."	Like many young children, Laura shows an inability to *delay gratification*. Her teacher is possibly *reinforcing* her tantrums with immediate attention. Perhaps Laura's mother or other caregivers have previously reinforced such tantrums, giving Laura little reason to learn to control her impulses or acquire other self-regulation skills.	Reinforce young children for appropriate behaviors (e.g., give a child one-on-one attention when she is engaged in a productive activity). Impose mild punishments for inappropriate behaviors (e.g., place an unruly child in a short "time-out" situation in which she gets no attention from others). Also teach strategies for delaying gratification (e.g., suggest that a child repeatedly tell herself, "I can play with the toy longer if I wait for my turn").

Developmental Trends Exercise (continued)

Age	A Youngster's Experience	Developmental Concepts *Identifying Motivational Phenomena*	Implications *Motivating Productive Behaviors*
Middle Childhood (6–10 Years)	After years of struggling with basic reading skills, 10-year-old Kellen becomes increasingly irritable and soon stops doing his homework. One day his mother finds him curled up under his desk, crying and saying, "I can't do this anymore." Mother takes him to a psychiatrist, who determines that Kellen has dyslexia.		Give children the guidance and support they need to be successful. Seek the advice of specialists when children show unusual delays in acquiring certain skills. Do *not* dismiss chronic problems as being just a "phase" that children will "grow out of."
Early Adolescence (10–14 Years)	During his third-period class, a middle school teacher often sees 12-year-old JoBeth passing notes to one or more of her classmates. Inevitably, the other students giggle after reading what she has written. Before class one day, the teacher takes JoBeth aside and tells her, "This note passing has to stop. It's getting to be a distraction to the entire class." JoBeth looks down sheepishly. "I'm sorry, Mr. Roberts," she says. "I'm just trying to make the other kids like me. Jeremy Smith tells jokes all the time, and he's one of the most popular kids in the school."	JoBeth's desire for popularity reflects a *social goal*. In observing Jeremy's success telling jokes, JoBeth is experiencing *vicarious reinforcement*, which leads to an increase in her own joke-telling behavior.	
Late Adolescence (14–18 Years)	Even as a preschooler, Emmanuel showed a keen interest in basketball, and throughout his childhood and early adolescence he spent many hours playing basketball with his friends at a nearby Boys' Club. Since beginning high school he's twice tried out for the varsity high school team but without success. "I'm just too short," he reasons. "Anyway, it's probably better that I focus on my schoolwork, which will help me get into a good college."	Emmanuel has a *personal interest* in basketball. However, his failure in making the varsity team decreases his *self-efficacy* for the sport. He places less *value* on it and instead turns his attention to academic achievement, which he perceives to be more useful in helping him achieve his long-term goal of attending a prestigious college.	Incorporate teenagers' personal interests into academic subject matter. Provide outlets through which *all* youngsters can pursue interest areas that are apt to promote their physical and psychological well-being (e.g., create nonselective intramural programs for all who want to participate in team sports).

Key Concepts

motivation (p. 482)
extrinsic motivation (p. 482)
intrinsic motivation (p. 482)
reinforcer (p. 482)
primary reinforcer (p. 482)
secondary reinforcer (p. 483)
delay of gratification (p. 483)
punishment (p. 483)
vicarious reinforcement (p. 483)
vicarious punishment (p. 483)

self-efficacy (p. 484)
sense of self-determination (p. 485)
situational interest (p. 485)
personal interest (p. 485)
value (p. 486)
internalized motivation (p. 486)
mastery goal (p. 488)
performance goal (p. 489)

performance-approach goal (p. 489)
performance-avoidance goal (p. 489)
social goal (p. 490)
attribution (p. 491)
incremental view (of ability) (p. 492)
entity view (of ability) (p. 492)
mastery orientation (p. 493)

learned helplessness (p. 493)
situated motivation (p. 497)
student at risk (p. 503)
self-regulation (p. 504)
self-reinforcement (p. 509)
self-monitoring (p. 511)
self-instructions (p. 511)
self-motivation (p. 511)
self-evaluation (p. 511)

MyEducationLab

Now go to Chapter 13 of MyEducationLab at www.myeducationlab.com, where you can:

· View instructional objectives for the chapter.
· Take a quiz to test your mastery of chapter objectives. Detailed feedback is provided to explain why your responses are correct or incorrect.
· Deepen your understanding of particular concepts and principles with Review, Practice, and Enrichment exercises.

· Complete Activities and Applications exercises that give you additional experience in interpreting artifacts, increase your understanding of how research contributes to knowledge about chapter topics, and encourage you to apply what you have learned about children's development.
· Apply what you have learned in the chapter to your work with children in Building Teaching Skills and Dispositions exercises.
· Observe children and their unique contexts in Video Examples.

Development of Morality and Interpersonal Behaviors

Alice Terry worked as a middle school teacher with gifted and talented students in a rural area of Georgia. Over the years, Alice had watched her students thrive when given a chance to work together on authentic activities, especially when they were allowed to address pressing needs in their community. Yet in her reading, she found that there was little systematic data on what adolescents learned from these activities. She decided to obtain evidence about adolescents' experiences in serving their community (Terry, 2000, 2001, 2003, 2008).

Adolescents in Alice's area had taken on several demanding projects, such as restoring buildings, preparing a solid waste management plan for their county, and designing a walking tour past historic buildings and monuments. When she asked current and former students about their experiences, they described the many challenges they surmounted. For example, they had had to reach consensus on a specific problem to tackle, convince community leaders of their seriousness, and determine how to get along with one another while performing their duties.

Students described numerous benefits as well, especially having a sense of purpose in their work. Now in high school, several adolescents who had renovated a theater as middle school students described their accomplishments:

> "Makes you feel like you have a—" Trina interrupted.
> "A place in life," Kevin continued. "We, like, have our—we have, like, a place. No, not a place, but we have a a—a mark."
> Anna blurted out, "We left our mark, yeah!"
> "Our mark. When we were eighth graders," Kevin added, "we really made a difference."
> "We'll go back," Ann responded, "and probably find some of our signatures somewhere."
> "Our footprints are in there," Kevin mused. "Our breath will still be there."[a] (Terry, 2000, p. 126)

Students' sense of purpose was also evident in the commitment they expressed. When asked about fulfilling their obligations, Anna responded:

> "It was important. We had deadlines. People were expecting it." Kevin followed up, "We were actually required to do it. They [letters to businesses] had to be mailed. It was our motivation, I think. It was like our job; we had to do it." (Terry, 2000, p. 128)

Students' realizations that they were effectively preserving their community's identity deepened their sense of purpose. Aaron put it this way:

> "I thought a community would be fine by itself, and then, after getting into this, it's like, I didn't realize how much it really needs. At the cemetery, a lot of the tombstones and everything are just decaying away—[there will] come a time when you won't even be able to tell—we'd be losing our history. Our history is there." (Terry, 2003, p. 303)

Along with gaining a sense of purpose, the adolescents acquired valuable social insights into relationships with peers and their own personal qualities. For example, students realized that they had to be aware of how their moods affected others:

> "You can't be in a grouchy mood and do stuff like this," Anna began, "'cause folks are just gonna get mad at you—you can't do that. . . . You got to have a good attitude about it."
> Kevin interjected, "Everybody has to have a good attitude."
> Anna added, "Or nothing will get done." (Terry, 2000, p. 124)

A related social insight was that cooperation was imperative to the group's progress. When asked to advise other adolescents who would be working on community service projects, the students emphasized teamwork:

> "Learn to . . . work together," Kevin advised.
> Anna added, "Work hard."
> "Get along. To just, um, use their time wisely so they can get the most out of the project," Trina remarked.
> Anna elaborated with a bit of sarcasm, "Cooperate. Do not try to be . . . [Sara]!
> Trina concluded, "To get along. To cooperate." (Terry, 2000, p. 126)

Case Study:
Changing the World, One City at a Time

Outline:

Case Study: Changing the World, One City at a Time

Moral Reasoning and Behavior

Interpersonal Behaviors

Summary

Applying Concepts in Child Development

In addition, students learned about themselves. Kat, now a young woman, had been impatient with her teammates and recalled lessons in self-control and tolerance:

> I used to just blow up at people. . . . I guess we were working in such close quarters that, you know, if somebody that you didn't like was there, they were going to breathe on you at some point. You were going to have to put up with it. (Terry, 2001, pp. 126–127)

Another adolescent, Latoya, appreciated that she was ultimately included on equal terms with the other students:

> I'm the only Black girl in there . . . when I first came, it was kinda different because I didn't have any friends, 'cause I was kinda shy in my other classes, you know? And, but, we kinda get closer, and now I think our experiences are the same now. . . . We're all pretty, uh, equal now. (Terry, 2003, p. 304)

- What did Alice Terry and her colleagues understand about the needs of young people?

- What skills did the adolescents learn as they participated in community service projects?

aExcerpts from Terry, A. W. (2000). An early glimpse: Service learning from an adolescent perspective. *Journal of Secondary Gifted Education, 11*(3), 115–134. Reprinted by permission.

Acquiring a sense of right and wrong, fairness and duty, and obligation to family, friends, and community entails a series of cognitive and emotional changes. Although most children and adolescents gain an increasing awareness of their moral responsibilities to others, now and again they do need guidance. In the introductory case study, Alice Terry understood that adolescents in her area could benefit from an opportunity to work together and serve their community. As a result of their experiences, these young people learned that their community needed them, that they had to compromise and act considerately in order to achieve common goals, and that they could derive considerable satisfaction from their collective accomplishments.

In this chapter, we examine children's moral development and interpersonal skills. We look specifically at children's reasoning about right and wrong, the qualities of their interactions with other people, and their tendencies to help and occasionally to hurt others. As we have discovered to be true about other aspects of development, teachers and other caring adults play a vital role in these emerging skills.

Moral Reasoning and Behavior

Moral development involves acquiring standards about right and wrong, analyzing moral issues thoughtfully, and increasingly engaging in helpful behaviors that reflect concern for other people's rights and needs. We begin with an influential theory that focuses on how children reason about people's rights and welfare.

Kohlberg's Theory of Moral Development

When the groundbreaking cognitive-developmental psychologist Lawrence Kohlberg first began to examine other early theorists' descriptions of children's moral development, he was disappointed with what he read (Kohlberg, 1963, 1964; also see Chapter 1). At the time, other theorists (e.g., Sigmund Freud, B. F. Skinner) had suggested that children behave morally only in response to pressure from others, and even then children frequently give in to their own self-serving impulses. Kohlberg rejected these ideas, instead proposing that children carefully think through the proper courses of action to take in various situations. Kohlberg argued that children construct their own standards about what is morally right and wrong, and they often revisit and revise these standards over time as they gain such advanced cognitive capabilities as abstract thought and social perspective-taking ability.

As you will soon find out, contemporary moral theorists quibble with specific aspects of Kohlberg's theory, but his basic idea that moral development is a constructive process has stood the test of time (Kurtines, Berman, Ittel, & Williamson, 1995; Nucci, 2006; Turiel, 2008).

moral development
Advancements in reasoning and behaving in accordance with culturally prescribed or self-constructed standards of right and wrong.

Kohlberg was the first researcher to look in depth at how people analyze hypothetical conflicts involving moral issues, and he discovered that children and adults often respond to such conflicts by pulling together their moral beliefs in unique ways. As an example, consider the following situation:

> In Europe, a woman was near death from a rare form of cancer. There was one drug that the doctors thought might save her, a form of radium that a druggist in the same town had recently discovered. The druggist was charging $2,000, ten times what the drug cost him to make. The sick woman's husband, Heinz, went to everyone he knew to borrow the money, but he could only get together about half of what the drug cost. He told the druggist that his wife was dying and asked him to sell it cheaper or let him pay later. But the druggist said no. So Heinz got desperate and broke into the man's store to steal the drug for his wife. (Kohlberg, 1984, p. 186)

Should Heinz have stolen the drug? What would you have done if you were Heinz? Which is worse, stealing something that belongs to someone else or letting another person die a preventable death, and why?

The story of Heinz and his dying wife is an example of a **moral dilemma,** a situation in which two or more people's rights or needs may be at odds and for which there is no clear-cut right or wrong solution. Following are three boys' responses to Heinz's dilemma. We have given the boys fictitious names so that we can talk about them more easily.

> *Andrew (a fifth grader):* Maybe his wife is an important person and runs a store, and the man buys stuff from her and can't get it any other place. The police would blame the owner that he didn't save the wife. He didn't save an important person, and that's just like killing with a gun or a knife. You can get the electric chair for that. (Kohlberg, 1981, pp. 265–266)

> *Bradley (a high school student):* If he cares enough for her to steal for her, he should steal it. If not he should let her die. It's up to him. (Kohlberg, 1981, p. 132)

> *Charlie (a high school student):* In that particular situation Heinz was right to do it. In the eyes of the law he would not be doing the right thing, but in the eyes of the moral law he would. If he had exhausted every other alternative I think it would be worth it to save a life. (Kohlberg, 1984, pp. 446–447)

Each boy offers a different reason to justify why Heinz should steal the lifesaving drug. In Andrew's response, the identity of the owner he refers to is not clear, but perhaps he means the druggist, in which case he is suggesting that the druggist needs to be punished for not saving a life. Bradley takes a self-serving view, proposing that the decision to either steal or not steal the drug depends on how much Heinz loves his wife. Only Charlie considers the value of human life in justifying why Heinz should break the law.

After obtaining hundreds of responses to moral dilemmas, Kohlberg proposed that the development of moral reasoning is characterized by a sequence of six stages grouped into three general *levels* of morality: preconventional, conventional, and postconventional (Colby, Kohlberg, Gibbs, & Lieberman, 1983; Kohlberg, 1963, 1976, 1984) (see Table 14-1). **Preconventional morality** is the earliest and least mature form of moral reasoning, in that a child has not yet adopted or internalized society's conventions regarding what is right or wrong—hence the label *preconventional.* Andrew's response to the Heinz dilemma is a good example of preconventional, Stage 1 thinking, in that he focuses on the consequences (death in the electric chair) of not providing the medicine. Kohlberg also classified Bradley's response as preconventional, in this case as a Stage 2 response. Bradley is beginning to recognize the importance of saving someone else's life, but the decision to do so ultimately depends on whether or not Heinz loves his wife. In other words, his decision depends on *his* feelings alone.

Conventional morality is characterized by an acceptance of society's conventions regarding right and wrong. At this level, an individual obeys rules and follows society's norms even when there are no consequences for obedience or disobedience. Adherence to rules and conventions is somewhat rigid, however, and a rule's appropriateness or fairness is seldom questioned. In contrast, people who exhibit **postconventional morality** view rules as useful but changeable mechanisms created to maintain the general social order and protect human rights, rather than as absolute dictates that must be obeyed without question. Postconventional individuals live by their own abstract principles about right and wrong—principles that typically include such basic human rights as life, liberty, and justice. They may

MyEducationLab

Listen to three young people give reasons for not spending money found in a lost wallet in the "Preconventional Reasoning," "Conventional Reasoning," and "Postconventional Reasoning" videos. (Find Video Examples in Chapter 14 of MyEducationLab.)

Table 14-1   Kohlberg's Three Levels and Six Stages of Moral Reasoning

Level	Age Range	Stage	Nature of Moral Reasoning
Level I: Preconventional Morality	Seen in preschool children, most elementary school students, some junior high school students, and a few high school students	Stage 1: Punishment-avoidance and obedience	People make decisions based on what is best for themselves, without regard for others' needs or feelings. They obey rules only if established by more powerful individuals; they may disobey if they aren't likely to get caught. "Wrong" behaviors are those that will be punished.
		Stage 2: Exchange of favors	People recognize that others also have needs. They may try to satisfy others' needs if their own needs are also met ("You scratch my back, I'll scratch yours"). They continue to define right and wrong primarily in terms of consequences to themselves.
Level II: Conventional Morality	Seen in a few older elementary school students, some junior high school students, and many high school students (Stage 4 typically does not appear until the high school years)	Stage 3: Good boy/good girl	People make decisions based on what actions will please others, especially authority figures and other individuals with high status (e.g., teachers, popular peers). They are concerned about maintaining relationships through sharing, trust, and loyalty, and they take other people's perspectives and intentions into account when making decisions.
		Stage 4: Law and order	People look to society as a whole for guidelines about right or wrong. They know rules are necessary for keeping society running smoothly and believe it is their "duty" to obey them. However, they perceive rules to be inflexible; they don't necessarily recognize that as society's needs change, rules should change as well.
Level III: Postconventional Morality	Rarely seen before college (Stage 6 is extremely rare even in adults)	Stage 5: Social contract	People recognize that rules represent agreements among many individuals about appropriate behavior. Rules are seen as potentially useful mechanisms that can maintain the general social order and protect individual rights, rather than as absolute dictates that must be obeyed simply because they are "the law." People also recognize the flexibility of rules; rules that no longer serve society's
		Stage 6: Universal ethical principles	Stage 6 is a hypothetical, "ideal" stage that few people ever reach. People in this stage adhere to a few abstract, universal principles (e.g., equality of all people, respect for human dignity, commitment to justice) that transcend specific norms and rules. They answer to a strong inner conscience and willingly disobey laws that violate their own ethical principles.

Sources: Colby & Kohlberg, 1984; Colby et al., 1983; Kohlberg, 1976, 1984, 1986; Reimer, Paolitto, & Hersh, 1983; Snarey, 1995.

disobey rules inconsistent with their principles, as we see in Charlie's Stage 5 response to the Heinz dilemma: "In the eyes of the law he would not be doing the right thing, but in the eyes of the moral law he would."

A great deal of research on moral development has followed on the heels of Kohlberg's work. Some of it supports Kohlberg's sequence of moral reasoning: Generally speaking, children and adolescents seem to make advancements in the order that Kohlberg proposed (Boom, Brugman, & van der Heijden, 2001; Colby & Kohlberg, 1984; Nucci, 2009; Stewart & Pascual-Leone, 1992). Nevertheless, contemporary psychologists have identified several weaknesses in Kohlberg's theory. One set of problems is related to how Kohlberg defined morality. For one thing, Kohlberg included both *moral issues* (e.g., causing harm) and *social conventions* (e.g., having rules to help society run smoothly) into his views of morality, but as you will soon see, children view these two domains differently. In addition, he largely overlooked one very important aspect of morality: that of helping and showing compassion for (as well as respecting the rights of) others (Gilligan, 1982, 1987). Furthermore, although Kohlberg acknowledged that moral thinking is closely intertwined with emotions, he emphasized cognitive factors. In contrast, contemporary researchers have found that emotions (e.g., empathy and guilt) exert powerful influences on both moral thought and action (Arsenio, Gold, & Adams, 2006; R. A. Thompson, Meyer, & McGinley, 2006; Turiel, 2006).

Another limitation of Kohlberg's theory is his proposal that environmental factors have only a modest impact on moral development. Kohlberg assumed that children's moral thinking is guided by their own introspection, largely without adult assistance. Yet recent research indicates that children are very much influenced by parents and other adults as well as by their many cultural experiences (Dunn, 2006; Grusec, 2006; J. G. Miller, 2006). Finally, Kohlberg largely overlooked situational factors that youngsters take into account when deciding what's morally right and wrong in specific contexts (Rest, Narváez, Bebeau, & Thoma, 1999). For example, children are more apt to think of lying as immoral if it causes someone else harm than if it has no adverse effect—that is, if it is just a "white lie" (Turiel, Smetana, & Killen, 1991).

Developmental Trends in Morality

Many contemporary developmental psychologists believe that moral development involves general *trends* rather than hard-and-fast stages. Contemporary psychologists have identified the following developmental changes in children's moral reasoning and behavior:

• ***Children begin using internal standards to evaluate behavior at a very early age.*** Children begin to apply their own standards for right and wrong even before age 2 (Dunn, 1988; Kochanska, Casey, & Fukumoto, 1995; S. Lamb, 1991; R. A. Thompson et al., 2006). For example, infants and toddlers may wince, cover their eyes or ears, or cry when they witness an aggressive interaction. And many toddlers distinguish between what's "good" and "bad" and what's "nice" and "naughty." For instance, they may look at a broken object and say "uh-oh!" (J. Kagan, 1984; S. Lamb & Feeny, 1995). You can see 16-month-old Corwin show concern when his block tower falls down in the "Intelligence: Infancy" video in MyEducationLab.

Sometime around age 3, children know that causing psychological harm, such as fear or embarrassment, is inappropriate. And by age 4, most children understand that causing physical harm to another person is wrong regardless of what authority figures might tell them and regardless of what consequences certain behaviors may or may not bring to themselves (Helwig, Zelazo, & Wilson, 2001; Laupa & Turiel, 1995; Smetana, 1981; Turiel, 2006).

• ***Children increasingly distinguish between moral transgressions and violations of cultural expectations.*** Mainstream Western culture discourages some behaviors—**moral transgressions**—because they cause damage or harm, violate human rights, or run counter to basic principles of equality, freedom, or justice. It discourages other behaviors—**conventional transgressions**—because, although not unethical, they violate widely held understandings about how one should act (e.g., children shouldn't talk back to adults or burp at meals). Conventional transgressions are usually specific to a particular culture. For instance, although burping is frowned on in mainstream Western culture, people in some cultures burp as a compliment to the cook. In contrast, many moral transgressions are universal across cultures (J. G. Miller, 2007; Nucci, 2001; Turiel, 2002, 2006). Children around the world realize it is wrong to hit others, steal their belongings, and call them nasty names.

Even preschoolers realize that not all actions are "wrong" in the same way and that violations of moral standards are more serious than other transgressions (Nucci & Weber, 1995; Turiel, 1983; Yau & Smetana, 2003). Children's awareness of social conventions is minimal in early childhood but increases throughout the elementary and secondary school years (Helwig & Jasiobedzka, 2001; Laupa & Turiel, 1995; Mullins & Tisak, 2006; Nucci & Nucci, 1982; Turiel, 2006). However, children and adults do not always agree about which behaviors constitute moral transgressions, which ones fall into the conventional domain, and which ones are simply matters of *personal choice*. For instance, from a fairly young age children believe their choices of friends and hairstyles are personal matters, whereas adults may disagree.

• ***Children's capacity to respond emotionally to others' harm and distress increases over the school years.*** Certain emotions tend to accompany and evoke moral actions, and these emotions emerge gradually as children grow older. Children begin to show signs of **guilt**—a feeling of discomfort when they know that they have inflicted damage or caused someone else pain or distress—as early as 22 months (Kochanska, Gross, Lin, & Nichols, 2002; see Chapter 11). By the time children reach the middle elementary grades, most of them occasionally feel **shame:** They feel embarrassed or humiliated when they fail to meet

MyEducationLab

See evidence that Corwin has emerging internal standards in the "Intelligence: Infancy" video. (Find Video Examples in Chapter 14 of MyEducationLab.)

moral transgression
Action that causes damage or harm or in some other way infringes on the needs and rights of others.

conventional transgression
Action that violates society's general guidelines (often unspoken) for socially acceptable behavior.

guilt
Feeling of discomfort when one inflicts damage or causes someone else pain or distress.

shame
Feeling of embarrassment or humiliation after failing to meet certain standards for moral behavior.

standards for moral behavior that either they or others have established (Damon, 1988; Harter, 1999; Hoffman, 1991).[1] Both guilt and shame, though unpleasant emotions, indicate that children are developing a sense of right and wrong and will work hard to correct their misdeeds (Eisenberg, 1995; Harter, 1999; Kochanska & Aksan, 2006; Narváez & Rest, 1995).

Guilt and shame emerge when children believe they have done something wrong. In contrast, *empathy,* the capacity to experience the same feelings as another person (see Chapter 11), and **sympathy,** a genuine feeling of sorrow and concern about another person's problems or distress, motivate moral behavior even in the absence of wrongdoing. These emotions emerge in early childhood and continue to develop throughout middle childhood and adolescence (S. Lamb & Feeny, 1995; Zahn-Waxler, Radke-Yarrow, et al., 1992). In the primary grades, children show empathy mostly for people they know, such as friends and classmates. But by the upper elementary school grades, they may also begin to feel empathy for people they *don't* know—perhaps for the poor, the homeless, or those in catastrophic circumstances (Damon, 1988; Eisenberg, 1982; Hoffman, 1991). In the opening case study, the adolescents felt empathic to people in their community generally, wishing to preserve historical landmarks and natural resources for everyone's benefit. Also during adolescence, young people become better able to disregard their own personal distress in order to attend to another's misfortune with sympathy (Eisenberg, Spinrad, & Sadovsky, 2006).

● ***Children's understanding of fairness evolves throughout early and middle childhood.*** The ability to share with others depends on children's sense of **distributive justice,** their beliefs about what constitutes everyone's fair share of a valued commodity (food, toys, playground equipment, etc.). Children's notions of distributive justice change over time (Damon, 1977; Gummerum, Keller, Takezawa, & Mata, 2008; Lapsley, 2006). In the preschool years, beliefs about what's fair are based on children's own needs and desires; for instance, it would be perfectly "fair" to give oneself a large handful of candy and give others smaller amounts. In the early elementary grades, children base their judgments about fairness on strict equality: A desired commodity is divided into equal portions. Sometime around age 8, children begin to take merit and special needs into account. For instance, they may think that people who contribute more to a group's efforts should reap a greater portion of the group's rewards and that people who are exceptionally poor might be given more resources than others.

● ***As children get older, they increasingly behave in accordance with self-chosen moral standards.*** Children's moral behaviors are correlated with their moral reasoning (Blasi, 1980; Eisenberg, Zhou, & Koller, 2001; Reimer et al., 1983; Turiel, 2008). For example, children and adolescents who, from Kohlberg's perspective, reason at higher stages are less likely to cheat or insult others, more likely to help people in need, and more likely to disobey orders that would cause someone harm (F. H. Davidson, 1976; Kohlberg, 1975; Kohlberg & Candee, 1984; P. A. Miller, Eisenberg, Fabes, & Shell, 1996).

Yet as children decide how to act in particular circumstances, factors in addition to moral reasoning come into play. For example, children's perspective-taking ability and emotions (shame, guilt, empathy, sympathy) influence their decisions to behave morally or otherwise (Batson, 1991; Damon, 1988; Eisenberg et al., 2001). Children's personal needs and goals typically come into play as well. For instance, although children may want to do the right thing, they may also be concerned about whether others will approve of their actions and about what positive or negative consequences might result. Children are more apt to behave in accordance with their moral standards if the benefits are high ("Will other people like me better?") and the personal costs are low ("How much will I be inconvenienced?") (M. L. Arnold, 2000; Batson & Thompson, 2001; Narváez & Rest, 1995). In the opening case study, the group solidarity and shared pride students experienced more than compensated for their hard work and the discomfort they felt in resolving interpersonal differences.

As you have learned, the full constellation of moral skills and understandings takes time to emerge in children. The Developmental Trends table "Moral Reasoning and Behavior at Different Age Levels" describes advancements you are likely to see in infancy, childhood, and adolescence.

sympathy
Feeling of sorrow and concern about another's problems or distress.

distributive justice
Beliefs about what constitutes people's fair share of a valued commodity.

[1]As you learned in Chapter 11, Erik Erikson suggested that shame may appear in the toddler years if adults try to impose unrealistic expectations on youngsters' behaviors. As a general rule, however, shame appears in the elementary years, as children become more cognitively able to consider how their behaviors might be consistent or inconsistent with society's standards (Harter, 1999).

Moral Reasoning and Behavior at Different Age Levels

Age	What You Might Observe	Diversity	Implications
Infancy (Birth–2 Years)	· Acquisition of some standards for behavior (e.g., saying "uh-oh!" after knocking over and breaking an object) · Reactions of distress when witnessing aggressive behavior	· In the second year, children begin to label objects and events in ways that reflect culture-specific standards (e.g., *good, bad, dirty, boo boo*). · Toddlers who are fearful and inhibited may experience considerable distress when parents respond harshly to their wrongdoings.	· Consistently discourage behaviors that cause harm or distress to others (e.g., hitting or biting peers). · Acknowledge undesirable events (e.g., spilled milk or a broken object), but don't communicate that children are somehow inadequate for having caused them.
Early Childhood (2–6 Years)	· Some awareness that behaviors causing physical or psychological harm are morally wrong · Guilt for some misbehaviors (e.g., damaging a valuable object) · Greater concern for one's own needs than for those of others; complaining "It's not fair" when one's own needs aren't met	· Some cultures emphasize early training in moral values; for example, in many Hispanic communities, a child who is *bien educado* (literally, "well educated") knows right from wrong and tries to behave accordingly. · Children who show greater evidence of guilt about transgressions are more likely to adhere to rules for behavior. · At ages 2 and 3, girls are more likely to show guilt than boys; boys catch up at about age 4.	· Make standards for behavior very clear. · When children misbehave, give reasons why such behaviors are unacceptable, focusing on the harm and distress they have caused others (see the discussion on *induction* in the upcoming section in this chapter, "Adults' reasons and rationales").
Middle Childhood (6–10 Years)	· Sense of distributive justice increasingly taking into account people's differing contributions, needs, and special circumstances (e.g., people with disabilities might get a larger share) · Increasing empathy for unknown individuals who are suffering or needy · Feelings of shame as well as guilt for moral wrongdoings	· Some cultures place greater emphasis on ensuring people's individual rights and needs, whereas others place greater value on the welfare of the community as a whole. · Children whose parents explain *why* certain behaviors are unacceptable show more advanced moral development.	· Talk about how rules enable classrooms and other group situations to run more smoothly. · Present simple moral dilemmas similar to circumstances children might encounter themselves (e.g., "What should a girl do when she has forgotten her lunch money and finds a dollar bill on the floor under a classmate's desk?").
Early Adolescence (10–14 Years)	· Some tendency to think of rules and conventions as standards that should be followed for their own sake · Tendency to believe that distressed individuals (e.g., the homeless) are entirely responsible for their own fate	· Sometime around puberty, some youngsters begin to incorporate moral traits into their overall sense of self. · Youngsters' religious beliefs (e.g., their beliefs in an afterlife) influence their judgments about what behaviors are morally right and wrong.	· Involve adolescents in group projects that will benefit their school or community. · Encourage adolescents to think about how society's laws and practices affect people in need (e.g., the poor, the sick, the elderly). · When imposing discipline for moral transgressions, point out harm caused to others (doing so is especially important when youngsters have deficits in empathy and moral reasoning).
Late Adolescence (14–18 Years)	· Understanding that rules and conventions help society run more smoothly · Increasing concern about doing one's duty and abiding by the rules of society as a whole rather than simply pleasing certain authority figures · Genuine empathy for people in distress · Belief that society has an obligation to help those in need	· For some older adolescents, high moral values are a central part of their overall identity; these individuals often show a strong commitment to helping those less fortunate than themselves. · Adolescents who have less advanced moral reasoning—especially those who focus on their own needs almost exclusively (i.e., preconventional reasoners)—are more likely to engage in antisocial activities.	· Explore moral issues in social studies, science, and literature. · Give teenagers a political voice in decision making about rules at school and elsewhere.

Sources: M. Chandler & Moran, 1990; Damon, 1988; Eisenberg, 1982; Eisenberg & Fabes, 1998; Farver & Branstetter, 1994; C. A. Flanagan & Faison, 2001; D. Hart & Fegley, 1995; Helwig & Jasiobedzka, 2001; Helwig et al., 2001; Hoffman, 1975, 1991; Kochanska et al., 1995, 2002; Kohlberg, 1984; D. L. Krebs & Van Hesteren, 1994; Kurtines et al., 1995; S. Lamb & Feeny, 1995; Laupa & Turiel, 1995; Nucci, 2001; Nucci & Weber, 1995; Rushton, 1980; Schonert-Reichl, 1993; Smetana & Braeges, 1990; Triandis, 1995; Turiel, 1983, 2006; Yates & Youniss, 1996; Yau & Smetana, 2003; Youniss & Yates, 1999; Zahn-Waxler, Radke-Yarrow, et al., 1992.

Factors Affecting Moral Development

Some prominent members of mainstream Western culture (e.g., certain politicians, religious leaders, and newspaper columnists) have suggested that society is in a sharp moral decline. Yet evidence does not necessarily support this idea. In fact, some indicators reveal *improvements* in people's moral behaviors. In the United States, for example, crime rates have gone down in the last few years, children are better protected under labor laws, race relations and women's rights have improved, and volunteerism in charities and public service organizations has increased (Ladd, 1999; Turiel, 2002, 2006).

To some degree, children's moral reasoning and behavior depends on their cognitive development and sense of self. But for better of worse, the sociocultural environment in which children grow up—including their interactions with peers and adults and their exposure to moral issues and religious teachings—also plays a significant role. In the following sections we look at six distinct factors associated with the development of moral reasoning and behavior: general cognitive development, sense of self, interactions with peers, adults' reasons and rationales, exposure to moral issues and dilemmas, and religious upbringing.

General cognitive development. Let's return once again to Charlie's response to the Heinz dilemma: "In the eyes of the law he would not be doing the right thing, but in the eyes of the moral law he would." Advanced moral reasoning—thoughtful reasoning about moral law and about such ideals as equality, justice, and basic human rights—requires considerable reflection about intangible ideas (Kohlberg, 1976; Turiel, 2002). Thus, moral development depends to some extent on cognitive development. For instance, children who are intellectually gifted are, on average, more likely than their peers to think about moral issues and to work hard to address injustices in the local community or the world at large (L. K. Silverman, 1994).

Yet cognitive development does not *guarantee* moral development. It is quite possible to think abstractly about academic subject matter and yet reason in a self-centered, "preconventional" manner (Kohlberg, 1976; L. K. Silverman, 1994). In other words, cognitive development is a necessary but insufficient condition for moral development.

Sense of self. Children are more likely to engage in moral behavior when they think they are actually capable of helping other people—in other words, when they have high self-efficacy about their ability to make a difference (Narváez & Rest, 1995). Furthermore, in adolescence some youngsters begin to integrate a commitment to moral values into their personal goals in life and overall sense of *identity* (M. L. Arnold, 2000; Blasi, 1995; Wentzel, Filisetti, & Looney, 2007; also see Chapter 12). These adolescents think of themselves as moral, caring individuals and place a high priority on acting in accordance with this self-perception. Their acts of altruism and compassion are not limited to their friends and acquaintances but also extend to the community at large, as was the case with the young people in the opening case study. In one investigation (D. Hart & Fegley, 1995), researchers conducted in-depth interviews with inner-city Hispanic and African American teenagers who demonstrated an exceptional commitment to helping others (by volunteering many hours at Special Olympics, a neighborhood political organization, a nursing home, etc.). These teens did not necessarily display more advanced moral reasoning (as defined by Kohlberg's stages) than others their age, but they were more likely to describe themselves in terms of moral traits and goals (e.g., being helpful to others) and to mention certain ideals toward which they were striving.

Interactions with peers. Children learn many moral lessons in their interactions with agemates. When infants and toddlers interact at home or in child care settings, such lessons begin quite early. Interactions among very young children should be monitored closely, because they often involve physical contact and a potential for physical harm. When adults scold children for aggressive actions and suggest alternative ways to resolve conflicts, children begin to develop an awareness of appropriate and inappropriate ways to treat others.

Beginning in the preschool years and continuing through adolescence, issues related to sharing, cooperation, and negotiation emerge in youngsters' group activities (Damon, 1981, 1988; Turiel, 2006). Furthermore, conflicts frequently arise as a result of physical harm, disregard for another's feelings, or mistreatment of possessions (Dunn & Munn, 1987; Killen & Nucci, 1995). To learn to resolve interpersonal conflicts successfully, children must engage in social perspective taking, show consideration for others' feelings and possessions, and try to satisfy others' needs in addition to their own (Killen & Nucci, 1995; Singer & Doornenbal, 2006). (We elaborate on socially helpful and hurtful behaviors later in this chapter.)

Adults' reasons and rationales. Certainly it is important to impose consequences for harmful actions and other immoral behaviors. However, punishment by itself often focuses children's attention primarily on their own distress (Hoffman, 1975; Nucci, 2001). Children are more likely to make gains in moral development when they think about the harm that certain behaviors have caused for *others*. Giving children reasons why certain behaviors are unacceptable, with a focus on other people's perspectives, is known as **induction** (Hoffman, 1975). Following are examples:

- "Having your hair pulled the way you just pulled Mai's can really be painful."
- "You probably hurt John's feelings when you call him names like that."
- "This science project you've just ridiculed may not be as fancy as yours, but I know that Michael spent many hours working on it and is quite proud of what he's done."

Consistent use of induction in disciplining children, especially when accompanied by *mild* punishment for misbehavior—for instance, insisting that children make amends for their wrongdoings—appears to promote compliance with rules and foster the development of empathy, compassion, and altruism (G. H. Brody & Shaffer, 1982; Hoffman, 1975; Nucci, 2001; Rushton, 1980; Turiel, 2006). In contrast, power-assertive techniques (e.g., "Do this because I say so!") are relatively *in*effective in promoting moral development (Damon, 1988; Kochanska et al., 2002; Nucci, 2001; Zhou et al., 2002).

Giving children reasons about why specific rules are necessary and holding them accountable for their transgressions can help promote their moral development.

Exposure to moral issues and dilemmas. Kohlberg proposed that children develop morally when they are challenged by moral dilemmas they cannot adequately deal with at their current stage of moral reasoning—in other words, when they encounter situations that create disequilibrium. Although most contemporary developmental psychologists reject Kohlberg's idea of discrete stages, they have confirmed his view that disequilibrium spurs moral development. For instance, discussions of controversial topics and moral issues appear to promote the development of moral reasoning, especially when children are exposed to reasoning that's slightly more advanced than their own (DeVries & Zan, 1996; Power, Higgins, & Kohlberg, 1989; Schlaefli, Rest, & Thoma, 1985).

Religion. Having a religious faith or other clear philosophical position about the meaning of life plays an integral role in the moral development of many children. Even though religious beliefs do not typically enhance moral reasoning as Kohlberg defined it, perhaps most of the time, these beliefs *do* contribute to moral development by providing a compelling rationale for acting humanely (L. J. Walker & Reimer, 2006). In Figure 14-1, you can see that children holding distinct religious and philosophical beliefs share a disposition to care for other people. Other productive developmental outcomes can occur as well. Youngsters who have religious beliefs tend to have good coping skills, look after their health (e.g., by exercising, following a good diet, and wearing seat belts), and participate in community service (P. E. King & Benson, 2006). However, in a few unfortunate cases, children are taught to use their faith as a justification for mistreating others, as has occurred, for example, in some white supremacy groups and certain terrorist organizations (P. E. King & Benson, 2006).

Diversity in Moral Development

The factors just described can lead to considerable diversity in the moral values and behaviors that young people acquire. Some disabilities also impact moral development; for instance, children with a *conduct disorder* show a general disregard for the rights and feelings of others (see Chapter 11). In addition, moral development may be somewhat different for youngsters of different genders and cultural backgrounds, as we now explain.

Gender differences. On average, girls are somewhat more likely than boys to feel guilt, shame, empathy, and sympathy—emotions associated with moral behavior (Alessandri &

induction
Act of explaining why a certain behavior is unacceptable, usually with a focus on the pain or distress that someone has caused another.

Thirteen-year-old Sajid, a Muslim boy from London, reflects on Allah's teachings as explained to him by his father:

> Either you give to the poor, to your neighbor, or you risk lots of trouble when you die ...[My father] said I should still try to be very good in school, in all that I do; but I should help my friends, too. You should be generous; you should give help to others. (Coles, 1990, pp. 240–41)

Seven-year-old Fred writes about the Christian values he has learned, and his 6-year-old brother, Ray, draws a nativity scene.

Eleven-year-old Sylvia comes from an agnostic family and articulates her beliefs:

> I didn't say there's nothing out there; I know there is a lot to live for. I love my family, and I love my friends. I love it when we go to a new place on a trip, and I can see new people, and you can stand there—like up in Vermont or New Hampshire—and look at all

the land, for miles (if you're up a mountain), and the trees, and you're nearer the clouds. (Coles, 1990, p. 299)

Five-year-old Lindsey has drawn a picture of Buddha. Her drawing and commentary are posted to an online Buddhist Web site:

If you look in the triangle, it will make you gooder ...because there are people doing nice things in there. And thinking about it will make you nice. First when you look it is just scribble—but if you look closer (that is why the Buddha is closing one eye) you can see them being nice. (The Online Buddhist Family Center, 2003; http://www.idsl.net/heather/onlinebuddhistcenter/welcome.html). Reprinted with permission of Heather K. Woollard.

On Yom Kippur, 12-year-old Maggie prepares for her Bat Mitzvah and learns moral lessons from her Rabbi:

> The rabbi explained that the point of coming together for Yom Kippur was to think about what we had done wrong in the past year and to think about our relationships with each other, with friends and family. She said that sometimes the services get boring and that's when we're meant to think about who we are as people and how to help in our communities.

Figure 14-1

Children use their religious and philosophical beliefs to help interpret family traditions and personal obligations.

Excerpts from Sajid and Sylvia from *The Spiritual Life of Children* by Robert Coles. Copyright © 1990 by Robert Coles. Reprinted by permission of Houghton Mifflin Company. All rights reserved.

Lewis, 1993; MacGeorge, 2003; Zahn-Waxler & Robinson, 1995). Girls' greater tendency to feel shame may be related to their general tendency to attribute failures to internal, personal qualities. In other words, girls are more likely than boys to take personal responsibility for their misdeeds (Alessandri & Lewis, 1993).

Although girls and boys may feel somewhat differently about situations with moral implications, do they also *reason* differently? In presenting a variety of moral dilemmas to young adults of both genders, Kohlberg found that females reasoned, on average, at Stage 3, whereas males were more likely to reason at Stage 4 (Kohlberg & Kramer, 1969). But psychologist Carol Gilligan has argued that Kohlberg's stages do not adequately describe female moral development (Gilligan, 1982, 1987; Gilligan & Attanucci, 1988). In particular, Gilligan has suggested that Kohlberg's stages reflect a **justice orientation**—an emphasis on fairness and equal rights—that characterizes males' moral reasoning. In contrast, she has proposed, females are socialized to take a **care orientation** toward moral issues—that is, to focus on

justice orientation
Focus on individual rights in moral decision making.

care orientation
Focus on nurturance and concern for others in moral decision making.

interpersonal relationships and take responsibility for others' well-being. The following dilemma can elicit either a justice orientation or a care orientation:

The Porcupine Dilemma

A group of industrious, prudent moles have spent the summer digging a burrow where they will spend the winter. A lazy, improvident porcupine who has not prepared a winter shelter approaches the moles and pleads to share their burrow. The moles take pity on the porcupine and agree to let him in. Unfortunately, the moles did not anticipate the problem the porcupine's sharp quills would pose in close quarters. Once the porcupine has moved in, the moles are constantly being stabbed. The question is, what should the moles do? (D. T. Meyers, 1987, p. 141, adapted from Gilligan, 1985)

Are girls more likely than boys to be socialized to take care of others? Carol Gilligan suggests that they are, but other researchers have found no significant differences in the care orientations of males and females.

People with a justice orientation are apt to look at this situation in terms of someone's rights being violated. They might point out that the burrow belongs to the moles, and so the moles can legitimately throw the porcupine out. If the porcupine refuses to leave, the moles might rightfully harm him, perhaps even kill him. In contrast, people with a care orientation are likely to show compassion when dealing with the porcupine. For instance, they might suggest that the moles cover the porcupine with a blanket so his quills won't annoy anyone (D. T. Meyers, 1987).

Gilligan has raised a good point: Males and females are often socialized quite differently, as you learned in previous chapters. Furthermore, by including compassion for other human beings as well as respect for others' rights, she has broadened our conception of what morality encompasses (Durkin, 1995; L. J. Walker, 1995). However, most research studies do not find major gender differences in moral reasoning (Nunner-Winkler, 1984; L. J. Walker, 1991, 2006). Minor differences (usually favoring females) sometimes emerge in early adolescence but disappear by late adolescence (Basinger, Gibbs, & Fuller, 1995). Furthermore, males and females typically incorporate both justice and care into their moral reasoning, applying different orientations (sometimes one, sometimes the other, sometimes both) to different moral problems (Rothbart, Hanley, & Albert, 1986; Smetana, Killen, & Turiel, 1991; L. J. Walker, 1995, 2006). Such findings are sufficiently compelling that Gilligan herself has acknowledged that both justice and care orientations are frequently seen in males and females alike (L. M. Brown, Tappan, & Gilligan, 1995; Gilligan & Attanucci, 1988).

Ethnic and cultural differences.   Different cultural groups have somewhat different standards regarding which behaviors are "right" and which behaviors are "wrong." For example, in mainstream Western culture, lying to avoid punishment for inappropriate behavior is considered wrong, but it is a legitimate way of saving face in certain other cultures (Triandis, 1995). Some cultures emphasize the importance of being considerate of other people (e.g., "Please be quiet so that your sister can study"), whereas others emphasize the importance of tolerating inconsiderate behavior (e.g., "Please try not to let your brother's radio bother you when you study") (Fuller, 2001; H. L. Grossman, 1994). And whereas many people in mainstream Western societies believe that males and females should have equal rights and opportunities, many Hindu people in India believe that a woman's obedience to her husband is integral to the social and moral order, and so a husband is justified in beating his wife if she disobeys him (Nucci, 2001; Shweder, Mahapatra, & Miller, 1987; Turiel, 2006).

Culture-specific religious beliefs sometimes enter into children's moral reasoning. Consider such simple behaviors as eating chicken and getting a haircut. Although these behaviors have no moral implications in mainstream Western culture, they can have dire consequences in Hindu culture. Some Hindu groups believe that if a family's eldest son eats chicken or gets a haircut soon after his father's death, he is preventing his father from having eternal salvation (Shweder et al., 1987). More broadly, the foremost moral values that children learn vary among cultures, with some societies teaching children to emphasize individual rights and justice, others promoting a sense of duty to family and society, and still others stressing adherence to a sacred order (Haidt, 2008; J. G. Miller, 2007; Turiel, 2006).

Cultural differences almost certainly affect the degree to which children, boys and girls alike, acquire various orientations toward morality (Markus & Kitayama, 1991; J. G. Miller, 1997, 2006; Shweder, Much, Mahapatra, & Park, 1997). At the same time, we must be careful not to overgeneralize about differences in moral reasoning across cultural groups. Most cultures place value on both individual rights and concern for others (Turiel, 2006; Turiel, Killen, & Helwig, 1987). Furthermore, moral decision making within any culture is often situation specific, calling for justice in some situations, compassion in other situations, and a balance between the two in still others (J. G. Miller, 2007; Turiel, 1998; Turiel et al., 1987).

Promoting Moral Development

Clearly children's moral reasoning and behavior are important components of their overall social-emotional development. Yet superficial attempts to "build character"—giving youngsters lectures about morally appropriate behavior, having them read stories with moral messages, or publicly rewarding them for displaying certain virtues—have little or no impact on moral development (Narváez, 2002; Nucci, 2001, 2009; Turiel, 2008). In fact, giving concrete reinforcers for moral actions may actually *undermine* moral development, in much the same way that extrinsic rewards undermine intrinsic motivation in certain situations (Nucci, 2001; also see Chapter 13).

Several other strategies can definitely promote more advanced moral reasoning and behavior, however. Research findings point to the following recommendations for teachers, parents, and other adults who interact regularly with children and adolescents:

• ***Clarify which behaviors are acceptable and which are not, and help children understand the reasons for various regulations and prohibitions.*** Adults must make it crystal clear that some behaviors (e.g., shoving, making racist remarks, bringing weapons to school) will not be acceptable under any circumstances. Adults should also explain that some behaviors may be quite appropriate in certain situations yet inappropriate in others. For example, copying a classmate's work may be permissible when a student is in the process of learning but is unacceptable (it constitutes fraud) during tests and other assessments of what a student has already learned (Thorkildsen, 1995).

Adults should accompany any disciplinary actions or discussions of rules with explanations about why certain behaviors cannot be tolerated, with a particular emphasis on potential or actual physical or psychological harm (recall our earlier discussion of *induction*). For example, a preschool teacher might say, "If we throw the blocks, someone may get hurt. Jane can come back to the block area when she is ready to use the blocks for building" (M. B. Bronson, 2000, p. 206; Riley et al., 2008). Similarly, an elementary school teacher might remind students, "We walk when we are in line so nobody gets bumped or tripped" (M. B. Bronson, 2000, p. 205). Adults might also ask children to describe to one another exactly how they feel when they're the victims of certain misbehaviors or to speculate about how they would feel in a situation where someone else has been victimized (Doescher & Sugawara, 1989; Hoffman, 1991). In addition, adults should encourage children to make amends for misdeeds (Nucci, 2001). For instance, a middle school teacher might say, "I'm sure you didn't mean to hurt Jamal's feelings, but he's pretty upset about what you said. Why don't you think about what you might do or say to make him feel better?"

• ***Engage children in discussions about moral issues.*** Moral issues and dilemmas often arise in conjunction with inappropriate behaviors (e.g., aggression, theft) that occur at school and in other group settings. One effective approach is a *just community,* in which students and their teachers hold regular "town meetings" to discuss recent interpersonal conflicts and moral violations and to establish rules that can help students be more productive and socially responsible (e.g., A. Higgins, 1995; Power et al., 1989). Another strategy is *peer mediation,* a technique we'll describe later in the chapter.

Moral issues arise in classroom subject matter as well. For instance, an English class studying works of Shakespeare might debate whether Hamlet was justified in killing Claudius to avenge the murder of his father. A social studies class might wrestle with the inhumane treatment that millions of people suffered during the Holocaust of World War II (see Figure 14-2). A science class might discuss the ethical issues involved in using laboratory rats to study the effects of cancer-producing agents.

Classroom discussions can also help young people learn how to distinguish among moral, conventional, and personal matters, perhaps within the context of analyzing historical events. For example, in American history a teacher might ask stu-

I tried to get the feeling of deep Sadness and Sorrow into my Picture. I whant the viewer to feel the emotion of what it was like for a Jew. I didn't add any color becaus for a Jew ther life was gray dull and very Painfull, that is what I want the Viewer to feel.

My Picture is titled

A Jewish life

Figure 14-2

Children's moral beliefs influence their interpretations of and reactions to school subject matter. Here Cody tries to imagine and capture the feelings of Jewish people during World War II in a seventh-grade unit on the Holocaust.

dents to reflect on why George Washington refused to accept a letter from King George II of England. In Washington's mind, the letter violated an important social convention because it was addressed to "Mr. George Washington" rather than "President George Washington," thereby failing to recognize his status as leader of a legitimate nation (Nucci, 2001, 2006). In comparison, students might discuss the moral dimensions of John Brown's 19th-century violent campaigns against slavery in the United States (Nucci, 2001, 2006).

Teachers and other adults can do several things to ensure that discussions about moral, conventional, and personal issues promote children's moral development (Nucci, 2001; Reimer et al., 1983). First, they should create a trusting and nonthreatening atmosphere in which children feel free to express their ideas without censure or embarrassment. Second, they can help children identify all aspects of a dilemma, including the needs and perspectives of the various individuals involved. Third, they can encourage children to explore the underlying bases for their thinking—that is, to clarify and examine the principles that their moral judgments reflect.

In discussions about misdeeds, adults must also help youngsters understand the diverse perspectives that some of their peers may bring to the conversation. Adults might encourage children to look at moral dilemmas from several different angles, perhaps considering the extent to which justice, care, social conventions, and personal choice are all involved (Nucci & Weber, 1991). For example, although classmates who deface their school building with graffiti might believe they are engaging in creative self-expression (personal choice), they are also breaking a rule (convention), disregarding other students' rights to study and learn in a clean and attractive setting (justice), and thumbing their noses to the needs of those around them (care).

• ***Challenge children's moral reasoning with slightly more advanced reasoning.*** Kohlberg's stages (see Table 14-1 on page 520) provide a useful framework for identifying moral arguments likely to create disequilibrium for youngsters. In particular, Kohlberg suggested that teachers offer reasoning that is one stage above a child's reasoning. For example, imagine that a teenage boy who is concerned primarily about gaining peer approval (Stage 3) often lets a popular cheerleader copy his homework. His teacher might present law-and-order logic (Stage 4), suggesting that homework assignments are designed to help students learn more effectively and so all students should complete them without classmates' assistance. If adults present arguments too much higher than children's current reasoning, however, children will have trouble understanding the logic and so will probably not reconsider their thinking (Boom et al., 2001; Narváez, 1998).

• ***Get children and adolescents actively involved in community service.*** As you've learned, youngsters are more likely to adhere to strong moral principles when they have high self-efficacy for helping others and when they have integrated a commitment to moral ideals into their general sense of identity. Such self-perceptions don't appear out of the blue, of course, as the teacher in our opening case study, Alice Terry, understood. Children are more likely to have high self-efficacy for particular behaviors (including moral ones) when they have the guidance, support, and feedback they need to carry out those behaviors successfully. And they are more likely to integrate moral values into their overall sense of self when they become actively involved in service to others even before they reach puberty (Nucci, 2001; Youniss & Yates, 1999). Through ongoing **service learning**—food and clothing drives, visits to homes for the elderly, community clean-up efforts, and so on—children and adolescents alike learn that they have the skills and the responsibility for helping those less fortunate than themselves and in other ways making the world a better place in which to live. In the process, they also begin to think of themselves as concerned, compassionate, and moral citizens (Nucci, 2001; Youniss & Yates, 1999). To gain full advantage from such experiences, students need to have some choice in the projects they take on and to reflect on what they have witnessed and accomplished by writing about their experiences or discussing them as a group (Hart, Atkins, Donnelly, 2006; Nucci, 2006).

• ***Foster a climate of religious tolerance.*** In the United States, the First Amendment to the Constitution requires that matters of church and state be kept separate. Many other nations offer similar protections. Public school teachers can certainly discuss religions within the context of curricula about history, culture, or other appropriate academic topics. But teachers and other public figures cannot incorporate religious ideas or practices into classroom activities or community events in any way that shows preference for one

service learning
Activity that promotes learning and skill development through volunteerism or community service.

religion over another, or even a preference for religion over atheism. Just as professionals foster respect for diverse cultural backgrounds, so, too, should they advance acceptance of diverse religious beliefs. If they are to work effectively in adult society, young people must learn that a variety of religious persuasions and nonreligious beliefs have value and that their nation guarantees citizens' right to religious freedom. Many school districts and other institutions for youngsters have specific policies that prohibit any name-calling that denigrates others' religious beliefs, practices, and affiliations.

Teaching respect for diverse religious perspectives does not necessarily mean communicating the message that all beliefs are equally acceptable. For instance, teachers should certainly not embrace beliefs that blatantly violate some people's basic human rights. It *does* mean, however, that teachers and their students should work hard to understand other groups' behaviors within the context of their religious beliefs and assumptions.

Interpersonal Behaviors

Considering other people's needs is an important way to express morality. Showing respect for others' needs and feelings is also an important ingredient in effective interpersonal interactions and relationships. As children grow older, they acquire an ever-expanding repertoire of **social skills,** the various strategies (including perspective taking) that enable them to interact effectively with others. Children vary considerably in their social competence, however. Some are courteous, know the right things to say in conversations, and willingly share and cooperate with peers. Others are less skilled, perhaps offending and alienating age-mates or perhaps feeling so anxious in social situations that they keep to themselves. Not surprisingly, young people's social skills affect the number and quality of their friendships, as well as their overall adjustment at school (Dishion, Andrews, & Crosby, 1995; Gottman, 1983; Pellegrini & Bohn, 2005; K. H. Rubin, Bukowski, & Parker, 2006).

Children develop social skills in large part by practicing these social skills with peers and adults (Gottman, 1986; Maccoby & Lewis, 2003). But they also acquire social abilities by observing what adults and peers do in interactions with others. For instance, children's parents may model a variety of interpersonal styles—perhaps being agreeable and respectful of others' needs, on the one hand, or hostile and aggressive, on the other (Dodge, Pettit, Bates, & Valente, 1995; Nix et al., 1999; Putallaz & Heflin, 1986).

Interpersonal Behaviors at Different Ages

Human beings acquire a wide variety of social skills in the first two decades of life. The unique aspects of infancy, childhood, and adolescence all offer important lessons and opportunities for practice.

Infancy (birth–age 2).   Interpersonal relationships begin with attachments to parents and other caregivers, with whom young infants often interact with eye contact, smiles, and cooing. In the second year, interactions with caregivers also increasingly involve a common focus on external objects (recall our discussions of *intersubjectivity* and *joint attention* in Chapter 7).

In the latter half of the first year, infants who are given appropriate opportunities can also practice their emerging social skills with peers. They may babble in response to one another, smile at another infant, or look where another child points (Eckerman, 1979; Mueller & Silverman, 1989; K. H. Rubin et al., 2006). As toddlers, they may imitate one another, offer one another toys, and cooperate with and assist others in simple tasks and play activities (P. L. Harris, 2006; Howes, 1992; Howes & Matheson, 1992). Their developing language skills in the second year, as well as games with older children and adults (e.g., peekaboo, pat-a-cake, hide-and-seek), allow increasingly sustained exchanges (W. C. Bronson, 1981).

Children show social skills even in infancy.

social skills
Strategies used to interact effectively with others.

Early childhood (ages 2–6).   With the capacity for coordinating attention with others well established by age 2, young children interact more with age-mates, especially within the context of play activities. One early researcher identified six different kinds of behaviors that preschool teachers and child care providers might observe in 2- to 5-year-olds (Parten, 1932). These categories, most of which reflect a continuum of increasing social interaction, are described in the Observation Guidelines table "Observing the Social Aspects of Young Children's Play." Several of the categories are also illustrated in MyEducationLab. If you are able to spend time in a preschool, you will find that younger and older preschoolers alike are apt to exhibit many or all of the behaviors at one time or another. However, most children become increasingly interactive and cooperative in play activities as they grow older (Gottman, 1983; Howes & Matheson, 1992; K. H. Rubin et al., 2006).

Parallel play, though seemingly nonsocial, has a definite social function: Children use it as a way to learn more about peers' interests, initiate conversations, and find common ground for subsequent social interactions (Bakeman & Brownlee, 1980; Gottman, 1983; K. H. Rubin et al., 2006). Yet the imagination and social coordination that characterize the last category—cooperative play—make it an especially important activity of early childhood. In Figure 14-3 you can see the result of a coordinated effort between friends Alex (age 5) and Davis (age 6). As they worked on the picture, they continually listened to each other, built on each other's ideas, and drew from their many past experiences together.

MyEducationLab

Observe onlooker behavior and three types of play (parallel, associative, and cooperative play) in the "Types of Play" video. (Find Video Examples in Chapter 14 of MyEducationLab.)

Observation Guidelines

Observing the Social Aspects of Young Children's Play

Characteristic	Look For	Example	Implication
Unoccupied Behavior	· Failure to engage in any activity, either with or without another individual · Aimless wandering · Quiet sitting and staring	During free-play time, Donald often retreats to a corner of the play yard, where he sits quietly either running his fingers through the dirt or staring off into space.	Try to engage the child with intriguing toys or other objects, or with a small-group activity. Consult with a specialist if unoccupied behavior is persistent and pervasive despite frequent attempts to engage the child.
Solitary Play	· Absorption in one's own playthings · Apparent lack of awareness of other children's presence	Although Laura and Erika are sitting next to each other in the sandbox, they are facing in opposite directions. Laura is digging a large hole ("to China," she says), and Erika is making "roads" with a toy bulldozer.	Keep in mind the value of children's independent play. On some occasions, present new toys or games that require the participation of two or more children.
Onlooker Behavior	· Unobtrusive observation of other children's play activities	As three of his classmates play "store," Jason quietly watches them from the side of the room.	Ask the child if he or she would like to play with the other children. If so, ask the others if the onlooker might join in.
Parallel Play	· Playing next to another child, but with little or no interaction · Similarities in the behaviors of two or more children who are playing independently near each other	Naticia and Leo are both making "skyscrapers" with wooden blocks. Sometimes one child looks at what the other is doing, and occasionally one child makes a tower similar to the other's.	Comment that both children are doing something similar. Suggest an enjoyable activity that incorporates what both children are doing.
Associative Play	· Some talking and sharing of objects with another child · Occasional comments about what another child is doing	Several children are working at the same table creating different animals from Play-Doh. They occasionally ask for a particular color ("Gimme the red") or make remarks about others' creations ("You made a kitty just like I did").	Keep in mind that associative play is often a productive way for children to get to know one another better. Once children feel comfortable together, suggest an activity that would encourage cooperative behaviors.
Cooperative Play	· Active sharing of toys and coordination of activities · Taking on specific roles related to a common theme	Sheldon sets up a "doctor's office" and Jan comes to visit him with her teddy bear, who has a "sore throat." Sheldon puts a tongue depressor to the bear's mouth and instructs it to "Say 'aahh.'"	Provide a variety of toys and other objects that are best used in group play—balls, props for playing "house" and "store," and so on.

Source: First two columns based on Parten, 1932.

Figure 14-3

Alex (age 5) and Davis (age 6) shared fantasies that guided them in drawing this picture together.

In one form of cooperative play, *sociodramatic play,* children assume complementary imagined roles and carry out a logical sequence of actions. In the following scenario, we see Eric and Naomi, long-time friends, assuming roles of husband and wife. Naomi is making plans to go shopping:

N: I'm buying it at a toy store, to buy Eric Fisher a record 'cause he doesn't have a. . . .
E: What happened to his old one?
N: It's all broken.
E: How did it get all broken?
N: Ah, a robber stealed it, I think. That's what he said, a robber stealed it.
E: Did he see what the action was? You know my gun is in here, so could you go get my gun? It's right over there, back there, back there, not paper . . . did you get it?
N: Yes, I found the robbers right in the closet.
E: Good, kill 'em.
N: I killed 'em.
E: Already?
N: Yes, so quick they can't believe it. (Gottman, 1986, p. 191)

Sociodramatic play activities contribute in many ways to children's growing social competence. Children must coordinate their actions and perspectives, sharing fantasies, taking turns, and in other ways considering what a playmate is doing (K. H. Rubin et al., 2006). They must agree on individual roles ("I'll be the warrior"; "Okay, I'll be the chief"), props ("The log can be our base"), and rules and guidelines that govern actions ("We'll let Frances play, but she has to be the horse") (Garvey, 1990; Howes & Matheson, 1992).

In the process of playing, children develop skills in assertiveness, negotiation, and conflict resolution (Göncü, 1993; Gottman, 1986; Howes, 1992). For instance, they become increasingly skillful and polite in making requests. Whereas a 3-year-old is apt to be a bit bossy ("Give me the red one"; "You hafta . . ."), 5- and 6-year-olds are more likely to use hints and suggestions ("Would you like . . . ?" "Let's . . .") (Parkhurst & Gottman, 1986, p. 329). Through negotiating roles and story lines, they discover the advantages of compromise ("I want to be the Mommy, you're the baby"; "No, you were the Mommy last time, so it's *my* turn"; "Okay, but next time I get to be the Mommy"). And children learn how to give one another emotional support, perhaps by voicing approval for one another's actions ("That's pretty") or expressing sympathy for a playmate's distress ("Don't worry about that, it'll come off") (Gottman, 1983, p. 58; K. H. Rubin et al., 2006).

In the "Physical Activity: Early Childhood" video in MyEducationLab, you can watch two 4-year-olds, Acadia and Cody, use a variety of strategies to nourish their relationship and prevent any disagreements from escalating. They make explicit reference to their friendship ("Let's go, Cody, my best friend"). They encourage one another to climb ("This is gonna be cool!"). They admit when they're wrong ("Silly me, I forget everything"). And eventually they come to agreement about which slide to go down ("Yeah. Let's do it"). Not all preschoolers are as skillful as Acadia and Cody, however. In some instances preschoolers cooperate more successfully when adults help them iron out their difficulties (Mize, Pettit, & Brown, 1995; Parke & Bhavnagri, 1989).

MyEducationLab

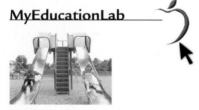

Observe Acadia and Cody coordinating their activities and resolving their differences in the "Physical Activity: Early Childhood" video. (Find Video Examples in Chapter 14 of MyEducationLab.)

Middle childhood (ages 6–10). Once children begin elementary school, about 30% of their social interactions are with peers (K. H. Rubin et al, 2006). As a result of their many social experiences, children become aware that some ways of behaving are acceptable to peers, whereas other ways are not (Gottman & Mettetal, 1986; J. R. Harris, 1998). For example, in the following gossip session, 8-year-old Erica and Mikaila reveal their shared belief that tattling on others is inappropriate:

E: Katie's just a. . . .
M: Tattletale.
E: Yeah, she tells on everything.
M: Yeah. (Gottman & Mettetal, 1986, p. 206; reprinted with permission of Cambridge University Press)

With their growing awareness of other people's opinions, most children become eager to behave in socially acceptable ways. They also become more concerned about equitably resolving conflicts and preserving friendships (Hartup, 1996; Newcomb & Bagwell, 1995). In

Figure 14-4, 10-year-old Jacob reveals his awareness that arguing with friends can be unpleasant, but that disputes often can be resolved to everyone's satisfaction. Not all attempts to resolve conflicts are successful, of course. Most children discover that such strategies as sulking ("I'm going home!"), threatening ("I'm never gonna play with you again!"), and hitting ("Take that!") rarely work. Through experimentation with a variety of strategies and through their growing capacity for social perspective taking, most children become proficient at maintaining amicable relationships with their age-mates.

Whereas younger children are apt to get together in groups of two or three and engage in free-flowing fantasy, elementary school children often convene in larger groups and choose games and other activities that have established rules. Verbal contests (e.g., "Twenty Questions," "I Spy"), board games, and team sports are common (Corsaro, 1985; Hartup, 1984). At this age, rules take on a certain immutable quality: They are permanent fixtures that cannot be altered by whim, and failure to follow them constitutes cheating—a serious breach from what is good and civilized. In the following conversation with 10-year-old Ben, an adult asks if it would be possible to change the rules in a game of marbles. Ben agrees (somewhat unwillingly) that he could formulate new rules but has doubts about their legitimacy:

Figure 14-4

Ten-year-old Jacob drew a child getting into an argument with a friend and then coming to a mutually acceptable solution.

> Ben: [I]t would be cheating.
> Adult: But all your pals would like to [play with the new rule], wouldn't they?
> Ben: Yes, they all would.
> Adult: Then why would it be cheating?
> Ben: Because I invented it: it isn't a rule! It's a wrong rule because it's outside of the rules. A fair rule is one that is in the game. (dialogue from Piaget, 1960b, p. 55; format adapted)

Children learn a great deal from participating in rule-governed games. They discover how to use rules to their own advantage ("If I put another house on Boardwalk, you have to pay me double the next time you land on it"). They learn how to form alliances with other children ("I'll run behind him, and then you pass me the ball over his head"). And they develop strategies for dealing with ambiguous situations ("It was *in!*" "Are you kidding? It was *out!*" "Okay, we'll say it's out, but next time *I* get to decide!"). Occasional bickering aside, the predominance of rule-governed activities in middle childhood seems to reflect children's growing motivation to learn and abide by the rules of society (DeVries, 1997).

Early adolescence (ages 10–14).   Once children reach puberty, they increasingly rely on their peers for emotional support as well as recreation (Levitt, Guacci-Franco, & Levitt, 1993; K. H. Rubin et al., 2006; R. M. Ryan et al., 1994). Some begin to reveal their innermost thoughts to others, especially peers (Basinger et al., 1995; Levitt et al., 1993). But even as their tendency for self-disclosure expands, young adolescents become increasingly self-conscious about what others might think of them. To some degree, their age-mates are apt to exert **peer pressure,** strongly encouraging them to behave in certain ways and not to behave in others. Youngsters who have poor relationships with their families and those whose self-esteem is largely contingent on other people's opinions seem to be especially vulnerable to peer pressure (Erwin, 1993; Hacker & Bol, 2004; Rudolph, Caldwell, & Conley, 2005; also see Chapter 12). A desire to be part of the "in" crowd can drive many young adolescents to do foolish things, as this reflection by one youngster reveals:

> There's all this crap about being accepted into a group and struggling and making an effort to make friends and not being comfortable about your own self-worth as a human being. You're trying very hard to show everyone what a great person you are, and the best way to do that is if everyone else is drinking therefore they think that's the thing to do, then you might do the same thing to prove to them that you have the same values that they do and therefore you're okay. At the same time, the idea of peer pressure is a lot of bunk. What I heard about peer

peer pressure
Tactics used to encourage some behaviors and discourage others in age-mates.

pressure all the way through school is that someone is going to walk up to me and say, "Here, drink this and you'll be cool." It wasn't like that at all. You go somewhere and everyone else would be doing it and you'd think, "Hey, everyone else is doing it and they seem to be having a good time—now why wouldn't I do this?" In that sense, the preparation of the powers that be, the lessons that they tried to drill into me, they were completely off. They had no idea what we are up against. (C. Lightfoot, 1992, p. 240)

Self-socialization plays a significant role in young adolescents' motivation to conform. In other words, much of the motivation to conform to peers' standards for behavior probably comes from within rather than from outside (Hartup, 1983; R. E. Owens, 1996). As you should recall from our discussion of the *imaginary audience* in Chapter 12, young adolescents often overestimate other people's interest in their appearance and behavior. This heightened concern for how others evaluate them can lead them to closely imitate their peers' choices in dress, music, slang, and so on.

Young adolescents have a tendency to categorize other people, especially their peers. They are apt to pigeonhole classmates into such groups as "brains," "jocks," "skaters," and "geeks" and to affiliate with the groups they perceive to be a close match with their own interests and values (J. R. Harris, 1995; Pipher, 1994). Often, too, young adolescents begin to divide into racial or ethnic groups, even if they have previously mingled freely with one another in the elementary school grades. To some extent, such self-imposed segregation reflects youngsters' desires to affiliate with peers who, in their eyes, can better understand and help them deal with the overt and subtle forms of discrimination they sometimes face (Tatum, 1997).

Late adolescence (ages 14–18).   Older adolescents spend almost a third of their waking hours interacting with peers (K. H. Rubin et al., 2006). They spend relatively little time with adults and very little time *exclusively* with an adult, such as a parent or teacher (Csikszentmihalyi, 1995; Csikszentmihalyi & Larson, 1984). In their efforts to develop a sense of identity, they often use peers as a forum for self-exploration and self-understanding (Gottman & Mettetal, 1986). For instance, in the following dialogue, two girls struggle with their beliefs about premarital sexual intercourse as they discuss one girl's recent breakup with her boyfriend Randy:

A: [*joking*] I think you should take Randy to court for statutory rape.
B: I don't. I'm to the point of wondering what "that kind of girl" . . . I don't know about the whole scene.
A: The thing is. . . .
B: It depends on the reasoning. And how long you've been going out with somebody.
A: Yeah, I'm satisfied with my morals.
B: As long as you're satisfied with your morals, that's cool.
A: Yeah, but other people. . . .
B: And I'm pretty, I'm pretty sturdy in mine.
A: Yeah [*giggle*], I know that. Mine tend to bend too easily. (Gottman & Mettetal, 1986, p. 218; reprinted with the permission of Cambridge University Press)

A greater capacity for abstract thought allows older adolescents to think of other people as unique individuals rather than as members of specific groups. Older teens also become increasingly aware of the characteristics they share with people from diverse backgrounds. Perhaps as a result, ties to specific peer groups dissipate, hostilities between groups soften, and youngsters become more flexible about the people with whom they associate (B. B. Brown et al., 1986; Gavin & Furman, 1989; Larkin, 1979; Shrum & Cheek, 1987). One recent graduate of a racially mixed high school put it this way:

Senior year was wonderful, when the black kids and the white kids got to be friends again, and the graduation parties where everyone mixed. . . . It was so much better. (T. Lewin, 2000, p. 20)

Development of Prosocial Behavior and Aggression

Two particular kinds of interpersonal behaviors—prosocial behavior and aggression—have an impact on other people's physical or psychological well-being and therefore have moral as well as social implications.

Cognitive advancements make it possible for older adolescents to see their peers more as individuals than as members of particular groups, and so most increasingly associate with peers from diverse backgrounds.

Prosocial behavior is an action intended to promote the well-being of another person, perhaps by sharing, teaching, or comforting. **Aggression** is an action intentionally taken to hurt another person either physically (e.g., hitting, shoving, or fighting) or psychologically (e.g., embarrassing, insulting, or ostracizing). Here we look at the effects of biology and environment and at basic trends and principles that characterize the development of these two behaviors.

Hereditary and other biological influences.
From an evolutionary perspective, both prosocial and aggressive tendencies have enabled human beings to survive and so may be part of humans' genetic endowment (Dodge, Coie, & Lynam, 2006; Hoffman, 1981; D. L. Krebs, 2008). Prosocial behavior promotes group cohesion, is essential for childrearing, and helps people pull together in harsh conditions. Some kinds of aggression, though antisocial in nature, also increase chances of survival. Squabbling and warfare cause people to spread apart (thereby improving people's chances of finding food and other essential resources) and, in times of battle, to compete such that the strongest members survive and give birth to future, stronger generations.

An evolutionary perspective of such behaviors is, of course, speculative at best. Twin studies provide more convincing evidence that both prosocial and aggressive behaviors have biological origins. Monozygotic (identical) twins tend to be more similar than dizygotic (fraternal) twins with respect to altruistic behavior, empathy for others, and aggression (Eisenberg, Fabes, & Spinrad, 2006; Ghodsian-Carpey & Baker, 1987; Rushton, Fulkner, Neal, Nias, & Eysenck, 1986; Zahn-Waxler, Robinson, & Emde, 1992).

Precisely how heredity affects children's tendencies to be especially helpful or hurtful is unknown, but genes probably determine the amount of chemicals in the brain and body that regulate empathic and aggressive tendencies. For example, certain substances involved in transmitting messages from one neuron to another affect the extent to which children attend to others' emotions and experience social contact as pleasant (Eisenberg et al., 2006; Panksepp, 1986). In addition, certain areas of the brain become active when people listen to sad stories, indicating that particular parts of the brain are devoted to empathic responses (Ruby & Decety, 2001). Possibly, such slight variations in both the structure of the brain and the amount of certain chemical substances within it contribute to individual differences in prosocial behavior.

A similar picture emerges with the biological bases of aggression. Aggressive behavior appears to be triggered partly by the male hormone testosterone. On average, males are more aggressive than females, and after puberty, males with high testosterone levels tend to be more aggressive than males with lower levels (J. Archer, 1991; Susman, Inoff-Germain, et al., 1987). Chemical substances in the brain also affect children's aggressive tendencies, perhaps by influencing children's ability to inhibit aggressive impulses (Dodge et al., 2006). Finally, children with damage to certain areas of the brain, especially an area of the frontal cortex involved in planning and behavior control, also display heightened aggression (Pennington & Bennetto, 1993; Raine & Scerbo, 1991).

Environmental influences.
One influential environmental factor is the presence of prosocial and aggressive models in children's lives. Children who observe sympathetic and generous models tend to be more helpful than those without such models (R. Elliott & Vasta, 1970; C. R. Owens & Ascione, 1991; Yarrow, Scott, & Waxler, 1973). Likewise, children who observe aggressive models—whether the models are adults, peers, or fictional characters in the media—show greater-than-average aggression (C. A Anderson et al., 2003; Brendgen et al., 2008; N. E. Goldstein, Arnold, Rosenberg, Stowe, & Ortiz, 2001; Margolin & Gordis, 2004).

Reinforcement also plays a role in both prosocial and aggressive behavior. Over the short run, children engage in more prosocial behavior if they are rewarded (e.g., with candy or praise) for such behavior (J. H. Bryan, Redfield, & Mader, 1971; Eisenberg, Fabes, Carlo, & Karbon, 1992; Rushton & Teachman, 1978). However, tangible rewards such as candy appear counterproductive over the long run, perhaps because children begin to perform prosocial actions primarily to benefit themselves ("I gave her my candy because I knew Dad would give me an even bigger treat for sharing") rather than to gain personal satisfaction from helping others (Eisenberg & Fabes, 1998; Szynal-Brown & Morgan, 1983). Aggressive behavior is often reinforced by its outcomes: It may enable children to gain desired objects or get revenge (Dodge et al., 2006; Crick & Dodge, 1996; Lochman, Wayland, & White, 1993). And some aggressive children find reinforcement in their victims' expressions of alarm and pain,

prosocial behavior
Action intended to benefit another person (for example, sharing with or helping another person).

aggression
Action intentionally taken to hurt another either physically or psychologically.

perhaps because these children gain a sense of power when they see others squirm under their cruel treatment (Bandura, 1991).

Families and cultures affect children's prosocial and aggressive tendencies as well. Children are more likely to imitate their parents' prosocial behaviors when parents exhibit an authoritative parenting style—that is, when parents are warm and loving, hold high standards for behavior, and explain why certain behaviors are unacceptable (Eisenberg, 1995; Eisenberg & Fabes, 1998; Hoffman, 1988). Children also tend to be more prosocial when their parents (mothers as well as fathers) have work obligations outside the home and give them numerous responsibilities (e.g., taking care of younger siblings) to help keep the household going (Carlo, Koller, Raffaelli, & de Guzman, 2007; Whiting & Whiting, 1975). Other family environments are breeding grounds for aggression. Authoritar*ian* (rather than authoritat*ive*) parenting, especially when accompanied by frequent physical punishment or abuse, appears to foster aggression and other antisocial behavior, but so, too, does very permissive parenting (P. L. Harris, 2006; Straus, 2000; also see Chapter 3). And in some cultures, families may teach children that aggression is an appropriate means of resolving conflicts or maintaining one's honor (D. Cohen & Nisbett, 1994; E. Staub, 1995).

Schools provide additional contexts in which children can learn either prosocial or aggressive behaviors. For example, children and adolescents are more likely to engage in prosocial behaviors, as well as to integrate qualities such as compassion and altruism into their overall sense of self, if teachers and other adults get them actively involved in public service to others (Youniss & Yates, 1999). Violent aggression at schools is rare, but milder forms—racial and sexual harassment, vandalization, and so on—are fairly common (Burstyn et al., 2001; DeVoe et al., 2003; Garbarino, Bradshaw, & Vorrasi, 2002; S. Graham, 2006a). At a few high schools (fortunately, only a few), it is acceptable practice to threaten or fight with a peer who tries to steal one's boyfriend or girlfriend, or students may believe that acting aggressively is the only way to ensure that they don't become victims of someone *else's* aggression (K. M. Williams, 2001a, 2001b).

As children grow, they blend the various factors we have examined into a personal style of responding to frustrating circumstances aggressively or, instead, with restraint. For example, in a study with middle school students, students tended to report using high levels of aggressive behaviors when several conditions occurred: Students had poor coping skills (e.g., they reported taking risks and were frequently angry with other people), received little social support from family and teachers, and were not taught at school how to get along with students of different races and cultures (Reis, Trockel, & Mulhall, 2007). Over time, the multiply determined styles of being aggressive or not aggressive seem to affect children's brains, priming children to act in similarly aggressive or nonaggressive ways in the future (Gollan, Lee, & Coccaro, 2005).

Development of prosocial behavior.   Even young infants seem to be attuned to others' distress, in that they may start to cry when they hear other babies crying (Eisenberg et al., 2006; Simner, 1971; also see Chapter 11). True prosocial behaviors—actions intended to help someone else—appear early in the second year (Farver & Branstetter, 1994; P. L. Harris, 2006; Zahn-Waxler et al., 1992). For example, toddlers may spontaneously give adults or peers assistance with everyday tasks, and they are apt to offer their favorite blanket or teddy bear to someone who seems to be unhappy or in pain. As a general rule, children behave more prosocially—for instance, they become increasingly generous—as they grow older (Eisenberg, 1982; Eisenberg et al., 2006; Rushton, 1980).

Age, of course, is not the only variable that determines whether children and adolescents act prosocially. In the process of putting themselves in someone else's shoes, children must experience some of the other person's feelings—that is, they must have *empathy*. Many children who behave prosocially also feel *sympathy* (Batson, 1991; Eisenberg, 1995; Eisenberg & Fabes, 1998). As we mentioned earlier, basic signs of empathy and sympathy are evident in young children. However, a deep concern for others' needs emerges only gradually over time. Psychologist Nancy Eisenberg and her colleagues have identified five different levels, or *orientations,* through which youngsters are apt to proceed over the course of childhood and adolescence. These orientations are described and illustrated in the Observation Guidelines table "Assessing Children's Prosocial Development." Children do not march through the orientations in a lock-step manner,

MyEducationLab

Learn more about the numerous factors associated with adolescents' aggression by completing an Understanding Research exercise in Chapter 14's Activities and Applications section in MyEducationLab.

Children tend to act more prosocially as they grow older. For example, they become increasingly empathic with age.

Observation Guidelines

Assessing Children's Prosocial Development

Characteristic	Look For	Example	Implication
Hedonistic Orientation (common in preschool and the early elementary grades)	· Tendency to help others only when one can simultaneously address one's own needs as well · Prosocial behaviors directed primarily toward familiar adults and peers	Several preschoolers are at a table drawing pictures. Peter is using the only black crayon at the table. Alaina asks him for the crayon so she can color her dog black, telling him, "I just need it for a second." Ignoring her, Peter continues to use the black crayon for several more minutes and then gives it to Alaina.	Point out that other people also have legitimate needs, and emphasize the importance of fairness and helping others. For example, ask children to be "reading buddies" for younger children, explaining that doing so will help them become better readers themselves.
Superficial Needs-of-Others Orientation (common in the elementary grades)	· Some willingness to help others even at personal sacrifice to oneself · Only superficial understanding of others' perspectives	During an annual holiday toy drive, many of the children in a third-grade class contribute some of their toys. They seem happy to do so, commenting that "Poor kids need toys too" and "This doll will be fun for somebody else to play with."	Commend youngsters for altruistic behaviors, and ask them to speculate on how their actions are apt to make others feel (e.g., "Can you imagine how these children must feel when they get your toys? Most of them escaped the flood with only the clothes on their backs. What must it be like to lose everything you own—your clothes, your books, your favorite toys—*everything*?!").
Stereotyped, Approval-Focused Orientation (seen in some elementary and secondary students)	· Tendency to behave prosocially as a means to gain others' approval · Simplistic, stereotypical views of what "good" and "bad" people do	When walking to school one day, Cari sees Stanley inadvertently stumble and drop his backpack in a puddle. She stops, asks him if he's okay, and helps him wipe off the backpack. As she describes the incident to her teacher later that morning, she says, "Maybe he'll be my friend now. Anyway, it's nice to help other people."	Provide numerous opportunities for youngsters to engage in prosocial activities. Choose activities that are apt to be enjoyable and in other ways rewarding in and of themselves.
Empathic Orientation (common in the secondary grades)	· Genuine empathy for other people's distress, even when one does not know the people personally · Willingness to help without regard for consequences for oneself	Members of a high school service club coordinate a schoolwide garage sale, with all proceeds going to a fund to help pay medical expenses of a classmate with a rare form of cancer. They spend several weekends collecting people's contributions to the sale, using their own money for the supplies they need to make the fund-raiser a success.	Alert youngsters to circumstances, both locally and around the globe, in which people's basic needs are not being met or in which basic human rights are being violated. Ask youngsters to brainstorm ways in which they might in some small way make a difference for people living in dire circumstances.
Internalized Values Orientation (seen in a small minority of high school students)	· Generalized concern for equality, dignity, human rights, and the welfare of society as a whole · Commitment to helping others integrated into one's overall sense of self	Franklin spends much of his free time working with Habitat for Humanity, which builds houses for low-income families. "This is as important as my schoolwork," he says. "It's the responsibility of all of us to help one another whenever we can."	Create opportunities—public service projects, fund-raisers, and so on—in which youngsters with an internalized-values orientation can share their enthusiasm for prosocial activities with their peers.

Sources: First two columns based on Eisenberg, 1982; Eisenberg et al., 1995; Eisenberg, Lennon, & Pasternack, 1986.

physical aggression
Action that can potentially cause bodily injury (for example, hitting or scratching another person).

relational aggression
Action that can adversely affect interpersonal relationships (for example, calling another person names or socially excluding the person).

proactive aggression
Deliberate aggression against another as a means of obtaining a desired goal.

reactive aggression
Aggressive response to frustration or provocation.

bully
Child or adolescent who frequently threatens, harasses, or causes physical or psychological injury to particular peers.

hostile attributional bias
Tendency to interpret others' behaviors as reflecting hostile or aggressive intentions.

MyEducationLab

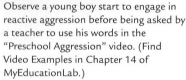

Observe a young boy start to engage in reactive aggression before being asked by a teacher to use his words in the "Preschool Aggression" video. (Find Video Examples in Chapter 14 of MyEducationLab.)

however. Their behavior is apt to reflect two or more orientations in any particular time period, but with age they increasingly exhibit more advanced orientations (Eisenberg et al., 1995; Eisenberg, Miller, Shell, McNalley, & Shea, 1991).

Other factors come into play as well. For example, children are more likely to help another individual if they themselves have been the cause of the person's pain or distress (Eisenberg, 1995). They are also more likely to behave prosocially if others' misfortunes are the result of an accident, disability, or other uncontrollable circumstance, rather than the result of something they think distressed people have brought upon themselves (Eisenberg & Fabes, 1998; S. Graham, 1997).

Finally, prosocial behaviors are more common when benefits outweigh the costs—for instance, when children think the beneficiary might eventually do them a favor in return (Eisenberg, Fabes, Schaller, Carlo, & Miller, 1991; L. Peterson, 1980). For some youngsters, however, the benefits of prosocial actions are strictly internal: A feeling of personal satisfaction about helping someone else more than makes up for any loss of time or convenience (see the "empathic" and "internalized values" orientations in the Observation Guidelines table on page 537). Unfortunately, some children believe that *aggression* yields more benefits than prosocial actions, as we shall see now.

Development of aggression.   Aggression takes a variety of forms. **Physical aggression** is an action that can potentially cause bodily injury. Examples are hitting, pushing, fighting, and using weapons. **Relational aggression** is an action that can adversely affect friendships and other interpersonal relationships. Examples are name-calling, spreading unflattering rumors, and ostracizing a peer from a desirable social group.

The capacity for aggression emerges fairly early. By the latter half of the first year, infants may show anger toward caregivers who prevent them from reaching desired objects (Stenberg & Campos, 1990). As they approach their first birthday, they may swat at age-mates who take their toys (M. Caplan, Vespo, Pedersen, & Hay, 1991; Dodge et al., 2006). Conflicts over possessions become fairly common during the preschool years (S. Jenkins, Bax, & Hart, 1980).

For most children, physical aggression declines after early childhood, partly because children learn to control their impulses, partly because they acquire better strategies for resolving conflicts, and partly because they become increasingly skillful at relational aggression (R. B. Cairns, Cairns, Neckerman, Ferguson, & Gariépy, 1989; Dodge et al., 2006; Loeber, 1982; Mischel, 1974; NICHD Early Childhood Research Network, 2004). This developmental decline in aggression is not universal, however. Researchers have identified two distinct groups of aggressive children and adolescents (Crick & Dodge, 1996; Poulin & Boivin, 1999; Vitaro, Gendreau, Tremblay, & Oligny, 1998). Those who engage in **proactive aggression** deliberately initiate aggressive behaviors—physical aggression, relational aggression, or both—as a means of obtaining desired goals. Those who engage in **reactive aggression** act aggressively primarily in response to frustration or provocation. Of the two groups, children who exhibit proactive aggression are more likely to have difficulty maintaining friendships with others (Poulin & Boivin, 1999). They may also direct considerable aggression toward particular peers, and those who do so are often known as **bullies.** Their hapless victims often are children who are immature, anxious, friendless, and lacking in self-confidence—some also have disabilities—and so are relatively defenseless (Bierman, 2004; L. Little, 2002; Marsh, Parada, Yeung, & Healey, 2001; Pellegrini, Bartini, & Brooks, 1999).

Social cognition clearly plays a role in aggressive behavior. Aggressive children tend to have one or more of the following characteristics:

- *Poor social perspective-taking ability.* Children who are highly aggressive tend to have limited ability to look at situations from other people's perspectives or to empathize with their victims (Dodge et al., 2006).
- *Misinterpretation of social cues.* Children who are either physically or relationally aggressive toward peers tend to interpret others' behaviors as reflecting hostile intentions, especially when such behaviors have ambiguous meanings. This **hostile attributional bias** is especially prevalent in children who are prone to *reactive* aggression (Crick & Dodge, 1996; Dodge et al., 2003; Orobio de Castro, Veerman, Koops, Bosch, & Monshouwer, 2002).
- *Prevalence of self-serving goals.* For most young people, establishing and maintaining interpersonal relationships is a high priority. For aggressive children, however, more self-serving goals—perhaps maintaining an inflated self-image, seeking revenge, or gaining

power and dominance—often take precedence (Bender, 2001; Crick & Dodge, 1996; Pellegrini, 2002).

- *Ineffective social problem-solving strategies.* Aggressive children often have little knowledge of how to persuade, negotiate, or compromise, and so they resort to hitting, shoving, barging into play activities, and using other ineffective strategies (Lochman & Dodge, 1994; Neel, Jenkins, & Meadows, 1990; D. Schwartz et al., 1998).
- *Beliefs about the appropriateness and effectiveness of aggression.* Many aggressive children believe that violence and other forms of aggression are acceptable ways of resolving conflicts and retaliating for others' misdeeds. For instance, they may believe they need to teach someone a "lesson." Those who display high rates of *proactive* aggression are also apt to believe that aggressive action will yield positive results—for instance, that it will enhance their social status. Aggressive children tend to associate with one another, thus confirming one another's beliefs that aggression is appropriate (Astor, 1994; Espelage, Holt, & Henkel, 2003; Farmer et al., 2002; Pellegrini & Bartini, 2000; E. Staub, 1995).

Children who are especially aggressive when they are young tend to be more aggressive in later years as well (C. A. Anderson et al., 2003; Kupersmidt & Coie, 1990; G. W. Ladd & Burgess, 1999). Furthermore, children who display proactive aggression (but not those who display only reactive aggression) are at increased risk for engaging in delinquent activities later on (Vitaro et al., 1998). And the victims of aggression—whether it be physical or relational—are apt to have low self-esteem and possibly suffer from depression (Crick, Casas, & Nelson, 2002). After being the victim of relational aggression from friends, 13-year-old Julie confides her distress in her diary (we've changed the names of her friends but left her original spelling intact):

> I feel like I need to tell somebody whats going on. Umm well the topic is friends. OK well I start off with Sonja and Dana. They make me so mad sometimes. Today I went and sat down @ lunch then I got up for a sec. When I came back Sonja was sitting right next to where I was sitting so I sat down next to her. Then Sonja says "Julie you can't sit there I'm saving it for someone important." "Who?" "Dana." I had already kinda known it was Dana those two have been inseperable the last month or so. So me, being angry at Sonja, goes to sit on the other side. The whole time at lunch Sonja was talking about me. I am not afraid to say that I am jealous because I am and I have already told Dana and Sonja this twice and they don't really get the point. They are both really great friends and I don't want to lose them.

Julie ends by saying that Dana and Sonja are both "really great friends," apparently trying to overlook their intentionally vindictive behavior. Some 13-year-olds might react differently, perhaps by actively confronting their peers about the transgression or by withdrawing from these particular relationships. But whatever tactic they use, many children and adolescents do become preoccupied with teasing, ridicule, and social exclusion by peers (Crick, Casas, & Nelson, 2002).

Both prosocial behavior and aggression can typically be seen at one time or another in youngsters of various ages and backgrounds. In addition to their universality across cultural groups, these seemingly opposite kinds of behavior have other similarities, as you can see in the Basic Developmental Issues table "Comparing Prosocial Behavior and Aggression."

Diversity in Interpersonal Behaviors

Youngsters' interpersonal behaviors tend to differ somewhat depending on their gender, ethnic and cultural background, and (in some cases) disabilities and other special educational needs.

Gender differences. At the preschool level, you are apt to see gender differences in children's play activities (Dunsmore, Noguchi, Garner, Casey, & Bhullar, 2008; Gallahue & Ozmun, 1998; Gottman, 1986; Paley, 1984). In sociodramatic play, girls tend to enact scenarios that are relatively calm and sedate (e.g., playing house or school). In contrast, boys often introduce elements of adventure and danger (e.g., playing cops and robbers or fighting intergalactic battles).

As boys grow older, they continue to place high priority on physical action. Girls spend much more time simply talking—sharing personal concerns, telling secrets, offering emotional support, and so on (Berndt, 1992; G. P. Jones & Dembo, 1989; McCallum & Bracken,

In his drawing of a superhero holding a weapon, 6-year-old Myron shows his understanding that aggression is a way of gaining power and dominance over others.

MyEducationLab

Listen to a girl talk about what it is like to be the target of a bully's aggression in the "Bullying" video. (Find Video Examples in Chapter 14 of MyEducationLab.)

Basic Developmental Issues

Comparing Prosocial Behavior and Aggression

Issue	Prosocial Behavior	Aggression
Nature and Nurture	The capacity for prosocial behavior appears to be a natural, inborn human characteristic, but individual children have unique genetic endowments (e.g., temperaments) that predispose them to varying degrees of altruism. Prosocial behavior is nurtured by affectionate caregiving, role modeling, reinforcement for prosocial actions, and explicit requests for children to consider the needs of others in unfortunate circumstances.	The capacity for aggression has a biological basis and is to some degree inherited. Aggressiveness in individual children is influenced by temperamental dispositions, hormone levels, and neurological structures in the brain. Yet the social environment influences how children express their aggressive impulses. Families, social institutions (e.g., schools), and communities may foster aggression either directly (e.g., through modeling and endorsement of aggression) or indirectly (e.g., through harsh punishment and unreasonable expectations).
Universality and Diversity	The capacity for prosocial behavior is universal in the human species. Furthermore, people in most cultures become increasingly prosocial as they get older. Significant diversity exists in the extent to which various cultural groups encourage prosocial activities (e.g., sharing, nurturing), as well as in children's exposure to adults who model prosocial behavior and articulate a commitment to caring for people in need.	Aggressive behavior is universal in human beings. Some general developmental sequences in aggressive expression, such as a gradual shift from physical aggression to verbal aggression, may also be universal. Substantial diversity is present in the ways that children and adolescents express aggression, in the amount of aggression young people encounter in their daily environments, and in the extent to which cultural groups condone aggression as a way of resolving conflict.
Qualitative and Quantitative Change	Qualitative changes may occur in children's understanding of why helping others is important and valuable. For instance, young children often give help primarily to gain rewards or approval, whereas older children and adolescents are more likely to have a genuine concern for people in need. Quantitative increases occur in children's knowledge of effective prosocial strategies and in their ability to carry out such strategies.	A gradual shift from physical aggression in early childhood to more verbal and relational forms of aggression in later years reflects qualitative change. The decline in physical aggression over childhood and adolescence reflects quantitative change.

Sources: Dodge, Coie, & Lyman, 2006; Eisenberg & Fabes, 1998.

1993; Underwood, 2007). Girls tend to form closer and more intimate relationships with others and are more sensitive to the subtle, nonverbal messages (body language) that others communicate (J. H. Block, 1983; Deaux, 1984). On average, girls are slightly more kind and considerate, but in many circumstances boys do show their "softer" sides, displaying affection and sympathy appropriate for the occasion (Eisenberg & Fabes, 1998).

The most pronounced gender difference in children's interpersonal behaviors is in physical aggression. Beginning in the preschool years, boys are more physically aggressive than girls (Collaer & Hines, 1995; Dodge et al., 2006; Eagly, 1987; Loeber & Stouthamer-Loeber, 1998; Underwood, 2007). This greater inclination toward physical aggression is probably the result of both biological factors (recall the link between testosterone and aggression) and socialization (parents are more likely to allow aggression in sons than in daughters) (Collaer & Hines, 1995; Condry & Ross, 1985; Eisenberg et al., 1996). However, girls are at least as aggressive as boys (and sometimes more so) in relational aggression—for example, by tattling, gossiping, and snubbing their peers (Crick, Grotpeter, & Bigbee, 2002; Dodge et al., 2006; D. C. French, Jansen, & Pidada, 2002; Pellegrini, 2002).

Boys also tend to be more assertive than girls. For example, in mixed-sex work groups, they are apt to dominate activities and take charge of needed equipment, and they are more likely to get their way when group members disagree (Jovanovic & King, 1998). Such assertiveness may be nurtured in same-sex activity groups over the years, as boys' friendships typically involve more conflict and competition than girls' friendships do (Eisenberg et al., 1996). In contrast, girls are more likely to acquiesce

Girls tend to form closer, more intimate relationships with one another than boys do.

to others' wishes, perhaps because they value group harmony more than boys do and so make frequent small concessions to keep the peace (Benenson et al., 2002; P. M. Miller, Danaher, & Forbes, 1986; Rudolph et al., 2005).

Ethnic and cultural differences.   Children may have more or fewer opportunities to interact with peers depending on the culture in which they grow up. Unlike in North America, where most children come into frequent contact with age-mates at an early age, children in some cultures in other parts of the world stay close to home and play primarily with parents and siblings, at least until they reach school age (Trawick-Smith, 2003; Whiting & Edwards, 1988). Some children whose primary language is different from that of the larger society in which they live (e.g., as is true for non–English-speaking immigrants to an English-speaking country) also have limited opportunities to interact with age-mates (A. Doyle, 1982).

To some degree, different cultural groups also model and teach different interpersonal behaviors. For instance, children in China are encouraged to be shy, whereas those in Israel are encouraged to be assertive (X. Chen, Rubin, & Li, 1995; Krispin, Sternberg, & Lamb, 1992). Smiling is a sign of agreement and friendliness in almost any cultural group, but in a few cultures (e.g., in some Japanese American families) it may also indicate embarrassment (Eckman, 1972).

Cultures differ, too, in the degree to which they encourage competition or cooperation with others. In North America and western Europe, many people see competition as desirable (e.g., parents may enter their children in dance contests, high school teachers sometimes grade on a curve), and children are more likely to be praised for their individual achievements than for group success. In contrast, many other cultures (e.g., most Asian and Hispanic societies) place a high premium on loyalty, trust, cooperation, and prosocial behavior (Greenfield, 1994; Kitayama et al., 2007; P. B. Smith & Bond, 1994; Triandis, 1995).

Children with special needs.   On average, children and adolescents with high intelligence (e.g., youngsters whom school personnel have identified as gifted) have good social skills. However, a few youngsters with highly advanced intellectual abilities have trouble establishing and maintaining effective interpersonal relationships with age-mates because they are in some ways so *very* different from their peers (A. E. Gottfried, Fleming, & Gottfried, 1994; Keogh & MacMillan, 1996; Winner, 1997).

Many children with disabilities, too, have good interpersonal skills. But some others do not. Children with significant physical disabilities may have few opportunities to practice social skills with their peers. And children who have impaired social cognition—for instance, children with a significant intellectual disability or one of the autism spectrum disorders— often have deficiencies in social skills as well (S. Greenspan & Granfield, 1992; Milch-Reich, Campbell, Pelham, Connelly, & Geva, 1999; Turnbull et al., 2007; also see Chapter 12). Youngsters with chronic emotional and behavioral problems (e.g., conduct disorders) typically have difficulty making and keeping friends, usually because of poor social problem-solving and other social skills (Asher & Coie, 1990; Cartledge & Milburn, 1995; DuPaul & Eckert, 1994).

As you have learned, social skills change steadily over the childhood years. In the Developmental Trends table "Interpersonal Skills at Different Age Levels," we present characteristics and behaviors that teachers and other practitioners are likely to see in infants, children, and adolescents, as well as common forms of diversity in the different age-groups.

Fostering effective interpersonal skills.   Teachers and other practitioners who work with young people in social settings have many opportunities to encourage good social skills and discourage inappropriate interpersonal behaviors. Following are strategies that researchers and experienced educators have found to be effective:

• ***Teach specific social skills and social problem-solving strategies.*** Through frequent interactions with adults and peers, many youngsters acquire effective social behaviors on their own. But many others—perhaps because of limited opportunities to interact with age-mates, poor role models at home, or a cognitive disability—know little about how to initiate conversations, exchange compliments, offer emotional support, or in other ways establish and maintain rewarding interpersonal relationships. Some also lack productive strategies for solving social problems. For example, they may barge into a game without asking if they can participate or respond to any provocation with aggression.

Interpersonal Skills at Different Age Levels

Age	What You Might Observe	Diversity	Implications
Infancy (Birth–2 Years) 	· Increasing engagement with other infants (e.g., watching and touching them, vocalizing, smiling at them and imitating them) · Appearance of simple prosocial behaviors (e.g., offering a teddy bear to a crying child) in the second year · Anger at caregivers who frustrate efforts toward desired goals · Conflicts with peers about toys and other desired objects · Occasional biting, hitting, or scratching of peers	· Infants who have frequent contact with age-mates (e.g., in group child care) tend to be more sociable. · Infants may be more inclined to show prosocial behaviors when caregivers model these behaviors. · Some children have "difficult" temperaments; they may be especially contrary in the second year, biting others or exhibiting frequent temper tantrums.	· Allow infants to interact with one another under your guidance and protection. · Verbalize expressions of empathy and sympathy toward a child within earshot of other children. · Warmly acknowledge infants' prosocial behaviors. · Set up the environment to reduce frustration and aggression; for instance, provide duplicates of favorite toys, and create separate areas for quiet play and active movement. · Explain to aggressive toddlers that some actions are unacceptable, and impose appropriate consequences (e.g., by placing a child in a short time-out after first comforting the target of the child's aggression).
Early Childhood (2–6 Years) 	· Some signs of empathy for people in distress · Increasing sharing and coordination of play activities (e.g., sociodramatic play) · Attempts to comfort people in distress, especially those whom children know well; comforting strategies not always effective · Some aggressive struggles with peers about possessions; increasing ability to inhibit aggressive impulses	· Children who are temperamentally fearful and inhibited may stay on the periphery of social interactions. · Children who are inclined to be impulsive may use more physical aggression than children who are more patient and self-regulating. · Children are more apt to behave prosocially if they are consistently reinforced for such behavior. · On average, boys are more physically aggressive than girls.	· Recognize that selfish and territorial behaviors are common in early childhood. · Model sympathetic responses; explain what you are doing and why you are doing it. · Encourage children to give one another comfort when they can. · Praise any gentle, controlled, and constructive responses to frustration or provocation. · Comfort the victims of aggression, and administer appropriate consequences for the perpetrators. Explain why aggressive behavior cannot be tolerated.
Middle Childhood (6–10 Years) 	· Growing repertoire of conflict-resolution skills · Expanding time in large social groups playing rule-governed games · Increasing empathy for unknown individuals who are suffering or needy · Increasing desire to help others as an objective in and of itself · Decrease in overt physical aggression, but with an increase in relational aggression and more covert antisocial behaviors (e.g., lying, stealing)	· Children whose parents value prosocial behavior are more likely to value it as well and to have genuine concern for others. · Some children consistently misinterpret peers' thoughts and motives (e.g., by interpreting accidents as deliberate attempts to cause harm). · Some children become increasingly aggressive in the elementary grades. · Some children are bullies who regularly victimize vulnerable peers (e.g., those without friends or those with disabilities).	· Assist children in their attempts to resolve interpersonal conflicts by asking them to consider one another's perspectives and develop a solution that addresses everyone's needs. · Draw attention to a comforted child's relief when another child helps ("Look how much better Sally feels now that you've apologized for hurting her feelings"). · Do not tolerate physical aggression or bullying. Make sure children understand rules for behavior, and follow through with appropriate consequences when children are aggressive. · Be on the lookout for children who seem to be frequent victims of others' aggression; help them form productive, supportive relationships with peers.
Early Adolescence (10–14 Years) 	· Increasing sensitivity to body language and other nonverbal cues · Decline in physical aggression · Frequent teasing and taunting of peers; emergence of sexual harassment · Rising tendency to be affected by peer pressure and desire to fit into particular social groups · Tendency to divide into separate social groups defined by race and ethnicity (more common in large schools with many students)	· Self-disclosure is more common in girls than in boys. · Beginning at puberty, an increased testosterone level in boys adds to their aggressive tendencies. · Some adolescents with social-emotional problems (e.g., those with conduct disorders) show deficits in empathy for others. · Bullying behavior in some youngsters may temporarily increase after the transition to middle school or junior high.	· Communicate that giving, sharing, and caring for others should be high priorities. · Keep a watchful eye on students' between-class and after-school activities; make it clear that aggression is *not* acceptable on school grounds. · Talk with adolescents about their peer relationships and the pressures they may feel to conform.

Developmental Trends (continued)

Age	What You Might Observe	Diversity	Implications
Late Adolescence (14–18 Years) 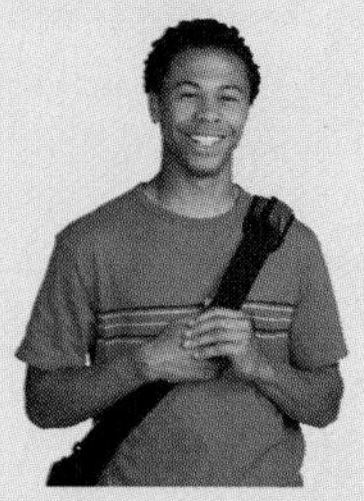	· For many, less motivation to engage in aggressive behavior, often as a result of forming more intimate and rewarding relationships with others · Frequent in-depth, heart-to-heart discussions with peers, during which adolescents explore who they are and what they stand for · New flexibility in peer groups; softening of peer-group boundaries	· Some high school students are exceptionally committed to making the world a better place (e.g., they may be active in Amnesty International, a group committed to preserving human rights around the world). · On average, youngsters who live in poor, violent neighborhoods are more apt to become aggressive. · Violence-prone adolescents often believe that hitting another person is reasonable retribution for unjust actions. · Substance abuse and sexual activity increase the probability of aggression.	· Encourage community service work so as to engender a commitment to helping others. Ask adolescents to reflect on their experiences through group discussions or written essays. · Enforce prohibitions against bringing weapons to school and other settings. · Provide intensive treatment to young people who exhibit especially aggressive tendencies.

Teachers, counselors, and other adults can teach effective interpersonal behaviors both through explicit verbal instructions (e.g., see Figure 14-5) and through encouragement and modeling of desired behaviors. The Development and Practice feature "Teaching Social Skills" presents several useful strategies.

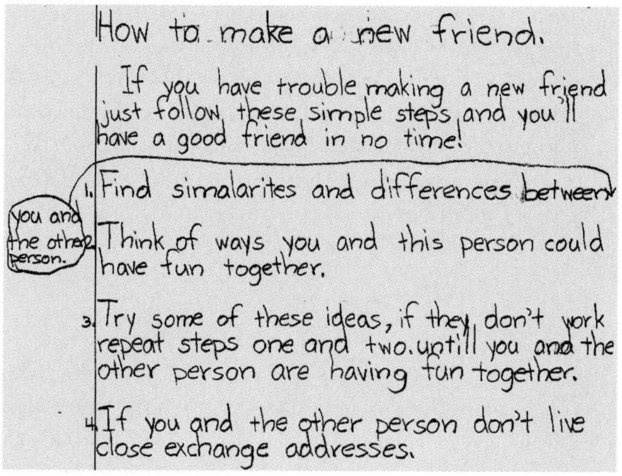
How to make a new friend.
If you have trouble making a new friend just follow these simple steps and you'll have a good friend in no time!
1. Find simalarites and differences between you and the other person.
2. Think of ways you and this person could have fun together.
3. Try some of these ideas, if they don't work repeat steps one and two. untill you and the other person are having fun together.
4. If you and the other person don't live close exchange addresses.

Figure 14-5

In this writing assignment, 9-year-old Mariel lists four strategies that her teacher has suggested for making a new friend.

Yet adults must also give children some leeway in their social lives. Following is one elementary school teacher's perspective on the advantages of letting children learn some social lessons on their own:

> Before, when problems came up, I think I was very quick to intervene. Certainly, I asked the kids involved to express themselves "very briefly" about what had happened. But I was quick to judge, to comment, to advise, and to try to reconcile them, for instance, by saying, "Well, now you must be friends." Thus, the students themselves were not active in the problem solution. It was usually I who found the solutions and I who controlled the situation. Now I am not as quick to intervene. I ask the children to stop and think, and to express themselves about what happened, and I withdraw more and listen to them. Certainly it is more effective if they themselves face and solve the problems. Then the solution and the whole experience are more likely to stay with them. (Adalbjarnardottir & Selman, 1997, p. 421)

• ***Label appropriate behaviors as they occur.*** Teachers can heighten children's awareness of effective social skills by identifying and praising behaviors that reflect those skills (Vorrath, 1985; Wittmer & Honig, 1994). For example, a teacher might say, "Thank you for *sharing* your art materials so helpfully," or, "I think that you two were able to write a more imaginative short story by *cooperating* on the project." Researchers have found, too, that describing children as having desirable characteristics (generosity, empathy, etc.) has beneficial effects (Grusec & Redler, 1980; R. S. L. Mills & Grusec, 1989). For example, 8-year-olds who are told, "You're the kind of person who likes to help others whenever you can," are more likely to share their belongings with others later on.

• ***Plan cooperative activities.*** When youngsters participate in cooperative games rather than in competitive ones, aggressive behaviors tend to decrease (Bay-Hinitz, Peterson, & Quilitch, 1994). In cooperative learning activities, youngsters can practice help-giving, help-seeking, and conflict-resolution skills (Damon, 1988; Lickona, 1991; Webb & Farivar, 1994). Furthermore, cooperative tasks that require a number of different skills and abilities foster an appreciation for the various strengths that children with diverse backgrounds are likely to contribute (E. G. Cohen, 1994; E. G. Cohen & Lotan, 1995; Lotan, 2006). Cooperative activities are usually most successful when children have a structure to follow (e.g., when each group member is given a specific role to perform) and are given some guidelines about appropriate group behavior (E. G. Cohen, 1994; Schofield, 1995; N. M. Webb & Palincsar, 1996; Webb et al., 2008).

Development and Practice

Teaching Social Skills

- **Explicitly teach skills that children may be lacking.**

  A counselor who is working with several very shy and socially isolated high school students teaches them several ways to initiate and maintain conversations with others. "One thing you might do," he says, "is give a compliment about something you like about a person. Then you can follow up with a question to get the person talking. For example, you might say, 'I really liked what you said about protecting the rain forests in class the other day. I didn't realize how quickly the earth's rain forests were being destroyed. Have you read a lot about the topic?' " After describing several additional strategies, the counselor has the students work in pairs to practice each one.

- **Ask children to brainstorm approaches to solving social dilemmas.**

  A middle school teacher presents this situation to his class: "Imagine that one of your classmates comes up to you and asks if she can copy your homework. You don't want to let her copy it. After all, she won't learn what her teacher wanted her to learn by copying someone else's work. But you also don't want to make her angry or upset. How might you refuse her request while also keeping her friendship?"

- **Encourage children and adolescents to think carefully before acting in difficult social situations.**

  A soccer coach finds that several of her 9- and 10-year-old players react impulsively to any provocation. For instance, they might hit or yell at a teammate or opposing player who unintentionally bumps into them on the playing field. The coach teaches the athletes four steps to follow in such situations: (a) *Think* about what just happened, (b) *list* three different ways to respond, (c) *predict* what might happen for each response, and (d) *choose* the best response.

- **Give concrete feedback about effective and ineffective interpersonal behaviors.**

  During a cooperative learning activity, a high school teacher notices that the members of one cooperative group are getting increasingly angry. After briefly eavesdropping on their discussion, the teacher reminds them, "As we agreed yesterday, it's okay to criticize ideas, but it's *not* okay to criticize people."

- **Communicate your concern for children who are hurt, and enlist the support of other children in caring for them.**

  A preschool teacher sympathizes with a child who has skinned his knee. She brings out the first aid kit and asks another child to find a bandage as she applies the antiseptic.

- **Acknowledge children's good deeds.**

  When a third-grade teacher notices a child helping a classmate who doesn't understand an assignment, she comments, "Thank you for helping Amanda, Jack. You're always ready to lend a hand!"

- ***Expose children to numerous models of prosocial behavior.*** Adults teach by what they do as well as by what they say. For example, when educators model compassion and consideration for others, children are likely to emulate such behaviors. Ideally, children should come into contact with other prosocial models as well. For instance, preschool teachers might encourage children to watch age-appropriate television programs that model prosocial behavior (e.g., *Sesame Street, Barney and Friends*) (D. R. Anderson, 2003; Jordan, 2003). In the elementary and secondary grades, teachers might invite public servants or members of charitable organizations to talk with students about the many intangible rewards of community service work. Teachers can also make use of prosocial models in literature (Nucci, 2001). One good example is Harper Lee's *To Kill a Mockingbird,* set in the highly segregated and racially charged Alabama of the 1930s. In this novel a lawyer defends an African American man falsely accused of raping a white woman and exemplifies a willingness to fight for social justice in the face of strong social pressure to convict the man.

- ***Give concrete guidelines for behavior.*** Children should consistently hear the message that they must be respectful and considerate of others. One way to communicate this message is to establish firm rules that prohibit physical aggression and possession of weapons. Behaviors that cause psychological harm—malicious gossip, prejudicial remarks, sexual harassment, intimidation, ostracism, and so on—must also be off-limits. And adults must consistently enforce these rules in the classroom, on the playground, in extracurricular activities, and elsewhere (Juvonen, Nishina, & Graham, 2000; Learning First Alliance, 2001).

- ***Develop a peer mediation program.*** Children and adolescents alike often benefit from **peer mediation** training that teaches them how to intervene effectively in their peers' interpersonal disputes (M. Deutsch, 1993; D. W. Johnson & Johnson, 1996, 2001; Schumpf, Crawford, & Usadel, 1991). In such training, youngsters learn how to help their peers resolve conflicts by asking opposing sides to express their differing points of view and then work together to devise a reasonable resolution. In one study (D. W. Johnson, Johnson, Dudley,

peer mediation
Approach to conflict resolution in which one child or adolescent (the mediator) asks peers in conflict to express their differing viewpoints and then work together to identify an appropriate compromise.

Ward, & Magnuson, 1995), students in grades 2 through 5 were trained to help peers resolve interpersonal conflicts by asking the opposing sides to do the following:

1. Define the conflict (the problem).
2. Explain their own perspectives and needs.
3. Explain the *other* side's perspectives and needs.
4. Identify at least three possible solutions to the conflict.
5. Reach an agreement that addresses the needs of both parties.

Students took turns serving as mediator for their classmates, such that everyone had experience resolving the conflicts of others. As a result, the students more frequently resolved their *own* interpersonal conflicts in ways that addressed the needs of both parties, and they were less likely to ask for adult intervention, than students who had not had mediation training.

Peer mediation is most effective when youngsters of diverse ethnic backgrounds, socioeconomic groups, and achievement levels all serve as mediators. Furthermore, it is typically most useful for relatively small, short-term interpersonal problems (hurt feelings, conflicts over use of limited academic resources, etc.). Even the most proficient of peer mediators may be ill prepared to handle conflicts that reflect deep-seated and emotionally charged attitudes and behaviors, such as conflicts that involve sexual harassment or homophobia (Casella, 2001; K. M. Williams, 2001b).

Creating a Safe School Environment

Students can learn and achieve at optimal levels only if they know they are both physically and psychologically safe at school. Furthermore, if they *don't* feel safe, they're at increased risk for dropping out of school before graduation (Rumberger, 1995). To be truly effective in combating aggression and violence at school, teachers and administrators must attack it on three levels, depicted graphically in Figure 14-6 (Dwyer & Osher, 2000; Hyman et al., 2006; H. M. Walker et al., 1996).[2]

Level I: Creating a nonviolent school environment. One-shot "antiviolence" campaigns have little lasting effect on school aggression and violence (Burstyn & Stevens, 2001). Instead, creating a peaceful, nonviolent school environment must be a long-term effort that includes the following strategies:

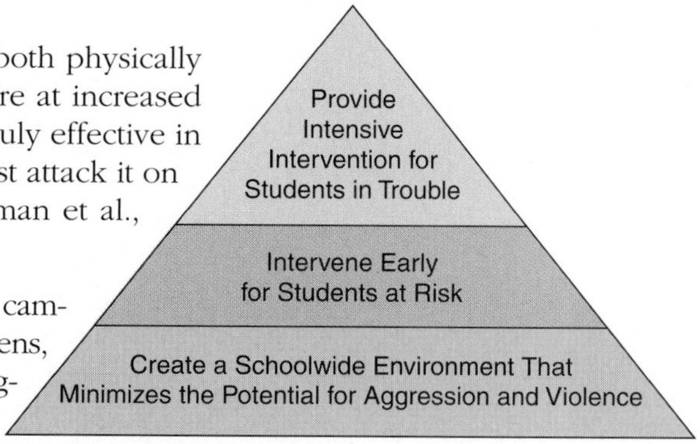

- Make a joint, schoolwide commitment to supporting all students' academic and social success.
- Provide a challenging and engaging curriculum.
- Form caring, trusting faculty–student relationships.
- Insist on genuine and equal respect—among students as well as faculty—for people of diverse backgrounds, races, and ethnicities.
- Establish schoolwide policies and practices that foster appropriate behavior (e.g., give clear guidelines for behavior, consistently apply consequences for infractions, provide instruction in effective social interaction and problem-solving skills).
- Involve students in decision making about school policies and procedures.
- Provide mechanisms through which students can communicate their concerns openly and without fear of reprisal.
- Emphasize prosocial behaviors (e.g., sharing, helping, cooperation).
- Establish close working relationships with community agencies and families.
- Openly discuss safety issues.

  (Burstyn & Stevens, 2001; Dwyer & Osher, 2000; Dwyer, Osher, & Warger, 1998; Learning First Alliance, 2001; Meehan, Hughes, & Cavell, 2003; G. M. Morrison, Furlong, D'Incau, & Morrison, 2004; Pellegrini, 2002)

Figure 14-6

A three-level approach to preventing aggression and violence in schools.

Based on a figure in *Safeguarding Our Children: An Action Guide* (p. 3) by K. Dwyer and D. Osher, 2000, Washington, DC: U.S. Departments of Education and Justice, American Institutes for Research.

---

[2]For a more in-depth discussion of the three levels, read *Safeguarding Our Children: An Action Guide* by K. Dwyer and D. Osher (2000). You can download a copy from a variety of Internet Web sites, such as www.ed.gov/admins/lead/safety/actguide/index.html.

Many of these strategies have surfaced at one place or another in this book (and we will build on these tactics further in Chapter 15). The final strategy on the list—an open discussion of safety issues—encompasses a variety of more specific strategies. For example, school faculty members should:

- Explain what bullying is (i.e., that it involves harassing and intimidating peers who cannot easily defend themselves) and why it is unacceptable.
- Solicit students' input on potentially unsafe areas (e.g., an infrequently used restroom or back stairwell) that require more faculty supervision.
- Convey willingness to hear students' complaints about troublesome classmates (such complaints can provide important clues about which students are most in need of assistance and intervention).

You can watch a middle school teacher talk openly with her students about bullying in a Building Teaching Skills and Dispositions exercise in MyEducationLab.

Level II: Intervening early for students at risk. Students are at risk for negative adjustment in school, as well as in life more generally, when peers reject them (a topic we explore further in Chapter 15). Perhaps 10 to 15 percent of students need some sort of intervention to help them interact effectively with peers, establish good working relationships with teachers, and become bona fide members of the school community (Dwyer & Osher, 2000; H. M. Walker et al., 1996). Such an intervention cannot be a one-size-fits-all approach but must instead be tailored to students' particular strengths and needs. For some students it might take the form of social skills training. In other cases it might mean getting students actively involved in school clubs or extracurricular activities. In still others it may require well-planned, systematic efforts to encourage and reinforce productive behaviors. But regardless of their nature, interventions are more effective when they occur *early* in the game—before students go too far down the path of antisocial behavior—and when they are developed by a multi-disciplinary team of teachers and other professionals who bring various areas of expertise to the planning table (Dryfoos, 1997; Dwyer & Osher, 2000).

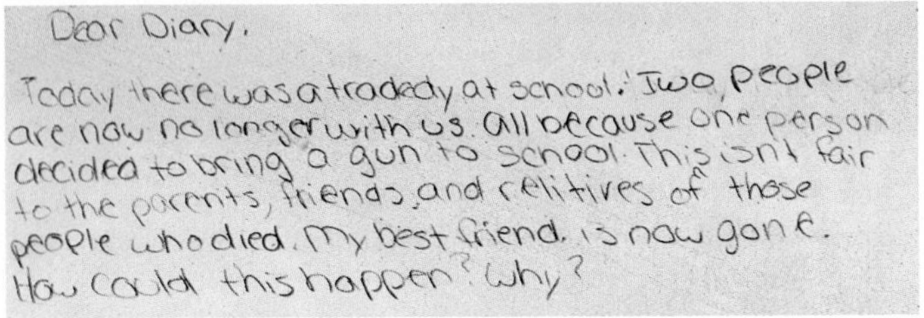

MyEducationLab

Go to the Building Teaching Skills and Dispositions section in Chapter 14 of MyEducationLab to learn how teachers can talk to children and adolescents about bullying.

Dear Diary,

Today there was a tradedy at school. Two people are now no longer with us. All because one person decided to bring a gun to school. This isn't fair to the parents, friends, and relitives of those people who died. My best friend is now gone. How could this happen? Why?

Figure 14-7

Occasionally physical aggression at school has tragic consequences, as shown in one child's diary entry.

Level III: Providing intensive intervention for students in trouble. When left unchecked, aggressive tendencies sometimes escalate into serious violence (see Figure 14-7). For a variety of reasons, minor interventions will not always be sufficient when students are predisposed to be exceptionally violent. For instance, some students have serious mental illnesses (e.g., schizophrenia, bipolar disorder) that interfere with their ability to cope appropriately with everyday frustrations (see Chapter 11). Typically, schools must work closely and collaboratively with other community groups—perhaps mental health clinics, police and probation officers, and social services—to help students at high risk for aggression and violence (Dwyer & Osher, 2000; Greenberg et al., 2003; Hyman et al., 2006).

Teachers' frequent interactions with students put teachers in an ideal position to identify those children and adolescents most in need of intensive intervention to get them back on track for academic and social success. Especially after working with a particular age-group for a period of time, teachers acquire a good sense of what characteristics are and are not normal for that age level. Teachers should especially be on the lookout for the early warning signs of violence presented in Figure 14-8.

Although teachers must be ever-vigilant about signs that a student may be planning to cause harm to others, it is essential that they keep several points in mind. First, despite media reports about school shootings, extreme violence is *very rare* in schools (DeVoe et al., 2003; Garbarino et al., 2002). Unreasonable paranoia about potential school violence will prevent teachers from working effectively with students. Second, the great majority of students who exhibit one or a few of the warning signs in Figure 14-8 will *not* become violent. And most importantly, a teacher must *never* use the warning signs as a reason to unfairly accuse, isolate, or punish a student (Dwyer et al., 1998). These signs provide a means of getting youngsters help if they need it, not of excluding them from the education that all children and adolescents deserve.

Experts have identified numerous warning signs that a child or adolescent may possibly be contemplating violent actions against others. By themselves, most of the signs are unlikely to signal a violent attack, but several of them in combination necessitate consultation with school administrators and specially trained professionals.

- **Social withdrawal.** Over time, a student interacts less and less frequently with teachers and with all or most peers.

- **Excessive feelings of isolation, rejection, or persecution.** A student may directly or indirectly express the belief that he or she is friendless, disliked, or unfairly picked on.

- **Rapid decline in academic performance.** A student shows a dramatic change in academic performance and seems unconcerned about doing well. Cognitive and physical factors (e.g., learning disabilities, ineffective study strategies, brain injury) have been ruled out as causes of the decline.

- **Poor coping skills.** A student has little ability to deal effectively with frustration, takes the smallest affront personally, and has trouble bouncing back after minor disappointments.

- **Lack of anger control.** A student frequently responds with uncontrolled anger to even the slightest injustice and may misdirect anger at innocent bystanders.

- **Sense of superiority, self-centeredness, and lack of empathy.** A student depicts himself or herself as smarter or in some other way better than peers, is preoccupied with his or her own needs, and has little regard for the needs of others.

- **Lengthy grudges.** A student is unforgiving of others' transgressions, even after considerable time has elapsed.

- **Violent themes in drawings and written work.** Violence predominates in a student's artwork, stories, and journal entries, and certain individuals (e.g., a parent or particular classmate) are regularly targeted in these fantasies. (Keep in mind that *occasional* violence in writing and art is not unusual, especially for boys.)

- **Intolerance of individual and group differences.** A student shows intense disdain for and prejudice toward people of a certain race, ethnicity, gender, sexual orientation, religion, or disability.

- **History of violence, aggression, and other discipline problems.** A student has a long record of seriously inappropriate behavior extending over several years.

- **Association with violent peers.** A student associates regularly with a gang or other antisocial peer group.

- **Inappropriate role models.** A student may speak with admiration about Satan, Hitler, Osama bin Laden, or some other malevolent figure.

- **Frequent alcohol or drug use.** A student who abuses alcohol or drugs may have reduced self-control; in some cases substance abuse signals significant mental illness.

- **Inappropriate access to firearms.** A student has easy access to guns and ammunition and may regularly practice using them.

- **Threats of violence.** A student has openly expressed an intent to harm someone else. *This warning sign alone requires immediate action.*

Figure 14-8

Early warning signs of violent behavior.

Sources: Dwyer et al., 1998; O'Toole, 2000. As published in Ormrod, Jeanne E. *Educational Psychology: Developing Learners, 6e.* Published by Merrill/Prentice Hall, Upper Saddle River, NJ. Copyright © 2008 by Pearson Education. Reprinted by permission of the publisher.

Gang-related problems. A frequent source of aggression at some schools is gang-related hostilities. Although gangs are more prevalent in low-income, inner-city schools, they are sometimes found in suburban and rural schools as well (Howell & Lynch, 2000).

The three-level approach to combating school aggression and violence just described can go a long way toward suppressing violent gang activities, but school personnel will often need to take additional measures as well. Recommended strategies include the following:

- Develop, communicate, and enforce clear-cut policies regarding potential threats to school safety.
- Identify the specific nature and scope of gang activity in the student population.
- Forbid clothing, jewelry, and behaviors that signify membership in a particular gang (e.g., bandanas, shoelaces in gang colors, certain hand signs).[3]
- Actively mediate between-gang and within-gang disputes. (Kodluboy, 2004)

In the last of these strategies—mediation—either adults or peers might serve as mediators, provided that they are familiar with the cultures and issues of the gang(s) involved (Kodluboy, 2004).

With help from caring adults, most young people develop the basic moral abilities and social skills they need to get along well with others. In the next and final chapter, we look more closely at children's social relationships in their friendships, peer groups, and schools and classrooms.

---

[3]A potential problem with this strategy is that it may violate students' civil liberties. For guidance on how to walk the line between ensuring students' safety and giving them reasonable freedom of expression, see Kodluboy (2004) and Rozalski and Yell (2004).

Summary

Moral Reasoning and Behavior

An ability to distinguish between right and wrong emerges early in life and continues to develop over time. Infants are clearly uncomfortable when they witness others being hurt. Most preschoolers have some awareness that actions that cause significant physical or psychological harm are wrong even if an authority figure tells them otherwise. As children get older, they progress in their understanding of fairness and develop an increasing capacity to feel guilt, shame, and empathy about moral wrongdoings. As they advance in cognitive skills, and especially as they become capable of abstract thought, they reason about moral issues and dilemmas in more sophisticated ways, and they are more likely to behave in accordance with general moral principles. Even at the high school level, however, youngsters do not always take the moral high road, as personal needs and self-interests often enter into their moral decisions.

To some degree, different cultures foster different moral values, but virtually all cultural groups recognize the importance of fairness, justice, and concern for others. Adults can promote young people's moral development by explaining why certain behaviors are unacceptable (in that they cause harm or distress to another or jeopardize another's rights and needs), engaging youngsters in discussions about moral issues and dilemmas, exposing them to diverse and slightly more advanced moral perspectives, and getting them actively involved in service to others.

Interpersonal Behaviors

Interpersonal behaviors begin in infancy, when children show an interest in other people and make simple social gestures. Youngsters continue to acquire and refine their social skills (e.g., cooperation, negotiation, conflict resolution) throughout childhood and adolescence, especially as they spend more and more of their time with peers rather than adults. Child care settings, schools, and other group environments provide important contexts in which effective interpersonal skills develop and can be nurtured.

Most children become increasingly prosocial and less aggressive over the years, with such changes being partly the result of their growing capacity for perspective taking, empathy, and sympathy. However, some children and adolescents display troublesome levels of physical or relational aggression, perhaps partly as a result of disabilities, aggressive role models at home or in the community, or counterproductive social information processing. These youngsters often need planned interventions to get them on the road to more productive relationships with others.

Applying Concepts in Child Development

The exercises in this section will help you increase your effectiveness in nurturing children's moral development and interpersonal skills.

Case Study

Gang Mediation

Read the case and then answer the questions that follow it.

At Washington Middle School, many students belonged to one of several gangs that seemed to "rule the school." Fights among rival gangs were common, and nongang members were frequent victims of harassment. School officials tried a variety of strategies to keep the gang-related behavior in check—mandating dress codes, conducting regular weapon searches, counseling or suspending chronic trouble makers, and so on—but without success.

In desperation, two school counselors suggested that the school implement a peer mediation program. The program began by focusing on the three largest gangs, which were responsible for most of the trouble on school grounds. Interpersonal problems involving two or more gangs would be brought to a mediation team, comprised of five school faculty members and three representatives from each of the three gangs. The team would abide by the following rules:

1. Really try to solve the problem.
2. No name-calling or put-downs.
3. No interrupting.
4. Be as honest as possible.

5. No weapons or acts of intimidation.
6. All sessions to be confidential until an agreement is reached or mediation is called off. (Sanchez & Anderson, 1990, p. 54)

All team members would have to agree to and sign off on any decisions that the team reached. However, participation in the process was voluntary, and students could withdraw at any time.

To lay the groundwork for productive discussions, faculty members of the mediation team met separately with each of the three gangs to establish feelings of rapport and trust and to explain how the mediation process would work. After considerable discussion and venting of hostile intergroup feelings, many gang members agreed to try the new approach. Meanwhile, the buzz throughout the student body was that "something unusual and special was happening" at Washington.

Mediation sessions were held in a conference room, with team members sitting around a large table so that they could maintain eye contact with one another. In the first session, common grievances were aired. Students agreed that they didn't like being put down or intimidated, that they worried about their physical safety, and that they all wanted one another's respect. Curiously, each gang also complained that the school administration showed preferential treatment for the *other* gangs. Through all of this, the students got one message loud and clear: They could speak freely and honestly at the meeting, without fear of reprisal from faculty members or other students.

In several additional meetings during the next 2 weeks, the team reached agreement that a number of behaviors would be unacceptable at school: There would be no put-downs, name-calling, hateful stares, threats, shoving, or gang graffiti. After the final meeting, each gang was separately called into the conference room. Its representatives on the mediation team explained the agreement, and other members of the gang were asked to sign it. Despite some skepticism, most members of all three gangs signed the agreement.

A month later, it was clear that the process had been successful, at least in improving the school's social climate over the short term. Members of rival gangs nodded pleasantly to one another or gave one another a "high five" sign as they passed in the hall. Gang members no longer felt compelled to hang out in groups for safety's sake. Members of two of the gangs were seen playing soccer together one afternoon. And there had been no gang-related fights all month. (case described in Sanchez & Anderson, 1990)[a]

· Why do you think the mediation approach was successful when other approaches had failed? Drawing on what you've learned about moral development and interpersonal skills, identify at least three possible reasons.

Once you have answered the question, compare your response with the one presented in Appendix A.

[a]Excerpt and case description from "Gang mediation: A process that works" by F. Sanchez and M. L. Anderson, 1990, *Principal, 69*(5), 54–56. Reprinted with permission. Copyright 1990 National Association of Elementary School Principals. All rights reserved.

Interpreting Children's Artifacts and Reflections

Consider chapter concepts as you analyze the following artifact from an adolescent.

Remembering 9/11

On September 11, 2001, several thousand innocent Americans lost their lives in a series of terrorist attacks. During the following months, scenes from the tragedy were shown repeatedly on television and in magazines. After seeing these images, many children expressed deep-seated concerns. Children wondered if they themselves were safe, asked a lot of questions, and wanted to help those who lost loved ones. In schools, teachers reassured children, answered their questions, kept up familiar routines, and, in some cases, arranged for the children to send artwork and cards to survivors and rescue workers.

Several months after the terrorists' attacks, elementary art teacher Jeanette Smith Anthos noticed that children in her school continued to be preoccupied with the events of September 11th (Anthos, 2004). She observed that children in her classes regularly drew pictures of explosions and destruction. She realized that the children needed an outlet to express their fears, sadness, and outrage about the injustices and horrors of the tragedy.

To structure her art lesson, Jeanette showed the children Pablo Picasso's *Guernica,* a painting of the 1937 bombings of a small Basque village,[4] and encouraged the children to talk about their present concerns about September 11th. She also showed the children how Picasso had conveyed the emotions of people affected by the bombing. She then asked the children to create their own drawings in memory of September 11th, communicating emotions and using symbols. Each child sat down with a regular pencil, a set of colored pencils, a black fine-tip marker, and a 12" × 18" piece of white drawing paper.

The children drew beautiful, poignant pictures. Third-grader Antonio Villanueva created the picture shown here. If you have seen Picasso's *Guernica,* you might notice that Antonio has closely emulated Picasso's way of depicting human faces. As you examine Antonio's drawing, consider these questions:

· Does Antonio seem to interpret the events of September 11th as primarily a moral or conventional transgression?
· What emotions does Antonio convey in his drawing?
· What symbols does Antonio include in his art?

[4]Picasso's *Guernica* can be found on many Internet sites. To locate one of them, type the keywords "Guernica" and "Picasso" into a search engine such as Google or Yahoo!

Once you have analyzed Antonio's art, compare your ideas with those presented in Appendix B. For further practice in analyzing children's artifacts and reflections, go to the Activities and Applications section in Chapter 14 of MyEducationLab.

Reprinted with permission. Anthos, J. S. (2004). The healing power of art. *School Arts, 103*(10), 46–47.

Developmental Trends Exercise

In this chapter you learned about how children interact with one another. The following table presents five examples of the social skills of groups of youngsters of various ages. For each example, the table presents one or more relevant developmental principles, offers an implication for working with youngsters in that age-group, or both. Go to the Activities and Applications section in Chapter 14 of MyEducationLab to apply what you've learned about interpersonal skills as you fill in the empty cells in the table.

Observing Interpersonal Skills in Children and Adolescents

Age	Youngsters' Experiences	Developmental Concepts *Identifying Interpersonal Skills*	Implications *Cultivating Productive Interpersonal Skills*
Infancy **(Birth–2 Years)**	In the infant room at a child care center, a group of infants spend time together daily. Occasionally, the infants seem very interested in one another, passing toys back and forth, looking intently at each other's faces, and smiling at each other. At other times they seem oblivious to the presence of peers, even crawling over one another's bodies and grabbing toys from others' hands as if their peers were storage shelves.	Infants show a tentative interest in one another and begin to make social gestures with familiar peers. Yet infants are not always attuned to one another's social cues or mindful of the impact of their actions on others.	Encourage infants' social interests in one another by regularly commenting on what everyone is doing and acknowledging the social gestures that infants make (e.g., "Look, Sandee, see how Berlinda is smiling at you"). Point out when infants hurt one another mistakenly or intentionally ("Oh, look, Andie, you pulled George's hair and he doesn't like that. Let's read a storybook with him on the beanbag chair to help him feel better.")
Early Childhood **(2–6 Years)**	The housekeeping area is a favorite spot for children at the Sunnyside Preschool. On any given day, individual children vary in their styles of playing, however. Some children play mostly by themselves, absorbed in their own thoughts and barely aware of the actions of peers. Some children stand at the sidelines of others' play, quietly watching and listening. Other children engage in common activities, for example, washing baby dolls side by side at the toy sink without saying a word. Still other children pass objects back and forth and occasionally comment about each other's activities. And a few children verbally negotiate reciprocal roles, such as being mommies and daddies.		Arrange group environments so children can choose to play alone or with others. Supply the room with toys and equipment that foster imagination and dialogue among children. For example, equip a play area with familiar household objects from a kitchen, and rotate theme-related props (e.g., tools from various jobs and activities) once a week. Observe the regular styles of play behavior of individual children and encourage their occasional entry into cooperative play.
Middle Childhood **(6–10 Years)**	Children at St. Mary Elementary School look forward to recess every day, during which time they typically play various pick-up games, including kickball and soccer. Children occasionally argue over rules and who is winning the game. Usually they are able to resolve their differences on their own, but every now and then a recess monitor intervenes as arguments escalate into shoving matches.		Allow children to play together in large groups with minimal supervision. Give children access to balls, fields and playgrounds, and during cold winter months, indoor recreational areas. When arguments escalate, discourage children from acting with malice and becoming physically aggressive. Use heated disagreements as opportunities to coach children in constructive conflict-resolution skills.
Early Adolescence **(10–14 Years)**	The hallways of Harrison Middle School come alive during transitions between classes. Crowds of young adolescents congregate around lockers, with individuals whispering secrets, talking about their day, and laughing. Most of their banter is good natured, but from time to time a few students call one another lewd names, push and shove, or touch one another inappropriately.	Young adolescents are eminently social creatures. They attend closely to one another's actions and statements and desperately want to be accepted by their peers. Teasing is common at this age, as is a heightened sensitivity to one another's remarks. Occasionally, teasing gets out of hand and becomes harassment.	Provide opportunities for young adolescents to aggregate and enjoy one another's company. Station an adult nearby to discourage inappropriate behaviors and watch out for youngsters being rejected by peers. Make sure young people are aware of policies prohibiting bullying and harassment at school.

Developmental Trends Exercise (continued)

Age	Youngsters' Experiences	Developmental Concepts _Identifying Interpersonal Skills_	Implications _Cultivating Productive Interpersonal Skills_
Late Adolescence (14–18 Years)	Members of the graduating class of Washington Irving High School are excited about finishing up school together and earning their diplomas. As freshmen, sophomores, and juniors, the students had rigidly divided themselves by racial and ethnic lines, but increasingly, the students have become more flexible in their social groupings. Heterogeneous service learning groups have also sparked a sense of common purpose, mutual respect, and unity among the students.		Organize numerous clubs and extracurricular activities that give adolescents a chance to affiliate with peers from different backgrounds. Create opportunities for service learning that allow adolescents to work together toward meaningful common goals.

Key Concepts

moral development (p. 518)
moral dilemma (p. 519)
preconventional morality (p. 519)
conventional morality (p. 519)
postconventional morality (p. 519)
moral transgression (p. 521)
conventional transgression (p. 521)

guilt (p. 521)
shame (p. 521)
sympathy (p. 522)
distributive justice (p. 522)
induction (p. 525)
justice orientation (p. 526)
care orientation (p. 526)

service learning (p. 529)
social skills (p. 530)
peer pressure (p. 533)
prosocial behavior (p. 535)
aggression (p. 535)
physical aggression (p. 538)
relational aggression (p. 538)

proactive aggression (p. 538)
reactive aggression (p. 538)
bully (p. 538)
hostile attributional bias (p. 538)
peer mediation (p. 544)

MyEducationLab

Now go to Chapter 14 of MyEducationLab at www.myeducationlab.com, where you can:

· View instructional objectives for the chapter.
· Take a quiz to test your mastery of chapter objectives. Detailed feedback is provided to explain why your responses are correct or incorrect.
· Deepen your understanding of particular concepts and principles with Review, Practice, and Enrichment exercises.

· Complete Activities and Applications exercises that give you additional experience in interpreting artifacts, increase your understanding of how research contributes to knowledge about chapter topics, and encourage you to apply what you have learned about children's development.
· Apply what you have learned in the chapter to your work with children in Building Teaching Skills and Dispositions exercises.
· Observe children and their unique contexts in Video Examples.

chapter 15

Peers, Schools, and Society

On a bright day in May, kindergarten teacher Pamela Bradshaw took her class on a field trip to the zoo. The visit went well, but as it was wrapping up, Pamela began to worry about getting the children back to school on time. The children and parent volunteers were not yet fully assembled, and Pamela still had to squeeze in a birthday celebration before they could leave the zoo. Feeling pressured as she stood at the zoo's gate, Pamela was baffled when 6-year-old Patrick asked her about "sharing," the class's version of show-and-tell. Here's how Pamela recalls the events:

> "What about sharing?" he [Patrick] asked. . . .
>
> Patrick wanted to share?—surely he could see that there was no way. He just had to be kidding. . . .
>
> Patrick asked again. . . .
>
> If time was normally limited, and tremendously limited for a trip to the zoo, on this particular day it was impossibly limited. Already Mary's dad held out a Tupperware container that held precious birthday cupcakes Mary had waited all day—all year—to present. I called Mary to me, positioning her before the handful of gathered children for her Happy Birthday song. If the children were ready to sing, we might still have just enough time to buckle seat belts and drive across the valley. . . .
>
> I was dumbfounded . . . that Patrick insisted on sharing at the zoo. Under the pressure of watching the time and gathering the group, I had held off his question. Now I had to explain the simple facts to him.
>
> "Patrick," I began as I kneeled to be at eye level with him, "there won't be time for sharing today. Could you maybe bring your sharing back on Monday instead?"
>
> Patrick's face answered what he didn't verbalize. His anxious expression was transformed to one of total dismay before I could convince him with reasons. Patrick was usually so happy-go-lucky, so willing to go with the flow, that I had to wonder what could make this sharing so important to him. Only then did I remember that his family needed to leave about a week before school ended to begin their summer jobs in Wyoming. This was, in fact, his last day at school, his last chance to share, his last opportunity to be a member of this bonded group.
>
> "Oh Patrick, I forgot!"
>
> He looked at me hopefully, as if I could manufacture more time. . . . One more glance at his face made the decision for me.
>
> "You can share after we sing to Mary," I told him.
>
> And he did, producing a plastic "frilled lizard" from his backpack, explaining its origins, then calling for the ritual questions or comments from his classmates.
>
> Even with the jostling and shouting crowd surrounding them, the children raised their hands. Patrick called on kids whose faces were smeared with chocolate cupcake icing; Patrick's frilled lizard, for the most part, was the focus of their attention. I checked my watch again, and just as I was hopeful that we could still make it through the exit turnstile and back to school in time, I was surprised to hear Patrick shout, "Next sharer!"
>
> According to custom, it was indeed Patrick's privilege to choose the next child for sharing time, but I smiled, knowing that only a child such as Patrick, aware that this was his last day, would remember to bring an item to the zoo for sharing. The other children who routinely took their turns on Thursdays wouldn't want to lug something around for three hours.
>
> There on the bright patch of lawn, four kindergartners tossed aside half-eaten cupcakes as their hands shot up, each competing for Patrick's attention while trying to unzip backpacks with the other hand. My jaw must have dropped as I watched them push aside their water bottles and crumpled lunch bags for the item they had indeed lugged around the zoo for three hours.
>
> While I caught up with my own astonishment, Patrick quickly chose Will. Before I could move, Will stood to tell the group about his "Nintendo guy" with a clear voice. . . .
>
> In spite of the noise, the commotion, and their own weariness at the zoo, my kindergartners conducted and participated in their own independent sharing circle. I stood in awe of their vitality and strong sense

Case Study:

Sharing at the Zoo

Outline:

Case Study:
Sharing at the Zoo

Peers

Schools

Society

Summary

Applying Concepts in Child
Development

of purpose. I was proud to see how integrated they were with one another. (Bradshaw, 2001, pp. 108–110)[a]

- What did the children in Pamela's class learn from participating in their kindergarten group?

- How were the children affected by Pamela's yearlong efforts to maintain a productive classroom environment?

[a]From "What About Sharing?" by P. Bradshaw, in B. Rogoff, C. G. Turkanis, and L. Bartlett (Eds.), *Learning Together: Children and Adults in a School Community* (pp. 108–110), 2001, New York: Oxford University Press. Copyright 2001 Barbara Rogoff et al. Used by permission of Oxford University Press, Inc.

s children grow, they spend an increasing amount of time in social groups outside the family—with peers, in schools, and in other community settings. Children learn a lot from participating in social groups, including how to get along with others and how welcome they are in particular settings. In the opening case study, Patrick and the other children knew that they belonged in Pamela's kindergarten—and that it belonged to them. Pamela had consistently fostered a productive classroom environment, and as a result, the children enjoyed kindergarten, invested in its customs, and listened respectfully to one another. In this chapter you will find that peers and teachers are catalysts for children's growth and that other elements of society, including the media and after-school programs, also strongly influence youngsters. You will see, too, that teachers and other adults can facilitate healthy relationships among peers, create productive learning environments at school, and help children and adolescents make good choices in society.

Peers

Throughout this book we have discussed many ways in which adults influence children and adolescents. *Peers*, people of approximately the same age and position within a social group, make equally important contributions to youngsters' development. In the next few pages, we examine the functions of peer relationships, the factors that affect children's acceptance by peers, and the nature of close friendships, larger social groups, and romantic relationships.

Functions of Peer Relationships

Companionship with peers is one of children's top priorities. From a developmental standpoint, peer relationships serve multiple functions.

- ***Peers offer emotional support.*** The presence of familiar peers helps children relax in new environments and cope with mild ridicule and physical aggression from other children (Asher & Parker, 1989; Ginsberg, Gottman, & Parker, 1986; Pellegrini & Bartini, 2000; Rothstein-Fisch & Trumbull, 2008; Wentzel, 1999). Although some youngsters adjust quite successfully on their own, as a general rule children and adolescents who have peers to turn to in times of trouble or uncertainty have higher self-esteem, fewer emotional problems (such as depression), and higher school achievement (Buhrmester, 1992; Guay et al., 1999; K. H. Rubin et al., 2006; D. Schwartz, Gorman, Duong, & Nakamoto, 2008).

Peers are desired companions beginning in early childhood. Art by Madison, age 7.

- ***Peers serve as partners for practicing social skills.*** When children interact with their peers, they enter social exchanges on a more or less equal footing: No single individual has absolute power or authority. By satisfying their own needs while also maintaining productive relationships with others, children acquire the fundamental personal and social skills you learned about in previous chapters: social perspective taking (Chapter 12), self-regulation (Chapter 13), and effective conflict-resolution skills (Chapter 14) (Bierman, 2004; Creasey, Jarvis, & Berk, 1998; Selman, 2003; Sutton-Smith, 1979).

- ***Peers socialize one another.*** Children and adolescents socialize one another in several ways (Erwin, 1993; Ginsberg et al., 1986; J. R. Harris, 1998; K. H. Rubin et al., 2006; A. M. Ryan, 2000). Peers define options for leisure time, perhaps jumping rope in a vacant lot, getting together in a study group, or smoking cigarettes on the corner. They offer new ideas and perspectives, whether demonstrating how to do an "Ollie" on a skateboard or presenting potent arguments for becoming a vegetarian. They serve as role models, showing what is possible and what is admirable. Peers reinforce one another for acting in ways deemed appropriate for their age, gender, ethnic group, and cultural background. And they sanction one another, perhaps through ridicule, gossip, or ostracism, for stepping beyond acceptable bounds.

Adolescents find it reassuring to talk with peers about everyday experiences.

- ***Peers contribute to a sense of identity.*** Association with a particular group of peers helps children and adolescents decide who they are and who they want to become (Clemens, Shipp, & Pisarik, 2008; Forthun et al., 2006; see Chapter 12). For instance, when Jeanne's son Alex was in middle school, he and his friends were avid skateboarders and spent long hours at a local skateboard ramp practicing and refining their technique. Alex proudly labeled himself a "skater" and wore the extra-large T-shirts and wide-legged pants that conveyed this identity.

- ***Peers help one another make sense of their lives.*** During daily conversations, children share ideas that help one another interpret confusing and troubling events. For example, children may talk about similar experiences in dealing with a difficult teacher or being punished by parents. Such informally instructive conversations occur throughout childhood but take on special significance during adolescence, when teenagers are changing rapidly and appreciate reassurance from peers facing similar challenges (Richard & Schneider, 2005; Seltzer, 1982; H. S. Sullivan, 1953).

Peer Acceptance

The functions of peer relationships we just described operate for most youngsters, and especially for youngsters who are reasonably well regarded by peers. By and large, children who believe that peers view them favorably achieve at higher levels academically, have higher self-esteem, are happier at school, exhibit fewer problem behaviors, and have better school attendance records (Guay et al., 1999; Harter, 1996; K. H. Rubin et al., 2006; Wentzel, 1999).

Developmental researchers often examine peer acceptance by asking children in a classroom or other setting to confidentially nominate individual children with whom they would like to interact and others whom they would prefer to avoid. Researchers then collect these nominations and classify the children into one of five groups: *popular, rejected, neglected, controversial,* and *average* (Coie, Dodge, & Coppotelli, 1982; K. H. Rubin et al., 2006). The researchers subsequently compare the typical social features of children in the five groups.

Children who are well liked by numerous peers are considered **popular.** When researchers ask children to identify classmates they would most like to do something with, the children don't necessarily choose those whom they and their teachers perceive to be the most admired members of the student body (Lafontana & Cillessen, 1998; Parkhurst & Hopmeyer, 1998). When we talk about *popular children* in terms of peer acceptance, we are describing young people who are well liked, kind, and trustworthy, rather than those who hold obvious high-status positions such as head cheerleader or football quarterback. Children who are well accepted by peers typically have good social skills. For instance, they know how to initiate and sustain conversations, refrain from talking excessively about themselves, show sensitivity to the subtle social cues that others give them, and adjust their behaviors to changing circumstances. They also tend to be quite prosocial, often helping, sharing, cooperating, and empathizing with others (Caprara, Barbaranelli, Pastorelli, Bandura, & Zimbardo, 2000; Crick & Dodge, 1994; Oortwijn, Boekaerts, Vedder, & Fortuin, 2008; K. H. Rubin et al., 2006; Wentzel & Asher, 1995).

Children who are frequently selected for exclusion by peers are known as **rejected children.** Rejected children often have poor social skills—for example, they may continually try to draw attention to themselves and may also be impulsive and disruptive in the classroom (Asher & Renshaw, 1981; Pellegrini, Bartini, & Brooks, 1999; Putallaz & Heflin,

popular children
Children whom many peers like and perceive to be kind and trustworthy.

rejected children
Children whom many peers identify as being unfavorable social partners.

1986; K. H. Rubin et al., 2006). Some rejected children are aggressive, placing a higher priority on acquiring objects and gaining power over others than on maintaining congenial interpersonal relationships (Dodge, Bates, & Pettit, 1990; Ladd & Burgess, 1999; Patrick, 1997). Other rejected children appear to peers to be immature, insensitive, inattentive, strange, or exceptionally timid (Bierman, 2004; K. H. Rubin et al., 2006). Rejected children's tendency to alienate others leaves them few opportunities to develop the social skills they so desperately need, and many consequently feel lonely and unhappy or become targets of other children's bullying behaviors (Bierman, 2004; Bullock, 1993; Coie & Cillessen, 1993; K. H. Rubin et al., 2006).

A third group of children are **neglected children,** those whom age-mates rarely select as peers they would either most like or least like to do something with (Asher & Renshaw, 1981). Neglected children tend to be quiet and keep to themselves. Some prefer to be alone, others may simply not know how to go about making friends, and still others may be quite content with one or two close friends (Guay et al., 1999; K. H. Rubin & Krasnor, 1986). Neglected status is often only a temporary situation; children categorized as neglected at one time are not always so categorized in follow-up assessments (K. H. Rubin et al., 2006).

A fourth category, **controversial children,** includes youngsters who are very well liked by some of their peers and intensely disliked by others. Controversial children are apt to have characteristics of both popular and rejected children. For example, they may be aggressive on some occasions and helpful and cooperative at other times (Coie & Dodge, 1988; K. H. Rubin et al., 2006). The fifth group consists of children who, for lack of a better term, are known simply as *average:* Some peers like them and others don't, but without the intensity of feelings shown for popular, rejected, or controversial children and also without the invisibility of neglected children.

Because of its important effects on the development of children and adolescents, peer acceptance is an important quality for adults to monitor. In the Observation Guidelines table "Noticing Children's Level of Peer Acceptance," we present common characteristics of popular, rejected, neglected, controversial, and average children, and we suggest some basic strategies for supporting children at varying levels of peer acceptance. A little later on, we offer more detailed recommendations for fostering relationships among children.

Friendships

Healthy friendships come in many forms. Some are brief liaisons; others last a lifetime. Some are relatively casual; others are deep and intimate. Some children have many friends; others invest steadfastly in a few close ones. Despite their varied types, friendships have four common qualities that distinguish them from other kinds of peer relationships:

My best friend is brian and we have had many fun times together with my other friends (anthony and anhuu) too. We have been friends since 1st grade, He has always been in my class those years, so has anhuu and anthony, We have had sad and happy times/adventures, We sometimes argued, We wanted play hide and seek and get soda and other things at the Noble home park, We both enjoyed hamsters as pets, Sometimes he came to my house to play

Figure 15-1

Ten-year-old Joseph explains that he has shared many experiences with his friend Brian.

neglected children
Children whom peers rarely select as someone they would either most like or least like to do something with.

controversial children
Children whom some peers really like and other peers strongly dislike.

- *Friendships are voluntary relationships.* Children often spend time with peers strictly through happenstance: Perhaps they ride the same school bus, are members of the same class, or join the same sports team. In contrast, children *choose* their friends. Two or more youngsters typically remain friends as long as they continue to enjoy one another's company and can successfully resolve their differences.

- *Friendships are powered by shared routines.* Friends find activities that are mutually meaningful and enjoyable, as can be seen in 10-year-old Joseph's essay on the many good times, as well as some difficult periods, he has experienced with his friend Brian (Figure 15-1). Over time, friends acquire a common set of experiences that enable them to share certain perspectives on life (Gottman, 1986; McDougall & Hymel, 2007; Suttles, 1970). As a result, they can easily communicate about many topics. Children talk, smile, and laugh more often with friends than with nonfriends; they also engage in more complex fantasy play with friends (J. G. Parker, 1986).

- *Friendships are reciprocal relationships.* In the time they spend together, friends address one another's needs (J. L. Epstein, 1986; K. H. Rubin et al., 2006). Although friends take on slightly different roles in their relationship, generally they are equal partners. For example, one friend may instigate fun activities, and the other friend may be an especially sympathetic listener, with both styles reflecting the children's mutual regard.

Observation Guidelines

Noticing Children's Level of Peer Acceptance

Characteristic	Look For	Example	Implication
Popular Children	· Good social and communication skills · Sensitivity and responsiveness to others' wishes and needs · Willingness to assimilate into ongoing activities · Signs of leadership potential	On the playground, 8-year-old Daequan moves easily from one group to another. Before joining a conversation, he listens to what others are saying and adds an appropriate comment. He doesn't draw much attention to himself but is well liked by most of his classmates.	Use popular children as leaders when trying to change other children's behavior. For example, when starting a recycling program, ask a well-regarded youngster to help get the program off the ground.
Rejected Children	· For some, high rates of aggression; for others, immature, anxious, or impulsive behavior; for still others, unusually shy and withdrawn behavior · For some, frequent disruptive behavior in class · Unwillingness of other children to play or work with them · In some cases, appearance to other children of being strange and annoying	Most children dislike 10-year-old Terra. She frequently calls other children insulting nicknames, threatens to beat them up, and noisily intrudes into their private conversations.	Help rejected children learn basic social skills, such as how to initiate a conversation. Place them in cooperative groups with children who are likely to be accepting. With aggressive children, give appropriate consequences and teach self-regulatory strategies for controlling impulses. Publicly compliment all youngsters (including rejected children) on things they do well. When rejected children fail to respond to informal interventions, consult counselors.
Neglected Children	· Tendency to be relatively quiet; little or no disruptive behavior · Fewer-than-average interactions with age-mates but possible friendships with one or two peers · For some, anxiety about interacting with others · Possible temporary nature of neglected status	Fourteen-year-old Sedna is initially a bit shy at her new school. Later in the year, however, she seems to be happier and more involved in school activities.	Identify group activities in which neglected children might feel comfortable and be successful. Arrange situations in which shy children with similar interests can get to know one another.
Controversial Children	· Acceptance by some peers, rejection by others · Possible aggression and disruptive behavior in some situations, yet helpfulness, cooperation, and social sensitivity in others	Thirteen-year-old Marcus is usually charming and cheerful, but occasionally he makes jokes at someone else's expense. His sunny personality impresses many classmates, yet his biting humor offends others.	Let controversial children know in no uncertain terms when their behaviors are inappropriate, but acknowledge their effective social skills as well.
Average Children	· Tendency to be liked by some peers but disliked by others · Average interpersonal skills (e.g., typical levels of prosocial behavior and aggression) · Ability to find a comfortable social niche	Five-year-old Joachim doesn't draw much attention to himself. He's made a few friends in kindergarten and seems to get along fairly well with them, but he sometimes has trouble handling disagreements.	Help average children refine their emerging social skills. Encourage them to be tactful, honest, and kind with peers.

Sources: Bierman, 2004; Coie & Dodge, 1988; Coie & Kupersmidt, 1983; Dodge, 1983; Dodge, Coie, & Brakke, 1982; Dodge, Schlundt, Schocken, & Delugach, 1983; Newcomb & Bukowski, 1984; Newcomb, Bukowski, & Pattee, 1993; Putallaz & Gottman, 1981; K. H. Rubin et al., 2006.

● ***Friendships ensure ongoing, dependable sources of support.*** Friends help each other cope with stressful events by providing emotional support (Berndt & Keefe, 1995; Ginsberg et al., 1986; McDougall & Hymel, 2007). In Figure 15-2, 7-year-old Jessica reveals her emerging understanding of the importance of a good friend. Because friends have an emotional investment in their relationship, they work hard to look at situations from each other's

Today Miranda walked me to school and she is going to walk me back. Miranda is my best friend we met egether afther lunch. Miranda is teching me lots of things she the best friend any boty cwold have.

Figure 15-2

Seven-year-old Jessica recognizes the value of a good friend.

point of view and resolve disputes that threaten to be divisive. As a result, they develop enhanced perspective-taking and conflict resolution skills (Basinger et al., 1995; DeVries, 1997).

Characteristics of friendships at different ages. Years ago, Jeanne asked her three children, "What are friends for?" Here are their responses:

Jeff (age 6):   To play with.
Alex (age 9):   Friends can help you in life. They can make you do better in school. They can make you feel better.
Tina (age 12):   To be your friend and help you in good times and bad times. They're there so you can tell secrets. They're people that care. They're there because they like you. They're people you can trust.

Like Jeff, young children describe friends primarily as recreational companions; thus, their understandings of friendship are simple and concrete. As children reach the upper elementary grades, they, like Alex, begin to understand that friends can help and depend on one another. Adolescents, like Tina, begin to share their innermost secrets with friends (Berndt, 1992; Gottman & Mettetal, 1986; McDougall & Hymel, 2007; Youniss, 1980). As we look more closely at the nature of friendship across the five developmental periods, we see that friendships begin with mutual enjoyment and gradually reflect such additional characteristics as loyalty, trust, compromise, and intimacy (Selman, 1980, 2003).

Infancy (birth–2 years). Primitive relationships among peers evolve slowly during infancy. In the beginning, social interests are fleeting, and infants are as likely to crawl over one another as to initiate social contact. Yet as infants grow and become familiar with one another, they smile and watch one another's faces and actions (K. H. Rubin et al., 2006). For example, when Teresa's son Connor was 9 months old, he became friendly with Patrick, another boy of the same age at his child care center. The two boys established familiar play routines, often laughing and chasing one another as they crawled around the room. Although they weren't yet speaking, and they certainly didn't swap secrets, they were clearly attuned to each other's behaviors. Such social interests solidify, and in their second year, toddlers make social overtures more consistently, carry on complex interactions, and display positive emotions with children whom they know (Howes, 1988).

Figure 15-3

Four-year-old Dana drew a picture of herself and her friend Dina. The two girls met in child care and became good friends.

Early childhood (ages 2–6 years). In the preschool years children infuse language, fantasy, and play into social interactions with familiar peers. When 3- and 4-year-olds interact with children they have gotten to know (rather than with children who are strangers), they are more likely to offer social greetings and carry on a conversation, engage in complex play, and exhibit good social skills (Charlesworth & LaFreniere, 1983; A. Doyle, 1982; Hinde, Titmus, Easton, & Tamplin, 1985). Figure 15-3 shows a picture drawn by 4-year-old Dana of herself and her friend Dina. The two girls met in child care and became close companions. Afterwards, they moved to separate towns but happily renewed their friendship when given the chance at summer camp.

Of course, early friendships also provide opportunities for disagreements and arguments (Hartup & Laursen, 1991). In the process of working through conflicts with friends, children learn to assert themselves while showing their regard for friends.

Middle childhood (ages 6–10 years). During the elementary school years, children continue to act differently with friends than with peers who are not friends. For example, with friends they are more likely to express their feelings and speculate about one another's emotional states (Newcomb & Bagwell, 1995; Newcomb & Brady, 1982). At this age friends develop a sense of loyalty to one another, and many of them, girls especially, use self-disclosure as a strategy for maintaining a friendship (Buhrmester, 1996; Diaz & Berndt, 1982; Flanagan, 2003; R. N. Turner, Hewstone, & Voci, 2007). Friendships are more stable in middle childhood than in earlier years, and children are more deliberate in selecting playmates with qualities similar to their own (Berndt & Hoyle, 1985; K. H. Rubin, Lynch, Coplan, Rose-Krasnor, & Booth, 1994). Youngsters typically choose friends of their own gender, perhaps in part because same-gender peers are more likely to share interests and pastimes (Gottman, 1986;

Kovacs, Parker, & Hoffman, 1996; Maccoby, 1990). However, numerous children of this age do have cross-gender friendships, and such relationships tend to promote social perspective taking and flexible communication skills (McDougall & Hymel, 2007).

Early adolescence (ages 10–14 years).   Differences in relationships between friends and nonfriends intensify during early adolescence (Basinger et al., 1995; J. G. Parker & Gottman, 1989). Many young adolescents let down their guard and reveal their weaknesses and vulnerabilities to close friends, even as they may try to maintain a demeanor of competence and self-confidence in front of other age-mates. Adolescents also confront feelings of possessiveness and jealousy about friends (J. G. Parker, Low, Walker, & Gamm, 2005). Gradually, young adolescents learn that friendships don't have to be exclusive, and friendship pairs converge into larger groups.

Late adolescence (ages 14–18 years).   Older adolescents tend to be quite selective in their choice of friends (J. L. Epstein, 1986). Gone are the days when they run out of fingers as they count off their "close" friends. Instead, older teenagers tend to nurture relationships with a few friends that they keep for some time, perhaps throughout their lives. They frequently turn to friends for emotional support in times of trouble or confusion, and they are likely to engage in lengthy discussions about personal problems and possible solutions (Asher & Parker, 1989; Buhrmester, 1992, 1996; Newcomb & Bagwell, 1995; J. G. Parker & Gottman, 1989; Seltzer, 1982). As they exchange their tales of trials and tribulations, adolescent friends often discover that they aren't as unique as they once thought, thereby weakening the *personal fable* that we discussed in Chapter 12 (Elkind, 1981a).

Fostering friendships and other productive peer relationships.   Group environments for children—classrooms, schools, after-school programs, and so forth—are excellent settings for fostering children's friendships and other constructive peer relationships. Thoughtful intervention is particularly important for youngsters who are socially isolated or rejected by their peers. We offer the following suggestions:

Many close friendships in the elementary and middle school years are among children of the same gender. Art by Andres, age 10.

• ***Help young children ease into social groups.***   Young children who are shy or new to a community can benefit from gentle intercession by teachers and caregivers. In the following anecdote, Mrs. Kusumoto, a Japanese preschool teacher, skillfully models desired behaviors and helps one child, Fumiko, enter a group of peers:

> Mrs. Kusumoto helps Fumiko put a cha-cha-cha tape in the portable cassette player, and calls a second girl to come over and join them on a small stage made of blocks. The two girls and Mrs. Kusumoto stand on the stage, singing and shaking their maracas. Then Mrs. Kusumoto steps down and faces them, singing along and encouraging them to continue. After a few minutes she attempts to melt away. The girls continue singing briefly, but when the song ends the second girl runs off, leaving Fumiko alone and unoccupied. She looks for Mrs. Kusumoto and begins following her around again. Mrs. Kusumoto approaches a small group of girls who are playing house, asking them: "Would you like to invite this girl over for dinner? After giving the concert, she is very hungry." One of the girls nods silently. Fumiko smiles and enters the "house." She stands there uncertainly, saying nothing. Mrs. Kusumoto inquires, "Fumiko-chan. Have you had your dinner? Why don't you join us? Don't you want something to eat? It looks good." Fumiko nods and the girls bring her a couple [of] dishes of clay "food." Mrs. Kusumoto looks on briefly, then moves quietly out of the scene. (Holloway, 2000, pp. 100–101)

• ***Set up situations in which youngsters can enjoy friendly interactions with one another.***   Teachers can do many simple things to encourage children to get to know one another. For example, teachers can arrange structured cooperative learning activities that require all group members to share equal responsibility, and they can provide play equipment such as balls and climbing structures that lend themselves to coordinated group activities (S. S. Martin, Brady, & Williams, 1991; Schofield, 1995; Slavin, 1990). They can also ask youngsters to read to a peer with a visual impairment, sign to a child with hearing loss, provide tutoring to a classmate with a learning disability, or take notes for a child

One effective way to foster productive peer relationships in children is to encourage children to pursue shared goals in cooperative activities.

with a physical impairment. In addition, teachers can acknowledge the mutual benefits of children's helpful gestures ("Thanks, Jamie, for helping Branson—he really appreciates your assistance, and you seemed to learn a lot yourself from explaining the assignment to him").

● *Be aware of family factors that affect children's relationships with peers.* Parents' beliefs and practices influence children's interactions with peers (Goudena, 2006). For example, some parents are quite protective, rarely allowing their children to play with children outside the family, whereas other parents actively arrange for children to affiliate with peers (Fletcher, Bridges, & Hunter, 2007). Children who have not had much experience with peers at home or in the neighborhood can gain valuable experience in social groups at school, particularly when teachers use subtle strategies that foster their inclusion. For example, a teacher might sit with a group of children at lunch and, when noticing a child eating alone, invite him or her to join them (e.g., "Sasha, would you like to join us? We're talking about our pets, and you can tell us about your new puppy").

● *Minimize or eliminate barriers to social interaction.* Children and adolescents are less likely to interact with peers when physical, linguistic, or social barriers stand in the way (Matheson, Olsen, & Weisner, 2007). For example, Jeanne recalls a junior high school student who could not negotiate the cafeteria steps with her wheelchair and frequently ended up eating lunch alone. Educators can be on the lookout for such physical impediments to interaction and campaign for their removal. They can also teach groups of youngsters who speak different languages (including American Sign Language) some basic vocabulary and simple phrases in one another's native tongues. At a deeper level, educators must actively address the prejudices and tensions that sometimes separate diverse ethnic groups (see Chapter 12).

● *Cultivate children's empathy for peers with special needs.* Some children feel resentment or anger because of their belief that peers with special needs should be able to control inappropriate behaviors (Juvonen, 1991; Juvonen & Weiner, 1993). Consequently, children are less likely to be tolerant of peers with cognitive difficulties or emotional and behavioral disorders than they are of peers with obvious physical disabilities (Madden & Slavin, 1983; Ysseldyke & Algozzine, 1984). Teachers and other practitioners must help nondisabled children understand the difficulties that peers may have as a result of a disability. At the same time, perhaps through paired or small-group activities, adults can show nondisabled youngsters that peers with disabilities have many of the same talents, thoughts, feelings, and desires that they have (D. Staub, 1998).

● *Provide the specific kinds of support rejected children need most.* An important first step in helping rejected children is to determine the reasons why other children find them unpleasant to be around. Some rejected children are aggressive, have limited social skills, and use coercive behaviors to get their way (Bierman, 2004). Other rejected children have trouble asserting their desires and opinions, and peers may occasionally call them names and victimize them (Salmivalli & Isaacs, 2005). Once educators understand exactly what is missing from rejected children's repertoires of social skills, they can take steps to help children acquire the missing competencies.

● *Help change the reputations of rejected children.* Unfortunately, bad reputations often live on long after people's behavior has changed for the better. Even after children show dramatic improvements in social behavior, peers may continue to dislike and reject them (Bierman, Miller, & Staub, 1987; Juvonen & Weiner, 1993). For example, when encountering formerly aggressive children, many peers assume "once a bully, always a bully." To improve children's reputations, adults can create structured cooperative learning groups and extracurricular activities in which children can use their newly developed social skills. In one way or another, adults must help previously annoying and abrasive children to show peers that they can be good companions.

● *Encourage a general feeling of respect for others.* Adults who effectively promote friendships among diverse groups of children are often those who consistently communicate that all members of their community deserve respect as human beings (Battistich et al., 1995; Osterman, 2000). Fernando Arias, a high school vocational education teacher, put it this way:

> In our school, our philosophy is that we treat everybody the way we'd like to be treated. . . . Our school is a unique situation where we have pregnant young ladies who go to our school. We have special education children. We have the regular kids, and we have the drop-out recovery program . . . we're all equal. We all have an equal chance. And we have members of every gang at our school, and we hardly have any fights, and there are close to about 300 gangs in our city. We all get along. It's one big family unit it seems like. (Turnbull, Pereira, & Blue-Banning, 2000, p. 67)

• *Encourage children to be honest and diplomatic during conflicts with friends.* When children argue with friends, they often find it difficult to express their personal feelings *and* accept the validity of their friends' perspectives. Role playing can be a useful way to give children practice with resolving disagreements. For instance, one fifth-grade teacher, Mrs. Burgos, asked her students to interpret a dispute between characters in a novel. During class Mrs. Burgos asked two girls, Marisol and Rosario, to simulate the conflict. In the scenario Marisol has been assigned a desirable part in the school's dramatic production of a Thanksgiving story but has not told her good friend Rosario about this honor. It takes extended discussion before the girls fully acknowledge both their perspectives:

Marisol: I think that you're just jealous because I got the best part and you couldn't get the part that you wanted to get.
Rosario: That's not true, I'm not jealous. I'm just mad at you because you didn't tell me.
Marisol: I just changed my mind when I went home and thought about it all over.
Rosario: Yeah, but best friends is for to share and tell secrets.
Marisol: When I went to look for you, you didn't want to talk to me or nothing.
Rosario: Because I was mad at you. (Selman, 2003, p. 205; reprinted with permission of Russell Sage Foundation)

• *Be a backup system when relationships with peers aren't going well.* Disruptions in peer relationships—perhaps because of interpersonal conflicts or a friend's relocation to a distant city—can trigger emotional distress in youngsters (Wentzel, 1999). Warm, supportive adults can lessen the pain in such circumstances, and ongoing gestures of affection can also bolster the spirits of other children who, for whatever reasons, have no close friends (Guay et al., 1999; Wentzel, 1999). Such sympathetic overtures may be especially important for children who have little support at home and might otherwise turn to deviant peer groups for attention (Parks, 1995).

As you have learned, adults can do many things to foster productive relationships among children. In the Building Teaching Skills and Dispositions exercise, you can listen to four young people of various ages talk about friends and consider specific ways for educators to support friendships.

Social Groups

In middle childhood children are motivated to interact with peers at school and in their neighborhoods. Adolescents are even more inclined to congregate with peers. As a result of their expanding social lives, youngsters come into contact with many peers and begin to form larger social groups that regularly fraternize (K. H. Rubin et al., 2006). Initially, these groups are comprised of single-sex friendships, but in adolescence they often include both boys and girls.

Youngsters' social groups vary considerably in size, function, and character. However, many have the following attributes:

• *Group members develop a common culture.* A social group works out a general set of rules (often unspoken), expectations, and interpretations—a **peer culture** —that influences how group members behave (P. Davidson & Youniss, 1995; Killeya-Jones, Costanzo, Malone, Quinlan, & Miller-Johnson, 2007). This shared culture gives group members a sense of community, belonging, and identity. Within a school the array of groups can be quite complex, as 14-year-old Connor shows in his representation of the groups of students he perceived during his freshman year in high school (Figure 15-4).

MyEducationLab

Go to Chapter 15's Building Teaching Skills and Dispositions section in MyEducationLab to learn more about children's views of friendship and the strategies teachers and practitioners can use to foster children's friendships.

peer culture
General set of rules, expectations, and interpretations that influence how members of a particular peer group behave.

Figure 15-4

Fourteen-year-old Connor diagrammed the groups of students he observed during his freshman year in high school. In his inner circle he labeled the different groups (e.g., *preps, jocks, gamers*), and in the outer circle he described each one (e.g., "wear nice clothes and usually cocky," "athletic, usually wear letter jackets," "Nintendo is a large part in their lives").

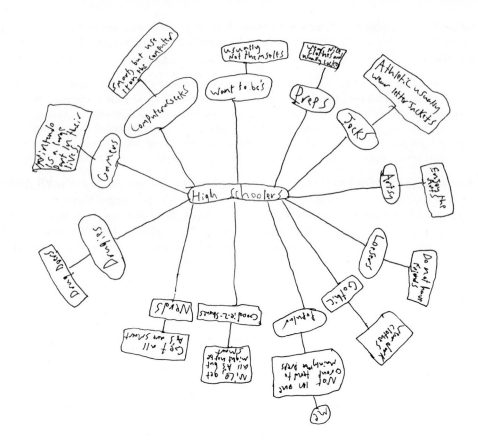

• *Group members socialize one another to follow the group's norms.* Group members encourage conformity by reinforcing behaviors that are appropriate in the eyes of the group and by discouraging behaviors that are not (Clasen & Brown, 1985; Killeya-Jones et al., 2007). Youngsters also affiliate with peers who have similar beliefs and then pressure themselves to adopt their group's norms and values; that is, they *self-socialize* (Gottman & Mettetal, 1986; Killeya-Jones et al., 2007). Fortunately, many peer groups embrace productive and prosocial behaviors, such as honesty, fairness, cooperation, academic achievement, and a sense of humor (Damon, 1988; Kindermann, 1993; McCallum & Bracken, 1993). Others, however, encourage unproductive behaviors, such as threatening and pushing classmates around; making fun of "brainy" students; and endorsing cheating, cutting class, skipping school, or using drugs (Berndt, 1992; B. B. Brown, 1993; B. C. Kelly, 2007; Knapp & Woolverton, 1995).

• *Group members influence youngsters more strongly in some areas of life than others.* Young people rarely accept a peer's suggestions without question (B. B. Brown, 1990; Padilla-Walker & Carlo, 2007). Instead, they typically evaluate what peers ask them to do and may consider advice they have previously received from people outside the peer group. Peer groups are particularly influential in matters of style—for example, in dress, music, and social activities. In contrast, parents, teachers, and other significant adults continue to be influential in most young people's views about education, morality, religion, and careers (J. R. Harris, 1998; Hartup, 1983; Sewald, 1986).

• *Group members have a sense of unity as a group.* Once youngsters gel as a group, they prefer other group members over nonmembers, and they develop feelings of loyalty to individuals within the group. In some cases they also feel hostility and rivalry toward members of other groups and view their competitors as unfriendly and incompetent (Griffiths & Nesdale, 2006; Rutland, Cameron, Bennett, & Ferrell, 2005; Sherif, Harvey, White, Hood, & Sherif, 1961). Such feelings toward *out-groups* are particularly intense when two or more groups actively compete for status or resources, as rival athletic teams and adolescent gangs often do.

• *Dominance hierarchies emerge within the group.* When children's groups continue for any length of time, a pecking order, or **dominance hierarchy**, gradually evolves (K. H. Rubin et al., 2006; Strayer, 1991). Some group members rise to the top, leading the

dominance hierarchy
Relative standing of group members in terms of such qualities as leadership and social influence.

way and making decisions for the entire group. Other group members are followers: They look to those around them for guidance about how to behave and assume lesser roles in the group's activities. Sometimes these less dominant individuals find unique niches within the group, perhaps becoming the clown, daredevil, or brain of the group.

Once youngsters reach puberty, social groups become a particularly prominent feature of their social worlds. Developmental researchers have described three group phenomena that are significant during the adolescent years: cliques, subcultures, and gangs.

Cliques. **Cliques** are moderately stable friendship groups of perhaps three to nine individuals; they provide the basis for many voluntary social interactions during adolescence (X. Chen, Chang, & He, 2003; K. H. Rubin et al., 2006). Clique boundaries tend to be fairly rigid and exclusive (some people are in, others are out), and membership in various cliques affects social status and dominance with peers. In early adolescence, cliques are usually comprised of a single sex; in later adolescence, cross-sex cliques become increasingly common (J. L. Epstein, 1986).

Although most middle school and high school students have friends, a smaller number of them belong to cliques (J. L. Epstein, 1986). Thus, the emergence of cliques in early adolescence heightens young people's concerns about acceptance (Gavin & Furman, 1989). Young adolescents wonder about their social standing: "Who likes me?" "Will I be popular at my new school?" "Why didn't Sal invite me to his party?" When they occasionally leave one clique to join another, they are apt to engender feelings of betrayal, hurt, and jealousy in the friends they leave behind (Kanner, Feldman, Weinberger, & Ford, 1987). Late in high school, adolescents feel freer to move in and out of groups, and suspicion and rivalry among groups dissipate (see Chapter 14).

Subcultures. Some adolescents affiliate with a well-defined **subculture,** a group that resists a powerful dominant culture by adopting a significantly different way of life (J. S. Epstein, 1998; J. Tanner, Asbridge, & Wortley, 2008). Such a group may be considerably larger than a clique and is defined by its common values, beliefs, and behavior patterns. Some subcultures are tightly knit groups, and others are loosely configured, with members coming and going. Some subcultures are relatively benign; for instance, a middle school skateboarders' subculture may simply espouse a particular mode of dress and a recreational pastime. Other subcultures, such as those that promote drug use, endorse racist and anti-Semitic behaviors (e.g., skinheads), or practice Satanic rituals, can be worrisome (B. C. Kelly, 2007; C. C. Clark, 1992).

Some adolescent subcultures, like this one, are distinguished by relatively superficial characteristics, such as mode of dress or preference for a particular kind of music. Other subcultures that endorse dangerous and violent behaviors are more worrisome.

Adolescents are apt to affiliate with subcultures when they feel alienated from the dominant culture (perhaps that of their school or that of society more generally) or pessimistic about their future (C. C. Clark, 1992; J. S. Epstein, 1998; J. R. Harris, 1998). Some young people feel not only disenfranchised from society but also rejected by their families, heightening their need for intimacy in the new group. For example, "street families" among groups of homeless youth offer one another protection and emotional support and share tangible resources (e.g., temporary shelter). One 16-year-old girl described her street family:

> Well, it's like we all just put what we have together and share. In our family, we all work together to make sure we are all taken care of. It's like someone will panhandle one day and someone else will do it the next. And whatever people get they will bring it back and share with everyone. . . . Mainly, I think street families provide these opportunities to help with food and shelter. (H. Smith, 2008, p. 764)

Gangs. A **gang** is a cohesive social group characterized by initiation rites, distinctive colors and symbols, alleged ownership of a specific territory, feuds with one or more rival groups, and criminal activity (A. Campbell, 1984; Kodluboy, 2004). Gangs have well-defined dominance hierarchies, strict rules, and stiff penalties for breaking them.

Once confined to a few neighborhoods in inner cities, gangs have now become widespread, and membership has grown substantially, especially in lower-income inner-city areas but also in suburbs and rural areas (National Drug Intelligence Center, 2008; Parks, 1995;

clique
Moderately stable friendship group of perhaps three to nine members.

subculture
Group that resists the ways of the dominant culture and adopts its own norms for behavior.

gang
Cohesive social group characterized by initiation rites, distinctive colors and symbols, territorial orientation, feuds with rival groups, and criminal activity.

Valdez, 2000). In one study, 7 percent of boys and 4 percent of girls in the United States reported that they were members of a gang (Gottfredson & Gottfredson, 2001).

Adolescents, and sometimes younger children as well, affiliate with gangs for a variety of reasons. Joining a gang enables young people to demonstrate their loyalty to friends and family, gain recognition for accomplishments, obtain financial rewards (through criminal activities), receive missing emotional support, and gain protection from victimization (A. Campbell, 1984; C. C. Clark, 1992; E. Jensen, 2005; Kodluboy, 2004; Parks, 1995).

In some instances gang members endorse prosocial behaviors, including caring for one another and encouraging one another's self-expression (Moje, 2000). But generally speaking, gangs do more harm than good. High rates of using and selling drugs, carrying destructive weapons, and intimidating peers make gangs a serious concern for law enforcement officers and community leaders (E. Jensen, 2005; Parks, 1995).

Many educators likewise recognize that gangs are a serious problem. Youth in gangs often intimidate classmates, defend the school as their own territory, and recruit new members from among the student body (National Youth Violence Prevention Center, 2001). As you learned in Chapter 14, effective educators try to address children's needs long before children are tempted to join gangs. When youngsters feel cared for by teachers and are confident in their own academic abilities, they are more likely to remain in school, avoid criminal activity, and resist the pressures of gangs (E. Jensen, 2005). Early childhood curricula that prepare young children with emergent literacy skills and a healthy self-confidence, and after-school programs that give children support and productive outlets for their time (e.g., Boys and Girls Clubs of America) are especially valuable *prevention strategies* (Howell, 2000; D. Peterson & Esbensen, 2004).

Teachers who become aware that their students have joined gangs can consult with police and community leaders about intervention and suppression programs in their area. *Intervention programs* entice youths to leave gangs by offering job training, adult mentoring, gang mediation, and counseling (Howell, 2000). *Suppression programs* try to reduce gang activities through weapon seizures and arrests for gang-related incidents near schools.

Romance and Sexuality

Awareness of romantic relationships first develops in early childhood. Many children, especially those living in traditional two-parent families, believe that getting married and having children is a normal, perhaps inevitable, part of growing up. They sometimes act out their fantasies in play, as this episode involving Eric and Naomi illustrates:

E: Hey, Naomi, I know what we can play today.
N: What?
E: How about, um, the marry game. You like that.
N: Marry?
E: How about baker or something? How about this. Marry you? OK, Naomi, you want to pretend that?
N: Yes.
E: OK, Naomi, do you want to marry me?
N: Yeah.
E: Good, just a minute, Naomi, we don't have any marry place.
N: We could pretend this is the marry place.
E: Oh, well, pretend this, ah, there'll have to be a cake.
N: The wedding is here first.
E: OK, but listen to this, we have to have a baby, oh, and a pet.
N: This is our baby. (Gottman, 1986, p. 157)

Most preschoolers are curious about courtship and marriage. Here Teresa's son Alex (age 5) depicts his image of his parents getting married.

Consistent with what we have learned about cognitive abilities at this age, young children's understandings of courtship and marriage are simple and concrete. For example, in the preceding scenario, the children focus on having a "marry place" and wedding cake. Nevertheless, by pretending to get married, young children anticipate their eventual entry into romantic relationships.

Dating.   As children grow, they gradually expand on their ideas about what it means to participate in romantic relationships, and many eventually begin to date. For instance, prior to puberty some children practice courtship behaviors, with girls vying for the attention of boys by using cosmetics and choosing clothing and hairstyles that make them look older and (they think) prettier, and boys flaunting whatever manly airs they can muster (Elkind, 1981b; Giordano, 2003). The early romances of late middle childhood and early adolescence often exist more in youngsters' minds than in reality, as the following conversation between two young teenage girls illustrates:

A: How's Lance [*giggle*]? Has he taken you to a movie yet?
B: No. Saw him today but I don't care.
A: Didn't he say anything to you?
B: Oh . . .
A: Lovers!
B: Shut up!
A: Lovers at first sight! [*Giggle.*]
B: [*Giggle.*] Quit it! (Gottman & Mettetal, 1986, p. 210; reprinted with the permission of Cambridge University Press)

As young people reach adolescence, many form into couples and regularly date. Relationships become increasingly serious and involve emotional intimacy and self-disclosure (K. H. Rubin et al., 2006). The biological changes associated with puberty usher in sexual desires as well (Larson, Clore, & Wood, 1999). In most Western cultures, social pressures mount to tempt, perhaps even push, young adolescents into dating and some degree of sexual activity (Larson et al., 1999; B. C. Miller & Benson, 1999).

In determining how to act in romantic relationships, adolescents turn to familiar people and institutions. Both sexes pay close attention to the romantic activities of those around them and absorb the many romantic images they see in the media (Connolly & Goldberg, 1999; Giordano, 2003; Larson et al., 1999). For example, youngsters learn from one another that they should strive for certain ideals in romantic relationships, such as being in love and dating only one person at a time, or alternatively, trying to "score" (have sex) with numerous partners (Giordano, 2003, p. 269). In addition, parents influence youngsters through the relationships they have established within the family (W. A. Collins & Sroufe, 1999). For example, adolescents with secure attachments to family members are likely to have successful dating experiences, perhaps because they have greater self-confidence, better social skills, and more experience in trusting relationships. Similarly, adolescents who are accustomed to a balanced give-and-take in decision making at home may use this same style with romantic partners, negotiating what movie to see, which party to attend, and so on. In contrast, teens who have seen family violence may hit and push dating partners or, conversely, tolerate partners' aggressive behavior ("He didn't mean it"; "She was drunk"; "He'll outgrow it") (Wolfe & Wekerle, 1997).

Romantic relationships benefit adolescents in several ways. Being in a relationship fulfills needs for companionship, affection, and security and may significantly enhance social status with peers (W. A. Collins & Sroufe, 1999; Furman & Simon, 1999; Giordano, 2003; B. C. Miller & Benson, 1999). Such relationships also provide opportunities for young people to experiment with new interpersonal behaviors and examine previously unexplored aspects of their own identity. With time and experience, many young people become adept at capturing and maintaining the affections of romantic partners.

At the same time, romantic relationships can wreak havoc on adolescents' emotions (W. A. Collins & van Dulmen, 2006). Adolescents can find it exciting and frustrating to enter (and exit) romantic liaisons with one another. In some cases the emotional highs and lows that come with romance—the roller-coaster ride between exhilaration and disappointment—cloud judgment, trigger depression, and distract young people from schoolwork (Davila, 2008; Larson et al., 1999; K. H. Rubin et al., 2006).

Sexual intimacy. Both genders have some capacity for sexual arousal even before puberty (Conn & Kanner, 1940; de Graaf & Rademakers, 2006). Children and preadolescents occasionally look at or touch one another in private places and play games (e.g., strip poker) that have sexual overtones (Dornbusch et al., 1981; Katchadourian, 1990). Except in cases of sexual abuse, however, sexuality before adolescence lacks the erotic features present in later development.

During puberty nature ensures that young people gain both the physical structures and the physiological impetus to become sexually active. Although sexual maturation is a natural process, it is not a simple matter to address. No one knows how best to handle adolescent sexuality—not parents, not teachers, and certainly not adolescents themselves. Many adults ignore the topic, assuming (or perhaps hoping) it's not yet relevant for the adolescents in their care. Even teenagers who have good relationships with their parents have few chances to talk about sex (Brooks-Gunn & Furstenberg, 1990; R. M. C. Leite, Buoncompagno, Leite, & Mergulhao, 1995). And when parents and teachers do broach the topic of sexuality, they often raise it in conjunction with problems, such as irresponsible behavior, substance abuse, disease, and unwanted pregnancy.

Adolescents, meanwhile, must come to terms with their emerging sexuality, either on their own or in collaboration with trusted peers. They must learn to accept their changing bodies, cope with unanticipated feelings of sexual desire, and try to reconcile the conflicting messages they get from various sources—home, school, religious groups, peers, the media—about whether and under what circumstances varying degrees of sexual intimacy are appropriate (Brooks-Gunn & Paikoff, 1993).

For many adolescents sexual intimacy goes hand in hand with, and is a natural outgrowth of, long-term romantic relationships (Graber, Britto, & Brooks-Gunn, 1999; B. C. Miller & Benson, 1999). For many others, however, it is something that should be saved for the "right moment," perhaps for marriage. And for a few, sexual intimacy is an activity completely separate from romantic involvement. For these individuals, it may be a means of enhancing social standings with peers, exploring possible sexual orientations, gaining others' attention and affection, or simply experiencing physical pleasure (W. A. Collins & Sroufe, 1999; L. M. Diamond, Savin-Williams, & Dubé, 1999; Gerbhardt, Kuyper, & Greunsven, 2003; Woody, D'Souza, & Russel, 2003).

Adolescents' intimate experiences sometimes add to their confusion about sexuality. Consider these varying recollections about a first kiss (Alapack, 1991):

> The experience was so gentle that I was in awe. I walked back to my cabin on weak knees. My girlfriends told me I was blushing furiously. I felt lightheaded, but oh so satisfied. (p. 58)

> I found myself mentally stepping back, thinking: "no rockets, fireworks, music or stars." I had to fake enjoyment, humor him. But I felt nothing! Later I sat on my bed and contemplated becoming a nun! (p. 60)

> He kissed me violently and pawed me over. When I started to cry, he let me go . . . I didn't want it to count. I wanted to wipe it off as I rubbed off the saliva. I couldn't. It couldn't be reversed; I couldn't be unkissed again. And the moisture, I could feel it, smell it, even though it was wiped. It made me nauseous. I felt like I was going to throw up. (p. 62)

These varied accounts have little in common, except perhaps a sense of discovery. Other first intimacies also reflect such variability: Some teens are moved by tenderness and shared pleasure, but others are disappointed, repulsed, or confused (Carns, 1973; Sorensen, 1983; Woody et al., 2003).

Most adolescents gradually add to their repertoire of sexual behaviors. As you might recall from Chapter 5, a sizable minority of adolescents (approximately 4 or 5 in 10) try sexual intercourse during the high school years (Centers for Disease Control and Prevention, 2006). Typically, adolescents initiate sexual intercourse only after several years of experience with less intimate contacts (DeLamater & MacCorquodale, 1979; Udry, 1988).

For quite a few adolescents, sexual activity has unintended physical consequences, including pregnancy and infection. Unfortunately, adolescents may hold beliefs that make them vulnerable to risk. For example, many teenagers do not consider oral or anal sexual contact to be "real" sex, and they believe (incorrectly) that sexually transmitted infections are not possible with such contact (Remez, 2000). Even when adolescents are aware that such consequences are possible, they sometimes discount these risks, focus on immediate pleasures, or use impaired judgment as a result of drugs or alcohol (see Chapter 5 for a discussion of adolescents' unsafe sexual behaviors).

Sexual orientation. By **sexual orientation**, we mean the particular sex(es) to whom an individual is romantically and sexually attracted. A small but significant percentage of adolescents find themselves sexually attracted to their own gender either instead of or in addition to the opposite gender. Although it has been difficult to establish precise figures, researchers have estimated that 2 to 3 percent of young people report being gay, lesbian, or bisexual, with an additional few percent either having some degree of same-sex attractions while continuing to identify primarily as heterosexual or realizing later in adulthood that they are homosexual or bisexual (Bailey, Dunn, & Martin, 2000; Savin-Williams, 2005; Savin-Williams & Diamond, 2004).

sexual orientation
Particular sex(es) to which an individual is romantically and sexually attracted.

The causes of sexual orientation remain uncertain, but many theorists suspect that both genetic and environmental factors contribute (Byne, 1997; De Cecco & Parker, 1995; Money, 1988; Savin-Williams & Diamond, 1997). Some evidence for a genetic component comes from twin studies: Monozygotic (identical) twins are more similar in their sexual orientation than dizygotic (fraternal) twins (Bailey et al., 2000; Bailey & Pillard, 1997; Gabard, 1999; see Chapter 4 for a description of the genetic similarity of twins). Nevertheless, even monozygotic twins are not always the same. For male twins, if one is homosexual, the other has a 50–50 chance of being so; for female twins, the probability is a bit lower. Other researchers have observed subtle differences between homosexual and heterosexual individuals in certain brain structures, and some investigators suggest that variations in hormones circulating in the prenatal environment may initiate a cascade of physiological effects that ultimately influence sexual orientation (Bailey & Pillard, 1997; Odent, 2005; Rahman & Wilson, 2003).

Regardless of the exact blend of nature and nurture that determines sexual orientation, this important aspect of sexuality does not appear to be a voluntary decision. Many homosexual and bisexual young people recall feeling "different" from peers in their childhood days and not initially understanding this feeling (D. A. Anderson, 1994; Carver et al., 2004; Savin-Williams, 1995). Adolescence is a particularly confusing time for them, as they struggle to form an identity while feeling different and isolated from peers (Morrow, 1997; C. J. Patterson, 1995). When their attractions to same-gender peers become stronger, they may initially work hard to ignore or discount such sentiments. At an older age, they may begin to accept some aspects of their homosexuality, and later still they may "come out" and identify fully and openly with other gay and lesbian individuals. In the following Interpreting Children's Artifacts and Reflections feature, "This Is Who I Am," consider the challenges that one young man faced when considering his homosexuality.

Interpreting Children's Artifacts and Reflections

This Is Who I Am

After a year of college, 19-year-old Michael wrote the following essay. As you read it, speculate about the factors that initially made it difficult for him to accept his homosexuality and feel good about himself.

As long as I can remember, I always felt a little different when it came to having crushes on other people. When I was in elementary school I never had crushes on girls, and when I look back on that time now, I was probably most attracted to my male friends. I participated in some of the typical "boy" activities, like trading baseball cards and playing video games, but I was never very interested in rough sports. I often preferred to play with the girls in more role-playing and cooperative games. Of course, I didn't understand much about sex or gender roles at the time. I just figured I would become more masculine and develop feelings for the opposite sex after going through puberty.

To my dismay, middle school and the onset of puberty only brought more attention to my lack of interest in girls. The first time I thought about being gay was when I was in 6th grade, so I was probably 11 or 12 years old at the time. But in my mind, being gay was not an option and I began to expend an incredible amount of energy repressing my developing homosexual urges. In 7th grade, I had my first experience with major depression. Looking back on it, I am almost positive that being gay was the immediate cause of the depression. . . . When I finally recovered from the episode a few months later, I did my best to move on with my life and forget about my problems with sexuality. I continued to repress my feelings through high school, a task that became more and more difficult as the years went by. I never really dated any girls and my group of friends in high school was highly female. When I was 16, a junior in high school, I had another more severe bout of

depression. . . . I continued to be ashamed of my feelings and refused to even tell my psychologist about concerns over my sexuality. After finally emerging from my depression, I came to somewhat of an agreement with myself. I decided that I would simply put my conflict on hold, hoping it would resolve itself. Unfortunately, I still held on to the hope that it would resolve itself in heterosexuality and I remained distraught by my feelings. I finally came out during my freshman year at [college] with the support of my friends and an extremely accepting social environment.

Having exposure to the homosexual lifestyle in college is what finally made me realize that I could have a normal life and that I would not have to compromise my dreams because of it. Even though my high school was relatively liberal and very supportive of different backgrounds, there was very little discussion about homosexuality, even in health class. We had visibly gay teachers, but it was rarely openly talked about. I think the reason it took me so long to accept my sexuality was simply because I had no exposure to it while growing up. It angers me that people refer to homosexuality as a lifestyle choice because I had no choice over my sexuality. I spent seven years of my life denying my homosexuality, and believe me, if there had ever been a choice between gay or straight during that time, I would have chosen straight in a second. Today I can't imagine my life without being gay and I would never choose to be straight.

Essay used with permission.

As Michael's experience suggests, the road to self-acceptance for a gay adolescent can be a rocky one, and anger and depression occasionally occur along the way (Elia, 1994; C. J. Patterson, 1995). The fact that no one talked openly about homosexuality made it difficult for Michael to accept the validity of his own feelings. The resulting emotional toll that he experienced was substantial. Happily, Michael eventually entered a supportive social climate, which fostered his self-acceptance.

Michael's experience raises the issue of how homosexuality and bisexuality are addressed at school. When the topic of homosexuality comes up in the school curriculum, it is usually within the context of acquired immune deficiency syndrome (AIDS) and other risks (Filax, 2007; Malinsky, 1997). Adolescents with a homosexual or bisexual orientation are frequently harassed by peers and occasionally become the victims of hate crimes (Elze, 2003; R. A. Friend, 1993; Savin-Williams, 1995). Under such circumstances some gay, lesbian, and bisexual youths become "silent, invisible, and fearful" (M. B. Harris, 1997, p. xxi), and a higher-than-average proportion drop out of school (Elia, 1994; Filax, 2007).

Despite these social hardships, most gay and lesbian youths are psychologically and socially healthy and find the social support they need (Savin-Williams, 1989; Savin-Williams & Ream, 2003). For example, one lesbian girl, Elise, joined a local support group with the help of her mother. Elise found contact with other gay and lesbian adolescents to be very reassuring:

> I was so happy to realize that—oh wow, it's very difficult to describe the feeling—realizing, feeling completely completely alone and then realizing that other people know exactly where you're at or what you're going through. I mean it was amazing. (Herr, 1997, p. 60)

Addressing adolescents' sexuality.   When young people reach puberty, the intrigue of romance saturates their social environments, and they become preoccupied with who harbors secret yearnings for whom, whether the targets of desire reciprocate with affection, and which friends have progressed to various points along the continuum of sexual exploration. As an educator or other practitioner potentially working with young people, you may find this undercurrent of romantic desire to be distracting. You cannot squash the instincts that energize adolescents' brains and bodies but you can be supportive in the following ways.

Adults who are open-minded and supportive can help adolescents navigate the highs and lows of romance.

- ***Remember how you felt as an adolescent.*** If romance was not a part of your own adolescence, we suspect that you longed for it or found yourself fantasizing about someone. If you dated occasionally or frequently, the sentiments from your first experiences undoubtedly left a trace (we wager you can remember your first date, first kiss, first rejection). Distracting as romantic desires might be, they are a natural, healthy part of coming-of-age.

- ***Expect diversity in adolescents' romantic relationships.*** Teenagers' romantic activities will, to some degree, reflect the cultural norms of the surrounding community. Yet within any given culture, individual differences are sizable. Some young people attract a series of steady admirers, whereas others may be inexperienced in, possibly even indifferent to, the world of romance. And, as mentioned earlier, a small percentage of adolescents will have yearnings for members of their own gender.

- ***Make information about human sexuality easily available.*** A conventional belief has held that education about human sexuality is the prerogative of parents and has no place in schools. Typically, if sex education is a part of the school curriculum at all, it focuses on the biological aspects of sexual intercourse and offers little information to help teens make sense of their conflicting thoughts and feelings about physical intimacy. Furthermore, adolescents' participation in a sex education curriculum usually requires parents' approval, and many parents are loath to give it. Less controversial alternatives include making literature about a variety of related issues accessible at school libraries and letting adolescents know that school counselors and nurses are always willing to talk with them about matters of health and sexuality.

- ***Create a supportive environment for all young people.*** To adults the romantic bonds and breakups of adolescents often seem trivial, but they may cause considerable stress in teenagers. For instance, adolescents may feel deep humiliation after rejection by a desired romantic partner or a profound sense of loss as a long-term relationship ends (Kaczmarek & Backlund, 1991). In such situations teachers and counselors can help adolescents sort through their feelings and look forward with optimism to brighter days and new relationships (Bannister, Jakubec, & Stein, 2003; Larson et al., 1999).

SEXUAL HARASSMENT: IT'S NO JOKE!

- **Sexual harassment is unwanted and unwelcomed sexual behavior** which interferes with your right to get an education or to participate in school activities. In school, sexual harassment may result from someone's words, gestures or actions (of a sexual nature) that make you feel uncomfortable, embarrassed, offended, demeaned, frightened, helpless or threatened. If you are the target of sexual harassment, it may be very scary to go to school or hard to concentrate on your school work.

- **Sexual harassment can happen once, several times, or on a daily basis.**

- **Sexual harassment can happen any time and anywhere** in school—in hallways or in the lunchroom, on the playground or the bus, at dances or on field trips.

- **Sexual harassment can happen to anyone!** Girls and boys both get sexually harassed by other students in school.

- **Agreement isn't needed.** The target of sexual harassment and the harasser do not have to agree about what is happening; sexual harassment is defined by the girl or boy who is targeted. The harasser may tell you that he or she is only joking, but if their words, gestures or actions (of a sexual nature) are making you uncomfortable or afraid, then you're being sexually harassed. You do not have to get others, either your friends, teachers or school officials, to agree with you.

- **No one has the right to sexually harass another person!** School officials are legally responsible to guarantee that all students, you included, can learn in a safe environment which is free from sexual harassment and sex discrimination. If you are being sexually harassed, your student rights are being violated. Find an adult you trust and tell them what's happening, so that something can be done to stop the harassment.

- **Examples of sexual harassment in school:**
  - touching, pinching, and grabbing body parts
  - being cornered
  - sending sexual notes or pictures
  - writing sexual graffiti on desks, bathroom walls or buildings
  - making suggestive or sexual gestures, looks, jokes, or verbal comments (including "mooing," "barking" and other noises)
  - spreading sexual rumors or making sexual propositions
  - pulling off someone's clothes
  - pulling off your own clothes
  - being forced to kiss someone or do something sexual
  - attempted rape and rape

REMEMBER: SEXUAL HARASSMENT IS SERIOUS AND AGAINST THE LAW!

Figure 15-5

Example of how teachers and school counselors might describe sexual harassment in language that children and adolescents understand.
Originally appeared as "Stop Sexual Harassment in Schools," by N. Stein, May 18, 1993, *USA Today*. Copyright 1993 by Nan Stein. Reprinted with permission of the author.

In addition, educators must make sure that adolescents with diverse sexual orientations feel welcome, respected, and safe at school. Teachers and other school personnel should prohibit verbal insults about sexual orientation, can listen sympathetically to youth who feel alienated or ostracized in the school environment because of their sexual orientation, and in general must create an overall culture of mutual respect for all members of the school community (Elze, 2003; Filax, 2007; Morrow, 1997).

- *Describe sexual harassment and indicate why it is prohibited.* **Sexual harassment** is any action that a target can reasonably construe as hostile, humiliating, or sexually offensive (Sjostrom & Stein, 1996; also see Chapter 14). It is a form of discrimination and therefore is prohibited by federal and state laws. Sexual harassment can be a problem at the late elementary, middle school, and high school levels, when youngsters are maturing and developing an interest in sexual matters. Youngsters must be advised that sexual harassment will not be tolerated. They should be informed that under no circumstances may they degrade one another—by words, gestures, or actions—with regard to physical traits or sexual orientation. An example of a description of sexual harassment, appropriate for students at varying grade levels, appears in Figure 15-5.

- *Make appropriate referrals when necessary.* Teachers occasionally learn unexpectedly about aspects of youngsters' personal lives. For instance, students may tell teachers they are pregnant, have a pregnant girlfriend, have been raped or sexually abused, or suspect they've contracted a sexually transmitted infection. Educators need to be prepared to make appropriate referrals to counselors and other officials and to encourage adolescents to talk with family members.

As you have learned, peer relationships change considerably over the childhood years. In the Developmental Trends table "Peer Relationships at Different Age Levels," you can review typical features and variations in peer relationships during the developmental periods of childhood and consider their implications for supporting youngsters of various ages.

sexual harassment
Form of discrimination in which a target individual perceives another's actions or statements to be hostile, humiliating, or offensive, especially pertaining to physical appearance or sexual matters.

Peer Relationships at Different Age Levels

Age	What You Might Observe	Diversity	Implications
Infancy (Birth–2 Years) 	· Growing interest in other infants in the same child care setting · Beginning attempts to make contact with familiar infants, such as looking at their faces and smiling at them · In second year, side-by-side play and awareness of one another's actions	· Some infants have not had social experiences with siblings or other children in child care; they may need time to adjust to the presence of other children. · Security of attachment to caregivers may affect children's interaction style with peers. · Infants who are temperamentally inclined to be shy, fearful, or inhibited may be wary of other children.	· Place small babies side by side when they are calm and alert. · Talk about what other children are doing (e.g., "Look at Willonda shaking that toy; let's go watch how she makes the beads spin"). · Supervise small children to prevent them from hurting one another. When they accidentally bump into others, redirect them to a different path (e.g., "Come this way, Tammy. Chloe doesn't like it when you bump into her").
Early Childhood (2–6 Years) 	· Increasing frequency and complexity of interactions with familiar peers · Developing preference for play activities with particular peers · Formation of rudimentary friendships based on proximity and easy access (e.g., formation of friendships with neighbors and preschool classmates) · Involved conversations and imaginative fantasies with friends	· Children with prior social experiences may find it easier to make friends in a new preschool or child care center. · Children who have sociable and easy-going temperaments tend to form and keep friends more easily than children who are shy, aggressive, anxious, or high-strung.	· Help shy children gain entry into groups, especially if they have previously had limited social experiences. · When necessary, help children resolve conflicts with friends, but encourage them to identify solutions that benefit everyone, and let them do as much of the negotiation as possible.
Middle Childhood (6–10 Years)	· Concern about being accepted by peers · Tendency to assemble in larger groups than in early childhood · Less need for adult supervision than in early childhood · Outdoor peer groups structured with games and sports · Increase in gossip as children show concern over friends and enemies · Some social exclusiveness, with friends being reluctant to have others join in their activities · Predominance of same-gender friendships (especially after age 7)	· Boys tend to play in larger groups than girls do. · Some children are temperamentally cautious and timid; they may stand at the periphery of groups and show little social initiative. · Some children are actively rejected by peers, perhaps because they are perceived as odd or have poor social skills.	· Supervise children's peer relationships from a distance; intervene when needed to defuse an escalating situation. · Tactfully facilitate the entry of isolated and rejected children into ongoing games, cooperative learning groups, and informal lunch groups. · Teach rejected children how to interact appropriately with peers.
Early Adolescence (10–14 Years)	· Variety of contexts (e.g., competitive sports, extracurricular activities, parties) in which to interact with peers · Heightened concern about acceptance and popularity among peers · Fads and conformity in dress and communication styles in peer groups · Same-gender cliques, often restricted to members of a single ethnic group · Increasing intimacy, self-disclosure, and loyalty among friends · New interest in members of the opposite gender; for gay and lesbian youths, new dimensions of interest in the same gender · For some, initiation of dating, often within the context of group activities	· Some young adolescents are very socially minded; others are more quiet and reserved. · Gossiping and social exclusion may continue in some groups. · Some young adolescents become involved in gangs and other delinquent social activities. · A few young adolescents are sexually active. · A small percentage begin to construct an identity as gay or lesbian individuals.	· Make classrooms, schools, and other settings friendly, affirming places for all adolescents. Create an atmosphere of acceptance and respect for diverse kinds of students. Do not tolerate name calling, insensitive remarks, or sexual harassment. · Provide appropriate places for adolescents to hang out before and after school. · Identify mechanisms (e.g., cooperative learning groups, public service projects) through which teenagers can fraternize productively as they work toward academic or prosocial goals. · On some occasions, decide which youngsters will work together in groups; on other occasions, let them choose their work partners. · Sponsor after-school activities (e.g., in sports, music, or academic interest areas).

Developmental Trends (continued)

Age	What You Might Observe	Diversity	Implications
Late Adolescence (14–18 Years)	· Emerging understanding that relationships with numerous peers do not necessarily threaten close friendships · Increasing dependence on friends for advice and emotional support, with adults remaining important in such matters as educational choices and career goals · Less cliquishness toward the end of high school; greater tendency to affiliate with larger, less exclusive crowds · Increasing amount of time spent in mixed-gender groups · Many social activities unsupervised by adults · Emergence of committed romantic couples, especially in the last 2 years of high school	· Some teenagers have parents who continue to monitor their whereabouts; others have little adult supervision. · Adolescents' choices of friends and social groups affect their leisure activities, risk-taking behaviors, and attitudes about schoolwork. Some adolescents actively seek out risky activities. · Teens who find themselves attracted to same-gender peers face additional challenges in constructing their adult identities, especially if others are not accepting of their sexual orientation.	· In literature and history, assign readings with themes of psychological interest to adolescents (e.g., loyalty among friends, self-disclosure of feelings, and vulnerability). · Encourage adolescents to join extracurricular activities and in other ways make them feel an integral part of their school. · Sponsor dances and other supervised social events that give adolescents opportunities to socialize.

Schools

You have learned in this book that teachers and other practitioners can nurture children and adolescents by providing age-appropriate instruction, adequate physical activity, good nutrition, affectionate care, clear rules, and appropriate discipline. When educators integrate such practices into warm, effectively governed classrooms and schools, youngsters truly stand to gain. Let's now consider three characteristics of schools that make them enriching environments for children and adolescents: a sense of community, affirming socialization messages, and sensitivity to developmental transitions.

The School as a Community

In our introductory case study, Pamela Bradshaw established a productive learning environment by being sympathetic, respectful, and knowledgeable about age-appropriate activities. As a result, children listened politely to one another and felt bonded to their kindergarten group. In other words, they functioned well together as a *community*.

Educators foster a **sense of community** in schools when students, teachers, and other school staff have shared goals, support one another's efforts, and believe that everyone makes an important contribution (Hom & Battistich, 1995; D. Kim, Solomon, & Roberts, 1995; Lickona, 1991; Osterman, 2000; also see Chapter 3). When schools cultivate a sense of community, students are more likely to exhibit prosocial behavior, express positive attitudes about school, be intrinsically motivated to learn, and achieve at high levels. Furthermore, a sense of community is associated with lower rates of disruptive classroom behavior, emotional distress, truancy, violence, drug use, and dropping out of school (Hom & Battistich, 1995; D. Kim et al., 1995; Osterman, 2000).

A sense of community is the outgrowth of hard work by teachers, other school staff, families, and students themselves. Teachers can do their part to cultivate a sense of community when they attend to three factors: (a) the climate of the classroom, (b) instructional methods, and (c) school traditions.

Classroom climate.   To begin with, teachers can foster a sense of community when they establish a warm, supportive atmosphere in the classroom, show that they care for children,

sense of community
In a classroom or school, a collection of widely shared beliefs that students, teachers, and other staff have common goals, support one another's efforts, and make important contributions to everyone's success.

MyEducationLab

This poster in a middle school corridor (shown in the "Environments: Early Adolescence" video in the Video Examples section of Chapter 15 in MyEducationLab) illustrates one important element of classroom climate: the feeling that one is physically and psychologically safe at school.

and express their support for children's learning. Children are apt to thrive personally and academically when their classrooms exhibit the following features:

- Teachers communicate genuine caring, respect, and support for all students.
- Students feel both physically and psychologically safe; for instance, they know that they can make mistakes without being ridiculed by their teacher or classmates and that they can seek help from others when they need it.
- Teachers adopt an *authoritative* approach to instruction and classroom management, setting clear guidelines for behavior but, in the process, also considering students' needs and involving students in decision making (such an approach incorporates the elements of authoritative parenting described in Chapter 3).
- Teachers provide sufficient order and structure to guide classroom assignments (such instructional strategies are summarized in Chapters 6, 7, and 10).
- Teachers give students opportunities to engage in appropriate self-chosen and self-directed activities (motivational principles underlying the benefits of children's independent choices are described in Chapter 13).

Classrooms that reflect these principles are, in general, productive ones: Students are motivated to learn new skills, perceive themselves as being reasonably capable, achieve at high academic levels, and act in a socially competent manner (G. A. Davis & Thomas, 1989; Juvonen, 2006; Roderick & Camburn, 1999; A. M. Ryan & Patrick, 2001; Scott-Little & Holloway, 1992; Wentzel, 1999; H. K. Wilson, Pianta, & Stuhlman, 2007). When other aspects of children's lives trouble them—for instance, when children's family relationships are strained, children live in dangerous and economically disadvantaged neighborhoods, or the community has recently experienced a natural disaster—perceived support from teachers is especially important in helping youngsters feel safe, competent, valued, and understood (McMahon, Parnes, Keys, & Viola, 2008; E. P. Smith, Boutte, Zigler, & Finn-Stevenson, 2004).

Instructional methods.   Teachers can also promote a sense of community by using instructional methods that are active, engaging, and cooperative (E. P. Smith et al., 2004). In one model, children form a **community of learners,** a classroom arrangement in which students help one another to achieve a common learning goal. A community of learners has characteristics such as these:

- All students are active participants in classroom activities.
- Discussion and collaboration among two or more students are common occurrences and play a key role in learning.
- Diversity in students' interests and rates of progress is expected and respected.
- Students and teacher coordinate their efforts at helping one another learn; no one has exclusive responsibility for teaching others.
- Everyone is a potential resource for the others; different individuals are likely to serve as resources on different occasions, depending on the topics and tasks at hand. (In some cases students may "major" in a particular topic and become local experts on it.)
- The teacher provides some guidance and direction for classroom activities, but students may also contribute to the course of activities.
- Students regularly critique one another's work.
- The process of learning is emphasized as much as, and sometimes more than, the finished product. (A. L. Brown & Campione, 1994, 1996; Campione, Shapiro, & Brown, 1995; Prawat, 1992; Rogoff, 1994; Rogoff, Matusov, & White, 1996; Rothstein-Fisch & Trumbull, 2008)

The outcomes of community-of-learners groups are often quite positive, especially when teachers encourage children to abide by age-appropriate rules for interaction. These groups tend to promote fairly complex thinking processes and are highly motivating for students (A. L. Brown & Campione, 1994; Turkanis, 2001). For instance, students in these groups often insist on going to school even when they are ill, and they are disappointed when summer vacation begins (Rogoff, 1994).

School traditions.   Teachers can also foster a sense of community by encouraging children to participate actively in school activities and day-to-day operations. Schools that operate as

community of learners
A classroom in which teacher(s) and students actively and collaboratively work to help one another learn.

true communities encourage everyone to work together as cooperative and productive citizens (Battistich et al., 1995; Battistich, Solomon, Watson, & Schaps, 1997; A. L. Brown & Campione, 1994; Rothstein-Fisch & Trumbull, 2008). Several strategies are helpful in creating this positive school spirit:

- Soliciting students' ideas about school activities, such as how Valentine's Day might be observed
- Creating mechanisms through which students can help make the school run smoothly and efficiently (e.g., assigning various helper roles to individual students on a rotating basis)
- Emphasizing prosocial values in school codes of conduct, in newsletters, and on bulletin boards
- Providing public recognition of students' contributions to the overall success of the classroom and school
- Creating schoolwide traditions that are fun for youngsters and their families, such as carnivals and field days (D. Kim et al., 1995; Lickona, 1991; Osterman, 2000)

Socialization in Schools

Beginning early in their lives, most children learn that there are certain things that they can or should do and other things that they definitely should not do. As you learned in Chapter 3, parents *socialize* young children to use certain behaviors (e.g., showing politeness by saying "please" and "thank you") and avoid others (e.g., hitting other children). Teachers, too, have expectations for children's behavior and classroom performance. Many of these expectations help children acquire the personal, social, and academic skills they will need to be successful adults in their society. Occasionally, however, teachers' expectations can be detrimental for children's long-term development, as you will soon see.

School values.   Teachers begin to socialize children the moment that children enter school. For example, teachers typically expect and encourage behaviors such as these:

- Showing respect for authority figures
- Controlling impulses
- Following instructions
- Completing assigned tasks in a timely manner
- Working independently
- Helping and cooperating with classmates
- Striving for academic excellence

Teachers' often unstated expectations for such behavior are sometimes known as the *hidden curriculum* of the classroom (Anyon, 1988; Chafel, 1997; Jackson, 1988; Solmon & Lee, 2008). Customs and values are considered "hidden" when teachers firmly expect them to be followed but rarely talk about them. A teacher's hidden curriculum may or may not be consistent with sound developmental and educational principles. For example, a teacher may emphasize the importance of always getting the right answer, doing tasks in a particular way, or, as the following dialogue between a teacher and several students illustrates, getting things done as quickly as possible:

Teacher:	I will put some problems on the board. You are to divide.
Child:	We got to divide?
Teacher:	Yes.
Several children:	[*Groan*] Not again, Mr. B., we done this yesterday.
Child:	Do we put the date?
Teacher:	Yes. I hope we remember we work in silence. You're supposed to do it on white paper. I'll explain it later.
Child:	Somebody broke my pencil. [*Crash*—a child falls out of his chair.]
Child:	[*repeats*] Mr. B., somebody broke my *pencil!*
Child:	Are we going to be here all morning? (Anyon, 1988, p. 367)

In this situation the teacher presents math problems merely as things that need to be done—not as tasks that might actually have some benefit—and the children clearly have little interest in the assignment.

Teachers can help students see their schoolwork as activities for achieving important knowledge and skills, not just as things to get done.

Children may or may not find it easy to live up to teachers' standards for behavior, but they are more likely to be successful in the classroom if they are at least *aware* of these standards. Teachers can do two things:

 • ***Explicitly tell children about expected behavior.*** Children come to school with their own ways of talking and acting and do not automatically decipher teachers' expectations for how children are supposed to communicate in groups, ask for help, express their confusion, and so forth. In general, children find it easier to act in acceptable ways when teachers explain their expectations and post important rules of behavior on a bulletin board or disseminate them in simple handouts (Gettinger & Kohler, 2006).

 • ***Offer extra help to students who find it especially difficult to identify unspoken social rules at school.*** Some youngsters, perhaps due to a cognitive or social-emotional disability, find it particularly challenging to determine which behaviors are appropriate and which are inappropriate in various situations. For example, students with Asperger syndrome, one of the autism spectrum disorders you read about in Chapter 12, may not distinguish the contexts that do and do not permit high-spirited vocalizations. Thus, a child may need to be told that although squealing on the playground is considered fun, shouting inside the classroom will annoy others (Myles & Simpson, 2001). Similarly, children with Asperger syndrome may not understand that some teachers allow students to talk during a lesson without first raising their hands and being called on, whereas other teachers find students' spontaneous interjections to be disruptive. Strategies that appear effective in making the hidden curriculum transparent for children with disabilities include role playing, asking children to speculate about proper courses of action in various situations, and conducting "social autopsies"—conversations between individual children and adults after children make a social mistake and need help in determining why they offended someone and how they might act differently next time (Myles & Simpson, 2001).

Teachers' expectations about the abilities of individual students. As we have seen, teachers have expectations for how their students should behave in the classroom. But teachers also form expectations about how individual students are *likely* to perform. In many instances teachers size up their students fairly accurately: They know which ones need help with reading skills, which ones have trouble working together in the same cooperative group, and so on, and they can adapt their instruction accordingly (Goldenberg, 1992; Good & Brophy, 1994; Good & Nichols, 2001; also see Chapter 2).

But teachers occasionally make inaccurate assessments. For instance, teachers often underestimate the abilities of students who

 • Are physically unattractive
 • Misbehave frequently in class
 • Speak in dialects other than Standard English
 • Are members of ethnic minority groups
 • Are recent immigrants
 • Come from low-income backgrounds (Amatea & West-Olatunji, 2007; R. E. Bennett et al., 1993; McKown & Weinstein, 2008; J. Oakes & Guiton, 1995; Ritts, Patterson, & Tubbs, 1992; G. Thompson, 2008)

Teachers with low expectations for certain students offer them few opportunities for speaking in class, ask them easy questions, give little feedback about their responses, and present them with few, if any, challenging assignments (Babad, 1993; Good & Brophy, 1994; S. Graham, 1990; Rosenthal, 1994). In contrast, teachers with high expectations for students create a warmer classroom climate, interact with students more frequently, provide more opportunities for students to respond, and give more positive feedback (Rubie-Davies, 2007).

Most children and adolescents are well aware of their teachers' differential treatment of individual students and use that treatment to draw inferences about their own and others' abilities (R. Butler, 1994; Good & Nichols, 2001; Weinstein, 1993). When teachers repeatedly give children low-ability messages, children may begin to see themselves as their teachers see them. Furthermore, students' behavior may mirror their self-perceptions. For example, students may exert little effort on academic tasks, or they may frequently misbehave in class (Marachi, Friedel, & Midgley, 2001; Murdock, 1999). In some cases, then, teachers' expectations lead to a **self-fulfilling prophecy:** What teachers expect students to achieve becomes what students actually do achieve.

Communicating high expectations. A characteristic consistently found in effective schools is high expectations for student performance (M. Phillips, 1997; Roderick & Camburn, 1999). Even if students' initial academic performance is low, educators and other professionals must remember that cognitive abilities and skills can and do change over time, especially when the environment is conducive to growth. We suggest two strategies to help teachers maintain a realistic yet optimistic outlook on what young people can accomplish.

* ***Learn more about students' backgrounds.*** Adults are most likely to develop low expectations for students' performance when they have rigid stereotypes about students from certain ethnic or socioeconomic groups (Amatea & West-Olatunji, 2007; Reyna, 2000). Such stereotypes are often the result of ignorance about students' home environments and cultures (K. Alexander et al., 1987; L. Wilson, 2007). Education is the key here: Teachers and other school personnel must learn as much as they can about students' backgrounds and local communities. With a clear picture of students' families, activities, and values, educators are far more likely to think of students as *individuals*—each with a unique set of talents and skills—than as stereotypical members of a particular group.

* ***Collaborate with colleagues to maximize academic success on a schoolwide basis.*** Educators are more likely to have high expectations for students when they are confident in their own ability to help students achieve academic and social success (Ashton, 1985; Weinstein, Madison, & Kuklinski, 1995; L. Wilson, 2007). Consider the case of one inner-city high school. For many years teachers at the school believed that their low-achieving students, most of whom were from low-income families, were simply unmotivated to learn. Teachers also saw themselves, their colleagues, and school administrators as ineffective in helping these students succeed. To counteract such tendencies, the school faculty began holding regular 2-hour meetings in which they

* Read research related to low-achieving and at-risk students
* Explored various hypotheses about why their students were having difficulty
* Developed, refined, and evaluated innovative strategies for helping their students succeed
* Established a collaborative atmosphere in which, working together, they could take positive action

Such meetings helped the teachers form higher expectations for their students' achievement and a better understanding of what they themselves could do to help the students achieve (Weinstein et al., 1995).

Transitions to New Schools

Entering any new school requires youngsters to adjust to unfamiliar peers and teachers, new academic expectations, and novel activities in a new building. In other respects, however, the experiences of adjusting to elementary and secondary school environments present distinct challenges to youngsters.

Elementary school. In most Western societies, children typically begin elementary school at the age of 5 or 6, when society declares them "ready" for serious learning. In reality children have been learning steadily since birth, and schools now build on this knowledge. For instance, children who have been encouraged to listen to stories and use complex language at home or in preschool have a solid foundation for a school's literacy curriculum. Likewise, children who have had many constructive experiences with peers are prepared for a classroom's social environment. In general, children who have participated in preschool tend to make good social adjustments and perform at reasonably high levels in first grade (W. S. Barnett, 1996; Consortium of Longitudinal Studies, 1983; Magnuson, Ruhm, & Waldfogel, 2007).

In addition to adjusting to the personalities of new teachers and peers, children must also adapt to the regulatory atmosphere of the classroom. Elementary classrooms tend to be more formal and regimented than the cozy settings of family, child care, and preschool. As a result, when children first enter elementary school, one of their challenges is learning and

self-fulfilling prophecy
Phenomenon in which an adult's expectations for a child's performance bring about that level of performance.

following the policies and procedures of the "big kids" school (Corsaro & Molinari, 2005). Here's how first grader Sofia described school rules to her mother and an interviewer:

Mother:	Do you know the rules? What are the rules in first grade?
Sofia:	You cannot run in the corridors, you cannot hurt anyone, you have to raise your hand before talking, you cannot lose toys.
Interviewer:	You know all the rules!
Sofia:	Then you cannot walk around, you cannot shout in the bathroom.
Interviewer:	You know everything.
Mother:	And then? Perhaps you must wait your turn.
Sofia:	And then, then, you have to be silent, write the date. That's all. (Corsaro & Molinari, 2005, pp. 74–75)

Of course, there is more to school than restrictions, and most children eventually settle in and enjoy the relationships and traditions of their classrooms. To help children adjust to new classrooms, teachers generally spend time establishing routines and offering lots of reassurance during those initial days (and sometimes weeks or months) when children feel uneasy. Many teachers and schools also offer orientations and encourage children and families to visit their classrooms before school begins (Corsaro & Molinari, 2005). We authors recall that all of our children had elementary teachers who invited them to visit their classrooms in the spring or summer when student placements were announced and who also sent the children friendly letters before the school year began.

To ease children's adjustment, elementary teachers also give careful consideration to those children who begin the year lacking age-typical intellectual or social skills. These children most certainly *are* ready to learn, but they may need individualized services to succeed academically. For example, kindergarten children who have had little exposure to books at home can begin to master essential literacy skills at school by listening regularly to simple stories in small groups, perhaps with the help of a parent volunteer or teacher's aide. Without focused enrichment and supportive relationships with teachers, however, children who begin school with cognitive delays are likely to fall further behind (Hamre & Pianta, 2005).

In the elementary grades, each child is one of 15 to 30 students whom a teacher gets to know fairly well. Eventually, most children adjust favorably and develop proficiency in basic academic and social skills. Youngsters will draw from these resources when they move into secondary school environments.

Secondary schools. There are often two major transitions at the secondary level. First, beginning at grade 5, 6, or 7, many students move from elementary to either middle school or junior high school. Second, at grade 9 or 10, students move from middle or junior high school to high school. And as they progress through these upper grade levels, students attend separate classes, each with its own teacher. The three secondary configurations—middle, junior high, and high school—have distinctive features but share qualities that distinguish them from elementary schools. A typical secondary school is unlike an elementary school in these ways:

- The school is larger and has more students.
- Teacher–student relationships are more superficial and less personal than they were in elementary school.
- There is more whole-class instruction, with less individualized instruction that takes into account each student's particular needs.
- Classes are less socially cohesive; students may not know their classmates very well and may be reluctant to call on peers for assistance.
- Competition among students (e.g., for popular classes or spots on an athletic team) is more common, especially in high school.
- Students have more independence and responsibility for their own learning; for instance, they sometimes have relatively unstructured assignments to be accomplished over a 2- or 3-week period and must take the initiative to seek help if they are struggling.
- Standards for assigning grades are more rigorous, so students may earn lower grades than they did in elementary school. Grades are often assigned on a comparative basis, with only the highest-achieving students getting As and Bs. (Darling-Hammond & Friedlaender, 2008; Eccles & Midgley, 1989; Futrell & Gomez, 2008; Harter, 1996; Hine & Fraser, 2002; Roderick & Camburn, 1999; Wentzel & Wigfield, 1998; Wigfield et al., 1996)

MyEducationLab

Learn more about research on supportive classroom environments by completing an Understanding Research exercise in Chapter 15's Activities and Applications section in MyEducationLab.

Development and Practice

Easing School Transitions

- **Make contact with children before the beginning of school.**

  In April a kindergarten teacher invites prospective students and their parents to come to an orientation in her classroom. The teacher arranges for snacks to be served and reserves time for a brief presentation and for independent exploration of the room.

- **Provide a means through which every student can feel a part of a small, close-knit group.**

  In September a ninth-grade math teacher establishes *base groups* of three or four students, who provide support and assistance to one another throughout the school year. At the beginning or end of every class period, the teacher gives students in the base groups 5 minutes to help one another with homework assignments.

- **Find time to meet one on one with every student.**

  Early in the school year, while his classes are working on a variety of cooperative learning activities, a middle school social studies

teacher holds individual meetings with each of his students. In these meetings he searches for common interests that he and his students share and encourages the students to seek him out whenever they need help with academic or personal problems. Throughout the semester he continues to touch base with individual students (often during lunch or before or after school) to see how they are doing.

- **Give children and adolescents the extra support that some may need to master subject matter and study skills.**

  A high school implements a homework hotline staffed by a teacher and a group of honor students, and teachers in the school make a point of encouraging students to keep up with their work (McCarthy & Kuh, 2005).

Many educators lament the apparent mismatch between the secondary environment and the needs of adolescents. At a time when adolescents are self-conscious, uncertain, and confronted with tumultuous changes in their bodies and social circumstances, they have relationships with teachers that are superficial, shallow, and sometimes adversarial. For many students secondary school environments lead to less self-confidence about mastering academic subject matter, lower overall self-esteem, and considerable anxiety. Some students withdraw emotionally from the school environment—a disengagement that may eventually result in their dropping out of school or committing criminal acts (Eccles & Midgley, 1989; Janosz, Le Blanc, Boulerice, & Tremblay, 2000; Seidman, Aber, & French, 2004; Urdan & Maehr, 1995; Wigfield et al., 1996).

Certainly, many dedicated secondary teachers are warm and supportive in their interactions with individual students, but teachers serve dozens and sometimes hundreds of students every year, making it virtually impossible to establish close relationships with all of them. One strategy that many high schools are now using is to have every teacher take responsibility for a small group of students whom the teacher gets to know individually. A second and related strategy is to separate out groups of students within the school building. These groups, sometimes known as *houses* or *schools within schools*, permit a reasonably small number of youngsters to become familiar with one another and with a few teachers (Nucci, 2009; Ready, Lee, & Welner, 2004; Seidman et al., 2004). Clusters of students may take some classes together, and they are sometimes located in separate areas of the school.

Fortunately, many secondary schools are finding ways to welcome entering students and personalize learning environments as students settle into classes. Students who make a smooth adjustment to secondary school are more likely to be successful there and, as a result, are more likely to graduate from high school (Roderick & Camburn, 1999; J. S. Smith, 2006; Wigfield et al., 1996). The Development and Practice feature "Easing School Transitions" illustrates several strategies for helping youngsters adjust to new schools.

Society

As you have learned, youngsters acquire many skills, beliefs, and attitudes during ongoing interactions with adults and other children in their families and schools. Others in **society**— an enduring group of people who are socially and economically organized into collective institutions and activities—also influence children's development. We now examine the effects of a society's services, the media, and interactive technologies.

society
Large, enduring group of people that is socially and economically organized and has collective institutions and activities.

Services for Children and Adolescents

In the following sections we examine the services offered by many societies to children and adolescents when they are not in school. We focus on child care, early intervention programs, and after-school programs and activities.

Child care. Many young children are in the care of adults other than their parents for a significant portion of the week. Children are attended to in a variety of settings, from family homes to commercial buildings, and by caregivers who differ in experience, education, and dedication to children (see Chapter 3). Such variations raise concerns about the degree to which children are cared for in a manner that is affectionate, safe, and age-appropriate (Brauner, Gordic, & Zigler, 2004; NICHD Early Child Care Research Network, 2006a).

Advocates for high standards in child care have two primary ways of defining quality. *Structural measures* include such objective indicators as caregivers' training and experience, child-to-caregiver ratios, staff turnover, and number and complexity of toys and equipment (Ghazvini & Mullis, 2002; M. E. Lamb & Ahnert, 2006). For example, early childhood specialists recommend that the child-to-caregiver ratio be no more than three infants or six toddlers for each adult (Bredekamp & Copple, 1997). *Process measures* of quality, which reflect children's social and cognitive experiences in child care, include adults' sensitive care of children, affectionate child–caregiver relationships, productive child–peer interactions, and developmentally appropriate activities (M. E. Lamb & Ahnert, 2006; NICHD Early Child Care Research Network, 2006a). For example, the schedules of activities in a toddler room might be fairly predictable from day to day but also flexible enough to be guided by children's individual and changing needs (Bredekamp & Copple, 1997). Thus, toddlers might be offered two snacks over the span of the morning, even though only a few choose to eat twice.

In reality, indicators of structure and process are closely related. Numerous studies show that lower child-to-staff ratios, smaller group sizes, and more caregiver education are associated with good child–caregiver interactions (e.g., Howes, Smith, & Galinsky, 1995; M. E. Lamb & Ahnert, 2006; NICHD Early Child Care Research Network, 2002). Conversely, when caregivers have too many children to care for, their style of interacting with individual children tends to become rushed and mechanical.

Young children often benefit from experiences in high-quality child care—that is, settings in which caregivers are sensitive and have appropriate training, child-to-staff ratios are low, and caregivers focus on children's individual needs.

In general, research confirms that child care in high-quality settings has beneficial effects on children's development. For example, infants and small children typically enjoy secure attachments to employed caregivers who are warm, sensitive, and consistently involved in the children's care (Barnas & Cummings, 1994; M. E. Lamb & Ahnert, 2006; also see Chapter 11). In addition, high-quality child care has been shown to enhance children's cognitive, linguistic, and social development, with the greatest benefits occurring for children whose home environments have been inattentive or unstimulating (M. E. Lamb & Ahnert, 2006; Sylva, Melhuish, Sammons, Siraj-Blatchford, & Taggart, 2004).

Children who spend long hours in child care from an early age do face risks, however. Exposure to child care at a young age and for long hours seems to trigger slight increases in children's aggression and noncompliance (Belsky & Eggebeen, 1991; M. E. Lamb & Ahnert, 2006; NICHD Early Child Care Research Network, 2002, 2005). These effects are not always seen and, when they are, are smaller for high-quality than for low-quality care.

Early childhood intervention programs. High-quality educational environments for young children have positive effects on children's intellectual growth and may be particularly beneficial for children from low-income backgrounds (Brooks-Gunn, 2003; M. E. Lamb & Ahnert, 2006; McLoyd, 1998a). **Early childhood intervention programs** typically combine an educational focus with other supports for children and their families, such as medical care, social services, and parenting guidance.

In the United States the best known model of early childhood intervention is Project Head Start. Established under federal legislation, Head Start was designed for 3- to 5-year-

early childhood intervention program Program designed to foster basic intellectual, social-emotional, and physical development in young children, especially those with developmental delays or those whose families are economically disadvantaged.

old, low-income children and their families. Since 1965 it has served millions of children, many of them from single-parent homes. A typical Head Start program includes preschool, health screening and referrals, mental health services, nutrition education, family support services, and parent involvement in decision making (Perkins-Gough, 2007; U.S. Department of Health and Human Services, Administration for Children and Families, 2008).

Many investigations have examined the effectiveness of Head Start and similar early childhood intervention programs. Children from these programs score higher on measures of cognitive ability and achieve at higher levels in school, but such advantages often disappear by the upper elementary grades (Ludwig & Phillips, 2007; McLoyd, 1998b; Ramey & Ramey, 1998; U.S. Department of Health and Human Services, Administration for Children and Families, 2005). Nonetheless, other long-term benefits have been observed: Low-income children who attend Head Start or similar preschool programs are less likely to require special educational services and more likely to graduate from high school than are similar children with no preschool experience (Lazar, Darlington, Murray, Royce, & Snipper, 1982; McLoyd, 1998a; A. J. Perry, 2005; Schweinhart & Weikart, 1983; also see Chapter 8). Longer and more intensive programs (e.g., 2 or more years of full-time preschool rather than a single year of part-time schooling), as well as programs in which teachers are well trained and parents are actively involved, yield the greatest benefits (Ramey & Ramey, 1998; Ripple, Gilliam, Chanana, & Zigler, 1999).

Some educators suggest that quality care and education should be more universally available and should start earlier than age 3. One model program, the Carolina Abecedarian Project, offers services to children of economically poor families beginning in infancy (F. A. Campbell et al., 2002). Rigorous research suggests that children who attended this early intervention program have higher intelligence scores from infancy through adolescence and are less likely to require special educational services than those who had no early intervention. In addition, individuals who participated in the program have higher reading and math scores as adults. In general, children from economically disadvantaged families make the most progress when interventions begin early (ideally in infancy) and continue throughout the school years (Brooks-Gunn, 2003; Perkins-Gough, 2007; A. Reynolds, 1994; E. Zigler & Muenchow, 1992).

After-school programs and extracurricular activities. Another way in which communities contribute to young people's development is through the programs they offer before and after school and during the summer—clubs, sports leagues, dance and martial arts lessons, scout troops, and so on. Twelve-year-old Colin gives a sense of his rich learning experiences, made possible by his community, in the "After School: Early Adolescence" video in MyEducationLab:

Interviewer:	So you play basketball?
Colin:	Yeah. Yeah.
Interviewer:	What other . . . is that your favorite sport?
Colin:	I like basketball and track about the same.
Interviewer:	Do you play any other sports?
Colin:	Yeah. I play, basically, I play football, baseball, hockey. . . .
Interviewer:	Wow. What do you like about sports?
Colin:	Well, they're fun and just something to do.
Interviewer:	What kinds of hobbies do you have?
Colin:	I like coin collecting and . . . I garden and I try to take sign language and really do sign language. Yeah.
Interviewer:	So what kinds of clubs do you belong to?
Colin:	I belong to . . . well, I used to belong to 4-H. And I'm in the chess club, Boy Scouts, and sign language club.

A growing body of research indicates that participation in structured after-school and summer activities fosters children's cognitive and social-emotional development. For instance, academically oriented programs appear to cultivate positive feelings about school, better school attendance, higher grades and achievement test scores, better classroom behavior, greater conflict resolution skills, and decreased tension with family members (Charles A. Dana Center, 1999; H. Cooper, Charlton, Valentine, & Muhlenbruck, 2000; Dryfoos, 1999; Granger, 2008;

MyEducationLab

Listen to 12-year-old Colin describe what he does outside school in the "After School: Early Adolescence" video. (Find Video Examples in Chapter 15 of MyEducationLab.)

Effective after-school programs typically offer a variety of activities through which young people can pursue their individual interests. Art by Brandon, age 11.

Vandell & Pierce, 1999). Nonacademic programs, too, seem to have benefits. For instance, high school students who participate in their school's extracurricular activities are more likely than nonparticipants to achieve at high levels and graduate from high school. They are also less likely to smoke, use alcohol or drugs, join gangs, engage in criminal activities, or become teenage parents (Biddle, 1993; H. Cooper, Valentine, Nye, & Lindsay, 1999; Donato et al., 1997; Eppright, Sanfacon, Beck, & Bradley, 1998; Gilman, Meyers, & Perez, 2004; Zill, Nord, & Loomis, 1995).

After-school and summer programs vary in their focus and services, yet most espouse a commitment to providing caring adult–child relationships. In addition, effective programs include these general features:

- A variety of activities, including recreation, academic and cultural enrichment, and opportunities for pursuit of individual interests
- Chances for meaningful participation in authentic activities, such as building a fort, reading to younger children, or registering voters
- Opportunities for success, perhaps in domains in which youngsters have previously unrecognized talents
- Positive interactions with both adults and peers
- Structure and clear limits, with youngsters' active participation in setting rules
- High regard and respect for young people's diverse cultural beliefs and practices (C. R. Cooper, Denner, & Lopez, 1999; Granger, 2008; Kerewsky & Lefstein, 1982; Lefstein & Lipsitz, 1995)

At the elementary level, after-school programs often provide supervision, academic support, and recreational activities for children of working parents. Many programs are delivered in school buildings, sometimes by school authorities and at other times with the cooperation of private vendors, community organizations, or government agencies (Dryfoos, 1999; Mahoney & Zigler, 2006; National Center for Education Statistics, 1997). In some cases schools become a hub of activities offering not only programs for school-age children but also care for younger children and nutritional support and counseling for families (Comer, 2005; B. M. Stern & Finn-Stevenson, 1999). When after-school programs help children with homework, regular communication between classroom teachers and after-school caregivers can align instructional objectives across the two environments (Caplan, McElvain, & Walter, 2001). Face-to-face meetings and two-way written forms, such as the one shown in Figure 15-6, are often effective means of coordinating educational objectives.

At the secondary level, most out-of-school programs take the form of school-affiliated *extracurricular activities*, such as athletic teams, performing arts groups, debating societies, and organizations for school leadership and school spirit. These school-based activities provide young people with opportunities to gain new skills and spend productive time with peers (P. A. Lauer et al., 2006; Peck, Roeser, Zarrett, & Eccles, 2008; Quane & Rankin, 2006). Additional programs are offered in the community and are especially appealing when they provide contact with caring adults and peers. In one study 75 percent of 10- to 18-year-olds who attended one of four inner-city Boys and Girls Clubs of America described the setting as being like a home to them (N. L. Deutsch & Hirsch, 2001). Sixteen-year-old Sammy described his feeling about his club:

> Some people do not have any home. I have been granted the gift of having two homes: my home and the Boys and Girls Club. [The club] allows me to express myself mentally, verbally, physically, and artistically. (p. 1)

As you discovered in Chapter 14, giving back to the community is another worthwhile activity for young people. Community service projects provide an opportunity for service learning, in which youngsters gain practical skills and increased self-confidence while assisting other people and contributing to the betterment of their community (Sheckley & Keeton, 1997; Sloan, 2008; Stukas, Clary, &

Directions: This form is to be used by the classroom teacher and after-school tutor to share information about an individual student's homework assignments and study habits. For each homework assignment, the teacher fills out the information in column one and gives the form to the tutor. After assisting the student, the tutor fills out the information in column two and returns the form to the teacher.

Today's Date:	
Student's Name:	
Teacher's Name:	
Tutor's Name:	
Completed by teacher.	**Completed by tutor.**
The homework for today is:	This student: ☐ Completed the homework easily and independently. ☐ Had difficulty *understanding* what was asked in the homework. ☐ Had difficulty *completing* the homework. ☐ Had difficulty *focusing* on the assignment.
Please pay special attention to:	This student required: ☐ No help with the assignment. ☐ A little help. ☐ Occasional help. ☐ A great deal of help. ☐ See comments on back.
This homework should take _____ minutes to complete.	The homework took _____ minutes to complete.

Figure 15-6

A homework sharing tool. Daytime teachers and after-school teachers who tutor children can use this form to communicate about homework.

From *Beyond the Bell: A Toolkit for Creating Effective After-School Programs* (2nd ed., p. 105), by Judith G. Caplan, Carol K. McElvain, and Katie E. Walter, 2001, Naperville, IL: NCREL. Copyright 2001 by the North Central Regional Educational Laboratory. All rights reserved. Reprinted with permission.

Development and Practice

Enhancing Students' Before- and After-School Experiences

- **Help children navigate transitions between school and after-school care.**

  After school a kindergarten teacher walks outside with children to make sure that each child successfully connects with family members or car pool drivers, gets on the appropriate bus or van, or begins walking home.

- **Sponsor after-school clubs at your school.**

  A middle school offers several clubs for students to participate in after school. Popular options include a Hispanic cultures club, several athletic teams, an honor society, a band, a community service group, and the yearbook staff.

- **Inform parents and other family members about nonschool programs in the area.**

  At a parent–teacher–student conference, a middle school teacher describes clubs and sports programs available at the school, as well as recreational and service opportunities in the local community.

- **Establish a team of school personnel and after-school providers to ensure that after-school programs use resources appropriately and meet children's physical, social-emotional, and academic needs.**

  Two teachers, the principal, and the director of an after-school program meet regularly to discuss space, resources, and ways that the after-school program can give children needed rest, relaxation, snacks, and tutoring.

Snyder, 1999). For example, 15-year-old Connor volunteered to become the football coach for his 7-year-old brother's team when none of the team parents were able to do so. Following is his description of what the experience meant to him:

> [I learned] just how to be a leader and a lot about football. You have to be nice to the little kids and when they make a good play, you gotta tell them about it and when they make a bad play, you gotta *not* tell them about it. I had fun doing it.

Many adolescents also structure their free time with part-time jobs. Adolescents can gain beneficial experiences in getting to work on time, following the requirements of a position, being courteous in a business setting, and managing money. With limited work hours (e.g., 10 to 15 hours per week), adolescents may have adequate time to study and stay involved in school activities (Charner & Fraser, 1988; Mortimer, Shanahan, & Ryu, 1994; Steinberg, Brown, Cider, Kaczmarek, & Lazzaro, 1988). However, some adolescents work long hours, leaving little time to do homework (Marsh & Kleitman, 2005).

After-school activities can foster young people's skills and dispositions to help others and serve the community.

We cannot be definite about the specific effects of extracurricular activities and after-school programs because youngsters who choose to participate in these services may be different from youngsters who decide not to take advantage of them. Nonetheless, because of the potential—and, we suggest, likely—benefits of extracurricular activities and after-school programs, they merit investment of time, energy, and financial resources until social scientists can determine their effects with more certainty. The Development and Practice feature "Enhancing Students' Before- and After-School Experiences" suggests strategies for educators and other practitioners to help young people make good use of their nonschool time.

Television and the Interactive Technologies

Many children and adolescents regularly view television and use a growing collection of **interactive technologies**—computers, CD-ROMs, the Internet, video games, talking books, and cell phones. These media are widely used by youngsters in part because of their accessibility. The majority of youngsters in the United States between 8 and 18 years of age live in households with one or more televisions, video players, radios, audio players, video game players, computers, and instant messaging programs; and most of these youngsters additionally have cable or satellite and Internet access in their homes (D. F. Roberts & Foehr, 2008). Contributing to the popularity of television and interactive technologies are their engaging qualities (such as colorful, fast-moving scenes), alluring themes (e.g., triumphing over bad guys or gyrating with teen idols), and in the cases of cell phones and the Internet, capabilities that enable youngsters to stay in touch with one another.

Content of programs and games.   Bells and whistles may grab children's attention, but it is the *content* of media programs that sticks in their minds (Brooks-Gunn & Donahue, 2008). Fortunately, many programs aired on television and built into interactive technologies have educationally worthwhile content. For example, educational television programs such as

interactive technology
Array of electronic, digitally based machines that are operated dynamically by a person whose commands determine emerging program sequences.

Sesame Street, The Magic School Bus, Dora the Explorer, Blue's Clues, Between the Lions, and *Bill Nye the Science Guy* teach children vocabulary, word recognition, reading concepts, problem-solving skills, and scientific principles (D. R. Anderson, 2003; Comstock & Scharrer, 2006; A. B. Jordan, 2003; Kirkorian, Wartella, & Anderson, 2008; Linebarger & Walker, 2005). Programs that model prosocial behaviors such as the television programs *Mister Rogers' Neighborhood* and *Saved by the Bell* and the video game *Smurfs* teach children valuable social skills (D. R. Anderson, 2003; Chambers & Ascione, 2001; A. B. Jordan, 2003).

Unfortunately, developmentally counterproductive content coexists with, and potentially overshadows, socially responsible material in the media. For example, television programs and video games are apt to show ethnic minorities infrequently and to include stereotypical characters—for instance, women as airheads, men as brutes, and people with dark skin as thugs (Eisenberg et al., 1996; Maher et al., 2008; T. Robinson, Callister, Magoffin, & Moore, 2006). Such offensive portrayals are ridiculous distortions of reality but may prompt impressionable children to develop misconceptions about gender and particular social groups. Similarly, when youngsters repeatedly view slender and athletically toned actors, actresses, and rock stars, they may develop a standard of physical attractiveness that is not realistic for their own body frame (D. R. Anderson, Huston, Schmitt, Linebarger, & Wright, 2001). In addition, advertisements on television and Internet Web sites may cultivate desires for particular cereals, fast food, clothing, toys, and digital devices—items that may or may not be in children's best interests (Buijzen & Valkenburg, 2003; Calvert, 2008; S. Reese, 1996; Wartella, Caplovitz, & Lee, 2004).

The excessively violent and gruesomely realistic scenes of many television programs and video games are another concern. In fact, violence can be found in a large percentage of television programs and video games (C. A. Anderson et al., 2003; Comstock & Scharrer, 2006; S. L. Smith & Donnerstein, 1998). Repeated exposure to violent acts on television seems to make children more aggressive and may be particularly harmful to those already predisposed to aggression (C. Anderson & Huesmann, 2005; Comstock & Scharrer, 2008; Eron, 1980; Huesmann, Moise-Titus, Podolski, & Eron, 2003). For example, young children inclined to solve conflicts in physically aggressive ways are apt to choose programs with violent content and become *more aggressive* after viewing such programs. In addition, heavy viewing of televised violence may *desensitize* children to acts of violence; that is, children's repeated viewing of televised violence seems to erode children's empathic responses to victims of real violent acts. Similarly, violent video games appear to increase child users' aggressive behavior and desensitize them to the suffering of actual victims of aggressive behavior (Cocking & Greenfield, 1996; Funk, Buchman, Jenks, & Bechtoldt, 2003; B. J. Wilson, 2008).

Television viewing.   On average, television viewing time increases rapidly during early childhood, continues to increase in middle childhood and early adolescence (reaching a peak of almost 3 hours a day), and then declines gradually after about age 14 (D. F. Roberts & Foehr, 2008). Children vary greatly in their television viewing habits, however: Some are glued to their TV sets for several hours a day while others rarely if ever watch television. Developmental scholars, health practitioners, and educators are especially concerned about heavy-viewing children because of their high exposure to inappropriate content, low levels of physical activity, and diminished time for interactions with peers (e.g., Caroli, Argentieri, Cardone, & Masi, 2004).

Electronic interactive games.   Interactive games played on game consoles, computers, and handheld devices are an especially popular source of entertainment among Western youth, especially boys in middle childhood and adolescence (Kutner, Olson, Warner, &

Gene drew this picture of his video game equipment from memory, showing his familiarity with the apparatus and a game's combat theme.

Children sometimes learn inappropriate lessons from television.

Hertzog, 2008; D. F. Roberts & Foehr, 2008). For example, video game systems are present in 83 percent of U.S. homes with youngsters between the ages of 8 and 18 (D. F. Roberts & Foehr, 2008). Youngsters with access to video games spend numerous hours clutching controllers as they engage in virtual punching matches, motorcycle races, and explorations of mythical environments. Six-year-old Brent shows his enthusiasm for video games in the "After School: Early Childhood" video in MyEducationLab. He says:

> I usually play video games. There's this army game and snowboard game and . . . and a game called "Smash Brothers." . . . They're cool.

The appeal of video games results largely from their use of strikingly effective instructional principles. Video games allow children to pursue a tangible goal, implement evolving strategies, make steady progress, experience success, use increasingly advanced tools, and obtain personalized feedback at every step (Gentile & Gentile, 2008). Playing video games can become a habit, however, and overuse is a concern when it leads children to curtail healthful physical activity. Also, as we indicated earlier, youngsters who play video games are likely to select at least some games that contain violent content and inappropriate social stereotypes.

Nonetheless, video games have the potential to exert some positive influences on children. For instance, numerous nonviolent and creative video games are available, and youngsters can improve their spatial and visual-attention skills as a result of playing these games (e.g., C. A. Anderson, 2002; De Lisi & Wolford, 2002; Greenfield, DeWinstanley, Kilpatrick, & Kaye, 1996). Particular games, such as those with health-promotion themes, can teach children valuable skills in caring for themselves and managing their health conditions (D. A. Lieberman, 1997). In addition, such games as Konami's *Dance Dance Revolution* and Nintendo's *Wii Fit* encourage many young people to engage in exercise (Olmsted, 2008).

Computers and the Internet. Personal computers and other electronic devices seem to be just about everywhere these days. Computer technologies are changing the ways that adults communicate, make decisions, spend money, and entertain themselves. Children and adolescents follow suit and in many cases actually lead the pack.

Computers and the Internet have many uses in the classroom. Well-constructed software can give students a carefully structured curriculum that permits personalized lessons and steady feedback. The rich, dynamic environment of the Internet makes resources available from around the world. Through such mechanisms as electronic mail (e-mail), Web-based chat rooms, and electronic bulletin boards, computer technology enables students to communicate with peers and subject matter experts, analyze data, exchange perspectives, build on one another's ideas, and solve problems (A. L. Brown & Campione, 1996; Fabos & Young, 1999; Hewitt & Scardamalia, 1996; McCombs & Vakili, 2005; Schachter, 2000; Winn, 2002).

Outside the classroom (and sometimes within it), youngsters increasingly use the Internet for their own personal communications. As youngsters make the transition from childhood to adolescence, many supplement or even replace interests in electronic games with social communication by e-mail and in chat rooms and Internet-based group games (e.g., Multiuser Dungeons, known as MUDs) (Greenfield & Subrahmanyam, 2003; Hellenga, 2002). In a recent survey the majority of teens who spent time online created content for the Internet, such as their own Web pages (Lehnhart & Madden, 2005).

Research on social relationships enabled by the Internet is still quite new, but a preliminary case can be made for some positive effects. For example, a shy teenager who forms relationships with a few individuals through regular e-mail and chat room exchanges may learn to express feelings of anger, fear, and frustration. Other adolescents may find like-minded individuals who support their interests and orientations (e.g., homosexuality). Adolescents even experiment with different personalities at a time when they are wrestling with identity issues; for instance, some young people intentionally project older images or accentuate their physical attractiveness (Clemens et al., 2008; Hellenga, 2002).

Some negative consequences are also possible, however. A teenager may withdraw from family and peers in favor of friends known only electronically. And this desire to stay connected electronically may lead to excessively long hours on the computer (Hellenga, 2002). Other youngsters develop bad habits, such as *flaming* (i.e., verbally ridiculing someone in a public electronic site), *trolling* in newsgroups (i.e., making an inflammatory remark to provoke an argument), *hacking* into secured sites to disrupt services or spread computer viruses, and plagiarizing the work of other people (Hellenga, 2002). Furthermore, adolescents who

MyEducationLab

Listen to Brent talk about video games in the "After School: Early Childhood" video. (Find Video Examples in Chapter 15 of MyEducationLab.)

MyEducationLab

Observe children using the Internet to learn about worms in the "Internet and Online Learning" video. (Find Video Examples in Chapter 15 of MyEducationLab.)

are regular users of the Internet often are sexually harassed or solicited (Finkelhor, Mitchell, & Wolak, 2000; Willard, 2007).

Implications of television and technology.   If utilized properly, electronic media and technologies have tremendous potential for educating children. We offer the following suggestions:

- ***Encourage parents to regulate children's television viewing.*** At meetings and school events and in newsletters, educators can encourage parents to set specific TV-viewing goals for their children. For instance, if parents find their children watching television many hours a day, they might want to set a 2-hour limit. Parents also may find it informative to watch television with their children. In the process they can discover how their children interpret what they watch and can provide a reality check when characters and story lines consistently violate norms for appropriate behavior ("Do you think people should really insult one another like that?").

- ***Teach critical viewing skills.*** Practitioners can teach youngsters how to watch television with a critical eye (Calvert, 2008). For example, elementary teachers can help young children understand that television commercials aim to persuade them to buy something, perhaps toys or hamburgers. Teachers can also point out more subtle advertising ploys, such as the use of color, images (e.g., sexual symbols), and endorsements by famous actors and athletes. And with any medium—television, computers, books, magazines, and so on—adults can help young people become more aware of stereotypes and negative portrayals of men and women, ethnic groups, and various professions.

- ***Educate youngsters about the aggression they see on television and in video games.*** Educators and social scientists have had some success in persuading children that the glamorous, humorous, successful, and pervasive manner in which violence is shown on television is misleading (Rosenkoetter, Rosenkoetter, Ozretich, & Acock, 2004). For example, you can point out that, contrary to typical television scenes, violence is usually *not* an effective way to handle disagreements and often creates additional problems. You can also explain to children that violence is an eye-catching and unrealistic mechanism that television producers use to attract audiences and make money.

- ***Use televised movies and computer programs that build on instructional units.*** Some television programs and videos can make print content more concrete and understandable. For instance, when Teresa and a coleader guided a group of sixth and seventh graders in a Great Books discussion of George Bernard Shaw's play *Pygmalion*, everyone struggled to make sense of characters' dialects. Afterward, the group watched segments of *My Fair Lady*, a movie based on the play, and found the dialects much easier to understand.

- ***Increase youngsters' familiarity and comfort with computers.*** Although many middle- and upper-income families now have personal computers, many lower-income families cannot afford them. But as we look to the future, we anticipate that computer expertise, including Internet use, will be increasingly critical for everyone's success. Adults in many settings can find ways to incorporate computers and the Internet into lessons and activities. For instance, a preschool teacher might teach children how to play computer games that give practice in emergent literacy skills, and an after-school tutor might show young people how they can use the Internet to look up information needed for homework.

- ***Teach young people to be critical users of the Internet.*** Young people need to learn how to navigate through countless electronic sites. Because information on many significant topics is expanding exponentially, youngsters must learn (perhaps with the assistance of adults) to find, retrieve, organize, and evaluate information they find on the Internet. As young people begin to use the Internet for activities in classrooms and clubs, teachers should give guidance in evaluating the quality of information on the World Wide Web. For example, data provided by government agencies and well-respected nonprofit organizations are fairly reliable, but opinion pieces on someone's personal Web page may not be.

- ***Advise parents of dangers on the Internet.*** Parents can familiarize themselves with Web sites their children visit and can consider using Internet filters or blocks. Parents can also talk with their children about who is on their buddy list for instant messaging communications and discourage any meetings with online acquaintances, in order to avoid exploitation by sexual predators. In addition, parents can learn common acronyms in contemporary use—for example, LOL, laugh out loud; PAW, parents are watching; A/S/L, age, sex, and location; and WTGP, want to go private? (National Center for Missing and Exploited Children, 2004).

- ***Discourage youngsters from using technologies for aggressive purposes.***
Teachers and other adults must advise children and adolescents to refrain from *cyberbullying*, the sending or posting of harmful messages over the Internet or with other interactive technologies (Willard, 2007). Adults should also discourage young people from posting racist messages or profanity in their blogs (interactive online personal journals) and from sending unflattering photographs or demeaning messages over cell phones. Some young people also need to be reminded to refrain from sending mocking or threatening statements as text messages (brief written messages over cell phones) or as instant messages (synchronous communications on cell phones or over the Internet to individuals on buddy lists) (Willard, 2007).

- ***Encourage use of a wide range of media.*** Television is the primary medium, and in some cases the only medium, through which many children and adolescents gain news and information about their region and country. Ideally, youngsters should learn to use the many other media available to them—not only the Internet but also books, newspapers, and newsmagazines—to gain the knowledge and skills they will need in the adult world.

As you have learned, children grow up in a complex social world. The Basic Developmental issues table "Social Contexts of Child Development" synthesizes the effects of peers, school, and society on children, from the perspective of nature and nurture, universality and diversity, and qualitative and quantitative change. Children's many social contacts and relationships at school and in the community accumulate in their developmental effects on children.

Basic Developmental Issues

Social Contexts of Child Development

Issue	Influences of Peers, School, and Society
Nature and Nurture	Peers, schools, and society are powerful agents of *nurture* in children's lives. In ideal circumstances, peers offer children emotional support, a safe forum for polishing social skills, and reassuring perspectives on confusing and troubling events. Teachers communicate expectations about children's abilities, implement classroom traditions, organize learning groups, and cultivate children's sense of belonging at school. Society has institutions that care for children, technological systems that enable widespread communication, and media that transmit messages about expected behaviors. *Nature* provides a necessary foundation for children's social development with a biologically based desire to interact with other people. Nature's maturational changes are evident in children's evolving peer relationships—for example, increases in language and the ability to take the perspective of others enhance children's ability to resolve differences with peers. Finally, individual differences that derive partly from genes (e.g., temperaments and some physical disabilities) can affect children's peer relationships and social acceptance.
Universality and Diversity	*Universality* is present in the benefits children experience from being liked by peers, having relationships with caring adults outside the family (e.g., teachers and child care providers), participating in a school setting where they are encouraged to achieve at high levels and feel that they belong, and having safe and interesting options for their free time. *Diversity* occurs in the particular social skills children develop, the extent to which peers find them likable social partners, the suitability of children's environments (e.g., the quality of child care centers), and the degree to which young people engage in risky behaviors with peers (e.g., committing crimes with fellow gang members, engaging in unprotected sexual contact).
Qualitative and Quantitative Change	Children undergo several *qualitative* transformations in their social relationships. For example, children form associations with peers that are fleeting social exchanges during infancy, but these ties change into rich language-based and stable relationships during early and middle childhood and then into close friendships, cliques, and romantic relationships during adolescence. Other qualitative overhauls occur in the onset of sexual feelings for peers of opposite gender (or in some instances, same gender) and in youngsters' uses of particular technologies (e.g., initially preferring television and video games and later choosing electronic mail and chat rooms). Children also exhibit more gradual, *quantitative* changes in their peer relationships, styles of behaving in schools, and uses of society's institutions and services. For example, children gradually refine their skills for interacting with peers, and once they adjust to a new school, children slowly learn to follow its rules and abide by its expectations.

Summary

Peers

Peers serve important functions in social-emotional development. Not only do they offer companionship, but they create contexts for practicing social skills, making sense of social experiences, and shaping habits and ideas. Peer relationships change systematically throughout childhood and adolescence; for instance, activities tend to shift from simple gestures and imitation (infancy), to pretend play (early childhood), to structured group games (middle childhood), to social activities within cliques (early adolescence), and finally to larger, mixed-gender groups (late adolescence). Friendships are especially important peer relationships that provide emotional support and foster motivation to resolve conflicts in mutually satisfying ways.

Although preschoolers and elementary school children have some understanding of romantic relationships, young people do not appreciate the multifaceted nature of romance until they reach adolescence. As they go through puberty, they must come to terms with their changing bodies, sexual drives, and increasing sexual attraction to peers. Romances, either actual or imagined, can delight youngsters but also wreak havoc on their emotions. Some adolescents experiment with sexual intimacy with only limited information about the potential risks; others wrestle with sexual feelings for same-gender peers. As adolescents experience confusing new feelings, they certainly appreciate sensitivity and understanding on the part of educators.

Schools

Schools are powerful contexts of development for children and adolescents. Schools not only prepare youngsters with essential academic skills but also serve as complex social environments that communicate to youngsters how welcome they are and how likely they are to succeed. Ideally, schools offer children a sense of community, deliver affirming messages about learning in general and individual abilities in particular, and support children as they transition into new academic environments.

Society

Society plays an important role through its provision of services to children. Groups of children spend time in child care settings that vary enormously in quality—from sensitive and developmentally appropriate to overcrowded and harsh. Child care has the potential to be a beneficial experience, and early childhood interventions—particularly those that begin during infancy and last for several years—can foster intellectual and social skills in young children. After-school programs and extracurricular activities also bolster the development of youngsters, especially through stable, affectionate relationships with adults and peers and their many options for productive pastimes.

Many children and adolescents spend after-school hours watching television and playing or working on the computer. Television, computers, and other media have considerable potential to foster children's cognitive development, but their benefits have not yet been fully realized. Violent and stereotypical content in the media is a definite risk factor for young people, although some child consumers may be more susceptible to harmful effects than others.

Applying Concepts in Child Development

The exercises in this section will help you increase your effectiveness in fostering children's ability to get along with peers, at school, and in society.

Case Study

Read the case and then answer the questions that follow it.

Aaron and Cole

Aaron and Cole became friends when they were both students in Mr. Howard's fifth-grade class. Although Aaron was in most respects a typical fifth grader, Cole had significant developmental delays. Special educator Debbie Staub (1998) described Cole's special educational needs and his strengths as follows:

> Cole has limited expressive vocabulary and uses one- or two-word sentences. He does not participate in traditional academic tasks, although he is included with his typically developing schoolmates for the entire school day. Cole has a history of behavioral problems that have ranged from mild noncompliance to adult requests to serious aggressive and destructive behavior such as throwing furniture at others. In spite of his occasional outbursts, however, it is hard not to like him. Cole is like an eager toddler who finds wonder in the world around him. The boys he has befriended in Mr. Howard's class bring him great joy. He appreciates their jokes and harmless teasing. Cole would like nothing better than to hang out with his friends all day, but if he had to choose just one friend, it would be Aaron. (D. Staub, 1998, p. 76)[a]

[a] Excerpts from *Delicate Threads: Friendships Between Children With and Without Special Needs in Inclusive Settings*, by D. Staub, 1998, Bethesda, MD: Woodbine House. Reprinted with permission.

Throughout their fifth- and sixth-grade years, Aaron was both a good friend and a caring mentor to Cole.

> Without prompting from adults, Aaron helped Cole with his work, included him in games at recess, and generally watched out for him. Aaron also assumed responsibility for Cole's behavior by explaining to Cole how his actions affected others. The following excerpt from a classroom observation illustrates Aaron's gentle way with Cole:
>
> > Cole was taking Nelle's [a classmate's] things out of her bag and throwing them on the floor. As soon as Aaron saw, he walked right over to Cole and started talking to him. He said, "We're making a new rule—no being mean." Then he walked with Cole to the front of the room and told him to tell another boy what the new rule was. Cole tapped the boy's shoulder to tell him but the boy walked away. Cole looked confused. Aaron smiled and put his hand on Cole's shoulder and told him, "It's okay. Just remember the rule." Then he walked Cole back to Nelle's stuff and quietly asked Cole to put everything back. (pp. 77–78)

But Aaron, too, benefited from the friendship, as his mother explained: "Our family has recently gone through a tough divorce and there are a lot of hurt feelings out there for everyone. But at least when Aaron is at school he feels good about being there and I think a big reason is because he has Cole and he knows that he is an important person in Cole's life" (pp. 90–91).

Dr. Staub observed that, despite their developmental differences, the boys' relationship was in many respects a normal one:

> I asked Mr. Howard once, "Do you think Cole's and Aaron's friendship looks different from others' in your class?" Mr. Howard thought for a moment before responding: "No, I don't think it looks that different. Well, I was going to say one of the differences is that Aaron sometimes tells Cole to be quiet, or 'Hey Cole, I gotta do my work!' But I don't know if that is any different than what he might say to Ben leaning over and interrupting him. I think I would say that Aaron honestly likes Cole and it's not because he's a special-needs kid." (p. 78)

Aaron and Cole remained close until Cole moved to a group home 30 miles away at the beginning of seventh grade.

· In what ways did the friendship of Aaron and Cole promote each boy's social-emotional development?
· Was the boys' friendship a reciprocal one? Why or why not?

Once you have answered these questions, compare your responses with those presented in Appendix A.

Interpreting Children's Artifacts and Reflections

Consider chapter concepts as you analyze the following artifacts from several children.

Teachers at Work

A group of researchers asked students in elementary and middle schools to draw pictures of their teachers working in the classroom (Haney, Russell, & Bebell, 2004). We've selected five of the students' pictures and have given the artists fictitious names to help you identify them individually in your response. As you examine the pictures below and on the following page, consider these questions:

· What do each of the students seem to be suggesting about how teachers *socialize* children?

· What might the students be communicating about the *hidden curriculum* in their school?

Once you have analyzed the artwork, compare your ideas with those presented in Appendix B. For further practice in analyzing children's artifacts and reflections, go to the Activities and Applications section in Chapter 15 of MyEducationLab.

Oscar

Ladarius

Excerpted from Walt Haney, Michael Russell, and Damian Bebell, "Drawing on Education: Using Drawings to Document Schooling and Support Change," *Harvard Educational Review, v74:3* (Fall 2004), pp. 241–272. Copyright © by the President and Fellows of Harvard College. All rights reserved. For more information, please visit www.harvardeducationalreview.org. Drawings are taken from pp. 245 (Luis), 248 (Oscar), 250 (Ladarius), and 255 (Evelyn and Jon). Children's names are fictitious.

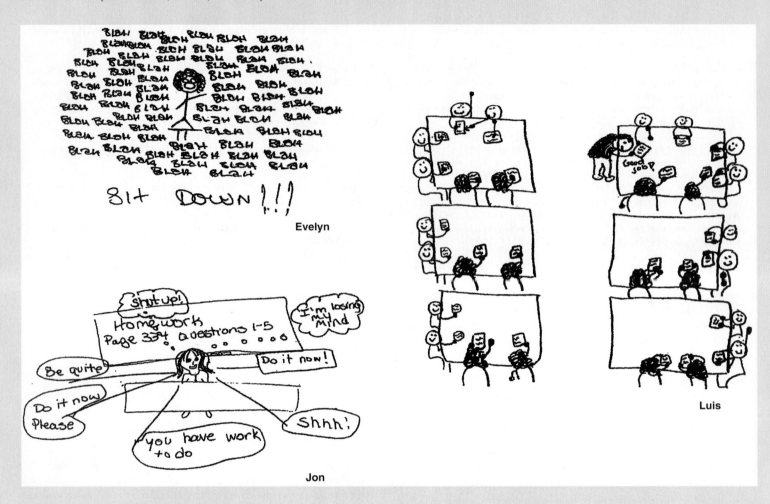

Developmental Trends Exercise

In this chapter you learned that children's social relationships with peers, teachers, and other adults in the community affect children's ability to get along with others. The following table describes behaviors of youngsters at different age levels related to their inclusion as social partners. For each example, the table presents one or more relevant developmental principles, offers an implication for working with youngsters in that age-group, or both. Go to the Activities and Applications section in Chapter 15 of MyEducationLab to apply what you've learned about interpersonal skills as you fill in the empty cells in the table.

Fostering Children's Acceptance by Peers

Age	A Youngster's Experience	Developmental Concepts Identifying Factors Affecting a Youngster's Acceptance by Peers	Implications Promoting Likability in Youngsters
Infancy (Birth–2 Years)	Noticing other infants in the child care center, 8-month-old Tyler reacts differently from one occasion to the next. Sometimes he smiles at other infants, reaches out to touch their faces, and babbles to them. At other times he seems oblivious to other infants, ignoring their gestures and looking past them as he crawls toward a new toy.	Tyler is beginning to show an interest in other children. As is typical for his young age, Tyler's curiosity about peers is fleeting but will slowly blossom into a full-fledged desire to interact with peers. With continued opportunities and support from perceptive adults, Tyler is likely to develop a genuine interest in interacting pleasantly with peers.	Talk with infants and toddlers about the activities and emotional states you notice in other young children. For example, when a few children are in high chairs, comment on the food you are placing on each tray and everyone's reaction to it ("I guess Ben doesn't want green beans today, but look at how much Hana is enjoying them!"). Gently point out the effect when infants accidentally hurt another child ("Brenda, please be careful. Soledad doesn't like it when you poke her eyes. Let's see if she likes having her arm rubbed instead.").

Developmental Trends Exercise (continued)

Age	A Youngster's Experience	Developmental Concepts *Identifying Factors Affecting a Youngster's Acceptance by Peers*	Implications *Promoting Likability in Youngsters*
Early Childhood (2–6 Years)	Five-year-old Finian and his family moved into a new community midway through Finian's kindergarten year. Having now spent 2 weeks in his new kindergarten class, Finian typically stands quietly at the periphery of other children's social interactions. None of the children encourage him to join their play.	Like Finian, children who *transition to a new school* need considerable time to adjust to the school's people and customs. Finian has yet to find a social niche among his peers and has some of the qualities of *neglected children*. That is, he is quiet, keeps to himself, and is not sought after by peers to join their social groups.	
Middle Childhood (6–10 Years)	Eight-year-old Kia has no friends in school. Other children find her bossy and rude. For example, on the playground Kia walks up to a group of children who are quietly inspecting a shiny stone, shoves her way into the group, and demands that the children admire her new shoes, which she claims are far nicer than theirs. When the other children appear annoyed and try to move away from her, Kia grabs one girl, insisting that the two of them play together on the monkey bars.		Identify and teach missing social skills to rejected children. In Kia's case it would be helpful to coach her in how to enter a social group. Kia could practice standing near other children, politely listening to the focus of their conversation, and then interjecting a comment that is relevant to the topic being discussed. Because rejected children generally have multiple social needs, consider offering ongoing support, including services from a school counselor or psychologist.
Early Adolescence (10–14 Years)	Twelve-year-old Frank is an energetic young man who takes his zeal for life into every setting he inhabits—his middle school classes, the school cafeteria, his after-school track team, and more. Frank has a good sense of humor but occasionally interrupts the class with off-color jokes and snide comments about peers. All the young people in his middle school know of Frank; many like him, but others find him abrasive, callous, and self-centered.	Frank shares the qualities of socially *controversial children*. He is well liked by some peers but avoided by others. Controversial children can be disruptive in some situations yet helpful, cooperative, and socially sensitive in others.	
Late Adolescence (14–18 Years)	As a 15-year-old, Tara seems fairly happy with her social life. She has three close friends, all girls, and she and they increasingly interact with boys at school football games and school dances. Every now and then, Tara becomes annoyed with one of her friends, calls her names, or tries to exclude her from a social event; usually, however, Tara is kind hearted and sensitive to her friends. Some students who are not Tara's friends think she's a bit snooty, but they do not perceive her to be overly objectionable.	In the parlance of social acceptance, Tara might be considered *average*: She is liked by some peers and moderately disliked by others. Children who are average in their likability tend to exhibit age-typical social skills, be reasonably concerned about other people's welfare, and show occasional lapses of tact and self-control.	Talk with young people about their social lives—how they get along with peers, who their friends are, and what trouble spots they encounter with peers. Encourage average youngsters to develop their prosocial skills, such as being diplomatic with other people, while also continuing to look after their own needs.

Key Concepts

popular children (p. 555)
rejected children (p. 555)
neglected children (p. 556)
controversial children (p. 556)
peer culture (p. 561)

dominance hierarchy (p. 562)
clique (p. 563)
subculture (p. 563)
gang (p. 563)
sexual orientation (p. 566)

sexual harassment (p. 569)
sense of community (p. 571)
community of learners (p. 572)
self-fulfilling prophecy (p. 575)
society (p. 577)

early childhood intervention
program (p. 578)
interactive technology (p. 581)

MyEducationLab

Now go to Chapter 15 of MyEducationLab at www.myeducationlab.com, where you can:

· View instructional objectives for the chapter.
· Take a quiz to test your mastery of chapter objectives. Detailed feedback is provided to explain why your responses are correct or incorrect.
· Deepen your understanding of particular concepts and principles with Review, Practice, and Enrichment exercises.

· Complete Activities and Applications exercises that give you additional experience in interpreting artifacts, increase your understanding of how research contributes to knowledge about chapter topics, and encourage you to apply what you have learned about children's development.
· Apply what you have learned in the chapter to your work with children in Building Teaching Skills and Dispositions exercises.
· Observe children and their unique contexts in Video Examples.

Appendix A

Analyses of the Ending Case Studies

chapter 1: Latisha (p. 29)

In what ways do we see the contexts of family, school, neighborhood, and culture affecting Latisha's development?

Latisha is strongly influenced by the settings in which she lives. Latisha doesn't say much about her mother, but it appears that her mother offers the loving care and stable home environment Latisha needs to become an optimistic and productive citizen. Her mother also demonstrates a strong work ethic and has exposed Latisha to the healing powers of modern medicine. Two men, Latisha's stepfather and an uncle, appear to take an interest in her well-being as well. Prevailing dangers in the neighborhood obviously bother Latisha, but her family serves as a safe haven. In addition, school seems to be a nurturing environment for Latisha; she achieves at sufficiently high levels that she is able to consider becoming a doctor. Finally, Latisha seems to have absorbed many of the principles of her culture, such as feeling obligated to help others.

Based on your own experiences growing up, what aspects of Latisha's development would you guess are probably universal? What aspects reflect diversity?

Latisha's natural human potential is nurtured by relationships and experiences. Like all other youngsters, Latisha can achieve her full potential only if she is loved and has adequate nutrition, a clean and toxin-free environment, opportunities for physical activity, and a reasonably challenging education. In other respects, however, Latisha's development is unique. She has a one-of-a-kind profile of individual traits and dispositions, and her particular genetic heritage probably contributes to her strong intellectual potential and her cheerful but cautious temperament. Every youngster's environment is ultimately distinctive as well; although Latisha's neighborhood is somewhat dangerous, fortunately her own family appears to be affectionate and protective.

What clues do we have that Latisha's teachers can almost certainly have a positive impact on her long-term development and success?

Latisha is an upbeat, motivated student who likes school and most of her teachers, and she has a career goal that requires extensive education. These characteristics reflect favorably on Latisha's ability to benefit from instruction. To help her reach her career goal, her teachers might instruct her in the use of effective study skills, encourage her interests in medicine, advise her to take challenging science and mathematics courses, and offer hands-on assistance when she is completing applications for college admission and financial aid.

chapter 2: The Study Skills Class (pp. 59–60)

What methods did Deborah use to collect her data? What were the potential strengths and limitations of each method?

Deborah conducted action research to learn why her 20 eighth-grade students were unprepared, disruptive, and seemingly unmotivated in the classroom. She observed the students' behavior and collected other information through questionnaires, interviews, and school records of grades and attendance. As sources of data, these methods tend to have the following advantages and disadvantages:

- Observations have the advantage of documenting actions that people may not be able or willing to articulate. However, it is not always clear whether actions are typical for a group, nor is it fully apparent what the actions mean. For example, might students be off task if the work is too simple, difficult, tedious, or unrelated to their prior experiences? Furthermore, the presence of observers—in this case Deborah herself—is likely to affect the behaviors of those being observed, and observers' interpretations are often affected by their expectations.

- Questionnaires allow researchers to collect and analyze a lot of information from a fairly large group of people over a short period of time. However, questionnaires exceed some respondents' reading abilities and do not permit follow-up or probing. In addition, when respondents are not honest or when items are out of sync with respondents' ideas, the data that questionnaires yield can be misleading. It is not apparent from Deborah's report whether she was sufficiently knowledgeable about her students to have been able to present them with meaningful questions and response choices.

- Interviews have the advantage of permitting respondents to describe their thoughts in depth, but they are time-consuming to conduct and require good rapport between the interviewer and respondents. It is possible that the students were not candid with Deborah when answering her questions about school.

- Records of grades and attendance can be accurate measures of students' academic achievement and enrollment. However, grades are often affected by teachers' subjective impressions of students, and records of attendance do not reveal *why* students attend or miss school.

Deborah tentatively concluded that her own teaching led to the dramatic drop in grades from the second quarter to the third. Is her conclusion justified? Why or why not?

Deborah's conclusion that her teaching was responsible for the drop in grades is not necessarily justified. A range of factors can affect students' grades, including other events occurring at school and in students' lives outside of school. And even if Deborah's teaching *was* the cause of students' academic decline, it would not be obvious which aspect or aspects of her behavior or instruction—such as her grading scheme, instructional methods, or relationships with students—were influential factors.

chapter 3: Four-Year-Old Sons (p. 105)

How do the two mothers interpret their sons' questions differently? How might their interpretations help us to predict their disciplinary styles?

Elizabeth interprets Charles's questions as acts of defiance. She believes that Charles is trying to provoke her with his questions. In contrast, Joyce sees Peter's questions as an outgrowth of his natural curiosity. We might expect that Elizabeth discourages Charles's questions and expects his immediate (and unquestioning) compliance. In contrast, we might expect that Joyce will actually encourage Peter's questioning by responding with patient and elaborate explanations and, in disciplinary situations, with reasons for following a certain course of action. In general, we might suspect that Elizabeth uses an authoritarian parenting style, whereas Joyce probably uses an authoritative one.

How might Elizabeth and Joyce have developed their particular parenting styles?

As they interact with their children, parents are affected by their cultural beliefs and previous experiences. It is possible that both Elizabeth and Joyce are using parenting styles that they themselves were exposed to as children; the two mothers might also be affected by child-rearing techniques they see friends and other family members typically using. Factors in the women's cultural groups and communities may be influential as well (e.g., many parents with advanced degrees encourage their children to think critically about school subject matter; many parents in dangerous neighborhoods insist on children's immediate compliance with safety rules).

What kinds of educational opportunities might these mothers create at home for their children? What might teachers do to encourage each mother's involvement at school?

Each mother would undoubtedly want her son to do well in school. The educational activities the two mothers arrange at home may be different, however. Possibly Elizabeth might provide information that she would expect Charles to accept at face value. In contrast, Joyce might engage Peter in activities that capitalize on his natural curiosity (e.g., trips to the library, zoo, or natural history museum) and encourage him to think critically about his experiences. Teachers can encourage both mothers (and other family members as well) to become involved at school by inviting them to take part in school events and visit their children's classrooms, by asking them to share their talents at school, by encouraging them to read daily to their children, and so on. In addition, teachers might make a point of explaining their educational philosophy and disciplinary strategies so that families can understand the nature and purpose of the curriculum and classroom procedures.

chapter 4: Understanding Adam (pp. 141–142)

Adam was eventually diagnosed with fetal alcohol syndrome (FAS). What characteristics do children with FAS have?

Children with fetal alcohol syndrome typically have mental retardation, delays in physical and motor development, and facial abnormalities. These children also tend to be impulsive and to exhibit other behavioral problems.

What conditions lead to FAS? In other words, how was it that Adam came to develop FAS?

Fetal alcohol syndrome can occur when a pregnant woman drinks alcohol, especially when she does so repeatedly. Alcohol that circulates in the woman's body disrupts the growth of structures in the body and brain of the fetus. Given the severity of Adam's symptoms and the fact that his birth mother died of acute alcohol poisoning, we can reasonably assume that Adam was exposed to consistently high levels of alcohol during his prenatal development.

Adam eventually learned many practical skills, such as how to read and hold down a simple job. What kinds of support would Adam have needed to achieve a good quality of life?

Like any child, Adam would have benefited from being in a loving family and receiving good nutrition, appropriate medical care, and opportunities for physical activity. As a result of his mental retardation and health problems, Adam would have needed many opportunities for practicing basic skills, such as tying his shoes and writing his name, and ongoing medical care to address his physical problems.

chapter 5: Lucy (pp. 187–188)

How did Lucy's illness affect her physical, social, and cognitive development?

Lucy had leukemia, a disease that triggers the uncontrolled proliferation of white blood cells and is often treated with chemotherapy and radiation. Lucy's disease and invasive medical treatments delayed her progress through puberty, caused her hair loss, weakened her immune system, and may have impaired the functioning of her internal organs, such as her spleen. The illness also affected Lucy's social development. Lucy would have seemed unusual to peers—she appeared young and frail, had missed many important social events, and savored rather than resisted her family's protective gestures. The effects of the illness on her cognitive development are less clear, but her extended absences from school and her diminished energy would have made it difficult for her to keep up with increasingly challenging academic work.

In some respects, Lucy probably developed more quickly than most students her age. What particular strengths might Lucy have had as a result of having combated a life-threatening illness?

Lucy's life-threatening illness and hospital stays would have given her an advanced perspective on human physiology and medical care and may have transformed her long-term priorities and goals. Although Lucy is apt to remain fearful about her health, she can be proud of the resilience she has shown in the face of adversity.

As a teacher working with this age-group, what strategies might you use to ease Lucy's return to school?

Lucy's teachers might try one of several strategies:

- *Talk with Lucy's parents.* Lucy's parents may advise her teachers of any remaining symptoms Lucy may have, such as nausea, and things teachers can do to help her, such as allowing her to snack on crackers during regular class time. Furthermore, Lucy's teachers cannot tell other students *anything* about Lucy's illness until they obtain permission from Lucy's parents to do so.

- *Prepare the other students for Lucy's return to school.* With permission from Lucy and her parents, teachers can explain to the other students what Lucy has been through and how they all can help her. For example, some students may need to be reassured that they will not catch leukemia from Lucy but that they can help her by reducing her chances of future infection by shielding her from their sneezes and coughs.
- *Encourage Lucy to take care of herself.* Children with chronic illnesses need to become conscientious about caring for themselves. They need to monitor their own symptoms, take prescribed medications on schedule, and carry out other health-protective measures, such as applying sunscreen when medications cause extreme sensitivity to sunlight.
- *Ease Lucy's reentry into school.* It can be difficult for children to return to school after lengthy hospitalizations or convalescence at home. Teachers should be attentive and supportive as returning students adjust to the classroom and their schoolwork ("It is great to see you catching up with your math, Lucy! You're really starting to blaze through those problems").
- *Teach missing skills.* When students have been too weak to study, they naturally fall behind in their course work. Teachers can help students master missing concepts and skills so that students can return to a productive learning track.

chapter 6: Adolescent Scientists (pp. 228–229)

In what ways does Mr. Sowell scaffold the students' efforts during the lab activity?

He asks several questions that encourage the students to reconsider and revise their findings. He points out that they have simultaneously changed both length and weight and asks, "Why can't you come to a conclusion by looking at the two frequencies?" He guides them toward identifying an error in their reasoning and then asks, "Can you think of a way to redesign your experiments so that you're only changing weight?" In general, he guides them in their thinking but does not specifically tell them the correct answer.

With which one of Piaget's stages is the students' reasoning most consistent? Explain your choice.

Their reasoning is consistent with Piaget's concrete operations stage, in which children have difficulty separating and controlling variables.

Use one or more of Piaget's ideas to explain why Marina persists in her belief that, despite evidence to the contrary, weight affects a pendulum's frequency.

Marina does not notice the inconsistency between what she has observed and what she believes to be true. In other words, she does not experience disequilibrium. Instead, she assimilates any new observations to her belief that weight is the most influential factor.

Drawing from current perspectives on Piaget's theory, identify a task for which the students might be better able to separate and control variables.

There are many possible answers to this question. In general, children are more likely to show formal operational reasoning with subject matter and tasks with which they are familiar. For example, you might present a task related to fishing (see Figure 6-4 on p. 204), growing sunflowers under varying conditions, or gaining proficiency in a particular athletic skill using various training regimens.

chapter 7: The Library Project (p. 269)

Initially, the intern realizes that her students will need some structure to complete the project successfully. In what ways do she and the librarian structure the assignment for the students?

The intern breaks the large project into several smaller pieces—gathering information at the library, writing rough drafts, and so on—and assigns each group member a particular topic to research. At the school library, the librarian locates appropriate resources, and the intern provides guidance as the students conduct their research. The following day, the intern gives suggestions about how the students might effectively use an index to find the information they need.

What specific strategies do the students use as they engage in their library research? In what ways are their strategies less effective than an adult's might be?

The students are using the index to find the information they need and taking notes on facts and data that might be helpful. However, their use of the index is relatively inflexible (e.g., a student looking for information on *economy* doesn't think to look under *commerce, imports,* or *exports*), and the students copy excerpts from the resources verbatim rather than rephrasing, condensing, or summarizing. Adults would presumably be more flexible in their index use and note taking.

How does the students' prior knowledge (or lack thereof) influence the effectiveness of their strategies?

The students have less knowledge than adults about the topics they are researching (*economy, culture, religion,* etc.). Their relative lack of knowledge undoubtedly limits their ability to use an index effectively, make sense of what they read, identify the ideas most relevant to their research topics, and paraphrase and summarize what they've learned.

chapter 8: Fresh Vegetables (p. 309)

Did Steven have mental retardation (an intellectual disability)? Why or why not?

It appears that Steven did *not* have mental retardation. Two characteristics must be present for a diagnosis of an intellectual disability: (a) significantly below-average general intelligence and (b) deficits in adaptive behavior. Although Steven's early IQ scores were low, the case revealed no evidence that he had deficits in adaptive functioning. Furthermore, he later earned a high grade point average in regular high school classes—an outcome that would be highly unlikely for a student with an intellectual disability.

The school psychologist recommended that Steven be placed in a special class for students with special needs. Was such a class an appropriate placement for Steven? Why or why not?

The class probably was appropriate as a short-term placement, although another option would have been to offer him enriching activities in the regular classroom. Whether Steven had an intellectual disability or not, his very limited knowledge and skills made it highly unlikely that he could initially succeed in a general education classroom without intensive instruction that addressed the areas in which he lagged behind his agemates. Once Steven mastered basic skills in reading, writing, and mathematics, he became better able to tackle age-appropriate learning tasks.

chapter 9: Boarding School (p. 351)

Why might Joseph prefer his native dialect to Standard English?

Joseph probably views his native dialect as an important part of his ethnic identity. Furthermore, he probably knows that his dialect is the preferred way of speaking in his local community and believes he can communicate most effectively when he uses it.

Is Joseph bilingual? Why or why not?

The answer to the question depends on one's definition of *bilingual.* Joseph can certainly speak both dialects fluently and knows the contexts in which he should use each one. However, both dialects are forms of English; they are not entirely different languages that have unique vocabularies, grammatical constructions, and so on. Perhaps a more accurate descriptor would be *bidialectical.*

The counselor told Joseph that he had "been cured." What beliefs about Joseph's native dialect does this statement reflect?

The counselor apparently believed that (a) Joseph's dialect was inferior to Standard English and (b) the dialect was a problem that needed to be corrected.

Is it important for Joseph and his classmates to master Standard English? Why or why not? What implications does your answer have for classroom instruction?

Yes, the students probably should master Standard English, and perhaps some, like Joseph, have already done so. Many people in mainstream Western cultures perceive people who speak distinct local dialects as having low social status. Thus, a lack of proficiency in Standard English will limit the students' social and professional options once they reach adulthood. Ultimately people from diverse ethnic groups are most successful when they can use both their local dialect and Standard English in appropriate settings. One effective instructional strategy would be to require Standard English in most written work and in formal oral presentations but to encourage the local dialect in creative writing and informal class discussions.

chapter 10: Beating the Odds (p. 399)

In what ways did nurture clearly play a role in the students' mathematical achievement? How might nature also have been involved?

To a considerable degree, the students' achievement was the result of nurture: Mr. Escalante provided intensive instruction, to the point that students knew calculus thoroughly and probably had automatized many basic calculus skills. He also communicated high expectations for students' performance (the importance of communicating high expectations will become clear in the discussion of the developing self in Chapter 12). From a nature perspective, the students' high ability levels were probably partly due to their genetic potential (see the discussion of hereditary influences on intelligence in Chapter 8).

The calculus class consisted of 10 boys and 8 girls. Are these numbers consistent or inconsistent with research related to gender differences in mathematics?

Average gender differences in math ability tend to be fairly small, but boys show greater *variability* in math ability, especially in adolescence. The slightly higher number of boys might be expected, given research findings. (If you have some knowledge of statistics, you might realize that the small difference in the number of boys vs. girls would not indicate a distinct male advantage in mathematics unless a similar difference was observed consistently across many advanced math classes.)

ETS employees based their suspicions about cheating partly on the similarity of answers they saw in students' responses. What other explanation for the similarity might there be?

The students were all in the same calculus class and so probably learned similar strategies for solving calculus problems. Furthermore, in their practice sessions, they may have solved many problems similar to those that appeared on the test and perhaps discussed the best approach for each one. If so, they would all have used similar approaches in solving the test problems.

chapter 11: The Girly Shirt (p. 439)

Considering what you have learned about trends in emotional development, is Tim's reaction typical for his age?

Children in middle childhood are increasingly able to regulate their emotions, but their coping strategies are hardly foolproof. Children in the elementary years are affected by self-conscious emotions (e.g., shame), and Tim may have become furious because he felt embarrassed and humiliated by his classmates' thoughtless remarks and derisive laughter. Thus, Tim's angry outburst is probably not unusual for his age, but if he persists in making explosive outbursts, he is at risk for losing friends and getting distracted from academic lessons.

What kind of plan might be effective in helping Tim control his anger?

Ms. Fox might, with Tim's help, formulate one or more plans to help Tim acquire skills for controlling his emotions. Together, they might target Tim's social-emotional skills and specifically focus on his ability to express his emotions productively. The plans might have a few objectives, such as (a) fostering Tim's social sensitivity and friendship skills so that he becomes a desirable social partner that other children genuinely care about; (b) helping Tim recognize and label his feelings as they occur (e.g., noticing when he is feeling happy, sad, embarrassed, disappointed, angry, ashamed, and so forth); and (c) asking Tim to use a strategy for coping with unpleasant feelings such as anger (e.g., initially stopping to recognize that he is angered by another child's rude remark, taking a deep breath, and considering several actions and their consequences before responding). Because Tim's explosive anger might, unchecked, jeopardize his social standing among peers, become a detrimental habit, and disrupt the entire class, Ms. Fox will need to monitor his emotional expressions. She can praise him when he shows restraint, and she can remove privileges from him (or apply another consequence) when he allows his temper to escalate. Ms. Fox might also ask a school counselor or psychologist for additional strategies she could use with Tim.

chapter 12: Joachín's Dilemma (p. 476)

What challenges did Joachín face in establishing his identity?

Forming an identity typically involves consideration of one's origins, abilities, convictions, and goals in life. For Joachín, the process of identity formation required him to reconcile society's negative stereotypes of young African American men with the many assets that he personally had in his life. For two years, he followed a torturous quest, responding to the pessimistic views he had absorbed from his friends and broader community. In the process he found that acting tough gained him respect from others. For a time he withdrew from his family, stumbled in his studies, and set aside the hobbies he had grown to enjoy.

What factors in Joachín's life ultimately helped him form a productive identity?

Joachín eventually realized that he could choose a different path. He knew that he had the skills he needed to succeed academically, a family that supported him, and good prospects for contributing to society. A seemingly likable young man, Joachín probably also made new friends who affirmed his academic, athletic, and musical talents.

chapter 13: Derrika (p. 513)

Given what you've learned about the development of self-regulation, how might you explain Derrika's sudden academic difficulties beginning in the eighth grade?

Derrika seemed to be motivated to do well in school, as she "liked to be challenged" and had plans to go to college. However, Derrika may have been poorly equipped to handle the increasing expectations for independence and self-regulation in the secondary grades. She showed limited ability to regulate her own behavior (she frequently cut class and often didn't get up in time for biology class). With such poor self-regulation about attending class, we can reasonably suspect that she also had trouble getting her assignments done in a timely fashion.

To what factors did Derrika's elementary school teachers apparently attribute any academic failures she had? To what factors did her high school teachers attribute her failures?

Derrika described her elementary school teachers this way: "If you don't want to learn, they are going to make you learn." Apparently those teachers attributed students' success to students' own hard work and effective instructional strategies—attributions that were internal, unstable, and controllable. In contrast, Derrika's high school teachers conveyed this message: "If you fail, you just fail. It ain't our fault. You're the one that's dumb." They were attributing failures to students' lack of intelligence—an attribution that, for Derrika, was internal, stable, and uncontrollable. Such an attribution is clearly not founded in reality but nevertheless potentially was influential in Derrika's expectations about her future performance and her willingness to exert effort at school.

What strategies might a teacher, counselor, or other practitioner use to help Derrika get back on the road to academic success?

A variety of strategies are possible here. Following are examples:

- Tailor assignments to Derrika's current knowledge and skills.
- Scaffold Derrika's efforts on challenging tasks.
- Teach Derrika specific self-regulation techniques (e.g., self-reinforcement for completing assignments, self-monitoring of progress, self-evaluating quality of work).
- Initiate an after-school homework program in which Derrika and other struggling students might have a regular time to complete assignments and receive guidance in basic self-regulation skills.

chapter 14: Gang Mediation (pp. 548–549)

Why do you think the mediation approach was successful when other approaches had failed? Drawing on what you've learned about moral development and interpersonal skills, identify at least three possible reasons.

Possible reasons include the following:

- The students were given concrete guidelines about acceptable and unacceptable interpersonal behaviors.
- Discussions with rival gang members probably promoted a better understanding of why rivals might act as they do and how rivals might interpret one another's behaviors (see Chapter 12's discussion of social perspective taking). Similarly, these discussions may have elicited empathy for the distress that others felt when faced with intimidation.
- Discussions may have appealed to the adolescents' sense of fairness and justice. Students may have come to appreciate that everyone at school is entitled to walk the school halls without fear of harassment.
- Participation in the meetings may have reminded the students of their personal moral standards, increasing the likelihood that they would act in accordance with these principles.
- Through the mediation sessions, students probably discovered alternative ways of processing social information. For instance, rather than interpret a rival gang member's facial expression as a hostile stare or an "attitude," a student might realize that the individual was simply deep in thought about a troubling personal matter.
- When members of rival gangs discussed a source of conflict, they may have acquired more effective social problem-solving skills (e.g., looking at a situation from all sides and trying to find a reasonable compromise that addresses everyone's needs).
- In conducting the mediation sessions, the counselors modeled effective interpersonal behaviors and social problem-solving skills.
- Prior to the peer mediation, school personnel instituted regulations (e.g., dress codes, weapon searches) that the students may have perceived as punishment. In contrast, the peer mediation approach used induction, giving reasons for why certain behaviors are unacceptable. Inductive discipline promotes compliance with rules and fosters empathy.
- From a Vygotskian perspective, when the students used particular social strategies in the group situation (with the counselors' scaffolding), they may have gradually internalized these strategies and become capable of using them independently.

chapter 15: Aaron and Cole (pp. 586–587)

In what ways did the friendship of Aaron and Cole promote each boy's social-emotional development?

Aaron and Cole's friendship gave both boys mutual encouragement and support. Other benefits differed slightly for the two boys. During the time Aaron's parents were getting divorced, Aaron felt sad, confused, and vulnerable. Cole helped Aaron feel needed and appreciated. Aaron also displayed leadership among his classmates by serving as a positive role model who interacted patiently and inclusively with a peer with a disability. Cole benefited from the reassurance, acceptance, and guidance he received from Aaron. Cole also was included in certain social groups because of Aaron's intercession.

Was the boys' friendship a reciprocal one? Why or why not?

The friendship between the two boys was reciprocal in that they both entered the association voluntarily and enjoyed its benefits. Although the two boys had different abilities and social standings, they each felt affection for the other.

Analyses of Ending Artifacts

chapter 1: James's Changes, Big and Small (p. 30)

James describes some of the changes as "small," and he seems to see these developments as reflections of incremental (quantitative) improvements. Examples include growing larger physically, gaining athletic skills, becoming better educated, and receiving more homework. Some modifications in his environment appear to have caused qualitative changes. James suggests that the opportunity to participate in sports at seventh grade, not possible by school policy the previous year, makes a big difference in life, at least in part because he must now use his time efficiently in order to complete his homework.

James also writes that his parents have new expectations of him, reflecting their faith in his character, which he enjoys but seems to perceive as demands for heightened maturity. At the same time, James feels that his parents misunderstand him, which is a common perception of young adolescents. James's insight that he is now having conversations with teachers instead of "just talking about school" may reflect a qualitative change in his thinking and behavior. James indicates that he is "a lot more concerned about . . . grades as the years pass," a statement that may indicate that his academic performance is becoming more salient to him or has taken a qualitatively new place in his value system. James's comments about relationships with girls may be addressing both qualitative dynamics (perhaps unprecedented in-depth conversation) and quantitative changes (possibly more contact).

chapter 2: I Went to Davis's House (p. 60)

Alex is inconsistent in his punctuation. Perhaps you noticed how he capitalizes the pronoun and one proper noun (*I* and *Alex*) and fails to capitalize the other proper noun (*davis*). He marks possession properly (*davis's*) and indents his name, as he might in a letter. Possibly, Alex's understanding of punctuation is emerging but incomplete. However, what if you learned that Alex's parents are lax about punctuation when they write informal notes yet conscientious in their punctuation in formal writing? Might Alex be imitating a *style* of informal writing rather than trying to follow all rules of punctuation? To answer that question, we would need additional writing samples from Alex, ideally with details of the circumstances in which he prepared them.

chapter 3: In My Neighborhood (pp. 105–106)

The adolescents seem to have benefited from several features of their neighborhoods. A large, quiet, and well-equipped park supported the youngsters' recreation and served as a sanctuary. The adolescents also appeared to have vigilant parents who directed their safe passage through nearby dangerous streets. Police officers were present and seen as protectors. On the negative side, adolescents encountered a lot of violence on the streets and viewed some of their neighbors as threatening. The physical surroundings could also be unpleasant, with trash dumped and buildings burning nearby.

chapter 4: Horses by Nadia (p. 142)

Children who are autistic have trouble expressing their thoughts verbally. Nadia used little language in her daily life and was unable to describe the sophisticated artwork she produced. Nadia's autism, limited language, and tendency to become absorbed by particular topics probably had a genetic basis. Nadia's autism might additionally have been due to exposure to an unknown teratogen during her prenatal development.

Despite her limited verbal abilities and tendency to withdraw from social interaction, Nadia showed extraordinary artistic ability as early as age 3. She adeptly represented the contours of moving animals, gave special attention to faces, legs, and hooves, and realistically captured depth and perspective. It is likely that her artistic talent also had some genetic basis. It seems that her brain allowed her to keep detailed images of horses in mind and impelled her to reproduce these images on paper.

The effects of the environment can be seen in the encouragement that Nadia received to draw. Once it became evident that she had this particular talent, she was given supplies to foster her artistic self-expression. Nadia's particular interest in horses was nurtured with exposure to pictures of animals, yet it is not clear why she chose horses from among other possible themes.

chapter 5: MyPyramid Worksheet by Alex (p. 188)

The U.S. Department of Agriculture (2008) recommends that children eat a diet that is rich in whole grains, fresh vegetables and fruits, low-fat milk products, and foods that are high in protein, including lean meat, poultry, fish, beans, peas, nuts, and seeds. Alex's worksheet included goals within the main categories of grains, vegetables, fruits, milk, and meat and beans. Alex came closest to achieving dietary goals related to grains, fruits, and meats and beans. He did not achieve goals related to vegetables and milk. Alex exceeded the goal related to physical activity. Alex seemed to have a fairly realistic sense of the value of his health behaviors. Alex may have been able to evaluate his health behaviors sensibly because he studied the well-constructed form, which makes it fairly apparent where the successes and gaps are in one's diet.

chapter 6: Fish in a Boat (p. 230)

Virtually any concept depicted in the cartoon—fish, boat, oar, leak, bailing water, and so on—is a cognitive tool that could help Brady conceptualize this situation. Brady's artistic techniques—shading the clouds with diagonal lines; depicting upward motion with short, curved lines below the two fish; putting one fish's comment in a "talk balloon"—are also cognitive tools that Western culture has passed down from previous generations. Furthermore, to the extent that the computer software facilitated Brady's ability to create the cartoon, it, too, may have been a cognitive tool as well as a physical tool.

The situation Brady portrays violates several basic principles of the physical world. For instance, air is lighter than water and so would hardly seep downward into the boat. Furthermore, of course, fish don't talk or row, nor are they even likely to sit in a rowboat. To create the cartoon, then, Brady had to engage in contrary-to-fact reasoning—an ability associated with Piaget's formal operations stage.

chapter 7: Interview with Aletha (p. 270)

Aletha knows that attention is critical for getting information into memory ("To learn new things you have to pay attention"). She also knows that paying attention involves more than just directing her eyes and ears in a particular direction—that it involves a certain amount of mental effort as well ("It's hard if you're not interested, but that's not how it works. You have to pay attention"). In her own way, she also knows that working memory has a limited capacity ("You can't read a book because it's hard to do both," ". . . it's hard because I had to write while I was listening"). Furthermore, by asking herself questions that she hopes her teacher will answer, she increases the odds that she will keep her attention focused on the lesson and can monitor her ongoing comprehension of the lesson—two signs of self-regulated learning. Aletha's metacognitive development is hardly complete, however: Her view of learning from an educational film is simply to "memorize" her notes.

chapter 8: Jermaine's Life (pp. 309–310)

Jermaine's story has two qualities that suggest he is exceptionally talented in verbal abilities. First, as a first-grader (when he would have been about 6 or 7 years old), Jermaine took the initiative to write a book, with the passage presented here being only a brief excerpt from it. Second, Jermaine used writing tools that are advanced for his age: a sophisticated vocabulary (e.g., *triton, saddled, nonsense, toothless*), a vivid and original plot (the outsmarting of fierce dragons), and well-constructed sentences (e.g., "I saddled up my dragon, grabbed my triton, and tried to escape"). For Jermaine's verbal skills to blossom further, he may benefit from continued encouragement at school, the availability of challenging literature, opportunities to discuss literature with teachers and at least a few peers with similar interests, additional outlets to share his inventive stories, and exposure to role models who make their livings as writers or other professionals who rely on strong verbal skills and imaginative abilities. The scholars who first described this case (Hebert & Beardsley, 2001) inform us that Jermaine's indentification as being gifted soon gives him access to instruction and resources that help him develop his extraordinary talent led to extensive support from educators.

chapter 9: Figure of Speech (p. 351)

Jeff clearly understands the literal meaning of the sentence, because the eyes in his drawing are quite a bit larger than the person's very narrow waistline. In addition, Jeff has mastered the correct spellings of the words in the sentence. The person he has drawn is an unrealistic, somewhat cartoonish one, so perhaps he has an inkling that the sentence is not intended to be taken entirely at face value. However, he misses the meaning that this common figure of speech usually conveys: that a person requests more food than he or she can possibly eat at a single sitting. Jeff's focus on the literal rather than figurative meaning of the sentence is hardly surprising. As you've learned, understanding figurative speech is far more common in adolescence than at younger ages.

chapter 10: The Pet Who Came to Dinner (p. 400)

Justin's misspellings reveal a great deal about his phonological awareness. He captures some but not all of the sounds in words—for example:

- He accurately (although incorrectly) captures all of the sounds in several words, including *done* ("dun"), *there* ("ther"), *water* ("wodr"), *were* ("wr"), and *newspaper* ("nuwspapr")—note that in the last three of these he uses the letter *r* to represent the "er" sound.
- *Once* is spelled as both "owans" and "ouns," in the first case adding an "a" vowel and in the second case omitting the "w" sound.
- *Drink* is spelled "briak," omitting the "n" sound (he has probably reversed the letter *d*, making it look like a *b*).
- *Dessert* is spelled "dasrt," which changes the initial vowel sound from short-*e* to short-*a*; again the *r* probably represents the "er" sound.
- *Having* is spelled "aving," omitting the *h* sound.
- *Rushed* is spelled "rust," changing the *sh* sound to an *s* sound.
- *Started* is spelled "stor did," changing the short-*a* to a long-*o* sound.
- *Snoring* is spelled "soreing," omitting the *n* sound.

It appears, then, that Justin's phonological awareness still needs some fine-tuning.

With the exception of lowercase *d* (which he occasionally reverses so that it looks like a *b*), Justin knows his uppercase and lowercase letters and can form them with reasonable smoothness and clarity. He also knows that sentences should begin with a capital letter and end with a period. He knows, too, that possessive nouns require an apostrophe ("mom's" and "dad's"). He hasn't completely mastered capitalization rules: He capitalizes "Came" and "Dinner" in the middle of a sentence, and he neglects to capitalize two proper nouns ("mom's" and "dad's"). He creates two run-on sentences: "Owans ther was a cat who came to Dinner he eat all the food," and "Owans he was dun he ask for dasrt for dasrt we wr aving cake." He is inconsistent in his use of past-tense verbs (e.g., "Came," "was") versus present-tense verbs (e.g., "eat," "ask") to tell his story. And he has not yet learned that the title of a story should appear in a line by itself, centered at the top of the page. In summary, Justin has mastered some but not all aspects of capitalization, punctuation, and grammar in written English.

Justin's narrative is simply a sequence of events strung together, without regard for cause-and-effect relationships and with no attention to characters' mental or emotional states. If this were an *oral* narrative, we would conclude that his story is more typical of a preschooler than of a 7-year-old (see the discussion of narratives in Chapter 9). However, Justin had to consider writing mechanics as well as the story line as he wrote, possibly stretching his working memory capacity and reducing the complexity of the story he could write.

If you were to see many other second graders' written short stories, you would probably conclude that Justin's story is fairly typical for a native English-speaking second grader.

chapter 11: **Paint Me Like I Am** (pp. 439–440)

Delia expresses a range of emotions in her poem. She communicates clearly and vividly about happiness, a pleasant emotion she associates with beauty in nature and a sense of freedom. Delia also writes about sadness and pain, emotions that she would prefer to keep to herself. Writing poems may be a therapeutic pastime for Delia because it allows her to reflect on the full range of her emotions and deal with them productively. As she imagines a painter who will render her face in good spirits, Delia seems to suggesting that her unpleasant feelings need not define who she is, either to herself or to others.

chapter 12: **Two Histories** (p. 477)

For Rachel, forming an ethnic identity took considerable work. She had to confront thoughtless and blatantly rude comments from other children (and possibly adults), who themselves were disturbed that Rachel possessed some features characteristic of people from Jewish backgrounds (e.g., light-colored skin) and other features characteristic of people from African American descent (e.g., broad facial features). Some people made remarks that criticized her for being multiethnic (e.g., "Looks more Latina than half-breed," "But that boy always called me mixed in such an ugly way"). A few responses were vehemently racist (e.g., "Some say, 'Nigga get off the swing'") or pitted one racial heritage against the other (e.g., "Act White," "Won't date Black men," "And I get told it's better to pretend I'm White").

Rachel struggles with being a "compromise," a blend of two heritages, when the norm in society is to come from a single ethnic group. Yet Rachel clearly rejects the ignorant interpretations she has heard over the years, and she enjoys the traditions of both cultural groups (e.g., their meals, styles of dance, and cultural symbols). She realizes she has qualities that are shared by her two heritages and have fused and intensified within her core: Although Rachel feels tormented, she also believes she has the strength of a warrior.

chapter 13: **Tears of Pearls** (pp. 513–514)

Writing an essay of this kind has several potential benefits. First, by knowing why homework was turned in late, the teacher can help Andrea develop a better strategy for future homework assignments (e.g., Andrea might make a point to check her social studies folder as soon as she arrives at class each day). Second, in writing the essay, Andrea must engage in some degree of self-monitoring and self-evaluation. And third, Andrea must describe a future course of action (how she intends to get future assignments in on time) to someone else. As you may recall from our discussion of Vygotsky's theory in Chapter 6, complex cognitive processes have their roots in social interactions. By describing her future plans to someone else, Andrea may begin to *internalize* such future planning and do it more regularly even in the absence of a teacher's required essay.

It is clear in Andrea's essay that she does have some ability to regulate her learning and behavior, albeit with assistance from her mother. In particular, she says, "Every night I do my homework and my mom checks it and it goes in my backpack." She also feels *guilt* about not getting her homework in on time, a reaction indicating that she is at least in the introjection phase of internalizing certain guidelines for behavior (look once again at Figure 13-2). Much as guilt is an unpleasant feeling, it can be an extremely powerful motivator in helping youngsters adhere to certain standards for behavior.

chapter 14: Remembering 9/11 (p. 549)

Antonio appears to interpret the events of September 11th as a moral transgression because he emphasizes the harm caused to American people. The characters in Antonio's drawing are obviously distressed. Antonio aptly portrays grief, disbelief, and possibly anger in the survivors of the September 11th attacks. He communicates such intense emotions using tears, open mouths, bared teeth, tilted heads, and flung-open arms. By drawing his characters in front of an American flag (a symbol of the United States), Antonio may be suggesting that the entire nation shared in the anguish and outrage.

chapter 15: Teachers at Work (pp. 587–588)

The pictures by Oscar, Evelyn, and Jon reveal that school can be a controlling and perhaps tedious place. Oscar shows his teacher, Mr. Smith, holding a piece of chalk in front of the board and commanding the attention of the children, who sit at their desks in rows. The children are anonymous, having no faces or individual features. Children are socialized to be quiet, still, and attentive. The hidden curriculum conveys the message that the teacher is in charge and the children are there to obey the teacher. Evelyn depicts an apparently dull and long-winded teacher who punctuates long speeches with demands for children to sit down. Once again, children are socialized to be quiet, still, and attentive. The hidden curriculum conveys that it is children's job to appease an insensitive teacher who is unaware that children are not understanding or even attending to her monologues. Jon shows a teacher sitting at her desk, presumably in the front of the room, uttering a string of directions that vary in mood and politeness (e.g., "Do it now, please," "Shut up!" and "I'm losing my mind"). The hidden curriculum conveys that children are to comply with an unstable and didactic teacher whose moods are unpredictable.

The pictures by Ladarius and Luis reveal a different spirit in the classroom: Children are happy and active in their learning. Ladarius shows a teacher surrounded by smiling, standing children. The hidden curriculum seems to be that children are to be engaged participants in interesting lessons. Luis shows a classroom with smiling children carrying out lessons in cooperative groups. The teacher is circulating among the groups and encouraging children in their work ("Good job"). The hidden curriculum seems to be that children are to work together and enjoy themselves in the process.

Glossary

accommodation Process of responding to a new event by either modifying an existing scheme or forming a new one.

acculturation Process of taking on the customs and values of a new culture.

action research Systematic study of an issue or problem by a teacher or other practitioner, with the goal of bringing about more productive outcomes for children.

adaptive behavior Behavior related to daily living skills and appropriate conduct in social situations.

addiction Physical and psychological dependence on a substance, such that increasing quantities must be taken to produce the desired effect and withdrawal produces adverse physiological and psychological effects.

African American English Dialect of some African American communities that includes pronunciations, idioms, and grammatical constructions different from those of Standard English.

aggression Action intentionally taken to hurt another either physically or psychologically.

alleles Genes located at the same point on corresponding (paired) chromosomes and related to the same physical characteristic.

amusia Inability to detect the small changes in pitch that are common in melodies; an extreme form of tone deafness.

androgyny Tendency to have some characteristics that are stereotypically female (e.g., nurturance) and others that are stereotypically male (e.g., assertiveness).

anorexia nervosa Eating disorder in which a person eats little or nothing for weeks or months and seriously jeopardizes health.

anxiety Emotional state characterized by worry and apprehension.

anxiety disorder Chronic emotional condition characterized by excessive, debilitating worry.

apprenticeship Mentorship in which a novice works intensively with an expert to learn how to accomplish complex tasks in a particular domain.

appropriation Gradual adoption of (and perhaps also adaptation of) other people's ways of thinking and behaving for one's own purposes.

assessment Task that children complete and researchers use to make judgments of children's understandings and skills.

assimilation Form of acculturation in which a person totally embraces a culture, abandoning a previous culture in the process. Also, in Piaget's theory, process of responding (either physically or mentally) to a new event in a way that is consistent with an existing scheme.

attachment An enduring emotional tie uniting one person to another.

attention-deficit hyperactivity disorder (ADHD) Disability characterized by inattention, by hyperactivity and impulsive behavior, or by all of these characteristics.

attribution Belief about the cause of one's own or another person's success or failure.

authentic activity Instructional activity similar to one that a child might eventually encounter in the outside world.

authoritarian parenting style Parenting style characterized by strict expectations for behavior and rigid rules that children are expected to obey without question.

authoritative parenting style Parenting style characterized by emotional warmth, high expecta-

tions and standards for behavior, consistent enforcement of rules, explanations regarding the reasons behind these rules, and the inclusion of children in decision making.

autism spectrum disorders Disorders marked by impaired social cognition, social skills, and social interaction, as well as by repetitive behaviors; extreme forms are often associated with significant cognitive and linguistic delays and highly unusual behaviors.

autobiographical self Mental "history" of important events in one's life.

automatization Process of becoming able to respond quickly and efficiently while mentally processing or physically performing certain tasks.

axon Armlike part of a neuron that sends information to other neurons.

babbling Repeating certain consonant-vowel syllables over and over (e.g., "mamamama"); common in the latter half of the first year.

behaviorism Theoretical perspective in which children's behavioral and emotional responses change as a direct result of particular environmental stimuli.

bicultural orientation Form of acculturation in which a person is familiar with two cultures and selectively draws from the values and traditions of one or both cultures depending on the context.

bilingual education Approach to second-language instruction in which students are instructed in academic subject areas in their native language while simultaneously being taught to speak, read, and write in the second language.

bilingualism Knowing and speaking two languages fluently.

biological theory Theoretical perspective that focuses on inherited physiological structures of the body and brain that support survival, growth, and learning.

bulimia Eating disorder in which a person, in an attempt to be thin, eats a large amount of food and then purposefully purges it from the body by vomiting or taking laxatives.

bully Child or adolescent who frequently threatens, harasses, or causes physical or psychological injury to particular peers.

canalization Tight genetic control of a particular aspect of development.

care orientation Focus on nurturance and concern for others in moral decision making.

case study Naturalistic research study in which investigators document a single person's or a small group's experiences in depth over a period of time.

central conceptual structure Integrated network of concepts and cognitive processes that forms the basis for much of one's thinking, reasoning, and learning in a specific content domain.

central executive Component of the human information processing system that oversees the flow of information throughout the system.

cephalocaudal trend Vertical ordering of motor skills and physical development; order is head first to feet last.

child development Study of the persistent, cumulative, and progressive changes in the physical, cognitive, and social-emotional development of children and adolescents.

child maltreatment Adverse treatment of a child in the form of neglect, physical abuse, sexual abuse, or emotional abuse.

chromosome Rodlike structure that resides in the nucleus of every cell of the body and contains genes that guide growth and development; each chromosome is made up of DNA and other biological instructions.

class inclusion Recognition that an object simultaneously belongs to a particular category and to one of its subcategories.

clinical method Procedure in which an adult probes a child's reasoning about a task or problem, tailoring questions in light of what the child has previously said or done in the interview.

clique Moderately stable friendship group of perhaps three to nine members.

codominance Situation in which the two genes of an allele pair, although not identical, both have some influence on a characteristic.

cognitive apprenticeship Mentorship in which an expert and a novice work together on a challenging task and the expert suggests ways to think about the task.

cognitive development Systematic changes in reasoning, concepts, memory, and language.

cognitive-developmental theory Theoretical perspective that focuses on major transformations to the underlying structures of thinking over the course of development.

cognitive process theory Theoretical perspective that focuses on the precise nature of human mental operations.

cognitive strategy Specific mental process that people intentionally use to acquire or manipulate information.

cognitive tool Concept, symbol, strategy, or other culturally constructed mechanism that helps people think more effectively.

collectivistic culture Cultural group that encourages obedience to and dependence on authority figures and being honorable, cooperative, and invested in group accomplishments.

community The neighborhood in which a child and his or her family live and the surrounding vicinity.

community of learners A classroom in which teacher(s) and students actively and collaboratively work to help one another learn.

comprehension monitoring Process of checking oneself to make sure one understands what is being studied.

conceptual change Revision of one's knowledge and understanding of a topic in response to new information about the topic.

conduct disorder Chronic emotional condition characterized by lack of concern for the rights of others.

conservation Realization that if nothing is added or taken away, amount stays the same regardless of any alterations in shape or arrangement.

constructivism Theoretical perspective proposing that learners construct a body of knowledge and beliefs, rather than absorbing information exactly as it is received.

context The broad social environments, including family, schools, neighborhoods, community organizations, culture, ethnicity, and society at large, that influence children's development.

contingent self-worth Overall sense of self that is highly dependent on others' opinions.

control group Group of participants in a research study who do not receive the treatment under investigation; often used in an experimental study.

controversial children Children whom some peers really like and other peers strongly dislike.

conventional morality Acceptance of society's conventions regarding right and wrong; behaving to please others or to live up to society's expectations for appropriate behavior.

conventional transgression Action that violates society's general guidelines (often unspoken) for socially acceptable behavior.

cooing Making and repeating vowel sounds (e.g., "oooooo"); common in early infancy.

coparents The two (or more) parents who share responsibility for rearing their children.

co-regulated learning Process through which an adult and child share responsibility for directing various aspects of the child's learning.

correlation Extent to which two variables are related to each other, such that when one variable increases, the other either increases or decreases in a somewhat predictable fashion.

correlational study Research study that explores relationships among variables.

cortex Part of the forebrain that enables conscious thinking processes, including executive functions.

cross-sectional study Research study in which the performance of individuals at different ages is compared at a single point in time.

crystallized intelligence Knowledge and skills accumulated from one's prior experience, schooling, and culture.

cultural bias Extent to which an assessment instrument offends or unfairly penalizes some individuals because of their ethnicity or cultural background, gender, or socioeconomic status.

culturally responsive teaching A teacher's use of particular instructional strategies based on knowledge of children's cultural backgrounds and individual characteristics.

culture Behaviors and belief systems that characterize a long-standing social group and provide a framework for how group members decide what is normal and appropriate.

culture shock Sense of confusion that occurs when one encounters an environment with expectations for behavior very different from those in one's home environment.

delay of gratification Forgoing small immediate rewards for larger ones at a future time.

dendrite Branchlike part of a neuron that receives information from other neurons.

depression Emotional condition characterized by significant sadness, discouragement, hopelessness, and, in children, irritability.

developmental systems theory Theoretical perspective that focuses on the multiple factors, including systems inside and outside children, that combine to influence children's development.

developmentally appropriate practice Instruction and other services adapted to the age, characteristics, and developmental progress of individual children.

dialect Form of a language that is characteristic of a particular geographic region or ethnic group.

differentiation A gradual transition from general to more specific functioning over the course of development.

disequilibrium State of being unable to address new events with existing schemes.

disorganized and disoriented attachment Attachment classification in which children lack a single coherent way of responding to attachment figures.

distributed intelligence Thinking facilitated by physical objects and technology, social support, and concepts and symbols of one's culture.

distributive justice Beliefs about what constitutes people's fair share of a valued commodity.

diversity In a particular aspect of human development, the varied ways in which individuals progress.

dizygotic twins Twins that began as two separate zygotes and so are as genetically similar as two siblings conceived and born at different times.

DNA A spiral-staircase–shaped molecule that guides the production of proteins needed by the body for growth and development; short for *deoxyribonucleic acid.*

dominance hierarchy Relative standing of group members in terms of such qualities as leadership and social influence.

dominant gene Gene that overrides any competing instructions in an allele pair.

dynamic assessment Systematic examination of how a child's knowledge or reasoning may change as a result of learning a specific task or performing it with adult guidance.

dyscalculia Inability to master basic numerical concepts and operations in a developmentally typical time frame despite normal instruction.

dyslexia Inability to master basic reading skills in a developmentally typical time frame despite normal reading instruction.

early childhood intervention program Program designed to foster basic intellectual, social-emotional, and physical development in young children, especially those with developmental delays or those whose families are economically disadvantaged.

egocentrism Inability of a child in Piaget's preoperational stage to view situations from another person's perspective.

elaboration Process of using prior knowledge to embellish on new information and thereby learn it more effectively.

embryo During prenatal weeks 2 through 8, the developing being that is in the process of forming major body structures and organs.

emergent literacy Knowledge and skills that lay a foundation for reading and writing; typically develops in the preschool years from early experiences with written language.

emotion Affective response to an event that is personally relevant to one's needs and goals.

emotional contagion Tendency for infants to cry spontaneously when they hear other infants crying.

emotional regulation Strategies to manage affective states.

empathy Capacity to experience the same feelings as another person, especially when the feeling is pain or distress.

English language learner (ELL) School-age child who is not fully fluent in English because his or her family speaks a language other than English at home.

entity view (of ability) Belief that ability is a "thing" that is relatively permanent and unchangeable.

epistemological beliefs Beliefs regarding the nature of knowledge and knowledge acquisition.

equilibration Movement from equilibrium to disequilibrium and back to equilibrium; a process that promotes the development of increasingly complex forms of thought and knowledge.

equilibrium State of being able to address new events using existing schemes.

ethnic identity Awareness of being a member of a particular ethnic or cultural group and willingness to adopt certain values and behaviors characteristic of that group.

ethnicity Membership in a group of people with a common cultural heritage and shared values, beliefs, and behaviors.

ethnography Naturalistic research study in which investigators spend an extensive period of time documenting the cultural patterns of a group of people in the group's everyday settings.

ethological attachment theory Theoretical perspective that emphasizes the benefits to children derived from close bonds with caregivers, particularly protection from harm and a secure base from which to explore the environment.

executive functions Purposeful and goal-directed intellectual processes (e.g., planning, decision making) made possible by higher brain structures.

expansion Repetition of a child's short utterances in more complete and grammatically correct forms.

experimental study Research study in which a researcher manipulates one aspect of the environment (a treatment), controls other aspects of the environment, and assesses the treatment's effects on participants' behavior.

expressive language Ability to communicate effectively through speaking and writing.

extrinsic motivation Motivation provoked by the external consequences that certain behaviors bring.

family Two or more people who live together and are related by such enduring factors as birth, marriage, adoption, or long-term mutual commitment.

family structure In a family with children, the family's makeup; specifically, the children in a family home and the adults who live with and care for the children.

fast mapping Inferring a word's general meaning after a single exposure.

fetus During prenatal week 9 until birth, the developing being that is growing in size and weight and in sensory abilities, brain structures, and organs needed for survival.

figurative speech Speech that communicates meaning beyond a literal interpretation of its words.

fine motor skills Small, precise movements of particular parts of the body, especially the hands.

fluid intelligence Ability to acquire knowledge quickly and thereby adapt effectively to new situations.

Flynn effect Gradual increase in intelligence test performance observed in many countries during the past several decades.

forebrain Part of the brain responsible for complex thinking, emotions, and motivation.

functionalism Theoretical perspective of language development that emphasizes the purposes language serves for human beings.

g General factor in intelligence that influences performance in a wide variety of tasks and content domains.

gamete Reproductive cell that, in humans, contains 23 chromosomes rather than the 46 chromosomes present in other cells in the body; a male gamete (sperm) and a female gamete (ovum) join at conception.

gang Cohesive social group characterized by initiation rites, distinctive colors and symbols, territorial orientation, feuds with rival groups, and criminal activity.

gender schema Self-constructed body of beliefs about the traits and behaviors of males or females.

gene Basic unit of heredity in a living cell; genes are made up of DNA and contained on chromosomes.

giftedness Unusually high ability in one or more areas, to the point where children require special educational services to help them meet their full potential.

glial cell Cell in the brain or other part of the nervous system that provides structural or functional support for one or more neurons.

goal-directed behavior Intentional behavior aimed at bringing about an anticipated outcome.

grammatical word Nonlexical word that affects the meanings of other words or the interrelationships among words in a sentence.

gross motor skills Large movements of the body that permit locomotion through and within the environment.

grounded theory study Naturalistic research study in which investigators develop and elaborate new theories while comparing data (such as interview statements from participants) to the researchers' emerging interpretations.

growth spurt Rapid increase in height and weight during puberty.

guided participation Active engagement in adult activities, typically with considerable direction and structure from an adult or other more advanced individual; children are given increasing responsibility and independence as they gain experience and proficiency.

guilt Feeling of discomfort when one inflicts damage or causes someone else pain or distress.

habituation Changes in children's physiological responses to repeated displays of the same stimulus, reflecting loss of interest.

hindbrain Part of the brain controlling the basic physiological processes that sustain survival.

holophrase A single word used to express a complete thought; commonly observed in children's earliest speech.

hostile attributional bias Tendency to interpret others' behaviors as reflecting hostile or aggressive intentions.

identity Self-constructed definition of who one is, what things one finds important, what one believes, and what goals one wants to accomplish in life.

imaginary audience Belief that one is the center of attention in any social situation.

immersion Approach to second-language instruction in which students hear and speak the second language almost exclusively in the classroom.

inclusion Practice of educating all students, including those with severe and multiple disabilities, in neighborhood schools and general education classrooms.

incremental view (of ability) Belief that ability can and does improve with effort and practice.

individual constructivism Theoretical perspective that focuses on how people independently construct meaning from their experiences.

individualistic culture Cultural group that encourages independence, self-assertion, competition, and expression of personal needs.

induction Act of explaining why a certain behavior is unacceptable, usually with a focus on the pain or distress that someone has caused another.

infant-directed speech Short, simple, high-pitched speech often used when talking to young children.

infantile amnesia General inability to recall events that have occurred in the early years of life.

information processing theory Theoretical perspective that focuses on the specific ways in which people mentally acquire, interpret, and remember information and how such cognitive processes change over the course of development.

inner speech "Talking" to oneself mentally rather than aloud as a way of guiding oneself through a task.

insecure-avoidant attachment Attachment classification in which children appear somewhat indifferent to attachment figures.

insecure-resistant attachment Attachment classification in which children are preoccupied with their attachment figures but gain little comfort from them when distressed.

integration An increasing coordination of body parts over the course of development.

intellectual disability Disability marked by significantly below-average general intelligence and deficits in adaptive behavior.

intelligence Ability to apply past knowledge and experiences flexibly to accomplish challenging new tasks.

intelligence test General measure of current cognitive functioning, used primarily to predict academic achievement over the short run.

intentionality Engagement in an action congruent with one's purpose or goal.

interactive technology Array of electronic, digitally based machines that are operated dynamically by a person whose commands determine emerging program sequences.

internalization In Vygotsky's theory, the gradual evolution of external, social activities into internal, mental activities.

internalized motivation Adoption of behaviors that others value, whether or not one's immediate environment reinforces those behaviors.

intersubjectivity Awareness of shared perceptions and understandings that provide the foundation for social interaction.

interview Data collection technique that obtains self-report data through face-to-face conversation.

intrinsic motivation Motivation resulting from personal characteristics or from factors inherent in the task being performed.

invented spelling A child's early, self-constructed word spelling, which may reflect only some of the word's phonemes.

IQ score Score on an intelligence test, determined by comparing one's performance with the performance of same-age peers.

IRE cycle Adult–child interaction pattern marked by adult *initiation*, child *response*, and adult *evaluation;* in Western cultures, such a pattern is often seen in instructional settings.

joint attention Phenomenon in which two people (e.g., a child and caregiver) simultaneously focus on the same object or event, monitor each other's attention, and coordinate their responses.

justice orientation Focus on individual rights in moral decision making.

knowledge base One's knowledge about specific topics and the world in general.

knowledge telling Writing down ideas in whatever order they come to mind, with little regard for communicating the ideas effectively.

knowledge transforming Writing about ideas in such a way as to intentionally help the reader understand them.

language acquisition device Biologically built-in mechanism hypothesized to facilitate language learning.

language socialization Direct and indirect means through which other people teach children the language and verbal behaviors deemed to be appropriate in their culture.

learned helplessness General belief that one is incapable of accomplishing tasks and has little or no control of the environment.

learning disability Significant deficit in one or more cognitive processes, to the point where special educational services are required.

left hemisphere Left side of the cortex; largely responsible for sequential reasoning and analysis, especially in right-handed people.

lexical word Word that in some way represents an aspect of one's physical, social, or psychological world.

longitudinal study Research study in which the performance of a single group of people is tracked over a period of time.

long-term memory Component of memory that holds knowledge and skills for a relatively long period of time.

mastery goal Desire to acquire additional knowledge or master new skills (also known as a *learning goal*).

mastery orientation General belief that one is capable of accomplishing challenging tasks, accompanied by an intent to master such tasks.

maturation Genetically guided changes that occur over the course of development.

mediated learning experience Discussion between an adult and a child in which the adult helps the child make sense of an event they have mutually experienced.

mediation In Vygotsky's theory, a process through which adults help children make culturally appropriate sense of their experiences, perhaps by attaching labels to objects or explaining the nature of certain phenomena.

meiosis The process of cell division and reproduction by which gametes are formed.

menarche First menstrual period in an adolescent female.

metacognition Knowledge and beliefs about one's own cognitive processes, as well as efforts to regulate those cognitive processes to maximize learning and memory.

metacognitive awareness Extent to which one is able to reflect on the nature of one's own thinking processes.

metalinguistic awareness Extent to which one consciously understands and thinks about the nature and functions of language.

midbrain Part of the brain that coordinates communication between the hindbrain and forebrain.

mitosis The process of cell duplication by which chromosomes are preserved and a human being or other biological organism can grow.

monozygotic twins Twins that began as a single zygote and so share the same genetic makeup.

moral development Advancements in reasoning and behaving in accordance with culturally prescribed or self-constructed standards of right and wrong.

moral dilemma Situation in which there is no clear-cut answer regarding the morally right thing to do.

moral transgression Action that causes damage or harm or in some other way infringes on the needs and rights of others.

motivation State that energizes, directs, and sustains behavior.

music literacy Ability to read and understand musical notation.

myelination The growth of a fatty sheath around neurons that allows them to transmit messages more quickly.

narrative Verbal account of logically interconnected events; a story.

native language The first language a child learns.

nativism Theoretical perspective proposing that some knowledge is biologically built-in and available at birth or soon thereafter.

nature Inherited characteristics and tendencies that affect development.

need for relatedness Fundamental need to feel socially connected to, and loved and respected by, other people.

neglected children Children whom peers rarely select as someone they would either most like or least like to do something with.

neo-Piagetian theory Theoretical perspective that combines elements of Piaget's theory with more contemporary research findings and suggests that development in specific content domains is often stagelike in nature.

neuron Cell that transmits information to other cells; also called nerve cell.

niche-picking Tendency to actively seek out environments that match one's inherited abilities.

nurture Environmental conditions that affect development.

obesity Condition in which a person weighs at least 20 percent more than his or her optimal weight for good health.

object permanence Realization that objects continue to exist even when they are out of sight.

observation Data collection technique whereby a researcher carefully observes and documents the behaviors of participants in a research study.

operation In Piaget's theory, an organized and integrated system of logical thought processes.

organization Process of identifying interrelationships among pieces of information as a way of learning them more effectively.

overextension   Overly broad meaning for a word, such that it is used in situations to which it doesn't apply.

overregularization   Use of a syntactic rule in situations where an exception to the rule applies.

parenting style   General pattern of behaviors that a parent uses to nurture and discipline his or her children.

peer culture   General set of rules, expectations, and interpretations that influence how members of a particular peer group behave.

peer mediation   Approach to conflict resolution in which one child or adolescent (the mediator) asks peers in conflict to express their differing viewpoints and then work together to identify an appropriate compromise.

peer pressure   Tactics used to encourage some behaviors and discourage others in age-mates.

perception   Interpretation of stimuli that the body has sensed.

performance goal   Desire to demonstrate high ability and make a good impression.

performance-approach goal   Desire to look good and receive favorable judgments from others.

performance-avoidance goal   Desire not to look bad or receive unfavorable judgments from others.

permissive parenting style   Parenting style characterized by emotional warmth but few expectations or standards for children's behavior.

personal fable   Belief held by many adolescents that they are unique beings invulnerable to normal risks and dangers.

personal interest   Long-term, relatively stable interest in a particular topic or activity.

personal space   A child's personally and culturally preferred distance from other people during social interaction.

personality   Characteristic way a person behaves, thinks, and feels.

phonemes   Smallest units of a spoken language that signify differences in meaning.

phonological awareness   Ability to hear the distinct sounds of which spoken words are comprised.

phonology   The sound system of a language; how words sound and are produced.

physical aggression   Action that can potentially cause bodily injury (e.g., hitting or scratching another person).

physical development   Systematic changes of the body and brain and age-related changes in motor skills and health behaviors.

physiological measure   Direct assessment of physical development or physiological functioning.

playing the dozens   Friendly, playful exchange of insults, common in some African American communities; also called *joaning* or *sounding*.

polygenic inheritance   Situation in which many genes combine in their influence on a particular characteristic.

popular children   Children whom many peers like and perceive to be kind and trustworthy.

postconventional morality   Behaving in accordance with self-developed abstract principles regarding right and wrong.

pragmatics   Conventions and strategies used in effective and socially acceptable verbal interactions.

preconventional morality   A lack of internalized standards about right and wrong; making decisions based on what is best for oneself, without regard for others' needs and feelings.

prejudice   Display of negative attitudes, feelings, and behaviors toward particular individuals because of their membership in a specific group.

premature infant   Infant born early (before 37 weeks of prenatal growth) and sometimes with serious medical problems.

prenatal development   Growth that takes place between conception and birth.

primary reinforcer   Stimulus or event that satisfies a built-in biological need.

proactive aggression   Deliberate aggression against another as a means of obtaining a desired goal.

prosocial behavior   Action intended to benefit another person (e.g., sharing with or helping another person).

proximodistal trend   Inside-outside ordering of motor skills and physical development; order is inside first and outside last.

psychodynamic theory   Theoretical perspective that focuses on how early experiences and internal conflicts affect social and personality development.

psychosocial stages   In Erikson's theory, eight periods of life that involve age-related challenges.

puberty   Physiological changes that occur during adolescence and lead to reproductive maturation.

punishment   Consequence of a response that leads to a decrease in the frequency of that response.

qualitative change   Relatively dramatic developmental change that reflects considerable reorganization or modification of functioning.

quantitative change   Developmental change that involves a series of minor, trendlike modifications.

quasi-experimental study   Research study in which one or more experimental treatments are administered but in which random assignment to groups is not possible.

questionnaire   Data collection technique that obtains self-report data through a paper-pencil inventory.

reactive aggression   Aggressive response to frustration or provocation.

receptive language   Ability to understand the language one hears or reads.

recessive gene   Gene that influences growth and development primarily when the other gene in the allele pair is identical to it.

reciprocal teaching   Approach to teaching reading comprehension in which students take turns asking teacher-like questions of their classmates.

recursive thinking   Thinking about what other people may be thinking about oneself, possibly through multiple iterations.

reflex   Automatic motor response to a particular kind of stimulus.

rehearsal   Attempt to learn and remember information by repeating it over and over.

reinforcer   Consequence of a response that leads to an increase in the frequency of that response.

rejected children   Children whom many peers identify as being unfavorable social partners.

rejection   Form of acculturation in which a person fails to learn or accept any customs and values from a new cultural environment.

relational aggression   Action that can adversely affect interpersonal relationships (e.g., calling another person names or socially excluding the person).

reliability   Extent to which a data collection technique yields consistent, dependable results—results that are only minimally affected by temporary and irrelevant influences.

resilience   Ability of some youngsters (often enhanced with environmental support) to thrive despite adverse environmental conditions.

right hemisphere   Right side of the cortex; largely responsible for simultaneous processing and synthesis, especially in right-handed people.

rough-and-tumble play   Playful physical "fighting" common in early and middle childhood.

sample   The specific participants in a research study; their performance is often assumed to indicate how a larger population of individuals would perform.

scaffolding   Support mechanism, provided by a more competent individual, that helps a child successfully perform a task within his or her zone of proximal development.

schema   Tightly integrated set of ideas about a specific object or situation.

scheme   In Piaget's theory, an organized group of similar actions or thoughts that are used repeatedly in response to the environment.

schizophrenia   A psychiatric condition characterized by irrational ideas and disorganized thinking.

scientific method   Multistep process of carefully defining and addressing a research question using critical thinking and analysis of the evidence.

scientific reasoning   Cognitive processes central to conducting scientific research and interpreting findings appropriately.

script   Schema that involves a predictable sequence of events related to a common activity.

secondary reinforcer   Stimulus or event that becomes reinforcing over time through its association with one or more other reinforcers.

secure attachment   Attachment classification in which children use attachment figures as a source of comfort in times of distress and as a secure base from which to explore.

selective adoption   Form of acculturation in which a person assumes some customs of a new culture while also retaining some customs of a previous culture.

self-conscious emotion   Affective state that reflects awareness of a community's social standards (e.g., pride, guilt, shame).

self-efficacy   Belief that one is capable of executing certain behaviors or reaching certain goals.

self-evaluation   Judging one's own performance in accordance with predetermined criteria.

self-fulfilling prophecy   Phenomenon in which an adult's expectations for a child's performance bring about that level of performance.

self-handicapping   Action that undermines one's own success as a way of protecting self-worth during difficult tasks.

self-instructions   Specific directions that one gives oneself while performing a complex behavior; a form of *self-talk*.

self-monitoring   Process of observing and recording one's own behavior.

self-motivation   Intentionally using certain strategies to keep oneself on task during a dull but important activity.

self-regulated learning   Directing and controlling one's own cognitive processes in order to learn successfully.

self-regulation   Process of directing and controlling one's personal actions and emotions.

self-reinforcement   Self-imposed pleasurable consequence for a desired behavior.

self-report   Data collection technique whereby participants are asked to describe their own characteristics and performance.

self-socialization   Tendency to integrate personal observations and others' input into self-constructed standards for behavior and to choose actions consistent with those standards.

self-talk   Talking to oneself as a way of guiding oneself through a task.

semantic bootstrapping   Using knowledge of word meanings to derive knowledge about syntactic categories and structures.

semantics   The meanings of words and word combinations.

sensation   Physiological detection of stimuli in the environment.

sense of community   In a classroom or school, a collection of widely shared beliefs that students, teachers, and other staff have common goals, support one another's efforts, and make important contributions to everyone's success.

sense of self   Knowledge, beliefs, judgments, and feelings about oneself as a person.

sense of self-determination   Belief that one has some choice and control regarding the future course of one's life.

sensitive period   A period in development when certain environmental experiences have a more pronounced influence than is true at other times.

sensory register Component of memory that holds incoming information in an unanalyzed form for a very brief time (2–3 seconds or less).

service learning Activity that promotes learning and skill development through volunteerism or community service.

sexual harassment Form of discrimination in which a target individual perceives another's actions or statements to be hostile, humiliating, or offensive, especially pertaining to physical appearance or sexual matters.

sexual orientation Particular sex(es) to which an individual is romantically and sexually attracted.

shame Feeling of embarrassment or humiliation after failing to meet certain standards for moral behavior.

sight vocabulary Words that a child can immediately recognize while reading.

situated motivation Phenomenon in which aspects of the immediate environment enhance motivation to learn particular things or behave in particular ways.

situational interest Interest evoked temporarily by something in the environment.

social cognition Process of thinking about how other people are likely to think, act, and react and choosing one's own interpersonal behaviors accordingly.

social-cognitive bias Mental shortcut in thinking about other people or social events.

social constructivism Theoretical perspective that focuses on people's collective efforts to impose meaning on the world.

social-emotional development Systematic changes in emotions, self-concept, motivation, social relationships, and moral reasoning and behavior.

social goal Goal related to establishing or maintaining relationships with other people.

social learning theory Theoretical perspective that focuses on how children's beliefs and goals influence their actions and how they often learn by observing others.

social perspective taking Imagining what someone else might be thinking or feeling.

social referencing Looking at someone else (e.g., a caregiver) for clues about how to respond to a particular object or event.

social skills Strategies used to interact effectively with others.

socialization Systematic efforts by other people and institutions to prepare youngsters to act in ways deemed by society to be appropriate and responsible.

society Large, enduring group of people that is socially and economically organized and has collective institutions and activities.

sociocognitive conflict Situation in which one encounters and has to wrestle with ideas and viewpoints different from one's own.

sociocultural theory Theoretical perspective that focuses on children's learning of tools, thinking processes, and communication systems through practice in meaningful tasks with other people.

sociodramatic play Play in which children take on specific roles and act out a scenario of imaginary events.

socioeconomic status (SES) One's general standing in an economically stratified society,

encompassing family income, type of job, and education level.

sociolinguistic behaviors Social conventions (often culture specific) that govern appropriate verbal interaction.

specific ability test Test designed to assess a specific cognitive skill or the potential to learn and perform in a specific content domain.

specific language impairment Disability characterized by abnormalities in producing or understanding spoken language, to the point where special educational services are required.

spermarche First ejaculation in an adolescent male.

stage A period of development characterized by a qualitatively distinct way of behaving or thinking.

stage theory Theory that describes development as involving a series of qualitatively distinct changes.

Standard English Form of English generally considered acceptable in school (as reflected in textbooks, grammar instruction, etc.) and in the media.

standards In education, general statements regarding the knowledge and skills that students should gain and the characteristics that their accomplishments should reflect.

state of arousal Physiological condition of sleepiness or wakefulness.

stepfamily Family created when one parent–child(ren) family combines with another parent figure and any children in his or her custody.

stereotype Rigid, simplistic, and erroneous characterization of a particular group.

stereotype threat Reduction in performance on a task (often unintentional) as a result of a belief that one's group typically performs poorly on the task.

story schema Knowledge of the typical elements and sequence of a narrative.

stranger anxiety Fear of unfamiliar adults in the latter half of the first year and into the second year of life.

student at risk Student who has a high probability of failing to acquire the minimal academic skills necessary for success in the adult world.

subculture Group that resists the ways of the dominant culture and adopts its own norms for behavior.

substance schema General view of all physical phenomena as being either touchable substances or properties of those substances.

subtractive bilingualism Phenomenon in which immersion in a new-language environment leads to deficits in one's native language.

sudden infant death syndrome (SIDS) Death of an infant in the first year of life, typically during sleep, that cannot be explained by a thorough medical examination; the risk of SIDS is highest between birth and 4 months.

symbol Mental entity that represents an external object or event, typically without reflecting its perceptual and behavioral qualities.

symbolic thought Ability to mentally represent and think about external objects and events.

sympathy Feeling of sorrow and concern about another's problems or distress.

synapse Junction between two neurons.

synaptic pruning A universal process in brain development whereby many previously formed synapses wither away, especially if they have not been used frequently.

synaptogenesis A universal process in brain development whereby many new synapses appear in the first few years of life.

syntax Rules consistently used to put words together into sentences.

telegraphic speech Short, grammatically incomplete sentences that include lexical (rather than grammatical) words almost exclusively; common in toddlers.

temperament A child's characteristic ways of responding to emotional events, novel stimuli, and personal impulses.

teratogen Potentially harmful substance that can cause damaging effects during prenatal development.

test Instrument designed to assess knowledge, abilities, or skills in a consistent fashion across individuals.

theory Organized system of principles and explanations regarding a particular phenomenon.

theory of mind Awareness that people have an inner, psychological life (thoughts, beliefs, feelings, etc.).

theory theory Theoretical perspective proposing that children construct increasingly integrated and complex understandings of physical and mental phenomena.

underextension Overly restricted meaning for a word, excluding some situations to which the word applies.

uninvolved parenting style Parenting style characterized by a lack of emotional support and a lack of standards regarding appropriate behavior.

universality In a particular aspect of human development, the commonalities seen in the way virtually all individuals progress.

validity Extent to which a data collection technique actually assesses what the researcher intends for it to assess.

value Belief that a particular activity has direct or indirect benefits.

vicarious punishment Phenomenon in which a child decreases a certain response after seeing someone else punished for that response.

vicarious reinforcement Phenomenon in which a child increases a certain response after seeing someone else reinforced for that response.

visual-spatial ability Ability to imagine and mentally manipulate two- and three-dimensional figures.

wait time The length of time a teacher pauses, after either asking a question or hearing a student's comment, before saying something.

working memory Component of memory that enables people to actively think about and process a small amount of information.

zone of proximal development (ZPD) Range of tasks that one cannot yet perform independently but can perform with the help and guidance of others.

zygote Cell formed when a male sperm joins with a female ovum; with healthy genes and nurturing conditions in the uterus, it may develop into a fetus and be born as a live infant.

References

Aalsma, M. C., Lapsley, D. K., & Flannery, D. J. (2006). Personal fables, narcissism, and adolescent adjustment. *Psychology in the Schools, 43,* 481–491.

Abe, J. A. A. (2005). The predictive validity of the five-factor model of personality with preschool age children: A nine year follow-up study. *Journal of Research in Personality, 39,* 423–442.

Abi-Nader, J. (1993). Meeting the needs of multicultural classrooms: Family values and the motivation of minority students. In M. J. O'Hair & S. J. Odell (Eds.), *Diversity and teaching: Teacher education yearbook I.* Fort Worth, TX: Harcourt Brace Jovanovich.

Abma, J. C., Martinez, G. M., Mosher, W. D., & Dawson, B. S. (2004). Teenagers in the United States: Sexual activity, contraceptive use, and childbearing, 2002. *Vital and Health Statistics, 23*(24), 1–48.

Aboud, F. E. (1988). *Children and prejudice.* New York: Basil Blackwell.

Aboud, F. E. (2005). The development of prejudice in childhood and adolescence. In J. F. Dovidio, P. Glick, & L. A. Rudman (Eds.), *On the nature of prejudice: Fifty years after Allport* (pp. 310–326). Malden, MA: Blackwell.

Abrams, D., Rutland, A., Cameron, L., & Ferrell, J. (2007). Older but wilier: In-group accountability and the development of subjective group dynamics. *Developmental Psychology, 43,* 134–148.

Ackerman, C. M., & Fifield, A. (2005). *Education policy brief: Gifted and talented education.* Retrieved March 3, 2008, from http://www.rdc .udel.edu/policy_briefs/v19_May.pdf

Ackerman, P. L., & Lohman, D. F. (2006). Individual differences in cognitive functions. In P. A. Alexander & P. H. Winne (Eds.), *Handbook of educational psychology* (2nd ed., pp. 139–161). Mahwah, NJ: Erlbaum.

Adalbjarnardottir, S., & Selman, R. L. (1997). "I feel I have received a new vision": An analysis of teachers' professional development as they work with students on interpersonal issues. *Teaching and Teacher Education, 13,* 409–428.

Adam, E. K. (2004). Beyond quality: Parental and residential stability and children's adjustment. *Current Directions in Psychological Science, 13,* 210–213.

Adam, E. K., Snell, E. K., & Pendry, P. (2007). Sleep timing and quantity in ecological and family context: A nationally representative time-diary study. *Journal of Family Psychology, 21,* 4–19.

Adams, G. R., Gullotta, T. P., & Markstrom-Adams, C. (1994). *Adolescent life experiences* (3rd ed.). Pacific Grove, CA: Brooks/Cole.

Adams, M. J. (1990). *Beginning to read: Thinking and learning about print.* Cambridge, MA: MIT Press.

Adams, R. J. (1987). An evaluation of color preference in early infancy. *Infant Behavior and Development, 10,* 143–150.

Adamson, L. B., & Bakeman, R. (1991). The development of shared attention during infancy. In R. Vasta (Ed.), *Annals of child development* (Vol. 8, pp. 1–41). London: Kingsley.

Adamson, L. B., & McArthur, D. (1995). Joint attention, affect, and culture. In C. Moore & P. J. Dunham (Eds.), *Joint attention: Its origins and role in development* (pp. 205–221). Hillsdale, NJ: Erlbaum.

Afflerbach, P., VanSledright, B., & Dromsky, A. (2003, April). *Reading and thinking like historians: Investigating a 4th grade performance assessment.* Paper presented at the annual meeting of the American Educational Research Association, Chicago.

Agency for Toxic Substances and Disease Registry. (1999, June). *ToxFAQs™ for lead.* Retrieved January 19, 2003, from http://www.atsdr.cdc.gov/tfacts13.html

Ahern, A. L., & Hetherington, M. M. (2006). The thin ideal and body image: An experimental study of implicit attitudes. *Psychology of Addictive Behaviors, 20,* 338–342.

Ahnert, L., Pinquart, M., & Lamb, M. E. (2006). Security of children's relationships with nonparental care providers: A meta-analysis. *Child Development, 74,* 664–679.

Ainsworth, M. D. S. (1963). The development of infant–mother interaction among the Ganda. In B. M. Foss (Ed.), *Determinants of infant behavior* (Vol. 2, pp. 67–104). New York: Wiley.

Ainsworth, M. D. S. (1973). The development of infant–mother attachment. In B. Caldwell & H. Ricciuti (Eds.), *Review of child development research* (Vol. 3, pp. 1–94). Chicago: University of Chicago Press.

Ainsworth, M. D. S., Blehar, M. C., Waters, E., & Wall, S. (1978). *Patterns of attachment.* Hillsdale, NJ: Erlbaum.

Aitchison, J. (1996). *The seeds of speech: Language origin and evolution.* Cambridge, England: Cambridge University Press.

Akhtar, N., Jipson, J., & Callanan, M. A. (2001). Learning words through overhearing. *Child Development, 72,* 416–430.

Akiskal, H. S., & McKinney, W. T. (1973). Depressive disorders: Toward a unified hypothesis. *Science, 162,* 20–29.

Alan Guttmacher Institute (2001). *Can more progress be made? Teenage sexual and reproductive behavior in developed countries.* Retrieved February 1, 2008, from http://www.guttmacher.org/pubs/summaries/euroteens_summ.pdf

Alapack, R. (1991). The adolescent first kiss. *Humanistic Psychologist, 19,* 48–67.

Alberts, A., Elkind, D., & Ginsberg, S. (2007). The personal fable and risk-taking in early adolescence. *Journal of Youth and Adolescence, 36,* 71–76.

Alderman, M. K. (1990). Motivation for at-risk students. *Educational Leadership, 48*(1), 27–30.

Aldous, J. (2006). Family, ethnicity, and immigrant youths' educational achievements. *Journal of Family Issues, 27,* 1633–1667.

Aldridge, M. A., Stillman, R. D., & Bower, T. G. R. (2001). Newborn categorization of vowel-like sounds. *Developmental Science, 4,* 220–232.

Alessandri, S. M., & Lewis, M. (1993). Parental evaluation and its relation to shame and pride in young children. *Sex Roles, 29,* 335–343.

Alexander, E. S. (2006, April). *Beyond S.M.A.R.T.? Integrating hopeful thinking into goal setting for adolescents at-risk of dropping out of high school.* Paper presented at the annual meeting of the American Educational Research Association, San Francisco.

Alexander, J. M., Johnson, K. E., Leibham, M. E., & Kelley, K. (2008). The development of conceptual interests in young children. *Cognitive Development, 23,* 324–334.

Alexander, K., Entwisle, D., & Thompson, M. (1987). School performance, status relations, and the structure of sentiment: Bringing the teacher back in. *American Sociological Review, 52,* 665–682.

Alexander, P. A., Graham, S., & Harris, K. R. (1998). A perspective on strategy research: Progress and prospects. *Educational Psychology Review, 10,* 129–154.

Alfassi, M. (1998). Reading for meaning: The efficacy of reciprocal teaching in fostering reading comprehension in high school students in remedial reading classes. *American Educational Research Journal, 35,* 309–332.

Alim, H. S., & Baugh, J. (Eds.). (2007). *Talkin black talk: Language, education, and social change.* New York: Teachers College Press.

Alland, A. (1983). *Playing with form.* New York: Columbia University Press.

Allison, K. W. (1998). Stress and oppressed social category membership. In J. K. Swim & C. Stangor (Eds.), *Prejudice: The target's perspective* (pp. 149–170). San Diego, CA: Academic Press.

Als, H., Lawhon, G., Duffy, F. H., McAnulty, G. B., Gibes-Grossman, R., & Blickman, J. G. (1994). Individualized developmental care for the very low-birth-weight preterm infant. Medical and neurofunctional effects. *Journal of the American Medical Association, 272,* 853–858.

Alvermann, D. E., & Moore, D. W. (1991). Secondary school reading. In R. Barr, M. L. Kamil, P. B. Mosenthal, & P. D. Pearson (Eds.), *Handbook of reading research* (Vol. II, pp. 951–983). New York: Longman.

Alvermann, D. E., Young, J. P., Green, C., & Wisenbaker, J. M. (1999). Adolescents' perceptions and negotiations of literacy practices in after-school read and talk clubs. *American Educational Research Journal, 36,* 221–264.

Amatea, E. S., & West-Olatunji, C. A. (2007). Joining the conversation about educating our poorest children: Emerging leadership roles for school counselors in high-poverty schools. *Professional School Counseling, 11*(2), 81–89.

Ambrose, D., Allen, J., & Huntley, S. B. (1994). Mentorship of the highly creative. *Roeper Review, 17,* 131–133.

American Academy of Pediatrics. (2005). Breastfeeding and the use of human milk. *Pediatrics, 115,* 496–506.

American Academy of Pediatrics Committee on Pediatric AIDS and Committee on Adolescence. (2001). Adolescents and human immunodeficiency virus infection: The role of the pediatrician in prevention and intervention. *Pediatrics, 107,* 188–190.

American Academy of Pediatrics Committee on Pediatric AIDS and Committee on Infectious Diseases. (1999). Issues related to human immunodeficiency virus transmission in schools, child care, medical settings, home, and community. *Pediatrics, 104,* 318–324.

American Academy of Pediatrics Committee on Sports Medicine and Fitness. (2000). Intensive training and sports specialization in young athletes. *Pediatrics, 106,* 154–157.

American Academy of Pediatrics Committee on Sports Medicine and Fitness and Committee on Injury and Poison Prevention. (2000). Swimming programs for infants and toddlers. *Pediatrics, 105,* 868–870.

American Academy of Pediatrics Task Force on Infant Sleep Position and Sudden Infant Death Syndrome. (2000). Changing concepts of sudden infant death syndrome: Implications for infant sleeping environment and sleep position. *Pediatrics, 105,* 650–656.

American Association on Intellectual and Developmental Disabilities. (2008). *Frequently asked questions on intellectual disability and the AAIDD definition.* Retrieved March 4, 2008, from http://www.aamr.org/Policies/faq_mental_retardation.shtml

American Educational Research Association. (2000). AERA position statement on high-stakes testing in pre-K–12 education. Retrieved October 15, 2007, from https://www.aera.net/policyandprograms/?id=378

American Psychiatric Association. (1994). *Diagnostic and statistical manual of mental disorders* (4th ed.). Washington, DC: Author.

American Psychological Association. (2002). Ethical principles of psychologists and code of conduct. *American Psychologist, 57,* 1060–1073.

American Speech-Language-Hearing Association (1993). Definitions of communication disorders and variations. *ASHA, 35*(Suppl. 10), 40–41.

Ames, C. (1984). Competitive, cooperative, and individualistic goal structures: A cognitive-motivational analysis. In R. Ames & C. Ames (Eds.), *Research on motivation in education: Vol. 1. Student motivation* (pp. 177–207). San Diego, CA: Academic Press.

Ames, C. (1992). Classrooms: Goals, structures, and student motivation. *Journal of Educational Psychology, 84*, 261–271.

Amirkhanian, Y. A., Tiunov, D. V., & Kelly, J. A. (2001). Risk factors for HIV and other sexually transmitted diseases among adolescents in St. Petersburg, Russia. *Family Planning Perspectives, 33*, 106–112.

Anastasi, A., & Urbina, S. (1997). *Psychological testing* (7th ed.). Upper Saddle River, NJ: Prentice Hall.

Anderman, E. M., Griesinger, T., & Westerfield, G. (1998). Motivation and cheating during early adolescence. *Journal of Educational Psychology, 90*, 84–93.

Anderman, E. M., & Maehr, M. L. (1994). Motivation and schooling in the middle grades. *Review of Educational Research, 64*, 287–309.

Anderman, L. H., & Anderman, E. M. (1999). Social predictors of changes in students' achievement goal orientation. *Contemporary Educational Psychology, 25*, 21–37.

Anderman, L. H., Patrick, H., Hruda, L. Z., & Linnenbrink, E. A. (2002). Observing classroom goal structures to clarify and expand goal theory. In C. Midgley (Ed.), *Goals, goal structures, and patterns of adaptive learning* (pp. 243–278). Mahwah, NJ: Erlbaum.

Anderson, C., & Huesmann, L. R. (2005). The evidence that media violence stimulates aggression in young viewers remains "unequivocal." *Observer, 18*(10), 7.

Anderson, C. A., Berkowitz, L., Donnerstein, E., Huesmann, L. R., Johnson, J. D., Linz, D., et al. (2003). The influence of media violence on youth. *Psychological Science in the Public Interest, 4*, 81–110.

Anderson, D. A. (1994). Lesbian and gay adolescents: Social and developmental considerations. *The High School Journal, 77*(1,2), 13–19.

Anderson, D. R. (2003). The Children's Television Act: A public policy that benefits children. *Applied Developmental Psychology, 24*, 337–340.

Anderson, D. R., Bryant, J., Wilder, A., Santomero, A., Williams, M., & Crawley, A. M. (2000). Researching *Blue's Clues:* Viewing behavior and impact. *Media Psychology, 2*, 179–194.

Anderson, D. R., Huston, A. C., Schmitt, K. L., Linebarger, D. L., & Wright, J. C. (2001). Early childhood television viewing and adolescent behavior: The recontact study. *Monographs of the Society for Research in Child Development, 66*(1, Serial No. 264).

Anderson, J. C. (1983). *The architecture of cognition.* Cambridge, MA: Harvard University Press.

Anderson, K. E., Lytton, H., & Romney, D. M. (1986). Mothers' interactions with normal and conduct-disordered boys: Who affects whom? *Developmental Psychology, 22*, 604–609.

Anderson, L. W., & Pellicer, L. O. (1998). Toward an understanding of unusually successful programs for economically disadvantaged students. *Journal of Education for Students Placed at Risk, 3*, 237–263.

Anderson, R. C., Nguyen-Jahiel, K., McNurlen, B., Archodidou, A., Kim, S.-Y., Reznitskaya, A., et al. (2001). The snowball phenomenon: Spread of ways of talking and ways of thinking across groups of children. *Cognition and Instruction, 19*, 1–46.

Anderson, R. C., Shirey, L., Wilson, P., & Fielding, L. (1987). Interestingness of children's reading materials. In R. Snow & M. Farr (Eds.), *Aptitude, learning, and instruction: III. Cognitive and affective process analyses* (pp. 287–299). Hillsdale, NJ: Erlbaum.

Andrews, G., Halford, G. S., Bunch, K. M., Bowden, D., & Jones, T. (2003). Theory of mind and relational complexity. *Child Development, 74*, 1476–1499.

Andrews, J. F., & Mason, J. M. (1986). Childhood deafness and the acquisition of print concepts. In D. B. Yaden, Jr., & S. Templeton (Eds.), *Metalinguistic awareness and beginning literacy: Conceptualizing what it means to read and write* (pp. 277–290). Portsmouth, NH: Heinemann.

Andriessen, J. (2006). Arguing to learn. In R. K. Sawyer (Ed.), *The Cambridge handbook of the learning sciences* (pp. 443–459). Cambridge, England: Cambridge University Press.

Anglin, J. M. (1977). *Word, object, and conceptual development.* New York: Norton.

Annett, R. D. (2004). Asthma. In R. T. Brown (Ed.), *Handbook of pediatric psychology in school settings* (pp. 149–167). Mahwah, NJ: Erlbaum.

Antelman, S., & Caggiula, A. (1977). Norepinephrine-dopamine interactions and behavior. *Science, 195*, 646–651.

Anthony, J. L., & Francis, D. J. (2005). Development of phonological awareness. *Current Directions in Psychological Science, 14*, 255–259.

Anthony, J. L., Lonigan, C. J., & Dyer, S. M. (1996, April). *The development of reading comprehension: Listening comprehension or basic language processes?* Paper presented at the annual meeting of the American Educational Research Association, New York.

Anthos, J. S. (2004). The healing power of art. *School Arts, 103*(10), 46–47.

Anyon, J. (1988). Social class and the hidden curriculum of work. In G. Handel (Ed.), *Childhood socialization* (pp. 357–382). New York: Aldine de Gruyter.

Arbib, M. (Ed.). (2005). *Action to language via the mirror neuron system.* New York: Cambridge University Press.

Arbona, C., Jackson, R. H., McCoy, A., & Blakely, C. (1999). Ethnic identity as a predictor of attitudes of adolescents toward fighting. *Journal of Early Adolescence, 19*, 323–340.

Archer, J. (1991). The influence of testosterone on human aggression. *British Journal of Psychology, 82*, 1–28.

Arcus, D. M. (1991). *Experiential modification of temperamental bias in inhibited and uninhibited children.* Unpublished doctoral dissertation, Harvard University, Cambridge, MA.

Arcus, D. M. (2001). Inhibited and uninhibited children: Biology in the social context. In T. D. Wachs & G. A. Kohnstamm (Eds.), *Temperament in context* (pp. 43–60). Mahwah, NJ: Erlbaum.

Arndt, T. L., Stodgell, C. J., & Rodier, P. M. (2005). The teratology of autism. *International Journal of Developmental Neuroscience, 23*, 189–199.

Arnett, J. J. (1999). Adolescent storm and stress, reconsidered. *American Psychologist, 54*, 317–326.

Arnold, M. L. (2000). Stage, sequence, and sequels: Changing conceptions of morality, post-Kohlberg. *Educational Psychology Review, 12*, 365–383.

Aronson, S. R., & Huston, A. C. (2004). The mother-infant relationship in single, cohabiting, and married families: A case for marriage? *Journal of Family Psychology, 18*, 5–18.

Arsenio, W. F., Gold, J., & Adams, E. (2006). Children's conceptions and displays of moral emotions. In M. Killen & J. G. Smetana (Eds.), *Handbook of moral development* (pp. 581–609). Mahwah, NJ: Erlbaum.

Artman, L., & Cahan, S. (1993). Schooling and the development of transitive inference. *Developmental Psychology, 29*, 753–759.

Asai, S. (1993). In search of Asia through music: Guidelines and ideas for teaching Asian music. In T. Perry & J. W. Fraser (Eds.), *Freedom's plow: Teaching in the multicultural classroom.* New York: Routledge.

Ashcraft, M. H. (1982). The development of mental arithmetic: A chronometric approach. *Developmental Review, 2*, 212–236.

Asher, S. R., & Coie, J. D. (Eds.). (1990). *Peer rejection in childhood.* Cambridge, England: Cambridge University Press.

Asher, S. R., & Parker, J. G. (1989). Significance of peer relationship problems in childhood. In B. H. Schneider, G. Attili, J. Nadel, & R. P. Weissberg (Eds.), *Social competence in developmental perspective.* Dordrecht, The Netherlands: Kluwer.

Asher, S. R., & Renshaw, P. D. (1981). Children without friends: Social knowledge and social skill training. In S. R. Asher & J. M. Gottman (Eds.), *The development of children's friendships* (pp. 273–296). Cambridge, England: Cambridge University Press.

Ashiabi, G. S. (2007). Play in the preschool classroom: Its socioemotional significance and the teacher's role in play. *Early Childhood Education Journal, 35*(2), 199–207.

Ashmead, D. H., Davis, D. L., Whalen, T., & Odom, R. D. (1991). Sound localization and sensitivity to interaural time differences in human infants. *Child Development, 62*, 1211–1226.

Ashmore, R., & DelBoca, F. (1976). Psychological approaches. In P. A. Katz (Ed.), *Elimination of racism.* New York: Pergamon.

Ashton, P. (1985). Motivation and the teacher's sense of efficacy. In C. Ames & R. Ames (Eds.), *Research on motivation in education: Vol. 2. The classroom milieu.* San Diego, CA: Academic Press.

Aslin, R. N. (1993). Perception of visual direction in human infants. In C. E. Granrud (Ed.), *Visual perception and cognition in infancy.* Hillsdale, NJ: Erlbaum.

Aslin, R. N., Saffran, J. R., & Newport, E. L. (1998). Computation of conditional probability statistics by 8-month-old infants. *Psychological Science, 9*, 321–324.

Asmussen, L., & Larson, R. (1991). The quality of family time among adolescents in single-parent and married-parent families. *Journal of Marriage and Family, 53*, 1021–1030.

Assor, A., & Connell, J. P. (1992). The validity of students' self-reports as measures of performance affecting self-appraisals. In D. H. Schunk & J. L. Meece (Eds.), *Student perceptions in the classroom.* Hillsdale, NJ: Erlbaum.

Astington, J. W. (1991). Intention in the child's theory of mind. In C. Moore & D. Frye (Eds.), *Children's theories of mind* (pp. 157–172). Hillsdale, NJ: Erlbaum.

Astington, J. W., & Pelletier, J. (1996). The language of mind: Its role in teaching and learning. In D. R. Olson & N. Torrance (Eds.), *The handbook of education and human development: New models of learning, teaching and schooling* (pp. 593–619). Cambridge, MA: Blackwell.

Astor, R. A. (1994). Children's moral reasoning about family and peer violence: The role of provocation and retribution. *Child Development, 65*, 1054–1067.

Atkinson, J. (1998). The "where and what" or "who and how" of visual development. In F. Simion & G. Butterworth (Eds.), *The development of sensory, motor and cognitive capacities in early infancy: From perception to cognition* (pp. 3–24). Hove, England: Psychology Press.

Atkinson, M. (1992). *Children's syntax: An introduction to principles and parameters theory.* Oxford, England: Blackwell.

Attie, I., Brooks-Gunn, J., & Petersen, A. (1990). A developmental perspective on eating disorders and eating problems. In M. Lewis & S. M. Miller (Eds.), *Handbook of developmental psychopathology* (pp. 409–420). New York: Plenum Press.

Atwater, E. (1996). *Adolescence.* Upper Saddle River, NJ: Prentice Hall.

Au, T. K., & Glusman, M. (1990). The principle of mutual exclusivity in word learning: To honor or not to honor? *Child Development, 61*, 1474–1490.

Avis, J., & Harris, P. L. (1991). Belief-desire reasoning among Baka children: Evidence for a universal conception of mind. *Child Development, 62*, 460–467.

Ayoub, C. C. (2006). Adaptive and maladaptive parenting: Influence on child development. In H. E. Fitzgerald, R. Zucker, & K. Freeark (Eds. in Chief), N. F. Watt, C. Ayoub, R. H. Bradley, J. E. Puma, & W. A. LeBouef (Vol. Eds.), *The crisis in youth mental health: Critical issues and effective programs: Vol. 1. Early intervention programs and policies* (pp. 121–413). Westport, CT: Praeger.

Babad, E. (1993). Teachers' differential behavior. *Educational Psychology Review, 5,* 347–376.

Bahrick, L. E., Gogate, L. J., & Ruiz, I. (2002). Attention and memory for faces and actions in infancy: The salience of actions over faces in dynamic events. *Child Development, 73,* 1629–1643.

Bailes, A., & Jackson, M. E. (2000). Shared responsibility in home birth practice: Collaborating with clients. *Journal of Midwifery and Women's Health, 45*(6), 537–543.

Bailey, J. M., Dunne, M. P., & Martin, N. G. (2000). Genetic and environmental influences on sexual orientation and its correlates in an Australian twin sample. *Journal of Personality and Social Psychology, 78,* 524–536.

Bailey, J. M., & Pillard, R. C. (1997). The innateness of homosexuality. In M. R. Walsh (Ed.), *Women, men, and gender: Ongoing debates* (pp. 184–187). New Haven, CT: Yale University Press.

Baillargeon, R. (1994). How do infants learn about the physical world? *Current Directions in Psychological Science, 3,* 133–140.

Baillargeon, R. (2004). Infants' physical worlds. *Current Directions in Psychological Science, 13,* 89–94.

Baillargeon, R. (2008). Innate ideas revisited: For a principle of persistence in infants' physical reasoning. *Perspectives on Psychological Science, 3,* 2–13.

Baird, J. A., & Astington, J. W. (2005). The development of the intention concept: From the observable world to the unobservable mind. In R. R. Hassin, J. S. Uleman, & J. A. Bargh (Eds.), *The new unconscious* (pp. 256–276). New York: Oxford University Press.

Bakari, R. (2000). *The development and validation of an instrument to measure preservice teachers' attitudes toward teaching African American students.* Unpublished doctoral dissertation, University of Northern Colorado, Greeley.

Bakeman, R., & Brownlee, J. R. (1980). The strategic use of parallel play: A sequential analysis. *Child Development, 51,* 873–878.

Baker, C. (1993). *Foundations of bilingual education and bilingualism.* Clevedon, England: Multilingual Matters.

Baker, L., Scher, D., & Mackler, K. (1997). Home and family influences on motivations for reading. *Educational Psychologist, 32,* 69–82.

Bakermans-Kranenburg, M. J., van IJzendoorn, M. H., & Juffer, F. (2003). Less is more: Meta-analyses of sensitivity and attachment interventions in early childhood. *Psychological Bulletin, 129,* 195–215.

Baldwin, D. A. (1993). Early referential understanding: Infants' ability to recognize referential acts for what they are. *Developmental Psychology, 29,* 832–843.

Baldwin, D. A. (2000). Interpersonal understanding fuels knowledge acquisition. *Current Directions in Psychological Science, 9,* 40–45.

Baldwin, M. W., Keelan, J. P. R., Fehr, B., Enns, V., & Koh-Rangarajoo, E. (1996). Social-cognitive conceptualization of attachment working models: Availability and accessibility effects. *Journal of Personality and Social Psychology, 71,* 94–109.

Baltes, P. B. (1997). On the incomplete architecture of human ontogeny: Selection, optimization, and compensation as a foundation of developmental theory. *American Psychologist, 52,* 366–380.

Baltes, P. B., Lindenberger, U., & Staudinger, U. M. (2006). Life span theory in developmental psychology. In W. Damon & R. M. Lerner (Eds. in Chief) & R. M. Lerner (Vol. Ed.), *Handbook of child psychology: Vol. 1. Theoretical models of human development* (6th ed., pp. 569–664). Hoboken, NJ: Wiley.

Bandura, A. (1965). Influence of models' reinforcement contingencies on the acquisition of imitative responses. *Journal of Personality and Social Psychology, 1,* 589–595.

Bandura, A. (1977). *Social learning theory.* Englewood Cliffs, NJ: Prentice Hall.

Bandura, A. (1982). Self-efficacy mechanism in human agency. *American Psychologist, 37,* 122–147.

Bandura, A. (1991). Social cognitive theory of moral thought and action. In W. M. Kurtines & J. L. Gewirtz (Eds.), *Handbook of moral behavior and development: Vol. 1. Theory.* Hillsdale, NJ: Erlbaum.

Bandura, A. (1997). *Self-efficacy: The exercise of control.* New York: Freeman.

Bandura, A. (2006). Toward a psychology of human agency. *Perspectives on Psychological Science, 1,* 164–180.

Bandura, A., Barbaranelli, C., Caprara, G. V., & Pastorelli, C. (2001). Self-efficacy beliefs as shapers of children's aspirations and career trajectories. *Child Development, 72,* 187–206.

Bandura, A., & Mischel, W. (1965). Modification of self-imposed delay of reward through exposure to live and symbolic models. *Journal of Personality and Social Psychology, 2,* 698–705.

Bandura, A., Ross, D., & Ross, S. A. (1963). Imitation of film-mediated aggressive models. *Journal of Abnormal and Social Psychology, 66,* 3–11.

Banks, J. A. (1994). *An introduction to multicultural education.* Needham Heights, MA: Allyn & Bacon.

Banks, J. A., & Banks, C. A. M. (Eds.). (1995). *Handbook of research on multicultural education.* New York: Macmillan.

Bannister, E. M., Jakubec, S. L., & Stein, J. A. (2003). "Like, what am I supposed to do?": Adolescents' health concerns in their dating relationships. *Canadian Journal of Nursing Research, 35*(2), 16–33.

Bao, X.-H., & Lam, S.-F. (2008). Who makes the choice? Rethinking the role of autonomy and relatedness in Chinese children's motivation. *Child Development, 79,* 269–283.

Barab, S. A., & Plucker, J. A. (2002). Smart people or smart contexts? Cognition, ability, and talent development in an age of situated approaches to knowing and learning. *Educational Psychologist, 37,* 165–182.

Barber, J. G., & Delfabbro, P. H. (2004). *Children in foster care.* New York: Routledge.

Barchfeld, P., Sodian, B., Thoermer, C., & Bullock, M. (2005, April). *The development of experiment generation abilities from primary school to late adolescence.* Poster presented at the biennial meeting of the Society for Research in Child Development, Atlanta, GA.

Barga, N. K. (1996). Students with learning disabilities in education: Managing a disability. *Journal of Learning Disabilities, 29,* 413–421.

Barker, G. P., & Graham, S. (1987). Developmental study of praise and blame as attributional cues. *Journal of Educational Psychology, 79,* 62–66.

Barkley, R. A. (1998). *Attention-deficit hyperactivity disorder: A handbook for diagnosis and treatment* (2nd ed.). New York: Guilford Press.

Barnas, M. V., & Cummings, E. M. (1994). Caregiver stability and toddlers' attachment-related behaviors towards caregivers in day care. *Infant Behavior and Development, 17,* 141–147.

Barnett, J. E. (2001, April). *Study strategies and preparing for exams: A survey of middle and high school students.* Paper presented at the annual meeting of the American Educational Research Association, Seattle, WA.

Barnett, W. S. (1996). Long-term effects of early childhood programs on cognitive and school outcomes. *The Future of Children, 5*(3), 25–50.

Baron-Cohen, S., Tager-Flusberg, H., & Cohen, D. J. (1993). *Understanding other minds: Perspectives from autism.* Oxford, England: Oxford University Press.

Baroody, A. J., Tiilikainen, S. H., & Tai, Y.-C. (2006). The application and development of an addition goal sketch. *Cognition and Instruction, 24,* 123–170.

Barrett, J. G. (2005). Conduct disorders. In C. B. Fisher & R. M. Lerner (Eds.), *Encyclopedia of applied developmental science* (Vol. 1, pp. 294–295). Thousand Oaks, CA: Sage.

Barringer, C., & Gholson, B. (1979). Effects of type and combination of feedback upon conceptual learning by children: Implications for research in academic learning. *Review of Educational Research, 49,* 459–478.

Barron, R. W. (1998). Proto-literate knowledge: Antecedents and influences on phonological awareness and literacy. In C. Hulme & R. M. Joshi (Eds.), *Reading and spelling: Development and disorders.* Mahwah, NJ: Erlbaum.

Barrow, F. H., Armstrong, M. I., Vargo, A., & Boothroyd, R. A. (2007). Understanding the findings of resilience-related research for fostering the development of African American adolescents. *Child and Adolescent Psychiatric Clinics of North America, 16,* 393–413.

Bartlett, E. J. (1982). Learning to revise: Some component processes. In M. Nystrand (Ed.), *What writers know: The language, process, and structure of written discourse.* New York: Academic Press.

Barton, K. C., & Levstik, L. S. (1996). "Back when God was around and everything": Elementary children's understanding of historical time. *American Educational Research Journal, 33,* 419–454.

Bartsch, K., & Wellman, H. M. (1995). *Children talk about the mind.* New York: Oxford University Press.

Basinger, K. S., Gibbs, J. C., & Fuller, D. (1995). Context and the measurement of moral judgment. *International Journal of Behavioral Development, 18,* 537–556.

Basso, K. (1972). To give up on words: Silence in western Apache culture. In P. Giglioli (Ed.), *Language and social context.* New York: Penguin Books.

Basso, K. H. (1984). Stalking with stories: Names, places, and moral narratives among the Western Apache. In E. M. Bruner & S. Plattner (Eds.), *Text, play and story: The construction and reconstruction of self and society* (pp. 19–55). Washington, DC: American Ethnological Society.

Bates, E., & MacWhinney, B. (1987). Competition, variation, and language learning. In B. MacWhinney (Ed.), *Mechanisms of language acquisition.* Hillsdale, NJ: Erlbaum.

Batshaw, M. L., & Shapiro, B. K. (1997). Mental retardation. In M. L. Batshaw (Ed.), *Children with disabilities* (4th ed.). Baltimore: Brookes.

Batson, C. D. (1991). *The altruism question: Toward a social-psychological answer.* Hillsdale, NJ: Erlbaum.

Batson, C. D., & Thompson, E. R. (2001). Why don't moral people act morally? Motivational considerations. *Current Directions in Psychological Science, 10,* 54–57.

Battin-Pearson, S., Newcomb, M. D., Abbott, R. D., Hill, K. G., Catalano, R. F., & Hawkins, J. D. (2000). Predictors of early high school dropout: A test of five theories. *Journal of Educational Psychology, 92,* 568–582.

Battistich, V. (2003). Effects of a school-based program to enhance prosocial development on children's peer relations and social adjustment. *Journal of Research in Character Education, 1*(1), 1–17.

Battistich, V., Solomon, D., Kim, D., Watson, M., & Schaps, E. (1995). Schools as communities, poverty levels of student populations, and students' attitudes, motives, and performance: A multilevel analysis. *American Educational Research Journal, 32,* 627–658.

Battistich, V., Solomon, D., Watson, M., & Schaps, E. (1997). Caring school communities. *Educational Psychologist, 32,* 137–151.

Bauer, P. J. (2002). Long-term recall memory: Behavioral and neuro-developmental changes in the first 2 years of life. *Current Directions in Psychological Science, 11,* 137–141.

Bauer, P. J. (2006). Event memory. In W. Damon, R. M. Lerner (Series Eds.), D. Kuhn, & R. Siegler (Vol. Eds.), *Handbook of child psychology: Vol. 2. Cognition, perception, and language* (6th ed., pp. 373–425). New York: Wiley.

Bauer, P. J. (2007). Recall in infancy: A neurodevelopmental account. *Current Directions in Psychological Science, 16,* 142–146.

Bauer, P. J., DeBoer, T., & Lukowski, A. F. (2007). In the language of multiple memory systems: Defining and describing developments in long-term declarative memory. In L. M. Oakes & P. J. Bauer (Eds.), *Short- and long-term memory in infancy and early childhood: Taking the first steps toward remembering* (pp. 240–270). New York: Oxford University Press.

Bauer, P. J., & Dow, G. A. (1994). Episodic memory in 16- and 20-month-old children: Specifics not generalized, but not forgotten. *Developmental Psychology, 30,* 403–417.

Baumeister, R. F., Campbell, J. D., Krueger, J. I., & Vohs, K. D. (2003). Does high self-esteem cause better performance, interpersonal success, happiness, or healthier lifestyles? *Psychological Science in the Public Interest, 4*(1), 1–44.

Baumrind, D. (1967). Child care practices anteceding three patterns of preschool behavior. *Genetic Psychology Monographs, 75,* 43–88.

Baumrind, D. (1971). Current patterns of parental authority. *Developmental Psychology Monographs, 4*(1, Pt. 2).

Baumrind, D. (1980). New directions in socialization research. *American Psychologist, 35,* 639–652.

Baumrind, D. (1982). An explanatory study of socialization effects on Black children: Some Black-White comparisons. *Child Development, 43,* 261–267.

Baumrind, D. (1989). Rearing competent children. In W. Damon (Ed.), *Child development today and tomorrow.* San Francisco: Jossey-Bass.

Baumrind, D. (1991). Parenting styles and adolescent development. In R. Lerner, A. C. Petersen, & J. Brooks-Gunn (Eds.), *The encyclopedia of adolescence.* New York: Garland Press.

Bay-Hinitz, A. K., Peterson, R. F., & Quilitch, H. R. (1994). Cooperative games: A way to modify aggressive and cooperative behaviors in young children. *Journal of Applied Behavior Analysis, 27,* 435–446.

Bayley, N. (2005). *Bayley Scales of Infant Development* (3rd ed.). San Antonio, TX: Psychological Corporation.

Beal, C. R. (1996). The role of comprehension monitoring in children's revision. *Educational Psychology Review, 8,* 219–238.

Bearison, D., & Levey, L. (1977). Children's comprehension of referential communication: Decoding ambiguous messages. *Child Development, 48,* 716–720.

Bearison, D. J. (1998). Pediatric psychology and children's medical problems. In W. Damon (Series Ed.), I. E. Sigel, & K. A. Renninger (Vol. Eds.), *Handbook of child psychology: Vol. 4. Child psychology in practice* (5th ed., pp. 635–711). New York: Wiley.

Beaty, J. J. (1998). *Observing development of the young child* (4th ed.). Upper Saddle River, NJ: Merrill/Prentice Hall.

Beaumont, R., & Sofronoff, K. (2008). A multicomponent social skills intervention for children with Asperger syndrome: The Junior Detective Training Program. *Journal of Child Psychology and Psychiatry, 49*(7), 743–753.

Bebko, J. M., Burke, L., Craven, J., & Sarlo, N. (1992). The importance of motor activity in sensorimotor development: A perspective from children with physical handicaps. *Human Development, 35*(4), 226–240.

Beck, M. (1999). *Expecting Adam: A true story of birth, rebirth, and everyday magic.* New York: Random House.

Beck, S. R., Robinson, E. J., Carroll, D. J., & Apperly, I. A. (2006). Children's thinking about counterfactuals and future hypotheticals as possibilities. *Child Development, 77,* 413–426.

Beeman, M. J., & Chiarello, C. (1998). Complementary right- and left-hemisphere language comprehension. *Current Directions in Psychological Science, 7,* 2–8.

Belenky, M. F., Bond, L. A., & Weinstock, J. S. (1997). *A tradition that has no name: Nurturing the development of people, families, and communities.* New York: Basic Books.

Belenky, M. F., Clinchy, B. M., Goldberger, N. R., & Tarule, J. M. (1986). *Women's ways of knowing: The development of self, voice, and mind.* New York: Basic Books.

Belfiore, P. J., & Hornyak, R. S. (1998). Operant theory and application to self-monitoring in adolescents. In D. H. Schunk and B. J. Zimmerman (Eds.), *Self-regulated learning: From teaching to self-reflective practice.* New York: Guilford Press.

Bell, L. A. (1989). Something's wrong here and it's not me: Challenging the dilemmas that block girls' success. *Journal for the Education of the Gifted, 12,* 118–130.

Bell, M. A., Wolfe, C. D., & Adkins, D. R. (2007). Frontal lobe development during infancy and childhood: Contributions of brain electrical activity, temperament, and language to individual differences in working memory and inhibitory control. In D. Coch, K. W. Fischer, & G. Dawson (Eds.), *Human behavior, learning, and the developing brain: Typical development* (pp. 247–276). New York: Guilford Press.

Bell, P., & Linn, M. C. (2002). Beliefs about science: How does science instruction contribute? In B. K. Hofer & P. R. Pintrich (Eds.), *Personal epistemology: The psychology of beliefs about knowledge and knowing* (pp. 321–346). Mahwah, NJ: Erlbaum.

Bell, R. Q. (1988). Contributions of human infants to caregiving and social interaction. In G. Handel (Ed.), *Childhood socialization* (pp. 103–122). New York: Aldine de Gruyter.

Bellugi, U., Järvinen-Pasley, A., Doyle, T. F., Reilly, J., Reiss, A. L., & Korenberg, J. R. (2007). Affect, social behavior, and the brain in Williams syndrome. *Current Directions in Psychological Science, 16,* 99–104.

Belsky, J., & Eggebeen, D. (1991). Early and extensive maternal employment and young children's socioemotional development: Children of the National Longitudinal Survey of Youth. *Journal of Marriage and Family, 53*(4), 1083–1098.

Belsky, J., Gilstrap, B., & Rovine, M. (1984). The Pennsylvania Infant and Family Development Project, I: Stability and change in mother–infant and father–infant interaction in a family setting at one, three, and nine months. *Child Development, 55,* 692–705.

Belzer, M. E., Rogers, A. S., Camarca, M., Fuschs, D., Peralta, L., Tucker, D., et al. (2001). Contraceptive choices in HIV infected and HIV at-risk adolescent females. *Journal of Adolescent Health, 29*(Suppl. 3), 93–100.

Bem, S. L. (1977). On the utility of alternative procedures for assessing psychological androgyny. *Journal of Consulting and Clinical Psychology, 45,* 196–205.

Bem, S. L. (1981). Gender schema theory: A cognitive account of sex typing. *Psychological Review, 88,* 354–364.

Bem, S. L. (1989). Genital knowledge and gender constancy in preschool children. *Child Development, 60,* 649–662.

Bembenutty, H., & Karabenick, S. A. (2004). Inherent association between academic delay of gratification, future time perspective, and self-regulated learning. *Educational Psychology Review, 16,* 35–57.

Benbow, C. P., Lubinski, D., Shea, D. L., & Eftekhari-Sanjani, H. (2000). Sex differences in mathematical reasoning ability at age 13: Their status 20 years later. *Psychological Science, 11,* 474–480.

Bender, G. (2001). Resisting dominance? The study of a marginalized masculinity and its construction within high school walls. In J. N. Burstyn, G. Bender, R. Casella, H. W. Gordon, D. P. Guerra, K. V. Luschen, et al., *Preventing violence in schools: A challenge to American democracy* (pp. 61–77). Mahwah, NJ: Erlbaum.

Benenson, J. F., Maiese, R., Dolenszky, E., Dolensky, N., Sinclair, N., & Simpson, A. (2002). Group size regulates self-assertive versus self-deprecating responses to interpersonal competition. *Child Development, 73,* 1818–1829.

Benes, F. (2001, May–June). Modern myelination: The brain at midlife. *Harvard Magazine, 103,* 9.

Bennett, A., Bridglall, B. L., Cauce, A. M., Everson, H. T., Gordon, E. W., Lee, C. D., et al. (2007). Task force report on the affirmative development of academic ability: All students reaching the top: Strategies for closing academic achievement gaps. In E. W. Gordon & B. L. Bridglall (Eds.), *Affirmative development: Cultivating academic ability* (pp. 239–275). Lanham, MD: Rowman.

Bennett, G. K., Seashore, H. G., & Wesman, A. G. (1982). *Differential Aptitude Tests.* San Antonio, TX: Psychological Corporation.

Bennett, R. E., Gottesman, R. L., Rock, D. A., & Cerullo, F. (1993). Influence of behavior perceptions and gender on teachers' judgments of students' academic skill. *Journal of Educational Psychology, 85,* 347–356.

Benoit, D., & Parker, K. C. (1994). Stability and transmission of attachment across three generations. *Child Development, 65,* 1444–1456.

Benton, S. L. (1997). Psychological foundations of elementary writing instruction. In G. D. Phye (Ed.), *Handbook of academic learning: Construction of knowledge.* San Diego, CA: Academic Press.

Benware, C., & Deci, E. L. (1984). Quality of learning with an active versus passive motivational set. *American Educational Research Journal, 21,* 755–765.

Bereiter, C. (1994). Implications of postmodernism for science, or, science as progressive discourse. *Educational Psychologist, 29,* 3–12.

Bereiter, C., & Scardamalia, M. (1987). *The psychology of written composition.* Hillsdale, NJ: Erlbaum.

Bereiter, C., & Scardamalia, M. (2006). Education for the Knowledge Age: Design-centered models of teaching and instruction. In P. A. Alexander & P. H. Winne (Eds.), *Handbook of educational psychology* (2nd ed., pp. 695–713). Mahwah, NJ: Erlbaum.

Berenstain, S., & Berenstain, J. (1990). *The Berenstain bears' trouble with pets.* New York: Random House.

Berger, R. (2000). Remarried families of 2000: Definitions, descriptions, and interventions. In W. C. Nichols, M. A. Pace-Nichols, D. S. Becvar, & A. Y. Napier (Eds.), *Handbook of family development* (pp. 371–390). New York: Wiley.

Bergeron, R., & Floyd, R. G. (2006). Broad cognitive abilities of children with mental retardation: An analysis of group and individual profiles. *American Journal on Mental Retardation, 111,* 417–432.

Berk, L. E. (1994). Why children talk to themselves. *Scientific American, 271,* 78–83.

Berkeley, S., Mastropieri, M., & Scruggs, T. (2008, March). *Reading comprehension strategy instruction and attribution retraining for secondary students with disabilities.* Paper presented at the annual meeting of the American Educational Research Association, New York.

Berliner, D. (2006). Our impoverished view of educational research. *Teachers College Record, 108,* 949–995.

Berliner, D. C. (2005, April). *Ignoring the forest, blaming the trees: Our impoverished view of educational reform.* Paper presented at the annual meeting of the American Educational Research Association, Montreal, Canada.

Bermejo, V. (1996). Cardinality development and counting. *Developmental Psychology, 32,* 263–268.

Berndt, T. J. (1992). Friendship and friends' influence in adolescence. *Current Directions in Psychological Science, 1,* 156–159.

Berndt, T. J., & Hoyle, S. G. (1985). Stability and change in childhood and adolescent friendships. *Developmental Psychology, 21,* 1007–1015.

Berndt, T. J., & Keefe, K. (1995). Friends' influence on adolescents' adjustment to school. *Child Development, 66,* 1312–1329.

Berndt, T. J., & Keefe, K. (1996). Friends' influence on school adjustment: A motivational analysis. In

J. Juvonen & K. R. Wentzel (Eds.), *Social motivation: Understanding children's school adjustment* (pp. 248–278). Cambridge, England: Cambridge University Press.

Berninger, V. W. (2004). Understanding the graphia in developmental dysgraphia: A developmental neuropsychological perspective for disorders in producing written language. In D. Dewey & D. Tupper (Eds.), *Developmental motor disorders: A neuropsychological perspective* (pp. 189–233). New York: Guilford Press.

Berninger, V. W., Fuller, F., & Whitaker, D. (1996). A process model of writing development across the life span. *Educational Psychology Review, 8,* 193–218.

Bernstein, R. (2003, June). *Two married parents are the norm.* United States Department of Commerce News, CB03-97. U.S. Census Bureau Public Information Office. Retrieved November 16, 2007, from http://www.census.gov/Press-Release/www/2003/cb03-97.html

Bertenthal, B. I. (1993). Infants' perception of biomechanical motions: Intrinsic image and knowledge-based constraints. In C. E. Granrud (Ed.), *Visual perception and cognition in infancy* (pp. 175–214). Hillsdale, NJ: Erlbaum.

Bertenthal, B. I., Campos, J. J., & Kermoian, R. (1994). An epigenetic perspective on the development of self-produced locomotion and its consequences. *Current Directions in Psychological Science, 3,* 140–145.

Berzonsky, M. D. (1988). Self-theorists, identity status, and social cognition. In D. K. Lapsley & F. C. Power (Eds.), *Self, ego, and identity: Integrative approaches* (pp. 243–261). New York: Springer-Verlag.

Bialystok, E. (1994a). Representation and ways of knowing: Three issues in second language acquisition. In N. C. Ellis (Ed.), *Implicit and explicit learning of languages.* London: Academic Press.

Bialystok, E. (1994b). Towards an explanation of second language acquisition. In G. Brown, K. Malmkjær, A. Pollitt, & J. Williams (Eds.), *Language and understanding.* Oxford, England: Oxford University Press.

Bialystok, E. (2001). *Bilingualism in development: Language, literacy, and cognition.* Cambridge, England: Cambridge University Press.

Bialystok, E., McBride-Chang, C., & Luk, G. (2005). Bilingualism, language proficiency, and learning to read in two writing systems. *Journal of Educational Psychology, 97,* 580–590.

Bialystok, E., & Senman, L. (2004). Executive processes in appearance–reality tasks: The role of inhibition of attention and symbolic representation. *Child Development, 75,* 562–579.

Bibace, R., & Walsh, M. E. (1981). Children's conceptions of illness. In R. Bibace & M. E. Walsh (Eds.), *New directions for child development: Children's conceptions of health, illness, and bodily functions* (pp. 31–48). San Francisco: Jossey-Bass.

Biddle, S. J. (1993). Children, exercise and mental health. *International Journal of Sport Psychology, 24,* 200–216.

Biemiller, A. (1994). Some observations on beginning reading instruction. *Educational Psychologist, 29,* 203–209.

Biemiller, A., Shany, M., Inglis, A., & Meichenbaum, D. (1998). Factors influencing children's acquisition and demonstration of self-regulation on academic tasks. In D. H. Schunk & B. J. Zimmerman (Eds.), *Self-regulated learning: From teaching to self-reflective practice* (pp. 203–224). New York: Guilford Press.

Bierman, K. L. (2004). *Peer rejection: Developmental processes and intervention strategies.* New York: Guilford Press.

Bierman, K. L., Miller, C. L., & Staub, S. D. (1987). Improving the social behavior and peer acceptance of rejected boys: Effect of social skill training with instructions and prohibitions. *Journal of Consulting and Clinical Psychology, 55,* 194–200.

Bigler, R. S., & Liben, L. S. (2007). Developmental intergroup theory: Explaining and reducing children's social stereotyping and prejudice. *Current Directions in Psychological Science, 16,* 162–166.

Bigner, B. J. (2006). *Parent–child relations: An introduction to parenting* (7th ed.). Upper Saddle River, NJ: Pearson Merrill Prentice Hall.

Bijeljac-Babic, R., Bertoncini, J., & Mehler, J. (1993). How do 4-day-old infants categorize multisyllable utterances? *Developmental Psychology, 29,* 711–721.

Binder, L. M., Dixon, M. R., & Ghezzi, P. M. (2000). A procedure to teach self-control to children with attention deficit hyperactivity disorder. *Journal of Applied Behavior Analysis, 33,* 233–237.

Birkas, E., Horváth, J., Lakatos, K., Nemoda, Z., Sasvari-Szekely, M., Winkler, I., et al. (2006). Association between dopamine D4 receptor (DRD4) gene polymorphisms and novelty-elicited auditory event-related potentials in preschool children. *Brain Research, 1103*(1), 150–158.

Birnbaum, D. W., & Croll, W. L. (1984). The etiology of children's stereotypes about sex differences in emotionality. *Sex Roles, 10,* 677–691.

Bishop, D. V. M. (2006). What causes specific language impairment in children? *Current Directions in Psychological Science, 15,* 217–221.

Bishop, E. G., Cherny, S. S., Corley, R., Plomin, R., DeFries, J. C., & Hewitt, J. K. (2003). Development genetic analysis of general cognitive ability from 1 to 12 years in a sample of adoptees, biological siblings, and twins. *Intelligence, 31,* 31–49.

Bivens, J. A., & Berk, L. E. (1990). A longitudinal study of the development of elementary school children's private speech. *Merrill-Palmer Quarterly, 36,* 443–463.

Bjorklund, D. F. (1987). How age changes in knowledge base contribute to the development of children's memory: An interpretive review. *Developmental Review, 7,* 93–130.

Bjorklund, D. F. (1997). In search of a metatheory for cognitive development (or, Piaget is dead and I don't feel so good myself). *Child Development, 68,* 144–148.

Bjorklund, D. F. (2003). Evolutionary psychology from a developmental systems perspective: Comment on Lickliter and Honeycutt (2003). *Psychological Bulletin, 129,* 836–841.

Bjorklund, D. F., & Brown, R. D. (1998). Physical play and cognitive development: Integrating activity, cognition, and education. *Child Development, 69,* 604–606.

Bjorklund, D. F., & Coyle, T. R. (1995). Utilization deficiencies in the development of memory strategies. In F. E. Weinert & W. Schneider (Eds.), *Research on memory development: State of the art and future directions.* Hillsdale, NJ: Erlbaum.

Bjorklund, D. F., & Ellis, B. J. (2005). Evolutionary psychology and child development: An emerging synthesis. In B. J. Ellis & D. F. Bjorklund (Eds.), *Origins of the social mind: Evolutionary psychology and child development* (pp. 3–18). New York: Guilford Press.

Bjorklund, D. F., & Green, B. L. (1992). The adaptive nature of cognitive immaturity. *American Psychologist, 47,* 46–54.

Blachford, S. L. (2002). *The Gale encyclopedia of genetic disorders.* Detroit, MI: Gale Group.

Black-Gutman, D., & Hickson, F. (1996). The relationship between racial attitudes and social-cognitive development in children: An Australian study. *Developmental Psychology, 32,* 448–456.

Blackson, T. C., Butler, T., Belsky, J., Ammerman, R. T., Shaw, D. S., & Tarter, R. E. (1999). Individual traits and family contexts predict sons' externalizing behavior and preliminary relative risk ratios for conduct disorder and substance use disorder outcomes. *Drug and Alcohol Dependence, 56,* 115–131.

Blackwell, L. S., Trzesniewski, K. H., & Dweck, C. S. (2007). Implicit theories of intelligence predict achievement across an adolescent transition: A longitudinal study and an intervention. *Child Development, 78,* 246–263.

Blades, M., & Spencer, C. (1987). Young children's strategies when using maps with landmarks. *Journal of Environmental Psychology, 7,* 201–217.

Blair, C. (2002). School readiness: Integrating cognition and emotion in a neurobiological conceptualization of children's functioning at school entry. *American Psychologist, 57,* 111–127.

Blair, C., & Razza, R. P. (2007). Relating effortful control, executive function, and false belief understanding to emerging math and literacy ability in kindergarten. *Child Development, 78,* 647–663.

Blakemore, C. (1976). The conditions required for the maintenance of binocularity in the kitten's visual cortex. *Journal of Physiology, 261,* 423–444.

Blakemore, S.-J. (2007). The social brain of a teenager. *The Psychologist, 20*(10), 600–602.

Blasi, A. (1980). Bridging moral cognition and moral action: A critical review of the literature. *Psychological Bulletin, 88,* 593–637.

Blasi, A. (1995). Moral understanding and the moral personality: The process of moral integration. In W. M. Kurtines & J. L. Gewirtz (Eds.), *Moral development: An introduction.* Boston: Allyn & Bacon.

Bleeker, M. M., & Jacobs, J. E. (2004). Achievement in math and science: Do mothers' beliefs matter 12 years later? *Journal of Educational Psychology, 96,* 97–109.

Block, J. H. (1979). Another look at sex differentiation in the socialization behaviors of mothers and fathers. In J. Sherman & F. L. Denmark (Eds.), *Psychology of women: Future of research.* New York: Psychological Dimensions.

Block, J. H. (1983). Differential premises arising from differential socialization of the sexes: Some conjectures. *Child Development, 54,* 1335–1354.

Block, N. (1999). How heritability misleads about race. In A. Montagu (Ed.), *Race and IQ* (expanded ed., pp. 444–486). New York: Oxford University Press.

Bloom, B. S. (1964). *Stability and change in human characteristics.* New York: Wiley.

Bloom, K., Russell, A., & Wassenberg, K. (1987). Turn taking affects the quality of infant vocalizations. *Journal of Child Language, 14,* 211–227.

Bloom, L., & Lahey, M. (1978). *Language development and language disorders.* New York: Wiley.

Bloom, L., & Tinker, E. (2001). The intentionality model and language acquisition. *Monographs of the Society for Research in Child Development, 66*(4, Serial No. 267).

Blyth, D. A., Simmons, R. G., & Zakin, D. F. (1985). Satisfaction with body image for early adolescent females: The impact of pubertal timing within different school environments. *Journal of Youth and Adolescence, 14,* 207–225.

Boccia, M., & Campos, J. J. (1989). Maternal emotional signals, social referencing, and infants' reactions to strangers. In N. Eisenberg (Ed.), *New directions for child development* (Vol. 44, pp. 25–49). San Francisco: Jossey-Bass.

Bochenhauer, M. H. (1990, April.) *Connections: Geographic education and the National Geographic Society.* Paper presented at the annual meeting of the American Educational Research Association, Boston.

Bodrova, E., & Leong, D. J. (1996). *Tools of the mind: The Vygotskian approach to early childhood education.* Upper Saddle River, NJ: Merrill/Prentice Hall.

Boekaerts, M. (1993). Being concerned with well-being and with learning. *Educational Psychologist, 28,* 149–167.

Boekaerts, M., de Koning, E., & Vedder, P. (2006). Goal-directed behavior and contextual factors in the classroom: An innovative approach to the study of multiple goals. *Educational Psychologist, 41,* 33–51.

Bohannon, J. N., MacWhinney, B., & Snow, C. (1990). No negative evidence revisited: Beyond learnability, or who has to prove what to whom. *Developmental Psychology, 26,* 221–226.

Bokhorst, C. L., Westenberg, P. M., Oosterlaan, J., & Heyne, D. A. (2008). Changes in social fears across childhood and adolescence: Age-related differences in the factor structure of the Fear Survey Schedule for Children—Revised. *Journal of Anxiety Disorders, 22,* 135–142.

Boling, C. J., & Evans, W. H. (2008). Reading success in the secondary classroom. *Preventing School Failure, 52*(2), 59–66.

Bong, M. (2001). Between- and within-domain relations of academic motivation among middle and high school students: Self-efficacy, task-value, and achievement goals. *Journal of Educational Psychology, 93,* 23–34.

Bong, M., & Skaalvik, E. M. (2003). Academic self-concept and self-efficacy: How different are they really? *Educational Psychology Review, 15,* 1–40.

Boom, J., Brugman, D., & van der Heijden, P. G. M. (2001). Hierarchical structure of moral stages assessed by a sorting task. *Child Development, 72,* 535–548.

Borkowski, J. G., Bisconti, T., Willard, C. C., Keogh, D. A., Whitman, T. L., & Weed, K. (2002). The adolescent as parent: Influences on children's intellectual, academic, and socioemotional development. In J. G. Borkowski, S. L. Ramey, & M. Bristol-Power (Eds.), *Parenting and the child's world: Influences on academic, intellectual, and social-emotional development* (pp. 161–184). Mahwah, NJ: Erlbaum.

Borkowski, J. G., & Burke, J. E. (1996). Theories, models, and measurements of executive functioning. In G. R. Lyon & N. A. Krasnegor (Eds.), *Attention, memory, and executive function* (pp. 235–261). Baltimore: Brookes.

Bornstein, M. H. (2006a). Parenting science and practice. In W. Damon & R. M. Lerner (Eds. in Chief) & K. A. Renninger & I. E. Sigel (Vol. Eds.), *Handbook of child psychology: Vol. 4. Child psychology in practice* (6th ed., pp. 893–949). Hoboken, NJ: Wiley.

Bornstein, M. H. (2006b). On the significance of social relationships in the development of children's earliest symbolic play: An ecological perspective. In A. Göncü & S. Gaskins (Eds.), *Play and development: Evolutionary, sociocultural, and functional perspectives* (pp. 101–129) Mahwah, NJ: Erlbaum.

Bornstein, M. H., & Cote, L. R., with Maital, S., Painter, K., Park, S., Pascual, L., et al. (2004). Cross-linguistic analysis of vocabulary in young children: Spanish, Dutch, French, Hebrew, Italian, Korean, and American English. *Child Development, 75,* 1115–1139.

Bornstein, M. H., Haynes, O. M., Pascual, L., Painter, K. M., & Galperin, C. (1999). Play in two societies: Pervasiveness of process, specificity of structure. *Child Development, 70,* 317–331.

Bortfeld, H., Morgan, J. L., Golinkoff, R. M., & Rathbun, K. (2005). Mommy and me: Familiar names help launch babies into speech-stream segmentation. *Psychological Science, 16,* 298–304.

Bortfeld, H., & Whitehurst, G. J. (2001). Sensitive periods in first language acquisition. In D. B. Bailey, Jr., J. T. Bruer, F. J. Symons, & J. W. Lichtman (Eds.), *Critical thinking about critical periods* (pp. 173–192). Baltimore: Brookes.

Bosacki, S. L. (2000). Theory of mind and self-concept in preadolescents: Links with gender and language. *Journal of Educational Psychology, 92,* 709–717.

Boscardin, C. K., Muthén, B., Francis, D. J., & Baker, E. L. (2008). Early identification of reading difficulties using heterogeneous developmental trajectories. *Journal of Educational Psychology, 100,* 192–208.

Botvin, G. J., & Scheier, L. M. (1997). Preventing drug abuse and violence. In D. K. Wilson, J. R. Rodrigue, & W. C. Taylor (Eds.), *Health-promoting and health-compromising behaviors among minority adolescents* (pp. 55–86). Washington, DC: American Psychological Association.

Bouchard, T. J., & McGue, M. (1981). Familial studies of intelligence: A review. *Science, 212,* 1056.

Bouchard, T. J., Jr. (1997). IQ similarity in twins reared apart: Findings and responses to critics. In R. J. Sternberg & E. L. Grigorenko (Eds.), *Intelligence, heredity, and environment* (pp. 126–160). Cambridge, England: Cambridge University Press.

Bouffard, T., Marcoux, M.-F., Vezeau, C., & Bordeleau, L. (2003). Changes in self-perceptions of competence and intrinsic motivation among elementary schoolchildren. *British Journal of Educational Psychology, 73,* 171–186.

Boutte, G. S., & McCormick, C. B. (1992). Authentic multicultural activities: Avoiding pseudomulticulturalism. *Childhood Education, 68*(3), 140–144.

Bowlby, J. (1951). *Maternal care and mental health.* Geneva, Switzerland: World Health Organization.

Bowlby, J. (1958). The nature of the child's tie to his mother. *International Journal of Psycho-Analysis, 39,* 350–373.

Bowlby, J. (1969/1982). *Attachment and loss: Vol. 1. Attachment* (2nd ed.). New York: Basic Books.

Bowlby, J. (1973). *Attachment and loss: Vol. 2. Separation: Anxiety and anger.* New York: Basic Books.

Bowlby, J. (1988). *A secure base: Parent–child attachment and healthy human development.* New York: Basic Books.

Bowman, B. T. (1989). Educating language-minority children: Challenges and opportunities. *Phi Delta Kappan, 71,* 118–120.

Boykin, A. W. (1994). Harvesting talent and culture: African-American children and educational reform. In R. J. Rossi (Ed.), *Schools and students at risk: Context and framework for positive change.* New York: Teachers College Press.

Brabham, E. G., & Lynch-Brown, C. (2002). Effects of teachers' reading-aloud styles on vocabulary acquisition and comprehension of students in the early elementary grades. *Journal of Educational Psychology, 94,* 465–473.

Bracken, B. A., & McCallum, R. S. (1998). *Universal Nonverbal Intelligence Test.* Itasca, IL: Riverside.

Bracken, B. A., McCallum, R. S., & Shaughnessy, M. F. (1999). An interview with Bruce A. Bracken and R. Steve McCallum, authors of the Universal Nonverbal Intelligence Test (UNIT). *North American Journal of Psychology, 1,* 277–288.

Bracken, B. A., & Walker, K. C. (1997). The utility of intelligence tests for preschool children. In D. P. Flanagan, J. L. Genshaft, & P. L. Harrison (Eds.), *Contemporary intellectual assessment: Theories, tests, and issues* (pp. 484–502). New York: Guilford Press.

Bradley, L., & Bryant, P. (1991). Phonological skills before and after learning to read. In S. A. Brady & D. P. Shankweiler (Eds.), *Phonological processes in literacy.* Hillsdale, NJ: Erlbaum.

Bradley, R. H., & Caldwell, B. M. (1984). The relation of infants' home environments to achievement test performance in first grade: A follow-up study. *Child Development, 55,* 803–809.

Bradley, R. H., Corwyn, R. F., McAdoo, H., & Coll, C. (2001). The home environments of children in the United States: Part I. Variations by age, ethnicity, and poverty status. *Child Development, 72,* 1844–1867.

Bradley-Johnson, S. (2001). Cognitive assessment for the youngest children: A critical review of tests. *Journal of Psychoeducational Assessments, 19,* 19–44.

Bradshaw, P. (2001). What about sharing? In B. Rogoff, C. G. Turkanis, & L. Bartlett (Eds.), *Learning together: Children and adults in a school community* (pp. 108–120). New York: Oxford University Press.

Braine, L. G., Schauble, L., Kugelmass, S., & Winter, A. (1993). Representation of depth by children: Spatial strategies and lateral biases. *Developmental Psychology, 29,* 466–479.

Brainerd, C. J. (2003). Jean Piaget, learning research, and American education. In B. J. Zimmerman & D. H. Schunk (Eds.), *Educational psychology: A century of contributions* (pp. 251–287). Mahwah, NJ: Erlbaum.

Brainerd, C. J., & Reyna, V. F. (2005). *The science of false memory.* Oxford, England: Oxford University Press.

Bramlett, M. D., & Mosher, W. D. (2002). Cohabitation, marriage, divorce, and remarriage in the United States. National Center for Health Statistics. *Vital and Health Statistics, 23*(22).

Branch, C. (1999). Race and human development. In R. H. Sheets & E. R. Hollins (Eds.), *Racial and ethnic identity in school practices: Aspects of human development* (pp. 7–28). Mahwah, NJ: Erlbaum.

Brannon, M. E. (2002). The development of ordinal numerical knowledge in infancy. *Cognition, 83,* 223–240.

Braswell, G. S., & Callanan, M. A. (2003). Learning to draw recognizable graphic representations during mother-child interactions. *Merrill-Palmer Quarterly, 49,* 471–494.

Brauner, J., Gordic, B., & Zigler, E. (2004). Putting the child back into child care: Combining care and education for children ages 3–5. *Social Policy Report, 18* (Society for Research in Child Development).

Brazelton Institute. (2008). *The Neonatal Behavioral Assessment Scale: What is it? Understanding the baby's language.* Retrieved February 29, 2008, from http://www.brazelton-institute.com/intro.html

Brazelton, T. B., & Nugent, J. K. (1995). *The Neonatal Behavioral Assessment Scale.* London, England: Mac Keith Press.

Bredekamp, S., & Copple, C. (Eds.). (1997). *Developmentally appropriate practice in early childhood programs* (3rd ed.). Washington, DC: National Association for the Education of Young Children.

Brendgen, M., Boivin, M., Vitaro, F., Bukowski, W. M., Dionne, G., Tremblay, R. E., & Pérusse, D. (2008). Linkages between children's and their friends' social and physical aggression: Evidence for a gene-environment interaction? *Child Development, 79,* 13–29.

Brendgen, M., Wanner, G., Vitaro, F., Bukowski, W. M., & Tremblay, R. E. (2007). Verbal abuse by the teacher during childhood and academic, behavioral, and emotional adjustment in young adulthood. *Journal of Educational Psychology, 99,* 26–38.

Brenner, E. M., & Salovey, P. (1997). Emotion regulation during childhood: Developmental, interpersonal, and individual considerations. In P. Salovey & D. J. Sluyter (Eds.), *Emotional development and emotional intelligence: Educational implications* (pp. 168–195). New York: Basic Books.

Brenner, L. A., Koehler, D. J., Liberman, V., & Tversky, A. (1996). Overconfidence in probability and frequency judgments: A critical examination. *Organizational Behavior and Human Decision Processes, 65,* 212–219.

Bretherton, I. (1991). Pouring new wine into old bottles: The social self as internal working model. In M. R. Gunnar & L. A. Sroufe (Eds.), *Self processes and development: The Minnesota Symposia on Child Development* (Vol. 23, pp. 1–42). Hillsdale, NJ: Erlbaum.

Bretherton, I., Fritz, J., Zahn-Waxler, C., & Ridgeway, D. (1986). Learning to talk about emotions: A functionalist perspective. *Child Development, 57,* 529–548.

Brett, D., Pospisil, H., Valcárcel, J., Reich, J., & Bork, P. (2002). Alternative splicing and genome complexity. *Nature Genetics, 30,* 29–30.

Brinton, B., & Fujiki, M. (1984). Development of topic manipulation skills in discourse. *Journal of Speech and Hearing Research, 27,* 350–358.

Britt, M. A., Rouet, J-F., Georgi, M. C., & Perfetti, C. A. (1994). Learning from history texts: From causal analysis to argument models. In G. Leinhardt, I. L. Beck, & C. Stainton (Eds.), *Teaching and learning in history.* Hillsdale, NJ: Erlbaum.

Broderick, P. C., & Korteland, C. (2004). A prospective study of rumination and depression in early adolescence. *Clinical Child Psychology and Psychiatry, 9,* 383–396.

Brody, G. H. (2004). Siblings' direct and indirect contributions to child development. *Current Directions in Psychological Science, 13,* 124–126.

Brody, G. H., Chen, Y.-F., Murry, V. M., Ge, X., Simons, R. L., Gibbons, F. X., et al. (2006). Perceived discrimination and the adjustment of African American youths: A five-year longitudinal analysis with contextual moderation effects. *Child Development, 77,* 1170–1189.

Brody, G. H., & Shaffer, D. R. (1982). Contributions of parents and peers to children's moral socialization. *Developmental Review, 2,* 31–75.

Brody, G. H., Stoneman, Z., & McCoy, J. K. (1994). Forecasting sibling relationships in early adolescence from child temperament and family processes in middle childhood. *Child Development, 65,* 771–784.

Brody, N. (1992). *Intelligence.* New York: Academic Press.

Brody, N. (1997). Intelligence, schooling, and society. *American Psychologist, 52,* 1046–1050.

Brody, N. (2006). Geocentric theory: A valid interpretation of Gardner's theory of intelligence. In J. A. Schaler (Ed.), *Howard Gardner under fire: The rebel psychologist faces his critics* (pp. 73–94). Chicago: Open Court.

Brodzinsky, D. M. (2006). Family structural openness and communication openness as predictors in the adjustment of adopted children. *Adoption Quarterly, 9*(4), 1–19.

Bronfenbrenner, U. (1979). *The ecology of human development: Experiments by nature and design.* Cambridge, MA: Harvard University Press.

Bronfenbrenner, U. (1999). Is early intervention effective? Some studies of early education in familial and extra-familial settings. In A. Montagu (Ed.), *Race and IQ* (expanded ed., pp. 343–378). New York: Oxford University Press.

Bronfenbrenner, U. (2001). The bioecological theory of human development. In N. J. Smelser & P. B. Baltes (Eds.), *International encyclopedia of the social and behavioral sciences* (Vol. 10, pp. 6963–6970). New York: Elsevier.

Bronfenbrenner, U. (2005). *Making human beings human: Bioecological perspectives on human development.* Thousand Oaks, CA: Sage.

Bronfenbrenner, U., Alvarez, W. F., & Henderson, C. R., Jr. (1984). Working and watching: Maternal employment status and parents' perceptions of their three-year-old children. *Child Development, 55,* 1362–1379.

Bronfenbrenner, U., & Morris, P. A. (2006). The bioecological model of human development. In W. Damon & R. M. Lerner (Eds. in Chief) & R. M. Lerner (Vol. Ed.), *Handbook of child psychology: Vol. 1. Theoretical models of human development* (6th ed., pp. 793–828). Hoboken, NJ: Wiley.

Bronson, M. B. (2000). *Self-regulation in early childhood: Nature and nurture.* New York: Guilford Press.

Bronson, W. C. (1981). Toddlers' behaviors with agemates: Issues of interaction, cognition, and affect. *Monographs of Infancy, 1,* 127.

Brooks-Gunn, J. (1989). Pubertal processes and the early adolescent transition. In W. Damon (Ed.), *Child development today and tomorrow* (pp. 155–176). San Francisco: Jossey-Bass.

Brooks-Gunn, J. (2003). Do you believe in magic? What we can expect from early childhood intervention programs. *Social Policy Report, 17*(1). Ann Arbor, MI: Society for Research in Child Development.

Brooks-Gunn, J., & Donahue, E. H. (2008). Introducing the issue. *Future of Children, 18*(1), 3–10.

Brooks-Gunn, J., & Furstenberg, F. F. (1990). Coming of age in the era of AIDS: Puberty, sexuality, and contraception. *Milbrank Quarterly, 68*(Suppl. 1), 59–84.

Brooks-Gunn, J., Klebanov, P. K., & Duncan, G. J. (1996). Ethnic differences in children's intelligence test scores: Role of economic deprivation, home environment, and maternal characteristics. *Child Development, 67,* 396–408.

Brooks-Gunn, J., & Paikoff, R. L. (1992). Changes in self-feelings during the transition toward adolescence. In H. R. McGurk (Ed.), *Childhood social development: Contemporary perspectives* (pp. 63–97). Hillsdale, NJ: Erlbaum.

Brooks-Gunn, J., & Paikoff, R. L. (1993). "Sex is a gamble, kissing is a game": Adolescent sexuality and health promotion. In S. G. Millstein, A. C. Petersen, & E. O. Nightingale (Eds.), *Promoting the health of adolescents: New directions for the twenty-first century* (pp. 180–208). New York: Oxford University Press.

Brophy, J. E. (2004). *Motivating students to learn* (2nd ed.). Mahwah, NJ: Erlbaum.

Brophy, J. E., & Alleman, J. (1996). *Powerful social studies for elementary students.* Fort Worth, TX: Harcourt Brace.

Brophy, J. E., & VanSledright, B. (1997). *Teaching and learning history in elementary schools.* New York: Teachers College Press.

Brown, A. L., & Campione, J. C. (1994). Guided discovery in a community of learners. In K. McGilly (Ed.), *Classroom lessons: Integrating cognitive theory and classroom practice.* Cambridge, MA: MIT Press.

Brown, A. L., & Campione, J. C. (1996). Psychological theory and the design of innovative learning environments: On procedures, principles, and systems. In L. Schauble & R. Glaser (Eds.), *Innovations in learning: New environments for education.* Mahwah, NJ: Erlbaum.

Brown, A. L., & Palincsar, A. S. (1987). Reciprocal teaching of comprehension strategies: A natural history of one program for enhancing learning. In J. Borkowski & J. D. Day (Eds.), *Cognition in special education: Comparative approaches to retardation, learning disabilities, and giftedness.* Norwood, NJ: Ablex.

Brown, B. B. (1990). Peer groups and peer culture. In S. S. Feldman & G. R. Elliott (Eds.), *At the threshold: The developing adolescent* (pp. 171–196). Cambridge, MA: Harvard University Press.

Brown, B. B. (1993). School culture, social politics, and the academic motivation of U.S. citizens. In T. M. Tomlinson (Ed.), *Motivating students to learn: Overcoming barriers to high achievement.* Berkeley, CA: McCutchan.

Brown, B. B., Eicher, S. A., & Petrie, S. (1986). The importance of peer group ("crowd") affiliation in adolescence. *Journal of Adolescence, 9,* 73–96.

Brown, J. D., & Siegel, J. D. (1988). Exercise as a buffer of life stress: A prospective study of adolescent health. *Health Psychology, 7,* 341–353.

Brown, J. R., & Dunn, J. (1996). Continuities in emotion understanding from three to six years. *Child Development, 67,* 789–802.

Brown, J. V., Bakeman, R., Coles, C. D., Platzman, K. A., & Lynch, M. E. (2004). Prenatal cocaine exposure: A comparison of 2-year-old children in parental and nonparental care. *Child Development, 75,* 1282–1295.

Brown, L. M., Tappan, M. B., & Gilligan, C. (1995). Listening to different voices. In W. M. Kurtines & J. L. Gewirtz (Eds.), *Moral development: An introduction.* Boston: Allyn & Bacon.

Brown, R. (1973). *A first language: The early stages.* Cambridge, MA: Harvard University Press.

Brown, R., & Hanlon, C. (1970). Derivational complexity and order of acquisition in child speech. In J. R. Hayes (Ed.), *Cognition and the development of language.* New York: Wiley.

Brown, R. T., Reynolds, C. R., & Whitaker, J. S. (1999). Bias in mental testing since *Bias in Mental Testing. School Psychology Quarterly, 14,* 208–238.

Brown-Mizuno, C. (1990). Success strategies for learners who are learning disabled as well as gifted. *Teaching Exceptional Children, 23*(1), 10–12.

Brownell, M. T., Mellard, D. F., & Deshler, D. D. (1993). Differences in the learning and transfer performance between students with learning disabilities and other low-achieving students on problem-solving tasks. *Learning Disabilities Quarterly, 16,* 138–156.

Bruer, J. T. (1999). *The myth of the first three years: A new understanding of early brain development and lifelong learning.* New York: Free Press.

Bruer, J. T., & Greenough, W. T. (2001). The subtle science of how experience affects the brain. In D. B. Bailey, Jr., J. T. Bruer, F. J. Symons, & J. W. Lichtman (Eds.), *Critical thinking about critical periods* (pp. 209–232). Baltimore: Brookes.

Bruner, J. S. (1966). *Toward a theory of instruction.* Cambridge, MA: Harvard University Press.

Bruner, J. S. (1972). The nature and uses of immaturity. *American Psychologist, 27,* 687–708.

Bruner, J. S. (1983). The acquisition of pragmatic commitments. In R. M. Golinkoff (Ed.), *The transition from prelinguistic to linguistic communication* (pp. 27–42). Hillsdale, NJ: Erlbaum.

Bruner, J. S., & Sherwood, V. (1976). Early rule structure: The case of "peekaboo." In R. Harre (Ed.), *Life sentences* (pp. 55–62). London: Wiley.

Bruni, M. (1998). *Fine-motor skills in children with Down syndrome: A guide for parents and professionals.* Bethesda, MD: Woodbine House.

Bryan, J. H., Redfield, J., & Mader, S. (1971). Words and deeds concerning altruism and subsequent reinforcement power of the model. *Child Development, 42,* 1501–1508.

Bryan, T., Burstein, K., & Bryan, J. (2001). Students with learning disabilities: Homework problems and promising practices. *Educational Psychologist, 36,* 167–180.

Bryant, J. B. (2001). Language in social contexts: Communicative competence. In J. B. Gleason (Ed.), *The development of language* (pp. 167–209). Boston: Allyn & Bacon.

Bryant, P., Nunes, T., & Aidinis, A. (1999). Different morphemes, same spelling problems: Cross-linguistic developmental studies. In M. Harris & G. Hatano (Eds.), *Learning to read and write: A cross-linguistic perspective.* Cambridge, England: Cambridge University Press.

Buchanan, C. M., Eccles, J. S., & Becker, J. B. (1992). Are adolescents the victims of raging hormones: Evidence for activational effects of hormones on moods and behaviors at adolescence. *Psychological Bulletin, 111,* 62–107.

Buchoff, T. (1990). Attention deficit disorder: Help for the classroom teacher. *Childhood Education, 67*(2), 86–90.

Budd, G. M., & Volpe. S. L. (2006). School-based obesity prevention: Research, challenges, and recommendations. *Journal of School Health, 76,* 485–495.

Budwig, N. (1995). *A developmental-functionalist approach to child language.* Mahwah, NJ: Erlbaum.

Buehl, M. M., & Alexander, P. A. (2006). Examining the dual nature of epistemological beliefs. *International Journal of Educational Research, 45,* 28–42.

Buhrmester, D. (1992). The developmental courses of sibling and peer relationships. In F. Boer & J. Dunn (Eds.), *Children's sibling relationships: Developmental and clinical issues.* Hillsdale, NJ: Erlbaum.

Buhrmester, D. (1996). Need fulfillment, interpersonal competence, and the developmental contexts of friendship. In W. M. Bukowski, A. F. Newcomb, & W. W. Hartup (Eds.), *The company they keep: Friendship during childhood and adolescence* (pp. 158–185). New York: Cambridge University Press.

Buijzen, M., & Valkenburg, P. M. (2003). The effects of television advertising on materialism, parent–child conflict, and unhappiness: A review of research. *Applied Developmental Psychology, 24,* 437–456.

Bullock, J. R. (1993). Children's loneliness and their relationships with family and peers. *Family Relations, 42,* 46–49.

Bullock, L. M., & Gable, R. A. (2006). Programs for children and adolescents with emotional and behavioral disorders in the United States: A historical overview, current perspectives, and future programs. *Preventing School Failure, 50,* 7–13.

Bullock, M., & Ziegler, A. (1999). Scientific reasoning: Developmental and individual differences. In F. E. Weinert & W. Schneider (Eds.), *Individual development from 3 to 12: Findings from the Munich longitudinal study.* New York: Cambridge University Press.

Burhans, K. K., & Dweck, C. S. (1995). Helplessness in early childhood: The role of contingent worth. *Child Development, 66,* 1719–1738.

Burkam, D. T., Lee, V. E., & Smerdon, B. A. (1997). Gender and science learning early in high school: Subject matter and laboratory experiences. *American Educational Research Journal, 34,* 297–331.

Burnett, P. (2001). Elementary students' preferences for teacher praise. *Journal of Classroom Interaction, 36,* 16–23.

Burns, C. E., Brady, M. A., Dunn, A. M., & Starr, N. B. (2000). *Pediatric primary care: A handbook for nurse practitioners,* (2nd ed.). Philadelphia: Saunders.

Burstyn, J. N., Bender, G., Casella, R., Gordon, H. W., Guerra, D. P., Luschen, K. V., et al. (2001). *Preventing violence in schools: A challenge to American democracy.* Mahwah, NJ: Erlbaum.

Burstyn, J. N., & Stevens, R. (2001). Involving the whole school in violence prevention. In J. N. Burstyn, G. Bender, R. Casella, H. W. Gordon, D. P. Guerra, K. V. Luschen, R. Stevens, & K. M. Williams (Eds.), *Preventing violence in schools: A challenge to American democracy* (pp. 139–158). Mahwah, NJ: Erlbaum.

Burton, L. M. (1992). Black grandparents rearing children of drug addicted parents: Stressors, outcomes, and social service needs. *The Gerontologist, 32,* 744–751.

Burton, S., & Mitchell, P. (2003). Judging who knows best about yourself: Developmental change in citing the self across middle childhood. *Child Development, 74,* 426–443.

Butler, D. L., & Winne, P. H. (1995). Feedback and self-regulated learning: A theoretical synthesis. *Review of Educational Research, 65,* 245–281.

Butler, R. (1994). Teacher communication and student interpretations: Effects of teacher responses to failing students on attributional inferences in two age groups. *British Journal of Educational Psychology, 64,* 277–294.

Butler, R. N. (1963). The life review: An interpretation of reminiscence in the aged. *Psychiatry, 26,* 65–76.

Butterfield, E. C., & Ferretti, R. P. (1987). Toward a theoretical integration of cognitive hypotheses about intellectual differences among children. In J. G. Borkowski & J. D. Day (Eds.), *Cognition in special children: Approaches to retardation, learning disabilities, and giftedness.* Norwood, NJ: Ablex.

Byne, W. (1997). Why we cannot conclude that sexual orientation is primarily a biological phenomenon. *Journal of Homosexuality, 34,* 73–80.

Byrne, B. M. (2002). Validating the measurement and structure of self-concept: Snapshots of past, present, and future research. *American Psychologist, 57,* 897–909.

Byrne, B. M., & Shavelson, R. J. (1986, April). *On gender differences in the structure of adolescent self concept.* Paper presented at the annual meeting of the American Educational Research Association, San Francisco.

Byrnes, J. P. (1996). *Cognitive development and learning in instructional contexts.* Boston: Allyn & Bacon.

Byrnes, J. P. (2001). *Minds, brains, and learning: Understanding the psychological and educational relevance of neuroscientific research.* New York: Guilford Press.

Cain, C. S. (2006). *Attachment disorders: Treatment strategies for traumatized children.* Lantham, MD: Jason Aronson Publishing.

Cain, K., & Oakhill, J. (1998). Comprehension skill and inference-making ability: Issues of causality. In C. Hulme & R. M. Joshi (Eds.), *Reading and spelling: Development and disorders.* Mahwah, NJ: Erlbaum.

Cairns, H. S. (1996). *The acquisition of language* (2nd ed.). Austin, TX: Pro-Ed.

Cairns, R. B., Cairns, B. D., Neckerman, H. J., Ferguson, L. L., & Gariépy, J.-L. (1989). Growth and aggression: 1. Childhood to early adolescence. *Developmental Psychology, 25,* 320–330.

Caldwell, M. S., Rudolph, K. D., Troop-Gordon, W., & Kim, D. (2004). Reciprocal influences among rela-

tional self-views, social disengagement, and peer stress during early adolescence. *Child Development, 75,* 1140–1154.

Calfee, R. C., & Masuda, W. V. (1997). Classroom assessment as inquiry. In G. D. Phye (Ed.), *Handbook of classroom assessment: Learning, achievement, and adjustment.* San Diego, CA: Academic Press.

Calin-Jageman, R. J., & Ratner, H. H. (2005). The role of encoding in the self-explanation effect. *Cognition and Instruction, 23,* 523–543.

Calkins, S. D., Hungerford, A., & Dedmon, S. E. (2004). Mothers' interactions with temperamentally frustrated infants. *Infant Mental Health Journal, 25,* 219–239.

Callaghan, T., Rochat, P., Lillard, A., Claux, M. L., Odden, H., Itakura, S., Tapanaya, S., & Singh, S. (2005). Synchrony in the onset of mental-state reasoning. *Psychological Science, 16,* 378–384.

Callanan, M. A., & Oakes, L. M. (1992). Preschoolers' questions and parents' explanations: Causal thinking in everyday activity. *Cognitive Development, 7,* 213–233.

Calvert, S. L. (2008). Children as consumers: Advertising and marketing. *Future of Children, 18*(1), 205–234.

Cameron, C. A., Hunt, A. K., & Linton, M. J. (1996). Written expression as recontextualization: Children write in social time. *Educational Psychology Review, 8,* 125–150.

Cameron, J. (2001). Negative effects of reward on intrinsic motivation—a limited phenomenon: Comment on Deci, Koestner, and Ryan (2001). *Review of Educational Research, 71,* 29–42.

Campbell, A. (1984). *The girls in the gang: A report from New York City.* New York: Basil Blackwell.

Campbell, D. T., & Stanley, J. C. (1963). Experimental and quasi-experimental designs for research on teaching. In N. L. Gage (Ed.), *Handbook of research on teaching* (pp. 171–246). Chicago: Rand McNally.

Campbell, D. W., Eaton, W. O., McKeen, N. A., & Mitsutake, G. (1999, April). *The rise and fall of motor activity: Evidence of age-related change from 7 to 14 years.* Paper presented at the biennial meeting of the Society for Research in Child Development, Albuquerque, NM.

Campbell, F. A., & Ramey, C. T. (1994). Effects of early intervention on intellectual and academic achievement: A follow-up study of children from low-income families. *Child Development, 65,* 684–698.

Campbell, F. A., Ramey, C. T., Pungello, E., Sparling, J., & Miller-Johnson, S. (2002). Early childhood education: Young adult outcomes from the Abecedarian Project. *Applied Developmental Science, 6,* 42–57.

Campbell, L., Campbell, B., & Dickinson, D. (1998). *Teaching and learning through multiple intelligences* (2nd ed.). Boston: Allyn & Bacon.

Campbell, T. F., Dollaghan, C. A., Rockette, H. E., Paradise, J. L., Feldman, H. M., Shriberg, L. D., et al. (2003). Risk factors for speech delay of unknown origin in 3-year-old children. *Child Development, 74,* 346–357.

Campione, J. C., Shapiro, A. M., & Brown, A. L. (1995). Forms of transfer in a community of learners: Flexible learning and understanding. In A. McKeough, J. Lupart, & A. Marini (Eds.), *Teaching for transfer: Fostering generalization in learning.* Mahwah, NJ: Erlbaum.

Campos, J. J., Bertenthal, B. I., & Kermoian, R. (1992). Early experiences and emotional development: The emergence of wariness of heights. *Psychological Science, 3,* 61–64.

Campos, J. J., Frankel, C. B., & Camras, L. (2004). On the nature of emotion regulation. *Child Development, 75,* 377–394.

Camras, L. A., Chen, Y., Bakeman, R., Norris, K., & Cain, T. R. (2006). Culture, ethnicity, and children's facial expressions: A study of European American, mainland Chinese, Chinese American, and adopted Chinese girls. *Emotion, 6,* 103–114.

Camras, L. A., Malatesta, C., & Izard, C. (1991). The development of facial expressions in infancy. In R. S. Feldman & B. Rime (Eds.), *Fundamentals of nonverbal behavior: Studies in emotion and social interaction* (pp. 73–105). New York: Cambridge University Press.

Canessa, E. (2007). Modeling of body mass index by Newton's second law. *Journal of Theoretical Biology, 248,* 646–656.

Canfield, R. L., & Smith, E. G. (1996). Number-based expectations and sequential enumeration by 5-month-old infants. *Developmental Psychology, 32,* 269–279.

Capelli, C. A., Nakagawa, N., & Madden, C. M. (1990). How children understand sarcasm: The role of context and intonation. *Child Development, 61,* 1824–1841.

Caplan, J. G., McElvain, C. K., & Walter, K. E. (2001). *Beyond the bell: A tool kit for creating after-school programs* (2nd ed.). Naperville, IL: North Central Regional Educational Laboratory.

Caplan, M., Vespo, J. E., Pedersen, J., & Hay, D. F. (1991). Conflict over resources in small groups of 1- and 2-year-olds. *Child Development, 62,* 1513–1524.

Caprara, G. V., Barbaranelli, C., Pastorelli, C., Bandura, A., & Zimbardo, P. G. (2000). Prosocial foundations of children's academic achievement. *Psychological Science, 11,* 302–306.

Capron, C., & Duyme, M. (1989). Assessment of effects of socio-economic status on IQ in a full cross-fostering study. *Nature, 340,* 552–554.

Cardelle-Elawar, M. (1992). Effects of teaching metacognitive skills to students with low mathematics ability. *Teaching and Teacher Education, 8,* 109–121.

Carey, S. (1978). The child as word learner. In M. Halle, J. Bresnan, & G. Miller (Eds.), *Linguistic theory and psychological reality.* Cambridge, MA: MIT Press.

Carey, S. (1985). *Conceptual change in childhood.* Cambridge, MA: MIT Press.

Carey, S., & Bartlett, E. (1978). Acquiring a single new word. *Papers and Reports on Child Language Development, 15,* 17–29.

Carey, S., Evans, R., Honda, M., Jay, E., & Unger, C. (1989). "An experiment is when you try it and see if it works": A study of grade 7 students' understanding of the construction of scientific knowledge. *International Journal of Science Education, 11,* 514–529.

Carlo, G., Koller, S., Raffaelli, M., & de Guzman, M. R. T. (2007). Culture-related strengths among Latin American families: A case study of Brazil. *Marriage and Family Review, 41*(3/4), 335–360.

Carlson, E. A., Sampson, M. C., & Sroufe, L. A. (2003). Implications of attachment theory and research for developmental-behavioral pediatrics. *Journal of Developmental and Behavioral Pediatrics, 24,* 364–379.

Carlson, N. R. (2007). *Physiology of behavior* (9th ed.). Boston: Pearson Allyn & Bacon.

Carns, D. (1973). Talking about sex: Notes on first coitus and the double sexual standard. *Journal of Marriage and Family, 35,* 677–688.

Caroli, M., Argentieri, L., Cardone, M., & Masi, A. (2004). Role of television in childhood obesity prevention. *International Journal of Obesity, 28,* S105–S108.

Caron, A. J., Caron, R. F., & MacLean, D. J. (1988). Infant discrimination of naturalistic emotional expressions: The role of face and voice. *Child Development, 59,* 604–616.

Carpenter, M., Nagell, K., & Tomasello, M. (1998). Social cognition, joint attention, and communicative competence from 9 to 15 months of age. *Monographs of the Society for Research in Child Development, 63*(4, Serial No. 255). Chicago: University of Chicago Press.

Carr, M., & Biddlecomb, B. (1998). Metacognition in mathematics from a constructivist perspective. In D. J. Hacker, J. Dunlosky, & A. C. Graesser (Eds.), *Metacognition in educational theory and practice* (pp. 69–91). Mahwah, NJ: Erlbaum.

Carr, M., & Schneider, W. (1991). Long-term maintenance of organizational strategies in kindergarten children. *Contemporary Educational Psychology, 16,* 61–72.

Carraher, T. N., Carraher, D. W., & Schliemann, A. D. (1985). Mathematics in the streets and in the schools. *British Journal of Developmental Psychology, 3,* 21–29.

Carranza, M. E. (2007). Building resilience and resistance against racism and discrimination among Salvadorian female youth in Canada. *Child and Family Social Work, 12,* 390–398.

Carroll, J. B. (1992). Cognitive abilities: The state of the art. *Psychological Science, 3,* 266–270.

Carroll, J. B. (1993). *Human cognitive abilities: A survey of factor-analytic studies.* New York: Cambridge University Press.

Carroll, J. B. (2003). The higher stratum structure of cognitive abilities: Current evidence supports *g* and about ten broad factors. *The scientific study of general intelligence: Tribute to Arthur Jensen* (pp. 5–21). Oxford, England: Elsevier.

Carter, D. E., Detine-Carter, S. L., & Benson, F. W. (1995). Interracial acceptance in the classroom. In H. C. Foot, A. J. Chapman, & J. R. Smith (Eds.), *Friendship and social relations in children* (pp. 117–143). New Brunswick, NJ: Transaction.

Carter, K. R. (1991). Evaluation of gifted programs. In N. Buchanan & J. Feldhusen (Eds.), *Conducting research and evaluation in gifted education: A handbook of methods and applications.* New York: Teachers College Press.

Carter, K., & Doyle, W. (2006). Classroom management in early childhood and elementary classrooms. In C. M. Evertson & C. S. Weinstein (Eds.), *Handbook of classroom management: Research, practice, and contemporary issues* (pp. 373–406). Mahwah, NJ: Erlbaum.

Carter, K. R., & Ormrod, J. E. (1982). Acquisition of formal operations by intellectually gifted children. *Gifted Child Quarterly, 26,* 110–115.

Cartledge, G., & Milburn, J. F. (1995). *Teaching social skills to children and youth: Innovative approaches* (3rd ed.). Needham Heights, MA: Allyn & Bacon.

Carver, P. R., Egan, S. K., & Perry, D. G. (2004). Children who question their heterosexuality. *Developmental Psychology, 40*(1), 43–53.

Case, R. (1985). *Intellectual development: Birth to adulthood.* Orlando, FL: Academic Press.

Case, R. (1991). *The mind's staircase: Exploring the conceptual underpinnings of children's thought and knowledge.* Hillsdale, NJ: Erlbaum.

Case, R., & Mueller, M. P. (2001). Differentiation, integration, and covariance mapping as fundamental processes in cognitive and neurological growth. In J. L. McClelland & R. S. Siegler (Eds.), *Mechanisms of cognitive development: Behavioral and neural perspectives* (pp. 185–219). Mahwah, NJ: Erlbaum.

Case, R., & Okamoto, Y., in collaboration with Griffin, S., McKeough, A., Bleiker, C., Henderson, B., & Stephenson, K. M. (1996). The role of central conceptual structures in the development of children's thought. *Monographs of the Society for Research in Child Development, 61*(1–2, Serial No. 246).

Case, R., Okamoto, Y., Henderson, B., & McKeough, A. (1993). Individual variability and consistency in cognitive development: New evidence for the existence of central conceptual structures. In R. Case & W. Edelstein (Eds.), *The new structuralism in cognitive development: Theory and research on individual pathways.* Basel, Switzerland: Karger.

Casella, R. (2001). The cultural foundations of peer mediation: Beyond a behaviorist model of urban school conflict. In J. N. Burstyn, G. Bender, R. Casella, H. W. Gordon, D. P. Guerra, K. V. Luschen, et al. *Preventing violence in schools: A challenge to American democracy* (pp. 159–179). Mahwah, NJ: Erlbaum.

Case-Smith, J. (1996). Fine motor outcomes in preschool children who receive occupational therapy services. *American Journal of Occupational Therapy, 50,* 52–61.

Casey, B. J., Giedd, J. N., & Thomas, K. M. (2000). Structural and functional brain development and its relation to cognitive development. *Biological Psychology, 54,* 241–257.

Caspi, A. (1998). Personality development across the life course. In W. Damon (Series Ed.) & N. Eisenberg (Vol. Ed.), *Handbook of child psychology: Vol. 3. Social, emotional, and personality development* (5th ed., pp. 311–388). New York: Wiley.

Caspi, A., Moffitt, T. E., Morgan, J., Rutter, M., Taylor, A., Arseneault, L., et al. (2004). Maternal expressed emotion predicts children's antisocial behavior problems: Using monozygotic-twin differences to identify environmental effects on behavioral development. *Developmental Psychology, 40,* 149–161.

Cassidy, M., & Berlin, L. J. (1994). The insecure/ambivalent pattern of attachment: Theory and research. *Child Development, 65,* 971–991.

Catania, J. A., Coates, T. J., Stall, R., Turner, H., Peterson, J., Hearst, N., et al. (1992). Prevalence of AIDS-related risk factors and condom use in the United States. *Science, 258,* 1101–1106.

Cattell, R. B. (1963). Theory of fluid and crystallized intelligence: A critical experiment. *Journal of Educational Psychology, 54,* 1–22.

Cattell, R. B. (1980). The heritability of fluid, *gf,* and crystallised, *gc,* intelligence, estimated by a least squares use of the MAVA method. *British Journal of Educational Psychology, 50,* 253–265.

Cattell, R. B. (1987). *Intelligence: Its structure, growth, and action.* Amsterdam: North-Holland.

Catts, H. W., Adlof, S. M., Hogan, T. P., & Weismer, S. E. (2005). Are specific language impairments and dyslexia distinct disorders? *Journal of Speech, Language and Hearing Research, 48,* 1378–1396.

Cavell, T. A., Hymel, S., Malcolm, K. T., & Seay, A. (2007). Socialization and interventions for antisocial youth. In J. E. Grusec & P. D. Hastings (Eds.), *Handbook of socialization: Theory and research* (pp. 42–67). New York: Guilford Press.

Cazden, C. B. (1968). The acquisition of noun and verb inflections. *Child Development, 39,* 433–448.

Cazden, C. B. (1976). Play with language and metalinguistic awareness: One dimension of language experience. In J. Bruner, A. Jolly, & K. Sylva (Eds.), *Play: Its role in development and evolution.* New York: Basic Books.

Ceci, S. J. (2003). Cast in six ponds and you'll reel in something: Looking back on 25 years of research. *American Psychologist, 58,* 855–864.

Ceci, S. J., & Roazzi, A. (1994). The effects of context on cognition: Postcards from Brazil. In R. J. Sternberg & R. K. Wagner (Eds.), *Mind in context: Interactionist perspectives on human intelligence.* Cambridge, England: Cambridge University Press.

Ceci, S. J., Rosenblum, T. B., & Kumpf, M. (1998). The shrinking gap between high- and low-scoring groups: Current trends and possible causes. In U. Neisser (Ed.), *The rising curve: Long-term gains in IQ and related measures* (pp. 287–302). Washington, DC: American Psychological Association.

Ceci, S. J., & Williams, W. M. (1997). Schooling, intelligence, and income. *American Psychologist, 52,* 1051–1058.

Centers for Disease Control and Prevention. (2002, Fall). *Planning for physical activity* (a BAM! Body and Mind Teacher's Corner resource). Retrieved January 19, 2003, from http://www.bam.gov/teachers/activities/planning.htm

Centers for Disease Control and Prevention. (2004). *Youth risk behavior surveillance—United States, 2003.* Atlanta: Author.

Centers for Disease Control and Prevention. (2005a). *Guidelines for effective school health education to prevent the spread of AIDS.* Retrieved June 19, 2005, from http://www.cdc.gov/HealthyYouth.sexual-behaviors/guidelines/guidelines.htm

Centers for Disease Control and Prevention. (2005b). *Making it happen: School nutrition success stories.* Retrieved May 25, 2005, from http://www.cdc.gov/HealthyYouth/nutrition/Making-It-Happen/success.htm

Centers for Disease Control and Prevention. (2005c). *Nutrition and the health of young people.* Atlanta: Author.

Centers for Disease Control and Prevention. (2005d). QuickStats: Total and primary cesarean rate and vaginal birth after previous cesarean (VBAC) rate—United States, 1989–2003. *Morbidity and Mortality Weekly Report, 54*(2), 46.

Centers for Disease Control and Prevention. (2006). *Youth risk behavior surveillance—United States, 2005. Morbidity and Mortality Weekly Report, 55* (No. SS-5). Atlanta: Author.

Centers for Disease Control and Prevention. (2007a). *Autism spectrum disorder fact sheet.* Retrieved January 22, 2008, from http://www.cdc.gov/ncbddd/autism/ActEarly/autism.html

Centers for Disease Control and Prevention. (2007b). *Overweight and obesity.* Retrieved January 31, 2008, from http://www.cdc.gov/nccdphp/dnpa/obesity/childhood/prevalence.htm

Cermak, L. S., & Craik, F. I. M. (Eds.). (1979). *Levels of processing in human memory.* Hillsdale, NJ: Erlbaum.

Certo, J., Cauley, K. M., & Chafin, C. (2002, April). *Students' perspectives on their high school experience.* Paper presented at the annual meeting of the American Educational Research Association, New Orleans, LA.

Chafel, J. A. (1991). The play of children: Developmental processes and policy implications. *Child & Youth Care Forum, 20,* 115–132.

Chafel, J. A. (1997). Schooling, the hidden curriculum, and children's conceptions of poverty. *Social Policy Report: Society for Research in Child Development, 11*(1), 1–18.

Chall, J. S. (1996). *Stages of reading development* (2nd ed.). Fort Worth, TX: Harcourt, Brace.

Chambers, J. H., & Ascione, F. R. (2001). The effects of prosocial and aggressive videogames on children's donating and helping. *Journal of Genetic Psychology, 148*(4), 499–505.

Champagne, A. B., & Bunce, D. M. (1991). Learning-theory-based science teaching. In S. M. Glynn, R. H. Yeany, & B. K. Britton (Eds.), *The psychology of learning science.* Hillsdale, NJ: Erlbaum.

Chandler, M., & Boyes, M. (1982). Social-cognitive development. In B. Wolman (Ed.), *Handbook of developmental psychology.* Upper Saddle River, NJ: Prentice Hall.

Chandler, M., & Moran, T. (1990). Psychopathy and moral development: A comparative study of delinquent and nondelinquent youth. *Development and Psychopathology, 2,* 227–246.

Chandler, M. J. (1987). The Othello effect: Essay on the emergence and eclipse of skeptical doubt. *Human Development, 30,* 137–159.

Chao, R. K. (1994). Beyond parental control and authoritarian parenting style: Understanding Chinese parenting through the cultural notion of training. *Child Development, 65,* 1111–1119.

Chao, R. K. (2000). Cultural explanations for the role of parenting in the school success of Asian-American children. In R. D. Taylor & M. C. Wang (Eds.), *Resilience across contexts: Family, work, culture, and community* (pp. 333–363). Mahwah, NJ: Erlbaum.

Chapman, M. (1988). *Constructive evolution: Origins and development of Piaget's thought.* Cambridge, England: Cambridge University Press.

Charity, A. H., Scarborough, H. S., & Griffin, D. M. (2004). Familiarity with school English in African American children and its relation to early reading achievement. *Child Development, 75,* 1340–1356.

Charles A. Dana Center. (1999). *Hope for urban education: A study of nine high-performing, high-poverty, urban elementary schools.* Washington, DC: U.S. Department of Education, Planning and Evaluation Service.

Charlesworth, W. R., & LaFreniere, P. (1983). Dominance, friendship, and resource utilization in preschool children's groups. *Ethology and Sociobiology, 4,* 175–186.

Charner, I., & Fraser, B. S. (1988). *Youth and work: What we know, what we don't know, what we need to know*. Washington, DC: Commission on Work, Family, and Citizenship. (ERIC Document Service No. ED 292 980)

Chase-Lansdale, P. L., Brooks-Gunn, J., & Zamsky, E. S. (1994). Young African-American multigenerational families in poverty: Quality of mothering and grandmothering. *Child Development, 65*, 373–393.

Chassin, L., Hussong, A., Barrera, M. Jr., Molina, B. S. G., Trim, R., & Ritter, J. (2004). Adolescent substance use. In R. M. Lerner & L. Steinberg (Eds.), *Handbook of adolescent psychology* (2nd ed., pp. 665–696). Hoboken, NJ: Wiley.

Chatterji, M. (2006). Reading achievement gaps, correlates, and moderators of early reading achievement: Evidence from the Early Childhood Longitudinal Study (ECLS) kindergarten to first grade sample. *Journal of Educational Psychology, 98*, 489–507.

Chavez, A., Martinez, C., & Soberanes, B. (1995). Effects of early malnutrition on late mental and behavioral performance. *Developmental Brain Dysfunction, 8*, 90–102.

Chavous, T. M., Bernat, D. H., Schmeelk-Cone, K., Caldwell, C. H., Kohn-Wood, L., et al. (2003). Racial identity and academic attainment among African American adolescents. *Child Development, 74*, 1076–1090.

Chazan-Cohen, R., Jerald, J., & Stark, D. R. (2001). A commitment to supporting the mental health of our youngest children. *Zero to Three, 22*(1), 4–12.

Chen, X., Anderson, R. C., Li, W., Hao, M., Wu, X., & Shu, H. (2004). Phonological awareness of bilingual and monolingual Chinese children. *Journal of Educational Psychology, 96*, 142–151.

Chen, X., Chang, L., & He, Y. (2003). The peer group as a context: Mediating and moderating effects on the relations between academic achievement and social functioning in Chinese children. *Child Development, 74*, 710–727.

Chen, X., Rubin, K. H., & Li, Z. (1995). Social functioning and adjustment in Chinese children. *Developmental Psychology, 31*, 531–539.

Chen, Z., Sanchez, R. P., & Campbell, T. (1997). From beyond to within their grasp: The rudiments of analogical problem solving in 10- and 13-month-olds. *Developmental Psychology, 33*, pp. 790–801.

Chi, M. T. H. (1978). Knowledge structures and memory development. In R. S. Siegler (Ed.), *Children's thinking: What develops?* Hillsdale, NJ: Erlbaum.

Chipman, S. F. (2005). Research on the women and mathematics issue: A personal case history. In A. M. Gallagher & J. C. Kaufman (Eds.), *Gender differences in mathematics: An integrative psychological approach* (pp. 1–24). Cambridge, England: Cambridge University Press.

Chisholm, K., Carter, M. C., Ames, E. W., & Morison, S. J. (1995). Attachment security and indiscriminately friendly behavior in children adopted from Romanian orphanages. *Development and Psychopathology, 7*, 283–297.

Chiu, M. M. (2007). Families, economies, cultures, and science achievement in 41 countries: Country-, school-, and student-level analyses. *Journal of Family Psychology, 21*, 510–519.

Choi, S., & McDonough, L. (2007). Adapting spatial concepts for different languages: From preverbal event schemas to semantic categories. In J. M. Plumert & J. P. Spencer (Eds.), *The emerging spatial mind* (pp. 142–167). New York: Oxford University Press.

Chomsky, C. S. (1969). *The acquisition of syntax in children from 5 to 10*. Cambridge, MA: MIT Press.

Chomsky, N. (1959). Review of B. F. Skinner's *Verbal Behavior. Language, 35*, 26–58.

Chomsky, N. (1965). *Aspects of the theory of syntax*. Cambridge, MA: MIT Press.

Chomsky, N. (1972). *Language and mind* (enlarged ed.). San Diego, CA: Harcourt Brace Jovanovich.

Chomsky, N. (1976). *Reflections on language*. London: Temple Smith.

Chomsky, N. (2006). *Language and mind* (3rd ed.). Cambridge, England: Cambridge University Press.

Chouinard, M. M. (2007). Children's questions: A mechanism for cognitive development. *Monographs of the Society for Research in Child Development, 72* (1; Serial No. 286).

Chow, B. W.-Y., McBride-Chang, C., & Burgess, S. (2005). Phonological processing skills and early reading abilities in Hong Kong Chinese kindergartners learning to read English as a second language. *Journal of Educational Psychology, 97*, 81–87.

Christenson, S. L., & Thurlow, M. L. (2004). School dropouts: Prevention, considerations, interventions, and challenges. *Current Directions in Psychological Science, 13*, 36–39.

Christie, J. F., & Johnsen, E. P. (1983). The role of play in social-intellectual development. *Review of Educational Research, 53*, 93–115.

Chu, Y.-W. (2000). *The relationships between domain-specific self-concepts and global self-esteem among adolescents in Taiwan*. Unpublished doctoral dissertation, University of Northern Colorado, Greeley.

Chukovsky, K. (1968). *From two to five* (M. Morton, Trans.). Berkeley: University of California Press.

Cicchetti, D., Rogosch, F. A., & Toth, S. L. (1997). Ontogenesis, depressotypic organization, and the depressive spectrum. In S. S. Luthar, J. A. Burack, D. Cicchetti, & J. R. Weisz (Eds.), *Developmental psychopathology: Perspectives on adjustment, risk, and disorder* (pp. 273–313). Cambridge, England: Cambridge University Press.

Cicchetti, D., & Toth, S. L. (1998). Perspectives on research and practice in developmental psychopathology. In W. Damon (Series Ed.), I. E. Sigel, & K. A. Renninger (Vol. Eds.), *Handbook of child psychology: Vol. 4. Child psychology in practice* (5th ed., pp. 479–583). New York: Wiley.

Cimpian, A., Arce, H.-M. C., Markman, E. M., & Dweck, C. S. (2007). Subtle linguistic cues affect children's motivation. *Psychological Science, 18*, 314–316.

Clark, B. (1997). *Growing up gifted* (5th ed.). Upper Saddle River, NJ: Merrill/Prentice Hall.

Clark, C. C. (1992). Deviant adolescent subcultures: Assessment strategies and clinical interventions. *Adolescence, 27*(106), 283–293.

Clark, D. B. (2006). Longitudinal conceptual change in students' understanding of thermal equilibrium: An examination of the process of conceptual restructuring. *Cognition and Instruction, 24*, 467–563.

Clark, R. M. (1983). *Family life and school achievement: Why poor Black children succeed or fail*. Chicago: University of Chicago Press.

Clasen, D. R., & Brown, B. B. (1985). The multidimensionality of peer pressure in adolescence. *Journal of Youth and Adolescence, 14*, 451–468.

Clemens, E. V., Shipp, A. E., & Pisarik, C. T. (2008). Myspace as a tool for mental health professionals. *Child and Adolescent Mental Health, 13*(2), 97–98.

Clifford, M. M. (1990). Students need challenge, not easy success. *Educational Leadership, 48*(1), 22–26.

Cochran, M., & Niego, S. (2002). Parenting and social networks. In M. H. Bornstein (Ed.), *Handbook of parenting: Vol. 4. Social conditions and applied parenting* (2nd ed., pp. 123–148). Mahwah, NJ: Erlbaum.

Cochran-Smith, M., & Lytle, S. (1993). *Inside out: Teacher research and knowledge*. New York: Teachers College Press.

Cocking, R. R., & Greenfield, P. M. (1996). Introduction. In P. M. Greenfield & R. Cocking (Eds.), *Interacting with video* (pp. 3–7). Norwood, NJ: Ablex.

Cody, H., & Kamphaus, R. W. (1999). Down syndrome. In S. Goldstein & C. R. Reynolds (Eds.), *Handbook of neurodevelopmental and genetic disorders* (pp. 385–405). New York: Guilford Press.

Cohen, D., & Nisbett, R. E. (1994). Self-protection and the culture of honor: Explaining Southern violence. *Personality and Social Psychology Bulletin, 20*, 551–567.

Cohen, E. G. (1994). Restructuring the classroom: Conditions for productive small groups. *Review of Educational Research, 64*, 1–35.

Cohen, E. G., & Lotan, R. A. (1995). Producing equal-status interaction in the heterogeneous classroom. *American Educational Research Journal, 32*, 99–120.

Cohen, L. B., & Cashon, C. H. (2006). Infant cognition. In W. Damon & R. M. Lerner (Eds. in Chief) & D. Kuhn & R. S. Siegler (Vol. Eds.), *Handbook of child psychology: Vol. 2. Cognition, perception, and language* (6th ed., pp. 214–251). Hoboken, NJ: Wiley.

Cohen, M. N. (1998, April 17). Culture, not race, explains human diversity. *The Chronicle of Higher Education*, p. B4.

Cohen, M. R. (1997). Individual and sex differences in speed of handwriting among high school students. *Perceptual and Motor Skills, 84*(3, Pt. 2), 1428–1430.

Coie, J. D., & Cillessen, A. H. N. (1993). Peer rejection: Origins and effects on children's development. *Current Directions in Psychological Science, 2*, 89–92.

Coie, J. D., & Dodge, K. A. (1988). Multiple sources of data on social behavior and social status. *Child Development, 59*, 815–829.

Coie, J. D., Dodge, K. A., & Coppotelli, H. (1982). Dimensions and types of social status: A cross-age perspective. *Developmental Psychology, 18*, 557–570.

Coie, J. D., Dodge, K. A., Terry, R., & Wright, V. (1991). The role of aggression in peer relations: An analysis of aggression episodes in boys' play groups. *Child Development, 62*, 812–826.

Coie, J. D., & Kupersmidt, J. (1983). A behavioral analysis of emerging social status in boys' groups. *Child Development, 54*, 1400–1416.

Coker, D. (2007). Writing instruction for young children: Methods targeting the multiple demands that writers face. In S. Graham, C. A. MacArthur, & J. Fitzgerald (Eds.), *Best practices in writing instruction: Solving problems in the teaching of literacy* (pp. 101–118). New York: Guilford.

Colby, A., & Kohlberg, L. (1984). Invariant sequence and internal consistency in moral judgment stages. In W. M. Kurtines & J. L. Gewirtz (Eds.), *Morality, moral behavior, and moral development*. New York: Wiley.

Colby, A., Kohlberg, L., Gibbs, J., & Lieberman, M. (1983). A longitudinal study of moral judgment. *Monographs of the Society for Research in Child Development, 48*(1–2, Serial No. 200).

Cole, D. A., Martin, J. M., Peeke, L. A., Seroczynski, A. D., & Fier, J. (1999). Children's over- and under-estimation of academic competence: A longitudinal study of gender differences, depression, and anxiety. *Child Development, 70*, 459–473.

Cole, D. A., Maxwell, S. E., Martin, J. M., Peeke, L. G., Seroczynski, A. D., Tram, J. M., et al. (2001). The development of multiple domains of child and adolescent self-concept: A cohort sequential longitudinal design. *Child Development, 72*, 1723–1746.

Cole, M. (1990). Cognitive development and formal schooling: The evidence from cross-cultural research. In L. C. Moll (Ed.), *Vygotsky and education* (pp. 89–110). New York: Cambridge University Press.

Cole, M. (2006). Culture and cognitive development in phylogenetic, historical and ontogenetic perspective. In W. Damon & R. M. Lerner (Series Eds.) & D. Kuhn & R. Siegler (Vol. Eds.), *Handbook of child psychology: Vol. 2. Cognition, perception, and language* (6th ed., pp. 636–683). New York: Wiley.

Cole, M., & Hatano, G. (2007). Cultural-historical activity theory: Integrating phylogeny, cultural history, and ontogenesis in cultural psychology. In S. Kitayama & D. Cohen (Eds.), *Handbook of cultural psychology* (pp. 109–135). New York: Guilford Press.

Cole, M., & Scribner, S. (1978). Introduction. In L. S. Vygotsky, *Mind in society: The development of higher psychological processes* (M. Cole, V. John-

Steiner, S. Scribner, & E. Souberman, Eds.). Cambridge, MA: Harvard University Press.

Cole, P. M. (1986). Children's spontaneous control of facial expression. *Child Development, 57,* 1309–1321.

Cole, P. M., & Tamang, B. L. (2001). Nepali children's ideas about emotional displays in hypothetical challenges. *Developmental Psychology, 34,* 640–646.

Cole, P. M., & Tan, P. Z. (2007). Emotion socialization from a cultural perspective. In J. E. Grusec & P. D. Hastings (Eds.), *Handbook of socialization: Theory and research* (pp. 516–542). New York: Guilford Press.

Coles, R. L. (2006). *Race and family: A structural approach.* Thousand Oaks, CA: Sage.

Coley, R. L., & Chase-Lansdale, P. L. (1998). Adolescent pregnancy and parenthood. *American Psychologist, 53,* 152–166.

Coll, C. G., Crnic, K., Lamberty, G., Wasik, B. J., Jenkins, R., García, H. V., et al. (1996). An integrative model for the study of developmental competencies in minority children. *Child Development, 67,* 1891–1914.

Collaer, M. L., & Hines, M. (1995). Human behavioral sex differences: A role for gonadal hormones during early development? *Psychological Bulletin, 118,* 55–107.

Collie, R., & Hayne, H. (1999). Deferred imitation by 6- and 9-month-old infants: More evidence for declarative memory. *Developmental Psychobiology, 35,* 83–90.

Collier, V. P. (1989). How long? A synthesis of research on academic achievement in a second language. *TESOL Quarterly, 23,* 509–523.

Collier, V. P. (1992). The Canadian bilingual immersion debate: A synthesis of research findings. *Studies in Second Language Acquisition, 14,* 87–97.

Collingwood, T. R. (1997). *Helping at-risk youth through physical fitness programming.* Champaign, IL: Human Kinetics.

Collins, A. (2006). Cognitive apprenticeship. In R. K. Sawyer (Ed.), *The Cambridge handbook of the learning sciences* (pp. 47–60). Cambridge, England: Cambridge University Press.

Collins, A., Brown, J. S., & Newman, S. E. (1989). Cognitive apprenticeship: Teaching the crafts of reading, writing, and mathematics. In L. B. Resnick (Ed.), *Knowing, learning, and instruction: Essays in honor of Robert Glaser.* Hillsdale, NJ: Erlbaum.

Collins, W. A. (1990). Parent–child relationships in the transition to adolescence: Continuity and change in interaction, affects, and cognition. In R. Montemayor, G. Adams, & T. Gullota (Eds.), *Advances in adolescent development* (Vol. 2). Beverly Hills, CA: Sage.

Collins, W. A., Maccoby, E. E., Steinberg, L., Hetherington, E. M., & Bornstein, M. H. (2000). Contemporary research on parenting: The case for nature and nurture. *American Psychologist, 55,* 218–232.

Collins, W. A., & Sroufe, L. A. (1999). Capacity for intimate relationships: A developmental construction. In W. Furman, B. B. Brown, & C. Feiring (Eds.), *The development of romantic relationships in adolescence* (pp. 125–147). Cambridge, England: Cambridge University Press.

Collins, W. A., & van Dulmen, M. (2006). "The course of true love(s). . .": Origins and pathways in the development of romantic relationships. In A. C. Crouter & A. Booth (Eds.), *Romance and sex in adolescence and emerging adulthood: Risks and opportunities* (pp. 53–86). Mahwah, NJ: Erlbaum.

Colombo, J. (1993). *Infant cognition: Predicting later intellectual functioning.* Newbury Park, CA: Sage.

Comeau, L., Cormier, P., Grandmaison, É., & Lacroix, D. (1999). A longitudinal study of phonological processing skills in children learning to read in a second language. *Journal of Educational Psychology, 91,* 29–43.

Comer, J. P. (2005, March). The rewards of parent participation. *Educational Leadership, 62*(6), 38–42.

Commons, M. L., Richards, F. A., & Armon, C. (Eds.) (1984). *Beyond formal operations.* New York: Praeger.

Comstock, G., & Scharrer, E. (2006). Media and popular culture. In W. Damon & R. M. Lerner (Series Eds.) & K. A. Renninger & I. E. Sigel (Vol. Eds.), *Handbook of child psychology: Vol. 3. Social, emotional, and personality development* (6th ed., pp. 817–863). New York: Wiley.

Condon, J. C., & Yousef, F. S. (1975). *An introduction to intercultural communication.* Indianapolis, IN: Bobbs-Merrill.

Condry, J. C., & Ross, D. F. (1985). Sex and aggression: The influence of gender label on the perception of aggression in children. *Child Development, 56,* 225–233.

Conel, J. L. (1939–1975). *Postnatal development of the human cerebral cortex* (Vols. 1–8). Cambridge, MA: Harvard University Press.

Conger, R. D., & Dogan, S. J. (2007). Social class and socialization in families. In J. E. Grusec & P. D. Hastings (Eds.), *Handbook of socialization: Theory and research* (pp. 433–460). New York: Guilford.

Conn, J., & Kanner, L. (1940). Spontaneous erections in childhood. *Journal of Pediatrics, 16,* 237–240.

Connell-Carrick, K. (2007). Methamphetamine and the changing face of child welfare: Practice principles for child welfare workers. *Child Welfare, 86*(3), 125–144.

Connolly, J., & Goldberg, A. (1999). Romantic relationships in adolescence: The role of friends and peers in their emergence and development. In W. Furman, B. B. Brown, & C. Feiring (Eds.), *The development of romantic relationships in adolescence* (pp. 266–290). Cambridge, England: Cambridge University Press.

Connor, P. D., Sampson, P. D., Streissguth, A. P., Bookstein, F. L., & Barr, H. M. (2006). Effects of prenatal alcohol exposure on fine motor coordination and balance: A study of two adult samples. *Neuropsychologia, 44,* 744–751.

Consortium of Longitudinal Studies. (Ed.). (1983). *As the twig is bent: Lasting effects of preschool programs.* Mahwah, NJ: Erlbaum.

Conway, M. B., Christensen, T. M., & Herlihy, B. (2003). Adult children of divorce and intimate relationships: Implications for counseling. *Family Journal: Counseling and Therapy for Couples and Families, 11,* 364–273.

Cook, V., & Newson, M. (1996). *Chomsky's universal grammar: An introduction* (2nd ed.). Oxford, England: Blackwell.

Cooney, J. B, & Ladd, S. F. (1992). The influence of verbal protocol methods on children's mental computation. *Learning and Individual Differences, 4,* 237–257.

Cooney, J. B., Swanson, H. L., & Ladd, S. F. (1988). Acquisition of mental multiplication skill: Evidence for the transition between counting and retrieval strategies. *Cognition and Instruction, 5,* 323–345.

Cooper, C. E., & Crosnoe, R. (2007). The engagement in schooling of economically disadvantaged parents and children. *Youth and Society, 38,* 372–291.

Cooper, C. R., Denner, J., & Lopez, E. M. (1999, Fall). Cultural brokers: Helping Latino children on pathways toward success. *The Future of Children: When School Is Out, 9,* 51–57.

Cooper, C. R., Jackson, J. F., Azmitia, M, Lopez, E., & Dunbar, N. (1995). Bridging students' multiple worlds: African American and Latino youth in academic outreach programs. In R. F. Macias & R. G. Garcia-Ramos (Eds.), *Changing schools for changing students: An anthology of research on language minorities* (pp. 211–234). Santa Barbara: University of California Linguistic Minority Research Institute.

Cooper, H., Charlton, K., Valentine, J. C., & Muhlenbruck, L. (2000). Making the most of summer school: A meta-analytic and narrative review. *Monographs of the Society for Research in Child Development, 65*(1, Serial No. 260).

Cooper, H., & Dorr, N. (1995). Race comparisons on need for achievement: A meta-analytic alternative to Graham's narrative review. *Review of Educational Research, 65,* 483–508.

Cooper, H., Robinson, J. C., & Patall, E. A. (2006). Does homework improve academic achievement? A synthesis of research, 1987–2003. *Review of Educational Research, 76,* 1–62.

Cooper, H., Valentine, J. C., Nye, B., & Lindsay, J. J. (1999). Relationships between five after-school activities and academic achievement. *Journal of Educational Psychology, 91,* 369–378.

Cooper, R. P., & Aslin, R. N. (1990). Preference for infant-directed speech in the first month after birth. *Child Development, 61,* 1584–1595.

Coopersmith, S. (1967). *The antecedents of self-esteem.* San Francisco: Freeman.

Corbin, J. M., & Strauss, A. (2008). *Basics of qualitative research: Techniques and procedures for developing grounded theory* (3rd ed.). Los Angeles: Sage.

Corcoran, C. B., & Parker, J. A. (2005). Powderpuff girls: Fighting evil gender messages or postmodern paradox? In J. L. Chin (Ed.), *The psychology of prejudice and discrimination: Bias based on gender and sexual orientation, Vol. 3: Race and ethnicity in psychology* (pp. 27–59). Westport, CT: Praeger.

Cornell, D. G., Pelton, G. M., Bassin, L. E., Landrum, M., Ramsay, S. G., Cooley, M. R., et al. (1990). Self-concept and peer status among gifted program youth. *Journal of Educational Psychology, 82,* 456–463.

Cornish, K., Burack, J. A., Rahman, A., Munir, F., Russo, N., & Grant, C. (2005). Theory of mind deficits in children with fragile X syndrome. *Journal of Intellectual Disability Research, 49,* 372–378.

Corno, L., & Mandinach, E. B. (2004). What we have learned about student engagement in the past twenty years. In D. M. McNerney & S. Van Etten (Eds.), *Big theories revisited* (pp. 299–328). Greenwich, CT: Information Age.

Corpus, J. H., McClintic-Gilberg, M. S., & Hayenga, A. O. (2006, April). *Understanding intrinsic and extrinsic motivation: Age differences and links to children's beliefs and goals.* Paper presented at the annual meeting of the American Educational Research Association, San Francisco.

Corriveau, K., Pasquini, E., & Goswami, U. (2007). Basic auditory processing skills and specific language impairment: A new look at an old hypothesis. *Journal of Speech, Language, and Hearing Research, 50,* 647–666.

Corsaro, W. A. (1985). *Friendship and peer culture in the early years.* Norwood, NJ: Ablex.

Corsaro, W. A., & Molinari, L. (2005). *I compagni: Understanding children's transition from preschool to elementary school.* New York: Teachers College Press.

Cosden, M., Morrison, G., Albanese, A. L., & Macias, S. (2001). When homework is not home work: After-school programs for homework assistance. *Educational Psychologist, 36,* 211–221.

Cossu, G. (1999). The acquisition of Italian orthography. In M. Harris & G. Hatano (Eds.), *Learning to read and write: A cross-linguistic perspective.* Cambridge, England: Cambridge University Press.

Cota-Robles, S., & Neiss, M. (1999, April). *The role of puberty in non-violent delinquency among Anglo-American, Hispanic, and African American boys.* Paper presented at the biennial meeting of the Society for Research in Child Development, Albuquerque, NM.

Côté, J. E. (2005). Erikson's theory. In C. B. Fisher & R. M. Lerner (Eds.), *Encyclopedia of applied developmental science* (Vol. 1, pp. 406–409). Thousand Oaks, CA: Sage.

Cotterell, J. L. (1992). The relation of attachments and supports to adolescent well-being and school adjustment. *Journal of Adolescent Research, 7,* 28–42.

Council for Exceptional Children. (1995). *Toward a common agenda: Linking gifted education and school reform.* Reston, VA: Author.

Courage, M. L., & Adams, R. J. (1990). Visual acuity assessment from birth to three years using the acuity card procedures: Cross-sectional and longitudinal samples. *Optometry and Vision Science, 67,* 713–718.

Courage, M. L., Reynolds, G. D., & Richards, J. E. (2006). Infants' attention to patterned stimuli: Developmental change from 3 to 12 months of age. *Child Development, 77,* 680–695.

Covington, M. V. (1987). Achievement motivation, self-attributions, and the exceptional learner. In J. D. Day & J. G. Borkowski (Eds.), *Intelligence and exceptionality.* Norwood, NJ: Ablex.

Covington, M. V. (1992). *Making the grade: A self-worth perspective on motivation and school reform.* Cambridge, England: Cambridge University Press.

Covington, M. V., & Müeller, K. J. (2001). Intrinsic versus extrinsic motivation: An approach/avoidance reformulation. *Educational Psychology Review, 13,* 157–176.

Cowan, W. M. (1979). The development of the brain. *Scientific American, 241,* 106–117.

Cox, C. B. (2000). Empowering grandparents raising grandchildren. New York: Springer.

Cox, M. E., Orme, J. G., & Rhoades, K. W. (2003). Willingness to foster children with emotional or behavioral problems. *Journal of Social Service Research, 29,* 23–51.

Craft, M. (1984). Education for diversity. In M. Craft (Ed.), *Educational and cultural pluralism.* London: Falmer Press.

Crago, M. B. (1988). *Cultural context in the communicative interaction of young Inuit children.* Unpublished doctoral dissertation, McGill University, Montreal, Canada.

Crago, M. B., Allen, S. E. M., & Hough-Eyamie, W. P. (1997). Exploring innateness through cultural and linguistic variation. In M. Gopnik (Ed.), *The inheritance and innateness of grammars.* New York: Oxford University Press.

Crago, M. B., Annahatak, B., & Ningiuruvik, L. (1993). Changing patterns of language socialization in Inuit homes. *Anthropology and Education Quarterly, 24,* 205–223.

Craig, L. (2006). Does father care mean fathers share? A comparison of how mothers and fathers in intact families spend time with their children. *Gender & Society, 20,* 259–281.

Crain, W. (2005). *Theories of development: Concepts and applications* (5th ed.). Upper Saddle River, NJ: Pearson Prentice Hall.

Crawley, A. M., Anderson, D. R., Wilder, A., Williams, M., & Santomero, A. (1999). Effects of repeated exposures to a single episode of the television program *Blue's Clues* on the viewing behaviors and comprehension of preschool children. *Journal of Educational Psychology, 91,* 630–637.

Creasey, G. L., Jarvis, P. A., & Berk, L. E. (1998). Play and social competence. In O. N. Saracho & B. Spodek (Eds.), *Multiple perspectives on play in early childhood education.* Albany: State University of New York Press.

Creswell, J. W. (2002). *Educational research: Planning, conducting, and evaluating quantitative and qualitative research.* Upper Saddle River, NJ: Merrill/Prentice Hall.

Crews, F., He, J., & Hodge, C. (2007). Adolescent cortical development: A critical period of vulnerability for addiction. *Pharmacology, Biochemistry, and Behavior, 86,* 189–199.

Crick, N. R., Casas, J. F., & Nelson, D. A. (2002). Toward a more comprehensive understanding of peer maltreatment: Studies of relational victimization. *Current Directions in Psychological Science, 11,* 98–101.

Crick, N. R., & Dodge, K. A. (1994). A review and reformulation of social information-processing mechanisms in children's social adjustment. *Psychological Bulletin, 115,* 74–101.

Crick, N. R., & Dodge, K. A. (1996). Social information-processing mechanisms in reactive and proactive aggression. *Child Development, 67,* 993–1002.

Crick, N. R., Grotpeter, J. K., & Bigbee, M. A. (2002). Relationally and physically aggressive children's intent attributions and feelings of distress for relational and instrumental peer provocation. *Child Development, 73,* 1134–1142. 73, 1220–1237.

Criss, M. M., Pettit, G. S., Bates, J. E., Dodge, K. A., & Lapp, A. L. (1992). Family adversity, positive peer relationships, and children's externalizing behavior: A longitudinal perspective on risk and resilience. *Child Development, 73,* 1220–1237.

Critten, S., Pine, K., & Steffler, D. (2007). Spelling development in young children: A case of representational redescription? *Journal of Educational Psychology, 99,* 207–220.

Crohn, H. M. (2006). Five styles of positive stepmothering from the perspective of young adult stepdaughters. *Journal of Divorce and Remarriage, 46(1/2),* 119–134.

Cromer, R. F. (1993). Language growth with experience without feedback. In P. Bloom (Ed.), *Language acquisition: Core readings.* Cambridge, MA: MIT Press.

Cromley, J. G., & Azevedo, R. (2007). Testing and refining the direct and inferential mediation model of reading comprehension. *Journal of Educational Psychology, 99,* 311–325.

Crosnoe, R., & Elder, G. H., Jr. (2004). Family dynamics, supportive relationships, and educational resilience during adolescence. *Journal of Family Issues, 25(5),* 571–602.

Crosnoe, R., & Huston, A. C. (2007). Socioeconomic status, schooling, and the developmental trajectories of adolescents. *Developmental Psychology, 43,* 1097–1110.

Cross, W. E., Jr., Strauss, L., & Fhagen-Smith, P. (1999). African American identity development across the life span: Educational implications. In R. H. Sheets & E. R. Hollins (Eds.), *Racial and ethnic identity in school practices: Aspects of human development* (pp. 29–47). Mahwah, NJ: Erlbaum.

Crouter, A. C., & Bumpus, M. F. (2001). Linking parents' work stress to children's and adolescents' psychological adjustment. *Current Directions in Psychological Science, 10,* 156–159.

Crowley, K., Callanan, M. A., Tenenbaum, H. R., & Allen, E. (2001). Parents explain more often to boys than girls during shared scientific thinking. *Psychological Science, 12,* 258–261.

Crowley, K., & Jacobs, M. (2002). Building islands of expertise in everyday family activity. In G. Leinhardt, K. Crowley, & K. Knutson (Eds.), *Learning conversations in museums* (pp. 333–356). Mahwah, NJ: Erlbaum.

Crystal, D. S., & Stevenson, H. W. (1991). Mothers' perceptions of children's problems with mathematics: A cross-national comparison. *Journal of Educational Psychology, 83,* 372–376.

Csikszentmihalyi, M. (1995). Education for the twenty-first century. *Daedalus, 124(4),* 107–114.

Csikszentmihalyi, M., & Larson, R. (1984). *Being adolescent: Conflict and growth in the teenage years.* New York: Basic Books.

Cullen, K. W., Zakeri, I., Pryor, E. W., Baranowski, T., Baranowski, J., & Watson, K. (2004). Goal setting is differentially related to change in fruit, juice, and vegetable consumption among fourth-grade children. *Health Education & Behavior, 31,* 258–269.

Cummins, J. (1981). Age on arrival and immigrant second language learning in Canada: A reassessment. *Applied Linguistics, 2,* 132–149.

Cummins, J. (1984). *Bilingualism and special education: Issues in assessment and pedagogy.* Clevedon, England: Multilingual Matters.

Cummins, J. (2000). *Language, power, and pedagogy: Bilingual children in the crossfire.* Clevedon, England: Multilingual Matters.

Cunningham, C. E., & Cunningham, L. J. (1998). Student-mediated conflict resolution programs. In R. A. Barkley (Ed.), *Attention-deficit hyperactivity disorder: A handbook for diagnosis and treatment* (2nd ed., pp. 491–509). New York: Guilford Press.

Cunningham, T. H., & Graham, C. R. (2000). Increasing native English vocabulary recognition through Spanish immersion: Cognate transfer from foreign to first language. *Journal of Educational Psychology, 92,* 37–49.

Curtiss, S. (1977). *Genie: A psycholinguistic study of a modern-day "wild child."* New York: Academic Press.

Dahl, R. E., & Lewin, D. S. (2002). Pathways to adolescent health: Sleep regulation and behavior. *Journal of Adolescent Health, 31*(6 Suppl.), 175–184.

Dahlberg, G., Moss, P., & Pence, A. (1999). *Beyond quality in early childhood education and care: Postmodern perspectives.* London: Falmer Press.

Dahlin, B., & Watkins, D. (2000). The role of repetition in the processes of memorizing and understanding: A comparison of the views of Western and Chinese secondary students in Hong Kong. *British Journal of Educational Psychology, 70,* 65–84.

d'Ailly, H. (2003). Children's autonomy and perceived control in learning: A model of motivation and achievement in Taiwan. *Journal of Educational Psychology, 95,* 84–96.

Daley, T. C., Whaley, S. E., Sigman, M. D., Espinosa, M. P., & Neumann, C. (2003). IQ on the rise: The Flynn effect in rural Kenyan children. *Psychological Science, 14,* 215–219.

Damon, W. (1977). *The social world of the child.* San Francisco: Jossey-Bass.

Damon, W. (1981). Exploring children's social cognitions on two fronts. In J. M. Flavell & L. Ross (Eds.), *Social cognitive development: Frontiers and possible futures* (pp. 154–175). Cambridge, England: Cambridge University Press.

Damon, W. (1984). Peer education: The untapped potential. *Journal of Applied Developmental Psychology, 5,* 331–343.

Damon, W. (1988). *The moral child: Nurturing children's natural moral growth.* New York: Free Press.

Damon, W. (1991). Putting substance into self-esteem: A focus on academic and moral values. *Educational Horizons, 70(1),* 12–18.

Damon, W., & Hart, D. (1988). *Self-understanding in childhood and adolescence.* New York: Cambridge University Press.

DanceSafe. (2000a). *What Is LSD?* Retrieved November 1, 2005, from http://www.dancesafe.org/documents/druginfo/lsd.php

DanceSafe. (2000b). *What is speed?* Oakland, CA: Author. Retrieved November 1, 2005, from http://www.dancesafe.org/documents/druginfo/speed.php

Dannemiller, J. L., & Stephens, B. R. (1988). A critical test of infant pattern preference models. *Child Development, 59,* 210–216.

Danner, F. W., & Day, M. C. (1977). Eliciting formal operations. *Child Development, 48,* 1600–1606.

Danthiir, V., Roberts, R. D., Schulze, R., & Wilhelm, O. (2005). Mental speed: On frameworks, paradigms, and a platform for the future. In O. Wilhelm & R. W. Engle (Eds.), *Handbook of understanding and measuring intelligence* (pp. 27–46). Thousand Oaks, CA: Sage.

Darling-Hammond, L. (1995). Inequality and access to knowledge. In J. A. Banks & C. A. M. Banks (Eds.), *Handbook of research on multicultural education.* New York: Macmillan.

Darling-Hammond, L., & Bransford, J. (Eds.). (2005). *Preparing teachers for a changing world: What teachers should learn and be able to do.* San Francisco: Jossey-Bass/Wiley.

Darling-Hammond, L., & Friedlaender, D. (2008, May). Creating excellent and equitable schools. *Educational Leadership, 65*(8), 14–21.

Davenport, E. C., Jr., Davison, M. L., Kuang, H., Ding, S., Kim, S., & Kwak, N. (1998). High school mathematics course-taking by gender and ethnicity. *American Educational Research Journal, 35,* 497–514.

Davidson, F. H. (1976). Ability to respect persons compared to ethnic prejudice in childhood. *Journal of Personality and Social Psychology, 34,* 1256–1267.

Davidson, M. R., London, M. L., & Ladewig, P. A. W. (2008). *Olds' maternal-newborn nursing and women's health across the lifespan.* Upper Saddle River, NJ: Pearson Prentice Hall.

Davidson, P., & Youniss, J. (1995). Moral development and social construction. In W. M. Kurtines & J. L. Gewirtz (Eds.), *Moral development: An introduction.* Boston: Allyn & Bacon.

Davies, C., & Uttal, D. H. (2007). Map use and the development of spatial cognition. In J. M. Plumert & J. P. Spencer (Eds.), *The emerging spatial mind* (pp. 219–247). New York: Oxford University Press.

Davila, J. (2008). Depressive symptoms and adolescent romance: Theory, research, and implications. *Child Development Perspectives, 2*(1), 26–31.

Davis, B. (2001). The restorative power of emotions in Child Protective Services. *Child and Adolescent Social Work Journal, 18,* 437–454.

Davis, G. A., & Rimm, S. B. (1998). *Education of the gifted and talented* (4th ed.). Boston: Allyn & Bacon.

Davis, G. A., & Thomas, M. A. (1989). *Effective schools and effective teachers.* Needham Heights, MA: Allyn & Bacon.

Davis, H. A. (2003). Conceptualizing the role and influence of student–teacher relationships on children's social and cognitive development. *Educational Psychologist, 38,* 207–234.

Davis, H. A., Schutz, P. A., & Chambless, C. B. (2001, April). *Uncovering the impact of social relationships in the classroom: Viewing relationships with teachers from different lenses.* Paper presented at the annual meeting of the American Educational Research Association, Seattle, WA.

Davis, J. H. (2008). *Why our schools need the arts.* New York: Teachers College Press.

Davis-Kean, P. E., & Sandler, H. M. (2001). A meta-analysis of measures of self-esteem for young children: A framework for future measures. *Child Development, 72,* 887–906.

De Cecco, J. P., & Parker, D. A. (1995). The biology of homosexuality: Sexual orientation or sexual preference. *Journal of Homosexuality, 28,* 1–27.

De Corte, E., Greer, B., & Verschaffel, L. (1996). Mathematics teaching and learning. In D. C. Berliner & R. C. Calfee (Eds.), *Handbook of educational psychology.* New York: Macmillan.

De Corte, E., Op't Eynde, P., & Verschaffel, L. (2002). "Knowing what to believe": The relevance of students' mathematical beliefs for mathematics education. In B. K. Hofer & P. R. Pintrich (Eds.), *Personal epistemology: The psychology of beliefs about knowledge and knowing* (pp. 297–320). Mahwah, NJ: Erlbaum.

de Graaf, H., & Rademakers, J. (2006). Sexual behavior of prepubertal children. *Journal of Psychology and Human Sexuality, 18*(1), 1–21.

de Jong, T., & van Joolingen, W. R. (1998). Scientific discovery learning with computer simulations of conceptual domains. *Review of Educational Research, 68,* 179–201.

De La Paz, S. (2005). Effects of historical reasoning instruction and writing strategy mastery in culturally and academically diverse middle school classrooms. *Journal of Educational Psychology, 97,* 139–156.

De Lisi, R., & Golbeck, S. L. (1999). Implications of Piagetian theory for peer learning. In A. M. O'Donnell & A. King (Eds.), *Cognitive perspectives on peer learning* (pp. 3–37). Mahwah, NJ: Erlbaum.

De Lisi, R., & Wolford, J. L. (2002). Improving children's mental rotation accuracy with computer game playing. *Journal of Genetic Psychology, 16*(3), 272–282.

de Muinck Keizer-Schrama, S. M. P. F., & Mul, D. (2001). Trends in pubertal development in Europe. *Human Reproduction Update, 7,* 287–291.

de Villiers, J. (1995). Empty categories and complex sentences: The case of wh- questions. In P. Fletcher & B. MacWhinney (Eds.), *The handbook of child language* (pp. 508–540). Oxford, England: Blackwell.

Deal, L. W., Gomby, D. S., Zippiroli, L., & Behrman, R. E. (2000). Unintentional injuries in childhood: Analysis and recommendations. *Future of Children, 10*(1), 4–22.

Deary, I. J. (2003). Reaction time and psychometric intelligence: Jensen's contributions. In H. Nyborg (Ed.), *The scientific study of general intelligence: Tribute to Arthur Jensen* (pp. 53–75). Oxford, England: Elsevier.

Deater-Deckard, K., Dodge, K., Bates, J., & Pettit, G. (1996). Physical discipline among African American and European American mothers: Links to children's externalizing behaviors. *Developmental Psychology, 32,* 1065–1072.

Deaux, K. (1984). From individual differences to social categories: Analysis of a decade's research on gender. *American Psychologist, 39,* 105–116.

DeBose, C. E. (2007). The Ebonics phenomenon, language planning, and the hegemony of Standard English. In H. S. Alim & J. Baugh (Eds.), *Talkin black talk: Language, education, and social change* (pp. 30–42). New York: Teachers College Press.

DeCapua, A., Smathers, W., & Tang, L. F. (2007). Schooling, interrupted. *Educational Leadership, 64*(6), 40–46.

DeCasper, A. J., & Fifer, W. P. (1980). Of human bonding: Newborns prefer their mothers' voices. *Science, 208,* 1174–1176.

DeCasper, A. J., & Spence, M. J. (1986). Prenatal maternal speech influences newborns' perception of speech sounds. *Infant Behavior and Development, 9,* 133–150.

Deci, E. L. (1992). The relation of interest to the motivation of behavior: A self-determination theory perspective. In K. A. Renninger, S. Hidi, & A. Krapp (Eds.), *The role of interest in learning and development.* Hillsdale, NJ: Erlbaum.

Deci, E. L., Koestner, R., & Ryan, R. M. (2001). Extrinsic rewards and intrinsic motivation in education: Reconsidered once again. *Review of Educational Research. 71,* 1–27.

Deci, E. L., & Moller, A. C. (2005). The concept of competence: A starting place for understanding intrinsic motivation and self-determined extrinsic motivation. In A. J. Elliot & C. S. Dweck (Eds.), *Handbook of competence and motivation* (pp. 579–597). New York: Guilford Publications.

Deci, E. L., & Ryan, R. M. (1985). *Intrinsic motivation and self-determination in human behavior.* New York: Plenum Press.

Deci, E. L., & Ryan, R. M. (1992). The initiation and regulation of intrinsically motivated learning and achievement. In A. K. Boggiano & T. S. Pittman (Eds.), *Achievement and motivation: A social-developmental perspective.* Cambridge, England: Cambridge University Press.

Deci, E. L., & Ryan, R. M. (1995). Human autonomy: The basis for true self-esteem. In M. H. Kernis (Ed.), *Efficacy, agency, and self-esteem.* New York: Plenum Press.

DeLamater, J., & MacCorquodale, P. (1979). *Premarital sexuality: Attitudes, relationships, behavior.* Madison: University of Wisconsin Press.

Delaney, K. R. (2006). Following the affect: Learning to observe emotional regulation. *Journal of Child and Adolescent Psychiatric Nursing, 19*(4), 175–181.

Delgado-Gaitan, C. (1994). Socializing young children in Mexican-American families: An intergenerational perspective. In P. M. Greenfield & R. R. Cocking (Eds.), *Cross-cultural roots of minority child development* (pp. 55–86). Hillsdale, NJ: Erlbaum.

DeLisi, R., & Gallagher, A. M. (1991). Understanding of gender stability and constancy in Argentinian children. *Merrill-Palmer Quarterly, 37,* 483–502.

DeLisle, J. R. (1984). *Gifted children speak out.* New York: Walker.

DeLoache, J. S., Cassidy, D. J., & Brown, A. L. (1985). Precursors of mnemonic strategies in very young children's memory. *Child Development, 56,* 125–137.

DeLoache, J. S., Miller, K. F., & Rosengren, K. S. (1997). The credible shrinking room: Very young children's performance with symbolic and nonsymbolic relations. *Psychological Science, 8,* 308–313.

DeLoache, J. S., & Todd, C. M. (1988). Young children's use of spatial categorization as a mnemonic strategy. *Journal of Experimental Child Psychology, 46,* 1–20.

Demarest, R. J., & Charon, R. (1996). *An illustrated guide to human reproduction and fertility control.* New York: Parthenon.

DeMarie-Dreblow, D., & Miller, P. H. (1988). The development of children's strategies for selective attention: Evidence for a transitional period. *Child Development, 59,* 1504–1513.

deMarrais, K. B., Nelson, P. A., & Baker, J. H. (1994). Meaning in mud: Yup'ik Eskimo girls at play. In J. L. Roopnarine, J. E. Johnson, & F. H. Hooper (Eds.), *Children's play in diverse cultures.* Albany, NY: SUNY Press.

Dempster, F. N., & Corkill, A. J. (1999). Interference and inhibition in cognition and behavior: Unifying themes for educational psychology. *Educational Psychology Review, 11,* 1–88.

Denckla, M. B. (2007). Executive function: Binding together the definitions of attention-deficit/hyperactivity disorder and learning disabilities. In L. Meltzer (Ed.), *Executive function in education: From theory to practice* (pp. 5–18). New York: Guilford Press.

Deshler, D. D., & Schumaker, J. B. (1988). An instructional model for teaching students how to learn. In J. L. Graden, J. E. Zins, & M. J. Curtis (Eds.), *Alternative educational delivery systems: Enhancing instructional options for all students.* Washington, DC: National Association of School Psychologists.

Deutsch, D., Henthorn, T., & Dolson, M. (2004). Absolute pitch, speech, and tone language: Some experiments and a proposed framework. *Music Perception, 21,* 339–356.

Deutsch, M. (1993). Educating for a peaceful world. *American Psychologist, 48,* 510–517.

Deutsch, N. L., & Hirsch, B. J. (2001, April). *A place to call home: Youth organizations in the lives of inner city adolescents.* Paper presented at the biennial meeting of the Society for Research in Child Development, Minneapolis, MN.

DeVault, G., Krug, C., & Fake, S. (1996, September). Why does Samantha act that way: Positive behavioral support leads to successful inclusion. *Exceptional Parent, 43*–47.

Devine, P. G. (1995). Prejudice and out-group perception. In A. Tesser (Ed.), *Advanced social psychology.* New York: McGraw-Hill.

Devlin, B., Daniels, M., & Roeder, K. (1997). The heritability of IQ. *Nature, 388*(6641), 468–471.

Devlin, B., Fienberg, S. E., Resnick, D. P., & Roeder, K. (1995). Galton redux: Intelligence, race, and society: A review of "The Bell Curve: Intelligence and Class Structure in American Life." *American Statistician, 90,* 1483–1488.

DeVoe, J. F., Peter, K., Kaufman, P., Ruddy, S. A., Miller, A. K., Planty, M., et al. (2003). *Indicators of school crime and safety: 2002* (NCES 2003-009/NCJ 196753). Washington, DC: U.S. Departments of Education and Justice.

DeVries, R. (1997). Piaget's social theory. *Educational Researcher, 26*(2), 4–17.

DeVries, R., & Zan, B. (1996). A constructivist perspective on the role of the sociomoral atmosphere in promoting children's development. In C. T. Fosnot (Ed.), *Constructivism: Theory, perspectives, and practice.* New York: Teachers College Press.

Deyhle, D., & LeCompte, M. (1999). Cultural differences in child development: Navajo adolescents in middle schools. In R. H. Sheets & E. R. Hollins (Eds.), *Racial and ethnic identity in school practices: Aspects of human development* (pp. 123–139). Mahwah, NJ: Erlbaum.

Diagram Group. (1983). *The human body on file.* New York: Facts on File.

Diamond, L. M., Savin-Williams, R. C., & Dubé, E. M. (1999). Sex, dating, passionate friendships, and romance: Intimate peer relations among lesbian, gay, and bisexual adolescents. In W. Furman, B. B. Brown, & C. Feiring (Eds.), *The development of romantic relationships in adolescence* (pp. 175–210). Cambridge, England: Cambridge University Press.

Diamond, M., & Hopson, J. (1998). *Magic trees of the mind*. New York: Dutton.

Diamond, S. C. (1991). What to do when you can't do anything: Working with disturbed adolescents. *Clearing House, 64*, 232–234.

Diaz, R. M. (1983). Thought and two languages: The impact of bilingualism on cognitive development. In E. W. Gordon (Ed.), *Review of research in education* (Vol. 10). Washington, DC: American Educational Research Association.

Diaz, R. M., & Berndt, T. J. (1982). Children's knowledge of best friend: Fact or fancy? *Developmental Psychology, 18*, 787–794.

Diaz, R. M., & Klingler, C. (1991). Toward an explanatory model of the interaction between bilingualism and cognitive development. In E. Bialystok (Ed.), *Language processing in bilingual children*. Cambridge, England: Cambridge University Press.

Dibbens, L. M., Heron, S. E., & Mulley, J. C. (2007). A polygenic heterogeneity model for common epilepsies with complex genetics. *Genes, Brain & Behavior, 6*, 593–597.

Dichele, A., & Gordon, M. (2007). Literacy in urban education: Problems and promises. In J. L. Kincheloe, k. hayes, K. Rose, & P. M. Anderson (Eds.), *Urban education: A comprehensive guide for educators, parents, and teachers* (pp. 263–273). Lanham, MD: Rowman & Littlefield Education.

Dick, D. M., Rose, R. J., Viken, R. J., & Kapriro, J. (2000). Pubertal timing and substance abuse: Associations between and within families across late adolescence. *Developmental Psychology, 36*, 180–189.

Dickens, W. T., & Flynn, J. R. (2001). Heritability estimates versus large environmental effects: The IQ paradox resolved. *Psychological Review, 108*, 346–369.

Dickinson, D., Wolf, M., & Stotsky, S. (1993). Words move: The interwoven development of oral and written language. In J. B. Gleason (Ed.), *The development of language*. Boston: Allyn & Bacon.

Dick-Read, G. (1944). *Childbirth without fear*. New York: Harper & Brothers.

Dien, T. (1998). Language and literacy in Vietnamese American communities. In B. Pérez (Ed.), *Sociocultural contexts of language and literacy*. Mahwah, NJ: Erlbaum.

Digman, J. M. (1989). Five robust trait dimensions: Development, stability, and utility. *Journal of Personality, 57*, 195–214.

Dilworth-Bart J. E., & Moore, C. F. (2006). Mercy mercy me: Social injustice and the prevention of environmental pollutant exposures among ethnic minority and poor children. *Child Development, 77*(2), 247–265.

Diorio, J., & Meaney, M. J. (2007). Maternal programming of defensive responses through sustained effects on gene expression. *Journal of Psychiatry & Neuroscience, 32*, 275–284.

DiPietro, J. A. (2004). The role of prenatal maternal stress in child development. Current Directions in Psychological Science, 13, 71–74.

diSessa, A. A. (1996). What do "just plain folk" know about physics? In D. R. Olson & N. Torrance (Eds.), *The handbook of education and human development: New models of learning, teaching, and schooling*. Cambridge, MA: Blackwell.

diSessa, A. A. (2006). A history of conceptual change research. In R. K. Sawyer (Ed.), *The Cambridge handbook of the learning sciences* (pp. 265–281). Cambridge, England: Cambridge University Press.

diSessa, A. A. (2007). An interactional analysis of clinical interviewing. *Cognition and Instruction, 25*, 523–565.

diSessa, A. A., Gillespie, N. M., & Esterly, J. B. (2004). Coherence versus fragmentation in the development in the concept of force. *Cognitive Science, 28*, 843–900.

Dishion, T. J., Andrews, D. W., & Crosby, L. (1995). Antisocial boys and their friends in early adolescence: Relationship characteristics, quality, and interactional process. *Child Development, 66*, 139–151.

Dix, T., Stewart, A. D., Gershoff, E. T., & Day, W. H. (2007). Autonomy and children's reactions to being controlled: Evidence that both compliance and defiance may be positive markers in early development. *Child Development, 78*, 1204–1221.

Dixon, J. A., & Kelley, E. (2007). Theory revision and redescription. *Current Directions in Psychological Science, 16*, 111–115.

Dixon, M. R., & Cummings, A. (2001). Self-control in children with autism: Response allocation during delays to reinforcement. *Journal of Applied Behavior Analysis, 34*, 491–495.

Dodge, K. A. (1983). Behavioral antecedents of peer social status. *Child Development, 54*, 1386–1399.

Dodge, K. A., Bates, J. E., & Pettit, G. S. (1990). Mechanisms in the cycle of violence. *Science, 250*, 1678–1683.

Dodge, K. A., Coie, J., & Lynam, D. (2006). Aggression and antisocial behavior in youth. In W. Damon & R. M. Lerner (Series Eds.) & N. Eisenberg (Vol. Ed.), *Handbook of child psychology: Vol. 3. Social, emotional, and personality development* (6th ed., pp. 719–788). New York: Wiley.

Dodge, K. A., Coie, J. D., & Brakke, N. P. (1982). Behavior patterns of socially rejected and neglected preadolescents: The role of social approach and aggression. *Journal of Abnormal Child Psychology, 10*, 389–410.

Dodge, K. A., Lansford, J. E., Burks, V. S., Bates, J. E., Pettit, G. S., Fontaine, R., et al. (2003). Peer rejection and social information-processing factors in the development of aggressive behavior problems in children. *Child Development, 74*, 374–393.

Dodge, K. A., Pettit, G. S., Bates, J. E., & Valente, E. (1995). Social information processing patterns partially mediate the effect of early physical abuse on later conduct problems. *Journal of Abnormal Psychology, 104*, 632–643.

Dodge, K. A., Schlundt, D. G., Schocken, I., & Delugach, J. D. (1983). Social competence and children's social status: The role of peer group entry strategies. *Merrill-Palmer Quarterly, 29*, 309–336.

Doescher, S. M., & Sugawara, A. I. (1989). Encouraging prosocial behavior in young children. *Childhood Education, 65*, 213–216.

Dohnt, H., & Tiggemann, M. (2006b). The contribution of peer and media influences to the development of body satisfaction and self-esteem in young girls: A prospective study. *Developmental Psychology, 42*, 929–936.

Dohnt, H. K., & Tiggemann, M. (2006a). Body image concerns in young girls: The role of peers and media prior to adolescence. *Journal of Youth and Adolescence, 35*(2), 141–151.

Domitrovich, C. E., Cortes, R. C., & Greenberg, M. T. (2007). Improving young children's social and emotional competence: A randomized trial of the preschool "PATHS" curriculum. *Journal of Primary Prevention, 28*, 67–91.

Donaldson, M. (1978). *Children's minds*. New York: Norton.

Donaldson, S. K., & Westerman, M. A. (1986). Development of children's understanding of ambivalence and causal theories of emotion. *Developmental Psychology, 22*, 655–662.

Donato, F., Assanelli, D., Chiesa, R., Poeta, M. L., Tomansoni, V., & Turla, C. (1997). Cigarette smoking and sports participation in adolescents: A cross-sectional survey among high school students in Italy. *Substance Use and Misuse, 32*, 1555–1572.

Donovan, C. A. (1999, April). *"Stories have a beginning, a middle, and an end. Information only has a beginning": Elementary school children's genre and writing development*. Paper presented at the annual meeting of the American Educational Research Association, San Diego, CA.

Dornbusch, S. M., Carlsmith, J. M., Gross, R. T., Martin, J. A., Jennings, D., Rosenberg, A., et al. (1981).

Sexual development, age, and dating: A comparison of biological and social influences upon one set of behaviors. *Child Development, 52*, 179–185.

Dornbusch, S. M., Ritter, P. L., Leiderman, P. H., Roberts, D. F., & Fraleigh, M. J. (1987). The relation of parenting style to adolescent school performance. *Child Development, 58*, 1244–1257.

Dorris, M. (1989). *The broken cord*. New York: HarperCollins.

Dovidio, J. F., & Gaertner, S. L. (1999). Reducing prejudice: Combating intergroup biases. *Current Directions in Psychological Science, 8*, 101–105.

Downey, J. (2000, March). *The role of schools in adolescent resilience: Recommendations from the literature*. Paper presented at the International Association of Adolescent Health, Washington, DC.

Dowson, M., & McInerney, D. M. (2001). Psychological parameters of students' social and work avoidance goals: A qualitative investigation. *Journal of Educational Psychology, 93*, 35–42.

Doyle, A. (1982). Friends, acquaintances, and strangers: The influence of familiarity and ethnolinguistic background on social interaction. In K. H. Rubin & H. S. Ross (Eds.), *Peer relationships and social skills in childhood* (pp. 229–252). New York: Springer-Verlag.

Doyle, P. A., Bird, B. C., Appel, S., Parisi, D., Rogers, P., Glarso, R., et al. (2006). Developing an effective communications campaign to reach pregnant women at high risk of late or no prenatal care. *Social Marketing Quarterly, 12*(4), 35–50.

Doyle, W. (1986). Classroom organization and management. In M. C. Wittrock (Ed.), *Handbook of research on teaching* (3rd ed.). New York: Macmillan.

Dreweke, J., & Wind, R. (2007, May). *Strong evidence favors comprehensive approach to sex ed*. Guttmacher Institute Media Center. Retrieved February 1, 2008, from http://www.guttmacher.org/media/nr/2007/05/23/index.html

Dryden, M. A., & Jefferson, P. (1994, April). *Use of background knowledge and reading achievement among elementary school students*. Paper presented at the annual meeting of the American Educational Research Association, New Orleans, LA.

Dryfoos, J. G. (1997). The prevalence of problem behaviors: Implications for programs. In R. P. Weissberg, T. P. Gullotta, R. L. Hamptom, B. A. Ryan, & G. R. Adams (Eds.), *Enhancing children's wellness* (Vol. 8, pp. 17–46). Thousand Oaks, CA: Sage.

Dryfoos, J. G. (1999, Fall). The role of the school in children's out-of-school time. *The Future of Children: When School Is Out, 9*, 117–134.

Dube, E. F. (1982). Literacy, cultural familiarity, and "intelligence" as determinants of story recall. In U. Neisser (Ed.), *Memory observed: Remembering in natural contexts*. San Francisco: Freeman.

Dube, M., Julien, D., Lebeau, E., & Gagnon, I. (2000). Marital satisfaction of mothers and the quality of daily interaction with their adolescents. *Canadian Journal of Behavioural Science, 32*, 18–28.

Duckworth, A. L., & Seligman, M. E. P. (2005). Self-discipline outdoes IQ in predicting academic performance of adolescents. *Psychological Science, 16*, 939–944.

Duckworth, A. L., & Seligman, M. E. P. (2006). Self-discipline gives girls the edge: Gender in self-discipline, grades, and achievement test scores. *Journal of Educational Psychology, 98*, 198–208.

Dufresne, A., & Kobasigawa, A. (1989). Children's spontaneous allocation of study time: Differential and sufficient aspects. *Journal of Experimental Child Psychology, 47*, 274–296.

Duncan, G. J., Dowsett, C. J., Claessens, A., Magnuson, K., Huston, A. C., Klebanov, P., et al. (2007). School readiness and later achievement. *Developmental Psychology, 43*, 1428–1446.

Duncan, P. D., Ritter, P. L., Dornbusch, S. M., Gross, R. T., & Carlsmith, J. M. (1985). The effects of pubertal timing on body image, school behavior, and deviance. *Journal of Youth and Adolescence,* *14,* 227–235.

Dunham, P. J., Dunham, F., & Curwin, A. (1993). Joint-attentional states and lexical acquisition at 18 months. *Developmental Psychology, 29,* 827–831.

Dunn, J. (1984). *Sisters and brothers.* Cambridge, MA: Harvard University Press.

Dunn, J. (1988). *The beginnings of social understanding.* Cambridge, MA: Harvard University Press.

Dunn, J. (2006). Moral development in early childhood and social interaction in the family. In M. Killen & J. G. Smetana (Eds.), *Handbook of moral development* (pp. 331–350). Mahwah, NJ: Erlbaum.

Dunn, J. (2007). Siblings and socialization. In J. E. Grusec & P. D. Hastings (Eds.), *Handbook of socialization: Theory and research* (pp. 309–327). New York: Guilford Press.

Dunn, J., Bretherton, I., & Munn, P. (1987). Conversations about feeling states between mothers and their young children. *Developmental Psychology, 23,* 132–139.

Dunn, J., Brown, J., & Beardsall, L. (1991). Family talk about feeling states and children's later understanding of others' emotions. *Developmental Psychology, 27,* 448–455.

Dunn, J., & Munn, P. (1985). Becoming a family member: Family conflict and the development of social understanding in the second year. *Child Development, 56,* 480–492.

Dunn, J., & Munn, P. (1987). Development of justification in disputes with mother and sibling. *Developmental Psychology, 23,* 791–798.

Dunsmore, J. C., Noguchi, R. J. P., Garner, P. W., Casey, E. C., & Bhullar, N. (2008). Gender-specific linkages of affective social competence with peer relations in preschool children. *Early Education and Development, 19*(2), 211–237.

DuPaul, G., & Hoff, K. (1998). Reducing disruptive behavior in general education classrooms: The use of self-management strategies. *School Psychology Review, 27,* 290–304.

DuPaul, G. J., & Eckert, T. L. (1994). The effects of social skills curricula: Now you see them, now you don't. *School Psychology Quarterly, 9,* 113–132.

Durand, V. M. (1998). *Sleep better: A guide to improving sleep for children with special needs.* Baltimore, MD: Brookes.

Durik, A., M., Vida, M., & Eccles, J. S. (2006). Task values and ability beliefs as predictors of high school literacy choices: A developmental analysis. *Journal of Educational Psychology, 98,* 382–393.

Durkin, K. (1995). *Developmental social psychology: From infancy to old age.* Cambridge, MA: Blackwell.

Durkin, K., & Conti-Ramsden, G. (2007). Language, social behavior, and the quality of friendships in adolescents with and without a history of specific language impairment. *Child Development, 78,* 1441–1457.

Dwairy, M., Achoui, M., Abouserie, R., Farah, A., Sakhleh, A. A., Fayad, M., et al. (2006). Parenting styles in Arab societies: A first cross-regional research study. *Journal of Cross Cultural Psychology, 37,* 230–247.

Dweck, C. S. (1975). The role of expectations and attributions in the alleviation of learned helplessness. *Journal of Personality and Social Psychology, 31,* 674–685.

Dweck, C. S. (1986). Motivational processes affecting learning. *American Psychologist, 41,* 1040–1048.

Dweck, C. S. (2000). *Self-theories: Their role in motivation, personality, and development.* Philadelphia: Psychology Press.

Dweck, C. S., & Elliott, E. S. (1983). Achievement motivation. In E. M. Hetherington (Ed.), *Handbook of child psychology: Vol. 4. Socialization, personality, and social development* (4th ed.). New York: Wiley.

Dweck, C. S., & Leggett, E. L. (1988). A social-cognitive approach to motivation and personality. *Psychological Review, 95,* 256–273.

Dweck, C. S., Mangels, J. A., & Good, C. (2004). Motivational effects on attention, cognition, and performance. In D. Y. Dai & R. J. Sternberg (Eds.), *Motivation, emotion, and cognition: Integrative perspectives on intellectual functioning and development* (pp. 41–55). Mahwah, NJ: Erlbaum.

Dwyer, K., & Osher, D. (2000). *Safeguarding our children: An action guide.* Washington, DC: U.S. Departments of Education and Justice, American Institutes for Research. Retrieved February 26, 2004, from http://www.ed.gov/pubs/edpubs.html

Dwyer, K., Osher, D., & Warger, C. (1998). *Early warning, timely response: A guide to safe schools.* Washington, DC: U.S. Department of Education. Retrieved February 26, 2004, from http://www.ed.gov/offices/OSERS/OSEP/earlywrn.html

Dyck, M. J., Piek, J. P., Hay, D., Smith, L., & Hallmayer, J. (2006). Are abilities abnormally interdependent in children with autism? *Journal of Clinical Child and Adolescent Psychology, 35,* 20–33.

Dykens, E. M., & Cassidy, S. B. (1999). Prader-Willi syndrome. In S. Goldstein & C. R. Reynolds (Eds.), *Handbook of neurodevelopmental and genetic disorders* (pp. 525–554). New York: Guilford Press.

Eacott, M. J. (1999). Memory for the events of early childhood. *Current Directions in Psychological Science, 8,* 46–49.

Eagly, A. H. (1987). *Sex differences in social behavior: A social-role interpretation.* Hillsdale, NJ: Erlbaum.

Eamon, M. K., & Mulder, C. (2005). Predicting antisocial behavior among Latino young adolescents: An ecological systems analysis. *American Journal of Orthopsychiatry, 75,* 117–127.

Early, D. M., Maxwell, K. L., Burchinal M., Alva, S., Bender, R. H., Bryant, D., et al. (2007). Teachers' education, classroom quality, and young children's academic skills: Results from seven studies of preschool programs. *Child Development, 78,* 558–580.

Eccles, J. S. (1989). Bringing young women to math and science. In M. Crawford & M. Gentry (Eds.), *Gender and thought: Psychological perspectives.* New York: Springer-Verlag.

Eccles, J. S. (2007). Families, schools, and developing achievement-related motivations and engagement. In J. E. Grusec & P. D. Hastings (Eds.), *Handbook of socialization: Theory and research* (pp. 665–691). New York: Guilford Press.

Eccles, J. S., Freedman-Doan, C., Frome, P., Jacobs, J., & Yoon, K. S. (2000). Gender-role socialization in the family: A longitudinal approach. In T. Eckes & H. M. Trautner (Eds.), *The developmental social psychology of gender* (pp. 333–360). Mahwah, NH: Erlbaum.

Eccles, J. S., & Midgley, C. (1989). Stage-environment fit: Developmentally appropriate classrooms for young adolescents. In C. Ames & R. Ames (Eds.), *Research on motivation in education: Vol. 3. Goals and cognition.* San Diego, CA: Academic Press.

Eccles, J. S., & Wigfield, A. (1985). Teacher expectations and student motivation. In J. B. Dusek (Ed.), *Teacher expectancies.* Hillsdale, NJ: Erlbaum.

Eccles, J. S., Wigfield, A., & Schiefele, U. (1998). Motivation to succeed. In W. Damon (Series Ed.) & N. Eisenberg (Vol. Ed.), *Handbook of child psychology: Vol 3. Social, emotional, and personality development* (5th ed., pp. 1017–1095). New York: Wiley.

Eccles (Parsons), J. S. (1983). Expectancies, values, and academic behaviors. In J. T. Spence (Ed.), *Achievement and achievement motivation.* San Francisco: Freeman.

Echols, L. D., West, R. F., Stanovich, K. E., & Kehr, K. S. (1996). Using children's literacy activities to predict growth in verbal cognitive skills: A longitudinal investigation. *Journal of Educational Psychology, 88,* 296–304.

Eckerman, C. O. (1979). The human infant in social interaction. In R. Cairns (Ed.), *The analysis of social interactions: Methods, issues, and illustrations* (pp. 163–178). Hillsdale, NJ: Erlbaum.

Eckman, P. (1972). Universals and cultural differences in facial expressions of emotion. In J. K. Cole (Ed.), *Nebraska symposium on motivation.* Lincoln: University of Nebraska Press.

Edens, K. M., & Potter, E. F. (2001). Promoting conceptual understanding through pictorial representation. *Studies in Art Education, 42,* 214–233.

Edmunds, A. L., & Edmunds, G. A. (2005). Sensitivity: A double-edged sword for the pre-adolescent and adolescent gifted child. *Roeper Review, 27*(2), 69–77.

Edwards, P. A., & Garcia, G. E. (1994). The implications of Vygotskian theory for the development of home-school programs: A focus on storybook reading. In V. John-Steiner, C. P. Panofsky, & L. W. Smith (Eds.), *Sociocultural approaches to language and literacy: An interactionist perspective.* Cambridge, England: Cambridge University Press.

Eeds, M., & Wells, D. (1989). Grand conversations: An explanation of meaning construction in literature study groups. *Research in the Teaching of English, 23,* 4–29.

Egan, L. C., Santos, L. R., & Bloom, P. (2007). The origins of cognitive dissonance: Evidence from children and monkeys. *Psychological Science, 18,* 978–983.

Ehri, L. C. (1991). Development of the ability to read words. In P. D. Pearson (Ed.), *Handbook of reading research* (Vol. II). New York: Longman.

Ehri, L. C. (1994). Development of the ability to read words: Update. In R. B. Ruddell, M. R. Ruddell, & H. Singer (Eds.), *Theoretical models and processes of reading* (4th ed.). Newark, DE: International Reading Association.

Ehri, L. C. (1998). Word reading by sight and by analogy in beginning readers. In C. Hulme & R. M. Joshi (Eds.), *Reading and spelling: Development and disorders.* Mahwah, NJ: Erlbaum.

Ehri, L. C., Dreyer, L. G., Flugman, B., & Gross, A. (2007). Reading Rescue: An effective tutoring intervention model for language-minority students who are struggling readers in first grade. *American Educational Research Journal, 44,* 414–448.

Ehri, L. C., Nunes, S. R., Stahl, S. A., & Willows, D. M. (2001). Systematic phonics instruction helps students learn to read: Evidence from the National Reading Panel's meta-analysis. *Review of Educational Research, 71,* 393–447.

Ehri, L. C., & Robbins, C. (1992). Beginners need some decoding skill to read words by analogy. *Reading Research Quarterly, 27,* 12–27.

Ehrler, D. J., Evans, J. G., & McGhee, R. L. (1999). Extending big-five theory into childhood: A preliminary investigation into the relationship between big-five personality traits and behavior problems in children. *Psychology in the Schools, 36,* 451–458.

Eigsti, I.-M., Zayas, V., Mischel, W., Shoda, Y., Ayduk, O., Dadlani, M. B., Davidson, M. C., Aber, J. L., & Casey, B. J. (2006). Predicting cognitive control from preschool to late adolescence and young adulthood. *Psychological Science, 17,* 478–484.

Eilam, B. (2001). Primary strategies for promoting homework performance. *American Educational Research Journal, 38,* 691–725.

Eilers, R. E., & Oller, D. K. (1994). Infant vocalizations and early diagnosis of severe hearing impairment. *Journal of Pediatrics, 124,* 199–203.

Eisenberg, N. (1982). The development of reasoning regarding prosocial behavior. In N. Eisenberg (Ed.), *The development of prosocial behavior.* New York: Academic Press.

Eisenberg, N. (1992). *The caring child.* Cambridge, MA: Harvard University Press.

Eisenberg, N. (1995). Prosocial development: A multifaceted model. In W. M. Kurtines & J. L. Gewirtz (Eds.), *Moral development: An introduction.* Boston: Allyn & Bacon.

Eisenberg, N. (2006). Emotion-related regulation. In H. E. Fitzgerald, B. M. Lester, & B. Zuckerman (Vol. Eds.), H. E. Fitzgerald, R. Zucker, & K. Freeark (Eds. in Chief), *The crisis in youth mental health: Critical issues and effective programs. Vol. 1: Childhood disorders* (pp. 133–155). Westport, CT: Praeger.

Eisenberg, N., Carlo, G., Murphy, B., & Van Court, N. (1995). Prosocial development in late adolescence: A longitudinal study. *Child Development, 66,* 1179–1197.

Eisenberg, N., Cumberland, A., & Spinrad, T. L. (1988). Parental socialization of emotion. *Psychological Inquiry, 9,* 241–273.

Eisenberg, N., & Fabes, R. A. (1998). Prosocial development. In W. Damon (Series Ed.) & N. Eisenberg (Vol. Ed.), *Handbook of child psychology: Vol. 3. Social, emotional, and personality development* (pp. 701–778). New York: Wiley.

Eisenberg, N., Fabes, R. A., Carlo, G., & Karbon, M. (1992). Emotional responsivity to others: Behavioral correlates and socialization antecedents. In N. Eisenberg & R. A. Fabes (Eds.), *New directions in child development* (No. 55, pp. 57–73). San Francisco: Jossey-Bass.

Eisenberg, N., Fabes, R. A., Schaller, M., Carlo, G., & Miller, P. A. (1991). The relations of parental characteristics and practices to children's vicarious emotional responding. *Child Development, 62,* 1393–1408.

Eisenberg, N., Fabes, R. A., & Spinrad, T. L. (2006). Prosocial development. In W. Damon & R. M. Lerner (Series Eds.) & N. Eisenberg (Vol. Ed.), *Handbook of child psychology: Vol. 3. Social, emotional, and personality development* (6th ed., pp. 646–718). New York: Wiley.

Eisenberg, N., Lennon, R., & Pasternack, J. F. (1986). Altruistic values and moral judgment. In N. Eisenberg (Ed.), *Altruistic emotion, cognition, and behavior.* Hillsdale, NJ: Erlbaum.

Eisenberg, N., Martin, C. L., & Fabes, R. A. (1996). Gender development and gender effects. In D. C. Berliner & R. C. Calfee (Eds.), *Handbook of educational psychology.* New York: Macmillan.

Eisenberg, N., Miller, P. A., Shell, R., McNalley, S., & Shea, C. (1991). Prosocial development in adolescence: A longitudinal study. *Developmental Psychology, 27,* 849–857.

Eisenberg, N., Smith, C. L., Sadovsky, A., & Spinrad, T. L. (2004). Effortful control: Relations with emotion regulation, adjustment, and socialization in childhood. In R. R. Baumeister & K. D. Vohs (Eds.), *Handbook of self-regulation: Research, theory, and applications* (pp. 259–282). New York: Guilford Press.

Eisenberg, N., Spinrad, T. L., Fabes, R. A., Reiser, M., Cumberland, A., Shepard, S. A., et al. (2004). The relations of effortful control and impulsivity to children's resiliency and adjustment. *Child Development, 75,* 25–46.

Eisenberg, N., Spinrad, T. L., & Sadovsky, A. (2006). Empathy-related responding in children. In M. Killen & J. G. Smetana (Eds.), *Handbook of moral development* (pp. 517–549). Mahwah, NJ: Erlbaum.

Eisenberg, N., Zhou, Q., & Koller, S. (2001). Brazilian adolescents' prosocial moral judgment and behavior: Relations to sympathy, perspective taking, gender-role orientation, and demographic characteristics. *Child Development, 72,* 518–534.

Eisenberger, R. (1992). Learned industriousness. *Psychological Review, 99,* 248–267.

Ekelin, M., Crang-Svalenius, E., & Dykes, A. K. (2004). A qualitative study of mothers' and fathers' experiences of routine ultrasound examination in Sweden. *Midwifery, 20,* 335–344.

Elbro, C., & Petersen, D. K. (2004). Long-term effects of phoneme awareness and letter sound training: An intervention study with children at risk for dyslexia. *Journal of Educational Psychology, 96,* 660–670.

Elder, A. D. (2002). Characterizing fifth grade students' epistemological beliefs in science. In B. K. Hofer & P. R. Pintrich (Eds.), *Personal epistemology: The psychology of beliefs about knowledge and knowing* (pp. 347–363). Mahwah, NJ: Erlbaum.

Elia, J. P. (1994). Homophobia in the high school: A problem in need of a resolution. *Journal of Homosexuality, 77*(1), 177–185.

Elias, G., & Broerse, J. (1996). Developmental changes in the incidence and likelihood of simultaneous talk during the first two years: A question of function. *Journal of Child Language, 23,* 201–217.

Elison, J., & Harter, S. (2007). Humiliation: Causes, correlates, and consequences. In J. L. Tracy, R. W. Robins, & J. P. Tangney (Eds.), *The self-conscious emotions: Theory and research* (pp. 310–329). New York: Guilford Press.

Elkind, D. (1981a). *Children and adolescents: Interpretive essays on Jean Piaget* (3rd ed.). New York: Oxford University Press.

Elkind, D. (1981b). *The hurried child: Growing up too fast too soon.* Reading, MA: Addison-Wesley.

Elkind, D. (1987). *Miseducation: Preschoolers at risk.* New York: Knopf.

Elkind, D. (2007). *The power of play: How spontaneous, imaginative activities lead to happier, healthier children.* Cambridge, MA: De Capo Press.

Elliot, A. J., & McGregor, H. A. (2000, April). Approach and avoidance goals and autonomous-controlled regulation: Empirical and conceptual relations. In A. Assor (Chair), *Self-determination theory and achievement goal theory: Convergences, divergences, and educational implications.* Symposium conducted at the annual meeting of the American Educational Research Association, New Orleans, LA.

Elliott, D. J. (1995). *Music matters: A new philosophy of music education.* New York: Oxford University Press.

Elliott, R., & Vasta, R. (1970). The modeling of sharing: Effects associated with vicarious reinforcement, symbolization, age, and generalization. *Journal of Experimental Child Psychology, 10,* 8–15.

Ellis, B. J. (2004). Timing of pubertal maturation in girls: An integrated life history approach. *Psychological Bulletin, 130,* 920–958.

Elze, D. E. (2003). Gay, lesbian, and bisexual youths' perceptions of their high school environments and comfort in school. *Children and Schools, 25*(4), 225–239.

Emde, R. N., & Buchsbaum, H. (1990). "Didn't you hear my mommy?" Autonomy with connectedness in moral self-emergence. In D. Cicchetti & M. Beeghly (Eds.), *The self in transition: Infancy to adulthood* (pp. 35–60). Chicago: University of Chicago Press.

Emde, R., Gaensbauer, T., & Harmon, R. (1976). *Emotional expression in infancy: A biobehavioral study* (Psychological Issues, Vol. 10, No. 37). New York: International Universities Press.

Emery, R. E., Laumann-Billings, L., Waldron, M. C., Sbarra, D. A., & Dillon, P. (2001). Child custody mediation and litigation: Custody, contact, and coparenting 12 years after initial dispute resolution. *Journal of Counseling and Clinical Psychology, 69,* 323–332.

Emmer, E. T., Evertson, C. M., & Worsham, M. E. (2000). *Classroom management for secondary teachers* (5th ed.). Boston: Allyn & Bacon.

Emmer, E. T., & Gerwels, M. C. (2006). Classroom management in middle and high school classrooms. In C. M. Evertson & C. S. Weinstein (Eds.), *Handbook of classroom management: Research, practice, and contemporary issues* (pp. 407–437). Mahwah, NJ: Erlbaum.

Empson, S. B. (1999). Equal sharing and shared meaning: The development of fraction concepts in a first-grade classroom. *Cognition and Instruction, 17,* 283–342.

Engle, P. L., & Breaux, C. (1998). Fathers' involvement with children: Perspectives from developing countries. *Social Policy Report: Society for Research in Child Development, 12*(1), 1–21.

English, D. J. (1998). The extent and consequences of child maltreatment. *The Future of Children: Protecting Children from Abuse and Neglect, 8*(1), 39–53.

Enkin, M., Keirse, M. J., Neilson, J., Crowther, C., Duley, L., Hodnett, E., et al. (2000). *A guide to effective care in pregnancy and childbirth* (3rd ed.). Oxford, England: Oxford University Press.

Enyedy, N. (2005). Inventing mapping: Creating cultural forms to solve collective problems. *Cognition and Instruction, 23,* 427–466.

Eppright, T. D., Sanfacon, J. A., Beck, N. C., & Bradley, S. J. (1998). Sport psychiatry in childhood and adolescence: An overview. *Child Psychiatry and Human Development, 28,* 71–88.

Epstein, J. A., Botvin, G. J., Diaz, T., Toth, V., & Schinke, S. P. (1995). Social and personal factors in marijuana use and intentions to use drugs among inner city minority youth. *Journal of Developmental and Behavioral Pediatrics, 16,* 14–20.

Epstein, J. L. (1986). Friendship selection: Developmental and environmental influences. In E. Mueller & C. Cooper (Eds.), *Process and outcome in peer relationships* (pp. 129–160). New York: Academic Press.

Epstein, J. L. (1996). Perspectives and previews on research and policy for school, family, and community partnerships. In A. Booth & J. F. Dunn (Eds.), *Family-school links: How do they affect educational outcomes?* Mahwah, NJ: Erlbaum.

Epstein, J. S. (1998). Introduction: Generation X, youth culture, and identity. In J. S. Epstein (Ed.), *Youth culture: Identity in a postmodern world* (pp. 1–23). Malden, MA: Blackwell.

Epstein, L. H., Wing, R. R., & Valoski, A. (1985). Childhood obesity. *Pediatric Clinics of North America, 32,* 363–379.

Epstein, S., & Morling, B. (1995). Is the self motivated to do more than enhance and/or verify itself? In M. H. Kernis (Ed.), *Efficacy, agency, and self-esteem.* New York: Plenum Press.

Epstein, T. (2000). Adolescents' perspectives on racial diversity in U.S. history: Case studies from an urban classroom. *American Educational Research Journal, 37,* 185–214.

Ericsson, K. A. (2003). The acquisition of expert performance as problem solving. In J. E. Davidson & R. J. Sternberg (Eds.), *The psychology of problem solving* (pp. 31–83). Cambridge, England: Cambridge University Press.

Erikson, E. H. (1963). *Childhood and society* (2nd ed.). New York: Norton.

Erikson, E. H. (1972). *Eight ages of man.* In C. S. Lavatelli & F. Stendler (Eds.), *Readings in child behavior and child development.* San Diego, CA: Harcourt Brace Jovanovich.

Eron, L. D. (1980). Prescription for reduction of aggression. *American Psychologist, 35,* 244–252.

Eron, L. D. (1987). The development of aggressive behavior from the perspective of a developing behaviorism. *American Psychologist, 42,* 435–442.

Erwin, P. (1993). *Friendship and peer relations in children.* Chichester, England: Wiley.

Espelage, D. L., Holt, M. K., & Henkel, R. R. (2003). Examination of peer-group contextual effects on aggression during early adolescence. *Child Development, 74,* 205–220.

Espinosa, L. (2007). English-language learners as they enter school. In R. Pianta, M. Cox, & K. Snow (Eds.), *School readiness and the transition to kindergarten in the era of accountability* (pp. 175–196). Baltimore, MD: Paul H. Brookes.

Espinosa, L. (2008). *Challenging common myths about young English language learners.* FCD Policy Brief: Advancing PK-3 (No. 8). New York: Foundation for Child Development.

Estes, D., Chandler, M., Horvath, K. J., & Backus, D. W. (2003). American and British college students' epistemological beliefs about research on psychological and biological development. *Applied Developmental Psychology, 23,* 625–642.

Estes, K. G., Evans, J. L., Alibali, M. W., & Saffran, J. R. (2007). Can infants map meaning to newly segmented words? Statistical segmentation and word learning. *Psychological Science, 18,* 254–260.

Etaugh, C., Grinnell, K., & Etaugh, A. (1989). Development of gender labeling: Effect of age of pictured children. *Sex Roles, 21,* 769–773.

Evans, E. M. (2001). Cognitive and contextual factors in the emergence of diverse belief systems: Creation versus evolution. *Cognitive Psychology, 42,* 217–266.

Evans, E. M., Schweingruber, H., & Stevenson, H. W. (2002). Gender differences in interest and knowledge acquisition: The United States, Taiwan, and Japan. *Sex Roles, 47,* 153–167.

Evans, G. W. (2004). The environment of childhood poverty. *American Psychologist, 59,* 77–92.

Evans, G. W., & Kim, P. (2007). Childhood poverty and health: Cumulative risk exposure and stress dysregulation. *Psychological Science, 18,* 953–957.

Evans, M. A., & Saint-Aubin, J. (2005). What children are looking at during shared storybook reading: Evidence from eye movement monitoring. *Psychological Science, 16,* 913–920.

Fabes, R. A., Eisenberg, N., Jones, S., Smith, M., Guthrie, I., Poulin, R., et al. (1999). Regulation, emotionality, and preschoolers' socially competent peer interactions. *Child Development, 70,* 432–442.

Fabos, B., & Young, M. D. (1999). Telecommunication in the classroom: Rhetoric versus reality. *Review of Educational Research, 69,* 217–259.

Fadiman, A. (1997). *The spirit catches you and you fall down: The Hmong child, her American doctors, and the collision of two cultures.* New York: Noonday Press/Farrar, Straus and Giroux.

Fagan, J. F., Holland, C. R., & Wheeler, K. (2007). The prediction, from infancy, of adult IQ and achievement. *Intelligence, 35,* 225–231.

Fagan, J. F., & Singer, L. T. (1983). Infant recognition memory as a measure of intelligence. In L. P. Lipsitt (Ed.), *Advances in infancy research* (Vol. 2). Norwood, NJ: Ablex.

Fahrmeier, E. D. (1978). The development of concrete operations among the Hausa. *Journal of Cross-Cultural Psychology, 9,* 23–44.

Fairchild, H. H., & Edwards-Evans, S. (1990). African American dialects and schooling: A review. In A. M. Padilla, H. H. Fairchild, & C. M. Valadez (Eds.), *Bilingual education: Issues and strategies.* Newbury Park, CA: Sage.

Falbo, T. (1992). Social norms and the one-child family: Clinical and policy implications. In F. Boer & J. Dunn (Eds.), *Children's sibling relationships* (pp. 71–82). Hillsdale, NJ: Erlbaum.

Falbo, T., & Polit, D. (1986). A quantitative review of the only child literature: Research evidence and theory development. *Psychological Bulletin, 100,* 176–189.

Fantini, A. E. (1985). *Language acquisition of a bilingual child: A sociolinguistic perspective.* Clevedon, England: Multilingual Matters. (Available from the SIT Bookstore, School for International Training, Kipling Road, Brattleboro, VT 05302)

Fantino, A. M., & Colak, A. (2001). Refugee children in Canada: Searching for identity. *Child Welfare, 80,* 587–596.

Farber, B., Mindel, C. H., & Lazerwitz, B. (1988). The Jewish American family. In C. H. Mindel, R. W. Habenstein, & R. Wright (Eds.), *Ethnic families in America: Patterns and variations.* New York: Elsevier.

Farmer, T. W., Leung, M.-C., Pearl, R., Rodkin, P. C., Cadwallader, T. W., & Van Acker, R. (2002). Deviant or diverse peer groups? The peer affiliations of aggressive elementary students. *Journal of Educational Psychology, 94,* 611–620.

Farran, D. C. (2001). Critical periods and early intervention. In D. B. Bailey, Jr., J. T. Bruer, F. J. Symons, & J. W. Lichtman (Eds.), *Critical thinking about critical periods* (pp. 233–266). Baltimore: Brookes.

Farrar, M. J., & Goodman, G. S. (1992). Developmental changes in event memory. *Child Development, 63,* 173–187.

Farrell, M. M., & Phelps, L. (2000). A comparison of the Leiter-R and the Universal Nonverbal Intelligence Test (UNIT) with children classified as language impaired. *Journal of Psychoeducational Assessment, 18,* 268–274.

Farrington-Flint, L., & Wood, C. (2007). The role of lexical analogies in beginning reading: Insights from children's self-reports. *Journal of Educational Psychology, 99,* 326–338.

Farver, J. A. M., & Branstetter, W. H. (1994). Preschoolers' prosocial responses to their peers' distress. *Developmental Psychology, 30,* 334–341.

Fausel, D. F. (1986). Loss after divorce: Helping children grieve. *Journal of Independent Social Work, 1*(1), 39–47.

Feather, N. T. (1982). *Expectations and actions: Expectancy-value models in psychology.* Hillsdale, NJ: Erlbaum.

Federal Interagency Forum on Child and Family Statistics. (2007). *America's children in brief: Key national indicators of well-being, 2007.* Washington, DC: U.S. Government Printing Office.

Feinberg, M. E., Kan, M. L., & Hetherington, E. M. (2007). The longitudinal influence of coparenting conflict on parental negativity and adolescent adjustment. *Journal of Marriage and Family, 69,* 687–702.

Feinman, S. (1992). *Social referencing and the social construction of reality in infancy.* New York: Plenum Press.

Feldhusen, J. F. (1989). Synthesis of research on gifted youth. *Educational Leadership, 26*(1), 6–11.

Feldhusen, J. F., Van Winkle, L., & Ehle, D. A. (1996). Is it acceleration or simply appropriate instruction for precocious youth? *Teaching Exceptional Children, 28*(3), 48–51.

Feldman, R., Sussman, A. L., & Zigler, E. (2004). Parental leave and work adaptation at the transition to parenthood: Individual, marital, and social correlates. *Applied Developmental Psychology, 25,* 459–470.

Feldman, S. S., & Wentzel, K. R. (1990). The relationship between parental styles, sons' self-restraint, and peer relations in early adolescence. *Journal of Early Adolescence, 10,* 439–454.

Feldman, S. S., & Wood, D. N. (1994). Parents' expectations for preadolescent sons' behavioral autonomy: A longitudinal study of correlates and outcomes. *Journal of Research on Adolescence, 4,* 45–70.

Felton, R. H. (1998). The development of reading skills in poor readers: Educational implications. In C. Hulme & R. M. Joshi (Eds.), *Reading and spelling: Development and disorders.* Mahwah, NJ: Erlbaum.

Fennell, C. T., Byers-Heinlein, K., & Werker, J. F. (2007). Using speech sounds to guide word learning: The case of bilingual infants. *Child Development, 78,* 1510–1525.

Fennema, E. (1987). Sex-related differences in education: Myths, realities, and interventions. In V. Richardson-Koehler (Ed.), *Educators' handbook: A research perspective.* White Plains, NY: Longman.

Fenson, L., Dale, P., Reznick, J., Bates, E., Thal, D., & Pethick, S. (1994). Variability in early communicative development. *Monographs of the Society for Research in Child Development, 59*(5, Serial No. 242), 1–173.

Fenson, L., Vella, D., & Kennedy, M. (1989). Children's knowledge of thematic and taxonomic relations at two years of age. *Child Development, 60,* 911–919.

Fernald, A. (1992). Human maternal vocalizations to infants as biologically relevant signals: An evolutionary perspective. In J. Barkow, L. Cosmides, & J. Tooby (Eds.), *Evolutionary psychology and the generation of culture.* New York: Oxford University Press.

Fernald, A., Swingley, D., & Pinto, J. P. (2001). When half a word is enough: Infants can recognize spoken words using partial phonetic information. *Child Development, 72,* 1003–1015.

Feuerstein, R. (1979). *The dynamic assessment of retarded performers: The Learning Potential Assessment Device, theory, instruments, and techniques.* Baltimore: University Park Press.

Feuerstein, R. (1980). *Instrumental enrichment: An intervention program for cognitive modifiability.* Baltimore: University Park Press.

Feuerstein, R. (1990). The theory of structural cognitive modifiability. In B. Z. Presseisen (Ed.), *Learning and thinking styles: Classroom interaction.* Washington, DC: National Education Association.

Feuerstein, R., Feuerstein, Ra., & Gross, S. (1997). The Learning Potential Assessment Device. In D. P. Flanagan, J. L. Genshaft, & P. L. Harrison (Eds.), *Contemporary intellectual assessment: Theories, tests, and issues* (pp. 297–313). New York: Guilford Press.

Fewell, R. R., & Sandall, S. R. (1983). Curricula adaptations for young children: Visually impaired, hearing impaired, and physically impaired. *Curricula in Early Childhood Special Education, 2*(4), 51–66.

Fiedler, E. D., Lange, R. E., & Winebrenner, S. (1993). In search of reality: Unraveling the myths about tracking, ability grouping and the gifted. *Roeper Review, 16*(1), 4–7.

Fiedler, K. (2008). Language: A toolbox for sharing and influencing social reality. *Perspectives on Psychological Science, 3,* 38–47.

Field, D. (1987). A review of preschool conservation training: An analysis of analyses. *Developmental Review, 7,* 210–251.

Field, S. L., Labbo, L. D., & Ash, G. E. (1999, April). *Investigating young children's construction of social studies concepts and the intersection of literacy learning.* Paper presented at the annual meeting of the American Educational Research Association, Montreal, Canada.

Field, T. (2001). Massage therapy facilitates weight gain in preterm infants. *Current Directions in Psychological Science, 10,* 51–54.

Field, T., Woodson, R., Greenberg, R., & Cohen, D. (1982). Discrimination and imitation of facial expressions by neonates. *Science, 218,* 179–81.

Fifer, W. P., & Moon, C. M. (1995). The effects of fetal experience with sound. In J. P. Lecanuet, W. P. Fifer, N. A. Krasnegor, & W. P. Smotherman (Eds.), *Fetal development: A psychobiological perspective.* Hillsdale, NJ: Erlbaum.

Filax, G. (2007). Queer in/visibility: The case of Ellen, Michel, and Oscar. In S. Books (Ed.), *Invisible children in the society and its schools* (3rd ed., pp. 213–234). Mahwah, NJ: Erlbaum.

Finders, M., & Lewis, C. (1994). Why some parents don't come to school. *Educational Leadership, 51*(8), 50–54.

Finkelhor, D., Mitchell, K. J., & Wolak, J. (2000). *Online victimization: A report on the nation's youth.* Durham, NH: Crimes Against Children Research Center. Retrieved March 7, 2003, from http://www.unh.edu/ccrc/pdf/Victimization_Online_Survey.pdf

Fiorello, C. A., & Primerano, D. (2005). Research into practice: Cattell-Horn-Carroll cognitive assessment in practice: Eligibility and program development issues. *Psychology in the Schools, 42*(5), 525–536.

Fischer, G., & Konomi, S. (2007). Innovative socio-technical environments in support of distributed intelligence and lifelong learning. *Journal of Computer Assisted Learning, 23,* 338–350.

Fischer, K. (2005, April). Dynamic skill development and integration of motivation, emotion, and cognition. In D. Y. Dai (Chair), *Beyond cognitivism: Where are we now?* Symposium presented at the annual meeting of the American Educational Research Association, Montreal, Canada.

Fischer, K. W., & Bidell, T. (1991). Constraining nativist inferences about cognitive capacities. In S. Carey & R. Gelman (Eds.), *The epigenesis of mind: Essays on biology and cognition.* Hillsdale, NJ: Erlbaum.

Fischer, K. W., & Bidell, T. R. (2006). Dynamic development of action and thought. In W. Damon & R. M. Lerner (Eds. in Chief) & R. M. Lerner (Vol. Ed.), *Handbook of child psychology: Vol. 1. Theoretical models of human development* (6th ed., pp. 313–399). Hoboken, NJ: Wiley.

Fischer, K. W., & Daley, S. G. (2007). Connecting cognitive science and neuroscience to education: Potentials and pitfalls in inferring executive processes. In L. Meltzer (Ed.), *Executive function in education: From theory to practice* (pp. 55–72). New York: Guilford Press.

Fischer, K. W., Daniel, D. B., Immordino-Yang, M. H., Stern, E., Battro, A., & Koizumi, H. (2007). Why *Mind, Brain, and Education?* Why now? *Mind, Brain, and Education, 1*(1), 1–2.

Fischer, K. W., & Immordino-Yang, M. H. (2006). Cognitive development and education: From dynamic general structure to specific learning and teaching. In W. Damon, R. M. Lerner (Series Eds.), D. Kuhn, & R. Siegler (Vol. Eds.), *Handbook of child psychology: Vol. 1. Cognition, perception, and language* (6th ed.). New York: Wiley.

Fischer, K. W., Knight, C. C., & Van Parys, M. (1993). Analyzing diversity in developmental pathways: Methods and concepts. In R. Case & W. Edelstein (Eds.), *The new structuralism in cognitive development: Theory and research on individual pathways*. Basel, Switzerland: Karger.

Fishbein, D. H., Hyde, C., Eldreth, D., Paschall, M. J., Hubal, R., Das, A., et al. (2006). Neurocognitive skills moderate urban male adolescents' responses to preventive intervention materials. *Drug and Alcohol Dependence, 82*(1), 47–60.

Fisher, C. B., Jackson, J. F., & Villarruel, F. A. (1998). The study of African American and Latin American children and youth. In W. Damon (Series Ed.) & R. M. Lerner (Vol. Ed.), *Handbook of child psychology: Vol. 1. Theoretical models of human development* (5th ed., pp. 1145–1207). New York: Wiley.

Fisher, D., & Frey, N. (2007). *Checking for understanding: Formative assessment techniques for your classroom*. Alexandria, VA: Association for Supervision and Curriculum Development.

Fisher, J. D., & Fisher, W. A. (1992). Changing AIDS-risk behavior. *Psychological Bulletin, 111,* 455–474.

Fitzgerald, J. (1987). Research on revision in writing. *Review of Educational Research, 57,* 481–506.

Fives, C. J., & Flanagan, R. (2002). A review of the Universal Nonverbal Intelligence Test (UNIT): An advance for evaluating youngsters with diverse needs. *School Psychology International, 23,* 425–448.

Fivush, R., Haden, C., & Adam, S. (1995). Structure and coherence of preschoolers' personal narratives over time: Implications for childhood amnesia. *Journal of Experimental Child Psychology, 60,* 32–56.

Fivush, R., Haden, C., & Reese, E. (1996). Remembering, recounting, and reminiscing: The development of autobiographical memory in social context. In D. C. Rubin (Ed.), *Remembering our past: Studies in autobiographical memory* (pp. 341–359). Cambridge, England: Cambridge University Press.

Fivush, R., Haden, C. A., & Reese, E. (2006). Elaborating on elaborations: Role of maternal reminiscing style in cognitive and socioemotional development. *Child Development, 77,* 1568–1588.

Fivush, R., & Nelson, K. (2004). Culture and language in the emergence of autobiographical memory. *Psychological Science, 15,* 573–577.

Flanagan, C. (2003). Trust, identity, and civic hope. *Applied Developmental Science, 7*(6), 165–171.

Flanagan, C. A., & Faison, N. (2001). Youth civic development: Implications of research for social policy and programs. *Social Policy Report of the Society for Research in Child Development, 15*(1), 1–14.

Flanagan, C. A., & Tucker, C. J. (1999). Adolescents' explanations for political issues: Concordance with their views of self and society. *Developmental Psychology, 35,* 1198–1209.

Flavell, J. H. (1994). Cognitive development: Past, present, and future. In R. D. Parke, P. A. Ornstein, J. J. Rieser, & C. Zahn-Waxler (Eds.), *A century of developmental psychology* (pp. 569–587). Washington, DC: American Psychological Association.

Flavell, J. H. (1996). Piaget's legacy. *Psychological Science, 7*(4), 200–203.

Flavell, J. H. (2000). Development of children's knowledge about the mental world. *International Journal of Behavioral Development, 24*(1), 15–23.

Flavell, J. H., Flavell, E. R., & Green, F. L. (2001). Development of children's understanding of connections between thinking and feeling. *Psychological Science, 12,* 430–432.

Flavell, J. H., Friedrichs, A. G., & Hoyt, J. D. (1970). Developmental changes in memorization processes. *Cognitive Psychology, 1,* 324–340.

Flavell, J. H., Green, F. L., & Flavell, E. R. (1995). Young children's knowledge about thinking. *Monographs of the Society for Research in Child Development, 60*(1, Serial No. 243).

Flavell, J. H., Green, F. L., & Flavell, E. R. (2000). Development of children's awareness of their own thoughts. *Journal of Cognitive Development, 1,* 97–112.

Flavell, J. H., & Miller, P. H. (1998). Social cognition. In W. Damon (Series Ed.), D. Kuhn, & R. S. Siegler (Vol. Eds.), *Handbook of child psychology: Vol. 2. Cognition, perception, and language* (5th ed.). New York: Wiley.

Flavell, J. H., Miller, P. H., & Miller, S. A. (2002). *Cognitive development* (4th ed.). Upper Saddle River, NJ: Prentice Hall.

Flay, B. R., & Allred, C. G. (2003). Long-term effects of the Positive Action program. *American Journal of Health Behavior, 27*(1), 6–21.

Flege, J. E., Munro, M. J., & MacKay, I. R. A. (1995). Effects of age of second-language learning on the production of English consonants. *Speech Communication, 16,* 1–26.

Fletcher, A. C., Bridges, T. H., & Hunter, A. G. (2007). Managing children's friendships through interparental relationships: Roles of ethnicity and friendship context. *Journal of Marriage and Family, 69,* 1135–1149.

Fletcher, A. C., Hunter, A. G., & Eanes, A. Y. (2006). Links between social network closure and child well-being: The organizing role of friendship context. *Developmental Psychology, 42,* 1057–1068.

Fletcher, J. M., Lyon, G. R., Fuchs, L. S., & Barnes, M. A. (2007). *Learning disabilities: From identification to intervention*. New York: Guilford Press.

Fletcher, K. L., & Bray, N. W. (1996). External memory strategy use in preschool children. *Merrill-Palmer Quarterly, 42,* 379–396.

Flieller, A. (1999). Comparison of the development of formal thought in adolescent cohorts aged 10 to 15 years (1967–1996 and 1972–1993). *Developmental Psychology, 35,* 1048–1058.

Floyd, R. G., Bergeron, R., & Alfonso, V. C. (2006). Cattell-Horn-Carroll cognitive ability profiles of poor comprehenders. *Reading and Writing, 19,* 427–456.

Flum, H., & Kaplan, A. (2006). Exploratory orientation as an educational goal. *Educational Psychologist, 41,* 99–110.

Flynn, J. R. (1987). Massive IQ gains in 14 nations: What IQ tests really measure. *Psychological Bulletin, 101,* 171–191.

Flynn, J. R. (1991). *Asian Americans: Achievement beyond IQ*. Hillsdale, NJ: Erlbaum.

Flynn, J. R. (2003). Movies about intelligence: The limitations of g. *Current Directions in Psychological Science, 12,* 95–99.

Flynn, J. R. (2007). *What is intelligence? Beyond the Flynn effect*. New York: Cambridge University Press.

Forbes, M. L., Ormrod, J. E., Bernardi, J. D., Taylor, S. L., & Jackson, D. L. (1999, April). *Children's conceptions of space, as reflected in maps of their hometown*. Paper presented at the annual meeting of the American Educational Research Association, Montreal, Canada.

Ford, D. Y. (1996). *Reversing underachievement among gifted Black students*. New York: Teachers College Press.

Ford, L., & Dahinten, V. S. (2005). Use of intelligence tests in the assessment of preschoolers. In D. P. Flanagan & P. L. Harrison (Eds.), *Contemporary intellectual assessment: Theories, tests, and issues* (2nd ed., pp. 487–503). New York: Guilford Press.

Ford, M. E. (1996). Motivational opportunities and obstacles associated with social responsibility and caring behavior in school contexts. In J. Juvonen & K. R. Wentzel (Eds.), *Social motivation: Understanding children's school adjustment* (pp. 126–153). Cambridge, England: Cambridge University Press.

Ford, M. E., & Smith, P. R. (2007). Thriving with social purpose: An integrative approach to the development of optimal human functioning. *Educational Psychologist, 42,* 153–171.

Forehand, R., Wierson, M., Thomas, A. M., Fauber, R., Armistead, L., Kempton, T., et al. (1991). A short-term longitudinal examination of young adolescent functioning following divorce: The role of family factors. *Journal of Abnormal Child Psychology, 19,* 97–111.

Forgey, M. A., Schinke, S., & Cole, K. (1997). School-based interventions to prevent substance use among inner-city minority adolescents. In D. K. Wilson, J. R. Rodrigue, & W. C. Taylor (Eds.), *Health-promoting and health-compromising behaviors among adolescents* (pp. 251–267). Washington, DC: American Psychological Association.

Forthun, L. F., Montgomery, M. J., & Bell, N. J. (2006). Identity formation in a relational context: A person-centered analysis of troubled youth. *Identity, 6*(2), 141–167.

Fowler, J. W., & Peterson, P. L. (1981). Increasing reading persistence and altering attributional style of learned helpless children. *Journal of Educational Psychology, 73,* 251–260.

Fowler, S. A., & Baer, D. M. (1981). "Do I have to be good all day?" The timing of delayed reinforcement as a factor in generalization. *Journal of Applied Behavior Analysis, 14,* 13–24.

Fox, N. A., Henderson, H. A., Rubin, K. H., Calkins, S. D., & Schmidt, L. A. (2001). Continuity and discontinuity of behavioral inhibition and exuberance: Psychophysiological and behavioral influences across the first 4 years of life. *Child Development, 72*(1), 1–21.

Francis, M., & McCutchen, D. (1994, April). *Strategy differences in revising between skilled and less skilled writers*. Paper presented at the annual meeting of the American Educational Research Association, New Orleans, LA.

Frank, A. (1967). *The diary of a young girl* (B. M. Mooyaart, Trans.). New York: Doubleday.

Frank, C. (1999). *Ethnographic eyes: A teacher's guide to classroom observation*. Portsmouth, NH: Heinemann.

Franklin, J. H. (2007). African American families: A historical note. In H. P. McAdoo (Ed.), *Black families* (4th ed., pp. 3–6). Thousand Oaks, CA: Sage.

Frederiksen, N. (1984). Implications of cognitive theory for instruction in problem-solving. *Review of Educational Research, 54,* 363–407.

Fredricks, J. A., Blumenfeld, P. C., & Paris, A. H. (2004). School engagement: Potential of the concept, state of the evidence. *Review of Educational Research, 74,* 59–109.

Freeark, K. (2006). Adoption and youth: Critical issues and strengths-based programming to address them. In K. Freeark & W. S. Davidson (Eds.), *The crisis in youth mental health: Critical issues and effective programs: Vol. 3. Issues for families, schools, and communities* (pp. 121–146). Westport, CT: Praeger/Greenwood.

Freedenthal, S. & Stiffman, A. R. (2007). "They might think I was crazy": Young American Indians' reasons for not seeking help when suicidal. *Journal of Adolescent Research, 22,* 58–77.

Freedman, B. A. (2003, April). *Boys and literacy: Why boys? Which boys? Why now?*. Paper presented at the annual meeting of the American Educational Research Association, Chicago.

Freedman, K. (2001). The social reconstruction of art education: Teaching visual culture. In C. A. Grant & M. L. Gomez, *Campus and classroom: Making schooling multicultural* (2nd ed.). Upper Saddle River, NJ: Merrill/Prentice Hall.

The Freedom Writers (with Gruwell, E.) (1999). *The Freedom Writers diary: How a teacher and 150 teens used writing to change themselves and the world around them*. New York: Broadway Books.

Freeman, K. E., Gutman, L. M., & Midgley, C. (2002). Can achievement goal theory enhance our understanding of the motivation and performance of African American young adolescents? In C. Midgley (Ed.), *Goals, goal structures, and patterns of adaptive learning* (pp. 175–204). Mahwah, NJ: Erlbaum.

Freitag, C. M. (2007). The genetics of autistic disorders and its clinical relevance: A review of the literature. *Molecular Psychiatry, 12,* 2–22.

French, D. C., Jansen, E. A., & Pidada, S. (2002). United States and Indonesian children's and adolescents' reports of relational aggression by disliked peers. *Child Development, 73,* 1143–1150.

French, L., & Brown, A. (1977). Comprehension of "before" and "after" in logical and arbitrary sequences. *Journal of Child Language, 4,* 247–256.

French, S. E., Seidman, E., Allen, L., & Aber, J. L. (2006). The development of ethnic identity during adolescence. *Developmental Psychology, 42,* 1–10.

Frensch, P. A., & Rünger, D. (2003). Implicit learning. *Current Directions in Psychological Science, 12,* 13–18.

Freud, S. (1905). *Three contributions to the theory of sex. The basic writings of Sigmund Freud* (A. A. Brill, trans.). New York: The Modern Library.

Freud, S. (1910). *The origin and development of psychoanalysis.* New York: Henry Regnery (Gateway Editions), 1965.

Freud, S. (1923). *The ego and the id* (J. Riviere, trans.). New York: Norton, 1960.

Freund, L. (1990). Maternal regulation of children's problem solving behavior and its impact on children's performance. *Child Development, 61,* 113–126.

Friedman, C. K., Leaper, C., & Bigler, R. S. (2007). Do mothers' gender-related attitudes or comments predict young children's gender beliefs? *Parenting: Science and Practice, 7,* 357–366.

Friedman, L. (1994, April). The role of spatial skill in gender differences in mathematics: Meta-analytic evidence. Paper presented at the annual meeting of the American Educational Research Association, New Orleans, LA.

Friend, R. A. (1993). Choices, not closets: Heterosexism and homophobia in schools. In L. Weis & M. Fine (Eds.), *Beyond silenced voices: Class, race, and gender in United States schools* (pp. 209–235). Albany, NY: SUNY Press.

Frosch, C. A., Mangelsdorf, S. C., & McHale, J. L. (2000). Marital behavior and the security of preschooler-parent attachment relationships. *Journal of Family Psychology, 14,* 144–161.

Frost, J. L., Shin, D., & Jacobs, P. J. (1998). Physical environments and children's play. In O. N. Saracho & B. Spodek (Eds.), *Multiple perspectives on play in early childhood education.* Albany: State University of New York Press.

Fry, A. F., & Hale, S. (1996). Processing speed, working memory, and fluid intelligence. *Psychological Science, 7,* 237–241.

Fuchs, D., Fuchs, L. S., Mathes, P. G., & Simmons, D. C. (1997). Peer-assisted learning strategies: Making classrooms more responsive to diversity. *American Educational Research Journal, 34,* 174–206.

Fuchs, L. S., Fuchs, D., Prentice, K., Burch, M., Hamlett, C. L., Owen, R., et al. (2003). Enhancing third-grade students' mathematical problem solving with self-regulated learning strategies. *Journal of Educational Psychology, 95,* 306–315.

Fujimura, N. (2001). Facilitating children's proportional reasoning: A model of reasoning processes and effects of intervention on strategy change. *Journal of Educational Psychology, 93,* 589–603.

Fukkink, R. G., & de Glopper, K. (1998). Effects of instruction in deriving word meanings from context: A meta-analysis. *Review of Educational Research, 68,* 450–469.

Fuligni, A. J. (1998). The adjustment of children from immigrant families. *Current Directions in Psychological Science, 7,* 99–103.

Fuller, M. L. (2001). Multicultural concerns and classroom management. In C. A. Grant & M. L. Gomez, *Campus and classroom: Making schooling multicultural* (pp. 109–134). Upper Saddle River, NJ: Merrill/Prentice Hall.

Funk, J. B., Buchman, D. D., Jenks, J., & Bechtoldt, H. (2003). Playing violent video games, desensitization, and moral evaluation in children. *Applied Developmental Psychology, 24,* 413–436.

Furman, W., & Simon, V. A. (1999). Cognitive representations of adolescent romantic relationships. In W. Furman, B. B. Brown, & C. Feiring (Eds.), *The development of romantic relationships in adolescence* (pp. 75–98). Cambridge, England: Cambridge University Press.

Furstenberg, F. F., Jr., Nord, C., Peterson, J. L., & Zill, N. (1983). The life course of children and divorce: Marital disruption and parental conflict. *American Sociological Review, 48,* 656–668.

Fuson, K. C., & Briars, D. J. (1990). Using a base-ten blocks learning/teaching approach for first- and second-grade place-value and multidigit addition and subtraction. *Journal for Research in Mathematics Education, 21,* 180–206.

Fuson, K. C., & Hall, J. W. (1983). The acquisition of early word meanings: A conceptual analysis and review. In H. P. Ginsburg (Ed.), *Children's mathematical thinking.* New York: Academic Press.

Fuson, K. C., & Kwon, Y. (1992). Korean children's understanding of multidigit addition and subtraction. *Child Development, 63,* 491–506.

Futrell, M. H., & Gomez, J. (2008, May). How tracking creates a poverty of learning. *Educational Leadership, 65*(8), 74–28.

Futterman, D., Chabon, B., & Hoffman, N. D. (2000). HIV and AIDS in adolescents. *Pediatric Clinics of North America, 47,* 171–188.

Gabard, D. L. (1999). Homosexuality and the Human Genome Project: Private and public choices. *Journal of Homosexuality, 37,* 25–51.

Gabriele, A. J. (2007). The influence of achievement goals on the constructive activity of low achievers during collaborative problem solving. *British Journal of Educational Psychology, 77,* 1221–141.

Gaines, D. (1991). *Teenage wasteland: Suburbia's dead end kids.* New York: Pantheon.

Galaburda, A. M., & Rosen, G. D. (2001). Neural plasticity in dyslexia: A window to mechanisms of learning disabilities. In J. L. McClelland & R. S. Siegler (Eds.), *Mechanisms of cognitive development: Behavioral and neural perspectives* (pp. 307–323). Mahwah, NJ: Erlbaum.

Galambos, N. L., Almeida, D. M., & Petersen, A. C. (1990). Masculinity, femininity, and sex role attitudes in early adolescence: Exploring gender intensification. *Child Development, 61,* 1905–1914.

Galambos, N. L., & Maggs, J. L. (1991). Children in self-care: Figures, facts and fiction. In J. V. Verner & N. L. Galambos (Eds.), *Employed mothers and their children* (pp. 131–157). New York: Garland Press.

Gallagher, A. M., & Kaufman, J. C. (Eds.) (2005). *Gender differences in mathematics: An integrative psychological approach.* Cambridge, England: Cambridge University Press.

Gallagher, J. J. (1991). Personal patterns of underachievement. *Journal for the Education of the Gifted, 14,* 221–233.

Gallahue, D. L., & Ozmun, J. C. (1998). *Understanding motor development: Infants, children, adolescents, adults.* Boston: McGraw-Hill.

Gallimore, R., & Goldenberg, C. (2001). Analyzing cultural models and settings to connect minority achievement and school improvement research. *Educational Psychologist, 36,* 45–56.

Gallimore, R., & Tharp, R. (1990). Teaching mind in society: Teaching, schooling, and literate discourse. In L. C. Moll (Ed.), *Vygotsky and education: Instructional implications and applications of socio-historical psychology.* Cambridge, England: Cambridge University Press.

Gallistel, C. R., Brown, A. L., Carey, S., Gelman, R., & Keil, F. C. (1991). In S. Carey & R. Gelman (Eds.), *Epigenesis of mind: Essays on biology and cognition.* Hillsdale, NJ: Erlbaum.

Gallistel, C. R., & Gelman, R. (1992). Preverbal and verbal counting and computation. *Cognition, 44,* 43–74.

Galotti, K. M., Komatsu, L. K., & Voelz, S. (1997). Children's differential performance on deductive and inductive syllogisms. *Developmental Psychology, 33,* 70–78.

Gambrell, L. B., & Bales, R. J. (1986). Mental imagery and the comprehension-monitoring performance of fourth- and fifth-grade poor readers. *Reading Research Quarterly, 21,* 454–464.

Ganea, P. A. Shutts, K., Spelke, E. S., & DeLoache, J. S. (2007). Thinking of things unseen: Infants' use of language to update mental representations. *Psychological Science, 18,* 734–739.

Garbarino, J., & Abramowitz, R. H. (1992). Sociocultural risk and opportunity. In J. Garbarino (Ed.), *Children and families in the social environment* (pp. 35–70). New York: Aldine de Gruyter.

Garbarino, J., Bradshaw, C. P., & Vorrasi, J. A. (2002). Mitigating the effects of gun violence on children and youth. *The Future of Children, 12*(2), 73–85.

García, E. E. (1994). *Understanding and meeting the challenge of student cultural diversity.* Boston: Houghton Mifflin.

García, E. E. (1995). Educating Mexican American students: Past treatment and recent developments in theory, research, policy, and practice. In J. A. Banks & C. A. M. Banks (Eds.), *Handbook of research on multicultural education.* New York: Macmillan.

García, E. E., & Jensen, B. (2007). Helping young Hispanic learners. Educational Leadership, 64(6), 34–39.

García Coll, C., Lamberty, G., Jenkins, R., McAdoo, H. P., Crnic, K., Wasik, B. H., et al. (1996). An integrative model for the study of developmental competencies in minority children. *Child Development, 67,* 1891–1914.

Gardiner, H. W., & Kosmitzki, C. (2008). *Lives across cultures: Cross-cultural human development* (4th ed.). Boston, MA: Pearson Allyn & Bacon.

Gardner, H. (1983). *Frames of mind: The theory of multiple intelligences.* New York: Basic Books.

Gardner, H. (1993). *Multiple intelligences: The theory in practice.* New York: Basic Books.

Gardner, H. (1995). Reflections on multiple intelligences: Myths and messages. *Phi Delta Kappan, 77,* 200–209.

Gardner, H. (1999). *Intelligence reframed: Multiple intelligences for the 21st century.* New York: Basic Books.

Gardner, H. (2000a). A case against spiritual intelligence. *International Journal of the Psychology of Religion, 10*(1), 27–34.

Gardner, H. (2000b). *The disciplined mind: Beyond facts and standardized tests, the K–12 education that every child deserves.* New York: Penguin Books.

Gardner, H. (2003). *Multiple intelligences after twenty years.* Paper presented at the annual meeting of the American Educational Research Association, Chicago, IL. Retrieved February 25, 2008, from http://www.pz.harvard.edu/PIs/HG_MI_after_20_years.pdf

Gardner, H. (2006). Replies to my critics. In J. A. Schaler (Ed.), *Howard Gardner under fire: The rebel psychologist faces his critics* (pp. 277–344). Chicago: Open Court.

Gardner, H., & Hatch, T. (1990). Multiple intelligences go to school: Educational implications of the theory of multiple intelligences. *Educational Researcher, 18*(8), 4–10.

Gardner, H., & Moran, S. (2006). The science of multiple intelligences theory: A response to Lynn Waterhouse. *Educational Psychologist, 41*(4), 227–232.

Gardner, H., Torff, B., & Hatch, T. (1996). The age of innocence reconsidered: Preserving the best of the progressive traditions in psychology and education. In D. R. Olson & N. Torrance (Eds.), *The handbook of education and human development: New models of learning, teaching and schooling* (pp. 28–55). Cambridge, MA: Blackwell.

Garland, A., Augustyn, M., & Stein, M. T. (2007). Disruptive and oppositional behavior in an 11-year-old boy. *Journal of Developmental and Behavioral Pediatrics, 28,* 406–408.

Garner, R. (1987). Strategies for reading and studying expository texts. *Educational Psychologist, 22,* 299–312.

Garner, R. (1998). Epilogue: Choosing to learn or not-learn in school. *Educational Psychology Review, 10,* 227–237.

Garrison, L. (1989). Programming for the gifted American Indian student. In C. J. Maker & S. W. Schiever (Eds.), *Critical issues in gifted education: Vol. 2. Defensible programs for cultural and ethnic minorities.* Austin, TX: Pro-Ed.

Gartrell, N., Deck, A., Rodas, C., Peyser, H., & Banks, A. (2005). The national lesbian family study: 4. Interviews with 10-year-old children. *American Journal of Orthopsychiatry, 75,* 518–524.

Garvey, C. (1990). *Play.* Cambridge, MA: Harvard University Press.

Garvey, C., & Berninger, G. (1981). Timing and turn taking in children's conversations. *Discourse Processes, 4,* 27–59.

Gaskins, I. W., Satlow, E., & Pressley, M. (2007). Executive control of reading comprehension in the elementary school. In L. Meltzer (Ed.), *Executive function in education: From theory to practice* (pp. 194–215). New York: Guilford Press.

Gaskins, S. (1999). Children's daily lives in a Mayan village: A case study of culturally constructed roles and activities. In A. Göncü (Ed.), *Children's engagement in the world: Sociocultural perspectives* (pp. 25–61). Cambridge, England: Cambridge University Press.

Gatzke-Kopp, L. M., & Beauchaine, T. P. (2007). Central nervous system substrates of impulsivity: Implications for the development of attention-deficit/hyperactivity disorder and conduct disorder. In D. Coch, G. Dawson, & K. W. Fischer (Eds.), *Human behavior, learning, and the developing brain: Atypical development* (pp. 239–263). New York: Guilford Press.

Gauvain, M. (2001). *The social context of cognitive development.* New York: Guilford Press.

Gauvain, M., & Perez, S. M. (2005). Parent–child participation in planning children's activities outside of school in European American and Latino families. *Child Development, 76,* 371–383.

Gauvain, M., & Perez, S. M. (2007). The socialization of cognition. In J. E. Grusec & P. D. Hastings (Eds.), *Handbook of socialization: Theory and research* (pp. 588–613). New York: Guilford Press.

Gavin, L. A., & Fuhrman, W. (1989). Age differences in adolescents' perceptions of their peer groups. *Developmental Psychology, 25,* 827–834.

Gay, G. (2006). Connections between classroom management and culturally responsive teaching. In C. M. Evertson & C. S. Weinstein (Eds.), *Handbook of classroom management: Research, practice, and contemporary issues* (pp. 343–370). Mahwah, NJ: Erlbaum.

Ge, X., Conger, R. D., Cadoret, R. J., Neiderhiser, J. M., Yates, W., Troughton, E., et al. (1996). The developmental interface between nature and nurture: A mutual influence model of child anti-social behavior and parent behaviors. *Developmental Psychology, 33,* 351–363.

Ge, X., Conger, R. D., & Elder, G. H. Jr. (2001). Pubertal transition, stressful life events, and the emergence of gender differences in adolescent depressive symptoms. *Developmental Psychology, 37,* 404–417.

Ge, X., Kim, I. J., Brody, G. H., Conger, R. D., Simons, R. L., Gibbons, F. X., et al. (2003). It's about timing and change: Pubertal transition effects on symptoms of major depression among African American youths. *Developmental Psychology, 39,* 430–439.

Geary, D. C. (1994). *Children's mathematical development: Research and practical applications.* Washington, DC: American Psychological Association.

Geary, D. C. (2005). Folk knowledge and academic learning. In B. J. Ellis & D. F. Bjorklund (Eds.), *Origins of the social mind: Evolutionary psychology and child development* (pp. 493–519). New York: Guilford Press.

Geary, D. C. (2006). Development of mathematical understanding. In W. Damon, R. M. Lerner (Series Eds.), D. Kuhn, & R. Siegler (Vol. Eds.), *Handbook of child psychology: Vol. 1. Cognition, perception, and language* (6th ed.). New York: Wiley.

Gee, C. B., & Rhodes, J. E. (2008). A social support and social strain measure for minority adolescent mothers: A confirmatory factor analytic study. *Child: Care, Health and Development, 34*(1), 87–97.

Geenen, S., & Powers, L. E. (2007). "Tomorrow is another problem": The experiences of youth in foster care during their transition into adulthood. *Children and Youth Services Review, 29,* 1085–1101.

Gelman, R., & Baillargeon, R. (1983). A review of some Piagetian concepts. In J. H. Flavell & E. M. Markman (Eds.), *Handbook of child psychology. Vol. 3. Cognitive development.* New York: Wiley.

Gelman, R., & Gallistel, C. R. (1978). *The child's understanding of number.* Cambridge, MA: Harvard University Press.

Gelman, S. A. (2003). *The essential child: Origins of essentialism in everyday thought.* New York: Oxford University Press.

Gelman, S. A., & Kalish, C. W. (2006). Conceptual development. In W. Damon, R. M. Lerner (Series Eds.), D. Kuhn, & R. Siegler (Vol. Eds.), *Handbook of child psychology: Vol. 1. Cognition, perception, and language* (6th ed.). New York: Wiley.

Gelman, S. A., & Markman, E. M. (1986). Categories and induction in young children. *Cognition, 23,* 183–209.

Gelman, S. A., & Raman, L. (2003). Preschool children use linguistic form class and pragmatic cues to interpret generics. *Child Development, 74,* 308–325.

Gelman, S. A., & Taylor, M. (1984). How two-year-old children interpret proper and common names for unfamiliar objects. *Child Development, 55,* 1535–1540.

Genesee, F. (1985). Second language learning through immersion: A review of U.S. programs. *Review of Educational Research, 55,* 541–561.

Gentile, D. A., & Gentile, J. R. (2008). Violent video games as exemplary teachers: A conceptual analysis. *Journal of Youth and Adolescence, 37,* 127–141.

Gentry, R. (1982). An analysis of the developmental spellings in *Gnys at Wrk. The Reading Teacher, 36,* 192–200.

George, L. (2005). Lack of preparedness: Experiences of first-time mothers. *MCN: The American Journal of Maternal/Child Nursing, 30*(4), 251–255.

Gerbhardt, W. A., Kuyper, L., & Greunsven, G. (2003). Need for intimacy in relationships and motives for sex as determinants of adolescent condom use. *Journal of Adolescent Health, 33,* 154–164.

Gerken, L. (1994). Child phonology: Past research, present questions, future directions. In M. A. Gernsbacher (Ed.), *Handbook of psycholinguistics* (pp. 781–820). San Diego, CA: Academic Press.

Gernsbacher, M. A., Stevenson, J. L., Khandakar, S., & Goldsmith, H. H. (2008). Why does joint attention look atypical in autism. *Child Development Perspectives, 2*(1), 38–45.

Gershoff, E. T., Aber, J. L., & Raver, C. C. (2005). Child poverty in the United States: An evidence-based conceptual framework for programs and policies. In R. M. Lerner, F. Jacobs, & D. Wertlieb (Eds.), *Applied developmental science: An advanced textbook* (pp. 269–324). Thousand Oaks, CA: Sage.

Gertner, Y., Fisher, C., & Eisengart, J. (2006). Learning words and rules: Abstract knowledge of word order in early sentence comprehension. *Psychological Science, 17,* 684–691.

Gesell, A. (1928). *Infancy and human growth.* New York: Macmillan.

Gettinger, M., & Kohler, K. M. (2006). Process-outcome approaches to classroom management and effective teaching. In C. M. Evertson & C. S. Weinstein (Eds.), *Handbook of classroom management: Research, practice, and contemporary issues* (pp. 73–95). Mahwah, NJ: Erlbaum.

Ghazvini, A., & Mullis, R. L. (2002). Center-based care for young children: Examining predictors of quality. *Journal of Genetic Psychology, 163,* 112–125.

Ghetti, S., & Alexander, K. W. (2004). "If it happened, I would remember it": Strategic use of event memorability in the rejection of false autobiographical events. *Child Development, 75,* 542–561.

Ghodsian-Carpey, J., & Baker, L. A. (1987). Genetic and environmental influences on aggression in 4- to 7-year-old twins. *Aggressive Behavior, 13,* 173–186.

Gibson, E. J., & Walk, R. D. (1960). The "visual cliff." *Scientific American, 202*(4), 64–71.

Gibson, J. J., (1979). *The ecological approach to visual perception.* Boston: Houghton-Mifflin.

Giedd, J. N., Blumenthal, J., Jeffries, N. O., Castellanos, F. X., Liu, H., Zijdenbos, A., et al. (1999). Brain development during childhood and adolescence: A longitudinal MRI study. *Nature Neuroscience, 2,* 861–863.

Gillam, R. B., & Johnston, J. R. (1992). Spoken and written language relationships in language/learning-impaired and normal achieving school-age children. *Journal of Speech and Hearing Research, 35,* 1303–1315.

Gillberg, I. C., & Coleman, M. (1996). Autism and medical disorders: A review of the literature. *Developmental Medicine and Child Neurology, 38,* 191–202.

Gillham, J. E., Reivich, K. J., Jaycox, L. H., & Seligman, M. E. P. (1995). Prevention of depressive symptoms in schoolchildren: Two-year follow-up. *Psychological Science, 6,* 343–351.

Gilligan, C. (1982). *In a different voice: Psychological theory and women's development.* Cambridge, MA: Harvard University Press.

Gilligan, C. F. (1985, March). Keynote address at the Conference on Women and Moral Theory, Stony Brook, NY.

Gilligan, C. F. (1987). Moral orientation and moral development. In E. F. Kittay & D. T. Meyers (Eds.), *Women and moral theory.* Totowa, NJ: Rowman & Littlefield.

Gilligan, C. F., & Attanucci, J. (1988). Two moral orientations. In C. F. Gilligan, J. V. Ward, & J. M. Taylor (Eds.), *Mapping the moral domain: A contribution of women's thinking to psychological theory and education.* Cambridge, MA: Center for the Study of Gender, Education, and Human Development (distributed by Harvard University Press).

Gilliland, H. (1988). Discovering and emphasizing the positive aspects of the culture. In H. Gilliland & J. Reyhner (Eds.), *Teaching the Native American.* Dubuque, IA: Kendall/Hunt.

Gilman, R., Meyers, J., & Perez, L. (2004). Structured extracurricular activities among adolescents: Findings and implications for school psychologists. *Psychology in the Schools, 41,* 31–41.

Ginsberg, D., Gottman, J. M., & Parker, J. G. (1986). The importance of friendship. In J. M. Gottman & J. G. Parker (Eds.), *Conversations of friends: Speculations on affective development* (pp. 3–48). Cambridge, England: Cambridge University Press.

Ginsburg, G. P., & Kilbourne, B. K. (1988). Emergence of vocal alternation in mother-infant interchanges. *Journal of Child Language, 15,* 221–235.

Ginsburg, H. P., Cannon, J., Eisenband, J., & Pappas, S. (2006). Mathematical thinking and learning. In K. McCartney & D. Phillips (Eds.), *Blackwell handbook of early childhood development* (pp. 208–229). Malden, MA: Blackwell.

Ginsburg, H. P., Lee, J. S., & Boyd, J. S. (2008). Mathematics education for young children: What it is and how to promote it. *Social Policy Report, 22*(1).

Ginsburg, H. P., Posner, J. K., & Russell, R. L. (1981). The development of mental addition as a function of schooling and culture. *Journal of Cross-Cultural Psychology, 12,* 163–178.

Giordano, P. C. (2003). Relationships in adolescence. *Annual Review of Sociology, 29,* 257–281.

Girotto, V., & Light, P. (1993). The pragmatic bases of children's reasoning. In P. Light & G. Butterworth (Eds.), *Context and cognition: Ways of learning and knowing.* Mahwah, NJ: Erlbaum.

Glaser, C., & Brunstein, J. C. (2007). Improving fourth-grade students' composition skills: Effects of strategy instruction and self-regulation procedures. *Journal of Educational Psychology, 99,* 297–310.

Glick, J. (1975). Cognitive development in cross-cultural perspective. In F. Horowitz (Ed.), *Review of child development research* (Vol. 4). Chicago: University of Chicago Press.

Glucksberg, S., & Krauss, R. M. (1967). What do people say after they have learned to talk? Studies of the development of referential communication. *Merrill-Palmer Quarterly, 13,* 309–316.

Glynn, S. M., Yeany, R. H., & Britton, B. K. (1991a). A constructive view of learning science. In S. M. Glynn, R. H. Yeany, & B. K. Britton (Eds.), *The psychology of learning science* (pp. 3–19). Mahwah, NJ: Erlbaum.

Glynn, S. M., Yeany, R. H., & Britton, B. K. (Eds.) (1991b). *The psychology of learning science.* Hillsdale, NJ: Erlbaum.

Gnepp, J. (1989). Children's use of personal information to understand other people's feelings. In C. Saarni & P. L. Harris (Eds.), *Children's understanding of emotion.* Cambridge, England: Cambridge University Press.

Goldberg, E., & Costa, L. D. (1981). Hemisphere differences in the acquisition and use of descriptive systems. *Brain and Language, 14,* 144–173.

Goldenberg, C. (1992). The limits of expectations: A case for case knowledge about teacher expectancy effects. *American Educational Research Journal, 29,* 517–544.

Goldin-Meadow, S. (1997). When gestures and words speak differently. *Current Directions in Psychological Science, 6,* 138–143.

Goldin-Meadow, S. (2006). Talking and thinking with our hands. *Current Directions in Psychological Science, 15,* 34–39.

Goldin-Meadow, S. (2007). Pointing sets the stage for learning language—and creating language. *Child Development, 78,* 741–745.

Goldin-Meadow, S., & Mylander, C. (1993). Beyond the input given: The child's role in the acquisition of language. In P. Bloom (Ed.), *Language acquisition: Core readings.* Cambridge, MA: MIT Press.

Goldin-Meadow, S., Nusbaum, H., Kelly, S. D., & Wagner, S. (2001). Explaining math: Gesturing lightens the load. *Psychological Science, 12,* 516–522.

Goldstein, A. P. (1999). Aggression reduction strategies: Effective and ineffective. *School Psychology Quarterly, 14,* 40–58.

Goldstein, M. H., & Schwade, J. A. (2008). Social feedback to infants' babbling facilitates rapid phonological learning. *Psychological Science, 19,* 515–523.

Goldstein, N. E., Arnold, D. H., Rosenberg, J. L., Stowe, R. M., & Ortiz, C. (2001). Contagion of aggression in day care classrooms as a function of peer and teacher responses. *Journal of Educational Psychology, 93,* 708–719.

Goldstein, S., & Brooks, R. B. (Eds.) (2006). *Handbook of resilience in children.* New York: Springer.

Goldstein, S., & Rider, R. (2006). Resilience and the disruptive disorders of childhood. In. S. Goldstein & R. B. Brooks (Eds.), *Handbook of resilience in children* (pp. 203–222). New York: Springer.

Goleman, D. (1995). *Emotional intelligence.* New York: Bantam Books.

Golinkoff, R. M., & Hirsh-Pasek, K. (2006). Baby wordsmith: From associationistic to social sophisticate. *Current Directions in Psychological Science, 15,* 30–33.

Golinkoff, R. M., Hirsh-Pasek, K., Bailey, L., & Wenger, N. (1992). Young children and adults use lexical principles to learn new nouns. *Developmental Psychology, 28,* 99–108.

Gollan, J. K., Lee, R., & Coccaro, E. F. (2005). Developmental psychopathology and neurobiology of aggression. *Development and Psychopathology, 17,* 1151–1171.

Gollnick, D. M., & Chinn, P. C. (2002). *Multicultural education in a pluralistic society* (6th ed.). Upper Saddle River, NJ: Merrill/Prentice Hall.

Golomb, C. (2004). *The child's creation of a pictorial world* (2nd ed.). Mahwah, NJ: Erlbaum.

Golombok, S., Perry, B., Burston, A., Murray, C., Mooney-Somers, J., Stevens, M., et al. (2003). Children with lesbian parents: A community study. *Developmental Psychology, 39,* 20–33.

Gomby, D. S., Culross, P. L., & Behrman, R. E. (1999). Home visiting: Recent program evaluations—Analysis and recommendations. *The Future of Children. Home Visiting: Recent Program Evaluations, 9*(1), 4–26.

Göncü, A. (1993). Development of intersubjectivity in the dyadic play of preschoolers. Early Childhood Research Quarterly, 8, 99–116.

Göncü, A., & Gaskins, S. (2006). An integrative perspective on play and development. In A. Göncü & S. Gaskins (Eds.), *Play and development: Evolutionary, sociocultural, and functional perspectives* (pp. 3–17) Mahwah, NJ: Erlbaum.

Gonzalez, A.-L., & Wolters, C. A. (2006). The relation between perceived parenting practices and achievement motivation in mathematics. *Journal of Research in Childhood Education, 21,* 203–217.

Gonzalez-Mena, J. (2002). *The child in the family and the community* (3rd ed.). Upper Saddle River, NJ: Merrill/Prentice Hall.

Good, T. L., & Brophy, J. E. (1994). *Looking in classrooms* (6th ed.). New York: HarperCollins.

Good, T. L., McCaslin, M. M., & Reys, B. J. (1992). Investigating work groups to promote problem solving in mathematics. In J. Brophy (Ed.), *Advances in research on teaching: Vol. 3. Planning and managing learning tasks and activities.* Greenwich, CT: JAI Press.

Good, T. L., & Nichols, S. L. (2001). Expectancy effects in the classroom: A special focus on improving the reading performance of minority students in first-grade classrooms. *Educational Psychologist, 36,* 113–126.

Goodman, K. S. (1989). Whole-language research: Foundations and development. *Elementary School Journal, 90,* 207–221.

Goodman, K. S., & Goodman, Y. M. (1979). Learning to read is natural. In L. B. Resnick & P. A. Weaver (Eds.), *Theory and practice of early reading* (Vol. 1). Hillsdale, NJ: Erlbaum.

Goodwin, M. H. (2006). *The hidden life of girls: Games of stance, status, and exclusion.* Malden, MA: Blackwell.

Goodwyn, S. W., & Acredolo, L. P. (1998). Encouraging symbolic gestures: A new perspective on the relationship between gesture and speech. In J. M. Iverson & S. Goldin-Meadow (Eds.), *Nature and functions of gesture in children's communication.* San Francisco: Jossey-Bass.

Goodwyn, S. W., Acredolo, L. P., & Brown, C. A. (2000). Impact of symbolic gesturing on early language development. *Journal of Nonverbal Behavior, 24,* 81–103.

Gopnik, M. (Ed.) (1997). *The inheritance and innateness of grammars.* New York: Oxford University Press.

Gordon, P. (2004). Numerical cognition without words: Evidence from Amazonia. *Science, 306,* 496–499.

Goswami, U. (1999). The relationship between phonological awareness and orthographic representation in different orthographies. In M. Harris & G. Hatano (Eds.), *Learning to read and write: A cross-linguistic perspective.* Cambridge, England: Cambridge University Press.

Goswami, U. (2007). Typical reading development and developmental dyslexia across languages. In D. Coch, G. Dawson, & K. W. Fischer (Eds.), *Human behavior, learning, and the developing brain: Atypical development* (pp. 145–167). New York: Guilford Press.

Gottfredson, G. D., & Gottfredson, D. C. (2001). *Gang problems and gang programs in a national sample of schools.* Ellicott City, MD: Gottfredson Associates.

Gottfredson, L. (2003). Dissecting practical intelligence theory: Its claims and evidence. *Intelligence, 31,* 343–397.

Gottfried, A. E., Fleming, J. S., & Gottfried, A. W. (1994). Role of parental motivational practices in children's academic intrinsic motivation and achievement. *Journal of Educational Psychology, 86,* 104–113.

Gottfried, A. E., Fleming, J. S., & Gottfried, A. W. (2001). Continuity of academic intrinsic motivation from childhood through late adolescence: A longitudinal study. *Journal of Educational Psychology, 93,* 3–13.

Gottfried, A. W., Gottfried, A. E., Bathurst, K., & Guerin, D. W. (1994). *Gifted IQ: Early developmental aspects.* New York: Plenum Press.

Gottlieb, G. (1991). Experiential canalization of behavioral development: Theory. *Developmental Psychology, 27,* 4–13.

Gottlieb, G. (1992). *Individual development and evolution: The genesis of novel behavior.* New York: Oxford University Press.

Gottlieb, G., Wahlsten, D., & Lickliter, R. (2006). The significance of biology for human development: A developmental psychobiological systems view. In W. Damon & R. M. Lerner (Eds. in Chief) & R. M. Lerner (Vol. Ed.), *Handbook of child psychology: Vol. 1. Theoretical models of human development* (6th ed., pp. 210–257). Hoboken, NJ: Wiley.

Gottman, J. M. (1983). How children become friends. *Monographs of the Society for Research in Child Development, 48*(3, Serial No. 201).

Gottman, J. M. (1986). The world of coordinated play: Same- and cross-sex friendship in young children. In J. M. Gottman & J. G. Parker (Eds.), *Conversations of friends: Speculations on affective development* (pp. 139–191). Cambridge, England: Cambridge University Press.

Gottman, J. M., & Mettetal, G. (1986). Speculations about social and affective development: Friendship and acquaintanceship through adolescence. In J. M. Gottman & J. G. Parker (Eds.), *Conversations of friends: Speculations on affective development* (pp. 192–237). Cambridge, England: Cambridge University Press.

Goudena, P. (2006). Real and symbolic entry of children in the social world of peers and parent–child interactions. In X. Chen, D. C. French, & B. H. Schneider (Eds.), *Peer relationships in cultural context* (pp. 247–263). New York: Cambridge University Press.

Gould, S. J. (1977). *Ontogeny and phylogeny.* Cambridge, MA: Harvard University Press.

Graber, J. A., Britto, P. R., & Brooks-Gunn, J. (1999). What's love got to do with it? Adolescents' and young adults' beliefs about sexual and romantic relationships. In W. Furman, B. B. Brown, & C. Feiring (Eds.), *The development of romantic relationships in adolescence* (pp. 364–395). Cambridge, England: Cambridge University Press.

Graesser, A., Golding, J. M., & Long, D. L. (1991). Narrative representation and comprehension. In R. Barr, M. L. Kamil, P. Mosenthal, & P. D. Pearson (Eds.), *Handbook of reading research* (Vol. II). New York: Longman.

Graham, S. (1989). Motivation in Afro-Americans. In G. L. Berry & J. K. Asamen (Eds.), *Black students: Psychosocial issues and academic achievement.* Newbury Park, CA: Sage.

Graham, S. (1990). Communicating low ability in the classroom: Bad things good teachers sometimes do. In S. Graham & V. S. Folkes (Eds.), *Attribution theory: Applications to achievement, mental health, and interpersonal conflict.* Hillsdale, NJ: Erlbaum.

Graham, S. (1991). A review of attribution theory in achievement contexts. *Educational Psychology Review, 3,* 5–39.

Graham, S. (1997). Using attribution theory to understand social and academic motivation in African American youth. *Educational Psychologist, 32,* 21–34.

Graham, S. (2006a). Peer victimization in school: Exploring the ethnic context. *Current Directions in Psychological Science, 15,* 317–321.

Graham, S. (2006b). Writing. In P. A. Alexander & P. H. Winne (Eds.), *Handbook of educational psychology* (2nd ed., pp. 457–478). Mahwah, NJ: Erlbaum.

Graham, S., Harris, K. R., & Fink, B. (2000). Is handwriting causally related to learning to write? Treatment of handwriting problems in beginning writers. *Journal of Educational Psychology, 92,* 620–633.

Graham, S., Harris, K. R., & Olinghouse, N. (2007). Addressing executive function problems in writing: An example from the self-regulated strategy development model. In L. Meltzer (Ed.), *Executive function in education: From theory to practice* (pp. 216–236). New York: Guilford Press.

Graham, S., & Perin, D. (2007). A meta-analysis of writing instruction for adolescent students. *Journal of Educational Psychology, 99,* 445–476.

Graham, S., Schwartz, S. S., & MacArthur, C. A. (1993). Knowledge of writing and the composing process, attitude toward writing, and self-efficacy for students with and without learning disabilities. *Journal of Learning Disabilities, 26,* 237–249.

Graham, S., & Weintraub, N. (1996). A review of handwriting research: Progress and prospects from 1980 to 1994. *Educational Psychology Review, 8,* 7–87.

Grandin, T. (1995). *Thinking in pictures and other reports of my life with autism.* New York: Random House.

Grandin, T., & Johnson, C. (2005). *Animals in translation: Using the mysteries of autism to decode animal behavior.* New York: Simon & Schuster.

Granger, R. C. (2008). After-school programs and academics: Implications for policy, practice, and research. *Social Policy Report, 22*(2). Society for Research in Child Development.

Granrud, C. E. (2006). Size constancy in infants: 4-month-olds' responses to physical versus retinal image size. *Journal of Experimental Psychology: Human Perception and Performance, 32,* 1398–1404.

Grant, C. A., & Gomez, M. L. (2001). *Campus and classroom: Making schooling multicultural* (2nd ed.). Upper Saddle River, NJ: Merrill/Prentice Hall.

Grant, H., & Dweck, C. (2001). Cross-cultural response to failure: Considering outcome attributions with different goals. In F. Salili & C. Chiu (Eds.), *Student motivation: The culture and context of learning* (pp. 203–219). Dordrecht, The Netherlands: Kluwer Academic.

Graue, M. E., & Walsh, D. J. (1998). *Studying children in context.* Thousand Oaks, CA: Sage.

Green, L., Fry, A. F., & Myerson, J. (1994). Discounting of delayed rewards: A life-span comparison. *Psychological Science, 5,* 33–36.

Greenberg, M. T. (1999). Attachment and psychopathology in childhood. In J. Cassidy & P. R. Shaver (Eds.), *Handbook of attachment: Theory, research, and clinical applications* (pp. 469–496). New York: Guilford Press.

Greenberg, M. T., Domitrovich, C., & Bumbarger, B. (2000). *Preventing mental disorders in school-age children: A review of the effectiveness of prevention programs.* University Park, PA: Prevention Research Center for the Promotion of Human Development, Pennsylvania State University.

Greenberg, M. T., Kusché, C. A., Cook, E. T., & Quamma, J. P. (1995). Promoting emotional competence in school-aged children: The effects of the PATHS curriculum. *Development and Psychopathology, 7,* 117–136.

Greenberg, M. T., Weissberg, R. P., O'Brien, M. U., Zins, J. E., Fredericks, L., Resnik, H., & Elias, M. J. (2003). Enhancing school-based prevention and youth development through coordinated social, emotional, and academic learning. *American Psychologist, 58,* 466–474.

Greene, J. P., & Forster, G. (2004). Sex, drugs, and delinquency in urban and suburban public schools. Education Working Paper. Manhattan Institute for Policy Research. Retrieved August 12, 2008, from www.manhattan-institute.org/html/ewp_04.htm

Greenfield, P. M. (1994). Independence and interdependence as developmental scripts: Implications for theory, research, and practice. In P. M. Greenfield & R. R. Cocking (Eds.), *Cross-cultural roots of minority child development.* Hillsdale, NJ: Erlbaum.

Greenfield, P. M. (1998). The cultural evolution of IQ. In U. Neisser (Ed.), *The rising curve: Long-term gains in IQ and related measures* (pp. 81–123). Washington, DC: American Psychological Association.

Greenfield, P. M., DeWinstanley, P., Kilpatrick, H., & Kaye, D. (1996). Action video games and informal education: Effects on strategies for dividing visual attention. In P. M. Greenfield & R. R. Cocking (Eds.), *Advances in applied developmental psychology: Vol. 11. Interacting with video* (pp. 187–205). Westport, CT: Ablex.

Greenfield, P. M., & Subrahmanyam, K. (2003). Online discourse in a teen chatroom: New codes and new modes of coherence in a visual medium. *Applied Developmental Psychology, 24,* 713–738.

Greenfield, P. M., Trumbull, E., Keller, H., Rothstein-Fisch, C., Suzuki, L. K., & Quiroz, B. (2006). Cultural conceptions of learning and development. In P. A. Alexander & P. H. Winne (Eds.), *Handbook of educational psychology* (2nd ed., pp. 675–692). Mahwah, NJ: Erlbaum.

Greeno, J. G. (2007). Toward the development of intellective character. In E. W. Gordon & B. L. Bridglall (Eds.), *Affirmative development: Cultivating academic ability* (pp. 17–47). Lanham, MD: Rowman.

Greeno, J. G., Collins, A. M., & Resnick, L. B. (1996). Cognition and learning. In D. C. Berliner & R. C. Calfee (Eds.), *Handbook of educational psychology.* New York: Macmillan.

Greenough, W. T., & Black, J. E. (1992). Induction of brain structure by experience: Substrates for cognitive development. In M. R. Gunnar & C. A. Nelson (Eds.), *Developmental behavioral neuroscience. The Minnesota Symposium on Child Psychology* (Vol. 24, pp. 155–200). Mahwah, NJ: Erlbaum.

Greenough, W. T., Black, J. E., & Wallace, C. S. (1987). Experience and brain development. *Child Development, 58,* 539–559.

Greenspan, D. A., Solomon, B., & Gardner, H. (2004). The development of talent in different domains. In L. V. Shavinina & M. Ferrari (Eds.), *Beyond knowledge: Extracognitive aspects of developing high ability* (pp. 119–135). Mahwah, NJ: Erlbaum.

Greenspan, S., & Granfield, J. M. (1992). Reconsidering the construct of mental retardation: Implications of a model of social competence. *American Journal of Mental Retardation, 96,* 442–453.

Greenspan, S. I., & Meisels, S. (1996). Toward a new vision for the developmental assessment of infants and young children. In S. J. Meisels & E. Fenichel (Eds.), *New visions for the developmental assessment of infants and young children.* Washington, DC: Zero to Three.

Gregg, M., & Leinhardt, G. (1994a, April). *Constructing geography.* Paper presented at the annual meeting of the American Educational Research Association, New Orleans, LA.

Gregg, M., & Leinhardt, G. (1994b). Mapping out geography: An example of epistemology and education. *Review of Educational Research, 64,* 311–361.

Greif, M. L., Kemler Nelson, D. G., Keil, F. C., & Gutierrez, F. (2006). What do children want to know about animals and artifacts? Domain-specific requests for information. *Psychological Science, 17,* 455–459.

Griffin, S., Case, R., & Capodilupo, A. (1995). Teaching for understanding: The importance of the central conceptual structures in the elementary mathematics curriculum. In A. McKeough, J. Lupart, & A. Marini (Eds.), *Teaching for transfer: Fostering generalization in learning.* Mahwah, NJ: Erlbaum.

Griffin, S. A., Case, R., & Siegler, R. S. (1994). Rightstart: Providing the central conceptual prerequisites for first formal learning of arithmetic to students at risk for school failure. In K. McGilly (Ed.), *Classroom lessons: Integrating cognitive theory and classroom practice.* Cambridge, MA: MIT Press.

Griffiths, J. A., & Nesdale, D. (2006). In-group and out-group attitudes of ethnic majority and minority children. *International Journal of Intercultural Relations, 30,* 735–749.

Griswold, K. S., & Pessar, L. F. (2000). Management of bipolar disorder. *American Family Physician, 62,* 1343–1356.

Gromko, J. E. (1994). Children's invented notations as measures of musical understanding. *Psychology of Music, 22,* 136–147.

Gromko, J. E. (1996, April). *Theorizing symbolic development in music: Interpretive interactions with preschool children.* Paper presented at the Music Educators National Conference, Kansas City, MO.

Gromko, J. E. (1998). Young children's symbol use: Common principles and cognitive processes. *Update: Applications of Research in Music Education, 16*(2), 3–7.

Gromko, J. E. (2004). Predictors of music sight-reading ability in high school wind players. *Journal of Research in Music Education, 52,* 6–15.

Gromko, J. E., & Poorman, A. S. (1998). Developmental trends and relationships in children's aural perception and symbol use. *Journal of Research in Music Education, 46,* 16–23.

Gronlund, N. E. (2004). *Writing instructional objectives for teaching and assessment* (7th ed.). Upper Saddle River, NJ: Merrill/Prentice Hall.

Gross, D., Fogg, L., Webster-Stratton, C., Garvey, C., Julion, W., & Grady, J. (2003). Parent training with multi-ethnic families of toddlers in day care in low-income urban communities. *Journal of Consulting and Clinical Psychology, 71,* 261–278.

Gross, R. H. (2004). Sports medicine in youth athletes. *Southern Medical Journal, 97,* 880.

Gross, R. T., & Duke, P. M. (1980). The effect of early versus late physical maturation in adolescent behavior. *Pediatric Clinics of North America, 27,* 71–77.

Grossman, H. L. (1994). *Classroom behavior management in a diverse society.* Mountain View, CA: Mayfield.

Grossmann, K. E., Grossmann, K., Huber, F., & Wartner, U. (1981). German children's behavior toward their mothers at 12 months and their fathers at 18 months in Ainsworth's Strange Situation. *International Journal of Behavioral Development, 4,* 157–181.

Grusec, J. (2006). The development of moral behavior and conscience from a socialization perspective. In M. Killen & J. G. Smetana (Eds.), *Handbook of moral development* (pp. 243–265). Mahwah, NJ: Erlbaum.

Grusec, J. E., & Davidov, M. (2007). Socialization in the family: The roles of parents. In J. E. Grusec & P. D. Hastings (Eds.), *Handbook of socialization: Theory and research* (pp. 284–308). New York: Guilford Press.

Grusec, J. E., & Redler, E. (1980). Attribution, reinforcement, and altruism. *Developmental Psychology, 16,* 525–534.

Guay, F., Boivin, M., & Hodges, E. V. E. (1999). Social comparison processes and academic achievement: The dependence of the development of self-evaluations on friends' performance. *Journal of Educational Psychology, 91,* 564–568.

Guberman, S. R., Rahm, J., & Menk, D. W. (1998). Transforming cultural practices: Illustrations from children's game play. *Anthropology and Education Quarterly, 29,* 419–445.

Gummerum, M., Keller, M., Takezawa, M., & Mata, J. (2008). To give or not to give: Children's and adolescents' sharing and moral negotiations in economic decision situations. *Child Development, 79,* 562–576.

Gustafsson, J., & Undheim, J. O. (1996). Individual differences in cognitive functions. In D. C. Berliner & R. C. Calfee (Eds.), *Handbook of educational psychology.* New York: Macmillan.

Guthrie, B. J., Caldwell, C. H., & Hunter, A. G. (1997). Minority adolescent female health: Strategies for the next millennium. In D. K. Wilson, J. R. Rodrigue, & W. C. Taylor (Eds.), *Health-promoting and health-compromising behaviors among minority adolescents* (pp. 153–171). Washington, DC: American Psychological Association.

Guthrie, J. T., Cox, K. E., Anderson, E., Harris, K., Mazzoni, S., & Rach, L. (1998). Principles of integrated instruction for engagement in reading. *Educational Psychology Review, 10,* 177–199.

Guthrie, J. T., Wigfield, A., Barbosa, P., Perencevich, K. C., Taboada, A., Davis, M. H., et al. (2004). Increasing reading comprehension and engagement through concept-oriented reading instruction. *Journal of Educational Psychology, 96,* 403–423.

Gutiérrez, K. D., & Rogoff, B. (2003). Cultural ways of learning: Individual traits or repertoires of practice. *Educational Researcher, 32*(5), 19–25.

Gutman, L. M., & Eccles, J. S. (2007). Stage-environment fit during adolescence: Trajectories of family relations and adolescent outcomes. *Developmental Psychology, 43,* 522–537.

Hacker, D. J. (1995, April). *Comprehension monitoring of written discourse across early-to-middle adolescence.* Paper presented at the annual meeting of the American Educational Research Association, San Francisco.

Hacker, D. J., & Bol, L. (2004). Metacognitive theory: Considering the social-cognitive influences. In D. M. McNerney & S. Van Etten (Eds.), *Big theories revisited* (pp. 275–297). Greenwich, CT: Information Age.

Hacker, D. J., Bol, L., Horgan, D. D., & Rakow, E. A. (2000). Test prediction and performance in a classroom context. *Journal of Educational Psychology, 92,* 160–170.

Haenan, J. (1996). Piotr Gal'perin's criticism and extension of Lev Vygotsky's work. *Journal of Russian and East European Psychology, 34*(2), 54–60.

Haenen, J., Schrijnemakers, H., & Stufkens, J. (2003). Sociocultural theory and the practice of teaching historical concepts. In A. Kozulin, B. Gindis, V. S. Ageyev, & S. M. Miller (Eds.), *Vygotsky's educational theory in cultural context* (pp. 246–266). Cambridge, England: Cambridge University Press.

Haerens, L., Deforche, B. Maes, L., Cardon, G., Stevens, V., & De Bourdeaudhuij, I. (2006). Evaluation of a 2-year physical activity and healthy eating intervention in middle school children. *Health Education Research, 21,* 911–921.

Hagen, J. W., & Stanovich, K. G. (1977). Memory: Strategies of acquisition. In R. V. Kail, Jr., & J. W. Hagen (Eds.), *Perspectives on the development of memory and cognition.* Hillsdale, NJ: Erlbaum.

Hagerman, R. J., & Lampe, M. E. (1999). Fragile X syndrome. In S. Goldstein & C. R. Reynolds (Eds.), *Handbook of neurodevelopmental and genetic disorders* (pp. 298–316). New York: Guilford Press.

Hagger, M. S., Chatzisarantis, N. L. D., Barkoukis, V., Wang, C. K. J., & Baranowski, J. (2005). Perceived autonomy support in physical education and leisure-time physical activity: A cross-cultural evaluation of the trans-contextual model. *Journal of Educational Psychology, 97,* 376–390.

Haidt, J. (2008). Morality. *Perspectives on Psychological Science, 3*(1), 65–72.

Haight, B. K. (1992). Long-term effects of a structured life review process. *Journal of Gerontology: Psychological Sciences, 47,* 312–315.

Haight, W. L. (1999). The pragmatics of caregiver-child pretending at home: Understanding culturally specific socialization practices. In A. Göncü (Ed.), *Children's engagement in the world: Sociocultural perspectives* (pp. 128–147). Cambridge, England: Cambridge University Press.

Hains, A. A., & Hains, A. H. (1988). Cognitive-behavioral training of problem-solving and impulse-control with delinquent adolescents. *Journal of Offender Counseling, Services & Rehabilitation, 12*(2), 95–113.

Haith, M. M. (1990). Perceptual and sensory processes in early infancy. *Merrill-Palmer Quarterly, 36,* 1–26.

Haith, M. M., Hazan, C., & Goodman, G. S. (1988). Expectation and anticipation of dynamic visual events by 3.5-month-old babies. *Child Development, 59,* 467–479.

Hale-Benson, J. E. (1986). *Black children: Their roots, culture, and learning styles.* Baltimore: Johns Hopkins University Press.

Halford, G. S. (1989). Cognitive processing capacity and learning ability: An integration of two areas. *Learning and Individual Differences, 1,* 125–153.

Halford, G. S., & Andrews, G. (2006). Reasoning and problem solving. In W. Damon, R. M. Lerner (Series Eds.), D. Kuhn, & R. Siegler (Vol. Eds.), *Handbook of child psychology: Vol. 2. Cognition, perception, and language* (6th ed.). New York: Wiley.

Halgunseth, L. C., Ispa, J. M., & Rudy, D. (2006). Parental control in Latino families: An integrated review of the literature. *Child Development, 77,* 1282–1297.

Hallenbeck, M. J. (1996). The cognitive strategy in writing: Welcome relief for adolescents with learning disabilities. *Learning Disabilities Research and Practice, 11,* 107–119.

Halpern, D. F. (1992). *Sex differences in cognitive abilities* (2nd ed.). Hillsdale, NJ: Erlbaum.

Halpern, D. F. (1998). Teaching critical thinking for transfer across domains. *American Psychologist, 53,* 449–455.

Halpern, D. F. (2004). A cognitive-process taxonomy for sex differences in cognitive abilities. *Current Directions in Psychological Science, 13,* 135–139.

Halpern, D. F. (2006). Assessing gender gaps in learning and academic achievement. In P. A. Alexander & P. H. Winne (Eds.), *Handbook of educational psychology* (2nd ed., pp. 635–653). Mahwah, NJ: Erlbaum.

Halpern, D. F., Bendow, C. P., Geary, D. C., Gur, R. C., Hyde, J. S., & Gernsbacher, M. A. (2007). The science of sex differences in science and mathematics. *Psychological Science in the Public Interest, 8*(1), 1–51.

Halpern, D. F., & LaMay, M. L. (2000). The smarter sex: A critical review of sex differences in intelligence. *Educational Psychology Review, 12,* 229–246.

Hamers, J. H. M., & Ruijssenaars, A. J. J. M. (1997). Assessing classroom learning potential. In G. D. Phye (Ed.), *Handbook of academic learning: Construction of knowledge.* San Diego, CA: Academic Press.

Hamill, P. V., Drizd, T. A., Johnson, C. L., Reed, R. B., Roche, A. F., & Moore, W. M. (1979). Physical growth: National Center for Health Statistics percentiles. *American Journal of Clinical Nutrition, 32,* 607–629.

Hammer, D. (1997). Discovery learning and discovery teaching. *Cognition and Instruction, 15,* 485–529.

Hamre, B. K., & Pianta, R. C. (2005). Can instructional and emotional support in the first-grade classroom make a difference for children at risk for school failure? *Child Development, 76,* 949–967.

Haney, W., Russell, M., & Bebell, D. (2004). Drawing on education: Using drawings to document schooling and support change. *Harvard Educational Review, 74,* 241–272.

Hanley, J. R., Tzeng, O., & Huang, H.-S. (1999). Learning to read Chinese. In M. Harris & G. Hatano (Eds.), *Learning to read and write: A cross-linguistic perspective.* Cambridge, England: Cambridge University Press.

Hannon, E. E., & Trehub, S. E. (2005). Metrical categories in infancy and adulthood. *Psychological Science, 16,* 48–55.

Harach, L., & Kuczynski, L. (2005). Construction and maintenance of parent–child relationships: Bidirectional contributions from the perspectives of parents. *Infant and Child Development, 14,* 327–343.

Harackiewicz, J. M., Barron, K. E., Pintrich, P. R., Elliot, A. J., & Thrash, T. M. (2002). Revision of achievement goal theory: Necessary and illuminating. *Journal of Educational Psychology, 94,* 638–645.

Hardy, I., Jonen, A., Möller, K., & Stern, E. (2006). Effects of instructional support within constructivist learning environments for elementary school students' understanding of "floating and sinking." *Journal of Educational Psychology, 98,* 307–326.

Hare, J. (1994). Concerns and issues faced by families headed by a lesbian couple. *Families in Society, 43,* 27–35.

Hareli, S., & Weiner, B. (2002). Social emotions and personality inferences: A scaffold for a new direction in the study of achievement motivation. *Educational Psychologist, 37,* 183–193.

Harlow, H. F., & Zimmerman, R. R. (1959). Affectional responses in the infant monkey. *Science, 130,* 421–432.

Harris, C. R. (1991). Identifying and serving the gifted new immigrants. *Teaching Exceptional Children, 23*(4), 26–30.

Harris, J. R. (1995). Where is the child's environment? A group socialization theory of development. *Psychological Review, 102,* 458–489.

Harris, J. R. (1998). *The nurture assumption: Why children turn out the way they do.* New York: Free Press.

Harris, K. R., & Graham, S. (1992). Self-regulated strategy development: A part of the writing process. In M. Pressley, K. R. Harris, & J. T. Guthrie (Eds.), *Promoting academic competence and literacy in school.* San Diego, CA: Academic Press.

Harris, L., Oman, R. F., Vesely, S. K., Tolma, E. L., Aspy, C. B., Rodine, S., et al. (2007). Associations between youth assets and sexual activity: Does adult supervision play a role? *Child: Care, Health and Development, 33,* 448–454.

Harris, M. (1992). *Language experience and early language development: From input to uptake.* Hove, England: Erlbaum.

Harris, M., & Giannouli, V. (1999). Learning to read and spell in Greek: The importance of letter knowledge and morphological awareness. In M. Harris & G. Hatano (Eds.). *Learning to read and write: A cross-linguistic perspective.* Cambridge, England: Cambridge University Press.

Harris, M., & Hatano, G. (Eds.). (1999). *Learning to read and write: A cross-linguistic perspective.* Cambridge, England: Cambridge University Press.

Harris, M. B. (1997). Preface: Images of the invisible minority. In M. B. Harris (Ed.), *School experiences of gay and lesbian youth: The invisible minority* (pp. xiv–xxii). Binghamton, NY: Harrington Park Press.

Harris, M. J., & Rosenthal, R. (1985). Mediation of interpersonal expectancy effects: 31 meta-analyses. *Psychological Bulletin, 97,* 363–386.

Harris, N. G. S., Bellugi, U., Bates, E., Jones, W., & Rossen, M. (1997). Contrasting profiles of language development in children with Williams and Down syndromes. *Developmental Neuropsychology, 13,* 345–370.

Harris, P. L. (1989). *Children and emotion: The development of psychological understanding.* Oxford, England: Basil Blackwell.

Harris, P. L. (2006). Social cognition. In W. Damon, R. M. Lerner (Series Eds.), D. Kuhn, & R. Siegler (Vol. Eds.), *Handbook of child psychology: Vol. 2. Cognition, perception, and language* (6th ed., pp. 811–858). New York: Wiley.

Harris, Y. R., & Graham, J. A. (2007). *The African American child: Development and challenges.* New York: Springer.

Harrison, A. O., Wilson, M. N., Pine, C. J., Chan, S. Q., & Buriel, R. (1990). Family ecologies of ethnic minority children. *Child Development, 61,* 347–362.

Harrison, C. (2004). Giftedness in early childhood: The search for complexity and connection. *Roeper Review, 26*(2), 78–84.

Harrison, K., & Cantor, J. (1997). The relationship between media consumption and eating disorders. *Journal of Communication, 47,* 40–67.

Hart, B., & Risley, T. R. (1995). *Meaningful differences in the everyday experiences of young American children.* Baltimore: Brookes.

Hart, B., & Risley, T. R. (1999). *The social world of children learning to talk.* Baltimore: Brookes.

Hart, D. (1988). The adolescent self-concept in social context. In D. K. Lapsley & F. C. Power (Eds.), *Self, ego, and identity: Integrative approaches* (pp. 71–90). New York: Springer-Verlag.

Hart, D., Atkins, R., & Donnelly, T. M. (2006). Community service and moral development. In M. Killen & J. G. Smetana (Eds.), *Handbook of moral development* (pp. 633–656). Mahwah, NJ: Erlbaum.

Hart, D., & Fegley, S. (1995). Prosocial behavior and caring in adolescence: Relations to self-understanding and social judgment. *Child Development, 66,* 1346–1359.

Hart, E. L., Lahey, B. B., Loeber, R., Applegate, B., & Frick, P. J. (1995). Developmental changes in attention-deficit hyperactivity disorder in boys: A four-year longitudinal study. *Journal of Abnormal Child Psychology, 23,* 729–750.

Harter, S. (1992). The relationship between perceived competence, affect, and motivational orientation within the classroom: Processes and patterns of change. In A. K. Boggiano & T. S. Pittman (Eds.), *Achievement and motivation: A social-developmental perspective.* Cambridge, England: Cambridge University Press.

Harter, S. (1996). Teacher and classmate influences on scholastic motivation, self-esteem, and level of voice in adolescents. In J. Juvonen & K. Wentzel (Eds.), *Social motivation: Understanding children's school adjustment.* New York: Cambridge University Press.

Harter, S. (1999). *The construction of the self.* New York: Guilford Press.

Harter, S. (2006). The self. In W. Damon & R. M. Lerner (Eds. in Chief) & N. Eisenberg (Vol. Ed.), *Handbook of child psychology, Vol. 3. Social, emotional, and personality development* (6th ed., pp. 505–570). Hoboken, NJ: Wiley.

Harter, S., Stocker, C., & Robinson, N. S. (1996). The perceived directionality of the link between approval and self-worth: The liabilities of a looking glass self-orientation among young adolescents. *Journal of Research on Adolescence, 6,* 285–308.

Harter, S., & Whitesell, N. R. (1989). Developmental changes in children's understanding of single, multiple, and blended emotion concepts. In C. Saarni & P. Harris (Eds.), *Children's understanding of emotion* (pp. 81–116). Cambridge, England: Cambridge University Press.

Harter, S., Whitesell, N. R., & Junkin, L. J. (1998). Similarities and differences in domain-specific and global self-evaluations of learning-disabled, behaviorally disordered, and normally achieving adolescents. *American Educational Research Journal, 35,* 653–680.

Harter, S., Whitesell, N. R., & Kowalski, P. (1992). Individual differences in the effects of educational transitions on young adolescents' perceptions of competence and motivational orientation. *American Educational Research Journal, 29,* 777–807.

Hartmann, D. P., & George, T. P. (1999). Design, measurement, and analysis in developmental research. In M. H. Bornstein & M. E. Lamb (Eds.), *Developmental psychology: An advanced textbook* (4th ed., pp. 125–195). Mahwah, NJ: Erlbaum.

Hartup, W. W. (1983). Peer relations. In P. H. Mussen (Ed.), *Handbook of child psychology: Vol. IV. Socialization* (4th ed.). New York: Wiley.

Hartup, W. W. (1984). The peer context in middle childhood. In A. Collins (Ed.), *Development during middle childhood: The years from six to twelve.* Washington, DC: National Academy Press.

Hartup, W. W. (1996). The company they keep: Friendships and their developmental significance. *Child Development, 67,* 1–13.

Hartup, W. W., & Laursen, B. (1991). Relationships as developmental contexts. In R. Cohen & W. A. Siegel (Eds.), *Context and development* (pp. 253–279). Hillsdale, NJ: Erlbaum.

Harwood, R. L., Miller, J. G., & Irizarry, N. L. (1995). *Culture and attachment: Perceptions of the child in context.* New York: Guilford Press.

Hatano, G., & Inagaki, K. (1991). Sharing cognition through collective comprehension activity. In L. B. Resnick, J. M. Levine, & S. D. Teasley (Eds.), *Perspectives on socially shared cognition.* Washington, DC: American Psychological Association.

Hatano, G., & Inagaki, K. (1996). Cognitive and cultural factors in the acquisition of intuitive biology. In D. R. Olson & N. Torrance (Eds.), *The handbook of education and human development: New models of learning, teaching, and schooling.* Cambridge, MA: Blackwell.

Hatfield, E., Cacioppo, J. T., & Rapson, R. L. (1994). *Emotional contagion.* Cambridge, England: Cambridge University Press.

Hattie, J., Biggs, J., & Purdie, N. (1996). Effects of learning skills interventions on student learning: A meta-analysis. *Review of Educational Research, 66,* 99–136.

Haviland, J. M., & Lelwica, M. (1987). The induced affect response: 10-week-old infants' responses to three emotional expressions. *Developmental Psychology, 23,* 97–104.

Hawkins, F. P. L. (1997). *Journey with children: The autobiography of a teacher.* Niwot: University Press of Colorado.

Hawley, C. A. (2005). Saint or sinner? Teacher perceptions of a child with traumatic brain injury. *Pediatric Rehabilitation, 8,* 117–129.

Hayes, C. D., & Hofferth, S. L. (1987). *Risking the future: Adolescent sexuality, pregnancy, and childbearing* (Vol. 2). Washington, DC: National Academy Press.

Hayes, D. P., & Grether, J. (1983). The school year and vacations: When do students learn? *Cornell Journal of Social Relations, 17*(1), 56–71.

Hayes, R. A., & Slater, A. (2008). Three-month-olds' detection of alliteration in syllables. *Infant Behavior and Development, 31,* 153–156.

Hayne, H. (2007). Infant memory development: New questions, new answers. In L. M. Oakes & P. J. Bauer (Eds.), *Short- and long-term memory in infancy and early childhood: Taking the first steps toward remembering* (pp. 209–239). New York: Oxford University Press.

Hayslip, B., Jr. (1994). Stability of intelligence. In R. J. Sternberg (Ed.), *Encyclopedia of human intelligence* (Vol. 2). New York: Macmillan.

Haywood, H. C., & Lidz, C. S. (2007). *Dynamic assessment in practice: Clinical and educational applications.* Cambridge, England: Cambridge University Press.

Healy, C. C. (1993). Discovery courses are great in theory, but. . . . In J. L. Schwartz, M. Yerushalmy, & B. Wilson (Eds.), *The geometric supposer: What is it a case of?* Hillsdale, NJ: Erlbaum.

Heath, S. B. (1980). Questioning at home and at school: A comparative study. In G. Spindler (Ed.), *The ethnography of schooling: Educational anthropology in action.* New York: Holt, Rinehart & Winston.

Heath, S. B. (1983). *Ways with words: Language, life, and work in communities and classrooms.* Cambridge, England: Cambridge University Press.

Heath, S. B. (1986). Taking a cross-cultural look at narratives. *Topics in Language Disorders, 7*(1), 84–94.

Heath, S. B. (1989). Oral and literate traditions among Black Americans living in poverty. *American Psychologist, 44,* 367–373.

Hébert, T. P., & Beardsley, T. M. (2001). Jermaine: A critical case study of a gifted black child living in rural poverty. *Gifted Child Quarterly, 45,* 85–103.

Hecht, S. A., Close, L., & Santisi, M. (2003). Sources of individual differences in fraction skills. *Journal of Experimental Child Psychology, 86,* 277–302.

Heckenhausen, H. (1984). Emergent achievement behavior: Some early developments. In J. Nicholls (Ed.), *Advances in achievement motivation.* Greenwich, CT: JAI Press.

Heckenhausen, H. (1987). Emotional components of action: Their ontogeny as reflected in achievement behavior. In D. Girlitz & J. F. Wohlwill (Eds.), *Curiosity, imagination, and play.* Hillsdale, NJ: Erlbaum.

Hedges, L. V., & Nowell, A. (1995). Sex differences in mental test scores, variability, and numbers of high-scoring individuals. *Science, 269,* 41–45.

Hegarty, M., & Kozhevnikov, M. (1999). Types of visual-spatial representations and mathematical problem solving. *Journal of Educational Psychology, 91,* 684–689.

Heibeck, T. H., & Markman, E. M. (1987). Word learning in children: An examination of fast mapping. *Child Development, 58,* 1021–1034.

Heine, S. J. (2007). Culture and motivation: What motivates people to act in the ways that they do? In S. Kitayama & D. Cohen (Eds.), *Handbook of cultural psychology* (pp. 714–733). New York: Guilford Press.

Hellenga, K. (2002). Social space, the final frontier: Adolescents on the Internet. In J. T. Mortimer & R. W. Larson (Eds.), *The changing adolescent experience: Societal trends and the transition to adulthood* (pp. 208–249). Cambridge, England: Cambridge University Press.

Hellings, P. J., & Burns, C. E. (2004). Genetic disorders. In C. E. Burns, A. M. Dunn, M. A. Brady, N. B. Starr, & C. G. Blosser (Eds.), *Pediatric primary care: A handbook for nurse practitioners* (3rd ed., pp. 1159–1183). St. Louis, MO: Saunders.

Helwig, C. C., & Jasiobedzka, U. (2001). The relation between law and morality: Children's reasoning about socially beneficial and unjust laws. *Child Development, 72,* 1382–1393.

Helwig, C. C., Zelazo, P. D., & Wilson, M. (2001). Children's judgments of psychological harm in normal and noncanonical situations. *Child Development, 72,* 66–81.

Hembree, R. (1988). Correlates, causes, effects, and treatment of test anxiety. *Review of Educational Research, 58,* 47–77.

Hemmings, A. B. (2004). *Coming of age in U.S. high schools: Economic, kinship, religious, and political crosscurrents.* Mahwah, NJ: Erlbaum.

Hemphill, L., & Snow, C. (1996). Language and literacy development: Discontinuities and differences. In D. R. Olson & N. Torrance (Eds.), *The handbook of education and human development: New models of learning, teaching, and schooling.* Cambridge, MA: Blackwell.

Henderson, N. D. (1982). Human behavior genetics. *Annual Review of Psychology, 33,* 403–440.

Hennessey, B. A. (1995). Social, environmental, and developmental issues and creativity. *Educational Psychology Review, 7,* 163–183.

Hennessey, M. G. (2003). Metacognitive aspects of students' reflective discourse: Implications for intentional conceptual change teaching and learning. In G. M. Sinatra & P. R. Pintrich (Eds.), *Intentional conceptual change* (pp. 103–132). Mahwah, NJ: Erlbaum.

Herbert, J., & Stipek, D. (2005). The emergence of gender differences in children's perceptions of their academic competence. *Applied Developmental Psychology, 26,* 276–295.

Herr, K. (1997). Learning lessons from school: Homophobia, heterosexism, and the construction of failure. In M. B. Harris (Ed.), *School experiences of gay and lesbian youth: The invisible minority* (pp. 51–64). Binghamton, NY: Harrington Park Press.

Herrell, A., & Jordan, M. (2004). *Fifty strategies for teaching English language learners* (2nd ed.). Upper Saddle River, NJ: Merrill/Prentice Hall.

Herrnstein, R. J., & Murray, C. (1994). *The bell curve: Intelligence and class structure in American life.* New York: Free Press.

Hersh, C. A., Stone, B. J., & Ford, L. (1996). Learning disabilities and learned helplessness: A heuristic approach. *International Journal of Neuroscience, 84,* 103–113.

Hess, R. D., & Azuma, M. (1991). Cultural support for learning: Contrasts between Japan and the United States. *Educational Researcher, 29*(9), 2–8.

Hess, R. D., Chang, C. M., & McDevitt, T. M. (1987). Cultural variations in family beliefs about children's performance in mathematics: Comparisons among People's Republic of China, Chinese-American, and Caucasian-American families. *Journal of Educational Psychology, 79,* 179–188.

Hess, R. D., & Holloway, S. D. (1984). Family and school as educational institutions. In R. D. Parke, R. N. Emde, H. P. McAdoo, & G. P. Sackett (Eds.), *Review of child development research: Vol. 7. The family* (pp. 179–222). Chicago: University of Chicago Press.

Hetherington, E. M., Bridges, M., & Insabella, G. M. (1998). What matters? What does not? Five perspectives on the association between marital transitions and children's adjustment. *American Psychologist, 53,* 167–184.

Hetherington, E. M., & Clingempeel, W. G. (1992). Coping with marital transitions: A family systems perspective. *Monographs of the Society for Research in Child Development, 57*(2–3, Serial No. 227).

Hetherington, E. M., Cox, M., & Cox, R. (1978). The aftermath of divorce. In J. H. Stevens, Jr., & M. Matthews (Eds.), *Mother–child, father–child relations* (pp. 110-155). Washington, DC: National Association for the Education of Young Children.

Hetherington, E. M., Henderson, S. H., Reiss, D., Anderson, E. R., Bridges, M., Chan, R. W., et al. (1999). Adolescent siblings in stepfamilies: Family functioning and adolescent adjustment. *Monographs of the Society for Research in Child Development, 64*(4, Serial No. 259).

Hettinger, H. R., & Knapp, N. F. (2001). Potential, performance, and paradox: A case study of J.P., a verbally gifted, struggling reader. *Journal for the Education of the Gifted, 24,* 248–289.

Hewitt, J., & Scardamalia, M. (1996, April). *Design principles for the support of distributed processes.* Paper presented at the annual meeting of the American Educational Research Association, San Francisco.

Hiatt, S., Campos, J., & Emde, R. (1979). Facial patterning and infant emotional expression: Happiness, surprise, and fear. *Child Development, 50,* 1020–1035.

Hickey, D. T. (1997). Motivation and contemporary socio-constructivist instructional perspectives. *Educational Psychologist, 32,* 175–193.

Hickey, D. T., & Granade, J. B. (2004). The influence of sociocultural theory on our theories of engagement and motivation. In D. M. McInerney & S. Van Etten (Eds.), *Big theories revisited* (pp. 223–247). Greenwich, CT: Information Age.

Hickey, T. L., & Peduzzi, J. D. (1987). Structure and development of the visual system. In P. Salapatek & L. Cohen (Eds.), *Handbook of infant perception: Vol. 1. From sensation to perception.* New York: Academic Press.

Hicks, L. (1997). Academic motivation and peer relationships—How do they mix in an adolescent world? *Middle School Journal, 28,* 18–22.

Hidalgo, N. M., Siu, S., Bright, J. A., Swap, S. M., & Epstein, J. L. (1995). Research on families, schools, and communities: A multicultural perspective. In J. A. Banks & C. A. M. Banks (Eds.), *Handbook of research on multicultural education.* New York: Macmillan.

Hidi, S., & Harackiewicz, J. M. (2000). Motivating the academically unmotivated: A critical issue for the 21st century. *Review of Educational Research, 70,* 151–179.

Hidi, S., & Renninger, K. A. (2006). The four-phase model of interest development. *Educational Psychologist, 41,* 111–127.

Hidi, S., Renninger, K. A., & Krapp, A. (2004). Interest, a motivational variable that combines affecting and cognitive functioning. In D. Y. Dai & R. J. Sternberg (Eds.), *Motivation, emotion, and cognition: Integrative perspectives on intellectual functioning and development* (pp. 89–115). Mahwah, NJ: Erlbaum.

Hiebert, E. H., & Fisher, C. W. (1992). The tasks of school literacy: Trends and issues. In J. Brophy (Ed.), *Advances in research on teaching: Vol. 3. Planning and managing learning tasks and activities.* Greenwich, CT: JAI Press.

Hiebert, E. H., & Raphael, T. E. (1996). Psychological perspectives on literacy and extensions to educational practice. In D. C. Berliner & R. C. Calfee (Eds.), *Handbook of educational psychology.* New York: Macmillan.

Hiebert, J., Carpenter, T. P., Fennema, E., Fuson, K. C., Wearne, D., Murray, H., et al. (1997). *Making sense: Teaching and learning mathematics with understanding.* Portsmouth, NH: Heinemann.

Hiebert, J., & Wearne, D. (1996). Instruction, understanding, and skill in multidigit addition and subtraction. *Cognition and Instruction, 14,* 251–283.

Higgins, A. (1995). Educating for justice and community: Lawrence Kohlberg's vision of moral education. In W. M. Kurtines & J. L. Gewirtz (Eds.), *Moral development: An introduction.* Boston: Allyn & Bacon.

Higgins, A. T., & Turnure, J. E. (1984). Distractibility and concentration of attention in children's development. *Child Development, 55,* 1799–1810.

Hill, J. P., Holmbeck, G. N., Marlow, L., Green, T. M., & Lynch, M. E. (1985). Menarchal status and parent–child relations in families of seventh-grade girls. *Journal of Youth and Adolescence, 14,* 301–316.

Hill, P. R., Hogben, J. H., & Bishop, D. V. M. (2005). Auditory frequency discrimination in children with specific language impairment: A longitudinal study. *Journal of Speech, Language and Hearing Research, 48,* 1136–1146.

Hilliard, A., & Vaughn-Scott, M. (1982). The quest for the minority child. In S. G. Moore & C. R. Cooper (Eds.), *The young child: Reviews of research* (Vol. 3). Washington, DC: National Association for the Education of Young Children.

Hillier, L., Hewitt, K. L., & Morrongiello, B. A. (1992). Infants' perception of illusions in sound localization: Reaching to sounds in the dark. *Journal of Experimental Child Psychology, 53,* 159–179.

Hilt, L. M. (2005, April). *The effects of attribution retraining on class performance, achievement motivation, and attributional style in high school students.* Poster presented at the biennial meeting of the Society for Research in Child Development, Atlanta, GA.

Hinde, R. A., Titmus, G., Easton, D., & Tamplin, A. (1985). Incidence of "friendship" and behavior with strong associates versus non-associates in preschoolers. *Child Development, 56,* 234–245.

Hine, P., & Fraser, B. J. (2002, April). *Combining qualitative and quantitative methods in a study of Australian students' transition from elementary to high school.* Paper presented at the annual meeting of the American Educational Research Association, New Orleans, LA.

Hinkley, J. W., McInerney, D. M., & Marsh, H. W. (2001, April). *The multi-faceted structure of school achievement motivation: A case for social goals.* Paper presented at the annual meeting of the American Educational Research Association, Seattle, WA.

Hirsh-Pasek, K., & Golinkoff, R. M. (1996). *The origins of grammar: Evidence from early language comprehension.* Cambridge, MA: MIT Press.

Hirsh-Pasek, K., Hyson, M., & Rescorla, L. (1990). Academic environments in preschool: Do they pressure or challenge young children? *Early Education and Development, 1*(6), 401–423.

Ho, C. S., & Fuson, K. C. (1998). Children's knowledge of teen quantities as tens and ones: Comparisons of Chinese, British, and American kindergartners. *Journal of Educational Psychology, 90,* 536–544.

Ho, D. Y. F. (1994). Cognitive socialization in Confucian heritage cultures. In P. M. Greenfield & R. R. Cocking (Eds.), *Cross-cultural roots of minority child development.* Hillsdale, NJ: Erlbaum.

Ho, H.-Z., Hinckley, H. S., Fox, K. R., Brown, J. H., & Dixon, C. N. (2001, April). *Family literacy: Promoting parent support strategies for student success.* Paper presented at the annual meeting of the American Educational Research Association, Seattle, WA.

Hobson, P. (2004). *The cradle of thought: Exploring the origins of thinking.* Oxford, England: Oxford University Press.

Hobson, P. R., Chidambi, G., Lee, A., & Meyer, J. (2006). Foundations for self-awareness: An exploration through autism. *Monographs of the Society for Research in Child Development, Serial No. 84, 71*(2), 1–166.

Hoekstra, R. A., Bartels, M., & Boomsma, D. I. (2007). Longitudinal genetic study of verbal and nonverbal IQ from early childhood to young adulthood. *Learning and Individual Differences, 17,* 97–114.

Hoerger, M. L., & Mace, F. C. (2006). A computerized test of self-control predicts classroom behavior. *Journal of Applied Behavior Analysis, 39,* 147–159.

Hoerr, T. R. (2003). Distributed intelligence and why schools need to foster it. *Independent School, 63,* 76–83.

Hofer, B. K. (2000). Dimensionality and disciplinary differences in personal epistemology. *Contemporary Educational Psychology, 25,* 378–405.

Hofer, B. K., & Pintrich, P. R. (1997). The development of epistemological theories: Beliefs about knowledge and knowing and their relation to learning. *Review of Educational Research, 67,* 88–140.

Hofer, B. K., & Pintrich, P. R. (Eds.). (2002). *Personal epistemology: The psychology of beliefs about knowledge and knowing.* Mahwah, NJ: Erlbaum.

Hofer, M. A. (2006). Psychobiological roots of early attachment. *Current Directions in Psychological Science, 15*(2), 84–87.

Hoff, E. (2003). The specificity of environmental influence: Socioeconomic status affects early vocabulary development via maternal speech. *Child Development, 74,* 1368–1378.

Hoff, E., & Naigles, L. (2002). How children use input to acquire a lexicon. *Child Development, 73,* 418–433.

Hoff-Ginsberg, E. (1997). *Language development.* Pacific Grove, CA: Brooks/Cole.

Hoffman, M. L. (1975). Altruistic behavior and the parent–child relationship. *Journal of Personality and Social Psychology, 31,* 937–943.

Hoffman, M. L. (1981). Is altruism part of human nature? *Journal of Personality and Social Psychology, 40,* 121–137.

Hoffman, M. L. (1988). Moral development. In M. H. Bornstein & M. E. Lamb (Eds.), *Developmental psychology: An advanced textbook* (2nd ed.). Hillsdale, NJ: Erlbaum.

Hoffman, M. L. (1991). Empathy, social cognition, and moral action. In W. M. Kurtines & J. L. Gewirtz (Eds.), *Moral behavior and development: Vol. 1. Theory.* Hillsdale, NJ: Erlbaum.

Hoffman, M. L. (1994). Discipline and internalization. *Developmental Psychology, 30,* 26–28.

Hogdon, L. A. (1995). *Visual strategies for improving communication: Vol. 1: Practical supports for school and home.* Troy, MI: Quirk Roberts.

Hokoda, A., & Fincham, F. D. (1995). Origins of children's helplessness and mastery achievement patterns in the family. *Journal of Educational Psychology, 87,* 375–385.

Holliday, B. G. (1985). Towards a model of teacher–child transactional processes affecting black children's academic achievement. In M. B. Spencer, G. K. Brookins, & W. R. Allen (Eds.), *Beginnings: The social and affective development of black children*. Hillsdale, NJ: Erlbaum.

Holloway, S. D. (2000). *Contested childhood: Diversity and change in Japanese preschools*. New York: Routledge.

Holloway, S. D., Fuller, B., Rambaud, M. F., & Eggers-Péirola, C. (1997). *Through my own eyes: Single mothers and the cultures of poverty*. Cambridge, MA: Harvard University Press.

Holm, A., Farrier, F., & Dodd, B. (2007). Phonological awareness, reading accuracy and spelling ability of children with inconsistent phonological disorder. *International Journal of Language and Communication Disorders, 43*, 300–322.

Holmes, R. M. (1998). *Fieldwork with children*. Thousand Oaks, CA: Sage.

Holmes, R. M., Pellegrini, A. D., & Schmidt, S. L. (2006). The effects of different recess timing regimens on preschoolers' classroom attention. *Early Child Development and Care, 176*, 735–743.

Hom, A., & Battistich, V. (1995, April). *Students' sense of school community as a factor in reducing drug use and delinquency*. Paper presented at the annual meeting of the American Educational Research Association, San Francisco.

Hong, Y., Chiu, C., & Dweck, C. S. (1995). Implicit theories of intelligence: Reconsidering the role of confidence in achievement motivation. In M. H. Kernis (Ed.), *Efficacy, agency, and self-esteem*. New York: Plenum Press.

Hong, Y., Morris, M. W., Chiu, C., & Benet-Martínez, V. (2000). Multicultural minds: A dynamic constructivist approach to culture and cognition. *American Psychologist, 55*, 709–720.

Hoover-Dempsey, K. V., & Sandler, H. M. (1997). Why do parents become involved in their children's education? *Review of Educational Research, 67*, 3–42.

Horn, J. L. (2008). Spearman, *g*, expertise, and the nature of human cognitive capability. In P. C. Kyllonen, R. D. Roberts, & L. Stankov (Eds.), *Extending intelligence: Enhancement and new constructs* (pp. 185–230). New York: Erlbaum/Taylor & Francis.

Horn, J. L., & Masunaga, H. (2000). New directions for research into aging and intelligence: The development of expertise. In T. J. Perfect & E. A. Maylor (Eds.), *Models of cognitive aging* (pp. 125–159). Oxford, England: Oxford University Press.

Horn, J. L., & Noll, J. (1997). Human cognitive capabilities: Gf-Gc theory. In D. P. Flanagan, J. L. Genshaft, & P. L. Harrison (Eds.), *Contemporary intellectual assessment: Theories, tests, and issues* (pp. 53–91). New York: Guilford Press.

Horowitz, F. D., Darling-Hammond, L., & Bransford, J. (with Comer, J., Rosebrock, K., Austin, K., & Rust, F.) (2005). Educating teachers for developmentally appropriate practice. In L. Darling-Hammond & J. Bransford (Eds.), *Preparing teachers for a changing world: What teachers should learn and be able to do* (pp. 88–125). San Francisco: Jossey-Bass/Wiley.

Horst, J. S., Oakes, L. M., & Madole, K. L. (2005). What does it look like and what can it do? Category structure influences how infants categorize. *Child Development, 76*, 614–631.

Howard, G. R. (2007). As diversity grows, so must we. *Educational Leadership, 64*(6), 16–22.

Howe, D. (2006). Disabled children, parent–child interaction and attachment. *Child and Family Social Work, 11*, 95–106.

Howe, M. L. (2003). Memories from the cradle. *Current Directions in Psychological Science, 12*, 62–65.

Howell, J. C. (2000, August). *Youth gang programs and strategies*. Washington, DC: U.S. Department of Justice, Office of Juvenile Justice and Delinquency Prevention.

Howell, J. C., & Lynch, J. P. (2000, August). Youth gangs in schools. *Juvenile Justice Bulletin* (OJJDP Publication NCJ-183015). Washington, DC: U.S. Department of Justice, Office of Juvenile Justice and Delinquency Prevention.

Howes, C. (1988). The peer interactions of young children. *Monographs of the Society for Research in Child Development, 53*(1, Serial No. 217).

Howes, C. (1992). *The collaborative construction of pretend*. Albany: State University of New York Press.

Howes, C. (1999). Attachment relationships in the context of multiple caregivers. In J. Cassidy & P. R. Shaver (Eds.), *Handbook of attachment: Theory, research, and clinical applications* (pp. 671–687). New York: Guilford Press.

Howes, C., & Matheson, C. C. (1992). Sequences in the development of competent play with peers: Social and social-pretend play. *Developmental Psychology, 28*, 961–974.

Howes, C., & Ritchie, S. (1998). Changes in child–teacher relationships in a therapeutic preschool program. *Early Education and Development, 9*, 411–422.

Howes, C., & Segal, J. (1993). Children's relationships with alternative caregivers: The special case of maltreated children removed from their homes. *Journal of Applied Developmental Psychology, 17*, 71–81.

Howes, C., Smith, E., & Galinsky, E. (1995). *The Florida child care quality improvement study*. New York: Families and Work Institute.

Howie, J. D. (2002, April). *Effects of audience, gender, and achievement level on adolescent students' communicated attributions and affect in response to academic success and failure*. Paper presented at the annual meeting of the American Educational Research Association, New Orleans, LA.

Huang, M.-H., & Hauser, R. M. (1998). Trends in Black-White test-score differentials: II. The WORDSUM vocabulary test. In U. Neisser (Ed.), *The rising curve: Long-term gains in IQ and related measures* (pp. 303–332). Washington, DC: American Psychological Association.

Hubel, D. H., & Wiesel, T. (1965). Binocular interaction in striate cortex of kittens reared with artificial squint. *Journal of Neurophysiology, 28*, 1041–1059.

Huesmann, L. R., Moise-Titus, J., Podolski, C. L., & Eron, L. D. (2003). Longitudinal relations between children's exposure to TV violence and their aggressive and violent behavior in young adulthood: 1977–1992. *Developmental Psychology, 39*(2), 201–221.

Hufton, N., Elliott, J., & Illushin, L. (2002). Achievement motivation across cultures: Some puzzles and their implications for future research. *New Directions for Child and Adolescent Development, 96*, 65–85.

Hughes, C., & Dunn, J. (2007). Children's relationships with other children. In C. A. Brownell & C. B. Kopp (Eds.), *Socioemotional development in the toddler years: Transitions and transformations* (pp. 177–200). New York: Guilford Press.

Hughes, D. (2003). Correlates of African American and Latino parents' messages to children about ethnicity and race: A comparative study of racial socialization. *American Journal of Community Psychology, 31*, 15–33.

Hughes, F. P. (1998). Play in special populations. In O. N. Saracho & B. Spodek (Eds.), *Multiple perspectives on play in early childhood education* (pp. 171–193). Albany: State University of New York Press.

Hughes, J., & Kwok, O. (2007). Influence of student–teacher and parent–teacher relationships on lower achieving readers' engagement and achievement in the primary grades. *Journal of Educational Psychology, 99*, 39–51.

Hughes, J. M., Bigler, R. S., & Levy, S. R. (2007). Consequences of learning about historical racism among European American and African American children. *Child Development, 78*, 1689–1705.

Huizink, A. C., Mulder, E. J. H., & Buitelaar, J. K. (2004). Prenatal stress and risk for psychopathology: Special effects or induction of general susceptibility? *Psychological Bulletin, 130*, 115–142.

Hulanicka, B., Gronkiewicz, L., & Koniarek, J. (2001). Effect of familial distress on growth and maturation of girls: A longitudinal study. *American Journal of Human Biology, 13*, 771–776.

Hulit, L. M., & Howard, M. R. (2006). *Born to talk* (4th ed.). Boston: Allyn & Bacon.

Hulme, C., & Joshi, R. M. (Eds.). (1998). *Reading and spelling: Development and disorders*. Mahwah, NJ: Erlbaum.

Humphreys, A. P., & Smith, P. K. (1987). Rough-and-tumble play, friendship, and dominance in school children: Evidence for continuity and change with age. *Child Development, 58*, 201–212.

Humphreys, L. G. (1992). What both critics and users of ability tests need to know. *Psychological Science, 3*, 271–274.

Hunt, E. (1997). Nature vs. nurture: The feeling of *vujà dé*. In R. J. Sternberg & E. L. Grigorenko (Eds.), *Intelligence, heredity, and environment* (pp. 531–551). Cambridge, England: Cambridge University Press.

Huntsinger, C. S., Jose, P. E., Larson, S. L., Krieg, D. B., & Shaligram, C. (2000). Mathematics, vocabulary, and reading development in Chinese American and European American children over the primary school years. *Journal of Educational Psychology, 92*, 745–760.

Hursh, D. (2007). Assessing No Child Left Behind and the rise of neoliberal education policies. *American Educational Research Journal, 44*, 493–518.

Husman, J., & Freeman, B. (1999, April). *The effect of perceptions of instrumentality on intrinsic motivation*. Paper presented at the annual meeting of the American Educational Research Association, Montreal, Canada.

Hussong, A., Chassin, L., & Hicks, R. (1999, April). *The elusive relation between negative affect and adolescent substance use: Does it exist?* Paper presented at the biennial meeting of the Society for Research in Child Development, Albuquerque, NM.

Huston, A. C. (1983). Sex typing. In E. M. Hetherington (Ed.), *Handbook of child psychology: Vol. 4. Socialization, personality, and social development* (4th ed., pp. 387–467). New York: Wiley.

Huston, A. C., Donnerstein, E., Fairchild, H., Feshbach, N. D., Katz, P. A., Murray, J. P., et al. (1992). *Big world, small screen: The role of television in American society*. Lincoln: University of Nebraska Press.

Hutt, S. J., Tyler, S., Hutt, C., & Christopherson, H. (1989). *Play, exploration, and learning: A natural history of the pre-school*. London: Routledge.

Huttenlocher, J., Jordan, N. C., & Levine, S. C. (1994). A mental model for early arithmetic. *Journal of Experimental Psychology: General, 123*, 284–296.

Huttenlocher, J., Newcombe, N., & Vasilyeva, M. (1999). Spatial scaling in young children. *Psychological Science, 10*, 393–398.

Huttenlocher, P. R. (1990). Morphometric study of human cerebral cortex development. *Neuropsychologia, 28*, 517–527.

Hwang, W.-C. (2006). Acculturative family distancing: Theory, research, and clinical practice. *Psychotherapy: Theory, Research, Practice, Training, 43*, 397–409.

Hyde, J. S., Mezulis, A. H., & Abramson, L. Y. (2008). The ABCs of depression: Integrating affective, biological, and cognitive models to explain the emergence of the gender difference in depression. *Psychological Review, 115*(2), 291–313.

Hyde, K. L., & Peretz, I. (2004). Brains that are out of tune but in time. *Psychological Science, 15*, 356–360.

Hyman, I., Kay, B., Tabori, A., Weber, M., Mahon, M., & Cohen, I. (2006). Bullying: Theory, research, and interventions. In C. M. Evertson & C. S. Weinstein (Eds.), *Handbook of classroom management: Research, practice, and contemporary issues* (pp. 855–884). Mahwah, NJ: Erlbaum.

Hyman, I., Mahon, M., Cohen, I., Snook, P., Britton, G., & Lurkis, L. (2004). Student alienation syndrome: The other side of school violence. In J. C. Conoley & A. P. Goldstein (Eds.), *School violence intervention* (2nd ed., pp. 483–506). New York: Guilford Press.

Hynd, C. (1998). Conceptual change in a high school physics class. In B. Guzzetti & C. Hynd (Eds.), *Perspectives on conceptual change: Multiple ways to understand knowing and learning in a complex world* (pp. 27–36). Mahwah, NJ: Erlbaum.

Hyson, M. C., Hirsh-Pasek, K., Rescorla, L., Cone, J., & Martell-Boinske, L. (1991). Ingredients of parental "pressure" in early childhood. *Journal of Applied Developmental Psychology, 12*(3), 347–365.

Hyvönen, P., & Kangas, M. (2007). From bogey mountains to funny houses: Children's desires for play environment. *Australian Journal of Early Childhood, 32*(3), 39–47.

Iacoboni, M., & Woods, R. P. (1999). Cortical mechanisms of human imitation. *Science, 286,* 2526–2528.

Igoa, C. (1995). *The inner world of the immigrant child.* Mahwah, NJ: Erlbaum.

Imhof, M. (2001, March). *In the eye of the beholder: Children's perception of good and poor listening behavior.* Paper presented at the annual meeting of the International Listening Association, Chicago.

Immerwahr, J. (2004). *Public attitudes on higher education: A trend analysis, 1993 to 2003.* New York: National Center for Public Policy and Higher Education and Public Agenda.

Immordino-Yang, M. H., & Damazio, A. (2007). We feel, therefore we learn: The relevance of affective and social neuroscience to education. *Mind, Brain, and Education, 1,* 3–10.

Information Center for Sickle Cell and Thalassemic Disorders. (2002). *Malaria and the red cell.* Retrieved December 29, 2007, from http://sickle.bwh.harvard.edu/malaria_sickle.html.

Inglis, A., & Biemiller, A. (1997, March). *Fostering self-direction in mathematics: A cross-age tutoring program that enhances math problem solving.* Paper presented at the annual meeting of the American Educational Research Association, Chicago.

Inhelder, B., & Piaget, J. (1958). *The growth of logical thinking from childhood to adolescence* (A. Parsons & S. Milgram, Trans.). New York: Basic Books.

Insel, T. R. (2000). Toward a neurobiology of attachment. *Review of General Psychology, 4,* 176–185.

Institute of Education Sciences. (2006). Character education. Retrieved October 9, 2007, from http://ies.ed.gov/ncee/wwc/reports/character_education/index.asp

International Human Genome Sequencing Consortium. (2004, October 21). Finishing the euchromatic sequence of human genome. *Nature, 431,* 931–945.

Irujo, S. (1988). An introduction to intercultural differences and similarities in nonverbal communication. In J. S. Wurzel (Ed.), *Toward multiculturalism: A reader in multicultural education.* Yarmouth, ME: Intercultural Press.

Isabella, R. A., & Belsky, J. (1991). Interactional synchrony and the origins of infant-mother attachment: A replication study. *Child Development, 62,* 373–384.

Isen, A., Daubman, K. A., & Gorgoglione, J. M. (1987). The influence of positive affect on cognitive organization: Implications for education. In R. E. Snow & M. J. Farr (Eds.), *Aptitude, learning and instruction: Vol. 3. Cognitive and affective process analysis.* Hillsdale, NJ: Erlbaum.

Iyengar, S. S., & Lepper, M. R. (1999). Rethinking the value of choice: A cultural perspective on intrinsic motivation. *Journal of Personality and Social Psychology, 76,* 349–366.

Jacklin, C. N. (1989). Female and male: Issues of gender. *American Psychologist, 44,* 127–133.

Jackson, P. W. (1988). The daily grind. In G. Handel (Ed.), *Childhood socialization.* New York: Aldine de Gruyter.

Jacob, B. A. (2007). The challenges of staffing urban schools with effective teachers. *Future of Children, 17*(1), 129–153.

Jacobs, J. E., Davis-Kean, P., Bleeker, M., Eccles, J. S., & Malanchuk, O. (2005). "I can, but I don't want to": The impact of parents, interests, and activities on gender differences in math. In A. M. Gallagher & J. C. Kaufman (Eds.), *Gender differences in mathematics: An integrative psychological approach* (pp. 246–263). Cambridge, England: Cambridge University Press.

Jacobs, J. E., Lanza, S., Osgood, D. W., Eccles, J. S., & Wigfield, A. (2002). Changes in children's self-competence and values: Gender and domain differences across grades one through twelve. *Child Development, 73,* 509–527.

Jacobsen, B., Lowery, B., & DuCette, J. (1986). Attributions of learning disabled children. *Journal of Educational Psychology, 78,* 59–64.

Jacoby, R., & Glauberman, N. (Eds.). (1995). *The Bell Curve debate: History, documents, opinions.* New York: Random House.

Jalongo, M. R. (2008). *Learning to listen, listening to learn: Building essential skills in young children.* Washington, DC: National Association for the Education of Young Children Press.

Jalongo, M. R., Isenberg, J. P., & Gerbracht, G. (1995). *Teachers' stories: From personal narrative to professional insight.* San Francisco: Jossey-Bass.

James, D. K., Spencer, C. J., & Stepsis, B. W. (2002). Fetal learning: A prospective randomized controlled study. *Ultrasound in Obstetrics and Gynecology, 20,* 431–438.

Janosz, M., Le Blanc, M., Boulerice, B., & Tremblay, R. E. (2000). Predicting different types of school dropouts: A typological approach with two longitudinal samples. *Journal of Educational Psychology, 92,* 171–190.

Jaswal, V. K., & Markman, E. M. (2001). Learning proper and common names in inferential versus ostensive contexts. *Child Development, 72,* 768–786.

Jelalian, E., Wember, Y. M., Bungeroth, H., & Birmaher, V. (2007). Practitioner review: Bridging review: Bridging the gap between research and clinical practice in pediatric obesity. *Journal of Child Psychology and Psychiatry, 48,* 115–127.

Jeltova, I., Birney, D., Fredine, N., Jarvine, L., Sternberg, R. J., & Grigorenko. E. L. (2007). Dynamic assessment as a process-oriented assessment in educational settings. *Advances in Speech-Language Pathology, 9*(4), 273–285.

Jencks, C. M., & Mayer, S. (1990). The social consequences of growing up in a poor neighborhood: A review. In M. McGreary & L. Lynn (Eds.), *Concentrated urban poverty in America.* Washington, DC: National Academy.

Jenkins, J. M., Turrell, S. L., Kogushi, Y., Lollis, S., & Ross, H. S. (2003). A longitudinal investigation of the dynamics of mental state talk in families. *Child Development, 74,* 905–920.

Jenkins, S., Bax, M., & Hart, H. (1980). Behavior problems in preschool children. *Journal of Child Psychology and Psychiatry, 21,* 5–18.

Jenlink, C. L. (1994, April). *Music: A lifeline for the self-esteem of at-risk students.* Paper presented at the annual meeting of the American Educational Research Association, New Orleans, LA.

Jensen, A. R. (2007). Book review: *Howard Gardner under fire: The Rebel psychologist faces his critics. Intelligence, 36,* 96–97.

Jensen, E. (2005). *Teaching with the brain in mind* (2nd ed.). Alexandria, VA: Association for Supervision and Curriculum Development.

Jensen, M. M. (2005). *Introduction to emotional and behavioral disorders: Recognizing and managing problems in the classroom.* Upper Saddle River, NJ: Merrill Prentice Hall.

Jessor, R., & Jessor, S. L. (1977). *Problem behavior and psychosocial development: A longitudinal study of youth.* San Diego, CA: Academic Press.

Jia, G., & Aaronson, D. (2003). A longitudinal study of Chinese children and adolescents learning English in the United States. *Applied Psycholinguistics, 24,* 131–161.

Jimerson, S., Egeland, B., & Teo, A. (1999). A longitudinal study of achievement trajectories: Factors associated with change. *Journal of Educational Psychology, 91,* 116–126.

Jipson, J. L., & Callanan, M. A. (2003). Mother-child conversation and children's understanding of biological and nonbiological changes in size. *Child Development, 74,* 629–644.

Joanisse, M. F. (2007). Phonological deficits and developmental language impairments: Evidence from connectionist models. In D. Mareschal, S. Sirois, G. Westermann, & M. H. Johnson (Eds.), *Neuroconstructivism: Vol. 2. Perspectives and prospects* (pp. 205–229). Oxford, England: Oxford University Press.

Johanning, D. I., D'Agostino, J. V., Steele, D. F., & Shumow, L. (1999, April). *Student writing, post-writing group collaboration, and learning in pre-algebra.* Paper presented at the annual meeting of the American Educational Research Association, Montreal, Canada.

John, O. P. (1990). The "Big Five" factor taxonomy: Dimensions of personality in the natural language and in questionnaires. In L. Pervin (Ed.), *Handbook of personality: Theory and research* (pp. 66–100). New York: Guilford Press.

John, O. P., Caspi, A., Robins, R. W., Moffitt, T. E., & Stouthamer-Loeber, M. (1994). The "Little Five": Exploring the five-factor model of personality in adolescent boys. *Child Development, 65,* 160–178.

Johnson, D. W., & Johnson, R. T. (1996). Conflict resolution and peer mediation programs in elementary and secondary schools: A review of the research. *Review of Educational Research, 66,* 459–506.

Johnson, D. W., & Johnson, R. T. (2001, April). *Teaching students to be peacemakers: A meta-analysis.* Paper presented at the annual meeting of the American Educational Research Association, Seattle, WA.

Johnson, D. W., Johnson, R., Dudley, B., Ward, M., & Magnuson, D. (1995). The impact of peer mediation training on the management of school and home conflicts. *American Educational Research Journal, 32,* 829–844.

Johnson, J. O. (2005, October). *Who's minding the kids? Child care arrangements: Winter 2002.* Current Population Reports, P70–101. Washington, DC: U.S. Department of Commerce, U.S. Census Bureau. Retrieved November 28, 2007, from http://www.census.gov/population/www/socdemo/childcare.html

Johnson, J. S., & Newport, E. L. (1989). Critical period effects in second language learning: The influence of maturational state on acquisition of English as a second language. *Cognitive Psychology, 21,* 60–99.

Johnson, K. E., Alexander, J. M., Spencer, S., Leibham, M. E., & Neitzel, C. (2004). Factors associated with the early emergence of intense interests within conceptual domains. *Cognitive Development, 19,* 325–343.

Johnson, M. H. (1999). Developmental neuroscience. In M. H. Bornstein & M. E. Lamb (Eds.), *Developmental psychology: An advanced textbook* (4th ed., pp. 199–230). Mahwah, NJ: Erlbaum.

Johnson, M. H., & de Haan, M. (2001). Developing cortical specialization for visual-cognitive function: The case of face recognition. In J. L. McClelland & R. S. Siegler (Eds.), *Mechanisms of cognitive development: Behavioral and neural perspectives* (pp. 253–270). Mahwah, NJ: Erlbaum.

Johnson, W., Bouchard, T. J. Jr., McGue, M., Segal, N. L., Tellegen, A., Keyes, M., et al. (2007). Genetic and environmental influences on the Verbal-Perceptual-Image Rotation (VPR) model of the structure of mental abilities in the Minnesota study of twins reared apart. *Intelligence, 35,* 542–562.

Johnson, W., te Nijenhuis, J., & Bouchard, T. J. Jr. (2007). Still just 1 *g*: Consistent results from five test batteries. *Intelligence, 36,* 81–95.

Johnston, J. R. (1997). Specific language impairment, cognition and the biological basis of language. In

M. Gopnik (Ed.), *The inheritance and innateness of grammars*. New York: Oxford University Press.

Johnston, L. D., O'Malley, P. M., Bachman, J. G., & Schulenberg, J. E. (2007). *Monitoring the Future national results on adolescent drug use: Overview of key findings, 2006* (NIH Publication No. 07-6202). Bethesda, MD: National Institute on Drug Abuse.

Johnston, P., & Afflerbach, P. (1985). The process of contruting main ideas from text. *Cognition and Instruction, 2,* 207–232.

Johnston, T. D., & Edwards, L. (2002). Genes, interactions, and the development of behavior. *Psychological Review, 109,* 26–34.

Jones, D., & Christensen, C. A. (1999). Relationship between automaticity in handwriting and students' ability to generate written text. *Journal of Educational Psychology, 91,* 44–49.

Jones, G. P., & Dembo, M. H. (1989). Age and sex role differences in intimate friendships during childhood and adolescence. *Merrill-Palmer Quarterly, 35,* 445–462.

Jones, H. F. (1949). Adolescence in our society. In *Anniversary papers of the Community Service Society of New York: The family in a democratic society* (pp. 70–82). New York: Columbia University Press.

Jordan, A. B. (2003). Children remember prosocial program lessons but how much are they learning? *Applied Developmental Psychology, 24,* 341–345.

Jordan, A. H., & Lovett, B. J. (2007). Stereotype threat and test performance: A primer for school psychologists. *Journal of School Psychology, 45,* 45–59.

Jordan, N. C., Hanich, L. B., & Kaplan, D. (2003). A longitudinal study of mathematical competencies in children with specific mathematics difficulties versus children with comorbid mathematics and reading difficulties. *Child Development, 74,* 834–850.

Josselson, R. (1988). The embedded self: I and Thou revisited. In D. K. Lapsley & F. C. Power (Eds.), *Self, ego, and identity: Integrative approaches* (pp. 91–106). New York: Springer-Verlag.

Jovanovic, J., & King, S. S. (1998). Boys and girls in the performance-based science classroom: Who's doing the performing? *American Educational Research Journal, 35,* 477–496.

Juel, C. (1991). Beginning reading. In R. Barr, M. Kamii, P. Mosenthal, & P. D. Pearson (Eds.), *Handbook of reading research* (Vol. II). New York: Longman.

Juel, C. (1998). What kind of one-on-one tutoring helps a poor reader? In C. Hulme & R. M. Joshi (Eds.), *Reading and spelling: Development and disorders*. Mahwah, NJ: Erlbaum.

Jusczyk, P. W. (1995). Language acquisition: Speech sounds and phonological development. In J. L. Miller & P. D. Eimas (Eds.), *Handbook of perception and cognition: Vol. 11. Speech, language, and communication*. Orlando, FL: Academic Press.

Jusczyk, P. W. (1997). Finding and remembering words: Some beginnings by English-learning infants. *Current Directions in Psychological Science, 6,* 170–174.

Jusczyk, P. W. (2002). How infants adapt speech-processing capacities to native-language structure. *Current Directions in Psychological Science, 11,* 15–18.

Jusczyk, P. W., & Aslin, R. N. (1995). Infants' detection of the sound patterns of words in fluent speech. *Cognitive Psychology, 29,* 1–23.

Juster, N. (1961). *The phantom tollbooth*. New York: Random House.

Jutta, K., Jutta, E., & Karbach, J. (2008). Verbal self-instructions in task switching: A compensatory tool for action-control deficits in childhood and old age? *Developmental Science, 11,* 223–236.

Juvonen, J. (1991). Deviance, perceived responsibility, and negative peer reactions. *Developmental Psychology, 27,* 672–681.

Juvonen, J. (2000). The social functions of attributional face-saving tactics among early adolescents. *Educational Psychology Review, 12,* 15–32.

Juvonen, J. (2006). Sense of belonging, social bonds, and school functioning. In P. A. Alexander & P. H.

Winne (Eds.), *Handbook of educational psychology* (2nd ed., pp. 655–674). Mahwah, NJ: Erlbaum.

Juvonen, J., Nishina, A., & Graham, S. (2000). Peer harassment, psychological adjustment, and school functioning in early adolescence. *Journal of Educational Psychology, 92,* 349–359.

Juvonen, J., & Weiner, B. (1993). An attributional analysis of students' interactions: The social consequences of perceived responsibility. *Educational Psychology Review, 5,* 325–345.

Kaczmarek, M. G., & Backlund, B. A. (1991). Disenfranchised grief: The loss of an adolescent romantic relationship. *Adolescence, 26,* 253–259.

Kaffman, A., & Meaney, M. J. (2007). Neurodevelopmental sequelae of postnatal maternal care in rodents: Clinical and research implications of molecular insights. *Journal of Child Psychology and Psychiatry, 48,* 224–244.

Kagan, J. (1981). *The second year: The emergence of self-awareness*. Cambridge, MA: Harvard University Press.

Kagan, J. (1984). *The nature of the child*. New York: Basic Books.

Kagan, J. K., & Fox, N. A. (2006). Biology, culture, and temperamental biases. In W. Damon & R. M. Lerner (Eds. in Chief) & N. Eisenberg (Vol. Ed.), *Handbook of child psychology, Vol. 3. Social, emotional, and personality development* (6th ed., pp. 167–225). Hoboken, NJ: Wiley.

Kagan, J., Snidman, N., Vahn, V., & Towsley, S. (2007). The preservation of two infant temperaments into adolescence. *Monographs of the Society for Research in Child Development, 72,* 1–80.

Kağitçibaşi, Ç. (2007). *Family, self, and human development across cultures: Theory and applications* (2nd ed.). Mahwah, NJ: Erlbaum.

Kahl, B., & Woloshyn, V. E. (1994). Using elaborative interrogation to facilitate acquisition of factual information in cooperative learning settings: One good strategy deserves another. *Applied Cognitive Psychology, 8,* 465–478.

Kail, R. (1990). *The development of memory in children* (3rd ed.). New York: Freeman.

Kail, R. V. (1998). *Children and their development*. Upper Saddle River, NJ: Prentice Hall.

Kail, R. V. (2007). Longitudinal evidence that increases in processing speed and working memory enhance children's reasoning. *Psychological Science, 18,* 312–313.

Kail, R. V., & Ferrer, E. (2007). Processing speed in childhood and adolescence: Longitudinal models for examining developmental change. *Child Development, 78,* 1760–1770.

Kaler, S. R., & Kopp, C. B. (1990). Compliance and comprehension in very young toddlers. *Child Development, 61,* 1997–2003.

Kamerman, S. B. (2000). Parental leave policies: An essential ingredient in early childhood education and care policies. *Social Policy Report, 14*(2). Ann Arbor, MI: Society for Research in Child Development.

Kanner, A. D., Feldman, S. S., Weinberger, D. A., & Ford, M. E. (1987). Uplifts, hassles, and adaptational outcomes in early adolescents. *Journal of Early Adolescence, 7,* 371–394.

Kaplan, A. (1998, April). *Task goal orientation and adaptive social interaction among students of diverse cultural backgrounds*. Paper presented at the annual meeting of the American Educational Research Association, San Diego, CA.

Kaplan, A., Middleton, M. J., Urdan, T., & Midgley, C. (2002). Achievement goals and goal structures. In C. Midgley (Ed.), *Goals, goal structures, and patterns of adaptive learning* (pp. 21–53). Mahwah, NJ: Erlbaum.

Kaplan, A., & Midgley, C. (1997). The effect of achievement goals: Does level of perceived academic competence make a difference? *Contemporary Educational Psychology, 22,* 415–435.

Kaplan, P. S., Goldstein, M. H., Huckeby, E. R., & Cooper, R. P. (1995). Habituation, sensitization, and

infants' responses to motherese speech. *Developmental Psychobiology, 28,* 45–57.

Kapp-Simon, K., & Simon, D. J. (1991). Meeting the challenge: Social skills training for teens with special needs. *Connections: The Newsletter of the National Center for Youth and Disabilities, 2*(2), 1–5.

Karabenick, S. A., & Sharma, R. (1994). Seeking academic assistance as a strategic learning resource. In P. R. Pintrich, D. R. Brown, & C. E. Weinstein (Eds.), *Student motivation, cognition, and learning: Essays in honor of Wilbert J. McKeachie*. Hillsdale, NJ: Erlbaum.

Karafantis, D. M., & Levy, S. R. (2004). The role of children's lay theories about the malleability of human attributes in beliefs about and volunteering for disadvantaged groups. *Child Development, 75,* 236–250.

Karenga, M., & Karenga, T. (2007). The *Nguzo Saba* and the black family: Principles and practices of well-being and flourishing. In H. P. McAdoo (Ed.), *Black families* (4th ed., pp. 7–28). Thousand Oaks, CA: Sage.

Kark, J. (2000). Sickle cell trait. Retrieved December 29, 2007, from http://sickle.bwh.harvard.edu/sickle_trait.html

Karmiloff-Smith, A. (1979). Language development after five. In P. Fletcher & M. Garman (Eds.), *Language acquisition: Studies in first language development*. Cambridge, England: Cambridge University Press.

Karmiloff-Smith, A. (1993). Innate constraints and developmental change. In P. Bloom (Ed.), *Language acquisition: Core readings*. Cambridge, MA: MIT Press.

Karpov, Y. V. (2003). Development through the lifespan. In A. Kozulin, B. Gindis, V. S. Ageyev, & S. M. Miller (Eds.), *Vygotsky's educational theory in cultural context* (pp. 138–155). Cambridge, England: Cambridge University Press.

Karpov, Y. V., & Haywood, H. C. (1998). Two ways to elaborate Vygotsky's concept of mediation: Implications for instruction. *American Psychologist, 53,* 27–36.

Kašek, M. (2004). Predicting later IQ from infant visual habituation and dishabituation: A meta-analysis. *Applied Developmental Psychology, 25,* 369–393.

Kaslow, F. W. (2000). Families experiencing divorce. In W. C. Nichols, M. A. Pace-Nichols, D. S. Becvar, & Y. A. Napier (Eds.), *Handbook of family development and intervention* (pp. 341–368). New York: Wiley.

Kassel, J. D., Weinstein, S., Skitch, S. A., Veilleux, J., & Mermelstein, R. (2005). The development of substance abuse in adolescence: Correlates, causes, and consequences. In J. D. Kassel, S. Weinstein, S. A. Skitch, J. Veilleux, & R. Mermelstein (Eds.), *Development of psychopathology: A vulnerability-stress perspective* (pp. 355–384). Thousand Oaks, CA: Sage.

Katchadourian, H. (1990). Sexuality. In S. S. Feldman & G. R. Elliott (Eds.), *At the threshold: The developing adolescent* (pp. 330–351). Cambridge, MA: Harvard University Press.

Katkovsky, W., Crandall, V. C., & Good, S. (1967). Parental antecedents of children's beliefs in internal-external control of reinforcements in intellectual achievement situations. *Child Development, 38,* 765–776.

Katz, E. W., & Brent, S. B. (1968). Understanding connectives. *Journal of Verbal Learning and Verbal Behavior, 7,* 501–509.

Katz, L. F., & Gottman, J. M. (1991). Marital discord and child outcomes: A social psychophysiological approach. In J. Garber & K. A. Dodge (Eds.), *The development of emotion regulation and dysregulation*. Cambridge, England: Cambridge University Press.

Katz, L. F., & Low, S. M. (2004). Marital violence, co-parenting, and family-level processes in relation to children's adjustment. *Journal of Family Psychology, 18,* 372–382.

Kazak, A. E. (2006). Pediatric psychosocial preventative health model (PPPHM): Research, practice, and collaboration in pediatric family systems medicine. *Family, Systems, & Health, 24,* 381–395.

Kazdin, A. E. (1997). Conduct disorder across the life-span. In S. S. Luthar, J. A. Burack, D. Cicchetti, & J. R. Weisz (Eds.), *Developmental psychopathology: Perspectives on adjustment, risk, and disorder* (pp. 248–272). Cambridge, England: Cambridge University Press.

Kearins, J. M. (1981). Visual spatial memory in Australian aboriginal children of desert regions. *Cognitive Psychology, 13,* 434–460.

Kedar, Y., Casasola, M., & Lust, B. (2006). Getting there faster: 18- and 24-month-old infants' use of function words to determine reference. *Child Development, 77,* 325–338.

Keil, F. C. (1989). *Concepts, kinds, and cognitive development.* Cambridge, MA: MIT Press.

Keil, F. C. (1994). The birth and nurturance of concepts by domains: The origins of concepts of living things. In L. A. Hirschfeld & S. A. Gelman (Eds.), *Mapping the mind: Domain specificity in cognition and culture.* New York: Cambridge University Press.

Keil, F. C., & Silberstein, C. S. (1996). Schooling and the acquisition of theoretical knowledge. In D. R. Olson & N. Torrance (Eds.), *The handbook of education and human development: New models of learning, teaching, and schooling.* Cambridge, MA: Blackwell.

Kelemen, D. (1999). Why are rocks pointy? Children's preference for teleological explanations of the natural world. *Developmental Psychology, 35,* 1440–1452.

Kelemen, D. (2004). Are children "intuitive theists"?: Reasoning about purpose and design in nature. *Psychological Science, 15,* 295–301.

Keller, H. (2003). Socialization for competence: Cultural models of infancy. *Human Development, 46,* 288–311.

Kellogg, R. (1967). *The psychology of children's art.* New York: CRM–Random House.

Kelly, B. C. (2007). Club drug use and risk management among "Bridge and Tunnel" youth. *Journal of Drug Issues, 37*(2), 425–444.

Kelly, J., & Emery, R. (2003). Children's adjustment following divorce: Risk and resilience perspectives. *Family Relations, 52,* 352–362.

Kelly, J. A. (1995). *Changing HIV risk behaviors: Practical strategies.* New York: Guilford Press.

Kelly, J. A., Murphy, D. A., Sikkema, K. J., & Kalichman, S. C. (1993). Psychological interventions to prevent HIV infection are urgently needed. *American Psychologist, 48,* 1023–1034.

Kelly, J. B. (2007). Children's living arrangements following separation and divorce: Insights from empirical and clinical research. *Family Process, 46,* 35–52.

Kelly, J. B., & Lamb, M. E. (2000). Using child development research to make appropriate custody and access decisions for young children. *Family and Conciliation Courts Review, 38*(3), 297–311.

Kemler Nelson, D. G., Egan, L. C., & Holt, M. B. (2004). When children ask, "What is it?" what do they want to know about artifacts? *Psychological Science, 15,* 384–389.

Kemper, S. (1984). The development of narrative skills: Explanations and entertainments. In S. Kuczaj (Ed.), *Discourse development: Progress in cognitive development research.* New York: Springer-Verlag.

Keogh, B. K. (2003). *Temperament in the classroom: Understanding individual differences.* Baltimore, MD: Brookes.

Keogh, B. K., & MacMillan, D. L. (1996). Exceptionality. In D. C. Berliner & R. C. Calfee (Eds.), *Handbook of educational psychology.* New York: Macmillan.

Kerewsky, W., & Lefstein, L. M. (1982). Young adolescents and their community: A shared responsibility. In L. M. Lefstein et al. (Eds.), *3:00 to 6:00 p.m.: Young adolescents at home and in the community.* Carrboro, NC: Center for Early Adolescence.

Kerns, L. L., & Lieberman, A. B. (1993). *Helping your depressed child.* Rocklin, CA: Prima.

Kiang, L., & Harter, S. (2005, April). *Integrated/fragmented selves in Chinese Americans: Do pieces of the personal puzzle fit?* Poster presented at the biennial meeting of the Society for Research in Child Development, Atlanta.

Killen, M., & Nucci, L. P. (1995). Morality, autonomy, and social conflict. In M. Killen & D. Hart (Eds.), *Morality in everyday life: Developmental perspectives* (pp. 52–86). Cambridge, England: Cambridge University Press.

Killeya-Jones, L. A., Costanzo, P. R., Malone, P., Quinlan, N. P., & Miller-Johnson, S. (2007). Norm-narrowing and self- and other-perceived aggression in early-adolescent same-sex and mixed-sex cliques. *Journal of School Psychology, 45,* 549–565.

Killgore, W. D., Oki, M., & Yurgelun-Todd, D. A. (2001). Sex-specific developmental changes in amygdala responses to affective faces. *Neuroreport, 12,* 427–433.

Killip, S., Bennett, J. M., & Chambers, M. D. (2007). Iron deficiency anemia. *American Family Physician, 75,* 671–678.

Kim, D., Solomon, D., & Roberts, W. (1995, April). *Classroom practices that enhance students' sense of community.* Paper presented at the annual meeting of the American Educational Research Association, San Francisco.

Kim, K. H., Relkin, N. R., Lee, K. M., & Hirsch, J. (1997). Distinct cortical areas associated with native and second languages. *Nature, 388,* 171–174.

Kim-Cohen, J., Moffitt, T. E., Caspi, A., & Taylor A. (2004). Genetic and environmental processes in young children's resilience and vulnerability to socioeconomic deprivation. *Child Development, 75,* 651–668.

Kindermann, T. A. (1993). Natural peer groups as contexts for individual development: The case of children's motivation in school. *Developmental Psychology, 29,* 970–977.

King, A. (1999). Discourse patterns for mediating peer learning. In A. M. O'Donnell & A. King (Eds.), *Cognitive perspectives on peer learning* (pp. 87–115). Mahwah, NJ: Erlbaum.

King, E. W. (1999). *Looking into the lives of children: A worldwide view.* Albert Park, Australia: James Nicholas.

King, P. E., & Benson, P. L. (2006). Spiritual development and adolescent well-being and thriving. In E. C. Roehlkepartain, P. E. King, L. Wagener, & P. L. Benson (Eds.), *The handbook of spiritual development in childhood and adolescence* (pp. 384–398). Thousand Oaks, CA: Sage.

Kingstone, A., Smilek, D., Ristic, J., Friesen, C. K., & Eastwood, J. D. (2003). Attention, researchers! It is time to take a look at the real world. *Current Directions in Psychological Science, 12,* 176–180.

Kirby, J. R., Parrila, R. K., & Pfeiffer, S. L. (2003). Naming speed and phonological awareness as predictors of reading development. *Journal of Educational Psychology, 95,* 453–464.

Kirkorian, H. L., Wartella, E. A., & Anderson, D. R. (2008). Media and young children's learning. *Future of Children, 18*(1), 39–61.

Kirschenbaum, R. J. (1989). Identification of the gifted and talented American Indian student. In C. J. Maker & S. W. Schiever (Eds.), *Critical issues in gifted education: Vol. 2. Defensible programs for cultural and ethnic minorities.* Austin, TX: Pro-Ed.

Kirschner, P. A., Sweller, J., & Clark, R. E. (2006). Why minimal guidance during instruction does not work: An analysis of the failure of constructivist, discovery, problem-based, experiential, and inquiry-based teaching. *Educational Psychologist, 41,* 75–86.

Kisilevsky, B. S., Hains, S. M. J., Lee, K., Xie, X., Huang, H., Ye, H. H., et al. (2003). Effects of experience on fetal voice recognition. *Psychological Science, 14,* 220–224.

Kitayama, S., Duffy, S., & Uchida, Y. (2007). Self as cultural mode of being. In S. Kitayama & D. Cohen (Eds.), *Handbook of cultural psychology* (pp. 136–174). New York: Guilford Press.

Klaczynski, P. (2000). Motivated scientific reasoning biases, epistemological beliefs, and theory polarization: A two-process approach to adolescent cognition. *Child Development, 71,* 1347–1366.

Klaczynski, P. A. (2001). Analytic and heuristic processing influences on adolescent reasoning and decision-making. *Child Development, 72,* 844–861.

Klahr, D. (1982). Non-monotone assessment of monotone development: An information processing analysis. In S. Strauss & R. Stavy (Eds.), *U-shaped behavioral growth* (pp. 63–86). New York: Academic Press.

Klahr, D., & Robinson, M. (1981). Formal assessment of problem solving and planning processes in children. *Cognitive Psychology, 13,* 113–148.

Klassen, T. P., MacKay, J. M., Moher, D., Walker, A., & Jones, A. L. (2000). Community-based injury prevention interventions. *The Future of Children, 10*(1), 83–110.

Klibanoff, R. S., Levine, S. C., Huttenlocher, J., Vasilyeva, M., & Hedges, L. V. (2006). Preschool children's mathematical knowledge: The effect of teacher "math talk." *Developmental Psychology, 42,* 59–69.

Kline, K., & Flowers, J. (1998, April). *A comparison of fourth graders' proportional reasoning in reform and traditional classrooms.* Paper presented at the annual meeting of the American Educational Research Association, San Diego, CA.

Klinnert, M. D. (1984). The regulation of infant behavior by maternal facial expression. *Infant Behavior and Development, 7,* 447–465.

Klinnert, M. D., Emde, R. N., Butterfield, P., & Campos, J. J. (1986). Social referencing: The infant's use of emotional signals from a friendly adult with mother present. *Developmental Psychology, 22,* 427–434.

Kluger, A. N., & DeNisi, A. (1998). Feedback interventions: Toward the understanding of a double-edged sword. *Current Directions in Psychological Science, 7,* 67–72.

Knafo, A., & Plomin, R. (2006). Prosocial behavior from early to middle childhood: Genetic and environmental influences on stability and change. *Developmental Psychology, 42,* 771–786.

Knapp, M. S., Turnbull, B. J., & Shields, P. M. (1990). New directions for educating the children of poverty. *Educational Leadership, 48*(1), 4–9.

Knapp, M. S., & Woolverton, S. (1995). Social class and schooling. In J. A. Banks & C. A. M. Banks (Eds.), *Handbook of research on multicultural education.* New York: Macmillan.

Knapp, N. F. (2002). Tom and Joshua: Perceptions, conceptions and progress in meaning-based reading instruction. Journal of Literacy Research, 34, 59–98.

Knauss, C., Paxton, S. J., & Alsaker, F. D. (2007). Relationships among body dissatisfaction, internalisation of the media body ideal and perceived pressure from media in adolescent girls and boys. *Body Image, 4,* 353–360.

Knickmeyer R. C., & Baron-Cohen, S. (2006). Fetal testosterone and sex differences. *Early Human Development, 82,* 755–760.

Knudson, R. E. (1992). The development of written argumentation: An analysis and comparison of argumentative writing at four grade levels. *Child Study Journal, 22,* 167–181.

Kochanska, G. (1993). Toward a synthesis of parental socialization and child temperament in early development of conscience. *Child Development, 64,* 325–347.

Kochanska, G., & Aksan, N. (1995). Mother-child mutually positive affect, the quality of child compliance to requests and prohibitions, and maternal control as correlates of early internalization. *Child Development, 66*, 236–254.

Kochanska, G., & Aksan, N. (2006). Children's conscience and self-regulation. *Journal of Personality, 74*, 1587–1618.

Kochanska, G., Casey, R. J., & Fukumoto, A. (1995). Toddlers' sensitivity to standard violations. *Child Development, 66*, 643–656.

Kochanska, G., Coy, K. C., & Murray, K. T. (2001). The development of self-regulation in the first four years of life. *Child Development, 72*, 1091–1111.

Kochanska, G., Gross, J. N., Lin, M.-H., & Nichols, K. E. (2002). Guilt in young children: Development, determinants, and relations with a broader system of standards. *Child Development, 73*, 461–482.

Kodluboy, D. W. (2004). Gang-oriented interventions. In J. C. Conoley & A. P. Goldstein (Eds.), *School violence intervention* (2nd ed., pp. 194–232). New York: Guilford Press.

Koegel, L. K. (1995). Communication and language intervention. In R. L. Koegel & L. K. Koegel (Eds.), *Strategies for initiating positive interactions and improving learning opportunities.* Baltimore, MD: Brookes.

Koenig, M. A., Clément, F., & Harris, P. L. (2004). Trust in testimony: Children's use of true and false statements. *Psychological Science, 15*, 694–698.

Koeppel, J., & Mulrooney, M. (1992). The Sister Schools Program: A way for children to learn about cultural diversity—when there isn't any in their school. *Young Children, 48*(1), 44–47.

Koestner, R., Ryan, R. M., Bernieri, F., & Holt, K. (1984). Setting limits in children's behavior: The differential effects of controlling versus informational styles on intrinsic motivation and creativity. *Journal of Personality, 52*, 233–248.

Kohlberg, L. (1963). Moral development and identification. In H. Stevenson (Ed.), *Child psychology: The sixty-second yearbook of the National Society for the Study of Education* (pp. 277–332). Chicago: University of Chicago Press.

Kohlberg, L. (1964). Development of moral character and moral ideology. In M. L. Hoffman & L. W. Hoffman (Eds.), *Review of child development research: Vol. 1* (pp. 383–432). New York: Russell Sage Foundation.

Kohlberg, L. (1969). Stage and sequence: The cognitive-developmental approach to socialization. In D. A. Goslin (Ed.), *Handbook of socialization theory and research* (pp. 347–480). Chicago: Rand McNally.

Kohlberg, L. (1975). The cognitive-developmental approach to moral education. *Phi Delta Kappan, 57*, 670–677.

Kohlberg, L. (1976). Moral stages and moralization: The cognitive-developmental approach. In T. Lickona (Ed.), *Moral development and behavior: Theory, research, and social issues.* New York: Holt, Rinehart & Winston.

Kohlberg, L. (1981). *The philosophy of moral development: Moral stages and the idea of justice.* San Francisco: Harper & Row.

Kohlberg, L. (1984). *The psychology of moral development: The nature and validity of moral stages.* San Francisco: Harper & Row.

Kohlberg, L. (1986). A current statement on some theoretical issues. In S. Modgil & C. Modgil (Eds.), *Lawrence Kohlberg: Consensus and controversy.* Philadelphia: Falmer Press.

Kohlberg, L., & Candee, D. (1984). The relationship of moral judgment to moral action. In W. M. Kurtines & J. L. Gewirtz (Eds.), *Morality, moral behavior, and moral development.* New York: Wiley.

Kohlberg, L., & Fein, G. G. (1987). Play and constructive work as contributors to development. In L. Kohlberg (Ed.), *Child psychology and childhood education: A cognitive-developmental view* (pp. 392–440). New York: Longman.

Kohlberg, L., & Kramer, R. (1969). Continuities and discontinuities in childhood and adult moral development. *Human Development, 12*, 93–120.

Kohlberg, L., Levine, C., & Hewer, A. (1983). Moral stages: A current formulation and a response to

critics. *Contributions to Human Development, 10*, 1–174.

Kohlberg, L., & Mayer, R. (1972). Development as the aim of education. *Harvard Educational Review, 42*, 449–496.

Kohler, F. W., Greteman, C., Raschke, D., & Highnam, C. (2007). Using a buddy skills package to increase the social interactions between a preschooler with autism and her peers. *Topics in Early Childhood Education, 27*, 155–163.

Kohn, M. L. (1977). *Class and conformity* (2nd ed.). Chicago: University of Chicago Press.

Kolb, B., & Fantie, B. (1989). Development of the child's brain and behavior. In C. R. Reynolds & E. F. Janzen (Eds.), *Handbook of clinical child neuropsychology* (pp. 17–40). New York: Plenum Press.

Kolb, B., Gibb, R., & Robinson, T. E. (2003). Brain plasticity and behavior. *Current Directions in Psychological Science, 12*, 1–5.

Kolb, B., & Whishaw, I. (1996). *Fundamentals of human neuropsychology* (3rd ed.). San Francisco: Freeman.

Kopp, C. B. (1982). Antecedents of self-regulation: A developmental perspective. *Developmental Psychology, 18*, 199–214.

Koren-Karie, N., Oppenheim, D., Dolev, S., Sher, E., & Etzion-Carasso, A. (2002). Mothers' insightfulness regarding their infants' internal experience: Relations with maternal sensitivity and infant attachment. *Developmental Psychology, 38*(4), 534–542.

Kornhaber, M., Fierros, E., & Veenema, S. (2004). *Multiple intelligences: Best ideas from research and practice.* Boston: Allyn & Bacon.

Koskinen, P. S., Blum, I. H., Bisson, S. A., Phillips, S. M., Creamer, T. S., & Baker, T. K. (2000). Book access, shared reading, and audio models: The effects of supporting the literacy learning of linguistically diverse students in school and at home. *Journal of Educational Psychology, 92*, 23–36.

Kovacs, D. M., Parker, J. G., & Hoffman, L. W. (1996). Behavioral, affective, and social correlates of involvement in cross-sex friendship in elementary school. *Child Development, 67*, 2269–2286.

Kovas, Y., Haworth, C. M. A., Dale, P. S., & Plomin, R. (2007). The genetic and environmental origins of learning abilities and disabilities in the early school years. *Monographs of the Society for Research in Child Development, 72*(3, Serial No. 288), 1–160.

Koza, J. E. (2001). Multicultural approaches to music education. In C. A. Grant & M. L. Gomez, *Campus and classroom: Making schooling multicultural* (2nd ed.). Upper Saddle River, NJ: Merrill/Prentice Hall.

Kozulin, A. (1986). Vygotsky in context. In A. S. Vygotsky, *Thought and language* (rev. ed.; A. Kozulin, Ed. and Trans.). Cambridge, MA: MIT Press.

Krampen, G. (1987). Differential effects of teacher comments. *Journal of Educational Psychology, 79*, 137–146.

Krashen, S. D. (1996). *Under attack: The case against bilingual education.* Culver City, CA: Language Education Associates.

Krebs, D. L. (2008). Morality: An evolutionary account. *Perspectives on Psychological Science, 3*, 149–172.

Krebs, D. L., & Van Hesteren, F. (1994). The development of altruism: Toward an integrative model. *Developmental Review, 14*, 103–158.

Krebs, P. L. (1995). Mental retardation. In J. P. Winnick (Ed.), *Adapted physical education and sport* (2nd ed., pp. 93–109). Champaign, IL: Human Kinetics.

Kreider, R. M., & Fields, J. (2005, July). *Living arrangements of children: 2001.* Current Population Reports, P70–104. Washington, DC: U.S. Department of Commerce, U.S. Census Bureau.

Kreutzer, M. A., Leonard, C., & Flavell, J. H. (1975). An interview study of children's knowledge about memory. *Monographs of the Society for Research in Child Development, 40*(1, Serial No. 159).

Krispin, O., Sternberg, K. J., & Lamb, M. E. (1992). The dimensions of peer evaluation in Israel: A cross-cultural perspective. *International Journal of Behavioral Development, 15*, 299–314.

Krivitski, E. C., McIntosh, D. E., Rothlisberg, B., & Finch, H. (2004). Profile analysis of deaf children using the Universal Nonverbal Intelligence Test. *Journal of Psychoeducational Assessment, 22*, 338–350.

Kroger, J. (2003). What transits in an identity status transition? *Identity: An International Journal of Theory and Research, 3*, 197–220.

Kroger, J. (2004). Identity in formation. In K. Hoover (Ed.), *The future of identity: Centennial reflections on the legacy of Erik Erikson* (pp. 61–76). Lanham, MD: Lexington Books.

Kroger, S. M., Schettler, T., & Weiss, B. (2005). Environmental toxicants and developmental disabilities. *American Psychologist, 60*(3), 243–255.

Kuczynski, L., & Parkin, C. M. (2007). Agency and bidirectionality in socialization: Interactions, transactions, and relational dialectics. In J. E. Grusec & P. D. Hastings (Eds.), *Handbook of socialization: Theory and research* (pp. 259–283). New York: Guilford Press.

Kufeldt, K., Simard, M., & Vachon, J. (2003). Improving outcomes for children in care: Giving youth a voice. *Adoptions and Fostering, 27*, 8–19.

Kugiumutzakis, G. (1999). Genesis and development of early infant mimesis to facial and vocal models. In J. Nadel & G. Butterworth (Eds.), *Imitation in infancy* (pp. 36–59). New York: Cambridge University Press.

Kuhl, P. K. (2004). Early language acquisition: Cracking the speech code. *Nature Reviews Neuroscience, 5*, 831–843.

Kuhl, P. K. (2007). Is speech learning "gated" by the social brain? *Developmental Science, 10*, 110–120.

Kuhl, P. K., Conboy, B. T., Padden, D., Nelson, T., & Pruitt, J. (2005). Early speech perception and later language development: Implications for the "critical period." *Language Learning and Development, 1*, 237–264.

Kuhl, P. K., & Meltzoff, A. N. (1997). Evolution, nativism and learning in the development of language and speech. In M. Gopnik (Ed.), *The inheritance and innateness of grammars.* New York: Oxford University Press.

Kuhlmeier, V., Wynn, K., & Bloom, P. (2003). Attribution of dispositional states by 12-month-olds. *Psychological Science, 14*, 402–408.

Kuhn, D. (1993). Connecting scientific and informal reasoning. *Merrill-Palmer Quarterly, 39*, 74–103.

Kuhn, D. (1997). Constraints or guideposts? Developmental psychology and science education. *Review of Educational Research, 67*, 141–150.

Kuhn, D. (2001a). How do people know? *Psychological Science, 12*, 1–8.

Kuhn, D. (2001b). Why development does (and does not) occur: Evidence from the domain of inductive reasoning. In J. L. McClelland & R. S. Siegler (Eds.), *Mechanisms of cognitive development: Behavioral and neural perspectives* (pp. 221–249). Mahwah, NJ: Erlbaum.

Kuhn, D. (2006). Do cognitive changes accompany developments in the adolescent brain? *Perspectives on Psychological Science, 1*, 59–67.

Kuhn, D. (2007). Is direct instruction an answer to the right question? *Educational Psychologist, 42*, 109–113.

Kuhn, D., Amsel, E., & O'Loughlin, M. (1988). *The development of scientific thinking skills.* San Diego, CA: Academic Press.

Kuhn, D., Daniels, S., & Krishnan, A. (2003, April). *Epistemology and intellectual values as core metacognitive constructs.* Paper presented at the annual meeting of the American Educational Research Association, Chicago.

Kuhn, D., & Dean, D., Jr. (2005). Is developing scientific thinking all about learning to control variables? *Psychological Science, 16*, 866–870.

Kuhn, D., & Franklin, S. (2006). The second decade: What develops (and how)? In W. Damon, R. M. Lerner (Series Eds.), D. Kuhn, & R. Siegler (Vol. Eds.), *Handbook of child psychology: Vol. 1. Cognition, perception, and language* (6th ed.). New York: Wiley.

Kuhn, D., Garcia-Mila, M., Zohar, A., & Andersen, C. (1995). Strategies of knowledge acquisition. *Monographs of the Society for Research in Child Development, 60*(4, Whole No. 245).

Kuhn, D., & Park, S.-H. (2005). Epistemological understanding and the development of intellectual values. *International Journal of Educational Research, 43,* 111–124.

Kuhn, D., & Pearsall, S. (2000). Developmental origins of scientific thinking. *Journal of Cognition and Development, 1,* 113–129.

Kuhn, D., Shaw, V., & Felton, M. (1997). Effects of dyadic interaction on argumentative reasoning. *Cognition and Instruction, 15,* 287–315.

Kuhn, D., & Udell, W. (2003). The development of argument skills. *Child Development, 74,* 1245–1260.

Kuhn, D., & Weinstock, M. (2002). What is epistemological thinking and why does it matter? In B. K. Hofer & P. R. Pintrich (Eds.), *Personal epistemology: The psychology of beliefs about knowledge and knowing* (pp. 121–144). Mahwah, NJ: Erlbaum.

Kulberg, A. (1986). Substance abuse: Clinical identification and management. *Pediatrics Clinics of North America, 33,* 325–361.

Kulik, J. A., & Kulik, C. C. (1997). Ability grouping. In N. Colangelo & G. Davis (Eds.), *Handbook of gifted education* (2nd ed., pp. 230–242). Boston: Allyn & Bacon.

Kunzinger, E. L., III (1985). A short-term longitudinal study of memorial development during early grade school. *Developmental Psychology, 21,* 642–646.

Kuo, L., & Anderson, R. C. (2006). Morphological awareness and learning to read: A cross-language perspective. *Educational Psychologist, 41,* 161–180.

Kupersmidt, J. B., & Coie, J. D. (1990). Preadolescent peer status, aggression, and school adjustment as predictors of externalizing problems in adolescence. *Child Development, 61,* 1350–1362.

Kurtines, W. M., Berman, S. L., Ittel, A., & Williamson, S. (1995). Moral development: A co-constructivist perspective. In W. M. Kurtines & J. L. Gewirtz (Eds.), *Moral development: An introduction.* Boston: Allyn & Bacon.

Kurtines, W. M., & Gewirtz, J. L. (Eds.). (1991). *Moral behavior and development: Vol. 2. Research.* Hillsdale, NJ: Erlbaum.

Kutner, L. A., Olson, C. K., Warner, D. E., & Hertzog, S. M. (2008). Parents' and sons' perspectives on video game play: A qualitative study. *Journal of Adolescent Research, 23*(1), 76–96.

Kwok, O.-M., Hughes, J. N., & Luo, W. (2007). Role of resilient personality on lower achieving first grade students' current and future achievement. *Journal of School Psychology, 45,* 61–82.

La Guardia, J. G., Ryan, R. M., Couchman, C. E., & Deci, E. L. (2000). Within-person variation in security of attachment: A self-determination theory perspective on attachment, need fulfillment, and well-being. *Journal of Personality and Social Psychology, 79,* 367–384.

La Paro, K. M., & Pianta, R. C. (2000). Predicting children's competence in the early school years: A meta-analytic review. *Review of Educational Research, 70,* 443–484.

LaBlance, G. R., Steckol, K. F., & Smith, V. L. (1994). Stuttering: The role of the classroom teacher. *Teaching Exceptional Children, 26*(2), 10–12.

Laboratory of Comparative Human Cognition. (1982). Culture and intelligence. In R. J. Sternberg (Ed.), *Handbook of human intelligence.* Cambridge, England: Cambridge University Press.

Ladd, E. C. (1999). *The Ladd report.* New York: Free Press.

Ladd, G. W., & Burgess, K. B. (1999). Charting the relationship trajectories of aggressive, withdrawn, and aggressive/withdrawn children during early grade school. *Child Development, 70,* 910–929.

Ladson-Billings, G. (1994). *The dreamkeepers: Successful teachers of African American children.* San Francisco: Jossey-Bass.

Lafontana, K. M., & Cillessen, A. H. N. (1998). The nature of children's stereotypes of popularity. *Social Development, 7,* 301–320.

Laible, D., & Thompson, R. A. (2007). Early socialization: A relationship perspective. In J. E. Grusec & P. D. Hastings (Eds.), *Handbook of socialization: Theory and research* (pp. 181–207). New York: Guilford Press.

Laird, J., Kienzl, G., DeBell, M., & Chapman, C. (2007). *Dropout rates in the United States: 2005* (Compendium Report, National Center for Education Statistics 2007-059). Washington: NCES.

Lajoie, S. P., & Derry, S. J. (Eds.). (1993). *Computers as cognitive tools.* Mahwah, NJ: Erlbaum.

Lakatos, K., Birkas, E., Nemoda, Z., & Gervai, J. (2007, March). *Genetic influence on the ability to delay gratification in childhood.* Paper presented at the biennial meeting of the Society for Research in Child Development, Boston.

Lalor, J., & Begley, C. (2006). Fetal anomaly screening: What do women *want* to know? *Journal of Advanced Nursing, 55*(1), 11–19.

Lamaze, F. (1958). *Painless childbirth.* London: Burke.

Lamb, M. E., & Ahnert, L. (2006). Nonparental child care: Context, concepts, correlates, and consequences. In W. Damon & R. M. Lerner (Series Eds.) & K. A. Renninger & I. E. Sigel (Vol. Eds.), *Handbook of child psychology: Vol. 3. Social, emotional, and personality development* (6th ed., pp. 950–1016). New York: Wiley.

Lamb, M. E., Chuang, S. S., & Cabrera, N. (2005). Promoting child adjustment by fostering positive paternal involvement. In R. M. Lerner, F. Jacobs, & D. Wertlieb (Eds.), *Applied developmental science: An advanced textbook* (pp. 179–200). Thousand Oaks, CA: Sage.

Lamb, M. E., Frodi, A. M., Hwang, C. P., Frodi, M., & Steinberg, J. (1982). Mother- and father-infant interactions involving play and holding in traditional and non-traditional Swedish families. *Developmental Psychology, 18,* 215–221.

Lamb, M. E., & Lewis, C. (2004). The development and significance of father-child relationships in two-parent families. In M. E. Lamb (Ed.), *The role of the father in child development* (4th ed., pp. 272–306). Hoboken, NJ: John Wiley.

Lamb, S. (1991). First moral sense: Aspects of and contributions to a beginning morality in the second year of life. In W. M. Kurtines & J. L. Gewirtz (Eds.), *Handbook of moral behavior and development: Vol. 2. Research.* Hillsdale, NJ: Erlbaum.

Lamb, S., & Feeny, N. C. (1995). Early moral sense and socialization. In W. M. Kurtines & J. L. Gewirtz (Eds.), *Moral development: An introduction.* Boston: Allyn & Bacon.

Lamborn, S. D., Mounts, N. S., Steinberg, L., & Dornbusch, S. M. (1991). Patterns of competence and adjustment among adolescents from authoritative, authoritarian, indulgent, and neglectful families. *Child Development, 62,* 1049–1065.

Lampert, M., Rittenhouse, P., & Crumbaugh, C. (1996). Agreeing to disagree: Developing sociable mathematical discourse. In D. R. Olson & N. Torrance (Eds.), *The handbook of education and human development: New models of learning, teaching, and schooling.* Cambridge, MA: Blackwell.

Landis, D., Gaylord-Harden, N. K., Malinowski, S. L., Grant, K. E., Carleton, R. A., & Ford, R. E. (2007). Urban adolescent stress and hopelessness. *Journal of Adolescence, 30,* 1051–1070.

Landrum, T. J., & Kauffman, J. M. (2006). Behavioral approaches to classroom management. In C. M. Evertson & C. S. Weinstein (Eds.), *Handbook of classroom management: Research, practice, and contemporary issues* (pp. 47–71). Mahwah, NJ: Erlbaum.

Lane, D. M., & Pearson, D. A. (1982). The development of selective attention. *Merrill-Palmer Quarterly, 28,* 317–337.

Langacker, R. (1986). An introduction to cognitive grammar. *Cognitive Science, 10,* 1–40.

Lange, G., & Pierce, S. H. (1992). Memory-strategy learning and maintenance in preschool children. *Developmental Psychology, 28,* 453–462.

Langlois, J. A., Rutland-Brown, W., & Thomas, K. E. (2004). *Traumatic brain injury in the United States: Emergency department visits, hospitalizations, and deaths.* Atlanta, GA: Centers for Disease Control and Prevention, National Center for Injury Prevention and Control.

Lansford, J. E., Chang, L., Dodge, K. A., Malone, P. S., Oburu, P., Palmérus, K., et al. (2005). Physical discipline and children's adjustment: Cultural normativeness as a moderator. *Child Development, 76,* 1234–1246.

Lapan, R. T., Tucker, B., Kim, S.-K., & Kosciulek, J. F. (2003). Preparing rural adolescents for post-high school transitions. *Journal of Counseling and Development, 81,* 329–342.

Lapsley, D. K. (1993). Toward an integrated theory of adolescent ego development: The "new look" at adolescent egocentrism. *American Journal of Orthopsychiatry, 63,* 562–571.

Lapsley, D. K. (2006). Moral stage theory. In M. Killen & J. G. Smetana (Eds.), *Handbook of moral development* (pp. 37–66). Mahwah, NJ: Erlbaum.

Lapsley, D. K., Jackson, S., Rice, K., & Shadid, G. (1988). Self-monitoring and the "new look" at the imaginary audience and personal fable: An ego-developmental analysis. *Journal of Adolescent Research, 3,* 17–31.

Lapsley, D. K., & Narvaez, D. (2006). Character education. In W. Damon & R. M. Lerner (Eds. in Chief) & K. A. Renninger & I. E. Sigel (Vol. Ed.), *Handbook of child psychology: Vol. 4. Child psychology in practice* (6th ed., pp. 248–296). Hoboken, NJ: Wiley.

Lareau, A. (1989). *Home advantage: Social class and parental intervention in elementary education.* New York: Falmer Press.

Larkin, R. W. (1979). *Suburban youth in cultural crisis.* New York: Oxford University Press.

Larner, M. B., Stevenson, C. S., & Behrman, R. E. (1998). Protecting children from abuse and neglect: Analysis and recommendations. *The Future of Children: Protecting Children from Abuse and Neglect, 8*(1), 4–22.

Larson, R. W. (2000). Toward a psychology of positive youth development. *American Psychologist, 55,* 170–183.

Larson, R. W., Clore, G. L., & Wood, G. A (1999). The emotions of romantic relationships: Do they wreak havoc on adolescents? In W. Furman, B. B. Brown, & C. Feiring (Eds.), *The development of romantic relationships in adolescence* (pp. 19–49). Cambridge, England: Cambridge University Press.

Last, C. G., Hersen, M., Kazdin, A. E., Francis, G., & Grubb, H. J. (1987). Psychiatric illness in the mothers of anxious children. *American Journal of Psychiatry, 144,* 1580–1583.

Lauer, P. A., Akiba, M., Wilkerson, S. B., Apthorp, H. S., Snow, D., & Martin-Glenn, M. L. (2006). Out-of-school-time programs: A meta-analysis of effects for at-risk students. *Review of Educational Research, 76,* 275–313.

Laupa, M., & Turiel, E. (1995). Social domain theory. In W. M. Kurtines & J. L. Gewirtz (Eds.), *Moral development: An introduction.* Boston: Allyn & Bacon.

Laursen, B., Bukowski, W. M., Aunola, K., & Nurmi, J. E. (2007). Friendship moderates prospective associations between social isolation and adjustment problems in young children. *Child Development, 78,* 1395–1404.

Lautrey, J. (1993). Structure and variability: A plea for a pluralistic approach to cognitive development. In R. Case & W. Edelstein (Eds.), *The new structuralism in cognitive development: Theory and research on individual pathways.* Basel, Switzerland: Karger.

Lave, J., & Wenger, E. (1991). *Situated learning: Legitimate peripheral participation.* Cambridge, England: Cambridge University Press.

Lavelli, M., & Fogel, A. (2005). Developmental changes in the relationship between the infant's attention and emotion during early face-to-face communication: The 2-month transition. *Developmental Psychology, 41,* 265–280.

Lazar, I., Darlington, R., Murray, H., Royce, J., & Snipper, A. (1982). Lasting effects of early education: A report from the Consortium for Longitudinal Studies. *Monographs of the Society for Research in Child Development, 47*(2–3, Serial No. 195).

Leakey, R. (1994). *The origin of humankind.* New York: Basic Books.

Leaper, C., & Friedman, C. K. (2007). The socialization of gender. In J. E. Grusec & P. D. Hastings (Eds.), *Handbook of socialization: Theory and research* (pp. 561–587). New York: Guilford Press.

Learning First Alliance. (2001). *Every child learning: Safe and supportive schools.* Washington, DC: Learning First Alliance and Association for Supervision and Curriculum Development.

Lee, C. D., & Slaughter-Defoe, D. T. (1995). Historical and sociocultural influences on African and American education. In J. A. Banks & C. A. M. Banks (Eds.), *Handbook of research on multicultural education.* New York: Macmillan.

Lee, J.-S., & Bowen, N. K. (2006). Parent involvement, cultural capital, and the achievement gap among elementary school children. *American Educational Research Journal, 43,* 193–218.

Lee, K., Cameron, C. A., Doucette, J., & Talwar, V. (2002). Phantoms and fabrications: Young children's detection of implausible lies. *Child Development, 73,* 1688–1702.

Lee, O. (1999). Science knowledge, world views, and information sources in social and cultural contexts: Making sense after a natural disaster. *American Educational Research Journal, 36,* 187–219.

Lee, S. (1985). Children's acquisition of conditional logic structure: Teachable? *Contemporary Educational Psychology, 10,* 14–27.

Lee, V. E., & Burkam, D. T. (2003). Dropping out of high school: The role of school organization and structure. *American Educational Research Journal, 40,* 353–393.

Lee-Pearce, M. L., Plowman, T. S., & Touchstone, D. (1998). Starbase-Atlantis, a school without walls: A comparative study of an innovative science program for at-risk urban elementary students. *Journal of Education for Students Placed at Risk, 3,* 223–235.

Lefstein, L. M., & Lipsitz, J. (1995). *3:00 to 6:00 p.m.: Programs for young adolescents.* Minneapolis, MN: Search Institute.

Legare, C. H., & Gelman, S. A. (2007, March). *Bewitchment, biology, or both: The co-existence of natural and supernatural explanatory frameworks across development.* Paper presented at the biennial meeting of the Society for Research in Child Development, Boston.

Lehman, D. R., & Nisbett, R. E. (1990). A longitudinal study of the effects of undergraduate training on reasoning. *Developmental Psychology, 26,* 952–960.

Lehmann, M., & Hasselhorn, M. (2007). Variable memory strategy use in children's adaptive intratask learning behavior: Developmental changes and working memory influences in free recall. *Child Development, 78,* 1068–1082.

Lehnhart, A., & Madden, M. (2005, November). *Teen content creators and consumers.* Washington, DC: Pew Internet and American Life Project.

Leichtman, M. D., & Ceci, S. J. (1995). The effects of stereotypes and suggestions on preschoolers' reports. *Developmental Psychology, 31,* 568–578.

Leichtman, M. D., Pillemer, D. B., Wang, Q., Koreishi, A., & Han, J. J. (2000). When Baby Maisy came to school: Mothers' interview styles and preschoolers' event memories. *Cognitive Development, 15,* 99–114.

Lein, L. (1975). Black American immigrant children: Their speech at home and school. *Council on Anthropology and Education Quarterly, 6,* 1–11.

Leinhardt, G. (1994). History: A time to be mindful. In G. Leinhardt, I. L. Beck, & C. Stainton (Eds.),

Teaching and learning in history. Hillsdale, NJ: Erlbaum.

Leite, R. M. C., Buoncompagno, E. M., Leite, A. C. C., & Mergulhao, E. A. (1995). Psychosexual characteristics of male university students in Brazil. *Adolescence, 30,* 363–380.

Leite, R. W., & McKenry, P. C. (2002). Aspects of father status and postdivorce father involvement with children. *Journal of Family Issues, 23,* 601–623.

Lemanek, K. L. (2004). Adherence. In R. T. Brown (Ed.), *Handbook of pediatric psychology in school settings* (pp. 129–148). Mahwah, NJ: Erlbaum.

Leming, J. S. (2000). Tell me a story: An evaluation of a literature-based character education programme. *Journal of Moral Education, 29,* 413–427.

Lennox, C., & Siegel, L. S. (1998). Phonological and orthographic processes in good and poor spellers. In C. Hulme & R. M. Joshi (Eds.), *Reading and spelling: Development and disorders.* Mahwah, NJ: Erlbaum.

Lens, W. (2001). How to combine intrinsic task motivation with the motivational effects of the instrumentality of present tasks for future goals. In Efklides, A., Kuhl, J., & Sorrentino, R. (Eds.), *Trends and prospects in motivation research* (pp. 37–52). Dordrecht, The Netherlands: Kluwer.

Lepper, M. R., Corpus, J. H., & Iyengar, S. S. (2005). Intrinsic and extrinsic motivational orientations in the classroom: Age differences and academic correlates. *Journal of Educational Psychology, 97,* 184–196.

Lerner, R. M. (2002). *Concepts and theories of human development* (3rd ed.). Mahwah, NJ: Erlbaum.

Leventhal, T., Xue, Y., & Brooks-Gunn, J. (2006). Immigrant differences in school-age children's verbal trajectories: A look at four racial/ethnic groups. *Child Development, 77,* 1359–1374.

Levine, L. (1983). Mine: Self-definition in 2-year-old boys. *Developmental Psychology, 19,* 544–549.

Levine, M. (2006). The price of privilege: How parental pressure and material advantage are creating a generation of disconnected and unhappy kids. New York: HarperCollins.

LeVine, R. A. (2004). Challenging expert knowledge: Findings from an African study of infant care and development. In U. P. Gielen & J. P. Roopnarine (Eds.), *Childhood and adolescence: Cross-cultural perspectives and applications* (pp. 149–165). Westport, CT: Praeger.

LeVine, R. A., & Norman, K. (2008). Attachment in anthropological perspective. In R. A. LeVine & R. S. New (Eds.), *Anthropology and child development: A cross-cultural reader* (pp. 127–142). Malden, MA: Blackwell Publishing.

Levitt, M. J., Guacci-Franco, N., & Levitt, J. L. (1993). Convoys of social support in childhood and early adolescence: Structure and function. *Developmental Psychology, 29,* 811–818.

Lewin, T. (2000, June 25). Growing up, growing apart: Fast friends try to resist the pressure to divide by race. *The New York Times,* pp. 1, 18–20.

Lewis, M. (1993). Self-conscious emotions: Embarrassment, pride, shame, and guilt. In M. Lewis & J. Haviland (Eds.), *The handbook of emotions* (pp. 563–573). New York: Guilford Press.

Lewis, M. (1995). Embarrassment: The emotion of self-exposure and evaluation. In J. Tangney & K. Fischer (Eds.), *Self-conscious emotions: The psychology of shame, guilt, embarrassment and pride* (pp. 198–218). New York: Guilford Press.

Lewis, M. (2000). The emergence of human emotions. In M. Lewis & J. M. Haviland-Jones (Eds.), *Handbook of emotions* (2nd ed., pp. 265–280). New York: Guilford Press.

Lewis, M. (2005). The child and its family: The social network model. *Human Development, 48,* 8–27.

Lewis, M., & Brooks-Gunn, J. (1979). *Social cognition and the acquisition of self.* New York: Plenum.

Lewis, M., Feiring, C., & Rosenthal, S. (2000). Attachment over time. *Child Development, 71,* 707–720.

Lewis, P., Abbeduto, L., Murphy, M., Richmond, E., Giles, N., Bruno, L., et al. (2006). Cognitive,

language and social-cognitive skills of individuals with fragile X with and without autism. *Journal of Intellectual Disability Research, 50,* 532–545.

Li, J. (2004). High abilities and excellence: A cultural perspective. In L. V. Shavinina & M. Ferrari (Eds.), *Beyond knowledge: Extracognitive aspects of developing high ability* (pp. 187–208). Mahwah, NJ: Erlbaum.

Li, J. (2005). Mind or virtue: Western and Chinese beliefs about learning. *Current Directions in Psychological Science, 14,* 190–194.

Li, J. (2006). Self in learning: Chinese adolescents' goals and sense of agency. *Child Development, 77,* 482–501.

Li, J., & Fischer, K. W. (2004). Thought and affect in American and Chinese learners' beliefs about learning. In D. Y. Dai & R. J. Sternberg (Eds.), *Motivation, emotion, and cognition: Integrative perspectives on intellectual functioning and development* (pp. 385–418). Mahwah, NJ: Erlbaum.

Li, S.-C. (2007). Biocultural co-construction of developmental plasticity across the lifespan. In S. Kitayama & D. Cohen (Eds.), *Handbook of cultural psychology* (pp. 528–544). New York: Guilford Press.

Liben, L. S., & Bigler, R. S. (2002). The developmental course of gender differentiation: Conceptualizing, measuring, and evaluating constructs and pathways. *Monographs of the Society for Research in Child Development, 67*(2, Serial No. 269).

Liben, L. S., & Downs, R. M. (1989a). Educating with maps: Part I, the place of maps. *Teaching Thinking and Problem Solving, 11*(1), 6–9.

Liben, L. S., & Downs, R. M. (1989b). Understanding maps as symbols: The development of map concepts in children. In H. W. Reese (Ed.), *Advances in child development and behavior* (Vol. 22). San Diego, CA: Harcourt Brace Jovanovich.

Liben, L. S., Kastens, K. A., & Stevenson, L. M. (2002). Real-world knowledge through real-world maps: A developmental guide for navigating the educational terrain. *Developmental Review, 22,* 267–322.

Liben, L. S., & Myers, L. J. (2007). Developmental changes in children's understanding of maps: What, when, and how? In J. M. Plumert & J. P. Spencer (Eds.), *The emerging spatial mind* (pp. 193–218). New York: Oxford University Press.

Liberman, A. M. (1998). Why is speech so much easier than reading and writing? In C. Hulme & R. M. Joshi (Eds.), *Reading and spelling: Development and disorders.* Mahwah, NJ: Erlbaum.

Lichtenberger, E. O., & Kaufman, A. S. (2003). *Essentials of WPPSI-III assessment.* New York: Wiley.

Lickona, T. (1991). Moral development in the elementary school classroom. In W. M. Kurtines & J. L. Gewirtz (Eds.), *Moral behavior and development: Vol. 3. Application.* Hillsdale, NJ: Erlbaum.

Lidz, C. S. (1991). Issues in the assessment of preschool children. In B. A. Bracken (Ed.), *The psychoeducational assessment of preschool children* (2nd ed., pp. 18–31). Boston: Allyn & Bacon.

Lidz, C. S., & Gindis, B. (2003). Dynamic assessment of the evolving cognitive functions in children. In A. Kozulin, B. Gindis, V. S. Ageyev, & S. M. Miller (Eds.), *Vygotsky's educational theory in cultural context* (pp. 99–116). Cambridge, England: Cambridge University Press.

Lieberman, A. (1993). *The emotional life of the toddler.* New York: Free Press.

Lieberman, D. A. (1997). Interactive video games for health promotion: Effects on knowledge, self-efficacy, social support, and health. In R. L. Street, Jr., W. R. Gold, & T. R. Manning (Eds.), *Health promotion and interactive technology: Theoretical applications and future directions* (pp. 103–120). Mahwah, NJ: Erlbaum.

Light, P., & Butterworth, G. (Eds.). (1993). *Context and cognition: Ways of learning and knowing.* Hillsdale, NJ: Erlbaum.

Lightfoot, C. (1992). Constructing self and peer culture: A narrative perspective on adolescent risk taking. In

L. T. Winegar & J. Valsiner (Eds.), *Children's development within social context: Vol. 2. Research and methodology* (pp. 229–245). Hillsdale, NJ: Erlbaum.

Lightfoot, D. (1999). *The development of language: Acquisition, change, and evolution*. Malden, MA: Blackwell.

Lillard, A. S. (1993). Pretend play skills and the child's theory of mind. *Child Development, 64*, 348–371.

Lillard, A. S. (1997). Other folks' theories of mind and behavior. *Psychological Science, 8*, 268–274.

Lillard, A. S. (1998). Playing with a theory of mind. In O. N. Saracho & B. Spodek (Eds.), *Multiple perspectives on play in early childhood education*. Albany: State University of New York Press.

Lillard, A. S. (1999). Developing a cultural theory of mind: The CIAO approach. *Current Directions in Psychological Science, 8*, 57–61.

Lindberg, M. (1991). A taxonomy of suggestibility and eyewitness memory: Age, memory process, and focus of analysis. In J. L. Doris (Ed.), *The suggestibility of children's recollections*. Washington, DC: American Psychological Association.

Linder, T. W. (1993). *Transdisciplinary play-based assessment: A functional approach to working with young children*. Baltimore: Brookes.

Lindfors, K., Elovainio, M., Wickman, S., Vuorinen, R., Sinkkonen, J., Dunkel, L., et al. (2007). Brief report: The role of ego development in psychosocial adjustment among boys with delayed puberty. *Journal of Research on Adolescence, 17*(4), 601–612.

Linebarger, D. L., & Walker, D. (2005). Infants' and toddlers' television viewing and language outcomes. *American Behavioral Scientist, 48*(5), 624–645.

Linn, M. C., Clement, C., Pulos, S., & Sullivan, P. (1989). Scientific reasoning during adolescence: The influence of instruction in science knowledge and reasoning strategies. *Journal of Research in Science Teaching, 26*, 171–187.

Linn, M. C., & Muilenburg, L. (1996). Creating lifelong science learners: What models form a firm foundation? *Educational Researcher, 25*(5), 18–24.

Linn, M. C., Songer, N. B., & Eylon, B. (1996). Shifts and convergences in science learning and instruction. In D. C. Berliner & R. C. Calfee (Eds.), *Handbook of educational psychology*. New York: Macmillan.

Linn, R. L., & Miller, M.D. (2005). *Measurement and assessment in teaching* (9th ed.). Upper Saddle River, NJ: Merrill/Prentice Hall.

Linnenbrink, E. A. (2005). The dilemma of performance-approach goals: The use of multiple goal contexts to promote students' motivation and learning. *Journal of Educational Psychology, 97*, 197–213.

Linnenbrink, E. A., & Pintrich, P. R. (2004). Role of affect in cognitive processing in academic contexts. In D. Y. Dia & R. J. Sternberg (Eds.), *Motivation, emotion, and cognition: Integrative perspectives on intellectual functioning and development* (pp. 57–87). Mahwah, NJ: Erlbaum.

Linscheid, T. R., & Fleming, C. H. (1995). Anorexia nervosa, bulimia nervosa, and obesity. In M. C. Roberts (Ed.), *Handbook of pediatric psychology* (pp. 676–700). New York: Guilford Press.

Linver, M. R., Brooks-Gunn, J., & Kohen, D. E. (2002). Family processes as pathways from income to young children's development. *Developmental Psychology, 38*, 719–734.

Lippa, R. A. (2002). *Gender, nature, and nurture*. Mahwah, NJ: Erlbaum.

Lipson, M. Y. (1983). The influence of religious affiliation on children's memory for text information. *Reading Research Quarterly, 18*, 448–457.

Lipton, J. S., & Spelke, E. S. (2005). Preschool children's mapping of number words to nonsymbolic numerosities. *Child Development, 76*, 978–988.

Little, L. (2000, June). *Peer victimization of children with Asperger-spectrum disorders*. Paper presented at the Youth and Victimization International Research Conference, Durham, NH.

Little, T. D., Oettingen, G., Stetsenko, A., & Baltes, P. B. (1995). Children's action-control beliefs about school performance: How do American children compare with German and Russian children? *Journal of Personality and Social Psychology, 69*, 686–700.

Littlewood, W. T. (1984). *Foreign and second language learning: Language-acquisition research and its implications for the classroom*. Cambridge, England: Cambridge University Press.

Liu, D., Wellman, H. M., Tardif, T., & Sabbagh, M. A. (2008). Theory of mind development in Chinese children: A meta-analysis of false-belief understanding across cultures and languages. *Developmental Psychology, 44*, 523–531.

Lobel, A. (1979). *Frog and Toad are friends*. New York: HarperCollins.

Lochman, J. E., & Dodge, K. A. (1994). Social-cognitive processes of severely violent, moderately aggressive, and nonaggressive boys. *Journal of Consulting and Clinical Psychology, 62*, 366–374.

Lochman, J. E., Wayland, K. K., & White, K. J. (1993). Social goals: Relationship to adolescent adjustment and to social problem solving. *Journal of Abnormal Child Psychology, 21*, 1993.

Locke, E. A., & Latham, G. P. (2006). New directions in goal-setting theory. *Current Directions in Psychological Science, 15*, 265–268.

Locke, J. L. (1993). *The child's path to spoken language*. Cambridge, MA: Harvard University Press.

Lockhart, K. L., Chang, B., & Story, T. (2002). Young children's beliefs about the stability of traits: Protective optimism? *Child Development, 73*, 1408–1430.

Lodewyk, K. R., & Winne, P. H. (2005). Relations among the structure of learning tasks, achievement, and changes in self-efficacy in secondary students. *Journal of Educational Psychology, 97*, 3–12.

Loeb, S., Fuller, B., Kagan, S. L., & Carrol, B. (2004). Child care in poor communities: Early learning effects of type, quality, and stability. *Child Development, 75*, 47–65.

Loeber, R. (1982). The stability of antisocial child behavior. *Annals of Child Development, 2*, 77–116.

Loeber, R., & Stouthamer-Loeber, M. (1998). Development of juvenile aggression and violence. *American Psychologist, 53*, 242–259.

Logan, K. R., Alberto, P. A., Kana, T. G., & Waylor-Bowen, T. (1994). Curriculum development and instructional design for students with profound disabilities. In L. Sternberg (Ed.), *Individuals with profound disabilities: Instructional and assistive strategies* (3rd ed.). Austin, TX: Pro-Ed.

Logsdon, B. J., Alleman, L. M., Straits, S. A., Belka, D. E., & Clark, D. (1997). *Physical education unit plans for grades 5–6* (2nd ed.). Champaign, IL: Human Kinetics.

London, M. L., Ladewig, P. W., Ball, J. W., & Bindler, R. C. (2007). *Maternal and child nursing care* (2nd ed.). Upper Saddle River, NJ: Pearson Prentice Hall.

Long, M. (1995). The role of the linguistic environment in second language acquisition. In W. C. Ritchie & T. K. Bhatia (Eds.), *Handbook of language acquisition: Vol. 2. Second language acquisition*. San Diego, CA: Academic Press.

Lonigan, C. J., Burgess, S. R., Anthony, J. L., & Barker, T. A. (1998). Development of phonological sensitivity in 2- to 5-year-old children. *Journal of Educational Psychology, 90*, 294–311.

Lopez, A. M. (2003). Mixed-race school-age children: A summary of census 2000 data. *Educational Researcher, 32*(6), 25–37.

Lopez, E. C. (1997). The cognitive assessment of limited English proficient and bilingual children. In D. P. Flanagan, J. L. Genshaft, & P. L. Harrison (Eds.), *Contemporary intellectual assessment: Theories, tests, and issues* (pp. 503–516). New York: Guilford Press.

López, G. R., Scribner, J. D., & Mahitivanichcha, K. (2001). Redefining parental involvement: Lessons from high-performing migrant-impacted schools. *American Educational Research Journal, 38*, 253–288.

Lopez, V. A., & Emmer, E. T. (2002). Influences of beliefs and values on male adolescents' decision to commit violent offenses. *Psychology of Men and Masculinity, 3*, 28–40.

Lord, H., & Mahoney, J. L. (2007). Neighborhood crime and self-care: Risks for aggression and lower academic performance. *Developmental Psychology, 43*, 1321–1333.

Losey, K. M. (1995). Mexican American students and classroom interaction: An overview and critique. *Review of Educational Research, 65*, 283–318.

Lotan, R. A. (2006). Managing groupwork in the heterogeneous classroom. In C. M. Evertson & C. S. Weinstein (Eds.), *Handbook of classroom management: Research, practice, and contemporary issues* (pp. 525–539). Mahwah, NJ: Erlbaum.

Lou, Y., Abrami, P. C., Spence, J. C., Poulsen, C., Chambers, B., & d'Apollonia, S. (1996). Within-class grouping: A meta-analysis. *Review of Educational Research, 66*, 423–458.

Louis, B., Subotnik, R. F., Breland, P. S., & Lewis, M. (2000). Establishing criteria for high ability versus selective admission to gifted programs: Implications for policy and practice. *Educational Psychology Review, 12*(3), 295–314.

Lovett, S. B., & Flavell, J. H. (1990). Understanding and remembering: Children's knowledge about the differential effects of strategy and task variables on comprehension and memorization. *Child Development, 61*, 1842–1858.

Lowry, R., Sleet, D., Duncan, C., Powell, K., & Kolbe, L. (1995). Adolescents at risk for violence. *Educational Psychology Review, 7*, 7–39.

Lubinski, D., & Bleske-Rechek, A. (2008). Enhancing development in intellectually talented populations. In P. C. Kyllonen, R. D. Roberts, & L. Stankov (Eds.), *Extending intelligence: Enhancement and new constructs* (pp. 109–132). New York: Erlbaum/Taylor & Francis.

Lucariello, J., Kyratzis, A., & Nelson, K. (1992). Taxonomic knowledge: What kind and when? *Child Development, 63*, 978–998.

Lucas-Thompson, R., & Clarke-Stewart, K. A. (2007). Forecasting friendship: How marital quality, maternal mood, and attachment security are linked to children's peer relationships. *Journal of Applied Developmental Psychology, 28*, 499–514.

Luckasson, R., Borthwick-Duffy, S., Buntinx, W. H. E., Coulter, D. L., Craig, E. M., Reeve, A., et al. (Eds.). (2002). *Mental retardation: Definition, classification, and systems of supports* (10th ed.). Washington, DC: American Association on Mental Retardation.

Ludwig, J., & Phillips, D. (2007). The benefits and costs of Head Start. *Social Policy Report, 21*(3). Society for Research in Child Development.

Lueptow, L. B. (1984). *Adolescent sex roles and social change*. New York: Columbia University Press.

Lumeng, J. (2006). Childhood obesity prevention: Responsibilities of the family, schools, and community. In K. Freeark & W. S. Davidson II (Vol. Eds.), H. E. Fitzgerald, R. Zucker, & K. Freeark (Eds. in Chief), *The crisis in mental health: Critical issues and effective programs. Vol. 3: Issues for families, schools, and communities* (pp. 55–77). Westport, CT: Praeger.

Luna, B., Garver, K. E., Urban, T. A., Lazar, N. A., & Sweeney, J. A. (2004). Maturation of cognitive processes from late childhood to adulthood. *Child Development, 75*, 1357–1372.

Luna, B., & Sweeney, J. A. (2004). The emergence of collaborative brain function: fMRI studies of the development of response inhibition. Annals of the New York Academy of Sciences, 1021, 296–309.

Lundy, B. L. (2003). Father- and mother-infant face-to-face interactions: Differences in mind-related comments and infant attachment? *Infant Behavior and Development, 26*, 200–212.

Lupart, J. L. (1995). Exceptional learners and teaching for transfer. In A. McKeough, J. Lupart, & A. Marini (Eds.), *Teaching for transfer: Fostering generalization in learning*. Mahwah, NJ: Erlbaum.

Luster, L. (1992). *Schooling, survival, and struggle: Black women and the GED*. Unpublished doctoral dissertation, Stanford University, School of Education, Stanford, CA.

Luthar, S. S., & Latendresse, S. J. (2005). Children of the affluent: Challenges to well-being. *Current Directions in Psychological Science, 14,* 49–53.

Lutke, J. (1997). Spider web walking: Hope for children with FAS through understanding. In A. Streissguth & J. Kanter (Eds.), *The challenge of fetal alcohol syndrome: Overcoming secondary disabilities* (pp. 181–188). Seattle: University of Washington Press.

Luyckx, K., Goossens, L., & Soenens, B. (2006). A developmental contextual perspective on identity construction in emerging adulthood: Change dynamics in commitment formation and commitment evaluation. *Developmental Psychology, 42,* 366–380.

Luykx, A., Lee, O., Mahotiere, M., Lester, B., Hart, J., & Deaktor, R. (2007). Cultural and home influences on children's responses to science assessments. *Teachers College Record, 109,* 897–926.

Lyman, E. T. (1981). The responsive classroom discussion: The inclusion of all students. In A. Anderson (Ed.), *Mainstreaming digest* (pp. 109–113). College Park, MD: University of Maryland Press.

Lyon, T. D., & Flavell, J. H. (1994). Young children's understanding of "remember" and "forget." *Child Development, 65,* 1357–1371.

MacArthur, C., & Graham, S. (1987). Learning disabled students' composing with three methods: Handwriting, dictation, and word processing. *Journal of Special Education, 21,* 22–42.

Maccoby, E. E. (1984). Middle childhood in the context of the family. In W. A. Collins (Ed.), *Development during middle childhood* (pp. 184–239). Washington, DC: National Academy Press.

Maccoby, E. E. (1990). Gender and relationships: A developmental account. *American Psychologist, 45,* 513–520.

Maccoby, E. E. (2007). Historical overview of socialization research and theory. In J. E. Grusec & P. D. Hastings (Eds.), *Handbook of socialization: Theory and research* (pp. 13–41). New York: Guilford.

Maccoby, E. E., & Hagen, J. W. (1965). Effects of distraction upon central versus incidental recall: Developmental trends. *Journal of Experimental Child Psychology, 2,* 280–289.

Maccoby, E. E., & Jacklin, C. N. (1974). *The psychology of sex differences*. Stanford, CA: Stanford University Press.

Maccoby, E. E., & Lewis, C. C. (2003). Less day care or different day care? *Child Development, 74,* 1069–1075.

MacDonald, S., Uesiliana, K., & Hayne, H. (2000). Cross-cultural and gender differences in childhood amnesia. *Memory, 8,* 365–376.

MacGeorge, E. L. (2003). Gender differences in attributions and emotions in helping contexts. *Sex Roles, 48,* 175–182.

Mackey, W. C. (2001). Support for the existence of an independent man-to-child affiliative bond: Fatherhood as a biocultural invention. *Psychology of Men and Masculinity, 2,* 51–66.

Macklem, G. L. (2008). *Practitioner's guide to emotion regulation in school-aged children*. New York: Springer Science + Business Media.

MacLean, D. J., Sasse, D. K., Keating, D. P., Stewart, B. E., & Miller, F. K. (1995, April). *All-girls' mathematics and science instruction in early adolescence: Longitudinal effects*. Paper presented at the annual meeting of the American Educational Research Association, San Francisco.

MacMaster, K., Donovan, L. A., & MacIntyre, P. D. (2002). The effects of being diagnosed with a learning disability on children's self-esteem. *Child Study Journal, 32,* 101–108.

MacWhinney, B., & Chang, F. (1995). Connectionism and language learning. In C. Nelson (Ed.), *Basic and applied perspectives on learning, cognition, and development: The Minnesota Symposia on Child Psychology* (Vol. 28). Mahwah, NJ: Erlbaum.

Madden, N. A., & Slavin, R. E. (1983). Mainstreaming students with mild handicaps: Academic and social outcomes. *Review of Educational Research, 53,* 519–569.

Madhubuti, H., & Madhubuti, S. (1994). *African-centered education*. Chicago: Third World Press.

Magnuson, K. (2007). Maternal education and children's academic achievement during middle childhood. *Developmental Psychology, 43,* 1497–1512.

Magnuson, K. A., Meyers, M. K., Ruhm, C. J., & Waldfogel, J. (2004). Inequality in preschool education and school readiness. *American Educational Research Journal, 41,* 115–157.

Magnuson, K. A., Ruhm, C., & Waldfogel, J. (2007). The persistence of preschool effects: Do subsequent classroom experiences matter? *Early Childhood Research Quarterly, 22,* 18–38.

Mahaffy, K. A., & Ward, S. K. (2002). The gendering of adolescents' childbearing and educational plans: Reciprocal effects and the influence of social context. *Sex Roles, 46,* 403–417.

Maher, J. K., Herbst, K. C., Childs, N. M., & Finn, S. (2008). Racial stereotypes in children's commercials. *Journal of Advertising Research, 48*(1), 80–93.

Mahoney, J. L., & Zigler, E. F. (2006). Translating science to policy under the No Child Left Behind Act of 2001: Lessons from the national evaluation of the 21st-Century Community Learning Centers. *Journal of Applied Developmental Psychology, 27,* 282–294.

Maier, M. A., Bernier, A., Pekrun, R., Zimmermann, P., & Grossmann, K. E. (2004). Attachment working models as unconscious structures: An experimental test. *International Journal of Behavioral Development, 28*(2), 180–189.

Main, M. (1995). Recent studies in attachment: Overview, with selected implications for clinical work. In S. Goldberg, R. Muir, & J. Kerr (Eds.), *Attachment theory: Social, developmental, and clinical perspectives* (pp. 407–474). Hillsdale, NJ: Analytic Press.

Main, M., & Cassidy, J. (1988). Categories of response to reunion with the parent at age 6: Predictable from infant attachment classification and stable over a 1-month period. *Developmental Psychology, 24,* 415–426.

Main, M., Kaplan, N., & Cassidy, J. (1985). Security in infancy, childhood, and adulthood: A move to the level of representation. *Monographs of the Society for Research in Child Development, 50,* 66–104.

Main, M., & Solomon, J. (1986). Discovery of an insecure-disorganized/disoriented attachment pattern. In T. B. Brazelton & M. W. Yogman (Eds.), *Affective development in infancy* (pp. 95–124). Norwood, NJ: Ablex.

Main, M., & Solomon, J. (1990). Procedures for identifying infants as disorganized/disoriented during the Ainsworth Strange Situation. In M. T. Greenberg, D. Cicchetti, & E. M. Cummings (Eds.), *Attachment in the preschool years* (pp. 121–160). Chicago: University of Chicago Press.

Maker, C. J. (1993). Creativity, intelligence, and problem solving: A definition and design for cross-cultural research and measurement related to giftedness. *Gifted Education International, 9*(2), 68–77.

Maker, C. J., & Schiever, S. W. (Eds.). (1989). *Critical issues in gifted education: Vol. 2. Defensible programs for cultural and ethnic minorities*. Austin, TX: Pro-Ed.

Malatesta, C. Z., & Haviland, J. M. (1982). Learning display rules: The socialization of emotion expression in infancy. *Child Development, 53,* 991–1003.

Malinsky, K. P. (1997). Learning to be invisible: Female sexual minority students in America's public high schools. In M. B. Harris (Ed.), *School experiences of gay and lesbian youth: The invisible minority* (pp. 35–50). Binghamton, NY: Harrington Park Press.

Maller, S. J. (2000). Item invariance of four subtests of the Universal Nonverbal Intelligence Test across groups of deaf and hearing children. *Journal of Psychoeducational Assessment, 18,* 240–254.

Mallick, S. K., & McCandless, B. R. (1966). A study of catharsis of aggression. *Journal of Personality and Social Psychology, 4,* 591–596.

Malmberg, L.-E., Stein, A., West, A., Simon, L., Barnes, J., Leach, P., et al. (2007). Parent–infant interaction: A growth model approach. *Infant Behavior and Development, 30,* 615–630.

Malone, D. M., Stoneham, Z., & Langone, J. (1995). Contextual variation of correspondences among measures of play and developmental level of preschool children. *Journal of Early Intervention, 18,* 199–215.

Mandel, D. R., Jusczyk, P. W., & Pisoni, D. B. (1995). Infants' recognition of the sound patterns of their own names. *Psychological Science, 6,* 314–317.

Manderson, L., Tye, L. C., & Rajanayagam, K. (1997). Condom use in heterosexual sex: A review of research, 1985–1994. In J. Catalan, L. Sherr, et al. (Eds.), *The impact of AIDS: Psychological and social aspects of HIV infection* (pp. 1–26). Singapore: Harwood Academic.

Mandler, J. M. (2007a). The conceptual foundations of animals and artifacts. In E. Margolis & S. Laurence (Eds.), *Creations of the mind: Theories of artifacts and their representation* (pp. 191–211). New York: Oxford University Press.

Mandler, J. M. (2007b). On the origins of the conceptual system. *American Psychologist, 62,* 741–751.

Mandler, J. M., Fivush, R., & Reznick, J. S. (1987). The development of contextual categories. *Cognitive Development, 2,* 339–354.

Mangelsdorf, S. C., Shapiro, J. R., & Marzolf, D. (1995). Developmental and temperamental differences in emotion regulation in infancy. *Child Development, 66,* 1817–1828.

Manis, F. R. (1996). Current trends in dyslexia research. In B. J. Cratty & R. L. Goldman (Eds.), *Learning disabilities: Contemporary viewpoints*. Amsterdam: Harwood Academic.

Mar, R. A., & Oatley, K. (2008). The function of fiction is the abstraction and simulation of social experience. *Perspectives on Psychological Science, 3,* 173–192.

Marachi, R., Friedel, J., & Midgley, C. (2001, April). *"I sometimes annoy my teacher during math": Relations between student perceptions of the teacher and disruptive behavior in the classroom*. Paper presented at the annual meeting of the American Educational Research Association, Seattle, WA.

Maraj, B. K. V., & Bonertz, C. M. (2007). Verbal-motor learning in children with Down syndrome. *Journal of Sport and Exercise Psychology, 29* (Supplement), 108.

Maratsos, M. (1998). Some problems in grammatical acquisition. In W. Damon (Series Ed.), D. Kuhn, & R. S. Siegler (Vol. Eds.), *Handbook of child psychology: Vol. 2. Cognition, perception, and language* (5th ed.). New York: Wiley.

Marcia, J. E. (1980). Identity in adolescence. In J. Adelson (Ed.), *Handbook of adolescent psychology*. New York: Wiley.

Marcia, J. E. (1988). Common processes underlying ego identity, cognitive/moral development, and individuation. In D. K. Lapsley & F. C. Power (Eds.), *Self, ego, and identity: Integrative approaches* (pp. 211–225). New York: Springer-Verlag.

Marcia, J. (1991). Identity and self-development. In R. M. Lerner, A. C. Petersen, & J. Brooks-Gunn (Eds.), *Encyclopedia of adolescence* (Vol. 1, pp. 529–533). New York: Garland.

Marcovitch, S., Goldberg, S., Gold, A., Washington, J., Wasson, C., Krekewich, K., et al. (1997). Determinants of behavioral problems in Romanian children adopted in Ontario. *International Journal of Behavioral Development, 20,* 17–31.

Marcus, G. F. (1996). Why do children say "breaked"? *Current Directions in Psychological Science, 5,* 81–85.

Marcus, G. F., Vijayan, S., Bandi Rao, S., & Vishton, P. M. (1999). Rule learning by seven-month-old infants. *Science, 283,* 77–80.

Marcus, R. F., & Sanders-Reio, J. (2001). The influence of attachment on school completion. *School Psychology Quarterly, 16,* 427–444.

Marean, G. C., Werner, L. A., & Kuhl, P. K. (1992). Vowel categorization by very young infants. *Developmental Psychology, 28,* 396–405.

Mareschal, D., Johnson, M. H., Sirois, S., Spratling, M. W., Thomas, M. S. C., & Westermann, G. (2007). *Neuroconstructivism: Vol. 1. How the brain constructs cognition.* Oxford, England: Oxford University Press.

Margolin, G., & Gordis, E. B. (2004). Children's exposure to violence in the family and community. *Current Directions in Psychological Science, 13,* 152–155.

Markman, E. M. (1977). Realizing that you don't understand: A preliminary investigation. *Child Development, 48,* 986–992.

Markman, E. M. (1979). Realizing that you don't understand: Elementary school children's awareness of inconsistencies. *Child Development, 50,* 643–655.

Markman, E. M. (1989). *Categorization and naming in children: Problems of induction.* Cambridge, MA: MIT Press.

Marks, H. M. (2000). Student engagement in instructional activity: Patterns in the elementary, middle, and high school years. *American Educational Research Journal, 37,* 153–184.

Marks, J. (1995). *Human biodiversity: Genes, race, and history.* New York: Aldine de Gruyter.

Markus, H. R., & Hamedani, M. G. (2007). Sociocultural psychology: The dynamic interdependence among self systems and social systems. In S. Kitayama & D. Cohen (Eds.), *Handbook of cultural psychology* (pp. 3–39). New York: Guilford Press.

Markus, H. R., & Kitayama, S. (1991). Culture and the self: Implications for cognition, emotion, and motivation. *Psychological Review, 98,* 224–253.

Marsh, H. W. (1989). Age and sex effect in multiple dimensions of self-concept: Preadolescence to early-adulthood. *Journal of Educational Psychology, 81,* 417–430.

Marsh, H. W. (1990a). Causal ordering of academic self-concept and academic achievement: A multiwave, longitudinal panel analysis. *Journal of Educational Psychology, 82,* 646–656.

Marsh, H. W. (1990b). A multidimensional, hierarchical model of self-concept: Theoretical and empirical justification. *Educational Psychology Review, 2,* 77–172.

Marsh, H. W., & Craven, R. (1997). Academic self-concept: Beyond the dustbowl. In G. D. Phye (Ed.), *Handbook of classroom assessment: Learning, achievement, and adjustment.* San Diego, CA: Academic Press.

Marsh, H. W., & Hau, K.-T. (2003). Big-fish–little-pond effect on academic self-concept: A cross-cultural (26-country) test of the negative effects of academically selective schools. *American Psychologist, 58,* 364–376.

Marsh, H. W., & Kleitman, S. (2005). Consequences of employment during high school: Character building, subversion of academic goals, or a threshold? *American Educational Research Journal, 42,* 331–369.

Marsh, H. W., Parada, R. H., Yeung, A. S., & Healey, J. (2001). Aggressive school troublemakers and victims: A longitudinal model examining the pivotal role of self-concept. *Journal of Educational Psychology, 93,* 411–419.

Marsh, H. W., Trautwein, U., Lüdtke, O., Köller, O., & Baumert, J. (2005). Academic self-concept, interest, grades, and standardize test scores: Reciprocal effects models of causal ordering. *Child Development, 76,* 397–416.

Marshall, N. L. (2004). The quality of early child care and children's development. *Current Directions in Psychological Science, 13,* 165–168.

Marshand, G., & Skinner, E. A. (2007). Motivational dynamics of children's academic help-seeking and concealment. *Journal of Educational Psychology, 99,* 65–82.

Martin, C. L. (2000). Cognitive theories of gender development. In T. Eckes & H. Trautner (Eds.), *The developmental social psychology of gender* (pp. 91–121). Mahwah, NJ: Erlbaum.

Martin, C. L., Ruble, D. N., & Szkrybalo, J. (2002). Cognitive theories of early gender development. *Psychological Bulletin, 128,* 903–933.

Martin, S. S., Brady, M. P., & Williams, R. E. (1991). Effects of toys on the social behavior of preschool children in integrated and nonintegrated groups: Investigation of a setting event. *Journal of Early Intervention, 15,* 153–161.

Martinez, C. R., & Forgatch, M. S. (2001). Preventing problems with boys' noncompliance: Effects of a parent-training intervention for divorcing mothers. *Journal of Consulting and Clinical Psychology, 69,* 416–428.

Martino, S. C., Ellickson, P. L., Klein, D. J., McCaffrey, D., & Edelen, M. O. (2008). Multiple trajectories of physical aggression among adolescent boys and girls. *Aggressive Behavior, 34,* 61–75.

Masataka, N. (1992). Pitch characteristics of Japanese maternal speech to infants. *Journal of Child Language, 19,* 213–224.

Mason, L. (2003). Personal epistemologies and intentional conceptual change. In G. M. Sinatra & P. R. Pintrich (Eds.), *Intentional conceptual change* (pp. 199–236). Mahwah, NJ: Erlbaum.

Massey, C. M., & Gelman, R. (1988). Preschoolers' ability to decide whether a photographed unfamiliar object can move itself. *Developmental Psychology, 24,* 307–317.

Massey, D. S., & Denton, N. A. (1993). *American apartheid: Segregation and the making of the underclass.* Cambridge, MA: Cambridge University Press.

Massimini, K. (2000). *Genetic disorders sourcebook* (2nd ed.). Detroit, MI: Omnigraphics.

Masten, A. S., Neemann, J., & Andenas, S. (1994). Life events and adjustment in adolescents: The significance of event independence, desirability, and chronicity. *Journal of Research on Adolescence, 4,* 71–97.

Masur, E. F., McIntyre, C. W., & Flavell, J. H. (1973). Developmental changes in apportionment of study time among items in a multitrial free recall task. *Journal of Experimental Child Psychology, 15,* 237–246.

Matheson, C., Olsen, R. J., & Weisner, T. (2007). A good friend is hard to find: Friendship among adolescents with disabilities. *American Journal on Mental Retardation, 112*(5), 319–329.

Mathews, J. (1988). *Escalante: The best teacher in America.* New York: Henry Holt.

Matthews, D., Lieven, E., & Tomasello, M. (2007). How toddlers and preschoolers learn to uniquely identify referents for others: A training study. *Child Development, 78,* 1744–1759.

Matthews, J. (1999). *The art of childhood and adolescence: The construction of meaning.* London: Falmer Press.

Mayall, B., Bendelow, G., Barker, S., Storey, P., & Veltman, M. (1996). *Children's health in primary schools.* London: Falmer Press.

Mayer, D. L., & Dobson, V. (1982). Visual acuity development in infants and young children, as assessed by operant preferential looking. *Vision Research, 22,* 1141–1151.

Mayer, R. E. (2004). Should there be a three-strikes rule against pure discovery learning? *American Psychologist, 59,* 14–19.

Mayes, L. C., & Bornstein, M. H. (1997). The development of children exposed to cocaine. In S. S. Luthar, J. A. Burack, D. Cicchetti, & J. R. Weisz (Eds.), *Developmental psychopathology: Perspectives on adjustment, risk, and disorder* (pp. 166–188). Cambridge, England: Cambridge University Press.

Maynard, A. E. (2002). Cultural teaching: The development of teaching skills in Maya sibling interactions. *Child Development, 73,* 969–982.

Mayseless, O. (2005). Ontogeny of attachment in middle childhood: Conceptualization of normative changes. In K. A. Kerns & R. A. Richardson (Eds.), *Attachment in middle childhood* (pp. 1–23). New York: Guilford Press.

McAdoo, H. P., & Martin, A. (2005). Families and ethnicity. In R. M. Lerner, F. Jacobs, & D. Wertlieb (Eds.), *Applied developmental science: An advanced textbook* (pp. 141–154). Thousand Oaks, CA: Sage.

McAlpine, L. (1992). Language, literacy and education: Case studies of Cree, Inuit and Mohawk communities. *Canadian Children, 17*(1), 17–30.

McAlpine, L., & Taylor, D. M. (1993). Instructional preferences of Cree, Inuit, and Mohawk teachers. *Journal of American Indian Education, 33*(1), 1–20.

McBride-Chang, C., & Ho, C. S. (2000). Developmental issues in Chinese children's character acquisition. *Journal of Educational Psychology, 92,* 50–55.

McBride-Chang, C., & Treiman, R. (2003). Hong Kong Chinese kindergartners learn to read English analytically. *Psychological Science, 14,* 138–143.

McBrien, J. L. (2005a). *Discrimination and academic motivation in adolescent refugee girls.* Unpublished doctoral dissertation, Emory University, Atlanta, GA. *Dissertation Abstracts International Section A: Humanities and Social Sciences, 66*(5-A), 2055, pp. 1602.

McBrien, J. L. (2005b). Educational needs and barriers for refugee students in the United States: A review of the literature. *Review of Educational Research, 75,* 329–364.

McCabe, M. P., & Ricciardelli, L. A. (2004). A longitudinal study of pubertal timing and extreme body change behaviors among adolescent boys and girls. *Adolescence, 39,* 145–166.

McCaleb, S. P. (1994). *Building communities of learners: A collaboration among teachers, students, families, and community.* New York: St. Martin's Press.

McCall, R. B. (1993). Developmental functions for general mental performance. In D. K. Detterman (Ed.), *Current topics in human intelligence* (Vol. 3). Norwood, NJ: Ablex.

McCall, R. B. (1994). Academic underachievers. *Current Directions in Psychological Science, 3,* 15–19.

McCall, R. B., Kennedy, C. B., & Applebaum, M. I. (1977). Magnitude of discrepancy and the distribution of attention in infants. *Child Development, 48,* 772–786.

McCall, R. B., & Plemons, B. W. (2001). The concept of critical periods and their implications for early childhood services. In D. B. Bailey, Jr., J. T. Bruer, F. J. Symons, & J. W. Lichtman (Eds.), *Critical thinking about critical periods* (pp. 267–287). Baltimore: Brookes.

McCallum, R. S. (1991). The assessment of preschool children with the Stanford-Binet Intelligence Scale: Fourth Edition. In B. A. Bracken (Ed.), *The psychoeducational assessment of preschool children* (2nd ed., pp. 107–132). Boston: Allyn & Bacon.

McCallum, R. S. (1999). A "baker's dozen" criteria for evaluating fairness in nonverbal testing. *The School Psychologist, 53,* 41–60.

McCallum, R. S., & Bracken, B. A. (1993). Interpersonal relations between school children and their peers, parents, and teachers. *Educational Psychology Review, 5,* 155–176.

McCallum, R. S., & Bracken, B. A. (1997). The Universal Nonverbal Intelligence Test. In D. P. Flanagan, J. L. Genshaft, & P. L. Harrison (Eds.), *Contemporary intellectual assessment: Theories, tests, and issues* (pp. 268–280). New York: Guilford Press.

McCallum, R. S., & Bracken, B. A. (2005). The Universal Nonverbal Intelligence Test: A multidimensional measure of intelligence. In D. P. Flanagan & P. L. Harrison (Eds.), *Contemporary intellectual assessment: Theories, tests, and issues* (2nd ed., pp. 425–440). New York: Guilford Press.

McCann, T. M. (1989). Student argumentative writing knowledge and ability at three grade levels. *Research in the Teaching of English, 23,* 62–72.

McCarthy, M., & Kuh, G. D. (2005, September 9). Student engagement: A missing link in improving high schools. *Teachers College Record.*

McCarty, T. L., & Watahomigie, L. J. (1998). Language and literacy in American Indian and Alaska Native communities. In B. Pérez (Ed.), *Sociocultural contexts of language and literacy.* Mahwah, NJ: Erlbaum.

McCaslin, M., & Good, T. L. (1996). The informal curriculum. In D. C. Berliner & R. C. Calfee (Eds.), *Handbook of educational psychology.* New York: Macmillan.

McClelland, J. L. (2001). Failures to learn and their remediation: A Hebbian account. In J. L. McClelland & R. S. Siegler (Eds.), *Mechanisms of cognitive development: Behavioral and neural perspectives* (pp. 97–121). Mahwah, NJ: Erlbaum.

McClelland, J. L., Fiez, J. A., & McCandliss, B. D. (2002). Teaching the /r/–/l/ discrimination to Japanese adults: Behavioral and neural aspects. *Physiology and Behavior, 77,* 657–662.

McCloskey, M. (1983). Naïve theories of motion. In D. Genter & A. L. Stevens (Eds.), *Mental models* (pp. 299–324). Hillsdale, NJ: Erlbaum.

McCombs, B. L., & Vakili, D. (2005). A learner-centered framework for e-learning. *Teachers College Record, 107*(8), 1582–1600.

McCourt, F. (2005). *Teacher man: A memoir.* New York: Scribner.

McCoy, K. (1994). *Understanding your teenager's depression.* New York: Perigee.

McCrae, R. R., Costa, P. T. Jr., & Busch, C. M. (1986). Evaluating comprehensiveness in personality systems: The California Q-Set and the five-factor model. *Journal of Personality, 54,* 430–446.

McCreary, M. L., Slavin, L. A., & Berry, E. J. (1996). Predicting problem behavior and self-esteem among African-American adolescents. *Journal of Adolescent Research, 11,* 216–234.

McCrink, K., & Wynn, K. (2004). Large-number addition and subtraction by 9-month-old infants. *Psychological Science, 15,* 776–781.

McCrink, K., & Wynn, K. (2007). Ratio abstraction by 6-month-old infants. *Psychological Science, 18,* 740–745.

McCutchen, D. (1987). Children's discourse skill: Form and modality requirements of schooled writing. *Discourse Processes, 10,* 267–286.

McCutchen, D. (1996). A capacity theory of writing: Working memory in composition. *Educational Psychology Review, 8,* 299–325.

McDermott, S., Durkin, M. S., Schupf, N., & Stein, Z. A. (2007). Epidemiology and etiology of mental retardation. In J. W. Jacobson, J. A. Mulick, & J. Rojahn (Eds.), *Handbook of intellectual and developmental disabilities* (pp. 3–40). New York: Springer.

McDevitt, M. (2005). The partisan child: Developmental provocation as a model of political socialization. *International Journal of Public Opinion, 18*(1), 67–88.

McDevitt, M., & Kiousis, S. (2007, August). *Political socialization upside down: The adolescent's contribution to civic parenting.* Paper presented at annual meeting of the Association for Education in Journalism and Mass Communication, Washington, DC.

McDevitt, T. M. (1990). Encouraging young children's listening skills. *Academic Therapy, 25,* 569–577.

McDevitt, T. M., & Ford, M. E. (1987). Processes in young children's communicative functioning and development. In M. E. Ford & D. H. Ford (Eds.), *Humans as self-constructing systems: Putting the framework to work.* (pp. 145–175). Hillsdale, NJ: Erlbaum.

McDevitt, T. M., Spivey, N., Sheehan, E. P., Lennon, R., & Story, R. (1990). Children's beliefs about listening: Is it enough to be still and quiet? *Child Development, 61,* 713–721.

McDougall, P., & Hymel, S. (2007). Same-gender versus cross-gender friendship conceptions. *Merrill-Palmer Quarterly, 53,* 347–380.

McGlothlin, H., & Killen, M. (2005). Children's perceptions of intergroup and intragroup similarity and the role of social experience. *Applied Developmental Psychology, 26,* 680–698.

McGrew, K. S. (2005). The Cattell-Horn-Carroll theory of cognitive abilities: Past, present, and future. In D. P. Flanagan & P. L. Harrison (Eds.), *Contemporary intellectual assessment: Theories, tests, and issues* (2nd ed., pp. 136–181). New York: Guilford Press.

McGrew, K. S., Flanagan, D. P., Zeith, T. Z., & Vanderwood, M. (1997). Beyond *g:* The impact of *Gf-Gc* specific cognitive abilities research on the future use and interpretation of intelligence tests in the schools. *School Psychology Review, 26,* 189–210.

McGue, M., Bouchard, T. J., Jr., Iacono, W. G., & Lykken, D. T. (1993). Behavioral genetics of cognitive ability: A life-span perspective. In R. Plomin & G. E. McClearn (Eds.), *Nature, nurture, and psychology.* Washington, DC: American Psychological Association.

McGuigan, F., & Salmon, K. (2004). The time to talk: The influence of the timing of adult-child talk on children's event memory. *Child Development, 75,* 669–686.

McHale, J. P., & Rasmussen, J. L. (1998). Coparental and family group-level dynamics during infancy: Early family precursors of child and family functioning during preschool. *Development and Psychopathology, 10,* 39–59.

McHale, S. M., Bartko, W. T., Crouter, A. C., & Perry-Jenkins, M. (1990). Children's housework and psychosocial functioning: The mediating effects of parents' sex-role behaviors and attitudes. *Child Development, 61,* 1413–1426.

McHale, S. M., & Crouter, A. C. (1996). The family context of children's sibling relationships. In G. Brody (Ed.), *Sibling relationships: Their causes and consequences* (pp. 173–195). Norwood, NJ: Ablex.

McKenzie, J. K. (1993). Adoption of children with special needs. *The Future of Children, 3*(1), 26–42.

McKeough, A. (1995). Teaching narrative knowledge for transfer in the early school years. In A. McKeough, J. Lupart, & A. Marini (Eds.), *Teaching for transfer: Fostering generalization in learning.* Mahwah, NJ: Erlbaum.

McKown, C., & Weinstein, R. S. (2003). The development and consequences of stereotype consciousness in middle childhood. *Child Development, 74,* 498–515.

McKown, C., & Weinstein, R. S. (2008). Teacher expectations, classroom context, and the achievement gap. *Journal of School Psychology, 46,* 235–261.

McLane, J. B., & McNamee, G. D. (1990). *Early literacy.* Cambridge, MA: Harvard University Press.

McLoyd, V. C. (1998a). Children in poverty: Development, public policy, and practice. In W. Damon (Series Ed.), I. E. Sigel, & K. A. Renninger (Eds.), *Handbook of child psychology: Vol. 4. Child psychology in practice* (5th ed., pp. 135–208). New York: Wiley.

McLoyd, V. C. (1998b). Socioeconomic disadvantage and child development. *American Psychologist, 53,* 185–204.

McLoyd, V. C., Aikens, N. L., & Burton, L. M. (2006). Childhood poverty, policy, and practice. In W. Damon & R. M. Lerner (Eds. in Chief) & K. A. Renninger & I. E. Sigel (Vol. Eds.), *Handbook of child psychology, Vol. 4. Child psychology in practice* (6th ed., pp. 700–775). Hoboken, NJ: Wiley.

McMahon, S. (1992). Book club: A case study of a group of fifth graders as they participate in a literature-based reading program. *Reading Research Quarterly, 27,* 292–294.

McMahon, S. D., Parnes, A. L., Keys, C. B., & Viola, J. J. (2008). School belonging among low-income urban youth with disabilities: Testing a theoretical model. *Psychology in the Schools, 45*(5), 387–401.

McMahon, S. D., Wernsman, J., & Parnes, A. L. (2006). Understanding prosocial behavior: The impact of empathy and gender among African American adolescents. *Journal of Adolescent Health, 39,* 135–137.

McNeill, D. (1966). Developmental psycholinguistics. In F. Smith & G. A. Miller (Eds.), *The genesis of language.* Cambridge, MA: MIT Press.

McNeill, D. (1970). *The acquisition of language: The study of developmental psycholinguistics.* New York: Harper & Row.

Mechelli, A., Crinion, J. T., Noppeney, U., O'Doherty, J., Ashburner, J., Frackowiak, R., & Price, C. J. (2004). Structural plasticity in the bilingual brain. *Nature, 431,* 757.

Meece, J. L. (1994). The role of motivation in self-regulated learning. In D. H. Schunk & B. J. Zimmerman (Eds.), *Self-regulation of learning and performance: Issues and educational applications.* Mahwah, NJ: Erlbaum.

Meece, J. L., & Holt, K. (1993). A pattern analysis of students' achievement goals. *Journal of Educational Psychology, 85,* 582–590.

Meehan, B. T., Hughes, J. N., & Cavell, T. A. (2003). Teacher–student relationships as compensatory resources for aggressive children. *Child Development, 74,* 1145–1157.

Mehan, H. (1979). *Social organization in the classroom.* Cambridge, MA: Harvard University Press.

Meichenbaum, D. (1977). *Cognitive-behavior modification: An integrative approach.* New York: Plenum Press.

Meichenbaum, D. (1985). Teaching thinking: A cognitive-behavioral perspective. In S. F. Chipman, J. W. Segal, & R. Glaser (Eds.), *Thinking and learning skills: Vol. 2. Research and open questions.* Hillsdale, NJ: Erlbaum.

Meichenbaum, D., & Goodman, J. (1971). Training impulsive children to talk to themselves: A means of developing self-control. *Journal of Abnormal Psychology, 77,* 115–126.

Meins, E., Fernyhough, C., Wainwright, R., Clark-Carter, D., Gupta, M. D., Fradley, E., et al. (2003). Pathways to understanding mind: Construct validity and predictive validity of maternal mind-mindedness. *Child Development, 74,* 1194–1211.

Mejía-Arauz, R., Rogoff, B., Dexter, A., & Najafi, B. (2007). Cultural variation in children's social organization. *Child Development, 78,* 1001–1014.

Meltzer, L. (Ed.). (2007). *Executive function in education: From theory to practice.* New York: Guilford Press.

Meltzer, L., & Krishnan, K. (2007). Executive function difficulties and learning disabilities: Understandings and misunderstandings. In L. Meltzer (Ed.), *Executive function in education: From theory to practice* (pp. 77–105). New York: Guilford Press.

Meltzer, L., Pollica, L. S., & Barzillai, M. (2007). Executive function in the classroom: Embedding strategy instruction into daily teaching practices. In L. Meltzer (Ed.), *Executive function in education: From theory to practice* (pp. 165–193). New York: Guilford Press.

Meltzoff, A. N. (1990). Foundations for developing a concept of self: The role of imitation in relating self to other and the value of social mirroring, social modeling, and self practice in infancy. In D. Cicchetti & M. Beeghly (Eds.), *The self in transition: Infancy to childhood* (pp. 139–164). Chicago: University of Chicago Press.

Mena, J, G., & Eyer, D. W. (2007). *Infants, toddlers, and caregivers: A curriculum of respectful, responsive care and education* (7th ed.). Boston: McGraw-Hill.

Menéndez, R. (Director). (1988). *Stand and deliver* [Motion picture]. United States: Warner Studios.

Mennella, J. A., Jagnow, C. P., & Beauchamp, G. K. (2001). Prenatal and postnatal flavor learning by human infants. *Pediatrics, 107,* 88.

Menyuk, P., & Menyuk, D. (1988). Communicative competence: A historical and cultural perspective. In J. S. Wurzel (Ed.), *Toward multiculturalism: A reader in multicultural education.* Yarmouth, ME: Intercultural Press.

Mercer, J. (2006). *Understanding attachment: Parenting, child care, and emotional development.* Westport, CT: Praeger.

Merzenich, M. M. (2001). Cortical plasticity contributing to child development. In J. L. McClelland & R. S. Siegler (Eds.), *Mechanisms of cognitive development: Behavioral and neural perspectives* (pp. 67–95). Mahwah, NJ: Erlbaum.

Metz, K. E. (1995). Reassessment of developmental constraints on children's science instruction. *Review of Educational Research, 65*, 93–127.

Metz, K. E. (1997). On the complex relation between cognitive developmental research and children's science curricula. *Review of Educational Research, 67*, 151–163.

Metz, K. E. (2004). Children's understanding of scientific inquiry: Their conceptualizations of uncertainty in investigations of their own design. *Cognition and Instruction, 22*, 219–290.

Meyer, C. F., & Rhoades, E. K. (2006). Multiculturalism: Beyond food, festival, folklore, and fashion. *Kappa Delta Pi Record, 42*(2), 82–87.

Meyer, D., Madden, D., & McGrath, D. J. (2005). English language learner students in U.S. public schools: 1994 and 2000. *Education Statistics Quarterly, 6*(3). Retrieved April 7, 2008, from http://nces.ed.gov/programs/quarterly/vol_6/6_3/3_4.asp

Meyer, D. K., Turner, J. C., & Spencer, C. A. (1994, April). *Academic risk taking and motivation in an elementary mathematics classroom.* Paper presented at the annual meeting of the American Educational Research Association, New Orleans, LA.

Meyer, D. K., Turner, J. C., & Spencer, C. A. (1997). Challenge in a mathematics classroom: Students' motivation and strategies in project-based learning. *Elementary School Journal, 97*, 501–521.

Meyers, D. T. (1987). The socialized individual and individual autonomy: An intersection between philosophy and psychology. In E. F. Kittay and D. T. Meyers (Eds.), *Women and moral theory.* Totowa, NJ: Rowman & Littlefield.

Meyerstein, I. (2001). A systemic approach to fetal loss following genetic testing. *Contemporary Family Therapy, 23*, 385–402.

Michaels, M. L. (2006). Factors that contribute to step-family success: A qualitative analysis. *Journal of Divorce and Remarriage, 44*(3/4), 53–66.

Michel, C. (1989). Radiation embryology. *Experientia, 45*, 69–77.

Micheli, L. J. (1995). Sports injuries in children and adolescents: Questions and controversies. *Clinics in Sports Medicine, 14*, 727–745.

Midgley, C. (Ed.). (2002). *Goals, goal structures, and patterns of adaptive learning.* Mahwah, NJ: Erlbaum.

Midgley, C., Feldlaufer, H., & Eccles, J. S. (1989). Change in teacher efficacy and student self- and task-related beliefs in mathematics during the transition to junior high school. *Journal of Educational Psychology, 81*, 247–258.

Midgley, C., Kaplan, A., & Middleton, M. (2001). Performance-approach goals: Good for what, for whom, under what circumstances, and at what cost? *Journal of Educational Psychology, 93*, 77–86.

Mikulincer, M., & Shaver, P. R. (2007). *Attachment in adulthood: Structure, dynamics, and change.* New York: Guilford Press.

Milch-Reich, S., Campbell, S. B., Pelham, W. E., Jr., Connelly, L. M., & Geva, D. (1999). Developmental and individual differences in children's on-line representations of dynamic social events. *Child Development, 70*, 413–431.

Miller, B. C., & Benson, B. (1999). Romantic and sexual relationship development during adolescence. In W. Furman, B. B. Brown, & C. Feiring (Eds.), *The development of romantic relationships in adolescence* (pp. 99–121). Cambridge, England: Cambridge University Press.

Miller, D. (1994). Suicidal behavior of adolescents with behavior disorders and their peers without disabilities. *Behavioral Disorders, 20*(1), 61–68.

Miller, G. A., & Gildea, P. M. (1987). How children learn words. *Scientific American, 257*, 94–99.

Miller, G. E., & Wrosch, C. (2007). You've gotta know when to fold 'em: Goal disengagement and systemic inflammation in adolescence. *Psychological Science, 18*, 773–777.

Miller, J. G. (1987). Cultural influences on the development of conceptual differentiation in person description. *British Journal of Developmental Psychology, 5*, 309–319.

Miller, J. G. (1997). A cultural-psychology perspective on intelligence. In R. J. Sternberg & E. L. Grigorenko (Eds.), *Intelligence, heredity, and environment* (pp. 269–302). Cambridge, England: Cambridge University Press.

Miller, J. G. (2006). Insights into moral development from cultural psychology. In M. Killen & J. G. Smetana (Eds.), *Handbook of moral development* (pp. 375–398). Mahwah, NJ: Erlbaum.

Miller, J. G. (2007). Cultural psychology of moral development. In S. Kitayama & D. Cohen (Eds.), *Handbook of cultural psychology* (pp. 477–499). New York: Guilford Press.

Miller, K. (1989). Measurement as a tool for thought: The role of measuring procedures in children's understanding of quantitative invariance. *Developmental Psychology, 25*, 589–600.

Miller, K. F., Smith, C. M., Zhu, J., & Zhang, H. (1995). Preschool origins of cross-national differences in mathematical competence: The role of number-naming systems. *Psychological Science, 6*, 56–60.

Miller, L. S. (1995). *An American imperative: Accelerating minority educational advancement.* New Haven, CT: Yale University Press.

Miller, N., & Maruyama, G. (1976). Ordinal position and peer popularity. *Journal of Personality and Social Psychology, 33*, 123–131.

Miller, P., & Seier, W. (1994). Strategy utilization deficiencies in children: when, where, and why. In H. Reese (Ed.), *Advances in child development and behavior* (Vol. 25). New York: Academic Press.

Miller, P. A., Eisenberg, N., Fabes, R. A., & Shell, R. (1996). Relations of moral reasoning and vicarious emotion to young children's prosocial behavior toward peers and adults. *Developmental Psychology, 32*, 210–219.

Miller, P. J., & Goodnow, J. J. (1995). Cultural practices: Toward an integration of culture and development. In J. J. Goodnow & P. J. Miller (Eds.), *Cultural practices as contexts for development* (New Directions for Child Development, No. 67; pp. 5–16). San Francisco, CA: Jossey-Bass.

Miller, P. M., Danaher, D. L., & Forbes, D. (1986). Sex-related strategies of coping with interpersonal conflict in children aged five to seven. *Developmental Psychology, 22*, 543–548.

Miller, R. B., & Brickman, S. J. (2004). A model of future-oriented motivation and self-regulation. *Educational Psychology Review, 16*, 9–33.

Miller, S. D., Heafner, T., Massey, D., & Strahan, D. B. (2003, April). *Students' reactions to teachers' attempts to create the necessary conditions to promote the acquisition of self-regulation skills.* Paper presented at the annual meeting of the American Educational Research Association, Chicago.

Mills, D. L., & Sheehan, E. A. (2007). Experience and developmental changes in the organization of language-relevant brain activity. In D. Coch, K. W. Fischer, & G. Dawson (Eds.), *Human behavior, learning, and the developing brain: Typical development* (pp. 183–218). New York: Guilford Press.

Mills, G. E. (2007). *Action research: A guide for the teacher researcher* (3rd ed.). Upper Saddle River, NJ: Pearson Merrill/Prentice Hall.

Mills, R. S. L., & Grusec, J. E. (1989). Cognitive, affective, and behavioral consequences of praising altruism. *Merrill-Palmer Quarterly, 35*, 299–326.

Milne, E., White, S., Campbell, R., Swettenham, J., Jansen, P., & Ramas, F. (2006). Motion and form coherence detection in autistic spectrum disorder: Relationship to motor control and 2:4 digit ratio. *Journal of Autism and Developmental Disorders, 36*, 225–237.

Milner, H. R. (2006). Classroom management in urban classrooms. In C. M. Evertson & C. S. Weinstein (Eds.), *Handbook of classroom management: Research, practice, and contemporary issues* (pp. 491–522). Mahwah, NJ: Erlbaum.

Milner, H. R., & Ford, D. Y. (2007). Cultural considerations of culturally diverse elementary students in gifted education. *Roeper Review, 29*(3), 166–173.

Minami, M., & McCabe, A. (1996). Compressed collections of experiences: Some Asian American traditions. In A. McCabe (Ed.), *Chameleon readers: Some problems cultural differences in narrative structure pose for multicultural literacy programs* (pp. 72–97). New York: McGraw-Hill.

Mingroni, M. A. (2007). Resolving the IQ paradox: Heterosis as a cause of the Flynn effect and other trends. *Psychological Review, 114*, 806–829.

Minskoff, E. H. (1980). Teaching approach for developing nonverbal communication skills in students with social perception deficits: II. Proxemic, vocalic, and artifactual cues. *Journal of Learning Disabilities, 13*, 203–208.

Minstrell, J., & Stimpson, V. (1996). A classroom environment for learning: Guiding students' reconstruction of understanding and reasoning. In L. Schauble & R. Glaser (Eds.), *Innovations in learning: New environments for education.* Mahwah, NJ: Erlbaum.

Mischel, W. (1974). Processes in delay of gratification. In L. Berkowitz (Ed.), *Advances in experimental social psychology* (Vol. 7, pp. 249–292). New York: Academic Press.

Mischel, W., & Ebbesen, E. (1970). Attention in delay of gratification. *Journal of Personality and Social Psychology, 16*, 329–337.

Mischel, W., Shoda, Y., & Rodriguez, M. L. (1989). Delay of gratification in children. *Science, 244*, 933–938.

Mitchem, K. J., & Young, K. R. (2001). Adapting self-management programs for classwide use. *Remedial and Special Education, 22*(2), 75–88.

Mithaug, D. K., & Mithaug, D. E. (2003). Effects of teacher-directed versus student-directed instruction on self-management of young children with disabilities. *Journal of Applied Behavior Analysis, 36*, 133–136.

Mitru, G., Millrood, D., & Mateika, J. H. (2002). The impact of sleep on learning and behavior of adolescents. *Teachers College Record, 104*, 704–726.

Miura, I. T., Okamoto, Y., Vlahovic-Stetic, V., Kim, C. C., & Han, J. H. (1999). Language supports for children's understanding of numerical fractions: Cross-national comparisons. *Journal of Experimental Child Psychology, 74*, 356–365.

Miyake, K., Campos, J., Kagan, J., & Bradshaw, D. (1986). Issues in socioemotional development in Japan. In H. Azuma, K. Hakuta, & H. Stevenson (Eds.), *Kodomo: Child development and education in Japan* (pp. 238–261). San Francisco: Freeman.

Miyake, K., Chen, S.-J., & Campos, J. J. (1985). Infant temperament, mother's mode of interaction, and attachment in Japan: An interim report. In I. Bretherton & E. Waters (Eds.), Growing points of attachment theory and research. *Monographs of the Society for Research in Child Development, 50*(1–2, Serial No. 209), 276–297.

Mize, J., Pettit, G. S., & Brown, E. G. (1995). Mothers' supervision of their children's peer play: Relations with beliefs, perceptions, and knowledge. *Developmental Psychology, 31*, 311–321.

Mohatt, G., & Erickson, F. (1981). Cultural differences in teaching styles in an Odawa school: A sociolinguistic approach. In H. T. Trueba, G. P. Guthrie, & K. H. Au (Eds.), *Culture and the bilingual classroom: Studies in classroom ethnography.* Rowley, MA: Newbury House.

Mohr, N. (1979). *Felita.* New York: Bantam Doubleday Dell.

Moje, E. B. (2000). "To be part of the story": The literacy practices of gangsta adolescents. *Teachers College Record, 102*(3), 651–690.

Money, J. (1988). *Gay, straight, and in-between: The sexology of erotic orientation.* New York: Oxford University Press.

Moni, K., & Jobling, A. (2000). Ignoring the frontiers: Poetry and young adults with Down syndrome. *Social Alternatives, 19*(3), 36–39.

Montagu, A. (1999a). Introduction. In A. Montagu (Ed.), *Race and IQ* (expanded ed., pp. 1–18). New York: Oxford University Press.

Montagu, A. (Ed.). (1999b). *Race and IQ* (expanded ed.). New York: Oxford University Press.

Montague, D. P. F., & Walker-Andrews, A. S. (2001). Peekaboo: A new look at infants' perceptions of emotion expressions. *Developmental Psychology, 37,* 826–838.

Montemayor, R. (1982). The relationship between parent–adolescent conflict and the amount of time adolescents spend with parents, peers, and alone. *Child Development, 53,* 1512–1519.

Montessori, M. (1936). *The secret of childhood* (M. J. Costelloe, Trans.). New York: Ballantine Books, 1966.

Montessori, M. (1949). *The absorbent mind* (M. J. Costelloe, Trans.). New York: Holt, Rinehart & Winston.

Montgomery, D. (1989). Identification of giftedness among American Indian people. In C. J. Maker & S. W. Schiever (Eds.), *Critical issues in gifted education: Vol. 2. Defensible programs for cultural and ethnic minorities.* Austin, TX: Pro-Ed.

Montgomery, J. W., & Windsor, J. (2007). Examining the language performances of children with and without specific language impairment: Contributions of phonological short-term memory and speed of processing. *Journal of Speech, Language, and Hearing Research, 50,* 778–797.

Moon, S. M., Feldhusen, J. F., & Dillon, D. R. (1994). Long term effects of an enrichment program based on the Purdue three-stage model. *Gifted Child Quarterly, 38,* 38–47.

Moore, C. (2007). Understanding self and others in the second year. In C. A. Brownell & C. B. Kopp (Eds.), *Socioemotional development in the toddler years: Transitions and transformations* (pp. 43–65). New York: Guilford Press.

Moore, C. F. (2005). An unhealthy start in life—What matters most? *Psychological Science in the Public Interest, 6*(3), i.

Moore, G. A., Cohn, J. F., & Campbell, S. B. (2001). Infant affective responses to mother's still face at 6 months differentially predict externalizing and internalizing behaviors at 18 months. *Developmental Psychology, 37,* 706–714.

Moore, K. L., & Persaud, T. V. N. (2008). *Before we are born: Essentials of embryology and birth defects* (7th ed.). Philadelphia: W. B. Saunders/Elsevier.

Moore, K. L., Persaud, T. V. N., & Shiota, K. (2000). *Color atlas of clinical embryology* (2nd ed.). Philadelphia: Saunders.

Moore, P. S., Whaley, S. E., & Sigman, M. (2004). Interactions between mothers and children: Impacts of maternal and child anxiety. *Journal of Abnormal Psychology, 113*(3), 471–476.

Moore, S. M., & Rosenthal, D. A. (1991). Condoms and coitus: Adolescents' attitudes to AIDS and safe sex behavior. *Journal of Adolescence, 14,* 211–227.

Moore-Brown, B., Huerta, M., Uranga-Hernandez, Y., & Peña, E. D. (2006). Using dynamic assessment to evaluate children with suspected learning disabilities. *Intervention in School and Clinic, 41*(4), 209–217.

Moran, C. E., & Hakuta, K. (1995). Bilingual education: Broadening research perspectives. In J. A. Banks & C. A. M. Banks (Eds.), *Handbook of research on multicultural education.* New York: Macmillan.

Moran, S., & Gardner, H. (2006). Extraordinary achievements: A developmental and systems analysis. In W. Damon, R. M. Lerner (Series Eds.), D. Kuhn, & R. Siegler (Vol. Eds.), *Handbook of child psychology: Vol. 2. Cognition, perception, and language* (6th ed.). New York: Wiley.

Morelli, G. A., & Rothbaum, F. (2007). Situating the child in context: Attachment relationships and self-regulation in different cultures. In S. Kitayama & D. Cohen (Eds.), *Handbook of cultural psychology* (pp. 500–527). New York: Guilford Press.

Morgan, J. L., Bonamo, K. M., & Travis, L. L. (1995). Negative evidence on negative evidence. *Developmental Psychology, 31,* 180–197.

Morgan, M. (1985). Self-monitoring of attained subgoals in private study. *Journal of Educational Psychology, 77,* 623–630.

Morris, D. (1977). *Manwatching: A field guide to human behaviour.* New York: Harry N. Abrams.

Morris, D., Tyner, B., & Perney, J. (2000). Early steps: Replicating the effects of a first-grade reading intervention program. *Journal of Educational Psychology, 92,* 681–693.

Morrison, G. M., Furlong, M. J., D'Incau, B., & Morrison, R. L. (2004). The safe school: Integrating the school reform agenda to prevent disruption and violence at school. In J. C. Conoley & A. P. Goldstein (Ed.), *School violence intervention* (2nd ed., pp. 256–296). New York: Guilford Press.

Morrongiello, B. A., Fenwick, K. D., Hillier, L., & Chance, G. (1994). Sound localization in newborn human infants. *Developmental Psychobiology, 27,* 519–538.

Morrow, S. L. (1997). Career development of lesbian and gay youth: Effects of sexual orientation, coming out, and homophobia. In M. B. Harris (Ed.), *School experiences of gay and lesbian youth: The invisible minority* (pp. 1–15). Binghamton, NY: Harrington Park Press.

Mortimer, J. T., Shanahan, M., & Ryu, S. (1994). The effects of adolescent employment on school-related orientation and behavior. In R. K. Silbereisen & E. Todt (Eds.), *Adolescence in context: The interplay of family, school, peers and work in adjustment.* New York: Springer-Verlag.

Mosborg, S. (2002). Speaking of history: How adolescents use their knowledge of history in reading the daily news. *Cognition and Instruction, 20,* 323–358.

Moses, L., Baldwin, D. A., Rosicky, J. G., & Tidball, G. (2001). Evidence for referential understanding in the emotions domain at twelve and eighteen months. *Child Development, 72,* 718–735.

Mueller, E., & Silverman, N. (1989). Peer relations in maltreated children. In D. Cicchetti & V. Carlson (Eds.), *Child maltreatment: Theory and research on the causes and consequences of child abuse and neglect* (pp. 529–579). New York: Cambridge University Press 7.

Muis, K. R. (2004). Personal epistemology and mathematics: A critical review and synthesis of research. *Review of Educational Research, 74,* 317–377.

Muis, K. R. (2007). The role of epistemic beliefs in self-regulated learning. *Educational Psychologist, 42,* 173–190.

Muis, K. R., Bendixen, L. D., & Haerle, F. C. (2006). Domain-generality and domain-specificity in personal epistemology research: Philosophical and empirical reflections in the development of a theoretical framework. *Educational Psychology Review, 18,* 3–54.

Mullen, M. K., & Yi, S. (1995). The cultural context of talk about the past: Implications for the development of autobiographical memory. *Cognitive Development, 10,* 407–419.

Mullins, D., & Tisak, M. S. (2006). Moral, conventional, and personal rules: The perspective of foster youth. *Journal of Applied Developmental Psychology, 27,* 310–325.

Mundy, P., Block, J., Delgado, C., Pomares, Y., Van Hecke, A. V., & Parlade, M. V. (2007). Individual differences and the development of joint attention in infancy. *Child Development, 78,* 938–954.

Mundy, P., & Newell, L. (2007). Attention, joint attention, and social cognition. *Current Directions in Psychological Science, 16,* 269–274.

Munroe, R. L., & Munroe, P. J. (1992). Fathers in children's environments: A four culture study. In B. S. Hewlett (Ed.), *Father-child relations: Cultural and biosocial contexts* (pp. 213–230). New York: Aldine de Gruyter.

Murdock, T. B. (1999). The social context of risk: Status and motivational predictors of alienation in middle school. *Journal of Educational Psychology, 91,* 62–75.

Muris, P., Meesters, C., & Rompelberg, L. (2006). Attention control in middle childhood: Relations to

psychopathological symptoms and threat perception distortions. *Behaviour Research and Therapy, 45,* 997–1010.

Murnane, R. J. (2007, Fall). Improving the education of children living in poverty. *The Future of Children, 17*(2), 161–182.

Murphy, D. A., Durako, S. J., Moscicki, A. B., Vermund, S. H., Ma, Y., Schwarz, D. F., et al. (2001). No change in health risk behaviors over time among HIV infected adolescents in care: Role of psychological distress. *Journal of Adolescent Health, 29*(Suppl. 3), 57–63.

Murphy, P. K. (2007). The eye of the beholder: The interplay of social and cognitive components in change. *Educational Psychologist, 42,* 41–53.

Murphy, P. K., & Alexander, P. A. (2008). Examining the influence of knowledge, beliefs, and motivation in conceptual change. In S. Vosniadou (Ed.), *International handbook of research on conceptual change* (pp. 583–616). Taylor and Francis.

Murphy, P. K., & Mason, L. (2006). Changing knowledge and beliefs. In P. A. Alexander & P. H. Winne (Eds.), *Handbook of educational psychology* (2nd ed., pp. 305–324). Mahwah, NJ: Erlbaum.

Mustanski, B. S., Viken, R. J., Kaprio, J., Pulkkinen, L., & Rose, R. (2004). Genetic and environmental influences on pubertal influences on pubertal development: Longitudinal data from Finnish twins at ages 11 and 14. *Developmental Psychology, 40,* 1188–1198.

Muter, V. (1998). Phonological awareness: Its nature and its influence over early literacy development. In C. Hulme & R. M. Joshi (Eds.), *Reading and spelling: Development and disorders.* Mahwah, NJ: Erlbaum.

Myles, B. M., & Simpson, R. L. (2001). Understanding the hidden curriculum: An essential social skill for children and youth with Asperger syndrome. *Intervention in School and Clinic, 36*(5), 279–286.

Naegele, J. R., & Lombroso, P. J. (2001). Genetics of central nervous system developmental disorders. *Child and Adolescent Psychiatric Clinics of North America, 10,* 225–239.

Nagy, W. E., Berninger, V., Abbott, R., Vaughan, K., & Vermeulen, K. (2003). Relationship of morphology and other language skills to literacy skills in at-risk second-grade readers and at-risk fourth-grade writers. *Journal of Educational Psychology, 95,* 730–742.

Nagy, W. E., Herman, P. A., & Anderson, R. C. (1985). Learning words from context. *Reading Research Quarterly, 20,* 233–253.

Nakata, N., & Trehub, S. E. (2004). Infants' responsiveness to maternal speech and singing. *Infant Behavior and Development, 27,* 455–464.

Nakazawa, C., Takahira, S., Muramatsu, Y., Kawano, G., Fujiwara, C., Takahashi, M., & Ikegami, T. (2001, April). *Gender issues in mathematics, science and technology.* Paper presented at the annual meeting of the American Educational Research Association, Seattle, WA.

Narayanan, U., & Warren, S. T. (2006). Neurobiology of related disorders: Fragile X syndrome. In S. O. Moldin & J. L. R. Rubenstein (Eds.), *Understanding autism: From basic neuroscience to treatment* (pp. 113–131). Boca Raton, FL: CRC Press.

Narváez, D. (1998). The influence of moral schemas on the reconstruction of moral narratives in eighth graders and college students. *Journal of Educational Psychology, 90,* 13–24.

Narváez, D. (2002). Does reading moral stories build character? *Educational Psychology Review, 14,* 155–171.

Narváez, D., & Rest, J. (1995). The four components of acting morally. In W. M. Kurtines & J. L. Gewirtz (Eds.), *Moral development: An introduction.* Boston: Allyn & Bacon.

Nasir, N. S., & Saxe, G. B. (2003). Ethnic and academic identities: A cultural practice perspective on emerging tensions and their management in the lives of minority students. *Educational Researcher, 32*(5), 14–18.

Nation, K., & Hulme, C. (1998). The role of analogy in early spelling development. In C. Hulme & R. M. Joshi (Eds.), *Reading and spelling: Development and disorders.* Mahwah, NJ: Erlbaum.

National Association for the Education of Young Children. (1997). *Developmentally appropriate practice in early childhood programs serving children from birth through age 8.* Washington, DC: Author.

National Association of Bilingual Education. (1993). Census reports sharp increase in number of non-English speaking Americans. *NABE News, 16*(6), 1, 25.

National Association of Secondary School Principals. (2004). *Breaking ranks II: Strategies for leading high school reform.* Reston, VA: Author.

National Campaign to Prevent Teen Pregnancy. (2005). *Teenage pregnancy rates in the United States, 1972–2000.* Retrieved June 22, 2005, from http://www.teenpregnancy.org/resources/data/national.asp

National Center for Education Statistics. (1997). *Issue brief: Schools serving family needs: Extended-day programs in public and private schools.* Washington, DC: Author.

National Center for Education Statistics. (2003). *Percentage of high school completers ages 16–24 who were enrolled in college the October after completing high school, by type of institution, family income, and race/ethnicity: October 1972–96.* Washington, DC: Author. Retrieved February 24, 2003, from http://nces.ed.gov/ quicktables/Detail. asp?Key5147

National Center for Education Statistics. (2006). *Status and trends in the education of racial and ethnic minorities. Table 1b. Population in the four U.S. regions, and in the 20 states with highest percentages of total minority population, by race/ethnicity and region/state: 2005.* Retrieved December 3, 2007, from http://nces.ed.gov/pubs2007/ minoritytrends/tables/table_1b.asp?referrer=report

National Center for Education Statistics. (2007). *Digest of education statistics. Table 183. Graduation rates and postsecondary attendance rates of recent high school students, by selected high school characteristics: 1999–2000.* National Center for Education Statistics, Institute of Education Sciences, U.S. Department of Education. Retrieved December 6, 2007, from http://nces.ed.gov/programs/digest/d05/tables/dt05_183.asp

National Center for Health Statistics. (2005). *NCHS Data on Adolescent Health.* Retrieved February 1, 2008, from http://www.cdc.gov/nchs/data/factsheets/adolescenthlth.pdf

National Center for Missing and Exploited Children. (2004). *HDOP: Help delete online predators.* Retrieved November 20, 2005, from http://www.missingkids.com/adcouncil

National Clearinghouse for English Language Acquisition. (2006). *Resources about secondary English language learners.* Washington, DC: Author. Retrieved December 3, 2007, from http://www.ncela.gwu.edu/resabout/ells/intro

National Council for Accreditation of Teacher Education. (2000). *Program standards for elementary teacher preparation.* Retrieved from http://www.ncate.org/elemstds.pdf

National Drug Intelligence Center. (2008). *Attorney General's report to Congress on the growth of violent street gangs in suburban areas.* Retrieved June 10, 2008, from http://www.usdoj.gov/ndic/pubs27/27612/estimate.htm

National Human Genome Research Institute. (2003). *From the blueprint to you* (NIH Publication No. 03–5377). Bethesda, MD: National Institutes of Health.

National Institute of Mental Health. (2008a). *Autism spectrum disorders (Pervasive developmental disorders).* Retrieved January 22, 2008, from http://www.nimh.nih.gov/health/publications/autism/summary.shtml

National Institute of Mental Health. (2008b). *Suicide in the U.S.: Statistics and prevention.* Retrieved April 28, 2008, from http://www.nimh.nih.gov/health/publications/suicide-in-the-us-statistics-and-prevention.shtml#races

National Institute on Drug Abuse. (2008). *Drugs, brains, and behavior: The science of addiction.* Retrieved February 1, 2008, from http://www.drugabuse.gov

National Joint Committee on Learning Disabilities. (1994). Learning disabilities: Issues on definition, a position paper of the National Joint Committee on Learning Disabilities. In *Collective perspectives on issues affecting learning disabilities: Position papers and statements.* Austin, TX: Pro-Ed.

National Middle School Association. (2003). *This we believe: Successful schools for young adolescents.* Columbus, OH: Author.

National Research Council. (1999). *How people learn: Brain, mind, experience, and school.* Washington, DC: Author.

National Science Foundation. (2007). *Women, minorities, and persons with disabilities in science and engineering: 2007.* Arlington, VA: Author. Retrieved July 12, 2007, from http://www.nsf.gov/statistics/wmpd

National Youth Violence Prevention Center. (2001). *Gangs.* Retrieved October 5, 2008, from http://www.safeyouth.org/scripts/facts/docs/gangs.pdf

Nayak, A., & Kehily, M. J. (2008). *Gender, youth and culture: Young masculinities and femininities.* Houndmills, Basingstoke, Hampshire, England: Palgrave Macmillan.

NCSS Task Force on Ethnic Studies Curriculum Guidelines. (1992). Curriculum guidelines for multicultural education. *Social Education, 56,* 274–294.

Neef, N. A., Marckel, J., Ferreri, S. J., Bicard, D. F., Endo, S., Aman, M. G., et al. (2005). Behavioral assessment of impulsivity: A comparison of children with and without attention deficit hyperactivity disorder. *Journal of Applied Behavior Analysis, 38,* 23–37.

Neel, R. S., Jenkins, Z. N., & Meadows, N. (1990). Social problem-solving behaviors and aggression in young children: A descriptive observational study. *Behavioral Disorders, 16,* 39–51.

Neinstein, L. S. (2004). Substance abuse—Stimulants/inhalants/opioids/anabolic steroids/designer and club drugs. Adolescent health curriculum. Retrieved February 1, 2008, from http://www.usc.edu/student-affairs/Health_Center/adolhealth/content/b8subs3.html

Neiss, M. B., Sedikides, C., & Stevenson, J. (2006). Genetic influences on level and stability of self-esteem. *Self and Identity, 5,* 247–266.

Neiss, M. B., Stevenson, J., Sedikides, C., Kumashiro, M., Finkel, E. J., & Rusbult, C. E. (2005). Executive self, self-esteem, and negative affectivity: Relations at the phenotypic and genotypic level. *Journal of Personality and Social Psychology, 89,* 593–606.

Neisser, U. (1998a). Introduction: Rising test scores and what they mean. In U. Neisser (Ed.), *The rising curve: Long-term gains in IQ and related measures* (pp. 3–22). Washington, DC: American Psychological Association.

Neisser, U. (Ed.). (1998b). *The rising curve: Long-term gains in IQ and related measures.* Washington, DC: American Psychological Association.

Neisser, U., Boodoo, G., Bouchard, T. J., Boykin, A. W., Brody, N., Ceci, S. J., et al. (1996). Intelligence: Knowns and unknowns. *American Psychologist, 51,* 77–101.

Nelson, C. A. (2005, April). *Brain development and plasticity: Examples from the study of early institutional rearing.* Invited address at the Developmental Science Teaching Institute at the biennial meeting of the Society for Research in Child Development, Atlanta.

Nelson, C. A., & Fivush, R. (2004). The emergence of autobiographical memory: A social cultural developmental theory. *Psychological Review, 111,* 486–511.

Nelson, C. A., III, Thomas, K. M., & de Haan, M. (2006). Neural bases of cognitive development. In D. Kuhn, R. Siegler (Vol. Eds.), W. Damon, & R. M. Lerner (Series Eds.), *Handbook of child psychology. Vol. 2: Cognition, perception, and language* (6th ed., pp. 3–57). New York: Wiley.

Nelson, K. (1973). Structure and strategy in learning to talk. *Monographs of the Society for Research in Child Development, 38*(1–2, Serial No. 149).

Nelson, K. (Ed.). (1986). *Event knowledge: Structure and function in development.* Hillsdale, NJ: Erlbaum.

Nelson, K. (1996a). *Language in cognitive development: The emergence of the mediated mind.* Cambridge, England: Cambridge University Press.

Nelson, K. (1996b). Memory development from 4 to 7 years. In A. J. Sameroff & M. M. Haith (Eds.), *The 5 to 7 shift* (pp. 141–160). Chicago: University of Chicago Press.

Nelson, K. (1997). Event representations then, now, and next. In P. van den Broek, P. J. Bauer, & T. Bourg (Eds.), *Developmental spans in event representation and comprehension: Bridging fictional and actual events* (pp. 1–26). Mahwah, NJ: Erlbaum.

Nelson, K. (2005). Evolution and development of human memory systems. In B. J. Ellis & D. F. Bjorklund (Eds.), *Origins of the social mind: Evolutionary psychology and child development* (pp. 354–382). New York: Guilford Press.

Nettelbeck, T., & Wilson, C. (2005). Intelligence and IQ: What teachers should know. *Educational Psychology, 25*(6), 609–630.

Nevid, J. S., Rathus, S. A., & Greene, B. (2006). *Abnormal psychology in a changing world* (6th ed.). Upper Saddle River, NJ: Pearson Prentice Hall.

Neville, H. J., & Bavelier, D. (2001). Variability of developmental plasticity. In J. L. McClelland & R. S. Siegler (Eds.), *Mechanisms of cognitive development: Behavioral and neural perspectives* (pp. 271–287). Mahwah, NJ: Erlbaum.

Newcomb, A. F., & Bagwell, C. L. (1995). Children's friendship relations: A meta-analysis review. *Psychological Bulletin, 117,* 306–347.

Newcomb, A. F., & Brady, J. E. (1982). Mutuality in boys' friendship relations. *Child Development, 53,* 392–395.

Newcomb, A. F., & Bukowski, W. M. (1984). A longitudinal study of the utility of social preference and social impact sociometric classification schemes. *Child Development, 55,* 1434–1447.

Newcomb, A. F., Bukowski, W. M., & Pattee, L. (1993). Children's peer relations: A meta-analytic review of popular, rejected, controversial, and average sociometric status. *Psychological Bulletin, 113,* 99–128.

Newcomb, N. S., Drummey, A. B., Fox, N. A., Lie, E., & Ottinger-Albergs, W. (2000). Remembering early childhood: How much, how, and why (or why not). *Current Directions in Psychological Science, 9,* 55–58.

Newcombe, N. S., Sluzenski, J., & Huttenlocher, J. (2005). Preexisting knowledge versus on-line learning: What do young infants really know about spatial location? *Psychological Science, 16,* 222–227.

Newell, G. E., Koukis, S., & Boster, S. (2007). Best practices in developing a writing across the curriculum program in the secondary school. In S. Graham, C. A. MacArthur, & J. Fitzgerald (Eds.), *Best practices in writing instruction: Solving problems in the teaching of literacy* (pp. 74–98). New York: Guilford.

Newkirk, T. (2002). *Misreading masculinity: Boys, literacy, and popular culture.* Portsmouth, NH: Heinemann.

Newman, L. S. (1990). Intentional and unintentional memory in young children: Remembering vs. playing. *Journal of Experimental Child Psychology, 50,* 243–258.

Newman, R. S., & Schwager, M. T. (1992). Student perceptions and academic help seeking. In D. Schunk & J. Meece (Eds.), *Student perceptions in the classroom.* Hillsdale, NJ: Erlbaum.

Newman, S. (2001). *Parenting and only child: The joys and challenges of raising your one and only.* New York: Broadway Books.

Newport, E. L. (1990). Maturational constraints on language learning. *Cognitive Science, 14,* 11–28.

Newson, J., & Newson, E. (1975). Intersubjectivity and the transmission of culture: On the origins of symbolic functioning. *Bulletin of the British Psychological Society, 28,* 437–446.

Ng, F. F., Kenney-Benson, G. A., & Pomerantz, E. M. (2004). Children's achievement moderates the effects of mothers' use of control and autonomy support. *Child Development, 75,* 764–780.

Nguyen, S. P., & Murphy, G. L. (2003). An apple is more than just a fruit: Cross-classification in children's concepts. *Child Development, 74,* 1783–1806.

Ni, Y., & Zhou, Y.-D. (2005). Teaching and learning fraction and rational numbers: The origins and implications of whole number bias. *Educational Psychologist, 40,* 27–52.

NICHD Early Child Care Research Network. (1997). The effects of infant child care on infant-mother attachment security: Results of the NICHD study of early child care. *Child Development, 68,* 860–879.

NICHD Early Child Care Research Network. (2002). Early child care and children's development prior to school entry: Results from the NICHD study of early child care. *American Educational Research Journal, 39*(1), 133–164.

NICHD Early Child Care Research Network. (2005). Early child care and children's development in the primary grades: Follow-up results from the NICHD study of early child care. *American Educational Research Journal, 42*(3), 537–570.

NICHD Early Child Care Research Network. (2006a). Child-care effect sizes for the NICHD Study of Early Child Care and Youth Development. *American Psychologist, 61,* 99–116.

NICHD Early Child Care Research Network. (2006b). Infant-mother attachment classification: Risk and protection in relation to changing maternal caregiving quality. *Developmental Psychology, 42,* 38–58.

Nicholls, J. G. (1984). Conceptions of ability and achievement motivation. In R. Ames & C. Ames (Eds.), *Research on motivation in education: Vol. 1. Student motivation.* San Diego, CA: Academic Press.

Nicholls, J. G. (1990). What is ability and why are we mindful of it? A developmental perspective. In R. J. Sternberg & J. Kolligian (Eds.), *Competence considered.* New Haven, CT: Yale University Press.

Nicholls, J. G., Cobb, P., Yackel, E., Wood, T., & Wheatley, G. (1990). Students' theories of mathematics and their mathematical knowledge: Multiple dimensions of assessment. In G. Kulm (Ed.), *Assessing higher order thinking in mathematics.* Washington, DC: American Association for the Advancement of Science.

Nichols, M. L., & Ganschow, L. (1992). Has there been a paradigm shift in gifted education? In N. Coangelo, S. G. Assouline, & D. L. Ambroson (Eds.), *Talent development: Proceedings from the 1991 Henry B. and Jocelyn Wallace National Research Symposium on Talent Development.* New York: Trillium.

Nichter, M., Nichter, M., Muramoto, M., Adrian, S., Goldade, K., Tesler, L., et al. (2007). Smoking among low-income pregnant women: An ethnographic analysis. *Health Education and Behavior, 34*(5), 748–764.

Nickerson, A. B., & Nagle, R. J. (2005). Parent and peer attachment in late childhood and early adolescence. *Journal of Early Adolescence, 25,* 223–249.

Nicolopoulou, A., & Richner, E. S. (2007). From actors to agents to persons: The development of character representation in young children's narratives. *Child Development, 78,* 412–429.

Nicolson, S., & Shipstead, S. G. (2002). *Through the looking glass: Observations in the early childhood classroom* (3rd ed.). Upper Saddle River, NJ: Merrill/Prentice Hall.

Nieto, S. (1995). *Affirming diversity* (2nd ed.). White Plains, NY: Longman.

Nievar, M. A., & Becker, B. J. (2008). Sensitivity as a privileged predictor of attachment: A second perspective on De Wolff and van IJzendoorn's meta-analysis. *Social Development, 17,* 102–114.

Nilsson, D. E., & Bradford, L. W. (1999). Neurofibromatosis. In S. Goldstein & C. R. Reynolds (Eds.), *Handbook of neurodevelopmental and genetic disorders* (pp. 350–367). New York: Guilford Press.

Nippold, M. A. (1988). The literate lexicon. In M. A. Nippold (Ed.), *Later language development: Ages nine through nineteen.* Boston: Little, Brown.

Nippold, M. A., & Taylor, C. L. (1995). Idiom understanding in youth: Further examination of familiarity and transparency. *Journal of Speech and Hearing Research, 38,* 426–433.

Nippold, M. A., Ward-Lonergan, J. M., & Fanning, J. L. (2005). Persuasive writing in children, adolescents, and adults: A study of syntactic, semantic, and pragmatic development. *Language, Speech, and Hearing Services in Schools, 36*(2), 125–138.

Nisbett, R. E. (2005). Heredity, environment, and race: Differences in IQ: A commentary on Rushton and Jensen. *Psychology, Public Policy, and Law, 11,* 302–310.

Nix, R. L., Pinderhughes, E. E., Dodge, K. A., Bates, J. E., Pettit, G. S., & McFadyen-Ketchum, S. A. (1999). The relation between mothers' hostile attribution tendencies and children's externalizing behavior problems: The mediating role of mothers' harsh discipline practices. *Child Development, 70,* 896–909.

Nixon, S. M. (2005). Mental state verb production and sentential complements in four-year-old children. *First Language, 25*(1), 19–37.

Noffke, S. (1997). Professional, personal, and political dimensions of action research. *Review of Research in Education, 22,* 305–343.

Noguera, P. A. (2003). "Joachín's dilemma": Understanding the link between racial identity and school-related behaviors. In M. Sadowski (Eds.), *Adolescents at school: Perspectives on youth, identity, and education* (pp. 19–30). Cambridge, MA: Harvard Education Press.

Nokes, J. D., Dole, J. A., & Hacker, D. J. (2007). Teaching high school students to use heuristics while reading historical texts. *Journal of Educational Psychology, 99,* 492–504.

Nolen-Hoeksema, S., Morrow, J., & Fredrickson, B. L. (1993). Response styles and the duration of episodes of depressed moods. *Journal of Abnormal Psychology, 102,* 20–28.

Nomura, Y., Fifer, W., & Brooks-Gunn, J. (2005). *The role of perinatal factors for risk of co-occurring psychiatric and medical disorders in adulthood.* Paper presented at the biennial meeting of the Society for Research in Child Development, Atlanta, GA.

Norenzayan, A., Choi, I., & Peng, K. (2007). Perception and cognition. In S. Kitayama & D. Cohen (Eds.), *Handbook of cultural psychology* (pp. 569–594). New York: Guilford Press.

North Central Regional Educational Laboratory. (2008). Implementing the No Child Left Behind Act: Implications for rural schools and districts. Retrieved August 12, 2008, from http://www.ncrel .org/policy/pubs/html/implicate/challenge.htm

Northrup, J. C., & Bean, R. A. (2007). Culturally competent family therapy with Latino/Anglo American adolescents: Facilitating identity formation. *American Journal of Family Therapy, 35,* 251–263.

Nucci, L. (2009). *Nice is not enough: Facilitating moral development.* Columbus, OH: Merrill Pearson.

Nucci, L. P. (2001). *Education in the moral domain.* Cambridge, England: Cambridge University Press.

Nucci, L. P. (2006). Education for moral development. In M. Killen & J. G. Smetana (Eds.), *Handbook of moral development* (pp. 657–681). Mahwah, NJ: Erlbaum.

Nucci, L. P., & Nucci, M. S. (1982). Children's social interactions in the context of moral and conventional transgressions. *Child Development, 53,* 403–412.

Nucci, L. P., & Weber, E. K. (1991). The domain approach to values education: From theory to practice. In W. M. Kurtines & J. L. Gewirtz (Eds.), *Handbook of moral behavior and development: Vol. 3. Application* (pp. 251–266). Hillsdale, NJ: Erlbaum.

Nucci, L. P., & Weber, E. K. (1995). Social interactions in the home and the development of young children's conceptions of the personal. *Child Development, 66,* 1438–1452.

Nunner-Winkler, G. (1984). Two moralities? A critical discussion of an ethic of care and responsibility versus an ethic of rights and justice. In W. M. Kurtines & J. L. Gewirtz (Eds.), *Morality, moral behavior, and moral development.* New York: Wiley.

Nuttall, R. L., Casey, M. B., & Pezaris, E. (2005). Spatial ability as mediator of gender differences on mathematics tests. In A. M. Gallagher & J. C. Kaufman (Eds.), *Gender differences in mathematics: An integrative psychological approach* (pp. 121–142). Cambridge, England: Cambridge University Press.

Oakes, J., & Guiton, G. (1995). Matchmaking: The dynamics of high school tracking decisions. *American Educational Research Journal, 32,* 3–33.

Oakes, L. M., & Bauer, P. J. (Eds.) (2007). *Short- and long-term memory in infancy and early childhood: Taking the first steps toward remembering.* New York: Oxford University Press.

Oakes, L. M., Kannass, K. N., & Shaddy, D. J. (2002). Developmental changes in endogenous control of attention: The role of target familiarity on infants' distraction latency. *Child Development, 73,* 1644–1655.

Oakes, L. M., & Rakison, D. H. (2003). Issues in the early development of concepts and categories: An introduction. In D. H. Rakison & L. M. Oakes (Eds.), *Early category and concept development: Making sense of the blooming, buzzing confusion* (pp. 3–23). Oxford, England: Oxford University Press.

Oatley, K., & Nundy, S. (1996). Rethinking the role of emotions in education. In D. R. Olson & N. Torrance (Eds.), *The handbook of education and human development: New models of learning, teaching, and schooling.* Cambridge, MA: Blackwell.

O'Boyle, M. W., & Gill, H. S. (1998). On the relevance of research findings in cognitive neuroscience to educational practice. *Educational Psychology Review, 10,* 397–409.

Ochs, E. (2002). Becoming a speaker of culture. In C. Kramsch (Ed), *Language acquisition and language socialization* (pp. 99–120). London: Continuum.

Ochs, E., & Schieffelin, B. (1995). The impact of language socialization on grammatical development. In P. Fletcher & B. MacWhinney (Eds.), *The handbook of child language.* Cambridge, MA: Blackwell.

O'Connor, E., & McCartney, K. (2006). Testing associations between young children's relationships with mothers and teachers. *Journal of Educational Psychology, 98,* 87–98.

O'Connor, T. G. (2006). Toward integrating behavioral genetics and family process. *Family Systems and Health, 24,* 416–424.

O'Connor, T. G., Deater-Deckard, K., Fulker, D., Rutter, M., & Plomin, R. (1998). Genotype-environment correlations in late childhood and early adolescence: Antisocial behavioral problems and coercive parenting. *Developmental Psychology, 34,* 970–981.

Odent, M. (2005). Genesis of sexual orientation: From Plato to Dorner. *Journal of Prenatal and Perinatal Psychology and Health, 20*(1), 49–57.

Office for Human Research Protections. (2007). *Special protections for children as research subjects.* Retrieved October 3, 2007, from http:// www.hhs.gov/ohrp/children

Ogbu, J. U. (1994). From cultural differences to differences in cultural frames of reference. In P. M.

Greenfield & R. R. Cocking (Eds.), *Cross-cultural roots of minority child development* (pp. 365–391). Hillsdale, NJ: Erlbaum.

Ogbu, J. U. (1999). Beyond language: Ebonics, proper English, and identity in a Black-American speech community. *American Educational Research Journal, 36,* 147–184.

Ogbu, J. U. (2003). *Black American students in an affluent suburb: A study of academic disengagement.* Mahwah, NJ: Erlbaum.

Ogden, E. H., & Germinario, V. (1988). *The at-risk student: Answers for educators.* Lancaster, PA: Technomic.

O'Grady, W. (1997). *Syntactic development.* Chicago: University of Chicago Press.

Okagaki, L. (2001). Triarchic model of minority children's school achievement. *Educational Psychologist, 36,* 9–20.

Okagaki, L. (2006). Ethnicity and learning. In P. A. Alexander & P. H. Winne (Eds.), *Handbook of educational psychology* (2nd ed., pp. 615–634). Mahwah, NJ: Erlbaum.

Okagaki, L., & Sternberg, R. J. (1993). Parental beliefs and children's school performance. *Child Development, 64,* 36–56.

Oldfather, P., & West, J. (1999). *Learning through children's eyes: Social constructivism and the desire to learn.* Washington, DC: American Psychological Association.

O'Leary, K. D., & O'Leary, S. G. (Eds.). (1972). *Classroom management: The successful use of behavior modification.* New York: Pergamon Press.

O'Leary, S. G., & Vidair, H. B. (2005). Marital adjustment, child-rearing disagreements, and overreactive parenting: Predicting child behavior problems. *Journal of Family Psychology, 19,* 208–216.

Olmsted, B. J. (2008). *The effects of interactive video (DDR) on heart rate, perceived exertion, step count, self-efficacy, and enjoyment in elementary school children.* Dissertation Abstracts International Section A: Humanities and Social Sciences, 68(8-A).

Olshansky, B. (1995). Picture this: An arts-based literacy program. *Educational Leadership, 53*(1), 44–47.

Olshansky, B., O'Connor, S., & O'Byrne, S. (2006, April). *Picture writing: Fostering literacy through art—diverse perspectives.* Paper presented at the annual meeting of the American Educational Research Association, San Francisco, CA.

Oltmanns, T. F., & Emery, R. E. (2007). *Abnormal psychology* (5th ed.). Upper Saddle River, NJ: Pearson Prentice Hall.

O'Malley, P. M., & Bachman, J. G. (1983). Self-esteem: Change and stability between ages 13 and 23. *Developmental Psychology, 19,* 257–268.

Oortwijn, M. B., Boekaerts, M., Vedder, P., & Fortuin, J. (2008). The impact of a cooperative learning experience on pupils' popularity, non-cooperativeness, and interethnic bias in multiethnic elementary schools. *Educational Psychology, 28*(2), 211–221.

Oppenheim, D., Koren-Karie, N., Dolev, S., & Yirmiya, N. (2008). Secure attachment in children with autism spectrum disorders. *Zero to Three, 28*(4), 25–30.

Oppenheimer, L. (1986). Development of recursive thinking: Procedural variations. *International Journal of Behavioral Development, 9,* 401–411.

O'Reilly, A. W. (1995). Using representations: Comprehension and production of actions with imagined objects. *Child Development, 66,* 999–1010.

Orme, J. G., & Buehler, C. (2001). Foster family characteristics and behavioral and emotional problems of foster children: A narrative review. *Family Relations, 50,* 3–15.

Ormrod, J. E. (2008a). *Educational psychology: Developing learners* (6th ed.). Upper Saddle River, NJ: Merrill/Prentice Hall.

Ormrod, J. E. (2008b). *Human learning* (5th ed.). Upper Saddle River, NJ: Merrill/Prentice Hall.

Ormrod, J. E., Jackson, D. L., Kirby, B., Davis, J., & Benson, C. (1999, April). *Cognitive development as reflected in children's conceptions of early*

American history. Paper presented at the annual meeting of the American Educational Research Association, Montreal, Canada.

Ormrod, J. E., & McGuire, D. J. (2007). *Case studies: Applying educational psychology* (2nd ed.). Upper Saddle River, NJ: Merrill/Prentice Hall.

Ornstein, R. (1997). *The right mind: Making sense of the hemispheres.* San Diego, CA: Harcourt Brace.

Orobio de Castro, B., Veerman, J. W., Koops, W., Bosch, J. D., & Monshouwer, H. J. (2002). Hostile attribution of intent and aggressive behavior: A meta-analysis. *Child Development, 73,* 916–934.

Ortony, A., Turner, T. J., & Larson-Shapiro, N. (1985). Cultural and instructional influences on figurative comprehension by inner city children. *Research in the Teaching of English, 19*(1), 25–36.

Oskamp, S. (Ed.). (2000). *Reducing prejudice and discrimination.* Mahwah, NJ: Erlbaum.

Osterman, K. F. (2000). Students' need for belonging in the school community. *Review of Educational Research, 70,* 323–367.

Otis, N., Grouzet, F. M. E., & Pelletier, L. G. (2005). Latent motivational change in an academic setting: A 3-year longitudinal study. *Journal of Educational Psychology, 97,* 170–183.

O'Toole, M. E. (2000). *The school shooter: A threat assessment perspective.* Quantico, VA: Federal Bureau of Investigation. Retrieved February 26, 2004, from http://www.fbi.gov/publications/school/school2.pdf

Owens, C. R., & Ascione, F. R. (1991). Effects of the model's age, perceived similarity, and familiarity on children's donating. *Journal of Genetic Psychology, 152,* 341–357.

Owens, R. E., Jr. (1996). *Language development* (4th ed.). Boston: Allyn & Bacon.

Owens, R. E., Jr. (2008). *Language development* (7th ed.). Boston: Allyn & Bacon.

Oyserman, D., & Lee, S. W.-S. (2007). Priming "culture": Culture as situated cognition. In S. Kitayama & D. Cohen (Eds.), *Handbook of cultural psychology* (pp. 255–279). New York: Guilford Press.

Oyserman, D., & Markus, H. R. (1993). The sociocultural self. In J. Suls (Ed.), *Psychological perspectives on the self* (Vol. 7, pp. 187–220). Mahwah, NJ: Erlbaum.

Padilla, A. M. (2006). Second language learning: Issues in research and teaching. In P. A. Alexander & P. H. Winne (Eds.), *Handbook of educational psychology* (2nd ed., pp. 571–591). Mahwah, NJ: Erlbaum.

Padilla, M. J. (1991). Science activities, process skills, and thinking. In S. M. Glynn, R. H. Yeany, & B. K. Britton (Eds.), *The psychology of learning science.* Hillsdale, NJ: Erlbaum.

Padilla-Walker, L. M., & Carlo, G. (2007). Personal values as a mediator between parent and peer expectations and adolescent behaviors. *Journal of Family Psychology, 21,* 538–541.

Paget, K. F., Kritt, D., & Bergemann, L. (1984). Understanding strategic interactions in television commercials: A developmental study. *Journal of Applied Developmental Psychology, 5,* 145–161.

Page-Voth, V., & Graham, S. (1999). Effects of goal setting and strategy use on the writing performance and self-efficacy of students with writing and learning problems. *Journal of Educational Psychology, 91,* 230–240.

Pahl, K., & Way, N. (2006). Longitudinal trajectories of ethnic identity among urban Black and Latino adolescents. *Child Development, 77,* 1403–1415.

Paikoff, R. L., & Brooks-Gunn, J. (1991). Do parent–child relationships change during puberty? *Psychological Bulletin, 110,* 47–66.

Pajares, F. (1996). Self-efficacy beliefs in academic settings. *Review of Educational Research, 66,* 543–578.

Pajares, F. (2005). Gender differences in mathematics self-efficacy beliefs. In A. M. Gallagher & J. C. Kaufman (Eds.), *Gender differences in mathematics: An integrative psychological approach* (pp. 294–315). Cambridge, England: Cambridge University Press.

Pajares, F., & Valiante, G. (1999). *Writing self-efficacy of middle school students: Relation to motivation constructs, achievement, gender, and gender orientation.* Paper presented at the annual meeting of the American Educational Research Association, Montreal, Canada.

Palacios, J., & Sánchez-Sandoval, Y. (2005). Beyond adopted/nonadopted comparisons. In D. M. Brodzinsky & J. Palacios (Eds.), *Psychological issues in adoption: Research and practice* (pp. 117–144). Westport, CT: Praeger/Greenwood.

Palermo, D. S. (1974). Still more about the comprehension of "less." *Developmental Psychology, 10,* 827–829.

Paley, V. G. (1984). *Boys and girls: Superheroes in the doll corner.* Chicago: University of Chicago Press.

Palincsar, A. S., & Brown, A. L. (1984). Reciprocal teaching of comprehension-fostering and comprehension-monitoring activities. *Cognition and Instruction, 1,* 117–175.

Palincsar, A. S., & Brown, A. L. (1989). Classroom dialogues to promote self-regulated comprehension. In J. Brophy (Ed.), *Advances in research on teaching* (Vol. 1). Greenwich, CT: JAI Press.

Palincsar, A. S., & Herrenkohl, L. R. (1999). Designing collaborative contexts: Lessons from three research programs. In A. M. O'Donnell & A. King (Eds.), *Cognitive perspectives on peer learning* (pp. 151–177). Mahwah, NJ: Erlbaum.

Pallotta, J., & Masiello, R. (Illustrator) (1992). *The icky bug counting book.* Watertown, MA: Charlesbridge.

Palmer, E. L. (1965). Accelerating the child's cognitive attainments through the inducement of cognitive conflict: An interpretation of the Piagetian position. *Journal of Research in Science Teaching, 3,* 324.

Pan, B. A., Rowe, M. L., Singer, J. D., & Snow, C. E. (2005). Maternal correlates of growth in toddler vocabulary production in low-income families. *Child Development, 76,* 763–782.

Pang, V. O. (1995). Asian Pacific American students: A diverse and complex population. In J. A. Banks & C. A. M. Banks (Eds.), *Handbook of research on multicultural education.* New York: Macmillan.

Panksepp, J. (1986). The psychobiology of prosocial behaviors: Separation distress, play, and altruism. In C. Zahn-Waxler, E. M. Cummings, & R. Iannotti (Eds.), *Altruism and aggression: Biological and social origins* (pp. 19–57). Cambridge, England: Cambridge University Press.

Panksepp, J. (1998). Attention deficit hyperactivity disorders, psychostimulants, and intolerance of childhood playfulness: A tragedy in the making? *Current Directions in Psychological Science, 7,* 91–98.

Panofsky, C. P. (1994). Developing the representational functions of language: The role of parent–child book-reading activity. In V. John-Steiner, C. P. Panofsky, & L. W. Smith (Eds.), *Sociocultural approaches to language and literacy: An interactionist perspective.* Cambridge, England: Cambridge University Press.

Paris, S. G. (1990, April). Discussant's comments. In B. McCombs (Chair), *Theoretical perspectives on socialization and children's development of self-regulated learning.* Symposium presented at the annual meeting of the American Educational Research Association, Boston.

Paris, S. G., & Ayres, L. R. (1994). *Becoming reflective students and teachers with portfolios and authentic assessment.* Washington, DC: American Psychological Association.

Paris, S. G., & Byrnes, J. P. (1989). The constructivist approach to self-regulation and learning in the classroom. In B. J. Zimmerman & D. H. Schunk (Eds.), *Self-regulated learning and academic achievement: Theory, research, and practice.* New York: Springer-Verlag.

Paris, S. G., & Cunningham, A. E. (1996). Children becoming students. In D. C. Berliner & R. C. Calfee (Eds.), *Handbook of educational psychology.* New York: Macmillan.

Paris, S. G., Morrison, F. J., & Miller, K. F. (2006). Academic pathways from preschool through elementary school. In P. A. Alexander & P. H. Winne (Eds.), *Handbook of educational psychology* (2nd ed., pp. 61–85). Mahwah, NJ: Erlbaum.

Paris, S. G., & Turner, J. C. (1994). Situated motivation. In P. R. Pintrich, D. R. Brown, & C. E. Weinstein (Eds.), *Student motivation, cognition, and learning: Essays in honor of Wilbert J. McKeachie.* Mahwah, NJ: Erlbaum.

Paris, S. G., & Upton, L. R. (1976). Children's memory for inferential relationships in prose. *Child Development, 47,* 660–668.

Parish, P., & Sweat, L. (2003). *Amelia Bedelia goes camping.* New York: HarperCollins.

Park, L. E., Crocker, J., & Kiefer, A. K. (2007). Contingencies of self-worth, academic failure, and goal pursuit. *Personality and Social Psychology Bulletin, 33,* 1503–1517.

Park, L. E., Crocker, J., & Vohs, K. D. (2006). Contingencies of self-worth and self-validation goals: Implications for close relationships. In K. D. Vohs & E. J. Finkel (Eds.), *Self and relationships: Connecting intrapersonal and interpersonal processes* (pp. 84–103). New York: Guilford Press.

Parke, R. D., & Bhavnagri, N. P. (1989). Parents as managers of children's peer relationships. In D. Belle (Ed.), *Children's social networks and social supports.* New York: Wiley.

Parke, R. D., & Buriel, R. (2006). Socialization in the family: Ethnic and ecological perspectives. In W. Damon & R. M. Lerner (Eds. in Chief) & N. Eisenberg (Vol. Ed.), *Handbook of child psychology: Vol. 3. Social, emotional, and personality development* (6th ed., pp. 429–504). Hoboken, NJ: Wiley.

Parke, R. D., Coltrane, S., Duffy, S., Buriel, R., Dennis, J., Powers, J., et al. (2004). Economic stress, parenting, and child adjustment in Mexican American and European American families. *Child Development, 75,* 1632–1656.

Parke, R. D., Ornstein, P. A., Rieser, J. J., & Zahn-Waxler, C. (1994). The past as prologue: An overview of a century of developmental psychology. In R. D. Parke, P. A. Ornstein, J. J. Rieser, & C. Zahn-Waxler (Eds.), *A century of developmental psychology* (pp. 1–70). Washington, DC: American Psychological Association.

Parker, J. G. (1986). Becoming friends: Conversational skills for friendship formation in young children. In J. M. Gottman & J. G. Parker (Eds.), *Conversations of friends: Speculations on affective development* (pp. 103–138). Cambridge, England: Cambridge University Press.

Parker, J. G., & Gottman, J. M. (1989). Social and emotional development in a relational context: Friendship interaction from early childhood to adolescence. In T. J. Berndt & G. W. Ladd (Eds.), *Peer relations in child development* (pp. 95–131). New York: Wiley.

Parker, J. G., Low, C. M., Walker, A. R., & Gamm, B. K. (2005). Friendship jealousy in young adolescents: Individual differences and links to sex, self-esteem, aggression, and social adjustment. *Developmental Psychology, 41,* 235–250.

Parker, W. D. (1997). An empirical typology of perfectionism in academically talented children. *American Educational Research Journal, 34,* 545–562.

Parkhurst, J., & Gottman, J. M. (1986). How young children get what they want. In J. M. Gottman & J. G. Parker (Eds.), *Conversations of friends: Speculations on affective development* (pp. 315–345). Cambridge, England: Cambridge University Press.

Parkhurst, J. T., & Hopmeyer, A. (1998). Socio-metric popularity and peer-perceived popularity: Two distinct dimensions of peer status. *Journal of Early Adolescence, 18,* 125–144.

Parks, C. P. (1995). Gang behavior in the schools: Reality or myth? *Educational Psychology Review, 7,* 41–68.

Parten, M. B. (1932). Social participation among preschool children. *Journal of Abnormal and Social Psychology, 27,* 243–269.

Pascarella, E. T., & Terenzini, P. T. (1991). *How college affects students: Findings and insights from twenty years of research.* San Francisco: Jossey-Bass.

Pascual-Leone, J. (1970). A mathematical model for the transition rule in Piaget's developmental stages. *Acta Psychologica, 32,* 301–345.

Patall, E. A., Cooper, H., & Wynn, S. (2008, March). *The importance of providing choices in the classroom.* Paper presented at the annual meeting of the American Educational Research Association, New York.

Pate, R. R., Long, B. J., & Heath, G. (1994). Descriptive epidemiology of physical activity in adolescents. *Pediatric Exercise Science, 6,* 434–447.

Patel, T. K., Snowling, M. J., & de Jong, P. F. (2004). A cross-linguistic comparison of children learning to read in English and Dutch. *Journal of Educational Psychology, 96,* 785–797.

Patrick, H. (1997). Social self-regulation: Exploring the relations between children's social relationships, academic self-regulation, and school performance. *Educational Psychologist, 32,* 209–220.

Patrick, H., Mantzicopoulos, Y., & Samarapungavan, A. (2009, March). *Sex differences in young children's motivation for science.* Poster presented at the annual meeting of the American Educational Research Association, New York.

Patterson, C. J. (1995). Sexual orientation and human development: An overview. *Developmental Psychology, 31,* 3–11.

Patterson, C. J. (2006). Children of lesbian and gay parents. *Current Directions in Psychological Science, 15,* 241–244.

Patterson, C. J., & Hastings, P. D. (2007). Socialization in the context of family diversity. In J. E. Grusec & P. D. Hastings (Eds.), *Handbook of socialization: Theory and research* (pp. 328–351). New York: Guilford.

Patterson, G. R., DeBaryshe, B. D., & Ramsey, E. (1989). A developmental perspective on antisocial behavior. *American Psychologist, 44,* 329–335.

Patterson, G. R., & Reid, J. B. (1970). Reciprocity and coercion: Two facets of social systems. In C. Neuringer & J. Michael (Eds.), *Behavior modification in clinical psychology.* New York: Appleton-Century-Crofts.

Patton, J. R., Blackbourn, J. M., & Fad, K. (1996). *Exceptional individuals in focus* (6th ed.). Upper Saddle River, NJ: Merrill/Prentice Hall.

Pauen, S. (2002). Evidence for knowledge-based category discrimination in infancy. *Child Development, 73,* 1016–1033.

Paul, R. (1990). Comprehension strategies: Interactions between world knowledge and the development of sentence comprehension. *Topics in Language Disorders, 10*(3), 63–75.

Paus, T. (2005). Brain mapping. In C. B. Fisher & R. M. Lerner (Eds.), *Encyclopedia of applied developmental science* (Vol. 1, pp. 178–181). Thousand Oaks, CA: Sage.

Paus, T., Zijdenbos, A., Worsley, K., Collins, D. I., Blumenthal, J., Giedd, J. N., et al. (1999). Structural maturation of neural pathways in children and adolescents: in vivo study. *Science, 283,* 1908–1911.

Pawlas, G. E. (1994). Homeless students at the school door. *Educational Leadership, 51*(8), 79–82.

Paxton, R. J. (1999). A deafening silence: History textbooks and the students who read them. *Review of Educational Research, 69,* 315–339.

Payne, R. K. (2005). *A framework for understanding poverty* (4th rev. ed.). Highlands, TX: aha! Process, Inc.

PE 4 Life (n.d.). The First Choice physical fitness program. Retrieved September 26, 2008, from http://www.pe4life.org/UserFiles/File/FirstChoice.pdf

Pea, R. D. (1993). Practices of distributed intelligence and designs for education. In G. Salomon (Ed.), *Distributed cognitions: Psychological and educational considerations.* Cambridge, England: Cambridge University Press.

Peak, L. (1993). Academic effort in international perspective. In T. M. Tomlinson (Ed.), *Motivating students to learn: Overcoming barriers to high achievement.* Berkeley, CA: McCutchan.

Pearson, P. D., Hansen, J., & Gordon, C. (1979). The effect of background knowledge on young children's comprehension of explicit and implicit information. *Journal of Reading Behavior, 11,* 201–209.

Peck, S. C., Roeser, R. W., Zarrett, N., & Eccles, J. S. (2008). Exploring the roles of extracurricular activity quantity and quality in the educational resilience of vulnerable adolescents: Variable- and pattern-centered approaches. *Journal of Social Issues, 64*(1), 135–155.

Pederson, D. R., Rook-Green, A., & Elder, J. L. (1981). The role of action in the development of pretend play in young children. *Developmental Psychology, 17,* 756–759.

Pedro-Carroll, J. L. (2005). Fostering resilience in the aftermath of divorce: The role of evidence-based programs for children. *Family Court Review, 43,* 52–64.

Peets, K., Hodges, E. V. E., Kikas, E., & Salmivalli, C. (2007). Hostile attributions and behavioral strategies in children. Does relationship matter? *Developmental Psychology, 43,* 889–900.

Pegg, P. O., & Plybon, L. E. (2005). Toward the theoretical measurement of ethnic identity. *Journal of Early Adolescence, 25,* 250–264.

Pellegrini, A. D. (1996). *Observing children in their natural worlds: A methodological primer.* Mahwah, NJ: Erlbaum.

Pellegrini, A. D. (2002). Bullying, victimization, and sexual harassment during the transition to middle school. *Educational Psychologist, 37,* 151–163.

Pellegrini, A. D. (2006). The development and function of rough-and-tumble play in childhood and adolescence: A sexual selection theory perspective. In A. Göncü & S. Gaskins (Eds.), *Play and development: Evolutionary, sociocultural, and functional perspectives* (pp. 77–98) Mahwah, NJ: Erlbaum.

Pellegrini, A. D., & Bartini, M. (2000). A longitudinal study of bullying, victimization, and peer affiliation during the transition from primary school to middle school. *American Educational Research Journal, 37,* 699–725.

Pellegrini, A. D., Bartini, M., & Brooks, F. (1999). School bullies, victims, and aggressive victims: Factors relating to group affiliation and victimization in early adolescence. *Journal of Educational Psychology, 91,* 216–224.

Pellegrini, A. D., & Bjorklund, D. F. (1997). The role of recess in children's cognitive performance. *Educational Psychologist, 32,* 35–40.

Pellegrini, A. D., & Bohn, C. M. (2005). The role of recess in children's cognitive performance and school adjustment. *Educational Researcher, 34*(1), 13–19.

Pellegrini, A. D., & Horvat, M. (1995). A developmental contextualist critique of attention deficit hyperactivity disorder. *Educational Researcher, 24*(1), 13–19.

Pence, K. L., & Justice, L. M. (2008). *Language development from theory to practice.* Upper Saddle River, NJ: Merrill/Prentice Hall.

Penner, A. M. (2003). International gender X item difficulty interactions in mathematics and science achievement tests. *Journal of Educational Psychology, 95,* 650–655.

Pennington, B. F., & Bennetto, L. (1993). Main effects of transactions in the neuropsychology of conduct disorder. Commentary on "The neuropsychology of conduct disorder." *Development and Psychopathology, 5,* 153–164.

Peralta, O. A., & Maita, M. D. R. (2007, March). *Teaching very young children the symbolic function of a map.* Paper presented at the biennial meeting of the Society for Research in Child Development, Boston.

Pérez, B. (Ed.). (1998). *Sociocultural contexts of language and literacy.* Mahwah, NJ: Erlbaum.

Perfetti, C. A. (1985). Reading ability. In R. J. Sternberg (Ed.), *Human abilities: An information-processing approach.* New York: Freeman.

Perfetti, C. A., & McCutchen, D. (1987). Schooled language competence: Linguistic abilities in reading and writing. In S. Rosenberg (Ed.), *Advances in applied psycholinguistics*. Cambridge, England: Cambridge University Press.

Perkins, D. N. (1992). *Smart schools: From training memories to educating minds*. New York: Free Press/Macmillan.

Perkins, D. N. (1995). *Outsmarting IQ: The emerging science of learnable intelligence*. New York: Free Press.

Perkins, D. N., & Grotzer, T. A. (1997). Teaching intelligence. *American Psychologist, 52*, 1125–1133.

Perkins, D., & Ritchhart, R. (2004). When is good thinking? In D. Y. Dai & R. J. Sternberg (Eds.), *Motivation, emotion, and cognition: Integrative perspectives on intellectual functioning and development* (pp. 351–384). Mahwah, NJ: Erlbaum.

Perkins-Gough, D. (2007, October). Giving intervention a Head Start: A conversation with Edward Zigler. *Educational Leadership, 65*(2), 8–14.

Perner, J., Lang, B., & Kloo, D. (2002). Theory of mind and self-control: More than a common problem of inhibition. *Child Development, 73*, 752–767.

Perner, J., & Wimmer, H. (1985). "John *thinks* that Mary *thinks* that . . .?" Attribution of second-order beliefs by 5- to 10-year-old children. *Journal of Experimental Child Psychology, 39*, 437–471.

Perry, A. J. (2005). Confirmatory program evaluation: Applications to early childhood interventions. *Teachers College Record, 107*(10), 2401–2425.

Perry, M. (2000). Explanations of mathematical concepts in Japanese, Chinese, and U.S. first- and fifth-grade classrooms. *Cognition and Instruction, 18*, 181–207.

Perry, N. E. (1998). Young children's self-regulated learning and contexts that support it. *Journal of Educational Psychology, 90*, 715–729.

Perry, N. E., Turner, J. C., & Meyer, D. K. (2006). Classrooms as contexts for motivating learning. In P. A. Alexander & P. H. Winne (Eds.), *Handbook of educational psychology* (2nd ed., pp. 327–348). Mahwah, NJ: Erlbaum.

Perry, N. E., VandeKamp, K. O., Mercer, L. K., & Nordby, C. J. (2002). Investigating teacher–student interactions that foster self-regulated learning. *Educational Psychologist, 37*, 5–15.

Perry, N. E., & Winne, P. H. (2004). Motivational messages from home and school: How do they influence young children's engagement in learning? In D. M. McInerney & S. Van Etten (Eds.), *Big theories revisited* (pp. 199–222). Greenwich, CT: Information Age.

Peters, A. M. (1983). *The units of language acquisition*. New York: Cambridge University Press.

Peterson, A. C., & Taylor, B. (1980). The biological approach to adolescence: Biological change and psychological adaptation. In J. Adelson (Ed.), *Handbook of adolescent psychology* (pp. 117–155). New York: Wiley.

Peterson, B. E., & Stewart, A. J. (1996). The antecedents and contexts of generativity motivation at midlife. *Psychology and Aging, 11*(1), 21–33.

Peterson, C. (1990). Explanatory style in the classroom and on the playing field. In S. Graham & V. S. Folkes (Eds.), *Attribution theory: Applications to achievement, mental health, and interpersonal conflict*. Hillsdale, NJ: Erlbaum.

Peterson, C., Maier, S. F., & Seligman, M. E. P. (1993). *Learned helplessness: A theory for the age of personal control*. New York: Oxford University Press.

Peterson, C. C. (2002). Drawing insight from pictures: The development of concepts of false drawing and false belief in children with deafness, normal hearing, and autism. *Child Development, 73*, 1442–1459.

Peterson, D., & Esbensen, F. A. (2004). The outlook is G.R.E.A.T.: What educators say about school-based prevention and the Gang Resistance Education and Training (G.R.E.A.T.) Program. *Evaluation Review, 28*(3), 218–245.

Peterson, K. A., Paulson, S. E., & Williams, K. K. (2007). Relations of eating disorder symptomology with perceptions of pressures from mother, peers, and media in adolescent girls and boys. *Sex Roles, 57*, 629–639.

Peterson, L. (1980). Developmental changes in verbal and behavioral sensitivity to cues of social norms of altruism. *Child Development, 51*, 830–838.

Petrill, S. A., Lipton, P. A., Hewitt, J. K., Plomin, R., Cherny, S. S., Corley, R., et al. (2004). Genetic and environmental contributions to general cognitive ability through the first 16 years of life. *Developmental Psychology, 40*, 805–812.

Petrill, S. A., & Wilkerson, B. (2000). Intelligence and achievement: A behavioral genetic perspective. *Educational Psychology Review, 12*, 185–199.

Pettito, A. L. (1985). Division of labor: Procedural learning in teacher-led small groups. *Cognition and Instruction, 2*, 233–270.

Pettito, L. A. (1997). In the beginning: On the genetic and environmental factors that make early language acquisition possible. In M. Gopnik (Ed.), *The inheritance and innateness of grammars*. New York: Oxford University Press.

Pfeifer, J. H., Brown, C. S., & Juvonen, J. (2007). Prejudice reduction in schools. Teaching tolerance in schools: Lessons learned since Brown v. Board of Education about the development and reduction of children's prejudice. *Social Policy Report, 21*(2), 1, 3–13, 20–23.

Pfeifer, M., Goldsmith, H. H., Davidson, R. J., & Rickman, M. (2002). Continuity and change in inhibited and uninhibited children. *Child Development, 73*, 1474–1485.

Phalet, K., Andriessen, I., & Lens, W. (2004). How future goals enhance motivation and learning in multicultural classrooms. *Educational Psychology Review, 16*, 59–89.

Phelan, P., Yu, H. C., & Davidson, A. L. (1994). Navigating the psychosocial pressures of adolescence: The voices and experiences of high school youth. *American Educational Research Journal, 31*, 415–447.

Phillips, D., & Zimmerman, M. (1990). The developmental course of perceived competence and incompetence among competent children. In R. Sternberg & J. Kolligian (Eds.), *Competence considered* (pp. 41–66). New Haven, CT: Yale University Press.

Phillips, M. (1997). What makes schools effective? A comparison of the relationships of communitarian climate and academic climate to mathematics achievement and attendance during middle school. *American Educational Research Journal, 34*, 633–662.

Phinney, J. S. (1989). Stages of ethnic identity development in minority group adolescents. *Journal of Early Adolescence, 9*, 34–49.

Phinney, J. S. (1990). Ethnic identity in adolescents and adults: Review of research. *Psychological Bulletin, 108*, 499–514.

Phinney, J. S., Cantu, C. L., & Kurtz, D. A. (1997). Ethnic and American identity as predictors of self-esteem among African American, Latino, and White adolescents. *Journal of Youth and Adolescence, 26*, 165–185.

Phinney, J. S., & Tarver, S. (1988). Ethnic identity search and commitment in Black and White eighth graders. *Journal of Early Adolescence, 8*, 265–277.

Piaget, J. (1928). *Judgment and reasoning in the child* (M. Warden, Trans.). New York: Harcourt, Brace.

Piaget, J. (1929). *The child's conception of the world*. New York: Harcourt, Brace.

Piaget, J. (1940). Le mécanisme du développement mental et les lois du groupement des opérations. *Archives de Psychologie, 28*, 215–285.

Piaget, J. (1950). *Introduction à l'épistémologie génétique*. Paris: Presses Universitaires de France.

Piaget, J. (1952a). *The child's conception of number* (C. Gattegno & F. M. Hodgson, Trans.). London: Routledge & Kegan Paul.

Piaget, J. (1952b). *The origins of intelligence in children*. New York: International Universities Press.

Piaget, J. (1954). *The construction of reality in the child*. New York: Basic Books.

Piaget, J. (1959). *The language and thought of the child* (3rd ed.; M. Gabain, Trans.). London: Routledge & Kegan Paul.

Piaget, J. (1960a). *The child's conception of physical causality* (M. Gabain, Trans.). Paterson, NJ: Littlefield, Adams.

Piaget, J. (1960b). The definition of stages of development. In J. M. Tanner & B. Inhelder (Eds.), *Discussions on child development: A consideration of the biological, psychological and cultural approaches to the understanding of human development and behavior: Vol. 4. The proceedings of the fourth meeting of the World Health Organization Study Group on the Psychobiological Development of the Child, Geneva, 1956* (pp. 116–135). New York: International Universities Press.

Piaget, J. (1960c). *The moral judgment of the child* (M. Gabain, Trans.). Glencoe, IL: Free Press. (First published in 1932)

Piaget, J. (1962). *Play, dreams, and imitation in childhood*. New York: W. W. Norton.

Piaget, J. (1971). The theory of stages in cognitive development. In D. R. Green (Ed.), *Measurement and Piaget* (pp. 1–11). New York: McGraw-Hill.

Piaget, J. (1985). *The equilibration of cognitive structures: The central problem of intellectual development*. Chicago: University of Chicago Press.

Pianta, R. C. (2006). Classroom management and relationships between children and teachers: Implications for research and practice. In C. M. Evertson & C. S. Weinstein (Eds.), *Handbook of classroom management: Research, practice, and contemporary issues* (pp. 685–709). Mahwah, NJ: Erlbaum.

Pianta, R. C., Belsky, J., Houts, R., & Morrison, F. (2007). Opportunities to learn in America's elementary classrooms. *Science, 315*(5820), 1795–1796.

Pianta, R. C., Hamre, B., & Stuhlman, M. (2003). Relationships between teachers and children. In W. M. Reynolds & G. E. Miller (Eds.), *Handbook of psychology: Educational psychology* (Vol. 7, pp. 199–234). New York: Wiley.

Pianta, R. C., & Steinberg, M. (1992). Teacher–child relationships and the process of adjusting to school. In R. C. Pianta (Ed.), *Beyond the parent: The role of other adults in children's lives* (pp. 61–80). San Francisco, CA: Jossey-Bass.

Piche, C., & Plante, C. (1991). Perceived masculinity, femininity, and androgyny among primary school boys: Relationships with the adaptation level of these students and the attitudes of the teachers towards them. *European Journal of Psychology of Education, 6*, 423–435.

Piirto, J. (1999). *Talented children and adults: Their development and education* (2nd ed.). Upper Saddle River, NJ: Merrill/Prentice Hall.

Pillow, B. H. (2002). Children's and adults' evaluation of the certainty of deductive inferences, inductive inferences, and guesses. *Child Development, 73*, 779–792.

Pillow, B. H., & Henrichon, A. J. (1996). There's more to the picture than meets the eye: Young children's difficulty understanding biased interpretation. *Child Development, 67*, 803–819.

Pinker, S. (1982). A theory of the acquisition of lexical interpretive grammars. In J. Bresnan (Ed.), *The mental representation of grammatical notions*. Cambridge, MA: MIT Press.

Pinker, S. (1984). *Language learnability and language development*. Cambridge, MA: Harvard University Press.

Pinker, S. (1987). The bootstrapping problem in language acquisition. In B. MacWhinney (Ed.), *Mechanisms of language acquisition*. Hillsdale, NJ: Erlbaum.

Pinker, S. (1997). Evolutionary biology and the evolution of language. In M. Gopnik (Ed.), *The inheritance and innateness of grammars*. New York: Oxford University Press.

Pintrich, P. R., & Schunk, D. H. (2002). *Motivation in education: Theory, research, and applications* (2nd ed.). Upper Saddle River, NJ: Merrill/Prentice Hall.

Pipher, M. (1994). *Reviving Ophelia: Saving the selves of adolescent girls*. New York: Putnam.

Pitner, R. O., Astor, R. A., Benbenishty, R., Haj-Yahia, M. M., & Zeira, A. (2003). The effects of group stereotypes on adolescents' reasoning about peer retribution. *Child Development, 74*, 413–425.

Plomin, R., Fulker, D. W., Corley, R., & DeFries, J. C. (1997). Nature, nurture, and cognitive development from 1 to 16 years: A parent– offspring adoption study. *Psychological Science, 8*, 442–447.

Plomin, R., Owen, M. J., & McGuffin, P. (1994). The genetic basis of complex human behaviors. *Science, 24*, 1733–1739.

Plomin, R., & Petrill, S. A. (1997). Genetics and intelligence: What's new? *Intelligence, 24*, 53–77.

Plomin, R., & Spinath, F. M. (2004). Intelligence: Genetics, genes, and genomics. *Journal of Personality and Social Psychology, 86*, 112–129.

Plumert, J. M. (1994). Flexibility in children's use of spatial and categorical organizational strategies in recall. *Developmental Psychology, 30*, 738–747.

Poel, E. W. (2007). Enhancing what students can do. *Educational Leadership, 64*, 64–66.

Polderman, T. J. C., Stins, J. F., Posthuma, D., Gosso, M. F., Verhulst, F. C., & Boomsma, D. I. (2006). The phenotypic and genotypic relation between working memory speed and capacity. *Intelligence, 34*, 549–560.

Pollack, W. (1998). *Real boys: Rescuing our sons from the myths of boyhood*. New York: Henry Holt.

Pollitt, E., & Oh, S. (1994). Early supplemental feeding, child development and health policy. *Food & Nutrition Bulletin, 15*, 208–214.

Pomerantz, E. M., Altermatt, E. R., & Saxon, J. L. (2002). Making the grade but feeling distressed: Gender differences in academic performance and internal distress. *Journal of Educational Psychology, 94*, 396–404.

Pomerantz, E. M., Moorman, E. A., & Litwack, S. D. (2007). The how, whom, and why of parents' involvement in children's academic lives: More is not always better. *Review of Educational Research, 77*, 373–410.

Ponterotto, J. G., Utsey, S. O., & Pedersen, P. B. (2006). *Preventing prejudice: A guide for counselors, educators, and parents* (2nd ed.). Thousand Oaks, CA: Sage.

Porat, D. A. (2004). *It's not written here, but this is what happened:* Students' cultural comprehension of textbook narratives on the Israeli-Arab conflict. *American Educational Research Journal, 41*, 963–996.

Poresky, R. H., Daniels, A. M., Mukerjee, J., & Gunnell, K. (1999, April). *Community and family influences on adolescents' use of alcohol and other drugs: An exploratory ecological analysis*. Paper presented at the biennial meeting of the Society for Research in Child Development, Albuquerque, NM.

Portes, P. R. (1996). Ethnicity and culture in educational psychology. In D. C. Berliner & R. C. Calfee (Eds.), *Handbook of educational psychology*. New York: Macmillan.

Posner, M. I., & Rothbart, M. K. (2007). *Educating the human brain*. Washington, DC: American Psychological Association.

Poulin, F., & Boivin, M. (1999). Proactive and reactive aggression and boys' friendship quality in mainstream classrooms. *Journal of Emotional and Behavioral Disorders, 7*, 168–177.

Poulin-Dubois, D., Frenkiel-Fishman, S., Nayer, S., & Johnson, S. (2006). Infants' inductive generalization of bodily, motion, and sensory properties to animals and people. *Journal of Cognition and Development, 7*(4), 431–453.

Powell, G. J. (1983). *The psychosocial development of minority children*. New York: Brunner/Mazel.

Powell, M. P., & Schulte, T. (1999). Turner syndrome. In S. Goldstein & C. R. Reynolds (Eds.), *Handbook of neurodevelopmental and genetic disorders* (pp. 277–297). New York: Guilford Press.

Power, F. C., Higgins, A., & Kohlberg, L. (1989). *Lawrence Kohlberg's approach to moral education*. New York: Columbia University Press.

Powers, L. E., Sowers, J. A., & Stevens, T. (1995). An exploratory, randomized study of the impact of mentoring on the self-efficacy and community-based knowledge of adolescents with severe physical challenges. *Journal of Rehabilitation, 61*(1), 33–41.

Pramling, I. (1996). Understanding and empowering the child as learner. In D. R. Olson & N. Torrance (Eds.), *The handbook of education and human development: New models of learning, teaching, and schooling*. Cambridge, MA: Blackwell.

Prawat, R. S. (1992). From individual differences to learning communities: Our changing focus. *Educational Leadership, 49*(7), 9–13.

Preedy, P. (1999). Meeting the educational needs of pre-school and primary aged twins and higher multiples. In A. C. Sandbank (Ed.), *Twin and triplet psychology: A professional guide to working with multiples* (pp. 70–99). London: Routledge.

Pressley, M. (1982). Elaboration and memory development. *Child Development, 53*, 296–309.

Pressley, M., Almasi, J., Schuder, T., Bergman, J., Hite, S., El-Dinary, P. B., et al. (1994). Transactional instruction of comprehension strategies: The Montgomery County Maryland SAIL program. *Reading and Writing Quarterly, 10*, 5–19.

Pressley, M., Borkowski, J. G., & Schneider, W. (1987). Cognitive strategies: Good strategy users coordinate metacognition and knowledge. In R. Vasta (Ed.), *Annals of child development* (Vol. 4). Greenwich, CT: JAI Press.

Pressley, M., El-Dinary, P. B., Marks, M. B., Brown, R., & Stein, S. (1992). Good strategy instruction is motivating and interesting. In K. A. Renninger, S. Hidi, & A. Krapp (Eds.), *The role of interest in learning and development*. Hillsdale, NJ: Erlbaum.

Pressley, M., & Harris, K. R. (2006). Cognitive strategies instruction: From basic research to classroom instruction. In P. A. Alexander & P. H. Winne (Eds.), *Handbook of educational psychology* (2nd ed., pp. 265–286). Mahwah, NJ: Erlbaum.

Pressley, M., & Hilden, K. (2006). Cognitive strategies: Production deficiencies and successful strategy instruction everywhere. In W. Damon, R. M. Lerner (Series Eds.), D. Kuhn, & R. Siegler (Vol. Eds.), *Handbook of child psychology: Vol. 2. Cognition, perception, and language* (6th ed.). New York: Wiley.

Preuss, L. J., & Dubow, E. F. (2004). A comparison between intellectually gifted and typical children in their coping responses to a school and a peer stressor. *Roeper Review, 26*(2), 105–111.

Pribilsky, J. (2001). Nervios and 'modern childhood': Migration and shifting contexts of child life in the Ecuadorian Andes. *Childhood, 8*(2), 251–273.

Price, J. R., Roberts, J. E., & Jackson, S. C. (2006). Structural development of the fictional narratives of African American preschoolers. *Language, Speech, and Hearing Services in Schools, 37*, 178–190.

Price, S., Noseworthy, J., & Thornton, J. (2007). Women's experience with social presence during childbirth. *MCN: The American Journal of Maternal/Child Nursing, 32*(3), 184–191.

Price-Williams, D. R., Gordon, W., & Ramirez, M. (1969). Skill and conservation. *Developmental Psychology, 1*, 769.

Pritchard, R. (1990). The effects of cultural schemata on reading processing strategies. *Reading Research Quarterly, 25*, 273–295.

Proctor, C. P., August, D., Carlo, M. S., & Snow, C. (2006). The intriguing role of Spanish language vocabulary knowledge in predicting English reading comprehension. *Journal of Educational Psychology, 98*, 159–169.

Proctor, R. W., & Dutta, A. (1995). *Skill acquisition and human performance*. Thousand Oaks, CA: Sage.

Provasnik, S., KewalRamani, A., Coleman, M. M., Gilbertson, L., Herring, W., & Xie, Q. (2007). *Status of education in rural America* (NCES 2007-040). Washington, DC: National Center for Education Statistics, Institute of Education Sciences, U.S. Department of Education.

Pruden, S. M., Hirsh-Pasek, K., Golinkoff, R. M., & Hennon, E. A. (2006). The birth of words: Ten-month-olds learn words through perceptual salience. *Child Development, 77*, 266–280.

Pulkkinen, L. (1982). Self-control and continuity from childhood to adolescence. In P. B. Baltes & O. G. Brim (Eds.), *Life-span development and behavior* (Vol. 4). Orlando, FL: Academic Press.

Pulos, S. (1997). Adolescents' implicit theories of physical phenomena: A matter of gravity. *International Journal of Behavioral Development, 20*, 493–507.

Pulos, S., & Linn, M. C. (1981). Generality of the controlling variables scheme in early adolescence. *Journal of Early Adolescence, 1*, 26–37.

Puntambekar, S., & Hübscher, R. (2005). Tools for scaffolding students in a complex learning environment: What have we gained and what have we missed? *Educational Psychologist, 40*, 1–12.

Purcell-Gates, V. (1995). *Other people's words: The cycle of low literacy*. Cambridge, MA: Harvard University Press.

Purcell-Gates, V., McIntyre, E., & Freppon, P. A. (1995). Learning written storybook language in school: A comparison of low-SES children in skills-based and whole language classrooms. *American Educational Research Journal, 32*, 659–685.

Purdie, N., & Hattie, J. (1996). Cultural differences in the use of strategies for self-regulated learning. *American Educational Research Journal, 33*, 845–871.

Purdie, N., Hattie, J., & Douglas, G. (1996). Student conceptions of learning and their use of self-regulated learning strategies: A cross-cultural comparison. *Journal of Educational Psychology, 88*, 87–100.

Putallaz, M., & Gottman, J. M. (1981). Social skills and group acceptance. In S. R. Asher & J. M. Gottman (Eds.), *The development of children's friendships* (pp. 116–149). New York: Cambridge University Press.

Putallaz, M., & Heflin, A. H. (1986). Toward a model of peer acceptance. In J. M. Gottman & J. G. Parker (Eds.), *Conversations of friends: Speculations on affective development* (pp. 292–314). Cambridge, England: Cambridge University Press.

Qian, G., & Pan, J. (2002). A comparison of epistemological beliefs and learning from science text between American and Chinese high school students. In B. K. Hofer & P. R. Pintrich (Eds.), *Personal epistemology: The psychology of beliefs about knowledge and knowing* (pp. 365–385). Mahwah, NJ: Erlbaum.

Quane, J. M., & Rankin, B. H. (2006). Does it pay to participate? Neighborhood-based organizations and the social development of urban adolescents. *Children and Youth Services Review, 28*, 1229–1250.

Quill, K. A. (1995). Visually cued instruction for children with autism and pervasive developmental disorders. *Focus on Autistic Behavior, 10*(3), 10–20.

Quinn, P. C. (2002). Category representation in young infants. *Current Directions in Psychological Science, 11*, 66–70.

Quinn, P. C. (2007). On the infant's prelinguistic conception of spatial relations: Three developmental trends and their implications for spatial language learning. In J. M. Plumert & J. P. Spencer (Eds.), *The emerging spatial mind* (pp. 117–141). New York: Oxford University Press.

Quinn, P. C., & Bhatt, R. S. (2006). Are some Gestalt principles deployed more readily than others during early development? The case of lightness versus form similarity. *Journal of Experimental*

Psychology: Human Perception and Performance, 32, 1221–1230.

Quittner, A. L., Modi, A. C., & Roux, A. L. (2004). Psychosocial challenges and clinical interventions for children and adolescents with cystic fibrosis: A developmental approach. In R. T. Brown (Ed.), *Handbook of pediatric psychology in school settings* (pp. 333–361). Mahwah, NJ: Erlbaum.

Radziszewska, B., & Rogoff, B. (1991). Children's guided participation in planning imaginary errands with skilled adult or peer partners. *Developmental Psychology, 27,* 381–389.

Raevuori, A., Dick, D. M., Keski-Rahkonen, A., Pulkkinen, L., Rose, R. J., Rissanen, A., et al. (2007). Genetic and environmental factors affecting self-esteem from age 14 to 17: A longitudinal study of Finnish twins. *Psychological Medicine, 37,* 1625–1633.

Rahman, Q., & Wilson, G. D. (2003). Sexual orientation and the 2nd to 4th finger length ratio: Evidence for organising[LP8] effects of sex hormones or developmental instability? *Psychoneuroendocrinology, 28,* 288–303.

Raikes, H., Pan, B. A., Luze, G., Tamis-LeMonda, C. S., Brooks-Gunn, J., Constantine, J., et al. (2006). Mother–child bookreading in low-income families: Correlates and outcomes during the first three years of life. *Child Development, 77,* 924–953.

Raine, A., Reynolds, C., & Venables, P. H. (2002). Stimulation seeking and intelligence: A prospective longitudinal study. *Journal of Personality and Social Psychology, 82,* 663–674.

Raine, A., & Scerbo, A. (1991). Biological theories of violence. In J. S. Milner (Ed.), *Neuropsychology of aggression* (pp. 1–25). Boston: Kluwer Academic Press.

Rakic, P. (1995). Corticogenesis in human and nonhuman primates. In M. S. Gazzaniga (Ed.), *The cognitive neurosciences* (pp. 127–145). Cambridge, MA: MIT Press.

Rakison, D. H. (2005). Infant perception and cognition: An evolutionary perspective on early learning. In B. J. Ellis & D. F. Bjorklund (Eds.), *Origins of the social mind: Evolutionary psychology and child development* (pp. 317–353). New York: Guilford Press.

Rallison, M. L. (1986). *Growth disorders in infants, children, and adolescents.* New York: Churchill Livingstone.

Ramani, G. B., & Siegler, R. S. (2008). Promoting broad and stable improvements in low-income children's numerical knowledge through playing number board games. *Child Development, 79,* 375–394.

Ramey, C. T., & Ramey, S. L. (1998). Early intervention and early experience. *American Psychologist, 53,* 109–120.

Ratner, H. H. (1984). Memory demands and the development of young children's memory. *Child Development, 55,* 2173–2191.

Raver, C. C. (2002). Emotions matter: Making the case for the role of young children's emotional development for early school readiness. *Social Policy Report of the Society for Research in Child Development, 16*(3), 1, 3–6, 8–10, 12–18.

Ravid, D., & Zilberbuch, S. (2003). Morphosyntactic constructs in the development of spoken and written Hebrew text production. *Journal of Child Language, 30,* 395–418.

Rayner, K., Foorman, B. R., Perfetti, C. A., Pesetsky, D., & Seidenberg, M. S. (2001). How psychological science informs the teaching of reading. *Psychological Science in the Public Interest, 2,* 31–74.

Rayport, S. G. (1992). Cellular and molecular biology of the neuron. In S. C. Yudofsky & R. E. Hales (Eds.), *The American Psychiatric Press textbook of neuropsychiatry* (2nd ed., pp. 3–28). Washington, DC: American Psychiatric Press.

Ready, D., Lee, V., & Welner, K. G. (2004). Educational equity and school structure: School size, overcrowding, and schools-within-schools. *Teachers College Record, 106*(10), 1989–2014.

Rees, S., Harding, R., & Inder, T. (2006). The developmental environment and the origins of neurological disorders. In P. Gluckman & M. Hanson (Ed.), *Developmental origins of health and disease* (pp. 379–391). New York: Cambridge University Press.

Reese, L., Garnier, H., Gallimore, R., & Goldenberg, C. (2000). Longitudinal analysis of the antecedents of emergent Spanish literacy and middle-school English reading achievement of Spanish-speaking students. *American Educational Research Journal, 37,* 633–662.

Reese, S. (1996). KIDMONEY: Children as big business. *Technos Quarterly, 5*(4), 1–7. Retrieved November 21, 2005, at http://www.ait.net/technos/tq_05/4reesephp

Reeve, J. (2006). Extrinsic rewards and inner motivation. In C. M. Evertson & C. S. Weinstein (Eds.), *Handbook of classroom management: Research, practice, and contemporary issues* (pp. 645–664.). Mahwah, NJ: Erlbaum.

Reeve, J., Bolt, E., & Cai, Y. (1999). Autonomy-supportive teachers: How they teach and motivate students. *Journal of Educational Psychology, 91,* 537–548.

Reeve, J., Deci, E. L., & Ryan, R. M. (2004). Self-determination theory: A dialectical framework for understanding sociocultural influences on student motivation. In D. M. McInerney & S. Van Etten (Eds.), *Big theories revisited* (pp. 31–60). Greenwich, CT: Information Age.

Reich, P. A. (1986). *Language development.* Englewood Cliffs, NJ: Prentice Hall.

Reid, N. (1989). Contemporary Polynesian conceptions of giftedness. *Gifted Education International, 6*(1), 30–38.

Reid, P. T. (1985). Sex-role socialization of Black children: A review of theory, family, and media influences. *Academic Psychology Bulletin, 7,* 201–212.

Reid, R., Gonzalez, J. E., Nordness, P. D., Trout, A., & Epstein, M. H. (2004). A meta-analysis of the academic status of students with emotional/behavioral disturbance. *The Journal of Special Education, 38,* 130–143.

Reimer, J., Paolitto, D. P., & Hersh, R. H. (1983). *Promoting moral growth: From Piaget to Kohlberg* (2nd ed.). White Plains, NY: Longman.

Reiner, M., Slotta, J. D., Chi, M. T. H., & Resnick, L. B. (2000). Naïve physics reasoning: A commitment to substance-based conceptions. *Cognition and Instruction, 18,* 1–34.

Reis, J., Trockel, M., & Mulhall, P. (2007). Individual and school predictors of middle school aggression. *Youth and Society, 38*(3), 322–347.

Reiss, D. (2005). The interplay between genotypes and family relationships: Reframing concepts of development and prevention. *Current Directions in Psychological Science, 14,* 139–143.

Reissland, N. (2006). Teaching a baby the language of emotions: A father's experience. *Zero to Three, 27*(1), 42–47.

Remez, L. (2000). Oral sex among adolescents: Is it sex or is it abstinence? *Family Planning Perspectives, 32*(6), 298–304.

Renninger, K. A., Hidi, S., & Krapp, A. (Eds.). (1992). *The role of interest in learning and development.* Hillsdale, NJ: Erlbaum.

Renzulli, J. S., & Reis, S. M. (1986). The enrichment triad/revolving door model: A schoolwide plan for the development of creative productivity. In J. Renzulli (Ed.), *Systems and models for developing programs for the gifted and talented.* Mansfield Center, CT: Creative Learning Press.

Repacholi, B. M., & Gopnik, A. (1997). Early reasoning about desires: Evidence from 14- and 18-month-olds. *Developmental Psychology, 33,* 12–21.

Rest, J. R., Narváez, D., Bebeau, M., & Thoma, S. (1999). A neo-Kohlbergian approach: The DIT and schema theory. *Educational Psychology Review, 11,* 291–324.

Reston, J. (2007). Reflecting on admission criteria. In G. E. Mills, *Action research: A guide for the teacher researcher* (3rd ed., pp. 141–142). Upper Saddle River, NJ: Pearson Merrill/Prentice Hall.

Reyna, C. (2000). Lazy, dumb, or industrious: When stereotypes convey attribution information in the classroom. *Educational Psychology Review, 12,* 85–110.

Reyna, V. F., & Farley, F. (2006). Risk and rationality in adolescent decision making: Implications for theory, practice, and public policy. *Psychological Science in the Public Interest, 7,* 1–44.

Reynolds, A. (1994). Effects of a preschool plus follow-on intervention for children at risk. *Developmental Psychology, 30,* 787–804.

Reynolds, R. E., Taylor, M. A., Steffensen, M. S., Shirey, L. L., & Anderson, R. C. (1982). Cultural schemata and reading comprehension. *Reading Research Quarterly, 17,* 353–366.

Reznick, J. S., & Goldfield, B. A. (1992). Rapid change in lexical development in comprehension and production. *Developmental Psychology, 28,* 408–414.

Ricciuti, H. N. (1993). Nutrition and mental development. *Current Directions in Psychological Science, 2,* 43–46.

Rice, M., Hadley, P. A., & Alexander, A. L. (1993). Social biases toward children with speech and language impairments: A correlative causal model of language limitations. *Applied Psycholinguistics, 14,* 445–471.

Rice, M. L., Huston, A. C., Truglio, R., & Wright, J. (1990). Words from "Sesame Street": Learning vocabulary while viewing. *Developmental Psychology, 26,* 421–428.

Richard, J. F., & Schneider, B. H. (2005). Assessing friendship motivation during preadolescence and early adolescence. *Journal of Early Adolescence, 25*(3), 367–385.

Richards, J. E., & Turner, E. D. (2001). Extended visual fixation and distractibility in children from six to twenty-four months of age. *Child Development, 72,* 963–972.

Richardson, R., & Hayne, H. (2007). You can't take it with you: The translation of memory across development. *Current Directions in Psychological Science, 16,* 223–227.

Ridderinkhof, K. R., & van der Molen, M. (1995). A psychophysiological analysis of developmental differences in the ability to resist interference. *Child Development, 60,* 1040–1056.

Rief, S. F., & Heimburge, J. A. (2007). *How to reach and teach all children through balanced literacy: User-friendly strategies, tools, activities, and ready-to-use materials (Grades 3–8).* San Francisco, CA: Jossey-Bass.

Riggs, J. M. (1992). Self-handicapping and achievement. In A. K. Boggiano & T. S. Pittman (Eds.), *Achievement and motivation: A social-developmental perspective.* Cambridge, England: Cambridge University Press.

Riggs, N. R., Greenberg, M. T., Kusché, C. A., & Pentz, M. A. (2006). The mediational role of neurocognition in the behavioral outcomes of a social-emotional prevention program in elementary school students: Effects of the PATHS curriculum. *Prevention Science, 7*(1), 91–102.

Riley, D., San Juan, R. R., Klinkner, J., & Ramminger, A. (2008). *Social and emotional development: Connecting science and practice in early childhood settings.* St. Paul, MN: Redleaf Press.

Rimm-Kaufman, S. E., Early, D. M., Cox, M. J., Saluja, G., Pianta, R. C., Bradley, R. H., et al. (2002). Early behavioral attributes and teachers' sensitivity as predictors of competent behavior in the kindergarten classroom. *Journal of Applied Developmental Psychology, 23*(4), 451–470.

Rindfuss, R. R., Liao, T. F., & Tsuya, N. O. (1992). Contact with parents in Japan: Effects on opinions toward gender and intergenerational roles. *Journal of Marriage and Family, 54,* 812–822.

Rinehart, S. D., Stahl, S. A., & Erickson, L. G. (1986). Some effects of summarization training on reading and studying. *Reading Research Quarterly, 21,* 422–438.

Ripple, C. H., Gilliam, W. S., Chanana, N., & Zigler, E. (1999). Will fifty cooks spoil the broth? The debate over entrusting Head Start to the states. *American Psychologist, 54,* 327–343.

Ris, M. D., Dietrich, K. N., Succop, P. A., Berger, O. G., & Bornschein, R. L. (2004). Early exposure to lead and neuropsychological outcome in adolescence. *Journal of the International Neuropsychological Society, 19,* 261–270.

Rittle-Johnson, B. (2006). Promoting transfer: Effects of self-explanation and direct instruction. *Child Development, 77,* 1–15. ng knowledge scaffolds to support mathematical problem solving. *Cognition and Instruction, 23,* 313–349.

Rittle-Johnson, B., & Koedinger, K. R. (2005). Designing knowledge scaffolds to support mathematical problem solving. *Cognition and Instruction, 23,* 313–349.

Rittle-Johnson, B., & Siegler, R. S. (1999). Learning to spell: Variability, choice, and change in children's strategy use. *Child Development, 70,* 332–348.

Rittle-Johnson, R. S., & Alibali, M. W. (2001). Developing conceptual understanding and procedural skill in mathematics: An iterative process. *Journal of Educational Psychology, 93,* 346–362.

Ritts, V., Patterson, M. L., & Tubbs, M. E. (1992). Expectations, impressions, and judgments of physically attractive students: A review. *Review of Educational Research, 62,* 413–426.

Robbins, W. J., Brody, S., Hogan, A. G., Jackson, C. M., & Green, C. W. (Eds.). (1928). *Growth.* New Haven, CT: Yale University Press.

Roberts, D. F., Christenson, P., Gibson, W. A., Mooser, L., & Goldberg, M. E. (1980). Developing discriminating consumers. *Journal of Communication, 30,* 94–105.

Roberts, D. F., & Foehr, U. G. (2008). Trends in media use. *Future of Children, 18*(1), 11–37.

Roberts, M. C., Brown, K. J., Boles, R. E., & Mashunkashey, J. O. (2004). Prevention of injuries: Concepts and interventions for pediatric psychology in the schools. In R. T. Brown (Ed.), *Handbook of pediatric psychology in school settings* (pp. 65–80). Mahwah, NJ: Erlbaum.

Roberts, T. A. (2005). Articulation accuracy and vocabulary size contributions to phonemic awareness and word reading in English language learners. *Journal of Educational Psychology, 97,* 601–616.

Roberts, T. A., & Meiring, A. (2006). Teaching phonics in the context of children's literature or spelling: Influences on first-grade reading, spelling, and writing and fifth-grade comprehension. *Journal of Educational Psychology, 98,* 690–713.

Robertson, J. S. (2000). Is attribution training a worthwhile classroom intervention for K–12 students with learning difficulties? *Educational Psychology Review, 12,* 111–134.

Robin, D. J., Berthier, N. E., & Clifton, R. K. (1996). Infants' predictive reaching for moving objects in the dark. *Developmental Psychology, 32,* 824–835.

Robins, R. W., & Trzesniewski, K. H. (2005). Self-esteem development across the lifespan. *Current Directions in Psychological Science, 14,* 158–162.

Robinson, D. R., Schofield, J. W., & Steers-Wentzell, K. L. (2005). Peer and cross-age tutoring in math: Outcomes and their design implications. *Educational Psychology Review, 17,* 327–362.

Robinson, T., Callister, M., Magoffin, D., & Moore, J. (2006). The portrayal of older characters in Disney animated films. *Journal of Aging Studies, 21,* 203–213.

Robinson, T. R., Smith, S. W., Miller, M. D., & Brownell, M. T. (1999). Cognitive behavior modification of hyperactivity-impulsivity and aggression: A meta-analysis of school-based studies. *Journal of Educational Psychology, 91,* 195–203.

Rochat, P., & Bullinger, A. (1994). Posture and functional action in infancy. In A. Vyt, H. Bloch, & M. H. Bornstein (Eds.), *Early child development in the French tradition: Contributions from current research.* Hillsdale, NJ: Erlbaum.

Rochat, P., & Goubet, N. (1995). Development of sitting and reaching in 5- to 6-month-old infants. *Infant behavior and development, 18,* 53–68.

Roderick, M., & Camburn, E. (1999). Risk and recovery from course failure in the early years of high school. *American Educational Research Journal, 36,* 303–343.

Roditi, B. N., & Steinberg, J. (2007). The strategy math classroom: Executive function processes and mathematics learning. In L. Meltzer (Ed.), *Executive function in education: From theory to practice* (pp. 237–260). New York: Guilford Press.

Roeser, R. W., Eccles, J. S., & Sameroff, A. J. (2000). School as a context of early adolescents' academic social-emotional development: A summary of research findings. *The Elementary School Journal, 100,* 443–471.

Roeser, R. W., Midgley, C., & Urdan, T. C. (1996). Perceptions of school psychological environment and early adolescents' psychological and behavioral functioning in school: The mediating role of goals and belonging. *Journal of Educational Psychology, 88,* 408–422.

Roffwarg, H. P., Muzio, J. N., & Dement, W. C. (1966). Ontogenetic development of the human sleep-dream cycle. *Science, 152,* 604–619.

Rogers, K. B. (2002). *Re-forming gifted education.* Scottsdale, AZ: Great Potential Press.

Rogoff, B. (1990). *Apprenticeship in thinking: Cognitive development in social context.* New York: Oxford University Press.

Rogoff, B. (1991). Social interaction as apprenticeship in thinking: Guidance and participation in spatial planning. In L. B. Resnick, J. M. Levine, & S. D. Teasley (Eds.), *Perspectives on socially shared cognition.* Washington, DC: American Psychological Association.

Rogoff, B. (1994, April). *Developing understanding of the idea of communities of learners.* Paper presented at the annual meeting of the American Educational Research Association, New Orleans, LA.

Rogoff, B. (1995). Observing sociocultural activity on three planes: Participatory appropriation, guided participation, and apprenticeship. In J. V. Wertsch, P. del Rio, & A. Alvarez (Eds.), *Sociocultural studies of mind.* Cambridge, England: Cambridge University Press.

Rogoff, B. (2003). *The cultural nature of human development.* Oxford, England: Oxford University Press.

Rogoff, B., Matusov, E., & White, C. (1996). Models of teaching and learning: Participation in a community of learners. In D. R. Olson & N. Torrance (Eds.), *The handbook of education and human development: New models of learning, teaching, and schooling.* Cambridge, MA: Blackwell.

Rogoff, B., Mistry, J., Göncü, A., & Mosier, C. (1993). Guided participation in cultural activity by toddlers and caregivers. *Monographs of the Society for Research in Child Development, 58*(8, Serial No. 236).

Rogoff, B., Moore, L., Najafi, B., Dexter, A., Correa-Chávez, M., & Solís, J. (2007). Children's development of cultural repertoires through participation in everyday routines and practices. In J. E. Grusec & P. D. Hastings (Eds.), *Handbook of socialization: Theory and research* (pp. 490–515). New York: Guilford Press.

Rogoff, B., & Morelli, G. (1989). Perspectives on children's development from cultural psychology. *American Psychologist, 44,* 343–348.

Rohner, R. P., & Rohner, E. C. (1981). Parental acceptance-rejection and parental control: Cross-cultural codes. *Ethnology, 20,* 245–260.

Roid, G. (2003). *Stanford-Binet Intelligence Scales* (5th ed.). Itasca, IL: Riverside.

Romero, A. J., & Roberts, R. E. (2003). The impact of multiple dimensions of ethnic identity on discrimination and adolescents' self-esteem. *Journal of Applied Social Psychology, 33,* 2288–2305.

Rondal, J. A. (1985). *Adult-child interaction and the process of language acquisition.* New York: Praeger.

Rondan, C., & Deruelle, C. (2007). Global and configural visual processing in adults with autism and Asperger syndrome. *Research in Developmental Disabilities, 28,* 197–206.

Root, M. P. P. (1999). The biracial baby boom: Understanding ecological constructions of racial identity in the 21st century. In R. H. Sheets & E. R. Hollins (Eds.), *Racial and ethnic identity in school practices: Aspects of human development* (pp. 67–89). Mahwah, NJ: Erlbaum.

Roseboom, T., de Rooij, S., & Painter, R. (2006). The Dutch famine and its long-term consequences for adult health. *Early Human Development, 82*(8), 485–491.

Rosenberg, M. (1986). Self-concept from middle childhood through adolescence. In S. Suls & A. Greenwald (Eds.), *Psychological perspectives on the self* (Vol. 3, pp. 107–135). Hillsdale, NJ: Erlbaum.

Rosenkoetter, L. I., Rosenkoetter, S. E., Ozretich, R. A., & Acock, A. C. (2004). Mitigating the harmful effects of violent television. *Applied Developmental Psychology, 25,* 25–47.

Rosenshine, B., & Meister, C. (1992). The use of scaffolds for teaching higher-level cognitive strategies. *Educational Leadership, 49*(7), 26–33.

Rosenshine, B., & Meister, C. (1994). Reciprocal teaching: A review of the research. *Review of Educational Research, 64,* 479–530.

Rosenshine, B., Meister, C., & Chapman, S. (1996). Teaching students to generate questions: A review of the intervention studies. *Review of Educational Research, 66,* 181–221.

Rosenstein, D., & Oster, H. (1988). Differential facial responses to four basic tastes in newborns. *Child Development, 59,* 1555–1568.

Rosenthal, R. (1994). Interpersonal expectancy effects: A 30-year perspective. *Current Directions in Psychological Science, 3,* 176–179.

Rosser, B. R. (1994). *Cognitive development: Psychological and biological perspectives.* Boston: Allyn & Bacon.

Rossman, B. R. (1992). School-age children's perceptions of coping with distress: Strategies for emotion regulation and the moderation of adjustment. *Journal of Child Psychology and Psychiatry, 33,* 1373–1397.

Rotenberg, K. J., & Mayer, E. V. (1990). Delay of gratification in Native and White children: A cross-cultural comparison. *International Journal of Behavioral Development, 13,* 23–30.

Roth, W., & Bowen, G. M. (1995). Knowing and interacting: A study of culture, practices, and resources in a grade 8 open-inquiry science classroom guided by a cognitive apprenticeship metaphor. *Cognition and Instruction, 13,* 73–128.

Rothbart, M. K. (2007). Temperament, development, and personality. *Current Directions in Psychological Science, 16,* 207–212.

Rothbart, M. K., & Bates, J. E. (2006). Temperament. In W. Damon & R. M. Lerner (Eds. in Chief) & N. Eisenberg (Vol. Ed.), *Handbook of child psychology, Vol. 3. Social, emotional, and personality development* (6th ed., pp. 99–225). Hoboken, NJ: Wiley.

Rothbart, M. K., Hanley, D., & Albert, M. (1986). Gender differences in moral reasoning. *Sex Roles, 15,* 645–653.

Rothbart, M. K., Posner, M. I., & Kieras, J. (2006). Temperament, attention, and the development of self-regulation. In K. McCartney & D. Phillips (Eds.), *Blackwell handbook of early childhood development* (pp. 338–357). Malden, MA: Blackwell.

Rothbart, M. K., Sheese, B. E., & Posner, M. I. (2007). Executive attention and effortful control: Linking temperament, brain networks, and genes. *Child Development Perspectives, 1,* 2–7.

Rothbaum, F., & Trommsdorff, G. (2007). Do roots and wings complement or oppose one another? The socialization of relatedness and autonomy in cultural context. In J. E. Grusec & P. D. Hastings (Eds.), *Handbook of socialization: Theory and research* (pp. 461–489). New York: Guilford Press.

Rothstein-Fisch, C. & Trumbull, E. (2008). *Managing diverse classrooms: How to build on students' strengths*. Alexandria, VA: Association for Supervision and Curriculum Development.

Rovee-Collier, C. (1999). The development of infant memory. *Current Directions in Psychological Science, 8,* 80–85.

Rowe, D. C., Almeida, D. M., & Jacobson, K. C. (1999). School context and genetic influences on aggression in adolescence. *Psychological Science, 10,* 277–280.

Rowe, D. C., Jacobson, K. C., & Van den Oord, E. J. C. G. (1999). Genetic and environmental influences on Vocabulary IQ: Parental education level as moderator. *Child Development, 70,* 1151–1162.

Rowe, D. W., & Harste, J. C. (1986). Metalinguistic awareness in writing and reading: The young child as curricular informant. In D. B. Yaden, Jr., & S. Templeton (Eds.), *Metalinguistic awareness and beginning literacy: Conceptualizing what it means to read and write*. Portsmouth, NH: Heinemann.

Rowe, D., Vazsonyi, A., & Flannery, D. (1994). No more than skin deep: Ethnic and racial similarity in developmental processes. *Psychological Review, 101,* 396–413.

Rowe, M. B. (1974). Wait-time and rewards as instructional variables, their influence on language, logic, and fate control: Part one—wait time. *Journal of Research in Science Teaching, 11,* 81–94.

Rowe, M. B. (1978). *Teaching science as continuous inquiry*. New York: McGraw-Hill.

Rowe, M. B. (1987). Wait-time: Slowing down may be a way of speeding up. *American Educator, 11,* 38–43, 47.

Rowland, T. W. (1990). *Exercise and children's health*. Champaign, IL: Human Kinetics.

Rowley, S. J., Cooper, S. M., & Clinton, Y. C. (2006). Family and school support for healthy racial identity development in African American youth. In K. Freeark & W. S. Davidson II (Vol. eds.), H. E. Fitzgerald, R. Zucker, & K. Freeark (Eds. in Chief), *The crisis in youth mental health. Vol. 3: Critical issues and effective programs* (pp. 79–98). Westport, CT: Praeger.

Rozalski, M. E., & Yell, M. L. (2004). Law and school safety. In J. C. Conoley & A. P. Goldstein (Eds.), *School violence intervention* (2nd ed., pp. 507–523). New York: Guilford Press.

Rubie-Davies, C. M. (2007). Classroom interactions: Exploring the practices of high- and low-expectation teachers. *British Journal of Educational Psychology, 77,* 289–306.

Rubin, K., Fein, G., & Vandenberg, B. (1983). Play. In E. M. Hetherington (Ed.), *Handbook of child psychology: Vol. 4. Socialization, personality, and social development* (pp. 693–774). New York: Wiley.

Rubin, K. H., Bukowski, W. M., & Parker, J. G. (2006). Peer interactions, relationships, and groups. In W. Damon & R. M. Lerner (Series Eds.) & N. Eisenberg (Vol. Ed.), *Handbook of child psychology: Vol. 3. Social, emotional, and personality development* (6th ed., pp. 571–645). New York: Wiley.

Rubin, K. H., & Krasnor, L. R. (1986). Social-cognitive and social behavioral perspectives on problem solving. In M. Perlmutter (Ed.), *Minnesota symposia on child psychology: Vol. 19. Cognitive perspectives on children's social and behavioral development*. Hillsdale, NJ: Erlbaum.

Rubin, K. H., Lynch, D., Coplan, R., Rose-Krasnor, L., & Booth, C. L. (1994). "Birds of a feather": Behavioral concordances and preferential personal attraction in children. *Child Development, 65,* 1778–1785.

Ruble, D. N., Martin, C. L., & Berenbaum, S. A. (2006). Gender development. In W. Damon & R. M. Lerner (Eds. in Chief) & N. Eisenberg (Vol. Ed.), *Handbook of child psychology, Vol. 3. Social, emotional, and personality development* (6th ed., pp. 858–932). Hoboken, NJ: Wiley.

Ruble, D. N., Taylor, L. J., Cyphers, L., Greulich, F. K., Lurye, L. E., & Shrout, P. E. (2007). The role of gender constancy in early gender development. *Child Development, 78,* 1121–1136.

Ruby, P., & Decety, J. (2001). Effect of subjective perspective taking during simulation of action: A PET investigation of agency. *Nature and Neuroscience, 4,* 546–550.

Rudlin, C. R. (1993). Growth and sexual development: What is normal, and what is not? *Journal of the American Academy of Physician Assistants, 6,* 25–35.

Rudolph, K. D., Caldwell, M. S., & Conley, C. S. (2005). Need for approval and children's well-being. *Child Development, 76,* 309–323.

Rudy, D., & Grusec, J. E. (2006). Authoritarian parenting in individualistic and collectivist groups: Associations with maternal emotion and cognition and children's self-esteem. *Journal of Family Psychology, 20,* 68–78.

Ruff, H. A., & Lawson, K. R. (1990). Development of sustained, focused attention in young children during free play. *Developmental Psychology, 26,* 85–93.

Ruff, H. A., & Rothbart, M. K. (1996). *Attention in early development: Themes and variations*. New York: Oxford University Press.

Ruffman, T., Perner, J., Olson, D. R., & Doherty, M. (1993). Reflecting on scientific thinking: Children's understanding of the hypothesis-evidence relation. *Child Development, 64,* 1617–1636.

Rumberger, R. W. (1995). Dropping out of middle school: A multilevel analysis of students and schools. *American Educational Research Journal, 32,* 583–625.

Rushton, J. P. (1980). *Altruism, socialization, and society*. Upper Saddle River, NJ: Prentice Hall.

Rushton, J. P., Fulkner, D. W., Neal, M. C., Nias, D. K. B., & Eysenck, H. J. (1986). Altruism and aggression: The heritability of individual differences. *Journal of Personality and Social Psychology, 50,* 1192–1198.

Rushton, J. P., & Teachman, G. (1978). The effects of positive reinforcement, attributions, and punishment on model induced altruism in children. *Personality and Social Psychology Bulletin, 4,* 322–325.

Russell, A., & Russell, G. (1994). Coparenting early school-age children: An examination of mother-father independence within families. *Developmental Psychology, 30,* 757–770.

Rutland, A., Cameron, L., Bennett, L., & Ferrell, J. (2005). Interracial contact and racial constancy: A multi-site study of racial intergroup bias in 3–5 year old Anglo-British children. *Applied Developmental Psychology, 26,* 699–713.

Rutter, M. (2005). Adverse preadoption experiences and psychological outcomes. In D. M. Brodzinsky & J. Palacios (Eds.), *Psychological issues in adoption: Research and practice* (pp. 67–92). Westport, CT: Praeger/Greenwood.

Rutter, M., & Garmezy, N. (1983). Developmental psychopathology. In P. H. Mussen (Series Ed.) & E. M. Hetherington (Vol. Ed.), *Handbook of child psychology: Vol. 4. Socialization, personality, and social development* (4th ed., pp. 775–911). New York: Wiley.

Rutter, M. L. (1997). Nature-nurture integration: The example of antisocial behavior. *American Psychologist, 52,* 390–398.

Ryan, A. M. (2000). Peer groups as a context for the socialization of adolescents' motivation, engagement, and achievement in school. *Educational Psychologist, 35,* 101–111.

Ryan, A. M., & Patrick, H. (2001). The classroom social environment and changes in adolescents' motivation and engagement during middle school. *American Educational Research Journal, 38,* 437–460.

Ryan, R. (2005, April). *Legislating competence: High stakes testing, school reform, and motivation from a self-determination theory viewpoint*. Paper

presented at the annual meeting of the American Educational Research Association, Montreal.

Ryan, R. M., Connell, J. P., & Grolnick, W. S. (1992). When achievement is *not* intrinsically motivated: A theory of internalization and self-regulation in school. In A. K. Boggiano & T. S. Pittman (Eds.), *Achievement and motivation: A social-developmental perspective*. Cambridge, England: Cambridge University Press.

Ryan, R. M., & Deci, E. L. (2000). Self-determination theory and the facilitation of intrinsic motivation, social development, and well-being. *American Psychologist, 55,* 68–78.

Ryan, R. M., & Kuczkowski, R. (1994). The imaginary audience, self-consciousness, and public individuation in adolescence. *Journal of Personality, 62,* 219–237.

Ryan, R. M., & Lynch, J. H. (1989). Emotional autonomy versus detachment: Revisiting the vicissitudes of adolescence and young adulthood. *Child Development, 60,* 340–356.

Ryan, R. M., Stiller, J. D., & Lynch, J. H. (1994). Representations of relationships to teachers, parents, and friends as predictors of academic motivation and self-esteem. *Journal of Early Adolescence, 14,* 226–249.

Rycus, J. S., Freundlich, M., Hughes, R. C., Keefer, B., & Oakes, E. J. (2006). Confronting barriers to adoption success. *Family Court Review, 44,* 210–230.

Saarni, C., Campos, J. J., Camras, L. A., & Witherington, D. (2006). Emotional development: Action, communication, and understanding. In W. Damon & R. M. Lerner (Eds. in Chief) & N. Eisenberg (Vol. Ed.), *Handbook of child psychology, Vol. 3. Social, emotional, and personality development* (6th ed., pp. 226–299). Hoboken, NJ: Wiley.

Sabbagh, M. A., Xu, F., Carlson, S. M., Moses, L. J., & Lee, K. (2006). The development of executive functioning and theory of mind: A comparison of Chinese and U.S. preschoolers. *Psychological Science, 17,* 74–81.

Sacks, C. H., & Mergendoller, J. R. (1997). The relationship between teachers' theoretical orientation toward reading and student outcomes in kindergarten children with different initial reading abilities. *American Educational Research Journal, 34,* 721–739.

Sadeh, A., Gruber, R., & Raviv, A. (2002). Sleep, neurobehavioral functioning, and behavior problems in school-age children. *Child Development, 73,* 405–417.

Sadler, T. W. (2006). *Hangman's medical embryology* (10th ed.). Philadelphia: Lippincott Williams & Wilkins.

Saffran, J. R. (2003). Statistical language learning: Mechanisms and constraints. *Current Directions in Psychological Science, 12,* 110–114.

Saffran, J. R., & Griepentrog, G. J. (2001). Absolute pitch in infant auditory learning: Evidence for developmental reorganization. *Developmental Psychology, 37,* 74–85.

Saffran, J. R., Aslin, R. N., & Newport, E. L. (1996). Statistical learning by 8-month-old infants. *Science, 274,* 1926–1928.

Salend, S. J., & Taylor, L. (1993). Working with families: A cross-cultural perspective. *Remedial and Special Education, 14,* 25–32, 39.

Salisbury, C. L., Evans, I. M., & Palombaro, M. M. (1997). Collaborative problem solving to promote the inclusion of young children with significant disabilities in primary grades. *Exceptional Children, 63,* 195–210.

Salmivalli, C., & Isaacs, J. (2005). Prospective relations among victimization, rejection, friendlessness, and children's self- and peer-perceptions. *Child Development, 76,* 1161–1171.

Salomon, G. (1993). No distribution without individual's cognition: A dynamic interactional view. In G. Salomon (Ed.), *Distributed cognition*. New York: Cambridge University Press.

Saltz, E. (1971). *The cognitive bases of human learning*. Homewood, IL: Dorsey.

Sameroff, A. J., Seifer, R., Baldwin, A., & Baldwin, C. (1993). Stability of intelligence from preschool to adolescence: The influence of social and family risk factors. *Child Development, 64,* 80–97.

Sanchez, F., & Anderson, M. L. (1990). Gang mediation: A process that works. *Principal, 69*(4), 54–56.

Sands, D. J., & Wehmeyer, M. L. (Eds.). (1996). *Self-determination across the life span: Independence and choice for people with disabilities*. Baltimore: Brookes.

Sarrazin, J., & Cyr, F. (2007). Parental conflicts and their damaging effects on children. *Journal of Divorce and Remarriage, 47,* 77–93.

Sattler, J. M. (2001). *Assessment of children: Cognitive applications* (4th ed.). San Diego, CA: Author.

Savin-Williams, R. C. (1989). Gay and lesbian adolescents. *Marriage and Family Review, 14*(3–4), 197–216.

Savin-Williams, R. C. (1995). Lesbian, gay male, and bisexual adolescents. In R. D'Augelli & C. J. Patterson (Eds.), *Lesbian, gay, and bisexual identities over the lifespan: Psychological perspectives* (pp. 165–189). New York: Oxford University Press.

Savin-Williams, R. C. (2005). *The new gay teenager*. Cambridge, MA: Harvard University Press.

Savin-Williams, R. C., & Diamond, L. M. (1997). Sexual orientation as a developmental context for lesbians, gays, and bisexuals: Biological perspectives. In N. L. Segal, G. E. Weisfeld, & C. C. Weisfeld (Eds.), *Uniting psychology and biology: Integrative perspectives on human development* (pp. 217–238). Washington, DC: American Psychological Association.

Savin-Williams, R. C., & Diamond, L. M. (2004). Sex. In R. M. Lerner & L. Steinberg (Eds.), *Handbook of adolescent psychology* (2nd ed., pp. 189–231). Hoboken, NJ: Wiley.

Savin-Williams, R. C., & Ream, G. L. (2003). Suicide attempts among sexual-minority male youth. *Journal of Clinical Child and Adolescent Psychology, 32*(4), 509–522.

Sawyer, R. J., Graham, S., & Harris, K. R. (1992). Direct teaching, strategy instruction, and strategy instruction with explicit self-regulation: Effects on the composition skills and self-efficacy of students with learning disabilities. *Journal of Educational Psychology, 84,* 340–352.

Saxe, G. B. (1981). Body parts as numerals: A developmental analysis of numeration among the Oksapmin in Papua New Guinea, *Child Development, 52,* 306–316.

Saxe, G. B., & Esmonde, I. (2005). Studying cognition in flux: A historical treatment of *fu* in the shifting structure of Oksapmin mathematics. *Mind, Culture, and Activity, 12,* 171–225.

Scarborough, H. (2001). Connecting early language and literacy to later reading (dis)abilities: Evidence, theory, and practice. In S. Neuman & D. Dickinson (Eds.), *Handbook of early literacy research* (pp. 97–110). New York: Guilford.

Scardamalia, M., & Bereiter, C. (1986). Research on written composition. In M. C. Wittrock (Ed.), *Handbook of research on teaching* (3rd ed.). New York: Macmillan.

Scarr, S. (1992). Developmental theories for the 1990s: Development and individual differences. *Child Development, 63,* 1–19.

Scarr, S. (1993). Biological and cultural diversity: The legacy of Darwin for development. *Child Development, 64,* 1333–1353.

Scarr, S., & McCartney, K. (1983). How people make their own environments: A theory of genotype environment effects. *Child Development, 54,* 424–435.

Scarr, S., & Weinberg, R. A. (1976). IQ test performance of Black children adopted by White families. *American Psychologist, 31,* 726–739.

Schachter, J. (2000). Does individual tutoring produce optimal learning? *American Educational Research Journal, 37,* 801–829.

Schaefer-McDaniel, N. (2007). "They be doing illegal things": Early adolescents talk about their inner-city neighborhoods. *Journal of Adolescent Research, 22,* 413–436.

Schaffer, H. R. (1996). *Social development*. Cambridge, MA: Blackwell.

Schaie, K. W., & Willis, S. L. (2000). A stage theory model of adult cognitive development revisited. In R. L. Rubinstein, M. Moss, & M. H. Klebans (Eds.), *The many dimensions of aging* (pp. 175–193). New York: Springer.

Schauble, L. (1990). Belief revision in children: The role of prior knowledge and strategies for generating evidence. *Journal of Experimental Child Psychology, 49,* 31–57.

Schauble, L. (1996). The development of scientific reasoning in knowledge-rich contexts. *Developmental Psychology, 32,* 102–119.

Schellenberg, E. G. (2004). Music lessons enhance IQ. *Psychological Science, 15,* 511–514.

Schellenberg, E. G. (2006). Long-term positive associations between music lessons and IQ. *Journal of Educational Psychology, 98,* 457–468.

Scherer, N., & Olswang, L. (1984). Role of mothers' expansions in stimulating children's language production. *Journal of Speech and Hearing Research, 27,* 387–396.

Schimmoeller, M. A. (1998, April). *Influence of private speech on the writing behaviors of young children: Four case studies*. Paper presented at the annual meeting of the American Educational Research Association, San Diego, CA.

Schinke, S. P., Moncher, M. S., & Singer, B. R. (1994). Native American youths and cancer risk prevention. *Journal of Adolescent Health, 15,* 105–110.

Schlaefli, A., Rest, J. R., & Thoma, S. J. (1985). Does moral education improve moral judgment? A meta-analysis of intervention studies using the defining issues test. *Review of Educational Research, 55,* 319–352.

Schleppenbach, M., Perry, M., Miller, K. F., Sims, L., & Fang, G. (2007). The answer is only the beginning: Extended discourse in Chinese and U.S. mathematics classrooms. *Journal of Educational Psychology, 99,* 380–396.

Schliemann, A. D., & Carraher, D. W. (1993). Proportional reasoning in and out of school. In P. Light and G. Butterworth (Eds.), *Context and cognition: Ways of learning and knowing*. Hillsdale, NJ: Erlbaum.

Schmidt, W. H. (2008, Spring). What's missing from math standards? *American Educator*. Retrieved March 3, 2008, from http://www.aft.org/pubs-reports/american_educator/issues/spring2008/schmidt.htm

Schneider, B., Atkinson, L., & Tardif, C. (2001). Child–parent attachment and children's peer relations: A quantitative review. *Developmental Psychology, 37,* 86–100.

Schneider, W., Korkel, J., & Weinert, F. E. (1989). Domain-specific knowledge and memory performance: A comparison of high- and low-aptitude children. *Journal of Educational Psychology, 81,* 306–312.

Schneider, W., & Lockl, K. (2002). The development of metacognitive knowledge in children and adolescents. In T. J. Perfect & B. L. Schwartz (Eds.), *Applied metacognition* (pp. 224–257). Cambridge, England: Cambridge University Press.

Schneider, W., & Pressley, M. (1989). *Memory development between 2 and 20*. New York: Springer-Verlag.

Schneider, W., Roth, E., & Ennemoser, M. (2000). Training phonological skills and letter knowledge in children at risk for dyslexia: A comparison of three kindergarten intervention programs. *Journal of Educational Psychology, 92,* 284–295.

Schneider, W., & Shiffrin, R. M. (1977). Controlled and automatic human information processing: I. Detection, search, and attention. *Psychological Review, 84,* 1–66.

Schnur, E., Brooks-Gunn, J., & Shipman, V. C. (1992). Who attends programs serving poor children? The case of Head Start attendees and nonattendees. *Journal of Applied Developmental Psychology, 13,* 405–421.

Schoenfeld, A. H. (1988). When good teaching leads to bad results: The disasters of "well-taught" mathematics courses. *Educational Psychologist, 23,* 145–166.

Schoenfeld, A. H. (1992). Learning to think mathematically: Problem solving, metacognition, and sense making in mathematics. In D. A. Grouws (Ed.), *Handbook of research on mathematics teaching and learning*. New York: Macmillan.

Schofield, J. W. (1995). Improving intergroup relations among students. In J. A. Banks & C. A. M. Banks (Eds.), *Handbook of research on multicultural education*. New York: Macmillan.

Schommer, M. (1994a). An emerging conceptualization of epistemological beliefs and their role in learning. In R. Garner & P. A. Alexander (Eds.), *Beliefs about text and instruction with text*. Hillsdale, NJ: Erlbaum.

Schommer, M. (1994b). Synthesizing epistemological belief research: Tentative understandings and provocative confusions. *Educational Psychology Review, 6,* 293–319.

Schommer, M., Calvert, C., Gariglietti, G., & Bajaj, A. (1997). The development of epistemological beliefs among secondary students: A longitudinal study. *Journal of Educational Psychology, 89,* 37–40.

Schonert-Reichl, K. A. (1993). Empathy and social relationships in adolescents with behavioral disorders. *Behavioral Disorders, 18,* 189–204.

Schoppe-Sullivan, S. J., Mangelsdorf, S. C., Frosch, C. A., & McHale, J. L. (2004). Associations between coparenting and marital behavior from infancy to the preschool years. *Journal of Family Psychology, 18,* 194–207.

Schratz, M. (1978). A developmental investigation of sex differences in spatial (visual-analytic) and mathematical skills in three ethnic groups. *Developmental Psychology, 14,* 263–267.

Schraw, G. (2006). Knowledge: Structures and processes. In P. A. Alexander & P. H. Winne (Eds.), *Handbook of educational psychology* (2nd ed., pp. 245–263). Mahwah, NJ: Erlbaum.

Schraw, G., Flowerday, T., & Lehman, S. (2001). Increasing situational interest in the classroom. *Educational Psychology Review, 13,* 211–224.

Schraw, G., Potenza, M. T., & Nebelsick-Gullet, L. (1993). Constraints on the calibration of performance. *Contemporary Educational Psychology, 18,* 455–463.

Schreibman, L. (2008). Treatment controversies in autism. *Zero to Three, 28*(4), 38–45.

Schuler, M. E., Nair, P., & Harrington, D. (2003). Developmental outcome of drug-exposed children through 30 months: A comparison of Bayley and Bayley II. *Psychological Assessment, 15*(3), 435–438.

Schultz, G. F., & Switzky, H. N. (1990). The development of intrinsic motivation in students with learning problems: Suggestions for more effective instructional practice. *Preventing School Failure, 34*(2), 14–20.

Schumpf, F., Crawford, D., & Usadel, H. C. (1991). *Peer mediation: Conflict resolution in schools*. Champaign, IL: Research Press.

Schunk, D. H. (1990, April). *Socialization and the development of self-regulated learning: The role of attributions*. Paper presented at the annual meeting of the American Educational Research Association, Boston.

Schunk, D. H. (1996). Goal and self-evaluative influences during children's cognitive skill learning. *American Educational Research Journal, 33,* 359–382.

Schunk, D. H., & Hanson, A. R. (1985). Peer models: Influence on children's self-efficacy and achievement. *Journal of Educational Psychology, 77,* 313–322.

Schunk, D. H., & Pajares, F. (2004). Self-efficacy in education revisited: Empirical and applied evidence. In D. M. McNerney & S. Van Etten (Eds.),

Big theories revisited (pp. 115–138). Greenwich, CT: Information Age.

Schunk, D. H., & Rice, J. (1989). Learning goals and children's reading comprehension. *Journal of Reading Behavior, 21,* 279–293.

Schunk, D. H., & Swartz, C. W. (1993). Goals and progress feedback: Effects on self-efficacy and writing achievement. *Contemporary Educational Psychology, 18,* 337–354.

Schutz, P. A. (1994). Goals as the transactive point between motivation and cognition. In P. R. Pintrich, D. R. Brown, & C. E. Weinstein (Eds.), *Student motivation, cognition, and learning: Essays in honor of Wilbert J. McKeachie.* Hillsdale, NJ: Erlbaum.

Schutz, P. A., & Davis, H. A. (2000). Emotions and self-regulation during test taking. *Educational Psychologist, 35,* 243–256.

Schwartz, B. L., & Perfect, T. J. (2002). Introduction: Toward an applied metacognition. In T. J. Perfect & B. L. Schwartz (Eds.), *Applied metacognition* (pp. 1–11). Cambridge, England: Cambridge University Press.

Schwartz, D., Dodge, K. A., Coie, J. D., Hubbard, J. A., Cillessen, A. H., Lemerise, E. A., et al. (1998). Social-cognitive and behavioral correlates of aggression and victimization in boys' play groups. *Journal of Abnormal Child Psychology, 26,* 431–440.

Schwartz, D., Gorman, A. H., Duong, M. T., & Nakamoto, J. (2008). Peer relationships and academic achievement as interacting predictors of depressive symptoms during middle childhood. *Journal of Abnormal Psychology, 117*(2), 289–299.

Schwartz, G. M., Izard, C. E., & Ansul, S. E. (1985). The 5-month-old's ability to discriminate facial expressions of emotion. *Infant Behavior and Development, 8*(1), 65–67.

Schwartz, J. L., Yarushalmy, M., & Wilson, B. (Eds.) (1993). *The geometric supposer: What is it a case of?* Hillsdale, NJ: Erlbaum.

Schwarz, C. V., & White, B. Y. (2005). Metamodeling knowledge: Developing students' understanding of scientific modeling. *Cognition and Instruction, 23,* 165–205.

Schweinhart, L. J., & Weikart, D. (1983). The effects of the Perry Preschool Program on youths through age 15: A summary. In Consortium for Longitudinal Studies (Ed.), *As the twig is bent: Lasting effects of preschool programs* (pp. 71–101). Hillsdale, NJ: Erlbaum.

Scott-Jones, D. (1991). Black families and literacy. In S. B. Silvern (Eds.), *Advances in reading/language research: Literacy through family, community, and school interaction* (pp. 173–200). Greenwich, CT: JAI Press.

Scott-Little, M., & Holloway, S. (1992). Child care providers' reasoning about misbehaviors: Relation to classroom control strategies and professional training. *Early Childhood Research Quarterly, 7,* 595–606.

Segal, B. M., & Stewart, J. C. (1996). Substance use and abuse in adolescence: An overview. *Child Psychiatry and Human Development, 26,* 193–210.

Segal, N. L. (2000). Virtual twins: New findings on within-family environmental influences on intelligence. *Journal of Educational Psychology, 92,* 442–448.

Segal, N. L., & Russell, J. M. (1992). Twins in the classroom: School policy issues and recommendations. *Journal of Educational and Psychological Consultation, 3,* 69–84.

Seidman, E., Aber, J. L., & French, S. E. (2004). The organization of schooling and adolescent development. In K. I. Maton, C. J. Schellenbach, B. J. Leadbeater, & A. L. Solarz (Eds.), *Investing in children, youth, families, and communities: Strengths-based research and policy* (pp. 233–250). Washington, DC: American Psychological Association.

Seixas, P. (1996). Conceptualizing the growth of historical understanding. In D. R. Olson & N. Torrance (Eds.), *The handbook of education and human development: New models of learning, teaching, and schooling.* Cambridge, MA: Blackwell.

Selfe, L. (1977). *Nadia: A case of extraordinary drawing ability in an autistic child.* London: Academic Press.

Selfe, L. (1995). Nadia reconsidered. In C. Golomb (Ed.), *The development of artistically gifted children: Selected case studies* (pp. 197–236). Hillsdale, NJ: Erlbaum.

Seligman, M. E. P. (1975). *Helplessness: On depression, development, and death.* San Francisco: Freeman.

Seligman, M. E. P. (1991). *Learned optimism.* New York: Knopf.

Selman, R. L. (1980). *The growth of interpersonal understanding: Developmental and clinical analysis.* New York: Academic Press.

Selman, R. L. (2003). *The promotion of social awareness: Powerful lessons from the partnership of developmental theory and classroom practice.* New York: Russell Sage Foundation.

Seltzer, V. C. (1982). *Adolescent social development: Dynamic functional interaction.* Lexington, MA: Heath.

Semb, G. B., Ellis, J. A., & Araujo, J. (1993). Long-term memory for knowledge learned in school. *Journal of Educational Psychology, 85,* 305–316.

Semrud-Clikeman, M., & Hynd, G. W. (1991). Specific nonverbal and social skills deficits in children with learning disabilities. In J. E. Obrzut & G. W. Hynd (Eds.), *Neuropsychological foundations of learning disabilities: A handbook of issues, methods, and practice* (pp. 603–630). San Diego, CA: Academic Press.

Sénéchal, M., & LeFevre, J.-A. (2002). Parental involvement in the development of children's reading skill: A five-year longitudinal study. *Child Development, 73,* 445–460.

Sénéchal, M., Thomas, E., & Monker, J. (1995). Individual differences in 4-year-old children's acquisition of vocabulary during storybook reading. *Journal of Educational Psychology, 87,* 218–229.

Senghas, A., & Coppola, M. (2001). Children creating language: How Nicaraguan Sign Language acquired a spatial grammar. *Psychological Science, 12,* 323–328.

Serpell, R., Baker, L., & Sonnenschein, S. (2005). *Becoming literate in the city: The Baltimore Early Childhood Project.* Cambridge, England: Cambridge University Press.

Sewald, H. (1986). Adolescents' shifting orientation toward parents and peers: A curvilinear trend over recent decades. *Journal of Marriage and the Family, 48,* 5–13.

Shah, J. Y. (2005). The automatic pursuit and management of goals. *Current Directions in Psychological Science, 14,* 10–13.

Shahinfar, A., Kupersmidt, J. B., & Matza, L. S. (2001). The relation between exposure to violence and social information processing among incarcerated adolescents. *Journal of Abnormal Psychology, 110,* 136–141.

Shanahan, L., McHale, S. M., Osgood, W., & Crouter, A. C. (2007). Conflict frequency with mothers and fathers from middle childhood to late adolescence: Within- and between-families comparisons. *Developmental Psychology, 43*(3), 539–550.

Shanahan, T., & Tierney, R. J. (1990). Reading-writing connection: The relations among three perspectives. In J. Zutell & S. McCormick (Eds.), *Literacy Theory and research: Analyses from multiple paradigms. Thirty-ninth yearbook of the National Reading Conference.* Chicago: National Reading Conference.

Shapiro, E. S., & Manz, P. H. (2004). Collaborating with schools in the provision of pediatric psychological services. In R. T. Brown (Ed.), *Handbook of pediatric psychology in school settings* (pp. 49–64). Mahwah, NJ: Erlbaum.

Shapka, J. D., & Keating, D. P. (2003). Effects of a girls-only curriculum during adolescence: Performance, persistence, and engagement in mathematics and science. *American Educational Research Journal, 40,* 929–960.

Share, D. L. (1995). Phonological recoding and self-teaching: Sine qua non of reading acquisition. *Cognition, 55,* 151–218.

Share, D. L., & Gur, T. (1999). How reading begins: A study of preschoolers' print identification strategies. *Cognition and Instruction, 17,* 177–213.

Shatz, M., & Gelman, R. (1973). The development of communication skills: Modifications in the speech of young children as a function of the listener. *Monographs of the Society for Research in Child Development, 38*(5, Serial No. 152).

Shavers, C. A. (2000). The interrelationships of exposure to community violence and trauma to the behavioral patterns and academic performance among urban elementary school-aged children. *Dissertation Abstracts International: Section B. The Physical Sciences and Engineering, 61*(4-B), 1876.

Shavinina, L. V., & Ferrari, M. (2004). Extracognitive facets of developing high ability: Introduction to some important issues. In L. V. Shavinina & M. Ferrari (Eds.), *Beyond knowledge: Extracognitive aspects of developing high ability* (pp. 3–13). Mahwah, NJ: Erlbaum.

Shaw, P., Eckstrand, K., Sharp, W., Blumenthal, J., Lerch, J. P., Greenstein, D., et al. (2007). Attention-deficit/hyperactivity disorder is characterized by a delay in cortical maturation. *Proceedings of the National Academy of Sciences, 104,* 19, 649–19, 654.

Shaywitz, S. E. (2004). *Overcoming dyslexia.* New York: Knopf.

Shaywitz, S. E., Mody, M., & Shaywitz, B. A. (2006). Neural mechanisms in dyslexia. *Current Directions in Psychological Science, 15,* 278–281.

Shea, D. L., Lubinski, D., & Benbow, C. P. (2001). Importance of assessing spatial ability in intellectually talented young adolescents: A 20-year longitudinal study. *Journal of Educational Psychology, 93,* 604–614.

Sheckley, B. G., & Keeton, M. T. (1997). Service learning: A theoretical model. In J. Schine (Ed.), *Service learning.* Chicago: National Society for the Study of Education.

Shedler, J., & Block, J. (1990). Adolescent drug use and psychological health. *American Psychologist, 45,* 612–630.

Sheehan, E. P., & Smith, H. V. (1986). Cerebral lateralization and handedness and their effects on verbal and spatial reasoning. *Neuropsychologia, 24,* 531–540.

Sheets, R. H. (1999). Human development and ethnic identity. In R. H. Sheets & E. R. Hollins (Eds.), *Racial and ethnic identity in school practices: Aspects of human development* (pp. 91–101). Mahwah, NJ: Erlbaum.

Sheets, R. H., & Hollins, E. R. (Eds.). (1999). *Racial and ethnic identity in school practices: Aspects of human development.* Mahwah, NJ: Erlbaum.

Sheffield, E., Stromswold, K., & Molnar, D. (2005, April). *Do prematurely born infants catch up?* Paper presented at the biennial meeting of the Society for Research in Child Development, Atlanta, GA.

Shellenberg, E. G., & Trehub, S. E. (2003). Good pitch memory is widespread. *Psychological Science, 14,* 262–266.

Shenfield, T., Trehub, S. E., & Nakata, T. (2003). Maternal singing modulates infant arousal. *Psychology of Music, 31,* 365–375.

Shenkin, S. D., Starr, J. M., & Deary, I. J. (2004). Birth weight and cognitive ability in childhood: A systematic review. *Psychological Bulletin, 130,* 989–1013.

Shepard, R. N., & Metzler, J. (1971). Mental rotation of three-dimensional objects. *Science, 171,* 701–703.

Sheridan, M. D. (1975). *Children's developmental progress from birth to five years: The Stycar Sequences.* Windsor, England: NFER.

Sherif, M., Harvey, O. J., White, B. J., Hood, W. R., & Sherif, C. (1961). *Inter-group conflict and cooperation: The Robbers Cave experiment.* Norman: University of Oklahoma Press.

Sherwen, L. N., Scoloveno, M. A., & Weingarten, C. T. (1999). *Maternity nursing: Care of the childbearing family* (3rd ed.). Stamford, CT: Appleton & Lange.

Shi, R., & Werker, J. F. (2001). Six-month-old infants' preference for lexical words. *Psychological Science, 12,* 70–75.

Shields, M. K., & Behrman, R. E. (2004). Children of immigrant families: Analysis and recommendations. *The Future of Children, 14*(2), 4–15.

Shim, S. S., & Ryan, A. M. (2006, April). *The nature and the consequences of changes in achievement goals during early adolescence.* Paper presented at the annual meeting of the American Educational Research Association, San Francisco, CA.

Shoda, Y., Mischel, W., & Peake, P. K. (1990). Predicting adolescent cognitive and self-regulatory competencies from preschool delay of gratification: Identifying diagnostic conditions. *Developmental Psychology, 26,* 978–986.

Shonkoff, J. P. & Phillips, D. A. (Eds.). (2000). *From neurons to neighborhoods: The science of early childhood development.* Washington, DC: National Academy of Sciences.

Short, E. J., & Ryan, E. B. (1984). Metacognitive differences between skilled and less skilled readers: Remediating deficits through story grammar and attribution training. *Journal of Educational Psychology, 76,* 225–235.

Short, E. J., Schatschneider, C. W., & Friebert, S. E. (1993). Relationship between memory and metamemory performance: A comparison of specific and general strategy knowledge. *Journal of Educational Psychology, 85,* 412–423.

Shrum, W., & Cheek, N. H. (1987). Social structure during the school years: Onset of the degrouping process. *American Sociological Review, 52,* 218–223.

Shultz, T. R. (1974). Development of the appreciation of riddles. *Child Development, 45,* 100–105.

Shultz, T. R., & Horibe, F. (1974). Development of the appreciation of verbal jokes. *Developmental Psychology, 10,* 13–20.

Shweder, R. A., Goodnow, J., Hatano, G., LeVine, R. A., Markus, H., & Miller, P. (1998). The cultural psychology of development: One mind, many mentalities. In W. Damon (Series Ed.) & R. M. Lerner (Vol. Ed.), *Handbook of child psychology: Vol. 1. Theoretical models of human development* (5th ed., pp. 865–937). New York: Wiley.

Shweder, R. A., Mahapatra, M., & Miller, J. G. (1987). Culture and moral development. In J. Kagan & S. Lamb (Eds.), *The emergence of morality in young children* (pp. 1–83). Chicago: University of Chicago Press.

Shweder, R. A., Much, N. C., Mahapatra, M., & Park, L. (1997). The "big three" of morality (autonomy, community, and divinity) and the "big three" explanations of suffering. In A. Brandt & P. Rozin (Eds.), *Morality and health* (pp. 119–169). Stanford, CA: Stanford University Press.

Sidel, R. (1996). *Keeping women and children last: America's war on the poor.* New York: Penguin Books.

Siegel, D. J. (1999). *The developing mind: How relationships and the brain interact to shape who we are.* New York: Guilford Press.

Siegel, D. J. (2001). Toward an interpersonal neurobiology of the developing mind: Attachment relationships, 'mindsight,' and neural integration. *Infant Mental Health Journal, 22,* 67–94.

Siegler, R. S. (1976). Three aspects of cognitive development. *Cognitive Psychology, 8,* 481–520.

Siegler, R. S. (1978). The origins of scientific reasoning. In R. S. Siegler (Ed.), *Children's thinking: What develops?* Hillsdale, NJ: Erlbaum.

Siegler, R. S. (1989). Mechanisms of cognitive growth. *Annual Review of Psychology, 40,* 353–379.

Siegler, R. S. (1994). Cognitive variability: A key to understanding cognitive development. *Current Directions in Psychological Science, 3,* 1–5.

Siegler, R. S. (1996). *Emerging minds: The process of change in children's thinking.* New York: Oxford University Press.

Siegler, R. S. (2006). Microgenetic analyses of learning. In W. Damon & R. M. Lerner (Eds. in Chief) & D. Kuhn & R. S. Siegler (Vol. Eds.), *Handbook of child psychology: Vol. 2. Cognition, perception, and language* (6th ed., pp. 464–510). Hoboken, NJ: Wiley.

Siegler, R. S., & Alibali, M. W. (2005). *Children's thinking* (4th ed.). Upper Saddle River, NJ: Prentice Hall.

Siegler, R. S., & Jenkins, E. (1989). *How children discover new strategies.* Hillsdale, NJ: Erlbaum.

Siegler, R. S., & Richards, D. D. (1982). The development of intelligence. In R. J. Sternberg (Ed.), *Handbook of human intelligence.* Cambridge, England: Cambridge University Press.

Siegler, R. S., & Robinson, M. (1982). The development of numerical understandings. In H. W. Reese & L. P. Lipsitt (Eds.), *Advances in child development and behavior* (Vol. 16). New York: Academic Press.

Siegler, R. S., & Svetina, M. (2006). What leads children to adopt new strategies? A microgenetic/cross-sectional study of class inclusion. *Child Development, 77,* 997–1015.

Siever, L., & Davis, K. (1985). Overview: Toward a dysregulation hypothesis of depression. *American Journal of Psychiatry, 142,* 1017–1031.

Sigman, M., & Whaley, S. E. (1998). The role of nutrition in the development of intelligence. In U. Neisser (Ed.), *The rising curve: Long-term gains in IQ and related measures* (pp. 155–182). Washington, DC: American Psychological Association.

Signorielli, N., & Lears, M. (1992). Children, television, and conceptions about chores: Attitudes and behaviors. *Sex Roles, 27,* 157–170.

Silk, J. S., Sessa, F. M., Morris, A. S., Steinberg, L., & Avenevoli, S. (2004). Neighborhood cohesion as a buffer against hostile maternal parenting. *Journal of Family Psychology, 18,* 135–146.

Silver, E. A., & Kenney, P. A. (1995). Sources of assessment information for instructional guidance in mathematics. In T. Romberg (Ed.), *Reform in school mathematics and authentic assessment.* Albany: State University of New York Press.

Silverman, I. W., & Ragusa, D. M. (1990). Child and maternal correlates of impulse control in 24-month-old children. *Genetic, Social, and General Psychology Monographs, 116,* 435–473.

Silverman, L. K. (1994). The moral sensitivity of gifted children and the evolution of society. *Roeper Review, 17*(2), 110–116.

Simmons, R. G., & Blyth, D. A. (1987). *Moving into adolescence: The impact of pubertal change in school context.* New York: Aldine de Gruyter.

Simmons, T., & O'Connell, M. (2003). *Married-couple and unmarried-partner households: 2000.* Census Special Reports, CENSR-5. Washington, DC: U.S. Census Bureau.

Simner, M. L. (1971). Newborn's response to the cry of another infant. *Developmental Psychology, 5,* 136–150.

Simons, J., Vansteenkiste, M., Lens, W., & Lacante, M. (2004). Placing motivation and future time perspective theory in a temporal perspective. *Educational Psychology Review, 16,* 121–139.

Simons, R. L., Robertson, J. F., & Downs, W. R. (1989). The nature of the association between parental rejection and delinquent behavior. *Journal of Youth and Adolescence, 18,* 297–310.

Simons, R. L., Whitbeck, L. B., Conger, R. D., & Conger, K. J. (1991). Parenting factors, social skills, and value commitments as precursors to school failure, involvement with deviant peers, and delinquent behavior. *Journal of Youth and Adolescence, 20,* 645–664.

Simons-Morton, B. G., Taylor, W. C., Snider, S. A., & Huang, I. W. (1993). The physical activity of fifth-grade students during physical education classes. *American Journal of Public Health, 83,* 262–264.

Simons-Morton, B. G., Taylor, W. C., Snider, S. A., Huang, I. W., & Fulton, J. E. (1994). Observed levels of elementary and middle school children's physical activity during physical education classes. *Preventive Medicine, 23,* 437–441.

Simonton, D. K. (2001). Talent development as a multidimensional, multiplicative, and dynamic process. *Current Directions in Psychological Science, 10,* 39–42.

Simos, P. G., Fletcher, J. M., Sarkari, S., Billingsley, R. L., Denton, C. & Papanicolaou, A. C. (2007). Altering the brain circuits for reading through intervention: A magnetic source imaging study. *Neuropsychology, 21,* 485–496.

Sims, M. (1993). How my question keeps evolving. In M. Cochran-Smith & S. L. Lytle (Eds.), *Inside/outside: Teacher research and knowledge* (pp. 283–289). New York: Teachers College Press.

Sinatra, G. M., & Pintrich, P. R. (2003). The role of intentions in conceptual change learning. In G. M. Sinatra & P. R. Pintrich (Eds.), *Intentional conceptual change* (pp. 1–18). Mahwah, NJ: Erlbaum.

Singer, E., & Doornenbal, J. (2006). Learning morality in peer conflict: A study of schoolchildren's narratives about being betrayed by a friend. *Childhood, 13*(2), 225–245.

Singer, J., Marx, R. W., Krajcik, J., & Chambers, J. C. (2000). Constructing extended inquiry projects: Curriculum materials for science education reform. *Educational Psychologist, 35,* 165–178.

Sinnott, J. D. (1998). *The development of logic in adulthood: Postformal thought and its applications.* New York: Plenum.

Sipe, R. B. (2006). Grammar matters. *English Journal, 95,* 15–17.

Sirois, S., Buckingham, D., & Shultz, T. R. (2000). Artificial grammar learning by infants: An auto-associator perspective. *Developmental Science, 3,* 442–456.

Sisk, D. A. (1989). Identifying and nurturing talent among American Indians. In C. J. Maker & S. W. Schiever (Eds.), *Critical issues in gifted education: Vol. 2. Defensible programs for cultural and ethnic minorities.* Austin, TX: Pro-Ed.

Sitko, B. M. (1998). Knowing how to write: Metacognition and writing instruction. In D. J. Hacker, J. Dunlosky, & A. C. Graesser (Eds.), *Metacognition in educational theory and practice* (pp. 93–115). Mahwah, NJ: Erlbaum.

Sjostrom, L., & Stein, N. (1996). *Bully proof: A teacher's guide on teasing and bullying for use with fourth and fifth grade students.* Wellesley, MA: Wellesley College Center for Women.

Skiba, R. J., & Rausch, M. K. (2006). Zero tolerance, suspension, and expulsion: Questions of equity and effectiveness. In C. M. Evertson & C. S. Weinstein (Eds.), *Handbook of classroom management: Research, practice, and contemporary issues* (pp. 1063–1089). Mahwah, NJ: Erlbaum.

Skinner, B. F. (1953). *Science and human behavior.* New York: Macmillan.

Skinner, B. F. (1957). *Verbal behavior.* New York: Appleton-Century-Croft.

Skinner, B. F. (1968). *The technology of teaching.* New York: Appleton-Century-Crofts.

Slater, A. M., Mattock, A., & Brown, E. (1990). Size constancy at birth: Newborn infants' responses to retinal and real size. *Journal of Experimental Child Psychology, 49,* 314–322.

Slater, A. M., & Morison, V. (1985). Shape constancy and slant perception at birth. *Perception, 14,* 337–344.

Slavin, R. E. (1990). *Cooperative learning: Theory, research, and practice.* Upper Saddle River, NJ: Prentice Hall.

Slavin, R. E., & Cheung, A. (2005). A synthesis of research on language of reading instruction for English language learners. *Review of Educational Research, 75,* 247–284.

Sleeter, C. E., & Grant, C. A. (1999). *Making choices for multicultural education: Five approaches to race, class, and gender* (3rd ed.). Upper Saddle River, NJ: Merrill/Prentice Hall.

Sloan, W. M. (2008). Serving the needs of learners. *Education Update, 50*(1) 1, 6–7.

Slonim, M. B. (1991). *Children, culture, ethnicity: Evaluating and understanding the impact.* New York: Garland.

Smart, C., Neale, B., & Wade, A. (2001). *The changing experience of childhood: Families and divorce.* Cambridge, England: Polity.

Smetana, J. G. (1981). Preschool children's conceptions of moral and social rules. *Child Development, 52,* 1333–1336.

Smetana, J. G., & Braeges, J. L. (1990). The development of toddlers' moral and conventional judgments. *Merrill-Palmer Quarterly, 36,* 329–346.

Smetana, J. G., Killen, M., & Turiel, E. (1991). Children's reasoning about interpersonal and moral conflicts. *Child Development, 62,* 629–644.

Smetana, J. G., Metzger, A., Gettman, D. C., & Campione-Barr, N. (2006). Disclosure and secrecy in adolescent–parent relationships. *Child Development, 77,* 201–217.

Smith, C. L. (2007). Bootstrapping processes in the development of students' commonsense matter theories: Using analogical mappings, thought experiments, and learning to measure to promote conceptual restructuring. *Cognition and Instruction, 25,* 337–398.

Smith, C. L., Maclin, D., Houghton, C., & Hennessey, M. G. (2000). Sixth-grade students' epistemologies of science: The impact of school science experiences on epistemological development. *Cognition and Instruction, 18,* 349–422.

Smith, E. P., Boutte, G. S., Zigler, E., & Finn-Stevenson, M. (2004). Opportunities for schools to promote resilience in children and youth. In K. I. Maton, C. J. Schellenbach, B. J. Leadbeater, & A. L. Solarz (Eds.), *Investing in children, youth, families, and communities: Strengths-based research and policy* (pp. 213–231). Washington, DC: American Psychological Association.

Smith, H. (2008). Searching for kinship: The creation of street families among homeless youth. *American Behavioral Scientist, 51*(6), 756–771.

Smith, H. L. (1998). Literacy and instruction in African American communities: Shall we overcome? In B. Pérez (Ed.), *Sociocultural contexts of language and literacy.* Mahwah, NJ: Erlbaum.

Smith, J., & Ross, H. (2007). Training parents to mediate sibling disputes affects children's negotiation and conflict understanding. *Child Development, 78,* 790–805.

Smith, J. S. (2006). Research summary: Transition from middle school to high school. Retrieved June 3, 2008, from http://www.nmsa.org/Research/ResearchSummaries/TransitionfromMStoHS/tabid/1087/Default.aspx

Smith, J. T. (1999). Sickle cell disease. In S. Goldstein & C. R. Reynolds (Eds.), *Handbook of neurodevelopmental and genetic disorders* (pp. 368–384). New York: Guilford Press.

Smith, L. (1994, February 16). Bad habits: Testament to the downward spiral of drugs and teen angst. *Los Angeles Times,* p. 1.

Smith, N. R., Cicchetti, L., Clark, M. C., Fucigna, C., Gordon-O'Connor, B., Halley, B. A., et al. (1998). *Observation drawing with children: A framework for teachers.* New York: Teachers College Press.

Smith, P. B., & Bond, M. H. (1994). *Social psychology across cultures: Analysis and perspectives.* Needham Heights, MA: Allyn & Bacon.

Smith, P. K. (2006). Evolutionary foundations and functions of play: An overview. In A. Göncü & S. Gaskins (Eds.), *Play and development: Evolutionary, sociocultural, and functional perspectives* (pp. 21–49) Mahwah, NJ: Erlbaum.

Smith, R. A., Martin, S. C., & Wolters, P. L. (2004). Pediatric and adolescent HIV/AIDS. In R. T. Brown (Ed.), *Handbook of pediatric psychology in school settings* (pp. 195–220). Mahwah, NJ: Erlbaum.

Smith, R. E., & Smoll, F. L. (1997). Coaching the coaches: Youth sports as a scientific and applied behavioral setting. *Current Directions in Psychological Science, 6,* 16–21.

Smith, S. L., & Donnerstein, E. (1998). Harmful effects of exposure to media violence: Learning of aggression, emotional desensitization, and fear. In R. G. Geen & E. Donnerstein (Eds.), *Human aggression: Theories, research, and implications for social policy* (pp. 167–202). New York: Academic Press.

Smitherman, G. (1994). "The blacker the berry the sweeter the juice": African American student writers. In A. H. Dyson & C. Genishi (Eds.), *The need for story: Cultural diversity in classroom and community.* Urbana, IL: National Council of Teachers of English.

Smitherman, G. (2007). The power of the rap: The Black idiom and the new Black poetry. In H. S. Alim & J. Baugh (Eds.), *Talkin black talk: Language, education, and social change* (pp. 77–91). New York: Teachers College Press.

Snarey, J. (1995). In a communitarian voice: The sociological expansion of Kohlbergian theory, research, and practice. In W. M. Kurtines & J. L. Gewirtz (Eds.), *Moral development: An introduction.* Boston: Allyn & Bacon.

Snedeker, J., Geren, J., & Shafto, C. L. (2007). Starting over: International adoption as a natural experiment in language development. *Psychological Science, 18,* 79–87.

Snow, C. E (1990). Rationales for native language instruction: Evidence from research. In A. M. Padilla, H. H. Fairchild, & C. M. Valadez (Eds.), *Bilingual education: Issues and strategies.* Newbury Park, CA: Sage.

Snow, C. E., & Kang, J. Y. (2006). Becoming bilingual, biliterate, and bicultural. In W. Damon & R. M. Lerner (Eds. in Chief) & R. M. Lerner (Vol. Ed.), *Handbook of child psychology: Vol. 4. Child psychology in practice* (6th ed., pp. 75–102). Hoboken, NJ: Wiley.

Snow, C. W., & McGaha, C. G. (2003). *Infant development* (3rd ed.). Upper Saddle River, NJ: Prentice Hall.

Snowling, M. J., Gallagher, A., & Frith, U. (2003). Family risk of dyslexia is continuous: Individual differences in the precursors of reading skill. *Child Development, 74,* 358–373.

Snyder, K. A. (2007). Neural mechanisms of attention and memory in preferential looking tasks. In L. M. Oakes & P. J. Bauer (Eds.), *Short- and long-term memory in infancy and early childhood: Taking the first steps toward remembering* (pp. 179–208). New York: Oxford University Press.

Society for Research in Child Development. (2007). *Ethical standards for research with children.* First published in the 1990–91 Directory and Fall 1991 Newsletter. Retrieved October 3, 2007, from http://www.srcd.org/ethicalstandards.html

Soderstrom, M., Kemler Nelson, D. G., & Jusczyk, P. W. (2005). Six-month-olds recognize clauses embedded in different passages of fluent speech. *Infant Behavior and Development, 28,* 87–94.

Soet, J. E., Brack, G. A., & DiIorio, C. (2003). Prevalence and predictors of women's experience of psychological trauma during childbirth. *Birth, 30* (1), 36–46.

Solmon, M. A., & Lee, A. M. (2008). Research on social issues in elementary school physical education. *Elementary School Journal, 108*(3), 229–239.

Solomon, D., Watson, M., Battistich, E., Schaps, E., & Delucchi, K. (1992). Creating a caring community: Educational practices that promote children's prosocial development. In F. K. Oser, A. Dick, & J. L. Patry (Eds.), *Effective and responsible teaching: The new synthesis.* San Francisco: Jossey-Bass.

Solomon, D., Watson, M. S., Delucchi, K. L., Schaps, E., & Battistich, V. (1988). Enhancing children's prosocial behavior in the classroom. *American Educational Research Journal, 25,* 527–554.

Sonnenschein, S. (1988). The development of referential communication: Speaking to different listeners. *Child Development, 59,* 694–702.

Sophian, C., & Vong, K. I. (1995). The parts and wholes of arithmetic story problems: Developing knowledge in the preschool years. *Cognition and Instruction, 13,* 469–477.

Sorensen, R. (1983). *Adolescent sexuality in contemporary society.* New York: World Books.

South, D. (2007). What motivates unmotivated students? In G. E. Mills, *Action research: A guide for the teacher researcher* (3rd ed., pp. 1–2). Upper Saddle River, NJ: Pearson Merrill/Prentice Hall.

Southerland, S. A., & Sinatra, G. M. (2003). Learning about biological evolution: A special case of intentional conceptual change. In G. M. Sinatra & P. R. Pintrich (Eds.), *Intentional conceptual change* (pp. 317–345). Mahwah, NJ: Erlbaum.

Sowell, E. R., Delis, D., Stiles, J., & Jernigan, T. L. (2001). Improved memory functioning and frontal lobe maturation between childhood and adolescence: A structural MRI study. *Journal of the International Neuropsychological Society, 7,* 312–322.

Sowell, E. R., Thompson, P. M., Holmes, C. J., Jernigan, T. L., & Toga, A. W. (1999). *In vivo* evidence for post-adolescent brain maturation in frontal and striatal regions. *Nature Neuroscience, 2,* 859–861.

Sowell, E. R., Thompson, P. M., Rex, D., Kornsand, D., Tessner, K. D., Jernigan, T. L., et al. (2002). Mapping sulcal pattern asymmetry and local cortical surface gray matter distribution *in vivo:* Maturation in the perisylvian cortices. *Cerebral Cortex, 12,* 17–26.

Spear, L. P. (2007). Brain development and adolescent behavior. In D. Coch, K. W. Fischer, & G. Dawson (Eds.), *Human behavior, learning, and the developing brain: Typical development* (pp. 362–396). New York: Guilford Press.

Spearman, C. (1904). General intelligence, objectively determined and measured. *American Journal of Psychology, 15,* 201–293.

Spearman, C. (1927). *The abilities of man: Their nature and measurement.* New York: Macmillan.

Spector, R. E. (2004). *Cultural diversity in health and illness* (6th ed.). Upper Saddle River, NJ: Prentice Hall.

Spelke, E. S. (1994). Initial knowledge: Six suggestions. *Cognition, 50,* 431–445.

Spelke, E. S. (2000). Core knowledge. *American Psychologist, 55,* pp. 1233–1243.

Spelke, E. S. (2005). Sex differences in intrinsic aptitude for mathematics and science? A critical review. *American Psychologist, 60,* 950–958.

Spelke, E. S., Breinlinger, K., Macomber, J., & Jacobson, K. (1992). Origins of knowledge. *Psychological Review, 99,* 605–632.

Spencer, M. B. (2006). Phenomenology and ecological systems theory: Development of diverse groups. In W. Damon & R. M. Lerner (Eds. in Chief) & R. M. Lerner (Vol. Ed.), *Handbook of child psychology, Vol. 1. Theoretical models of human development* (6th ed., pp. 829–893). Hoboken, NJ: Wiley.

Spencer, M. B., & Markstrom-Adams, C. (1990). Identity processes among racial and ethnic minority children in America. *Child Development, 61,* 290–310.

Spencer, M. B., Noll, E., Stoltzfus, J., & Harpalani, V. (2001). Identity and school adjustment: Revisiting the "acting White" assumption. *Educational Psychologist, 36,* 21–30.

Spera, C. (2005). A review of the relationship among parenting practices, parenting styles, and adolescent school achievement. *Educational Psychology Review, 17,* 125–146.

Sperling, M. (1996). Revisiting the writing-speaking connection: Challenges for research on writing and writing instruction. *Review of Educational Research, 66,* 53–86.

Spicker, H. H. (1992). Identifying and enriching: Rural gifted children. *Educational Horizons, 70*(2), 60–65.

Spinath, F. M., Price, T. S., Dale, P. S., & Plomin, R. (2004). The genetic and environmental origins of language disability and ability. *Child Development, 75,* 445–454.

Spirito, A., Valeri, S., Boergers, J., & Donaldson, D. (2003). Predictors of continued suicidal behaviors in adolescents following a suicide attempt. *Journal of Clinical Child and Adolescent Psychology, 32,* 284–289.

Spivey, N. N. (1997). *The constructivist metaphor: Reading, writing, and the making of meaning.* San Diego, CA: Academic Press.

Sprafkin, C., Serbin, L. A., Denier, C., & Connor, J. M. (1983). Sex-differentiated play: Cognitive consequences and early interventions. In M. B. Liss (Ed.), *Social and cognitive skills: Sex roles and children's play.* San Diego, CA: Academic Press.

Sroufe, L. A. (1983). Infant-caregiver attachment and patterns of adaptation in preschool: The roots of maladaptation and competence. In M. Perlmutter (Ed.), Development and policy concerning children with special needs. *Minnesota Symposium on Child Psychology, 16,* 41–83. Hillsdale, NJ: Erlbaum.

Sroufe, L. A., Egeland, B., Carlson, E., & Collins, W. (2005). *Minnesota study of risk and adaptation from birth to maturity: The development of the person.* New York: Guilford Press.

St. James-Roberts, I., & Plewis, I. (1996). Individual differences, daily fluctuations, and developmental changes in amounts of infant waking, fussiness, crying, feeding, and sleeping. *Child Development, 67,* 2527–2540.

Stack, C. B., & Burton, L. M. (1993). Kinscripts. *Journal of Comparative Family Studies, 24,* 157–170.

Stahl, S. A., & Miller, P. D. (1989). Whole language and language experience approaches for beginning reading: A quantitative research synthesis. *Review of Educational Research, 59,* 87–116.

Stahl, S. A., & Shanahan, C. (2004). Learning to think like a historian: Disciplinary knowledge through critical analysis of multiple documents. In T. L. Jetton & J. A. Dole (Eds.), *Adolescent literacy research and practice* (pp. 94–115). New York: Guilford.

Stanley, J. C. (1980). On educating the gifted. *Educational Researcher, 9*(3), 8–12.

Stanovich, K. E. (2000). *Progress in understanding reading: Scientific foundations and new frontiers.* New York: Guilford Press.

Staples, M. (2007). Supporting whole-class collaborative inquiry in a secondary mathematics classroom. *Cognition and Instruction, 25,* 161–217.

Starke, M., Wikland, K. A., & Möller, A. (2003). Parents' descriptions of development and problems associated with infants with Turner syndrome: A retrospective study. *Journal of Paediatrics and Child Health, 39,* 293–298.

Stattin, H., & Magnusson, D. (1989). The role of early aggressive behavior in the frequency, seriousness, and types of later crime. *Journal of Consulting and Clinical Psychology, 57,* 710–718.

Staub, D. (1998). *Delicate threads: Friendships between children with and without special needs in inclusive settings.* Bethesda, MD: Woodbine House.

Staub, E. (1995). The roots of prosocial and antisocial behavior in persons and groups: Environmental influence, personality, culture, and socialization. In W. M. Kurtines & J. L. Gewirtz (Eds.), *Moral development: An introduction.* Boston: Allyn & Bacon.

Staudt, M. M. (2001). Use of services prior to and following intensive family preservation services. *Journal of Child and Family Studies, 10,* 101–114.

Steele, C. M. (1997). A threat in the air: How stereotypes shape intellectual identity and performance. *American Psychologist, 52,* 613–629.

Stein, J. A., & Krishnan, K. (2007). Nonverbal learning disabilities and executive function: The challenges of effective assessment and teaching. In L. Meltzer (Ed.), *Executive function in education: From theory to practice* (pp. 106–132). New York: Guilford Press.

Stein, N. (1993, May). Stop sexual harassment in schools. *USA Today.*

Stein, N., Trabasso, T., & Liwag, M. (2000). A goal appraisal theory of emotional understanding: Implications for development and learning. In M. Lewis & J. Haviland (Eds.), *Handbook of emotions* (2nd ed., pp. 436–457). New York: Guilford Press.

Stein, N. L. (1982). What's in a story: Interpreting the interpretations of story grammars. *Discourse Processes, 5,* 319–335.

Steinberg, L. (1986). Latchkey children and susceptibility to peer pressure: An ecological analysis. *Developmental Psychology, 22,* 433–439.

Steinberg, L. (1996). *Beyond the classroom: Why school reform has failed and what parents need to do.* New York: Touchstone.

Steinberg, L. (2007). Risk taking in adolescence: New perspectives from brain and behavioral science. *Current Directions in Psychological Science, 16,* 55–59.

Steinberg, L., Blinde, P. L., & Chan, K. S. (1984). Dropping out among language minority youth. *Review of Educational Research, 54,* 113–132.

Steinberg, L., Brown, B. B., Cider, M., Kaczmarek, N., & Lazzaro, C. (1988). *Noninstructional influences on high school student achievement: The contributions of parents, peers, extracurricular activities, and part-time work.* Madison, WI: National Center on Effective Secondary Schools. (ERIC Document Reproduction Service No. ED 307 509)

Steinberg, L., Elmen, J., & Mounts, N. (1989). Authoritative parenting, psychosocial maturity, and academic success among adolescents. *Child Development, 60,* 1424–1436.

Steinberg, L., Lamborn, S., Darling, N., Mounts, S., & Dornbusch, S. (1994). Over time change in adjustment and competence among adolescents from authoritative, authoritarian, indulgent, and neglectful families. *Child Development, 65,* 754–770.

Steiner, H. H., & Carr, M. (2003). Cognitive development in gifted children: Toward a more precise understanding of emerging differences in intelligence. *Educational Psychology Review, 15,* 215–246.

Stenberg, C. R., & Campos, J. J. (1990). The development of anger expressions in infancy. In N. L. Stein, B. Leventhal, & T. Trabasso (Eds.), *Psychological and biological approaches to emotion* (pp. 247–282). Hillsdale, NJ: Erlbaum.

Stephan, K. E., Fink, G. R., & Marshall, J. C. (2007). Mechanisms of hemispheric specialization: Insights from analyses of connectivity. *Neuropsychologia, 45,* 209–228.

Stephenson, K. A., Parrila, R. K., Georgiou, G. K., & Kirby, J. R. (2008). Effects of home literacy, parents' beliefs, and children's task-focused behavior on emergent literacy and word reading skills. *Scientific Studies of Reading, 12*(1), 24–50.

Stern, B. M., & Finn-Stevenson, M. (1999). Preregistered for success: The Comer/Zigler initiative. In J. P. Comer, M. Ben-Avie, N. M. Haynes, & E. T. Joyner (Eds.), *Child by child: The Comer process for change in education* (pp. 63–77). New York: Teachers College Press.

Stern, D. N. (1977). *The first relationship: Mother and infant.* Cambridge, MA: Harvard University Press.

Stern, W. (1912). *Die psychologischen Methoden der Intelligenzprüfung.* Leipzig, Germany: Barth.

Sternberg, R. J. (1985). *Beyond IQ: A triarchic theory of human intelligence.* Cambridge, England: Cambridge University Press.

Sternberg, R. J. (1996). Myths, countermyths, and truths about intelligence. *Educational Researcher, 25*(2), 11–16.

Sternberg, R. J. (1997). The concept of intelligence and its role in lifelong learning and success. *American Psychologist, 52,* 1030–1037.

Sternberg, R. J. (1998). Abilities are forms of developing expertise. *Educational Researcher, 27*(3), 11–20.

Sternberg, R. J. (2002). Raising the achievement of all students: Teaching for successful intelligence. *Educational Psychology Review, 14,* 383–393.

Sternberg, R. J. (2003a). *Wisdom, intelligence, and creativity synthesized.* Cambridge, England: Cambridge University Press.

Sternberg, R. J. (2003b). "My house is a very very very fine house"—But it is not the only house. In H. Nyborg (Ed.), *The scientific study of general intelligence: Tribute to Arthur Jensen* (pp. 373–395). Oxford, England: Elsevier.

Sternberg, R. J. (2004). Culture and intelligence. *American Psychologist, 59,* 325–338.

Sternberg, R. J. (2005). The triarchic theory of successful intelligence. In D. P. Flanagan & P. L. Harrison (Eds.), *Contemporary intellectual assess-*

ment: Theories, tests, and issues (2nd ed., pp. 103–119). New York: Guilford Press.

Sternberg, R. J. (2007). Who are the bright children? The cultural context of being and acting intelligent. *Educational Researcher, 36,* 148–155.

Sternberg, R. J., Forsythe, G. B., Hedlund, J., Horvath, J. A., Wagner, R. K., Williams, W. M., et al. (2000). *Practical intelligence in everyday life.* Cambridge, England: Cambridge University Press.

Sternberg, R. J., & Grigorenko, E. L. (2000). Theme-park psychology: A case study regarding human intelligence and its implications for education. *Educational Psychology Review, 12,* 247–268.

Sternberg, R. J., Grigorenko, E. L., & Bridglall, B. L. (2007). Intelligence as a socialized phenomenon. In E. W. Gordon & B. L. Bridglall (Eds.), *Affirmative development: Cultivating academic ability* (pp. 49–72). Lanham, MD: Rowman.

Sternberg, R. J., & Zhang, L. (1995). What do we mean by giftedness? A pentagonal implicit theory. *Gifted Child Quarterly, 39,* 88–94.

Stevens, G. (2004). Using census data to test critical-period hypothesis for second-language acquisition. *Psychological Science, 15,* 215–216.

Stevens, R. J., & Slavin, R. E. (1995). The cooperative elementary school: Effects of students' achievement, attitudes, and social relations. American *Educational Research Journal, 32,* 321–351.

Stevenson, H. W., Chen, C., & Uttal, D. H. (1990). Beliefs and achievement: A study of Black, White, and Hispanic children. *Child Development, 61,* 508–523.

Stewart, L., & Pascual-Leone, J. (1992). Mental capacity constraints and the development of moral reasoning. *Journal of Experimental Child Psychology, 54,* 251–287.

Stiggins, R. (2007). Assessment through students' eyes. *Educational Leadership, 64*(8), 22–26.

Stiles, J., & Thal, D. (1993). Linguistic and spatial cognitive development following early focal brain injury: Patterns of deficit and recovery. In M. Johnson (Ed.), *Brain development and cognition.* Oxford, England: Blackwell.

Stipek, D. (2002). At what age should children enter kindergarten? A question for policy makers and parents. *Social Policy Report, 16,* 1, 3–16. Ann Arbor, MI: Society for Research in Child Development.

Stipek, D. J. (1984). Sex differences in children's attributions for success and failure on math and spelling tests. *Sex Roles, 11,* 969–981.

Stipek, D. J. (1993). *Motivation to learn: From theory to practice* (2nd ed.). Needham Heights, MA: Allyn & Bacon.

Stipek, D. J. (1996). Motivation and instruction. In D. C. Berliner & R. C. Calfee (Eds.), *Handbook of educational psychology.* New York: Macmillan.

Stipek, D. J., & Kowalski, P. S. (1989). Learned helplessness in task-orienting versus performance-orienting testing conditions. *Journal of Educational Psychology, 81,* 384–391.

Stipek, D. J., Recchia, S., & McClintic, S. M. (1992). Self-evaluation in young children. *Monographs of the Society for Research in Child Development, 57*(2, Serial No. 226).

Stormont, M. (2001). Social outcomes of children with AD/HD: Contributing factors and implications for practice. *Psychology in the Schools, 38,* 521–531.

Stormont, M., Stebbins, M. S., & Holliday, G. (2001). Characteristics and educational support needs of underrepresented gifted adolescents. *Psychology in the Schools, 38*(5), 413–423.

Strapp, C. M., & Federico, A. (2000). Imitations and repetitions: What do children say following recasts? *First Language, 20,* 273–290.

Strauch, B. (2003). The primal teen: What the new discoveries about the teenage brain tells us about our kids. New York: Doubleday.

Straus, M. A. (2000). The benefits of never spanking: New and more definitive evidence. In M. A. Straus, *Beating the devil out of them: Corporal punishment by American families and its effects on children.* New Brunswick, NJ: Transaction Publications.

Strayer, F. F. (1991). The development of agonistic and affiliative structures in preschool play groups. In J. Silverberg & P. Gray (Eds.), *To fight or not to fight: Violence and peacefulness in humans and other primates*. Oxford, England: Oxford University Press.

Streissguth, A. P., Barr, H. M., Sampson, P. D., & Bookstein, F. L. (1994). Prenatal alcohol and offspring development: The first fourteen years. *Drug and Alcohol Dependence, 36,* 89–99.

Striano, T. (2004). Direction of regard and the still-face effects in the first year: Does intention matter? *Child Development, 75,* 468–479.

Striano, T., & Berlin, E. (2004). Contribution of facial and vocal cues in the still-face response of 4-month-old infants. *Infant Behavior and Development, 27,* 499–508.

Stright, A. D., Neitzel, C., Sears, K. G., & Hoke-Sinex, L. (2001). Instruction begins in the home: Relations between parental instruction and children's self-regulation in the classroom. *Journal of Educational Psychology, 93,* 456–466.

Strike, K. A., & Posner, G. J. (1992). A revisionist theory of conceptual change. In R. A. Duschl & R. J. Hamilton (Eds.), *Philosophy of science, cognitive psychology, and educational theory and practice.* Albany: State University of New York Press.

Strozer, J. R. (1994). *Language acquisition after puberty.* Washington, DC: Georgetown University Press.

Stukas, A. A., Jr., Clary, E. G., & Snyder, M. (1999). Service learning: Who benefits and why. *Social Policy Report, Society for Research in Child Development, 13*(4), 1–19.

Styne, D. M. (2003). The regulation of pubertal growth. *Hormone Research, 60*(Suppl.1), 22–26.

Sudhalter, V., & Braine, M. D. (1985). How does comprehension of passives develop? A comparison of actional and experiential verbs. *Journal of Child Language, 12,* 455–470.

Sue, D. W. (1990). Culture-specific strategies in counseling: A conceptual framework. *Professional Psychology: Research and Practice, 21,* 424–433.

Suh, S., Suh, J., & Houston, I. (2007). Predictors of categorical at-risk high school dropouts. *Journal of Counseling & Development, 85,* 196–203.

Suhr, D. D. (1999). *An investigation of mathematics and reading achievement of 5- through 14-year-olds using latent growth curve methodology.* Unpublished doctoral dissertation, University of Northern Colorado, Greeley.

Suina, J. H., & Smolkin, L. B. (1994). From natal culture to school culture to dominant society culture: Supporting transitions for Pueblo Indian students. In P. M. Greenfield & R. R. Cocking (Eds.), *Cross-cultural roots of minority child development.* Mahwah, NJ: Erlbaum.

Sullivan, F. M., & Barlow, S. M. (2001). Review of risk factors for sudden infant death syndrome. *Paediatric and Perinatal Epidemiology, 15,* 144–200.

Sullivan, H. S. (1953). *The interpersonal theory of psychiatry.* New York: Norton.

Sullivan, J. R., & Conoley, J. C. (2004). Academic and instructional interventions with aggressive students. In J. C. Conoley & A. P. Goldstein (Eds.), *School violence intervention* (2nd ed., pp. 235–255). New York: Guilford Press.

Sullivan, M. W., & Lewis, M. (2003). Contextual determinants of anger and other negative expressions in young infants. *Developmental Psychology, 39,* 693–705.

Sullivan, R. C. (1994). Autism: Definitions past and present. *Journal of Vocational Rehabilitation, 4,* 4–9.

Sullivan-DeCarlo, C., DeFalco, K., & Roberts, V. (1998). Helping students avoid risky behavior. *Educational Leadership, 56*(1), 80–82.

Sulzby, E. (1985). Children's emergent reading of favorite storybooks: A developmental study. *Reading Research Quarterly, 20,* 458–481.

Sulzby, E. (1986). Children's elicitation and use of metalinguistic knowledge about *word* during literacy

interactions. In D. B. Yaden, Jr., & S. Templeton (Eds.), *Metalinguistic awareness and beginning literacy: Conceptualizing what it means to read and write.* Portsmouth, NH: Heinemann.

Suskind, R. (1998). *A hope in the unseen: An American odyssey from the inner city to the Ivy League.* New York: Broadway Books.

Susman, E. J., Inoff-Germain, G., Nottelmann, E. D., Loriaux, D. L., Cutler, J., Gordon, B., et al. (1987). Hormones, emotional dispositions, and aggressive attributes in young adolescents. *Child Development, 58,* 1114–1134.

Susman, E. J., Nottelmann, E. D., Inoff-Germain, G. E., Dorn, L. D., Cutler, G. B., Jr., Loriaux, D. L., et al. (1985). The relation of development and social-emotional behavior in young adolescents. *Journal of Youth and Adolescence, 14,* 245–264.

Suttles, G. D. (1970). Friendship as a social institution. In G. J. McCall, M. McCall, N. K. Denzin, G. D. Scuttles, & S. Kurth (Eds.), *Social relationships* (pp. 95–135). Chicago: Aldine de Gruyter.

Sutton-Smith, B. (1986). The development of fictional narrative performances. *Topics in Language Disorders, 7*(1), 1–10.

Sutton-Smith, B. (Ed.). (1979). *Play and learning.* New York: Gardner Press.

Svirsky, M. A., Robbins, A. M., Kirk, K. I., Pisoni, D. B., & Miyamoto, R. T. (2000). Language development in profoundly deaf children with cochlear implants. *Psychological Science, 11,* 153–158.

Swanborn, M. S. L., & de Glopper, K. (1999). Incidental word learning while reading: A meta analysis. *Review of Educational Research, 69,* 261–285.

Swann, W. B., Jr. (1997). The trouble with change: Self-verification and allegiance to the self. *Psychological Science, 8,* 177–180.

Swanson, H. L., & Jerman, O. (2006). Math disabilities: A selective meta-analysis of the literature. *Review of Educational Research, 76,* 249–274.

Swanson, H. L., Jerman, O., & Zheng, X. (2008). Growth in working memory and mathematical problem solving in children at risk and not at risk for serious math difficulties. *Journal of Educational Psychology, 100,* 343–379.

Swanson, H. L., & Lussier, C. M. (2001). A selective synthesis of the experimental literature on dynamic assessment. *Review of Educational Research, 71,* 321–363.

Swanson, H. L., Mink, J., & Bocian, K. M. (1999). Cognitive processing deficits in poor readers with symptoms of reading disabilities and ADHD: More alike than different? *Journal of Educational Psychology, 91,* 321–333.

Swim, J. K., & Stangor, C. (Eds.). (1998). *Prejudice: The target's perspective* (pp. 220–241). San Diego, CA: Academic Press.

Sylva, K., Melhuish, E., Sammons, P., Siraj-Blatchford, I., & Taggart, B. (2004). *Effective pre-school education.* London: Institute of Education, University of London.

Sylvester, R. (1995). *A celebration of neurosis: An educator's guide to the human brain.* Alexandria, VA: Association for Supervision and Curriculum Development.

Szynal-Brown, C., & Morgan, R. R. (1983). The effects of reward on tutor's behaviors in a cross-age tutoring context. *Journal of Experimental Child Psychology, 36,* 196–208.

Tager-Flusberg, H. (1993). Putting words together: Morphology and syntax in the preschool years. In J. Berko-Gleason (Ed.), *The development of language* (3rd ed.). Upper Saddle River, NJ: Merrill/Prentice Hall.

Tager-Flusberg, H., & Skwerer, D. P. (2007). Williams syndrome: A model developmental syndrome for exploring brain-behavior relationships. In D. Coch, G. Dawson, & K. W. Fischer (Eds.), *Human behavior, learning, and the developing brain: Atypical development* (pp. 87–116). New York: Guilford Press.

Takahashi, K. (1990). Are the key assumptions of the "Strange Situation" procedure universal? A view

from Japanese research. *Human Development, 33,* 23–30.

Takeuchi, A. H., & Hulse, S. H. (1993). Absolute pitch. *Psychological Bulletin, 113,* 345–361.

Tallal, P. (2003). Language learning disabilities: Integrating research approaches. *Current Directions in Psychological Science, 12,* 206–211.

Tamburrini, J. (1982). Some educational implications of Piaget's theory. In S. Modgil & C. Modgil (Eds.), *Jean Piaget: Consensus and controversy.* New York: Praeger.

Tannen, D. (1990). *You just don't understand: Talk between the sexes.* New York: Ballantine.

Tanner, J. M. (1990). *Foetus into man: Physical growth from conception to maturity* (Rev. ed.). Cambridge, MA: Harvard University Press.

Tanner, J., Asbridge, M., & Wortley, S. (2008). Our favorite melodies: Musical consumption and teenage lifestyles. *British Journal of Sociology, 59*(1), 117–144.

Tattersall, I. (2006). How we came to be human. *Scientific American, 16*(2), 66–73.

Tatum, B. D. (1997). *Why are all the Black kids sitting together in the cafeteria? and other conversations about race.* New York: Basic Books.

Taumoepeau, M., & Ruffman, T. (2008). Stepping stones to others' minds: Maternal talk relates to child mental state language and emotion understandings at 15, 24, and 33 months. *Child Development, 79,* 284–302.

Taylor, D., & Lorimer, M. (2002–2003). Helping boys succeed. *Educational Leadership, 60*(4), 68–70.

Taylor, J. M. (1994). *MDMA frequently asked questions list.* Retrieved from http://ibbserver.ibb.uu.nl/jboschma/ecstasy/xtc01

Taylor, M., Esbensen, B. M., & Bennett, R. T. (1994). Children's understanding of knowledge acquisition: The tendency for children to report that they have always known what they have just learned. *Child Development, 65,* 1581–1604.

Taylor, R. D., Casten, R., Flickinger, S. M., Roberts, D., & Fulmore, C. D. (1994). Explaining the school performance of African American adolescents. *Journal of Research on Adolescence, 4,* 21–44.

Taylor, R. D., & Roberts, D. (1995). Kinship support and maternal and adolescent well-being in economically disadvantaged African-American families. *Child Development, 66,* 1585–1597.

Taylor, S. M. (1994, April). *Staying in school against the odds: Voices of minority adolescent girls.* Paper presented at the annual meeting of the American Educational Research Association, New Orleans, LA.

Taylor, W. C., Beech, B. M., & Cummings, S. S. (1998). Increasing physical activity levels among youth: A public health challenge. In D. K. Wilson, J. R. Rodrigue, & W. C. Taylor (Eds.), *Health-promoting and health-compromising behaviors among minority adolescents* (pp. 107–128). Washington, DC: American Psychological Association.

Teale, W. H. (1978). Positive environments for learning to read: What studies of early readers tell us. *Language Arts, 55,* 922–932.

Teeter, P. A., & Semrud-Clikeman, M. (1997). *Child neuropsychology: Assessment and interventions for neurodevelopmental disorders.* Boston: Allyn & Bacon.

Tellegren, A., Lykken, D. T., Bouchard, T. J., & Wilcox, K. J. (1988). Personality similarity in twins reared apart and together. *Journal of Personality and Social Psychology, 54,* 1031–1039.

Tennenbaum, H. R., & Leaper, C. (2002). Are parents' gender schemas related to their children's gender-related cognitions? A meta-analysis. *Developmental Psychology, 38,* 615–630.

Tenenbaum, H. R., & Leaper, C. (2003). Parent–child conversations about science: Socialization of gender inequities. *Developmental Psychology, 39,* 34–47.

Tennyson, R. D., & Cocchiarella, M. J. (1986). An empirically based instructional design theory for teaching concepts. *Review of Educational Research, 56,* 40–71.

Terman, L. M. (1916). *The measurement of intelligence.* Boston: Houghton Mifflin.

Terman, L. M., & Merrill, M. A. (1972). *Stanford-Binet Intelligence Scale* (3rd ed.). Boston: Houghton Mifflin.

Terry, A. W. (2000). An early glimpse: Service learning from an adolescent perspective. *Journal of Secondary Gifted Education, 11*(3), 115–134.

Terry, A. W. (2001). A case study of community action service learning on young, gifted adolescents and their community (Doctoral dissertation, University of Georgia, 2000). *Dissertation Abstracts International, 61*(08), 3058.

Terry, A. W. (2003). Effects of service learning on young, gifted adolescents and their community. *Gifted Child Quarterly, 47*(4), 295–308.

Terry, A. W. (2008). Student voices, global echoes: Service-learning and the gifted. *Roeper Review, 30,* 45–51.

Teti, D. M., Gelfand, D., Messinger, D. S., & Isabella, R. (1995). Maternal depression and the quality of early attachment: An examination of infants, preschoolers and their mothers. *Developmental Psychology, 31,* 564–576.

Tharp, R. G. (1989). Psychocultural variables and constants: Effects on teaching and learning in schools. *American Psychologist, 44,* 349–359.

Tharp, R. G. (1994). Intergroup differences among Native Americans in socialization and child cognition: An ethnogenetic analysis. In P. M. Greenfield & R. R. Cocking (Eds.), *Cross-cultural roots of minority child development* (pp. 87–105). Hillsdale, NJ: Erlbaum.

Thelen, E., & Smith, L. B. (1998). Dynamic systems theories. In W. Damon (Series Ed.) & R. M. Lerner (Vol. Ed.), *Handbook of child psychology: Vol. 1. Theoretical models of human development* (5th ed., pp. 563–634). New York: Wiley.

Thelen, E., & Smith, L. B. (2006). Dynamic systems theories. In W. Damon & R. M. Lerner (Eds. in Chief) & R. M. Lerner (Vol. Ed.), *Handbook of child psychology: Vol. 1. Theoretical models of human development* (6th ed., pp. 258–312). Hoboken, NJ: Wiley.

Théoret, H., Halligan, E., Kobayashi, M., Fregni, F., Tager-Flusberg, H., & Pascual-Leone, A. (2005). Impaired motor facilitation during action observation in individuals with autism spectrum disorder. *Current Biology, 15,* 84–85.

Thiede, H., Romero, M., Bordelon, K., Hagan, H., & Murrill, C. S. (2001). Using a jail-based survey to monitor HIV and risk behaviors among Seattle area injection users. *Journal of Urban Health, 78,* 264–287.

Thomas, A., & Chess, S. (1977). *Temperament and development.* New York: Brunner/Mazel.

Thomas, H. (2006). Obesity prevention programs for children and youth: Why are their results so modest? *Health Education Research, 21,* 783–795.

Thomas, J. W. (1993). Promoting independent learning in the middle grades: The role of instructional support practices. *Elementary School Journal, 93,* 575–591.

Thomas, R. M. (2005). *High-stakes testing: Coping with collateral damage.* Mahwah, NJ: Erlbaum.

Thomas, S., & Oldfather, P. (1997). Intrinsic motivations, literacy, and assessment practices: "That's my grade. That's me." *Educational Psychologist, 32,* 107–123.

Thompson, G. (2008, March). Beneath the apathy. *Educational Leadership, 65*(6), 50–54.

Thompson, H., & Carr, M. (1995, April). *Brief metacognitive intervention and interest as predictors of memory for text.* Paper presented at the annual meeting of the American Educational Research Association, San Francisco.

Thompson, M., & Grace, C. O. (with L. J. Cohen) (2001). *Best friends, worst enemies: Understanding the social lives of children.* New York: Ballantine.

Thompson, P. M., Giedd, J. N., Woods, R. P., MacDonald, D., Evans, A. C., & Toga, A. W. (2000). Growth patterns in the developing brain detected by using continuum mechanical tensor maps. *Nature, 404,* 190–193.

Thompson, R. A. (1994a). Emotion regulation: A theme in search of a definition. *Monographs of the Society for Research in Child Development, 59*(2–3, Serial No. 240), 25–52.

Thompson, R. A. (1994b). The role of the father after divorce. *The Future of Children: Children and Divorce, 4*(1), 210–235.

Thompson, R. A. (2006). The development of the person: Social understanding, relationships, conscience, self. In W. Damon & R. M. Lerner (Eds. in Chief) & N. Eisenberg (Vol. Ed.), *Handbook of child psychology, Vol. 3. Social, emotional, and personality development* (6th ed., pp. 24–98). Hoboken, NJ: Wiley.

Thompson, R. A., Easterbrooks, M. A., & Padilla-Walker, L. M. (2003). In R. M. Lerner, M. A. Easterbrooks, & J. Mistry (Vol. Eds.), I. B. Weiner (Editor-in-Chief), *Handbook of psychology. Vol.6: Developmental psychology* (pp. 91–112). Hoboken, NJ: John Wiley & Sons.

Thompson, R. A., Meyer, S., & McGinley, M. (2006). Understanding values in relationships: The development of conscience. In M. Killen & J. G. Smetana (Eds.), *Handbook of moral development* (pp. 267–297). Mahwah, NJ: Erlbaum.

Thompson, R. F. (1975). *Introduction to physiological psychology.* New York: Harper & Row.

Thompson, R. H., Cotnoir-Bichelman, N. M., McKerchar, P. M., Tate, T. L., & Dancho, K. A. (2007). Enhancing early communication through infant sign training. *Journal of Applied Behavior Analysis, 40,* 15–23.

Thompson, R. H., McKerchar, P. M., & Dancho, K. A. (2004). The effects of delayed physical prompts and reinforcement on infant sign language acquisition. *Journal of Applied Behavior Analysis, 37,* 379–383.

Thorkildsen, T. A. (1995). Conceptions of social justice. In W. M. Kurtines & J. L. Gewirtz (Eds.), *Moral development: An introduction.* Boston: Allyn & Bacon.

Thorndike, R., Hagen, E., & Sattler, J. (1986). *Stanford-Binet Intelligence Scale* (4th ed.). Chicago: Riverside.

Thorndike-Christ, T. (2008, March). Profiles in failure: The etiology of maladaptive beliefs about mathematics. Paper presented at the annual meeting of the American Educational Research Association, New York.

Tiedemann, J. (2000). Parents' gender stereotypes and teachers' beliefs as predictors of children's concept of their mathematical ability in elementary school. *Journal of Educational Psychology, 92,* 144–151.

Tiggemann, M. (2003). Media exposure, body dissatisfaction, and disordered eating: Television and magazines are not the same! *European Eating Disorders Review, 11,* 418–430.

Timler, G. R., Olswang, L. B., & Coggins, L. E. (2005). "Do I know what I need to do?" A social communication intervention for children with complex clinical profiles. *Language, Speech, and Hearing Services in Schools, 36,* 73–85.

Timlin-Scalera, R. M., Ponterotto, J. G., Blumberg, F. C., & Jackson, M. A. (2003). A grounded theory study of help-seeking behaviors among White male high school students. *Journal of Counseling Psychology, 50,* 339–350.

Tincoff, R., & Jusczyk, P. W. (1999). Some beginnings of word comprehension in 6-month-olds. *Psychological Science, 10,* 172–175.

Tinglof, C. B. (2007). *Parenting school-age twins and multiples.* New York: McGraw-Hill.

Tobias, S. (1977). A model for research on the effect of anxiety on instruction. In J. E. Sieber, H. F. O'Neil, Jr., & S. Tobias (Eds.), *Anxiety, learning, and instruction.* Hillsdale, NJ: Erlbaum.

Tobin, J. J., Wu, D. Y. H., & Davidson, D. H. (1989). *Preschool in three cultures: Japan, China, and the United States.* New Haven, CT: Yale University Press.

Toga, A. W., & Thompson, P. M. (2003). Mapping brain asymmetry. *Nature Review Neuroscience, 4,* 37–48.

Tolani, N., & Brooks-Gunn, J. (2006). Are there socioeconomic disparities in children's mental health? In H. E. Fitzgerald, B. M. Lester, & B. Zuckerman (Vol. Eds.), H. E. Fitzgerald, R. Zucker, & K. Freeark (Eds. in Chief), *The crisis in youth mental health: Critical issues and effective programs* (Vol. 1, pp. 277–303). Westport, CT: Praeger.

Tomasello, M. (1999). *The cultural origins of human cognition.* Cambridge, MA: Harvard University Press.

Tomasello, M., Carpenter, M., & Liszkowski, U. (2007). A new look at infant pointing. *Child Development, 78,* 705–722.

Tompkins, G. E., & McGee, L. M. (1986). Visually impaired and sighted children's emerging concepts about written language. In D. B. Yaden, Jr., & S. Templeton (Eds.), *Metalinguistic awareness and beginning literacy: Conceptualizing what it means to read and write.* Portsmouth, NH: Heinemann.

Tong, S., Baghurst, P., Vimpani, G., & McMichael, A. (2007). Socioeconomic position, maternal IQ, home environment, and cognitive development. *Journal of Pediatrics, 151*(3), 284–288.e1.

Torquati, J. C. (2002). Personal and social resources as predictors of parenting in homeless families. *Journal of Family Issues, 23,* 463–485.

Torrance, E. P. (1995). Insights about creativity: Questioned, rejected, ridiculed, ignored. *Educational Psychology Review, 7,* 313–322.

Torres-Guzmán, M. E. (1998). Language, culture, and literacy in Puerto Rican communities. In B. Pérez (Ed.), *Sociocultural contexts of language and literacy.* Mahwah, NJ: Erlbaum.

Tourniaire, F., & Pulos, S. (1985). Proportional reasoning: A review of the literature. *Educational Studies in Mathematics, 16,* 181–204.

Touwen, B. C. L. (1974). The neurological development of the infant. In J. A. Davis & J. Dobbing (Eds.), *Scientific foundations of pediatrics.* Philadelphia: Saunders.

Trainor, L. J., Austin, C. M., & Desjardins, R. N. (2000). Is infant-directed speech prosody a result of the vocal expression of emotion? *Psychological Science, 11,* 188–195.

Trainor, L. J., & Trehub, S. E. (1992). A comparison of infants' and adults' sensitivity to Western tonal structure. *Journal of Experimental Psychology: Human Perception and Performance, 19,* 615–626.

Trautner, H. M. (1992). The development of sex-typing in children: A longitudinal analysis. *German Journal of Psychology, 16,* 183–199.

Trawick-Smith, J. (2003). *Early childhood development: A multicultural perspective* (3rd ed.). Upper Saddle River, NJ: Merrill/Prentice Hall.

Treffert, D. A., & Wallace, G. L. (2002). Islands of genius. *Scientific American, 286*(6), 76–85.

Treiman, R. (1998). Beginning to spell in English. In C. Hulme & R. M. Joshi (Eds.), *Reading and spelling: Development and disorders.* Mahwah, NJ: Erlbaum.

Treiman, R., Cohen, J., Mulqueeny, K., Kessler, B., & Schechtman, S. (2007). Young children's knowledge about printed names. *Child Development, 78,* 1458–1471.

Trelease, J. (1982). *The read-aloud handbook.* New York: Penguin Books.

Trevarthen, C., & Hubley, P. (1978). Secondary intersubjectivity: Confidence, confiding and acts of meaning in the first year. In A. Lock (Ed.), *Action, gesture, and symbol: The emergence of language.* London: Academic Press.

Triandis, H. C. (1995). *Individualism and collectivism.* Boulder, CO: Westview Press.

Triandis, H. C. (2007). Culture and psychology: A history of the study of their relationship. In S. Kitayama & D. Cohen (Eds.), *Handbook of cultural psychology* (pp. 59–76). New York: Guilford Press.

Tronick, E. Z., Als, H., Adamson, L., Wise, S., & Brazelton, B. (1978). The infants' response to entrapment between contradictory messages in face-to-face interaction. *American Academy of Child Psychiatry, 1,* 1–13.

Tronick, E. Z., Cohn, J., & Shea, E. (1986). The transfer of affect between mother and infant. In T. B. Brazelton & M. W. Yogman (Eds.), *Affective development in infancy* (pp. 11–25). Norwood, NJ: Ablex.

Trout, J. D. (2003). Biological specializations for speech: What can the animals tell us? *Current Directions in Psychological Science, 12,* 155–159.

Tsai, Y.-M., Kunter, M., Lüdtke, O., Trautwein, U., & Ryan, R. M. (2008). What makes lessons interesting? The role of situational and individual factors in three school subjects. *Journal of Educational Psychology, 100,* 460–472.

Tse, L. (2001). *Why don't they learn English: Separating fact from fallacy in the U.S. language debate.* New York: Teachers College Press.

Tsui, J. M., & Mazzocco, M. M. M. (2007). Effects of math anxiety and perfectionism on timed versus untimed math testing in mathematically gifted sixth graders. *Roeper Review, 29*(2), 132–139.

Tunmer, W. E., Pratt, C., & Herriman, M. L. (Eds.). (1984). *Metalinguistic awareness in children: Theory, research, and implications.* Berlin, Germany: Springer-Verlag.

Turiel, E. (1983). *The development of social knowledge: Morality and convention.* Cambridge, England: Cambridge University Press.

Turiel, E. (1998). The development of morality. In W. Damon (Series Ed.) & N. Eisenberg (Vol. Ed.), *Handbook of child psychology: Vol. 3. Social, emotional, and personality development* (pp. 863–932). New York: Wiley.

Turiel, E. (2002). *The culture of morality: Social development, context, and conflict.* Cambridge, England: Cambridge University Press.

Turiel, E. (2006). The development of morality. In W. Damon & R. M. Lerner (Eds. in Chief) & N. Eisenberg (Vol. Ed.), *Handbook of child psychology, Vol. 3. Social, emotional, and personality development* (6th ed., pp. 789–857). Hoboken, NJ: Wiley.

Turiel, E. (2008). The development of children's orientations toward moral, social, and personal orders: More than a sequence in development. *Human Development, 51,* 21–39.

Turiel, E., Killen, M., & Helwig, C. C. (1987). Morality: Its structure, function, and vagaries. In J. Kagan & S. Lamb (Eds.), *The emergence of morality in young children* (pp. 155–243). Chicago: University of Chicago Press.

Turiel, E., Smetana, J. G., & Killen, M. (1991). Social contexts in social cognitive development. In W. M. Kurtines & J. L. Gewirtz (Eds.), *Moral behavior and development: Vol. 2. Research.* Hillsdale, NJ: Erlbaum.

Turkanis, C. G. (2001). Creating curriculum with children. In B. Rogoff, C. G. Turkanis, & L. Bartlett (Eds.), *Learning together: Children and adults in a school community* (pp. 91–102). New York: Oxford University Press.

Turkheimer, E. (2000). Three laws of behavior genetics and what they mean. *Current Directions in Psychological Science, 9,* 160–164.

Turkheimer, E., Haley, A., Waldron, M., D'Onofrio, B., & Gottesman, I. I. (2003). Socioeconomic status modifies heritability of IQ in young children. *Psychological Science, 14,* 623–628.

Turnbull, A. P., Pereira, L., & Blue-Banning, M. (2000). Teachers as friendship facilitators: Respeto and personalismo. *Teaching Exceptional Children, 32*(5), 66–70.

Turnbull, A. P., Turnbull, R., & Wehmeyer, M. L. (2007). *Exceptional lives: Special education in today's schools* (5th ed.). Upper Saddle River, NJ: Merrill/Prentice Hall.

Turner, J. C. (1995). The influence of classroom contexts on young children's motivation for literacy. *Reading Research Quarterly, 30,* 410–441.

Turner, J. C., Meyer, D. K., Cox, K. E., Logan, C., DiCintio, M., & Thomas, C. T. (1998). Creating contexts for involvement in mathematics. *Journal of Educational Psychology, 90,* 730–745.

Turner, K. L., & Brown, C. S. (2007). The centrality of gender and ethnic identities across individuals and contexts. *Social Development, 16,* 700–719.

Turner, M. A., Freiberg, F., Godfrey, E., Herbig, C., Levy, D. K., & Smith, R. R. (2002). *All other things being equal: A paired testing study of mortgage lending institutions.* Washington, DC: Urban Institute.

Turner, R. N., Hewstone, M., & Voci, A. (2007). Reducing explicit and implicit outgroup prejudice via direct and extended contact: The mediating role or self-disclosure and intergroup anxiety. *Journal of Personality and Social Psychology, 94,* 369–388.

Tusing, M. E., & Ford, L. (2004). Examining preschool cognitive abilities using a CHC framework. *International Journal of Testing, 4,* 91–114.

Tversky, A., & Kahneman, D. (1990). Judgment under uncertainty: Heuristics and biases. In P. K. Moser (Ed.), *Rationality in action: Contemporary approaches* (pp. 171–188). New York: Cambridge University Press.

Tynes, B. M. (2007). Role taking in online "classrooms": What adolescents are learning about race and ethnicity. *Developmental Psychology, 43*(6), 1312–1320.

Tzuriel, D. (2000). Dynamic assessment of young children: Educational and intervention perspectives. *Educational Psychology Review, 12,* 385–435.

Udall, A. J. (1989). Curriculum for gifted Hispanic students. In C. J. Maker & S. W. Schiever (Eds.), *Critical issues in gifted education: Vol. 2. Defensible programs for cultural and ethnic minorities.* Austin, TX: Pro-Ed.

Udry, J. R. (1988). Biological predispositions and social control in adolescent sexual behavior. *American Sociological Review, 53*(5), 709–722.

Ullrich-French, S. & Smith, A. L. (2006). Perceptions of relationships with parents and peers in youth sport: Independent and combined prediction of motivational outcome. *Psychology of Sport and Exercise, 7,* 193–214.

Umaña-Taylor, A. J., & Alfaro, E. C. (2006). Ethnic identity among U.S. Latino adolescents: Theory, measurement, and implications for well-being. In K. Freeark & W. S. Davidson II (Vol. Eds.), H. E. Fitzgerald, R. Zucker, & K. Freeark (Eds. in Chief), *The crisis in youth mental health: Vol. 3: Critical issues and effective programs* (pp. 195–211). Westport, CT: Praeger.

Underwood, M. K. (2007). Do girls' and boys' friendships constitute different peer cultures, and what are the trade-offs for development? *Merrill-Palmer Quarterly, 53,* 319–324.

Upchurch, D. M., & McCarthy, J. (1990). The timing of first birth and high school completion. *American Sociological Review, 55,* 224–234.

Urban, J., Carlson, E., Egeland, B., & Sroufe, L. A. (1991). Patterns of individual adaptation across childhood. *Development and Psychopathology, 3,* 445–460.

Urdan, T. (1997). Achievement goal theory: Past results, future directions. In M. L. Maehr & P. R. Pintrich (Eds.), *Advances in motivation and achievement* (Vol. 10). Greenwich, CT: JAI Press.

Urdan, T. (2004). Predicators of academic self-handicapping and achievement: Examining achievement goals, classroom goal structures, and culture. *Journal of Educational Psychology, 96,* 251–264.

Urdan, T., Ryan, A. M., Anderman, E. M., & Gheen, M. H. (2002). Goals, goal structures, and avoidance behaviors. In C. Midgley (Ed.), *Goals, goal structures, and patterns of adaptive learning* (pp. 55–83). Mahwah, NJ: Erlbaum.

Urdan, T. C., & Maehr, M. L. (1995). Beyond a two-goal theory of motivation and achievement: A case for social goals. *Review of Educational Research, 65,* 213–243.

U.S. Census Bureau. (2004, September). National adoption month. Facts for features. CB04-FFSE.12. Retrieved November 16, 2007, from http://www. census.gov/Press-Release/www/releases/archives/facts_for_features_special_ editions/002683.html

U.S. Census Bureau. (2007a). *American fact finder: Table B11009. Unmarried-partner households by sex of partner.* Retrieved November 20, 2007, from http://factfinder.census.gov/servlet/DTTable?_bm=y&-geo_id=01000US&-ds_name=ACS_2006_EST_G00_&-_lang=en&-_caller=geoselect&-state=dt&-format=&-mt_name=ACS_2006_EST_G2000_B11009

U.S. Census Bureau. (2007b). *American families and living arrangements: 2006. Table C3. Living arrangements of children under 18 years and marital status of parents, by age, gender, race, and Hispanic origin of the child for all children: 2006.* Retrieved November 15, 2007, from http://www.census.gov/population/www/socdemo/hh-fam/cps2006.html

U.S. Census Bureau. (2007c). *Table FG1. Married couple family groups, by labor force status of both spouses, and race and Hispanic origin/1 of the reference person: 2006.* Retrieved November 28, 2007, from http://www.census.gov/population/www/socdemo/hh-fam/cps2006.html

U.S. Census Bureau. (2007d). *Table FG5. One-parent family groups with own children under 18, by labor force status, and race and hispanic origin/1 of the reference person: 2006.* Retrieved November 28, 2007, from http://www.census.gov/population/www/socdemo/hh-fam/cps2006.html

U.S. Department of Agriculture. (2008). *MyPyramid Plan.* Retrieved January 16, 2008, from http://wwww.mypyramid.gov

U.S. Department of Agriculture Food and Nutrition Service. (2008). *Research: WIC Nutrition Education Demonstration Study final report: Prenatal intervention.* Retrieved January 2, 2008, from http://www.fns.usda.gov/oane/MENU/Published/WIC/FILES/PrenatalExSum.htm

U.S. Department of Education. (1993). *National excellence: A case for developing America's talent.* Washington, DC: Office of Educational Research and Improvement.

U.S. Department of Education. (2005). *The condition of education, 2000–2005.* Washington, DC: U.S. Printing Office.

U.S. Department of Education, Office of Civil Rights. (1993). *Annual report to Congress.* Washington, DC: Author.

U.S. Department of Health and Human Services. (2000). *Eating disorders.* Retrieved January 31, 2008, from http://4women.gov/owh/pub/factsheets/eatingdis.htm

U.S. Department of Health and Human Services. (2007a). *The AFCARS Report: Preliminary FY 2005 estimates as of September 2006.* Retrieved November 19, 2007, from http://www.acf.hhs.gov/programs/cb/stats_research/afcars/tar/report13.htm

U.S. Department of Health and Human Services. (2007b). *Child maltreatment 2005.* Washington, DC: U.S. Government Printing Office.

U.S. Department of Health and Human Services. (2007c). *Welcome to communities that care.* Retrieved October 15, 2006, from http://www.preventionplatform.samhsa.gov

U.S. Department of Health and Human Services, Administration for Children and Families. (2005). *Head Start impact study: First year findings.* Retrieved June 3, 2008, from http://www.acf.hhs.gov/programs/opre/hs/impact_study/reports/first_yr_execsum/first_yr_execsum.pdf

U.S. Department of Health and Human Services, Administration for Children and Families. (2008). *Head Start: A child development program.* Retrieved June 3, 2008, from http://www.head-start.lane.or.us/general/HHS-brochure.html

U.S. Drug Enforcement Administration. (2002). *Team up: A drug prevention manual for high school athletic coaches.* Washington, DC: U.S. Department of Justice Drug Enforcement Administration.

Uttal, D. H., Marzolf, D. P., Pierroutsakos, S. L., Smith, C. M., Troseth, G. L., Scudder, K. V., et al. (1998). Seeing through symbols: The development of children's understanding of symbolic relations. In O. N. Saracho & B. Spodek (Eds.), *Multiple perspectives on play in early childhood education*. Albany: State University of New York Press.

Vadasy, P. F., Sanders, E. A., & Peyton, J. A. (2006). Code-oriented instruction for kindergarten students at risk for reading difficulties: A randomized field trial with paraeducator implementers. *Journal of Educational Psychology, 98*, 508–528.

Valdés, G., Bunch, G., Snow, C., & Lee, C. (with Matos, L.). (2005). Enhancing the development of students' language(s). In L. Darling-Hammond & J. Bransford (Eds.), *Preparing teachers for a changing world: What teachers should learn and be able to do* (pp. 126–168). San Francisco: Jossey-Bass/Wiley.

Valdez, A. J. (2000). *Gangs: A guide to understanding street gangs* (3rd ed.). San Clemente, CA: LawTech.

Valentine, J. C., Cooper, H., Bettencourt, B. A., & DuBois, D. L. (2002). Out-of-school activities and academic achievement: The mediating role of self-beliefs. *Educational Psychologist, 37*, 245–256.

Valentine, J. C., DuBois, D. L., & Cooper, H. (2004). The relation between self-beliefs and academic achievement: A meta-analytic review. *Educational Psychologist, 39*, 111–133.

Valiente, C., Fabes, R., Eisenberg, N., & Spinrad, T. (2004). The relations of parental expressivity and support to children's coping with daily stress. *Journal of Family Psychology, 18*, 97–106.

Valli, L., & Buese, D. (2007). The changing roles of teachers in an era of high-stakes accountability. *American Educational Research Journal, 44*, 519–558.

Van den Bergh, B. R. H., & Marcoen, A. (2004). High antenatal maternal anxiety is related to ADHD symptoms, externalizing problems, and anxiety in 8- and 9-year-olds. *Child Development, 75*, 1085–1097.

van den Broek, P., Bauer, P. J., & Bourg, T. (Eds.). (1997). *Developmental spans in event comprehension and representation: Bridging fictional and actual events*. Mahwah, NJ: Erlbaum.

van den Broek, P., Lynch, J. S., Naslund, J., Ievers-Landis, C. E., & Verduin, K. (2003). The development of comprehension of main ideas in narratives: Evidence from the selection of titles. *Journal of Educational Psychology, 95*, 707–718.

Van Dooren, W., De Bock, D., Hessels, A., Janssens, D., & Verschaffel, L. (2005). Not everything is proportional: Effects of age and problem type on propensities for overgeneralization. *Cognition and Instruction, 23*, 57–86.

van Hof-van Duin, J., & Mohn, G. (1986). The development of visual acuity in normal full-term and preterm infants. *Vision Research, 26*, 909–916.

Van Hoorn, J., Nourot, P. M., Scales, B., & Alward, K. R. (1999). *Play at the center of the curriculum* (2nd ed.). Upper Saddle River, NJ: Merrill/ Prentice Hall.

Van Hulle, C. A., Goldsmith, H. H., & Lemery, K. S. (2004). Genetic, environmental, and gender effects on individual differences in toddler expressive language. *Journal of Speech, Language, and Hearing Research, 47*, 904–912.

van IJzendoorn, M. H., Goldberg, S., Kroonenberg, P. M., & Frenkel, O. J. (1992). The relative effects of maternal and child problems on the quality of attachment: A meta-analysis of attachment in clinical samples. *Child Development, 63*, 840–858.

van IJzendoorn, M. H., Sagi, A., Lambermon, M. (1992). The multiple caregiver paradox: Data from Holland and Israel. In R. C. Pianta (Ed.), *New directions for child development: No. 57. Beyond the parent: The role of other adults in children's lives* (pp. 5–27). San Francisco, CA: Jossey-Bass.

van Kraayenoord, C. E., & Paris, S. G. (1997). Children's self-appraisal of their worksamples and academic progress. *Elementary School Journal, 97*, 523–537.

van Laar, C. (2000). The paradox of low academic achievement but high self-esteem in African American students: An attributional account. *Educational Psychology Review, 12*, 33–61.

Vandell, D. L., & Pierce, K. M. (1999, April). *Can after-school programs benefit children who live in high-crime neighborhoods?* Paper presented at the biennial meeting of the Society for Research in Child Development, Albuquerque, NM.

vanSledright, B., & Limón. M. (2006). Learning and teaching social studies: A review of cognitive research in history and geography. In P. A. Alexander & P. H. Winne (Eds.), *Handbook of educational psychology* (2nd ed., pp. 545–570). Mahwah, NJ: Erlbaum.

Vansteenkiste, M., Lens, W., & Deci, E. L. (2006). Intrinsic versus extrinsic goal contents in self-determination theory: Another look at the quality of academic motivation. *Educational Psychologist, 41*, 19–31.

Vansteenkiste, M., Zhou, M., Lens, W., & Soenens, B. (2005). Experiences of autonomy and control among Chinese learners: Vitalizing or immobilizing? *Journal of Educational Psychology, 97*, 468–483.

Varela, R. E., Vernberg, E. M., Sanchez-Sosa, J. J., Riveros, A., Mitchell, M., & Mashunkashey, J. (2004). Parenting style of Mexican, Mexican American, and Caucasian-Non-Hispanic families: Social context and cultural influences. *Journal of Family Psychology, 18*, 651–657.

Vasquez, J. A. (1990). Teaching to the distinctive traits of minority students. *Clearing House, 63*, 299–304.

Vaughn, B. E., Egeland, B., Sroufe, L. A., & Waters, E. (1979). Individual differences in infant-mother attachment at twelve and eighteen months: Stability and change in families under stress. *Child Development, 50*, 971–975.

Vaughn, B. E., Kopp, C. B., & Krakow, J. B. (1984). The emergence and consolidation of self-control from eighteen to thirty months of age: Normative trends and individual differences. *Child Development, 55*, 990–1004.

Vavra, E. (1987). Grammar and syntax: The student's perspective. *English Journal, 76*, 42–48.

Veale, A. (2006). Child-centered research with ethnic minority populations: Methodological, ethical, and practical challenges. *Irish Journal of Psychology, 27*, 25–36.

Venter, J. C., et al. (2001). The sequence of the human genome. *Science, 291*, 1304–1351.

Vermeer, H. J., Boekaerts, M., & Seegers, G. (2000). Motivational and gender differences: Sixth-grade students' mathematical problem-solving behavior. *Journal of Educational Psychology, 92*, 308–315.

Vignau, J., Bailly, D., Duhamel, A., Vervaecke, P., Beuscart, R., & Collinet, C. (1997). Epidemiologic study of sleep quality and troubles in French secondary school adolescents. *Journal of Adolescent Health, 21*, 343–350.

Villegas, A. M., & Lucas, T. (2002). *Educating culturally responsive teachers: A coherent approach*. Albany, NY: State University of New York Press.

Villegas, A. M., & Lucas, T. (2007). The culturally responsive teacher. *Educational Leadership, 64*(6), 28–33.

Vitaro, F., Gendreau, P. L., Tremblay, R. E., & Oligny, P. (1998). Reactive and proactive aggression differentially predict later conduct problems. *Journal of Child Psychology and Psychiatry and Allied Disciplines, 39*, 377–385.

Voelkl, K. E., & Frone, M. R. (2000). Predictors of substance use at school among high school students. *Journal of Educational Psychology, 92*, 583–592.

Vogel, G. (1997). Cocaine wreaks subtle damage on developing brains. *Science, 278*, 38–39.

Volker, M. A., Lopata, C., & Cook-Cottone, C. (2006). Assessment of children with intellectual giftedness and reading disabilities. *Psychology in the Schools, 43*, 855–869.

Volling, B. L. (2001). Early attachment relationships as predictors of preschool children's emotion regula-

tion with a distressed sibling. *Early Education and Development, 12*(2), 185–207.

Vollmer, T. R., & Hackenberg, T. D. (2001). Reinforcement contingencies and social reinforcement: Some reciprocal relations between basic and applied research. *Journal of Applied Behavior Analysis, 34*, 241–253.

Volterra, V., Caselli, M. C., Capirci, O., & Pizzuto, E. (2005). Gesture and the emergence and development of language. In M. Tomasello & D. I. Slobin (Eds.), *Beyond nature–nurture: Essays in honor of Elizabeth Bates* (pp. 3–40). Mahwah, NH: Erlbaum.

Vorrath, H. (1985). *Positive peer culture*. New York: Aldine de Gruyter.

Vosniadou, S. (1991). Conceptual development in astronomy. In S. M. Glynn, R. H. Yeany, & B. K. Britton (Eds.), *The psychology of learning science*. Hillsdale, NJ: Erlbaum.

Vosniadou, S. (1994). Universal and culture-specific properties of children's mental models of the earth. In L. A. Hirschfeld & S. A. Gelman (Eds.), *Mapping the mind: Domain specificity in cognition and culture*. Cambridge, England: Cambridge University Press.

Vosniadou, S. (2003). Exploring the relationships between conceptual change and intentional learning. In G. M. Sinatra & P. R. Pintrich (Eds.), *Intentional conceptual change* (pp. 377–406). Mahwah, NJ: Erlbaum.

Vosniadou, S., & Brewer, W. F. (1987). Theories of knowledge restructuring in development. *Review of Educational Research, 57*, 51–67.

Vygotsky, L. S. (1934/1986). *Thought and language* (rev. ed.; A. Kozulin, Ed. and Trans.). Cambridge, MA: MIT Press. (Original work published 1934)

Vygotsky, L. S. (1962). *Thought and language* (E. Haufmann & G. Vakar, Eds. and Trans.). Cambridge, MA: MIT Press.

Vygotsky, L. S. (1978). *Mind in society: The development of higher psychological processes* (M. Cole, V. John-Steiner, S. Scribner, & E. Souberman, Eds.).Cambridge, MA: Harvard University Press.

Vygotsky, L. S. (1987). Thinking and speech. In R. W. Rieber & A. S. Carton (Eds.), *The collected works of L. S. Vygotsky*. New York: Plenum Press.

Vygotsky, L. S. (1997). *Educational psychology*. Boca Raton, FL: St. Lucie Press.

Waddington, C. H. (1957). *The strategy of the genes*. London: Allyn & Bacon.

Wagner, L. S., Carlin, P. L., Cauce, A. M., & Tenner, A. (2001). A snapshot of homeless youth in Seattle: Their characteristics, behaviors and beliefs about HIV protective strategies. *Journal of Community Health, 26*, 219–232.

Wagner, M. (1995). *The contributions of poverty and ethnic background to the participation of secondary school students in special education*. Washington, DC: U.S. Department of Education.

Wahlsten, D., & Gottlieb, G. (1997). The invalid separation of effects of nature and nurture: Lessons from animal experimentation. In R. J. Sternberg & E. L. Grigorenko (Eds.), *Intelligence, heredity, and environment* (pp. 163–192). Cambridge, England: Cambridge University Press.

Wainright, J. L., Russell, S. T., & Patterson, C. J. (2004). Psychosocial adjustment and school outcomes of adolescents with same-sex parents. *Child Development, 75*, 1886–1898.

Waisbren, S. E. (1999). Phenylketonuria. In S. Goldstein & C. R. Reynolds (Eds.), *Handbook of neurodevelopmental and genetic disorders* (pp. 433–458). New York: Guilford Press.

Walczyk, J. J., Marsiglia, C. S., Johns, A. K., & Bryan, K. S. (2004). Children's compensations for poorly automated reading skills. *Discourse Processes, 37*(1), 47–66.

Waldman, I. D., Weinberg, R. A., & Scarr, S. (1994). Racial-group differences in IQ in the Minnesota Transracial Adoption Study: A reply to Levin and Lynn. *Intelligence, 19*, 29–44.

Walker, E., & Tessner, K. (2008). Schizophrenia. *Perspectives on Psychological Science, 3*, 30–37.

Walker, H. M., Horner, R. H., Sugai, G., Bullis, M., Sprague, J. R., Bicker, D., & Kaufman, M. J. (1996). Integrated approaches to preventing antisocial behavior patterns among school-age children and youth. *Journal of Emotional and Behavioral Disorders, 4,* 194–209.

Walker, L. J. (1991). Sex differences in moral reasoning. In W. M. Kurtines & J. L. Gewirtz (Eds.), *Handbook of moral behavior and development: Vol. 2. Research* (pp. 333–364). Hillsdale, NJ: Erlbaum.

Walker, L. J. (1995). Sexism in Kohlberg's moral psychology? In W. M. Kurtines & J. L. Gewirtz (Eds.), *Moral development: An introduction.* Boston: Allyn & Bacon.

Walker, L. J. (2006). Gender and morality. In M. Killen & J. G. Smetana (Eds.), *Handbook of moral development* (pp. 93–115). Mahwah, NJ: Erlbaum.

Walker, L. J., & Reimer, K. S. (2006). The relationship between moral and spiritual development. In E. C. Roehlkepartain, P. E. King, L. Wagener, & P. L. Benson (Eds.), *The handbook of spiritual development in childhood and adolescence* (pp. 224–238). Thousand Oaks, CA: Sage.

Walker, S. P., Wachs, T. D., Gardner, J. M., Lozoff, B., Wasserman, G. A., Pollitt, et al. (2007). Child development: Risks factors for adverse outcomes in developing countries. *Lancet, 369*(9556), 145–157.

Wallander, J. L., Eggert, K. M., & Gilbert, K. K. (2004). Adolescent health-related issues. In R. T. Brown (Ed.), *Handbook of pediatric psychology in school settings* (pp. 503–520). Mahwah, NJ: Erlbaum.

Wallerstein, J., & Lewis, J. M. (2007). Sibling outcomes and disparate parenting and stepparenting after divorce: Report from a 10-year longitudinal study. *Psychoanalytical Psychology, 24,* 445–458.

Wallerstein, J. S. (1984). Children of divorce: The psychological tasks of the child. In S. Chess (Ed.), *Annual Progress in Child Psychiatry and Child Development* (pp. 263–280). Philadelphia: Brunner-Routledge.

Wallerstein, J. S., & Kelly, J. B. (1980). *Surviving the break-up: How children and parents cope with divorce.* New York: Basic Books.

Wallerstein, J. S., Lewis, J. M., & Blakeslee, S. (2001). *The unexpected legacy of divorce: A twenty-five year landmark study.* New York: Hyperion Press.

Walls, T. A., & Little, T. D. (2005). Relations among personal agency, motivation, and school adjustment in early adolescence. *Journal of Educational Psychology, 97,* 23–31.

Walsh, C. E. (1999). *Enabling academic success for secondary students with limited formal schooling: A study of the Haitian Literacy Program at Hyde Park High School in Boston.* Providence, RI: Northeast and Islands Laboratory.

Walters, G. C., & Grusec, J. E. (1977). *Punishment.* San Francisco: Freeman.

Walton, G. E., Bower, N. J. A., & Bower, T. G. R. (1992). Recognition of familiar faces by newborns. *Infant Behavior and Development, 15,* 265–269.

Wang, J., & Lin, E. (2005). Comparative studies on U.S. and Chinese mathematics learning and the implications for standards-based mathematics teaching reform. *Educational Researcher, 34*(5), 3–13.

Wang, P. P., & Baron, M. A. (1997). Language and communication: Development and disorders. In M. L. Batshaw (Ed.), *Children with disabilities* (4th ed.). Baltimore: Brookes.

Wang, Q. (2006). Culture and the development of self-knowledge. *Current Directions in Psychological Science, 15,* 182–187.

Wang, Q., & Ross, M. (2007). Culture and memory. In S. Kitayama & D. Cohen (Eds.), *Handbook of cultural psychology* (pp. 645–667). New York: Guilford Press.

Want, S. C., & Harris, P. L. (2001). Learning from other people's mistakes: Causal understanding in learning to use a tool. *Child Development, 72,* 431–443.

Ward, R. A., & Spitze, G. (1998). Sandwiched marriages: The implications of child and parent relations for marital quality in midlife. *Social Forces, 77,* 647–666.

Warren, A. R., & McCloskey, L. A. (1993). Pragmatics: Language in social contexts. In J. Berko-Gleason (Ed.), *The development of language* (3rd ed.). New York: Macmillan.

Warren-Leubecker, A., & Bohannon, J. N. (1989). Pragmatics: Language in social contexts. In J. Berko-Gleason (Ed.), *The development of language* (2nd ed.). Upper Saddle River, NJ: Merrill/Prentice Hall.

Wartella, E., Caplovitz, A. G., & Lee, J. H. (2004). From Baby Einstein to Leapfrog, from Doom to The Sims, from instant messaging to Internet chat rooms: Public interest in the role of interactive media in children's lives. *Social Policy Report, 18*(4) (Society for Research in Child Development).

Warton, P. M., & Goodnow, J. J. (1991). The nature of responsibility: Children's understanding of "Your Job." *Child Development, 62,* 156–165.

Waschbusch, D. A., Craig, R., Pelham, W. E. Jr., & King, S. (2007). Self-handicapping prior to academic-oriented tasks in children with Attention Deficit/Hyperactivity Disorder (ADHD): Medication effects and comparisons with controls. *Journal of Abnormal and Child Psychology, 35,* 275–286.

Wasik, B. A., & Bond, M. A. (2001). Beyond the pages of a book: Interactive book reading and language development in preschool classrooms. *Journal of Educational Psychology, 93,* 243–250.

Wasik, B. A., Karweit, N., Burns, L., & Brodsky, E. (1998, April). *Once upon a time: The role of rereading and retelling in storybook reading.* Paper presented at the annual meeting of the American Educational Research Association, San Diego, CA.

Waters, E., Merrick, S., Treboux, D., Crowell, J., & Albersheim, L. (2000). Attachment security in infancy and early adulthood: A twenty-year longitudinal study. *Child Development, 71,* 684–689.

Waters, H. S. (1982). Memory development in adolescence: Relationships between metamemory, strategy use, and performance. *Journal of Experimental Child Psychology, 33,* 183–195.

Watson, J. D., Baker T. A., Bell S. P., Gann, A., Levine, M., & Losick, R (2004). *Molecular biology of the gene* (5th ed.), San Francisco, CA: Pearson/Benjamin Cummings (Cold Spring Harbor Laboratory Press).

Watson, M., & Battistich, V. (2006). Building and sustaining caring communities. In C. M. Evertson & C. S. Weinstein (Eds.), *Handbook of classroom management: Research, practice, and contemporary issues* (pp. 253–279). Mahwah, NJ: Erlbaum.

Watson, R. (1996). Rethinking readiness for learning. In D. R. Olson & N. Torrance (Eds.), *The handbook of education and human development: New models of learning, teaching and schooling* (pp. 148–172). Cambridge, MA: Blackwell.

Waxman, S. R. (1990). Linguistic biases and the establishment of conceptual hierarchies: Evidence from preschool children. *Cognitive Development, 5,* 123–150.

Way, N. (1998). *Everyday courage: The lives and stories of urban teenagers.* New York: New York University Press.

Weaver, C. (1990). *Understanding whole language: From principles to practice.* Portsmouth, NH: Heinemann.

Weaver, C. A., III, & Kintsch, W. (1991). Expository text. In R. Barr, M. L. Kamil, P. B. Mosenthal, & P. D. Pearson (Eds.), *Handbook of reading research* (Vol. II). New York: Longman.

Weaver-Hightower, M. (2003). The "boy turn" in research on gender and education. *Review of Educational Research, 73,* 471–498.

Webb, N. M., & Farivar, S. (1994). Promoting helping behavior in cooperative small groups in middle school mathematics. *American Educational Research Journal, 31,* 369–395.

Webb, N. M., Franke, M. L., Ing, M., Chan, A., De, T., Freund, D., et al. (2008). The role of teacher instructional practices in student collaboration. *Contemporary Educational Psychology, 33,* 360–381.

Webb, N. M., & Palincsar, A. S. (1996). Group processes in the classroom. In D. C. Berliner & R. C. Calfee (Eds.), *Handbook of educational psychology.* New York: Macmillan.

Webber, J., Scheuermann, B., McCall, C., & Coleman, M. (1993). Research on self-monitoring as a behavior management technique in special education classrooms: A descriptive review. *Remedial and Special Education, 14*(2), 38–56.

Webster-Stratton, C., & Hammond, M. (1999). Marital conflict management skills, parenting style, and early-onset conduct problems: Processes and pathways. *Journal of Child Psychology & Psychiatry & Allied Disciplines, 40,* 917–927.

Wechsler, D. (2002). *Wechsler Preschool and Primary Scale of Intelligence–Third Edition.* San Antonio, TX: Psychological Corporation.

Wechsler, D. (2003). *Wechsler Intelligence Scale for Children* (4th ed.). San Antonio, TX: Psychological Corporation.

Weinberg, R. A. (1989). Intelligence and IQ: Landmark issues and great debates. *American Psychologist, 44,* 98–104.

Weiner, B. (1984). Principles for a theory of student motivation and their application within an attributional framework. In R. Ames & C. Ames (Eds.), *Research on motivation in education: Vol. 1. Student motivation.* San Diego, CA: Academic Press.

Weiner, B. (1986). *An attributional theory of motivation and emotion.* New York: Springer-Verlag.

Weiner, B. (2000). Intrapersonal and interpersonal theories of motivation from an attributional perspective. *Educational Psychology Review, 12,* 1–14.

Weiner, B. (2004). Attribution theory revisited: Transforming cultural plurality into theoretical unity. In D. M. McNerney & S. Van Etten (Eds.), *Big theories revisited* (pp. 13–29). Greenwich, CT: Information Age.

Weinstein, R. S. (1993). Children's knowledge of differential treatment in school: Implications for motivation. In T. M. Tomlinson (Ed.), *Motivating students to learn: Overcoming barriers to high achievement.* Berkeley, CA: McCutchan.

Weinstein, R. S., Madison, S. M., & Kuklinski, M. R. (1995). Raising expectations in schooling: Obstacles and opportunities for change. *American Educational Research Journal, 32,* 121–159.

Weintraub, M., Horvath, D. L., & Gringlas, M. B. (2002). Single parenthood. In M. H. Bornstein (Ed.), *Handbook of parenting: Vol. 3. Being and becoming a parent* (pp. 109–140). Mahwah, NJ: Erlbaum.

Weisgram, E. S., Bigler, R. S., & Liben, L. S. (2007, March). *Altruism, money, power, and family: How values and gender shape occupational judgments and aspirations.* Paper presented at the biennial meeting of the Society for Research in Child Development, Boston.

Weisner, M. & Ittel, A. (2002). Relations of pubertal timing and depressive symptoms to substance abuse in early adolescence. *Journal of Early Adolescence, 22,* 5–23.

Weisner, T. S., & Gallimore, R. (1977). My brother's keeper: Child and sibling caregiving. *Current Anthropology, 18,* 169–190.

Weiss, M. J., & Hagen, R. (1988). A key to literacy: Kindergartners' awareness of the functions of print. *The Reading Teacher, 41,* 574–578.

Wellman, H. M. (1990). *The child's theory of mind.* Cambridge, MA: MIT Press.

Wellman, H. M., Cross, D., & Watson, J. (2001). Meta-analysis of theory-of-mind development: The truth about false belief. *Child Development, 72,* 655–684.

Wellman, H. M., & Estes, D. (1986). Early understanding of mental entities: A reexamination of childhood realism. *Child Development, 57,* 910–923.

Wellman, H. M., Fang, F., Liu, D., Zhu, L., & Zhu, G. (2006). Scaling of theory-of-mind understandings in Chinese children. *Psychological Science, 17,* 1075–1081.

Wellman, H. M., & Gelman, S. A. (1998). Knowledge acquisition in functional domains. In W. Damon (Series Ed.), D. Kuhn, & R. S. Siegler (Vol. Eds.), *Handbook of child psychology: Vol. 2. Cognition, perception, and language* (5th ed., pp. 523–573). New York: Wiley.

Wellman, H. M., Harris, P. L., Banerjee, M., & Sinclair, A. (1995). Early understanding of emotion: Evidence from natural language. *Cognition and Emotion, 9,* 117–149.

Wellman, H. M., & Hickling, A. K. (1994). The mind's "I": Children's conception of the mind as an active agent. *Child Development, 65,* 1564–1580.

Wellman, H. M., Phillips, A. T., & Rodriguez, T. (2000). Young children's understanding of perception, desire, and emotion. *Child Development, 71,* 895–912.

Welsh, M. C. (1991). Rule-guided behavior and self-monitoring on the tower of Hanoi disk-transfer task. *Cognitive Development, 4,* 59–76. *Journal of Educational Psychology, 91,* 76–97.

Wentzel, K. R. (1999). Social-motivational processes and interpersonal relationships: Implications for understanding motivation at school. *Journal of Educational Psychology, 91,* 76–97.

Wentzel, K. R. (2000). What is it that I'm trying to achieve? Classroom goals from a content perspective. *Contemporary Educational Psychology, 25,* 105–115.

Wentzel, K. R., & Asher, S. R. (1995). The academic lives of neglected, rejected, popular, and controversial children. *Child Development, 66,* 754–763.

Wentzel, K. R., Filisetti, L., & Looney, L. (2007). Adolescent prosocial behavior: The role of self-processes and contextual cues. *Child Development, 78,* 895–910.

Wentzel, K. R., & Wigfield, A. (1998). Academic and social motivational influences on students' academic performance. *Educational Psychology Review, 10,* 155–175.

Werker, J. F., & Lalonde, C. E. (1988). Cross-language speech perception: Initial capabilities and developmental change. *Developmental Psychology, 24,* 672–683.

Werker, J. F., & Tees, R. C. (1999). Influences on infant speech processing: Toward a new synthesis. *Annual Review of Psychology, 50,* 509–535.

Werner, E. E., & Smith, R. S. (2001). *Journeys from childhood to midlife: Risk, resilience, and recovery.* Ithaca, NY: Cornell University Press.

Wertsch, J. V. (1984). The zone of proximal development: Some conceptual issues. *Children's learning in the zone of proximal development: New directions for child development* (No. 23). San Francisco: Jossey-Bass.

Wertsch, J. V., & Tulviste, P. (1994). Lev Semyonovich Vygotsky and contemporary developmental psychology. In R. D. Parke, P. A. Ornstein, J. J. Rieser, & C. Zahn-Waxler (Eds.), *A century of developmental psychology* (pp. 333–355). Washington, DC: American Psychological Association.

Whalen, C. K., Jamner, L. D., Henker, B., Delfino, R. J., & Lozano, J. M. (2002). The ADHD spectrum and everyday life: Experience sampling of adolescent moods, activities, smoking, and drinking. *Child Development, 73,* 209–227.

Whipple, E. E. (2006). Child abuse and neglect: Consequences of physical, sexual, and emotional abuse of children. In H. E. Fitzgerald, R. Zucker, & K. Freeark (Eds. in Chief), H. E. Fitzgerald, B. M. Lester, & B. Zuckerman (Vol. Eds.), *The crisis in youth mental health: Critical issues and effective programs: Vol. 1. Childhood disorders* (pp. 205–229). Westport, CT: Praeger.

White, B. Y., & Frederiksen, J. (2005). A theoretical framework and approach for fostering metacognitive development. *Educational Psychologist, 40,* 211–223.

White, B. Y., & Frederiksen, J. R. (1998). Inquiry, modeling, and metacognition: Making science accessible to all students. *Cognition and Instruction, 16,* 3–118.

White, J. J., & Rumsey, S. (1994). Teaching for understanding in a third-grade geography lesson. In J. Brophy (Ed.), *Advances in research on teaching: Vol. 4. Case studies of teaching and learning in social studies* (pp. 33–69). Greenwich, CT: JAI Press.

White, R. (1959). Motivation reconsidered: The concept of competence. *Psychological Review, 66,* 297–333.

Whitehurst, G. J., Arnold, D. S., Epstein, J. N., Angell, A. L., Smith, M., & Fischel, J. E. (1994). A picture book reading intervention in day care and home for children from low-income families. *Developmental Psychology, 30,* 679–689.

Whiting, B. B., & Edwards, C. P. (1988). *Children of different worlds.* Cambridge, MA: Harvard University Press.

Whiting, B. B., & Whiting, J. W. M. (1975). *Children of six cultures: A psycho-cultural analysis.* Cambridge, MA: Harvard University Press.

Whitley, B. E., Jr., & Frieze, I. H. (1985). Children's causal attributions for success and failure in achievement settings: A meta-analysis. *Journal of Educational Psychology, 77,* 608–616.

Wickens, A. (2005). *Foundations of biopsychology* (2nd ed.) Harlow, England: Pearson Prentice Hall.

Wieder, S., Greenspan, S., & Kalmanson, B. (2008). Autism assessment and intervention: The developmental individual-difference, relationship-based DIR®/Floortime™ model. *Zero to Three, 28*(4), 31–37.

Wigfield, A. (1994). Expectancy-value theory of achievement motivation: A developmental perspective. *Educational Psychology Review, 6,* 49–78.

Wigfield, A., Byrnes, J. P., & Eccles, J. S. (2006). Development during early and middle adolescence. In P. A. Alexander & P. H. Winne (Eds.), *Handbook of educational psychology* (2nd ed., pp. 87–113). Mahwah, NJ: Erlbaum.

Wigfield, A., & Eccles, J. S. (1994). Children's competence beliefs, achievement values, and general self-esteem: Change across elementary and middle school. *Journal of Early Adolescence, 14,* 107–138.

Wigfield, A., & Eccles, J. (2000). Expectancy-value theory of achievement motivation. *Contemporary Educational Psychology, 25,* 68–81.

Wigfield, A., Eccles, J., Mac Iver, D., Reuman, D., & Midgley, C. (1991). Transitions at early adolescence: Changes in children's domain-specific self-perceptions and general self-esteem across the transition to junior high school. *Developmental Psychology, 27,* 552–565.

Wigfield, A., Eccles, J. S., & Pintrich, P. R. (1996). Development between the ages of 11 and 25. In D. C. Berliner & R. C. Calfee (Eds.), *Handbook of educational psychology.* New York: Macmillan.

Wigfield, A., Tonks, S., & Eccles, J. S. (2004). Expectancy value theory in cross-cultural perspective. In D. M. McInerney & S. Van Etten (Eds.), *Big theories revisited* (pp. 165–198). Greenwich, CT: Information Age.

Wiig, E. H., Gilbert, M. F., & Christian, S. H. (1978). Developmental sequences in perception and interpretation of ambiguous sentences. *Perceptual and Motor Skills, 46,* 959–969.

Wilcox, S. (1994). Struggling for a voice: An interactionist view of language and literacy in Deaf education. In V. John-Steiner, C. P. Panofsky, & L. W. Smith (Eds.), *Sociocultural approaches to language and literacy: An interactionist perspective.* Cambridge, England: Cambridge University Press.

Willard, N. E. (2007). *Cyberbullying and cyberthreats: Responding to the challenge of online social aggression, threats, and distress.* Champaign, IL: Research Press.

Willats, J. (1995). An information-processing approach to drawing development. In C. Lange-Kuttner & G. V. Thomas (Eds.), *Drawing and looking: Theoretical approaches to pictorial representation in children* (pp. 27–43). New York: Harvester Wheatsheaf.

Willatts, P. (1990). Development of problem solving strategies in infancy. In D. F. Bjorklund (Ed.), *Children's strategies* (pp. 23–66). Hillsdale, NJ: Erlbaum.

Williams, D. (1996). *Autism: An inside-outside approach.* London: Kingsley.

Williams, D. E., & D'Alessandro, J. D. (1994). A comparison of three measures of androgyny and their relationship to psychological adjustment. *Journal of Social Behavior and Personality, 9,* 469–480.

Williams, D. L. (2008). What neuroscience has taught us about autism. *Zero to Three, 28*(4), 38–45.

Williams, J. (2004). Seizure disorders. In R. T. Brown (Ed.), *Handbook of pediatric psychology in school settings* (pp. 221–239). Mahwah, NJ: Erlbaum.

Williams, J., & Williamson, K. (1992). "I wouldn't want to shoot nobody": The out-of-school curriculum as described by urban students. *Action in Teacher Education, 14*(2), 9–15.

Williams, K. M. (2001a). "Frontin' it": Schooling, violence, and relationships in the 'hood. In J. N. Burstyn, G. Bender, R. Casella, H. W. Gordon, D. P. Guerra, K. V. Luschen et al. (Eds.), *Preventing violence in schools: A challenge to American democracy* (pp. 95–108). Mahwah, NJ: Erlbaum.

Williams, K. M. (2001b). What derails peer mediation? In J. N. Burstyn, G. Bender, R. Casella, H. W. Gordon, D. P. Guerra, K. V. Luschen, et al. *Preventing violence in schools: A challenge to American democracy* (pp. 199–208). Mahwah, NJ: Erlbaum.

Williams, P. E., Weiss, L. G., & Rolfhus, E. L. (2003a). *WISC-IV technical report #2: Clinical validity.* San Antonio, TX: Harcourt Assessment. Retrieved September 6, 2005, from http://www.harcourtassessment.com

Williams, P. E., Weiss, L. G., & Rolfhus, E. L. (2003b). *WISC-IV technical report #2: Psychometric properties.* San Antonio, TX: Harcourt Assessment. Retrieved September 6, 2005, from http://www.harcourtassessment.com

Williams, R. W., & Herrup, K. (1998). The control of neuron number. *Annual Review of Neuroscience, 11,* 423–453.

Willig, A. C. (1985). A meta-analysis of selected studies on the effectiveness of bilingual education. *Review of Educational Research, 55,* 269–317.

Wilson, A. J., & Dehaene, S. (2007). Number sense and developmental dyscalculia. In D. Coch, G. Dawson, & K. W. Fischer (Eds.), *Human behavior, learning, and the developing brain: Atypical development* (pp. 212–238). New York: Guilford Press.

Wilson, B. (1997). Types of child art and alternative developmental accounts: Interpreting the interpreters. *Human Development, 40,* 155–168.

Wilson, B. J. (2008). Media and children's aggression, fear, and altruism. *Future of Children, 18*(1), 87–118.

Wilson, B. L., & Corbett, H. D. (2001). *Listening to urban kids: School reform and the teachers they want.* Albany, NY: State University of New York Press.

Wilson, D. K., Nicholson, S. C., & Krishnamoorthy, J. S. (1998). The role of diet in minority adolescent health promotion. In D. K. Wilson, J. R. Rodrigue, & W. C. Taylor (Eds.), *Health-promoting and health-compromising behaviors among minority adolescents* (pp. 129–151). Washington, DC: American Psychological Association.

Wilson, H. K., Pianta, R. C., & Stuhlman, M. (2007). Typical classroom experiences in first grade: The role of classroom climate and functional risk in the development of social competencies. *Elementary School Journal, 108*(2), 81–96.

Wilson, L. (2007). Great American schools: The power of culture and passion. *Educational Horizons, 86*(1), 33–44.

Wimmer, H., Landerl, K., & Frith, U. (1999). Learning to read German: Normal and impaired acquisition. In M. Harris & G. Hatano (Eds.), *Learning to read and write: A cross-linguistic perspective.* Cambridge, England: Cambridge University Press.

Wimmer, H., Mayringer, H., & Landerl, K. (2000). The double-deficit hypothesis and difficulties in learning to read a regular orthography. *Journal of Educational Psychology, 92,* 668–680.

Wimmer, H., & Perner, J. (1983). Beliefs about beliefs: Representation and constraining function of wrong beliefs in young children's understanding of deception. *Cognition, 13,* 103–128.

Winberg, J. (2005). Mother and newborn baby: Mutual regulation of physiology and behavior—a selective review. *Developmental Psychobiology, 47,* 219–229.

Wineburg, S. S. (1994). The cognitive representation of historical texts. In G. Leinhardt, I. L. Beck, & C. Stainton (Eds.), *Teaching and learning in history.* Hillsdale, NJ: Erlbaum.

Winn, W. (2002). Current trends in educational technology research: The study of learning environments. *Educational Psychology Review, 14,* 331–351.

Winne, P. H. (1995a). Inherent details in self-regulated learning. *Educational Psychologist, 30,* 173–187.

Winne, P. H. (1995b). Self-regulation is ubiquitous but its forms vary with knowledge. *Educational Psychologist, 30,* 223–228.

Winner, E. (1988). *The point of words.* Cambridge, MA: Harvard University Press.

Winner, E. (1996). The rage to master: The decisive role of talent in the visual arts. In K. A. Ericcson (Ed.), *The road to excellence: The acquisition of expert performance in the arts, sciences, sports and games* (pp. 271–301). Mahwah, NJ: Erlbaum.

Winner, E. (1997). Exceptionally high intelligence and schooling. *American Psychologist, 52,* 1070–1081.

Winner, E. (2000). The origins and ends of giftedness. *American Psychologist, 55,* 159–169.

Winner, E. (2006). Development in the arts: Drawing and music. In W. Damon, R. M. Lerner (Series Eds.), D. Kuhn, & R. Siegler (Vol. Eds.), *Handbook of child psychology: Vol. 2. Cognition, perception, and language* (6th ed.). New York: Wiley.

Winsler, A., Díaz, R. M., Espinosa, L., & Rodriguez, J. L. (1999). When learning a second language does not mean losing the first: Bilingual language development in low-income, Spanish-speaking children attending bilingual preschool. *Child Development, 70,* 349–362.

Winsler, A., & Naglieri, J. (2003). Overt and covert verbal problem-solving strategies: Developmental trends in use, awareness, and relations with task performance in children aged 5 to 17. *Child Development, 74,* 659–678.

Winston, P. (1973). Learning to identify toy block structures. In R. L. Solso (Ed.), *Contemporary issues in cognitive psychology: The Loyola Symposium.* Washington, DC: V. H. Winston.

Witkow, M. R., & Fuligni, A. J. (2007). Achievement goals and daily school experiences among adolescents with Asian, Latino, and European American backgrounds. *Journal of Educational Psychology, 99,* 584–596.

Wittmer, D. S., & Honig, A. S. (1994). Encouraging positive social development in young children. *Young Children, 49*(5), 4–12.

Wolcott, H. F. (1999). *Ethnography: A way of seeing.* Walnut Creek, CA: AltMira.

Wolf, M., & Bowers, P. G. (1999). The double-deficit hypothesis for the developmental dyslexias. *Journal of Educational Psychology, 91,* 415–438.

Wolfe, D. A., & Wekerle, C. (1997). Pathways to violence in teen dating relationships. In D. Cicchetti & S. L. Toth (Eds.), Developmental perspectives on trauma: Theory, research, and intervention. *Rochester Symposium on Developmental Psychology, 8,* 315–341. Rochester, NY: University of Rochester Press.

Wolfe, M. B. W., & Goldman, S. R. (2005). Relations between adolescents' text processing and reasoning. *Cognition and Instruction, 23,* 467–502.

Wolff, P. G. (1966). The causes, controls, and organization of behavior in the neonate. *Psychological Issues, 5*(1, Serial No. 17).

Wolters, C. A. (2003). Regulation of motivation: Evaluating an underemphasized aspect of self-regulated learning. *Educational Psychologist, 38,* 189–205.

Wolock, I., Sherman, P., Feldman, L. H., & Metzger, B. (2001). Child abuse and neglect referral patterns: A longitudinal study. *Children and Youth Services Review, 23,* 21–47.

Wong, S. C. (1993). Promises, pitfalls, and principles of text selection in curricular diversification: The Asian-American case. In T. Perry & J. W. Fraser (Eds.), *Freedom's plow: Teaching in the multicultural classroom.* New York: Routledge.

Wood, A., & Wood, B. (2001). *Alphabet adventure.* New York: Scholastic Books.

Wood, A. C., Saudino, K. J., Rogers, H., Asherson, P., & Kuntsi, J. (2007). Genetic influences on mechanically-assessed activity level in children. *Journal of Child Psychology and Psychiatry, 48,* 695–702.

Wood, D., Bruner, J. S., & Ross, G. (1976). The role of tutoring in problem-solving. *Journal of Child Psychology and Psychiatry, 17,* 89–100.

Wood, E., Willoughby, T., McDermott, C., Motz, M., Kaspar, V., & Ducharme, M. J. (1999). Developmental differences in study behavior. *Journal of Educational Psychology, 91,* 527–536.

Wood, J. W. (1998). *Adapting instruction to accommodate students in inclusive settings* (3rd ed.). Upper Saddle River, NJ: Merrill/Prentice Hall.

Woodring, L. A., Cancelli, A. A., Ponterotto, J. G., & Keitel, M. A. (2005). A qualitative investigation of adolescents' experiences with parental HIV/AIDS. *American Journal of Orthopsychiatry, 75,* 658–675.

Woodward, A. L., Markman, E. M., & Fitzsimmons, C. M. (1994). Rapid word learning in 13- and 18-month-olds. *Developmental Psychology, 30,* 553–566.

Woodward, A. L., & Sommerville, J. A. (2000). Twelve-month-old infants interpret action in context. *Psychological Science, 11,* 73–77.

Woody, J. D., D'Souza, H. J., & Russel, R. (2003). Emotions and motivations in first adolescent intercourse: An exploratory study based on object relations theory. *Canadian Journal of Human Sexuality, 12*(1), 35–51.

Woolfe, T., Want, S. C., & Siegal, M. (2002). Signposts to development: Theory of mind in deaf children. *Child Development, 73,* 768–778.

Woolley, J. D. (1995). The fictional mind: Young children's understanding of pretense, imagination, and dreams. *Developmental Review, 15,* 172–211.

World Health Organization. (2000). Obesity: Preventing and managing the global epidemic, WHO. Geneva, Switzerland, Report of a WHO consultation, Report No. 894.

Wright, S. C., Taylor, D. M., & Macarthur, J. (2000). Subtractive bilingualism and the survival of the Inuit language: Heritage- versus second-language education. *Journal of Educational Psychology, 92,* 63–84.

WritersCorps. (2003). *Paint me like I am: Teen poems from WritersCorps.* New York: HarperTempest.

Wynbrandt, J., & Ludman, M. D. (2000). *The encyclopedia of genetic disorders and birth defects* (2nd ed.). New York: Facts on File.

Wynn, K. (1990). Children's understanding of counting. *Cognition, 36,* 155–193.

Wynn, K. (1992). Addition and subtraction by human infants. *Nature, 358,* 749–750.

Wynn, K. (1995). Infants possess a system of numerical knowledge. *Current Directions in Psychological Science, 4,* 172–177.

Xu, F., & Spelke, E. S. (2000). Large number discrimination in 6-month-old infants. *Cognition, 74,* B1–B11.

Xue, Y., & Meisels, S. J. (2004). Early literacy instruction and learning in kindergarten: Evidence from the early childhood longitudinal study—kindergarten class of 1998–1999. *American Educational Research Journal, 41,* 191–229.

Yaden, D. B., Jr., & Templeton, S. (Eds.). (1986). *Metalinguistic awareness and beginning literacy: Conceptualizing what it means to read and write.* Portsmouth, NH: Heinemann.

Yakovlev, P. I., & Lecours, A. R. (1967). The myelogenetic cycles of regional maturation of the brain. In A. Minkowski (Ed.), *Regional development of the brain in early life* (pp. 3–70). Oxford, England: Blackwell Scientific.

Yarrow, M. R., Scott, P. M., & Waxler, C. Z. (1973). Learning concern for others. *Developmental Psychology, 8,* 240–260.

Yates, M., & Youniss, J. (1996). A developmental perspective on community service in adolescence. *Social Development, 5,* 85–111.

Yau, J., & Smetana, J. G. (2003). Conceptions of moral, social-conventional, and personal events among Chinese preschoolers in Hong Kong. *Child Development, 74,* 647–658.

Yeager, E. A., Foster, S. J., Maley, S. D., Anderson, T., Morris, J. W., III, & Davis, O. L., Jr. (1997, March). *The role of empathy in the development of historical understanding.* Paper presented at the annual meeting of the American Educational Research Association, Chicago.

Yilmaz, K. (2007). Historical empathy and its implications for classroom practices in schools. *History Teacher, 40,* 331–337.

Ying, Y.-W., & Han, M. (2007). The longitudinal effect of intergenerational gap in acculturation on conflict and mental health in Southeast Asian American adolescents. *American Journal of Orthopsychiatry, 77,* 61–66.

Yip, T., & Fuligni, A. J. (2002). Daily variation in ethnic identity, ethnic behaviors, and psychological well-being among American adolescents of Chinese descent. *Child Development, 73,* 1557–1572.

Young, E. L., & Assing, R. (2000). Review of The Universal Nonverbal Intelligence Test. *Journal of Psychoeducational Assessment, 18,* 280–288.

Young, J. M., Howell, A. N., & Hauser-Cram, P. (2005, April). *Predictors of mastery motivation in children with disabilities born prematurely.* Paper presented at the biennial meeting of the Society for Research in Child Development, Atlanta, GA.

Youngblood, J. II, & Spencer, M. B. (2002). Integrating normative identity processes and academic support requirements for special needs adolescents: The application of an identity-focused cultural ecological (ICE) perspective. *Applied Developmental Science, 6,* 95–108.

Young-Hyman, D. (2004). Diabetes and the school-age child and adolescent: Facilitating good glycemic control and quality of life. In R. T. Brown (Ed.), *Handbook of pediatric psychology in school settings* (pp. 169–193). Mahwah, NJ: Erlbaum.

Youniss, J. (1980). *Parents and peers in social development.* Chicago: University of Chicago Press.

Youniss, J. (1983). Social construction of adolescence by adolescents and their parents. In H. D. Grotevant & C. R. Cooper (Eds.), *Adolescent development in the family: New directions for child development* (No. 22). San Francisco: Jossey-Bass.

Youniss, J., & Yates, M. (1999). Youth service and moral-civic identity: A case of everyday morality. *Educational Psychology Review, 11,* 361–376.

Ysseldyke, J. E., & Algozzine, B. (1984). *Introduction to special education.* Boston: Houghton Mifflin.

Zachry, E. (2005). Getting my education: Teen mothers' experiences in school before and after motherhood. *Teachers College Record, 107,* 2566–2598 (1–19 online paging).

Zahn-Waxler, C., Friedman, R. J., Cole, P., Mizuta, I., & Hiruma, N. (1996). Japanese and United States preschool children's responses to conflict and distress. *Child Development, 67,* 2462–2477.

Zahn-Waxler, C., Radke-Yarrow, M., Wagner, E., & Chapman, M. (1992). Development of concern for others. *Developmental Psychology, 28,* 126–136.

Zahn-Waxler, C., & Robinson, J. (1995). Empathy and guilt: Early origins of feelings of responsibility. In J. P. Tangney & K. W. Fischer (Eds.), *Self-conscious emotions: The psychology of shame, guilt, embarrassment, and pride* (pp. 143–173). New York: Guilford Press.

Zahn-Waxler, C., Robinson, J., & Emde, R. N. (1992). The development of empathy in twins. *Developmental Psychology, 28,* 1038–1047.

Zajonc, R. B., & Mullally, P. R. (1997). Birth order: Reconciling conflicting effects. *American Psychologist, 52,* 685–699.

Zambo, D. (2003, April). *Thinking about reading: Talking to children with learning disabilities.* Paper presented at the annual meeting of the American Educational Research Association, Chicago.

Zambo, D., & Brem, S. K. (2004). Emotion and cognition in students who struggle to read: New insights and ideas. *Reading Psychology, 25,* 1–16.

Zeanah, C. H. (2000). Disturbances of attachment in young children adopted from institutions. *Journal of Developmental and Behavioral Pediatrics, 21,* 230–236.

Zelazo, P. D., Müller, U., Frye, D., & Marcovitch, S. (2003). The development of executive function in early childhood. *Monographs of the Society for Research in Child Development, 68*(3, Serial No. 274).

Zero to Three: National Center for Infants, Toddlers, and Families. (2002). *Temperament.* Retrieved January 16, 2003, from http://www.zerotothree.org/Archive/TEMPERAM.HTM

Zervigon-Hakes, A. (1984). Materials mastery and symbolic development in construction play: Stages of development. *Early Child Development and Care, 17,* 37–47.

Zhou, Q., Eisenberg, N., Losoya, S. H., Fabes, R. A., Reiser, M., Guthrie, I. K., et al. (2002). The relations of parental warmth and positive expressiveness to children's empathy-related responding and social functioning: A longitudinal study. *Child Development, 73,* 893–915.

Ziegert, D. I., Kistner, J. A., Castro, R., & Robertson, B. (2001). Longitudinal study of young children's responses to challenging achievement situations. *Child Development, 72,* 609–624.

Ziegert, J. C., & Hanges, P. J. (2005). Employment discrimination: The role of implicit attitudes, motivation, and a climate or racial bias. *Journal of Applied Psychology, 90,* 553–562.

Ziegler, J. C., Tan, L. H., Perry, C., & Montant, M. (2000). Phonology matters: The phonological frequency effect in written Chinese. *Psychological Science, 11,* 234–238.

Ziegler, S. G. (1987). Effects of stimulus cueing on the acquisition of groundstrokes by beginning tennis players. *Journal of Applied Behavior Analysis, 20,* 405–411.

Zigler, E. (2003). Forty years of believing in magic is enough. *Social Policy Report, 17*(1), 10.

Zigler, E., & Muenchow, S. (1992). *Head Start: The inside story of America's most successful educational experiment.* New York: Basic Books.

Zigler, E. F., & Finn-Stevenson, M. (1992). Applied developmental psychology. In M. H. Bornstein & M. E. Lamb (Eds.), *Developmental psychology: An advanced textbook.* Hillsdale, NJ: Erlbaum.

Zill, N., Nord, C., & Loomis, L. (1995, September). *Adolescent time use, risky behavior, and outcomes: An analysis of national data.* Rockville, MD: Westat.

Zimmerman, B. J. (1998). Developing self-fulfilling cycles of academic regulation: An analysis of exemplary instructional models. In D. H. Schunk & B. J. Zimmerman (Eds.), *Self-regulated learning: From teaching to self-reflective practice* (pp. 1–19). New York: Guilford Press.

Zimmerman, B. J. (2004). Sociocultural influence and students' development of academic self-regulation: A social-cognitive perspective. In D. M. McNerney & S. Van Etten (Eds.), *Big theories revisited* (pp. 139–164). Greenwich, CT: Information Age.

Zimmerman, B. J., & Schunk, D. H. (2004). Self-regulatory dimensions of academic learning and motivation. In G. D. Phye (Ed.), *Handbook of academic learning: Construction of knowledge.* San Diego, CA: Academic Press.

Zimmerman, B. J., & Schunk, D. H. (2004). Self-regulating intellectual processes and outcomes; A social cognitive perspective. In D. Y. Dai & R. J. Sternberg (Eds.), *Motivation, emotion, and cognition: Integrative perspectives on intellectual functioning and development* (pp. 323–349). Mahwah, NJ: Erlbaum.

Zimmerman, M. A., Bingenheimer, J. B., & Notaro, P. C. (2002). Natural mentors and adolescent resiliency: A study with urban youth. *American Journal of Community Psychology, 30,* 221–243.

Zuckerman, G. A. (1994). A pilot study of a ten-day course in cooperative learning for beginning Russian first graders. *Elementary School Journal, 94,* 405–420.

Zuckerman, M. U. (2007). *Sensation seeking and risky behavior.* Washington, DC: American Psychological Association.

Zwaan, R. A., Langston, M. C., & Graesser, A. C. (1995). The construction of situation models in narrative comprehension: An event-indexing model. *Psychological Science, 6,* 292–297.

Aalsma, M. C., 451
Aaronson, D., 316
Abbott, R., 359
Abe, J. A. A., 433
Aber, J. L., 102, 457, 577
Abi-Nader, J., 299, 503
Abma, J. C., 178
Aboud, F. E., 457, 469
Abramowitz, R. H., 71
Abrams, D., 468
Abramson, L. Y., 424
Ackerman, C. M., 303
Ackerman, P. L., 275
Acock, A. C., 584
Acredolo, L. P., 332
Adalbjarnardottir, S., 543
Adam, E. K., 19, 75
Adam, S., 248
Adams, E., 521
Adams, G. R., 177
Adams, M. J., 36
Adams, R. J., 139, 236, 237
Adamson, L., 421
Adamson, L. B., 258, 259
Adkins, D. R., 316
Adolf, S. M., 348
Afflerbach, P., 363, 390
Agency for Toxic Substances
   and Disease Registry, 184
Ahern, A. L., 169
Ahnert, L., 80, 415, 578
Aidinis, A., 368
Aikens, N. L., 35
Ainsworth, M. D. S., 18, 64, 407,
   410, 411, 412, 414
Aitchison, J., 315, 327
Akhtar, N., 323
Akiskal, H. S., 435
Aksan, N., 79, 522
Alan Guttmacher Institute, 180
Alapack, R., 566
Albanese, A. L., 268
Albersheim, L., 416
Albert, M., 527
Alberto, P. A., 185
Alberts, A., 451
Alderman, M. K., 504
Aldous, J., 95
Aldridge, M. A., 328
Alessandri, S. M., 525, 526
Alexander, A. L., 348
Alexander, E. S., 500
Alexander, J. M., 485, 495
Alexander, K., 296, 575
Alexander, K. W., 259
Alexander, P. A., 210, 249,
   252, 263
Alfaro, E. C., 459
Alfassi, M., 221
Alfonso, V. C., 276
Algozzine, B., 560
Alibali, M. W., 14, 205, 240, 249,
   264, 279, 318, 323, 328, 378
Alim, H. S., 347
Alland, A., 393
Alleman, J., 390
Alleman, L. M., 163
Allen, E., 93
Allen, J., 306
Allen, L., 457
Allen, S. E. M., 315
Allison, K. W., 472
Allred, C. G., 46, 48
Almeida, D. M., 7, 454
Als, H., 137, 421
Alsaker, F. D., 423
Altermatt, E. R., 386

Alvarez, W. F., 78
Alvermann, D. E., 360, 366
Alward, K. R., 223
Amatea, E. S., 574, 575
Ambrose, D., 306
American Academy of Pediatrics
   (AAP), 166
American Academy of Pediatrics
   (AAP) Committee on
   Adolescence, 178
American Academy of Pediatrics
   (AAP) Committee on
   Infectious Diseases, 186
American Academy of Pediatrics
   (AAP) Committee on Injury
   and Poison Prevention, 172
American Academy of Pediatrics
   (AAP) Committee on
   Pediatric AIDS, 178, 186
American Academy of Pediatrics
   (AAP) Committee on Sports
   Medicine and Fitness,
   172, 174
American Academy of Pediatrics
   (AAP) Task Force on Infant
   Sleep Position and Sudden
   Infant Death Syndrome, 174
American Association on
   Intellectual and
   Developmental Disabilities,
   305, 306
American Educational Research
   Association, 55
American Psychiatric
   Association, 266, 435,
   436, 473
American Psychological
   Association, 34
American Speech-Language-
   Hearing Association, 348
Ames, C., 173, 489, 501
Ames, E. W., 418
Amirkhanian, Y. A., 179
Amsel, E., 203
Anastasi, A., 285, 286, 287
Andenas, S., 423
Anderman, E. M., 445, 489, 490
Anderman, L. H., 462, 490
Andersen, C., 251
Anderson, C., 582
Anderson, C. A., 535, 539,
   582, 583
Anderson, D. A., 567
Anderson, D. R., 254, 544, 582
Anderson, J. C., 245
Anderson, K. E., 78
Anderson, L. W., 102, 103,
   104, 504
Anderson, M. L., 548, 549, 549n
Anderson, R. C., 242, 321,
   359, 366
Andrews, D. W., 530
Andrews, G., 204, 205, 226, 469
Andrews, J. F., 361
Andriessen, I., 339
Andriessen, J., 219
Anglin, J. M., 322
Annahatak, B., 338
Annett, R. D., 184
Ansul, S. E., 419
Antelman, S., 435
Anthony, J. L., 330, 340, 357
Anthos, J. S., 549
Anyon, J. S., 573
Apperly, I. A., 203
Applebaum, M. I., 238
Applegate, B., 267

Araujo, J., 219
Arbib, M., 258, 314
Arbona, C., 459
Arce, H.-M. C., 493
Archer, J., 535
Arcus, D. M., 7, 430
Argentieri, L., 582
Armon, C., 203
Armstrong, M. I., 458
Arndt, T. L., 142
Arnett, J. J., 423
Arnold, D. H., 535
Arnold, M. L., 522, 524
Aronson, S. R., 74
Arsenio, W. F., 521
Artman, L., 204
Asai, S., 99
Asbridge, M., 563
Ascione, F. R., 535, 582
Ash, G. E., 360
Ashcraft, M. H., 375
Asher, S. R., 437, 541, 554, 555,
   556, 559
Asherson, P., 119
Ashiabi, G. S., 469
Ashmead, D. H., 236–237
Ashmore, R., 471
Ashton, P., 575
Aslin, R. N., 237, 316, 322, 328
Asmussen, L., 70
Assing, R., 285
Assor, A., 446
Astington, J. W., 252, 253,
   467, 469
Astor, R. A., 469, 539
Atkins, R., 529
Atkinson, J., 236
Atkinson, L., 415
Atkinson, M., 316
Attanucci, J., 526, 527
Attie, I., 448
Atwater, E., 177
Au, T. K., 316, 323
August, D., 366
Augustyn, M., 438
Aunola, K., 46
Austin, C. M., 320
Avenevoli, S., 66
Avis, J., 467
Ayoub, C. C., 83
Ayres, L. R., 257, 511
Azevedo, R., 359, 360
Azmitia, M., 458
Azuma, M., 496

Babad, E., 574
Bachman, J. G., 177, 449
Backlund, B. A., 568
Backus, D. W., 252
Baer, D. M., 503
Baer, Donald, 18
Baghurst, P., 290
Bagwell, C. L., 532, 558, 559
Bahrick, L. E., 238
Bailes, A., 109, 109n
Bailey, J. M., 566, 567
Bailey, L., 323
Baillargeon, R., 203, 243, 261,
   383, 384, 386
Baird, J. A., 467
Bajaj, A., 252
Bakari, R., 97, 364
Bakeman, R., 131, 259, 336, 531
Baker, C., 341, 343
Baker, E. L., 357
Baker, J. H., 372
Baker, L., 356, 357

Baker, L. A., 535
Bakersman-Kranenburg,
   M. J., 417
Baldwin, A., 295
Baldwin, C., 295
Baldwin, D. A., 258, 317, 466
Baldwin, M. W., 416
Bales, R. J., 361
Ball, J. W., 128
Baltes, P. B., 8, 16, 19, 407, 464
Bandi Rao, S., 326
Bandura, A., 18, 42, 243, 386,
   387, 483, 484, 490, 496, 499,
   500, 507, 536, 555
Banerjee, M., 421
Banks, A., 75
Banks, C. A. M., 98, 336, 339,
   456, 465
Banks, J. A., 98, 99, 336, 339,
   456, 465
Bannister, E. M., 568
Bao, X.-H., 496
Barab, S. A., 280, 302
Baranowski, J., 499
Barbaranelli, P., 387, 555
Barber, J. G., 74
Barchfeld, P., 384
Barchfield, P., 385, 386
Barga, N. K., 266, 503
Barker, G. P., 494
Barker, S., 166
Barker, T. A., 340, 357
Barkley, R. A., 266, 267
Barkoukis, V., 499
Barlow, S. M., 174
Barnas, M. V., 578
Barnes, M. A., 266, 370
Barnett, J. E., 248
Barnett, W. S., 575
Baron, M. A., 348
Baron-Cohen, S., 455, 472
Baroody, A. J., 374
Barr, H. M., 161, 290
Barrett, J. G., 436
Barringer, C., 324
Barron, K. E., 489
Barron, R. W., 357
Barrow, F. H., 458, 459
Bartels, M., 293
Bartini, M., 538, 539, 554, 555
Bartko, W. T., 93
Bartlett, E., 323
Bartlett, E. J., 370
Bartlett, L., 554
Barton, K. C., 209, 389
Bartsch, K., 467
Barzillai, M., 158
Basinger, K. S., 527, 533,
   558, 559
Basso, K., 336
Basso, K. H., 98
Bates, E., 318, 327
Bates, J., 77
Bates, J. E., 6, 16, 67, 428, 430,
   430n, 530, 556
Bathurst, K., 302
Batshaw, M. L., 306–307
Batson, C. D., 522, 536
Battin-Pearson, S., 415
Battistich, E., 426
Battistich, V., 46, 49, 103, 487,
   561, 571, 573
Bauer, P. J., 239, 240, 241, 259,
   260, 333, 450
Baugh, J., 347
Baumeister, R. F., 451, 465, 466
Baumert, J., 446

Baumrind, D., 77
Bavelier, D., 315
Bax, M., 538
Bay-Hinitz, A. K., 543
Bayley, N., 287, 294
Beal, C. R., 370, 371
Bean, R. A., 93
Beardsall, L., 424
Beardsley, T. M., 309, 310
Bearison, D., 329
Bearison, D. J., 182
Beaty, J. J., 391
Beauchaine, T. P., 267
Beauchamp, G. K., 124
Beaumont, R., 474
Bebeau, M., 521
Bebell, Damian, 587, 588
Bebko, J. M., 207
Beck, M., 308
Beck, Martha, 307, 308
Beck, N. C., 580
Beck, S. R., 203
Becker, B. J., 411
Becker, J. B., 424
Beech, B. M., 172
Beeman, M. J., 315
Begley, C., 130
Behrman, R. E., 84, 91, 103, 184
Belenky, M. F., 83, 105
Belfiore, P. J., 503, 506, 509
Belka, D. E., 163
Bell, L. A., 499
Bell, M. A., 316
Bell, N. J., 454
Bell, P., 257
Bell, R. Q., 81
Bellugi, U., 318
Belsky, J., 69, 396, 411, 578
Belzer, M. E., 181
Bem, S. L., 454, 455
Bembenutty, H., 483
Benbenishty, R., 469
Benbow, C. P., 285, 296
Bendelow, G., 166
Bender, G., 539
Bendixen, L. D., 252
Benenson, J. F., 541
Benes, F., 154
Benet-Martínez, V., 94
Bennett, A., 279, 300
Bennett, G. K., 381
Bennett, J. M., 168
Bennett, L., 562
Bennett, R. E., 424, 574
Bennett, R. T., 250
Bennetto, L., 535
Benoit, D., 418
Benson, B., 565, 566
Benson, C., 389
Benson, F. W., 469
Benson, P. L., 525
Benton, S. L., 372, 373
Benware, C., 219
Bereiter, C., 222, 369, 370, 385
Berenbaum, S. A., 93
Berenstain, J., 474
Berenstain, S., 474
Bergemann, L., 468
Berger, O. G., 290
Berger, S., 72
Bergeron, R., 276
Berk, L. E., 213, 505, 554
Berkeley, S., 502
Berlin, L., 421
Berlin, L. J., 411
Berliner, D., 102

Berliner, D. C., 296
Berman, S. L., 518
Bermejo, V., 374
Bernardi, J. D., 241
Berndt, T. J., 490, 539, 557, 558, 562
Bernier, A., 415
Bernieri, F., 499
Berninger, G., 336
Berninger, V., 359
Berninger, V. W., 368, 370, 371
Bernstein, R., 72
Berry, E. J., 95
Bertenthal, B. I., 237
Berthier, N. E., 371
Bertoncini, J., 236
Berzonsky, M. D., 453
Bettencourt, B. A., 498
Bhatt, R. S., 247
Bhavnagri, N. P., 532
Bhullar, N., 539
Bialystok, E., 316, 343, 366
Bibace, R., 182
Biddle, S. J., 580
Biddlecomb, B., 378, 380, 383
Bidell, T., 205
Bidell, T. R., 10, 16
Biemiller, A., 219, 366, 380, 505
Bierman, K. L., 538, 554, 556, 557, 560
Bigbee, M. A., 540
Biggs, J., 256
Bigler, R. S., 390, 455, 469, 496
Bigner, S. J., 72, 73
Bijeljac-Babic, R., 236
Bijou, Sidney, 18
Binder, L. M., 503
Bindler, R. C., 128
Binet, Alfred, 280, 284n
Bingenheimer, J. B., 66
Birkas, E., 506
Birmaher, V., 169
Birnbaum, D. W., 424
Bishop, D. V. M., 348
Bishop, E. G., 288, 289
Bivens, J. A., 213
Bjorklund, D. F., 12, 18, 27, 171, 172, 211, 239, 241, 247, 250, 450, 451
Blachford, S. L., 117
Black, J. E., 156, 237
Blackbourn, J. M., 307
Black-Gutman, D., 469, 471
Blackson, T. C., 437
Blackwell, L. S., 492
Blades, M., 390
Blair, C., 158, 257, 505
Blakely, C., 459
Blakemore, C., 7
Blakemore, S.-J., 469
Blakeslee, S., 70
Blasi, A., 522, 524
Bleeker, M., 486
Bleeker, M. M., 380
Blehar, M. C., 407
Bleiker, C., 392
Bleske-Rechek, A., 304
Blinde, P. L., 503
Block, J., 178
Block, J. H., 424, 455, 540
Block, N., 298
Bloom, B. S., 295
Bloom, K., 334
Bloom, L., 318, 348
Bloom, P., 466, 484
Blue-Banning, M., 561
Blumenfeld, P. C., 504
Blyth, D. A., 164, 165, 451
Boccia, M., 421
Bochenhauer, M. H., 390
Bocian, K. M., 363
Bodrova, E., 215
Boekaerts, M., 381, 425, 490, 555
Boergers, J., 438
Bohannon, J. N., 315, 336
Bohn, C. M., 171, 172, 268, 530

Boivin, M., 447, 538
Bokhorst, C. L., 423
Bol, L., 252, 533
Boles, R. E., 185
Boling, C. J., 503
Bolt, E., 506
Bonamo, K. M., 327
Bond, L. A., 105
Bond, M. A., 346
Bond, M. H., 541
Bonertz, C. M., 161
Bong, M., 446, 500
Bookstein, F. L., 161, 290
Boom, J., 520, 529
Boomsma, D. I., 293
Booth, C. L., 558
Boothroyd, R. A., 458
Bordeleau, L., 450
Bordelon, K., 177
Bork, P., 110
Borkowski, J. G., 74, 75, 306, 492
Bornschein, R. L., 290
Bornstein, M. H., 78, 79, 157, 215, 289, 294, 321
Bortfeld, H., 316
Bortfield, H., 322
Bosacki, S. L., 474
Boscardin, C. K., 357
Bosch, J. D., 538
Boster, S., 373
Botvin, G. J., 178, 179
Bouchard, T. J., 289, 430
Bouchard, T. J., Jr., 274, 289
Bouffard, T., 450, 451
Boulerice, B., 577
Bourg, T., 260
Boutte, G. S., 99, 572
Bowden, D., 469
Bowen, G. M., 218
Bowen, N. K., 90
Bower, N. J. A., 237
Bower, T. G. R., 237, 328
Bowers, P. G., 363
Bowlby, J., 18, 64, 407, 414, 415, 416
Bowman, B. T., 339
Boyd, J. S., 382
Boyes, M., 468
Boykin, A. W., 300
Brabham, E. G., 324
Brack, G. A., 133
Bracken, B. A., 278, 283, 285, 288, 539–540, 562
Bradford, L. W., 117
Bradley, L., 340
Bradley, R. H., 77, 290
Bradley, S. J., 580
Bradley-Johnson, S., 287
Bradshaw, C. P., 536
Bradshaw, D., 430
Bradshaw, P., 553, 554
Brady, J. E., 558
Brady, M. A. 117
Brady, M. P., 559
Braeges, J. L., 523
Braine, L. G., 392
Braine, M. D., 326
Brakke, N. P., 557
Bramlett, M. D., 70
Branch, C., 465, 471
Brannon, M. E., 373, 380
Bransford, J., 28, 221
Branstetter, W. H., 523, 536
Braswell, G. S., 161
Brauner, J., 578
Bray, N. W., 307
Brazelton, B., 421
Brazelton, T. B., 287
Brazelton Institute, 287
Breaux, C., 69, 73
Bredekamp, S., 168, 578
Breinlinger, K., 261
Breland, P. S., 303
Brem, S. K., 484, 485, 495
Brendgen, M., 483, 535

Brenner, E. M., 422
Brenner, L. A., 469
Brent, S. B., 322
Bretherton, I., 421, 446
Brett, D., 110
Brewer, W. F., 262
Briars, D. J., 382
Brickman, S. J., 490, 500
Bridges, M., 70
Bridges, T. H., 560
Bridglall, B. L., 279
Bright, J. A., 86
Brinton, B., 332
Britt, M. A., 257
Britto, P. R., 566
Britton, B. K., 262, 389
Broderick, P. C., 455
Brodsky, E., 331
Brody, G. H., 82, 95, 525
Brody, N., 275, 278, 279, 285, 289, 293, 297
Brody, S., 159
Brodzinsky, D. M., 73
Broerse, J., 341
Bronfenbrenner, U., 16, 17, 19, 64, 65, 66, 68, 78, 137, 148, 291
Bronson, M. B., 172, 252, 484, 504, 506, 507, 508, 510, 528
Bronson, W. C., 530
Brooks, F., 538, 555
Brooks, R. B., 504
Brooks-Gunn, J., 73, 88, 97, 102, 137, 162, 291, 294, 296, 298, 425, 435, 448, 450, 566, 578, 579, 581
Brophy, J. E., 390, 456, 497, 503, 500, 502, 574
Brown, A., 330
Brown, A. L., 7, 19, 219, 221, 247, 572, 573, 583
Brown, B. B., 490, 501, 534, 562, 581
Brown, C. A., 332
Brown, C. S., 457, 469
Brown, E., 236
Brown, E. G., 532
Brown, J., 424
Brown, J. D., 171
Brown, J. H., 365
Brown, J. R., 424
Brown, J. S., 222
Brown, K. J., 185
Brown, L. M., 527
Brown, R., 256, 314, 325
Brown, R. D., 171
Brown, R. T., 297
Brown, John, 529
Brownell, M. T., 120, 266
Brownlee, J. R., 531
Brown-Mizuno, C., 305
Bruer, J. T., 7, 153, 154, 156, 237, 316, 341, 343, 350
Brugman, D., 520
Bruner, J. S., 19, 27, 208, 215, 217, 341
Bruni, M., 161
Brunstein, J. C., 371, 373
Bryan, J., 268
Bryan, J. H., 535
Bryan, K. S., 360
Bryan, T., 268
Bryant, J. B., 336
Bryant, P., 340, 368, 369
Buchanan, C. M., 424
Buchman, D. D., 582
Buchoff, T., 268
Buchsbaum, H., 450
Buckingham, D., 327
Budd, G. M., 169, 170
Budwig, N., 318
Buehl, M. M., 252
Buehler, C., 73
Buese, D., 396, 397

Buhrmester, D., 554, 558, 559
Buijzen, M., 582
Buitelaar, J. K., 128
Bukowski, W. M., 46, 483, 530, 557
Bullinger, A., 371
Bullock, J. R., 556
Bullock, L. M., 437
Bullock, M., 384, 386
Bumbarger, B., 426
Bumpus, M. F., 80
Bunce, D. M., 210
Bunch, G., 344
Bunch, K. M., 469
Bungeroth, H., 169
Buoncompagno, E. M., 566
Burgess, K. B., 539, 556
Burgess, S., 357
Burgess, S. R., 340, 357
Buriel, R., 69, 73, 82, 93
Burkam, D. T., 387, 388, 503
Burke, J. E., 306
Burke, L., 207
Burnett, P., 502
Burns, C. E., 115, 117
Burns, L., 331
Burstein, K., 268
Burstyn, J. N., 536, 545
Burton, L. M., 35, 72, 73
Burton, S., 448
Busch, C. M., 431
Butler, D. L., 253
Butler, R., 574
Butler, R. N., 407
Butterfield, E. C., 306
Butterfield, P., 258
Butterworth, G., 218
Byers-Heinlein, K., 343
Byne, W., 567
Byrne, B. M., 380, 445
Byrnes, J. P., 153, 209, 328, 360, 369, 371, 374, 378, 380, 381, 384, 385, 387, 388, 389, 390, 492, 499

Cabrera, N., 69
Cacioppo, J. T., 419
Caggiula, A., 435
Cahan, S., 204
Cai, Y., 506
Cain, C. S., 419
Cain, K., 363
Cain, T. R., 336
Cairns, B. D., 538
Cairns, H. S., 316, 325, 327
Cairns, R. B., 538
Caldwell, B. M., 290
Caldwell, C. H., 165
Caldwell, M. S., 446, 533
Calfee, R. C., 221
Calin-Jageman, R. J., 383
Calkins, S. D., 81, 430
Callaghan, T., 472
Callanan, M. A., 93, 161, 263, 323, 383, 386, 484
Callister, M., 582
Calvert, C., 252
Calvert, S. L., 331, 582, 584
Camburn, E., 89, 503, 508, 513, 572, 575, 576, 577
Cameron, C. A., 331, 370, 371
Cameron, J., 494, 503
Cameron, L., 468, 562
Campbell, A., 563, 564
Campbell, B., 278
Campbell, D. T., 42
Campbell, D. W., 171
Campbell, F. A., 37, 297, 579
Campbell, J. D., 451
Campbell, L., 278, 301
Campbell, S. B., 421, 541
Campbell, T., 254
Campbell, T. F., 348
Campione, J. C., 572, 573, 583
Campione-Barr, N., 69

Campos, J., 419, 430
Campos, J. J., 237, 258, 408, 411, 419, 421, 422, 538
Camras, L., 422
Camras, L. A., 336, 408, 424, 434
Cancelli, A. A., 47
Candee, D., 522
Canessa, E., 146
Canfield, R. L., 373
Cannon, J., 203
Cantor, J., 456
Cantu, C. L., 459
Capelli, C. A., 329
Capirci, O., 332
Caplan, J. G., 580
Caplan, M., 538
Caplovitz, A. G., 582
Capodilupo, A., 373
Caprara, G. V., 387, 555
Capron, C., 290
Cardelle-Elawar, M., 378, 380
Cardone, M., 582
Carey, S., 7, 168, 203, 321, 322, 323, 388
Carlin, P. L., 179
Carlo, G., 468, 535, 536, 538, 562
Carlo, M. S., 366
Carlsmith, J. M., 164
Carlson, E., 415
Carlson, E. A., 414
Carlson, N. R., 149, 150, 151, 152, 157, 174
Carlson, S. M., 267
Carns, D., 566
Caroli, M., 582
Caron, A. J., 419
Caron, R. F., 419
Carpenter, M., 258, 321
Carr, M., 254, 303, 361, 378, 380, 383
Carraher, D. W., 204, 218
Carraher, T. N., 218
Carranza, M. E., 472
Carrol, B., 291
Carroll, D. J., 203, 275
Carroll, J. B., 274, 275
Carter, D. E., 469
Carter, K., 432, 505
Carter, K. R., 303, 304
Carter, M. C., 418
Cartledge, G., 437, 541
Carver, P. R., 455, 567
Casas, J. F., 539
Casasola, M., 325
Case, R., 10, 18, 19, 205, 206, 373, 375, 376, 377, 378, 380, 382, 393
Casella, R., 545
Caselli, M. C., 332
Case-Smith, J., 161
Cashon, C. H., 38, 203, 243, 261, 386
Caspi, A., 102, 114, 431
Cassidy, D. J., 247
Cassidy, J., 409, 418
Cassidy, M., 411
Cassidy, S. B., 117
Casten, R., 471–472
Castro, R., 493
Catania, J. A., 179
Cattell, R. B., 275, 276, 281
Catts, H. W., 348
Cauce, A. M., 179
Cauley, K. M., 462
Cavell, T. A., 81, 545
Cazden, C. B., 326, 340
Ceci, S. J., 10, 259, 292, 297, 298
Centers for Disease Control and Prevention, 136, 142, 166, 168, 169, 171, 173, 177, 178, 180, 566

Cermak, L. S., 247
Certo, J., 462, 490
Cerullo, F., 424
Chabon, B., 178
Chafel, J. A., 215, 223, 573
Chafin, C., 462
Chall, J. S., 360, 361, 363
Chambers, J. C., 388
Chambers, J. H., 582
Chambers, M. D., 168
Chambless, C. B., 462
Champagne, A. B., 210
Chan, K. S., 503
Chan, S. Q., 73
Chanana, N., 579
Chance, C., 236
Chandler, M., 252, 468, 523
Chandler, M. J., 468
Chang, B., 450
Chang, C. M., 93
Chang, F., 327
Chang, L., 563
Chapman, C., 503
Chapman, M., 197, 203, 205, 227
Chapman, S., 257
Charity, A. H., 347
Charles A. Dana Center, 579
Charlesworth, W. R., 558
Charlton, K., 579
Charner, I., 581
Charon, R., 135
Chase-Lansdale, P. L., 73, 179
Chassin, L., 178
Chatterji, M., 95, 96
Chatzisarantis, N. L. D., 499
Chavez, A., 147
Chavous, T. M., 459
Chazan-Cohen, R., 20
Cheek, N. H., 534
Chen, C., 96
Chen, S.-J., 411
Chen, X., 340, 541, 563
Chen, Y., 336
Chen, Z., 254
Chess, S., 294, 430, 431
Cheung, A., 344, 345, 366
Chi, M. T. H., 240–241, 241, 384
Chiarello, C., 315
Chidambi, G., 472
Childs, N. M., 471
Chinn, P. C., 364
Chipman, S. F., 380, 496
Chisholm, K., 418
Chiu, C., 94, 493
Chiu, M. M., 82
Choi, I., 205
Choi, S., 323
Chomsky, N., 314, 315, 316, 324, 341
Chouinard, M. M., 263
Chow, B. W.-Y., 357, 364
Christensen, C. A., 368
Christensen, T. M., 70
Christenson, P., 331
Christenson, S. L., 503, 504
Christian, S. H., 342
Christie, J. F., 215, 334, 340
Christopherson, H., 207
Chu, Y.-W., 162
Chuang, S. S., 69
Chukovsky, K., 322
Cicchetti, D., 423, 435
Cider, M., 581
Cillessen, A. H. N., 555, 556
Cimpian, A., 493, 502
Clark, B., 302, 304
Clark, C. C., 563, 564
Clark, D., 163
Clark, D. B., 262, 263
Clark, R. E., 264
Clark, R. M., 89, 425
Clarke-Stewart, K. A., 415
Clary, E. G., 580–581
Clasen, D. R., 562
Clemens, E. V., 555, 583
Clement, C., 204

Clément, F., 331
Clifford, M. M., 462, 492
Clifton, R. K., 371
Clinchy, B. M., 83
Clingempeel, W. G., 71, 77
Clinton, Y. C., 458, 459
Clore, G. L., 565
Close, L., 378
Cobb, P., 489
Coccaro, E. F., 536
Cocchiarella, M. J., 324
Cochran, M., 65
Cochran-Smith, M., 56
Cocking, R. R., 582
Cody, H., 117
Coggins, L. E., 475
Cohen, D., 237, 536
Cohen, D. J., 472
Cohen, E. G., 543
Cohen, J., 356
Cohen, L. B., 38, 203, 243, 261, 386
Cohen, M. N., 100
Cohen, M. R., 161
Cohn, J. F., 421
Coie, J., 535
Coie, J. D., 44, 437, 539, 541, 555, 556, 557
Coker, D., 356
Colak, A., 465
Colby, A., 519, 520
Cole, D. A., 455, 495
Cole, K., 179
Cole, M., 19, 65, 205, 210, 262, 292, 387
Cole, P., 507
Cole, P. M., 413, 423, 424, 507
Coleman, M., 473, 511
Coles, C. D., 131
Coles, R. L., 93, 94, 95
Coles, Robert, 526
Coley, R. L., 179
Coll, C., 77
Coll, C. G., 35
Collaer, M. L., 540
Collie, R., 450
Collier, V. P., 316, 343, 344
Collingwood, T. R., 179
Collins, A., 217, 218, 222
Collins, A. M., 380
Collins, W., 415
Collins, W. A., 88, 289, 292, 565, 566
Colombo, J., 294
Comeau, L., 345
Comer, J. P., 580
Commons, M. L., 203
Comstock, G., 582
Conboy, B. T., 153
Condon, J. C., 338
Condry, J. C., 540
Cone, J., 425
Conel, Jesse LeRoy, 153
Conger, K. J., 77
Conger, R. D., 67, 77, 80, 164
Conley, C. S., 533
Conn, J., 565
Connell, J. P., 446, 486
Connell-Carrick, K., 73
Connelly, L. M., 541
Connolly, J., 565
Connor, J. M., 382
Connor, P. D., 161
Conoley, J. C., 511
Consortium of Longitudinal Studies, 575
Conti-Ramsden, G., 348
Conway, M. B., 70
Cook, E. T., 425
Cook, V., 314, 327
Cook-Cottone, C., 276
Cooney, J. B., 375, 380
Cooper, C. E., 79
Cooper, C. R., 458, 465, 580
Cooper, H., 446, 457, 497, 498, 499, 508, 579, 580

Cooper, R. P., 316
Cooper, S. M., 458, 459
Coopersmith, S., 77
Copland, R., 558
Copple, C., 168, 578
Coppola, M., 318
Coppotelli, H., 555
Corbett, H. D., 55, 252, 490, 508
Corbin, J. M., 45
Corcoran, C. B., 471
Corkill, A. J., 238, 266, 306, 505
Corley, R., 289
Cormier, P., 345
Cornell, D. G., 451
Cornish, K., 472
Corno, L., 508
Corpus, J. H., 486, 499
Corsaro, W. A., 533, 576
Cortes, R. C., 425
Corwyn, R. F., 77
Cosden, M., 268, 504
Cossu, G., 361
Costa, L. D., 151
Costa, P. T., Jr., 431
Costanzo, P. R., 561
Cota-Robles, S., 164
Côté, J. E., 406
Cote, L. R., 321
Cotner, Keli, 20n
Cotnoir-Bichelman, N. M., 334
Cotterell, J. L., 415
Couchman, C. E., 416
Council for Exceptional Children, 303
Courage, M. L., 139, 237, 485
Covington, M. V., 305, 445, 446, 489, 493
Cowan, W. M., 152, 157
Cox, C. B., 73
Cox, M., 70
Cox, M. E., 73
Cox, R., 70
Coy, K. C., 505
Coyle, T. R., 247
Crago, M. B., 274, 315, 338
Craig, L., 69
Craig, R., 445
Craik, F. I. M., 247
Crain, W., 404, 406
Crandall, V. C., 500
Crang-Svalenius, M., 129n
Craven, J., 207
Craven, R., 449, 450, 462
Crawford, D., 544
Crawley, A. M., 254
Creasey, G., 554
Creswell, J. W., 45
Crews, F., 164
Crick, N. R., 535, 538, 539, 540, 555
Criss, M. M., 16, 67
Critten, S., 369
Crocker, J., 407, 445
Crohn, H. M., 72
Croll, W. L., 424
Cromer, R. F., 316
Cromley, J. G., 359, 360
Crosby, L., 530
Crosnoe, R., 16, 36, 67, 79
Cross, D., 261
Cross, W. E., Jr., 457, 458
Crouter, A. C., 80, 82, 93, 423
Crowell, J., 416
Crowley, K., 93, 193, 216
Crumbaugh, C., 383
Crystal, D. S., 93
Csikszentmihalyi, M., 534
Cullen, K. W., 18
Culross, P. L., 91
Cumberland, A., 422
Cummings, A., 503
Cummings, E. M., 578
Cummings, J., 345
Cummings, S. S., 172

Cunningham, A. E., 356, 450, 464, 493, 499
Cunningham, C. E., 268
Cunningham, L. J., 268
Cunningham, T. H., 343, 344
Curtiss, S., 316
Curwin, A., 323
Cyr, F., 69, 70, 71

D'Agostino, J. V., 383
Dahinten, V. S., 287
Dahl, R. E., 175
Dahl, Roald, 265
Dahlberg, G., 27
Dahlin, B., 253, 254
d'Ailly, H., 496
Dale, P. S., 266, 348
D'Alessandro, J. D., 455
Daley, S. G., 207
Daley, T. C., 292
Damazio, A., 158
Damon, W., 210, 226, 423, 446, 450, 462, 522, 523, 524, 525, 543, 562
Danaher, D. L., 541
DanceSafe, 177
Dancho, K. A., 334
Daniels, A. M., 178
Daniels, M., 290
Daniels, S., 254
Dannemiller, J. L., 237
Danner, F. W., 203
Danthiir, V., 275
Darling, N., 77
Darling-Hammond, L., 28, 221, 576
Darlington, R., 579
Darwin, Charles, 18
Daubman, K. A., 425
Davenport, E. C., Jr., 95, 380
Davidov, M., 64, 78
Davidson, A. L., 339, 491
Davidson, D. H., 507
Davidson, F. H., 469, 522
Davidson, M. R., 125, 126, 128, 132, 133, 134, 135, 136
Davidson, P., 561
Davidson, R. J., 507
Davies, C., 390, 391
Devine, P. G., 475
Davila, J., 424, 565
Davis, B., 426
Davis, D. L., 236–237
Davis, G. A., 294, 305, 572
Davis, H. A., 415, 417, 432, 462, 505
Davis, J., 389
Davis, J. H., 394
Davis, K., 435
Davis-Kean, P., 486
Davis-Kean, P. E., 447
Dawson, B. S., 178
Day, M. C., 203
Day, W. H., 485
Deal, L. W., 184
Dean, D., Jr., 204, 388
Deary, I. J., 137, 275
Deater-Deckard, K., 77, 120–121
Deaux, K., 474, 496, 540
DeBaryshe, B. D., 437
DeBell, M., 503
De Bock, D., 203
DeBoer, T., 240
DeBose, C. E., 347
DeCapua, A., 92
De Casper, A., 237, 240, 316
De Cecco, J. P., 567
Decety, J., 535
Deci, E. L., 219, 407, 416, 462, 464, 484, 485, 486, 487, 497, 502, 505
Deck, A., 75
De Corte, E., 222, 374, 378, 380
Dedmon, S. E., 81
DeFalco, K., 511
DeFries, J. C., 289
de Glopper, K., 324

de Graaf, H., 565
de Guzman, M. R. T., 536
de Haan, M., 151, 237
Dehaene, S., 379–380
dc Jong, P. F., 364
de Jong, T., 208
de Koning, E., 490
Delamater, J., 165, 566
DeLaney, K. R., 427
De La Paz, S., 373
DelBoca, F., 471
Delfabbro, P. H., 74
Delfino, R. J., 267
Delgado-Gaitan, C., 94, 329, 336
Delis, D., 38
De Lisi, R., 583
DeLisi, R., 210, 454
DeLisle, J. R., 305
DeLoach, J. S., 242
DeLoache, J. S., 242, 247, 318
Delucchi, K., 426
Delucchi, K. L., 46
Delugach, J. D., 557
Demarest, R. J., 135
DeMarie-Dreblow, D., 238
deMarrais, K. B., 372
Dembo, M. H., 539
Dement, W. C., 174
Dempster, F. N., 238, 266, 306, 505
de Muinck Keizer-Schrama, S. M. P. F., 164
Denckla, M. B., 266
Denier, C., 382
DeNisi, A., 500
Denner, J., 580
Denton, N. A., 101
de Rooij, S., 147
Derry, S. J., 222
Deruelle, C., 473
Deshler, D. D., 266, 499
Desjardins, R. N., 320
Detine-Carter, S. L., 469
Deutsch, D., 394
Deutsch, M., 544
Deutsch, N. L., 580
DeVault, G., 120
de Villiers, J., 325, 326
Devine, P. G., 475
Devlin, B., 290
DeVoe, J. F., 536, 546
DeVries, R., 525, 533, 558
DeWinstanley, P., 583
Dexter, A., 299
Deyhle, D., 496
Diamond, L. M., 566, 567
Diamond, M., 152, 153, 157
Diamond, S. C., 437
Díaz, R. M., 345
Diaz, R. M., 340, 342, 343, 558
Diaz, T., 178
Dibbens, L. M., 115
Dichele, A., 101
Dick, D. M., 164
Dickens, W. T., 298
Dickinson, D., 278, 358, 371
Dick-Read, G., 133
Dien, T., 371, 372, 503
Dietrich, K. N., 290
Digman, J. M., 431
Dillon, D. R., 306
Dillon, P., 70
Dilorio, C., 133
Dilworth-Bart, J. E., 290
D'Incau, B., 545
Diorio, J., 119
DiPietro, J. A., 128
diSessa, A. A., 197, 208, 262
Dishion, T. J., 530
Dix, T., 485
Dixon, C. N., 365
Dixon, J. A., 261
Dixon, M. R., 503
Dobson, V., 139
Dodd, B., 368
Dodge, K., 77

Dodge, K. A., 16, 44, 67, 436, 530, 535, 538, 539, 540, 555, 556, 557
Doescher, S. M., 528
Dogan, S. J., 67, 80
Doherty, M., 203
Dohnt, H. K., 162, 456
Dole, J. A., 390
Dolev, S., 417, 472
Dolson, M., 394
Domitrovich, C., 426
Domitrovich, C. E., 425
Donahue, E. H., 581
Donaldson, D., 438
Donaldson, M., 203, 243, 329
Donaldson, S. K., 422, 468
Donato, F., 580
Donnelly, T. M., 529
Donnerstein, E., 582
D'Onofrio, B., 292
Donovan, C. A., 369
Donovan, L. A., 266
Doorenbal, J., 525
Dornbusch, S., 77
Dornbusch, S. M., 77, 164, 565
Dorr, N., 457, 499
Dorris, M., 142
Doucette, J., 331
Douglas, G., 252
Dovidio, J. F., 475
Dow, G. A., 241
Downey, J., 103
Downs, R. M., 391
Downs, W. R., 78
Dowson, M., 490, 501
Doyle, A., 343, 541, 558
Doyle, P. A., 131
Doyle, W., 432, 489, 505
Dreweke, J., 180
Dreyer, L. G., 365
Dromsky, A., 390
Drummey, A. B., 240
Dryden, M. A., 363
Dryfoos, J. G., 546, 579, 580
D'Souza, H. J., 566
Dube, E. F., 254
Dubé, E. M., 566
Dube, M., 69
DuBois, D. L., 446, 498
Dubow, E. F., 303
DuCette, J., 495
Duckworth, A. L., 257, 300, 495
Dudley, B., 544–545
Duffy, S., 65
Dufresne, A., 252
Duke, P. M., 164
Dulmen,, 565
Dunbar, N., 458
Dunbar, Paul Laurence, 367
Duncan, C., 451
Duncan, G. J., 288, 294
Duncan, P. D., 164
Dunham, F., 323
Dunham, P. J., 323
Dunn, A. M., 117
Dunn, J., 82, 409, 421, 424, 467, 521, 524
Dunn, M. P., 566
Dunsmore, J. C., 539
Duong, M. T., 554
DuPaul, G., 511
DuPaul, G. J., 541
Durand, V. M., 175
Durik, A. M., 486
Durkin, K., 178, 348, 499, 527
Durkin, M. S., 290
Dutta, A., 173
Duyme, M., 290
Dwairy, M., 77
Dweck, C., 253
Dweck, C. S., 424, 447, 448, 450, 455, 462, 464, 465, 469, 486, 487, 489, 489n, 492, 493, 494, 495, 499, 502
Dwyer, K., 545, 545n, 546, 547
Dyck, M. J., 473
Dyer, S. M., 330

Dykens, E. M., 117
Dykes, A. K., 129n

Eacott, M. J., 216, 240
Eagly, A. H., 540
Eamon, M. K., 66
Eanes, A. Y., 67
Early, D. M., 28
Easterbrooks, M. A., 411
Easton, D., 558
Eastwood, J. D., 258
Eaton, W. O., 171
Ebbesen, E., 505
Eccles, J. S., 38, 47, 79, 93, 297, 363, 381, 415, 424, 445, 451, 455, 462, 486, 489, 492, 493, 495, 497, 499, 502, 576, 577, 580
Eccles [Parsons], J. S., 486
Echols, L. D., 295
Eckerman, C. O., 530
Eckert, T. L., 541
Eckman, P., 541
Edelen, M. O., 164
Edens, K. M., 394
Edmunds, A. L., 303
Edmunds, G. A., 303
Edwards, C. P., 103, 541
Edwards, L., 112
Edwards, P. A., 296, 365
Edwards-Evans, S., 347
Eeds, M., 36
Eftekhari-Sanjani, H., 296
Egan, L. C., 263, 484
Egan, S. K., 455
Egeland, B., 363, 415
Eggebeen, D., 578
Eggers-Péirola, C., 89
Eggert, K. M., 165
Ehle, D. A., 305
Ehri, L. C., 358, 359, 363, 365, 366
Ehrler, D. J., 433
Eicher, S. A., 501
Eigsti, I.-M., 483, 507
Eilam, B., 509
Eilers, R. E., 341
Eisenband, J., 203
Eisenberg, N., 77, 158, 387, 419, 422, 423, 424, 462, 468, 507, 522, 523, 535, 536, 537, 538, 540, 540–541, 582
Eisengart, J., 325
Ekelin, M., 129n
Elbro, C., 365, 366
Elder, A. D., 385
Elder, G. H., Jr., 16, 67, 164
Elder, J. L., 215
El-Dinary, P. B., 256
Elia, J. P., 568
Elias, G., 341
Elison, J., 423
Elkind, D., 18, 157, 263, 291, 451, 559, 565
Ellickson, P. L., 164
Elliot, A. J., 489
Elliott, D. J., 218, 393, 394
Elliott, E. S., 486, 487, 489, 489n, 502
Elliott, J., 496
Elliott, R., 535
Ellis, B. J., 27, 164
Ellis, J. A., 219
Elmen, J., 77
Elze, D. E., 568, 569
Emde, R., 419
Emde, R. N., 258, 450, 535
Emery, R., 71
Emery, R. E., 70, 435, 436, 437
Emmer, E. T., 45, 432, 499
Empson, S. B., 203, 374, 380
Engels, Friedrich, 210
Engle, R., 69, 73
English, D. J., 83
Enkin, M., 135
Ennemoser, M., 366
Enns, V., 416

Entwisle, D., 296
Enyedy, N., 391
Eppright, T. D., 580
Epstein, J. A., 178
Epstein, J. L., 86, 89, 556, 559, 563
Epstein, L. H., 169
Epstein, M. H., 437
Epstein, S., 449
Epstein, T., 390
Erickson, F., 338
Erickson, L. G., 361
Ericsson, K. A., 7
Erikson, E. H., 18, 113, 404, 406, 407, 452, 522n
Erlbaum, Lawrence, 377
Eron, L. D., 44, 582
Erwin, P., 533, 555
Esbensen, B. M., 250
Esbensen, F. A., 564
Esmonde, I., 382
Espelage, D. L., 539
Espinosa, L., 345, 425
Espinosa, M. P., 292
Esterly, J. B., 262
Estes, D., 252, 467
Estes, K. G., 323
Etaugh, A., 454
Etaugh, C., 454
Etzion-Carasso, A., 417
Evans, E. M., 262, 386, 387, 454
Evans, G. W., 101, 102
Evans, I. M., 185
Evans, J. G., 433
Evans, J. L., 323
Evans, M. A., 363
Evans, R., 388
Evans, W. H., 503
Everson, C. M., 432
Eyer, D. W., 23
Eylon, B., 253
Eysenck, H. J., 535

Fabes, R., 422
Fabes, R. A., 387, 422, 504, 522, 523, 535, 536, 537, 538, 540
Fabos, B., 583
Fad, K., 307
Fadiman, A., 136
Fagan, J. F., 287, 297
Fahrmeier, E. D., 205
Fairchild, H. H., 347
Faison, N., 523
Fake, S., 120
Falbo, T., 82
Fang, F., 472
Fang, G., 381
Fanning, J. L., 369
Fantie, B., 155
Fantini, A. E., 313, 314, 317, 321, 328, 332, 335, 335n, 336, 339, 341, 342
Fantino, A. M., 465
Farber, B., 338
Farivar, S., 543
Farley, F., 155, 157, 159, 168
Farmer, T. W., 539
Farran, D. C., 291
Farrar, M. J., 241
Farrell, M. M., 285
Farrier, F., 368
Farrington-Flint, L., 359
Farver, J. A. M., 523, 536
Fausel, D. F., 70
Feather, N. T., 486
Federal Interagency Forum on Child and Family Statistics, 68, 72, 92, 92n, 96, 101, 168, 179, 344
Federico, A., 327
Feeny, N. C., 521, 522, 523
Fegley, S., 523, 524
Fehr, B., 416
Fein, G., 215
Fein, G. G., 426
Feinberg, M. E., 69
Feinman, S., 258

Feiring, C., 416
Feldhusen, J. F., 305, 306
Feldlaufer, H., 297
Feldman, L. H., 84
Feldman, R., 80
Feldman, S. S., 177, 506, 563
Felton, M., 257
Felton, R. H., 363, 365
Fennell, C. T., 343
Fennema, E., 495
Fenson, L., 247, 321, 341
Fenwick, K. D., 236
Ferguson, L. L., 538
Fernald, A., 316, 328
Ferrari, M., 304
Ferrell, J., 468, 562
Ferrer, E., 239
Ferretti, R. P., 306
Feuerstein, R., 216, 286, 307, 286
Feuerstein, Ra., 286
Fewell, R. R., 499
Fhagen-Smith, P., 457
Fiedler, E. D., 306
Fiedler, K., 226
Field, D., 204
Field, S. L., 360
Field, T., 137, 237
Fielding, L., 366
Fields, J., 82
Fienberg, S. E., 290
Fier, J., 455
Fierros, E., 278
Fiez, J. A., 345
Fifer, W., 137
Fifer, W. P., 237, 316, 341
Fifield, A., 303
Filax, G., 568, 569
Filisetti, L., 524
Finch, H., 284
Fincham, F. D., 494
Finders, M., 89, 90
Fink, B., 368
Fink, G. R., 152
Finkelhor, D., 584
Finn, S., 471
Finn-Stevenson, M., 298, 572, 580
Fiorella, C. A., 276
Fischer, G., 280
Fischer, K., 19, 195, 445
Fischer, K. W., 10, 16, 155, 205, 206, 207, 253, 305, 496, 497
Fishbein, D. H., 437
Fisher, C., 325
Fisher, C. B., 92, 94, 95, 415
Fisher, C. W., 222
Fisher, D., 54, 55
Fisher, J. D., 179
Fisher, W. A., 179
Fitzgerald, J., 370
Fitzsimmons, C. M., 323
Fives, C. J., 285
Fivush, R., 240, 247, 248, 259, 260, 450
Flanagan, C., 558
Flanagan, C. A., 468, 523
Flanagan, D. P., 274
Flanagan, R., 285
Flannery, D., 77
Flannery, D. J., 451
Flavell, E. R., 249, 250, 468
Flavell, J. H., 8, 10, 18, 19, 203, 205, 215, 236, 241, 249, 250, 251, 261, 329, 386, 466, 467, 468
Flay, B. R., 46, 48
Flege, J. E., 316
Fleming, C. H., 169
Fleming, J. S., 482, 541
Fletcher, A. C., 67, 560
Fletcher, J. M., 266, 370, 371
Fletcher, K. L., 307
Flickinger, S. M., 471–472
Flieller, A., 203, 204, 292
Flowerday, T., 497
Flowers, J., 383
Floyd, R. G., 276
Flugman, B., 365

Flum, H., 484
Flynn, J. R., 95, 292, 293, 297, 298
Foehr, U. G., 581, 582, 583
Fogel, A., 408
Foorman, B. R., 328
Forbes, D., 541
Forbes, M. L., 241, 391
Ford, D. Y., 306, 445
Ford, L., 281, 287, 495
Ford, M. E., 316, 332, 487, 490, 501, 563
Forehand, R., 70
Forgatch, M. S., 78
Forgey, M. A., 179
Forster, G., 101
Forthun, L. F., 454, 555
Fortuin, J., 555
Fowler, J. W., 502
Fowler, S. A., 503
Fox, K., 365
Fox, N. A., 7, 240, 428, 430
Fraleigh, M. J., 77
Francis, D. J., 357
Francis, G., 436
Francis, M., 370
Frank, A., 162
Frank, C., 52, 52n
Frankel, C. B., 422
Franklin, J. H., 93
Franklin, S., 205, 243, 253, 384, 385, 386
Fraser, B. J., 576
Fraser, B. S., 581
Frederiksen, J. R., 207, 208, 386
Frederiksen, N., 208
Fredricks, J. A., 504
Fredrickson, B. L., 424
Fredu, A., 18
Freeark, K., 73
Freedenthal, S., 438
Freedman, B. J., 363
Freedman, K., 99
Freedman-Doan, C., 38
Freeman, B., 500
Freeman, K. E., 496
Freitag, C. M., 142
French, D. C., 540
French, L., 330
French, S. E., 457, 577
Frenkel, O. J., 414
Frenkiel-Fishman, S., 466
Frensch, P. A., 264
Freppon, P. A., 366
Freud, S., 13, 18, 518
Freund, L., 259
Freundlich, M., 73
Frey, N., 54, 55
Frick, P. J., 267
Friebert, S. E., 251
Friedel, J., 574
Friedlaender, D., 576
Friedman, C. K., 296, 386, 387, 454, 455, 496, 499
Friedman, L., 387
Friedman, R. J., 507
Friedrichs, A. G., 250
Friend, R. A., 568
Friesen, C. K., 258
Frieze, I. H., 492
Frith, U., 361, 363
Fritz, J., 421
Frodi, A. M., 69
Frome, P., 38
Frone, M. R., 179
Frosch, C. A., 69
Frost, J. L., 172, 223
Fry, A. F., 239, 275, 483
Frye, D., 239
Fuchs, D., 219
Fuchs, L. S., 219, 266, 370, 378
Fujiki, M., 332
Fujimura, N., 382
Fukkink, R. G., 324
Fukumoto, A., 521
Fuligni, A. J., 36, 95, 458
Fulker, D., 120–121
Fulker, D. W., 289

Fulkner, D. W., 535
Fuller, B., 89, 291
Fuller, D., 527
Fuller, F., 370
Fuller, M. L., 527
Fulmore, C. D., 471–472
Fulton, J. E., 171
Funk, J. B., 582
Furlong, M. J., 545
Furman, W., 534, 563, 565
Furstenberg, F. F., 566
Furstenberg, F. F., Jr., 72
Fuson, K. C., 373, 375, 380,
    381, 382
Futrell, M. H., 576
Futterman, D., 178

Gabard, D. L., 567
Gable, R. A., 437
Gabriele, A. J., 489
Gaensbauer, T., 419
Gaertner, S. L., 475
Gagnon, I., 69
Gaines, D., 101
Galaburda, A. M., 361
Galambos, N. L., 80, 454
Galinsky, E., 578
Gallagher, A., 361
Gallagher, A. M., 296, 380, 454
Gallagher, J. J., 304
Gallahue, D. L., 147, 148, 168,
    173, 174, 539
Gallimore, R., 82, 217, 222, 363,
    364, 365, 496
Gallistel, C. R., 7, 38, 373
Galotti, K. M., 243
Galperin, C., 215
Gambrell, L. B., 361
Gamm, B. K., 559
Ganea, P. A., 318
Ganschow, L., 305
Garbarino, J., 71, 536, 546
Garcia, Delia, 439
García, E. E., 92, 93, 95, 98, 101,
    336, 343, 345, 475
Garcia, G. E., 296, 365
García Coll, C., 27, 95
Garcia-Mila, M., 251
Gardiner, H. W., 148
Gardner, H., 275, 277, 277n,
    278, 299, 301, 303, 305, 308,
    391, 392, 394
Gariépy, J.-L., 538
Gariglietti, G., 252
Garland, A., 438
Garmezy, N., 423
Garner, P. W., 539
Garner, R., 360, 372
Garnier, H., 363
Garrison, L., 98, 351
Gartrell, N., 75
Garver, K. E., 239
Garvey, C., 336, 532
Gaskins, I. W., 359, 360, 361
Gaskins, S., 157, 217
Gatzke-Kopp, L. M., 267
Gauvain, M., 15, 19, 79, 215,
    217, 217n, 218, 227, 258, 259,
    260, 260n, 264
Gavin, L. A., 534, 563
Gay, G., 336
Ge, X., 120, 164
Geary, D. C., 261, 373, 374, 375,
    378, 379, 380, 383
Gee, C. B., 423
Gee, Michael, 510
Geenen, S., 74
Gelfand, D., 418
Gelman, R., 7, 38, 203, 243, 332,
    373, 383, 386
Gelman, S. A., 18, 19, 261, 262,
    321, 323, 327, 383, 386, 387
Gendreau, P. L., 538
Genesee, F., 344
Gentile, D. A., 583
Gentile, J. R., 583
Gentry, R., 369, 371

George, L., 138
George, T. P., 41
Georgi, M. C., 257
Georgiou, G. K., 356
Gerbhardt, W. A., 566
Gerbracht, G., 4
Geren, J., 315
Gerken, L., 328
Germinario, V., 102
Gernsbacher, M. A., 473
Gershoff, E. T., 102, 485
Gertner, Y., 325
Gervai, J., 506
Gerwels, M. C., 499
Gesell, A., 8, 12, 18
Gettinger, M., 574
Gettman, D. C., 69
Geva, D., 541
Gewirtz, J. L., 10
Ghazvini, A., 578
Gheen, M. H., 445
Ghezzi, P. M., 503
Ghodsian-Carpey, J., 535
Gholson, B., 324
Giannouli, V., 357
Gibb, R., 156
Gibbs, J., 519
Gibbs, J. C., 527
Gibson, E. J., 237
Gibson, J. J., 237
Gibson, W. A., 331
Giedd, J. N., 154, 155
Gilbert, K. K., 165
Gilbert, M. F., 342
Gildea, P. M., 321
Gill, H. S., 296
Gillam, R. B., 369
Gillberg, I. C., 473
Gillespie, N. M., 262
Gillham, J. E., 437
Gilliam, W. S., 579
Gilligan, C., 407, 520, 526, 527
Gilligan, C. F., 526, 527
Gilliland, H., 98, 337, 338
Gilman, R., 580
Gilstrap, B., 69
Gindis, B., 286
Ginsberg, S., 451
Ginsburg, D., 554, 555, 557
Ginsburg, G. P., 334
Ginsburg, H. P., 203, 207, 373,
    374, 378, 380, 382
Giordano, P. C., 565
Girotto, V., 204
Glaser, C., 371, 373
Glauberman, N., 297
Glick, J., 10
Glucksberg, S., 332
Glusman, M., 316, 323
Glynn, S. M., 262, 389
Gnepp, J., 468
Gogate, L. J., 238
Golbeck, S. L., 210
Gold, J., 521
Goldberg, A., 565
Goldberg, E., 151
Goldberg, M. E., 331
Goldberg, S., 414
Goldberger, N. R., 83
Goldenberg, C., 363, 364, 365,
    496, 574
Goldfield, B. A., 346
Golding, J. M., 360
Goldin-Meadow, S., 243, 244,
    320–321, 349
Goldman, S. R., 390
Goldsmith, H. H., 346, 473, 507
Goldstein, A. P., 13
Goldstein, H., 314, 316
Goldstein, N. E., 535
Goldstein, S., 267, 504
Goleman, D., 419
Golinkoff, R. M., 316, 317, 322,
    323, 325
Gollan, J. K., 536
Gollnick, D. M., 364
Golomb, C., 391, 392, 393

Golombok, S., 74
Gomby, D. S., 91, 184
Gomez, J., 576
Gomez, M. L., 98, 329, 336, 338
Göncü, A., 157, 215, 226, 532
Gonzales, A.-L., 77
Gonzalez, J. E., 437
Gonzalez-Mena, J., 425
Good, C., 489
Good, S., 500
Good, T. L., 210, 222, 257, 260,
    490–491, 574
Goodman, G. S., 238, 241
Goodman, J., 268
Goodman, K. S., 365
Goodman, Y. M., 365
Goodnow, J. J., 88, 96
Goodwin, M. H., 333
Goodwyn, S. W., 332,
    334, 341
Goossens, L., 453
Gopnik, A., 467
Gopnik, M., 315
Gordic, B., 578
Gordis, E. B., 535
Gordon, C., 360
Gordon, M., 101
Gordon, P., 381, 393
Gordon, W., 204
Gorgoglione, J. M., 425
Gorman, A. H., 554
Goswami, U., 348, 357, 363, 364
Gottesman, I. I., 292
Gottesman, R. L., 424
Gottfredson, D. C., 564
Gottfredson, G. D., 564
Gottfredson, L., 279
Gottfried, A. E., 302, 482, 541
Gottfried, A. W., 302, 303,
    304, 482, 541
Gottlieb, G., 12, 19, 112, 118,
    289, 293
Gottman, J. M., 78, 530, 531,
    532, 534, 539, 554, 556, 557,
    558, 559, 562, 564, 565
Goubet, N., 371
Goudena, P., 560
Gould, S. J., 27
Graber, J. A., 566
Grace, C. O., 501
Graesser, A., 360
Graesser, A. C., 360
Graham, C. R., 343, 344
Graham, J. A., 148
Graham, S., 249, 367, 368, 369,
    370, 371, 372, 373, 457, 493,
    494, 497, 499, 500, 502, 536,
    538, 544, 574
Granade, J. B., 497
Grandin, T., 393, 473
Grandin, Temple, 473
Grandmaison, É., 345
Granfield, J. M., 541
Granger, R. C., 579, 580
Granrud, C. E., 38
Grant, C. A., 97, 98, 99, 329,
    336, 338
Grant, H., 253
Graue, M. E., 54
Green, B. L., 27, 239, 250,
    450, 451
Green, C., 366
Green, C. W., 159
Green, F. L., 249, 250, 468
Green, L., 483, 499
Green, T. M., 165
Greenberg, M. T., 412, 425,
    426, 546
Greenberg, R., 237
Greene, B., 435, 436
Greene, Evie, 248
Greene, J. P., 101
Greenfield, P. M., 19, 274, 297,
    541, 582, 583
Greeno, J. G., 280, 380, 382
Greenough, W. T., 153, 156, 237
Greenspan, D. A., 303

Greenspan, S., 473, 541
Greenspan, S. I., 294
Greer, B., 222
Gregg, M., 222, 391
Greif, M. L., 261
Greteman, C., 474
Grether, J., 367
Greunsven, G., 566
Griepentrog, G. J., 394
Griesinger, T., 445
Griffin, D. M., 347
Griffin, S., 373, 376, 380, 382
Griffin, S. A., 375
Griffiths, J. A., 562
Grigorenko, E. L., 275, 279
Gringlas, M. B., 71
Grinnell, K., 454
Griswold, K. S., 435
Grolnick, W. S., 486
Gromko, J. E., 303, 393, 394
Gronkiewicz, L., 164
Gronlund, N. E., 54
Gross, A., 365
Gross, D., 78
Gross, J. N., 521
Gross, R. H., 174
Gross, R. T., 164
Gross, S., 286
Grossman, H. L., 527
Grossmann, K., 413
Grossmann, K. E., 413, 415
Grotpeter, J. K., 540
Grotzer, T. A., 301
Grouzet, F. M. E., 486
Grubb, H. J., 436
Gruber, R., 175
Grusec, J. E., 64, 77, 78, 483, 543
Guacci-Franco, N., 533
Guay, F., 447, 554, 555, 556, 561
Guberman, S. R., 215, 218, 219
Guerin, D. W., 302
Guiton, G., 574
Gulotta, T. P., 177
Gummerum, M., 522
Gunnell, K., 178
Gur, T., 358, 363
Gustafsson, J., 285
Guthrie, B. J., 165
Guthrie, J. T., 366
Gutierrez, F., 261
Gutiérrez, K. D., 336
Gutman, L. M., 47, 496

Hackenberg, T. D., 483
Hacker, D. J., 252, 360, 390, 533
Haden, C., 248, 259
Haden, C. A., 259
Hadley, P. A., 348
Haenan, J., 215
Haenen, J., 252
Haerens, L., 169
Haerle, F. C., 252
Hagan, H., 177
Hagen, E., 282
Hagen, J. W., 238, 239
Hagen, R., 356
Hagerman, R. J., 110
Hagger, M. S., 499
Haidt, J., 527
Haight, B. K., 407
Haight, W. L., 215
Hains, A. A., 511
Hains, A. H., 511
Haith, M. M., 237, 238
Haj-Yahia, M. M., 469
Hakuta, K., 342, 343
Hale, S., 239, 275
Hale-Benson, J. E., 78, 330, 333,
    335, 338, 341, 496
Haley, A., 292
Halford, G. S., 204, 205, 226,
    240, 469
Halgunseth, L. C., 364
Hall, J. W., 373, 380
Hallenbeck, M. J., 370
Hallmayer, J., 473

Halpern, D. F., 293, 295, 296,
    331, 346, 371, 372, 380, 386,
    387, 495, 499
Hamedani, M. G., 15, 65, 219,
    413, 456
Hamers, J. H. M., 286
Hamill, P. V., 146
Hammer, D., 207
Hammond, M., 437
Hamre, B., 84
Hamre, B. K., 397, 501, 504, 576
Han, J. H., 381
Han, J. J., 260
Han, M., 94
Haney, Walt, 587, 588
Hanges, P. J., 95
Hanich, L. B., 379
Hanley, D., 527
Hanley, J. R., 364
Hanlon, C., 314
Hannon, E. E., 394
Hansen, J., 360
Hanson, A. R., 498
Harach, L., 69
Harackiewicz, J. M., 489
Harding, R., 147
Hardy, I., 208
Hare, J., 75
Hareli, S., 493
Harlow, H. F., 483
Harmon, R., 419
Harpalani, V., 95
Harrington, D., 290
Harris, C. R., 305
Harris, J. R., 334, 532, 534, 555,
    562, 563
Harris, K. R., 249, 360, 368,
    370, 373
Harris, L., 80
Harris, M., 316, 321, 349, 357,
    363, 364, 371
Harris, M. B., 568
Harris, M. J., 447
Harris, N. G. S., 318
Harris, P. L., 254, 331, 421, 466,
    467, 468, 469, 472, 530, 536
Harris, Y. R., 148
Harrison, A. O., 73, 456
Harrison, C., 304
Harrison, K., 456
Harste, J. C., 358
Hart, B., 323, 346
Hart, D., 447, 448, 450, 451, 452,
    523, 524, 529
Hart, E. L., 267
Hart, H., 538
Harter, S., 162, 407, 422, 423,
    445, 446, 447, 448, 449, 450,
    451, 452, 453, 454, 455, 456,
    458, 464, 468, 487, 490, 499,
    501, 522, 522n, 555, 576
Hartmann, D. P., 41
Hartup, W. W., 532, 533, 534,
    558, 562
Harvey, O. J., 562
Harwood, R. L., 430
Hasselhorn, M., 247
Hastings, P. D., 65, 71, 72, 74
Hatano, G., 210, 262, 363, 364,
    371, 386, 387
Hatch, T., 277, 391
Hatfield, E., 419
Hattie, J., 252, 254, 256
Hau, K.-T., 447, 451
Hauser, R. M., 298
Hauser-Cram, P., 137
Haviland, J. M., 419, 424
Hawkins, F. P. L., 196, 358
Hawley, C. A., 507
Haworth, C. M. A., 266
Hay, D., 473
Hay, D. F., 538
Hayenga, A. O., 499
Hayes, C. D., 164
Hayes, D. P., 367
Hayes, R. A., 7
Hayne, H., 240, 254, 450

Haynes, O. M., 215
Hayslip, B., Jr., 287
Haywood, H. C., 221, 226, 286
Hazen, C., 238
He, J., 164
He, Y., 563
Heafner, T., 509
Healey, J., 538
Healy, C. C., 383
Heath, G., 171
Heath, S. B., 98, 297, 320, 333, 338, 367
Hébert, T. P., 309, 310
Hecht, S. A., 378
Heckenhausen, H., 506
Hedges, L. V., 296, 363, 371, 380
Heflin, A. H., 530, 555
Hegarty, M., 296, 380
Heibeck, T. H., 323
Heimburge, J. A., 366
Heine, S. J., 496
Hellenga, K., 583
Hellings, P. J., 115
Helwig, C. C., 521, 523, 528
Hembree, R., 437
Hemmings, A. B., 490
Hemphill, L., 335, 369, 371
Henderson, B., 206, 376
Henderson, C. R., Jr., 78
Henderson, H. A., 430
Henderson, N. D., 430
Henkel, R. R., 539
Henker, B., 267
Hennessey, B. A., 497
Hennessey, M. G., 210, 257
Hennon, E. A., 316
Henrichon, A. J., 468
Henthorn, T., 394
Herbert, J., 455
Herbst, K. C., 471
Herlihy, B., 70
Herman, P. A., 321
Heron, S. E., 115
Herr, K., 568
Herrell, A., 345
Herrenkohl, L. R., 219, 256
Herriman, M. L., 340
Herrnstein, Richard, 297
Herrup, K., 149
Hersen, M., 436
Hersh, C. A., 495
Hersh, R. H., 520
Hertzog, S. M., 582–583
Hess, R. D., 79, 93, 496
Hessels, A., 203
Hetherington, E. M., 69, 70, 71, 72, 77, 289
Hetherington, M. M., 169
Hettinger, H. R., 305
Hewer, A., 9
Hewitt, J., 583
Hewitt, K. L., 237
Hewstone, M., 558
Heyne, D. A., 423
Hiatt, S., 419
Hickey, D. T., 208, 497
Hickey, T. L., 237
Hickling, A. K., 250, 254
Hicks, L., 490
Hicks, R., 178
Hickson, F., 469, 471
Hidalgo, N. M., 86
Hidi, S., 482, 485, 489, 497
Hiebert, E. H., 222, 365, 366
Hiebert, J., 216, 383
Higgins, A., 504, 525, 528
Higgins, A. T., 238
Highnam, C., 474
Hilden, K., 247
Hill, J. P., 165
Hill, P. R., 348
Hilliard, A., 339
Hillier, L., 236, 237
Hilt, L. M., 502
Hinckley, H. S., 365
Hinde, R. A., 558

Hine, P., 576
Hines, M., 540
Hinkley, J. W., 490
Hirsch, B. J., 580
Hirsch, J., 343
Hirsh-Pasek, K., 223, 316, 317, 323, 325, 425
Hiruma, N., 507
Ho, C. S., 364, 380, 381
Ho, D. Y. F., 254, 507
Ho, H.-Z., 365
Hobson, P., 258, 260, 317, 349, 472
Hobson, P. R., 472
Hodge, C., 164
Hodges, E. V. E., 43, 447
Hoekstra, R. A., 293
Hoerger, M. L., 495
Hoerr, T. R., 280
Hofer, B. K., 252, 253
Hofer, M. A., 415
Hoff, E., 323, 346
Hoff, K., 511
Hoff-Ginsburg, E., 343
Hoffman, L. W., 559
Hoffman, M. L., 78, 423, 510, 522, 523, 525, 528, 535, 536
Hoffman, N. D., 178
Hogan, A. G., 159
Hogan, T. P., 348
Hogben, J. H., 348
Hogdon, L. A., 473
Hoke-Sinex, L., 506
Hokoda, A., 494
Holland, C. R., 287
Holliday, B. G., 96, 497
Holliday, G., 305
Hollins, E. R., 457
Holloway, S., 572
Holloway, S. D., 79, 89, 559
Holm, A., 368
Holmbeck, G. N., 165
Holmes, C. J., 155
Holmes, R. M., 18, 54
Holt, K., 489, 499
Holt, M. B., 263
Holt, M. K., 539
Hom, A., 571
Honda, M., 388
Hong, Y., 94, 493
Honig, A. S., 543
Hood, W. R., 562
Hoover-Dempsey, K. V., 86, 89, 101
Hopkins, Betsy, 250
Hopmeyer, A., 555
Hopson, J., 152, 153, 157
Horgan, D. D., 252
Horibe, F., 342
Horn, J. L., 275, 278
Hornyak, R. S., 503, 506, 509
Horowitz, F. D., 221, 224, 266, 382
Horst, J. S., 247
Horvat, M., 268
Horvath, D. L., 71
Horvath, K. J., 252
Hough-Eyamie, W. P., 315
Houghton, C., 257
Houston, I., 503
Houts, R., 396
Howard, G. R., 68, 97, 99, 100, 465
Howard, M. R., 332, 347, 348
Howe, D., 414, 418
Howe, M. L., 450
Howell, A. N., 137
Howell, J. C., 547, 564
Howell, K. L., 253
Howes, C., 409, 414, 415, 416, 418, 530, 531, 532, 558, 578
Howie, J. D., 493
Hoyle, S. G., 558
Hoyt, J. D., 250

Hruda, L. Z., 462
Huang, H.-S., 364
Huang, I. W., 171
Huang, M.-H., 298
Hubel, D., 7
Huber, F., 413
Hubley, P., 258
Hübscher, R., 217
Huckeby, E. R., 316
Huerta, M., 286
Huesmann, L. R., 582
Hufton, N., 496
Hughes, C., 409
Hughes, D., 457
Hughes, F. P., 306
Hughes, J., 89
Hughes, J. M., 390
Hughes, J. N., 433, 545
Hughes, R. C., 73
Huizink, A. C., 128
Hulit, L. M., 332, 347, 348
Hulme, C., 363, 369
Hulse, S. H., 394
Humphreys, A. P., 171
Humphreys, L. G., 295
Hungerford, A., 81
Hunt, A. K., 370
Hunt, E., 289
Hunter, A. G., 67, 165, 560
Huntley, S. B., 306
Huntsinger, C. S., 381
Hursh, D., 396
Husman, J., 500
Hussong, A., 178
Huston, A. C., 36, 74, 296, 471, 582
Hutt, C., 207
Hutt, S. J., 207
Huttenlocher, J., 80, 242, 261, 374, 380, 390
Huttenlocher, P. R., 152, 153, 157
Hwang, C. P., 69
Hwang, W.-C., 94
Hyde, J. S., 424
Hyde, K. L., 394
Hyman, I., 483, 545, 546
Hymel, S., 81, 556, 557, 558, 559
Hynd, G. W., 151
Hyson, M., 223
Hyson, M. C., 425
Hyvönen, P., 45

Iacoboni, M., 258
Iacono, W. G., 289
Ievers-Landis, C. E., 360
Igoa, C., 345, 459, 503
Illushin, L., 496
Imhof, M., 329, 341
Immerwahr, J., 93
Immordino-Yang, M. H., 158, 206, 207
Inagaki, K., 210, 386, 387
Inder, T., 147
Information Center for Sickle Cell and Thalassemic Disorders, 115
Inglis, A., 219, 380
Inhelder, B., 18, 195, 197
Inoff-Germain, G., 535
Insabella, G. M., 70
Insel, T. R., 158
Institute of Education Sciences, 46–47, 49
International Human Genome Sequencing Consortium, 110
Irizarry, N. L., 430
Irujo, S., 98, 336, 338
Isaacs, J., 560
Isabella, R., 418
Isabella, R. A., 411
Isen, A., 425
Isenberg, J. P., 4
Ispa, J. M., 364

Ittel, A., 164, 518
Iyengar, S. S., 486, 496
Izard, C., 408
Izard, C. E., 419

Jacklin, C. N., 296
Jackson, C. M., 159
Jackson, D. L., 241, 389
Jackson, Dinah, 233
Jackson, J. F., 92, 458
Jackson, M. E., 109, 109n
Jackson, P. W., 573
Jackson, R. H., 459
Jackson, S., 452
Jackson, S. C., 335
Jacob, B. A., 101
Jacobs, J., 38
Jacobs, J. E., 380, 445, 484, 486, 495, 496, 499
Jacobs, M., 216
Jacobs, P. J., 172, 223
Jacobsen, B., 495, 499
Jacobson, K., 261
Jacobson, K. C., 7
Jacoby, R., 297
Jagnow, C. P., 124
Jakubec, S. L., 568
Jalongo, M. R., 3–4, 4n, 13, 16, 331
James, D. K., 124
Jamner, L. D., 267
Janosz, M., 577
Jansen, E. A., 540
Janssens, D., 203
Jarvis, P. A., 554
Jasiobedzka, U., 521, 523
Jaswal, V. K., 323
Jay, E., 388
Jaycox, L. H., 437
Jefferson, P., 363
Jelalian, E., 169
Jeltova, I., 286
Jencks, C. M., 66
Jenkins, E., 374, 375, 380
Jenkins, J. M., 469
Jenkins, S., 538
Jenkins, Z. N., 539
Jenks, J., 582
Jenlink, C. L., 394, 504
Jensen, A. R., 278
Jensen, B., 92, 95
Jensen, E., 155, 564
Jensen, M. M., 438
Jerald, J., 20
Jerman, O., 266, 382
Jernigan, T. L., 38, 39, 155
Jessor, R., 178
Jessor, S. L., 178
Jia, G., 316
Jimerson, S., 363
Jipson, J., 323
Jipson, J. L., 383, 386
Joanisse, M. F., 348
Johanning, D. I., 383
John, O. P., 431
Johns, A. K., 360
Johnsen, E. P., 215, 334, 340
Johnson, C., 393
Johnson, D. W., 544–545
Johnson, J. O., 80
Johnson, J. S., 316
Johnson, K. E., 485, 495, 499
Johnson, M. H., 154, 157, 237
Johnson, R., 544–545
Johnson, R. T., 544
Johnson, S., 466
Johnson, W., 274, 289
Johnston, J. R., 348, 369
Johnston, L. D., 177
Johnston, P., 363
Johnston, T. D., 112
Jonen, A., 208
Jones, A. L., 184
Jones, D., 368
Jones, G. P., 539
Jones, H. F., 164

Jones, T., 469
Jones, W., 318
Jordan, A. B., 544, 582
Jordan, A. H., 298
Jordan, M., 345
Jordan, N. C., 374, 379
Jose, P. E., 381
Joshi, R. M., 363
Josselson, R., 406, 407, 454
Jovanovic, J., 540
Juel, C., 358, 366
Juffer, F., 417
Julien, D., 69
Junkin, L. J., 447
Jusczyk, P. W., 7, 321, 322, 323, 328
Juster, N., 342
Justice, L. M., 326, 332, 341
Jutta, E., 511
Jutta, K., 511
Juvonen, J., 469, 492, 493, 499, 501, 544, 560, 572

Kaczmarek, M. G., 568
Kaczmarek, N., 581
Kaffman, A., 119
Kagan, J., 407, 430, 450, 521
Kagan, J. K., 7, 428, 430
Kagan, S. L., 291
Kağitçibaşi Ç., 65, 77, 86, 94, 97, 98, 254, 291, 406, 407, 413
Kahl, B., 256
Kahneman, D., 469
Kail, R., 240
Kail, R. V., 239, 306
Kaler, S. R., 505
Kalichman, S. C., 179
Kalish, C. W., 262, 321, 327
Kalmanson, B., 473
Kamerman, S. B., 80
Kamphaus, R. W., 117
Kan, M. L., 69
Kana, T. G., 185
Kang, J. Y., 35
Kangas, M., 45
Kannass, K. N., 238
Kanner, A. D., 563
Kanner, L., 565
Kaplan, A., 484, 489, 492, 496
Kaplan, D., 379
Kaplan, N., 418
Kaplan, P. S., 316
Kapp-Simon, K., 182, 186
Kaprio, J., 164
Karabenick, S. A., 483, 509
Karafantis, D. M., 469
Karbach, J., 511
Karbon, M., 535
Kardash, C. A. M., 253
Karenga, M., 93
Karenga, T., 93
Kark, J., 115
Karmiloff-Smith, A., 326, 327
Karpov, Y. V., 215, 226
Karweit, N., 331
Kašek, M., 275
Kaslow, F. W., 70
Kassel, J. D., 178
Kastens, K. A., 391
Katchadourian, H., 565
Katkovsky, W., 500
Katz, E. W., 322
Katz, L. F., 69, 78
Kauffman, J. M., 483
Kaufman, A. S., 287
Kaufman, J. C., 296, 380
Kaye, D., 583
Kazak, A. E., 148
Kazdin, A. E., 436, 437
Kearins, J. M., 254
Keating, D. P., 387
Kedar, Y., 325
Keefe, K., 490, 557
Keefer, B., 73
Keelan, J. P. R., 416
Keeton, M. T., 580

Kehily, M. J., 456
Kehr, K. S., 295
Keil, F. C., 7, 261, 386, 388
Keitel, M. A., 47
Kelemen, D., 262
Keller, H., 274
Keller, M., 522
Kelley, E., 261
Kelley, K., 485
Kellogg, R., 161, 371, 391, 393
Kelly, B. C., 562, 563
Kelly, J., 71
Kelly, J. A., 179
Kelly, J. B., 70, 418
Kelly, S. D., 243
Kemler Nelson, D. G., 7, 261, 263, 484
Kemper, S., 333
Kennedy, C. B., 238
Kennedy, M., 247
Kenney, P. A., 257
Kenney-Benson, G. A., 485
Keogh, B. K., 121, 288, 306, 431, 432, 433, 495, 541
Kerewsky, W., 580
Kermoian, R., 237
Kerns, L. L., 438
Kessler, B., 356
Keys, C. B., 572
Khandakar, S., 473
Kiang, L., 458
Kiefer, A. K., 445
Kienzl, G., 503
Kieras, J., 119
Kikas, E., 43
Kilbourne, B. K., 334
Killen, M., 469, 521, 524, 525, 527, 528
Killeya-Jones, L. A., 561, 562
Killgore, W. D., 155, 157
Killip, S., 168
Kilpatrick, H., 583
Kim, C. C., 381
Kim, D., 446, 487, 571, 573
Kim, K. H., 343
Kim, P., 101, 102
Kim, S.-K., 496
Kim-Cohen, J., 102
Kindermann, T. A., 562
King, A., 256
King, E. W., 93
King, P. E., 525
King, S., 445
King, S. S., 540
Kingstone, A., 258
Kintsch, W., 359
Kiousis, S., 82
Kirby, B., 389
Kirby, J. R., 356, 357
Kirk, K. I., 350
Kirkorian, H. L., 582
Kirschenbaum, R. J., 98
Kirschner, P. A., 264
Kisilevsky, B. S., 240
Kistner, J. A., 493
Kitayama, S., 65, 456, 527, 541
Klaczynski, P., 385, 386
Klaczynski, P. A., 205, 243
Klahr, D., 19, 197, 248
Klassen, T. P., 184
Klebanov, P. K., 294
Klein, D. J., 164
Kleitman, S., 581
Klibanoff, R. S., 380, 382
Kline, K., 383
Klingler, C., 340, 342, 343
Klinkner, J., 426
Klinnert, M. D., 258
Kloo, D., 469
Kluger, A. N., 500
Knafo, A., 114
Knapp, M. S., 104, 504, 562
Knapp, N. F., 305, 446
Knauss, C., 423
Knickmeyer, R. C., 455
Knight, C. C., 207

Knudson, R. E., 369
Knutson, K., 193
Kobasigawa, A., 252
Kochanska, G., 79, 407, 505, 521, 522, 523, 525
Kodluboy, D. W., 547, 547n, 563, 564
Koedinger, K. R., 217, 383
Koegel, L. K., 473
Koehler, D. J., 469
Koenig, M. A., 331
Koeppel, J., 475
Koestner, R., 498, 497
Kogushi, Y., 469
Kohen, D. E., 102
Kohlberg, L., 9, 14, 18, 23, 81, 426, 518, 519, 520, 522, 523, 524, 525, 526, 529
Kohler, F. W., 474
Kohler, K. M., 574
Kohn, M. L., 80
Koh-Rangarajoo, E., 416
Kolb, B., 155, 156, 316
Kolbe, L., 451
Köller, O., 446
Koller, S., 522, 536
Komatsu, L. K., 243
Koniarek, J., 164
Konomi, S., 280
Koops, W., 538
Kopp, C. B., 483, 505
Koreishi, A., 260
Koren-Karie, N., 417, 472
Korkel, J., 241
Kornhaber, M., 278, 301
Kornsand, D., 39, 155
Korteland, C., 455
Kosciulek, J. F., 496
Koskinen, P. S., 367
Kosmitzki, C., 148
Koukis, S., 373
Kovacs, D. M., 559
Kovas, Y., 266, 275, 290, 292
Kowalski, P., 487
Kowalski, P. S., 501
Koza, J. E., 99
Kozhevnikov, M., 296, 380
Kozulin, A., 211
Krajcik, J., 388
Krakow, J. B., 483
Kramer, R., 526
Krampen, G., 462
Krapp, A., 482, 485
Krashen, S. D., 345
Krasnor, L. R., 556
Krauss, R. M., 332
Krebs, D. L., 523, 535
Krebs, P. L., 184
Kreider, R. M., 82
Kreutzer, M. A., 251
Krieg, D. B., 381
Krishnan, A., 254
Krishnan, K., 251, 257, 260, 266, 268
Krishnmoorthy, J. S., 170
Krispin, O., 541
Kritt, D., 468
Krivitski, E. C., 284, 285
Kroger, J., 9, 406
Kroger, S. M., 184
Kroonenberg, P. M., 414
Krueger, J. I., 451
Krug, C., 120
Kuczkowski, R., 451
Kuczynski, L., 68, 69
Kufeldt, K., 74
Kugelmass, S., 392
Kugiumutzakis, G., 258
Kuh, G. D., 577
Kuhl, P. K., 7, 153, 315, 317, 320, 343
Kuhlmeier, V., 466
Kuhn, D., 19, 203, 204, 205, 208, 239, 243, 251, 252, 253, 254, 257, 263, 300, 384, 385, 386, 387, 388, 496

Kuklinski, M. R., 575
Kulberg, A., 177
Kulik, C. C., 306
Kulik, J. A., 306
Kumpf, M., 298
Kunter, M., 485
Kuntsi, J., 119
Kunzinger, E. L., III, 247
Kuo, L., 359
Kupersmidt, J., 557
Kupersmidt, J. B., 539
Kupersmidt, J. G., 437
Kurtines, W. M., 10, 518, 523
Kurtz, D. A., 459
Kusché, C. A., 425, 426
Kutner, L. A., 582–583
Kuyper, L., 566
Kwok, O., 89
Kwok, O.-M., 433
Kwon, Y., 375, 380, 381
Kyratzis, A., 247

Labbo, L. D., 360
LaBlance, G. R., 348
Laboratory of Comparative Human Cognition, 274
Lacante, M., 490
Lacroix, D., 345
Ladd, E. C., 524
Ladd, G. W., 539, 556
Ladd, S. F., 375, 380
Ladewig, P. A. W., 125
Ladewig, P. W., 128
Ladson-Billings, G., 96, 103, 347, 465
Lafontana, K. M., 555
LaFreniere, P., 558
La Guardia, J. G., 416
Lahey, B. B., 267
Lahey, M., 348
Laible, D., 77
Laird, J., 503
Lajoie, S. P., 222
Lakatos, K., 506
Lalonde, C. E., 328
Lalor, J., 130
Lam, S.-F., 496
LaMay, M. L., 293, 296, 346
Lamaze, F., 133
Lamb, M. E., 69, 80, 414, 415, 418, 541, 578
Lamb, S., 521, 522, 523
Lambermon, M., 414
Lamborn, S., 77
Lamborn, S. D., 77, 78
Lampe, M. E., 118
Lampert, M., 383
Landerl, K., 363
Landis, D., 423
Landrum, T. J., 483
Lane, D. M., 238
Lang, B., 469
Lang, D J., 215
Langacker, R., 318
Lange, G., 254
Lange, R. E., 306
Langlois, J. A., 184
Langone, J., 306
Langston, M. C., 360
Lansford, J. E., 483
Lapan, R. T., 496
La Paro, K. M., 288
Lapp, A. L., 16, 67
Lapsley, D. K., 451, 452, 454, 522
Lareau, A., 89
Larkin, R. W., 534
Larner, M. B., 84
Larson, R., 70, 534
Larson, R. W., 487, 565, 568
Larson, S. L., 381
Larson-Shapiro, N., 330
Last, C. G., 436
Latendresse, S. J., 101
Latham, G. P., 487, 489n
Lauer, P. A., 580
Laumann-Billings, L., 70

Laupa, M., 521, 523
Laursen, B., 46, 558
Lautrey, J., 205
Lave, J., 217, 218, 447
Lavelli, M., 408
Lawson, K. R., 238
Lazar, I., 579
Lazar, N. A., 239
Lazerwitz, B., 338
Lazzaro, C., 581
Leakey, R., 27
Leaper, C., 93, 296, 386, 387, 454, 455, 496, 498
Learning First Alliance, 544, 545
Lears, M., 471
Lebeau, E., 69
Le Blanc, M., 577
LeCompte, M., 496
Lecours, A. R., 153, 154, 157
Lee, A., 472
Lee, A. M., 573
Lee, C., 344
Lee, C. D., 475
Lee, Harper, 544
Lee, J. H., 582
Lee, J. S., 382
Lee, J.-S., 90
Lee, K., 267, 331, 468
Lee, K. M., 343
Lee, O., 262, 386, 387
Lee, R., 536
Lee, S., 204
Lee, S. W.-S., 65, 98, 413
Lee, V., 577
Lee, V. E., 387, 503
Lee-Pearce, M. L., 104, 386, 504
LeFevre, J.-A., 357
Lefstein, L. M., 580
Legare, C. H., 386, 387
Leggett, E. L., 492
Lehman, D. R., 204
Lehman, S., 499
Lehmann, M., 247
Lehnart, A., 583
Leibham, M. E., 485
Leichtman, M. D., 259, 260
Leiderman, P. H., 77
Lein, L., 336
Leinhardt, G., 193, 222, 257, 391
Leite, A. C. C., 566
Leite, R. M. C., 566
Leite, R. W., 70
Lelwica, M., 419
Lemanek, K. L., 184
Lemery, K. S., 346
Leming, J. S., 46, 48
Lemke, Leslie, 394
Lennon, R., 252, 537
Lennox, C., 368
Lens, W., 339, 490, 496, 497, 500
Leonard, C., 251
Leong, D J., 215
Lepper, M. R., 486, 496
Lerner, R. M., 16, 19, 406
Leventhal, T., 97
Levey, L., 329
Levine, C., 9
Levine, L., 450
Levine, M., 425
LeVine, R. A., 413
Levine, S. C., 374, 380
Levitt, J. L., 533
Levitt, M. J., 533
Levstik, L. S., 209, 389
Levy, S. R., 390, 469
Lewin, D. S., 175
Lewin, T., 534
Lewis, C., 89, 90, 414
Lewis, C. C., 530
Lewis, J. M., 18, 70
Lewis, M., 303, 415, 416, 419, 421, 450, 485, 525, 526
Lewis, P., 472
Li, J., 253, 274, 305, 496, 497
Li, S. -C., 10
Li, Z., 541

Liao, T. F., 94
Liben, L. S., 212, 242–243, 356, 391, 455, 469, 496
Liberman, A. M., 356
Liberman, V., 469
Lichtenberger, E. O., 287
Lickliter, R., 12
Lickona, T., 543, 571, 573
Lidz, C. S., 221, 286, 288
Lie, E., 240
Lieberman, A., 484, 499
Lieberman, A. B., 438
Lieberman, D. A., 583
Lieberman, M., 519
Lieven, E., 332, 334
Light, P., 204, 218
Lightfoot, C., 534
Lightfoot, D., 314, 315, 328
Lillard, A. S., 214, 215, 469, 472, 497, 499
Limón, M., 390, 397
Lin, E., 381
Lin, M.-H., 521
Lindberg, M., 241
Lindenberger, U., 8
Linder, T. W., 499
Lindfors, K., 164
Lindsay, J. J., 580
Linebarger, D. L., 582
Linn, M. C., 204, 253, 257, 385, 386, 388
Linn, R. L., 297
Linnenbrink, E. A., 425, 462, 489
Linscheid, T. R., 169
Linton, M. J., 370
Linver, M. R., 102, 296
Lippa, R. A., 93, 380, 454, 455, 496
Lipsitz, J., 580
Lipson, M. Y., 242, 359
Lipton, J. S., 373
Liszkowski, U., 321
Little, L., 538
Little, T. D., 464, 486, 487
Littlewood, W. T., 320
Litwack, S. D., 89
Liu, D., 467, 472
Liwag, M., 422
Lobel, A., 426
Lochman, J. E., 535, 539
Locke, E. A., 487, 489n
Locke, J. L., 315, 316, 331, 339, 341, 348
Lockhart, K. L., 450, 492, 493, 499
Lockl, K., 251, 252
Lodewyk, K. R., 217, 497, 499
Loeb, S., 291, 300
Loeber, R., 267, 538, 540
Logan, K. R., 185
Logsdon, B. J., 163, 181
Lohman, D. F., 275
Lollis, S., 469
Lombroso, P. J., 149
London, M. L., 125, 128, 129, 166, 169
Long, B. J., 171
Long, D. L., 360
Long, M., 343
Lonigan, C. J., 330, 340, 357
Loomis, L., 580
Looney, L., 524
Lopata, C., 276
Lopez, A. M., 458, 465
Lopez, E., 458
Lopez, E. C., 297
Lopez, E. M., 580
López, G. R., 91
Lopez, V. A., 45
Lord, H., 80
Lorenz, Konrad, 18
Lorimer, M., 363
Losey, K. M., 95, 98, 338
Lotan, R. A., 543
Lou, Y., 222
Louis, B., 303

Lovett, B. J., 298
Lovett, S. B., 251
Low, C. M., 559
Low, S. M., 69
Lowery, B., 495
Lowry, R., 451
Lozano, J. M., 267
Lubinski, D., 285, 296, 304
Lucariello, J., 247
Lucas, T., 96, 97, 100, 465
Lucas-Thompson, R., 415
Luckasson, R., 294
Ludman, M. D., 117
Lüdtke, O., 446, 485
Ludwig, J., 291, 579
Lueptow, L. B., 496
Luk, G., 366
Lukowski, A. F., 240
Lumeng, J., 169, 170
Luna, B., 154, 239
Lundy, B. L., 414
Luo, W., 433
Lupart, J. L., 302, 306
Luria, A. R., 19
Lussier, C. M., 286
Lust, B., 325
Luster, L., 95
Luthar, S. S., 101
Lutke, J., 158
Luyckx, K., 453
Luykx, A., 56
Lykken, D. T., 289, 430
Lyman, E. T., 55
Lynam, D., 535
Lynch, D., 558
Lynch, J. H., 415, 454
Lynch, J. P., 547
Lynch, J. S., 360
Lynch, M. E., 131, 165
Lynch-Brown, C., 324
Lyon, G. R., 266, 370
Lyon, T. D., 250
Lytle, S., 56
Lytton, H., 78

MacArthur, C., 370, 371
MacArthur, C. A., 370
Macarthur, J., 344
Maccoby, E. E., 64, 77, 78, 79,
   88, 238, 239, 289, 296,
   530, 559
MacCorquodale, P., 165, 566
MacDonald, S., 254
Mace, F. C., 495
Macias, S., 268
MacIntyre, P. D., 266
Mac Iver, D., 489
MacKay, I. R. A., 316
MacKay, J. M., 184
Mackey, W. C., 69
Macklem, G. L., 422, 437
Mackler, S., 357
MacLean, D. J., 387, 419
Maclin, D., 257
MacMaster, K., 266
MacMillan, D. L., 288, 306, 541
Macomber, J., 261
MacWhinney, B., 315, 327
Madden, C. M., 329
Madden, D., 344
Madden, M., 583
Madden, N. A., 560
Mader, S., 535
Madhubuti, H., 79
Madhubuti, S., 79
Madison, S. M., 575
Madole, K. L., 247
Maehr, M. L., 489, 577
Maggs, J. L., 80
Magnuson, D., 544–545
Magnuson, K., 79
Magnuson, K. A., 297, 575
Magnusson, D., 165
Magoffin, D., 582
Mahaffy, K. A., 496
Mahapatra, M., 527

Maher, J. K., 471, 582
Mahitivanichcha, K., 91
Mahoney, J. L., 80, 580
Maier, M. A., 415
Maier, S. F., 493
Main, M., 409, 411, 412, 415, 418
Maita, M. D. R., 390
Maker, C. J., 302, 305
Malanchuk, O., 486
Malatesta, C., 408
Malatesta, C. Z., 424
Malcolm, K. T., 81
Malinsky, K. P., 568
Maller, S. J., 284
Mallick, S. K., 13
Malmberg, L.-E., 414
Malone, D. M., 306
Malone, P., 561
Mandel, D. R., 328
Manderson, L., 180
Mandinach, E. B., 508
Mandler, J. M., 247, 261, 466
Mangels, J. A., 489
Mangelsdorf, S. C., 69, 409, 422
Manis, F. R., 266
Mantzicopoulos, Y., 387
Manz, P. H., 182, 184, 186
Mar, R. A., 426
Marachi, R., 574
Maraj, B. K. V., 161
Maratsos, M., 318
Marcia, J. E., 407, 452, 453,
   454, 490
Marcoen, A., 128
Marcoux, M.-F., 450
Marcovitch, S., 239, 418
Marcus, G. F., 326
Marcus, R. F., 415
Marean, G. C., 7
Mareschal, D., 258, 317
Margolin, G., 535
Markman, E. M., 252, 323, 360,
   383, 386, 493
Marks, H. M., 297, 495
Marks, M. B., 256
Markstrom-Adams, C., 177,
   457, 475
Markus, H. R., 15, 65, 219, 413,
   456, 490, 527
Marlow, L., 165
Marsh, H. W., 446, 447, 449,
   450, 451, 455, 462, 490, 492,
   538, 581
Marshall, J. C., 152
Marshall, N. L., 296
Marsiglia, C. S., 360
Martell-Boinske, L., 425
Martin, A., 95
Martin, C. L., 93, 387, 454, 455
Martin, J. M., 455
Martin, N. G., 566
Martin, S. C., 184
Martin, S. S., 559
Martinez, C., 147
Martinez, C. R., 78
Martinez, G. M., 178
Martino, S. C., 164
Maruyama, G., 82
Marx, Karl, 210
Marx, R. W., 388
Marzolf, D., 409
Masataka, N., 334
Mashunkashey, J. O., 185
Masi, A., 582
Masiello, R., 39
Mason, J. M., 361
Mason, L., 262, 263, 385
Massey, C. M., 383, 386
Massey, D., 509
Massey, D. S., 101
Massimini, K., 117
Mastropieri, M., 502
Masuda, W. V., 221
Masunaga, H., 275
Masur, E. F., 251

Mata, J., 522
Mateika, J. H., 175
Mathes, P. G., 219
Matheson, C., 560
Matheson, C. C., 530, 531, 532
Mathews, J., 399
Matthews, D., 332, 334
Matthews, J., 391
Mattock, A., 236
Matusov, E., 572
Matza, L. S., 437
Mayall, B., 166, 171
Mayer, D. L., 139
Mayer, E. V., 483, 499
Mayer, R., 23
Mayer, R. E., 208
Mayer, S., 66
Mayes, L. C., 294
Maynard, A. E., 218
Mayringer, H., 363
Mayseless, O., 410
Mazzocco, M. M. M., 303
McAdoo, H., 77
McAdoo, H. P., 95
McAlpine, L., 98, 347
McArthur, D., 258
McBride-Chang, C., 357, 363,
   364, 366
McBrien, J. L., 344, 345, 457
McCabe, A., 274
McCabe, M. P., 164
McCaffrey, D., 164
McCaleb, S. P., 372
McCall, C., 511
McCall, R. B., 238, 287, 291,
   295, 495
McCallum, R. S., 278, 283,
   284, 285, 287, 297, 298,
   539–540, 562
McCandless, B. D., 345
McCandless, B. R., 13
McCann, T. M., 369
McCarthy, J., 179
McCarthy, M., 577
McCartney, K., 8, 119, 293, 415
McCarty, T. L., 335, 343
McCaslin, M., 257, 260, 490–491
McCaslin, M. M., 210
McClelland, J. L., 345, 377
McClintic, S. M., 505
McClintic-Gilberg, M. S., 499
McCloskey, L. A., 347
McCloskey, M., 262
McCombs, B. L., 583
McCormick, C. B., 99
McCourt, F., 372
McCoy, A., 459
McCoy, J. K., 82
McCoy, K., 438
McCrae, R. R., 431
McCreary, M. L., 95
McCrink, K., 374, 380
McCutchen, D., 369, 370
McDermott, S., 290
McDevitt, M., 82
McDevitt, T. M., 93, 252, 316,
   329, 332, 341
McDonough, L., 323
McDougall, P., 556, 557,
   558, 559
McElvain, C. K., 580
McGaha, C. G., 140
McGee, L. M., 361
McGhee, R. L., 433
McGinley, M., 521
McGlothlin, H., 469
McGrath, D. J., 344
McGregor, H. A., 489
McGrew, K. S., 274, 275,
   276, 276n
McGue, M., 289, 292, 293
McGuffin, P., 119
McGuigan, F., 240
McGuire, D. J., 175
McGuire, Dinah, 309
McHale, J. L., 69

McHale, J. P., 69
McHale, S. M., 82, 93, 423
McInerney, D. M., 490, 501
McIntosh, D. E., 284
McIntyre, C. W., 251
McIntyre, E., 366
McKeen, N. A., 171
McKenry, P. C., 70
McKenzie, J. K., 74
McKeough, A., 206, 332, 333,
   335, 376
McKerchar, P. M., 334
McKinney, W. T., 435
McKown, C., 298, 574
McLane, J. B., 355, 356, 358,
   363, 367, 368, 370, 371, 373
McLane, Joan Brooks, 355
McLoyd, V. C., 35, 78, 96, 101,
   102, 294, 296, 298, 306, 425,
   496, 578, 579
McMahon, S., 366
McMahon, S. D., 49, 572
McMichael, A., 290
McNalley, S., 537
McNamee, G. D., 355, 356, 358,
   363, 367, 368, 370, 371, 373
McNamee, Gillian Dowley, 355
McNeill, D., 315, 325
Meadows, N., 539
Meaney, M. J., 119
Mechelli, A., 343
Meece, J. L., 489, 502
Meehan, B. T., 545
Meesters, C., 433
Mehan, H., 338
Mehler, J., 236
Meichenbaum, D., 219, 221, 222,
   268, 511
Meins, E., 469
Meiring, A., 366
Meisels, S., 294
Meisels, S. J., 366
Meister, C., 221, 222, 257
Mejía-Arauz, R., 299
Melhuish, E., 578
Mellard, D. F., 266
Mellor, D. J., 344
Meltzer, L., 158, 251, 256, 257,
   260, 266, 268, 507, 508
Meltzoff, A. N., 315, 320, 450
Mena, J. G., 23
Menéndez, R., 399
Menk, D. W., 215
Mennella, J. A., 124
Menyuk, D., 336
Menyuk, P., 336
Mercer, C. S., 418
Mercer, J., 419
Mercer, L. K., 509
Mergendoller, J. R., 366
Mergulhao, E. A., 566
Mermelstein, R., 178
Merrick, S., 416
Merrill, M. A., 294
Merzenich, M. M., 317
Messinger, D. S., 418
Mettetal, G., 532, 534, 558,
   562, 565
Metz, K. E., 10, 203, 208, 384, 386
Metzger, A., 69
Metzger, B., 84
Metzler, J., 380
Meyer, C. F., 97
Meyer, D., 344
Meyer, D. K., 481, 484, 488,
   491, 499
Meyer, J., 472
Meyer, S., 521
Meyers, D. T., 527
Meyers, J., 580
Meyers, M. K., 297
Meyerstein, I., 126
Mezulis, A. H., 424
Michaels, M. L., 72
Michel, C., 174, 290
Middleton, M., 489
Middleton, M. J., 492

Midgley, C., 297, 415, 451,
   489, 491, 492, 496, 499,
   574, 576, 577
Mikulincer, M., 416, 417
Milburn, J. F., 437, 541
Milch-Reich, S., 541
Miller, B. C., 565, 566
Miller, C. L., 560
Miller, D., 436
Miller, F. K., 387
Miller, G. A., 321
Miller, G. E., 500
Miller, J. G., 10, 205, 297, 430,
   472, 521, 527, 528
Miller, K., 375, 380
Miller, K. F., 242, 358, 380, 381
Miller, L. S., 95, 98, 296, 503
Miller, M. D., 120, 297
Miller, N., 82
Miller, P., 238
Miller, P. A., 522, 537, 538
Miller, P. D., 366
Miller, P. H., 203, 238, 468
Miller, P. J., 96
Miller, P. M., 541
Miller, R. B., 490, 500
Miller, S. A., 203
Miller, S. D., 509
Miller-Johnson, S., 37, 561
Millrood, D., 175
Mills, D. L., 318
Mills, G. E., 33n, 56, 59n
Mills, R. S. L., 543
Milne, E., 161
Milner, H. R., 306, 504
Minami, M., 274
Mindel, C. H., 338
Mingroni, M. A., 292
Mink, J., 363
Minskoff, E. H., 474
Minstrell, J., 208, 385, 388, 389
Mischel, W., 483, 505,
   507, 538
Mistry, J., 226
Mitchell, E., 584
Mitchell, P., 448
Mitchem, K. J., 511
Mithaug, D. E., 506
Mithaug, D. K., 506
Mitru, G., 175
Mitsutake, G., 171
Miura, I. T., 381
Miyake, K., 411, 430
Miyamoto, R. T., 350
Mize, J., 532
Mizuta, I., 507
Modi, A. C., 184
Mody, M., 361
Moffitt, T. E., 102, 431
Mohatt, G., 338
Moher, D., 184
Mohn, G., 139
Mohr, N., 443
Moise-Titus, J., 582
Moje, E. B., 564
Molinari, L., 576
Möller, A., 161
Moller, A. C., 407
Möller, K., 208
Molnar, D., 137
Moncher, M. S., 170
Money, J., 567
Monker, J., 323
Monshouwer, H. J., 538
Montagu, A., 284n, 297
Montague, D. P. F., 421
Montant, M., 364
Montemayor, R., 88
Montessori, M., 12, 18
Montgomery, D., 336
Montgomery, J. W., 348
Montgomery, M. J., 454
Moon, C. M., 316, 341
Moon, S. M., 306
Moore, C., 450
Moore, C. F., 148, 290

Moore, D. W., 360
Moore, G. A., 421
Moore, J., 582
Moore, K. L., 112, 114, 117, 118, 121, 122, 123, 124, 126, 127, 128, 129, 130
Moore, P. S., 436
Moore, S. M., 179
Moore-Brown, B., 286
Moorman, E. A., 89
Mooser, L., 331
Moran, C. E., 342, 343
Moran, S., 277, 305, 392
Moran, T., 523
Morelli, G., 338
Morelli, G. A., 64, 406, 407, 413, 414, 415, 424, 456, 507
Morgan, J. L., 322, 327
Morgan, M., 257
Morgan, R. R., 535
Morison, S. J., 418
Morison, V., 236
Morling, B., 449
Morris, A. S., 66
Morris, D., 215, 366
Morris, M. W., 94
Morris, P. A., 16, 17, 66, 68
Morrison, F., 396
Morrison, F. J., 358
Morrison, G., 268
Morrison, G. M., 545
Morrison, R. L., 545
Morrongiello, B. A., 236, 237
Morrow, J., 424
Morrow, S. L., 567, 569
Mortimer, J. T., 88, 581
Mosborg, S., 390
Moses, L., 466
Moses, L. J., 267
Mosher, W. D., 70, 178
Mosier, C., 226
Moss, P., 27
Mounts, N., 77
Mounts, N. S., 77
Mounts, S., 77
Much, N. C., 527
Mueller, E., 530
Müeller, K. J., 489
Mueller, M. P., 375, 377
Muenchow, S., 579
Muhlenbruck, L., 579
Muilenburg, L., 386, 388
Muis, K. R., 251, 252, 253, 257, 378
Mukerjee, J., 178
Mul, D., 164
Mulder, C., 66
Mulder, E. J. H., 128
Mullally, P. R., 82
Mullen, M. K., 259
Müller, U., 239
Mulley, J. C., 115
Mullhall, P., 536
Mullins, D., 521
Mullis, R. L., 578
Mulqueeny, K., 356
Mulrooney, M., 475
Mundy, P., 258, 317, 409
Munn, P., 421, 467, 524
Munro, M. J., 316
Munroe, P. J., 69
Munroe, R. L., 69
Murdock, T. B., 574
Muris, P., 433
Murnane, R. J., 102
Murphy, B., 468
Murphy, D. A., 179, 181
Murphy, G. L., 247
Murphy, P. K., 210, 219, 262, 263
Murray, Charles, 297
Murray, H., 579
Murray, K. T., 505
Murrill, C. S., 177
Mustanski, B. S., 164
Muter, V., 357

Muthén, B., 357
Muzio, J. N., 174
Myers, L. J., 212, 242–243, 356, 391
Myerson, J., 483
Mylander, C., 349
Myles, B. M., 574

Naegele, J. R., 149
Nagell, K., 258
Nagle, R. J., 410
Naglieri, J., 213
Nagy, W. E., 321, 359, 363
Naigles, L., 323
Nair, P., 290
Najafi, B., 299
Nakagawa, N., 329
Nakamoto, J., 554
Nakata, N., 393
Nakata, T., 393
Nakazawa, C., 386
Narayanan, U., 118
Narváez, D., 521, 522, 524, 528, 529
Nasir, N. S., 457
Naslund, J., 360
Nation, K., 369
National Association for the Education of Young Children (NAEYC), 20, 21n
National Association of Bilingual Education, 344
National Association of Secondary School Principals, 23
National Campaign to Prevent Teen Pregnancy, 179
National Center for Education Statistics, 101, 102, 580
National Center for Health Statistics, 184
National Center for Missing and Exploited Children, 585
National Clearinghouse for English Language Acquisition, 96
National Council for Accreditation of Teacher Education, 21
National Drug Intelligence Center, 563
National Human Genome Research Institute, 111
National Institute of Mental Health, 459
National Institute on Drug Abuse, 177, 178
National Joint Committee on Learning Disabilities, 266
National Middle School Association (NMSA), 22
National Research Council, 154, 157
National Science Foundation, 495
National Youth Violence Prevention Center, 564
Nayak, A., 456
Nayer, S., 466
NCSS Task Force on Ethnic Studies Curriculum Guidelines, 99
Neal, M. C., 535
Neale, B., 76
Nebelsick-Gullet, L., 257
Neckerman, H. J., 538
Neef, N. A., 495
Neel, R. S., 539
Neemann, J., 423
Neinstein, L. S., 177
Neiss, M., 164
Neiss, M. B., 447
Neisser, U., 274, 275, 289, 292, 293, 295, 297, 298, 301
Neitzel, C., 485, 506
Nelson, C. A., 152, 153, 154, 155, 156, 157, 240, 291, 473, 506

Nelson, C. A., III, 151
Nelson, D. A., 539
Nelson, K., 195, 212, 219, 240, 241, 242, 247, 260, 262, 264, 317, 332, 334, 341, 346, 450
Nelson, P. A., 372
Nelson, T., 153
Nemoda, Z., 506
Nesdale, D., 562
Nettelbeck, T., 292
Neumann, C., 292
Nevid, J. S., 435, 436
Neville, H. J., 315
Newcomb, A. F., 532, 557, 558, 559
Newcombe, N., 242
Newcombe, N. S., 240, 261
Newell, G. E., 373
Newell, L., 258, 317
Newkirk, T., 363
Newman, L. S., 247
Newman, R. S., 509
Newman, S., 82
Newman, S. E., 222
Newport, E. L., 316, 322, 328, 349, 350
Newson, E., 216
Newson, J., 216
Newson, M., 314, 327
Ng, F. F., 485
Nguyen, S. P., 247
Ni, Y., 374
Nias, D. K. B., 535
NICHD Early Child Care Research Network, 291, 416, 538, 578
Nicholls, J. G., 489, 489n, 492, 499
Nichols, K. E., 521
Nichols, M. L., 305
Nichols, S. L., 574
Nicholson, S. C., 170
Nichter, M., 131
Nickerson, A. B., 410
Nicolopoulou, A., 333, 341
Nicolson, S., 52, 53
Niego, S., 65
Nieto, S., 344
Nievar, M. A., 411
Nilsson, D. E., 117
Ningiuruvik, L., 338
Nippold, M. A., 321, 322, 329, 333, 340, 369
Nisbett, R. E., 204, 297, 536
Nishina, A., 544
Nix, R. L., 530
Nixon, S. M., 467
Noguchi, R. J. P., 539
Noguera, Pedro A., 476
Nokes, J. D., 390
Nolen-Hoeksema, S., 424
Noll, E., 95
Noll, J., 278
Nomura, Y., 137
Nord, C., 72, 580
Nordby, C. J., 508
Nordness, P. D., 437
Norenzayan, A., 205
Norman, K., 413
Norris, K., 336
North Central Regional Educational Library, 101
Northrup, J. C., 93
Noseworthy, J., 136
Notaro, P. C., 66
Nourot, P. M., 223
Nowell, A., 296, 363, 371, 380
Nucci, L., 520, 577
Nucci, L. P., 518, 521, 523, 524, 525, 527, 528, 529, 544
Nucci, M. S., 521
Nugent, J. K., 287
Nundy, S., 425
Nunes, S. R., 365
Nunes, T., 368
Nunner-Winkler, G., 527

Nurmi, J.-E., 46
Nusbaum, H., 243
Nuttal, R. L., 382
Nye, B., 580

Oakes, E. J., 73
Oakes, J., 574
Oakes, L. M., 226, 238, 239, 247, 263, 484
Oakhill, J., 363
Oatley, K., 425, 426
O'Boyle, M. W., 296
O'Byrne, S., 394
Ochs, E., 317, 320, 339
O'Connell, M., 74
O'Connor, E., 415
O'Connor, S., 394
O'Connor, T. G., 81, 120–121
Odent, M., 567
Odom, R. D., 236–237
Oettingen, G., 464
Office for Human Research Protections, 34
Ogbu, J. U., 95, 98, 294, 297, 298, 347
Ogden, E. H., 102
O'Grady, W., 314, 315, 320, 321, 325, 326, 341
Oh, S., 290
Okagaki, L., 93, 299, 381, 486, 496
Okamoto, Y., 10, 205, 206, 373, 375, 376, 380, 381, 382, 393
Oki, M., 155
Oldfather, P., 161, 491
O'Leary, K. D., 483
O'Leary, S., 69, 483
Oligny, P., 538
Olinghouse, N., 370
Oller, D. K., 341
Olmstead, B. J., 583
O'Loughlin, M., 203
Olsen, R. J., 560
Olshansky, B., 394
Olson, C. K., 582–583
Olson, D. R., 203
Olswang, L., 327
Olswang, L. B., 475
Oltmanns, T. F., 435, 436, 437
O'Malley, P. M., 177, 449
Oortwijn, M. B., 555
Oosterlaan, J., 423
Oppenheim, D., 417, 472
Oppenheimer, L., 468
Op't Eynde, P., 378
O'Reilly, A. W., 215
Orme, J. G., 73
Ormrod, J. E., 175, 241, 244, 264, 268, 303, 309, 389, 501
Ornstein, P. A., 10
Ornstein, R., 315, 316
Orobio de Castro, B., 538
Ortiz, C., 535
Ortony, A., 330, 334, 341
Osgood, W., 423
Osher, D., 545, 545n, 546
Osgood, W., 423
Osterman, K. F., 561, 571, 573
Otis, N., 486, 487, 490, 499, 508
O'Toole, M. E., 547
Ottinger-Albergs, W., 240
Owen, M. J., 119
Owens, C. R., 535
Owens, R. E., 213, 320, 321, 322, 325, 326, 327, 329, 330, 332, 333, 336, 340, 341, 346, 363, 369, 370, 371, 534
Oyserman, D., 65, 98, 413, 490
Ozmun, J. C., 147, 148, 168, 173, 174, 539
Ozretich, R. A., 584

Padden, D., 153
Padilla, A. M., 343, 344, 345
Padilla, M. J., 388

Padilla-Walker, L. M., 411, 562
Paget, K. F., 468
Page-Voth, V., 373, 500
Pahl, K., 457
Paikoff, R. L., 88, 162, 566
Painter, K. M., 215
Painter, R., 147
Pajares, F., 372, 462, 494, 495, 499
Palacios, J., 73
Palermo, D. S., 322
Paley, V. G., 539
Palincsar, A. S., 219, 221, 226, 256, 543
Pallotta, J., 39
Palmer, E. L., 208
Palombaro, M. M., 185
Pan, B. A., 323
Pan, J., 254, 386, 387, 496
Pang, V. O., 89, 99, 499
Panksepp, J., 268, 535
Panofsky, C. P., 357
Paolitto, D. P., 520
Pappas, S., 203
Parada, R. H., 538
Paris, A. H., 504
Paris, S. G., 257, 356, 358, 360, 363, 450, 464, 492, 493, 499, 502, 506, 511
Parish, P., 340
Park, L., 527
Park, L. E., 407, 445
Park, S.-H., 253, 254, 496
Parke, R. D., 10, 69, 82, 93, 102, 532
Parker, D. A., 567
Parker, J. A., 471
Parker, J. G., 530, 554, 556, 559
Parker, K. C., 418
Parker, W. D., 303, 306
Parkhurst, J., 532
Parkhurst, J. T., 555
Parkin, C. M., 68, 69
Parks, C. P., 561, 563, 564
Parnes, A. L., 49, 572
Parrila, R. K., 356, 357
Parten, M. B., 530
Pascarella, E. T., 203
Pascual, L., 215
Pascual-Leone, J., 206, 520
Pasquini, E., 348
Pasternack, J. F., 537
Pastorelli, C., 387, 555
Patall, E. A., 497, 508
Pate, R. R., 171
Patel, T. K., 364
Patrick, H., 386, 387, 462, 504, 556, 572
Pattee, L., 557
Patterson, C. J., 65, 71, 72, 74, 567, 568
Patterson, G. R., 81, 437
Patterson, M. L., 574
Patton, J. R., 307, 348, 509
Pauen, S., 247
Paul, R., 329
Paulson, S. E., 448
Paus, T., 38, 155, 157
Pavlov, Ivan, 18
Pawlas, G. E., 102, 104
Paxton, R. J., 390
Paxton, S. J., 423
Payne, R. K., 503
PE 4 Life, 179
Pea, R. D., 279, 280, 302
Peak, L., 499
Peake, P. K., 483
Pearsall, S., 385
Pearson, D. A., 238
Pearson, P. D., 360
Peck, S. C., 580
Pederson, D. R., 215
Pederson, J., 538
Pederson, P. B., 457
Pedro-Carroll, J. L., 71, 76
Peduzzi, J. D., 237

Peeke, L. A., 455
Peets, K., 43
Pegg, P. O., 459
Pekrun, R., 415
Pelham, W. E., Jr., 445, 541
Pellegrini, A. D., 18, 38, 53, 54,
    171, 172, 268, 530, 538, 539,
    540, 545, 554, 555
Pelletier, J., 252, 253, 467, 469
Pelletier, L. G., 486
Pellicer, L. O., 102, 103, 104, 504
Peña, E. D., 286
Pence, A., 27
Pence, K. L., 326, 332, 341
Pendry, P., 19
Peng, K., 205
Penner, A. M., 380
Pennington, B. F., 535
Pentz, M. A., 426
Peralta, O. A., 390
Pereira, L., 561
Peretz, I., 394
Pérez, B., 97, 344, 345, 356, 364
Perez, L., 580
Perez, S. M., 19, 79
Perfect, T. J., 250
Perfetti, C. A., 257, 328, 359, 369
Perin, D., 371, 373
Perkins, D., 253
Perkins, D. N., 218, 279, 280,
    300, 301, 302, 307
Perkins-Gough, D., 579
Perner, J., 203, 467, 468, 469
Perney, J., 366
Perry, A. J., 579
Perry, C., 364
Perry, D. G., 455
Perry, M., 381
Perry, N. E., 257, 499, 500,
    508, 511
Perry-Jenkins, M., 93
Persaud, T. V. N., 112, 114, 117,
    118, 121, 122, 123, 124, 126,
    127, 128
Pesetsky, D., 328
Pessar, L. F., 435
Peters, A. M., 323
Petersen, A., 448
Petersen, A. C., 454
Peterson, A. C., 165
Peterson, B. E., 407
Peterson, C., 493, 499
Peterson, C. C., 472, 473
Peterson, D., 564
Peterson, D. K., 365, 366
Peterson, J. L., 72
Peterson, K. A., 448
Peterson, L., 538
Peterson, P. L., 502
Peterson, R. F., 543
Petrie, S., 501
Petrill, S. A., 6, 7, 289, 293
Pettit, G., 77
Pettit, G. S., 16, 67, 530,
    532, 556
Pettito, A. L., 214
Pettito, L. A., 315, 341,
    344, 349
Peyser, H., 75
Peyton, J. A., 366
Pezaris, E., 382
Pfeifer, J. H., 469, 471, 475
Pfeifer, M., 507
Pfeiffer, S. L., 357
Phalet, K., 339, 496
Phelan, P., 339, 423, 491, 503
Phelps, L., 285
Phillips, A. T., 467
Phillips, D., 291, 446, 579
Phillips, D. A., 300
Phillips, M., 297, 575
Phinney, J. S., 95, 447, 457,
    459, 471
Piaget, Jean, 8, 14, 18, 193, 194,
    195, 196, 196n, 197, 199, 203,
    205, 224, 226, 227, 228, 234,

242, 260, 262, 277n, 329n,
    467n, 484, 487, 533
Pianta, R. C., 84, 288, 396, 397,
    415, 424, 501, 504, 572, 576
Picasso, Pablo, 549
Piche, C., 455
Pidada, S., 540
Piek, J. P., 473
Pierce, K. M., 579
Pierce, S. H., 254
Pierson, Greg, 20n
Piirto, J., 306, 361
Pillard, R. C., 567
Pillemer, D. B., 260
Pillow, B. H., 243, 468
Pine, C. J., 73
Pine, K., 369
Pinker, S., 316, 317, 323, 327
Pinquart, M., 415
Pinto, J. P., 328
Pintrich, P. R., 252, 253, 363,
    425, 445, 450, 464, 484,
    489, 494
Pipher, M., 88, 162, 187, 188,
    455, 534
Pisarik, C. T., 555
Pisoni, D. B., 328, 350
Pitner, R. O., 469
Pizzuto, E., 332
Plante, C., 455
Platzman, K. A., 131
Plemons, B. W., 291
Plewis, I., 174
Plomin, R., 7, 8, 18, 114, 119,
    120–121, 266, 289, 292, 348
Plowman, T. S., 104
Plucker, J. A., 280, 302
Plumert, J. M., 247
Plybon, L. E., 459
Podolski, C. L., 582
Poel, E. W., 185
Polderman, T. J. C., 288
Polit, D., 82
Pollack, W., 145, 424
Pollica, L. S., 158
Pollitt, E., 290
Pomerantz, E. M., 89, 386, 485
Ponterotto, J. G., 47, 457
Poorman, A. S., 393, 394
Porat, D. A., 390
Poresky, R. H., 178
Portes, P. R., 96, 102, 296,
    363, 499
Posner, G. J., 253
Posner, J. K., 382
Posner, M. I., 119, 158, 505
Pospisil, H., 110
Potenza, M. T., 257
Potter, E. F., 394
Poulin, F., 538
Poulin-Dubois, D., 466
Powell, G. J., 406, 407
Powell, K., 451
Powell, M. P., 117
Power, F. C., 525, 528
Powers, J. E., 74, 499
Pramling, I., 54
Pratt, C., 340
Prawat, R. S., 572
Preedy, P., 83
Pressley, M., 247, 248, 256, 257,
    359, 360, 361, 492
Preuss, L. J., 303
Pribilsky, J., 410
Price, J. R., 335
Price, S., 136
Price, T. S., 348
Price-Williams, D. R., 204
Primerano, D., 276
Pritchard, R., 242
Proctor, C. P., 366
Proctor, R. W., 173
Provasnik, S., 101
Pruden, S. M., 316, 323
Pruitt, J., 153
Pulkkinen, L., 78, 164

Pulos, S., 204, 209, 384, 386
Pungello, E., 37
Puntambekar, S., 217
Purcell-Gates, V., 328, 347, 366
Purdie, N., 252, 254, 256
Putallaz, M., 530, 555, 557

Qian, G., 254, 386, 387, 496
Quamma, J. P., 425
Quane, J. M., 580
Quilitch, H. R., 543
Quill, K. A., 473
Quinlan, N. P., 561
Quinn, P. C., 247, 322
Quittner, A. L., 184

Rademakers, J., 565
Radke-Yarrow, M., 522, 523
Radziszewska, B., 227
Raevuori, A., 447, 449
Raffaelli, M., 536
Ragusa, D. M., 506
Rahm, J., 215
Rahman, Q., 567
Raikes, H., 323, 363
Raine, A., 484, 535
Rajanayagam, K., 180
Rakic, P., 152, 157
Rakison, D. H., 226, 237, 262
Rakow, E. A., 252
Rallison, M. L., 169
Raman, L., 323
Ramani, G. B., 382
Rambaud, M. F., 89
Ramey, C. T., 37, 297, 579
Ramey, S. L., 579
Ramirez, M., 204
Ramminger, A., 426
Ramsey, E., 437
Rankin, B. H., 580
Raphael, T. E., 365, 366
Rapport, N. S., 90
Rapson, R. L., 419
Raschke, D., 474
Rasmussen, J. L., 69
Rathbun, K., 322
Rathus, S. A., 435, 436
Ratner, H. H., 259, 383
Rausch, M. K., 483
Raver, C. C., 102, 425
Ravid, D., 369
Raviv, A., 175
Rayner, K., 328, 359, 364,
    365, 366
Rayport, S. G., 152
Razza, R. P., 257
Ready, D., 577
Ream, G. L., 568
Recchia, S., 505
Redfield, J., 535
Redler, E., 543
Rees, S., 147
Reese, E., 259
Reese, L., 363
Reese, S., 582
Reeve, J., 482, 486, 506
Reich, P. A., 322, 325, 343
Reid, J. B., 81
Reid, N., 98, 299
Reid, P. T., 94
Reid, R., 437
Reimer, J., 520, 522, 529
Reimer, K. S., 525
Reiner, M., 384, 386, 388
Reis, J., 536
Reis, S. M., 303
Reiss, D., 119, 120
Reissland, N., 413
Reivich, K. J., 437
Relkin, N. R., 343
Remez, L., 566
Renninger, K. A., 482, 485, 497
Renshaw, P. D., 555, 556
Renzulli, J. S., 303
Repacholi, B. M., 467

Rescorla, L., 223, 425
Resnick, D. P., 290
Resnick, L. B., 380, 384
Rest, J., 522, 524
Rest, J. R., 521, 525
Reston, J., 33, 33n, 34, 56
Reuman, D., 489
Rex, D., 39, 155
Reyna, C., 575
Reyna, V. F., 155, 157, 159,
    168, 259
Reynolds, A., 579
Reynolds, C., 484
Reynolds, C. R., 297
Reynolds, G. D., 485
Reynolds, R. E., 242
Reys, B. J., 210
Reznick, J. S., 247, 346
Rhoades, E. K., 97
Rhoades, K. W., 73
Rhodes, J. E., 423
Ricciardelli, L. A., 164
Ricciuti, H. N., 290
Rice, J., 500
Rice, K., 452
Rice, M., 348
Richard, J. F., 555
Richards, D. D., 203
Richards, F. A., 203
Richards, J. E., 238, 485
Richardson, R., 240
Richner, E. S., 333, 341
Rickman, M., 507
Ridderinkhof, K. R., 238
Rider, R., 267
Ridgeway, D., 421
Rief, S. F., 366
Rieser, J. J., 10
Riggs, J. M., 445
Riggs, N. R., 426
Riley, D., 426, 528
Rimm, S. B., 294, 305
Rimm-Kaufman, S. E., 433
Rindfuss, R. R., 94
Rinehart, S. D., 361
Ripple, C. H., 579
Ris, M. D., 290
Risemberg, R., 252
Risley, T. R., 323, 346
Ristic, J., 258
Ritchhart, R., 253
Ritchie, S., 416
Rittenhouse, P., 383
Ritter, P. L., 77, 164
Rittle-Johnson, B., 217, 369, 371,
    378, 382, 383
Ritts, V., 574
Roazzi, A., 10
Robbins, A. M., 350
Robbins, C., 359
Robbins, W. J., 159
Roberts, D., 73, 471
Roberts, D. F., 77, 331, 581,
    582, 583
Roberts, J. E., 335
Roberts, M. C., 185, 186
Roberts, R. D., 275
Roberts, R. E., 459
Roberts, T. A., 340, 347, 363, 366
Roberts, V., 511
Roberts, W., 571
Robertson, B., 493
Robertson, J. F., 78
Robertson, J. S., 502
Robin, D. J., 371
Robins, R. W., 431, 449, 451
Robinson, D. R., 219
Robinson, E. J., 203
Robinson, J., 526, 535
Robinson, J. C., 508
Robinson, M., 248, 373
Robinson, N. S., 448
Robinson, T., 582
Robinson, T. E., 156
Robinson, T. R., 120
Rochat, P., 371

Rock, D. A., 424
Rodas, C., 75
Roderick, M., 89, 503, 508, 513,
    572, 575, 576, 577
Rodier, P. M., 142
Roditi, B. N., 378, 383
Rodriguez, J. L., 345
Rodriguez, M. L., 505
Rodriquez, T., 467
Roeder, K., 290
Roeser, R. W., 415, 580
Roffwarg, H. P., 174
Rogers, H., 119
Rogers, K. B., 304
Rogoff, B., 8, 10, 19, 64, 65, 79,
    95, 204, 205, 217, 218, 222,
    226, 227, 254, 292, 299, 336,
    338, 339, 554, 554n, 572
Rogosch, F. A., 435
Rohner, E. C., 77
Rohner, R. P., 77
Roid, G., 282
Rolfhus, E. L., 285
Romero, A. J., 459
Romero, M., 177
Romney, D. M., 78
Rompelberg, L., 433
Rondal, J. A., 320
Rondan, C., 473
Rook-Green, A., 215
Root, M. P. P., 465
Rose, R., 164
Rose, R. J., 164
Roseboom, T., 147
Rose-Krasnor, L., 558
Rosen, G. D., 361
Rosenberg, J. L., 535
Rosenberg, M., 448, 451
Rosenblum, T. B., 298
Rosengren, K. S., 242
Rosenkoetter, L. I., 584
Rosenkoetter, S. E., 584
Rosenshine, B., 221, 222, 257
Rosenstein, D., 236
Rosenthal, D. A., 179
Rosenthal, R., 296, 447, 574
Rosenthal, S., 416
Rosicky, J. G., 466
Ross, D., 42
Ross, D. F., 540
Ross, G., 217
Ross, H., 46
Ross, H. S., 469
Ross, M., 254, 259
Ross, S. A., 42
Rossen, M., 318
Rosser, B. R., 203
Rossman, B. R., 422
Rotenberg, K. J., 483, 499
Roth, E., 366
Roth, W., 218
Rothbart, M. K., 6, 119, 158, 238,
    428, 430, 430n, 505, 527
Rothbaum, F., 64, 406, 407, 413,
    414, 415, 424, 456, 496, 507
Rothlisberg, B., 284
Rothstein-Fisch, C., 554, 572, 573
Rouet, J.-F., 257
Roux, A. L., 184
Rovee-Collier, C., 240, 487, 499
Rovine, M., 69
Rowe, D., 77
Rowe, D. C., 7
Rowe, D. W., 358
Rowe, M. B., 338, 349, 385, 386
Rowe, M. L., 323
Rowland, T. W., 171, 172
Rowley, S. J., 458, 459
Royce, J., 579
Rubie-Davies, C. M., 574
Rubin, K., 215
Rubin, K. H., 430, 530, 531, 532,
    533, 534, 541, 554, 555, 556,
    557, 558, 561, 562, 563, 565
Ruble, D. N., 93, 424, 454,
    455, 456

Ruby, P., 535
Rudlin, C. R., 173
Rudolph, K. D., 446, 533, 541
Rudy, D., 77, 364
Ruff, H. A., 238
Ruffman, T., 203, 469
Ruhm, C., 575
Ruhm, C. J., 297
Ruijssenaars, A. J. J. M., 286
Ruiz, I., 238
Rumberger, R. W., 503, 545
Rumsey, S., 244
Rünger, D., 264
Rushton, J. P., 523, 525, 535, 536
Russel, R., 566
Russell, A., 334
Russell, J. M., 83
Russell, Michael, 587, 588
Russell, R. L., 382
Russell, S. T., 74
Rutland, A., 468, 562
Rutland-Brown, W., 184
Rutter, M., 73, 120–121, 423
Rutter, M. L., 7, 292
Ryan, A. M., 178, 445, 496, 555, 572
Ryan, E. B., 361
Ryan, R., 396
Ryan, R. M., 415, 416, 451, 454, 462, 464, 484, 485, 486, 487, 497, 499, 505, 533
Rycus, J. S., 73
Ryu, S., 88, 581

Saarni, C., 408, 411, 413, 419, 421, 422, 423, 431, 474
Sabbagh, M. A., 267, 467
Sacks, C. H., 366
Sadeh, A., 175
Sadler, T. W., 112, 124, 125, 126, 128, 129, 137
Sadovsky, A., 77, 522
Saffran, J. R., 322, 323, 327, 328, 394
Sagi, A., 414
Saint-Aubin, J., 363
St. James-Roberts, I., 174
Salend, S. J., 89
Salisbury, C. L., 185
Salmivalli, C., 43, 560
Salmon, K., 240
Salomon, G., 224
Salovey, P., 422
Saltz, E., 322
Samarapungavan, A., 387
Sameroff, A., 19
Sameroff, A. J., 295, 415
Sammans, P., 578
Sampson, M. C., 414
Sampson, P. D., 161, 290
Sanchez, F., 548, 549, 549n
Sanchez, R. P., 254
Sánchez-Sandoval, Y., 73
Sandall, S. R., 499
Sanders, E. A., 366
Sanders-Reio, J., 415
Sandler, H. M., 86, 89, 101, 447
Sands, D. J., 495, 508
Sanfacon, J. A., 580
San Juan, R. R., 426
Santisi, M., 378
Santomero, A., 254
Santos, L. R., 484
Sarlo, N., 207
Sarrazin, J., 69, 70, 71
Sasse, D. K., 387
Satlow, E., 359
Sattler, J., 282
Sattler, J. M., 278, 279, 285, 287, 292, 293, 295, 297
Saudino, K. J., 119
Savin-Williams, R. C., 566, 567, 568
Sawyer, R. J., 370
Saxe, G. B., 381, 382, 457
Saxon, J. L., 386

Sbarra, D. A., 70
Scales, B., 223
Scarborough, H., 357
Scarborough, H. S., 347
Scardamalia, M., 222, 369, 370, 583
Scarr, S., 8, 18, 77, 81, 119, 290, 293
Scerbo, A., 535
Schacter, J., 583
Schaefer-McDaniel, N., 101, 105, 105n
Schaffer, H. R., 408, 409
Schaie, K. W., 203
Schaller, M., 538
Schaps, E., 46, 426, 487, 573
Scharrer, E., 582
Schatschneider, C. W., 251
Schauble, L., 203, 204, 207, 385, 386, 392
Schechtman, S., 356
Scheier, L. M., 178, 179
Schellenberg, E. G., 295, 394
Scher, D., 357
Scherer, N., 327
Schettler, T., 184
Scheuermann, B., 511
Schiefele, U., 93
Schieffelin, B., 317, 320
Schiever, S. W., 302, 305
Schimmoeller, M. A., 213
Schinke, S., 179
Schinke, S. P., 170, 178
Schlaefli, A., 525
Schleppenbach, M., 381
Schliemann, A. D., 204, 218
Schlundt, D. G., 557
Schmidt, L. A., 430
Schmidt, S. L., 18
Schmidt, W. H., 397
Schmitt, K. L., 582
Schneider, B., 415
Schneider, B. H., 555
Schneider, W., 241, 245, 248, 251, 252, 254, 366, 492
Schnocken, I., 557
Schnur, E., 291
Schoenfeld, A. H., 252, 378, 380
Schofield, J. W., 219, 543, 559
Schommer, M., 252, 253, 257
Schonert-Reichl, K. A., 437, 523
Schoppe-Sullivan, S. J., 69
Schratz, M., 296
Schraw, G., 7, 257, 497
Schreibman, L., 473
Schrijnemakers, H., 252
Schulenberg, J. E., 177
Schuler, M. E., 290
Schulte, T., 117
Schultz, G. F., 499
Schulze, R., 275
Schumaker, J. B., 499
Schumpf, F., 544
Schunk, D. H., 251, 445, 450, 464, 494, 498, 500, 501
Schupf, N., 290
Schutz, P. A., 462, 487, 490, 505
Schwade, J. A., 314
Schwager, M. T., 509
Schwartz, B. L., 250
Schwartz, D., 539, 554
Schwartz, G. M., 419
Schwartz, J. L., 382
Schwartz, S. S., 370
Schwarz, C. V., 389
Schweingruber, H., 454
Schweinhart, L. J., 579
Scoloveno, M. A., 133
Scott, P. M., 535
Scott-Jones, D., 79
Scott-Little, M., 572
Scribner, J. D., 91
Scruggs, T., 502
Sears, K. G., 506
Seashore, H. G., 381

Seay, A., 81
Sedikides, C., 447
Seegers, G., 381
Segal, B. M., 178
Segal, J., 418
Segal, N. L., 83, 291
Seidenberg, M. S., 328
Seidman, E., 457, 577
Seier, W., 238
Seifer, R., 295
Seixas, P., 390
Selfe, L., 142
Seligman, M. E. P., 257, 300, 306, 437, 493, 495, 499
Selman, R. L., 18, 422, 443, 444, 466, 468, 543, 554, 558, 561
Seltzer, V. C., 555, 559
Semb, G. B., 219
Semrud-Clikeman, M., 151
Sénéchal, M., 323, 357
Senghas, A., 318
Senman, L., 343
Serbin, L. A., 382
Seroczynski, A. D., 455
Serpell, R., 356, 357, 358, 363, 365
Sessa, F. M., 66
Sewald, H., 562
Shaddy, D. J., 238
Shadid, G., 452
Shaffer, D. R., 525
Shafto, C. L., 315
Shah, J. Y., 487
Shahinfar, A., 437
Shaligram, C., 381
Shanahan, C., 390
Shanahan, L., 423
Shanahan, M., 88, 581
Shanahan, T., 371
Shany, M., 219
Shapiro, A. M., 572
Shapiro, B. K., 306–307
Shapiro, E. S., 182, 184, 186
Shapiro, J. R., 409
Shapka, J. D., 387
Share, D. L., 358, 363, 365
Sharma, R., 509
Shatz, M., 332
Shaughnessy, M. F., 278
Shavelson, R. J., 380
Shaver, P. R., 416, 417
Shavers, C. A., 43
Shavinina, L. V., 304
Shaw, George Bernard, 584
Shaw, P., 267
Shaw, V., 257
Shaywitz, B. A., 361
Shaywitz, S. E., 361, 365
Shea, C., 537
Shea, D. L., 285, 296
Sheckley, B. G., 580
Shedler, J., 178
Sheehan, E. A., 318
Sheehan, E. P., 151, 252
Sheese, B. E., 505
Sheets, R. H., 457
Sheffield, E., 137
Shell, R., 522, 537
Shellenberg, E. G., 394
Shenfield, T., 393
Shenkin, S. D., 137
Shepard, R. N., 380
Sher, E., 417
Sheridan, M. D., 176
Sherif, C., 562
Sherif, M., 562
Sherman, P., 84
Sherwen, L. N., 133, 135, 136, 137
Sherwood, V., 215
Shi, R., 321
Shields, M. K., 103
Shields, P. M., 504
Shiffrin, R. M., 245
Shim, S. S., 496
Shin, D., 172, 223

Shiota, K., 122
Shipman, V. C., 291
Shipp, A. E., 555
Shipstead, S. G., 52, 53
Shirey, L., 366
Shirey, L. L., 242
Shoda, Y., 483, 505
Shonkoff, J. P., 300
Short, E. J., 251, 361
Shrum, W., 534
Shultz, T. R., 327, 342
Shumow, L., 383
Shutts, K., 318
Shweder, R. A., 65, 98, 174, 527
Sidel, R., 102
Siegal, M., 469
Siegel, D. J., 158, 507
Siegel, J. D., 171
Siegel, L. S., 368
Siegler, R. S., 14, 19, 44, 203, 204, 205, 240, 249, 264, 279, 318, 326, 328, 373, 374, 375, 380, 383
Siever, L., 435
Sigman, M., 290, 436
Sigman, M. D., 292
Signorielli, N., 471
Sikkema, K. J., 179
Silberstein, C. S., 388
Silk, J. S., 66
Silver, E. A., 257
Silverman, I. W., 506
Silverman, L. K., 524
Silverman, N., 530
Simard, M., 74
Simmons, D. C., 219
Simmons, R. G., 164, 165, 451
Simmons, T., 74
Simner, M. L., 536
Simon, D. J., 182, 186
Simon, V. A., 565
Simons, J., 490
Simons, R. L., 77, 78
Simons-Morton, B. G., 171
Simonton, D. K., 293
Simos, P. G., 158
Simpson, R. L., 574
Sims, L., 381
Sims, M., 57, 58
Sinatra, G. M., 387, 484
Sinclair, A., 421
Singer, B. R., 170
Singer, E., 525
Singer, J., 388
Singer, J. D., 323
Singer, L. T., 297
Sinnott, J. D., 203
Sipe, R. B., 340
Siraj-Blatchford, I., 578
Sirois, S., 327
Sisk, D. A., 336
Sitko, B. M., 373
Siu, S., 86
Sjostrom, L., 569
Skaalvik, E. M., 446
Skiba, R. J., 483
Skinner, B. F., 12, 18, 314, 482, 518
Skitch, S. A., 178
Skwerer, D. P., 318
Slater, A., 7
Slater, A. M., 236
Slaughter-Defoe, D. T., 475
Slavin, L. A., 95
Slavin, R. E., 222, 344, 345, 366, 501, 559, 560
Sleet, D., 451
Sleeter, C. E., 97, 99
Sloan, W. M., 580
Slonim, M. B., 338
Slotta, J. D., 384
Sluzenski, J., 261
Smart, C., 76
Smerdon, B. A., 387
Smetana, J. G., 69, 521, 523, 527

Smilek, D., 258
Smith, A. L., 171
Smith, C. L., 77, 157, 207, 208, 210, 257, 263, 389
Smith, C. M., 380
Smith, E., 578
Smith, E. G., 373
Smith, E. P., 572
Smith, H., 563
Smith, H. L., 328, 330, 334, 341, 347
Smith, H. V., 151
Smith, J., 46
Smith, J. S., 577
Smith, J. T., 117
Smith, L., 177, 473
Smith, L. B., 16, 148, 237
Smith, N. R., 392
Smith, P. B., 541
Smith, P. K., 171
Smith, P. R., 487, 490, 501
Smith, R. A., 184
Smith, R. E., 172
Smith, R. S., 403, 404
Smith, S. L., 582
Smith, S. W., 120
Smith, V. L., 348
Smitherman, G., 333, 334, 371
Smolkin, L. B., 503
Smoll, F. L., 172
Snedeker, J., 315
Snell, E. K., 19
Snider, S. A., 171
Snidman, N., 430
Snipper, A., 579
Snow, C., 315, 335, 344, 366, 369, 371
Snow, C. E., 35, 323, 344
Snow, C. W., 140
Snowling, M. J., 361, 364
Snyder, K. A., 238
Snyder, M., 580–581
Soberanes, B., 147
Society for Research in Child Development, 34
Soderstrom, M., 7
Sodian, B., 384
Soenens, B., 453, 496
Soet, J. E., 133
Sofronoff, K., 474
Solmon, M. A., 573
Solomon, B., 303
Solomon, D., 46, 48, 426, 487, 571, 573
Solomon, J., 411, 412
Sommerville, J. A., 466
Songer, N. B., 253
Sonnenschein, S., 332, 356
Sophian, C., 374
Sorensen, R., 566
South, D., 59, 59n
Southerland, S. A., 387
Sowell, E. R., 38, 39, 154, 155
Sowers, J. A., 499
Sparling, J., 37
Spear, L. P., 506
Spearman, C., 274
Spector, R. E., 136
Spelke, E. S., 261, 262, 295, 296, 318, 373, 380, 383, 386
Spence, M. J., 240
Spencer, C., 390
Spencer, C. A., 481
Spencer, C. J., 124
Spencer, M. B., 16, 35, 68, 95, 98, 447, 457, 459, 461, 465, 475
Spencer, S., 485
Spera, C., 364
Sperling, M., 373
Spicker, H. H., 306
Spinath, F. M., 8, 114, 348
Spinrad, T. L., 77, 422, 522, 535
Spirito, A., 438
Spitze, G., 69
Spivey, N., 252

Spivey, N. N., 328, 370, 371
Sprafkin, C., 382
Sroufe, L. A., 414, 415, 565, 566
Stack, C. B., 73
Stahl, S. A., 361, 365, 366, 390
Stangor, C., 472
Stanley, J. C., 42, 306
Stanovich, K. E., 295, 324, 357, 363, 365, 366, 367
Stanovich, K. G., 238
Staples, M., 383
Stark, D. R., 20
Starke, M., 161
Starr, N. B., 117
Starr, J. M., 137
Stattin, H., 165
Staub, D., 560, 586, 586n, 587
Staub, Debbie, 586
Staub, E., 536, 539
Staub, S. D., 560
Staudinger, U. M., 8
Staudt, M. M., 91
Stebbins, M. S., 305
Steckol, K. F., 348
Steele, C. M., 294, 298
Steele, D. F., 383
Steers-Wentzell, K. L., 219
Steffensen, M. S., 242
Steffler, D., 369
Stein, J. A., 266, 268, 568
Stein, M. T., 438
Stein, N., 422, 569
Stein, N. L., 360
Stein, S., 256
Stein, Z. A., 290
Steinberg, J., 69, 378, 383
Steinberg, L., 66, 77, 80, 149, 155, 157, 159, 168, 289, 457, 490, 496, 503, 581
Steinberg, M., 415
Steiner, H. H., 303
Stenberg, C., 419, 538
Stephan, K. E., 152
Stephens, B. R., 237
Stephenson, K. A., 356
Stephenson, K. M., 376
Stepsis, B. W., 124
Stern, B. M., 580
Stern, D. N., 411
Stern, E., 208
Stern, W., 284
Sternberg, K. J., 541
Sternberg, R. J., 93, 274, 275, 278, 279, 285, 286, 295, 297, 298, 299, 300, 301, 303, 308
Stetsenko, A., 464
Stevens, G., 343
Stevens, R., 545
Stevens, R. J., 222, 501
Stevens, T., 499
Stevenson, C. S., 84
Stevenson, H. W., 93, 96, 454, 457
Stevenson, J., 447
Stevenson, J. L., 473
Stevenson, L. M., 391
Stewart, A. D., 485
Stewart, A. J., 407
Stewart, B. E., 387
Stewart, J. C., 178
Stewart, L., 520
Stiffman, A. R., 438
Stiggins, R., 55
Stiles, J., 38, 316
Stiller, J. D., 415
Stillman, R. D., 328
Stimpson, V., 208, 385, 388, 389
Stipek, D., 224, 288, 455
Stipek, D. J., 437, 462, 494, 495, 497, 501, 505
Stocker, C., 448
Stodgell, C. J., 142
Stoltzfus, J., 95
Stone, B. J., 495
Stoneham, Z., 306
Stoneman, Z., 82

Storey, P., 166
Stormont, M., 305, 472
Story, R., 252
Story, T., 450
Stotsky, S., 358
Stouthamer-Loeber, M., 431, 540
Stowe, R. M., 535
Strahan, D. B., 509
Straits, S. A., 163
Strapp, C. M., 327
Strauch, B., 154, 155
Straus, M. A., 536
Strauss, A., 45
Strauss, L., 457
Strayer, F. F., 562
Streissguth, A. P., 161, 290, 306
Striano, T., 421, 489
Stright, A. D., 506
Strike, K. A., 253
Stromswold, K., 137
Strozer, J. R., 315, 343, 344
Stufkens, J., 252
Stuhlman, M., 84, 572
Stukas, A. A., Jr., 580–581
Styne, D. M., 162
Subotnik, R. F., 303
Subrahmanyam, K., 583
Succop, P. A., 290
Sudhalter, V., 326
Sue, D. W., 338
Sugawara, A. I., 528
Suh, J., 503
Suh, S., 503
Suhr, D. D., 44
Suina, J. H., 503
Sullivan, F. M., 174
Sullivan, H. S., 555
Sullivan, J. R., 511
Sullivan, M. W., 485
Sullivan, P., 204
Sullivan, R. C., 473
Sullivan-DeCarlo, C., 511
Sulzby, E., 358, 367
Suskind, R., 63, 64n, 71, 71n
Susman, E. J., 164, 535
Sussman, A. L., 80
Suttles, G. D., 556
Sutton-Smith, B., 215, 332, 554
Svetina, M., 204
Svirsky, M. A., 350
Swanborn, M. S. L., 324
Swann, W. B., Jr., 449
Swanson, H. L., 266, 286, 363, 375, 382
Swap, S. M., 86
Swartz, C. W., 501
Sweat, L., 340
Sweeney, J. A., 154, 239
Sweller, J., 264
Swim, J. K., 472
Swingley, D., 328
Switzky, H. N., 499
Sylva, K., 578
Sylvester, R., 425
Szbrybalo, J., 454
Szynal-Brown, C., 535

Tager-Flusberg, H., 318, 472
Taggart, B., 578
Tai, Y.-C., 374
Takahashi, K., 411
Takeuchi, A. H., 394
Takezawa, M., 522
Tallal, P., 348
Talwar, V., 331
Tamang, B. L., 507
Tamburrini, J., 386
Tamplin, A., 558
Tan, L. H., 364
Tan, P. Z., 413, 424
Tang, L. F., 92
Tannen, D., 346
Tanner, J., 563
Tanner, J. M., 118, 146, 147, 168
Tanner, M., 115
Tappan, M. B., 527

Tardif, C., 415
Tardiff, T., 467
Tarule, J. M., 83
Tarver, S., 471
Tate, T. L., 334
Tatum, B. D., 347, 458, 472, 534
Taumoepeau, M., 469
Taylor, A., 102
Taylor, B., 165
Taylor, C. L., 340
Taylor, D., 363
Taylor, D. M., 98, 344
Taylor, J. M., 177
Taylor, L., 89
Taylor, M., 250, 323
Taylor, M. A., 242
Taylor, R. D., 73, 471–472
Taylor, S. L., 241
Taylor, S. M., 104
Teachman, G., 535
Teale, W. H., 356
Tees, R. C., 328, 394
Teeter, P. A., 151
Tellegren, A., 430
Templeton, S., 340, 363, 371
Tenenbaum, H. R., 93
te Nijenhuis, J., 274
Tennenbaum, H. R., 455
Tenner, A., 179
Tennyson, R. D., 324
Teo, A., 363
Terenzini, P. T., 203
Terman, L. M., 284, 284n, 294
Terry, A. W., 517, 518, 529
Terry, R., 44
Tessner, C., 258
Tessner, K. D., 39, 155
Teti, D. M., 418
Thal, D., 316
Tharp, R., 217, 222
Tharp, R. G., 98, 338
Thelen, E., 16, 19, 148, 237
Théoret, H., 473
Thiede, H., 177
Thoermer, C., 384
Thoma, S., 521
Thoma, S. J., 525
Thomas, A., 294, 430, 431
Thomas, E., 323
Thomas, H., 169, 170
Thomas, J. W., 251
Thomas, K. E., 184
Thomas, K. M., 151, 154
Thomas, M. A., 572
Thomas, R. M., 396
Thomas, S., 491
Thompson, E. R., 522
Thompson, G., 574
Thompson, H., 361
Thompson, M., 296, 501
Thompson, P. M., 39, 151, 155, 157, 414, 422
Thompson, R. A., 70, 71, 77, 409, 410, 411, 412, 414, 416, 422, 449, 450, 521
Thompson, R. F., 149
Thompson, R. H., 334, 341
Thorkildsen, T. A., 528
Thorndike, R., 282, 294
Thorndike-Christ, T., 501
Thornton, J., 136
Thrash, T. M., 489
Thurlow, M. L., 503, 504
Tidball, G., 466
Tiedemann, J., 380
Tierney, R. J., 371
Tiggemann, M., 162, 456
Tiilikainen, S. H., 374
Timler, G. R., 475
Tincoff, R., 321
Tinglof, C. B., 83
Tinker, E., 318
Tisak, M. S., 521
Titmus, G., 558

Tiunov, D. V., 179
Tobias, S., 437
Tobin, J. J., 507
Todd, C. M., 247
Toga, A. W., 39, 151, 155
Tolani, N., 425, 435
Tomasello, M., 258, 317, 321, 332, 334
Tompkins, G. E., 361
Tong, S., 290
Tonks, S., 486
Torff, B., 391
Torquati, J. C., 86
Torrance, E. P., 298, 302
Torres-Guzmán, M. E., 98, 337, 344
Tossey, Sally, 426
Toth, S. L., 423, 435
Toth, V., 178
Touchstone, D., 104
Tourniaire, F., 209
Touwen, B. C. L., 159
Towsley, S., 430
Trabasso, T., 422
Trainor, L. J., 320, 393, 430
Trautner, H. M., 455
Trautwein, U., 446, 485
Travis, L. L., 327
Trawick-Smith, J., 98, 333, 336, 337, 338, 363, 371, 391, 393, 541
Treboux, D., 416
Treffert, D. A., 142, 393, 394, 473
Trehub, S. E., 393, 394
Trelease, J., 363
Tremblay, R. E., 483, 538, 577
Trevarthen, C., 258
Triandis, H. C., 65, 98, 413, 523, 527, 541
Trockel, M., 536
Trommsdorff, G., 496
Tronick, E. Z., 421
Troop-Gordon, W., 446
Trout, A., 437
Trout, J. D., 318
Trumbull, E., 554, 572, 573
Trzesniewski, K. H., 449, 451, 492
Tsai, Y.-M., 485
Tse, L., 345
Tsui, J. M., 303
Tubbs, M. E., 574
Tucker, B., 496
Tucker, C. J., 468
Tulviste, P., 8
Tunmer, W. E., 340
Turiel, E., 518, 521, 522, 523, 524, 525, 527, 528
Turkanis, C. G., 554, 572
Turkheimer, E., 289, 292
Turnbull, A. P., 182, 184, 302, 303, 306, 307, 348, 361, 363, 370, 437, 473, 474, 541, 561
Turnbull, B. J., 504
Turnbull, R., 182
Turner, E. D., 238
Turner, J. C., 365, 378, 481, 497, 499
Turner, K. L., 457
Turner, M. A., 95
Turner, R. N., 558
Turner, T. J., 330
Turnure, J. E., 238
Turrell, S. L., 469
Tusing, M. E., 281
Tversky, A., 469
Tye, L. C., 180
Tyler, S., 207
Tyner, B., 366
Tynes, B. M., 468
Tzeng, O., 364
Tzuriel, D., 286

Uchida, Y., 65
Udall, A. J., 305
Udell, W., 19

Udry, J. R., 566
Uesiliana, K., 254
Ullrich-French, S., 171
Umaña-Taylor, A. J., 459
Underwood, M. K., 540
Undheim, J. O., 285
Unger, C., 388
Upchurch, D. M., 179
Upton, L. R., 360
Uranga-Hernandez, Y., 286
Urban, J., 415
Urban, T. A., 239
Urbina, S., 285, 286, 287
Urdan, T., 445, 446, 489, 492, 500
Urdan, T. C., 415, 577
Usadel, H. C., 544
U.S. Census Bureau, 70, 71, 73, 74, 80
U.S. Department of Agriculture Food and Nutrition Service, 131
U.S. Department of Education, 179, 303, 344
U.S. Department of Education, Office of Civil Rights, 307
U.S. Department of Health and Human Services, 56, 74, 84
U.S. Department of Health and Human Services, Administration for Children and Families, 169, 579
U.S. Drug Enforcement Administration, 180
Utsey, S. O., 457
Uttal, D. H., 96, 242, 390, 391

Vachon, J., 74
Vadsay, P. F., 366
Vahn, V., 430
Vakili, D., 583
Valcárcel, J., 110
Valdés, G., 344, 345
Valdez, A. J., 564
Valente, E., 530
Valentine, J. C., 446, 498, 579, 580
Valeri, S., 438
Valiante, G., 372, 495, 499
Valiente, C., 422
Valkenburg, P. M., 582
Valli, L., 396, 397
Valoski, A., 169
Van Court, N., 468
VandeKamp, K. O., 508
Vandell, D. L., 579
Vandenberg, B., 215
Van den Bergh, B. R. H., 128
van den Broek, P., 260, 360
Van den Oord, E. J. C. G., 7
van der Heijden, P. G. M., 520
van der Molen, M., 238
Vanderwood, M., 274
Van Dooren, W., 203, 374, 380
van Dulmen, M., 565
Van Hesteren, F., 523
van Hof-van Duin, J., 139
Van Hoorn, J., 223
Van Hulle, C. A., 346
van Ijzendoorn, M. H., 414, 417
van Joolingen, W. R., 208
van Kraayenoord, C. E., 506
van Laar, C., 457, 497
Van Parys, M., 207
vanSledright, B., 390, 397
Vansteenkiste, M., 490, 496, 497
Van Winkle, L., 305
Varela, R. E., 95
Vargo, A., 458
Vasilyeva, M., 242, 380
Vasquez, J. A., 299
Vasta, R., 535
Vaughan, K., 359
Vaughn, B. E., 415, 483, 499
Vaughn-Scott, M., 339
Vavra, E., 340

Vazsonyi, A., 77
Veale, A., 54
Vedder, P., 490, 555
Veenema, S., 278
Veerman, J. W., 538
Veilleux, J., 178
Vella, D., 247
Veltman, M., 166
Venables, P. H., 484
Venter, J. C., 111
Verduin, K., 360
Vermeer, H. J., 381, 495
Vermeulen, K., 359
Verschaffel, L., 203, 222, 378
Vespo, J. E., 538
Vezeau, C., 450
Vida, M., 486
Vidair, H. B., 69
Vignau, J., 175
Vijayan, S., 326
Viken, R. J., 164
Villaruel, F. A., 92
Villegas, A. M., 96, 97, 100, 465
Vimpani, G., 290
Viola, J. J., 572
Vishton, P. M., 326
Vitaro, F., 483, 538, 539
Vlahovic-Stetic, V., 381
Voci, A., 558
Voelkl, K. E., 179
Voelz, S., 243
Vogel, G., 306
Vohs, K. D., 407, 451
Volker, M. A., 276
Volling, B. L., 418
Vollmer, T. R., 483
Volpe, S. L., 169, 170
Volterra, V., 332
Vong, K. I., 374
Vorrasi, J. A., 536
Vorrath, H., 543
Vosniadou, S., 262, 386
Vygotsky, L. S., 15, 19, 44, 193, 210, 211, 212, 213, 214, 215, 224, 226, 227, 228, 234, 260, 286, 388, 391, 448, 505

Waddington, C. H., 118
Wade, A., 76
Wagner, L. S., 179
Wagner, M. M., 307
Wagner, S., 243
Wahlsten, D., 12, 289
Wainright, J. L., 74
Waisbren, S. E., 117
Walczyk, J. J., 360
Waldfogel, J., 297, 575
Waldman, I. D., 290
Waldron, M., 292
Waldron, M. C., 70
Walk, R. D., 237
Walker, A., 184
Walker, A. R., 559
Walker, E., 152
Walker, H. M., 545, 546
Walker, K. C., 288
Walker, L. J., 525, 527
Walker, S. P., 160
Walker-Andrews, A. S., 421
Wall, S., 407
Wallace, C. S., 156
Wallace, G. L., 142, 393, 394, 473
Wallander, J. L., 165, 184
Wallerstein, J., 18
Wallerstein, J. S., 70
Walls, T. A., 486, 487

Walsh, D. J., 54
Walsh, M. E., 182
Walter, K. E., 580
Walters, G. C., 483
Walton, G. E., 237
Wang, C. K. J., 499
Wang, J., 381
Wang, P. P., 348
Wang, Q., 254, 259, 260, 456
Wanner, G., 483
Want, S. C., 254, 469
Ward, M., 544–545
Ward, R. A., 69
Ward, S. K., 496
Ward-Lonergan, J. M., 369
Warger, C., 545
Warner, D. E., 582–583
Warren, A. R., 347
Warren, S. T., 118
Warren-Leubecker, A., 336
Wartella, E., 582
Wartella, E. A., 582
Wartner, U., 413
Warton, P. M., 88
Waschbusch, D. A., 445, 446
Washington, George, 529
Wasik, B. A., 331, 346
Wassenberg, K., 334
Watahomigie, L. J., 335, 343
Waters, E., 407, 415, 416
Waters, H. S., 251
Watkins, D., 253, 254
Watson, J., 261
Watson, J. B., 18
Watson, J. J., 244
Watson, J. D., 110
Watson, M., 103, 487, 573
Watson, M. S., 46, 426
Watson, R., 224
Waxler, C. Z., 535
Waxman, S. R., 323
Way, N., 457
Wayland, K. K., 535
Waylor-Bowen, T., 185
Wearne, D., 383
Weaver, C., 365
Weaver, C. A., III, 359
Weaver-Hightower, M., 363, 372
Webb, N. M., 219, 226, 543
Webber, J., 511
Weber, E. K., 521, 523, 529
Webster-Stratton, C., 437
Wechsler, D., 282, 287, 294
Wehmeyer, M. L., 182, 495, 508
Weikart, D., 579
Weinberg, R. A., 290, 292
Weinberger, D. A., 563
Weiner, B., 491, 493, 494, 497, 501, 560
Weinert, F. E., 241
Weingarten, C. T., 133
Weinstein, R. S., 298, 574, 575
Weinstein, S., 178
Weinstock, J. S., 105
Weinstock, M., 252, 253, 257
Weintraub, M., 71
Weintraub, N., 367, 368, 371
Weisgram, E. S., 496
Weisman, S. E., 348
Weisner, M., 164
Weisner, T., 560
Weisner, T. S., 82
Weiss, B., 184
Weiss, L. G., 285
Weiss, M. J., 356
Wekerle, C., 565
Wellman, H. M., 18, 19, 250, 254, 261, 421, 467, 468, 472

Wells, D., 36
Welner, K. G., 577
Welsh, M. C., 248
Wember, Y. M., 169
Wenger, E., 217, 218, 447
Wenger, N., 323
Wentzel, K. R., 431, 487, 500, 501, 506, 524, 554, 555, 561, 572, 576
Werker, J. F., 321, 328, 343, 394
Werner, E. E., 403, 404
Werner, L. A., 7
Wernsman, J., 49
Wertsch, J. V., 8, 19, 215
Wesman, A. G., 381
West, J., 161
West, R. F., 295
Westenberg, P. M., 423
Westerfield, G., 445
Westerman, M. A., 422, 468
Whalen, C. K., 267
Whalen, T., 236–237
Whaley, S. E., 290, 292, 436
Wheatley, G., 489
Wheeler, K., 287
Whipple, E. E., 83
Whishaw, I., 316
Whitaker, D., 370
Whitaker, J. S., 297
Whitbeck, L. B., 77
White, B. J., 562
White, B. Y., 207, 208, 386, 389
White, C., 572
White, J. J., 244
White, K. J., 535
White, R., 484
Whitehurst, G. J., 316, 357, 365
Whitesell, N. R., 422, 447, 468, 487
Whiting, B. B., 103, 536, 541
Whiting, J. W. M., 536
Whitley, B. E., Jr., 492
Wickens, A., 149, 150, 151
Wieder, S., 473
Wiesel, T., 7
Wigfield, A., 93, 363, 381, 386, 445, 447, 450, 451, 452, 454, 462, 486, 487, 489, 492, 495, 496, 499, 501, 502, 576, 577
Wiig, E. H., 342
Wikland, K. A., 161
Wilcox, K. J., 430
Wilcox, S., 349
Wilder, A., 254
Wilhelm, O., 275
Wilkerson, B., 289, 293
Wilkerson, B., 289, 293
Willard, N. E., 584, 585
Willatts, J., 392
Willatts, P., 248
Williams, D., 473
Williams, D. E., 455
Williams, D. L., 473
Williams, J., 29, 184
Williams, K. K., 448
Williams, K. M., 536, 545
Williams, M., 254
Williams, P. E., 285
Williams, R. E., 559
Williams, R. W., 149
Williams, W. M., 292
Williamson, K., 29
Williamson, S., 518
Willig, A. C., 344
Willis, S. L., 203
Willows, D. M., 365
Wilson, A. J., 379–380
Wilson, B., 382, 393

Wilson, B. J., 582
Wilson, B. L., 55, 252, 490, 508
Wilson, C., 292
Wilson, D. K., 170
Wilson, G. D., 567
Wilson, H. K., 572
Wilson, L., 575
Wilson, M., 521
Wilson, M. N., 73
Wilson, P., 366
Wimmer, H., 363, 467, 468
Winberg, J., 236
Wind, R., 180
Windsor, J., 348
Wineberg, S. S., 390
Winebrenner, S., 306
Wing, R. R., 169
Winn, W., 583
Winne, P. H., 217, 253, 257, 462, 498, 497, 500
Winner, E., 142, 302, 303, 304, 305, 306, 330, 367, 391, 392, 393, 394, 473, 541
Winsler, A., 213, 345
Winston, P., 324
Winter, A., 392
Wise, S., 421
Wisenbaker, J. M., 366
Witherington, D., 408
Witkow, M. R., 36
Wittmer, D. S., 543
Wolak, J., 584
Wolcott, H. F., 44
Wolf, M., 358, 363
Wolfe, C. D., 316
Wolfe, D. A., 565
Wolfe, M. B. W., 390
Wolff, P. G., 140, 174
Wolford, J. I., 583
Wolock, I., 84
Woloshyn, V. E., 256
Wolters, C. A., 251, 446, 511
Wolters, P. L., 184
Wong, S. C., 465
Wood, A., 359
Wood, A. C., 119
Wood, B., 359
Wood, C., 359
Wood, D., 217, 222
Wood, D. N., 177
Wood, E., 256
Wood, G. A., 565
Wood, J. W., 509
Wood, T., 489
Woodring, L. A., 47
Woods, R. P., 258
Woodson, R., 237
Woodward, A. L., 323, 466
Woody, J. D., 566
Woolfe, T., 469
Woolley, J. D., 467
Woolverton, S., 104, 562
World Health Organization, 169
Worsham, M. E., 432
Wortley, S., 563
Wright, J. C., 582
Wright, S. C., 344
Wright, V., 44
WritersCorps, 439, 440, 477
Wrosch, C., 500
Wu, D. Y. H., 507
Wynbrandt, J., 117
Wynn, K., 373, 374, 380, 466
Wynn, S., 497

Xu, F., 267, 373, 380
Xue, Y., 97, 366

Yackel, E., 489
Yaden, D. B., Jr., 340, 363, 371
Yakolev, P. I., 153, 154, 157
Yarrow, M. R., 535
Yarushalmy, M., 382
Yates, M., 523, 529, 536
Yau, J., 521, 523
Yeager, E. A., 390, 474
Yeany, R. H., 262, 389
Yeung, A. S., 538
Yi, S., 259
Yilmaz, K., 474
Ying, Y.-W., 94
Yip, T., 458
Yirmiya, N., 472
Yoon, K. S., 38
Young, E. L., 285
Young, J. M., 137
Young, J. P., 366
Young, K. R., 511
Young, M. D., 583
Youngblood, J., II, 465
Young-Hyman, D., 184
Youniss, J., 88, 523, 529, 536, 558, 561
Yousef, F. S., 338
Ysseldyke, J. E., 560
Yu, H. C., 339, 491
Yurgelun-Todd, D. A., 155

Zachry, E., 75
Zahn-Waxler, C., 10, 421, 507, 522, 523, 526, 535, 536
Zajonc, R. B., 82
Zakin, D. F., 165
Zambo, D., 464, 484, 485, 495
Zamsky, E. S., 73
Zan, B., 525
Zarrett, N., 580
Zeanah, C. H., 412
Zeira, A., 469
Zeith, T. Z., 274
Zelazo, P. D., 239, 521
Zero to Three, 431
Zervigon-Hakes, A., 215
Zhang, H., 380
Zhang, L., 303
Zheng, X., 382
Zhou, M., 496
Zhou, Q., 423, 522, 525
Zhou, Y.-D., 374
Zhu, G., 472
Zhu, J., 380
Zhu, L., 472
Ziegert, D. I., 493, 499
Ziegert, J. C., 95
Ziegler, A., 384, 386
Ziegler, J. C., 364
Ziegler, S. G., 222
Zigler, E., 80, 291, 572, 578, 579
Zigler, E. F., 298, 580
Zilberbuch, S., 369
Zill, N., 72, 580
Zimbardo, P. G., 555
Zimmerman, B. J., 251, 252, 506, 507, 508
Zimmerman, M., 446
Zimmerman, M. A., 66
Zimmerman, R. R., 483
Zimmermann, P., 415
Zippiroli, L., 184
Zohar, A., 251
Zuckerman, G. A., 257
Zuckerman, M. U., 119
Zwaan, R. A., 360

Subject Index

Absolute pitch, 394
Abstract thought
  brain development and, 155
  cognitive-developmental theories
    and, 14
  formal operations stage and, 202, 203
  history and, 390
  intelligence tests and, 297
  interpersonal behaviors and, 534
  listening comprehension and, 330
  mathematics and, 374
  observations of, 209
  science and, 384
  speaking skills and, 334
Abstract words, 322–323
Academic achievement
  culture and, 93, 95–96
  elaboration and, 248
  epistemological beliefs and, 253
  family involvement and, 89
  giftedness and, 303, 304, 305
  intelligence and, 274
  IQ scores and, 285, 295
  late adolescence and, 23
  learning disabilities and, 266
  metacognitive awareness and, 251
  motivation and, 495
  peer relationships and, 555
  rest and sleep, 175
  second-language learning and, 343
  sense of self and, 447
Academic domains. See also Mathematics;
    Reading; Science; Writing
  art, 391–393
  case studies, 355, 399
  developmental issues and, 395–396
  epistemological beliefs and, 252, 253
  geography, 390–391
  history, 389–390
  intrinsic motivation and, 486–487
  motivation and, 495
  music, 393–394
  neo-Piagetian theories and, 206–207
  physical activity integrated into, 163
  sense of self and, 464
  standards in, 394, 396–397
Accommodation
  definition of, 196
  Piaget's cognitive development theory
    and, 196, 238
Acculturation, 94
Achievement goals, 488–489
Action research
  data collection and, 56–57
  definition of, 56
  ethical conduct and, 58
  professional practice and, 49–58
Active gene-environment relation, 120
Activity level, observation of, 429
Actual developmental level, 213, 286
Acupuncture, 134
Adaptability, observation of, 429
Adaptation, 273, 274, 278
Adaptive behavior, 306
Addiction, 178
Adolescence. See also Early adolescence;
    Late adolescence
  art and, 392
  attachment and, 410
  attention-deficit hyperactivity disorder
    and, 267
  brain development and, 154–155, 157
  cigarette smoking and, 177
  cognitive development and, 202–203
  comprehension monitoring and, 252
  eating disorders and, 169

eating habits and, 168
elaboration and, 248, 251
emotional development and, 422, 423
emotional regulation and, 422
epistemological beliefs and, 252
Erikson's psychosocial stages and, 405
gangs and, 564
gender and, 455–456
handwriting and, 368
health-compromising behavior and,
    177–178
injuries and, 184
language development and, 321, 326,
    332, 333, 333–334, 336
learned helplessness and, 493
long-term goals and, 490, 500
maps and, 391
mathematics and, 378, 382
metacognitive awareness and, 250
metalinguistic awareness and, 340
moral development and, 521, 522
peer relationships and, 333–334, 405
personalities and, 428
physical activity and, 171, 172
physical needs of, 165
reading development and, 356,
    360, 364
reciprocal influences and, 81
rest and sleep, 174–175
risky behaviors and, 155, 159, 164,
    165, 166
science and, 384, 388
self-handicapping and, 446
sense of self and, 447
sexual intimacy and, 565–566
thinking/reasoning skills and, 243
transition to secondary schools and,
    576–577
video games and, 582–583
writing and, 369, 370
Adolescent parents, 74–75, 131
Adoption
  family structure and, 73
  foster care and, 73–74, 76
Adoption studies, 289, 290–291, 292, 293
Adult activities, participation in,
    217–218, 219
Adults and adulthood
  attributions and, 494
  children's interacting with, 329, 336,
    337
  collaborative use of cognitive strategies
    and, 259–260
  communities and, 66
  Erikson's psychosocial stages and,
    405–406
  health-compromising behavior and, 178
  infant-directed speech and, 320
  language development and, 323
  moral development and, 521,
    525, 528
  personalities and, 431
  postformal stage and, 203
  scaffolding and, 217
  self-regulation and, 507
  sense of self and, 446
  social construction of meaning
    and, 216
  social construction of memory and, 259
  social skills and, 530
  Vygotsky's cognitive development
    theory and, 211–212, 213–214, 216,
    226–227
Affective states, 419, See also Emotions
Africa, 254
African American English, 346–347

African Americans
  confidence-building strategies of, 95
  culture and, 242
  dialects and, 346–347
  discrimination and, 95
  ethnic identity and, 457, 459
  figurative language and, 330, 334
  gender and, 94
  history and, 390
  intelligence and, 274, 297
  moral development and, 524
  motivation and, 298, 496
  narratives and, 333
  percentages of children as, 92
  reading and, 363
  socioeconomic status and, 298
  sociolinguistic behaviors and, 336,
    337–338
  students at risk and, 503
Afterbirth, 135
After-school programs, 163, 179, 579–581
Aggression
  beliefs about, 539
  child care and, 578
  child maltreatment and, 83
  conduct disorder and, 436, 437
  correlational studies and, 43
  cyberbullying and, 585
  definition of, 535
  developmental issues of, 540
  development of, 538–539
  emotional development and, 425
  experimental studies and, 42, 44
  gender and, 424, 535, 540
  interpersonal behaviors and, 534–539
  longitudinal studies of, 44
  naturalistic studies and, 45
  parenting styles and, 78, 536
  peer relationships and, 555–556
  physical aggression, 538, 540, 554
  puberty and, 164
  rest and sleep, 175
  self-care and, 80
  television and, 582, 584
  video games and, 582, 584
  violence and, 536, 546
Agreeableness, 431, 433
Alcohol
  brain development and, 151, 158
  fetal alcohol syndrome, 128, 158,
    290, 306
  health-compromising behavior and,
    177–178
  late adolescence and, 165
  motor skills and, 161
  puberty and, 164
  self-handicapping and, 445
  as teratogen, 128, 130, 131
Alice's Adventures in Wonderland
    (Carroll), 342
Alleles, 115
Amelia Bedelia Goes Camping
    (Parish), 340
American Alliance for Health, Physical
    Education, Recreation and Dance, 185
American Educational Research
    Journal, 49
American Journal of Health Behavior, 49
American Psychiatric Association, 435
American Sign Language, 315, 335, 344,
    349, 361
Amniocentesis, 129, 130
Amusia, 394
Analgesics, 136
Analysis, left hemisphere and, 151
Analytical intelligence, 278

Androgyny, 455
Anecdotal records, 52, 53
Anesthetics, 136
Angelman syndrome, 116
Anger, 419, 420, 422
Anorexia nervosa, 169, 170
Anxiety
  chronic illness and, 182
  definition of, 426
  emotional development and, 420, 423,
    424, 426
  emotional problems and, 436, 437
  IQ scores and, 298
  stranger anxiety, 409, 419
Anxiety disorders, 436, 437
Apgar Scale, 287
Apprenticeships, 218
Appropriation, 213
Aptitude tests, 285
Arab Americans, 336
Arithmetic operations, 374–378
Art, 391–393, 395–396
Articulation, 347
Asian Americans
  academic achievement and, 93, 95
  birth and, 136
  culture and, 65
  families and, 86, 93
  gender and, 94
  intelligence and, 274, 297
  interpersonal behaviors and, 541
  mathematics and, 381
  metacognition and, 254
  motivation and, 496
  parenting styles and, 77
  percentages of children as, 92
  questions and, 329
  sociolinguistic behaviors and, 336, 338
Asian Indians, 94
Asperger syndrome, 472–473, 574
Assessment of learning potential, 286
Assessments. See also Observations
  cultural bias in, 56, 297–298, 299
  as data collection technique, 37
  definition of, 37
  developmental assessments, 287
  distortions of information and, 41
  dynamic assessment, 286
  interpreting children's artifacts and
    actions and, 55–56
  varying conditions and, 221
Assimilation (cognitive)
  definition of, 94n, 196, 196n
  Piaget's cognitive development theory
    and, 196
Assimilation (culture), definition of, 94,
    94n, 196n
Associations, research design and, 43, 46
Associative play, 531
Athletics. See also Organized sports
  charting progress, 173
  individual athletic activities, 172
  sense of self and, 447, 455
Attachments
  attachment security and later
    development, 415–416
  attachment security origins, 411,
    413–414
  definition of, 407
  depression and, 435, 436
  developmental course of, 408–410
  developmental issues and, 427
  disorganized and disoriented
    attachment, 411, 412
  emotional development and, 407–419
  individual differences in, 410–411

Attachments, *continued*
  infant-caregiver relationship and, 407–411, 416
  insecure-avoidant attachment, 410, 412, 415
  insecure-resistant attachment, 410–411, 412, 415
  multiple attachments, 414–415, 418
  observation of, 412, 419
  research implications, 416–419
  secure attachment, 410, 412, 415, 418, 450, 565
  sense of self and, 450
Attention
  distractions and, 238
  exceptionalities in information processing and, 266, 267–268
  information processing theory and, 236, 238–239, 243–244, 258
  joint attention, 258, 530
  language development and, 316, 317, 331
  observation of, 265
  purposeful nature of, 238–239
Attention-deficit hyperactivity disorder (ADHD), 266–267, 472, 495
Attitudes towards books, 358
Attribution retraining, 502
Attributions
  attribution retraining, 502
  definition of, 491
  development of, 491–494
  distinguishing among, 492
  gender and, 495
  origins of, 493–494
  success and, 491, 492, 501–502
Audience
  composition skills and, 369
  imaginary audience, 451, 452, 468, 506, 534
Auditory processing, 276
Australia, 254
Authentic activities
  definition of, 222
  reading and, 357, 365
  science and, 388
  writing and, 372
Authoritarian parenting style
  collectivist culture and, 77
  definition of, 77
  prosocial and aggressive behavior, 536
Authoritative parenting style
  definition of, 77
  individualistic culture and, 78
  self-regulation and, 506
Authority figures, behavior towards, 98
Autism
  art and, 393, 473
  interpreting children's artifacts and actions, 142
  music and, 394
  social cognition and, 473–474
Autism spectrum disorders, 118, 142, 472–474, 541
Autobiographical self, 389, 450, 460
Automatization
  definition of, 239
  language development and, 317
  mathematics and, 379
  observation of, 265
  practice and, 245, 365
  reading and, 239, 359, 365, 366
  spelling and, 369
  word recognition and, 359
  working memory and, 239
  writing and, 368, 369
Autonomy
  autonomy versus shame and doubt stage, 405, 406, 407
  culture and, 496
  motivation and, 485, 488
Average children (peer acceptance), 555, 556, 557
Axons, 149

Babbling, 331, 349, 413, 530
Bar mitzvahs, 165

Barney & Friends, 544
Bat mitzvahs, 165
Bayley Scales of Infant Development (Bayley), 287
Behaviorism
  definition of, 12
  theoretical positions of, 18
Behaviors. *See also* Health-compromising behaviors; Interpersonal behaviors; Prosocial behavior; Sociolinguistic behaviors
  communities and, 66
  culture and, 65
  guidelines for, 544
Behaviors with books, 358
Beliefs. *See also* Epistemological beliefs
  culture and, 65
  false beliefs, 467
  theory theory and, 263
Bell Curve, The (Herrnstein & Murray), 297
Berenstain Bears' Trouble with Pets, The (Berenstain and Berenstain), 474
Between the Lions, 582
Bias. *See also* Prejudice; Stereotypes
  confirmation bias, 384–385, 389
  cultural bias, 56, 297–298, 299
  family communication and, 89
  hostile attributional bias, 436, 538
  social-cognitive biases, 469
Bicultural orientation, 94, 100
Bilingual education, 344–345
Bilingualism
  definition of, 343
  families and, 90
  language development and, 314, 332
  metalinguistic awareness and, 340, 342
  second language development and, 343–344
  sign language and, 349
  subtractive bilingualism, 345
Bill Nye the Science Guy, 582
Bioecological perspective, 16, 66, 68, 148–149
Biofeedback, 134
Biological theories
  children's theories of biology, 383–384
  definition of, 11
  theoretical positions of, 11–12, 18
Bipolar disorder, 435, 436, 546
Birth
  birth process, 134–135
  case studies, 109–110
  medical interventions, 135–137
  preparation for, 133–134
Birth order, 82
Bisexual individual, 455, 566, 567, 568
Black English Vernacular, 346–347
Blacks. *See* African Americans
Blastocyst, 122
Blended families, 72n
Blindness. *See* Visual impairments
Blue's Clues, 254, 582
Bodily-kinesthetic intelligence, 277
Body language, right hemisphere and, 151
Body proportions, 146, 161
Bosnia, 474
Boys. *See* Gender
Brain
  autism and, 473
  developmental changes in, 152–157
  development of, 38, 149–159, 205, 206, 211, 224, 240, 304, 469
  educational applications of research on, 155–159
  injuries to, 184, 277, 507
  malformations in, 151–152
  neural commitments and, 317
  prosocial behavior and, 535
  rest and sleep and, 174
  specific language impairments and, 348
  structures and functions of, 150–152
  temperament and, 430
Braxton Hicks contractions, 134
Brazil, 336, 381
Breastfeeding, 166
Breathing, 159

Broca's area, 315
Bronfenbrenner's bioecological model, 16, 66, 68, 148–149
Bulimia, 169
Bullies, 538, 560
Bullying behavior, 538, 546

Canalization, 118–119
Cardinal principle, 373
Caregivers. *See also* Professional practice
  attachment and, 411, 414, 415, 416
  eating habits and, 166, 168
  infant-caregiver relationship, 20, 137, 258, 291, 407–411, 416, 430, 489, 578
  joint attention, 258
  physical needs of infants, 163
  sense of self and, 446, 450
  sensitive periods and, 119
  teachers' communication with, 85–86
Caregiver speech, 320
Care orientation, 526–527
Caring School Community, 46, 48, 49
Carolina Abecedarian Project, 579
Case studies
  academic domains, 355, 399
  birth, 109–110
  child development, 3–4, 29
  cognitive development, 193, 228–229
  disabilities, 141–142
  emotional development, 403–404, 439
  families, 63–64, 105
  as form of naturalistic study, 44–45
  intelligence, 273, 309
  interpersonal behaviors, 517–518, 548–549
  language development, 313, 351
  moral development, 517–518, 548–549
  motivation, 481, 513
  physical development, 145, 187–188
  productive classroom environment, 553–554, 587–589
  research methods, 33, 59–60
  sense of self, 443–444, 476
Cattell-Horn-Carroll (CHC) theory of cognitive abilities, 275–277, 281
Causal relationships
  formal operations stage and, 202
  goal-directed behavior and, 198
  long-term memory and, 241
  narratives and, 332–333
  play and, 214–215
  research design and, 42–43, 46
  science and, 388
Cell phones, 581
Cells, 111
Central conceptual structures
  definition of, 206
  number and, 206, 375–378
Central executive. *See also* Cognitive strategies; Metacognition
  definition of, 236
  information processing theory and, 236, 239
Cephalocaudal trends, 159
Cesarean delivery, 134, 136
Challenging tasks
  learned helplessness and, 493
  memory limitations and, 250
  Piaget's cognitive development theory and, 224
  scaffolding and, 221, 222, 497
  self-efficacy and, 446
  sense of self and, 462
  Vygotsky's cognitive development theory and, 210–211, 213–214, 224, 250
Change. *See also* Qualitative/quantitative change
  conceptual change, 263, 389
Character education, evaluation of programs in, 46–49
Chat rooms, 583
CHC (Cattell-Horn-Carroll) theory of cognitive abilities, 275–277, 281
Checklists, 52, 54
Child abuse
  adoption and, 73
  brain development and, 158

child maltreatment, 83–84, 85, 91, 435
  eating disorders and, 169
  rest and sleep, 175
Child care
  attachment and, 415
  parents' employment and, 80
  physical activity and, 171
  services for children and, 578
Child development
  basic issues in, 5–11
  case studies, 3–4, 29
  definition of, 4
  developmental periods, 17, 19–23
  eclectic approach to, 16
  as field of inquiry, 4–5, 6
  professional practice and, 10–11, 23, 26–28
  theories of, 11–16, 18–19
Childhelp USA, 83
Childhood. *See also* Early childhood; Middle childhood
  brain development and, 157
  eating habits and, 168
  epistemological beliefs and, 252
  language development and, 316
  overweight youth and, 168–169
  physical development and, 159–165
  reading development and, 356
  rest and sleep, 174–175
Child maltreatment, 83–84, 85, 91, 435
Child Protective Services, 83, 84
Children who are gifted, 93, 303–305
Children with intellectual disabilities, 305–308
Children with special needs. *See also* Exceptionalities
  attachment and, 418
  empathy for, 560
  interpersonal behaviors and, 541
  physical activity and, 173
  rest and sleep, 175
  social cognition and, 472–474
China, 364, 387, 393, 424, 456, 458–459, 496, 541
Choices, self-regulation and, 508–509
Chorionic villus sampling (CVS), 129, 130
Chromosome abnormalities, 115, 116, 118, 129, 130, 137
Chromosomes, 110, 111, 112, 114, 114n, 121
Chronic illnesses, 182, 183–184, 185, 186
Cigarette smoking
  health-compromising behavior and, 176–177, 179
  puberty and, 164
Circuits, of neurons, 150, 151
Class inclusion, 195, 201, 203, 329n
Classroom climate
  routines and, 55, 432, 508
  sense of community and, 571–572
Cleft palate, 118
Clinical method, 194
Cliques, 563
Cocaine, 128, 131, 158, 177
Codominance, 115
Cognitive apprenticeships, 218
Cognitive development. *See also* Cognitive processes; Intelligence; Language development; Literacy; Piaget's cognitive development theory; Vygotsky's cognitive development theory
  case studies, 193, 228–229
  critique of contemporary approaches to, 263–264
  definition of, 5
  developmental trends, 24–25, 205, 236
  families' concerns about, 87–88
  information processing theory and, 236
  language development and, 318
  listening skills and, 330
  moral development and, 524
  nature/nurture and, 11, 264
  puberty and, 162
  qualitative/quantitative change and, 11, 264
  universality/diversity and, 8, 11, 264

Cognitive-developmental theories
  definition of, 13
  stage progressions of, 14
  theoretical positions of, 13–14, 18
Cognitive modeling, 221
Cognitive processes
  bodily sensations and, 158–159
  case studies, 233, 269
  facilitating, 243–245, 267–268
  information processing theory and,
    205, 234–245
  intelligence tests and, 297
  learning disabilities and, 266
  speed of, 239
  triarchic theory and, 278, 279
  Vygotsky's cognitive development
    theory and, 211
Cognitive processing speed, 276
Cognitive process theories
  definition of, 14
  theoretical positions of, 14–15, 19
Cognitive strategies
  collaborative use of, 259–260
  definition of, 245
  developmental trends in, 255–256
  group activities and, 219–221
  intelligence and, 301, 302
  learning strategies and, 247–248
  problem-solving strategies and,
    248–249, 256
  promoting development of, 254, 256–257
Cognitive tools
  of cultures, 212, 213
  definition of, 212
  maps and, 391
  social interactions and, 213
  Vygotsky's cognitive development
    theory and, 210–211, 212, 391
Cohabiting families, 68, 74
Cohort-sequential design, 44
Collaborative learning, 256
Collectivistic cultures, 65, 77, 93, 98, 414,
    424, 456, 496
Communities
  definition of, 65
  developmental issues and, 67
  influence of, 65–66
  knowledge of, 241
  resources of, 100–102
  types of, 100–101
Community of learners, 572
Community service activities, 529, 580–581
Compassion, 520, 527, 536, 544
Competence
  attributions and, 492
  emotional development and, 425
  motivation and, 484, 495
  social competence, 279, 532
Competition
  culture and, 541
  organized sports and, 171–172, 173
  secondary schools and, 576
  siblings and, 82
Composition skills, 369–370
Comprehension monitoring
  definition of, 251
  self-regulated learning and, 251–252
Computer metaphors, 234
Computers, 583–584
Conceptual change, 263, 389
Conclusions, ethical conduct and, 58
Concrete operations stage, 198, 199,
    201–202, 204
Concrete thought, 209
Conduct disorder, 436–437, 525, 541
Confidentiality, 58, 76
Confirmation bias, 384–385, 389
Conflict resolution
  aggression and, 536, 538
  interpersonal behaviors and,
    532–533, 544
  peer relationships and, 554, 558, 561
  play and, 532
Conscientiousness, 431, 433
Conservation
  concrete operations stage and, 201
  cultural effects on, 212

  definition of, 201
  preoperational stage and, 201, 203, 204
Conservation of liquid, 201, 244
Conservation of number, 201, 374
Conservation of weight, 201, 202
Constructivism
  definition of, 224
  information processing theory and, 234
  Kohlberg's moral development theory
    and, 518–519
  Piaget's cognitive development theory
    and, 195, 224, 234, 260
  reading comprehension and, 359
  sense of self and, 446
  syntactic development and, 327
  Vygotsky's cognitive development
    theory and, 224, 260
Content domains. See Academic domains
Contentment, 419
Contexts. See also Communities; Culture;
    Ethnic minority groups; Families; Media;
    Neighborhoods; Religion and religious
    groups; Socioeconomic status (SES)
  definition of, 5
  developmental issues and, 67
  developmental systems theories and,
    16, 17
  intelligence and, 299
  language development and, 328–329
  naturalistic studies and, 44–45, 47
  social contexts of development, 585
  triarchic theory and, 278–279
Contingent self-worth, 448, 454
Contrary-to-fact ideas, formal operations
    stage and, 202
Control groups, 42, 291
Controllable attributions, 491
Controversial children (peer acceptance),
    555, 556, 557
Conventional morality, 519
Conventional transgressions, 521
Cooing, 320, 331, 408, 413
Cooperation
  culture and, 299, 541
  play and, 531–532
  school traditions and, 573
  social skills and, 544
Cooperative activities
  interpersonal behaviors and, 543
  peer relationships and, 559
Cooperative play, 531–532
Coparents, 69, 70
Coping mechanisms, 95, 457, 458, 459,
    472, 536, 546
Core goals, 487
Co-regulated learning, 260
Correlational studies
  definition of, 43
  intelligence and, 290, 297
Correlation coefficients, 43, 46
Correlations, definition of, 43
Cortex
  adolescence and, 154, 155
  aggression and, 535
  attention and, 238
  definition of, 150
  early adolescence and, 162
  early childhood and, 237, 238
  infancy and, 153
  language development and, 315
  middle childhood and, 154
  specialization within, 150–151
Counting, 373–374, 382
Covert self-instruction, 221
Crack, 177
Creative intelligence, 278
Critical listening, 331
Critical periods, environmental factors
    and, 7, 8
Crossing-over of genetic material, 112, 114
Cross-linguistic differences, reading
    and, 364
Cross-sectional studies, 44, 49
Crying
  attachments and, 408, 413
  caregivers' response to, 425
  emotional regulation and, 422

  language development and, 320
  physical development and, 152
Crystallized intelligence, 275–276
Cultural bias, in assessments, 56,
    297–298, 299
Culturally responsive teaching, 97, 99
Culture. See also Ethnic minority groups;
    Sociocultural theories
  apprenticeships, 218
  art and, 393
  attachment security and, 411, 413–414
  birth and, 136
  cognitive development and, 204–205
  collectivistic cultures, 65, 77, 93, 98,
    414, 424, 456, 496
  definition of, 65
  depression and, 435
  developmental issues of, 67
  diversity and, 8
  dynamic assessment, 286
  emotional development and, 424, 426
  families and, 84, 86, 89
  gender and, 296
  history and, 390
  individualistic cultures, 65, 77–78, 98,
    413, 424, 456
  intelligence and, 274, 275, 292
  intelligence tests and, 296, 299
  interpersonal behaviors and, 541
  intersubjectivity and, 259
  language development and, 226,
    318, 320
  maps and, 391
  mathematics and, 381–382
  moral development and, 527–528
  motivation and, 496–497
  multiple intelligences and, 277–278
  music and, 394
  narratives and, 333
  play and, 215
  prosocial and aggressive behavior, 536
  puberty and, 165
  questions and, 329
  rest and sleep and, 174
  schemas and scripts and, 242
  science and, 387
  self-regulation and, 507
  sense of self and, 456–457, 465
  social cognition and, 472
  social construction of memory and, 259
  sociolinguistic behaviors and, 336–338
  teacher expectations and, 96–97
  theory theory and, 262
  Vygotsky's cognitive development
    theory and, 212, 227
  writing and, 372
Culture shock, 339
Curiosity, 302, 484
CVS (chorionic villus sampling), 129, 130
Cyberbullying, 585
Cystic fibrosis (CF), 117, 182

Dance Dance Revolution, 583
Data collection
  accuracy in, 40, 42, 50
  action research and, 56–57
  distortions in, 41
  interpreting assessments and, 55–56
  listening to children and, 54–55
  observations and, 38–40, 50–53
  physiological measures, 38
  self-reports, 36–37
  teachers and, 49–58
  techniques of, 36–42
  tests and assessment tasks, 37
Dating, 564–565
Decision/reaction speed, 276
Definitions, fostering semantic
    development, 324
Delay of gratification, 483, 495, 503, 504
Delinquency
  aggression and, 539
  parenting styles and, 78
Dendrites, 149
Depression
  child maltreatment and, 83
  chronic illness and, 182

  definition of, 435–436
  eating disorders and, 169
  emotional development and, 424,
    435–436
  gender and, 424, 435, 456
  romantic relationships and, 565
  sleep and rest, 175
  suicide and, 436, 438
  victims of aggression and, 539
Depth perception, 156, 237
Despair, 406, 407
Developmental assessments, 287
Developmental domains, organization of, 5
Developmentally appropriate practice. See
    also Professional practice
  action research and, 57
  attention and, 245
  before- and after-school programs
    and, 581
  children from culturally and linguistically
    diverse backgrounds, 96
  commitment to, 28
  definition of, 23
  discovery learning and, 208
  elementary/secondary school transition
    and, 577
  English language learners, 345
  family communication and, 91
  giftedness and, 306
  guidelines for, 26
  hearing impairments and, 350
  infant and toddler care and, 417
  infant stimulation, 244
  intellectual disabilities and, 307
  listening skills and, 331
  newborn infants' needs and, 138
  phonological awareness and letter
    recognition, 359
  physical needs of adolescents, 165
  physical needs of infants and
    children, 163
  reading comprehension and, 361
  scaffolding and, 222
  self-regulation skills and, 512
  social goals and, 501
  social perspective taking and, 474
  social skills and, 544
  specific language impairments and, 348
  students at risk and, 504
Developmental periods. See also
    Adolescence; Adults and adulthood;
    Childhood; Early adolescence; Early
    childhood; Infancy; Late adolescence;
    Middle childhood
  child development and, 17, 19–23
Developmental strengths, 27
Developmental studies, 44
Developmental systems theories
  contexts and, 16, 17
  definition of, 15
  Spencer's identity development model
    and, 459, 461–462
  theoretical positions of, 15–16, 19
Developmental trends
  accomplishments and diversity of,
    24–25
  chronic health conditions, 183–184
  cognitive development and, 24–25,
    205, 236
  in cognitive strategies, 255–256
  emotional and personal development
    and, 434
  families' concerns for children, 87–88
  in interpersonal behaviors, 530–534,
    542–543
  in intrinsic motivation, 485–487
  in IQ scores, 293, 294, 295
  language skills, 340–341
  in mathematics, 379–380
  in metacognition, 255–256
  in moral development, 521–522, 523
  in motivation, 498–499
  in peer relationships, 570–571
  in perception, 236–237
  physical development and, 24–25,
    167–168
  in prenatal development, 132

Developmental trends, *continued*
   quantitative changes and, 9
   in reading, 362–363
   in science, 386
   in self-regulation, 504–506
   in sensation, 236–237
   sense of self and, 463
   social cognition and, 470
   social-emotional development and,
      24–25
   thinking/reasoning skills, 225, 242–243
   in writing, 371
Dialects, 346–347, 348
Differentiation
   definition of, 146
   physical development and, 146–147
Disabilities. *See also* Children with special
      needs; Intellectual disabilities; Learning
      disabilities; Special physical needs
   attachment security and, 414
   case studies, 141–142
   chromosome abnormalities and, 115
   motivation and, 495
   nature/nurture and, 120
   peer relationships and, 186
   poverty and, 102
Discovery learning, 207–208
Discrimination
   culture and, 27
   ethnic minority groups and, 95, 97,
      100, 457–458, 459
   intelligence and, 298
   interpersonal behaviors and, 534
   neighborhoods and, 95, 100–101
   sexual harassment as, 569
   social cognition and, 471–472
Disequilibrium
   challenge and, 224, 263
   definition of, 197
   discovery learning and, 208
   moral development and, 525, 529
   motivation and, 209–210, 484
   social interaction and, 226
Disgust, 420
Disorganized and disoriented attachment,
   411, 412
Dispositions, intelligence tests and,
   299–300
Distractions, 238
Distress, 419
Distributed intelligence, 279–280, 281,
   301–302
Distributive justice, 522
Diversity. *See also* Ethnic minority groups;
      Gender; Socioeconomic status (SES);
      Universality/diversity
   chronic health conditions and, 183–184
   in cognitive strategies, 255–256
   cognitive tools and, 212
   definition of, 8
   in development, 8–9
   developmentally appropriate practice
      and, 27
   early adolescence and, 22
   families and, 75–76
   giftedness and, 303
   in information processing abilities, 246
   in interpersonal behaviors, 539–541
   in IQ scores, 294
   in language development, 340–341,
      346–347
   in mathematics development, 379–382
   in metacognition, 253–254
   in moral development, 523, 525–528
   in motivation, 495–497
   physical activity and, 172–173
   in physical development, 167–168
   prenatal development and, 132
   in reading development, 361, 363–364
   of research participants, 35, 47, 49
   in romantic relationships, 568
   in science development, 385, 386, 387
   in self-regulation, 507–508
   in sense of self, 454–459, 461–462
   in social cognition, 472–474

in theory of mind, 472–473
   thinking/reasoning skills and, 225
Divorce
   attachment and, 418
   family structure and, 70–71, 75–76
Dizygotic twins, 114, 288–289, 535, 567
DNA, 110, 111, 121
Dominance hierarchies, 562–563
Dominant genes, 115
Dora the Explorer, 582
Down syndrome
   attachment and, 418
   genetics and, 115, 116
   injuries and, 184
   intellectual disabilities and, 306, 307–308
   IQ scores and, 288
   Williams syndrome compared to,
      318, 320
Drugs
   brain development and, 151, 158
   health-compromising behavior and,
      177–178, 179, 180
   late adolescence and, 165
   puberty and, 164
   rest and sleep, 175
   self-handicapping and, 445
   as teratogens, 128, 131, 132
Dual-immersion programs, 344
Duchenne muscular dystrophy, 117
Dynamic assessment, 221, 286
Dyscalculia, 379
Dyslexia, 361, 363, 464

Early adolescence
   after-school programs and, 80
   attachment and, 415
   chronic health conditions in, 183
   cognitive development and, 25,
      202–203
   cognitive strategies and, 255
   developmental features of, 17, 22
   developmentally appropriate practice
      and, 26
   emotional development and, 434
   ethnic identity and, 457
   families' concerns about, 88
   friendships and, 559
   information processing abilities
      and, 246
   interpersonal behaviors and,
      533–534, 542
   IQ scores and, 294
   language development and, 316
   language skills and, 341
   mathematics and, 380
   metacognitive awareness and, 255
   moral development and, 523
   motivation and, 499
   peer relationships and, 533–534, 570
   physical development and, 22, 25,
      162–165, 167
   professional viewpoints on, 22
   reading and, 362
   science and, 386
   sense of self and, 451–452, 463
   social cognition and, 470
   social-emotional development and, 25
   television viewing and, 582
   theory of mind and, 468
   thinking and reasoning skills, 225
   writing and, 371
Early childhood
   aggression and, 538, 540
   art and, 391–392, 393
   attachment and, 409, 415
   attention and, 238
   brain development and, 152–154
   chronic health conditions in, 183
   cognitive development and, 24, 203
   cognitive strategies and, 255
   concepts of illness, 182
   developmental features of, 17,
      20–21, 21n
   developmentally appropriate practice
      and, 26

elaboration and, 248
emotional development and, 421,
   422, 434
emotional regulation and, 423
Erikson's psychosocial stages and, 405
families' concerns about, 87
friendships and, 558
geography and, 390
giftedness and, 304
information processing abilities
   and, 246
intelligence tests and, 286–288
interpersonal behaviors and, 530–532,
   539, 542
IQ scores and, 294
language development and, 8, 20, 119,
   321, 325, 326, 328, 332, 336
language skills and, 341
learned helplessness and, 493
long-term memory and, 240
mathematics and, 375–378, 379, 382
metacognitive awareness and, 249–250,
   254, 255
metalinguistic awareness and, 340
moral development and, 521, 522, 523
motivation and, 485, 498
music and, 393, 394
overweight youth and, 69
peer relationships and, 570
phonological awareness and, 357
physical activity and, 171, 172, 173
physical development and, 20, 24,
   159–161, 167
Piaget's cognitive development theory
   and, 196, 199–201
play and, 223
professional viewpoints on, 20–21
reading and, 357, 362
reciprocal influences and, 81
rest and sleep, 174–175
romantic relationship awareness
   and, 564
science and, 386, 387
self-regulation and, 503–512
sense of self and, 450, 463
siblings and, 82
social cognition and, 470
social-emotional development and, 24
television viewing and, 582
theory of mind and, 467
theory theory and, 262, 383
thinking and reasoning skills, 225, 243
toxic substances and, 290
writing and, 367–368, 371, 372
Early childhood intervention programs,
   37, 291, 297, 300, 578–579
Early-maturing boys, 164, 165
Early-maturing girls, 164, 165
Eating disorders, 164, 169–170, 456
Eating habits. *See also* Nutrition
   infancy and, 160, 166
   late adolescence and, 23
   observation guidelines, 181
   overweight youth and, 168–169
   physical well-being and, 166, 168–171
   promoting good eating habits, 170–171
Ebonics, 346–347
Ecstasy (drug), 177
Education. *See also* Schools
   bilingual education, 344–345
   character education, 46–49
   family's involvement in, 79, 89–90,
      91, 93
   sex education, 566, 568
Effortful control, 430, 431
Egocentrism
   language development and, 332
   preoperational stage and, 200, 200n, 226
   theory of mind and, 467n
Elaboration
   definition of, 248
   giftedness and, 304
   as learning strategy, 248, 251, 256
   long-term memory and, 236
   modeling of, 257

Elementary schools, transitions to, 575–576
ELLs (English language learners), 97, 344,
   345, 366
E-mail, 90, 583
Embryonic period, 122–123, 126
Embryos, 121, 122–123, 132
Emergent literacy, 356–357, 358, 363, 366
Emotional abuse, 83
Emotional contagion, 419, 421
Emotional development. *See also* Emotions
   attachments and, 407–419
   case studies, 403–404, 439
   developmental issues in, 427
   Erikson's psychosocial development
      theory, 404–407
   problems in, 435–438
   promotion of, 425–427
   temperament and personality, 428–434
Emotional intensity, observation of, 429
Emotional regulation
   development of, 422–423
   modeling of, 427
   self-regulation and, 504
Emotional support, 554, 557–558, 568
Emotions
   age-appropriate outlets for, 426
   brain development and, 155, 158
   definition of, 419
   developmental changes in, 419,
      421–423
   gender and, 93, 423–424
   group differences in, 423–425
   moral development and, 520–521, 522
   physical development and, 165
   promoting emotional development,
      425–427
   puberty and, 162
   reciprocal influences and, 81
   right hemisphere and, 151
   romantic relationships and, 565
   self-conscious emotions, 161, 165, 421
   siblings and, 82
Empathic orientation, 537
Empathy
   emotional development and, 423
   moral development and, 522
   peer relationships and, 560
   prosocial behavior and, 536
England, 424
English language
   cultural bias and, 297
   English language development
      standards, 396
   intelligence tests and, 284
   language barriers and, 96
   limited proficiency in, 92, 503
   listening skills and, 328
   parents and, 90, 91
   questions in, 325–326
English language learners (ELLs), 97, 344,
   345, 366
Entity view of ability, 492, 495
Environmental factors. *See also*
      Nature/nurture
   anxiety disorders and, 436
   assessment of, 56
   behaviorism and, 12
   bioecological perspective and, 16
   children's natural tendencies affecting, 8
   depression and, 435
   emotional development and, 425
   gender and, 455
   genetic expression influenced by, 111,
      112, 114, 119–120, 292–293
   infancy and, 20
   information processing theory and,
      234–235
   intelligence and, 290–292
   interaction with heredity, 7–8, 111, 114,
      119–121, 292–293
   mathematics and, 380–381
   moral development and, 521
   physical development and, 148–149
   prosocial and aggressive behavior,
      535–536

self-regulation and, 506–507
sexual orientation and, 567
temperament and, 430
theory of mind and, 469
Epidural analgesia, 136
Epistemological beliefs
attributions and, 492
definition of, 252
developmental changes in, 253
geography and, 390
metacognition and, 252–253, 378
observation of, 265
promoting development of, 257
science and, 383, 385, 387
Equilibration, 197
Equilibrium, 197
Erikson's psychosocial development
theory
contemporary perspectives on, 406
developmental research related to, 407
emotional development and, 404–407
as psychodynamic theory, 13, 404
psychosocial stages of, 404–406
as stage theory, 9
Ethical conduct
action research and, 58
experimental studies and, 42–43, 42n
research methods and, 34
Ethics Curriculum for Children, 46, 48, 49
Ethnic identity
coping mechanisms and, 95, 457, 458,
459, 472
definition of, 95, 457
multiethnic identity, 93, 458–459, 465
observation of, 461
social cognition and, 472
Spencer's identity development model
and, 459, 461–462
Ethnicity
definition of, 92
families and, 93, 457
influence of, 92–93
race compared to, 93
socialization and, 93
Ethnic minority groups
academic achievement and, 95–96
challenges facing, 95
cigarette smoking and, 177
creating supportive environment for,
96–100
diversity within, 97
interpersonal behaviors and, 541
IQ scores and, 297–298, 299
language development and, 346–347
mathematics and, 381–382
moral development and, 527–528
motivation and, 496–497
percentages of children belonging
to, 92
reading and, 363–364
respect for, 99, 100
science and, 387
self-efficacy and, 498–499
sense of self and, 457–459, 465
social cognition and, 471, 472
stereotypes and, 89
television and, 582
Ethnographies, 44, 49
Ethological attachment theory, 407, 483
Etiquette, 336, 339
European Americans
academic achievement and, 93
cigarette smoking and, 176–177
culture and, 65, 242
ethnicity and, 457
history and, 390
intelligence and, 297
motivation and, 496
percentages of children as, 92
as research participants, 35
sense of self and, 456, 457
socioeconomic status and, 298
sociolinguistic behaviors and, 336–338
Evocative gene-environment relation,
119–120

Evolution, concept of, science and, 387
Evolutionary perspectives
language development and, 317–318
perceptual development and, 237
prosocial and aggressive behavior, 535
Examples, fostering semantic
development, 324
Exceptionalities. See also Children with
special needs
giftedness and, 303–305
in information processing, 266–268
in intelligence, 303–308
in language development, 347–350
Executive functions
brain development and, 158
definition of, 150
information processing theory
and, 236
learning disabilities and, 266
self-regulation and, 506
theory of mind and, 469
Existential intelligence, 277, 277n
Expansion, definition of, 327
Expecting Adam (Beck), 307–308
Experiences
effects of, 12, 203–204
knowledge base and, 241
listening to children and, 54–55
perceptual development and, 237
Piaget's cognitive development theory
and, 195, 226
speaking skills and, 334
talking with children about, 260
triarchic theory and, 278, 279
Vygotsky's cognitive development
theory and, 226
Experimental studies
definition of, 42
ethical conduct and, 42–43, 42n
research design and, 42–43
Experimentation
Piaget's cognitive development theory
and, 207–208
sensorimotor stage and, 200
Exploration of objects, 200, 207
Exploratory play, 223
Expressive language, 320
Extended families, 72–73
External attributions, 491
Extracurricular activities, 75, 99–100, 101,
175, 579–581
Extraversion, 431, 433
Extraversion/surgency, 428, 430, 431
Extrinsic motivation
appropriate use of, 502–503
definition of, 482
developmental issues of, 494
factors affecting, 482–483
Eye contact, 316, 336–337

Facial expressions, 421–422, 450
Faded, overt self-guidance, 221
Failures, 424, 446, 491, 492, 500–502
Fairness, 522
Fallopian tubes, 121
False beliefs, 467
Familiarity
attention and, 238
reasoning skills and, 210
triarchic theory and, 279
Families. See also Parents
case studies, 63–64, 105
children's influences on families, 80–83
definition of, 64
developmental issues in, 67
developmental trends and, 87–88
diversity in family structure, 75–76
eating habits and, 168
emotional development and, 424
ethnicity and, 93, 457
extended families, 72–73
families' influences on children,
76–80, 86
family processes, 76–91
heads of, 74–75

homeless families, 86, 101, 104, 168
peer relationships and, 560
prosocial and aggressive behavior
and, 536
risk factors in, 83–84
siblings and, 82–83
socioeconomic status of, 101
stepfamilies, 71–72, 72n
structure of, 68–76
teachers' partnerships with, 84–86,
89–91
transitions in, 75–76
Family structure, 68–76, 84
Fast mapping, 323
Fathers. See also Parents
attachment and, 413, 414
divorce and, 70
family structure and, 69
prenatal development and, 126, 128, 131
teachers' communication with, 75
Fear, 237, 408–409, 414, 419, 420, 428
Feedback
biofeedback, 134
language development and, 324,
328, 334
self-determination and, 502
self-regulation and, 508
sense of self and, 464
sociolinguistic behaviors and, 339
Fetal alcohol syndrome (FAS), 128, 158,
290, 306
Fetal period, 126
Fetoscope, 130
Fetuses, 121, 123–124, 132, 139
Field trips, 104, 387
Figurative speech, 329–330, 333, 334
Fine motor skills, 160, 161, 163, 372
First Amendment, 529–530
First Choice program, 179
First stage of labor, 134, 135
Flaming, 583
Fluency, 347
Fluid intelligence, 275–276
Flynn effect, 290, 292
Forebrain, 150
Foreclosure, identity and, 452–453
Formal operations stage, 198, 199,
202–203, 204, 374
Formal schooling
intelligence and, 291–292
mathematics and, 382
Vygotsky's cognitive development
theory and, 212, 292
Foster care, 73–74, 76, 291, 418
Fourth stage of labor, 135
Fragile X syndrome, 118, 472
Fraternal twins, 114, 288–289, 535, 567
Friendships, 556–561, See also Peer
relationships
Frog and Toad Are Friends (Lobel), 426
Functionalism
definition of, 318
language development and,
317–318, 319
Functions (in Vygotsky's theory), 211
Function words, 321
Future selves, 445, 490

g
Cattell-Horn-Carroll theory of cognitive
abilities, 275
definition of, 275
intelligence theories compared to, 281
IQ scores and, 277
theoretical perspective of, 274–275
Gametes, 112–114
Gang prevention programs, 564
Gangs, 547, 548–549, 563–564
Gardner's multiple intelligences, 277–278,
281, 300–301
Gay and lesbian individuals. See
Homosexual individuals
Gay parents, 74, 75
Gender
depression and, 424, 435, 456

emotional development and, 93,
423–424
emotional regulation and, 423
Erikson's psychosocial development
theory and, 406
genetics and, 114
giftedness and, 93, 305
intelligence tests and, 295–296
interpersonal behaviors and, 539–541
language development and, 346
mathematics and, 296, 380–381
moral development and, 524, 525–527
motivation and, 495–496
physical development and, 146, 161
puberty and, 22, 162, 163
reading and, 363
science and, 93, 387
sense of self and, 451, 454–456, 464
socialization and, 93–94, 540
stereotypes of, 93, 380, 424,
455–456, 495–496
verbal ability and, 295, 296
video games and, 582–583
writing and, 372
Gender schemas, 454, 460
General factor, intelligence and, 274–275
Generalized anxiety disorder, 436
Generativity versus stagnation stage,
405, 407
Genes
definition of, 110
dominant and recessive genes, 115
influence of, 118–119
operation of, 111–112
structure of, 110–111
Genetic counseling, 126, 130
Genetic disorders, 115, 116–117, 118
Genetics. See also Heredity
autism and, 473
children's natural tendencies affecting, 8
depression and, 435
environmental factors influencing, 111,
112, 114, 119–120, 292–293
formation of reproductive cells and,
112–114
individual traits and, 114–115, 118
influence of genes, 118–119
intellectual disabilities and, 306
motivation and, 495
nature/nurture and, 120–121, 125
operation of genes, 111–112
physical development and, 146
puberty and, 164
sense of self and, 447
sexual orientation and, 567
structure of genes, 110–111
temperament and, 430
Geography, 390–391, 395–396
Germany, 413
Germ cells, 112
Gestures, 243, 244, 316, 320, 332, 334, 335
Giftedness
characteristics of children with, 303–304
definition of, 303
fostering development of children with,
304–305
gender and, 93, 305
interpersonal behaviors and, 541
reading and, 361
writing and, 370
Girls. See Gender
Glial cells, 150
Goal-directed behavior
definition of, 198
motivation and, 487
Goals
achievement goals, 488–489
long-term goals, 490, 500
mastery goals, 488–489, 491, 492,
496, 500
motivation and, 487–491, 500
multiple goals, 490–491
self-handicapping and, 445
self-regulation and, 504
social goals, 489–490, 501

Grammatical rules, 328, 347, 369
Grammatical words, 321, 322, 325
Grandparents, 72–73, 80
Gravity, children's understanding of, 384
Gross motor skills, 159–161
Grounded theory studies, 45
Group activities, 219–221, 431–432, 559
Group discussions, 366, 383
Group play, 223
Growth curves, 147
Growth spurts, 146, 162
Guided participation
    culture and, 217–218
    definition of, 79, 217
Guilt
    definition of, 521
    emotional development and, 421
    initiative versus guilt stage and,
        405, 407
    moral development and, 521–522

Habituation
    definition of, 38
    interest and, 247, 275
    language development and, 327
    mathematics and, 374
Hacking, 583
Handwriting, 161, 368
Happiness, 419, 420
Hatha yoga, 134
Heads of family, 74–75, 79, 80, 86, See
    also Parents
Head Start, 291, 578–579
Health care, 101, 296
Health-compromising behaviors
    addressing, 179–181
    cigarette smoking and, 176–177, 179
    observation guidelines, 181
    physical well-being and, 176–181
    sexual activity and, 177, 178–181
    substance abuse and, 177–178, 179
Health emergencies, 186
Hearing loss/impairments
    intelligence tests and, 284
    language development and, 315, 349
    reading development and, 361
Hedonistic orientation, 537
Heredity. See also Genetics
    gender and, 455
    intelligence and, 288–289, 293
    interaction with environmental factors,
        7–8, 111, 114, 119–121, 292–293
    maturation and, 6
    prosocial and aggressive behavior, 535
    specific language impairments and, 348
Heroin, 128
Herpes simplex, 128
Heterosexuals, 566, 567
Hidden curriculum, 573, 587
Hierarchical stages
    neo-Piagetian theories and, 207
    stage theories and, 9, 10, 197
Higher mental functions, 211
High-interest literature, 366
Hindbrain, 150
Hindu culture, 527
Hispanic Americans
    birth and, 136
    confidence-building strategies of, 95
    ethnic identity of, 457, 459
    families and, 93
    intelligence and, 297
    moral development and, 524
    motivation and, 298
    percentages of children as, 92
    questions and, 329
    reading and, 363–364
    socioeconomic status and, 298
    sociolinguistic behaviors and, 336,
        337–338
    students at risk and, 503
Historical time, 209, 389
History, 389–390, 395–396, 426, 529
HIV/AIDS, 128, 131, 166, 177, 178–181,
    182, 568
Hmong, 136

Holophase, 325
Home environments. See also Families;
    Parents
    intelligence and, 290–291
Homeless families, 86, 101, 104, 168
Home visiting programs, 91
Homework completion, 175
Homosexual individual, 455, 566, 567–568
Homosexual parents, 74, 75
Hormones
    aggression and, 535, 540
    birth process and, 134
    depression and, 435
    emotional development and, 424
    environmental/hereditary interaction
        and, 120
    gender and, 455
    intelligence tests and, 296
    mathematical development and, 380
    prenatal development and, 122, 123
    puberty and, 162, 164
    rest and sleep and, 174
Hostile attributional bias, 436, 538
Housing, 101
Huntington disease (HD), 117
Hurricane Katrina, 474
Hyperactivity, 266, 268
Hyperbole, 330, 333, 335
Hypothesis testing, 202, 384–385
Hypothetical ideas, formal operations
    stage and, 202, 203

Idealism, 202, 209
Identical twins, 114, 288–289, 290, 293,
    535, 567
Identification phase, 505
Identity. See also Ethnic identity; Sense of
    self
    definition of, 452
    Erikson's psychosocial development
        theory and, 9, 406
    moral development and, 524
    motivation and, 485
    observation of, 460
    peer relationships and, 555
    Spencer's model of identity
        development, 459, 461–462
Identity achievement, 452
Identity diffusion, 452
Identity versus role confusion stage,
    405, 407
Imaginary audience
    definition of, 451
    interpersonal behaviors and, 534
    self-perception and, 451, 452, 506
    theory of mind and, 468
Imitation
    language development and, 314
    mirror neurons and, 258
    sense of self and, 450
    sensorimotor stage and, 200
    sociolinguistic behaviors and, 339
Immersion
    definition of, 344
    teaching second language and,
        344–345
Immigrants
    academic achievement and, 95
    bicultural orientation and, 94, 100
    diversity among, 97
    emotional development and, 425
    immigration patterns, 92
    interpersonal behaviors and, 541
    orienting to mainstream society, 96
    prenatal care and, 131
    reading and, 363–364
    social change and, 94
    socioeconomic status and, 103
Impulse control, 504, 538
Impulsivity, 266, 268
Inclusion, 185
Incremental view of ability, 492, 495
Independence, self-regulation and,
    508–509
Independent learning, 256–257, 295
Individual constructivism, 224

Individualistic cultures, 65, 77–78, 98, 413,
    424, 456
Inducing labor, 135
Induction, 525, 528
Industry versus inferiority stage, 405, 407
Infancy
    aggression and, 538
    attachments and, 407–409, 415–416
    attention and, 238, 258, 316
    babies at risk, 136–137, 139–140
    brain development and, 152–154,
        156, 174
    chronic health conditions in, 183
    cognitive development and, 24,
        200, 203
    cognitive strategies and, 255
    developmental features of, 17, 19–20
    developmentally appropriate practice
        and, 26
    eating habits and, 160, 166
    emotional development and, 419,
        422, 434
    Erikson's psychosocial stages and,
        404–405
    families' concerns about, 87
    friendships and, 558
    goals and, 487
    information processing abilities
        and, 246
    injury prevention, 186
    intelligence tests and, 286–287, 293
    interpersonal behaviors and, 530, 542
    IQ scores and, 294
    language development and, 119, 314,
        316, 320–323, 326–327, 328,
        331–332, 334, 346
    language skills and, 340
    long-term memory and, 240
    mathematics and, 373, 374, 379
    moral development and, 521, 523
    motivation and, 485, 498
    music and, 393, 394
    parents' sensitivity to newborn infants,
        138–139
    peer relationships and, 570
    physical activity and, 171, 172
    physical development and, 24,
        147–148, 159, 160, 167
    physical needs and, 163
    Piaget's cognitive development theory
        and, 196, 197–199, 203
    play and, 215
    problem-solving strategies, 248
    professional viewpoints on, 20
    prosocial behavior and, 536
    reading and, 362
    reciprocal influences and, 81
    rest and sleep, 160, 174, 175
    science and, 386
    sense of self and, 408, 446, 449–450, 463
    sensory and perceptual capabilities
        and, 138–139, 236–237
    social cognition and, 470
    social-emotional development and, 24
    social interaction and, 260
    social referencing and, 258, 421, 466
    social stimuli and, 237
    temperament and, 428, 429–430, 431
    theory of mind and, 466–467
    theory theory and, 261, 383, 384
    thinking and reasoning skills, 225, 243
    toxic substances and, 290
    Vygotsky's cognitive development
        theory, 212
    writing and, 371, 372
Infant-directed speech, 320, 322, 393
Infantile amnesia, 240, 259
Inferences
    language development and, 330
    logic and, 243
    observation and, 51–52
    reading comprehension and, 360
    theory of mind and, 468
Inferiority, 405, 407
Infinity, 201, 202
Informal interactions, 212

Information processing
    developmental trends in, 246
    exceptionalities in, 266–268
    social interaction and, 260
    speed of, 275, 288, 363
Information processing theory
    attention and, 236, 238–239,
        243–244, 258
    cognitive processes and, 205, 234–245
    cognitive strategies and, 249
    critique of, 263–264
    definition of, 234
    intersubjectivity and, 258–259
    key ideas in, 234–236
    language development and, 316–317,
        318, 319
    long-term memory and, 235–236,
        240–242
    model of human information
        processing system, 235
    perception and, 234–237
    sensation and, 234–237, 243
    sociocultural element of, 258–260
    thinking/reasoning skills and, 242–243
    working memory and, 235–236,
        239, 264
Inhalants, 177
Initiative, appealing to children's sense
    of, 68
Initiative versus guilt stage, 405, 407
Injuries, 166, 171, 172, 174, 184, 277
Inner speech
    cognitive development and, 212–213,
        221, 226
    definition of, 212
    self-regulation and, 505
Inquisitiveness, 302, 488
Insecure-avoidant attachment, 410,
    412, 415
Insecure-resistant attachment, 410–411,
    412, 415
Instructional strategies
    cognitive process theories and, 15
    community of learners and, 572
    culturally responsive teaching and,
        97, 99
Integration
    definition of, 147
    of knowledge, 241–242
    physical development and, 147
Integration phase, 505
Integrity versus despair stage, 406, 407
Intellectual disabilities
    characteristics of children with, 305–308
    definition of, 305
    fostering development of children with,
        307–308
    interpersonal behaviors and, 541
    motivation and, 495
    reading and, 361
    self-regulation and, 508–509
Intelligence
    case studies, 273, 309
    Cattell-Horn-Carroll theory of cognitive
        abilities, 275–277, 281
    conceptions of, 273–274
    critique of current perspectives on,
        298–300
    definition of, 274
    demonstration of, 300–301
    developmental trends in IQ scores,
        293, 294, 295
    development versus assessment of, 300
    distributed intelligence, 279–280, 281,
        301–302
    environmental factors and, 290–292
    exceptionalities in, 303–308
    Gardner's multiple intelligences,
        277–278, 281, 300–301
    group differences in, 295–298
    hereditary influences on, 288–289, 293
    implications of theories and research,
        300–302
    measurement of, 280, 282–288
    nature/nurture and, 281, 292–293
    qualitative/quantitative change and, 281

Spearman's g, 274–275, 277, 281
Sternberg's triarchic theory, 278–279, 281
theoretical perspectives of, 274–280
universality/diversity, 281
Intelligence quotient scores. *See* IQ scores
Intelligence tests
abstract thought and, 297
critique of, 299
culture and, 296, 299
definition of, 280
dynamic assessment, 286
early childhood and, 286–288
general intelligence tests, 280, 282–285
infancy and, 286–287, 293
metacognition and, 299–300
observations used with, 288
specific ability tests, 285
Intentionality, 466, 467, 468
Interactive technologies
definition of, 581
implications of, 584–585
video games, 582–583
Interest
emotional development and, 419
habituation and, 247, 275
high-interest literature, 366
motivation and, 485, 488
Internal attributions, 491
Internalization
cognitive strategies and, 256, 259–260
definition of, 213
language development and, 317, 318
self-regulation and, 505
sense of self and, 448
Internalized motivation, 486
Internalized values orientation, 537
International adoption, 73
Internet, 581, 582, 583–584
Interpersonal behaviors
aggressive behavior and, 534–539
case studies, 517–518, 548–549
developmental trends in, 530–534, 542–543
diversity in, 539–541
fostering effective skills, 541, 543–545
prosocial behavior and, 534–539
Interpersonal intelligence, 277
Interpersonal relationships. *See* Peer relationships; Romantic relationships; Social interaction
Interpretation
attributions and, 491–492
ethical guidelines for, 58
peer relationships and, 555
reading and, 366–367
of standardized tests, 55
theory of mind and, 468
Interpreting children's artifacts and actions
arithmetic errors and, 375
assessments and, 55–56
attachment and, 409
autism and, 142
brain development and, 154–155
cognitive processes and, 270
cognitive tools and, 230
data collection and, 55–56
emotions and, 439–440
ethnic identity and, 477
figurative speech and, 351
giftedness and, 303–304
homosexuality and, 567
intelligence, 309–310
learning disabilities and, 267
moral development and, 549
multiple intelligences and, 301
neighborhoods and, 105–106
observations and, 60
physical activity and, 173, 188
pseudowriting and, 368
qualitative/quantitative change and, 30
self-perception and, 449, 453
self-regulation and, 513–514

teachers and, 587–588
ultrasound examinations and, 129
writing and, 400
Interrupting, 338
Intersubjectivity
definition of, 258
information processing theory and, 258–259
interpersonal relationships and, 530
language development and, 317
observation of, 265
theory of mind and, 466
Intervention programs (gangs), 564
Interviews
as data collection technique, 36, 37
definition of, 36
interviewing skills, 54
Intimacy, intimacy versus isolation stage, 405, 407
Intrapersonal intelligence, 277
Intrinsic motivation
culture and, 496
definition of, 482
developmental issues of, 494
developmental trends in, 485–487
factors affecting, 483–487
observation guidelines, 488
Piaget's cognitive development theory and, 195
promotion of, 497, 508
school environment and, 571
Introjection phase, 505
Invented spellings, 369
IQ scores
accuracy of, 284–285, 295, 300
adoption studies and, 289, 290–291
age and, 287–288
definition of, 284
developmental trends in, 293, 294, 295
distribution of, 284, 284n
environmental factors and, 290–292
gender and, 295–296
giftedness and, 303
heredity and, 288–289, 293
information processing speed and, 275, 288
intelligence tests and, 282, 284
interpretation of, 299
predictive nature of, 287, 293
socioeconomic status and, 290, 291, 296–297, 298
stability of, 287, 293, 295
twin studies and, 288–289, 289n
IRE cycle (Initiation-Response-Evaluation cycle), 338
Irrational number, 374
Irregular verbs, 327
Isolation, 405, 407
Israel, 414–415, 541

Japan, 328, 364, 393, 411, 415, 424, 430, 496
Joint attention, 258, 530
Joint custody, 70
Journal of Moral Education, 49
Just community, 528
Justice orientation, 526–527

Kenya, 413
Keyboarding, 368
Kids Voting USA, 81–82
Klinefelter syndrome, 116
Knowledge
integration of, 241–242
long-term memory and, 240–241
neo-Piagetian theories and, 205–206
prior knowledge, 203–204, 208, 216, 274, 332
quantitative knowledge, 276
of written language's purpose, 358
Knowledge acquisition, 279
Knowledge base
accuracy of, 262
definition of, 240
gaps in, 102, 300
long-term memory and, 240–241

reading comprehension and, 359–360
relating new information to, 244
Knowledge telling, definition of, 370
Knowledge transforming, definition of, 370
Kohlberg's moral development theory
justice orientation of, 526
key ideas in, 14, 518–521
moral dilemmas and, 519, 525
stages of, 520, 529

Language acquisition device, 315, 316, 318
Language comprehension, 320
Language development
brain development and, 153, 157
case studies, 313, 351
cognitive development and, 318
critiquing theories of, 318, 320
developmental issues of, 319
diversity in, 340–341, 346–347
early theories of, 314–315
exceptionalities in, 347–350
functionalism and, 317–318, 319
information processing theory and, 316–317, 318, 319
listening skills and, 328–331
long-term memory and, 240
metalinguistic awareness and, 336, 339–340, 342
nativism and, 262n, 315–316, 318, 319, 346
nature/nurture and, 7, 319
Piaget's cognitive development theory and, 199, 201, 226, 332
pragmatics and, 314, 318, 336–339
second language development, 316, 317, 342–345
semantic development, 321–324
sensitive periods and, 119, 316
sociocultural theories and, 317, 318, 319
speaking skills and, 331–336
syntactic development, 324–328
theoretical perspectives of, 314–320
trends in, 320–342
Vygotsky's cognitive development theory, 212–213, 226, 317
Language production, 320
Language skills
developmental trends, 340–341
history and, 389
oral language skills, 302, 331–336
Language socialization, 317
Late adolescence
attachment and, 415
chronic health conditions in, 184
cognitive development and, 25
cognitive strategies and, 256
developmental features of, 17, 22–23
developmentally appropriate practice and, 26
emotional development and, 434
ethnic identity and, 457
families' concerns about, 88
friendships and, 559
information processing abilities and, 246
interpersonal behaviors and, 534, 543
IQ scores and, 294
language skills and, 341
mathematics and, 380
metacognitive awareness and, 256
moral development and, 523
motivation and, 499
peer relationships and, 23, 571
physical development and, 25, 165, 168
professional viewpoints on, 23
reading and, 363
science and, 386
sense of self and, 452–454, 463
social cognition and, 470
social-emotional development and, 25
theory of mind and, 468–469
thinking and reasoning skills, 225
writing and, 371
Late-maturing boys, 164, 165

Late-maturing girls, 164, 165
Leadership, observation of, 302
Learned helplessness, 493, 495, 497
Learning ability
intelligence and, 273, 302
middle childhood and, 157
prenatal development and, 124
spontaneous learning and, 156–157
zone of proximal development and, 214
Learning disabilities
brain development and, 158
chronic illnesses and, 186
definition of, 266
intelligence tests and, 284
mathematics and, 379
motivation and, 495
reading and, 361, 363
self-regulation and, 507
students at risk and, 503
writing and, 370
Learning strategies
giftedness and, 304
metacognition and, 247–248
metacognitive awareness and, 251
modeling of, 254, 256
motivation and, 488
observation of, 265
Left hemisphere
definition of, 151
speech and language comprehension and, 315
Lesbian parents, 74, 75
Letter recognition, 357, 358, 359, 366
Level of potential development, 213, 286
Lexical words, 321–322, 325
Libraries, 367
Linguistic creativity, 335–336
Linguistic intelligence, 277
Listening skills, 328–331
Listening to children, data collection and, 54–55
Literacy, 90, 91, 356, 364, *See also* Reading; Writing
Literature-based curriculum, 426
Lobes, 150
Logic
concrete operational stage and, 201
information processing theory and, 243
Piaget's cognitive development theory and, 226, 243
preoperational stage and, 200–201
prior knowledge and, 203–204
Logical-mathematical intelligence, 277
Longitudinal studies, 44
Long-term goals, 490, 500
Long-term memory
capacity of, 236, 240
definition of, 235
information processing theory and, 235–236, 240–242
working memory and, 264
Long-term storage and retrieval, Cattell-Horn-Carroll theory of cognitive abilities, 276
Low-achieving peers, 490
Lower mental functions, 211
Lysergic acid diethylamide (LSD), 177

Magic School Bus, The, 582
Magnetic resonance imaging (MRI), 38, 39
Manipulatives, 382
Maps, 390
Marijuana, 177
Massage therapy, 134
Mastery goals, 488–489, 491, 492, 496, 500
Mastery orientation, 493
Mathematical reasoning skills, 209
Mathematics
advanced problem-solving procedures, 378
basic arithmetic operations, 374–378
concepts and principles of, 374
concrete operations stage and, 201
developmental progressions in, 395–396
developmental trends in, 379–380

Mathematics, *continued*
development of, 373–383
gender and, 296, 380–381
metacognition in, 249, 378, 383
number sense and counting, 373–374
promoting development in, 382–383
social construction of meaning and, 216
Maturation
biological theories and, 12
birth process and, 134
brain development and, 154, 155, 205, 206, 211, 224, 240, 469
definition of, 6
developmentally appropriate practice and, 27
different rates of, 146
genetic expression and, 112, 118
language development and, 316, 330
perceptual development and, 237
physical development and, 161, 176
puberty and, 565
qualitative/quantitative change and, 10
sexual maturation, 165, 565
universality and, 8
Meaning
language development and, 321–324, 329–330, 332, 333
metalinguistic awareness and, 340, 342
reading and, 239, 359
social construction of, 216, 357
Vygotsky's cognitive development theory and, 211–212, 216
Media
encouraging wide use of, 585
reading and, 366–367
television and interactive technologies, 581–585
Mediated learning experiences, 216
Mediation, 211, 528, 544–545, 547
Meditation, 134
Meetings with parents, 90
Meiosis
chromosome abnormalities and, 115
definition of, 112
process of, 112–114, 114n
Melting pot, 94
Memory. *See also* Long-term memory; Working memory
brain development and, 154
information processing theory and, 235
metacognitive awareness and, 250
social construction of, 259
Men. *See* Caregivers; Fathers; Gender; Parents
Menarche, 162, 165
Mental age, 284
Mental representations, 415, 416
Mental retardation. *See also* Intellectual disabilities
brain development and, 151–152
fetal alcohol syndrome and, 290
gender and, 295
IQ scores and, 299
motivation and, 495
Mercury, 128
Metacognition
central executive and, 239
definition of, 245
diversity in, 253–254
epistemological beliefs and, 252–253, 378
intelligence tests and, 299–300
learning strategies and, 247–248
in mathematics, 249, 378, 383
metacognitive awareness and, 249–251, 254
observations of, 265
problem-solving strategies and, 248–249
promoting development of, 254, 256–257
in reading, 360–361
in science, 385
self-regulated learning and, 251–252, 256–257
triarchic theory and, 279
in writing, 370

Metacognitive awareness
definition of, 249
developmental trends in, 255–256
of learning strategies, 251
of memory, 250
metacognition and, 249–251, 254
of thought, 249–250
Metalinguistic awareness
definition of, 339
development of, 340, 342
language development and, 336, 339–340, 342
promoting, 342
second language development and, 340, 342, 343
sign language and, 349
Metaphors, 330, 335
Methamphetamine (speed), 177
Methylene dioxymethamphetamine (MDMA), 177
Mexico, 425
Microgenetic methods, 44
Midbrain, 150
Middle childhood
after-school programs and, 80
art and, 392, 393
attachment and, 410, 415
attention and, 238
brain development and, 154
chronic health conditions in, 183
cognitive development and, 25, 201, 203
cognitive strategies and, 255
comprehension monitoring and, 251–252
developmental features of, 17, 21, 21n
developmentally appropriate practice and, 26
emotional development and, 421, 422, 434
Erikson's psychosocial stages and, 405
families' concerns about, 88
friendships and, 558–559
geography and, 390–391
history and, 389–390
information processing abilities and, 246
interpersonal behaviors and, 532–533, 539–540, 542
IQ scores and, 294
language development and, 321, 322, 328, 332, 333, 336
language skills and, 341
learned helplessness and, 493
learning abilities and, 157
mathematics and, 373, 374, 375–378, 379, 382, 383
metacognitive awareness and, 250, 255
metalinguistic awareness and, 340
moral development and, 521, 522, 523
motivation and, 485, 498
music and, 393
peer relationships and, 21, 532–533, 570
personalities and, 428
phonological awareness and, 357
physical activity and, 171, 172
physical development and, 25, 161–162, 167
professional viewpoints on, 21
reading and, 360, 362, 364–365
reciprocal influences and, 81
rehearsal and, 247
science and, 384, 386, 387–388
self-handicapping and, 446
sense of self and, 450–451, 463
siblings and, 82
social cognition and, 470
social-emotional development and, 25
television viewing and, 582
theory of mind and, 468
theory theory and, 261, 262, 383–384
thinking/reasoning skills, 225, 242, 243
video games and, 582–583
writing and, 368, 369–370, 371
Middle East, 77
Mirror neurons, 258

Misconceptions
language development and, 324
mathematics and, 378
poverty and, 102
science and, 389
sociocognitive conflict and, 210
theory theory and, 262, 263
Mister Rogers' Neighborhood, 582
Mistrust, 404–405, 407
Mitosis, 121–122
Modeling
aggression and, 535
androgyny and, 455
attachment security and, 417
cognitive modeling, 221
cognitive strategies and, 254, 256
communities and, 66
of elaboration, 257
emergent literacy and, 357
emotional regulation and, 427
ethnic minority groups and, 96, 498–499
family structure and, 69
interactions with infants, 139
language development and, 314–315
parents' employment and, 80
peer relationships and, 555
prosocial behavior and, 535, 544
reading and, 365
self-efficacy and, 498–499
siblings and, 82
Moderate correlations, 43
Monozygotic twins, 114, 288–289, 290, 293, 535, 567
Moral compass, 474
Moral development
case studies, 517–518, 548–549
definition of, 518
developmental trends in, 521–522, 523
diversity in, 523, 525–528
factors affecting, 524–525
Kohlberg's theory of, 14, 518–521, 525, 526, 529
language development and, 318
promotion of, 528–530
Moral dilemmas, 519, 524, 525, 528–529
Moral issues, 520, 525, 528–529
Moral transgressions, 521
Moratorium, identity and, 452
Mosaic of cultural and ethnic pieces, 94
Motherese, 320
Mothers. *See also* Parents
attachment and, 411, 414, 416
emotional development and, 424
family structure and, 69
language development and, 346
music and, 393
newborn infants and, 138–139, 237
prenatal development and, 125–130
social referencing and, 258
temperament and, 430
Motivation. *See also* Extrinsic motivation; Intrinsic motivation
attributions and, 491–494
case studies, 481, 513
definition of, 482
developmental trends in, 498–499
diversity in, 495–497
Erikson's psychosocial development theory and, 406
giftedness and, 303, 304
goals and, 487–491, 500
IQ scores and, 295, 298
language development and, 318
Piaget's cognitive development theory and, 195
promoting motivation, 497–503
Motor skills
adolescence and, 155
canalization and, 118–119
early childhood and, 159–161
fine motor skills, 160, 161, 163, 372
gross motor skills, 159–161
infancy and, 159, 160
middle childhood and, 161
nature/nurture and, 176
physical development and, 147–148, 159

qualitative/quantitative change and, 147, 148, 176
universality/diversity and, 176
writing and, 367
MUDs (Multiuser Dungeons), 583
Multiethnic children, 93, 458–459, 465
Multiple attachments, 414–415, 418
Multiple-clause sentences, 326
Multiple intelligences, theoretical perspective of, 277–278, 281, 300–301
Multiuser Dungeons (MUDs), 583
Music, 393–396
Musical intelligence, 277
Music literacy, 393–394
Muslim cultures, 94, 136, 457
Myelination, 153, 154, 155, 166, 239

Narratives
definition of, 332
language development and, 332–335
story schemas and, 360
writing and, 369
National Association for the Education of Young Children, 20
National Child Abuse Hotline, 83
National Consortium for Physical Education and Recreation for Individuals with Disabilities, 185
National Middle School Association (NMSA), 22
Native Americans
bilingualism and, 343
birth and, 136
diversity of, 97
families and, 86, 89, 93
intelligence and, 274
motivation and, 496
percentages of children as, 92
sociolinguistic behaviors and, 336, 337, 338
students at risk and, 503
Native language. *See also* Bilingualism
definition of, 314
listening skills and, 328
reading and, 366
semantic development and, 323
speaking skills and, 331
Nativism
children's theories about physical world and, 262, 315n, 383
definition of, 262, 315
language development and, 262n, 315–316, 318, 319, 346
science development and, 387
Naturalistic studies, 44–45, 49n
Naturalist intelligence, 277
Nature
definition of, 5
as developmental issue, 5–6
developmental systems theories and, 16
Nature/nurture
academic domains and, 395
aggression and, 540
attachment and, 427
biological theories and, 12, 18
brain development and, 152, 153
child development theories and, 18–19
cognitive development and, 11, 264
communities and, 67
contexts and, 67
culture and, 67
as developmental issue, 4, 5–8, 10, 11
emotional development and, 427
Erikson's psychosocial development theory and, 406
families and, 67
genetics and, 120–121, 125
information processing theory and, 264
intelligence and, 281, 292–293
intelligence theories and, 281
language development theories and, 7, 319
motivation and, 494
obesity and, 169

perceptual development and, 237
physical development and, 11, 176
Piaget and Vygotsky contrasted, 227
prenatal development and, 124, 125
prosocial behavior and, 540
puberty and, 164
sense of self and, 471
sexual orientation and, 567
social cognition and, 471, 472
social context of development
    and, 585
temperament and, 7, 119, 120–121
theory theory and, 264
NCLB (No Child Left Behind) Act of
    2001, 396
Need for relatedness, 407, 489
Negative affectivity, 430, 430n, 431
Negative correlations, 43
Negative numbers, 201, 202, 209
Negative reinforcement, 483n
Neglect, child maltreatment, 83
Neglected children (peer acceptance),
    555, 556, 557
Neighborhoods
    conduct disorder and, 437
    discrimination and, 95, 100–101
    interpreting children's artifacts and
        actions, 105–106
Neonatal Behavioral Assessment Scale
    (Brazelton Institute), 287
Neo-Piagetian theories
    central conceptual structures and, 206
    definition of, 205
    information processing theory
        and, 205
    key ideas in, 205–207
    thinking/reasoning skills and, 208
Nepal, 424
Neural commitments, 153, 317
Neural tube defects, 129
Neurofibromatosis, 116
Neurons, 149–150, 152, 239, 258, 293
Neuroticism, 431, 433
Nicaragua, 318
Niche-picking, 293, 304
Nicotine, 128, 131
NMSA (National Middle School
    Association), 22
No Child Left Behind (NCLB) Act of
    2001, 396
Nonexamples, fostering semantic
    development, 324
Nonverbal behaviors, observation of, 50
Nonverbal communication, 336, 540
Nonverbal cues, 332, 474
Number, central conceptual structures
    and, 206, 375–378
Number sense, 373–374, 382
Nurture. See also Nature/nurture
    definition of, 5
    as developmental issue, 6–7
    developmental systems theories
        and, 16
    Vygotsky's cognitive development
        theory and, 211
Nutrition. See also Eating habits
    environmental/hereditary interaction
        and, 7, 111, 120
    growth curves and, 147
    intellectual disabilities and, 306
    intelligence and, 290, 292, 296
    physical development and, 176
    poverty and, 101
    pregnancy and, 125, 130, 131
    promoting good eating habits,
        170–171
    puberty and, 164
    socioeconomic status and, 298

Obesity, 169, 170
Object permanence, 198, 203
Observations
    attachment security assessment, 412
    cognitive development and, 200
    of cultural practices and beliefs, 98
    data collection and, 38–40, 50–53

definition of, 38
distortions of information and, 41
emergent literacy and, 358
emotions and, 420–421
family conditions and, 84–85
of general characteristics, 51
health behaviors assessment, 181
indicators of health in newborns, 140
inferences and, 51–52
intelligence and, 302
intelligence tests used with, 288
intrinsic motivation and, 488
of metacognition, 265
of peer acceptance, 557
physical development and, 167–168
physical development in infancy
    and, 160
of play activities, 223, 531
of prosocial behavior, 537
reasoning processes, 209
self-perceptions and, 460–461
social aspects of play and, 531
sociolinguistic behaviors and, 337
of temperament, 429–430
types of, 52–54
One-one principle, 373
Onlooker behavior, 531
Only children, 82
Open adoption, 73
Openness, 431, 433
Operant conditioning, 482
Operations
    definition of, 195
    Piaget's cognitive development theory
        and, 195
Opioids, 136
Oral language skills, 302, 331–336
Order-irrelevance principle, 373
Organic mercury, 128
Organization
    definition of, 247
    as learning strategy, 247–248
    Piaget's cognitive development theory
        and, 195
Organized sports
    cognitive development and, 215
    gender and, 93
    parents and, 80
    physical activity and, 171–172
Orientations, of prosocial behavior, 536,
    537, 538
Out-groups, 562
Ova, 112, 114, 114n, 121
Overextension, 322
Overhand throwing, 147, 148
Overlapping waves, 249, 375
Overregularization, 326, 327
Overt, external guidance, 221
Overt self-guidance, 221
Overweight youth, 168–169

Paper-pencil tests, advantages and
    limitations of, 55
Papua New Guinea, 381–382
Parallel play, 531
Parent discussion groups, 90
Parenting styles
    definition of, 77
    family processes and, 76–79
    observation of, 85
    sense of self and, 454
Parents. See also Families; Fathers;
    Mothers
    adolescent parents, 74–75, 131
    adoptive parents, 73, 289
    attachments and, 407–409, 410, 413,
        414, 415, 416, 417, 418–419
    babies at risk and, 137
    bioecological perspective and, 16
    birth preparation and, 133–134
    children's effects on, 80–82
    communities and, 65
    coparents, 69, 70
    daily activities and, 79
    divorcing parents, 70–71, 75–76, 418
    eating habits and, 168

emergent literacy and, 356–357
emotional development and, 425, 438
employment of, 80, 296
ethnic identity and, 457
gender and, 93–94
health-compromising behavior and, 178
interactive technologies and, 584–585
moral development and, 521
peer relationships and, 560
prenatal development and, 130–132
reading to children and, 357, 365, 367
sense of self and, 446, 450, 454
sensitivity to newborn infants, 138–139
sex education and, 566
single parents, 71, 73, 296, 503
stepparents, 71
television viewing time and, 584
ultrasound examinations and, 129
Parent-teacher-student conferences, 90
Part-time employment, 175, 581
Part-whole principle, 374
Passive aggressive, 474
Passive gene-environment relation, 119
Passive sentences, 326, 328
Peer culture, 561
Peer mediation, 528, 544–545, 547
Peer pressure, 180, 533–534
Peer relationships
    adolescence and, 333–334, 405
    attachments and, 409, 410, 416
    attributions and, 493
    birth order and, 82
    case studies, 553–554, 586–587
    developmental trends in, 570–571
    early adolescence and, 533–534, 570
    emotional development and, 423
    emotional regulation and, 422
    ethnicity and, 457, 458
    families and, 560
    foster care and, 74
    fostering, 559–561
    friendships and, 556–561
    functions of, 554–555
    gender and, 540–541
    giftedness and, 305
    goals and, 500
    health-compromising behavior and, 178
    late adolescence and, 23, 571
    middle childhood and, 21, 532–533, 570
    moral development and, 524–525
    obesity and, 169
    peer acceptance and, 555–556, 557
    Piaget's cognitive development theory
        and, 210, 226–227
    romantic relationships, 564–569
    sense of self and, 447, 450, 451
    social goals and, 489–490
    social groups and, 559, 561–564
    social skills and, 530, 554, 555
    specific language impairments and, 348
Perception. See also Self-perception
    definition of, 138
    depth perception, 156, 237
    developmental trends in, 236–237
    information processing theory and,
        234–237
    sensitive periods and, 119
    visual perception, 237
Performance-approach goals, 489
Performance-avoidance goals, 489
Performance goals, 489, 491, 500
Permissive parenting style
    aggression and, 536
    definition of, 78
Persistence, observation of, 430
Personal choice, 521
Personal fable
    definition of, 451
    late adolescence and, 451–452, 559
Personal interest, 485
Personal investment, 482
Personalities
    complexities of, 433
    definition of, 428
    elements of, 431
    facilitating development of, 431–433

Personal space, 337–338
Perspective taking. See also Social
    perspective taking
    language development and, 332, 334
    moral development and, 522
    peer relationships and, 558
    play and, 215
    social interaction and, 226
Peru, 336
Phantom Tollbooth, The (Juster), 342
Phenylkentonuria (PKU), 117
Phonemes
    definition of, 328
    metalinguistic awareness and, 340
    phonological awareness and,
        357, 357n
    speaking skills and, 331, 332
    spelling and, 369
Phonological awareness
    definition of, 357
    dyslexia and, 363
    promoting, 359, 365
    reading and, 357, 364, 366
    spelling and, 368–369
Phonology, definition of, 314
Physical abuse, 83
Physical activity. See also Athletics;
    Organized sports
    developmental issues, 176
    encouraging of, 163, 172–174, 179
    observation guidelines, 181
    overweight youth and, 169
    physical development and, 176
    physical well-being and, 171–174
Physical aggression, 538, 540, 554
Physical appearance
    eating disorders and, 169
    middle childhood and, 161–162
    self-esteem and, 161–162, 164
    sense of self and, 447, 451, 455
Physical development. See also Brain;
    Genetics; Motor skills
    case studies, 145, 187–188
    childhood and, 159–165
    definition of, 5
    developmental issues and, 176
    developmental trends and, 24–25,
        167–168
    early adolescence and, 22, 25,
        162–165, 167
    early childhood and, 20, 24,
        159–161, 167
    families' concerns about, 87–88
    infancy and, 24, 147–148, 159, 160, 167
    late adolescence and, 25, 165, 168
    middle childhood and, 25, 161–162, 167
    nature/nurture and, 11, 176
    physical well-being and, 165–166,
        168–182
    principles of, 146–149
    qualitative/quantitative change and, 11,
        147, 176
    special physical needs, 182–186
    universality/diversity and, 8, 11, 176
Physical disabilities, 185, 508–509, 541
Physical environment
    Piaget's cognitive development theory
        and, 196
    play and, 186
Physical growth
    developmental issues, 176
    rest and sleep and, 174
Physical well-being
    awareness of, 165–166
    developmental issues, 176
    eating habits and, 166, 168–171
    health-compromising behaviors and,
        176–181
    observations and, 181
    physical activity and, 171–174
    promoting, 185–186
    rest and sleep and, 174–176
Physical world
    children's theories of, 261–262, 383–384
    hands-on exploration of, 207–208
    play and, 215

Physiological measures
    definition of, 38
    distortions of information and, 41
Pi, children's understanding of, 201, 209, 374
Piaget's cognitive development theory
    applying ideas of, 207–210
    clinical method, 194, 208
    constructivism and, 195, 224, 234, 260
    current perspectives on, 203–206
    key ideas in, 13–14, 195–197
    language development and, 199, 201,
        226, 332
    nature/nurture and, 227
    neo-Piagetian theories, 205–207
    qualitative/quantitative change and, 227
    schemes and, 195, 198
    stages of cognitive development,
        197–203, 208–209, 236, 243, 374
    as stage theory, 9, 197, 205
    stimuli and, 238
    universality/diversity and, 227
    Vygotsky compared to, 224, 226–227
PKU (phenylkentonuria) (PKU), 117
Placenta, 122, 130
Place value, 209, 375
Planning
    brain development and, 158
    central executive and, 239
Play. See also Pretend play
    emotional development and, 426
    interpersonal behaviors and, 531,
        532, 539
    metalinguistic awareness and, 340, 342
    observation guidelines, 223, 531
    rough-and-tumble play, 171
    social skills and, 214
    symbolic thought and, 199, 223
    Vygotsky's cognitive development
        theory and, 214–215
Playing the dozens, 242n, 333
Polygenic inheritance, 115
Polynesia, 299
Popular children (peer acceptance),
    555, 557
Popularity, 447, 555
Positive Action program, 46, 48, 49
Positive correlations, 43
Postconventional morality, 519–520
Postformal stage, 203
Poverty. See also Socioeconomic status
    (SES)
    challenges of, 101–102
    depression and, 435
    early childhood intervention
        programs, 291
    eating habits and, 168, 170–171
    emotional development and, 424–425
    intellectual disabilities and, 306–307
    IQ scores and, 296
    as risk factor, 68
    students at risk and, 503
    teenage pregnancy and, 179
Practical intelligence, 278
Practical problem-solving ability, 278–279
Practice, automatization and, 245, 365
Prader-Willi syndrome, 116
Pragmatics
    definition of, 314
    development of, 336–339
    language development and, 314, 318,
        336–339
    specific language impairments and, 348
Prayer, 134
Preconventional morality, 519
Pregnancy
    avoiding harmful substances, 126–128
    implementing medical procedures,
        128–130
    nutrition and, 125, 130, 131
    preparation for, 125–126, 130, 300
    teenage pregnancy, 131, 178, 179, 180,
        566, 569
Prejudice
    breaking down, 27, 475, 544
    definition of, 469
    learned helplessness and, 497

peer relationships and, 457
social cognition and, 469, 471–472
Premature infants, 136
Prenatal development
    brain development during, 152, 156
    definition of, 121
    developmental trends and, 132
    environmental factors and, 7, 118
    medical care and, 125–130, 130
    parents and, 130–132
    phases of prenatal growth, 121–124
    sensitive periods in, 119, 126, 127
Preoperational stage, 198, 199–201, 203
Prepared childbirth classes, 133
Prescription medications, 177
Pretend play
    emotional development and, 426
    motor skills and, 160–161
    preoperational stage and, 199
    sensorimotor stage and, 200
    social cognition and, 473
    Vygotsky's cognitive development
        theory and, 215
Pride, 421
Primary reinforcers
    definition of, 482
    extrinsic motivation and, 482–483
Priorities, motivation and, 488
Prior knowledge, 203–204, 208, 216,
    274, 332
Private speech, 212
Proactive aggression, 538, 539
Problem solving
    cognitive strategies and, 248–249, 256
    intelligence and, 301, 302
    mathematics and, 378, 381, 382–383
    modeling of, 254
    Piaget's clinical method and, 194, 208
    practical problem-solving ability,
        278–279
    social problem-solving strategies, 539,
        541, 543
    zone of proximal development and, 214
Process measures, of child care, 578
Professional organizations, 28
Professional practice. See also
    Developmentally appropriate practice
    action research and, 49–58
    attachment security and, 416–419
    brain development research, 155–159
    child development and, 10–11, 23,
        26–28
    childhood and, 163
    children from diverse groups and,
        96–100
    cognitive processes and, 243–245
    diverse family structures and, 75–76
    early adolescence and, 22, 26
    early childhood and, 20–21, 26
    eating habits and, 170–171
    emotional development and, 425–427
    emotional problems and, 437–438
    health-compromising behaviors and,
        179–181
    infancy and, 20, 26, 163
    information processing and social
        interaction, 260
    information processing exceptionalities
        and, 267–268
    intelligence and, 300–302
    interpersonal skill promotion and, 541,
        543–545
    language development and, 323–324,
        327–328
    late adolescence and, 23, 26
    listening comprehension and, 330–331
    mathematics development and,
        382–383
    metacognitive and strategic
        development, 254, 256–257
    metalinguistic development and, 342
    middle childhood and, 21, 26
    moral development and, 528–530
    motivation and, 497–503
    nature/nurture and, 120–121
    parents' sensitivity to newborns, 138–139

peer relationships and, 559–561
physical activity and, 172–174
physical well-being and, 185–186
Piaget's cognitive development theory
    and, 207–210
prenatal development and, 130–132
reading development promotion,
    364–367
research and, 45–49
rest and sleep needs, 175–176
science development and, 387–389
self-regulation and, 508–511
sense of self and, 462, 464–466
social cognition development and,
    474–475
socioeconomic status and, 102–104
speaking skills and, 334–336
teachers addressing adolescents'
    sexuality, 568–569
television and technology, 584–585
temperaments and personality
    development, 431–433
theory theory and, 263
Vygotsky's cognitive development
    theory and, 219–223
writing development and, 372–373
Promoting Alternative Thinking Strategies
    (PATHS), 425
Pronunciation, 332
Proportional reasoning
    formal operations stage and, 202,
        203, 374
    maps and, 391
    mathematics and, 374
Prosocial behavior
    definition of, 535
    developmental issues of, 540
    development of, 536, 538
    gangs and, 564
    interpersonal behaviors and, 534–539
    modeling and, 535, 544
    observation of, 537
Protective factors, 68
Proximodistal trends, 159
Pseudowriting, 367–368
Psychodynamic theories
    definition of, 13
    theoretical positions of, 18
Psychosocial stages, 404–406
Puberty
    cognitive development and, 202–203
    definition of, 162
    eating disorders and, 169
    gender and, 22, 162, 163
    physical development and, 22, 161,
        162–165
    sense of self and, 454–455
Punishment
    aggression and, 536
    definition of, 483
    moral development and, 525
    negative reinforcement distinguished
        from, 483n
Pygmalion (Shaw), 584

Qualitative change
    definition of, 9
    Piaget's cognitive development theory
        and, 197
Qualitative/quantitative change
    academic domains and, 396
    aggression and, 540
    attachment and, 427
    child development theories and, 18–19
    cognitive-developmental perspective
        and, 11, 264
    communities and, 67
    contexts and, 67
    culture and, 67
    as developmental issue, 9–10, 11
    emotional development and, 427
    families and, 67
    genetics and, 125
    information processing theory
        and, 264
    intelligence theories and, 281

interpreting children's artifacts and
    actions, 30
language development theories
    and, 319
motivation and, 494
physical development and, 11, 147, 176
Piaget and Vygotsky contrasted, 227
prenatal development and, 124, 125
prosocial behavior and, 540
sense of self and, 471
social cognition and, 471
social context of development and, 585
theory theory and, 264
Quantitative change, definition of, 9
Quantitative knowledge, 276
Quasi-experimental studies, 42
Questionnaires, 36, 37
Questions
    close-ended questions, 54
    cognitive strategies and, 256
    culture and, 329
    ethnic minority groups and, 95
    language development and, 325–326
    leading questions, 259
    open-ended questions, 54
    Piaget's clinical method and, 208
    science and, 388
    sociolinguistic behavior and, 337, 338
    wait time and, 338
    why and how questions, 263
Quinceañeras, 165

Race. See also African Americans; Ethnic
    minority groups
    ethnicity compared to, 93
    history and, 390
    IQ scores and, 297–298, 299
    lack of biological basis for, 297
    moral development and, 524
    stereotypes and, 27
Racial harassment, 536
Randomness, experimental studies and, 42
Rating scales, 52–53, 54
Reactive aggression, 538
Readiness, Piaget/Vygotsky compared, 224
Reading
    automatization and, 239, 359, 365, 366
    Cattell-Horn-Carrol theory of cognitive
        abilities, 276
    developmental progressions in, 395–396
    developmental trends in, 362–363
    development of, 356–367
    diversity in, 361, 363–364
    emergent literacy and, 356–357,
        358, 363
    language development and, 324
    metacognition in, 360–361
    metalinguistic awareness and, 340, 342
    parents reading to children, 357,
        365, 367
    phonological awareness and, 357,
        364, 366
    promoting reading development,
        364–367
    reading comprehension and,
        359–360, 366
    reciprocal teaching and, 219–221
    specific language impairments and, 348
    Standard English and, 347
    word recognition and, 358–359
Reading comprehension, 359–360, 366
Reasoning skills. See also
    Thinking/reasoning skills
    culture and, 227
    familiarity and, 210
    language development and, 316
    scientific reasoning skills, 202, 209,
        384–385
Receptive language, 320, 347
Recessive genes, 115
Reciprocal influences, 80–82
Reciprocal relationships, 556
Reciprocal teaching
    definition of, 219
    reading comprehension and, 360
    reading instruction and, 219–221

Reconstituted families, 72n
Recursive thinking, 468
Reflexes, 124, 139, 140, 159, 198
Rehearsal
    definition of, 247
    as learning strategy, 247, 254
    long-term memory and, 236
Reinforcement
    language development and, 314–315
    prosocial and aggressive behavior,
        535–536
Reinforcers
    extrinsic motivation and, 482
    responses to, 495
Rejected children (peer acceptance),
    555–556, 557, 560
Rejection (culture), 94
Relational aggression, 538, 539, 540
Reliability
    assessments and, 55–56
    data collection and, 40, 50
    definition of, 40
    dynamic assessment and, 286
    evaluation of research methods and, 49
    intelligence tests and, 284–285
Religion and religious groups
    moral development and, 525, 526, 527,
        529–530
    science and, 387
Religious tolerance, 529–530
Repetition of gratifying actions, 200
Reproductive cells, formation of, 112–114
Research design
    associations and, 43, 46
    causal relationships and, 42–43, 46
    data analysis illustrations, 46–47
    developmental change and stability
        and, 44, 47
    evaluation of, 47
    natural contexts and, 44–45, 47
Research methods
    analyzing developmental research,
        36–49
    case studies, 33, 59–60
    data collection techniques, 36–42,
        49–58
    evaluation of, 45–49
    principles of, 34–36
    research designs, 42–45
Research participants, 35
Resilience, definition of, 102
Respect, 560–561
Response cost, 483
Rest and sleep
    accommodating children's needs for,
        175–176
    infancy and, 160, 174, 175
    observation guidelines, 181
    physical development and, 163, 176
    physical well-being and, 174–176
Reviving Ophelia (Pipher), 162
Right hemisphere
    definition of, 151
    giftedness and, 304
    language development and, 315–316
Risk factors
    in children's environment, 68
    in families, 83–84
Risky behaviors, 101, 155, 159, 164, 165,
    166, 175
Role confusion, 405, 407
Role taking, play and, 223
Romania, 291
Romantic relationships
    attachment and, 410, 416
    dating and, 564–565
    diversity in, 568
    peer relationships, 564–569
    sexual intimacy and, 565–566
    sexual orientation and, 566–567
    teachers addressing adolescents'
        sexuality, 568–569
Rote memorization, 254, 489
Rough-and-tumble play, 171
Routines, 432
Rubella, 128, 151–152

Rules
    conduct disorder and, 436
    conventional morality and, 519
    grammatical rules, 328, 347, 369
    interpersonal behaviors and, 533
    middle childhood and, 21
    moral development and, 528
    parenting styles and, 78
    problem-solving strategies and, 249
    self-determination and, 499–500
    self-regulation and, 505
    sign language and, 349
    syntactic rules, 324–326, 327
    unspoken social rules, 574
Running records, 52, 53
Rural areas
    communities of, 101
    gangs and, 547, 563
    social cognition and, 472
Russia, 496
Rwanda, 474

Sadness, 419, 420
Safe haven, 408
Samples
    definition of, 35
    evaluation of research methods and, 47
Savant syndrome, 473
Saved by the Bell, 582
Scaffolding
    acquisition of teaching skills and, 219
    challenging tasks and, 221, 222, 497
    collaborative learning and, 256
    definition of, 217
    exceptionalities in information
        processing and, 268
    learning disabilities and, 266
    mathematics and, 382–383
    reciprocal teaching and, 221
    science and, 388
    self-regulation and, 257, 509–510
    writing and, 372–373
Schemas
    definition of, 241
    gender schemas, 454, 460
    long-term memory and, 241–242
    story schemas, 360
    substance schemas, 384
Schemes
    definition of, 195
    schemas compared to, 241
    sensorimotor stage and, 198, 241
Schizophrenia, 151, 152, 546
School psychologists, 339
School readiness tests, 288
Schools. *See also* Academic achievement;
    Formal schooling
    eating habits and, 169, 170
    gangs and, 547
    guided participation and, 218
    intervention for students at risk, 546
    intervention for students in trouble, 546
    nonviolent school environment,
        545–546
    poverty and, 102
    prosocial and aggressive behavior, 536
    role in development, 5
    safe school environment, 545–547
    sense of community in, 571–573
    socialization and, 573–574
Schools within schools, 577
School traditions, 573
School values, 573
Science
    children's theories and, 383–384
    developmental progressions in,
        395–396
    developmental trends in, 386
    development of, 383–389
    diversity in, 385, 386, 387
    gender and, 93, 387
    metacognition in, 385
    moral development and, 528
    promoting development in, 387–389
    scientific reasoning skills, 202, 209,
        384–385

Scientific method
    definition of, 34
    research methods and, 34–35
    scientific reasoning skills and, 384
Scientific reasoning, definition of, 384
Scientific reasoning skills, 202, 209,
    384–385
Scripts
    definition of, 241
    long-term memory and, 241–242
Secondary reinforcers, 483
Secondary schools, transitions to, 576–577
Second language development
    bilingualism and, 343–344
    language development and, 342–345
    sensitive periods and, 316, 317, 343
    teaching second language, 344–345
    timing of, 342–343
Second stage of labor, 134–135
Secure attachment, 410, 412, 415, 418,
    450, 565
Secure base, 408, 410
Segregation, 101
Selective adoption (culture), 94
Self-care, 80, 163
Self-concept
    ethnic identity and, 457
    observation of, 460
    sense of self and, 444
Self-conscious emotions
    definition of, 421
    physical development and, 161, 165
Self-determination
    culture and, 496
    goals and, 500
    motivation and, 485, 487, 499–500
    self-regulation and, 503–504
Self-efficacy
    challenging tasks and, 446
    definition of, 484
    moral development and, 529
    motivation and, 484–485, 487, 498–499
    observation of, 488
Self-esteem
    factors influencing, 447
    interplay with behavior, 462
    learning disabilities and, 266
    peer relationships and, 555
    physical appearance and, 161–162, 164
    sense of self and, 444–445, 448,
        465–466
    stability of, 449
    victims and, 539
Self-evaluation
    promotion of, 257, 511
    self-regulation and, 505–506
    sense of self and, 448
    writing and, 370
Self-fulfilling prophecy, 575
Self-handicapping, 445–446
Self-hypnosis, 134
Self-improvement, 173
Self-instructions, 511
Self-monitoring, 257, 511
Self-motivation, 504, 511
Self-perception
    abstract conceptions and, 448–449
    children's behavior mirroring, 446
    contradictions in, 452
    ethnic minority groups and, 457–459
    factors influencing, 446–447
    imaginary audience and, 451, 452, 506
    moral development and, 524, 529
    multifaceted understandings of,
        447, 461
    observation guidelines, 460–461
    stability of, 449
    teachers' influence on, 465
Self-recognition, 450
Self-regulated learning
    definition of, 251
    giftedness and, 304
    metacognition and, 251–252, 256–257
    observation of, 265
    self-regulation and, 504
    social interaction and, 260

Self-regulation
    conditions fostering, 158, 506–507
    definition of, 77, 504
    developmental trends in, 504–506
    diversity in, 507–508
    emotional development and, 422
    peer relationships and, 554
    promotion of, 508–511, 512
    self-determination and, 503–504
Self-reinforcement, 509
Self-reports
    as data collection technique, 36–37
    definition of, 36
    distortions of information and, 41
Self-serving goals, 538–539
Self-socialization, 455, 504, 534, 562
Self-talk
    cognitive development and, 212, 226
    definition of, 212
    exceptionalities in information
        processing and, 268
    scaffolding and, 221
    self-regulation and, 505
    sign language and, 349
Self-worth
    contingent self-worth, 448, 454
    gender and, 454–455
    observation of, 460
    peer relationships and, 447, 448
    self-handicapping and, 446
    sense of self and, 444–445
Semantic bootstrapping, 327
Semantics
    definition of, 314
    language development and, 314, 318,
        321–324, 334
    semantic development, 321–324, 330–331
    sensory impairments and, 349
    specific language impairments and, 347
Sensation
    cognitive processes and, 158–159
    definition of, 138
    developmental trends in, 236–237
    information processing theory and,
        234–237, 243
Sense of community, 103, 561, 571–573
Sense of self
    case studies, 443–444, 476
    changing nature of, 449–454
    definition of, 444
    developmental issues of, 471
    developmental trends in, 463
    diversity in, 454–459, 461–462
    effects of, 445–446
    enhancement of, 462, 464–466
    factors influencing, 446–447
    general trends in, 447–449
    goals and, 490
    infancy and, 408, 446, 449–450, 463
    internalized motivation and, 486
    moral development and, 524
Sense of self-determination, 485
Sensitive periods
    definition of, 7
    language development and, 119, 316
    maturation and, 12, 119
    nature/nurture and, 7–8
    in prenatal development, 119, 126, 127
Sensitivity to physical input, observation
    of, 429
Sensorimotor schemes, 198, 241
Sensorimotor stage, 197–199, 203
Sensory impairments
    language development and, 349
    reading development and, 361
    science development and, 385
Sensory register, 235
Sentence structure, 325, 326, 327–328
Service learning, 529
SES. *See* Socioeconomic status (SES)
Sesame Street, 544, 582
Sex education, 566, 568
Sexual abuse, 83, 565
Sexual activity
    dating and, 565
    early-maturing girls and, 164

Sexual activity, *continued*
    health-compromising behavior and,
        177, 178–181
    late adolescence and, 23, 165
    risky behavior and, 166
    self-care and, 80
    sexual intimacy and, 565–566
Sexual harassment, 165, 536, 544, 569
Sexually transmitted infections (STIs),
    178–181
Sexual maturation, 165, 565
Sexual orientation, 74, 75, 455,
    566–567, 569
Shame
    autonomy versus shame and doubt
        stage, 405, 406, 407
    definition of, 521
    emotional development and, 420, 421
    moral development and, 521–522, 522n
Shared routines, 556
Short-term memory, 235, 235n, 276, *See
    also* Working memory
Siblings
    attachments and, 414, 415
    correlations between IQ scores, 289
    emotional regulation and, 422
    influences of, 82–83
Sickle cell disease, 115, 117
SIDS (sudden infant death syndrome), 174
Sight vocabulary, 359
Sign language
    American Sign Language, 315, 335, 344,
        349, 361
    language development and, 315, 318
    sensory impairments and, 349
lence
    intelligence and, 274
    sociolinguistic behaviors and, 336
miles, 330, 335
gle-gene defects, 116–117, 118
le parents, 71, 73, 296, 503
ated motivation, 497
ational interest, 485
ep. *See* Rest and sleep
ll-group learning, 256
rfs, 582
ks, 170
bility, observation of, 429
l cognition
    finition of, 466
    velopmental trends in, 470
    velopment issues of, 471
    ersity in, 472–474
    ors promoting, 469, 471–472
    ering development of, 474–475
    ry of mind and, 466–469
    ognitive biases, definition of, 469
    cognitive theory, 12n
    ompetence, 279, 532
    onstruction of meaning, 216, 357
    onstructivism, 224
    nventions, 520, 521
    es, 538
    otional development. *See also*
        nal development; Interpersonal
        ors; Moral development;
        ion; Self-regulation
    on of, 5
    mental trends, 24–25
    concerns about, 87–88
    development and, 318
    urture and, 11
    ynamic theories and, 13
    e/quantitative change and, 11
    ty/diversity and, 8, 11
    489–490, 501
    , peer relationships and, 559,

    ion. *See also* Interpersonal
        Peer relationships; Social

    barriers to, 560
    nformation processing
    260
    velopment and, 317
    ships and, 559–560

    Piaget's cognitive development theory
        and, 196, 200, 226
    Vygotsky's cognitive development
        theory and, 213, 226, 256, 260
Socialization
    aggression and, 540
    culture and, 424
    definition of, 64
    ethnicity and, 93
    families and, 76
    gender differences and, 93–94, 540
    language socialization, 317
    peer relationships and, 555
    reciprocal influences on, 80–82
    schools and, 573–574
    self-socialization, 455, 504, 534, 562
    sociolinguistic behaviors and, 339
    temperament and, 430
Social learning theories
    children's beliefs and goals and, 12–13
    definition of, 12
    motivation and, 483
    social cognitive theory and, 12n
    theoretical positions of, 18
Social perspective taking
    aggression and, 538
    definition of, 466
    encouragement of, 474
    interpersonal behaviors and, 533
    moral development and, 524–525
    peer relationships and, 554
    theory of mind and, 466–467, 467n, 469
Social referencing
    definition of, 258
    infancy and, 258, 421, 466
    theory of mind and, 466
Social skills
    chronic illness and, 182, 186
    definition of, 530
    emotional problems and, 437
    environmental factors and, 119
    exceptionality in information
        processing and, 268
    intelligence and, 302
    labeling behaviors, 543
    peer relationships and, 530, 554, 555
    play and, 214
    sense of self and, 453
    teaching of, 541, 543, 544
Social stimuli, 237, 258
Social studies, concrete operations stage
    and, 201–202
Social systems, 66–67, 76, 78
Social thought, 206
Society. *See also* Socialization
    definition of, 577
    immigrants orienting to mainstream
        society, 96
    services for children and adolescents
        and, 578–581
    television and interactive technologies,
        581–585
Sociocognitive conflict
    definition of, 210
    social interaction and, 226–227
Sociocultural theories. *See also* Culture
    definition of, 15, 211
    information processing theory and,
        258–260
    language development and, 317, 318,
        319
    theoretical positions of, 19
    Vygotsky's cognitive development
        theory and, 15, 211, 258
Sociodramatic play
    definition of, 215
    interpersonal behaviors and, 532, 539
Socioeconomic status (SES). *See also*
    Poverty
    computers and, 584
    definition of, 101
    eating habits and, 168, 170–171
    emotional development and, 424–425
    families and, 71
    IQ scores and, 290, 291, 296–297, 298
    language development and, 346

    narratives and, 333
    parents' employment and, 80
    pregnancy and, 131
    professional practice and, 102–104
    reading and, 363
    self-regulation and, 507–508
    stereotypes and, 89
Sociolinguistic behaviors
    accounting for differences in, 339
    culture and, 336–338
    definition of, 336
    development of, 339
    observations of, 337
Solitary play, 531
Southeast Asians, 456
Spatial intelligence, 277, 278
Spatial relationships, central conceptual
    structures and, 206
Speaking skills
    language development and, 331–336
    promoting, 334–336
Spearman's g, 274–275, 277, 281
Special physical needs
    chronic illness, 182, 183–184
    physical disabilities, 183
    promoting physical well-being and,
        185–186
    serious injuries, 184
Special Supplemental Nutrition Program
    for Women, Infants, and Children
    (WIC), 131
Specific ability tests, 285
Specific factors, intelligence and, 274–275
Specific language impairments, 347–348
Speech-language pathologists, 339
Speed (methamphetamine), 177
Spelling, 364, 368–369
Spencer's identity development model,
    459, 461–462
Sperm, 112, 114, 114n, 121
Spermarche, 162
Spina bifida, 118
Spontaneous learning, 156–157
Sports. *See* Organized sports
Stable attributions, 491
Stages
    cognitive-developmental theories
        and, 14
    definition of, 9, 9n
    Erikson's psychosocial development
        theory, 404–406
    Kohlberg's moral development theory
        and, 520, 529
    neo-Piagetian theories and, 207
    Piaget's cognitive development theory
        and, 197–203, 208–209, 236, 243, 374
Stage theories
    definition of, 9
    Piaget's cognitive development theory
        as, 9, 197, 205
    research on, 9–10
Stagnation, 405, 407
Standard English
    definition of, 346
    dialects and, 346–347
Standardized tests, interpretation of, 55
Standards
    of academic domains, 394, 396–397
    definition of, 396
Stanford-Binet Intelligence Scales, 282,
    285, 287
States of arousal, 139, 140
Stepfamilies, 71–72, 72n
Stepparents, 71
Stereotyped, approval-focused
    orientation, 537
Stereotypes
    breaking down, 27, 457, 475
    of culture, 97
    ethnic minority groups and, 89
    of family structure, 68
    of gender, 93, 380, 424, 455–456,
        495–496
    only children and, 82
    social cognition and, 469, 471
    teacher expectations and, 89, 575

Stereotype threat, definition of, 298
Sternberg's triarchic theory, 278–279, 281
Stimuli
    attention and, 238, 268
    autism and, 473
    social stimuli, 237, 258
STIs (sexually transmitted infections),
    178–181
Storybook reading skills, 365
Storyknifing, 372
Story schemas, 360
Stranger anxiety, 409, 419
Strange Situation, 410–411
Strata, of intelligence, 275–276
Stress
    attachment security and, 414, 416
    birth and, 133
    emotional development and, 425
    environmental/hereditary interaction
        and, 119, 120
    ethnic minority groups and, 96
    parenting styles and, 78
    physical activity and, 171
    poverty and, 102
    prenatal development and, 128, 131, 131
    puberty, 164
    rest and sleep, 175
    siblings and, 82
Strong correlations, 43
Structural measures, of child care, 578
Students at risk, 300, 503, 504, 546
Subcultures, 453
Substance abuse. *See also* Alcohol; Drugs
    eating disorders and, 169
    health-compromising behavior and,
        177–178, 179
    intellectual disabilities and, 306
    pregnancy and, 132
    risky behavior and, 166
Substance schemas, 384
Subtractive bilingualism, 345
Suburban areas
    communities of, 101
    gangs and, 547, 563
Success
    attributions and, 491, 492, 501–502
    intelligence and, 274
    literacy and, 364
    motivation and, 484–485, 496
    sense of self and, 462
Sudden infant death syndrome (SIDS), 174
Suicide, 169, 436, 438, 459
Superficial needs-of-others orientation, 537
Super Why!, 254
Suppression programs (gangs), 564
Symbolic thought
    definition of, 198
    play and, 199, 223
    preoperational stage and, 199, 200
    sensorimotor stage and, 198–199
    thinking/reasoning skills and, 242
Symbolic tools, 280
Symbols
    definition of, 242
    language development and, 318
    literacy and, 356
    maps and, 391
    Piaget's cognitive development theory
        and, 199, 242
    thinking/reasoning skills and, 242–243
Sympathy
    attachments and, 418
    definition of, 522
    moral development and, 522
    prosocial behavior and, 536
Synapses, 149, 152–153, 155
Synaptic pruning
    brain development and, 153, 154, 155
    definition of, 153
Synaptogenesis
    brain development and, 152, 153
    definition of, 152
Syntax
    definition of, 314
    language development and, 314, 318,
        324–328, 334

Photo Credits

Dennis Lane/Jupiter Images–BananaStock, p. 2; Mary Kate Denny/PhotoEdit Inc., pp. 7, 34, 86, 114, 332; Scott Cunningham/Merrill, pp. 9, 93, 291, 416; © Catherine Karnow/ Corbis, p. 15; David J. Sams/Getty Images, Inc.–Stone Allstock, p. 20 (top); Laima Druskis/PH College, pp. 20 (bottom), 119, 360, 364; Anthony Magnacca/Merrill, pp. 21, 252, 474, 502; Michael Newman/PhotoEdit Inc., pp. 22, 102, 120, 174, 418, 457, 560; Mark Anderson/Jupiter Images–Rubberball, p. 32; David Young-Wolff/Getty Images, Inc.–Stone Allstock, p. 50 (top); Hunter Freeman/Getty Images, Inc.–Stone Allstock, p. 50 (bottom); © Tracy Kahn/Corbis All Rights Reserved, p. 62; Ryan McVay/Getty Images, Inc.–PhotoDisc, p. 64; Tony Freeman/PhotoEdit Inc., pp. 65, 78, 164, 179, 215, 323, 408, 534, 555; Page Poore/PH College, p. 68; Paul Conklin/PhotoEdit Inc., pp. 73, 218; S. Gazin/The Image Works, p. 75; Laura Dwight/PhotoEdit Inc., pp. 79, 287; Corbis Digital Stock, p. 80; Elizabeth Zuckerman/PhotoEdit Inc., p. 89; Deborah Davis/PhotoEdit Inc., p. 95; Bob Daemmrich Photography, Inc., pp. 97, 446; Getty Images–Stockbyte, p. 108; Lauren Shear/ Photo Researchers, Inc., p. 115; Don W. Fawcett/Photo Researchers, Inc., p. 121 (top left); Dr. Yorgos Nikas/Photo Researchers, Inc., 121 (top right); Anatomical Travelogue/Photo Researchers, Inc., p. 121 (bottom left); Neil Bromhall/Photo Researchers, Inc., p. 121 (bottom right); Blair M. Seitz/Creative Eye/Mira.com, p. 126; Barros & Barros/Getty Images, Inc.–Image Bank, p. 135; Carol Ann Harrigan/PH College, p. 137; David Young-Wolff/ PhotoEdit Inc., pp. 144, 185, 343, 385, 405 (bottom), 410, 482, 489, 525, 536, 573; Teresa M. McDevitt, p. 147 (all); Billy E. Barnes/PhotoEdit Inc., p. 168; Arthur Tilley/Getty Images, Inc.–Taxi, pp. 171, 464; Jacqueline Mia Foster/PhotoEdit Inc., p. 192; David Mager/Pearson Learning Photo Studio, pp. 196, 359; © Ariel Skelley/Corbis, pp. 206 (left), 211, 442; Getty Images, Inc.–PhotoDisc, p. 206 (center); Richard Hutchings/Photo Researchers, Inc., p. 206 (right); © Jake Warga, p. 217; B2M Productions/Getty Images/Digital Vision, p. 232; Mark Richards/PhotoEdit/Courtesy of Joe Campus & Rosanne Kermoian, p. 237; Mike Provost/Silver Burdett Ginn, p. 241; Jeff Greenberg/PhotoEdit Inc., p. 256; Elena Rooraid/PhotoEdit Inc., p. 259; Richard Heinzen/SuperStock, Inc., p. 266; SuperStock, Inc., p. 272; Novastock/PhotoEdit Inc., p. 275; Silver Burdett Ginn, pp. 280, 298; Rachel Epstein/The Image Works, p. 289; Will Hart/PhotoEdit Inc., p. 295; Tim Davis/Corbis–Davis/Lynn Images, p. 299; John Paul Endress/Silver Burdett Ginn, p. 305; JGI/AGE Fotostock America, Inc.–Royalty-free, p. 312; Robert Brenner/PhotoEdit Inc., p. 315; Amy Etra/PhotoEdit Inc., p. 316; Krista Greco/Merrill, p. 322; © LWA–Dann Tardif/Corbis All Rights Reserved, p. 324; Phoebe Dunn/Stock Connection, p. 325; Spencer Grant/PhotoEdit Inc., p. 327; Richard Hutchings/PhotoEdit Inc., p. 334; Robert Burke/Getty Images, Inc.–Stone Allstock, p. 339; © Ellen B. Senisi, p. 354; Myrleen Ferguson Cate/PhotoEdit Inc., p. 375; Rudi Von Briel/PhotoEdit Inc., p. 387; © Ed Bock/Corbis All Rights Reserved, p. 402; Elie Bernager/Getty Images, Inc.–Stone Allstock, p. 405 (top); Leanne Temme/Photolibrary.com, p. 415; SW Productions/Getty Images, Inc.–Photodisc, p. 423; Jonathan Nourok/PhotoEdit Inc., p. 424; Andy Saks/Getty Images, Inc.–Stone Allstock, p. 427; Ken Straiter/Corbis/Stock Market, p. 431; Nancy Richmond/The Image Works, p. 438; EyeWire Collection/Getty Images, Inc.–Photodisc, pp. 450, 516; Michael Malyszko/Getty Images, Inc.–Taxi, p. 456; © Dorling Kindersley, p. 473; Tom Watson/Merrill, p. 475; Masterfile Royalty Free Division, p. 480; Renzo Mancini/Getty Images Inc.–Image Bank, p. 527; Laurence Monneret/Getty Images Inc.–Stone Allstock, p. 530; Richard Lord/The Image Works, p. 540; Image 100, p. 552; Catherine Karnow/Woodfin Camp & Associates, Inc., p. 563; Comstock Royalty Free Division, p. 568; Frank Siteman, p. 578; Mark Richards/PhotoEdit Inc., p. 581.

Child Development and Education

Fourth Edition

Teresa M. McDevitt
University of Northern Colorado

Jeanne Ellis Ormrod
University of Northern Colorado (Emerita)
University of New Hampshire

Merrill
Upper Saddle River, New Jersey
Columbus, Ohio

nsory impairments and, 349
sign language and, 349
specific language impairments and, 347
syntactic development, 324–328, 330–331
writing and, 369
Synthesis, right hemisphere and, 151

Taiwan, 364
Talkativeness
intelligence and, 274
sociolinguistic behaviors and, 336, 337
Task complexity, 27–28
Tay-Sachs disease, 117, 129
Teachers. See also Developmentally appropriate practice; Observations; Professional practice
attachments and, 415
bioecological perspective and, 16
collaboration of, 575
data collection and, 49–58
emotions of, 426–427
expectations of, 89, 95, 96–97, 103, 104, 296, 432, 437, 511, 573–575
family communication and, 85–86, 89, 90, 91
partnerships with families and, 84–86, 89–91
self-regulation and, 511
sense of self and, 446–447
temperament and, 431
Teaching skills, acquisition of, 218–219
Teenage pregnancy, 131, 178, 179, 180, 566, 569
Teen lingo, 333–334
Telegraphic speech
definition of, 325
expanding on, 327
Telephone conversations, 90, 91
Television
content of programs, 581–582
implications of, 584–585
popularity of, 581
viewing time, 582, 584
Temperament
bioecological perspective and, 16
definition of, 6
elements of, 428, 430–431
group activities and, 431–432
motivation and, 495
nature/nurture and, 7, 119, 120–121
observation of, 429–430
reciprocal influences and, 81
self-regulation and, 507
Teratogens, 126–128, 130, 131, 137
Testosterone, 162, 535, 540
Tests. See also Intelligence tests
administration of, 58
as data collection technique, 37
definition of, 37
distortions of information and, 41
Thalassemia (Cooley's anemia), 117
Themes, naturalistic studies, 47
Theories. See also specific theories
children's construction of, 260–263
definition of, 11
Theory of mind
definition of, 466
diversity in, 472–473
factors promoting development of, 469, 471–472
Theory theory
critique of, 263–264
definition of, 260
infancy and, 261, 383, 384
physical world theories, 261–263, 383–384
Thinking/reasoning skills. See also Abstract thought; Symbolic thought
cognitive process theories and, 14
concrete thought, 209

developmental trends in, 225, 242–243
information processing theory and, 242–243
language development and, 316
neo-Piagetian theories and, 208
Think–Pair–Share discussion strategy, 55
Third stage of labor, 135
Thought. See also Abstract thought; Symbolic thought
concrete thought, 209
language interdependent with, 212–213
metacognitive awareness and, 249–250
Through the Looking Glass (Carroll), 342
Time
conceptions of, 98
cultural effects on, 212
genetic expression affected by, 112
historical time, 209, 389
wait time, 337, 338
Toddlers. See Infancy
To Kill a Mockingbird (Lee), 544
Tone of voice, 316
Topic depth, composition skills and, 369
Toxic substances
fathers and, 126
genetics affected by, 111, 118
as health hazards, 184
intellectual disabilities and, 306–307
intelligence and, 290, 296
motor skills and, 118
poverty and, 102
prenatal development and, 126, 128
sensitive periods and, 119
Transitions
to elementary schools, 575–576
to secondary schools, 576–577
Treatments, 42
Triarchic theory, 278–279, 281
Trolling, 583
Trust versus mistrust stage, 404–405, 407
Turner syndrome, 116, 161
Twins, 83, 114
Twin studies
heredity/environment interaction and, 114
intelligence and, 288–289, 290, 292, 293
prosocial and aggressive behavior, 535
sexual orientation and, 567
temperament and, 430

Ultrasound examination, 128
Umbilical cord, 123
Uncontrollable attributions, 491, 492
Underextension, 321
Uninvolved parenting style, 78, 83
Universal Grammar, 315
Universality
art and, 393
definition of, 8
of prosocial and aggressive behaviors, 539
stage theories and, 197
Universality/diversity. See also Diversity
academic domains and, 395
aggression and, 540
attachment and, 427
child development theories and, 18–19
cognitive development and, 11, 264
communities and, 67
contexts and, 67
culture and, 67
as development issue, 8–9, 10, 11
emotional development and, 427
families and, 67
genetics and, 125
information processing theory and, 264
intelligence theories and, 281
language development theories and, 319
motivation and, 494
physical development and, 8, 11, 176

Piaget and Vygotsky contrasted, 227
prenatal development and, 124, 125
prosocial behavior and, 540
sense of self and, 471
social cognition and, 471
social context of development and, 585
stage theories and, 9, 10
theory theory and, 264
Universal Nonverbal Intelligence Test (UNIT), 282–284, 285, 298
Unoccupied behavior, 531
Unstable attributions, 491
Urban areas
communities of, 100–101
gangs and, 547, 563

Validity
assessments and, 55–56
data collection and, 40, 50
definition of, 40
dynamic assessment and, 286
evaluation of research methods and, 49
intelligence tests and, 284–285
Value, definition of, 486
Valued activities, 98
Variables
in correlational studies, 43
mathematics and, 374
separation and control of, 202, 203, 384, 388
Verbal ability
gender and, 295, 296
triarchic theory and, 279
Vicarious punishment, 483
Vicarious reinforcement, 483
Victims, 535–536, 539
Video games, 581–583
Violence
aggression and, 536, 546
correlational studies and, 43
television and, 582
video games and, 582
warning signs of, 546, 547
Visual acuity, 237, 383
Visual aids, 382
Visual cliff, 237
Visual impairments
language development and, 349
reading development and, 361
Visual perception, 156, 237
Visual-spatial ability
Cattell-Horn-Carroll theory of cognitive abilities, 276
definition of, 380
diversity in, 385, 387
gender and, 296, 380
multiple intelligences and, 301
promoting development in mathematics, 382
tasks requiring, 381
Vocabulary development
early childhood and, 321
parents reading to children and, 365
promoting, 323
reading and, 324
second-language learning and, 343, 345
sight vocabulary, 359
socioeconomic status and, 346
visual impairments and, 349
Voluntary relationships, 556
Vygotsky's cognitive development theory. See also Zone of proximal development (ZPD)
applying ideas of, 219–223
challenging tasks and, 210–211, 213–214, 224, 250
cognitive tools and, 210–211, 212, 391
current perspectives on, 215–219
dynamic assessment and, 286
formal schooling and, 212, 292
key ideas in, 211–215

language development, 212–213, 226, 317
nature/nurture and, 227
Piaget compared to, 224, 226–227
qualitative/quantitative change and, 227
sociocultural theories and, 15, 211, 258
universality/diversity and, 227

Wait time, 337, 338
Walking, 147, 148
Weak correlations, 43
Web sites/pages, 90, 397, 582, 583, 584
Wechsler Intelligence Scale for Children (Wechsler), 282, 285
Wechsler Preschool and Primary Scale of Intelligence (Wechsler), 287
Wernicke's area, 315
Whip Around technique, 55
Whole language instruction, 365–366
WIC (Special Supplemental Nutrition Program for Women, Infants, and Children), 131
Wii Fit, 583
Williams syndrome, 318, 320
WISC-IV (Wechsler), 282, 285, 287
Women. See Caregivers; Gender; Mothers; Parents
Word endings, 326
Word order, 325
Word recognition, 358–359, 366
Working memory
capacity of, 205, 235, 239, 244, 266, 276n, 363, 368, 384, 468
definition of, 205, 235
gestures and, 243, 244
information processing theory and, 235–236, 239, 264
language development and, 316–317
learning disabilities and, 266
long-term memory and, 264
neo-Piagetian theories and, 205
writing and, 368
WPPSI-III (Wechsler), 287
Writing
authentic writing activities, 222
Cattell-Horn-Carroll theory of cognitive abilities, 276
children's early efforts at, 358, 367
composition skills and, 369–370
developmental progressions in, 395–396
developmental trends in, 371
development of, 356, 367–373
diversity in, 370, 372
handwriting, 161, 368
metacognition in, 370
promoting writing development, 372–373
specific language impairments and, 348
spelling and, 368–369
syntax and grammatical rules, 369
Written communications, 90, 91
Written language, 356, 358, 361

X-chromosome-linked disorders, 118, 129
X chromosomes, 114

Y chromosomes, 114

Zone of proximal development (ZPD)
adult activities and, 218
challenging tasks and, 221, 224
definition of, 214
giftedness and, 304
mathematics and, 382
readiness and, 224
scaffolding and, 217
social interaction and, 226
Zygotes, 114, 121–122, 126, 132